精选常见词缀词根　详解常用英语词汇
目录索引方便快捷　英汉双解清楚明白

英语常用单词记法词典

——词缀词根记单词

主　编　朱振斌

ZHEJIANG UNIVERSITY PRESS
浙江大学出版社
·杭州·

图书在版编目(CIP)数据

英语常用单词记法词典：词缀词根记单词 / 朱振斌
主编. 一杭州：浙江大学出版社，2022. 8
ISBN 978-7-308-20908-3

I. ①英… II. ①朱… III. ①英语－词汇－记忆术－
高中－教学参考资料 IV. ①G634.413

中国版本图书馆 CIP 数据核字(2020)第 248044 号

英语常用单词记法词典——词缀词根记单词

YINGYU CHANGYONGDANCI JIFA CIDIAN——CIZHUICIGEN JIDANCI

朱振斌 主编

责任编辑 陶 杭

责任校对 董齐琪

封面设计 刘依群

责任印制 范洪法

出版发行 浙江大学出版社

（杭州天目山路 148 号 邮政编码 310007）

（网址: http://www.zjupress.com）

排 版 杭州隆盛图文制作有限公司

印 刷 杭州杭新印务有限公司

开 本 880mm×1230mm 1/16

印 张 26

字 数 1350 千

版 印 次 2022 年 8 月第 1 版 2022 年 8 月第 1 次印刷

书 号 ISBN 978-7-308-20908-3

定 价 88.00 元

版权所有 翻印必究 印装差错 负责调换

浙江大学出版社市场运营中心 联系方式：（0571）88273666；（0571）88925591；http://zjdxcbs.tmall.com

前　言

　　单词对于英语学习的重要性就像砖瓦对于盖房子一样。要想学好英语，就必须有一定的词汇量。许多同学怕记单词，他们付出了很大努力，记住了，但很快又忘光了。

　　英语单词真的那么难记吗?其实，记单词不但容易，而且很有趣。我们可以先想想我们是怎样学习汉字的。以记"学好英语"这四个字为例。"学"上面为学字头，下面是一个"子"。"好"字的左边为"女"，右边为"子"。"英"上面为草字头，下面为"央"。"语"的左边为言字旁，右边上面为"五"，下边为"口"。可以看出，我们在记汉字的时候，是按汉字的偏旁部首等组成部分来记的，所以记起来比较快。如果我们按笔画去记这些汉字，如记"学"，点、点、短撇、左点、横钩…，这样记不晕才怪！

　　正确的记英语单词的方法也应该按照"偏旁部首"来记，不过英语中的"偏旁部首"叫作"前缀"、"后缀"和"词根"。

　　如：cover（意为"盖住"）。在其前面加上 un-（表相反动作），构成 uncover（"盖住"的相反动作是"揭开"。如 uncover the pan"揭开平底锅"）。在 cover 前面加上 re-（又，再），构成 recover（"又盖住"，即受伤后皮肤又覆盖住伤口，因此 recover 意为"恢复健康"等）。在 cover 前面加上 dis-（意为"不"），构成 discover（原来被盖着看不见的东西，现在不再被盖了，那就是"发现原来存在的事物"。如：They discovered human remains there. 他们在那里发现了人的遗骸）。un-（表相反动作）、re-（又，再）、dis-（意为"不"）等加在 cover 的前面构成了具有不同词义的单词。un-、re-、dis-叫作前缀，而 cover 叫作词根。前缀通常是用来改变单词的词义的。

　　再如：careful（adj. 小心的，仔细的），careless（adj. 粗心大意的）。它们中的 care（n.小心）是词根，本身是名词。-ful（充满…的）和-less（缺少…的）加在词根 care 的后面，它们是后缀。后缀通常改变单词的词性。再如：friend（n. 朋友），friendly（adj. 友好的）。

　　英语中大部分单词都可以根据词缀、词根知识来记忆。可是我们在接受正规学校教育的过程中,教材中很少给我们讲解词缀、词根这方面知识，而老师上课也很少提这方面知识。我们该怎么办呢? 本书就是帮助你解决这个问题的。

　　本书在编排上有以下特点：

　　1. 系统地列出了常见的前缀、词根和后缀，并按字母顺序排列，在前面有详细的目录，便于查找和记忆词缀、词根的含义。

　　2. 所列例词尽可能全，因此适合不同水平的英语学习者使用。所选词汇没有偏词、怪词。高中英语词汇标有实线下划线；大学英语四、六级及考研英语词汇标有虚线下划线；其他没标下划线。

　　3. 本书单词释义详略得当。简单单词的释义一带而过，难理解的单词用英汉双解来释义。单词用法上挑重要的、常用的讲。

　　4. 书的最后有单词索引，索引按字母顺序排列。如果要查一个单词的用法，可以在索引中先找到这个单词，然后根据单词后面的页码来找到其在本书中的位置。因此，本书可以作为派生词（由词缀和词根构成的单词）词典来使用。

5. 本书内容丰富。书中许多例句是从近年来的英语新闻中选取的，更有利于读者理解词义、体会该词的常用性。书中不仅配有一些图片，还通过"小贴士"的形式补充了许多相关知识。有的单词还给出了"反义词""同义词""形近词"等。

6. 使用本书可以快速扩大词汇量，同时提高猜词能力。除去当作派生词词典来查生词记法之外，本书还可以当作词汇书来读记。在记单词的过程中，会掌握相当多的词缀和词根，这样可以提高我们猜生词的能力。根据词缀、词根来记单词，会对单词的词义把握得更准确。

本书主要体例说明

1. 带有实线下划线的单词（如：<u>conductor</u>）为高中学生要掌握的单词；带有虚线下划线的单词（如：missionary）为超出高考要求且又在考研范围之内的单词；没有下划线的单词（如：fresco）为超出考研和大学英语六级要求的单词，适合备考英语专业八级和 GRE 的学生读记。

2. 当一个单词在前缀、后缀和词根中多次出现时，一般只在一个地方（一般是在其词根所出现的地方）给出详细的词义和用法讲解，在其他地方出现时会在其后面的括号内给出其词义详解所在的页码。如：

<u>current</u> [ˈkʌrənt] adj. 当前的 n. 水流；气流；电流 <P146>

3. 汉语释义不能完全解释清楚的单词，配有英语释义。如：

❷ 逐渐形成，培养（某种态度、形象或技能）

If you cultivate an attitude, image, or skill, you try hard to develop it and make it stronger or better.

4. 单词音标后面的词性标示：vt.只能作及物动词；vi.只能作不及物动词；v.可作及物、不及物动词。

读者在使用本书时，可以先熟记本书上的单词，然后再在阅读中巩固这些单词。这样更能掌握单词的精准词义、更高效地扩大词汇量。当然，也可以根据前面的目录来查某个词缀或词根的意思，根据后面的索引查某个单词的记法。

本书编写历时近两年，谨以此书献给那些有志于学好英语的人，希望以我的辛苦铺平你通往成功的路。由于是初版，中间难免会出现这样那样的问题和不足，希望各位朋友多提宝贵意见。

编　者

2022 年 8 月

目 录

第一部分　根据词缀词根记单词

第1讲　根据前缀记单词

1. afloat [əˈfləʊt] adj. 漂浮的
『a在/到…的+float漂浮→漂浮的』

2. ahead [əˈhed] adv. 向前；在将来（a+head头）
『a在/到…的+head前端→向前』

3. alive 活的 [əˈlaɪv] adj. 活着的；有生气的
『a在/到…的+live活→活的』

4. asleep [əˈsliːp] adj. 睡着的
『a在/到…的+sleep睡觉→睡着的』

5. aside [əˈsaɪd] adv. 在旁边；到旁边
『a在/到…的+side→旁边』

1. amoral [ˌeɪˈmɒrəl] adj. 不遵守道德准则的，不分是非的
『a不，无，非+moral道德的→非道德性的→不分是非的』

not following any moral rules and not caring about right and wrong

He is an amoral person, with no sense of right or wrong.
他是一个没有道德观念的人，没有是非对错的分辨能力。

小贴士 immoral [ɪˈmɒrəl] 表示"不道德的，邪恶的"，im- 表示"不"。It's immoral to steal. 偷盗是不道德的。

2. apolitical [ˌeɪpəˈlɪtɪkl] adj. 不关心政治的；无关政党的
『a不，无，非+political政治的→不关心政治的』

I'm a completely apolitical man. 我对政治毫无兴趣。

3. atypical [ˌeɪˈtɪpɪkl] adj. 非典型的
『a不，无，非+typical典型的→非典型的』

4. asymptomatic [ˌeɪsɪmptəˈmætɪk] adj. 无症状的
『a不，无，非+symptom症状+atic…的→无症状的』

On April 1, Shenzhen reported 2 asymptomatic COVID-19 cases. 4月1日，深圳市报告2例无症状COVID-19（新冠肺炎）病例。

5. anonymous [əˈnɒnɪməs] adj. 匿名的，无名的 ⟨P237⟩
『an无+onym名称，名字+ous…的→没有名称的→匿名的』

6. anarchic [əˈnɑːkɪk] adj. 无政府主义的 ⟨P115⟩
『an无+arch统治者+ic…的→无统治者的→无政府主义的』

1. absent [ˈæbsənt] adj. 缺席的；不在场的
『abs相反+ent存在→不在→缺席的』

❶ 缺席的 be ~ from 缺席，不在
to be absent from work 缺勤

❷ 不存在的 be ~ from 不存在，缺少
Love was totally absent from his childhood.
他童年时根本没有得到过爱。

❸ 心不在焉的，出神的
an absent expression 心不在焉的神情

反义词 **present** [ˈpreznt] adj. 出席的，出现的

▶ **absence** [ˈæbsəns] n.不在场；缺少

❶ [U, C] ~ (from…)（某人）缺席，不在
He took my place **during my absence**.
在我缺勤期间他代替了我。
The decision was made **in my absence**.
这个决定是我不在的时候做出的。

❷ [U]缺乏，缺少，无
In the absence **of** a will, the court decides who the guardian is.
在没有遗嘱的情况下，由法庭指定监护人。
The case was dismissed in the absence of any definite proof.
此案因缺乏确凿证据而不予受理。

反义词 **presence** [ˈprezns] n. 出席；出现

2. absorb [əbˈsɔːb] v. 吸收
『ab去掉，离去+ sorb吸收→吸收掉→吸收』

❶ [VN] 吸收（液体、气体、热、光、能，等等）
Plants absorb oxygen. 植物吸收氧气。
Black walls absorb a lot of heat during the day.
黑色墙壁在白天吸收大量的热。

❷ [VN] 减轻（打击、碰击等）
This tennis racket absorbs shock on impact.
这个网球拍能减轻撞击所产生的剧烈震动。

❸ [VN] 理解；掌握（吸收知识）
It's a lot of information to absorb all at once.
要一下子消化这么多资料，真是很难。

❹ [VN] 吸引全部注意力；使全神贯注
This work had absorbed him for several years.
这项工作曾使他沉迷了好几年。
He was completely absorbed in reading and forgot even to take his meal. 他完全沉迷于阅读，连饭都忘了吃。

3. abuse [əˈbjuːs] v. & n. 滥用；谩骂；虐待
『ab离开+use用→脱离了正常的使用→滥用，辱骂』

❶ [VN] 滥用（酒、毒品）；滥用，妄用（权力等）
to abuse alcohol/drugs 酗酒；嗜毒
He showed how the rich and powerful can abuse their position.
他让我们看到有钱有势的人是如何滥用其地位的。

❷ [VN] 虐待，伤害；辱骂，诋毁
All the children had been physically and emotionally abused.
所有这些儿童的身心都受到了摧残。
The referee had been threatened and abused.
裁判遭到了恐吓和谩骂。

❸ n. 滥用；虐待，谩骂
alcohol/drug abuse 酗酒；嗜毒
He was arrested on charges of corruption and abuse of power.
他因被控贪污腐化和滥用职权而遭逮捕。
to scream/hurl/shout abuse 高声谩骂；破口大骂；大声辱骂
She suffered years of physical abuse.
她遭受了多年的肉体摧残。

▶ **abusive** [əˈbjuːsɪv] adj. 谩骂的；虐待的

『abuse谩骂；虐待（去e)+ive…的→谩骂的；虐待的』

He was alleged to have used abusive language.
他被指称使用过侮辱性语言。
He became violent and abusive toward Ben's mother.
他对本的妈妈动起粗来。

4. abduct [æbˈdʌkt] v. 诱拐；劫持 <P156>
『ab离开+ duct引导：带来→引开→诱拐』

5. abnormal [æbˈnɔːml] adj. 反常的 <P234>
『ab离开+normal正常的→离开正常的→不正常的』

6. abrupt [əˈbrʌpt] adj. 突然的；（言行）粗鲁、莽撞的 <P283>
『ab离去+rupt破，断裂→断开离去→突然的；粗鲁的』

7. abstract [ˈæbstrækt] adj. 抽象的；v. 抽取；抽取 n. 摘要 <P336>
『abs去掉，离去+tract拉→将（许多具体的事物中相同的部分）拉出来→抽象的』

8. abject [ˈæbdʒekt] adj. 凄惨的；自卑的 <P197>
『ab离开+ject投掷，扔→被扔掉的→被抛弃的→凄惨；自卑的』

9. abstain [əbˈsteɪn] vi. 戒除，节制；(投票时)弃权 <P324>
『abs离开+tain(=hold)坚持住，把持得住→（面对诱惑）把持得住，离开了→戒除；ab离开+stain(=hold)握着→握着（选票）离开→（投票时）弃权』

前缀4. acro- =top，表示"顶点，高点"

1. acrobat [ˈækrəbæt] n. 杂技演员
『acro顶点，高点+bat打→在高处表演打斗→杂技演员』

▶ **acrobatics** [ˌækrəˈbætɪks] n. 杂技

2. acme [ˈækmi] n. 顶峰
『ac(=acro)顶点+me→（成就的）顶点→顶峰』

His work is considered the acme of cinematic art.
他的作品被认为是电影艺术的巅峰之作。

3. acrophobia [ˌækrəˈfəʊbɪə] n. 恐高症 <P254>
『acro顶点，高点+phob恐惧，厌恶+ia某种病→恐高症』

4. acronym [ˈækrənɪm] n. 首字母缩略词 <P238>
『acro顶点，高点+(o)nym名字→顶点（也就是每个单词的第一个字母）构成的名字→首字母缩略词』

前缀5. acu-, acr(i)- =sharp，表示"敏锐；尖"

1. acute [əˈkjuːt] adj. 严重的；急性的；敏锐的；锐角的
『acu敏锐+te→严重的，敏锐的』

❶ 十分严重的，剧烈的；（疾病）急性的
There is an acute shortage of water. 水严重短缺。
Competition for jobs is acute. 求职竞争非常激烈。
acute pain 剧痛
acute appendicitis 急性阑尾炎

❷ （感官）灵敏的；敏锐的
Dogs have an acute sense of smell. 狗的嗅觉灵敏。
He is an acute observer of the social scene.
他是个敏锐的社会现状观察者。

❸ 锐角的

2. acumen [ˈækjəmən] n. 精明，敏锐
『acu敏锐+men表名词→敏锐』

Acumen is the ability to make good judgments and quick decisions.

His sharp business acumen meant he quickly rose to the top.
他精明的商业头脑令其青云直上。

3. acuity [əˈkjuːəti] n.（思维、视力、听力）敏锐度，敏锐
『acu敏锐+ity表名词→敏锐』

We work on improving visual acuity.
我们致力于提高视觉的敏锐度。

4. acupuncture [ˈækjupʌŋktʃə(r)] n. 针刺疗法，针灸
『acu尖+punct刺+ure表行为→用尖（针）刺→针灸

5. acrid [ˈækrɪd] adj. （气、味）难闻的，刺激的
『acr尖+ id有…的性质→刺激的』

The room filled with the acrid smell of tobacco.
房间里弥漫着刺鼻的烟草味。

6. acrimony [ˈækrɪməni] n.（态度、言辞）尖刻，讥讽
『acri尖+mony表名词→尖刻』

angry bitter feelings or words
The dispute was settled without acrimony.
没有唇枪舌剑，这场纠纷就解决了。

前缀6. ad-(ab-, ac-, af-, ag-, al-, an-, ap-, ar-, as-, at-)=to，表示"到…"；有时表示加强语气

ad-在 b, f, g, l, n, p, r, s, t 之前，受同化作用，要变为 ab-, af-, ag-, al-, an-, ap-, ar-, as-和 at-；ad-在 c, k, q 之前，要变为 ac-

1. accompany [əˈkʌmpəni] v. 陪伴，陪同；伴奏
『ac相当于to+company陪伴→陪伴到…→陪同』

❶ [VN] 陪同；陪伴 to travel or go somewhere with sb
During this spring festival, I will accompany my father to visit his hometown. 今年春节，我陪父亲归省。

❷ [VN] 伴随；与…同时发生
strong winds accompanied by heavy rain 狂风夹着暴雨

❸ （尤指用钢琴）为…伴奏
He sang and Alice accompanied him on the piano.
他一边唱，艾丽斯一边为他钢琴伴奏。

小贴士 作"陪伴"讲时，accompany是动词，company是不可数名词，companion是可数名词。

▶ **company** [ˈkʌmpəni] n. 公司；陪伴；连队

❶ [C + sing./pl. v.] (abbr. Co.) (often in names 常用于名称)
公司；商号；商行
the largest computer company in the world
全球最大的计算机公司
She joined the company in 2002.
她于 2002 年加盟这家公司。
词义辨析 <P369第38> 公司 company, corporation, firm

❷ [U] 陪伴；做伴
I enjoy Jo's company (= I enjoy being with Jo).
我喜欢和乔在一起。
He's coming with me for company. 他要陪伴我一起来。
I'll keep you company while you're waiting.
你等待时我会陪伴你。
Two's company, three's a crowd. 两人成伴，三人不欢。

❸ [U] (formal) 在一起的一群人
She told the assembled company what had happened.
她把发生的事告诉了聚会的人。
I didn't realize you had company. 我不知道你有客人。
Judging by the company he kept, Mark must have been a

wealthy man.

根据马克所交往的人来判断，他一定是位富翁。

❹ [C + sing./pl. v.] 连队

▶**companion** [kəmˈpæniən] n. 同伴；伴侣；同行者

❶ [C] 同伴；伴侣；同行者

A companion is someone whom you spend time with or whom you are travelling with.

Fred had been her constant companion for the last six years of her life.

在她生命的最后6年，弗雷德一直是她忠实的伴侣。

Fear was the hostages' constant companion.

人质一直都感到恐惧不安。

❷ [C]（爱好、志趣等相投的）伙伴，同伴

His younger brother is not much of a companion for him.

他的弟弟和他志趣不太相投。

They're drinking companions (= they go out drinking together).

他们是酒友。

2. appoint [əˈpɔɪnt] vt. 任命，委派；约定，指定

『ap相当于to+point点，指→指向某人/某个日子→任命；指定，约定』

❶ ~ sb (to sth) | ~ sb (as) sth 任命；委任

They appointed him (as) captain of the English team.

他们任命他为英国队队长。

It made sense to appoint a banker to this job.

指派一位银行家做这份工作是明智之举。

❷ [VN] [usually passive] 安排，确定（时间、地点）

A date for the meeting is still to be appointed.

会议日期尚待确定。

Everyone was assembled at the appointed time.

全体人员均按规定时间召集到场。

▶**appointment** [əˈpɔɪntmənt] n. 任命；约定；职位

『appoint 任命；约定+ment 表名词→任命，约定』

❶ [C] ~ (with sb) 约会；预约；约定

She **made an appointment** for her son to see the doctor.

她为儿子约定了看医生的时间。

You may **cancel or rearrange the appointment**.

你可以取消约会或是重新安排约会时间。

❷ [C, U] ~ (as/to sth) 任命；委任；职位

Mr Fay is to take up an appointment as a researcher with the Royal Society. 费伊先生将担任皇家学会研究员的职务。

The club also offers its congratulations to D. Brown on his appointment as president.

俱乐部也对 D.布朗被任命为主席表示祝贺。

▶**disappoint** [ˌdɪsəˈpɔɪnt] vt. 使失望

『dis不+appoint指派→没（被）指派→使失望』

▶**disappointed** [ˌdɪsəˈpɔɪntɪd] adj. 失望的

~ (at/by sth) | ~ (in/with sb/sth)

They were bitterly disappointed at the result of the game.

他们对比赛结果极为失望。

I was very disappointed with myself.

我对自己感到非常失望。

3. arrange [əˈreɪndʒ] v. 安排；排列

『ar相当于to+range排列→使达到排列好的状态→排列；安排』

❶ 安排；筹备 to plan or organize sth in advance

[VN] Can I **arrange an appointment** for Monday?

我可以安排星期一约见吗？

arrange for sb/sth to do sth 安排做某事

We arranged for a car to collect us from the airport.

我们安排了一辆轿车到机场接我们。

❷ [VN] 整理；排列；布置

arrange the books on the shelves 整理书架上的书

arrange some flowers in a vase 插好花瓶里的花

▶**arrangement** [əˈreɪndʒmənt] n.安排；排列

❶ make arrangements for 安排（arrangement常用复数）

I'll make arrangements for you to be met at the airport.

我会安排人到机场接你。

She's happy with her unusual living arrangements.

她对自己不同寻常的生活安排方式感到很得意。

❷ [C, U] 整理好的东西；整理；排列；布置

the art of flower arrangement 插花艺术

plans of the possible seating arrangements

几种可行的座次安排方案

▶**range** [reɪndʒ] n. 范围；vt. 排列

❶ [C, usually sing.] ~ (of sth) 一系列

There is a full range of activities for children.

这里有给孩子们提供的各种活动。

A wide range of colours and patterns are available.

各种颜色和样式都有。

❷ [C, usually sing.]（变动或浮动的）范围，界限，区间

It's difficult to find a house in our price range.

在我们的价格范围以内，很难找到房子。

This was outside the range of his experience.

这超出了他的阅历。

He shouted angrily at anyone within range.

他看见谁，就对谁生气地吼叫。

❸ [C] 山脉

the great mountain range of the Alps 雄伟的阿尔卑斯山脉

❹ [V] ~ from A to B | ~ between A and B

（在一定的范围内）变化，变动

Accommodation ranges from tourist class to luxury hotels.

住宿条件从经济旅馆至豪华宾馆不等。

Courses offered range from playwriting to directing to set design, always reflecting a commitment to diverse aesthetics.

课程设置包括从剧本创作到戏剧导演，再到布景设计等内容，总是体现了戏剧美学的多样性。

❺ [VN + adv./prep.] [usually passive] (formal)

（按一定位置或顺序）排列，排序

These books are ranged in order of the date of publication.

这些书是按出版日期的前后排列的。

▶**ranger** [ˈreɪndʒə(r)] n. 园林管理员；护林人

a person whose job is to take care of a park, a forest or an area of countryside

4. arrest [əˈrest] vt. 逮捕，拘捕

『ar相当于to+rest休息→使达到休息（不能自由走动）状态→逮捕』

[VN] [often passive] ~ sb (for sth)

A man has been arrested in connection with the robbery.

一名男子因与这桩抢劫案有关已被逮捕。

5. accustom [əˈkʌstəm] vt. 使习惯于〈P148〉

『ac相当于to+custom习惯→达到成为习惯→使习惯于』

6. assure [əˈʃʊə(r)] vt. 向…保证；使…确信〈P321〉

『as相当于to+sure确信→使达到确信的地步→使确信』

7. adapt [əˈdæpt] v.（使）适应；改编 <P114>

『ad相当于to + apt适当的→使达到适当→使适应；改编』

8. adjust [əˈdʒʌst] vt.& vi.（改变…以）适应，调整 <P199>

『ad到+just正确→使达到正确→调整』

9. adopt [əˈdɒpt] vt. 收养，采用 <P238>

『ad相当于to+opt选择→选择到→采纳；收养』

10. allocate [ˈæləkeɪt] vt.分配；分派；划拨 <P210>

『al 相当于to+ loc地方+ate表动词→（正式把某物）划拨到某个地方→分配；划拨』

11. attach [əˈtætʃ] vt. & vi. 附上；贴上；系上 <P322>

『at相当于to+tach接触→使…接触到…→系上；附上』

12. attract [əˈtrækt] v. 吸引；诱惑 <P336>

『at相当于to+tract拉→拉到→吸引』

13. aggressive [əˈgresɪv] adj. 有闯劲的；进攻性的 <P189>

『ag相当于to+gress走+ive有…性质的→（憋足劲）向（目标）走过去→有闯劲的；具有进攻性的』

14. attribute [əˈtrɪbjuːt, ˈætrɪbjuːt] vt. 把…归于 n. 属性 <P338>

『at相当于to+tribute给予→把（原因）给…→归因于』（v. [əˈtrɪbjuːt]; n. [ˈætrɪbjuːt]）

15. attain [əˈteɪn] vt. & vi. 达到，获得 <P323>

『at相当于to+tain拿住→拿到→获得』

前缀7. aero-=air，表示"空气"

1. aeroplane [ˈeərəpleɪn] n. 飞机

『aero空气+plane飞机→飞机』

(BrE) (also airplane especially in NAmE)

2. aerobatics [ˌeərəˈbætɪks] n. 特技飞行 (also plane BrE, NAmE)

『aero空气+bat打+ics…学，…术→（驾飞机）在空中打斗的技术→特技飞行』

▶**aerobatic** [ˌeərəˈbætɪk] adj. 特技飞行的

an aerobatic display 一场特技飞行表演

3. aerobics [eəˈrəʊbɪks] n. 有氧运动

『aero空气+bics→（吸进大量）空气（的运动）→有氧运动』

physical exercises intended to make the heart and lungs stronger, often done in classes with music

I'd like to join an aerobics class to improve my fitness.
我想参加有氧运动训练班来增强体质。

4. aerodynamics [ˌeərəʊdaɪˈnæmɪks] n. 空气动力（特性）；空气动力学

『aero空气+dynamics动力→空气动力学』

▶**aerodynamic** [ˌeərəʊdaɪˈnæmɪk] adj.（汽车等）流线型的

The secret of the machine lies in the aerodynamic shape of the frame. 该机器的精妙之处在于其构架呈流线型。

5. aerosol [ˈeərəsɒl] n.（喷油漆、头发定型剂等的）喷雾器；气雾剂；气溶胶

『aero空气+sol(=solution)溶解；溶液→溶解于空气中→气雾剂；气溶胶』

a metal container in which liquids are kept under pressure and forced out in a spray

ozone-friendly aerosols 对臭氧无损的气雾剂

an aerosol can/spray 喷雾罐；气雾喷雾器

The novel coronavirus can spread through aerosol transmission. 新型冠状病毒可以通过气溶胶传播。

6. aerospace [ˈeərəʊspeɪs] n. 航空航天（工业）

『aero空气+space空间，太空→大气层内外空间→航空航天』

7. aeronautics [ˌeərəˈnɔːtɪks] n. 航空学；飞机制造学

『aero空气+naut船（引申为航行）→研究在空气中航行的学科→航空学』

Aeronautics is the science of designing and building aeroplanes.

前缀8. ante-=before，表示"前，在前"

1. anteroom [ˈæntiruːm] n. 前厅，接待室

『ante前，在前+room房间→前厅』

He had been patiently waiting in the anteroom for an hour.
他在前厅耐心地等了一个小时。

2. antebellum [ˌæntiˈbeləm] adj. 战前的（尤指美国南北战争前的）

『ante前，在前+bell战争+um→战前的』

As the voice of the antebellum South, he was slavery's most ardent defender.
作为内战前南方的声音，他是奴隶制度最热烈的拥护者。
There are many antebellum houses in the area.
这个地区有许多南北战争以前的房屋。

3. antenna [ænˈtenə] n. 天线；触角，触须

『ante前面+nna→（昆虫头的）前面→触角（老式电视自带的两根天线与昆虫的触角相似，因此又指天线）』

❶ 天线（pl. antennae [ænˈteniː]）（=aerial）
They erected a television antenna on the roof.
他们在屋顶上架起了电视天线。

❷ 触角（pl. antennas or antennae）
either of the two long thin parts on the heads of some insects and some animals that live in shells, used to feel and touch things with
(figurative) The minister was praised for his acute political antennae. 这位部长以政治触觉敏锐而为人称道。
Its antenna has reached every aspect of social life.
它的触角已经伸向社会生活的每个方面。

4. ante [ˈænti] n. 赌注 v. 下赌注

『ante前面→来赌先下赌注→赌注』

up/raise the ante 提高要求；增加金额

If you up the ante or raise the ante, you increase your demands when you are in dispute or fighting for something.
We raised the ante so that only the richest companies could compete with us for the contract.
我们增加预付金额，这样一来就只有那些资金最雄厚的公司才能和我们竞争这份合同。

5. antecedent [ˌæntɪˈsiːdnt] n. 先行词；祖先；前事 adj. 先前的 <P127>

『ante前面+cede行走，前进+(e)nt表形容词或名词→走在

前面→先行的；先行词』

6. antenatal [ˌæntiˈneɪtl] adj. 产前的〈P232〉
『ante前，在前+nate出生（去e)+al…的→产前的』
(BrE) (also prenatal NAmE, BrE)

7. anterior [ænˈtɪəriə(r)] adj. （身体部位）前部的〈P80〉
『anter(=ante前面)+ior较…的，属于→于…的→较早的』

前缀9. ant-, anti- 表示"反对；相反；抗"

1. Antarctic [ænˈtɑːktɪk] adj. 南极的 n.(A-)南极洲
『ant相反+arctic北极的→南极的』

2. antiaircraft [ˌæntiˈeəkræft] adj. 防空的 n. 高射炮
『anti反对+aircraft飞机→反抗飞机（空袭)的→防空的』

3. antibacterial [ˌæntibækˈtɪəriəl] adj. 抗菌的
『anti抗+ bacterial细菌的→抗菌的』

4. antibody [ˈæntibɒdi] n. <医>抗体
『anti抗+ body身体→抗体』

5. anticlockwise [ˌæntiˈklɒkwaɪz] adv. & adj. 逆时针地
『anti相反+ clockwise顺时针的→逆时针的』

6. antidote [ˈæntidəʊt] n. 解药，解毒剂
『anti抗+dote (=dose) 药剂→抗（毒）药→解毒药』

7. antisocial [ˌæntiˈsəʊʃl] adj. 反社会的
『anti反对+ social社会的→反社会的』

8. antitank [ˈæntitæŋk] adj.对抗战车用的
『anti抗+ tank坦克→反坦克的』

9. antiwar [ˈæntiwɔː] adj. 反战的，反对战争的
『anti反对+war战争→反战的』

10. antonym [ˈæntənɪm] n. 反义词 〈P238〉
『ant相反+onym名字→名称相对→反义词』

11. antibiotic [ˌæntibaɪˈɒtɪk] n. 抗生素 adj. 抗生素的
〈P119〉
『anti抗+bio生命，生物+tic有…性质的→抗生素的』

12. antipathy [ænˈtɪpəθi] n. 厌恶；反感 〈P245〉
『anti反对+pathy感情→反对的感情→反感』

前缀10. aqu(a)-=water，表示"水"

1. aquarium [əˈkweəriəm] n. 水族馆；养鱼缸
『aqu水+arium场所，地点→水族馆』

2. aquamarine [ˌækwəməˈriːn] n. 海蓝宝石；海蓝色
『aqua水+ marine海的→如海水般→海蓝宝石』

3. aquatic [əˈkwætɪk] adj. 水生的，水栖的；水的
『aqu水+atic有…性质的→水的；水中的』

Our country has rich offshore aquatic resources.
我国近海有丰富的水产资源。

4. aqueduct [ˈækwɪdʌkt] n. 渡槽，高架渠
『aque(=aqua)水+duct引导→引导水→引水槽』

前缀11. aut-, auto-= self，表示"自己的"

1. autism [ˈɔːtɪzəm] n. 自闭症；孤独症
『aut自己+ ism表主义→自我中心主义→自闭症』

▶ **autistic** [ɔːˈtɪstɪk] adj. 患自闭症的

2. automatic [ˌɔːtəˈmætɪk] adj. 自动的；无意识的
『auto自己+ mat（= mob 动）+ ic…的→自动的』

❶ adj. (of a machine, device, etc. 机器、装置等）自动的
The gunmen opened fire with automatic weapons.
歹徒用自动武器开火了。
an automatic washing-machine 自动洗衣机

❷ adj. 无意识的；不假思索的
Breathing is an automatic function of the body.
呼吸是一种无意识的身体功能。
My reaction was automatic. 我的反应是不由自主的。

❸ n. 自动手枪（或步枪）；(BrE)自动挡汽车

▶ **automation** [ˌɔːtəˈmeɪʃn] n. 自动化
Automation meant the loss of many factory jobs.
自动化意味着许多工厂工人失业。

3. automobile [ˈɔːtəməbiːl] n. 汽车〈P226〉
『auto自己+mob移动+ile物体→自己（能）移动的物体→
汽车』

4. autobiography [ˌɔːtəbaɪˈɒɡrəfi] n.自传；自传文学
〈P187〉
『auto自己+bio人生+graphy描述，呈现→描述呈现自己的
人生→自传』

5. autograph [ˈɔːtəɡrɑːf] n.亲笔签名； v. 签名〈P187〉
『auto自己+graph写，画→自己写的字→亲笔字』

6. autocrat [ˈɔːtəkræt] n. 独裁者；专横的人〈P139〉
『auto自己+crat统治者→自己做统治者（不听别人)→独
裁者』

7. autonomy [ɔːˈtɒnəmi] n. 自治；自主权〈P234〉
『auto自己+nomy法则→按自己的法则办事→自治；自主
权』

前缀12. bene- 表示"善，好"

1. benefit [ˈbenɪfɪt] n. 利益，好处; vt. 有益于
『bene好+fit做→所做的好处→好处，利益』

❶ [U, C] 优势；益处；成效
I **enjoyed** the **great benefit** of his instructions concerning the
matter. 在这一问题上他的指教使我受益匪浅。
The new regulations will **be of benefit** to everyone concerned.
新规章将使所有有关人员受益。
It will be **to your benefit** to arrive early.
早到将会对你有利。
Don't go to any trouble **for my benefit**! 别为我费工夫!

❷ [VN] 对（某人）有用；使受益
We should spend the money on something that will benefit
everyone. 我们应该把这笔钱花在大家都能得益的事上。

❸ [V] ~ (from/by sth) 得益于；得利于
I am sure you'll **benefit a lot from** the activity.
我相信你会从这次活动中大受裨益。

▶ **beneficial** [ˌbenɪˈfɪʃl] adj. 有利的，有益的
『bene好+fic做→ial构成形容词→能带来好处的』

adj. ~ (to sth/sb) 有利的；有裨益的

He did a lot of work that was beneficial to us.
他做了很多对我们有益的工作。

While a moderate amount of stress can be beneficial, too much stress can exhaust you.
适度的压力是有好处的，但是压力太大会把人压垮。

2. benign [bɪˈnaɪn] adj. （人）和善的；（肿瘤）良性的；没有危害的；（环境）宜人的
『ben(=bene)善，好+ign→（肿瘤等）良性的；善良的』

They are normally a more benign audience.
他们通常是更为和善的观众。

It wasn't cancer, only a benign tumour.
这不是癌症，只是良性肿瘤。

We're taking relatively benign medicines and we're turning them into poisons.
我们服的药相对来说药性温和，但是我们却在把它们变成毒药。

They enjoyed an especially benign climate.
他们享受着特别温和的气候。

反义词 **malignant** [məˈlɪgnənt] adj. （肿瘤）恶性的；（人）恶意的，恶毒的 <P20>
『mal坏，恶+ign+ant…的→恶性的』

3. benediction [ˌbenɪˈdɪkʃn] n.（基督教的）祝福，祝祷 <P150>
『bene善，好+diction措辞→好的措辞→祝福』

4. beneficiary [ˌbenɪˈfɪʃəri] n. 受益人 <P165>
『bene善，好+ fici(=fic)做+ary人→得到（做）好处的人→受益者』

5. benevolent [bəˈnevələnt] adj. （当权者）仁慈的，乐善好施的 <P358>
『bene好+vol意愿+ent具有…性质的→意愿是好的→仁慈的，乐善好施的』

6. benefactor [ˈbenɪfæktə(r)] n. 捐款人；赞助人 <P161>
『bene善，好+ fact做+or表人→做好事的人→行善者』

前缀13. bi-=two，表示"两个"

1. bicycle [ˈbaɪsɪkl] n. 自行车 v. 骑自行车
『bi二+ cycle圆，环→两个轮子→自行车』

2. biweekly [baɪˈwiːkli] adj. & adv. 两周一次的/地 n. 双周刊
『bi 二+ weekly→一周一次的→双周刊』

3. biannual [baɪˈænjuəl] adj. 一年两次的 <P113>
『bi二+ annu年，一年+al…的→一年两次的』

4. biennial [baɪˈeniəl] adj. （事件）两年一次的 <P113>
『bi二+enn年+ial具有…的→两年（一次）的』

5. bilingual [ˌbaɪˈlɪŋgwəl] adj. 双语的 <P208>
『bi二，两+ lingu语言+al…的→双语种的』

6. bilateral [ˌbaɪˈlætərəl] adj. 双边的 <P201>
『bi二+ later边+al…的→双边的』

前缀14. by- 表示"在旁边；副的"

1. byproduct [ˈbaɪˌprɒdʌkt] n. 副产品；意外结果
（by副的+ product产品→副产品）

The raw material for the tyre is a byproduct of petrol refining.
制造轮胎的原材料是提炼汽油时产生的一种副产品。

Becoming a baseball fan was a byproduct of my research into sport on TV.
成为一个棒球迷，是我研究电视体育节目的意外结果。

2. passer-by [ˈpɑːsəˈbaɪ] n. 过路人，行人
『pass经过+er人+by旁边→从旁边经过的人→过路人的』
（其复数形式为passers-by。）

前缀15. cent(i)=hundred，表示"一百"

1. centimeter [ˈsentɪˌmiːtə] n. 厘米
『centi百+meter米→百分之一米→厘米』

2. centigram [ˈsentɪgræm] n. 厘克
『centi百+gram克→百分之一克→厘克』

3. centiliter [ˈsentɪliːtə(r)] n. 厘升
『centi百+liter升→百分之一升→厘升』

4. century [ˈsentʃəri] n. 百年，世纪
『cent百+ury表名词→百年，世纪』

5. centigrade [ˈsentɪgreɪd] adj. 摄氏度的 <P186>
『centi百+grade度，级→百分之一度的→摄氏度』

6. centipede [ˈsentɪpiːd] n. 蜈蚣 <P247>
『centi百+pede脚→百脚之虫→蜈蚣』

7. percent [pəˈsent] n. 百分比；百分之一 <P31>
『per(every)每一个+cent（一百）→一百中的每一个→百分之一』

小贴士 常见的量的表示法

倍数、分数	计量单位	词头符号	英文	参看页码
10^6	兆	M	mega	P22前缀48
10^3	千	k	kilo	P20前缀41
10^2	百	h	hect	P17前缀32
10	十	da	deca	P9前缀21
10^{-1}	分	d	deci	P9前缀22
10^{-2}	厘	c	centi	P6前缀15
10^{-3}	毫	m	milli	P22前缀47
10^{-6}	微	μ	micro	P22前缀46

前缀16. circum- 表示"环绕，周围"

1. circumference [səˈkʌmfərəns] n. 圆周
『circum环绕，周围+ fer从…到…+ence表状态→来环绕一圈→周长』

[C, U] 圆周；圆周长
The tree has a circumference of 6 feet. 这棵树周长6英尺。
The lake is 12 kilometers in circumference.
湖的周长（为）12千米。

2. circumstance [ˈsɜːkəmstəns] n. 环境；境遇 <P312>
『circum环绕，周围+ stance站→置身在其中→环境；状况』

3. circumvent [ˌsɜːkəmˈvent] vt. 规避（规则或限制）；躲避（障碍或危险） <P347>
『circum环绕+vent来→绕过（规则、障碍或危险）』

前缀17. co- (col-, cor-, com-, con-)=with, together, 表示"共同，一起"

① co- 表示"共同，一起"，通常放在元音词根前

1. co-author [kəʊˈɔːθə] n. 合著者；v. 合著
『co共同+author作者→合著者』

2. coexist [ˌkəʊɪɡˈzɪst] vi. 同时共存，和平共处
『co共同+exist存在→共存』

[V] ~ (with sb/sth) (formal) 共存；（尤指）和平共处
Different traditions coexist successfully side by side.
不同的传统和谐地共存着。

▶**coexistence** [ˌkəʊɪɡˈzɪstəns] n. 共存

3. coincidence [kəʊˈɪnsɪdəns] n. 巧合
『co共同+incidence发生→（两个）事件同时发生→巧合』

[C, U] （令人吃惊的）巧合，巧事
"I'm going to Paris next week." "What a coincidence! So am I." "我准备下周去巴黎。""真巧! 我也去。"

By (sheer) coincidence, I met the person we'd been discussing the next day.
真是巧了，我在第二天遇见了我们一直在谈论的那个人。

▶**coincide** [ˌkəʊɪnˈsaɪd] vi. 相符；巧合
Our holidays don't coincide. 我们的假期不在同一时间。
It's a pity our trips to New York don't coincide.
真遗憾我们不能同一时间去纽约旅行。
Her arrival coincided with our departure.
她来到时我们正好离开。

4. cooperate [kəʊˈɒpəreɪt] v. 合作；配合
『co共同+operate操作→一起工作→合作』
（BrE also co-operate）

❶ [V] ~ (with sb) (in/on sth) 合作，协作
The two groups agreed to cooperate with each other.
这两个组同意相互协作。

❷ [V] ~ (with sb) (in/on sth) 配合
Their captors told them they would be killed unless they cooperated. 抓住他们的人说如果他们不配合就杀掉他们。

▶**cooperation** [kəʊˌɒpəˈreɪʃn] n. 合作；配合

▶**cooperative** [kəʊˈɒpərətɪv] adj. 合作的；配合的

② col-, cor- 用在同辅音词根前，表示"共同，一起"

1. colleague [ˈkɒliːg] n. 同事；同行
『col共同+league团，联盟→同在一个联盟里→同事』

2. collate [kəˈleɪt] vt. 校对，核对；整理
『col共同+late放→放到一起看→校对』

to collect information together from different sources in order to examine and compare it
If you collate the latter with the earlier edition, you will find many parts have been rewritten.
你若将新版与旧版对照，会发现许多部分都改写了。
They have begun to collate their own statistics on racial abuse. 他们已经开始整理自己有关种族虐待的统计数据。

3. collaborate [kəˈlæbəreɪt] vi. 合作，协作〈P200〉
『col共同+labor劳动+ate表动词→一起工作→合作』

4. collateral [kəˈlætərəl] n. 担保物；adj. 附带的〈P201〉
『col共同，一起+later边+al…的→边挨着边的→并列的→附带的』

5. corrupt [kəˈrʌpt] adj. 贪污的；腐败的〈P283〉
『cor一起+rupt破，断裂→（行贿人和受贿人）一起使（制度）破裂→贪污的；腐败的』

③ com- 用在唇音 m, b, p 前，表示"共同，一起"

1. combine [kəmˈbaɪn] v.（使）结合；混合
『com一起+bine捆→捆在一起→结合』

❶ ~ (sth) (with sth) | ~ A and B (together)
Several factors had combined to ruin our plans.
几种因素加在一起毁了我们的计划。
Combine the eggs with a little flour.
把蛋和少量的面粉搅匀。

❷ [VN] ~ A and/with B 兼有，兼备；使融合（或并存）
The hotel combines comfort with convenience.
这家旅馆既舒适又方便。
This model combines a telephone and fax machine.
这种型号同时具备电话机和传真机的功能。

❸ [VN] ~ A and/with B 兼做，兼办
The trip will combine business with pleasure.
此次旅行将把出差和娱乐结合起来。

2. commemorate [kəˈmeməreɪt] vt. 纪念〈P218〉
『com一起，共同+ memor记忆+ ate表动词→纪念』

3. compassion [kəmˈpæʃn] n. 怜悯，同情〈P244〉
『com共同+passion强烈情感→有共同的感情→同情』

4. component [kəmˈpəʊnənt] n. 组成部分〈P261〉
『com共同+pone放，放置（去e)+ent表形容词或名词→共同放到一起→组成的；成分』

5. compress [kəmˈpres , ˈkɒmpres] v. 压缩；精简〈P269〉
『com一起+press压→压到一起→压缩；精简』

④ con- 用于其他情况，表示"共同，一起"

1. concentrate [ˈkɒnsntreɪt] v. 集中；专心
『con一起+centr中心+ate表动词→一起在中心上→集中』

~ (sth) (on sth/on doing sth) 集中（注意力，精力）做某事
to spend more time doing one particular thing than others
I can't concentrate with all that noise going on.
吵闹声不绝于耳，我无法集中精神。
It was up to him to **concentrate on** his studies and make something of himself.
是否能专心学习并取得一定成就就要靠他自己。
I decided to concentrate all my efforts on finding somewhere to live. 我决定全力以赴找个住的地方。

▶**concentration** [ˌkɒnsnˈtreɪʃn] n. 关注

2. consolidate [kənˈsɒlɪdeɪt] v. 巩固
『con一起+solid坚固+ate表动词→使坚固到一起→巩固』

to make a position of power or success stronger so that it is more likely to continue
With this new movie he has consolidated his position as the country's leading director.
他新执导的影片巩固了他作为全国最佳导演的地位。

3. contact [ˈkɒntækt] n. & vt. 联系，联络〈P321〉
『con一起+tact接触→接触到一起→联络，联系』

4. context [ˈkɒntekst] n. 语境，上下文〈P332〉
『con一起+text编织→编织在一起（来理解）→语境』

5. conclude [kənˈkluːd] v. 推断；结束；达成〈P136〉

『con一起+clude关闭→（把前面的内容）关闭到一起→推断；结束』

6. confirm [kənˈfɜːm] v. 证实；确认〈P173〉
『con一起+firm坚定→一起坚定（某事）→证实；确认』

7. conflict [ˈkɒnflɪkt] n. & v. 冲突〈P174〉
『con一起+flict打击→（两边）一起打斗→冲突』

8. confuse [kənˈfjuːz] v. 使困惑；混淆〈P181〉
『con共同+fuse流→流到一起→混合到一起分不开→困惑』

9. congress [ˈkɒŋgres] n. （美）国会；议会〈P189〉
『con一起+gress行走→走到一起（商量国家大事）→国会』

前缀18. contra- 表示"反对，相反"

1. contrary [ˈkɒntrəri] adj. 相反的
『contra相反+ry…的→相反的』

❶ 相反的
Contrary to popular belief, many cats dislike milk.
与普通的看法相反，许多猫不喜欢牛奶。
contrary advice/opinions/arguments
完全相反的建议/观点/论点

❷ **on the contrary** 与此相反；恰恰相反
"It must have been terrible." "On the contrary, I enjoyed every minute." "那一定很糟糕。" "恰恰相反，我非常喜欢。"

❸ **quite the contrary** 恰恰相反，正相反
I don't find him funny at all. Quite the contrary.
正相反，我觉得他一点儿也不可笑。

❹ **to the contrary** 相反的
Show me some evidence to the contrary.
给我看看有什么相反的证据吧。

2. contraband [ˈkɒntrəbænd] n. 禁运品，走私货
『contra相反+band(=ban)禁止→不顾禁止（携带）→走私货』

The ship was found not to be carrying any contraband.
并未发现这艘船上载有任何违禁物品。

3. contradict [ˌkɒntrəˈdɪkt] v. 反驳；相矛盾〈P149〉
『contra相反+ dict说→说相反的话→相矛盾；反驳』

4. contravene [ˌkɒntrəˈviːn] v. 违犯，违反（法律或规则）〈P346〉
『contra相反+vene来→向相反的方向来→违反』

前缀19. counter- 表示"反对；相反"

1. counteract [ˌkaʊntərˈækt] vt. 抵消；抵抗
『counter相反+act行动→相反的行动→抵消』

To counteract something means to reduce its effect by doing something that produces an opposite effect.
These exercises aim to counteract the effects of stress and tension. 这些训练旨在抵消压力与紧张的影响。
Our bodies produce antibodies to counteract disease.
我们的身体能产生抗体以抵抗疾病。

2. counterattack [ˈkaʊntərəˌtæk] n. & v. 反攻，反击
『counter相反+attack攻击→对着攻击→反攻』

3. counterclockwise [ˌkaʊntəˈklɒkwaɪz] adv. & adj. 逆时针方向地（的）
『counter相反+ clockwise顺时针地（的）→逆时针地（的）』

4. counterpart [ˈkaʊntəpɑːt] n. 职位（或作用）相当的人
『counter相反+part部分→相对应的部分→对应的人或物』

a person or thing that has the same position or function as sb/sth else in a different place or situation
The Foreign Minister held talks with the Chinese counterpart.
外交部长与中国外交部长举行了会谈。

5. counterfeit [ˈkaʊntəfɪt] adj. 仿造的 vt. & n.仿造
『counter相反+feit做→做的与原物不同的东西→仿造』

He admitted possessing and delivering counterfeit currency.
他供认持有并散播假币。

6. counterstrike [ˈkaʊntəstraɪk] n. & v. 反攻，反击
『counter相反+strike攻击→对着攻击→反攻』

小贴士 游戏"反恐精英"的英文名称为CS，是counter strike的首字母缩写，其字面意思为"反攻"。

前缀20. de- 表示"去掉；离开；毁坏""向下；下降""相反动作"

① 相当于"away, off"，表示 "去掉；离开；毁坏"

1. decapitate [dɪˈkæpɪteɪt] vt. 杀头，斩首〈P122〉
『de去掉+capit头+ate表动词→去掉头→斩首』

2. decode [ˌdiːˈkəʊd] vt. 译（码），解（码）
『de去掉+ code密码→去掉密码→破译』
反义词 **encode** [ɪnˈkəʊd] vt. 编码

3. deforest [ˌdiːˈfɒrɪst] vt. 清除…上的树林
『de去掉+forest树林→清除树林』

4. desalt [diːˈsɔːlt] vt. 脱盐，除去盐分
『de去掉+ salt 盐→除去盐分』

5. decease [dɪˈsiːs] n. (law or formal) 死亡；亡故
『de离开+cease停止→（生命）停止离开→死亡』

6. derail [dɪˈreɪl] v. (使)脱轨；使离开正常进程
『de离开+ rail铁轨→使（火车）脱轨』

[V] The train derailed and plunged into the river.
火车脱轨栽进了河里。
But the interest rate proposed could still derail the plan.
不过，方案中提议的利率仍可能使该计划流产。

7. depart [dɪˈpɑːt] v. 离开；离职〈P243〉
『de离开+part分开→离开→离开；离职』

8. detach [dɪˈtætʃ] v. 拆卸〈P322〉
『de去掉；离开+tach接触→使不接触→拆开』

9. defame [dɪˈfeɪm] vt. 诬蔑，诽谤，中伤
『de去掉；取消；毁+ fame名声→毁掉名声→诽谤』

[VN] (formal) 诬蔑，诽谤，中伤
to harm sb by saying or writing bad or false things about them
The article is an attempt to defame an honest man.
这篇文章旨在诋毁一个正直的人。

▶**defamatory** [dɪˈfæmətri] adj. 诽谤的，中伤的
『defame诽谤，中伤（去e）+atory有…性质的→诽谤的，中伤的』

10. deform [dɪˈfɔːm] v. 改变或损坏…的外形；使成畸形
〈P178〉
『de去掉；取消；毁+form形状→把形状弄坏→损坏外形；使畸形』

11. deface [dɪˈfeɪs] vt. 损伤…的外貌（尤指乱涂、乱写）
〈P161〉
『de去掉；取消；毁+face表面→把表面弄坏→损伤表面』

② 相当于"down"，表示"下降，降低，减少"

1. delay [dɪˈleɪ] n. & v. 耽搁；推迟；磨蹭
『de向下+lay放置→向后面放→推迟』

❶ ~(doing) sth. 推迟（做某事）
For sentimental reasons I wanted to delay my departure until June.
因为感情方面的原因，我想把离开的日期延迟至6月。
Big companies often delay paying their bills.
大的公司总是延期付账单。

❷ vt. (usually passive) 耽搁
Can you delay him in some way?
你能想办法拖住他一会儿吗？
Thousands of commuters were delayed for over an hour.
数千名乘车上下班的人被耽搁了一个多小时。

❸ vi. （故意）拖延，磨蹭
If he delayed any longer, the sun would be up.
如果他再拖延，太阳就要出来了。

❹ n. 耽搁；推迟；磨蹭
We apologise for the delay in answering your letter.
来信收悉，迟复为歉。
Report it to the police without delay (= immediately).
赶快将此事报告警方。

词义辨析 〈P365第22〉
推迟，延期 delay, postpone, put off, defer, adjourn

2. design [dɪˈzaɪn] n. & v. 设计
『de向下+ sign标记→向下做标记→设计』

3. devalue [ˌdiːˈvæljuː] v. 贬值；贬低
『de向下；降低，减少+value价值→减少价值→ 贬值』

They spread tales about her in an attempt to devalue her work.
他们散布一些有关她的流言，企图贬低她的工作。
India has devalued the rupee by about eleven percent.
印度已将卢比贬值了约 11%。

4. decline [dɪˈklaɪn] n. & vi. 减少；下降；衰落〈P135〉
『de向下+cline倾斜→向下倾斜→下降；衰落』

5. decrease [dɪˈkriːs] v. 减少，减小，降低〈P141〉
『de向下+crease增长→向下增加→减少』

6. demote [ˌdiːˈməʊt] vt.使降职；使（球队）降级〈P225〉
『de向下+mote→向下动→降级』

7. deposit [dɪˈpɒzɪt] n. 定金；存款；沉淀物〈P264〉
『de向下+posit放，放置→先放下去的钱→定金，存款』

8. depress [dɪˈpres] vt. 使抑郁；使减少〈P269〉
『de向下+ press压→（感到心情）向下压→压抑』

9. descend [dɪˈsend] v. 降临；下来〈P287〉
『de向下+scend 爬，攀→向下爬→下来』

③ 表示"相反"

1. deactivate [ˌdiːˈæktɪveɪt] v. 使停止工作

『de相反+activate使活动→使处于不活动的状态→使停止工作』

Do you know how to deactivate the alarm?
你知道如何让闹钟不响吗？

2. decompose [ˌdiːkəmˈpəʊz] v. 腐烂；（使）分解
『de相反+compose组成→分解』

[V] a decomposing corpse 正在腐烂的尸体
[VN] a decomposed body 已经腐烂的尸体

3. decentralize [ˌdiːˈsentrəlaɪz] v. 分散；下放（权力）
『de相反+centralize使中心化→分散』

If you were a manager, would you decentralize authority?
如果你是一位管理者，你愿意实行分权吗？
It is necessary to decentralize traffic flow.
治理交通拥堵需要分散交通流。

4. denationalize [ˌdiːˈnæʃnəlaɪz] vt. 使私有化；使非国有化
『de相反+nationalize国有化→使非国有化』

5. denuclearization [diːˌnjuːklɪərɪˈzeʃən] n.无核化
『de相反+nuclear核+ize构成动词（去e）+ation, 构成名词→无核化』

6. destruction [dɪˈstrʌkʃn] n. 破坏〈P318〉
『de相反+struct建设+ion 表动作→破坏』

前缀21. deca-=ten，表示"十"

1. decade [ˈdekeɪd] n. 十年
『deca十+（a）de表名词→十年』

As many as ten-million children will have been infected with the virus by the end of the decade.
到这个十年结束时，多达千万的儿童将会感染上这种病毒。

小贴士 decade "十年"，只用于表示时间，two decades "二十年"，decade要用复数。
dozen "十二"、 score "二十" 表示数量，表示具体数字时不用复数。three dozen 三打；two score 四十个。

2. decagon [ˈdekəgən] n. 十角形，十边形
『deca十+ gon角→十角形』

3. decagram [ˈdekəgræm] n. 十克
『deca十+ gram克→十克』

4. decameter [ˈdekəˌmiːtə] n. 十米
『deca十+ meter米→十米』

小贴士 常见的数量的表示法参看P6前缀15

前缀22. deci- 表示"十分之一"

1. decibel [ˈdesɪbel] n. <物>分贝
『deci十分之一+ bel贝→十分之一贝→分贝』

2. decigram [ˈdesɪgræm] n. 分克
『deci十分之一+ gram克→十分之一克→分克』

3. deciliter [ˈdesɪˌliːtə] n. 分升
『deci十分之一+ liter升→十分之一升→分升』

4. decimeter [ˈdesɪˌmiːtə] n. 分米
『deci十分之一+ meter米→十分之一米→分米』

小贴士 常见的数量的表示法参看P6前缀15

前缀23. di- 表示"两个"或"离开，分开"

① di- 表示"两个"

1. dilemma [dɪˈlemə] n. 进退两难，困境

『di二，两+lemma争论→两种争论不知咋办→困境』

He was faced with the dilemma of whether or not to return to his country. 要不要回国，他进退两难。

2. dioxide [daɪˈɒksaɪd] n. [化]二氧化物

『di二，两+ox氧+ide化合物→二氧化物』

▶**carbon dioxide** [ˈkɑːbən daɪˈɒksaɪd] n. 二氧化碳

3. diploma [dɪˈpləʊmə] n. 毕业文凭；学位证书

『di二，两+pl折叠的+oma名词后缀→折叠成两部分的→毕业证』

4. diphthong [ˈdɪfθɒŋ] n. 双元音

『di二，两+phthong声音→双元音』

5. disyllable [dɪˈsɪləbl] n. 双音节词

『di二，两+syllable音节→双音节词』

② di- 相当于"away, off"，表示"离开，分开"

1. divorce [dɪˈvɔːs] n. & v. 离婚

『di分开，离开+vorce (= vert转)→从（配偶）身边转开→离婚』

The marriage ended in divorce in 1996.
这桩婚姻在1996年以离婚告终。
They're getting divorced. 他们要离婚了。

2. differ [ˈdɪfə(r)] vi. 不同 <P167>

『dif分开+fer带来，拿来→带向不同（的方向）→不同』

3. digress [daɪˈgres] vi. 离题 <P189>

『di分开，离开+ gress走→离开（话题）→离题』

4. diminish [dɪˈmɪnɪʃ] v.（不断）减小，减弱 <P21>

『di离开+min小+ish使→使小下去→缩小，减弱』

前缀24. dia-=through, between, across，表示"穿过；两者之间"

1. diameter [daɪˈæmɪtə(r)] n. 直径

『dia穿过；两者之间+ meter测量→穿过（圆心）测量→直径』

2. diagonal [daɪˈægənl] n. 对角线 adj. 对角线的 <P185>

『dia穿过；两者之间+gon角+al表物→穿过两个对角（的线）→对角线』

3. diagram [ˈdaɪəgræm] n. 图表；示意图；图解 <P187>

『dia穿过；两者之间+gram写，画+交叉着画→图表』

4. dialect [ˈdaɪəlekt] n. 方言 <P204>

『dia二者之间+lect讲，读→在一部分人之间说→方言』

5. dialogue [ˈdaɪəlɒg] n. 对话 <P210>

『dia穿过；两者之间+ logue说话→两人对讲→对话』

前缀25. dis- 表示"离开，分开""不"或"相反动作"

① dis- 相当于"away, off"，表示"离开，分开"

1. disguise [dɪsˈgaɪz] n. & v. 假扮，伪装

『dis离开+guise引导→向别的地方引导→伪装』

❶ [VN]~ sb (as sb/sth) 假扮；装扮；伪装
She disguised herself as a boy. 她女扮男装。
They got in disguised as security guards.
他们装扮成安保人员混了进去。

❷ [VN] 掩蔽；掩饰
to hide sth or change it, so that it cannot be recognised
She made no attempt to disguise her surprise.
她毫不掩饰自己的惊奇。
She couldn't disguise the fact that she felt uncomfortable.
她无法掩饰她那不安的心情。

❸ [C, U] 伪装物
She wore glasses and a wig as a disguise.
她戴着眼镜和假发作为伪装。
The star travelled in disguise (= wearing a disguise) .
这位明星化了装去旅行。

2. disburse [dɪsˈbɜːs] vt.（从资金中）支付

『dis离开+burse(=purse)钱包→支付』

to pay money to sb from a large amount that has been collected for a purpose
The World Bank and the IMF have agreed to disburse financial aid to the country.
世界银行和国际货币基金组织已同意给该国拨援助款。

3. discard [dɪˈskɑːd] vt. 丢弃

『dis离开+card卡片→使卡片离开→丢弃』

to get rid of sth that you no longer want or need
The room was littered with discarded newspapers.
那房间里到处是丢弃的报纸。

4. dissipate [ˈdɪsɪpeɪt] v.（使）消散，消失；挥霍，浪费

『dis离开+sip扔+ate表动词→（使）离开→消失；浪费』

❶（使）消散，消失；驱散
to gradually become or make sth become weaker until it disappears
[V] Eventually, his anger dissipated. 他的愤怒终于平息了。
[VN] Her laughter soon dissipated the tension in the air.
她的笑声很快消除了紧张气氛。

❷ [VN] 浪费（金钱、时间或精力）；挥霍
When someone dissipates money, time, or effort, they waste it in a foolish way.（同义词 squander）
He's not the first young aristocrat to dissipate his fortune in gambling.
他不是第一个在赌场上把财产挥霍一空的年轻贵族。

5. dispel [dɪˈspel] v. 驱散；消除 <P248>

『dis离开+pel驱动；推→推开→驱散』

6. disrupt [dɪsˈrʌpt] vt. 扰乱，打乱 <P283>

『dis离开+rupt破，断裂→断开（使不能正常进行）→扰乱』

7. distract [dɪˈstrækt] vt. 使分心 <P336>

『dis离开+tract拉→把（心）拉开→分心』

8. distribute [dɪˈstrɪbjuːt] vt. 分发 <P338>

『dis离开+tribute给予→（分别）给出去→分配；分散』

9. dismiss [dɪsˈmɪs] v. 解雇；解散 <P224>

『dis离开+miss(=send)送，放出→把（人）送走→解雇；解散』

② dis- 意为"不，无"，表示否定或相反

1. disappear [ˌdɪsəˈpɪə(r)] vi. 不见，消失

『dis表相反+ appear出现→消失』

词义辨析 <P379第88>

消失 vanish, disappear, evaporate

2. disapprove [ˌdɪsəˈpruːv] v. 不赞成；反对
『dis表相反+ approve赞成→不赞成』

3. disarm [dɪsˈɑːm] v. 解除武装；裁军
『dis表相反+ arm武装→解除武装』

❶ [VN] 解除（某人）的武装
Most of the rebels were captured and disarmed.
大部分叛乱分子被俘获并解除了武装。

❷ [V] 裁军

4. discharge [dɪsˈtʃɑːdʒ] n. & v. 允许离开（医院、军队）；放出（液体、气体、电流等）；开（枪、炮等）
『dis表相反+ charge充（电）；装（弹药）→放出（电流）；开（枪炮等）』

❶ v. 允许…离开（医院、军队）；从（监狱）释放
The accused man was found not guilty and discharged.
被告男子被判无罪而获释。
He has a broken nose but may be discharged today.
他鼻梁断了，但或许今天就能出院。

❷ v. 放出（液体、气体、电流等）；排放
Lightning is caused by clouds discharging electricity.
闪电是由云层放电产生的。
The factory was fined for discharging chemicals into the river.
这家工厂因往河里排放化学物质而被罚款。

❸ [VN] (formal) 射出；开火
Arrows discharged at the enemy. 箭射向敌人。
The rifle was discharged accidently. 步枪走火了。

▶**charge** [tʃɑːdʒ] vt. & n. 收费；控告；负责

❶ [VN] ~ (sb/sth) for sth | ~ (sb) sth (for sth) 收费
What did they charge for the repairs?
他们收了多少修理费？

❷ [VN] ~ sb (with sth/with doing sth) 控告；指责
He was charged with murder. 他被指控犯有谋杀罪。
Opposition MPs charged the minister with neglecting her duty. 反对党议员指责女部长玩忽职守。

❸ [V] 猛攻；向…冲去
We charged at the enemy. 我们向敌人发起冲锋。
The children charged down the stairs. 孩子们冲下了楼梯。

❹ [VN] ~ (sth) (up) 给…充电
Before use, the battery must be charged.
电池使用前必须充电。

❺ [VN] 为（枪）装弹药

❻ [VN] 使负责，使管理
The committee has been charged with the development of sport in the region.
委员会已被赋予在该地区发展体育运动的职责。

❼ [C, U] ~ (for sth) （商品和服务所需的）要价，收费
Delivery is free of charge. 免费送货。

❽ [C, U] 指控；控告
They decided to drop the charges against the newspaper and settle out of court.
他们已决定撤销对那家报纸的指控，在庭外和解。

❾ [U] 主管；掌管
He **took charge of** the farm after his father's death.
他在父亲去世后掌管了这片农场。
Who's in charge here? 这儿谁管事啊？
Mother puts the baby **in the charge of** the baby-sitter while she is out. 母亲外出时，将婴儿交给临时保姆照顾。

5. discomfort [dɪsˈkʌmfət] n. 不舒服；不自在
『dis表相反+ comfort舒服→不舒服』

❶ [U] 轻微的病痛；不舒服
You will experience some minor discomfort during the treatment. 治疗中你会稍感不适。

❷ [U] 不安；不自在
John's presence caused her considerable discomfort.
约翰在场使她颇为尴尬。

❸ [C] (formal) 使人不舒服的事物；痛苦

6. disconnect [ˌdɪskəˈnekt] vt. 断开
『dis表相反+ connect连接→断开』

❶ [VN] ~ sth (from sth) 切断（煤气、水或电的供应）
First, disconnect the boiler from the water mains.
先将锅炉与供水总管断开。

❷ [VN] ~ sth (from sth) 使分离；使脱离
The ski had become disconnected from the boot.
滑雪板与靴子脱离了。

❸ [VN] [usually passive] 使（电话线路）中断
We were suddenly disconnected.
我们的电话突然断了。

❹ ~ (sb) (from sth) [often passive] （与互联网）断开
[VN] I keep getting disconnected when I'm online.
我上网时不断掉线。

7. discount [ˈdɪskaʊnt] n. & v. 折扣
『dis表相反+ count算在内→不算在内→打折』

[C, U] ~ on/off sth 折扣
They're offering a 10% discount on all sofas this month.
本月他们给沙发售价统统打九折。
They were selling everything at a discount.
他们销售的所有商品都打折。

8. discourage [dɪsˈkʌrɪdʒ] v. 阻拦；阻止
『dis不；无+courage勇气→使没有勇气（做事）』

❶ ~ sth | ~ sb from doing sth 阻拦；阻止；劝阻
His parents tried to discourage him from being an actor.
他的父母试图阻止他去当演员。

❷ [VN] ~ sb (from doing sth) 使灰心，使丧失信心
Don't be discouraged by the first failure—try again!
不要因第一次失败就灰心丧气——再试一次吧！
反义词 **encourage** [ɪnˈkʌrɪdʒ] vt. 鼓励

9. disease [dɪˈziːz] n. 疾病
『dis表相反+ease 舒适；缓和→不舒适→有疾病』

词义辨析 <P366第26> **疾病 illness, disease, disorder, infection, condition, bug, sickness**

10. dishonest [dɪsˈɒnɪst] adj. 不诚实的
『dis表相反+ honest诚实的→不诚实的』

11. dislike [dɪsˈlaɪk] v. 厌恶；不喜欢
『dis表相反+ like喜欢→不喜欢』

12. disorder [dɪsˈɔːdə(r)] n. 混乱；骚乱；失调
『dis表相反+order有序→无秩序无条理→混乱』

❶ [U] 杂乱，凌乱 a situation in which things or people are very untidy or disorganized
Everything was in disorder, but nothing seemed to be missing.
一切都乱七八糟，但似乎没有丢失什么东西。

❷ [C, U] 骚乱；动乱 violent behaviour of large groups of people
He called on the authorities to stop public disorder.
他呼吁当局制止公众骚乱。

❸ [C] (身心机能的)失调，紊乱
mental disorders 精神错乱
a rare nerve disorder 一种罕见的精神疾病

词义辨析 <P366第26> 疾病 illness, disease, disorder, infection, condition, bug, sickness

词义辨析 <P366第29> 混乱 disorder, chaos, confusion, mess

13. disclose [dɪsˈkləʊz] vt. 揭露 <P136>
『dis表相反+ close关闭→揭发；泄露』

14. discover [dɪˈskʌvə(r)] vt. 发现 <P138>
『dis表相反+ cover遮，盖→揭开→发现』

前缀26. e-, ec-, ef-, es-, ex-, extra-=out，表示"出来；向外；外面的"

① e-=out，表示"出，出来"

1. enormous [ɪˈnɔːməs] adj. 巨大的 <P234>
『e超出+norm正常+ous表形容词→超出正常的→巨大的』

2. elect [ɪˈlekt] vt. 选举 adj. 候任的 <P201>
『e出来+lect选择→（把某一职务的人）选择出来→选举』

3. eject [iˈdʒekt] v. 弹出；喷出；驱逐 <P196>
『e出来+ject投掷，扔→投掷出来→弹出；喷出；驱逐』

4. emerge [iˈmɜːdʒ] vi. 浮现 <P218>
『e出来+merge沉没→从沉没中露出了→浮现』

5. eliminate [ɪˈlɪmɪneɪt] vt. 排除；除掉 <P207>
『e出+limin限制+ate表动词→限制在外→消除』

② ec-, ef-, es-=out，表示"向外"（ef用在词根以 f 开头的词前；es-用在词根以 c, s 开头的词前）

1. eccentric [ɪkˈsentrɪk] adj. 古怪的；n.古怪的人
『ec(=e)出+centr中心+ic表形容词→偏离中心的→古怪的』

considered by other people to be strange or unusual
eccentric behaviour/clothes 古怪的行为/奇装异服
Most people considered him a harmless eccentric.
多数人都认为他是一个无伤大雅的怪人。

2. escape [ɪˈskeɪp] v. & n. 逃脱；泄露
『es出来+cape捕获→从捕获中出来→逃脱』

❶ [V] ~ (from sb/sth) （从监禁或管制中）逃出
He escaped from prison this morning.
他今天早上从监狱里逃跑了。

❷ ~ (from sth) 逃脱或逃避（不愉快或危险处境）
[V] She managed to escape from the burning car.
她设法从燃烧的汽车里逃了出来。
[VN] She was lucky to escape punishment.
她逃脱惩罚真是幸运。

❸ [V] （气体、液体等）漏；泄漏；渗出
Put a lid on to prevent heat escaping.
盖上盖子，以免热气跑了。

❹ [C, U] ~ (from sth) 逃跑；逃脱；逃避；泄漏
I had a narrow escape. 我是死里逃生。
There was no hope of escape from her disastrous marriage.

她无望从不幸的婚姻中解脱出来。
an escape of gas 漏气

❺ Esc键，退出键
Press escape to get back to the menu.
按Esc键，退回到菜单。

3. efface [ɪˈfeɪs] vt. 抹去；擦掉 <P161>
『ef出去+face脸，表面→使从表面出去→擦掉』

4. effect [ɪˈfekt] n. 效果，影响；v. 实施 <P163>
『ef出来+ fect做→所做的出了效果→影响』

③ ex-=out，表示"出去，出来；外面的"

1. exact [ɪɡˈzækt] vt. 强求；勒索；强迫
『ex出来+act行动→通过行动强行向别人要出自己所需→强求，勒索』

When someone exacts something, they demand and obtain it from another person, especially because they are in a superior or more powerful position.
Already he has exacted a written apology from the chairman of the commission.
他已经强行要求委员会主席作出书面道歉。

►**exacting** [ɪɡˈzæktɪŋ] adj. （人或事）要求苛刻的
You use exacting to describe something or someone that demands hard work and a great deal of care.
The Duke was not well enough to carry out such an exacting task. 公爵身体不太好，无法执行那么艰巨的任务。
He was an exacting man to work for.
他是个苛刻的人。

2. exile [ˈeksaɪl] n. 流放；流放者 vt. 流放；流亡
『ex出来+ile→拿、带、召集→流放；流亡』

❶ [U, sing.] 流放；流亡；放逐
the state of being sent to live in another country that is not your own, especially for political reasons or as a punishment
He returned after 40 years of exile. 他流放40年后归来。
He is now living in exile in Egypt. 他目前流亡埃及。

❷ [C] 被流放者；流亡者
political exiles 政治流亡者

❸ [VN] 流放；流亡
the party's exiled leaders 该党的流亡领袖

3. exotic [ɪɡˈzɒtɪk] adj. 具有异国情调的；外来的
『exo(=ex)外面的+tic具有…性质的→具有异国情调的』
Something that is exotic is unusual and interesting, usually because it comes from or is related to a distant country.
She travels to all kinds of exotic locations all over the world.
她走遍了全世界所有具有奇异风情的地方。

4. external [ɪkˈstɜːnl] adj. 外面的；国外的；外部的
『ex外面的+tern+al…的→外面的』

❶ 外部的，外面的
connected with or located on the outside of sth/sb
the external walls of the building 建筑物的外墙

The lotion is for external use only. 此涂液仅限外用。

❷ 对外的，与外国有关的

The government is committed to reducing the country's external debt. 政府决心减少本国的外债。

the Minister of State for External Affairs 外交大臣

❸ 外界的，外部的

happening or coming from outside a place, an organization, your particular situation, etc.

A combination of internal and external factors caused the company to close down.

内外因结合导致了这家公司的倒闭。

Many external influences can affect your state of mind.

许多外在因素都可能影响人的心情。

反义词 **internal** [ɪnˈtɜːnl] adj. 里面的；国内的；内部的

『in里面+tern+al…的』

❶ 内部的；里面的

inside something rather than outside

the internal structure of a building 大楼的内部结构

❷ 国内的，内部事务的

internal affairs/trade/markets 内政；国内贸易/市场

an internal flight 一架国内航班

❸（机构）内部的；体内的；内心的

internal divisions within the company 公司内部的各部门

internal organs/injuries 内脏；内伤

The medicine is not for internal use. 这种药不可内服。

5. **express** [ɪkˈspres] v. 表达；adj. 特快的〈P268〉

『ex出+press挤压→把（思想）挤出来→表达』

6. **export** vt. [ɪkˈspɔːt] n. & vt. 出口〈P266〉

『ex出去+port港口→（货物）出港→出口』

（vt. [ɪkˈspɔːt]　n. [ˈekspɔːt]　）

7. **expose** [ɪkˈspəʊz] vt. 揭露；露出；使接触〈P263〉

『ex出来+pose放置→放出来→暴露』

8. **exclude** [ɪkˈskluːd] vt. 不包括〈P137〉

『ex出去，外面+ clude关闭→关在外面→不包括』

9. **exhume** [eksˈhjuːm] vt. 挖出，发掘出〈P192〉

『ex出去+ hume土→出土→挖出』

10. **expel** [ɪkˈspel] vt. 开除；驱逐；排出〈P248〉

『ex出去+ pel驱动，推→推出去→开除』

11. **extract** [ˈekstrækt] vt. 提取；摘录；拔出〈P336〉

『ex出+tract拉→拉出来→提炼出；拔；摘录』

12. **exceed** [ɪkˈsiːd] vt. 超过〈P126〉

『ex出去+ceed走→走出固定范围→ 超出』

④ ex- 还可表示"前面的，前任的"

1. **ex-president** [ˈeksˈprezɪdənt] n. 前总统

『ex前面的，前任的+president总统→前总统』

2. **ex-wife** [ˈekswaɪf] n. 前妻

『ex前面的，前任的+wife妻子→前妻』

⑤ extra-=out，表示"以外，额外"

1. **extraordinary** [ɪkˈstrɔːdnri] adj. 非凡的

『extra以外+ordinary普通的→超出普通的→格外的』

❶ adj. 意想不到的；令人惊奇的；奇怪的

unexpected, surprising or strange

It's extraordinary that he managed to sleep through the party.

真想不到他竟然从聚会开始一直睡到结束。

❷ 非凡的，卓越的

She was a truly extraordinary woman.

她是位非常杰出的女性。

2. **extrasolar** [ˌekstrəˈsəʊlə(r)] adj.（存在于或来自）太阳系以外的

『extra以外+solar太阳的→太阳系以外的』

3. **extracurricular** [ˌekstrəkəˈrɪkjʊlə] adj. 课外的（学校课程以外的）〈P147〉

『extra以外+curricular课程的→课外的』

前缀27. eco- 表示"生态"

1. **ecology** [iˈkɒlədʒi] n. 生态学；生态

『eco生态+logy…学→生态学』

❶ [C, U] 生态（环境），生态系统

When you talk about the ecology of a place, you are referring to the pattern and balance of relationships between plants, animals, people, and the environment in that place.

Development has been guided by a concern for the ecology of the area. 该地区的发展以注重生态为指导原则。

❷ [U] 生态学

▶ **ecologist** [iˈkɒlədʒɪst] n. 生态学家

In the opinion polls the ecologists reached 20 percent.

在民意调查中，生态学家的比例达到了20%。

2. **ecosystem** [ˈiːkəʊsɪstəm] n. 生态系统

『eco生态+system系统→生态系统』

all the plants and living creatures in a particular area considered in relation to their physical environment

Poyang Lake wetland ecosystem is a complex, open and interactive system.

鄱阳湖湿地生态系统是一个复杂、开放的交互系统。

3. **ecotourism** [ˈiːkəʊtʊərɪzəm] n. 生态旅游

『eco生态+tourism旅游→生态旅游』

Ecotourism is the business of providing holidays and related services which are not harmful to the environment of the area.

前缀28. en-（em-, -en），表示"（使）进入…当中；（使）进入…状态"

（em-是 en-的变体，在双唇音 p, b, m 前用 em-）

① en-, em- 相当于in，表示"（使）进入…当中"

1. **embed** [ɪmˈbed]　v. 嵌入

『em进入…之中+ bed温床→进入温床→嵌入』

~ sth (in sth) 把…牢牢地嵌入（或插入、埋入）

The bullet embedded itself in the wall. 子弹射进了墙里。

There is glass embedded in the cut.

有一片玻璃扎在伤口里。

2. **embody** [ɪmˈbɒdi] vt. 体现；包含

『em进入…之中+ body实体→（思想或品质）进入某个实体中→（实体）体现（思想或品质）』

❶ 体现，代表（思想或品质）

[VN] They embody traditional Chinese culture and history.

它们体现了中国的传统文化和历史。

❷ 包括，包含

[VN] The proposal has been embodied in a draft resolution.
那项提案包含在一份决议草案中。

3. embrace [ɪmˈbreɪs] n. & v. 拥抱；欣然接受 〈P119〉
『em进入…之中+ brace手臂；支架→进入手臂中→拥抱』

4. encounter [ɪnˈkaʊntə(r)] v. 遭遇；偶然碰到
『en使进入…里面+ counter相反→进入相反的（环境；方向）→遭遇；偶然碰到』

❶ [VN] 遭遇，遇到（尤指令人不快或困难的事）
We encountered a number of difficulties in the first week.
我们在第一周遇到了一些困难。
I had never encountered such resistance before.
我以前从未遇到过这么大的阻力。

❷ [VN] 偶然碰到
to meet sb, or discover or experience sth, especially sb/sth new, unusual or unexpected
She was the most remarkable woman he had ever encountered.
她是他所见到过的最出色的女性。

❸ noun ~ (with sb/sth) | ~ (between A and B)
（意外、突然或暴力的）相遇，邂逅；遭遇；冲突
The story describes the extraordinary encounter between a man and a dolphin.
这个故事描述了一个男人与一只海豚之间的奇遇。

词义辨析〈P368第35〉 **偶遇；遭遇 encounter, meet with, run across, run into, come across**

5. enlighten [ɪnˈlaɪtn] vt.启发，启蒙
『en使进入…之中+light光+en使进入…之中→进入光明→启发』

[VN] (formal) 启发；开导；阐明
to give sb information so that they understand sth better
If you know what is wrong with her, please enlighten me.
如果你知道她出什么问题了，请告诉我。
Nobody seemed to be anxious to enlighten me about the events that led up to the dispute.
没有人急于使我明白导致这场争执的事件。

小贴士 有light（光）才能看见事物，才能了解事物。
throw/shed light on 使了解； in the light of 鉴于，由于；
keep sb in the dark 使蒙在鼓里； highlight 高光；强调

6. enlist [ɪnˈlɪst] v. 参加，入伍；取得（帮助）
『en进入…之中+ list名单→进入（军队）名单→入伍』

❶ ~ (sb) (in/into/for sth) | ~ (sb) (as sth) （使）入伍；征募
[V] They both enlisted in 1915. 他俩都是1915年入伍的。
[VN] He was enlisted into the US Navy.
他应征加入了美国海军。

❷ ~ sth/sb (in sth) | ~ sb (as sth) 谋取（帮助、支持或参与）
[VN] They hoped to enlist the help of the public in solving the crime. 他们希望寻求公众协助破案。
We were enlisted as helpers. 我们应邀协助。

7. enrol [ɪnˈrəʊl] v. 招收（学生）；报名（学课程）
『en相当于on+roll名单→写到名单上→注册』
（美语拼作 enroll. enrolling; enrolled, enrolled）

If you **enrol** or **are enrolled** at an institution or on a course, you officially join it and pay a fee for it.

This school plans to enroll 100 students every year.

该校计划每年只招收100名学生。
She enrolled on a local Women Into Management course.
她报名参加了当地女性管理课程。
I thought I'd enrol you with an art group at the school.
我想我会在学校给你报一个艺术团体。

▶ **roll** [rəʊl] v. 滚动 n. 名册；卷

❶ （使）翻滚，滚动
[V] The ball rolled down the hill. 球滚下了山。
[VN] Delivery men were rolling barrels across the yard.
送货人正把桶滚到院子一边。
The traffic rolled slowly forwards. 车流缓缓地向前挪动。
rock'n roll music 摇滚音乐 (rock n. 岩石；v. 摇动)
a rolling stone gathers no moss
(saying) 滚石不生苔，频迁不聚财
roll up your sleeves 捋起袖子；准备动手；摩拳擦掌

❷ [C] ~ (of sth) 卷；卷轴
Wallpaper is sold in rolls. 壁纸论卷销售。
a chicken/cheese, etc. roll 鸡肉卷、奶酪卷等

❸ [C] 花名册；名单
The chairman called/took the roll. 主席点了名。

8. enclose [ɪnˈkləʊz] vt. （用墙、篱笆等）把…围起来；把…装入信封〈P119〉
『en使进入…里面+ close关闭→关闭到里面→围住；装入』

② en-(em-) 表示"（使）进入…状态"

1. enable [ɪˈneɪbl] vt. 使能够
『en使进入…状态+able有能力的→使能够』

enable sb to do sth 使某人能够做某事
The new test should enable doctors to detect the disease early.
新的检测手段应该能够使医生们尽早查出这种疾病。
This will enable the audience to sit in comfort while watching the shows. 这样能够让观众舒舒服服地坐着看表演。

2. enchant [ɪnˈtʃɑːnt] vt.使着迷；使陶醉
『en使进入…状态+chant咒语→（用咒语）使进入迷惑（状态）→使迷醉』

❶ [VN] 使着迷；使陶醉
You made me laugh, and in the evening, you'd enchant me with your stories.
你让我开怀大笑，晚上，你的故事让我那么着迷。

❷ [VN] 对…施魔法；使着魔
King Arthur hid his treasures here and Merlin enchanted the cave so that nobody should ever find them.
亚瑟王将他的财宝藏在这里，梅林对洞穴施了魔法，这样永远不会有人找到那些财宝。

▶ **chant** [tʃɑːnt] n. & v. 反复唱，反复喊

❶ [C] 反复呼喊的话语；重复唱的歌词
words or phrases that a group of people shout or sing again and again
The crowd broke into chants of "Out! Out!".
人群突然爆发出"下台！下台！"的反复呼喊声。

❷ [C, U] 圣歌；反复吟咏的祷文；单调的吟唱

❸ [V, VN] 反复唱（呼喊）；反复吟咏祷文
Demonstrators chanted slogans. 示威者们反复喊着口号。
Muslims chanted and prayed. 穆斯林们诵经、祈祷。

3. encode [ɪnˈkəʊd] vt. （将文字等）译成密码；编码
『en使进入…状态+code代码→使成为代码→编码』

The two parties encode confidential data in a form that is not directly readable by the other party.
双方将机密资料加密，这样对方就无法直接读取资料。

4. encourage [ɪnˈkʌrɪdʒ] vt. 鼓励
『en使进入···状态+ courage勇气→使进入有勇气做某事的状态→鼓励』

❶ [VN] ~ sb (in sth)｜encourage sb to do sth 鼓励，鼓动
We were greatly encouraged by the positive response of the public. 公众所持的肯定态度给了我们极大的鼓舞。
We want to encourage people to go fishing, not put them off.
我们希望鼓励人们去垂钓，而不是打消他们的热情。

❷ 刺激；助长
[VN] They claim that some computer games encourage violent behaviour in young children.
他们声称有些电脑游戏助长儿童的暴力行为。

反义词 **discourage** [dɪsˈkʌrɪdʒ] vt. 阻拦；阻止 〈P11〉

5. endanger [ɪnˈdeɪndʒə(r)] vt. 危及，使遭受危险
『en使进入···状态+ danger危险→使进入危险处境』

[VN] 使遭危险；危及；危害
The health of our children is being endangered by exhaust fumes. 我们孩子们的健康正受到排放出的废气的危害。
It is illegal and could endanger other people's lives.
这是非法的，可能会危及他人的生命。

6. enforce [ɪnˈfɔːs] vt. 强制执行；强行实施
『en使进入···状态+force力量→使用力量→强行实施』

❶ [VN] 强制执行（法律、规定等）
It's the job of the police to enforce the law.
警察的工作就是执法。
United Nations troops enforced a ceasefire in the area.
联合国军队在该地区强制执行停火命令。

❷ [VN]强迫；迫使
You can't enforce cooperation between the players.
你不能强迫玩家之间的合作。

7. enjoy [ɪnˈdʒɔɪ] v. 享受···的乐趣；享有
『en使进入···状态+joy快乐→使进入快乐状态→享受』

❶ enjoy (doing) sth 享受···的乐趣（常跟动名词作宾语）
We thoroughly enjoyed our time in New York.
我们在纽约的时间过得十分快活。
I enjoy playing tennis. 我喜欢打网球。

❷ ~ yourself 过得快活，玩得痛快
They all enjoyed themselves at the party.
他们在聚会上都玩得非常痛快。

❸ [VN] (formal) 享有
People in this country enjoy a high standard of living.
这个国家的人民享有很高的生活水平。
He's always enjoyed good health. 他一直都很健康。

8. enlarge [ɪnˈlɑːdʒ] v. 扩大，放大
『en使进入···状态+large大的→使变大→扩大』

9. enrich [ɪnˈrɪtʃ] vt. 使富有；使丰富
『en使进入···状态+rich富有的；丰富的→使富有；使丰富』

❶ [VN] 使富有
He used his position to enrich himself.
他利用职位之便敛财。

❷ [VN] 使丰富

The study of science has enriched all our lives.
科学研究丰富了我们的整个生活。

10. ensure [ɪnˈʃʊə(r)] vt. 确保；保证
『en使进入···状态+sure确信→使确信→保证』
（also **insure** especially in NAmE）

to make sure that sth happens or is definite
[VN] The book ensured his success.
这本书保证了他的成功。
[V (that)] Please ensure (that) all lights are switched off.
请确保所有的灯都关了。

11. entitle [ɪnˈtaɪtl] vt. 使有权利；命名
『en使+title标题→使成为标题→命名』
『en使+title头衔→使有···的头衔→使有权利做某事』

❶ [often passive] ~ sb to (do) sth 使享有权利；使有资格
Everyone's entitled to their own opinion.
人人都有权发表自己的意见。
This ticket does not entitle you to travel first class.
你拿这张票不能坐头等舱。

❷ [VN-N] [usually passive] 给···命名（或提名）
Her first novel was entitled "More Innocent Times".
她的第一部小说名叫《更天真的时代》。

12. enact [ɪˈnækt] vt. 通过（法律）；演出
『en使进入···状态+act法案；表演→使成为法律；使表演→通过（法律）；演出』

The authorities have failed so far to enact a law allowing unrestricted emigration.
到目前为止，当局未能通过允许自由移民的法律。
She often enacted the stories told to her by her father.
她经常把她父亲讲给她的那些故事表演出来。

13. endure [ɪnˈdjʊə(r)] vt. 忍耐，容忍 〈P156〉
『en使进入···状态+dure持续→使持续→忍耐』

③ -en位于词尾，表示"使进入···状态"

1. frighten [ˈfraɪtn] v. 使惊恐；害怕
『fright害怕+ en使进入···状态→使害怕』

to make sb suddenly feel afraid 使惊吓；使惊恐
[VN] Sorry, I didn't mean to frighten you.
对不起，我没有吓唬你的意思。
[V] She doesn't frighten easily. 她不是轻易能吓倒的。

▶**frightened** [ˈfraɪtnd] adj. 受惊的；害怕的
The child felt frightened when he saw the big fire.
见到大火，那孩子感到恐惧。

▶**frightening** [ˈfraɪtnɪŋ] adj. 令人恐惧的
I had a frightening encounter with a poisonous snake.
我曾意外地遇到过一条毒蛇，吓得我要命。

▶**fright** [fraɪt] n. 惊骇
❶ [U] 惊骇；恐怖
He was shaking with fright. 他吓得发抖。

❷ [C] 使人惊吓的经历
You gave me a fright jumping out at me like that.
你这样跳起来扑向我，把我吓了一大跳。

词义辨析 〈P368第36〉 害怕 fright, fear, alarm, afraid
词义辨析 〈P368第37〉 惊吓 frighten, scare, alarm

2. sadden [ˈsædn] v. 使悲伤
『sad悲伤的+ en使进入···状态→使悲伤』

3. strengthen ['streŋθn] v. 加强；变强

『strength强壮+ en使进入…状态→使强壮→加强』

The wind had strengthened overnight. 夜里，风更大了。

The move is clearly intended to strengthen the President's position as head of state.

这一举措显然意在加强总统作为国家元首的地位。

4. tighten ['taɪtn] v. 变紧；收紧

『tight紧的+ en使进入…状态→使变紧→变紧；收紧』

❶ ~ (sth) (up)

[V] The rope holding the boat suddenly tightened and broke.

系船的绳子突然绷断了。

[VN] She tightened her grip on his arm.

她抓他的手臂抓得更紧了。

❷ [VN] 使更加严格；加强

Laws on gambling have tightened up recently.

有关赌博的法律最近变得更加严格。

5. widen ['waɪdn] v. 放宽，加宽

『wide宽的+ en使进入…状态→使变宽』

6. worsen ['wɜːsn] v. 变得更糟，恶化

『worse更糟+(e)n使进入…状态→变得更糟，恶化』

[V] The political situation is steadily worsening.

政治局势在持续恶化。

[VN] Staff shortages were worsened by the flu epidemic.

由于流感，职员短缺的情况更加严重了。

7. heighten ['haɪtn] v. 加强，提高

『height高（high的名词）+en使进入…状态→加强，提高』

if a feeling or an effect heightens, or sth heightens it, it becomes stronger or increases

[V] Tension has heightened after the recent bomb attack.

最近的炸弹袭击之后，情势更加紧张。

前缀29. epi- 表示"在…上、周围或中间；在…后面"

1. epicenter ['epɪsentə] n. 中心；震中

『epi在…上+center中心→中心』

The expectation is that the epicenter of the next big earthquake will be in or around Istanbul.

人们预计下一次大地震的震中将在伊斯坦布尔或其周围。

Europe was identified by the World Health Organization as the new "epicenter" of the ongoing COVID-19 pandemic last week.

上周，世界卫生组织将欧洲确定为正在发生的COVID-19（新冠肺炎）大流行病的新"震中"。

2. episode ['epɪsəʊd] n. 一段经历；（小说的）片段；（电视剧的）一集

『epi在…上+sode（路）→在（发展的）路上（的一段经历）→一段经历；（小说的）片段；（电视剧的）一集』

❶ [C]（人生的）一段经历；（小说的）片段，插曲

an event, a situation, or a period of time in sb's life, a novel, etc. that is important or interesting in some way

I'd like to try and forget the whole episode.

我倒想尽量把那段经历全部忘掉。

One of the funniest episodes in the book occurs in Chapter 6.

书中最有趣的片段之一在第6章。

❷ [C]（电视连续剧或无线电广播剧的）一集

The final episode will be shown next Sunday.

下周日将播出最后一集。

3. epidemic [ˌepɪ'demɪk] n. 流行病 〈P148〉

『epi(=upon)之上+dem人们+ic…的→在超过（某类、某地）人们之外的→流行性的』

4. epigram ['epɪgræm] n. 诙谐短诗，警句，隽语 〈P187〉

『epi在+gram写→（因为智慧幽默）在（人们之间流传）的写出的话→警句，隽语』

5. epigraph ['epɪgrɑːf] n. （建筑物或雕塑的）刻文，铭文；（书籍卷首或章节前的）引言，题词 〈P187〉

『epi在+graph写→在（建造物、雕塑、书）上写的字』

6. epilogue ['epɪlɒg] n. （书、电影等）收场白，后记 〈P210〉

『epi在…后面+logue说话→在（故事结束后）说的话→收场白，后记』

前缀30. eu- 表示"好的，优秀的"

1. eugenic [ju'dʒenɪk] adj. 优生的

『eu好的，优秀的+gen出生→出生好的→优生的』

In China today each couple is required to carry out a eugenic plan strictly.

在今天的中国，每对夫妇都被严格执行优生计划。

2. euphoria [ju'fɔːriə] n. 狂喜，兴高采烈

『eu好的+phor带来+ia表名词→带来好的→狂喜』

Euphoria is a feeling of intense happiness and excitement.

After the euphoria of yesterday's celebrations, the country will come down to earth today.

经过昨天的热烈庆祝之后，这个国家今天将回到现实中来。

▶ **euphoric** [ju'fɒrɪk] adj. 狂喜的，兴高采烈的

3. euphemism ['juːfəmɪzəm] n. 委婉语，委婉说法

『eu好的+pheme讲话+ism学术或行为→讲好（听）的话语→委婉语』

4. euthanasia [ˌjuːθə'neɪziə] n. 安乐死

『eu好的+thanasia死→安乐死』

5. eulogy ['juːlədʒi] n. 颂词，颂文；祷词 〈P211〉

『eu好的+log说话+y表名词→说好话→颂辞；祷词』

前缀31. fore- 表示"前面；预先"

1. forecast ['fɔːkɑːst] n. & vt. 预报；预测

『fore前面+ cast投→向前投→预报；预测』

（过去式、过去分词可以是forecast，也可以是forecasted）

❶ vt. 预报；预测

Experts are forecasting a recovery in the economy.

专家预测经济将复苏。

Snow is forecast for tomorrow. 预报明天有雪。

❷ n. 预报；预测

He delivered his election forecast.

他公布了自己对选举的预测。

According to the weather forecast, there will be a rain tomorrow. 据气象台预报，明天将会有雨。

2. forearm ['fɔːrɑːm] n. 前臂

『fore前面的+arm手臂→前臂』

3. forefather ['fɔːfɑːðə(r)] n. 祖先，祖宗

『fore前面+father父亲→先辈→祖先』

近义词 **ancestor** ['ænsestə(r)] n. 祖先，祖宗

4. forefinger [ˈfɔ:fɪŋgə(r)] n. 食指

『fore前面+finger指头→（除拇指外）前一个手指→食指』

小贴士　五指用英语怎么说？

拇指 thumb；食指 index finger, first finger或forefinger

中指 middle finger；无名指 ring finger

小拇指 little finger

5. forehead [ˈfɔ: (r) hed] n. 前额

『fore前面的+head头→头的前面→前额』

6. foresee [fɔ:ˈsi:] vt. 预知，预见

『fore前面；预先+see看见→预先看见→预见』

近义词　forecast 预报，预言；predict 预言

7. foremost [ˈfɔ:məʊst] adj. 最重要的；最好的 adv. 首先

❶ 最重要的；最好的

the world's foremost authority on the subject

该学科全世界首屈一指的权威

This question has been foremost in our minds recently.

近来我们的心目中一直认为这个问题最重要。

❷ first and foremost 首要的是

You use first and foremost to emphasize the most important quality of something or someone.

It is first and foremost a trade agreement.

这首先是一个贸易协议。

He does a little teaching, but first and foremost he's a writer.

他干一点教学，但首要的是写作。

前缀32. hect- 表示"百"

1. hectare [ˈhekteə(r)] n. 公顷

『hect百+ are公亩→一百公亩→公顷』

前缀33. hemi- 表示"半"

1. hemicycle [ˈhemɪˌsaɪkl] n. 半圆形

『hemi半+ cycle圆，环→半圆形』

2. hemisphere [ˈhemɪsfɪə(r)] n. 半球；地球的半球；[解] 大脑半球

『hemi半+sphere球→半球』

the northern hemisphere 北半球

前缀34. hetero- 表示"其他的；不同的"

1. heterosexual [ˌhetərəˈsekʃuəl] adj. 异性恋的 n. 异性恋者

『hetero其他的；不同+sexual性别的→异性的』

2. heterodox [ˈhetərədɒks] adj. 异端的，非正统的 ⟨P153⟩

『hetero其他的；不同+dox观点→异类观点的→异端邪说的』

3. heterogeneous [ˌhetərəˈdʒi:niəs] adj. 由不同成分组成的，成分混杂的 ⟨P183⟩

『hetero其他的，不同+gen产生+eous充满…的→由不同成分组成的→成分混杂的』

前缀35. homo- 表示"相同的，同类的；相似的"

1. homograph [ˈhɒməɡrɑ:f] n. 同形异义词（拼写相同，意义不同，读音可能不同）

『homo相同的+graph 写，画→写起来相同（但意义不同）的词→同形异义词』

2. homophone [ˈhɒməfəʊn] n. 同音异形词，同音异义词

（读音相同，写法或意义不同）

『homo相同的+phone声音→发音相同的字→同音字』

3. homosexual [ˌhəʊməˈsekʃuəl] n. 同性恋者（通常指男性）；同性恋的

4. homogeneous [ˌhɒməˈdʒi:niəs] adj. 由相同（或同类型）事物（或人）组成的 ⟨P183⟩

『homo相同的+gen产生+eous充满…的→由相同（成分）产生的→由相同事物或人组成的』

5. homonym [ˈhɒmənɪm] n. 同形（同音）异义词 ⟨P237⟩

『homo相同的+(o)nym名字→名字相同（但意义不同）的词→同音异义词』

前缀36. hyper- 表示"超过，过多"

1. hypertension [ˌhaɪpəˈtenʃn] n. 高血压

『hyper超过+tension紧张→（血流）过度紧张→高血压』

Obesity correlates with increased risk for hypertension and stroke. 肥胖会增加高血压和中风发作的概率。

2. hyperlink [ˈhaɪpəlɪŋk] n. & v. 超级链接

『hyper超过+link链接→链接的内容超过（本文档或内容）→超级链接』

When you click on a graphic and a video clip buttons, you have clicked on a hyperlink.

当你点击一个图形和一个视频剪辑播放按钮的时候，你在点击一个超链接。

3. hyperactive [ˌhaɪpərˈæktɪv] adj. 过分活跃的；多动的

『hyper超过+active活跃的→过分活跃的』

（尤指儿童及其行为）过分活跃的；多动

too active and only able to keep quiet and still for short periods

His research was used in planning treatments for hyperactive children.

他的研究被用来为患有多动症的儿童设计治疗方案。

▶ **hyperactivity** [ˌhaɪpərækˈtɪvɪti] n. 多动症

4. hyperbole [haɪˈpɜ:bəli] n. 夸张；夸张法

『hyper超过+bole抛→把（话）抛得超高→夸张』

But on Tuesday he played down the remarks, describing them as "a bit of hyperbole".

但本周二，他淡化了这些评论，称其"有点夸张"。

▶ **hyperbolic** [ˌhaɪpəˈbɒlɪk] adj. 夸张的

5. hypercritical [ˈhaɪpəˈkrɪtɪkəl] adj. （尤指对小错误）吹毛求疵的，过于苛刻的

『hyper超过+critical批评的→批评过头的→吹毛求疵的』

These are usually overbearing, negative people who are hypercritical of every decision you make.

这些人通常专横傲慢，不受欢迎，他们对你做的任何决定都吹毛求疵。

6. hypersensitive [ˌhaɪpəˈsensətɪv] adj. 非常敏感的；极度过敏的

『hyper超过+sensitive敏感的→过敏的→非常敏感的；极度过敏的』

He's hypersensitive to any kind of criticism.

他对任何批评都受不了。

Her skin is hypersensitive. 她的皮肤过敏。

7. hyper [ˈhaɪpə(r)] adj. 亢奋的；精力旺盛的

If someone is hyper, they are very excited and energetic.

I was incredibly hyper. I couldn't sleep.

我太亢奋了，根本无法入睡。

8. hyperopia [ˌhaɪpəˈroʊpiə] n. 远视 〈P238〉

『hyper超过+op视力+ia某种病→超过正常视力→远视』

前缀37. hypo- 下，低；次等

1. hypotension [ˌhaɪpoʊˈtenʃən] n. 低血压

『hypo低，下+tension压力→（血的）压力低→低血压』

2. hypocrite [ˈhɪpəkrɪt] n. 伪君子，虚伪的人 〈P142〉

『hypo下，低；次等+crite判断→（经）判断（实际水平）低于（所装出来的）人→伪君子』

3. hypodermic [ˌhaɪpəˈdɜːmɪk] n. 皮下注射器 adj. 皮下注射的 〈P149〉

『hypo下+derm皮肤+ic…的→皮下的→皮下注射的』

4. hypothesis [haɪˈpɒθəsɪs] n. 假说；假设 〈P333〉

『hypo下+thes放置+is表情况→放在下面（还不能作为正式理论）→假说』

5. hypothermia [ˌhaɪpəˈθɜːmiə] n. 体温过低 〈P333〉

『hypo低+therm热（引申为温度）+ia表疾病→体温低于（正常值的）病→体温过低』

前缀38. in- (im-, il-, ir-) 有时相当于"in"，表示"向内，进入"；有时相当于"not"，表示"不，无"

（in- 在双唇音 p, b, m 前用 im-，在 l 前用 il-，在 r 前用 ir-）

① in- (im-, il-, ir-)=in, 表示"向内，进入"

1. imprison [ɪmˈprɪzn] vt. 关押，监禁

『im进入+prison监狱→进入监狱→监禁』

They were imprisoned for possession of drugs.

他们因拥有毒品而被监禁。

同义词 **jail** [dʒeɪl] n. 监狱；vt. 监禁

2. import [ˈɪmpɔːt, ɪmˈpɔːt] n. 进口；进口商品 vt. 进口

『im进入+port港口→从港口进来→进口』

The import of cotton goods went up sharply.

棉织品的进口大大增加了。

In the UK visible imports have traditionally been greater than visible exports.

在英国，传统上有形产品的进口一直大于出口。

The country has to import most of its raw materials.

这个国家大多数原料均依赖进口。

3. indoor [ˈɪndɔː(r)] adj. 室内的

『in里面+door门→门里面的→室内的』

an indoor swimming pool 室内游泳池

indoor games 室内游戏

▶ **indoors** [ˌɪnˈdɔːz] adv. 在室内

to go/stay indoors 进入/留在屋里

Many herbs can be grown indoors.

很多草本植物能在室内种植。

▶ **outdoors** [ˌaʊtˈdɔːz] adv.在户外 n. 户外，野外

❶ adv. 在户外

The rain prevented them from eating outdoors.

雨天使他们无法在户外用餐。

❷ n. the outdoors [sing.] 野外，旷野，郊外

the countryside, away from buildings and busy places

They both have a love of the outdoors.

他们俩都喜爱郊外的环境。

Come to Canada and enjoy the great outdoors.

到加拿大来享受蓝天碧野吧！

4. inspire [ɪnˈspaɪə(r)] vt. 激励；给人灵感 〈P310〉

『in进入+spire呼吸→吸进（新鲜空气）（顿时来了灵感）→吸气』

5. illustrate [ˈɪləstreɪt] vt. 给…加插图；（用示例、图画等）说明；表明 〈P212〉

『il(=in)进入+lustr光+ate表动词→让光亮照进（模糊的事物）内部→使明白→说明』

② in- (im-, il-, ir-) =not, 表示"不，无"

1. illegal [ɪˈliːgl] adj. 非法的

『il不+ legal合法的→不合法的』

2. illogical [ɪˈlɒdʒɪkl] adj. 不合逻辑的

『il不+ logical逻辑的→不合逻辑的』

3. immoral [ɪˈmɒrəl] adj. 不道德的

『im不+ moral道德的→不道德的』

It's immoral to steal. 偷盗是不道德的。

There's nothing immoral about wanting to earn more money.

想多赚点钱没什么不道德。

4. impatient [ɪmˈpeɪʃnt] adj. 没有耐心的

『im不+patient有耐心的→没有耐心的』

▶ **impatience** [ɪmˈpeɪʃns] n. 没有耐心，急躁

▶ **patient** [ˈpeɪʃnt] adj. 有耐心的 n. 病人

5. impolite [ˌɪmpəˈlaɪt] adj. 不礼貌的，粗鲁的

『im不+ polite礼貌的→不礼貌的』

6. impossible [ɪmˈpɒsəbl] adj. 不可能的

『im不+ possible可能的→不可能的』

7. indifferent [ɪnˈdɪfrənt] adj. 漠不关心的

『in不+different不同→（不管发生什么事情，对他来说）没有什么不同→漠不关心』

People have become indifferent to the suffering of others.

人们对别人的痛苦已经变得无动于衷。

▶ **indifference** [ɪnˈdɪfrəns] n. 漠不关心

8. inevitable [ɪnˈevɪtəbl] adj. 不可避免的

『in不+evitable可以避免的→不可避免的』

It was inevitable that there would be job losses.

裁员已是不可避免的。

9. irregular [ɪˈregjələ(r)] adj. 不规则的

『ir不+ regular规则的→不规则的』

10. irrelative [ɪˈrelətɪv] adj. 不相关的

『ir不+ relative相关的→不相关的』

11. irresistible [ˌɪrɪˈzɪstəbl] adj.不可抗拒；诱人的 〈P302〉

『ir不+resist抵抗+ible可…的→不可抗拒的』

12. illiterate [ɪˈlɪtərət] adj. 文盲的；n. 目不识丁者 〈P209〉

『il不+ liter文字，字母+ate表形容词→不识字的，文盲的』

▶ **illiteracy** [ɪˈlɪtərəsi] n. 文盲；无知〈P209〉

13. immortal [ɪˈmɔːtl] adj. 不死的；流芳百世的 〈P229〉

『im不+ mortal死→不朽的』

14. impartial [ɪmˈpɑːʃl] adj. 公正的，中立的 <P243>
『im不+ part+ial偏袒的→不偏袒的→ 中立的』

15. incapable [ɪnˈkeɪpəbl] adj. 无能力的；软弱无能的 <P122>
『in不，无，非+capable有能力的→无能力的』

16. inglorious [ɪnˈglɔːriəs] adj. 不光彩的 <P95>
『in不+glorious光荣的→不光彩的』

17. injustice [ɪnˈdʒʌstɪs] n. 不公正 <P199>
『in不+ justice公正→不公正』

前缀39. infra- 相当于 "below" 表示 "下，低"

1. infrared [ˌɪnfrəˈred] adj. 红外线的
『infra (=below) 以下+ red 红色的→红外线的』
Infrared detectors have many uses.
红外探测器有多种用途。

2. infrastructure [ˈɪnfrəstrʌktʃə(r)] n. 基础设施 <P319>
『infra (=below) 以下+structure结构体→基础设施』

前缀40. inter- 表示 "相互；在…之间"

1. interact [ˌɪntərˈækt] vi. 互动；相互作用
『inter相互之间+act行动→互动，相互作用』

❶ ~ (with sb) 互动，交流，沟通
Teachers have a limited amount of time to interact with each child. 教师和每个孩子沟通的时间有限。

❷ 相互影响；相互作用
You have to understand how cells interact.
你必须明白细胞是怎样相互作用的。

▶ **interaction** [ˌɪntərˈækʃn] n. 互动，相互影响

▶ **interactive** [ˌɪntərˈæktɪv] adj. 互动的；互相作用的

2. interchange [ˈɪntətʃeɪndʒ] n. & v. 交换
『inter在…之间+change交换→在两者间变换→交换』

❶ （思想、信息等的）交换，互换
a continuous interchange of ideas 不断的思想交流

❷ ~A with B | ~ A and B
to interchange the front tyres with the rear ones
将前后轮胎对调

词义辨析 <P369第40>
交换 interchange, exchange, switch, trade

3. international [ˌɪntəˈnæʃnəl] adj.国际的
『inter相互之间+nation国家+al表形容词→国家相互之间的→国际的』

4. Internet [ˈɪntənet] n. 互联网
『inter相互之间+net网→相互之间连接的网→互联网』
互联网一般要用 "the Internet"。
All the rooms have access to the Internet.
所有的房间都可以接入互联网。

5. interpersonal [ˌɪntəˈpɜːsənl] adj. [名词前]人际关系的
『inter相互之间+person人+al…的→人际关系的』
Training in interpersonal skills is essential.
人际交往技巧的培训非常必要。

6. interstate [ˈɪntəsteɪt] adj.<美>州际的； n. 州际公路

『inter相互之间+state州→州际之间的』

7. interface [ˈɪntəfeɪs] n. （软件的用户）界面；（计算机或电子设备的）接口 v. （使通过界面或接口）连接
『inter在…之间+face面→在计算机和人或其他设备之间交互的面或东西→界面；接口』
The new version of the program comes with a much better user interface than the original.
新版程序的用户界面比原来程序的好得多。
the interface between computer and printer
计算机和打印机之间的接口
[V] The new system interfaces with existing telephone equipment. 新系统与现有的电话设备相连接。

8. interim [ˈɪntərɪm] adj. 过渡的 n. 过渡期间
『inter在…之间+im→在两件事之间→过渡期间』

❶ adj. 过渡的
intended to last for only a short time until sb/sth more permanent is found
She was sworn in as head of an interim government in March.
她3月份宣誓就任过渡政府首脑。

❷ in the interim 在过渡期间；在此期间
Despite everything that had happened in the interim, they had remained good friends.
不管在此间发生了什么，他们还是好朋友。

9. interval [ˈɪntəvl] n. （时间上的）间隔；幕间休息；（其他事情）穿插出现的间隙
『inter在…之间+val→在两个时间或事件之间；在两场表演之间→间隔；幕间休息』
The ferry service has restarted after an interval of 12 years.
时隔12年之后，轮渡服务又重新开通了。
During the interval, wine was served.
幕间休息时有葡萄酒供应。
Buses to the city leave at regular intervals.
开往城里的公共汽车每隔一定时间发出一班。

10. interfere [ˌɪntəˈfɪə(r)] vi. 干涉；妨碍
『在…之间+fere(=strike)攻击→在事情运行期间攻击→干涉；妨碍』

❶ [V] 干涉
to get involved in and try to influence a situation that does not concern you, in a way that annoys other people
I wish my mother would stop interfering and let me make my own decisions. 我希望我母亲不再干预，让我自己拿主意。
The police are very unwilling to interfere in family problems.
警方很不情愿插手家庭问题。

❷ [V] (sth) ~ with sth 妨碍
Drug problems frequently interfered with his work.
吸毒问题频频干扰他的工作。

▶ **interference** [ˌɪntəˈfɪərəns] n. 干涉；（电波的）干扰

11. interrogate [ɪnˈterəgeɪt] vt. 讯问，审问，盘问 <P282>
『inter在…之间+rog要求+ate表动词→在询问期间要求（说出真相）→讯问，审问，盘问』

12. interstellar [ˌɪntəˈstelə(r)] adj. 星际的 <P314>
『inter在…之间+stell星星+ar…的→星际的』

13. intercede [ˌɪntəˈsiːd] vi. 向…说情；调解，斡旋 <P127>
『inter在…之间+cede走→在两者之间走（防止发生冲突）→调停』

14. intercept [ˌɪntəˈsept] v. 拦截 〈P129〉
『inter在…之间+ cept(=take, hold, seize)抓，拿→在（路程间）被拿下→拦截』

15. interpose [ˌɪntəˈpəʊz] vt. 插进；插入 〈P264〉
『inter在…之间+pose放，放置→插入』

16. interrupt [ˌɪntəˈrʌpt] v. 插嘴；使暂停 〈P283〉
『inter在…之间+rupt断裂→在（讲话）中间打断→打断』

17. intersection [ˌɪntəˈsekʃn] n. 十字路口；交叉 〈P291〉
『inter相互之间+sect切割→相互切割→+(t)ion表行为或结果→十字路口』

18. interview [ˈɪntəvjuː] n. & v. 面试；采访 〈P353〉
『inter相互+view看→面对面相互看→面试；采访』

前缀41. kilo- 表示"一千"

1. kilocalorie [ˈkɪləʊˌkælərɪ] n. 千卡；大卡
『kilo千+calorie卡路里→千卡路里（热量单位）』

2. kilogram [ˈkɪləgræm] n. 千克，公斤
『kilo千+gram克→千克』

3. kilometer [ˈkɪləˌmiːtə] n. 千米，公里
『kilo千+meter米→千米』

4. kilovolt [ˈkɪləvəʊlt] n. 千伏特

5. kilowatt [ˈkɪləwɒt] n. 千瓦
『kilo千+watt瓦→千瓦』

小贴士 常见的数量的表示法参看P6前缀15

前缀42. mal-, male- 表示"坏，恶"

1. malfunction [ˌmælˈfʌŋkʃn] vi. & n. 出故障；功能失常
『mal坏，恶+function运转→运转出错了→出故障』

This was caused by a malfunction of the generator.
这是因为发电机故障引起的。
Some of the keys on the keyboard have started to malfunction.
键盘上的一些键开始出现故障。

2. maltreat [ˌmælˈtriːt] vt. 虐待
『mal坏，恶+treat对待→对待（某人）很坏→虐待』

He had been badly maltreated as a child.
他小时候受到虐待。

3. malicious [məˈlɪʃəs] adj. 怀有恶意的，恶毒的
『mal坏，恶+icious表形容→怀有恶意的』

These are not necessarily hateful, malicious people.
这些人不一定心怀仇恨，恶意伤人。

4. malpractice [ˌmælˈpræktɪs] n. 渎职，玩忽职守
『mal坏，恶+practice→做事，实践→不好好做事→玩忽职守』

The doctor has no more patients because of malpractice.
由于玩忽职守，大夫不再有病人了。

5. malign [məˈlaɪn] vt. 公开诽谤 adj. （作定语）有害的
『mal坏，恶+ign恶意伤害→公开诽谤』

She feels she has been much maligned by the press.
她觉得她遭到了新闻界的恣意诽谤。
a malign force/influence/effect 有害的势力/影响/作用

6. malignant [məˈlɪgnənt] adj. （肿瘤）恶性的；（人）恶意的，恶毒的

『mal坏，恶+ign+ant …的→恶性的』

She developed a malignant breast tumour.
她长了一个恶性的乳房肿瘤。
He said that we were evil, malignant and mean.
他说我们既邪恶又恶毒，还非常卑鄙。

反义词 **benign** [bɪˈnaɪn] adj. （人）和善的；（肿瘤）良性的；没有危害的；（环境）宜人的 〈P6〉
『ben(=bene)善，好+ign→（肿瘤等）良性的；善良的』

7. malevolent [məˈlevələnt] adj. 恶意的 〈P359〉
『male坏+vol意愿+ent具有…性质的→坏意愿→恶意的』

8. malnutrition [ˌmælnjuːˈtrɪʃn] n. 营养不良 〈P236〉
『mal坏+nutrition营养；滋养→营养不良』

前缀43. man(i) -, manu-=hand，表示"手"

1. manual [ˈmænjuəl] adj. 用手的，体力的；手动操作的 n. 使用手册
『manu手+al…的→用手的→用手的；手动操作的』

❶ [C]使用手册，说明书，指南
a computer/car/instruction manual
电脑 / 汽车产品说明书；用法指南

❷ adj. 用手的，体力的
Manual workers need a good breakfast for high-energy output. 体力劳动者身体能量消耗巨大，早餐要丰盛一些。

❸ adj. 手动的，用手操作的
There is a manual pump to get rid of the water.
有一只手摇水泵用来排水。
Leave the controls on manual. 让操纵杆处于手动状态。
It has no manual focus facility. 它没有手动调焦功能。

2. manipulate [məˈnɪpjuleɪt] vt. 操作；操纵
『mani手+pul拉+ate表动词→用手拉→操作』

❶ （熟练地）操作，使用
to manipulate the gears and levers of a machine
熟练地操纵机器的排挡和变速杆
Computers are very efficient at manipulating information.
计算机在处理信息方面效率极高。

❷ （暗中）控制，操纵
to control or influence sb/sth, often in a dishonest way so that they do not realize it
As a politician, he knows how to manipulate public opinion.
身为一位政客，他知道如何左右公众舆论。

3. manuscript [ˈmænjuskrɪpt] n. 手稿，原稿 〈P290〉
『manu手+script写→手写的→手稿；原稿』

4. manufacture [ˌmænjuˈfæktʃə(r)] v. & n. 大量生产 〈P161〉
『manu手+fact做，制作+ ure行为→用手做→制造』

5. manacle [ˈmænəkl] n. 手铐；脚镣 vt. 给…戴上镣铐 〈P48〉
『man手+acle表物→戴在手上的东西→手铐』

6. emancipate [ɪˈmænsɪpeɪt] vt. 解放，使不受束缚 〈P123〉
『e出+man手+cip(=take)拿+ate表动词→把（被束缚的）手释放出来→解放』

7. manicure [ˈmænɪkjʊə(r)] n. & v. 修指甲，手部护理 〈P146〉
『mani手+cure(=care)照料→手部护理』

8. manifest [ˈmænɪfest] vt. 显露 adj. 显而易见的 〈P169〉
『mani手+ fest仇恨→（因为）仇恨想（动手）打 →（情感）显而易见的；显露』

前缀44. max- 表示"大"

1. maximum [ˈmæksɪməm] adj. 最大值的 n. 最大的量、体积、强度等

❶ adj. [only before noun] (abbr. max) 最高的；最多的；最大极限的
the maximum speed/temperature/volume
最快速度；最高气温；最大音量

❷ n. (abbr. max) 最大量；最大限度；最高限度
a maximum of 30 children in a class
每班至多30名学生
The job will require you to use all your skills to the maximum.
这项工作将要求你最大限度地发挥你的技能。

▶ **maximize** [ˈmæksɪmaɪz] vt. 最大化，使增至最大限度；充分利用

In order to maximize profit the firm would seek to maximize output. 为了获得最大利润，这家公司会把产量增至最大。
Click on the square icon to maximize the window.
点击方形图标，把（计算机）窗口最大化。

▶ **maximal** [ˈmæksɪml] adj. 最大的；最高的

小贴士 一些家电的音量调节按钮上，max表示"音量最大"，min表示"音量最小"，max就是maximum的缩写，min就是minimum的缩写。另外，手机型号名称中的max也是表示"大"的意思，如"小米Max"，就是小米手机中的大屏手机。

2. climax [ˈklaɪmæks] n. 高潮，极点，顶点
『cli(m)攀爬+max大→发展到最大→高潮』

The story reaches a climax in chapter eight.
故事在第八章达到高潮。
This battle marked the climax of his career as a soldier.
这场战役标志着他军人生涯的顶峰。

前缀45. min(i)-=small，表示"小"

小贴士 汉语中的"迷你"实际上就是mini(小)的音译，如：miniskirt 迷你裙；minicamera 迷你相机

1. minibus [ˈmɪnɪbʌs] n. 小型公共汽车，中巴

2. minicab [ˈmɪnɪkæb] n. 微型出租汽车

3. minicamera [mɪnɪkæməˈrə] n. 小型照相机

4. minimum [ˈmɪnɪməm] adj. 最小值的 n. 最小值、最小量、最低限度

The work was done with the minimum amount of effort.
做这项工作没费什么劲。
Office machinery is kept to a minimum.
办公室的机器数量维持在最低限度。
minimum wage 最低工资

▶ **minimize** [ˈmɪnɪmaɪz] vt. 使减少到最低限度

Concerned people want to minimize the risk of developing cancer. 相关人员希望尽可能降低罹癌风险。

Click the square icon again to minimize the window.
再次点击方形图标，把（计算机）窗口最小化。

▶ **minimal** [ˈmɪnɪməl] adj. 最小的；最低限度的

5. miniskirt [ˈmɪnɪskɜːt] n. 迷你短裙，超短裙
『mini小+skirt裙子→短裙子，迷你裙』

6. miniature [ˈmɪnətʃə(r)] adj. 微型的 n. 缩微模型
『mini小+ature行为，行为的结果→缩小之后的结果』

❶ adj. 微型的，微缩版的
He looked like a miniature version of his handsome and elegant big brother.
他看上去就像是他那个英俊儒雅的哥哥的迷你版。

❷ n. 小画像；缩微模型；微型复制品
He showed me the miniature of the mansion.
他给我展示了大厦的模型。
The new solar system seems to be a miniature of our own.
新的太阳系好像是我们自己的一个缩略图。

7. minor [ˈmaɪnə(r)] adj. 较小的；次要的；轻微的
『min小+ or表比较级后缀→较小的；较少的』

[usually before noun] 较小的；次要的；轻微的
not very large, important or serious
There may be some minor changes to the schedule.
时间安排也许会有些小小的变动。
Women played a relatively minor role in the organization.
在这个组织中，妇女发挥着相对次要的作用。

▶ **minority** [maɪˈnɒrəti] n. 少数；少数派；少数民族

The nation wants peace; only a minority want the war to continue. 国家要和平，只有少数人希望战争继续下去。
Members of 21 minorities live in this area.
这个地区居住有21个少数民族的成员。

8. diminish [dɪˈmɪnɪʃ] v. （不断）减小，减弱
『di离开+min小+ish使→使小下去→缩小，减弱』

❶ v.（不断）减小；（不断）减弱
[V] The world's resources are rapidly diminishing.
世界资源正在迅速减少。
His influence has diminished with time.
随着时间的推移，他的影响已不如从前了。

❷ v. 贬低（某事物的重要性或价值）
I don't wish to diminish the importance of their contribution.
我并不想贬低他们所作贡献的重要性。

9. minute [ˈmɪnɪt] n. 分钟 [maɪˈnjuːt] adj. 微小的；详细的
『min小+ ute→微小的，细微的』

The kitchen on the boat is minute. 小船上的厨房小极了。
She remembered everything in minute detail.

她记得每一件事的细节。

前缀46. micro- 表示"微小"

1. microbiology [ˌmaɪkrəʊbaɪˈɒlədʒi] n. 微生物学
『micro微小+ biology生物学→微生物学』

2. microeconomics [ˌmaɪkrəiːkəˈnɒmɪks] n.微观经济学
『micro微小+economics经济学→微观经济学』

3. microphone [ˈmaɪkrəfəʊn] n. 话筒；麦克风
『micro小+phone声音→使小声音变大的东西→麦克风』

4. Microsoft [ˈmaɪkrəʊˌsɒft] n. （美国）微软公司
『micro微小+ soft柔软的→微软』

5. microwave [ˈmaɪkrəweɪv] n. 微波；微波炉
『micro微小+wave声波→微波』

6. microscope [ˈmaɪkrəskəʊp] n. 显微镜〈P289〉
『micro微小+scope镜→看微小东西的镜→显微镜』

小贴士 常见的数量的表示法参看P6前缀15

前缀47. milli- 表示"千分之一"

1. milligram [ˈmɪlɪɡræm] n. 毫克
『milli千分之一+gram克→千分之一克→毫克』

2. milliliter [ˈmɪlɪˌliːtə] n. 毫升
『milli千分之一+liter升→千分之一升→毫升』

小贴士 millilitre（英式拼写）；ml 毫升；cubic centimeter=cc
立方厘米

3. millimeter [ˈmɪlɪˌmiːtə] n. 毫米
『milli千分之一+meter米→千分之一米→毫米』

小贴士 millimeter→mm 毫米； centimeter→cm 厘米；
kilometer →km 千米

4. millivolt [ˈmɪlivəʊlt] n. 毫伏(特)，千分之一伏特
『milli千分之一+volt伏特→千分之一伏特→毫伏』

5. millisecond [ˈmɪlisekənd] n. 毫秒，千分之一秒
『milli千分之一+second秒→千分之一秒→毫秒』

小贴士 常见的数量的表示法参看P6前缀15

前缀48. mega- 表示"兆"；"大的"

1. megabyte [ˈmeɡəbaɪt] n. 兆字节
『mega兆+byte字节→兆字节』

小贴士 MB，为英文"MByte"的简写，是计算机中的一种储存单位，读作"兆"。比其大的储存单位是G。

2. megawatt [ˈmeɡəwɒt] n. 兆瓦
『mega兆+watt瓦特→兆瓦』

3. megahertz [ˈmeɡəhɜːts] n. 兆赫
『mega兆+hertz赫兹→兆赫』

小贴士 常见的数量的表示法参看P6前缀15

4. mega [ˈmeɡə] adj. & adv. 巨大的；极佳的；非常

The song was a mega hit last year.
这首歌是去年最热门的歌曲。
They're mega rich. 他们极其富有。

5. megaphone [ˈmeɡəfəʊn] n. 扩音器，喇叭筒
『mega巨大+phone声音→让声音变大→扩音器』

6. megastar [ˈmeɡəstɑː(r)] n. 演艺巨星
『mega大的+star影星、歌星等→演艺巨星』

7. megacity [ˈmeɡəˌsɪti] n. （人口超过1000万的）大城市

前缀49. mis-=wrong, bad, ill，表示"错误；坏的"

1. miscalculate [ˌmɪsˈkælkjuleɪt] v. 误算；对…判断错误
『mis错的+calculate计算→错误计算』

2. miscarry [ˌmɪsˈkæri] vi. （指妇女）流产；（指计划等）失败
『mis错的+carry运载→胎儿在孕妇肚中carry过程中出错→流产』

3. mislead [ˌmɪsˈliːd] vt. 误导
『mis错的+lead引导→误导』
（misled, misled）

[VN] ~ sb (about sth) | ~ sb (into doing sth) 误导
He deliberately misled us about the nature of their relationship.
关于他们究竟是什么关系，他故意给我们留下错误印象。

4. misspell [ˌmɪsˈspel] vt. 拼错
『mis错误+ spell拼写→拼错』

5. mistake [mɪˈsteɪk] n. & v.错误
『mis错的+take拿→拿错的→错误』
（mistook, mistaken）

词义辨析 <P369第41> 错误 mistake, error

6. misunderstand [ˌmɪsʌndəˈstænd] vt. 误会，误解
『mis错误+ understand理解→理解错误→误解』
（misunderstood, misunderstood）

[VN] I completely misunderstood her intentions.
我完全误会了她的意图。
[V] I thought he was her husband—I must have misunderstood.
我以为他是她丈夫——我一定是误会了。

▶**misunderstanding** [ˌmɪsʌndəˈstændɪŋ] n. 误解；不和

❶ [U, C] ~ (of/about sth) | ~ (between A and B) 误解；误会
There must be some misunderstanding—I thought I ordered the smaller model.
一定是搞错了——我以为我订的是更小型号的。

❷ [C] 意见不一；不和
We had a little misunderstanding over the bill.
我们对这个提案的看法有点分歧。

7. misfortune [ˌmɪsˈfɔːtʃuːn] n. 厄运，不幸
『mis坏的+fortune运气→不幸』

We had the misfortune to run into a violent storm.
我们不幸遭遇了猛烈的暴风雨。
She bore her misfortunes bravely.
她勇敢地承受不幸的遭遇。

8. mischief ['mɪstʃɪf] adj. 淘气，恶作剧

『mis坏的+chief头目→坏（孩子的）头目→淘气，恶作剧』

[U] 淘气，恶作剧，顽皮

bad behaviour (especially of children) that is annoying but does not cause any serious damage or harm

It's very quiet upstairs; they must be up to some mischief !

楼上很安静，他们一定在搞什么恶作剧。

Her eyes were full of mischief. 她眼睛里满是使坏的神情。

▶ **mischievous** ['mɪstʃɪvəs] adj. 顽皮的，捣蛋的

She rocks back and forth on her chair like a mischievous child. 她像个顽皮的孩子似的，坐在椅子上来回摇晃。

前缀50. mono- 表示"单个，一个"

1. monotone ['mɒnətəʊn] n. (说话或唱歌) 单调 adj.单调的

『mono单个，一个+tone声音→只有一种声音→单调』

❶ n. [sing.] 单调，单调的声音

The evidence was read out to the court in a dull monotone.

证据被当庭呆板地宣读了一遍。

❷ adj. (声音或外表) 单调的，无变化的

He spoke in a monotone drawl.

他用慢吞吞又单调的语气说话。

▶ **monotonous** [mə'nɒtənəs] adj. 单调乏味的

never changing and therefore boring

It's monotonous work, like most factory jobs.

与工厂大部分工作一样，这份工作也很单调乏味。

2. monosyllable ['mɒnəsɪləbl] n. 单音节词

『mono单个，一个+syllable音节→单音节词』

3. monorail ['mɒnəʊreɪl] n. 单轨铁路；单轨列车

『mono单个，一个+rail铁轨→单轨』

4. monopoly [mə'nɒpəli] n. 垄断，专营

『mono单个+poly卖→垄断，专营』

❶ ~ (in/of/on sth)

(business 商) 垄断；专营服务；被垄断的商品（或服务）

the complete control of trade in particular goods or the supply of a particular service; a type of goods or a service that is controlled in this way

In the past central government had a monopoly on television broadcasting. 过去，中央政府对电视节目播放实行垄断。

Electricity, gas and water were considered to be natural monopolies.

电、煤气和水的垄断经营过去被认为是理所当然的。

❷ [usually sing.] ~ in/of/on sth 独占；专利；专利品

the complete control, possession or use of sth; a thing that belongs only to one person or group and that other people cannot share

Managers do not have a monopoly on stress.

并不只是经营管理者有压力。

A good education should not be the monopoly of the rich.

良好的教育不应该成为富人的专利。

▶ **monopolize** [mə'nɒpəlaɪz] vt. 独占，垄断

Men traditionally monopolized jobs in the printing industry.

在传统上，男人包揽了印刷行业中的所有工作。

5. monologue ['mɒnəlɒg] n. 长篇大论；独白，独角戏 <P210>

『mono单个，一个+logue→一个人说→独白』

6. monarch ['mɒnək] n. 君主，帝王 <P115>

『mon单个，一个+arch统治者→一个人统治→君主』

前缀51. multi- 表示"很多"

1. multicultural [ˌmʌlti'kʌltʃərəl] adj. 多元文化的

『multi多种的+cultural文化的→多元文化的』

We live in a multicultural society.

我们生活在一个多元文化的社会中。

2. multimedia [ˌmʌlti'miːdiə] n. & adj. 多媒体

『multi多种的+media媒体→多媒体』

3. multiple ['mʌltɪpl] adj. 数量多的 n. 倍数

『multi多的+ple倍→多倍的，数量多的』

❶ adj. [only before noun] 数量多的；多种多样的

He died of multiple injuries. 他死于多处受伤。

❷ n. 倍数

14, 21 and 28 are all multiples of 7.

14、21和28都是7的倍数。

▶ **multiple-choice** 多项选择

▶ **multiply** ['mʌltɪplaɪ] v. 乘；成倍增加；繁殖

『multiple的动词形式』

❶ ~ (A by B) | ~ A and B (together) 乘；乘以

[V] The children are already learning to multiply and divide.

孩子们已经开始学习乘法和除法了。

❷ 成倍增加；迅速增加

[V] Our problems have multiplied since last year.

自去年以来，我们的问题成倍增加。

[VN] Cigarette smoking multiplies the risk of cancer.

抽烟会大大增加得癌症的风险。

❸ (biology 生) （使）繁殖，增殖

[V] Rabbits multiply rapidly. 兔子繁殖迅速。

[VN] It is possible to multiply these bacteria in the laboratory.

在实验室里繁殖这些细菌是可能的。

4. multipolar [ˌmʌlti'pəʊlə] adj. 多极的

『multi多种的+pol极+ar表形容词→多极的』

The future world order would be multipolar.

未来的世界秩序将是多极的。

▶ **multipolarization** [mʌltiːpəʊləraɪ'zeɪʃən] n.多极化

5. multitude ['mʌltɪtjuːd] n. 众多；大量；人群

『multi多种的+itude（去i）表状态、性质→众多，大量』

❶ [C] ~ (of sth/sb) 众多；大量

an extremely large number of things or people

These elements can be combined in a multitude of different ways. 这些因素可以通过无数不同的方式进行组合。

❷ the multitude 民众，群众

Political power has been placed in the hands of the multitude.

政治权力一直在民众手中。

❸ 人群，一大群人

The assembled multitude cheered and whistled as the political leaders arrived.

当政治领袖到达的时候，聚集的人群欢呼起来，并吹起了口哨。

6. multilateral [ˌmʌlti'lætərəl] adj.多边（国）的 <P201>

『multi多种的+lateral边的→多边的，多方面的』

7. multilingual [ˌmʌlti'lɪŋgwəl] adj. 使用多种语言的 <P208>

『multi多+ lingu语言+al…的→（使用）多种语言的』

前缀52. neo-=new，表示"新"

1. neoclassical [ˌniːəʊˈklæsɪkl] adj. 新古典主义的
『neo新的+classical古典的→新古典主义的』

2. neofascism ['nɪ(:)əʊ'fæʃɪzm] n. 新法西斯主义
『neo新的+fascism法西斯主义→新法西斯主义』

3. neocolonialism [ˌniːəʊkəˈləʊniəlɪzəm] n. 新殖民主义
『neo新的+colonialism殖民主义→新殖民主义』

4. Neolithic [ˌniːəˈlɪθɪk] adj. 新石器时代的
『neo新的+lith石的+ic…的→新石器时代的』

前缀53. non- 表示"不，非"

1. nonexistent [ˌnɒnɪgˈzɪstənt] adj. 不存在的
『non不+ existent存在的→不存在的』

2. nonfiction [ˌnɒnˈfikʃən] n. 非小说类文学作品
『non不，非+ fiction小说→非小说类写实文学』

[U] The series will include both fiction and non-fiction.
本系列丛书将包括小说和非小说类纪实文学作品。

3. nonsense ['nɒnsns] n.胡扯；胡闹；毫无意义的话或文章
『non不，非+ sense意义→无意义的』

❶ [U, C] 胡扯（指所言、所想、所信荒谬或不正确）
Reports that he has resigned are nonsense.
有关他已经辞职的报道是无稽之谈。
You're talking nonsense! 你在胡说八道！
I'm not buying any of that nonsense. 我才不信那些废话呢。

❷ [U] 胡闹（指愚蠢或不可接受的行为）
silly or unacceptable behaviour
The new teacher won't stand for any nonsense.
这位新教师不会容忍任何胡闹行为。

❸ [U] 毫无意义的话；没有意义的文章
Most of the translation he did for me was complete nonsense.
他给我翻译的大多数文章完全不知所云。

4. non-smoking [nɒn 'sməʊkɪŋ] adj. （公共场所）禁止吸烟的；（人）不吸烟的
『non不，非+ smoking吸烟→不吸烟的』

More and more restaurants are providing non-smoking areas.
越来越多的餐厅开辟出无烟区。
She's a non-smoking, non-drinking fitness fanatic（[fəˈnætɪk] 狂热者）.
她不吸烟，不喝酒，热衷健身。

5. nonstop [nɒn'stɒp] adj.不停的；adv.不停地
『non不，非+ stop停止→不停的/地』

❶ adj. 不停的；直达的
Many US cities now have non-stop flights to Aspen.
美国很多城市现在都有直达阿斯彭的航班。
He was exhausted from over ten hours of nonstop work.
他连续工作十余小时，十分疲乏。

❷ adv. 不停地；直达地
The plane will fly nonstop to Kunming.
飞机将径直飞往昆明。
Every day for the next three months, we would leave class together and talk nonstop.
在随后的三个月里，我们每天一起离开教室，不停地交谈。

前缀54. ob- (of-, op-) =against, toward, over，表示"反对；相对"

1. offer ['ɒfə(r)] n. & vt. 主动提出；提供
『of (=toward)+fer (=bring)带来，拿来→拿来给某人→提供』

2. object ['ɒbdʒɪkt, əb'dʒekt] vi. 反对 vt. 提出…作为反对的理由 n. 物体；目标；宾语；客体，对象〈P196〉
『ob对着+ject投掷→向…扔东西→目标；反对』
（n. ['ɒbdʒɪkt]; v. [əb'dʒekt])

3. offend [ə'fend] v. 得罪；冒犯〈P166〉
『of(=against)+fend 打击→打击（别人）→得罪』

4. opponent [ə'pəʊnənt] n. 对手；反对者〈P261〉
『op(=against)+pon放置+ent表人→位于对面→对手』

5. oppose [ə'pəʊz] vt. 反对〈P262〉
『op对着+pose放→放在（某物）的对立面→反对』

6. opposite ['ɒpəzɪt] adj. 对面的；相反的 adv.对面 n. 对立面，反义词 prep. 在…对面〈P262〉
『op对着+pose放（去e）+ite…的→放在（某物）的对立面的→对立的』

7. oppress [ə'pres] vt. 压迫；使压抑〈P269〉
『op(=against)对着+press压→对着压→压迫』

8. obstacle ['ɒbstəkl] n. 障碍（物）〈P312〉
『ob逆+st站+acle表物→逆向站的东西→障碍』

9. obstruct [əb'strʌkt] vt. 阻挡，阻塞；妨碍；阻挠〈P319〉
『ob(=against)对着+struct建造→对着（通道）建造→阻塞』

前缀55. out- 表示"超过"或"外来的；出去；过时的；完全地"

out- 表示"超过，过度"

1. outdo [ˌaʊtˈduː] vt. 胜过，优于
『out超出+do (做，表现)→表现超出→胜过』

Sometimes small firms can outdo big businesses when it comes to customer care.
在顾客服务方面，有时小企业可能优于大企业。

2. outlive [ˌaʊtˈlɪv] vt. 比…长寿；度过…而健在
『out超出+live 活→活得超出…→比…长寿』

He will not outlive this night. 他活不过今晚。
He outlived his wife by three years. 他比妻子多活了三年。
He'd outlived his purpose. 他已经失去了存在的价值。

3. outnumber [ˌaʊtˈnʌmbə(r)] vt. 数量多于
『out超出+number数量→数量上超出』

The demonstrators were heavily outnumbered by the police.
示威者人数远不及警察人数。

4. outshine [ˌaʊtˈʃaɪn] vt. 比…更出色，更优异
『out超出+shine闪亮→比…闪亮→更出色』

Jesse has begun to outshine me in sports.
杰西在体育方面开始超过我。

5. outweigh [ˌaʊtˈweɪ] vt.比…重要，胜过
『out超出+weight重→重于…→比…重要』

If one thing outweighs another, the first thing is of greater importance, benefit, or significance than the second thing.

The advantages far outweigh the disadvantages. 利远大于弊。

The medical benefits of an X-ray far outweigh the risk of having it. X光片在医学上的益处远甚于它带来的风险。

6. outwit [ˌaʊtˈwɪt] vt.（智力上）超过，胜过
『out超出+wit机智→智力上超过』
（outwitted, outwitted）

Somehow he always manages to outwit his opponents.
他反正总能设法智胜对手。

7. outrage [ˈaʊtreɪdʒ] n. 义愤；暴行 vt. 使震怒
『out过分+rage暴怒→（因义愤而）过度暴怒→义愤』

❶ [U] 愤怒；义愤；愤慨
a strong feeling of shock and anger
The judge's remarks caused public outrage.
裁判的话引起了公愤。
Environmentalists have expressed outrage at the ruling.
环境保护主义者对这一裁决表示愤慨。

❷ [C] 暴行；骇人听闻的事
an act or event that is violent, cruel or very wrong and that shocks people or makes them very angry
No one has yet claimed responsibility for this latest bomb outrage. 迄今还没有人宣称对最近的爆炸丑行负责。

❸ [VN] [often passive] 使震怒；激怒
to make sb very shocked and angry
He was outraged at the way he had been treated.
他对所遭受的待遇感到非常愤怒。

▶ **outrageous** [aʊtˈreɪdʒəs] adj. 无法容忍的；骇人的
It is outrageous that the figures are not in the public domain.
让人愤慨的是那些数字并未公开。

▶ **rage** [reɪdʒ] n. 暴怒 v. 发怒；激烈进行；迅速蔓延
❶ [U, C] 暴怒；狂怒
a feeling of violent anger that is difficult to control
His face was dark with rage. 他气得面色铁青。
Sue stormed out of the room in a rage.
休怒气冲冲地走了出去。

❷ [U] (in compounds 构成复合词)（某情况引起的)愤怒，暴力行为
anger and violent behaviour caused by a particular situation
a case of trolley rage in the supermarket
超市里一起由手推车引起的暴力事件

❸ **the rage or all the rage** 风靡一时，非常流行
When something is popular and fashionable, you can say that it is the rage or all the rage.
The 1950s look is all the rage at the moment.
目前，20世纪50年代的装扮正流行。

❹ ~ (at/against/about sb/sth) 发怒；怒斥
to show that you are very angry about sth or with sb, especially by shouting
[V] He raged against the injustice of it all.
这一切不公正使他大发怒火。
[V speech] "That's unfair!" she raged.
"这不公平！"她愤怒地喊道。

❺ [V] ~ (on)（暴风雨、战斗、争论等）猛烈地继续；激烈进行
to continue in a violent way
The riots raged for three days. 暴乱持续了三天。
The blizzard was still raging outside. 外面暴风雪仍在肆虐。

❻ [V , usually + adv./prep.]（疾病、火焰等）迅速蔓延，

快速扩散
Forest fires were raging out of control.
森林大火迅速蔓延，失去了控制。
A flu epidemic raged through Europe. 流感在整个欧洲肆虐。

小贴士 rage与outrage的区别
Rage is uncontrollable or deep anger. Outrage is indignation （义愤）. Something that causes indignation is also an outrage— "You rigged the game—this is an outrage!" When groups protest, it's because they find the cause they're fighting against to be an outrage that must be addressed and changed. Someone who is filled with rage might become very aggressive and prone to starting fights because they are so angry.

▶ **enrage** [ɪnˈreɪdʒ] vt. 使异常愤怒，激怒，触怒
『en使+rage暴怒→激怒』
He was enraged by news of plans to demolish the pub.
看到计划拆除酒馆的新闻，他非常愤怒。

② out- 表示"外来的；出去；过时的；完全地"

1. outcome [ˈaʊtkʌm] n. 结局，结果
『outcome使我们想到come out→最终结果（出来）』
The outcome of an activity, process, or situation is the situation that exists at the end of it.
We are waiting to hear the final outcome of the negotiations.
我们在等待谈判的最终结果。

词义辨析 <P367第32>
结果 effect, outcome, consequence, result, aftermath

2. outcry [ˈaʊtkraɪ] n. 强烈的抗议
『out出来+cry因生气而尖叫→呐喊，抗议』
[C, U] An outcry is a reaction of strong disapproval and anger shown by the public or media about a recent event.
The killing caused an international outcry.
这起谋杀引起了国际社会的强烈抗议。
All these things have aroused a huge outcry from the Internet.
所有的这些事情在网络上引起了强烈的抗议。（杨澜演讲）

3. outdated [ˌaʊtˈdeɪtɪd] adj. 过时的
『out外面的+dated日期的→过时的』
Some students think traditional things are outdated.
有些学生认为传统的东西过时了。

小贴士 "你out了。" out是现代的一种常用的网络语言,意思为"淘汰"或者"落伍"。

4. outgoing [ˈaʊtɡəʊɪŋ] adj. 外向的，爱交际的
『out外面+go走+ing表形容词→（喜欢）走出去的→外向的』
"I am outgoing, and like talking with people, " he wrote.
"我很外向，喜欢和人交谈，"他写道。

▶ **easygoing** [ˈiːzɪˌɡəʊɪŋ] adj. 脾气随和的，温和的

5. outline [ˈaʊtlaɪn] v. & n. 概述；轮廓
『out外面的+line线→外面的线→轮廓』
❶ n. 概要；提纲
This is a brief outline of the events. 这就是事件的简要情况。

You should draw up an outline for the essay.
你应该为文章草拟个提纲。

❷ vt. 概述
[VN] We outlined our proposals to the committee.
我们向委员会提纲挈领地讲了讲我们的提案。

❸ n. 轮廓线；略图
She drew the figures in outline.
她简略地勾勒出人物的轮廓。

❹ vt.（因背后的光线）显示…的轮廓
They saw the huge building outlined against the sky.
他们看见了在天空的映衬下那座巨大建筑的轮廓。

6. outlook [ˈaʊtlʊk] n. 人生观；前景；景色
『out外面+look看→向外看（人生；事情；景色）→人生观；前景；景色』

❶ [usually sing.] ~ (on sth) 人生观，世界观，观点
the attitude to life and the world of a particular person, group or culture
He had a practical outlook on life. 他的人生观很实际。

❷ [usually sing.] 展望；前景
The outlook for the economy is still uncertain.
经济前景仍不明朗。

小贴士 中央电视台"希望英语"节目的英文名称是outlook。"希望英语"主题歌是 *Making your Outlook brighter*（让你的前途更辉煌）。

❸ 景色；景致；景观
a view from a particular place
The house has a pleasant outlook over the valley.
房子俯瞰山谷，景色宜人。

7. outskirts [ˈaʊtskɜːts] n. 郊区
『out外面的+skirts(裙子外衣的)下摆；位于…的边缘→在（市镇）的边缘之外→郊区』

They live on the outskirts of Milan. 他们住在米兰市郊。
Hours later we reached the outskirts of New York.
我们几小时后到达了纽约市郊。

8. outstanding [aʊtˈstændɪŋ] adj. 优秀的；突出的
『out外面的+stand站→站出来的→显眼的→优秀的；突出的』

❶ 优秀的
He is an outstanding athlete and deserved to win.
他是位优秀的运动员，赢得比赛也是理所当然。

❷ 突出的，明显的
The company is an outstanding example of a small business that grew into a big one.
该公司是小企业成长为大企业的突出例子。

小贴士 excellent 优秀的；outstanding 杰出的；perfect 完美的；superb 极佳的；marvellous 极好的；exceptional 卓越的

9. outlaw [ˈaʊtlɔː] n. 逃犯 vt. 宣布…不合法
『out外面→law法律→（逃避）法律→逃犯』

❶ [VN] 宣布…不合法；使…成为非法
plans to outlaw the carrying of knives

宣布携带刀具为非法的方案

❷ [C] 逃犯；草莽英雄
(used especially about people in the past) a person who has done sth illegal and is hiding to avoid being caught; a person who is not protected by the law
Robin Hood, the world's most famous outlaw
罗宾汉，蜚声世界的绿林好汉

10. outlet [ˈaʊtlet] n. 出口；发泄途径；经销店；媒体
『out外面+let让→让（情感、污水、商品、电、信息）出来的（地方）→发泄途径；排放；插座；媒体』

❶ [C]（情感的）发泄途径；（思想的）表达方式
Sport became the perfect outlet for his aggression.
运动成为他攻击性心理的最佳出路。
Her father had found an outlet for his ambition in his work.
她父亲在工作中找到了施展抱负的机会。

❷ [C] 出口，排放管
a sewage outlet 污水排放口
an outlet pipe 排水管道

❸ [C] 专营店，经销店；折扣品经销店
The business has 34 retail outlets in this state alone.
那家商号仅在本州就有34个零售店。

❹ [C]（通常指墙上的）电源插座（BrE socket）

❺ [C] 媒体
a media/ news/ TV etc. outlet is a newspaper, television station, website, etc. that makes information or other services available to the public.
Details about the facility have been reported by many outlets in the past two weeks.
在过去的两周里，许多媒体都报道了该设施的详细情况。

11. output [ˈaʊtpʊt] n. 产量；（计算机、文字处理器等的）输出信息，输出文件
『out外面+put放→放出来→产量；输出』

Manufacturing output has increased by 8%.
工业产量增长了8%。
Once you specify the input and output types, click the Next button. 一旦您指定了输入和输出类型，单击Next按钮。

12. outfit [ˈaʊtfɪt] n. 全套服装，装束；机构；组织；全套装备 vt. 提供衣服或装备
『outfit→fit out完全合适→完全合适达到一个目的→全套衣服（为某个场合）；团队，小组（完成某项任务）；全套装备（达到某个目的）』

❶ [C] 全套服装，装束（尤指为某场合或目的）
a cowboy/Superman outfit 一套牛仔/超人服装
She bought a new outfit for the party. 她为聚会买了一套新衣服。

❷ [C] 团队；小组；分队
a group of people who work together as a team or organization
He works for a private security outfit.
他在一家私人保安公司工作。

❸ [C] 全套装备；成套工具（BrE；同义词 kit）
a set of equipment that you need for a particular purpose
a bicycle repair outfit 修自行车的整套工具

❹ [VN] 供给服装；配置设备
To outfit someone or something means to provide them with equipment for a particular purpose.

Police had been outfitted with protective riot gear.
警察配备了防暴装备。
They outfitted him with artificial legs. 他们为他安了假腿。

① over- 表示"过分，过度；超过"

1. overcharge [ˌəʊvəˈtʃɑːdʒ] v. 要价过高
『over过度+charge收费→收费过高』

Make sure they don't overcharge you for the drinks.
注意别让他们多收饮料费。
We were overcharged by £5.
我们被多收了5英镑。

2. overcrowded [ˌəʊvəˈkraʊdɪd] adj. 过度拥挤的
『over过度+crowded拥挤的→过度拥挤的』

3. overestimate [ˌəʊvərˈestɪmeɪt] vt. 过高估计
『over过度+estimate估计→过高估计』

They overestimated his ability when they promoted him.
他们提拔他的时候高估了他的能力。
The importance of these findings cannot be overestimated.
这些发现的重要性是无法充分估量的。

反义词 **underestimate** [ˌʌndərˈestɪmeɪt] vt. 低估

We underestimated the time it would take to get there.
我们低估了抵达那里所需的时间。
Never underestimate your opponent. 千万不可低估你的对手。

▶**estimate** [ˈestɪmət, ˈestɪmeɪt] n. & vt. 估计；估价
（n. [ˈestɪmət]; vt. [ˈestɪmeɪt]）

to form an idea of the cost, size, value, etc. of sth, but without calculating it exactly
[VN] The satellite will cost an estimated £400 million.
这颗卫星估计要耗资4亿英镑。
[V (that)] We estimated (that) it would cost about €5,000.
我们估计要花费大约 5000 欧元。
I can give you a rough estimate of the amount of wood you will need. 我可以粗略估计一下你所需要的木材量。

4. overreact [ˌəʊvəriˈækt] vi. 反应过度
『over过度+react反应→反应过度』

[V] ~ (to sth) 反应过激，反应过火（尤指对不愉快的事情）
to react too strongly, especially to sth unpleasant
Don't overreact if your partner has a poor attitude.
如果你的伴侣态度不好，不要反应过度。
You must learn not to overreact to criticism.
你必须学会不要对批评反应太强烈。

5. overwork [ˌəʊvəˈwɜːk] n. & v. 过度劳累
『over过度+work工作→工作过多，过度劳累』

6. overwhelm [ˌəʊvəˈwelm] vt. 难以承受，压垮
『over过度+whelm淹没→难以承受』

[VN] [often passive]
❶ 使难以承受
to have such a strong emotional effect on sb that it is difficult for them to resist or know how to react
She was overwhelmed by feelings of guilt. 她感到愧疚难当。

❷ 压垮；使应接不暇
to be so bad or so great that a person cannot deal with it; to give too much of a thing to a person

We were overwhelmed by requests for information.
问讯使我们应接不暇。

7. overqualified [ˌəʊvəˈkwɒlɪfaɪd] adj. 资历过高的；大材小用的
『over过度+qualified合格的→资历过高的』

They didn't give me the job because they said I was overqualified.
他们没有给我这份工作，因为他们说我大材小用了。

8. overtime [ˈəʊvətaɪm] n. 加班；加班费；加时赛
『over超出+time时间→超出（正常）时间→加班；加时赛』

❶ [U] 加班；加班费
The union announced a ban on overtime.
工会宣布禁止加班。
They pay $150 a day plus overtime.
他们支付每天150美元的报酬，外加加班费。
He would work overtime, without pay, to finish a job.
他会为了完成工作无偿加班。

❷ [U] 加时赛 （BrE extra time）
Denver had won the championship by defeating the Cleveland Browns 23 : 20 in overtime.
丹佛队在加时赛中以23比20击败克利夫兰布朗队夺得冠军。

❸ **be working overtime** (informal) 非常活跃；过分活跃
There was nothing to worry about. It was just her imagination working overtime.
没什么可担心的。那只是她的想象力太丰富了。

② over- 表示"在…之上；那边"

1. overhead [ˌəʊvəˈhed, ˈəʊvəhed] adj. 头顶上的 adv. 在头顶上
『over在…之上+head头→头上的；头顶上的』
（adv. [ˌəʊvəˈhed]; adj. [ˈəʊvəhed]）
Planes flew overhead constantly. 飞机不断从头顶上飞过。
overhead power lines 高架输电线

2. overpass [ˈəʊvəpɑːs] n. 天桥；跨线桥；上跨式立交桥
『over在…之上+pass经过→从（另外一条路）之上经过→天桥；跨线桥』
（BrE flyover）
The city built a pedestrian overpass over the highway.
这个城市在公路上建了一座过街天桥。

3. overcome [ˌəʊvəˈkʌm] vt. 战胜，克服（困难）
『over在…之上+come过来→（从困难上面）过来→克服（困难）』
Find a way to overcome your difficulties.
找出办法战胜困难。

4. overlook [ˌəʊvəˈlʊk] vt. 忽视；忽略；俯视
『over在…之上+look→从（某物）上面看过去→（无意或有意）没看到→忽视；忽略』
❶ 忽略；未注意到
to fail to see or notice sth
He seems to have overlooked one important fact.
他好像忽略了一个重要的事实。

❷（对不良现象等）不予理会，视而不见
to see sth wrong or bad but decide to ignore it
We could not afford to overlook such a serious offence.
对这样严重的违法行为，我们决不能视若无睹。

❸ 俯视；眺望

if a building, etc. overlooks a place, you can see that place from the building

Pretty and comfortable rooms overlook a flower-filled garden.
漂亮舒适的房间俯视着花团锦簇的花园。

5. overall [ˌəʊvərˈɔːl , ˈəʊvərɔːl] adj. 总体的，全面的 adv. 总体地 n. 罩衣；（连体）工作服
『over在…之上；在外边+all所有的→总的，整体的；（穿在其他衣服外面的）罩衣，工作服』
（adj. & adv. [ˌəʊvərˈɔːl]；n. [ˈəʊvərɔːl]）

❶ adj. [only before noun] 总的；总体的；全面的
You use overall to indicate that you are talking about a situation in general or about the whole of something.
When she finished painting, she stepped back to admire the overall effect. 画完以后，她退后一步，以审视总体效果。
The overall situation is good, despite a few minor problems.
总的情况是好的，尽管有一些小问题。
The overall winner, after ten games, will receive $250,000.
10场比赛后，总冠军将获得25万美元。

❷ adv. 总计，总体上
Overall, it has been a good year.
总的来说，今年是个好年景。
The company will invest $1.6m overall in new equipment.
这个公司将总计投资160万美元购置新设备。

❸ overalls [pl.] （吊带）工装裤；（上下连身的）工装服（NAmE coveralls）
a loose piece of clothing like a shirt and trousers/pants in one piece, made of heavy cloth and usually worn over other clothing by workers doing dirty work
The mechanic was wearing a pair of blue overalls.
机修工穿着一件蓝色工装连衣裤。

❹ [C]（工作时穿的）罩衣
An overall is a piece of clothing shaped like a coat that you wear over your clothes in order to protect them while you are working.

6. overcoat [ˈəʊvəkəʊt] n. 大衣，外套
『over在…之上+coat上衣，外套→穿在外面的上衣→大衣，外套』

7. overseas [ˌəʊvəˈsiːz] adj.海外的 adv. 在海外
『over那边的+seas海洋→海洋那边的→海外的』

❶ adj. 海外的，外国的
Every year nine million overseas visitors come to London.
每年有900万外国游客来伦敦观光。
overseas development/markets/trade　海外发展/市场/贸易

❷ adv. 在国外，在海外
The product is sold both at home and overseas.
这个产品行销国内外。

8. overtake [ˌəʊvəˈteɪk] vt. 赶上，超过
『over在…之上+take带到→带到…之上→超过』

❶ (especially BrE) 超过，赶上
to go past a moving vehicle or person ahead of you because you are going faster than they are
[VN] He pulled out to overtake a truck.
他驶出车流，以超过一辆卡车。
[V] It's dangerous to overtake on a bend.
在弯道强行超车是危险的。

❷ [VN] 赶上，超越
Nuclear energy may overtake oil as the main fuel.
核能可能会超过石油成为主要燃料。
We mustn't let ourselves be overtaken by our competitors.
我们决不能让竞争对手超过我们。

9. overlap [ˌəʊvəˈlæp, ˈəʊvəlæp] n. & v. 重叠
『over在…之上+lap一圈，一段→重叠』
（v. [ˌəʊvəˈlæp]; n. [ˈəʊvəlæp]）

[VN] A fish's scales overlap each other.
鱼鳞一片片上下交叠。
[V] The floor was protected with overlapping sheets of newspaper. 地板用一张搭着一张的报纸保护着。
There is (a) considerable overlap between the two subjects.
两门科目之间有相当多的共通之处。

▶ **lap** [læp] n. （人坐着时的）大腿部；（比赛中的）一圈；一段行程
She waited quietly with her hands in her lap.
她双手放在腿上静静等候。
My dream job just fell into my lap.
我没费劲就找到了梦寐以求的工作。
He was overtaken on the final lap.
他在最后一圈被超过。
They're off on the first lap of their round-the-world tour.
他们踏上环游世界的第一段行程。

10. override [ˌəʊvəˈraɪd] vt. （以权力）否决；凌驾于
『over在…之上+ride乘→从上面过去→（以权力）否决；凌驾于』

❶ [VN] （以权力）否决，推翻；不理会
The chairman overrode the committee's objections and signed the agreement. 主席不顾委员会的反对，径行签署了协议。

❷ [VN] 比…更重要；凌驾
Considerations of safety override all other concerns.
对安全的考虑高于一切。

❸ [VN] 使自动控制暂时失效，改用手工控制
A special code is needed to override the time lock.
这定时锁要用特定密码才能打开。

11. overhear [ˌəʊvəˈhɪə(r)] vt. 偶然听到；无意中听到
『over那边+hear听到→（经过时）听到了从那边传过来的声音→偶然听到』

[VN] We talked quietly so as not to be overheard.
我们低声交谈，以免别人听到。
[VN] I overheard a conversation between two boys on the bus. 我在公共汽车上无意中听到两个男孩的谈话。

③ over- 表示"翻转；翻过"

1. overthrow [ˌəʊvəˈθrəʊ] vt. & n. 推翻（政权）
『over翻转+throw扔→扔后翻转→推翻』

Security forces have uncovered a plot to overthrow the government. 安全部队揭露了一起推翻政府的阴谋。

2. overturn [ˌəʊvəˈtɜːn] v. 倾覆，弄翻 vt. 推翻，撤销（判决等）
『over翻转+turn转→倾覆，弄翻』

[V] The car skidded and overturned. 汽车打滑翻倒了。
[VN] He stood up quickly, overturning his chair.
他猛然站起来，弄翻了椅子。
His sentence was overturned by the appeal court.

上诉法庭撤销了对他的判决。

3. overhaul [ˈəʊvəˈhɔːl , ˌəʊvəˈhɔːl] n. & vt. 检修；修订　vt.（体育比赛中）赶上，超过

『over翻转+haul用力拉→又翻转又拉→检修；修订』

（n. [ˈəʊvəhɔːl]; v. [ˈəʊvəˈhɔːl]）

❶ [C] 检修，大修；修订

an examination of a machine or system, including doing repairs on it or making changes to it

A radical overhaul of the tax system is necessary.
有必要彻底改革税制。

This engine needs an overhaul. 这台发动机需要检修。

❷ [VN] 彻底检修；全面修订

The engine has been completely overhauled.
发动机已彻底检修过了。

The government said it wanted to overhaul the employment training scheme to make it cost effective.
政府表示希望彻底改革就业培训计划以实现高效益。

❸ [VN]（尤指在体育比赛中）赶上，超过

Argentina need to beat Peru by at least four goals to overhaul Brazil and reach the final itself.
阿根廷队至少要赢秘鲁队4球才能超越巴西队进入决赛。

▶ **haul** [hɔːl] vt.（用力地）拉，拖　使出庭受审

The wagons were hauled by horses. 那些货车是马拉的。

He reached down and hauled Liz up onto the wall.
他俯身把利兹拉上墙头。

He was hauled up before the local magistrates for dangerous driving. 他因危险驾驶而被移交地方法庭审判。

4. overflow [ˌəʊvəˈfləʊ , ˈəʊvəfləʊ] v. 溢出；挤满　n. 溢出，溢出的液体；容纳不下的人（或物）

『over翻过+flow流→流翻过→溢出』

（v. [ˌəʊvəˈfləʊ]; n. [ˈəʊvəfləʊ]）

❶ [V, VN] 漫出，溢出；挤满

Plates overflowed with party food.
聚会上的食物碟满盘盈。

(figurative) Her heart overflowed with love.
她的心里充满了爱。

Kenneth overflowed with friendliness and hospitality.
肯尼思满怀友善好客之情。

The river overflowed its banks. 河水漫出了堤岸。

The streets were overflowing with the crowds.
街上人群拥挤。

The meeting overflowed into the street.
集会的人群延伸到了大街上。

❷ [U, sing.] 溢出；溢出的液体；容纳不下的人（或物）

an overflow of water from the lake 漫出的湖水

Tents have been set up next to hospitals to handle the overflow. 医院旁搭起了帐篷以安置容纳不下的人员。

1. Pan-American [pæn əˈmerɪkən] adj. 泛美的；全美洲（各国）的

『pan全部的+American美洲的→全美洲的』

Where is the counter of Pan-American?
泛美（航空公司）的柜台在哪里？

2. panorama [ˌpænəˈrɑːmə] n. 全景；(某专题或事件的)全面叙述

『pan全+orama观看；景→全部看得到→全景』

There is a superb panorama of the mountains from the hotel.
从旅馆可饱览峰峦叠嶂的雄伟景观。

3. pantheism [ˈpænθiɪzəm] n. 泛神论（认为神存在于万事万物）

『pan全部+the神+ism主义→泛神论』

4. pandemic [pænˈdemɪk] n.（全国或全球性）流行病 〈P148〉

『pan全部+dem人们+ic…的→在广泛的（所有的）人群中的→广泛流行的』

1. parachute [ˈpærəʃuːt] n. 降落伞

『para防避+chute降落→降落伞』

2. parasol [ˈpærəsɒl] n. 太阳伞；（海滩上、餐馆外等处的）大遮阳伞 〈P303〉

『para防避+sol太阳→防避太阳→太阳伞』

3. paradox [ˈpærədɒks] n. 矛盾的人或事物；悖论 〈P153〉

『para相对立+dox观点→相对立的观点→自相矛盾』

② para-=beside，表示"在旁边；辅助"

1. parallel [ˈpærəlel] adj. 平行的；相应的

『para旁边+llel线→旁边的线→平行线』

❶ adj. 平行的；同时发生的；类似的

The road and the canal are parallel to each other.
道路与运河平行。

a parallel case 同类型事例

parallel trends 并行发展的趋势

❷ [C]（存在或发生在不同地点或时间的）相似之物；（两者间的）近似之处

This is an achievement without parallel in modern times.
这是现代无可比拟的成就。

Detailed study of folk music from a variety of countries reveals many close parallels.
仔细研究各国民间音乐后发现了许多非常相似之处。

❸ [C] 纬线，纬圈 （also parallel of latitude）

❹ [VN] 与…相似；与…同时发生；比得上

Their legal system parallels our own.
他们的法律制度与我们的相似。

The rise in unemployment is paralleled by an increase in petty crime. 在失业率上升的同时，轻度犯罪也跟着增长。

a level of achievement that has never been paralleled
绝无仅有的最高成就

▶ **unparalleled** [ʌnˈpærəleld] adj. 无比的，无双的

It was an unparalleled opportunity to develop her career.
这是她发展事业的绝好机会。

2. parameter [pəˈræmɪtə(r)] n. 规范；范围；参数

『para旁边+meter计量，测量→在计量的旁边（不能超过）→规范；范围』

[usually pl.] 规范；范围；参数

something that decides or limits the way sth can be done

That would be enough to make sure we fell within the parameters of our loan agreement.
那就足以确保我们符合贷款协议的范围。

This parameter specifies the size of this workspace.

该参数指定该工作空间的大小。

形近词 **perimeter** [pəˈrɪmɪtə(r)] n. （土地的）外缘；周长 <P219>

『peri周围的+meter测量→周长；（土地）外缘』

3. **paralyze** [ˈpærəlaɪz] vt. 使瘫痪

『para旁边+lyze分开→使相邻（相联系的）分开→相互间不能联动→瘫痪』

❶ 使瘫痪；使麻痹

to make sb unable to feel or move all or part of their body

The accident left him paralysed from the waist down.

那场事故使他腰部以下都瘫痪了。

❷ 使不能正常工作

to prevent sth from functioning normally

The airport is still paralysed by the strike.

机场仍因罢工而陷于瘫痪。

4. **paramedic** [ˌpærəˈmedɪk] n. <美>护理人员，医务辅助人员

『para辅助+medic医生→医务辅助人员』

5. **paralegal** [ˌpærəˈliːgl] n. 律师助理

『para辅助+legal法律的→辅助法律的→律师的助手』

6. **paramilitary** [ˌpærəˈmɪləteri] adj. 准军事的；辅助军事的

『para辅助+military军事的→准军事的』

7. **parasite** [ˈpærəsaɪt] n. 寄生虫；寄生植物

『para旁边+site位置，场所→在某个位置旁边（白吃白喝的）→寄生虫』

8. **paraphrase** [ˈpærəfreɪz] v. （用更容易理解的文字）解释，释义

『para辅助+phrase短语→用其他短语来辅助释义』

Baxter paraphrased the contents of the press release.

巴克斯特解释了新闻发布的内容。

9. **paradigm** [ˈpærədaɪm] n. 典范，范例；词形变化表

『para旁边+digm显示→在旁边显示（让学习）→典范，范例；词形变化表』

a typical example or pattern of sth

The war was a paradigm of the destructive side of human nature. 那场战争尽显人性中具有破坏性的一面。

He had become the paradigm of the successful man.

他已经成为成功人士的典范。

verb paradigms 动词词形变化表

▶ **paradigmatic** [ˌpærədɪɡˈmætɪk] adj. 典型的；范例的

10. **parable** [ˈpærəbl] n. 寓言故事

『para旁边+(a)ble能够的→能够和身边的事相比较（而有哲理性质的）→寓言故事』

A parable is a short story, which is told in order to make a moral or religious point, like those in the Bible.

近义词 **fable** [ˈfeɪbl] n. 寓言故事；谣传 <P159>

③ para-=beyond，表示"超过"

1. **paragraph** [ˈpærəɡrɑːf] n. 段落

『para超过+graph写→在超过（原来的地方）写→另起一段→（文章的）段落』

词义辨析 <P373 第61> 文章，段落 **paragraph, passage, article, essay, paper, novel, fiction, story**

2. **paragon** [ˈpærəɡən] n. 完人；典范

『para超过+gon角；尖→超出顶尖的→完人；典范』

a person who is perfect or who is a perfect example of a particular good quality

I make no claim to be a paragon.

我没有说过自己是完人。

He wasn't the paragon of virtue she had expected.

他不是她想象中的那种美德典范。

3. **paranormal** [ˌpærəˈnɔːml] adj. 超自然的

『para超出+normal正常的→超自然的』

that cannot be explained by science or reason and that seems to involve mysterious forces

Science may be able to provide some explanations of paranormal phenomena.

科学也许能够解释某些超自然现象。

4. **paramount** [ˈpærəmaʊnt] adj. 最重要的；权力最大的 <P229>

『para超过+mount山→超过山顶的→最重要的』

④ para-=parachute，意为"降落伞"

1. **paradrop** [ˈpærədrɒp] n. & v. 利用降落伞空投

『para降落伞+drop丢下→利用降落伞空投』

2. **paraglide** [ˈpærəɡlaɪd] v. 进行滑翔伞运动

『para降落伞+glide滑翔→进行滑翔伞运动』

3. **paratrooper** [ˈpærətruːpə(r)] n. 伞兵，空降兵

『para降落伞+troop军队+er人→伞兵』

前缀59. per-=through, thoroughly, 表示"自始至终；彻底"；还可以表示"每；假；坏"

① per-=through, 表示"自始至终；穿过"

1. **permanent** [ˈpɜːmənənt] adj. 永久的，长久的

『per自始至终+man停留+ent表形容词→始终停留的→永久的』

a permanent job 固定工作

The accident has not done any permanent damage.

那场事故没有造成什么永久性损伤。

The stroke left his right side permanently damaged.

中风使他的右半身永久受损。

She had decided to settle permanently in France.

她已经决定永久定居法国。

▶ **permanence** [ˈpɜːmənəns] n. 永久，持久性

The spoken word is immediate but lacks permanence.

口头之言便捷，但缺乏持久性。

2. **permeate** [ˈpɜːmieɪt] v. （液体、气体等）渗透，弥漫；（思想、情感等）扩散，感染

『per(=through)遍及+meate(=pass)传递→传递到所有地方→弥漫；感染』

[VN] The smell of leather permeated the room.

屋子里弥漫着皮革的气味。

[V + adv./prep.] rainwater permeating through the ground

渗入地下的雨水

[VN] a belief that permeates all levels of society

深入社会各阶层的看法

3. **persevere** [ˌpɜːsɪˈvɪə(r)] vi. 坚持不懈；锲而不舍 <P54>

『per自始至终+severe严厉的→自始至终对自己要求很严厉→坚持不懈』

4. persist [pəˈsɪst] vi. 执意；坚持；持续存在 〈P302〉
『per自始至终+sist (stand) 站立→始终站着→坚持到底』

5. perspective [pəˈspektɪv] n. 观点，看法，视角 〈P307〉
『per穿过+spect看+ive…的→（从某个地方）穿过（时空）来看→视角』

6. perspire [pəˈspaɪə(r)] vi. 出汗，流汗 〈P311〉
『per穿过+spire呼吸→（汗）穿过（毛孔）呼吸→出汗』

7. perceive [pəˈsiːv] vt. 注意到，察觉到 〈P128〉
『per通过+ceive抓住→通过（某个细节）抓到（某种情况）→注意到，觉察到』

8. perennial [pəˈreniəl] adj. 长久的；（植物）多年生的　n. 多年生植物 〈P113〉
『per贯穿+enn年+ial…的→贯穿整年的→长久的』

② per-=thoroughly, 表示"彻底地，完全地"

1. peruse [pəˈruːz] vt. 细读，研读
『per彻底地+use使用→彻底地、充分地使用（阅读材料）→细读，研读』

[VN] (formal or humorous) 细读；研读
to read sth, especially in a careful way
A copy of the report is available for you to peruse at your leisure. 现有一份报告，供你闲暇时细读。

▶**perusal** [pəˈruːzl] n. 阅读，读

I have sent you the papers for your perusal.
我把这些文件寄给你供翻阅。

2. peremptory [pəˈremptəri] adj. 强硬的，不容分辩的 〈P158〉
『per彻底地+empt(=take)拿+ory有…性质的→彻底拿走（决定权）的→强硬的，不容分辩的』

3. perfect [ˈpɜːfɪkt，pəˈfekt] adj. 完美的，极好的；十足的 vt.使完美 〈P163〉
『per彻底地+fect做→做得很彻底→完美的』
（adj. [ˈpɜːfɪkt]；v. [pəˈfekt]）

4. perplex [pəˈpleks] vt.使迷惑；使复杂化 〈P258〉
『per彻底地+plex折叠→彻底地折叠在一起（使看不清）→使迷惑；使复杂化』

5. perturb [pəˈtɜːb] vt. 使焦虑；使不安 〈P339〉
『per彻底地+turb搅动→（心思）被彻底搅动了→使焦虑；使不安』

③ per-，表示"假；坏"

1. perfunctory [pəˈfʌŋktəri] adj. 敷衍的
『per假+funct(=perform)执行+ory…的→假执行的→敷衍的』

They only made a perfunctory effort. 他们只是敷衍了事。

2. perpetrate [ˈpɜːpətreɪt] vt. 犯（罪），做（错事），干（坏事）
『per坏+pertrate(=perform)做→做坏事』

A high proportion of crime in any country is perpetrated by young males in their teens and twenties.
在任何国家的犯罪者中，十几二十岁的青年男性都占了很高的比例。

3. pervert [pəˈvɜːt，ˈpɜːvɜːt] v. 使走样；使堕落　n. 性变态者 〈P350〉

『per坏+vert转变→使向坏处转变→使走样；使堕落』
（v. [pəˈvɜːt]；n. [ˈpɜːvɜːt]）

4. perjure [ˈpɜːdʒə(r)] vt. 作伪证；发假誓 〈P199〉
『per害，假+jure发誓→发假誓→作伪证』

5. perfidy [ˈpɜːfədi] n. 背叛，背信弃义 〈P170〉
『per假+fid相信；信念+y表名词→假装相信→不忠诚』

④ per-=every，表示"每"

1. per [pə(r)] prep. 每；每一
Rooms cost £50 per person, per night.
房价每人每晚50英镑。

2. percent [pəˈsent] n. 百分比；百分之一
『per每一个+cent一百→一百中的每一个→百分之一』

前缀60. peri- 表示"周围；靠近"

1. periphery [pəˈrɪfəri] n. 外围；边缘
『peri周围+pher(=fer)带来+y表名词→带到周围→外围』

❶ [C]周围，外围
the outer edge of a particular area
Geographically, the UK is on the periphery of Europe, while Paris is at the heart of the continent.
从地理位置上讲，英国处于欧洲边缘，而巴黎却位于（欧洲）大陆的中心位置。

❷ [C] 边缘，次要部分
the less important part of sth, for example of a particular activity or of a social or political group
The crisis in the eurozone's periphery is not an accident；it is inherent in the system.
欧元区外围成员国所出现的危机不是偶然的，而是该体系固有的结果。

▶**peripheral** [pəˈrɪfərəl] adj. 周边的；次要的　n. 外围设备
『peri周围+pher(= fer)带来+al表形容词或名词→周边的』

❶ adj. 周边的，外围的；次要的
peripheral vision 周边视觉
Fund-raising is peripheral to their main activities.
对他们的主要活动而言，筹集资金是次要的。

❷ n.（计算机）外围设备
monitors, printers and other peripherals
显示器、打印机及其他外围设备

2. periscope [ˈperɪskəʊp] n. 潜望镜 〈P289〉
『peri周围+scope镜→（伸出水面）观察四周情况的镜→潜望镜』

3. perimeter [pəˈrɪmɪtə(r)] n.（土地的）外缘；周长 〈P219〉
『peri周围的+meter测量→周长；（土地）外缘』

前缀61. post-=behind, after，表示"在…之后"；还可表示"邮寄"

① post-=behind, after，表示"在…之后"

1. postdate [ˌpəʊstˈdeɪt] vt. 填迟…的日期
『post之后+date日期→把日期向后填→填迟…的日期』
反义词 **antedate**[ˌæntiˈdeɪt] vt. 填早…的日期

2. posterity [pɒˈsterəti] n. 子孙；后裔
『post之后+er人+ity表性质状况→后面的人→后代』

[U]You can refer to everyone who will be alive in the future as posterity.

Their music has been preserved for posterity.
他们的音乐已为后世保存起来。
Posterity will remember him as a great man.
后人将会记住他是个伟人。

3. postgraduate [ˌpəʊstˈgrædʒuət] adj. 研究生的 n. 研究生
『post之后+graduate毕业→大学毕业后→研究生』

He failed again in this year's postgraduate entrance examination. 今年考研他又落了第。
Take myself as an example, I changed my major when I became a postgraduate.
以自己作为一个例子，当我成为一个研究生时我改变了我的专业。

小贴士 **undergraduate** [ˌʌndəˈgrædʒuət] n. 在校本科生（还没有毕业）

4. post-war [ˈpəʊstˈwɔː] adj. 战后的
『post之后+ war 战争→战后的』

He really was one of the finest boxers in post-war Britain.
他确实是战后不列颠最优秀的拳击手之一。

5. posthumous [ˈpɒstjʊməs] adj. 死后的 ⟨P192⟩
『post之后+hum土+ous…的→在入土之后的→死后的』

6. postpone [pəˈspəʊn] n. 延迟；延期 ⟨P261⟩
『post之后+pone放置→向后面放→延迟』

7. postscript [ˈpəʊstskrɪpt] n.（信末签名后的）附言；（正文后的）补充说明 ⟨P290⟩
『post 之后+script写，稿子→在稿子之后又写上去的内容→附言』

8. posterior [pɒˈstɪəriə(r)] adj.（身体部位）后部的 n. 臀部，屁股 ⟨P80⟩
『post后，后面+er+ior较…的→（在时间、次序上）较后的』

② post- 表示"邮政，邮寄"

1. postage [ˈpəʊstɪdʒ] n. 邮费，邮资
『post邮寄+age费用，表名词→邮费』
[U] 邮资；邮费
This dictionary is 100 *yuan*, postage included.
这本词典连邮费共100元。

2. postcard [ˈpəʊstkɑːd] n. 明信片

前缀62. pre- 相当于"before"，表示"之前，预先"

1. prefix [ˈpriːfɪks] n. 前缀
『pre (before)之前+fix固定→固定在单词前面以改变其词义→前缀』
反义词 **suffix** [ˈsʌfɪks] n. 后缀

2. prehistory [ˌpriːˈhɪstri] n. 史前时期
『pre (before)之前+history历史→在有历史之前的时期→史前时期』
▶ **prehistoric** [ˌpriːhɪˈstɒrɪk] adj. 史前的

3. preposition [ˌprepəˈzɪʃn] n. 介词
『pre之前+position位置→放在（名词或代词）位置的前面→介词』
生词表中prep.就是preposition的缩写。

4. preschool [ˈpriːskuːl] adj. 学龄前的 n. 学前班
『pre之前+school学校→在上学前的→学龄前的』

Looking after preschool children is very tiring.
照顾学龄前的孩子非常辛苦。

5. precaution [prɪˈkɔːʃn] n. 预防措施
『pre事先+caution谨慎→事先很谨慎（而采取预防措施）→预防措施』

~ (against sth)   [usually pl.]

precautions against fire 防火措施
You must take all reasonable precautions to protect yourself and your family.
你必须采取一切合理的预防措施，保护自己和家人。
Could he not, just as a precaution, move to a place of safety?
就算仅仅是为了以防万一，难道他就不能挪到安全的地方吗？

▶ **caution** [ˈkɔːʃn] n. 小心，谨慎； vt. 告诫；警告
❶[U] 谨慎；小心；慎重
care that you take in order to avoid danger or mistakes; not taking any risks
You should proceed with the utmost caution.
你应该小心行事。
I threw caution to the wind and rode as fast as I could.
我不顾一切，骑得飞快。
❷ ~ (sb) against sth | ~ sb about sth 警告；告诫；提醒
[V] I would caution against getting too involved.
我要提出警告，别介入得太深。
山姆告诫他不要草率作出决定。

▶ **cautious** [ˈkɔːʃəs] adj. 小心的；谨慎的
being careful about what you say or do, especially to avoid danger or mistakes; not taking any risks
The government has been cautious in its response to the report. 政府对此报道反应谨慎。
They expressed cautious optimism about a solution to the crisis. 他们对解决危机持谨慎的乐观态度。

词义辨析 ⟨P361第2⟩ 小心的 cautious, careful

6. preview [ˈpriːvjuː] n. & vt. 预言；预先评论 ⟨P353⟩
『pre事先+view（看）→预演；预先评述』

7. precise [prɪˈsaɪs] adj. 准确的；确切的；精确的 ⟨P132⟩
『pre事先+cise切割→事先切好的→精确的』

8. preclude [prɪˈkluːd] vt. 使行不通；妨碍，阻止 ⟨P137⟩
『pre事先+clude关闭→（做某事的可能性）事先关闭→妨碍，阻止』

9. predict [prɪˈdɪkt] vt. 预言 ⟨P149⟩
『pre之前+dict说→在（发生）之前说→预言』

10. prescribe [prɪˈskraɪb] vt. 开药方；规定，指定 ⟨P289⟩
『pre预先+scribe写→（抓药之前要）预先写（处方）；预先写（规则）→开处方；（法律、规则）指定』

11. preface [ˈprefəs] n.（书的）前言，序言 vt. 为…写序言；作…的开场白 ⟨P161⟩
『pre前面+face面，脸→（书内容之前的）面→前言』

12. prejudice [ˈpredʒudɪs] n. 偏见 ⟨P197⟩
『pre之前+judice判断→事先已经判断好→偏见』

13. preliminary [prɪˈlɪmɪnəri] adj.预备的；初步的 n. 准备工作，初步行动；预赛，初赛 ⟨P207⟩
『pre事先+limin门槛，引申为"限制"+ary…的→入门前的→初步的，预备的』

前缀63. pro- 相当于"before"，表示"之前，预先"

① pro- 相当于"before，forth, forward"表示"向前"

1. prolong [prə'lɒŋ] vt. 延长
『pro向前+long长→向前拉长→延长』

[VN] 延长
The operation could prolong his life by two or three years.
这次手术可使他多活两三年。
To save time is to prolong life. 节省时间等于延长寿命。

2. profile ['prəʊfaɪl] n. 侧面像；人物简介 vt. 写简介
『pro向前+file纱线→向前拉的线条→侧面像』

❶ [C] 侧面像；侧影像
a picture of the president in profile 总统的侧面画像

❷ [C] 人物简介；传略
A newspaper published profiles of the candidates' wives.
一家报纸刊登了几位候选人夫人的简介。

❸ [VN] 写简介
His career is profiled in this month's journal.
这期月刊概述了他的工作生涯。

❹ **a high/low profile** 高/低调
If someone has a high profile, people notice them and what they do. If you keep a low profile, you avoid doing things that will make people notice you.

I advised her to keep a low profile for the next few days.
我建议她未来几天低调一点。

▶**file** [faɪl] n. 文件；文件夹 v. 提起（诉讼）；排成一行行走

❶ [C] 文件箱，文件夹；(计算机的)文件
He sat behind a table on which were half a dozen files.
他坐在一张放有6个文件夹的桌子后面。
to access/copy/create/delete/download/save a file
打开/复制/新建/删除/下载/保存文件

❷ [VN] 提起（诉讼）；提出（投诉、请求等）
to present sth so that it can be officially recorded and dealt with
A number of them have filed formal complaints against the police. 他们中的许多人都对警方提出了正式控告。

❸ [C] 排成一行的人（或物）
a line of people or things, one behind the other
They set off in file behind the teacher.
他们跟在教师后面鱼贯出发。

❹ [V + adv./prep.] 排成一行行走
The doors of the museum opened and the visitors began to file in. 博物馆开门了，参观者鱼贯而入。

3. prodigy ['prɒdədʒi] n. 天才，奇才，神童
『pro向前+digy所说的事情→（因为奇才）广为流传』

A prodigy is someone young who has a great natural ability for something such as music, mathematics, or sports.
She was a child prodigy, giving concerts before she was a teenager. 她是个神童，十来岁不到就举办音乐会了。

▶**prodigious** [prə'dɪdʒəs] adj. 巨大的，大得惊人的
[usually before noun] (formal) 巨大的；伟大的
very large or powerful and causing surprise or admiration
a prodigious achievement/memory/talent
惊人的成就/记忆力/才华

Laser discs can store prodigious amounts of information.
激光磁盘能够贮存大量信息。

4. progress ['prəʊgres] n. & v. 进步；前进 <P188>
『pro (forward)前+gress (walk)走→向前走→前进；进步』
(n. 英['prəʊgres]; 美 ['prɑːgres]; vi. [prə'gres]）

5. project ['prɒdʒekt] n. 工程；课题 vt. 投射 <P195>
『pro向前+ject投掷→向前投掷→投射；引申为工程项目』
(n. ['prɒdʒekt]; v. [prə'dʒekt]）

6. provoke [prə'vəʊk] vt. 激起，引起；挑衅，激怒 <P357>
『pro向前+voke喊→向前面喊→激起，引起；挑衅，激怒』

7. proceed [prə'siːd] v. 前进，继续进行 <P126>
『pro向前+ceed行走，前进→向前走；继续做』

8. produce [prə'djuːs] vt. 生产；制造；出示 n. 农产品 <P154>
『pro向前+ duce引导；带来→向前产出→生产』
(n. ['prɒdjuːs]; v. [prə'djuːs]）

9. promote [prə'məʊt] vt. 促进；促销；提升 <P225>
『pro向前+mote移动→使向前移动→提拔；促进；促销』

10. propose [prə'pəʊz] vt. 提议，建议；求婚 <P263>
『pro向前+pose放→（把建议）放到别人前面（供考虑）→提议』

11. prospect ['prɒspekt] n. 希望；前景；前途 <P307>
『pro向前+spect看→向前看→前景』

② pro- 表示"代理"

1. pro-consul n. 代理领事

2. pronoun ['prəʊnaʊn] n. 代词
『pro代理+noun名词→代理名词→代词』

③ pro- 表示"亲；赞同"

1. pro-American adj. 亲美的

2. pro-British adj. 亲英的

3. the pros and cons [prəʊs], [kɒns]事物的利与弊
『pro赞同；con 反对』
the advantages and disadvantages of sth
We weighed up the pros and cons.
我们权衡了利弊得失。
They sat for hours debating the pros and cons of setting up their own firm.
他们在一起坐了数小时，讨论自己创办公司的利弊。

④ pro- 表示"很多"

1. procreate ['prəʊkrieɪt] v. 生育，生殖
『pro多+create创造→创造很多→生育，生殖』
[V , VN] to produce children or baby animals
We procreate because that's the desire of the goddess.
我们生育因为这是神的愿望。

2. proliferate [prə'lɪfəreɪt] vi. 激增，剧增
『pro多+life生命+r+ate表动词→产生很多→激增，剧增』
Books and articles on the subject have proliferated over the last year.
过去一年以来，论及这一问题的书和文章大量涌现。
Computerized databases are proliferating fast.
计算机化的数据库正在激增。

▶ **prolific** [prə'lɪfɪk] adj. 多产的；众多的

❶ （作家、画家或作曲家）多产的；（人、动物、植物）多育的，多产的，高产的

She is a prolific writer of novels and short stories.
她是一位多产的作家，写了很多小说和短篇故事。

Rabbits and other rodents are prolific.
兔子和其他啮齿动物是多产的。

❷ （动物）众多的，大批的

If animals are prolific somewhere, there are a lot of them there.

All the big game congregate here；and birdlife is particularly prolific. 所有的大型野兽都聚集在这里，鸟类尤其丰富。

3. **profuse** [prə'fjuːs] adj. 大量的，丰富的 〈P182〉
『pro多+fuse流→多得流了出来→大量的，丰富的』

前缀64. pseud(o)- 表示"假；伪"

1. **pseudonym** ['suːdənɪm] n. 笔名；假名
『pseud假；伪+onym名字→假名；笔名』

Both plays were published under the pseudonym of Philip Dayre. 两个剧本都是以菲利普·戴尔的笔名出版的。

2. **pseudoscience** [ˌsjuːdəʊ'saɪəns] n. 伪科学；假科学
『pseud假；伪+（o）science科学→伪科学；假科学』

前缀65. re-=back; again，表示"返回；又"

① re-=back，表示"返回"

1. **return** [rɪ'tɜːn] n. & v. 返回；归还
『re返回+turn转动→向后转→返回』

2. **react** [ri'ækt] vi. 作出反应
『re返回+act做→回应；反应』

❶ ~ (to sth) (by doing sth)
Local residents have reacted angrily to the news.
当地居民对这一消息表示愤怒。

The market reacted by falling a further two points.
股市的反应是再下跌两个百分点。

❷ （对食物等）有不良反应，过敏
People can react badly to certain food additives.
人们对某些食品添加剂会严重过敏。

❸ ~ (with sth) | ~ (together) 产生化学反应
Iron reacts with water and air to produce rust.
铁和水及空气发生反应产生铁锈。

▶ **overreact** [ˌəʊvəri'ækt] vi. 反应过度 〈P27〉
『over过度+react反应→反应过度』

3. **recall** [rɪ'kɔːl] v. 记起；召回
『re返回+call喊，叫→（把过去的记忆）喊回来→回忆起』

❶ (formal) （不用于进行时）记起，回忆起，回想起
[VN] She could not recall his name. 她想不起他的名字。
[V-ing] I can't recall meeting her before.
我想不起以前曾经见过她。
[V that] He recalled that she always came home late on Wednesdays. 他回想起她星期三总是很晚回家。

❷ [VN] （不用于进行时）使想起
The music recalls memories of childhood.
音乐唤起了童年的回忆。

❸ [VN] 召回（某人）
Both countries recalled their ambassadors.

两个国家都召回了各自的大使。
He was recalled to military duty.
他被召回执行军事任务。

❹ [VN] 收回，召回（残损货品等）
The company has recalled all the faulty hairdryers.
公司回收了所有有问题的吹风机。

词义辨析 〈P362第7〉
记起 remember, memorise, recall, recollect

4. **recollect** [ˌrekə'lekt] v. （努力）记起，想起 〈P202〉
『re返回+collect收集→（把过去的记忆）一点一点地收集回来→（努力）回忆起』

5. **refresh** [rɪ'freʃ] vt. 使恢复精力
『re返回+fresh新鲜的→使回到新鲜的状态→恢复精力』

❶ [VN] 使恢复精力；使凉爽
The long sleep had refreshed her.
一场酣睡使她重又精力充沛。
He refreshed himself with a cool shower.
他冲了个凉水澡来提神。

❷ （computing 计）刷新

▶ **refreshing** [rɪ'freʃɪŋ] adj. 提神的；令人耳目一新的

❶ 使人精力充沛的，提神的；使人凉爽的
A refreshing breeze is blowing gently. 清风徐来。
He had a refreshing drink. 他喝了一杯提神的饮料。

❷ 令人耳目一新的；别具一格的
His work was deeply refreshing, and all of it shot through with humour. 他的作品令人耳目一新，充满幽默元素。
What is refreshing is the author's easy, conversational style.
让人耳目一新的是作者轻松的会话式写作风格。

▶ **refreshment** [rɪ'freʃmənt] n.提神；食物；点心

❶ [pl.] （在公共活动场所供应或销售的）饮料，小食
（可以理解为为了提神而喝的饮料或吃的小吃）

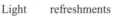

Light refreshments will be served during the break. 中间休息时有点心供应。

❷ [U] (formal) 食物和饮料
Can we offer you some refreshment? 您要吃点什么吗？

词义辨析 〈P362第8〉 小吃，点心 snack, refreshment

6. **remind** [rɪ'maɪnd] vt. 提醒；使想起
『re返回+mind心里→（使某事）返回到心里→使想起』

❶ 提醒某人使其回想起某事
~ sb (about/of sth)
If someone reminds you of a fact or event that you already know about, they say something which makes you think about it.
I can't think of his name—can you remind me?
我记不起他的名字了——你提醒我一下好吗？
She reminded me that we had in fact met before.
她提醒我实际上我们以前见过面。

❷ 提醒某人要做某事
~ sb about sth | ~ sb to do sth
Remind Jenny to bring her laptop when she comes.
提醒詹妮在她来的时候带上她的笔记本电脑。

Can you remind me about my dentist's appointment tomorrow? 你能提醒我明天牙医的预约吗？

❸ （因为相似或有联系）而使人不自觉地联想到
~ sb of sth

That song always reminds me of our holiday in Mexico.
那首歌总能让我想起我们在墨西哥度假的情景。

She was tall and dark, and reminded me of my cousin Sarah.
她又高又黑，让我想起了我的表妹莎拉。

▶ **reminder** [rɪˈmaɪndə(r)] n.使人回忆起某事；提示信

❶ [C] 使人回忆起某事

The cold served as a reminder that winter wasn't quite finished. 寒冷提醒人们冬天还没有完全结束。

❷ [C]（告知该做某事的）通知单，提示信

I stuck a reminder on the bulletin board.
我在告示牌上贴了一个提示语。

7. replace [rɪˈpleɪs] vt. 代替；更换
『re返回+place放→放回（原处）；放回（另外一个原来所在的地方）→放回；取代』

❶ [VN] 取代

The new design will eventually replace all existing models.
新的设计最终将会取代所有现有的型号。

Teachers will never be replaced by computers in the classroom. 课堂上电脑永远不会取代老师。

❷ [VN] 以…替换；以…接替

If you replace one thing or person with another, you put something or someone else in their place to do their job.

He will be difficult to replace when he leaves.
他离开后，他的位置很难有人接替。

It is not a good idea to miss meals and **replace them with** snacks. 不吃正餐，改吃点心，这不是什么好主意。

❸ [VN] 换下（坏的）；以新的替换

The shower that we put in a few years back has broken and we cannot afford to replace it.
我们几年前安装的淋浴器坏了，但买不起新的来换。

❹ [VN] 把…放回（原处）

I replaced the cup carefully in the saucer.
我小心翼翼地将杯子放回茶碟。

词义辨析 <P363第11> 替代 replace, substitute

▶ **replacement** [rɪˈpleɪsmənt] n. 替代；替代者
『replace替代+ment表名词→替代；替代者』

Replacement is guaranteed if the products are not up to the standard.

We undertake to replace the specifications.
产品不合规格，保证退换。

Taylor has nominated Adams as his replacement.
泰勒提名亚当斯接替他。

8. restore [rɪˈstɔː(r)] v. 修复；恢复；复原
『re返回++store贮存→又贮存了回来→恢复，修复』

❶ 恢复（秩序、和平、电力、信心、职位等）

to bring back a situation or feeling that existed before

The measures are intended to restore public confidence in the economy. 这些举措旨在恢复公众对经济的信心。

Order was quickly restored after the riots.
暴乱过后秩序很快得到了恢复。

The operation restored his sight. 手术使他恢复了视力。

By Sunday, electricity had been restored.

到星期日，电力已经恢复。

We will restore her to health but it may take time.
我们会让她恢复健康，但可能需要一些时间。

❷ 修复（艺术品、建筑等）

to repair a building, work of art, piece of furniture, etc. so that it looks as good as it did originally

Her job is restoring old paintings. 她的工作是修复旧画。

❸ ~ sth (to sb/sth) 归还（丢失或被盗的东西）

The police have now restored the painting to its rightful owner. 警察已经把这幅油画归还给了它的合法主人。

▶ **store** [stɔː(r)] n.商店；仓库 v. 贮存

❶ [C]商店（英国英语中主要指大型百货商店，而美国英语中可指任何规模的商店）

❷ [C] 贮存物；仓库

I handed over my secret store of chocolate biscuits.
我交出了自己偷偷藏起来的巧克力饼干。

❸ [VN] 贮存

He hoped the electronic equipment was safely stored away.
他希望那些电子设备得到妥善保存。

Thousands of pieces of data are stored in a computer's memory. 在计算机的存储器中存有成千上万条数据。

❹ in store (for sb)
即将发生（在某人身上）；等待着（某人）

We don't know what life holds in store for us.
我们不知道等待我们的将是什么样的生活。

If she had known what lay in store for her, she would never have agreed to go.
要是她事先知道会有什么遭遇的话，她是决不会同意去的。

There were also surprises in store for me.
也有一些令人吃惊的事在等着我。

9. reinstate [ˌriːɪnˈsteɪt] vt. 恢复原职；恢复（法律、做法等）；修复（设施等）
『re返回+in进入+state状态→返回原来的状态→复职；恢复』

The governor is said to have agreed to reinstate five senior workers who were dismissed.
据说州长已同意给5名被解雇的高级雇员复职。

There have been repeated calls to reinstate the death penalty.
不断有人呼吁恢复死刑。

10. reduce [rɪˈdjuːs] vt. 减少；使陷入 <P154>
『re返回+duce（引导）→返回引导→减少』

11. recreation [ˌrekriˈeɪʃn] n. 消遣；休闲 <P140>
『re返回+creation创造→创造（可理解为"工作"）后回来（做点别的事情消遣一下）→消遣』

12. recycle [ˌriːˈsaɪkl] vt. 回收利用；循环利用 <P132>
『re返回+cycle圆，环→再回到循环中→回收利用』

13. refer [rɪˈfɜː(r)] vi. 提及；参看；关系到；请教 <P167>
『re返回+fer带来→回到（原出处）；再到（另外一个地方）→查阅，参看；推荐，指引』
（注意：referred; referred; referring）

14. refuse [rɪˈfjuːz] v. 拒绝 <P182>
『re返回+fuse流→往回流→拒绝』

15. reject [rɪˈdʒekt, ˈriːdʒekt] vt. 拒绝；不录用；排斥 <P195>

16. reflect [rɪˈflekt] v. 反射；反映；反思〈P174〉

『re返回+ flect弯曲→（光线）往回弯曲→反射』

17. recover [rɪˈkʌvə(r)] v. 恢复（健康）；恢复（常态）〈P139〉

『re返回+cover覆盖→又覆盖回来→恢复；找到』

② re-=again，表示"又，再"

1. reappear [ˌriːəˈpɪə(r)] vi. 再（出）现

『re又+appear出现→再现』

2. rebuild [ˌriːˈbɪld] vt. 重建

『re又+build建设→又建设→重建』

3. remove [rɪˈmuːv] vt. 移开；脱下

『re又+move移动→又移动→移走』

❶ ~ sth (from sth) 移开

He removed his hand from her shoulder.
他将手从她的肩膀上拿开。
Illegally parked vehicles will be removed.
非法停放的车辆将被拖走。

❷ [VN] 脱下（衣服）

She removed her glasses and rubbed her eyes.
她摘下眼镜，揉了揉眼睛。
He removed his jacket. 他脱下了夹克。

▶**removal** [rɪˈmuːvl] n. 移去；免职
Clearance of the site required the removal of a number of trees. 清理这一场所需要移走不少树。

词义辨析〈P365第24〉

解雇 dismiss, fire, lay off, remove, sack

4. renew [rɪˈnjuː] vt. 重新开始；更新；续签

『re又+new新的→重新开始→更新』

❶ [VN] 重新开始；中止后继续

He renewed his attack on government policy towards Europe.
他重新开始对政府的欧洲政策进行抨击。

❷ [VN] 延长（执照、合同等）的有效期；使续签

How do I go about renewing my passport?
我该如何去续签护照？
I'd like to renew these library books (= arrange to borrow them for a further period of time) .
我想续借这几本图书馆的书。

5. reproduce [ˌriːprəˈdjuːs] v. 翻印；再现；繁殖

『re又+produce制造→再制造→复制；繁殖』

❶ [VN] 翻印；复制

We are grateful to you for permission to reproduce this article.
非常感谢您允许我们复印这篇文章。

❷ [VN] 再现，复制

The atmosphere of the novel is successfully reproduced in the movie. 小说的氛围在电影中得到了成功的再现。

❸ 繁殖；生育

Most plants reproduce by seeds. 多数植物靠种子繁殖。

▶**reproductive** [ˌriːprəˈdʌktɪv] adj. 生殖的，繁殖的

▶**reproduction** [ˌriːprəˈdʌkʃn] n. 繁殖；复制

6. reunion [riːˈjuːniən] n. 团聚；团圆

『re又+union合并；联盟→又合并到一起→团聚』

❶ 团聚，聚会

a social occasion or party attended by a group of people who have not seen each other for a long time

The whole family was there for this big family reunion.
全家人都来参加了这次盛大的家庭聚会。

❷ [C, U] ~ (with sb) | ~ (between A and B) 相聚；团圆

the act of people coming together after they have been apart for some time

Their reunion after a long separation brought mixed feelings of joy and sorrow to them both. 两人久别重逢，悲喜交集。

7. rewrite [ˌriːˈraɪt] vt. 重写，改写

『re再+write写→再写→重写，改写』

I intend to rewrite the story for younger children.
我想为年纪更小的孩子改写这篇故事。
This essay will have to be completely rewritten.
这篇文章得全部重写。

8. reiterate [riˈɪtəreɪt] vt. 重申

『re再+iterate(=to do)做→再做→重申』

to repeat sth that you have already said, especially to emphasize it

[V that] Let me reiterate that we are fully committed to this policy. 我再说一遍，我们完全拥护这项政策。
[VN] He reiterated his opposition to the creation of a central bank. 他重申了自己反对成立央行的立场。

9. reform [rɪˈfɔːm] n. & vt. 改革〈P177〉

『re再+form形成→重新形成→改革』

10. remark [rɪˈmɑːk] n. & vi. 评述，评论〈P215〉

『re一再+mark标记→反复做标记→评论』

11. review [rɪˈvjuː] n. & vt. 评论；审查；复习〈P353〉

『re又+view看→再看→复习；审查』

12. revise [rɪˈvaɪz] vt. 修订，修正；复习〈P354〉

『re又+vise看→再看→修订；复习』

13. reassure [ˌriːəˈʃʊə(r)] vt. 使安心；使消除疑虑〈P321〉

『re又+assure使放心→一再让人放心→消除（某人）疑虑』

14. refine [rɪˈfaɪn] vt. 提炼；改进〈P172〉

『re又+fine范围→又（缩小）范围→提炼；改进』

15. resume [rɪˈzjuːm] v. 重新开始，继续；恢复（职位）〈P320〉

『re又，再+sume拿，取→继续；恢复（职位）』

前缀66. retro-相当于"back"，表示"向后；往回"

1. retrogress [ˌretrəˈgres] vi. 倒退；退化

『retro往回+gress走→倒退；退化』

2. retrograde [ˈretrəgreɪd] adj. 倒退的，退化的

『retro往回+grade级别→倒退的』

3. retrospect [ˈretrəspekt] n. 回顾，回想〈P309〉

『retro往回+spect看→回顾，回想』

前缀67. se- 相当于"away; apart"，表示"离开；分开"

1. sedition [sɪˈdɪʃn] n. 煽动叛乱的言论（或行动）

『sed(=se)分开+it走+ion表名词→使与（政府）分开走→煽动叛乱』

[U] the use of words or actions that are intended to encourage people to oppose a government

Under the proposals, those found guilty of treason, secession, subversion or sedition could face life imprisonment.
在建议下，被判叛国、分裂国家、颠覆、煽动叛乱等罪者，可面临终身监禁。

▶ **seditious** [sɪˈdɪʃəs] adj. 煽动性的

He fell under suspicion for distributing seditious pamphlets.
他因散发反政府手册而遭到怀疑。

2. **secure** [sɪˈkjʊə(r)] adj. 安心的；安全的 v. 获得；使安全 〈P145〉
『se分开+cure(care)关心，在乎→远离忧虑→安心的』

3. **select** [sɪˈlekt] vt. 选拔；挑选 adj.精选的；优等的 〈P202〉
『se (apart)分开+lect选择→分开选→选择』

4. **secede** [sɪˈsiːd] v. 退出，脱离 〈P127〉
『se分开，离开+cede走→走开→退出』

5. **seclude** [sɪˈkluːd] vt. 与…隔绝；(使)隐居，独处 〈P137〉
『se分开+clude→关上〔门与尘世〕分开→使隔绝』

6. **seduce** [sɪˈdjuːs] vt. 引诱；诱奸 〈P155〉
『se离开+duce引导→引开→引诱』

7. **segregate** [ˈsegrɪgeɪt] vt. (种族、宗教、性别等)隔离，分开 〈P188〉
『se分开+greg群，聚集+ate表动词→分开聚集→隔离』

前缀68. semi- 相当于"half"，表示"一半"

1. **semicircle** [ˈsemisɜːkl] n. 半圆形
『semi一半+circle圆，环→半圆』

2. **semiconductor** [ˌsemikənˈdʌktə(r)] n. 半导体
『semi一半+conductor导体→半导体』

3. **semifinal** [ˌsemɪˈfaɪnəl] n. 半决赛
『semi一半+final决赛→半决赛』

前缀69. step- 表示"继，后"

1. **stepbrother** [ˈstepbrʌðə(r)] n. (同父异母或同母异父的)哥哥，弟弟 (也可以说half-brother)

2. **stepdaughter** [ˈstepdɔːtə(r)] n. 继女

3. **stepfather** [ˈstepfɑːðə(r)] n. 继父

4. **stepmother** [ˈstepmʌðə(r)] n. 继母，后母

5. **stepson** [ˈstepsʌn] n. 继子

6. **stepparent** [ˈstepˌpeərənt] n. 继父(母)

前缀70. stereo- 表示"立体"

1. **stereo** [ˈsteriəʊ] n. 立体声

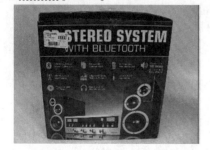

2. **stereophonic** [ˌsteriəˈfɒnɪk] adj. 立体声的；有立体声效果的
『stereo立体+phonic声音的→立体声的』

I'm wondering if the Hi-Fi stereophonic set is very dear.
我想知道这高保真立体声音响是不是很贵。

3. **stereotype** [ˈsteriətaɪp] n. 模式化的形象
『stereo立体+type类型→(已形成)立体的类型(形象)→形象已经固化→模式化的形象』

❶ 模式化的形象
a fixed idea or image that many people have of a particular type of person or thing
There's always been a stereotype about successful businessmen. 人们对于成功商人一直都有一种固定印象。

❷ [VN] [often passive] ～ sb (as sth) 使形象模式化
Children from certain backgrounds tend to be stereotyped by their teachers.
教师往往对来自特定背景的学生形成模式化的印象。

前缀71. sub- (suc-, suf-, sug-, sum-, sup-, sur-, sus-), 相当于"under", 表示"在下面"

1. **sub** [sʌb] n.潜艇；替补队员，替代者 v. 替代
❶ =**submarine** n. 潜艇 〈P 215〉
❷ =**substitute** v. 替代 n. 替代者 〈P 316〉

2. **subway** [ˈsʌbweɪ] n. 地铁
『sub下面+way路→(在地)下面的路→地铁』
词义辨析 〈P363第10〉
地铁 subway, underground, tube, metro

3. **subcontinent** [ˌsʌbˈkɒntɪnənt] n. 次大陆
『sub下面，次，亚+continent洲，大陆→次大陆』

4. **subdue** [səbˈdjuː] vt. 制服，征服；克制
『sub下面+ due (duce)引导→引导到下面→克制』
(subdued, subdued, subduing)

❶ [VN] 克制(感情)
to calm or control your feelings
She subdued the urge to run after him.
她克制住了去追他的冲动。
He forced himself to subdue and overcome his fears.
他强迫自己克制并战胜恐惧心理。
近义词 **suppress** [səˈpres] v.镇压；控制

❷ [VN] 制服；征服；控制
to bring sb/sth under control, especially by using force
Troops were called in to subdue the rebels.
军队被调来镇压反叛者。
It took three police officers to subdue him.
三名警察才制服了他。

5. **substance** [ˈsʌbstəns] n. 物质；实质
『sub下面+stance (stand)站→站在(表面)下面→实质』

❶ [C] 物质；物品；东西
a type of solid, liquid or gas that has particular qualities
a chemical/radioactive, etc. substance
化学/放射性等物质
a sticky substance 一种黏糊糊的东西

❷ [U] 实质性东西；基本内容；事实根据；重要的
the most important or main part of sth
Love and guilt form the substance of his new book.
他的新书主要讲爱情与罪孽。

I agreed with what she said in substance, though not with every detail.

对于她所说的，虽然不是每个细节我都同意，但基本内容却是赞同的。

There is some substance in what he says.

他的话是有一定根据的。

Nothing of any substance was achieved in the meeting.

会议没有取得任何实质性成果。

▶**substantial** [səbˈstænʃl] adj. 大量的；结实的

❶ 大量的；价值巨大的；重大的

large in amount, value or importance

Substantial numbers of people support the reforms.

相当多的人支持这些改革措施。

A substantial reward is being offered for the recovery of a painting by Turner.

为追回特纳的一幅画，已发布了重金悬赏令。

同义词 **considerable** [kənˈsɪdərəbl] adj.数量巨大的

❷ （建筑物）大而坚固的，结实的

On the site were a number of substantial timber buildings.

那块场地上建有若干大而结实的原木建筑物。

词义辨析 <P363第13>

物质 material, matter, stuff, substance

6. **subtitle** [ˈsʌbtaɪtl] n.小标题，副标题；（电影）字幕

『sub下面+title标题→（在大标题）下面的标题→副标题；sub下面+title标题→（在屏幕）下面的标题→字幕』

7. **subtropical** [ˌsʌbˈtrɒpɪkl] adj. 亚热带的

『sub下面+tropical热带的→在热带下面的→亚热带的』

▶**tropical** [ˈtrɒpɪkl] adj. 热带的；热带气候的

『tropic回归线+al有关…的→有关回归线的→热带的』

I had deliberately picked a city with a tropical climate.

我特意选了一个热带气候的城市。

▶**tropic** [ˈtrɒpɪk] n. 回归线；热带（the tropics 热带地区）

8. **supplant** [səˈplɑːnt] vt. 替代，取代（年老或落后事物）

『sup下面+plant种植→种植到…下面→替代，取代』

He may be supplanted by a younger man.

他可能会被一个年龄比他小的人取代。

By the 1930s the wristwatch had almost completely supplanted the pocket watch.

到了20世纪30年代，手表几乎完全取代了怀表。

9. **suppress** [səˈpres] vt. 镇压；抑制 <P269>

『sup(=sub)下面+press压→被压到下面→镇压；抑制』

10. **suspect** [səˈspekt] v. 怀疑 n. 犯罪嫌疑人 <P309>

『sus(=sub)下面+spect看→从下面看→怀疑』

（v. [səˈspekt]; n. & adj. [ˈsʌspekt]）

11. **sustain** [səˈsteɪn] v. 维持；保持 <P324>

『sus(=sub)下面+tain保持；坚持→在下面保持着→维持；保持』

12. **subscribe** [səbˈskraɪb] vi. 订阅；捐款 <P289>

『sub下面+scribe→在（单子）下面写上（名字）→订阅；认购』

13. **suburb** [ˈsʌbɜːb] n. 郊区 <P341>

『sub下面+urb城市→在城市下面→郊区』

14. **succeed** [səkˈsiːd] v. 成功；接替 < P125>

『suc(=sub)下面+ceed走→走到（目标）下面；走到（前任）的下面→成功；接替』

15. **subconscious** [ˌsʌbˈkɒnʃəs] adj. 下意识的 <P288>

『sub下面+ conscious有意识的→下意识的』

16. **submerge** [səbˈmɜːdʒ] v. 淹没，沉没；沉浸 <P219>

『sub下面+merge下沉→沉下去→沉没』

17. **submit** [səbˈmɪt] v. 呈递；屈从 <P222>

『sub下面+mit送→从下面送→呈递；屈从』

18. **subordinate** [səˈbɔːdɪnət , səˈbɔːdɪneɪt] adj. 从属的；次要的 n. 下属 vt. 使处于次要位置 <P239>

『sub下面+ordin顺序+ate表形容词或动词→顺序在下面的→从属的；下属』

19. **subside** [səbˈsaɪd] vi. 下沉；下降；减弱 <P297>

『sub下+side坐→向下坐→下沉』

20. **subsidy** [ˈsʌbsədi] n. 补贴；补助金 <P297>

『sub向下+side坐（去e）+y构成名词→位于其下→支撑；支持→补贴』

21. **subliminal** [ˌsʌbˈlɪmɪnl] adj. 下意识的，潜意识的 <P207>

『sub下面+limin限制+al…的→限制在（意识）下面的→下意识的』

前缀72. super-=above, over，表示"在上面；超级的，超过的"

①super-=above，表示"在…上面"

1. **super** [ˈsuːpə(r)] adj. 极好的 adv. 非常，格外

『super上面→极好的』

We had a super time in Italy. 我们在意大利过得十分惬意。

The message was super clear. 传递的信息非常清楚。

2. **superb** [suːˈpɜːb] adj. 极佳的；卓越的；质量极高的

『super上面+b（=be）→上面的→极佳的』

excellent; of very good quality

The car's in superb condition. 这辆车车况极好。

His performance was absolutely superb.

他的表演精彩绝伦。

3. **superstitious** [ˌsuːpəˈstɪʃəs] adj. 迷信的

『super上面+stit(set up)建立+ious…的→上层的人（喜欢把自己的决定）建立在（迷信之上）→迷信的』

Jean was extremely superstitious and believed the colour green brought bad luck.

琴非常迷信，认为绿色会带来厄运。

▶**superstition** [ˌsuːpəˈstɪʃn] n. 迷信；迷信行为

Your fears were grounded on nothing but superstition.

你的恐惧只不过是以迷信为依据的。

"I call it a pleasurable tradition, not a superstition，" said Mr Cohen, who lives in Atlanta.

住在亚特兰大的科恩说："我把它称作让人愉快的惯例，它不是迷信行为。"

4. **supreme** [suːˈpriːm] adj. 最高的；最大的

『supr(=super)上面的+eme表最高级→最上面的→最高的』

❶ [usually before noun]（级别或地位）最高的

The campaigners held a sit-in outside the Supreme Court.

运动参与者在最高法院门外举行了静坐示威。

❷ [usually before noun]（程度）最大的
very great or the greatest in degree
Her approval was of supreme importance.
她的认可是至关重要的。

5. superficial [ˌsuːpəˈfɪʃl] adj. 表面的；肤浅的
『super上面+fic(=face)表面+ial…的→表面的』

❶（伤势或伤害）表层的，表皮的
The 69-year-old clergyman escaped with superficial wounds.
这位69岁的牧师幸免于难，只受了点皮外伤。

❷ 表面的，乍看起来的（尤指实际并非如此）
Many of these killers are frequently glib and superficially charming. 这些杀手中，多数都是能说会道、外表迷人。

❸（行动、情感、关系）浅薄的，肤浅的
a superficial friendship 浅薄的交情
The guests engaged in superficial chatter. 客人们闲聊起来。

❹ 肤浅的，浅薄的
If you describe someone as superficial, you disapprove of them because they do not think deeply, and have little understanding of anything serious or important.
The book shows only a superficial understanding of the historical context. 这部书表现出对历史背景肤浅的理解。
This guy is a superficial yuppie with no intellect whatsoever.
这个家伙是个肤浅的雅皮士，没有什么头脑。

6. superior [suːˈpɪəriə(r)] adj. 级别更高的；更好的 〈P80〉
『super上面+ior较…的，属于…的→上面的→级别高的』

7. supervise [ˈsuːpəvaɪz] vt. 监督；管理 〈P354〉
『super在上面+vise看→在上面看着→监管』

8. superstructure [ˈsuːpəstrʌktʃə(r)] n. 上层建筑 〈P319〉
『super上面的+structure结构→上面的结构→上层建筑』

② super-=over，表示"超级的，超过的"

1. superman [ˈsuːpəmæn] n. 超人

2. supermarket [ˈsuːpəmɑːkɪt] n. 超市
『super超级的+market市场→超级市场』

3. supernatural [ˌsuːpəˈnætʃrəl] adj. 超自然的，不可思议的
『super超级的+natural自然的→超自然的』
that cannot be explained by the laws of science and that seems to involve gods or magic
supernatural events, forces, or creatures
超自然的事件、力量或生物
These are the devices you'll need to hunt for and expose all things supernatural.
这些就是你搜寻和揭露所有超自然现象所需的装置。

4. superstar [ˈsuːpəstɑː(r)] n. 巨星；超级明星
『super 超级的+star明星→超级明星』

5. supersonic [ˌsuːpəˈsɒnɪk] adj. 超声速的 〈P306〉
『super 超过的+sonic声速的→超过声速的→超声速的』

前缀73. sur- 是 super-的变体，相当于"above；over"，表示"在上面；超过"

1. surname [ˈsɜːneɪm] n. 姓
『sur (over) 在上面+name名字→加在名字上面→姓』

2. surpass [səˈpɑːs] v. 超过，胜过

『sur在上面+pass经过→pass over→超过』
to do or be better than sb/sth
Its success has surpassed all expectations.
它所取得的成功远远超出了预期。
Her cooking was always good, this time she had surpassed herself.
她的厨艺向来不错，这一次她更是胜过以往。

词义辨析 <P368第34> 超出 exceed, surpass, excel

3. surplus [ˈsɜːpləs] n. 过剩；顺差 adj. 过剩的
『sur超过+ plus (more)额外的→超出的』

❶ [C, U] 过剩；过剩量
Germany suffers from a surplus of teachers.
德国遭遇了教师过剩的问题。

❷ adj. 过剩的
I sell my surplus birds to a local pet shop.
我把多余的鸟卖给当地的宠物商店。

❸ [C]（贸易）顺差
Japan's annual trade surplus is in the region of 100 billion dollars. 日本每年的贸易顺差额在1000 亿美元左右。

反义词 deficit [ˈdefɪsɪt] n. 赤字；不足额

❶ [C] 赤字；逆差；亏损
The trade balance has been in deficit for the past five years.
过去五年来贸易状况一直是逆差。

❷ [C] 不足额；缺款额
There's a deficit of $3 million in the total needed to complete the project. 完成这项工程所需资金中有300万元的亏空。

4. surcharge [ˈsɜːtʃɑːdʒ] n. & vt. 额外费用；收额外费用
『sur超过+charge收费→超出（正常的）收费→额外费用』
Exclude airport tax, fuel surcharge and insurance.
价格不包括所有机场税、燃油附加费和保险费。
[VNN] We were surcharged £50 for travelling on a Friday.
因为在星期五旅行，我们多付了50英镑。

5. surrender [səˈrendə(r)] v. 投降；（被迫）交出 〈P281〉
『sur (above) 在上面+render给→（被迫把武器）交给上面→投降；交出』

6. surround [səˈraʊnd] vt. 围绕；包围
『sur (above) 在上面+round围绕→围绕在上面→环绕；包围』

❶ ~ sth/sb (with sth)
Tall trees surround the lake. 高树环绕着这个湖。
The lake is surrounded with/by trees.
这个湖被树环绕。

❷ sb/sth (with sb/sth) 包围，围住
Police surrounded the building.
警方包围了那栋房子。

▶ **surrounding** [səˈraʊndɪŋ] adj. 周围的
The hotel is ideally located for visiting the city and the surrounding area.
这个酒店坐落于参观这个城市及周边地区的理想位置。

▶ **surroundings** [səˈraʊndɪŋz] n. [pl.]（周围的）环境；周围的事物
everything that is around or near sb/sth
And the surroundings in the canteen have also been improved.
而且食堂环境也已经改善了。
Our new surroundings are a lot more friendly than we

expected. 我们的新环境比我们预期的要友好得多。

7. surveillance [sɜːˈveɪləns] n. 盯梢，监视

『sur (over) 上面+veil (1) 面纱→（脸上或监控）上面（蒙着）面纱（以免被发现）+ance表名词→（暗中）监视（某人）』

The police are keeping the suspects under constant surveillance. 警方正对嫌疑人实施不间断监视。

Police keep track of the kidnapper using electronic surveillance equipment.

警方利用电子监视设备跟踪绑架者。

8. survive [səˈvaɪv] v. 幸存；比…长寿 〈P356〉

『sur (over) 过来+vive (life) 活→活过来→幸存』

9. surface [ˈsɜːfɪs] n. 表面；vi. 浮出水面 〈P161〉

『sur上面+ face表面→表面上面→表面』

10. surmount [səˈmaʊnt] vt. 克服（困难）；置于顶端 〈P229〉

『sur (over) 上面+mount山→（攀登或放置于）山的上面→克服（困难）；置于顶端』

前缀74. syn-, sym-=together, with, 表示"同时；相同"（在双唇音 p, b, m 前用 sym-，其他情况用 syn-）

1. symptom [ˈsɪmptəm] n. 症状

『sym同时+ptom (fall) 降落→（症状）同时降落到（某人）身上）→症状』

❶ [C]（疾病的）症状

Look out for symptoms of depression.
留心看有无抑郁症状。

Symptoms include a headache and sore throat.
症状包括头痛和咽喉疼痛。

❷ [C]（不好事情的）征兆，迹象

In his speech the Bishop labelled these crimes as a symptom of society's moral decline.
主教在讲话中把这些罪行称为社会道德滑坡的征兆。

2. syndrome [ˈsɪndrəʊm] n. 综合症状；典型表现

『syn同时+drome (run) 跑→（多种症状）同时跑过来→综合症状』

❶ [C] 综合症状

The syndrome is more likely to strike those whose immune systems are already below par.
这种综合征更容易对那些免疫系统已经低于正常水平的人构成威胁。

❷ [C] 典型表现

It's a bit like the exam syndrome where you write down everything you know regardless of what has been asked.
不论问题是什么就把所知道的统统写上，这有些像典型的考试心理。

小贴士

AIDS 艾滋病，全写为 Acquired Immune Deficiency Syndrome，获得性免疫缺陷综合征

Down's syndrome 唐氏综合征

SARS 严重急性呼吸综合征，全写为 Severe Acute Respiratory Syndrome

3. synonym [ˈsɪnənɪm] n. 同义词 〈P238〉

『syn共同+onym名称，名字→（不同的单词所指的内容）同名→同义词』

4. synthesis [ˈsɪnθəsɪs] n. 综合；合成〈P333〉

『syn同时+thes放+is表名词→同时放到一起→综合；合成』

5. synchronize [ˈsɪŋkrənaɪz] v. （使）时间同步〈P131〉

『syn同时+chron时间+ize使…→使时间同步→同时发生』

6. symmetry [ˈsɪmətri] n. 对称；相仿〈P219〉

『sym相同的+meter测量（去e）+y构成名词→（两边）测量相同的→对称；相仿』

7. sympathy [ˈsɪmpəθi] n. 同情；赞同〈P244〉

『sym相同+pathy感情→感情相同→同情；赞同』

8. symphony [ˈsɪmfəni] n. 交响乐〈P254〉

『sym同时+phone声音（去e）+y构成名词→同时奏出的美妙的声音→交响乐』

9. symbiosis [ˌsɪmbaɪˈəʊsɪs] n. （生物）共生关系；互惠互利关系〈P119〉

『sym共同+bio生活+sis表现象→共生』

10. symposium [sɪmˈpəʊziəm] n. 专题讨论会〈P265〉

『sym共同+pose放（去e）+ium场所，地点→共同放在一起（讨论）的场所→专题讨论会』

前缀75. tele-=far off, 表示"远处"

1. telegram [ˈtelɪɡræm] n. 电报

『tele远处+gram写，画→从远处传来的写的东西→电报』

2. telegraph [ˈtelɪɡrɑːf] n. 电报

『tele远处+graph写，画→从远处传来的写的东西→电报』

词义辨析 〈P364第16〉 电报 telegraph, telegram

3. television [ˈtelɪvɪʒn] n. 电视

『tele远处+vision映像→从远处传来的映像→电视』

4. telephone [ˈtelɪfəʊn] n. 电话 v. 打电话〈P254〉

『tele远处+phone声音→从远处传来的声音→电话』

5. telescope [ˈtelɪskəʊp] n. 望远镜〈P288〉

『tele远处+scope镜→观察远处用的镜→望远镜』

前缀76. trans-=through, across, over, 表示"从…到…"

1. transact [trænˈzækt] v. 做交易，做业务

『trans从…到…+ act做→在两者之间转移→做交易』

~ (sth) (with sb) （与人或组织）做业务，做交易

A lot of our business is transacted over the Internet.
我们的很多生意都是通过互联网进行的。

▶ **transaction** [trænˈzækʃn] n. 交易，业务，买卖

Neither side would disclose details of the transaction.
双方均不肯披露交易细节。

They have made huge profit out of the transaction.
他们从这笔交易中获得了巨额利润。

2. transatlantic [ˌtrænzətˈlæntɪk] adj. 横渡大西洋的；大西洋彼岸的

『trans从…到…+atlantic大西洋→从大西洋这边到那边的→横渡大西洋的』

3. transcontinental [ˌtrænzˌkɒntɪˈnentl] adj. 横贯大陆的，大陆那边的

『trans从…到…+continent大陆，洲+ al表形容词→从大陆这端到大陆那端的→横贯大陆的』

4. translate [trænsˈleɪt] v. 翻译
『trans从…到…+late (bring out) 拿出→从一种（语言）到另一种（语言）→翻译』

~ (sth) (from sth) (into sth) | ~ sth (as sth)　翻译
He translated the letter into English.
他把这封信译成了英文。
Her books have been translated into 24 languages.
她的书被译成了24种语言。

近义词　**interpret** [ɪnˈtɜːprɪt] v. 口译；解释

❶ [V] ~ (for sb)　口译
She couldn't speak much English so her children had to interpret for her.
她讲不了几句英语，所以她的孩子们得给她翻译。

❷ [VN] 解释；说明；阐释
I didn't know whether to interpret her silence as acceptance or refusal. 我不知道该把她的沉默看作是接受还是拒绝。
The students were asked to interpret the poem.
学生们被要求诠释那首诗的意义。

词义辨析 <P364第17> **翻译 translate, interpret**

▶ **translator** [trænsˈleɪtə(r)] n. 翻译家；翻译者

5. transplant [trænsˈplɑːnt] vt. 移植
『trans从…到…+plant种植+从一个地方种植到另一个地方→移植』

❶ ~ sth (from sb/sth) (into sb/sth)　移植（器官、皮肤等）
Surgeons have successfully transplanted a liver into a four-year-old boy.
外科医生成功地给一个四岁的男孩移植了肝脏。

❷ 使迁移；使移民；移种
To transplant someone or something means to move them to a different place.
Some plants do not transplant well. 有些植物不宜移植。
Marriage had transplanted Rebecca from London to Manchester. 因为结婚，丽贝卡从伦敦移居到了曼彻斯特。

6. transport [ˈtrænspɔːt] n. & vt. 运输
『trans从…到…+port港口→从一个港口到另一个港口→运输』

❶ [U] (BrE) 交通运输系统；运输车辆；运输（NAmE transportation）
air/freight/road transport 空运；货运；路运
Applicants must have their own transport.
申请人必须有自己的交通工具。
The goods were damaged during transport.
货物在运输期间受损。

❷ [VN]（用交通工具）运输；（以自然方式）运输
to transport goods/passengers 运送货物/旅客
Blood transports oxygen around the body.
血把氧气输送到全身。

▶ **transportation** [ˌtrænspɔːˈteɪʃn] n. 交通；运输
especially NAmE = transport (BrE)

7. transitive [ˈtrænzətɪv] adj. 及物的
『trans从…到…+it走+ive具有…性质的→（动词）具有从（主语）走到（宾语）性质的→及物的』

▶ **intransitive** [ɪnˈtrænzətɪv] adj. 不及物的
『in不+transitive及物的→不及物的』

8. transfuse [trænsˈfjuːz] v. 输血 <P182>

『trans从…到…+fuse流→（让血）从…流到…→输血』

9. transmit [trænsˈmɪt] v. 传送；输送；发射；传染<P222>
『trans从…到…+mit (send) 送→从一个地方发送到另一个地方→传送；传染』

10. transparent [trænsˈpærənt] adj. 透明的；清澈的；易识破的；显而易见的 (P242)
『trans从…到…+parent能看见的（如：apparent明显的）→从一边到另一边能看见的→透明的』

11. transfer [trænsˈfɜː(r)] v. & n. 转移；调动〈P168〉
『trans从…到…+fer(carry) 运输→从一个地方到另一个地方→转移；调动』
（v. [trænsˈfɜː(r)] n. [ˈtrænsfɜː]; transferred, transferred, transferring）

12. transform [trænsˈfɔːm] v.改变，改观〈P176〉
『trans 从…到…+form形式→从一种形式转变为另一种形式→改变』

前缀77. tri-=three，表示"三"

1. triangle [ˈtraɪæŋgl] n. 三角形
『tri三+angle角→三个角→三角形』

▶ **triangular** [traɪˈæŋgjələ(r)] adj. 三角的；三角形的

2. tricycle [ˈtraɪˌsɪkəl] n. 三轮车
『tri三+cycle圆，环→三个环形→三轮车』

3. trio [ˈtriːəʊ] n. 三人组；三重唱；三重奏
『tri三+o音乐术语→三重奏，三重唱』
The trio had denied the charges.
三名被告均否认了该指控。
The violinist walked on the stage and the duo became a trio.
那位小提琴家走上台，二重奏变成了三重奏组。

4. triple [ˈtrɪpl] adj. 三倍的 v. 成为三倍
『tri三+ple倍→三倍的』

❶ adj. 三倍的；三部分的
The amount of alcohol in his blood was triple the legal maximum.
他血液中的酒精含量为法定最高限量的三倍。

❷ v. 成为三倍
[V] I got a fantastic new job and my salary tripled.
我得到了一份非常好的新工作，薪水涨到了原来的三倍。

前缀78. twi-=two，表示"二，两"

1. twilight [ˈtwaɪlaɪt] n. 暮色，黄昏；没落时期 adj. 朦胧的；界限模糊的
『twi两+light→在黑光和白光过渡时期→暮色，黄昏』

❶ [U] 暮色，黄昏；没落时期
It was hard to see him clearly in the twilight.
在朦胧的暮色中很难看清他。
We went for a walk along the beach at twilight.
黄昏时分我们沿着海滩散步。
Now both men are in the twilight of their careers.
现在两人的事业都到了没落期。

❷ adj. 朦胧的；界限模糊的
A twilight state or a twilight zone is a situation of confusion or uncertainty, which seems to exist between two different states or categories.
They fell into that twilight zone between military personnel

and civilian employees.
他们成了军队人员与平民雇员之间身份界定不清的人。

前缀79. ultra-=beyond，表示"超过"

1. ultrasound [ˈʌltrəsaʊnd] n. 超声；超声波
『ultra超出+sound声音→超声波』

I had an ultrasound scan to see how the pregnancy was progressing. 我进行了超声检查，看看妊娠情况如何。

▶**ultrasonic** [ˌʌltrəˈsɒnɪk] adj. 超声的 〈P306〉
『ultra超出+sonic声音的→超声波的』

2. ultraviolet [ˌʌltrəˈvaɪələt] adj. 紫外线的
『ultra超出，以外+violet紫色的→紫外线的』

The sun's ultraviolet rays are responsible for both tanning and burning. 阳光中的紫外线是皮肤晒黑和灼伤的根源。

▶**violet** [ˈvaɪələt] n. 紫罗兰；紫罗兰色

▶**infrared** [ˌɪnfrəˈred] adj. 红外线的 〈P19〉

前缀80. un- 表示否定或相反动作

① un- 表示否定

1. unable [ʌnˈeɪbl] adj. 不能的，不会的
『un不+able能够的→不能的』

▶**inability** [ˌɪnəˈbɪləti] n. 无能力

Some families go without medical treatment because of their inability to pay.
有些家庭因无力支付医疗费用而得不到医治。

2. uncharted [ˌʌnˈtʃɑːtɪd] adj. 未知的；图上未标明的
『un没有+chart图表，绘制地图+ed表被动→地图上还没有标明的→未知的，不熟悉的』

The party is sailing in uncharted waters.
这个党面临一种崭新的局势。
This type of work is uncharted territory for us.
我们从未涉足过这类工作。

3. uncivilized [ʌnˈsɪvəlaɪzd] adj. 不文明的；野蛮的
『un不+civilized文明的→不文明的』

You can knock her down, which is uncivilized.
你可以迫使她屈服，但这太不文明了。
It's not real sport. It's just fighting to entertain people. It's so uncivilized.
它不是真正的运动。它只是通过打架来娱乐大众。那太不文明了。

4. uneasy [ʌnˈiːzi] adj. 心神不安的，忧虑的
『un不+easy安逸的→（因着急而）心神不安的』

feeling worried or unhappy about a particular situation, especially because you think that sth bad or unpleasant may happen or because you are not sure that what you are doing is right

He was beginning to feel distinctly uneasy about their visit.
他对他们的造访明显地感到不安起来。
She felt uneasy about leaving the children with them.
把孩子们托付给他们，她心里七上八下的。

▶**ease** [iːz] n. 安逸，舒适
at ease 舒适；自由自在；无拘无束
I never feel completely at ease with him.
我跟他在一起总感到不是很自在。

小贴士
stand at ease 稍息；**stand at attention** 立正

▶**easy** [ˈiːzi] adj. 舒适的；安逸的；安心的
I'll agree to anything for an easy life.
只要有安逸舒适的生活我什么都同意。
I don't feel easy about letting the kids go out alone.
让这些孩子单独出去我不放心。

5. unequal [ʌnˈiːkwəl] adj. 不平等的
『un不+equal平等的→不平等的』

▶**inequality** [ˌɪnɪˈkwɒləti] n. 不平等
『in不，无+ equality平等→不平等』

People are concerned about social inequality.
人们很关注社会不平等问题。

6. unfair [ˌʌnˈfeə(r)] adj. 不公正的，不公平的
『un不+fair公正的→不公正的』

7. unjust [ˌʌnˈdʒʌst] adj. 不公正的
『un不+just公正的→不公正的』

The attack on Charles was deeply unjust.
对查尔斯的攻击甚为不公。

▶**injustice** [ɪnˈdʒʌstɪs] n. 不公正，不公平 〈P199〉
『in不，无+ justice公正→不公正』

② un- 表示相反动作

1. unbutton [ˌʌnˈbʌtn] vt. 解开纽扣
『un表相反动作+ button扣紧→解开纽扣』

Would you like to unbutton your jacket for checking?
您能解开上衣的扣子让我们检查一下吗？

2. undo [ʌnˈduː] vt. 撤销；解开
『un表相反动作+ do做→撤销；解开』

❶ [VN] 打开；解开；拆开
to open sth that is fastened, tied or wrapped
to undo a button/knot/zip, etc.
解开纽扣、解开绳结、拉开拉锁等
to undo a jacket/shirt, etc. 解开上衣、衬衫等
I undid the package and took out the books.
我打开包裹取出书来。

❷ [VN] 消除，取消，废止（某事的影响）
to cancel the effect of sth
He undid most of the good work of the previous manager.
他把前任经理的大部分功绩都毁掉了。
A heavy-handed approach from the police could undo that good impression.
警方采取高压手段可能会毁掉之前留下的好印象。

3. undress [ʌnˈdres] v. 脱衣服
『un表相反动作+ dress穿衣→脱衣服』

She undressed and got into bed. 她解衣上床了。
I helped to undress the children for bed.
我帮孩子们脱衣就寝。

4. unearth [ʌnˈɜːθ] vt. 挖掘；发现
『un表相反动作+ earth土地→从土地内挖出来→挖掘』

They will unearth the buried treasure here.
他们将在这儿挖掘地下宝藏。
I unearthed my old diaries when we moved house.
我们搬家时，我偶然发现了自己的旧日记。

5. unfold [ʌnˈfəʊld] v. 展开，打开
『un表相反动作+ fold折叠→展开，打开』

He quickly unfolded the blankets and spread them on the mattress. 他迅速展开毯子，铺在床垫上。
to unfold a map 展开地图
She unfolded her arms. 她张开双臂。
The audience watched as the story unfolded before their eyes. 观众注视着剧情逐渐地展开。

6. unload [ˌʌnˈləʊd] v. （从车、船上）卸，取下
『un表相反动作+load装载→卸载』

[VN] Everyone helped to unload the luggage from the car.
大家都帮着从汽车上卸行李。
[V] The truck driver was waiting to unload.
卡车司机在等着卸货。

7. unlock [ˌʌnˈlɒk] vt. 开锁
『un表相反动作+ lock上锁→开锁』

8. unpack [ʌnˈpæk] v. 打开包取出
『un表相反动作+ pack 打包→打开包取出』

I unpacked my bags as soon as I arrived.
我一到达就打开行李，整理衣物。

9. unrest [ʌnˈrest] n. 骚乱；动荡
『un表相反动作+ rest 休息→骚乱』

[U] 动乱；骚乱；动荡
If there is unrest in a particular place or society, people are expressing anger and dissatisfaction about something, often by demonstrating or rioting.

There is growing unrest in the south of the country.
这个国家的南方日益动荡不安。

▶**restless** [ˈrestləs] adj. 焦躁不安的；难以入睡的
『rest休息；放松+less不…的→焦躁的；没有休息的』

❶ 坐立不安的；不耐烦的
unable to stay still or be happy where you are, because you are bored or need a change
The audience was becoming restless. 观众开始不耐烦了。
After five years in the job, he was beginning to feel restless.
这份工作干了五年以后，他开始厌烦了。

❷ 没有真正休息的；没有睡眠的
without real rest or sleep
a restless night 不眠之夜

10. unsettle [ʌnˈsetl] vt. 使心神不宁
『un表相反动作+settle安静下来→使心神不宁』

The presence of the two policemen unsettled her.
两名警察的出现让她感到不安。

▶**unsettled** [ʌnˈsetld] adj. 心神不宁的
They all felt restless and unsettled.
他们都感到焦躁不安。

▶**settle** [ˈsetl] v. 解决；安顿；安居；坐定；栖息；将就；（使）平静

❶ 解决（分歧、纠纷等）
[VN] to settle a dispute/an argument/a matter
解决争端/争论/事情
It's time you settled your differences with your father.
现在你该解决同你父亲之间的分歧了。

❷ 安排好（某事）

If something is settled, it has all been decided and arranged.
As far as we're concerned, the matter is settled.
我们这边已经安排妥当了。

❸（在某地）定居下来，过安定的生活
She settled in Vienna after her father's death.
父亲死后，她就在维也纳定居了。
Find a girl, settle down, if you want you can marry.
如果你想结婚，找一个女孩，安定下来。（歌曲father and son 中歌词）

❹（舒服地）坐定或躺下
[V] Ellie settled back in her seat.
埃莉舒适地靠着椅背坐下。
[VN] He settled himself comfortably in his usual chair.
他在自己惯常坐的椅子上舒舒服服地坐下来。

❺（鸟、昆虫）降落，栖息
Two birds settled on the fence. 两只鸟落在篱笆上。

❻ settle for sth 将就
We reached the hotel late and had to settle for a room without a view.
我们到旅馆时很晚，只好勉强要了一间看不到风景的房间。
The only way to do great work is to love what you do. If you haven't found it yet, keep looking. Don't settle.
做伟大工作的唯一方法就是热爱你所做的事情。如果你还没有找到，继续寻找。不要将就。（乔布斯斯坦福大学演讲）

❼（使）平静下来，安静下来
The baby wouldn't settle. 婴儿安静不下来。

▶**settlement** [ˈsetlmənt] n. 解决；定居点

❶ [C, U]（解决纷争的）协议；解决，处理
Our objective must be to secure a peace settlement.
我们一定要达成和平协议。
the settlement of a dispute 争端的解决

❷ [C]（尤指拓荒安家的）定居点
The village is a settlement of just fifty houses.
这个村子里只住了 50 户人家。

11. unveil [ʌnˈveɪl] vt. 揭幕；推出
『un表相反动作+veil面纱，隐瞒→揭开（幕布）→揭幕→推出（新产品，新计划）』

❶ [VN] 为…揭幕
If someone formally unveils something such as a new statue or painting, they draw back the curtain which is covering it.

❷ [VN] 介绍，推出
to show or introduce a new plan, product, etc. to the public for the first time
They will be unveiling their new models at the Motor Show.
他们将在汽车大展上首次推出自己的新型汽车。

▶**veil** [veɪl] n. 面纱；薄薄的遮盖层；掩饰，掩盖
a bridal veil 新娘的面纱
The mountain tops were hidden beneath a veil of mist.
山顶笼罩在薄雾中。
It would be better to draw a veil over what happened next.
最好把之后发生的事情掩盖起来。

12. unravel [ʌnˈrævl] v. 解开；瓦解；揭开（迷）
『un表相反动作+ravel（线绳等）缠在一起→解开』

❶ [VN, V]（把缠或织在一起的线）解开
I unravelled the string and wound it into a ball.
我把绳子解开并绕成一个球。

❷ [V]（系统、计划、关系等）解体，失败

His government began to unravel because of a banking scandal. 他的政府由于一起金融丑闻而开始瓦解。

❸ [VN, V] 揭开；揭示

If you unravel a mystery or puzzle, or if it unravels, it gradually becomes clearer and you can work out the answer to it.

A young mother has flown to Iceland to unravel the mystery of her husband's disappearance.
一位年轻的母亲飞抵冰岛，要揭开她丈夫失踪之谜。

13. uncover [ʌnˈkʌvə(r)] vt. 揭开盖子；揭露，发现 〈P138〉

『un表相反动作+ cover覆盖→揭开（隐藏的或被覆盖的）』

前缀81. under- 表示"在下面；不足，不够"

① under- 表示"在下面"

1. undergo [ˌʌndəˈɡəʊ] vt. 经受（变化）；遭受（不愉快）

『under下面+go走→从下面走→经受；遭受』

（undergo, underwent, undergone）

尤指经历坎坷、变化或不愉快的事情，也可指接受测试、培训等。

Did that professor undergo a major surgery last year?
那位教授去年动过大手术吗？

New employees have to undergo some career training.
新员工要参加一些职业培训。

She underwent much suffering during her childhood.
她小时候受了许多苦。

2. undergraduate [ˌʌndəˈɡrædʒuət] n. 在校大学生

『under在…下面+graduate毕业→在毕业下面→还没有毕业，仍在校学习的→在校大学生』

For this reason, only advanced undergraduate and graduate students usually participate in seminars.
因此通常参加讨论会的只是高年级本科生和研究生。

3. underground [ˈʌndəɡraʊnd] adj. 地下的 n. 地铁

『under下面+ground地面→地面下面的→地下的；地铁』

4. underline [ˌʌndəˈlaɪn] vt. 在…下面画线；强调

『under下面+line线→在下面画线；强调』

Underline the following that apply to you.
在符合自身情况的项下画线。

[VN] The report underlines the importance of pre-school education. 这份报告强调学前教育的重要性。

5. underlie [ˌʌndəˈlaɪ] vt. 构成…的基础；作为…的原因

『under下面+lie位于→位于某事的下面→构成…的基础；作为…的原因』

（underlying, underlay, underlain）

Try to figure out what feeling underlies your anger.
努力找出你愤怒的原因。

It is a principle that underlies all the party's policies.
这是贯穿该党各项政策的一条准则。

6. underneath [ˌʌndəˈniːθ] prep. & adv. 隐藏（或掩盖）在…下面 n.（物体的）下表面，底面

❶ prep. & adv. 在…底下；隐藏（或掩盖）在下面

under or below sth else, especially when it is hidden or covered by the thing on top

The coin rolled underneath the piano. 硬币滚到了钢琴底下。

This jacket is too big, even with a sweater underneath.
即使里面穿一件毛衣，这件外套也太大了。

Underneath her cool exterior she was really very frightened.
她外表冷静，其实内心十分害怕。

❷ n. the underneath [sing.]（物体的）下表面，底面

She pulled the drawer out and examined the underneath carefully. 她拉开抽屉仔细查看底部。

7. undermine [ˌʌndəˈmaɪn] vt. 挖墙脚；逐渐削弱

『under下面+mine挖矿→在下面挖→挖墙脚；破坏』

Our confidence in the team has been seriously undermined by their recent defeats.
该队最近的几次失败已严重动摇了我们对他们的信心。

This crisis has undermined his position.
这场危机已损害了他的地位。

8. undertake [ˌʌndəˈteɪk] vt. 承担，着手；承诺

『under在…下面+ take拿→把（任务）拿到自己下面→承担做；着手做；承诺做』

❶ [VN] 承担，着手

to make yourself responsible for sth and start doing it

to undertake a task/project 承担一个任务/项目

The company has announced that it will undertake a full investigation into the accident.
公司已经宣布将对这次事故进行全面调查。

❷ 承诺，允诺；答应

[V to inf] He undertook to finish the job by Friday.
他答应星期五或之前完成这一工作。

▶ **undertaking** [ˌʌndəˈteɪkɪŋ] n. 任务，事业；保证

❶ [C]（重大或艰巨的）任务，项目，事业

a task or project, especially one that is important and/or difficult

In those days, the trip across country was a dangerous undertaking. 那个时期，越野旅行是一件危险的事情。

Organizing the show has been a massive undertaking.
组织那场演出是一项浩大的工程。

❷ [C] 保证，承诺

The landlord gave a written undertaking that the repairs would be carried out. 房东书面保证将进行维修。

9. underwear [ˈʌndəweə(r)] n. 衬衣，内衣

『under下面+wear穿→穿在其他衣服下面（贴着皮肤）的衣服→内衣』

② under- 表示"不足，不够"

1. undernourishment [ˌʌndəˈnʌrɪʃmənt] n. 营养不良

『under不足+nourishment营养→营养不足→营养不良』

2. underplay [ˌʌndəˈpleɪ] vt. 低调处理，降低…的重要性

『under不足+ play表演→表演角色不充分→低调处理』

If you underplay something, you make it seem less important than it really is.

President Trump was determined to underplay the threat presented by COVID-19 because he was afraid it would negatively impact his reelection prospects.
特朗普总统决心低调处理COVID-19（新冠肺炎）带来的威胁，因为他担心这会对他的连任前景造成负面影响。

3. underestimate [ˌʌndərˈestɪmeɪt] v. 低估 〈P27〉

『under不足+estimate估计→估计不足→低估』

前缀82. uni-=one，表示"一个，单一"

1. unique [juˈniːk] adj. 唯一的；独特的；独有的

『uni一个+que→唯一的』

❶ 唯一的，独一无二的

Everyone's fingerprints are unique.

每个人的指纹都是独一无二的。

❷ 独特的；无与伦比的

You can use unique to describe things that you admire because they are very unusual and special.

The preview offers a unique opportunity to see the show without the crowds.

预展提供了看展览但不挤挤的难得机会。

As a writer he has his unique style.

作为作家，他有自己独特的风格。

❸ ~ (to sb/sth)（某人、地或事物）独具的，特有的

The problem is not unique to British students.

这个问题并不是英国学生独有的。

2. unit [ˈjuːnɪt] n. 装置；单位；单元

『uni一个+t→作为一个整体的→装置；单位；单元』

The present perfect is covered in Unit 8.

现在完成时在第8单元讲解。

The basic unit of society is the family.

社会的基本单位是家庭。

Medical units were operating in the disaster area.

医疗小组正在灾区工作。

3. unite [juˈnaɪt] v.（使）联合；（使）团结

『uni一个+(i)te使→（在事情面前）成为一个整体→联合；团结』

[V, VN]（使）团结；（使）联合

If a group of people or things unite or if something unites them, they join together and act as a group.

Local resident groups have united in opposition to the plan.

当地居民团体已联合起来反对这项计划。

Will they unite behind the new leader?

他们会团结支持新领导人吗？

A special bond unites our two countries.

一种特殊的纽带把我们两国联结起来。

▶ **unity** [ˈjuːnəti] n. 联合，统一；团结

❶ [U] 联合（状态）；统一（状态）

Unity is the state of different areas or groups being joined together to form a single country or organization.

European unity 欧洲的统一

❷ [U] 团结；一致

When there is unity, people are in agreement and act together for a particular purpose.

a plea for unity within the party 要求党内团结的呼吁

The design lacks unity. 这项设计整体不够协调。

❸ [C] 统一体

If society is to exist as a unity, its members must have shared values.

社会若要成为一个统一的群体，它的成员就必须有共同的价值观。

4. unify [ˈjuːnɪfaɪ] vt. 统一；使成为一体

『uni一个+fy使→使…成为一个→统一』

The new leader hopes to unify the country.

新领袖希望把国家统一起来。

a unified transport system 统一的运输体系

▶ **unification** [ˌjuːnɪfɪˈkeɪʃn] n. 统一，联合

the process of general European unification

欧洲一体化进程

5. union [ˈjuːniən] n. 工会；协会；联盟

『uni一个+on→（为了共同目的而组成的）一个组织→联盟；协会；工会』

I've joined the union. 我已经加入工会。

the European Union 欧洲联盟

6. unanimous [juˈnænɪməs] adj. 一致同意的〈P114〉

『un(=uni)一个的+anim (mind) 心思+ous充满→一个心思的→想法一致的→一致同意的』

7. uniform [ˈjuːnɪfɔːm] n. 制服 adj. 一致的；统一的〈P177〉

『uni一个的+form形式→（许多个体）一个形式→制服；统一的』

8. unilateral [ˌjuːnɪˈlætrəl] adj. 单边的；单方的〈P201〉

『uni一个的+later边+al…的→单边的』

前缀83. vice- 表示"副"

1. vice-president [vaɪs ˈprezɪdənt] n. 副总裁；副总统；副校长

2. vice-manager [vaɪsˈmænɪdʒə(r)] n. 副经理

前缀84. with-=against; back，表示"向后；对着"

1. withdraw [wɪðˈdrɔː] vt. 撤回；取（款）；退出

『with (=back) 向后+draw拉→向后拉→撤回』

（withdraw, withdrew, withdrawn）

❶ ~ (sb/sth) (from sth) 撤回；收回；停止提供

Government troops were forced to withdraw.

政府部队被迫撤走了。

The drug was withdrawn from sale after a number of people suffered serious side effects.

这药因许多人服后产生严重副作用而被停止销售。

He withdrew his remarks and explained what he had meant to say. 他收回所说的话，然后又解释他本来想说什么。

❷ 提，取（银行账户中的款）

I'd like to withdraw £250 please. 劳驾，我想提取250英镑。

❸ 退出（活动或组织）

On June 1, 2017 Donald Trump withdrew the United States from the Paris Agreement.

2017年6月1日，唐纳德·特朗普让美国退出巴黎协议。

▶ **withdrawal** [wɪðˈdrɔːəl] n. 撤回；收回；退出

Parliament adopted a resolution calling for the complete withdrawal of troops. 议会采纳了要求全部撤军的决议。

2. withhold [wɪðˈhəʊld] vt. 拒绝给予

『with (=back) +hold→hold back→保留下来→拒绝给予』

（withhold, withheld, withheld）

[VN] ~ sth (from sb/sth) (formal) 拒绝给；不给

to refuse to give sth to sb

She was accused of withholding information from the police.

她被指控对警方知情不报。

It's never wise to withhold evidence.

藏匿证据绝非明智之举。

3. withstand [wɪðˈstænd] vt. 耐得住；经受得住

『with (=against)对着+stand站立→面对着攻击仍能站立→经受得住』

（withstand, withstood, withstood）

to be strong enough not to be hurt or damaged by extreme conditions, the use of force, etc.

The materials used have to be able to withstand high temperatures. 所使用的材料必须能够耐高温。

They can withstand extremes of temperature and weather without fading or cracking.
它们能够经受极端的气温和天气状况而不褪色、不破裂。

As a politician, he is able to withstand public criticism.
作为一名政治家，他经得住公众批评。

They are designed to withstand earthquakes and violent storms. 它们被设计成能经受地震与猛烈的暴风雨。

第2讲　根据后缀记单词

后缀1. -a 表名词复数，以-um, -on 结尾的名词复数词尾为-a

1. datum [ˈdeɪtəm] n. 数据

▶**data** [ˈdeɪtə] n. 数据；资料 （datum的复数形式）

[U, pl.] 数据；资料；材料

This data was collected from 69 countries.
这资料是从69个国家收集来的。

These data have been collected from various sources.
这些数据是从各方面搜集来的。

2. medium [ˈmiːdiəm] adj. 中等的；n. 媒介

『med(= middle)中间的+ium部分→中间部分→中等的；媒介』

（pl. media）

❶ adj. [usually before noun] (abbr. M) 中等的；中号的

a man of medium height/build 中等身材的人

There are three sizes－small, medium and large.
有三种尺寸——小号、中号和大号。

Cook over a medium heat for 15 minutes. 用中火煮15分钟。

小贴士 衣服标签上的S是小码，M是中码，L是大码，XL是特大码，XXL是超特大码。

衣服标签上的S指代的是英文单词SMALL，M指代英文单词MEDIUM，L指代英文单词LARGE，XL指代英文单词EXTRA LARGE，XXL指代英文单词EXTRA EXTRA LARGE。

❷ [C]（传播信息的）媒介，手段，方法

Television is the modern medium of communication .
电视是现代传媒。

A T-shirt can be an excellent medium for getting your message across.
T恤衫可以成为一种极好的表达信息的媒介。

❸ n.（文艺创作中使用的）材料，形式

Watercolour is his favourite medium.
水彩画是他最喜欢的表现方式。

❹ n.（biology 生物学）介质；培养基；环境

a substance that sth exists or grows in or that it travels through

The bacteria were growing in a sugar medium.
细菌在糖基中生长。

▶**media** [ˈmiːdiə] n. 媒体 （medium的复数）

『medium媒体→变um为a→media』

the media [U + sing./pl. v.] 媒体；大众传播媒介，大众传播工具（指电视、广播、报纸、互联网）

The trial was fully reported in the media.

媒体对这次审判进行了全面报道。

The media was/were accused of influencing the final decision.
人们指责媒体左右了终审判决。

3. phenomenon [fəˈnɒmɪnən] n. 现象；奇迹

❶ 现象

a fact or an event in nature or society, especially one that is not fully understood

They see the shift to the right as a worldwide phenomenon.
他们认为政治上的右翼倾向是一个世界现象。

❷ 杰出的人；非凡的人（或事物）

▶**phenomena** [fəˈnɒmɪnə] n. 现象 （phenomenon的复数形式）

后缀2. -able, -ible 形容词后缀，表示"能够的，可以的"；名词形式为-ability, -ibility

1. able [ˈeɪbl] adj. 有能力的；有才干的

❶ ~ to do sth 能够做某事

The older child should be able to prepare a simple meal.
那个年纪稍大的孩子应当会做一顿简单的饭菜。

❷ 聪明能干的

Someone who is able is very clever or very good at doing something.

We aim to help the less able in society to lead an independent life. 我们的宗旨是帮助社会上能力较弱的人独立生活。

▶**ability** [əˈbɪləti] n. 能力；才能

❶ [sing.] ~ to do sth 能力

The system has the ability to run more than one program at the same time. 该系统能够同时运行一个以上的程序。

❷ [C, U] 才能；本领

He was a man of extraordinary abilities. 他才干卓著。

A woman of her ability will easily find a job.
有她那样才能的女性找工作不难。

❸ to the best of one's abilities/ability 尽…所能地

I take care of them to the best of my abilities.
我尽我所能地照顾他们。

词义辨析 <P370第45>
有能力的；能够的 able, capable, competent

词义辨析 <P370第46>
能力 capacity, capability, competence, ability

2. available [əˈveɪləbl] adj.（物）可得到的；（人）有空的

『avail利用+able能够的→能够利用的→可得到的；有空的』

❶（东西）可使用的；可获得的；可购得的
Further information is available on request. 详情备索。
This was the only room available. 这是唯一可用的房间。
A wide range of colours and patterns are available.
各种颜色和样式都有。

❷（人）有空的
Will she be available this afternoon?
今天下午她有空吗？

▶**avail** [əˈveɪl] n. 用处 vt. 利用

❶ to little/no avail 没有用，不成功
The doctors tried everything to keep him alive but to no avail.
医生千方百计想使他活下来，但无济于事。

❷ avail yourself of sth 利用
Guests are encouraged to avail themselves of the full range of hotel facilities. 旅馆鼓励旅客充分利用各种设施。

3. **comfortable** [ˈkʌmftəbl] adj. 舒服的；自在的
『comfort舒服+able能够的→能够带来舒服的→舒服的』

▶**comfort** [ˈkʌmfət] n. 舒服；安慰 vt.安慰

❶ [U] 舒服，安逸，舒适
The hotel offers a high standard of comfort and service.
这家旅馆提供高标准的舒适享受和优质服务。
They had enough money to live in comfort in their old age.
他们有足够的钱舒舒服服地安度晚年。

❷ [U] 安慰
I tried to offer a few words of comfort.
我试图说上几句安慰的话。
If it's any comfort to you, I'm in the same situation.
就当是一句安慰的话——我的情况也跟你一样。

❸ [sing.] 令人感到安慰的人（或事物）
The children have been a great comfort to me through all of this.
在我经历这一切的日子里，孩子们一直是我的一个巨大安慰。
It's a comfort to know that she is safe.
知道她安然无恙是令人宽慰的事。

❹ [C, usually pl.] 舒适的设施（或条件）
The hotel has all modern comforts/every modern comfort.
这家旅馆拥有各种现代化的舒适设施。

❺ [VN]安慰
She comforted herself with the thought that it would soon be spring. 她想到春天很快就要来临，以此来宽慰自己。

4. **desirable** [dɪˈzaɪərəbl] adj. 令人向往的；值得拥有的
『desire渴望(去e)+able能够的→可以渴望的→值得拥有的』
~ (that)… | ~ (for sb) (to do sth)令人向往的；值得拥有的
that you would like to have or do; worth having or doing

It is desirable that interest rates (should) be reduced.
渴望利率下调。
The house has many desirable features.
这栋房子有许多吸引人的特点。

5. **disabled** [dɪsˈeɪbld] adj. 残疾的
『dis不+able能够的+(e)d表形容→不能够的→残疾的』

physically/mentally disabled
有生理残疾的；有心理缺陷的
He was born disabled. 他天生残疾。
the disabled/ disabled people 残疾人

▶**disability** [ˌdɪsəˈbɪləti] n. 残疾
[U] Living with disability is frustrating and challenging.
残疾人的生活充满挫折和挑战。
[C]She swims well despite her disabilities.
她虽然身有残疾，却是个游泳好手。

近义词 **handicap** [ˈhændikæp] n. 残疾；不利条件

❶ [C, U] (becoming old-fashioned, sometimes offensive)
生理缺陷；智障者；残疾
Despite her handicap, Jane is able to hold down a full-time job. 简尽管有生理缺陷，却能够保住一份全职工作。

❷ [C] 障碍；不利条件
A handicap is an event or situation that places you at a disadvantage and makes it harder for you to do something.
Not speaking the language proved to be a bigger handicap than I'd imagined.
事实证明不会讲这种语言造成的障碍比我想象的大。

▶**handicapped** [ˈhændikæpt] adj. 残疾的
The accident left him physically handicapped.
那次事故使他落下了残疾。

小贴士 此词源于一古赛马游戏，原形是hand in cap。赛马前把手放在帽子中进行抽签，常给优胜的抽签者以不利条件；优胜者要礼让他人少跑几码或自己多跑几码。

词义辨析 <P370第44> 残疾的 disabled, handicapped

6. **probable** [ˈprɒbəbl] adj. 很可能的
▶**probability** [ˌprɒbəˈbɪləti] n. 可能性

7. **reasonable** [ˈriːznəbl] adj. 合理的；公道的
『reason原因；推理+able能够的→可以推理原因的→合理的；公道的』

It is reasonable to assume that he knew beforehand that this would happen.
有理由认为他事先就知道会发生这样的事。
We sell good quality food at reasonable prices.
我们以公道的价格出售优质食品。

8. **unforgettable** [ˌʌnfəˈgetəbl] adj. 难忘的
『un不+forget忘记→able能够的→不能忘记的→难忘的』
（重音在get上，双写t后再加able）

9. **possible** [ˈpɒsəbl] adj. 可能的
▶**possibility** [ˌpɒsəˈbɪləti] n. 可能，可能性

10. **visible** [ˈvɪzəbl] adj. 看得见的；注意得到的
『vis看+ible能够的→能够看得见的→看得见的』

Most stars are not visible to the naked eye.
大多数星星肉眼看不见。
He showed no visible sign of emotion. 他丝毫不露声色。

▶**invisible** [ɪnˈvɪzəbl] adj. 看不见的
『in不+vis看+ible能够的→不能够看见的→看不见的』

▶**visibility** [ˌvɪzəˈbɪləti] n. 能见度；引人注目的程度
Visibility was down to about 100 meters in the fog.
雾中的能见距离降到了大约100米。
The advertisements were intended to increase the company's visibility in the marketplace.
那些广告旨在使这家公司在市场中更加引人注目。

11. **edible** [ˈedəbl] adj. 可食用的；（无毒）能吃的
『ed(=eat)吃+ible能够的→能够吃的→可食用的』

The food at the hotel was barely edible.
这家旅馆的食物简直不能入口。
edible snails/flowers 可食用的蜗牛/花

后缀3. -acle 构成名词，表示"物或抽象概念"

1. pinnacle [ˈpɪnəkl] n. 尖顶；顶峰
『pinn尖+acle表物→尖顶；顶峰』

❶ [C]（建筑物）小尖顶；（尤指山顶的）尖岩
A walker fell 80ft from a rocky pinnacle.
一位徒步者从一块80英尺高的尖锥形岩石上摔了下来。

❷ [C]顶峰，顶点
If someone reaches the pinnacle of their career or the pinnacle of a particular area of life, they are at the highest point of it.
He has reached the pinnacle of his career.
他已经登上事业的顶峰。
The Olympics represent the pinnacle of competition and achievement. 奥运会代表竞争和成就的顶峰。

2. manacle [ˈmænəkl] n. 手铐；脚镣 vt. 给…戴上镣铐
『man手+acle表物→戴在手上的东西→手铐』

His hands were manacled behind his back.
他的双手被铐在了身后。
Carleson locked the manacles around the man's wrists.
卡尔森给这个人锁上了手铐。

3. spectacle [ˈspektəkl] n. 眼镜；奇观 <P308>
『spect看+acle表物或抽象概念→看的东西；看到的（好东西）→眼镜；奇观』

4. miracle [ˈmɪrəkl] n. 奇迹 <P222>
『mire(=wonder)惊奇（去e）+acle表抽象概念→令人惊奇的事情→奇迹』

5. obstacle [ˈɒbstəkl] n. 障碍（物）<P312>
『ob逆+st站+acle表物→逆向站的东西→障碍』

6. receptacle [rɪˈseptəkl] n. 容器 <P128>
『re一再+cept拿+acle物→接收（东西）的物体→容器』

7. tentacle [ˈtentəkl] n. 触须，触角；束缚 <P328>
『tent伸展+acle物→伸展出去探的东西→触角』

后缀4. -ade 构成名词，表示"饮料；材料制成物；动作或动作结果；行动的人或集体"；重音在-ade音节上

① -ade 表示某些水果制成的饮料

1. lemonade [ˌleməˈneɪd] n. 柠檬味汽水；柠檬饮料
『lemon柠檬+ade表饮料→柠檬饮料』

2. orangeade [ˌɒrɪndʒˈeɪd] n. 橘子水，橙汁
『orange橘子；橙子+ade表饮料→橘子水，橙汁』

② -ade 表示某种材料制成物

1. arcade [ɑːˈkeɪd] n. 拱廊；室内（购物）商场 <P115>
『arc拱形+ade某种材料的制成物→拱廊』

2. colonnade [ˌkɒləˈneɪd] n. 石柱廊
『colon(=column)柱子（双写n）+ade某种材料的制成物→石柱廊』

a row of stone columns with equal spaces between them, usually supporting a roof
Greek houses included a walled court or garden usually surrounded by a colonnade.

希腊的住宅包括一个一般由柱廊围合的有围墙的庭院或花园。

③ -ade 表示动作，动作的结果

1. blockade [blɒˈkeɪd] n. 封锁 vt. 实施封锁
『block堵塞+ade表动作或动作的结果→封锁』

❶ [C]（尤指对港口的）包围，封锁；障碍物
the action of surrounding or closing a place, especially a port, in order to stop people or goods from coming in or out

to impose/lift a blockade 实行/解除封锁
an economic blockade 经济封锁
The police set up blockades on highways leading out of the city. 警察在城市出口的公路上设下路障。

❷ [VN] 包围，封锁
Truck drivers have blockaded roads to show their anger over new driving regulations.
卡车司机通过阻塞道路来表达他们对新机动车交通法规的不满。

▶**block** [blɒk] n. 大块；街区；大楼 vt. 堵塞；阻止
❶ [C] 大块（with straight sides）；（英）大楼；（美）一段街区的距离；障碍物
a block of ice/concrete/stone 一方冰/混凝土/石头
an office block 一栋办公大楼
She took the dog for a walk around the block.
她带着狗绕街区散步。
His apartment is three blocks away from the police station.
他住在和警察局相隔三个街区的公寓里。

❷ [VN] 堵塞
(also block up) to prevent anything moving through a space by being or placing something across it or in it
A fallen tree is blocking the road.
一棵倒下的树挡住了道路。
The sink's blocked up. 水池堵塞了。

❸ [VN] 阻碍，阻止
The Senate blocked publication of the report.
参议院阻止了该报告的发表。

▶**unblock** [ˌʌnˈblɒk] vt. 疏通（管道等）；清除障碍
『un表相反动作+ block堵塞→取消堵塞』

If you unblock the pipe, the water will run back into the house. 如果堵不住管道，水就会流回到屋里。
If you don't have any, then contact your network administrator and ask him or her to unblock those connections.
如果没有，请与网络管理员联系，要求他或她清除这些连接。

2. cascade [kæˈskeɪd] n. 小瀑布 v. 倾斜
『casc(=cas)落下+ade表动作或动作的结果→小瀑布；倾斜』

❶ [C] 小瀑布（尤指一连串瀑布中的一支）；倾泻；大簇的下垂物；倾泻（或涌出）的东西
a cascade of rainwater 如注的雨水
Her hair tumbled in a cascade down her back.
她的长发瀑布般地倾泻在后背上。
He crashed to the ground in a cascade of oil cans.
他随着一连串的油桶跌落坠地。

❷ [V+adv./prep.] 倾泻；大量落下或悬垂
Water cascaded down the mountainside.
水从山腰倾泻而下。

Blonde hair cascaded over her shoulders.
她的金发像瀑布似的披落在肩头。

3. barricade [ˌbærɪˈkeɪd] n. 路障 vt. 设路障阻挡 <P117>
『bar禁止，阻挡（双写r）+ic+ade表示动作或结果→路障；设路障阻挡』

④ 表示做某种行动的个人或集体

1. crusade [kruːˈseɪd] n.十字军东征；运动；参与斗争或运动
『crus(=cross)十字形；交叉+ ade 表行动的个人或团体→十字军』

❶ n.（发生于11世纪至13世纪的）十字军东征

❷ [C] ~ (for/against sth) | ~ (to do sth)（长期坚定不移的）斗争，运动

They led an unsuccessful crusade against government corruption.
他们领导了一场不成功的反对政府腐败的运动。

❸ [V] 长期坚定不移地奋斗

He headed the troops to crusade against the rebellion.
他率领军队讨伐叛乱。

2. motorcade [ˈməʊtəkeɪd] n.（载有重要人物的）车队，汽车行列
『motor马达，汽车+c+ade表行动的个人或团体→车队』

At times the president's motorcade slowed to a crawl.
有时总统车队放慢速度缓缓而行。

3. renegade [ˈrenɪɡeɪd] n. 变节者，背叛者 <P233>
『re又，再+neg否认+ade表行动的个人或团体→一再否认自己信仰的人』

4. cavalcade [ˌkævlˈkeɪd] n. 骑兵队 <P125>
『caval马+c+ade表行动的个人或团体→骑马的团体→骑兵队』

后缀5. -age 构成名词，表"总称；场所；费用；行为或结果"

① -age 构成集合名词，表总称

1. bandage [ˈbændɪdʒ] n. 绷带 vt. 用绷带绑扎
『band带子+ age集合名词，总称→绷带』

▶**band** [bænd] n. 乐队；带，箍

❶ [C] 乐队

❷ [C] 带，箍
a thin flat strip or circle of any material that is put around things, for example to hold them together or to make them stronger
All babies in the hospital have name bands on their wrists.
医院里所有新生儿手腕上都套着写有名字的手箍。

2. beverage [ˈbevərɪdʒ] n.（除水以外的）饮料
『bever喝+ age表总称→饮料』

Alcoholic beverages are served in the hotel lounge.
酒店的公共休息室出售酒精饮料。

小贴士 **soft drink** 软饮料，指不含酒精的饮料。

3. foliage [ˈfəʊliɪdʒ] n.（植物的）叶；枝叶
『foli树叶+age集合名词，总称→树叶』

Dark foliage clothes the hills. 浓密的树叶覆盖着群山。

4. mileage [ˈmaɪlɪdʒ] n. 英里数，里程；（一升油行驶的）里程数
『mile英里+age集合名词，总称→英里数』

We checked the mileage on the vehicle.
我们检查了车子的里程数。
Will you recommend one with good mileage?
你能推荐一个有好的英里数的吗？

5. plumage [ˈpluːmɪdʒ] n.（鸟的）全身羽毛
『plume羽毛（去e）+age集合名词，总称→羽衣』

The bright plumage of many male birds has evolved to attract females. 很多雄鸟进化出鲜艳的羽毛是为了吸引雌鸟。

▶**plume** [pluːm] n. 羽毛；（一）股，（一）缕

❶ [C] 羽毛，大羽；（战士头盔等的）羽饰
a black hat with an ostrich plume
装着一根鸵鸟羽毛的黑帽子

❷（烟、火等升起的）（一）股，（一）团，（一）缕
A plume of smoke, dust, fire, or water is a large quantity of it that rises into the air in a column.
A plume of smoke rose from the chimney.
从烟囱里冒出一缕轻烟。

6. tonnage [ˈtʌnɪdʒ] n.（船舶的）吨位
『ton一吨+age集合名词，总称→吨位』

The ship has a tonnage of twenty thousand.
这艘船的吨位是2万吨。

7. voltage [ˈvəʊltɪdʒ] n. 电压，伏特数
『volt伏特+ age集合名词，总称→电压，伏特数』

The voltage of an electrical current is its force measured in volts.
The systems are getting smaller and using lower voltages.
这些系统变得更小，使用的电压也更低。

8. heritage [ˈherɪtɪdʒ] n.遗产；传统 <P190>
『her继承人+it（=go）走+age集合名词，总称→继承的东西的总称→遗产』

② -age 构成名词，表场所

1. village [ˈvɪlɪdʒ] n. 村庄
『villa别墅（去a）+ age场所→别墅一般都在郊外→村庄』

2. anchorage [ˈæŋkərɪdʒ] n. 停泊处
『anchor铁锚；抛锚+age场所→抛锚的场所→停泊地』

The ship remained in anchorage for a month.
船在锚地停了一个月。

▶**anchor** [ˈæŋkə(r)] n. 锚；（电视节目）主持人 vt. 固定 v. 抛锚

❶ [C] 锚
The ship lay at anchor two miles off the rocky coast.
船在离岩岸两英里处抛锚停泊。

❷ [V] We anchored off the coast of Spain.
我们在西班牙沿海抛锚停泊。

❸ [VN] 使固定，扣牢；扎根于
Make sure the table is securely anchored.
务必要把桌子固定好。
Her novels are anchored in everyday experience.
她的小说取材于日常生活经验。

❹ (NAmE) n.（电视、广播节目的新闻）主持人 v. 主持
[VN] She anchored the evening news for seven years.
她主持了七年晚间新闻报道。
[C] Dan Rather, anchor of the CBC Evening News
丹·拉瑟，CBC晚间新闻的主播

3. hermitage [ˈhɜːmɪtɪdʒ] n. 隐居处；修道院

『hermit隐士+age场所→隐士住处』

I think she will be pleased with the hermitage.
我想，她一定会喜欢我们这个幽静的小地方。

► **hermit** [ˈhɜːmɪt] n. 隐士

③ -age 构成名词，表费用

1. **postage** [ˈpəʊstɪdʒ] n. 邮费，邮资
『post邮政+age费用→邮资』

All prices include postage and packing.
所有的价格都包括邮资和包装费。

2. **towage** [ˈtəʊɪdʒ] n. 拖（车、船）费
『tow拖+age费用→拖（车、船）费』

④ -age 构成名词，表示行为或行为的结果

1. **marriage** [ˈmærɪdʒ] n. 婚姻
『marry结婚+age行为或行为的结果→婚姻』

2. **usage** [ˈjuːsɪdʒ] n. 使用；用法
『use使用（去e）+age行为或行为的结果→使用』

3. **drainage** [ˈdreɪnɪdʒ] n. 排水系统；排水
『drain排干+age行为或行为的结果→排水』

► **drain** [dreɪn] v. （使液体）排空，流干，喝空；使（精力、金钱等）耗尽 n. 下水道
『记法：d谐音为"地"+rain雨水→（排空）地里的雨水→排空；下水道』

The marshes have been drained. 沼泽地里的水已排干。
[V] The swimming pool drains very slowly.
游泳池里的水排得很慢。
[VN] We had to drain the oil out of the engine.
我们必须把发动机里的机油全部放掉。
She quickly drained the last of her drink.
她一下子就把最后一点酒喝掉了。
I felt drained of energy. 我感到筋疲力尽。
We had to call in a plumber to unblock the drain.
我们只得叫个管道工来疏通下水道。

4. **wreckage** [ˈrekɪdʒ] n.（车辆等的）残骸；（建筑物等的）废墟
『wreck毁坏，失事+age行为或行为的结果→残骸，废墟』

[U] （车辆等的）残骸；（建筑物等的）废墟
the parts of a vehicle, building, etc. that remain after it has been badly damaged or destroyed
A few survivors were pulled from the wreckage.
从废墟中扒出了几个幸存者。
Pieces of wreckage were found ten miles away from the scene of the explosion.
在离爆炸现场十英里外的地方发现了残骸碎片。

► **wreck** [rek] n. 严重损毁的船（车辆或飞机）vt. 毁坏
❶ [C] 沉船；严重损毁的船（车辆或飞机）
Two passengers are still trapped in the wreck.
有两名乘客仍被困在失事的车辆里。

❷ [C]（身体或精神上）受到严重损伤的人
The interview reduced him to a nervous wreck.
这次面试使得他的精神高度紧张。

❸ [C] 状况非常糟糕的车辆（或建筑物等）
The house was a wreck when we bought it.
我们买下这座房子时，它破烂不堪。

❹ [VN] 破坏，毁坏

The building had been wrecked by the explosion.
那座楼房被炸毁了。
The road was littered with wrecked cars.
路上到处都弃置着被撞坏的汽车。
The weather wrecked all our plans.
天气把我们的计划全都毁了。

5. **storage** [ˈstɔːrɪdʒ] n. 贮存，贮藏
『store贮存（去e）+age行为或行为的结果→贮存，贮藏』

❶ [U] 贮存，贮藏；贮存空间
tables that fold flat for storage 便于存放的折叠桌
We need more storage now. 现在我们需要更多的贮存场所。

❷ [U] （计）存储
data storage 数据存储

6. **appendage** [əˈpendɪdʒ] n. 附加物，附属物〈P249〉
『append附加，增补+age行为或行为的结果→附加物』

7. **barrage** [ˈbærɑːʒ] n. 弹幕，火力网；连珠炮似的（质问、抱怨等）〈P117〉
『bar阻拦；长条；一束光线（双写r）+age表示行为或行为的结果→（用连射的炮弹形成许多）光束般的长条来阻拦→弹幕，火力网』

后缀6. -al 表名词，指"人；物；行为"；也可表形容词

① -al 表名词，指"行为"

1. **refusal** [rɪˈfjuːzl] n. 拒绝
『refuse拒绝（去e）+al表名词→拒绝』

His refusal to discuss the matter is very annoying.
他拒绝商量这件事，令人很恼火。

2. **trial** [ˈtraɪəl] n. 审判；尝试
『try审判；尝试+（变y为i）al表名词→审批；尝试』

❶ [U, C] （法院的）审讯，审理，审判
He's on trial for murder. 他因涉嫌谋杀罪而受审。

❷ [C, U] （对能力、质量、性能等的）试验，试用
The new drug is undergoing clinical trials.
这种新药正在进行临床试验。
She agreed to employ me for a trial period.
她同意试用我一段时间。

❸ **trial and error** 反复试验；不断摸索
Children learn to use computer programs by trial and error.
儿童通过反复摸索才学会运用计算机程序。

3. **arrival** [əˈraɪvl] n. 到达；到达者
『arrive到达（去e）+al表名词→到达』

Guests receive dinner on/upon arrival at the hotel.
旅客一到旅馆即可就餐。

4. **approval** [əˈpruːvl] n. 赞成；批准（计划；产品）
『approve赞成（去e）+al表名词→赞成；批准』

❶ [U] 赞成，同意
She desperately wanted to win her father's approval.
她急不可待地想赢得父亲的赞同。

❷ [U, C] ~ (for sth) (from sb) 批准，通过（计划、要求等）
The plan will be submitted to the committee for official approval. 该计划将送交委员会正式批准。

► **approve** [əˈpruːv] vi. 赞成 vt. 批准；通过
（approve作"赞成、同意"讲时，是不可数名词，常和of连用；作"批准"讲时是不及物动词）

❶ [V] ~ (of sb/sth) 赞成；同意
to think that sb/sth is good, acceptable or suitable
I told my mother I wanted to leave school but she didn't approve.
我告诉母亲我不想继续上学，但是母亲不同意。
Do you approve of my idea?
你同意我的想法吗？
She doesn't approve of me leaving school this year.
她不同意我今年离校。

❷ [VN] 批准（计划、要求等）
to officially agree to a plan, request, etc.
The committee unanimously approved the plan.
委员会一致通过了计划。

❸ [VN] [often passive] 批准、核准（产品、人选等）
If a product or person is approved by an official organization, they are declared to be of a good enough standard to be used or employed.
The course is approved by the Department for Education.
课程已获教育部核准。

5. burial [ˈberiəl] n. 葬礼；埋葬
『bury埋+（变y为i）al表名词→埋葬；葬礼』
Her body was sent home for burial.
她的尸骨已运回家乡安葬。
His family insisted he should be given a proper burial.
他的家人坚持要为他举行适当的葬礼。

▶ **bury** [ˈberi] vt. 埋葬；掩埋；掩盖；掩藏

❶ [VN] 埋葬；安葬
He was buried in Highgate Cemetery.
他被安葬在海格特墓地。

❷ [VN] 把（某物）掩埋在地下
He buried the box in the garden.
他把那个箱子埋在花园里。

❸ [VN]掩藏（感情、错误等）；掩盖
She had learnt to bury her feelings.
她已经学会了感情不外露。
He buried his face in his hands and wept.
他双手掩面而泣。

❹ **bury yourself in sth** 专心致志于某事
Since she left, he's buried himself in his work.
自从她走后，他全心扑在工作上。

6. denial [dɪˈnaɪəl] n. 否认；拒绝
『deny否认；拒绝+（变y为i）al表名词→否认；拒绝』

▶ **deny** [dɪˈnaɪ] vt. 否认；拒绝给予

❶ 否认（to say that sth is not true）
There's no denying (the fact) that quicker action could have saved them.
无可否认，如果行动快一点，本来是救得了他们的。
[VN] to deny a claim/a charge/an accusation
否认某种说法/指控/谴责
[V -ing] He **denies attempting** to murder his wife.
他否认企图谋杀妻子。

❷ ~ (sb) (sth) | ~ sth (to sb)
It would spoil a child if you denied him nothing.
如果你对一个孩子有求必应，这样会宠坏他。
They were denied access to the information.
他们被拒绝接触这些信息。

7. survival [səˈvaɪvl] n. 幸存；幸存物 ‹P356›
『survive幸存（去e）+al表名词→幸存』

8. withdrawal [wɪðˈdrɔːəl] n. 撤回；收回；退出‹P45›
『withdraw撤回；收回+al表名词→撤回；收回』

② -al 表形容词，译为"…的"

1. digital [ˈdɪdʒɪtl] adj. 数字的
『digit数字+al表形容词→数字的』

2. exceptional [ɪkˈsepʃənl] adj. 杰出的；例外的
『exception例外+al表形容词→例外的；杰出的』

❶ 杰出的，优秀的
unusually good
At the age of five he showed exceptional talent as a musician.
他五岁时就表现出非凡的音乐才能。

❷ 异常的，特别的
This deadline will be extended only in exceptional circumstances. 只有在特殊情况下才会延长最后期限。

▶ **exception** [ɪkˈsepʃn] n. 例外
『except除外+ion表名词→例外』
Most of the buildings in the town are modern, but the church is an exception.
城里大多是现代建筑，不过教堂是个例外。
There are always a lot of exceptions to grammar rules.
语法规则总是有很多例外。

3. global [ˈɡləʊbl] adj. 全球的
『globe全球，世界（去e）+al表形容词→全球的』

▶ **globalization** [ˌɡləʊbəlaɪˈzeɪʃn] n. 全球化

4. natural [ˈnætʃrəl] adj. 自然的；天生的
『nature自然（去e）+al表形容词→自然的』

❶ [only before noun] 自然的；天然的
natural disasters 自然灾害
a country's natural resources 一国的自然资源

❷ 正常的，自然的，合乎常情的
It is natural for the shopkeeper to feel annoyed when the supermarket is set up close to his shop.
当超市挨着这家商店建立起来时，店主感到苦恼是正常的。

❸ （能力或技能）天赋的，天生的
She has a natural ability to understand the motives of others.
她有一种洞察他人动机的天赋。

5. universal [ˌjuːnɪˈvɜːsl] adj. 普遍的；全体的；全球的
『universe宇宙（去e）+al表形容词→全宇宙的→普遍的』

❶ 普遍的；全体的
Something that is universal relates to everyone in the world or everyone in a particular group or society.
Such problems are a universal feature of old age.
这类问题是老年人的通病。
The new reforms have not met with universal approval within the government.
新的改革没有得到政府的普遍认可。

❷ 全球性的
Something that is universal affects or relates to every part of the world or the universe.
universal diseases 全球性的疾病
Climate change is a universal problem.
气候变化是个世界性的问题。

6. <u>racial</u> ['reɪʃl] adj. 种族的
『race种族（去e）+ial…的→种族的』
They have pledged to end racial discrimination in areas such as employment.
他们已经保证在诸如就业等方面停止种族歧视。

7. <u>formal</u> ['fɔːml] adj. 正式的 <P177>
『form形式+al表形容词→（重视）形式上的→正式的』

③ -al 表名词，指"人或物"

1. <u>criminal</u> ['krɪmɪnl] n. 罪犯，犯人
『crimin(=crime)犯罪+al表人→犯罪的人→罪犯』

▶<u>crime</u> [kraɪm] n. 罪行，犯罪
commit a serious crime 犯重罪
The criminal has been arrested. 罪犯已经被逮捕。

2. <u>national</u> ['næʃnəl] adj. 全国的；国家的 n. 某国国民
『nation国家+al表人或形容词→国家的；某国国民』

❶ adj. 国家的，全国的
Ruling parties have lost ground in national and local elections.
执政党在全国和地区选举中均败北。

❷ adj. 国民的，民族的
National means typical of the people or customs of a particular country or nation.
They are afraid of losing their national identity.
他们担心会失去他们的民族特色。

❸ n. 国民；国人
You can refer to someone who is legally a citizen of a country as a national of that country.
Foreign nationals have begun leaving because of a sharp rise in violence.
因为暴力活动的急剧增加，外国人已经开始离开这个国家。

▶<u>nationality</u> [ˌnæʃəˈnæləti] n. 国籍；民族
What's your nationality? 你的国籍是什么？
Kazakhstan alone contains more than a hundred nationalities.
单是哈萨克斯坦就有一百多个民族。

3. <u>aboriginal</u> [ˌæbəˈrɪdʒənl] adj. 土著的 n.(尤指澳大利亚的）土著居民<P240>
『ab+origin起源→al表人或形容词→起源的（人）→土著居民；土著的』

4. <u>original</u> [əˈrɪdʒənl] adj. 起初的；原创的；原作的 n. 原件；原著 <P240>
『origin起源+al表名词或形容词→原件；起源的』

5. <u>editorial</u> [ˌedɪˈtɔːriəl] adj. 编辑的 n. 社论，评论
『editor编者+i+al表形容词或表物→编辑的；社论，评论』

后级7. -an 表示"…人；…的"

1. <u>African</u> ['æfrɪkən] n. 非洲人 adj. 非洲的
『Africa非洲+(a)n…人；…的→非洲人；非洲的』

2. <u>American</u> [əˈmerɪkən] n. 美国人 adj. 美国的
『America美国+(a)n…人；…的→美国人；美国的』

3. <u>European</u> [ˌjʊərəˈpiːən] n. 欧洲人 adj. 欧洲的
『Europe ['jʊərəp]欧洲+an…人；…的→欧洲人；欧洲的』

4. <u>Tibetan</u> [tɪ'betn] n. 藏族人 adj. 西藏的
『Tibet['taɪbet, tɪ'bet]西藏+an…人；…的→藏族人；藏族的』

后级8. -ian, -arian，表示"…人；…的"；以-ian 结尾，重音在其前面的那个音节上

① -ian 表示"…人；…的"

1. <u>Arabian</u> [əˈreɪbiən] adj. 阿拉伯的（常用于描述地方）
『Arab['ærəb]阿拉伯人+ian…的→阿拉伯的』
Arabian means belonging or relating to Arabia, especially to Saudi Arabia. （Arabian指属于或关于阿拉伯半岛的，尤指沙特阿拉伯的。）
The Arabian Desert and Antarctica also are considered wilderness areas.
阿拉伯沙漠和南极洲也被认为是荒野地区。

▶<u>Arab</u> ['ærəb] n. 阿拉伯人 adj. 阿拉伯人的（常用于描述人）

❶ n. 阿拉伯人
The Arabs wear robes. 阿拉伯人穿长袍。

❷ adj. 阿拉伯人的
Arab means belonging or relating to Arabs or to their countries or customs.
On the surface, it appears little has changed in the Arab world.
表面上，阿拉伯世界好像没什么变化。

▶<u>Arabia</u> [əˈreɪbiə] n. 阿拉伯半岛

▶<u>Arabic</u> ['ærəbɪk] n. 阿拉伯语 adj. 阿拉伯语的

2. <u>Asian</u> ['eɪʃn] n. 亚洲人 adj. 亚洲的
『Asia ['eɪʒə]亚洲+(a)n…人；…的→亚洲人；亚洲的』

3. <u>Canadian</u> [kəˈneɪdiən] n. 加拿大人 adj. 加拿大的
『Canada ['kænədə]加拿大+(a)n…人；…的→加拿大人；加拿大的』

4. <u>Egyptian</u> [ɪˈdʒɪpʃn] n. 埃及人 adj. 埃及人的
『Egypt ['iːdʒɪpt]埃及+ian…的→埃及人；埃及的』

5. <u>historian</u> [hɪˈstɔːriən] n. 历史学家
『history ['hɪstri]历史（变y为i)+ian…人→历史学家』

6. <u>Italian</u> [ɪˈtæliən] n. 意大利人；意大利语 adj. 意大利的
『Italy ['ɪtəli]意大利（变y为i)+ian…人；…的→意大利人；意大利的』

7. <u>librarian</u> [laɪˈbreəriən] n. 图书管理员
『library ['laɪbrəri]图书馆（变y为i)+ian…人→图书管理员』

8. <u>magician</u> [məˈdʒɪʃn] n. 魔术师
『magic ['mædʒɪk]魔法+ian…人→魔术师』

9. <u>musician</u> [mjuˈzɪʃn] n. 音乐家
『music ['mjuːzɪk]音乐+ian…人→音乐家』

10. <u>physician</u> [fɪˈzɪʃn] n. 内科医生
『physical身体的（去al)+ian→内科医生』

▶<u>physics</u> ['fɪzɪks] n. 物理学

▶<u>physical</u> ['fɪzɪkl] adj. 身体的；有形的，物质的

❶ 身体的
connected with a person's body rather than their mind
Their life styles are bad for both their physical and mental health.
这种生活方式实在有碍身心健康。

❷ 有形的，物质的
connected with things that actually exist or are present and can be seen, felt, etc. rather than things that only exist in a person's mind
Physical books will surely become much rarer in the marketplace.
有形书（也就是纸质书，与电子书相对应）在市场上一定

会更加稀少。

11. politician [ˌpɒləˈtɪʃn] n. 政治家；政客
『politics[ˈpɒlətɪks]政治（去s）+ian…人→政治家；政客』

12. technician [tekˈnɪʃn] n. 技术员；技师
『technic[ˈteknɪk]技术，手法+ian…人→技术员；技师』

13. Christian [ˈkrɪstʃən] n. 基督徒 adj. 基督教的
『Christ基督+ ian表人→信基督的人→基督徒』

▶ **Christ** [kraɪst] n. 基督

▶ **Christmas** [ˈkrɪsməs] n. 圣诞节
『Christ基督+mass弥撒（去s）→为基督出生而做宗教仪式→圣诞节』

② -arian 表示"…人；…的"

1. vegetarian [ˌvedʒəˈteəriən] n. 素食者 adj. 素食的
『veget植物+arian…人；…的→只吃植物的人→素食者』

▶ **vegetable** [ˈvedʒtəbl] n. 蔬菜

▶ **vegetation** [ˌvedʒəˈteɪʃn] n.（统称）植物

The lake was almost solid with silt and vegetation.
湖里几乎快被淤泥和植物填满了。
Birds are abundant in the tall vegetation.
高大的植被中有着大量的鸟类。

2. totalitarian [təʊˌtæləˈteəriən] adj. 极权主义的 n. 极权主义者
『total全部+it行走+arian…的；…人→全部权力归于一身的→极权主义的；极权主义者』

A totalitarian political system is one in which there is only one political party which controls everything and does not allow any opposition parties.

3. disciplinarian [ˌdɪsəplɪˈneəriən] n. 严格纪律信奉者
『discipline纪律（去e）+arian…的；…人→严格纪律信奉的；严格纪律信奉者』

a person who believes in using rules and punishments for controlling people
He has a reputation for being a strict disciplinarian.
他因是个严格纪律执行者而闻名遐迩。

▶ **disciple** [dɪˈsaɪpl] n. 信徒，门徒；（耶稣的）门徒

▶ **discipline** [ˈdɪsəplɪn] n. 纪律；自制力 vt. 惩罚；管教
『disciple门徒（去e）+ine表抽象名词→门徒要守纪→纪律』

❶ [U] 纪律；自制力
The school has a reputation for high standards of discipline.
这所学校因纪律严格而闻名遐迩。
He'll never get anywhere working for himself—he's got no discipline.
他为自己工作是不会有什么成就的——他毫无自制力。

❷ [VN] 惩罚；管教，严格要求
The officers were disciplined for using racist language.
这些军官因使用种族歧视性语言而受到惩罚。
a guide to the best ways of disciplining your child
管教子女最佳方法指南
[VN to inf] He disciplined himself to exercise at least three times a week. 他规定自己每周至少锻炼三次。

4. authoritarian [ɔːˌθɒrɪˈteəriən] adj. 权威主义的，专制的 n. 权威主义者，专制者
『authority权力（去y）+arian…人；…的→独裁主义的；专制者』

His speech provides further evidence of his increasingly authoritarian approach.
他的讲话更加证明了他变得越来越独裁。

▶ **authority** [ɔːˈθɒrəti] n. 权力；权力部门；权威；权威人士

❶ [U] 权力，当权地位
She now has authority over the people who used to be her bosses. 她现在管辖着过去是她上司的那些人。

❷ [C, usually pl.] 当局；官方；当权者
The health authorities are investigating the problem.
卫生当局正在调查这个问题。

❸ [U] 权威
He spoke with authority on the topic.
他就这个课题发表权威意见。

❹ [C] 权威人士
She's an authority on criminal law. 她是刑法专家。

5. humanitarian [hjuːˌmænɪˈteəriən] adj. 人道主义的；人道主义者 <P192>
『human人+it+arian…的；…人→人道主义的；人道主义者』

6. utilitarian [ˌjuːtɪlɪˈteəriən] adj. 实用的；实用主义的 n. 实用主义者 <P341>
『util用+it+arian…的；…者→以实用为主的→实用主义的；实用主义者』

后缀9. -ain 表示"…人"

1. villain [ˈvɪlən] n. 恶棍，坏蛋；（小说、电影或戏剧中的）主要反面人物
『vill(=vile)邪恶+ain人→邪恶的人→恶棍，坏蛋』

2. chieftain [ˈtʃiːftən] n. 酋长，部落首领
『chief主要的+t+ain人→（部落中）主要的人→部落首领』

3. captain n. 上尉；船长；机长；（运动队）队长 <P122>
『capt拿，抓+ain表人→掌握（一群人）的人→首领』

后缀10. -ant 构成名词，表示"…人"，"…剂"

1. accountant [əˈkaʊntənt] n. 会计师
『account账+ant人→管账的人→会计师』

2. deodorant [diˈəʊdərənt] n. 除臭剂
『de去除+odor气味+ant剂』

▶ **odor** [ˈəʊdə] n. 臭味

Inside the room there was the unmistakable odor of sweaty feet. 房间里有一股明显的脚汗味。

3. lubricant [ˈluːbrɪkənt] n. 润滑剂
『lubric润滑+ant剂→润滑剂』

▶ **lubricate** [ˈluːbrɪkeɪt] vt. 润滑

Mineral oils are used to lubricate machinery.
矿物油被用来润滑机器。

4. inhabitant [ɪnˈhæbɪtənt] n.（某地）居民，栖息动物 <P189>
『inhabit在…居住+ant人→在某地居住的人』

5. disinfectant [ˌdɪsɪnˈfektənt] n. 消毒剂；杀菌剂<P163>
『dis不+infect感染，传染+ant剂→使不能感染（病毒）的药剂→消毒剂；杀菌剂』

6. stimulant [ˈstɪmjələnt] n. 兴奋剂；引起兴奋的药物 〈P316〉

『stimul刺激+ant剂→兴奋剂』

后缀11. -ance, -ancy; -ence, -ency 常和动词结合构成名词，-ant, -ent 是其对应的形容词形式

小贴士 来源于拉丁语及法语的名词后缀-ence(-ency)的用法与-ance(-ancy)基本相同。它们加在动词或动词词根后，意为the act or fact of ~ing或者the quality or condition of ~ing，即表示行为或该行为的性质、状态等。这些名词往往有与之对应的以-ent、-ant结尾的形容词。

-ence、-ency与形容词后缀-ent相对应（如 difference—different；urgency—urgent），表示性质、状态、行为，后缀-ence和-ency意同，有些英语单词具有-ence和-ency两种形式（如 innocence = innocency ; persistency = persistence）。-ance、-ancy与形容词后缀-ant相对应。

① -ance, -ancy加在动词或动词词根后构成名词，表示"行为或该行为的性质状态"，其对应的形容词常以-ant结尾

a. -ance, -ant加在动词后面分别构成名词和形容词

1. acquaint [əˈkweɪnt] vt. 使熟悉，使了解

『ac(=to)+quaint(=know)知道→使知道→使熟悉，使了解』

▶**acquaintance** [əˈkweɪntəns] n. 熟人；认识，了解

❶ [C] 认识的人；泛泛之交

a person that you know but who is not a close friend

He's just a business acquaintance. 他只是业务上认识的人。

❷ [U, C] 认识，了解

He hoped their acquaintance would develop further.
他希望他们的交情会进一步发展。

I had little acquaintance with modern poetry.
我对现代诗所知甚少。

❸ make sb's acquaintance/make the acquaintance of sb (formal) 与某人初次相见；结识某人

I am delighted to make your acquaintance, Mrs Baker.
贝克太太，我很高兴与您相识。

2. ignore [ɪɡˈnɔ: (r)] vt. 不理睬，不理会，忽视

『i (= im不)+gnore知道→（假装）不知道→不理睬』

❶ 忽视；对…不予理会

He ignored all the "No Smoking" signs and lit up a cigarette.
他无视所有"禁止吸烟"的警示，点了根烟。

❷ 佯装未见；不理睬

She ignored him and carried on with her work.
她没理他，继续干她的活。

▶**ignorance** [ˈɪɡnərəns] n. 无知；愚昧

a lack of knowledge or information about sth

She was kept in ignorance of her husband's activities.
关于丈夫的活动，她一直蒙在鼓里。

Children often behave badly out of/through ignorance.
儿童往往出于无知而不守规矩。

▶**ignorant** [ˈɪɡnərənt] adj. 不了解的；无知的；无礼的

❶ （对某事物）不了解的；无学识的

People don't like to ask questions for fear of appearing ignorant. 人们不喜欢问问题，因为害怕自己会显得无知。

Never make your students feel ignorant.
千万别让你的学生感到自己一无所知。

❷ 很无礼的；十分不懂规矩的

with very bad manners

I met some very ignorant people who called me all kinds of names.
我碰到了一些非常粗鲁的家伙，他们用各种脏话骂我。

词义辨析 〈P373 第60〉

忽视，无视 ignore, neglect, disregard

3. persevere [ˌpɜːsɪˈvɪə(r)] vi. 坚持

『per始终+severe严厉的→（为了做某事）始终对自己很严厉』

[V] ~ (in sth/in doing sth) | ~ (with sth/sb) (approving) 坚持；孜孜以求

Despite a number of setbacks, they persevered in their attempts to fly around the world in a balloon.
虽屡遭挫折，他们仍不断尝试乘气球环游世界。

She persevered with her violin lessons.
她孜孜不倦地学习小提琴。

▶**perseverance** [ˌpɜːsɪˈvɪərəns] n. 毅力，韧性，不屈不挠的精神

『persevere坚持（去e）+ance表性质→毅力，韧性』

They showed great perseverance in the face of difficulty.
他们面对困难表现了坚强的毅力。

▶**perseverant** [ˌpɜːsɪˈvɪərənt] adj. 有毅力的，不屈不挠的

『persevere坚持（去e）+ant表形容→有毅力的』

▶**persevering** [ˌpɜːsɪˈvɪərɪŋ] adj. 坚忍的；固执的

He is a persevering, approachable family man.
他是一个有毅力、平易近人的居家男人。

4. rely [rɪˈlaɪ] vi. 依靠，倚赖；信任，信赖

❶ 依赖，依靠

If you rely on someone or something, you need them and depend on them in order to live or work properly.

We had to rely on a compass and a lot of luck to get here.
我们不得不依靠指南针和不错的运气找到这儿来。

❷ 信赖，信任

If you can rely on someone to work well or to behave as you want them to, you can trust them to do this.

I know I can rely on you to sort it out.
我相信你会把它解决好的。

▶**reliance** [rɪˈlaɪəns] n. 依赖；信任

Heavy reliance on one client is risky when you are building up a business. 创业时过分依赖某一个客户是有风险的。

I wouldn't place too much reliance on (= trust) these figures.
我不会太相信这些数字的。

▶**reliant** [rɪˈlaɪənt] adj. 依赖的，依靠的

These people are not wholly reliant on Western charity.
这些人并非完全依赖西方慈善团体。

▶**reliable** [rɪˈlaɪəbl] adj. 可以信赖的，可靠的

We are looking for someone who is reliable and hard-working. 我们正在物色可靠而又勤奋的人。

5. resist [rɪˈzɪst] vt. 抵制；抵抗；抵挡（诱惑）〈P302〉

▶**resistance** [rɪˈzɪstəns] n. 抵制；抵抗；阻力；电阻

▶**resistant** [rɪˈzɪstənt] adj. 抵抗的；抵制的

6. assist [əˈsɪst] vt. 帮助，协助 〈P302〉

『as相当于to+sist站立→站立到（旁边）→帮助』

▶**assistance** [əˈsɪstəns] n. 帮助；援助

▶ **assistant** [əˈsɪstənt] n. 助手 adj. 助理的

b. -ance加在动词后面构成名词表行为或结果

1. annoy [əˈnɔɪ] vt. 使恼怒，使生气；打扰，骚扰

His constant joking was beginning to annoy her.
他不停地开玩笑，已开始惹她生气。

▶ **annoyance** [əˈnɔɪəns] n. 恼怒；使人烦恼的事
Much to our annoyance , they decided not to come after all.
他们终于决定不来，使我们很生气。
Inconsiderate neighbours can be more than an annoyance.
不为他人着想的邻居会非常惹人厌。

2. appear [əˈpɪə(r)] v. 显得；出现

▶ **appearance** [əˈpɪərəns] n. 外貌；出现

3. enter [ˈentə(r)] v. 进入；参加

▶ **entrance** [ˈentrəns] n. 入口；进入；参加

4. guide [gaɪd] vt. 指导；引路

▶ **guidance** [ˈgaɪdns] n. 指导
Activities all take place under the guidance of an experienced tutor. 所有活动都在经验丰富的导师指导下进行。

5. perform [pəˈfɔːm] v. 执行；表演；表现

▶ **performance** [pəˈfɔːməns] n. 执行；表演；表现

6. surveil [sɜːˈveɪl] vt. 监视
『sur表面+veil面纱→表面覆上面纱（以便监视）→监视』

▶ **surveillance** [sɜːˈveɪləns] n. （对犯罪嫌疑人或可能发生犯罪的地方的）监视

The police are keeping the suspects under constant surveillance. 警方正对嫌疑人实施不间断监视。
surveillance cameras/equipment 监视摄像机/设备

7. utter [ˈʌtə(r)] vt. 发出（声音）adj. 完全的，十足的

❶ [VN] 发出（声音）；说；讲
She did not utter a word during lunch.
午餐时，她一言未发。

❷ adj. 完全的，彻底的，十足的
This, of course, is utter nonsense.
这当然是一派胡言。
A look of utter confusion swept across his handsome face.
他英俊的脸上掠过一丝大惑不解的神情。

▶ **utterance** [ˈʌtərəns] n. 言语；吐露；表达

❶ [U] 用言语的表达；说话
the act of expressing sth in words
Upon the utterance of this word, Dan and Harry exchanged a quick, meaningful look.
这句话一出口，丹和哈里马上交换了一个意味深长的眼神。

❷ [C] 话语；言论
something that you say
A sentence is a (relatively) complete and independent human utterance.
一个句子是一个（相对地）完整和独立的人类的表达。

8. assure [əˈʃʊə(r)] vt. 向…保证；使…确信 <P321>
『as相当于to+ sure确信→使达到确信的地步→使确信』

▶ **assurance** [əˈʃʊərəns] n. 保证，确保；（人寿）保险

9. attend [əˈtend] v. 出席；参加；注意 <P328>

▶ **attendance** [əˈtendəns] n. 出席；出现人数

10. clear [klɪə(r)] vt. 清理；批准 <P134>

▶ **clearance** [ˈklɪərəns] n. 清理

11. inherit [ɪnˈherɪt] v. 继承（财产、某种状况、遗传特征等）；经遗传获得 <P190>

▶ **inheritance** [ɪnˈherɪtəns] n. 遗产；继承物

c. -ance, -ant加在词根后面分别构成名词和形容词

1. important [ɪmˈpɔːtnt] adj. 重要的

▶ **importance** [ɪmˈpɔːtns] n. 重要性

2. brilliant [ˈbrɪliənt] adj. 极好的；明亮的

❶ 聪颖的；技艺高超的；出色的
She had a brilliant mind. 她头脑聪明。
It is a very high quality production, brilliantly written and acted. 其制作水准很高，剧本和表演都很精彩。
If you get a chance to see the show, do go — it's brilliant.
如果你有机会去看那个演出，就一定要去——棒极了！

❷ （颜色）鲜明的，绚丽的；（光线等）明亮的
The event was held in brilliant sunshine.
这一活动是在阳光明媚的日子举办的。
The woman had brilliant green eyes.
这个女子有双明亮的碧眼。

▶ **brilliance** [ˈbrɪliəns] n. （卓越的）才华；光亮

He was a deeply serious musician who had shown his brilliance very early.
他是个很严肃的音乐家，很早就展露出非凡的才华。
His eyes became accustomed to the dark after the brilliance of the sun outside.
从耀眼的室外走进来后，他的双眼开始适应了黑暗。

3. distant [ˈdɪstənt] adj. 遥远的
『dis(=away)离开+（s）tant站→（两地）相离而站的→遥远的』

▶ **distance** [ˈdɪstəns] n. 距离；间距

❶ [C, U] 距离；间距
What's the distance between New York City and Boston?
纽约市离波士顿有多远？
We spotted them at a distance of two hundred yards.
我们在相距200码处就看到他们。

❷ **at/from a distance** 在远处
She had loved him at a distance for years.
她曾经暗恋了他好多年。
The only way I can cope with my mother is at a distance.
我可以和我妈妈相处的唯一方法就是保持距离。

❸ **in/into the distance** 在远方
We saw lights in the distance.
我们看到了远处的点点灯火。
Alice stood staring into the distance.
艾丽斯站着凝视远方。

4. significant [sɪgˈnɪfɪkənt] adj. 有重要意义的 <P300>
『sign记号，标志+i+ficant…的→具有标志意义的→有重大意义的』

▶ **significance** [sɪgˈnɪfɪkəns] n. 重要意义

5. arrogant [ˈærəgənt] adj. 傲慢的，自大的 <P282>
『ar加强+rog要求+ant…的→无理要求（别人）的→傲慢的』

▶ **arrogance** [ˈærəgəns] n. 傲慢，自大

d. -ant加在词根后构成形容词，对应的名词为-ancy（或-ance、-ancy两种形式），这两种名词形式意思相同

1. constant [ˈkɒnstənt] adj. 不断的，一直的；恒定的
『con强调+stant站→一直站（在那里）→不断的；恒定的』

❶ 连续发生的；重复的
happening all the time or repeatedly
Babies need constant attention. 婴儿一刻也离不开人。
This entrance is in constant use. 此入口经常使用。

❷ 不变的，固定的，恒定的
The average speed of the winds remained constant.
平均风速保持稳定。

▶ **constancy** [ˈkɒnstənsi] n. 恒定性

2. hesitate [ˈhezɪteɪt] v. 犹豫，踌躇

❶ ~ (about/over sth) （对某事）犹豫，迟疑不决
I didn't hesitate for a moment about taking the job.
我毫不犹豫地接受了那份工作。

❷ [V to inf] 顾虑，疑虑
Please do not hesitate to contact me if you have any questions.
如果有疑问就请尽管和我联系。

▶ **hesitant** [ˈhezɪtənt] adj. 犹豫的，迟疑的
~ (about sth) | ~ (to do sth) 犹豫的
She's hesitant about signing the contract.
她对是否签这个合同犹豫不决。

▶ **hesitance** [ˈhezɪtəns] n. 踌躇，犹豫

▶ **hesitancy** [ˈhezɪtənsi] n. 踌躇，犹豫

3. pregnant [ˈpregnənt] adj. 怀孕的
I was pregnant with our third child at the time.
当时我正怀着我们的第三个孩子。
She's six months pregnant. 她怀孕六个月了。

▶ **pregnancy** [ˈpregnənsi] n. 怀孕；孕期
Many women experience sickness during pregnancy.
许多妇女在怀孕期间都会有恶心现象。
She had a normal pregnancy and delivered a healthy child.
她正常妊娠，生了个健康的孩子。

② -ence, -ency加在动词或动词词根后构成名词，表示"行为或该行为的性质状态"，其对应的形容词常以-ent结尾

a. -ence, -ent加在动词后面分别构成名词和形容词

1. depend [dɪˈpend] vi. 依赖；依靠
▶ **dependent** [dɪˈpendənt] adj. 依靠的，依赖的；取决于
▶ **dependence** [dɪˈpendəns] n. 依靠；依赖

2. exist [ɪgˈzɪst] vi. 存在
▶ **existent** [ɪgˈzɪstənt] adj. 存在的
▶ **existence** [ɪgˈzɪstəns] n. 存在

3. occur [əˈkɜː(r)] vi. 发生；出现 〈P146〉
▶ **occurrence** [əˈkʌrəns] n. 发生；发生的事件

4. compete [kəmˈpiːt] vi. 竞争；参加比赛 〈P251〉
▶ **competent** [ˈkɒmpɪtənt] adj. 有能力的；能胜任的
▶ **competence** [ˈkɒmpɪtəns] n. 能力；胜任

5. differ [ˈdɪfə(r)] vi. 不同；意见不同 〈P167〉
▶ **different** [ˈdɪfrənt] adj. 不同的

▶ **difference** [ˈdɪfrəns] n. 不同，差别

6. persist [pəˈsɪst] vi. 执意；坚持；持续存在 〈P302〉
▶ **persistent** [pəˈsɪstənt] adj. 执着的，持续的
▶ **persistence** [pəˈsɪstəns] n. 坚持不懈；持续

b. -ence, -ent加在词根后面分别构成名词和形容词

1. convenient [kənˈviːniənt] adj. 方便的，便利的
▶ **convenience** [kənˈviːniəns] n. 方便；便利

2. diligent [ˈdɪlɪdʒənt] adj. 勤奋的，用功的
▶ **diligence** [ˈdɪlɪdʒəns] n. 勤奋，用功

3. evident [ˈevɪdənt] adj. 明显的
▶ **evidence** [ˈevɪdəns] n. 证据

4. patient [ˈpeɪʃnt] adj. 有耐心的
▶ **patience** [ˈpeɪʃns] n. 耐心

5. present [ˈpreznt] n. 出席的，在场的
▶ **presence** [ˈprezns] n. 出席，在场

6. silent [ˈsaɪlənt] adj. 沉默的；无声的
▶ **silence** [ˈsaɪləns] n. 沉默；无声

7. violent [ˈvaɪələnt] adj. 暴力的；剧烈的
『viol(=strength)强壮+ent表形容词→强壮了（容易使用暴力）→暴力的』
Students were involved in violent clashes with the police.
学生和警察发生了暴力冲突。
A violent storm had struck the area.
一场猛烈的暴风雨席卷了该地区。

▶ **violence** [ˈvaɪələns] n. 暴力，暴行；激烈的力量
形近词 **violate** [ˈvaɪəleɪt] vt. 违反（协议、法律或承诺）；侵犯（隐私）
『viol(=strength)强壮+ate表动词→强壮使用（暴力违法）→违反』
They went to prison because they violated the law.
他们触犯了法律，因此坐了牢。
These men were violating her family's privacy.
这些人侵犯了她的家庭隐私。
形近词 **violet** [ˈvaɪələt] n. 紫罗兰；紫罗兰色 〈P42〉

8. excellent [ˈeksələnt] adj. 优秀的，杰出的
▶ **excellence** [ˈeksələns] n. 优秀，杰出
▶ **excel** [ɪkˈsel] vi. 擅长，善于 vt. 超出

❶ [V] ~ in/at sth 擅长
As a child he excelled at music and art.
他小时候擅长音乐和美术。

❷ [VN] ~ yourself (BrE) 胜过平时
词义辨析 〈P368第34〉 超出 exceed, surpass, excel

9. absent [ˈæbsənt] adj. 缺席的，不在场的 〈P1〉
▶ **absence** [ˈæbsəns] n. 缺席；不存在

10. confident [ˈkɒnfɪdənt] adj. 自信的 〈P170〉
▶ **confidence** [ˈkɒnfɪdəns] n. 信心

11. consistent [kənˈsɪstənt] adj. 前后一致的；不矛盾的 〈P302〉

► **consistency** [kən'sɪstənsi] n. 一致性；连贯性

12. innocent ['ɪnəsnt] adj. 清白的；无辜的；天真的 <P233>

　► **innocence** ['ɪnəsns] n. 清白；无辜；单纯

13. intelligent [ɪn'telɪdʒənt] adj. 聪明的；有灵性的；智能的 <P203>

　► **intelligence** [ɪn'telɪdʒəns] n. 智力；情报

14. permanent ['pɜ:mənənt] adj. 永久的，长久的 <P30>

　► **permanence** ['pɜ:mənəns] n. 永久，持久

c. 后缀-ent构成的名词表示人或事，-ence构成的名词表示行为、处所、状态

1. correspondent [ˌkɒrə'spɒndənt] n. 通讯（尤指专门报道某一类新闻的）记者；写信的人

　『cor共同，一起+respond回应+ent表人→共同回应的人→你来我往写信的人→写信的人；（过去记者发稿主要是通过写信，所以"写信的人"也可指记者』

the BBC's political correspondent
英国广播公司的政治新闻记者
a foreign/war/sports, etc. correspondent
驻外、战地、体育等记者
I'm not a very good correspondent. 我不是一个善于写信的人

　► **correspondence** [ˌkɒrə'spɒndəns] n. 通信；信件

　『cor共同，一起+respond回应+ence表名词→你来我往回应→写信→写信；信件』

❶ [U] ~ (with sb) 往来的书信
The editor welcomes correspondence from readers on any subject. 编辑欢迎读者有关任何问题的来信。

❷ [U] ~ (with sb) 通信；通信联系
the activity of writing letters
We have been in correspondence for months.
我们通信几个月了。

2. resident ['rezɪdənt] n. 居民

　► **residence** ['rezɪdəns] n. 住处，住宅

❶ [C] 住所；住房；（尤指）宅第，豪宅
10 Downing Street is the British Prime Minister's official residence. 唐宁街10号是英国首相的官邸。

❷ [U] 居住，定居
Please state your occupation and place of residence.
请说明你的职业和住址。

3. incident ['ɪnsɪdənt] n. （不寻常的、不愉快的、暴力、冲突等）事件

One particular incident sticks in my mind.
有一件事我总忘不了。
There was a shooting incident near here last night.
昨夜这附近发生了枪击事件。
a border/diplomatic incident　边境／外交冲突

　词义辨析 <P370第47>
　事件 accident, incident, event, occurrence

　► **incidence** ['ɪnsɪdəns] n. （疾病等坏事的）发生，发生率

There have been quite a few incidences of bullying in the school this year. 今年学校里发生了不少欺凌事件。
The incidence of breast cancer increases with age.
乳腺癌的发病率随年龄增长而递增。

　► **incidentally** [ˌɪnsɪ'dentli] adv. 顺便提一下；附带地
　『incident偶发事件+al表形容词+ly表副词→偶然想到的→顺便提一下；附带地』

I didn't ask you to come. Incidentally, why have you come?
我没有叫你来。顺便问一下,你为什么过来?
The letter mentioned my great-aunt and uncle only incidentally. 信中仅附带提到了我的姑奶奶和叔叔。

d. -ent 加在词根后构成形容词，对应的名词为-ency

1. decent ['di:snt] adj. 像样的；正直的；得体的

❶ （物）像样的，尚好的，过得去的
Decent is used to describe something which is considered to be of an acceptable standard or quality.
Nearby is a village with a decent pub.
附近的村子里有一家还不错的酒馆。

❷ （人）正派的，正直的，规矩的
The majority of people around here are decent people.
这里的大多数人都很正派。

❸ （事）合宜的，得体的，适当的
considered by most people to be moral, good, or reasonable
It's not decent to get married again so soon after your husband has died.
你丈夫死后这么快又结婚是不体面的。

　► **decency** ['di:snsi] n. 正派；体面；正直

❶ [U] 正派；得体
honest, polite behaviour that follows accepted moral standards and shows respect for others
Her behaviour showed a total lack of common decency.
她的举止显示她连起码的礼节都不懂。
His sense of decency forced him to resign.
他顾及颜面，不得不辞了职。

❷ did not have the decency to do something
（出于礼貌）应该做（但没做）
Nobody had the decency to inform me of what was planned.
竟然没有一个人最起码地通知我一声计划了些什么。
His sense of decency and fair play made him refuse the offer.
他的正直感和公平竞争意识使他拒绝了这一提议。

2. frequent ['fri:kwənt] adj. 频繁的，时常发生的

　► **frequency** ['fri:kwənsi] n. 频率

3. urge [ɜ:dʒ] v. 催促；力劝 n. 冲动

❶ ~ sb to do sth
She urged him to stay. 她力劝他留下。

❷ ~ that （从句用虚拟语气）
The report urged that all children be taught to swim.
这份报告呼吁给所有的儿童教授游泳。

　► **urgent** ['ɜ:dʒənt] adj. 紧迫的，紧急的
There is an urgent need for food and water.
现在亟需食物和水。

　► **urgency** ['ɜ:dʒənsi] n. 紧迫，急迫
She was surprised at the urgency in his voice.
他语调中透着急迫，这让她很吃惊。

4. proficient [prə'fɪʃnt] adj. 精通的，熟练的 <P164>

　► **proficiency** [prə'fɪʃnsi] n. 熟练，精通

5. transparent [trænsˈpærənt] adj. 透明的；清澈的；易识破的；显而易见的 〈P242〉

▶ **transparency** [trænsˈpærənsi] n. 透明度，透明

6. emergent [iˈmɜːdʒənt] adj. 新兴的；处于发展初期的 〈P219〉

▶ **emergency** [iˈmɜːdʒənsi] n. 紧急情况；突发事件

7. current [ˈkʌrənt] adj. 当前的 n. 水流；气流；电流 〈P146〉

▶ **currency** [ˈkʌrənsi] n. 货币，通货；通用

8. efficient [ɪˈfɪʃnt] adj. 高效率的；高效能的 〈P164〉

▶ **efficiency** [ɪˈfɪʃnsi] n. 效率

后缀12. -ar 构成名词，表示"人或物"；-ar, -ular 构成形容词，表示"有…形状或性质的"

① -ar 构成名词，表示"人或物"；也可构成形容词，表示"有…形状或性质的"

1. beggar [ˈbegə(r)] n. 乞丐
『beg乞求（双写g）+ar人→乞丐』

2. liar [ˈlaɪə(r)] n. 说谎者
『lie说谎（去e）+ar人→说谎者』

3. scholar [ˈskɒlə(r)] n. 学者
『school学校（去o）+ar人→上过学的人→学者』

4. registrar [ˌredʒɪˈstrɑː(r)] n. （英国的）户籍管理员；（英国学院或大学的）注册主任，教务主任
『register注册（去e）+ar人→负责注册的人员』

5. cellar [ˈselə(r)] n. 地窖；地下室
『cell小房子+ar物→地下的小房子→地窖』

The box of papers had been stored in a cellar at the family home.
那箱文件一直藏在家中的地窖里。

▶ **cell** [sel] n. 单间牢房；细胞；电池（cellphone手机）；（计算机电子表格的）单元格

6. altar [ˈɔːltə(r)] n. 祭坛，圣坛 〈P112〉
『alt高+ar表物→高出的东西→祭坛』

7. vulgar [ˈvʌlgə(r)] adj. 粗俗的；不雅的；下流的
『vulg人群+ar…的→具有凡人性质的→粗俗的』

❶ 粗俗的，庸俗的，俗气的
If you describe something as vulgar, you think it is in bad taste or of poor artistic quality.
I think it's a very vulgar house. 我觉得这所房子很俗气。
a vulgar man 粗俗的男人
vulgar decorations 俗气的装饰

❷ 下流的
The women laughed coarsely at some vulgar jokes.
那些女人听了一些下流的笑话后粗俗地大笑起来。

8. linear [ˈlɪniə(r)] adj. （发展或运动）沿直线的；利用线条的 〈P207〉
『line直线+ar…的→直线的』

② -ular 构成形容词，表示"有…形状或性质的"

1. titular [ˈtɪtjulə(r)] adj. 名义上的
『title称号，头衔（去le）+ular有…形状或性质的→称号的，名义上的』

having a particular title or status but no real power or authority

He is titular head, and merely signs laws occasionally.
他是名义上的首脑，不过偶尔签字批准法律法规。

2. granular [ˈgrænjələ(r)] adj. 颗粒的
『grain谷物，颗粒（去i）+ular有…形状或性质的→颗粒的』

▶ **grain** [greɪn] n. 谷物；颗粒
America's grain exports 美国的谷物出口
a grain of salt/sand/sugar 一粒盐/沙/糖
There isn't a grain of truth in those rumours.
那些谣传一点也不可靠。

3. globular [ˈglɒbjələ(r)] adj. 球形的；球体的；由小球组成的
『globle球状（去e）+ular有…形状或性质的→球形的』

4. jocular [ˈdʒɒkjələ(r)] adj. 开朗的，爱开玩笑的
『joc笑话+ular有…形状或性质的→爱开玩笑的』

If you say that someone has a jocular manner, you mean that they are cheerful and often make jokes or try to make people laugh.
She said she had called him an idiot in a jocular fashion and had not meant to offend him.
她说她以打趣的方式叫他白痴，并不想冒犯他。

5. cellular [ˈseljələ(r)] adj. 细胞的；由细胞组成的
『cell细胞+ular有…形状或性质的→细胞的』

6. vascular [ˈvæskjələ(r)] adj. 血管的；（植物）维管的
『vasc(=vessel)血管+ular有…形状或性质的→血管的』

▶ **vessel** [ˈvesl] n. 大船，轮船；（盛液体的）容器，器皿；（人或动物的）血管，脉管；（植物的）导管

7. circular [ˈsɜːkjələ(r)] adj. 圆形的；环形的 〈P132〉
『circ圆，环+ular有…形状或性质的→圆形的』

后缀13. -ard 构成名词，多表示"不好的人"

1. coward [ˈkaʊəd] n. 胆小鬼，懦夫
『cow威胁+ ard人→容易受到威胁的人→胆怯者』

If you call someone a coward, you disapprove of them because they are easily frightened and avoid dangerous or difficult situations.
She accused her husband of being a coward.
她指责丈夫胆小懦弱。

▶ **cowardice** [ˈkaʊədɪs] n. 懦弱，胆怯
『coward胆小鬼+ice表性质→具有胆小鬼的性质→懦弱』

The terrorist action has been condemned as an act of barbarism and cowardice.
人们谴责恐怖主义行径是野蛮和懦弱的行为。

2. drunkard [ˈdrʌŋkəd] n. 酒鬼，经常酗酒者
『drunk醉的+ ard人→经常喝醉的人→酒鬼』

The author portrayed his father as a vicious drunkard.
作者把他父亲描绘成一个可恶的酒鬼。

3. steward [ˈstjuːəd] n. （私人家中的）管家；（飞机、火车、轮船上的）乘务员
『stew炖+ ard人→炖菜的人→管家』

小贴士 以前被雇来看守猪圈的人被称为steward，后来演变为指私人家中的管家。为了便于记忆，可以把乘务员理解为飞机、火车、轮船上的管家。

▶ **stewardess** [ˌstjuːəˈdes] n. （船舶、飞机或火车上的）女服务员，女乘务员

▶ **stew** [stjuː] vt. & vi. 炖，煨；n. 炖的菜，煨的菜（有肉和蔬菜）

4. bastard [ˈbɑːstəd] n. 私生子；混蛋
『bast原指"马鞍"，代指和旅行者生的孩子+ard人→私生子』

❶ [C] 私生子（可能具冒犯意味）

❷ [C] 杂种，坏蛋，混蛋

Bastard is an insulting word which some people use about a person, especially a man, who has behaved very badly.

❸ [C] （走运或倒霉的）家伙

后缀14. -arium, -orium 表名词，"地点，场所"

1. oceanarium [ˌəʊʃəˈneəriəm] n. 海洋馆
『ocean海洋+arium场所，地点→海洋馆』

2. planetarium [ˌplænɪˈteəriəm] n. 天文馆
『planet星球+arium场所，地点→（观察）星球的场所→天文馆』

3. crematorium [ˌkreməˈtɔːriəm] n. 火葬场
『cremat焚烧+orium场所，地点→火葬场』
（=crematory [ˈkrɛmətəri]）

4. sanatorium [ˌsænəˈtɔːriəm] n. 疗养院〈P286〉
『sanat(=sane)健康+orium地点，场所→（让人重获）健康的场所→疗养院』

5. aquarium [əˈkweəriəm] n. 水族馆；养鱼缸〈P5〉
『aqu水+arium场所，地点→水族馆』

6. auditorium [ˌɔːdɪˈtɔːriəm] n.（剧院或音乐厅的）观众席；会堂，礼堂，音乐厅〈P116〉
『audit听+orium地点，场所→听宣讲的地方→礼堂』

后缀15. -ary 可以构成形容词，表示具有某种性质，也可构成名词，表示"人" "物" 或 "场所"

① -ary 构成形容词，表示"具有…性质的"

1. elementary [ˌelɪˈmentri] adj. 初级的；基础的
『element要素，基本组成部分+ary有…性质的→基本组成部分的→基础的；基本的』

❶ 初级的；基础的
in or connected with the first stages of a course of study
an elementary English course 基础英语课程
a book for elementary students 初学者课本

❷ 基本的
of the most basic kind
the elementary laws of economics 基本经济法则
an elementary mistake 根本性错误

小贴士 **elementary school/ primary school** 小学

▶ **element** [ˈelɪmənt] n. 元素；要素；基本部分

❶ （化学中的）元素

❷ 要素；基本组成部分；典型部分；因素
Cost was a key element in our decision.
价钱是我们决策时考虑的主要因素。
The story has all the elements of a soap opera.
这个故事是非常典型的肥皂剧题材。
Customer relations is an important element of the job.
与客户的关系是这个工作的重要部分。

I suppose people do it because there is that element of danger and risk.
我想人们这样做是因为其中存在危险和风险的因素。

词义辨析〈P370第48〉
组成部分 element, component, ingredient

2. exemplary [ɪɡˈzempləri] adj. 典范的；惩戒性的
『example例子（变a为e，去后面e)+ary有…性质的→具有例子性质（让别人照着做或让别人不要照着做）→典范的；警戒性的』

❶ 典范的，可作榜样的
If you describe someone or something as exemplary, you think they are extremely good.
Those we have employed have been exemplary employees.
我们聘用的那些人员都成了模范员工。

❷ 惩戒性的；警戒性的
An exemplary punishment is unusually harsh and is intended to stop other people from committing similar crimes.
He demanded exemplary sentences for those behind the violence.
他要求对这起暴力事件的幕后指使者作出惩戒性判决。

3. honorary [ˈɒnərəri] adj. 荣誉上的；名誉上的
『honor荣誉+ary有…性质的→具有荣誉性质的→荣誉上的；名誉上的』

❶ （大学学位、级别等）荣誉的
an honorary doctorate/degree
荣誉博士学位；荣誉学位

❷ （机构中的职位）名誉上的，无报酬的
the honorary president 名誉校长

4. imaginary [ɪˈmædʒɪnəri] adj. 想象中的，假象的
『imagine想象（去e）+ary有…性质的→具有想象性质的→想象中的，假设的』

Lots of children have imaginary friends.
许多孩子都会凭空想象一些朋友。

5. monetary [ˈmʌnɪtri] adj. 货币的，钱的
『money钱（去y加t）+ary与…有关的→货币的』

Some countries tighten monetary policy to avoid inflation.
一些国家实行紧缩银根的货币政策，以避免通货膨胀。

6. planetary [ˈplænətri] adj. 行星的
『planet行星+ary与…有关的→行星的』

7. secondary [ˈsekəndri] adj. 次要的；间接引发的
『second第二；次于的+ary有…性质的→次要的』

❶ ~ (to sth) 第二位的，次要的
Experience is what matters—age is of secondary importance.
重要的是经验——年龄是次要的。
Raising animals was only secondary to other forms of farming.
与其他农业生产相对而言，动物饲养只是次要的。

❷ （疾病、感染）间接引发的；继发性的
He had kidney cancer, with secondary tumours in the brain and lungs.
他患有肾癌，还有脑部和肺部的继发性肿瘤。

❸ [only before noun] 中等教育的；中学的
the secondary curriculum 中学课程

8. legendary [ˈledʒəndri] adj. 传奇的；极其著名的〈P204〉
『legend传说，传奇+ary有…性质的→传奇的』

▶**legend** [ˈledʒənd] n. 传说；传奇故事；传奇人物

② **-ary** 构成名词，表示"…的人"

1. secretary [ˈsekrətri] n. 秘书
『secret秘密+ary从事…的人→从事与秘密有关的工作的人→秘书』

2. beneficiary [ˌbenɪˈfɪʃəri] n. 受益人 <P165>
『bene善，好+ fici(=fic)做+ary人→得到好处的人→受益者』

3. contemporary [kənˈtemprəri] n. 同代人 adj. 同时代的；当代的 <P326>
『con 共同+tempor时间+ary表示人 →同时间的人→同代人』

4. missionary [ˈmɪʃənri] n. 传教士 <P224>
『mission传教，布道+ary从事…的人→从事传教的人→传教士』

5. adversary [ˈædvəsəri] n. （辩论或战斗中的）敌手，对手 <P349>
『ad相当于to+vers转+ary表人→转到（自己对面的）人→对手』

③ **-ary** 构成名词，表示"场所，地点"

1. boundary [ˈbaʊndri] n. 分界线；范围
『bound形成边界+ary场所，地点→分界线』

[C] 边界；界限；分界线
a real or imagined line that marks the limits or edges of sth and separates it from other things or places; a dividing line
national boundaries 国界
boundary changes/disputes 边界变化/争端
The fence marks the boundary between my property and hers.
那道篱笆是我和她的住宅之间的分界。
Scientists continue to push back the boundaries of human knowledge. 科学家不断扩大人类知识的范围。

▶**bound** [baʊnd] vt. 形成边界 <P372第58>

词义辨析 <P372第57> 边界 **border, boundary, frontier**

2. granary [ˈɡrænəri] n. 谷仓，粮仓
『gran颗粒，谷粒+ ary场所→放谷粒的地方→粮仓』

The granaries containing last year's harvest are nearly empty.
贮存去年收割的粮食的谷仓几乎空了。

3. dictionary [ˈdɪkʃənri] n. 字典
『diction措辞；用词，用语+ary场所，地点→放用词用语的地方→字典』

4. library [ˈlaɪbrəri] n. 图书馆
『libr书籍+ary场所，地点→图书馆』

5. penitentiary [ˌpenɪˈtenʃəri] n. 监狱 <P249>
『penitent后悔的，忏悔的+i+ary表地点→让（犯罪的人）忏悔的地方→监狱』

6. sanctuary [ˈsæŋktʃuəri] n. 避难所；禁猎区；圣所 <P284>
『sanctu(=sanct)神圣+ary场所，地点→圣地；避难所』

7. mortuary [ˈmɔːtʃəri] n. 太平间，停尸房 <P229>
『mortu(= mort)死+ary场地→放死尸的地方→停尸室』

小贴士 -ery, -ory和-ury都可以表示地点。

④ **-ary** 构成名词，表示"物"

1. commentary [ˈkɒməntri] n. 现场解说；评论
『comment注释；评论+ary物→实况报道；评论』

❶ [C, U] （尤指电台或电视台所作的）实况报道，现场解说
He gave the listening crowd a running commentary.
他给这一大群听众进行了现场报道。

❷ [C] 评论性文章（或著作）
Mr Rich will be writing a twice-weekly commentary on American society and culture.
里奇先生每周将就美国社会与文化发表两篇评论文章。

2. documentary [ˌdɒkjuˈmentri] n. （电视、广播等）纪实节目，纪录片 adj. （证据）有文件记录的
『document文件+ary物→纪录片，纪实节目』

This great battle was vividly recorded in the documentary film. 这部纪录片生动地再现了这场伟大的战役。
We have documentary evidence that they were planning military action.
我们有书面证据证明他们正在策划军事行动。

▶**document** [ˈdɒkjumənt] n. 公文；（计算机）文档

❶ A document is one or more official pieces of paper with writing on them.
The foreign ministers of the two countries signed the documents today.
两国的外交大臣今天签署了文件。

❷ （计算机）文件，文档
When you are finished typing, remember to save your document. 完成录入后，记得将文档存盘。

小贴士 电脑中word文档的后缀名".doc"代表的就是document这个单词。

高中英语词汇通霸.doc

3. summary [ˈsʌməri] n. 总结；概括
『sum总；加（双写m）+ary表物→总结；概括』

[C]总结；概括；概要
The following is a summary of our conclusions.
现将我们的几点结论综述如下。
In summary , this was a disappointing performance.
总的来说，这场演出令人失望。

▶**summarize** [ˈsʌməraɪz] v. 总结；概括
『summary总结；概括（变y为i）+ize表动词→总结；概括』

The results of the research are summarized at the end of the chapter. 在这一章末尾对研究结果作了总结。

4. tributary [ˈtrɪbjətri] n. 支流 adj. 支流的 <P338>
『tribute给予（去e）+ ary…的→给（大河水）的→支流的』

后缀16. **-ate** 可以构成形容词、动词和名词

① **-ate**构成动词，表示"做，造成，使…"，有时拼作-iate, -uate

1. differentiate [ˌdɪfəˈrenʃieɪt] v. 区分，辨别
『different不同的+iate做，造成，使→区分，辨别』

❶ ~ (between) A and B | ~ A (from B) 区分；区别；辨别

[V] It's difficult to differentiate between the two varieties.
这两个品种很难辨别。

[VN] I can't differentiate one variety from another.
我无法将这几个品种区别开来。

❷ [VN] ~ sth (from sth)

表明…间的差别；构成…间差别的特征

The male's yellow beak differentiates it from the female.
雄鸟黄色的喙是与雌鸟相区别的主要特征。

▶ **differential** [ˌdɪfəˈrenʃl] n. 差额 adj. 差别的

❶ n. ~ (between A and B) 差额；差价；工资级差

an amount of difference between things which are compared

During the Second World War, industrial wage differentials in Britain widened.
第二次世界大战期间，英国的劳工工资级差进一步拉大了。

❷ adj. [only before noun] (formal) 差别的；以差别而定的

showing or depending on a difference; not equal

the differential treatment of prisoners based on sex and social class 按性别和社会阶层区别对待犯人

2. **activate** [ˈæktɪveɪt] vt. 使运作；使起作用；激活
『active活动的（去e）+ate使…→使进入活动状态→激活』

If a device or process is activated, something causes it to start working.

Video cameras with night vision can be activated by movement. 带夜视镜的摄像机一有动静就会启动。

▶ **active** [ˈæktɪv] adj. 积极的；活跃的；活动的 <P86>

deactivate [ˌdiːˈæktɪveɪt] v. 使停止工作
『de相反+activate使活动→使处于不活动的状态→使停止工作』

3. **impersonate** [ɪmˈpɜːsəneɪt] vt. 冒充；假扮；扮演
『im(=in)以…+ person人+ate表动词→以某人的身份→扮演』

to pretend to be sb in order to trick people or to entertain them

He was returned to prison in 1977 for impersonating a police officer. 他1977年因冒充警官而再次入狱。

4. **evaporate** [ɪˈvæpəreɪt] v. 蒸发；（逐渐）消失
『e出去+vapor蒸汽+ate使→使像蒸汽一样出去→蒸发；（逐渐）消失』

❶ （使）蒸发，挥发

[V] Heat until all the water has evaporated.
加热直至水全部蒸发。

[VN] The sun is constantly evaporating the earth's moisture.
太阳使地球上的湿气不断蒸发。

❷ [V] （逐渐）消失

If a feeling, plan, or activity evaporates, it gradually becomes weaker and eventually disappears completely.

My anger evaporated and I wanted to cry.
我的怒气渐渐消失，想大哭一场。

Your dreams always seem to evaporate, and nothing ever quite matches expectations.
你的梦想似乎总是逐渐破灭，从来没有什么事情能完全符合你的预期。

▶ **vapor** [ˈveɪpə(r)] n. 蒸汽，水汽

词义辨析 <P379第88> 消失 vanish, disappear, evaporate

② -ate构成形容词，表示"具有…的，有…性质的"

1. **considerate** [kənˈsɪdərət] adj. 关心的，体贴的 <P104>
『consider考虑+ate具有…性质的→具有考虑（别人）性质的→关心的，体贴的』

2. **fortunate** [ˈfɔːtʃənət] adj. 幸运的 <P179>
『fortune运气（去e）+ate具有…性质的→具有运气性质的→幸运的』

3. **passionate** [ˈpæʃənət] adj. 热诚的；感情强烈的 <P244>
『passion强烈感情+ate具有…性质的→感情强烈的』

4. **affectionate** [əˈfekʃənət] adj. 表示关爱的；表示爱的；充满深情的；满怀柔情的 <P163>
『affection喜爱，钟爱+ate具有…性质的→表示爱的』

5. **literate** [ˈlɪtərət] adj. 有读写能力的；有文化的 <P209>
『liter文字，字母+ate具有…的→有读写能力的』

③ -ate构成名词，表示"人"

1. **candidate** [ˈkændɪdət] n. 候选人；考生；求职者
『candid (=cand)白；发光+ate表人→古希腊人穿白袍候选→候选人』

❶ ~ (for sth) （竞选或求职的）候选人，申请人
There were a large number of candidates for the job.
有许多求职者申请这份工作。

The Democratic candidate is still leading in the polls.
这位民主党候选人的得票数依然领先。

❷ 考生，应试者
A candidate is someone who is taking an examination.

▶ **candidacy** [ˈkændɪdəsi] n. 候选人资格；候选人身份

2. **advocate** [ˈædvəkeɪt , ˈædvəkət] v. 提倡；拥护 n. 提倡者，拥护者 <P357>
『ad相当于to→voc叫喊；声音+ate表动词或表人→向（众人）喊（呼吁支持或参与）→提倡；拥护者』
（v. [ˈædvəkeɪt]; n. [ˈædvəkət]）

④ -ate构成名词，表示"职位，职权，总称"

1. **doctorate** [ˈdɒktərət] n. 博士学位，博士头衔
『doctor博士+ate职位，职权，总称→博士学位』

He worked hard at English literature and obtained a doctorate.
他努力攻读英国文学，并获得了博士学位。

2. **electorate** [ɪˈlektərət] n. （某国或某地区）全体选民 <P202>
『elect选举+or做某动作的人+ate表总称→全体选民』

后缀17. -cy 以表示职位、任期或表示性质、状态、行为（用来改变以 t, te 结尾的名词或形容词的词义

① 以-t, -te结尾的表示职务的名词，常把t, te变为cy以表示其职位、任期

1. **infant** [ˈɪnfənt] n. 婴儿，幼儿；初期的

▶ **infancy** [ˈɪnfənsi] n. 婴儿期，幼儿期；初期

The child died in infancy. 那孩子在婴儿期夭折了。

Computing science was still in its infancy.
计算科学仍然处于初期阶段。

2. **captain** [ˈkæptɪn] n. 上尉；船长；机长；（运动队）队长 <P122>

▶ **captaincy** [ˈkæptənsi] n. 队长职位（或任期）

3. **candidate** [ˈkændɪdət] n. 候选人；考生；求职者 <P61>
   ▶ **candidacy** [ˈkændɪdəsi] n. 候选人资格；候选人身份

4. **president** [ˈprezɪdənt] n. 总统；总裁；校长 <P297>
   ▶ **presidency** [ˈprezɪdənsi] n. 总统（总裁、主席）职位或任期

② 以-t, -te结尾的表示职业特征的名词，常把t, te变为cy，表示行为、性质

1. **consultant** [kənˈsʌltənt] n. 顾问；会诊医师
   ▶ **consultancy** [kənˈsʌltənsi] n. 咨询公司；咨询
   You work for a management consultancy that only has a canteen? 你所在的管理咨询公司只有一个食堂？
   The project provides both consultancy and training.
   这个项目既提供咨询服务也提供培训。

2. **diplomat** [ˈdɪpləmæt] n. 外交官
   ▶ **diplomacy** [dɪˈpləʊməsi] n. 外交；外交手段
   Today's Security Council resolution will be a significant success for American diplomacy.
   今天的安理会决议将是美国外交取得的一个重大成功。
   He stormed off in a fury, and it took all Minnelli's powers of diplomacy to get him to return.
   他愤然离去，米内利使出了浑身解数才把他劝了回来。
   ▶ **diplomatic** [ˌdɪpləˈmætɪk] adj. 外交的

3. **idiot** [ˈɪdiət] n. 白痴，傻瓜
   ▶ **idiocy** [ˈɪdiəsi] n. 愚蠢行为
   But I'll not believe this idiocy!
   可我不能相信这件蠢事！

4. **pirate** [ˈpaɪrət] n. 海盗；盗版者 vt. 盗印，窃用
   ▶ **piracy** [ˈpaɪrəsi] n. 海上抢劫；盗版行为

5. **occupant** [ˈɒkjəpənt] n. 居住者；（房屋、建筑等的）使用者 <P123>
   ▶ **occupancy** [ˈɒkjəpənsi] n. 占用，使用

6. **advocate** [ˈædvəkeɪt] v. 提倡；拥护 n. 提倡者，拥护者 <P357>
   ▶ **advocacy** [ˈædvəkəsi] n. 提倡，拥护

7. **agent** [ˈeɪdʒənt] n. 代理人；经纪人；间谍 <P110>
   『ag做+ent表人或物→做某事的人或物→代理人；动因』
   ▶ **agency** [ˈeɪdʒənsi] n. 代理机构；(especially NAmE)（政府的）专门机构

③ 以-t, -te结尾的形容词，常把t, te变为cy或加cy以表示性质、状态

1. **intimate** [ˈɪntɪmət] adj. 亲密的；密切的 vt. 透露
   『intim(= inmost)内心的+ate表动词或形容词→（关系）达到内心深处的→亲密的』
   ❶ adj. 亲密的，密切的
   We're not on intimate terms with our neighbours.
   我们和邻居来往不多。
   I discussed with my intimate friends whether I would immediately have a baby.
   我与密友们讨论是否我要马上生孩子。
   ❷ vt. ~ sth (to sb) 透露；（间接）表示，暗示
   He has already intimated to us his intention to retire.
   他已经向我们透露了他要退休的打算。

▶ **intimacy** [ˈɪntɪməsi] n. [U]亲密，密切；[C, usually pl.]亲密行为

2. **private** [ˈpraɪvət] adj. 私有的；个人的 <P271>
   ▶ **privacy** [ˈprɪvəsi] [ˈpraɪvəsi] n. 隐私，秘密

3. **accurate** [ˈækjərət] adj. 精确的，准确的 <P146>
   ▶ **accuracy** [ˈækjʊrəsi] n. 准确（性）；精确（程度）

4. **bankrupt** [ˈbæŋkrʌpt] adj. 破产的，倒闭的 <P283>
   ▶ **bankruptcy** [ˈbæŋkrʌptsi] n. 破产，倒闭

5. **adequate** [ˈædɪkwət] adj. 足够的，合乎需要的 <P158>
   ▶ **adequacy** [ˈædɪkwəsi] n. 足够，充分

6. **legitimate** [lɪˈdʒɪtɪmət] adj. 合法的；合理的；合法婚姻所生的 <P204>
   ▶ **legitimacy** [lɪˈdʒɪtɪməsi] n. 合法（性）；合理

7. **literate** [ˈlɪtərət] adj. 有读写能力的；有文化的 <P209>
   ▶ **literacy** [ˈlɪtərəsi] n. 有读写能力

后缀18. -dom 构成名词，表示"具有…性质"

1. **boredom** [ˈbɔːdəm] n. 厌烦，厌倦，无聊
   『bore无聊的，厌倦的+dom表名词→无聊，厌烦』

2. **freedom** [ˈfriːdəm] n. 自由
   『free自由的+dom表名词→自由』

3. **kingdom** [ˈkɪŋdəm] n. 王国
   『king国王+dom表名词→王国』

4. **wisdom** [ˈwɪzdəm] n. 智慧，才智
   『wise智慧的（去e）+dom表名词→智慧，才智』

5. **random** [ˈrændəm] adj. 随机的
   『ran运转+dom表名词→运转（的转盘停下来）来选择→随机的』
   ❶ 随机的，随意的
   The information is processed in a random order.
   信息是按随机顺序处理的。
   The winning numbers are randomly selected by computer.
   中奖号码是由电脑随机选取的。
   ❷ at random 随意，随机
   The terrorists fired into the crowd at random.
   恐怖分子胡乱地向人群开枪。
   Names were chosen at random from a list.
   名字是从名单中随便点的。

后缀19. -ed 接于名词之后，构成形容词，表示"具有…的；如…的"

1. **aged** [eɪdʒd] adj. 年迈的，老年的
   『age年龄+ed具有…的，充满…→…岁的；老年的』
   ❶ …岁的
   They have two children aged six and nine.
   他们有两个小孩，一个六岁，一个九岁。
   ❷ 年迈的
   She has an aged parent. 她有一个年迈的父亲/母亲。
   He is aged, but his memory is still good.
   他已年老，但记忆力仍然好。
   ❸ the aged 老年人
   The aged were well taken care of and respected in that

mountain village.
在那个山村里，老年人得到很好的照顾和尊敬。

2. bearded ['bɪədɪd] adj.（男子）有胡须的
『beard胡须+ed具有…的→有胡须的』

Do you only see that bearded and long-haired man?
您只看见那留胡子和长头发的人吗？

3. colored ['kʌləd] adj. 彩色的，有色的；有色人种的
『color颜色+ed具有…的→有色的，彩色的』

❶ （often in compounds 常构成复合词）有…色的；色彩…的

She was wearing a cream-coloured suit.
她身着一身米色套装。
The cages were full of brightly- coloured tropical birds.
笼子里满是色彩鲜艳的热带鸟。

❷ (old-fashioned or offensive) 有色人种的

4. gifted ['gɪftɪd] adj. 有天赋的，有才华的
『gift天赋，才能+ed具有…的→有天赋的』

5. hooked [hʊkt] adj. 钩状的
『hook钩+ed具有…的，如…的→钩状的』

He was thin and tall, with a hooked nose.
他又瘦又高，长着鹰钩鼻。

6. horned [hɔ:nd] adj. 有角的，有角状物的
『horn角+ed具有…的→有角的』

The first thing that stands out about the Amazon horned frog is its size.
亚马孙角蛙让人首先注意它的地方是它的大小。

7. legged [legd] adj. 有腿的
『leg腿+ed具有…的→有腿的』

having legs of a specified kind or number
In conclusion, I want to say that pets are my four legged brothers. 总之，我想说宠物是我的四条腿兄弟。
I dreamed about this one-legged seaman for many nights afterwards.
那以后我经常梦到他说的那个一条腿的水手。

8. pointed ['pɔɪntɪd] adj. 尖的；尖锐的，尖刻的
『point尖端+ed具有…的；如…的→尖的；尖锐的』

❶ 尖的，有尖头的
Use a pointed object such as a broken matchstick.
用一个有尖的东西，比如折断的火柴棍。

❷ 尖锐的，尖刻的，一针见血的，批评性的
Pointed comments or behaviour express criticism in a clear and direct way.
a pointed comment/remark 一针见血的评论/说话

9. talented ['tæləntɪd] adj. 天资聪颖的，天赋高的
『talent天才，天资+ed具有…的→天资聪颖的』

后缀20. -ed 用在动词后面构成形容词，表示人"感到…"；-ing 用在动词后面构成形容词，表示"令人…"

小贴士 -ed形容词和-ing形容词是由过去分词和现在分词在长期的使用过程中演变而来的。-ed形容词不仅保留有过去分词的大部分特征，还含有被动的意味，表示"被…"，常译为"感到…"。现在分词保留有现在分词的大部分特征，含有主动意味，常译作"令人…"。

1. moving ['mu:vɪŋ] adj. 令人感伤（或同情）的

If something is moving, it makes you feel strongly an emotion such as sadness, pity, or sympathy.
It is very moving to see how much strangers can care for each other.
看到陌生人之间这般彼此关照，实在令人感动。

▶**moved** [mu:vd] adj. 被感动的

The film was so sad that everyone was moved.
影片情节十分悲惨，观众无不为之感动。

2. touching ['tʌtʃɪŋ] adj. 令人同情的，感人的，动人的（同义词 moving）

causing feelings of pity or sympathy; making you feel emotional
It was a touching story that moved many of us to tears.
那是一个让我们许多人落泪的动人故事。

▶**touched** [tʌtʃt] adj. 感激的，受感动的

feeling happy and grateful because of what someone has done
She was touched by their warm welcome.
她对他们的热烈欢迎十分感动。
I was touched that he still remembered me.
他仍然记得我，使我十分感动。

3. astonishing [ə'stɒnɪʃɪŋ] adj. 使人吃惊的

He stated the market situation with astonishing clarity.
他极其清晰地陈述了市场行情。

▶**astonished** [ə'stɒnɪʃt] adj. 吃惊的

He was astonished to learn he'd won the competition.
他听说他比赛赢了，感到很惊讶。

后缀21. -eer 表示"专门从事某种工作或职业的人"；单词重音在-eer 所构成的音节上

1. engineer [ˌendʒɪ'nɪə(r)] n. 工程师 vt. 设计，制造
『engine发动机+eer从事某种工作的人→工程师』

▶**engineering** [ˌendʒɪ'nɪərɪŋ] n. 工程，工程学
『engineer 设计，制造+ ing表名词→与设计制造有关的→工程，工程学』

The percentage of girls in engineering has increased substantially. 学工科的女孩的比例已经大大增加了。
▶**engine** ['endʒɪn] n. 发动机，引擎；火车头，机车

2. mountaineer [ˌmaʊntə'nɪə(r)] n. 登山者
『mountain山+eer从事某种工作的人→从事登山的人→登山者』

The mountaineer broke a leg while climbing a cliff and was hospitalized for a month.
登山运动员在攀登悬崖时摔断了一条腿，住院治疗了一个月。

3. pioneer [ˌpaɪə'nɪə(r)] n. 先驱，先锋；开拓者 vt. 开创
『pion (= ped脚)+eer从事某种工作的人→走在前面的人→先驱』

❶ n. 先锋；先驱；带头人
Mr Jobs co-founded the company in 1976 and helped establish it as a technology pioneer.
乔布斯在1976年与他人共同创立了（苹果）公司，并把该公司建设成技术领域的先驱。
He is a pioneer in modern medical practice.
他是现代医学实践的先驱。

❷ n. 拓荒者

Pioneers are people who leave their own country or the place where they were living, and go and live in a place that has not been lived in before.

❸ vt. 开创；倡导

The method they pioneered remains fundamental to research into the behaviour of nerve cells.
他们首创的方法在神经细胞活动的研究中一直是不可或缺的。

❹ a Young Pioneer 一个少先队员

4. **volunteer** [ˌvɒlənˈtɪə(r)] n. 志愿者；自告奋勇者 〈P358〉
『volunt意愿+eer从事某种工作的人→自愿去做的人→志愿者』

后缀22. -el 表名词

① -el 表示"小"

1. **parcel** [ˈpɑːsl] n. 包裹，小包
『parc(=part)部分+el小→将一小部分包起来→小包，包裹』

(especially BrE) NAmE usually package

something that is wrapped in paper or put into a thick envelope so that it can be sent by mail, carried easily, or given as a present

There's a parcel and some letters for you.
有你的一个包裹和几封信。
She was carrying a parcel of books under her arm.
她腋下夹着一包书。

2. **morsel** [ˈmɔːsl] n. 一点点，一小份（尤指食物）〈P228〉
『mors咬+el小→咬一小口→一点点（食物）』

② -el 表示"人或物"

1. **personnel** [ˌpɜːsəˈnel] n. 全体人员；人事部门
『person人（双写n）+el人→全体人员』

❶ [pl.]（组织中的）人员，职员
Five other US military personnel were killed in various incidents. 另有5名美军士兵死于各种事件。

❷ [U + sing./pl. v.] 人事部门
She works in personnel. 她在人事部工作。
Personnel is/are currently reviewing pay scales.
人事部现在正审核工资级别。

2. **colonel** [ˈkɜːnl] n. 上校
『colon+el人→上校』

3. **model** [ˈmɒdl] n. 模型；模范；型号；模特儿
『mod方式，模式+el表物或人→其他都按这种方式进行的→模型；范例；模范』

4. **funnel** [ˈfʌnl] n. 漏斗；漏斗状物
『funn(=fuse)流+el表示物→让东西流进→漏斗』

❶ [C] 漏斗；漏斗状物

❷（使）通过狭窄空间；传送（金钱、货物或信息）
[V] Wind was funnelling through the gorge. 风吹过峡谷。
[VN] Huge pipes funnel the water down the mountainside.
巨大的管道把水沿山坡输送下山。
Its Global Programme on AIDS funnelled money from donors to governments.
其全球艾滋病项目把捐款发放给各国政府。

5. **novel** [ˈnɒvl] n. 小说 adj. 新颖的，新奇的 〈P237〉
『nov新的+el表物→小说；novel小说（有新颖、新奇的故

事情节的小说才会受欢迎）→新颖的，新奇的』

③ -el 表示"地点或场所"

1. **channel** [ˈtʃænl] n. 水渠；航道；频道；海峡
『chann（希腊语）管道+el地点，场所→航道』

2. **kennel** [ˈkenl] n. 狗窝
『kenn(=canine)狗+el地点，场所→狗窝』

3. **tunnel** [ˈtʌnl] n. 隧道
『tunn+el地点，场所→隧道』

后缀23. -en 可以构成形容词，表示"由…制成；似…的"，还可构成名词，表示"小；人"

① -en 表示"由…制成的；似…的"

1. **earthen** [ˈɜːθn] adj.（地面或墙）泥土制的；陶制的
『earth泥土+en由…制成；似…的→由泥土制成的』
Despite the mud outside, the earthen floor was clean.
尽管外面泥泞，屋内的泥土地面还是很干净。
After that the earthen pot floated away.
之后，陶罐漂走了。

2. **golden** [ˈɡəʊldən] adj. 金（黄）色的；金质的；美好的
『gold金子+en由…制成；似…的→由金子制成的；似金子的→金质的；金黄色的；美好的』

❶ 金质的，金的
a golden crown 金冠

❷ 金色的；金黄色的
golden hair 金发
miles of golden beaches 数英里的金色海滩

❸ 特别的；美好的
golden memories 美好的记忆
Businesses have a golden opportunity to expand into new markets. 商界有开拓新市场的良机。

❹ kill the goose that lays the golden egg/eggs 杀鹅（鸡）取卵

❺ silence is golden 沉默是金

小贴士 a heart of gold 金子般的心。不能说 a golden heart
She started to get a reputation as an unselfish girl with a heart of gold.
她开始被人们赞誉为有一颗金子般的心的无私女孩。

3. **wooden** [ˈwʊdn] adj. 木制的；呆板的
『wood木头+en由…制成；似…的→由木头制成的；似木头的→木制的；呆板的』
a wooden box 木箱
The actor playing the father was too wooden.
饰演父亲的演员太呆板。

4. **woollen** [ˈwʊlən] adj. 毛料的；羊毛制的
『wool羊毛（双写l）+en由…制成的→由羊毛制成的→毛料的』（NAmE woolen 美语中拼作woolen）
It's too warm to wear woollen sweaters now.
天热了，毛衣穿不住了。

5. **silken** [ˈsɪlkən] adj. 丝质的；柔软光洁的；柔和的
『silk丝绸+en由…制成；似…的→由丝绸制成的；似丝绸的→丝质的；柔软光洁的；柔和的』
silken ribbons 丝带
silken hair 柔软光滑的头发
her silken voice 她那柔和的嗓音

6. <u>barren</u> [ˈbærən] adj. 贫瘠的，不毛的，荒芜的；不结果的，不育的 〈P118〉
『bar棒，杆（双写r）+en似…的→（草木似乎都是由）光杆组成的（枝叶不茂盛）→贫瘠的，荒芜的→不生育的，不结果的』

② -en 表示"小"

1. <u>chicken</u> [ˈtʃɪkɪn] n. 小鸡；鸡肉；胆小鬼 adj. 胆小的
『chick小鸡+en小→小鸡』

I'm scared of the dark. I'm a big chicken.
我怕黑，是个十足的胆小鬼。
Why are you so chicken? 你怎么就这么胆小呢？

2. <u>kitten</u> [ˈkɪtn] n. 小猫
『kit (=cat)猫（双写t）+en小→小猫』

3. <u>maiden</u> [ˈmeɪdn] n. 少女 adj. 初次的
『maid女仆；未婚女子+en小→少女』

❶ n. 少女，未婚女子

❷ adj. （航行、飞行等）初次的，首次的
In 1912, the Titanic sank on her maiden voyage.
1912年，"泰坦尼克"号在处女航中失事沉没。

▶ <u>maid</u> [meɪd] n. （家庭）女佣；（旅馆）侍女

A maid brought me breakfast at half past eight.
8点半女佣给我送来了早餐。

③ -en 表示"人"

1. <u>citizen</u> [ˈsɪtɪzn] n. 市民，公民
『city城市（变y为i）+en人→市民，公民』

2. <u>warden</u> [ˈwɔːdn] n. 管理员；监狱长；看守人
『ward守卫，保卫+ en人→看守人』

A traffic warden asked him to move his car.
交通管理员让他把车开走。
A new warden took over the prison.
一位新的监狱长接管了这所监狱。

▶ <u>ward</u> [wɔːd] n. 病房；v. 挡住，防止

❶ [C] 病房
He worked as a nurse on the children's ward.
他在儿科病房当护士。

❷ ward off 避开，挡住，防止（危险、疾病等）
She raised her hand to ward off a blow.
她抬起手来挡开拳头。
Such a thin padded coat cannot ward off the cold mountain wind. 这么薄的棉衣在高山上挡不住寒风。

后缀24. en-（em-，-em）表示"（使）进入…状态"〈P13 前缀28〉

后缀25. -er 放在动词后，表示动作的执行者；-ee 放在动词后，表示动作的承受者，重音在-ee 所构成的音节上

1. <u>examine</u> [ɪgˈzæmɪn] vt. 考试；检查
　▶ <u>examiner</u> [ɪgˈzæmɪnə(r)] n. 主考人；检查人
　▶ <u>examinee</u> [ɪgˌzæmɪˈniː] n. 应试者

2. <u>train</u> [treɪn] v. 训练
　▶ <u>trainer</u> [ˈtreɪnə(r)] n. 教练员；驯兽师
　▶ <u>trainee</u> [ˌtreɪˈniː] n. 受培训者

3. <u>appointee</u> [əˌpɔɪnˈtiː] n. 被任命者
『appoint任命+ee被…者→被任命者』

4. <u>employ</u> [ɪmˈplɔɪ] vt. 雇用〈P258〉
　▶ <u>employer</u> [ɪmˈplɔɪə(r)] n. 雇主，老板
　▶ <u>employee</u> [ɪmˈplɔɪiː] n. 雇工，雇员

5. <u>devotee</u> [ˌdevəˈtiː] n. （狂热的）爱好者；（某一宗教团体的）教徒〈P104〉
『devote献身于（去e）+ee被…的人→爱好者』

6. <u>nominee</u> [ˌnɒmɪˈniː] n. 被提名者，候选人〈P234〉
『nomin(=name)名称，名字+ee被…者→被提名者』

7. <u>committee</u> [kəˈmɪti] n. 委员会〈P224〉
『commit（委托）（双写t）+ee被…者→被委托给的人→委员会』

8. <u>interview</u> [ˈɪntəvjuː] vt. 面试；采访〈P353〉
　▶ <u>interviewer</u> [ˈɪntəvjuːə(r)] n. 主持面试者；采访者
　▶ <u>interviewee</u> [ˌɪntəvjuːˈiː] n. 被面试者；被采访者

9. <u>refer</u> [rɪˈfɜː(r)] vt. 参考，参看 〈P167〉
　▶ <u>referee</u> [ˌrefəˈriː] n. 裁判员；仲裁人
『refer参看+ee被…的人→被参看的人→裁判员』

> 小贴士 -ee有时候表示"人"，并没有被动的意思

1. <u>absentee</u> [ˌæbsənˈtiː] n. 缺席者
『absent缺席的+ee…的人→缺席者』

2. <u>refugee</u> [ˌrefjuˈdʒiː] n. 避难者，难民〈P181〉
『refuge避难+(e)e表人→避难的人→难民』

后缀26. -er 构成动词，表示"反复的动作"；还可构成名词，表示"人或物"

① -er构成动词，表示"反复的动作"

1. <u>chatter</u> [ˈtʃætə(r)] vi. 喋喋不休；（牙齿）打战
『chat聊天（双写t）+er表反复→喋喋不休』

❶ [V] ~ (away/on) (to sb) (about sth) 喋喋不休；唠叨
to talk quickly and continuously, especially about things that are not important
They chattered away happily for a while.
他们高兴地闲扯了一会儿。
The children chattered to each other excitedly about the next day's events.
孩子们很兴奋，没完没了地谈论着第二天的活动。

❷ [V] （牙齿）打战，咯咯响
She was so cold her teeth chattered. 她冻得牙齿咯咯响。

2. <u>waver</u> [ˈweɪvə(r)] vi. 动摇，犹豫；摇曳
『wave飘动，起伏+(e)r表反复→动摇，犹豫』

❶ [V] 动摇，犹豫
Her determination never wavered. 她的决心从未动摇过。
She's wavering between buying a house in the city or moving away. 她举棋不定，不知是在这个城市买所房子，还是迁居他处。

❷ [V] 摇曳；闪烁
The shadows of the dancers wavered continually.
舞者们的身影在轻轻晃动着。

3. <u>shiver</u> [ˈʃɪvə(r)] v. （因寒冷、恐惧）颤抖，哆嗦
『shiv（谐音为"水雾"）+er表反复→因寒冷而哆嗦』

指因寒冷、害怕等而轻微和快速地颤抖。
Don't stand outside shivering—come inside and get warm!
别站在外面冻得打哆嗦了——进来暖暖身子吧！

He shivered at the thought of the cold, dark sea.
那寒冷黑暗的大海，他想想都吓得发抖。

4. quiver [ˈkwɪvə(r)] vi. & n. 轻微颤动

指树叶、鸟的翅膀等抖动，也指人因恐惧、紧张等而嘴唇、声音等颤动，侧重于轻微、急速、连续不断，有时令人难以察觉，在程度上弱于 tremble。（qui可以使我们联想到 quick）

Her lip quivered and then she started to cry.
她嘴唇微微一颤就哭了起来。

Jane couldn't help the quiver in her voice. 简不禁声音颤抖。

5. batter [ˈbætə(r)] v. 连续猛击；殴打〈P118〉
『bat打（双写t）+er表反复→连续猛击』

② -er 放在名词或形容词后面构成名词，表示"人"，也可放在动词后面，表示做该动作的"物"

1. banker [ˈbæŋkə(r)] n. 银行家
『bank银行+er人→银行家』

2. villager [ˈvɪlɪdʒə(r)] n. 村民
『village村庄+（e)r人→住在村庄的人→村民』

3. teenager [ˈtiːneɪdʒə(r)] n. 青少年
『teenage青少年的+（e)r人→青少年』

4. lighter [ˈlaɪtə(r)] n. 打火机
『light点燃+er物→打火机』

5. heater [ˈhiːtə(r)] n. 加热器；炉子
『heat加热+er物→加热器；炉子』

后缀27. -ern 构成形容词，表示"…方向的"，还可构成名词，表"…场所"

① -ern 表示"…方向的"

1. northern [ˈnɔːðən] adj. 北方的，北部的
『north [nɔːθ]北方+ern表形容词→北方的』
（注意：th的读音发生了变化）

2. southern [ˈsʌðən] adj. 南方的，南部的
『south [saʊθ]南方+ern表形容词→南方的』
（注意：ou和th的读音都发生了变化）

3. eastern [ˈiːstən] adj. 东方的
『east东方+ern表形容词→东方的』

4. western [ˈwestən] adj. 西方的；欧美的
『west西方+ern表形容词→西方的』

5. northeastern [ˌnɔːθˈiːstən] adj. 东北方的
『northeast东北方+ern表形容词→东北方的』

6. northwestern [ˈnɔːθˈwestən] adj. 西北方的
『northwest西北方+ern表形容词→西北方的』

7. southeastern [saʊθˈiːstən] adj. 东南方的
『southeast东南方+ern表形容词→东南方的』

8. southwestern [saʊθˈwestən] adj. 西南方的
『southwest西南方+ern表形容词→西南方的』

小贴士 汉语里"东南西北"的先后顺序到英语里就变成了north，south，east，west。汉语中的"东北，东南，西北，西南"以"东""西"为着眼点，而英语中则以"北north"和"南south"为着眼点：northeast 东北，northwest 西北，southeast东南，southwest西南。

小贴士 用时间表示方向：

一般是军事行动时用的，在没有参照物的情况下，想象一下自己面前有一个机械表盘，以自己为中心，以自己当时面对的正前方为12点钟方向，每夹角30°为一点，其他就此类推。如3点钟方向，就是自己的正右侧，9点钟方向就是自己的正左侧，1点钟方向就是自己的正前偏右30°的方向。

② -ern 表示"…场所"

1. lectern [ˈlektən] n. （教堂中的）诵经台；（演讲的）讲台
『lect讲，读+ern表场所→讲的地方→诵经台；讲台』

He turned over one of his note cards on the lectern.
他翻过一张放在演讲台上的笔记卡片。

Can I bring my notes to the lectern?
我可以带笔记到讲台去吗？

2. cavern [ˈkævən] n. 大洞穴，大山洞〈P125〉
『cave洞+（e)rn场所，地点→洞穴』

A cavern is a large deep cave.

后缀28. -ery 构成名词，表"地点，场所；总称；行为"

① -ery 构成名词，表"地点，场所"。部分词可看作"表示人的名词+y表场所"。如bake烤→baker面包师→bakery面包房

1. bakery [ˈbeɪkəri] n. 面包房，面包店
『bake烤，烘焙+ery→表场所→bakery面包房』

2. grocery [ˈɡrəʊsəri] n. 食品杂货店；杂货店
『grocer食品杂货商+y表场所→食品杂货店』
（NAmE usually grocery store）

3. ministry [ˈmɪnɪstri] n. （政府的）部
『minister部长（去er)+y表场所→部长工作的场所→部』

4. nursery [ˈnɜːsəri] n. 托儿所；幼儿园；育儿室
『nurse护理+（e)ry表场所→托儿所；幼儿园』

小贴士 **nursing home** 养老院；疗养所
a small private hospital, especially one where old people live and are cared for
He died in a nursing home at the age of 87.
他在一家养老院去世，享年87岁。

5. fishery [ˈfɪʃəri] n. 渔场
『fish鱼+ery表场所→渔场』

6. surgery [ˈsɜːdʒəri] n. 门诊处；外科手术
『surg外科+ery表场所或行为→门诊处；外科手术』

❶ [U] 外科手术；外科学
She had three surgeries over ten days.
她十天进行了三次手术。
His father has just recovered from heart surgery.
他父亲刚刚从心脏外科手术中康复过来。

❷ 诊疗室，诊所 （US, use doctor's office, dentist's office）
He had to wait for what seemed like ages in the doctor's surgery.
在诊所里，他不得不等待很长时间。

▶ **surgeon** [ˈsɜːdʒən] n. 外科医生

7. cemetery [ˈsemətri] n. 墓地，坟地，公墓
『cemet(=cem)躺+ery场所，地点→死人躺着的地方→坟墓』

His remains have been exhumed from a cemetery in Queens, New York City.
他的遗体被从纽约市皇后区的墓地里挖了出来。

8. refinery [rɪˈfaɪnəri] n. 精炼厂，提炼厂 〈P172〉

『refine精炼，提炼+(e)ry表场所→精炼厂，提炼厂』

② -ery 构成不可数名词，表总称。也可看作"表示人的名词+y表总称"。如jewel珠宝→jeweller珠宝商→jewellery珠宝

1. jewellery [ˈdʒuːəlri] n. 珠宝，首饰

『jewel 宝石，珠宝（双写l）+ery表总称→珠宝首饰』

（NAmE jewelry）

[U] 珠宝；首饰

objects such as rings and necklaces that people wear as decoration

She has some lovely pieces of jewellery.
她有几件漂亮的首饰。

▶ **jewel** [ˈdʒuːəl] n. 宝石；珍宝

▶ **jeweller** [ˈdʒuːələ(r)] n. 珠宝商；钟表匠；宝石匠；珠宝店

（NAmE jeweler）

a person who makes, repairs or sells jewellery and watches

2. machinery [məˈʃiːnəri] n.（统称）机器；（尤指）大型机器

『machine机器+(e)ry表总称→machiner操作机器者+y表总称→机器（统称）』

3. pottery [ˈpɒtəri] n. 陶器（尤指手工制的）

『pot茶壶；锅（双写t）+ery表总称→陶器（统称）』

▶ **pot** [pɒt] n. 锅；茶壶；咖啡壶；罐；花盆

4. scenery [ˈsiːnəri] n. 风景，景色，风光

『scene景色+(e)ry表总称→风景（统称）』

[U] 风景，景色，风光

The scenery in a country area is the land, water, or plants that you can see around you.

Whoever passes here would stop to admire the scenery.
但凡过路的人，都要停下一览这儿的风光。

▶ **scene** [siːn] n. 场面，现场；（戏剧的）一场；景色

❶ [C, usually sing.] ~ (of sth) （尤指不愉快事件发生的）地点，现场

Firefighters were on the scene immediately.
消防队立刻赶到现场。

❷ [C] ~ (of sth) 场面，情景

an event or a situation that you see, especially one of a particular type

The team's victory produced scenes of joy all over the country. 球队的胜利使举国上下出现一派欢乐的场面。

❸ [C] （电影，书等）镜头，场面；（戏剧）场

The movie opens with a scene in a New York apartment.
电影开头的一场戏发生在纽约的一套公寓里。

❹ [C] 景象；景色；风光

a view that you see

It's a scene of complete devastation.
那是一幅满目疮痍的景象。

❺ make a scene （尤指当众、有失体面的）争吵，吵闹

I'm sorry I made such a scene. 对不起，我失态了。

She had made a scene in the middle of the party.
她在聚会时大闹了一场。

5. shrubbery [ˈʃrʌbəri] n. 灌木丛

『shrub灌木（双写b）+ery表总称→灌木丛』

The voice seemed to be coming from the shrubbery.
声音似乎是从灌木丛里传来的。

The mountains are sparsely covered with shrubbery and trees.
山上有稀疏的灌木和树覆盖。

6. greenery [ˈɡriːnəri] n. 绿色植物

『green绿色+ery表总称→绿色植物』

Plants that make a place look attractive are referred to as greenery.

The room was decorated with flowers and greenery.
屋里装点着花卉和绿叶植物。

③ -ery 构成名词，表行为、性质或制度

1. robbery [ˈrɒbəri] n. 抢劫

『rob抢劫（双写b）+ery+表行为或性质→抢劫』

2. slavery [ˈsleɪvəri] n. 奴隶制度

『slave奴隶+(e)ry表制度→奴隶制度』

3. bravery [ˈbreɪvəri] n. 勇敢，勇气

『brave勇敢面对+(e)ry表行为→勇敢，勇气』

Bravery is brave behaviour or the quality of being brave.

He deserves the highest praise for his bravery.
他的英勇行为应该获得最高的赞誉。

4. butchery [ˈbʊtʃəri] n. 残杀；屠宰

『butcher屠杀+(er)y表行为→残杀；屠宰』

小贴士 the butcher's 肉店

In her view, war is simply a legalised form of butchery.
在她看来，战争只不过是一种合法化的屠杀。

5. archery [ˈɑːtʃəri] n. 箭术，弓箭运动

『arch弓+ery表行为→弓箭运动』

Horse riding, pool, table tennis, archery and fishing are also available. 骑马、游泳池、乒乓球、射箭和钓鱼也可。

6. trickery [ˈtrɪkəri] n. 欺骗，欺诈，耍花招

『trick诡计+ery行为→欺诈』

[U] the use of dishonest methods to trick people in order to achieve what you want

They are notorious for resorting to trickery in order to impress their clients.
他们为了打动客户不惜坑蒙拐骗，因而声名狼藉。

7. effrontery [ɪˈfrʌntəri] n. 厚颜无耻 〈P181〉

『ef出来+front面，脸+ery表行为→（不顾羞耻）把脸伸出去→厚颜无耻』

后缀29. -escent=grow, become，表示"变得"

1. adolescent [ˌædəˈlesnt] n. 青少年 adj. 青少年的

『adol(=adult, old)成年+escent变得→转变为成年的时期→青少年的，青春期的』

Young adolescents are happiest with small groups of close friends.
青少年在和自己小圈子里的好友待在一起时最为开心。

Most adolescent problems are temporary.
多数青少年问题是暂时性的。

▶ **adolescence** [ˌædəˈlesns] n. 青春期

Some people become very self-conscious in adolescence.
有些人在青春期会变得异常害羞。

2. incandescent [ˌɪnkænˈdesnt] adj. 炽热的；活力四射

的；暴怒的

『in使…+cand白；发光+escent变得→（遇热）变得发光的→炽热的；暴怒的』

incandescent lamps 白炽灯

Gill had an extraordinary, incandescent personality.
吉尔个性鲜明，热情洋溢。

It makes me incandescent with fury. 它令我极其愤怒。

3. evanescent [ˌevəˈnesnt] adj. (literary) 瞬息即逝的；迅速遗忘的 〈P342〉

『e出去+van空+escent变得→刚出现就变空了→迅速消失的』

4. convalescent [ˌkɒnvəˈlesnt] adj. 正在康复的；康复期的 n. 恢复期的病人 〈P345〉

『con加强+val强壮+escent变得→（开始）变强壮的→逐渐恢复的』

后缀30. -esque 构成形容词，表示"如…的"

1. picturesque [ˌpɪktʃəˈresk] adj. 风景如画的；（语言）生动形象的 〈P255〉

『picture图画+(e)sque像…的→像图画的→风景如画的』

2. statuesque [ˌstætʃuˈesk] adj. （女性）高挑的，挺拔的

『statue雕塑+(e)sque如…的→如雕塑般的→（女性）又高又美的』

She was a statuesque brunette.
她有着一头深褐色头发，身材高挑。

3. grotesque [grəʊˈtesk] adj. 怪诞的；丑陋奇异的 n. 丑八怪

『grot岩洞+(e)sque如…的→如岩洞里的（画）一样→怪诞的』

❶ adj. 怪诞的；荒唐的；荒谬的

strange in a way that is unpleasant or offensive

It's grotesque to expect a person of her experience to work for so little money.
想让她那样有经验的人为这点钱工作真是荒唐。

the grotesque disparities between the wealthy few and nearly everyone else
少数富人与几乎所有其他人之间悬殊的贫富差距

❷ adj. 丑陋奇异的，奇形怪状的

extremely ugly in a strange way that is often frightening or amusing

tribal dancers wearing grotesque masks
戴着奇异面具的部落跳舞者

They tried to avoid looking at his grotesque face and his crippled body.
他们尽量不去看他那张奇丑无比的脸和残疾的身体。

❸ [C] （尤指小说或绘画中的）怪异的人，丑八怪

4. burlesque [bɜːˈlesk] n. 滑稽讽刺表演（或作品）adj. 滑稽剧的

『burl嬉笑+esque如…的→滑稽讽刺表演的』

❶ [C] 滑稽讽刺表演（或作品）

❷ [U] (NAmE) 滑稽娱乐（曾经风靡美国,常伴有脱衣舞）

后缀31. -ess 表示阴性

1. actor [ˈæktə(r)] n. 演员（尤指男演员）

▶**actress** [ˈæktrəs] n. 女演员

2. emperor [ˈempərə(r)] n. 皇帝，君主 〈P157〉

▶**empress** [ˈemprəs] n. 女皇；皇后

3. god [gɒd] n. 上帝；神

▶**goddess** [ˈgɒdes] n. 女神；被崇拜的女人

4. host [həʊst] n. 主人；主办方；主持人 v. 做东；主办；主持

❶ [C] 主人

a person who invites guests to a meal, a party, etc. or who has people staying at their house

Ian, our host, introduced us to the other guests.
主人伊恩把我们介绍给了其他客人。

❷ [C] 东道主；主办国（或城市、机构）

Guangzhou is the host city of the 2010 Asian Games.
广州是2010年亚运会的举办城市。

❸ [C] （电视或广播的）节目主持人

I am a host of a live radio programme.
我是一个电台直播节目的主持人。

❹ [VN] 作为主人组织（聚会）；做东

Tonight she hosts a ball for 300 guests.
今晚她做东举办一场有300名客人参加的舞会。

❺ [VN] （国家、城市或机构）主办（活动）

Cannes hosts the annual film festival.
戛纳每年主办电影节。

❻ [VN] 主持（广播、电视节目）

She also hosts a show on St Petersburg Radio.
她还在圣彼得堡电台主持一个节目。

▶**hostess** [ˈhəʊstəs] n. 女主人

5. lion [ˈlaɪən] n. 狮子

▶**lioness** [ˈlaɪənes] n. 母狮

6. prince [prɪns] n. 王子

▶**princess** [ˌprɪnˈses] n. 公主；王妃

7. waiter [ˈweɪtə(r)] n. 服务员

▶**waitress** [ˈweɪtrəs] n. 女服务员，女侍者

8. poet [ˈpəʊɪt] n. 诗人

▶**poetess** [ˈpəʊətes] n. 女诗人

9. steward [ˈstjuːəd] n. （私人家中的）管家；（飞机、火车、轮船上的）乘务员 〈P58〉

▶**stewardess** [ˌstjuːəˈdes] n. （船舶、飞机或火车上的）女服务员，女乘务员

10. heir [eə(r)] n. 继承人 〈P190〉

▶**heiress** [ˈeəres] n. 女继承人

后缀32. -ette 构成名词，表示"小的东西或状态"

1. statuette [ˌstætʃuˈet] n. 小雕像

『statue雕像+(e)tte小→小雕像』

2. cigarette [ˌsɪgəˈret] n. 香烟

『cigar雪茄+ette小的东西→香烟』

3. palette [ˈpælət] n. 调色板；（画家使用的）主要色彩

『pal盘，板+ette小→小的（调色用的）盘子→调色板』

Greens and browns are typical of Ribera's palette.
绿色和棕色是里贝拉的主色调。

4. cassette [kəˈset] n. 盒式磁带

『cass(=case)盒子+ette小→小的盒子→盒式磁带』
a cassette recorder/player 盒式磁带录音机/放音机

后缀33. **-fold** 构成形容词或副词，表示"…倍，…重"

1. twofold [ˈtuːfəʊld] adj. 有两部分的 adv. 两倍的（地）
『two二+fold…倍，…重→两倍的（地）』

The case against is twofold: too risky and too expensive.
反对理由有两点：太冒险并且太昂贵。

2. tenfold [ˈtenfəʊld] adj. & adv. 十倍的（地）
『ten十+fold…倍，…重→十倍地（的）』

The two companies grew tenfold in the ensuing ten years.
在随后的十年中，两个公司的规模扩大为原来的十倍。

后缀34. **-ful** 表示"充满…的"，**-less** 表示"无…的"；-ful
还可构成名词，表示"量"

① **-ful** 表示"充满…的"，**-less** 表示"无…的"

1. care [keə(r)] n. 照料；小心 v. 关心；在乎

❶ **would you care for…/ would you care to…**
(formal) （礼貌用语）您喜欢，您愿意，您要
used to ask sb politely if they would like sth or would like to do sth, or if they would be willing to do sth
Would you care for another drink? 您再来一杯好吗？
If you'd care to follow me, I'll show you where his office is.
如果您愿意跟我走，我会把您领到他的办公室去。

❷ **care for sb** 照顾，照料；深深地爱，非常喜欢
She moved back home to care for her elderly parents.
她搬回家住，以便照料年迈的双亲。

He cared for her more than she realized.
她不知道他是多么在乎她。

词义辨析 <P371第49>
照料 **take care of, look after, care for**

▶ **careful** [ˈkeəfl] adj. 小心的，仔细的
『care小心，谨慎+ful充满…的→充满小心的→小心的』

▶ **careless** [ˈkeələs] adj. 粗心的
『care小心，谨慎+less缺少…的→缺少谨慎的→粗心的』

2. help [help] n. 帮助

▶ **helpful** [ˈhelpfl] adj. 有帮助的；乐意帮忙的
『help帮助+ful充满…的→充满帮助的→有帮助的』

❶ 有帮助的，有益的
Role-play is helpful in developing communication skills.
角色扮演有助于提高沟通技巧。
The booklet should be very helpful to parents of disabled children. 这本小册子对于残疾儿童的父母会很有用。

❷ （人）愿意帮忙的
James is a very helpful and cooperative lad.
詹姆斯是个肯帮忙、好合作的小伙子。

▶ **helpless** [ˈhelpləs] adj. 无助的
『help帮助+less缺少…的→缺少帮助的→无助的』

unable to take care of yourself or do things without the help of other people
It's natural to feel helpless against such abuse.
对这种虐待感到无能为力是自然的。
Their son watched helplessly as they vanished beneath the waves. 他们的儿子无助地看着他们消失在大浪中。

3. hope [həʊp] n. 希望 v. 希望

▶ **hopeful** [ˈhəʊpfl] adj. 抱有希望的；使人感到有希望的
『hope希望+ful充满…的→充满希望的→有希望的』

❶ （人）抱有希望的，满怀希望的
I feel hopeful that we'll find a suitable house very soon.
我对很快找到合适的房子抱有希望。
He is not very hopeful about the outcome of the interview.
他对面试的结果不抱很大希望。

❷ 使人感到有希望的
The latest trade figures are a hopeful sign.
最新贸易数字令人鼓舞。

▶ **hopefully** [ˈhəʊpfəli] adv. 抱有希望地；但愿

❶ 抱有希望地
"Are you free tonight?" she asked hopefully.
"你今晚有空吗？"她抱着希望地问。
He looked at her hopefully. 他满怀希望地看着她。

❷ 但愿，希望
used for saying that you hope something will happen
Hopefully, we'll get more news next week.
希望我们下周会得到更多的消息。

▶ **hopeless** [ˈhəʊpləs] adj. 没有希望的
『hope希望+less缺少…的→缺少希望的→没有希望的』

❶ （所做的某事）没有成功希望的，没有成功可能的
We tried to stop the flames from spreading, but we knew it was hopeless.
我们试图阻止火焰蔓延，但我们知道它是无望的。

❷ （某个情形）没有希望的
The situation is not as hopeless as it might seem.
情况并不像看上去那么无望。

❸ （especially BrE）（人）没有希望做好某事的
I'm hopeless with machinery.
对于机械我一窍不通。
I've got a hopeless memory. 我的记忆力糟透了。

4. breathless [ˈbreθləs] adj. 气喘吁吁的；屏息的
『breath呼吸+less缺少…的→缺少呼吸的→气喘吁吁的』

❶ （令人）气喘吁吁的，上气不接下气的
He arrived breathless at the top of the stairs.
他爬上楼梯顶时气喘吁吁的。

❷ ~ (with sth) （令人）屏息的，目瞪口呆的
You use breathless for emphasis when you are describing feelings of excitement or exciting situations.
That one kiss had left her breathless with excitement.
那一吻使她激动得屏住了呼吸。
Watching him climb up the precipice, everybody was breathless with anxiety.
看着他往悬崖上爬，大家都捏一把汗。

近义词 **breathtaking** [ˈbreθteɪkɪŋ] adj. 壮观的，美得令人窒息的；惊人的
『breath呼吸+take带走（去e）+ing表形容词→带走呼吸的→（美得）令人窒息的』

If you say that something is breathtaking, you are emphasizing that it is extremely beautiful or amazing.
The scenery along the coast was just breathtaking.
沿着海岸的景色简直令人叹为观止。

▶ **take one's breath away** 非常美丽的，美得让人室息的
to be extremely beautiful or exciting

It's really beyond description and it can take your breath away. 简直无法用语言来描述！它让你惊叹不已。

It is said that life is not measured by the breaths you take, but by the moments that take your breath away.

有人说，衡量生命的不是你呼吸的次数，而是让你屏住呼吸的时刻。

5. cheer [tʃɪə(r)] n. 欢快；欢呼 v. 欢呼；鼓舞

❶ [U] 欢快，愉快

They were impressed by his steadfast good cheer.
他整天笑呵呵的样子给他们留下很深的印象。

❷ [C] 欢呼声；喝彩声

A great cheer went up from the crowd.
观众爆发出一阵热烈的欢呼声。

cheers of encouragement 鼓励的喝彩声

❸ v. 欢呼；喝彩；加油

[V] We all cheered as the team came on to the field.
球队入场时我们都为之欢呼。

[VN] The crowd cheered the President as he drove slowly by.
当总统的车缓缓经过时，群众向他欢呼致意。

❹ [VN] [usually passive] 鼓励；鼓舞

She was cheered by the news from home.
来自家里的消息使她受到鼓舞。

❺ **cheer sb on** （赛跑、比赛等中）以喝彩声鼓励，为（某人）加油

His shots were very precise, and the crowd cheered him on with rounds and rounds of applause.
他的投篮非常准确，观众用一轮又一轮的掌声为他加油。

❻ **cheer (sb) up** （使）变得更高兴，振奋起来

Oh, come on—cheer up! 噢，得了，高兴起来吧！

Give Mary a call; she needs cheering up.
给玛丽打个电话，她需要人安慰。

❼ **cheers** （祝酒语）干杯，干

▶**cheerful** [ˈtʃɪəfl] adj. 快乐的；令人快乐的
『cheer快乐+ ful充满…的→充满快乐的→快乐的』

❶ 快乐的；高兴的

happy, and showing it by the way that you behave

They are both very cheerful in spite of their colds.
他们俩虽然感冒了，可都兴高采烈的。

❷ 令人愉快的，令人开心的

The nursery is bright and cheerful, with plenty of toys.
托儿所明亮宜人，还有许多玩具。

6. harm [hɑːm] n. & v. 伤害；损害

❶ **mean no harm** 没有什么恶意

He may look fierce, but he means no harm.
他可能看上去很凶，但并无恶意。

❷ **do harm to sb | do sb harm** 对某人有害处

The scandal did his career a lot of harm.
这件丑闻给他的事业造成了很大的危害。

The court case will do serious harm to my business.
这起诉讼案件将严重损害我的生意。

小贴士 **do good to sb | do sb good** 对某人有好处

The outing will do me good. 这次远足对我会有所助益。

It will do us a lot of good to take part in more social activities.
多参加一些社会活动对我们大有好处。

Sports and games do a lot of good to our health.

体育运动对我们的健康有很大好处。

❸ **there is no harm in (sb's) doing sth**
it does no harm (for sb) to do sth
it wouldn't do sb any harm (to do sth)
做某事没有什么坏处；做某事也无妨

He may say no, but there's no harm in asking.
他可能拒绝，但问一问也无妨。

It does no harm to ask. 问一问也无妨。

There's no harm in leaving a little earlier. 不妨早点动身。

It wouldn't do you any harm to smarten yourself up.
你不妨打扮一下。

小贴士 **it won't hurt to do sth**
it never hurts to do sth
做某事也无妨

It won't hurt to wait a bit longer. 再等一会儿没关系。

❹ **someone or something will come to no harm**
no harm will come to them
不会受损害；不会受到伤害

There is always a lifeguard to ensure that no one comes to any harm. 总是有一个救生员在场以确保无人受到伤害。

❺ **in harm's way** 处于危险中
out of harm's way 没有危险

These men were never told how they'd been put in harm's way. 从来没人告诉这些人他们是如何被置于险境的。

❻ **there is no harm done** 没有产生危害

He spilled wine on the carpet but there was no harm done.
他把酒洒在地毯上,但没有造成损害。

❼ [VN] 伤害；损害

He would never harm anyone. 他永远不会伤害任何人。

▶**harmful** [ˈhɑːmfl] adj. 有害的；（尤指）有损健康的
『harm危害+ ful充满…的→充满危害的→有害的』

be harmful to sb/sth 对…有害

Fruit juices can be harmful to children's teeth.
果汁可能损坏儿童的牙齿。

▶**harmless** [ˈhɑːmləs] adj. 无害的
『harm危害+less无…的→无危害的→无害的』

be harmless to sb/sth 对…无害

This pesticide is harmless to people. 这种农药对人体无害。

7. use [juːs] n. 用处

▶**useful** [ˈjuːsfl] adj. 有用的
『use用处+ ful充满…的→充满用处的→有用的』

▶**useless** [ˈjuːsləs] adj. 无用的
『use用处+less无…的→无用处的→无用的』

~ (to do sth) | ~ (doing sth)

He knew it was useless to protest. 他知道抗议是徒劳的。

It's useless worrying about it. 为这事担心无济于事。

8. regard [rɪˈgɑːd] n. 重视，关注 vt. 看待

❶ [VN] （尤指以某种方式）注视，凝视，看

He regarded us suspiciously. 他以怀疑的眼光看着我们。

❷ [VN] ~ sb/sth (with sth) | ~ sb/sth as sth
看待；把…视为

Capital punishment was regarded as inhuman and immoral.
死刑过去被认为是非人道且不道德的。

I regard his behavior with suspicion.
我对他的行为感到怀疑。

词义辨析 <P361第3> **认为，看作 consider, regard, view**

❸ [U] ~ to/for sb/sth（formal）注意；关注；关心

He was driving without regard to speed limits.

他开着车，根本不理会速度限制。

Social services should pay proper regard to the needs of inner-city areas.

社会服务机构应该对市中心贫民区的需要给予应有的关注。

❹ [U] ~ (for sb/sth) (formal) 尊重；尊敬；敬佩

I had great regard for his abilities. 我非常敬佩他的能力。

❺ regards [pl.]（用于信函结尾或转达问候）致意，问候

With kind regards, Yours… 谨此致意，…敬上

Give your brother my regards when you see him.

看到你哥哥时，代我向他问好。

❻ **in/with regard to sb/sth** 关于，至于

The company's position with regard to overtime is made clear in their contracts.

公司关于加班的立场在合同中有明确说明。

In regard to your request for information, I regret to inform you that I am unable to help you.

关于你需要情报的事，我遗憾地告诉你我没法帮助你。

❼ **in this/that regard** (formal) 在这方面；在这一点上

I have nothing further to say in this regard.

在这方面，我没什么要说的了。

▶ **regardless** [rɪˈɡɑːdləs] adv. 不顾地，不理会地

『regard重视，关注+less无…的→不重视→不顾地』

❶ adv. 不顾地，不理会地

Despite her recent surgery she has been carrying on regardless.

尽管最近做了手术，她还是不顾一切地进行下去。

❷ regardless of 不管，不顾

He went to the rescue of a drowning child regardless of his personal safety.

他为了抢救落水儿童，把个人安危置之度外。

▶ **regarding** [rɪˈɡɑːdɪŋ] prep. 关于

She has said nothing regarding your request.

关于你的要求，她什么也没说。

Call me if you have any problems regarding your work.

你如果还有什么工作方面的问题就给我打电话。

小贴士 下面表示"关于，至于"的介词或介词短语，意思是相同的。

with/in regard to

with respect to （in respect to是错误的, in respect of虽然词典中有，也是正确的，但使用不多）

in/with reference to

regarding, concerning

② **-ful 构成名词，表示"量"**

1. **handful** [ˈhændfʊl] n. 一把（的量）；少数人（或物）

『hand手+ful量→一把（的量）』

2. **mouthful** [ˈmaʊθfʊl] n. 一口（的量）；又长又拗口的词（或短语）

『mouth口+ful量→一口（的量）』

She took a mouthful of water. 她喝了一大口水。

It's called the Pan-Caribbean Disaster Preparedness and Prevention Project, which is quite a mouthful.

它被称为泛加勒比豆备灾防灾项目，名称相当冗长拗口。

3. **spoonful** [ˈspuːnfʊl] n. 一勺（的量）

『spoon匙+ful量→一勺(的量)』

后缀35. -fy 构成动词，表示"使…化，使…变得"，其名词形式为-fication

1. **simplify** [ˈsɪmplɪfaɪ] vt. 简化

『simple简单的（去e加i）+fy使…变得→使变得简单』

More needs to be done to simplify the process of registering to vote. 需要进一步简化投票注册程序。

▶ **simplification** [ˌsɪmplɪfɪˈkeɪʃn] n. 简单化

2. **classify** [ˈklæsɪfaɪ] vt. 分类，归类

『class类别（加i）+fy使…化→使类别化→分类』

The books in the library are classified according to subject.

图书馆的书按学科分类。

▶ **classified** [ˈklæsɪfaɪd] adj.（信息）机密的，保密的

He has a security clearance that allows him access to classified information.

他获得了安全许可，可以接触机密信息。

▶ **classification** [ˌklæsɪfɪˈkeɪʃn] n. 分类，归类

▶ **classical** [ˈklæsɪkl] adj. 古典的；古文的；典型的

❶ adj.（音乐）古典的

He plays classical music, as well as pop and jazz.

他演奏流行音乐和爵士乐，同时也演奏古典音乐。

❷ adj. 和古希腊与古罗马文化相关的

classical studies

古希腊与古罗马文化研究

a classical scholar (= an expert in Latin and Greek)

（研究拉丁文与希腊文的）古典学者

❸ adj. 古文的；文言文的

❹ adj. 典型的（also classic）

▶ **classic** [ˈklæsɪk] adj. 经典的；典型的；典雅的 n. 文学经典；经典

❶ adj.（电影、著作、音乐）经典的；最优秀的

the classic children's film *Huckleberry Finn*

经典儿童电影《哈克贝利·费恩（历险记）》

❷ [C] 文学经典，名著

A classic is a book which is well-known and considered to be of a high literary standard. You can refer to such books generally as the classics .

As I grow older, I like to reread the classics regularly.

随着年龄渐长，我喜欢经常重读经典著作。

❸ adj. 典型的（also classical）

She displayed the classic symptoms of depression.

她显现出了忧郁症的典型症状。

❹ [C] 典范

a thing that is an excellent example of its kind

That match was a classic. 那场比赛堪称经典。

❺ adj.（风格或设计）典雅的，古朴的；传统的

elegant, but simple and traditional in style or design; not affected by changes in fashion

classic design 古朴典雅的设计

3. **satisfy** [ˈsætɪsfaɪ] vt. 满足

『satis饱，满+fy使…的→使饱的→使满足』

❶ [VN] 使满意

The proposed plan will not satisfy everyone.
拟议中的计划不会让所有人都满意。

❷ [VN] 满足（要求、需要等）

The food wasn't enough to satisfy his hunger.
这食物不足以让他解饿。

She failed to satisfy all the requirements for entry to the college. 她没有达到进入那所学院的全部要求。

▶**satisfied** [ˈsætɪsfaɪd] adj. 感到满意的

be satisfied with 对…感到满意

We are not satisfied with these results.
我们对这些结果并不满意。

▶**satisfying** [ˈsætɪsfaɪɪŋ] adj. 令人满意的

giving pleasure because it provides sth you need or want

It's satisfying to play a game really well.
一种游戏玩得特别好是一桩惬意的事。

We will provide qualified products and satisfying service for you. 我们将竭诚为您提供最优异的产品和最满意的服务。

▶**satisfactory** [ˌsætɪsˈfæktəri] adj. （因符合要求而）令人满意的

I never got a satisfactory answer.
我从未得到令我满意的答复。

What you have done is far from satisfactory.
你做得很不到位。

Neither solution seemed satisfactory.
两个解决方案似乎都不合适。

▶**satisfaction** [ˌsætɪsˈfækʃn] n. 满足；满意

She looked back on her career with great satisfaction.
回顾自己的事业，她深感欣慰。

She didn't want to give him the satisfaction of seeing her cry.
她不愿当着他的面哭，让他幸灾乐祸。

to sb's satisfaction 使某人满意

The affair was settled to the complete satisfaction of the client. 问题解决了，客户十分满意。

To my satisfaction, we have settled everything in connection with this transaction.
我们已谈妥了这笔交易的所有事项，我感到很满意。

4. purify [ˈpjʊərɪfaɪ] vt. 使（某物）洁净，净化
『pure纯净的+fy使…化→使变得纯净→净化』

One tablet will purify a litre of water.
一丸即可净化一升水。

▶**pure** [pjʊə(r)] adj. 纯的；纯净的；纯粹的

❶ [usually before noun] 纯的

not mixed with anything else; with nothing added

These shirts are 100% pure cotton.
这些衬衫是百分之百的纯棉。

One movie is classified as pure art, the other as entertainment.
一部电影被列为纯艺术片，另一部被列为娱乐片。

❷ 干净的，不含有害物质的

a bottle of pure water 一瓶纯净水

The air was sweet and pure. 空气清新而纯净。

❸ 完全的，纯粹的

They met by pure chance. 他们相遇纯属偶然。

▶**purification** [ˌpjʊərɪfɪˈkeɪʃn] n. 净化

a water purification plant 水净化工厂

5. qualify [ˈkwɒlɪfaɪ] v. （使）有资格

『quality品质（去ty）+fy使→使具有某种要求的品质→使有资格』

❶ ~ sb (for sth) 使具备资格

This training course will qualify you for a better job.
本培训课程将使你能胜任更好的工作。

Paying a fee doesn't automatically qualify you for membership. 交纳会费并不能使你自动成为会员。

❷ [V] ~ (as sth) 合格，取得资格

He qualified as a doctor last year.
他去年获得了医生的资格。

▶**qualified** [ˈkwɒlɪfaɪd] adj. 合格的

be qualified for sth | be qualified to do sth 有资格做某事

She's extremely well qualified for the job.
她完全符合担任这项工作的条件。

I don't know much about it, so I don't feel qualified to comment. 关于此事我所知不多，所以觉得没资格评论。

▶**qualification** [ˌkwɒlɪfɪˈkeɪʃn] n. 资格；资历

❶ [C, usually pl.] (BrE) （通过考试或学习课程取得的）资格；学历

He left school with no formal qualifications.
他离开学校没有获得正式学历。

At the end of the course, you will have all the qualifications you need to get a job as a First Officer in a commercial jet airliner.
到课程结束的时候，你将获得成为一个商用喷气式飞机副驾驶所必须具有的一切证书。

❷ [C] （经验、技能等）资格；资历

Previous teaching experience is a necessary qualification for this job. 教学经验是担任这项工作的必备条件。

These young worker-technicians have all the qualifications we can hope for.
这些年轻的工人技术员具备一切我们期望具备的条件。

❸ [U] 获得资格，达到标准

Nurses in training should be given a guarantee of employment following qualification.
接受培训的护士取得资格后应有工作保障。

▶**quality** [ˈkwɒləti] n. 质量，品质

▶**qualitative** [ˈkwɒlɪtətɪv] adj. 质量的，性质的

There are qualitative differences between the two products.
这两种产品存在着质的差别。

6. quantify [ˈkwɒntɪfaɪ] vt. 以数量表达，量化
『quantity量（去ty）+fy使→使…量化→量化』

The risks to health are impossible to quantify.
健康的风险是无法用数量表示的。

▶**quantification** [ˌkwɒntɪfɪˈkeɪʃn] n. 量化

My grades were a quantification of my unhappiness.
从我的成绩中可以看出我的苦恼。

▶**quantity** [ˈkwɒntəti] n. 量，数量

The police found a quantity of drugs at his home.
警察在他家发现了大量毒品。

▶**quantitative** [ˈkwɒntɪtətɪv] adj. 数量上的

There is no difference between the two in quantitative terms.
两者在数量上毫无差别。

7. identify [aɪˈdentɪfaɪ] vt. 认出；确认

『identity身份（去ty）+fy使→使…的身份清楚→认出，确认』

❶ [VN] ~ sb/sth (as sb/sth) 确认；认出

The bodies were identified as those of two suspected drug dealers. 那两具尸体被辨认出原是两名贩毒嫌疑人。

She was able to identify her attacker.
她认出了袭击她的人。

❷ [VN] 发现，确认

Scientists claim to have identified natural substances with cancer-combating properties.
科学家们声称已经发现自然界的某些物质具有抗癌特性。

They are trying to identify what is wrong with the present system. 他们正试图弄清现行制度的弊端所在。

❸ [VN] ~ sb/sth (as sb/sth) 是…的标志，显示出

In many cases, the clothes people wear identify them as belonging to a particular social class.
很多情况下，人们的穿着显示出他们特定的社会阶层。

❹ identify with sb 与某人产生共鸣，认同，理解

She would only play a role if she could identify with the character. 她只愿意扮演她能认同的角色。

❺ identify sth with sth 认为某事物等同于某事物

You should not identify wealth with happiness.
你不应该认为财富等同于幸福。

She hates playing the sweet, passive women that audiences identify her with.
她讨厌扮演那些漂亮可爱、消极被动的女人，观众们已把她定型为这类角色。

▶ **identification** [aɪˌdentɪfɪˈkeɪʃn] n. 鉴定；确定

❶ [U, C] 鉴定；辨认

the process of showing, proving or recognizing who or what sb/sth is

The identification of the crash victims was a long and difficult task.
鉴别坠机意外伤亡者的工作费时而且困难重重。

Each product has a number for easy identification.
每件产品都有号码以便于识别。

❷ [U] 确认，确定

Early identification of a disease can prevent death and illness.
病症的及早诊断可避免死亡与病痛。

❸ [U] 身份证明

The woman who was on passport control asked me if I had any further identification.
检查护照的女士问我是否有进一步的身份证明。

小贴士 身份证 ID card （abbr. identification card）

▶ **identity** [aɪˈdentəti] n. 身份；特征

『ident相同+ity表名词→（与某人某物特征）完全相同的人或物→身份』

❶ [C, U] (abbr. ID) 身份；本身；本体
The police are trying to discover the identity of the killer.
警方正努力调查杀人凶手的身份。

Do you have any proof of identity? 你有身份证明吗？

❷ [C, U] 特征
the characteristics, feelings or beliefs that distinguish people from others

a sense of national/cultural/personal/group identity
民族/文化/个人/群体认同感

After years of performing, he felt that in some ways he had

lost his identity.
经过几年的演出，他觉得在某些方面失去了他的个性特征。

a plan to strengthen the corporate identity of the company
加强公司企业形象的计划

▶ **identical** [aɪˈdentɪkl] adj. 完全相同的
『ident相同+ical…的→相同的』

~ (to/with sb/sth)

Her dress is almost identical to mine.
她的连衣裙和我的几乎一模一样。

The two pictures are similar, although not identical.
这两幅图很相似，虽然不完全相同。

8. **horrify** [ˈhɒrɪfaɪ] vt. 使震惊，使感到恐怖
『horr颤抖；害怕+i+fy使…变得→使震惊』

[VN] The whole country was horrified by the killings.
全国都对这些凶杀案感到大为震惊。

[VN to inf] It horrified her to think that he had killed someone. 一想到他杀过人，她就感到毛骨悚然。

9. **fortify** [ˈfɔːtɪfaɪ] vt. 加强，增强
『fort强壮，牢固；堡垒+i+fy使…变得→使变得牢固→加强』

The town was heavily fortified. 这个城镇加强了防御。

Her position was fortified by election successes and economic recovery.
她的地位因选举成功和经济复苏而得到加强。

10. **justify** [ˈdʒʌstɪfaɪ] v. 证明（决定、行为或想法）正当 〈P199〉
『just正确+i+fy使…→使…正确→证明』

11. **clarify** [ˈklærəfaɪ] vt. 使清楚；澄清 〈P135〉
『clear清楚的（去e加i）+fy使…变得→使变得清楚』

12. **diversify** [daɪˈvɜːsɪfaɪ] v. （使）多样化 〈P351〉
『diverse多样的（去e加i）+fy使…化→使多样化』

13. **signify** [ˈsɪɡnɪfaɪ] v. 表示，表明 〈P299〉
『sign标志+i+fy使…→使成为…的标志』

后缀36. -hood 构成名词，表示"年纪；身份；状态"

① -hood表示"年纪，时期；身份"

1. **boyhood** [ˈbɔɪhʊd] n. 童年；男孩时代
『boy男孩+hood时期→童年』

2. **childhood** [ˈtʃaɪldhʊd] n. 童年，儿童时代
『child孩子+hood时期→儿童时期』

3. **manhood** [ˈmænhʊd] n. 成年；成年时期；男子气概
『man男子；男子汉+hood时期；性质→成年；男子气概』

Adolescence is the transition period between childhood and manhood. 青春期是儿童和成人阶段的过渡时期。

I believed that manhood required that I stand up to him, even if it meant fists.
我相信，男人气概要求我勇敢面对他，即使这意味着打架。

② -hood表示"性质，状态"

1. **neighbourhood** [ˈneɪbəhʊd] n. 地区；临近地区，临近街坊
『neighbour临近+hood表性质→临近地区，临近地区的人』

❶ （城镇中的）居住区，地段，地区
A neighbourhood is one of the parts of a town where people live.

She grew up in a quiet neighborhood of Boston.
她在波士顿一个安静的地方长大。

❷ the neighbourhood 周边地区；周边居民

the area around you or around a particular place, or the people who live there

Be quiet! You'll wake up the whole neighbourhood!
安静点！你会吵醒整个街区的！

Is there a good Chinese restaurant in the neighbourhood?
这附近有好的中国餐馆吗？

2. likelihood [ˈlaɪklihʊd] n. 可能，可能性
『likely可能的（变y为i）+hood表性质→可能性』

There is very little likelihood of that happening.
几乎没有发生那种事情的可能。

In all likelihood (= very probably) the meeting will be cancelled. 这次会议十有八九要被取消。

3. livelihood [ˈlaɪvlihʊd] n. 生计，谋生之道
『lively生机勃勃的（变y为i）+hood表状态→（使保持）生机勃勃的状态（的东西）→生计』

[C, usually sing., U] 赚钱谋生的手段；生计
a means of earning money in order to live

Communities on the island depended on whaling for their livelihood. 岛上的居民靠捕鲸为生。

As a result of this conflict he lost both his home and his means of livelihood.
这场冲突使他同时失去了住所和生计来源。

4. brotherhood [ˈbrʌðəhʊd] n. 兄弟情谊；兄弟会
『brother兄弟+hood表性质→兄弟情谊』

❶ [U] 兄弟情谊，手足之情
They live and work together in complete equality and brotherhood.
他们完全平等和兄弟般地在一起生活和工作。

❷ [C + sing./pl. v.] 宗教（或政治等）组织，兄弟会

后缀37. -ia 构成名词，表示"病"，还可表示"总称；状态"

1. dyslexia [dɪsˈleksɪə] n. 阅读障碍
『dys困难的+lex词+ia某种病→读词困难的病→阅读障碍』

[U] a slight disorder of the brain that causes difficulty in reading and spelling, for example, but does not affect intelligence

Until comparatively recently, dyslexia remained largely unrecognised.
诵读困难症一直没有引起太多的注意，这种情形直到最近才有所改观。

▶dyslexic [dɪsˈleksɪk] adj. 阅读障碍的

He was diagnosed as severely dyslexic but extraordinarily bright. 他被诊断患有严重的阅读困难症,但是却绝顶聪明。

2. hysteria [hɪˈstɪərɪə] n. 歇斯底里；癔症
『hyster子宫+ia某种病→古人认为妇女患歇斯底里症是子宫机能失调所致→歇斯底里症』

a state of extreme excitement, fear or anger in which a person, or a group of people, loses control of their emotions and starts to cry, laugh, etc.

There was mass hysteria when the band came on stage.
乐队登台时观众一片疯狂。

By now, she was screaming, completely overcome with hysteria. 现在她正在尖叫，完全处于癔症发作状态。

▶hysterical [hɪˈsterɪkl] adj. 歇斯底里的,情绪狂暴不可抑制的

He became almost hysterical when I told him.
我告诉他时，他几乎要发疯了。

▶hysteric [hɪˈsterɪk] n. 癔症患者 adj. 癔症的；歇斯底里的

3. anemia [əˈniːmɪə] n. 贫血；贫血症
『a无+nem血+ia某种病→贫血症』

4. pneumonia [njuːˈməʊnɪə] n. 肺炎
『pneumon肺+ia某种病→肺炎』

She nearly died of pneumonia. 她差点儿死于肺炎。

5. utopia [juːˈtəʊpɪə] n. 乌托邦，空想的完美境界
『u无+top地方+ia表名词→现实中没有的地方→乌托邦』

6. myopia [maɪˈəʊpɪə] n. 近视 <P238>
『my近+op视力+ia某种病→近视』

7. phobia [ˈfəʊbɪə] n. 恐怖；（构成名词）对…的恐惧症 <P253>
『phobe恐惧症患者（去e）+ia某种病→恐惧症』

8. hypothermia [ˌhaɪpəˈθɜːmɪə] n. 体温过低 <P333>
『hypo低+therm热（引申为温度）+ia表疾病→体温低于（正常值的）病→体温过低』

9. insomnia [ɪnˈsɒmnɪə] n. 失眠（症）<P306>
『in不+somn睡眠+ia某种病→睡不着觉的病→失眠症』

10. euphoria [juːˈfɔːrɪə] n. 狂喜，兴高采烈 <P16>
『eu好的+phor带来+ia表名词→带来好的→狂喜』

11. militia [məˈlɪʃə] n. 民兵组织；国民卫队 <P221>
『milit士兵+ia总称→（像）士兵（一样作战的）人→民兵』

12. insignia [ɪnˈsɪɡnɪə] n.（常指军队的)徽章，标志 <P300>
『in里面+sign标志+ia表名词→里面是（身份或组织的）标志→徽章，标志』

后缀38. -ic（-tic, -atic, -etic）构成形容词，表示性质；还可构成名词，表示"人；学科；药"
单词重音一般在其前一个音节上

① 构成形容词，表示"有…性质的，属于…的，具有…的"

a. -ic 表示"有…性质的，属于…的，具有…的"

1. idiotic [ˌɪdiˈɒtɪk] adj. 十分愚蠢的，白痴般的
『idiot白痴，傻瓜+ic有…性质的→白痴般的』

The child's idiotic deeds caused his family much trouble.
那小孩愚蠢的行为给家庭带来许多麻烦。

2. athletic [æθˈletɪk] adj. 身体健壮的；运动的
『athlete运动员（去e）+ic有…性质的→健壮的』

❶ adj. 健壮的
physically strong, fit and active
He can play any sport. He's naturally athletic.
他可以参加任何运动。他天生健壮。

❷ adj. (BrE) 体育运动的
Most athletic activities are about individual effort.
大多数体育项目是靠个人的拼搏。

▶athlete [ˈæθliːt] n. 运动员

▶athletics [æθˈletɪks] n. (BrE) 田径运动（NAmE track

and field）；(NAmE) 体育运动
『athlete运动员（去e）+ics…术→体育运动』

As the modern Olympics grew in stature, so too did athletics.
随着现代奥林匹克运动会声名远扬，田径运动也越来越受关注。

students involved in all forms of college athletics
参加各种大学体育运动的学生

3. gigantic [dʒaɪˈgæntɪk] adj. 巨大的，庞大的
『giant巨人，巨大（在gi后加g）+ic有…性质的→巨大的』

If you describe something as gigantic, you are emphasizing that it is extremely large in size, amount, or degree.

A gigantic task of national reconstruction awaits us.
重建国家的艰巨任务等待着我们去完成。

They made a gigantic demonstration against the government.
他们举行了一次声势浩大的反政府示威。

▶ **giant** [ˈdʒaɪənt] n. 巨人；伟人　adj. 巨大的

❶ [C]（尤指古代传说中虚构的）巨人

❷ [C] 伟人，卓越人物，大师；才华超群的人

He was without question one of the giants of Japanese literature. 毋庸置疑，他是日本的文学巨匠之一。

❸ [C] 大公司；大企业；大国

Japanese electronics giant Sony 日本电子业巨头索尼（公司）

❹ adj. 巨大的；特大的；极其重要的

Something that is described as giant is much larger or more important than most others of its kind.

Fewer than a thousand giant pandas still live in the wild.
只有不到1000只大熊猫仍然在野外生活。

He is a manager of a giant electronics company.
他是一家特大型电子产品公司的经理。

4. academic [ˌækəˈdemɪk] adj. 学业的，学术的
『academy专科学校（去y）+ic有…性质的→学业的』

Academic is used to describe things that relate to the work done in schools, colleges, and universities, especially work which involves studying and reasoning rather than practical or technical skills.

I was only average academically, but was good at sports.
我学习成绩平平，但体育方面很出色。

This college has a good academic reputation.
这所大学有良好的学术声誉。

▶ **academy** [əˈkædəmi] n. 专科学校；学会

❶ 专科院校，学院

Academy is sometimes used in the names of schools and colleges, especially those specializing in particular subjects or skills, or private high schools in the United States.

The website of the military academy has opened a military forum, where students can talk about military science.
军校网站上开设了军事论坛，让学生们自由讨论军事兵法。

❷（艺术、文学、科学等的）研究院，学会

a type of official organization which aims to encourage and develop art, literature, science, etc.

It is the custom of this academy to make an annual award for outstanding researchers in chemistry.
每年向杰出的化学研究人员发奖是这个学会的惯例。

The Royal Swedish Academy of Sciences announced the

winners this week. 瑞典皇家科学院这周宣布了获奖者名单。

The film won four Academy Awards for its Sound, Visual Effects, Makeup, and Sound Effects Editing.
影片赢得了音响、视觉效果、化妆和音效剪辑4项奥斯卡大奖。

小贴士 美国电影艺术与科学学院奖（Academy Awards），别称奥斯卡奖（Oscars），是由美国电影艺术与科学学院主办的电影类奖项，创办于1929年。该奖项是美国历史最为悠久、最具权威性和专业性的电影类奖项，也是全世界最具影响力的电影类奖项。

5. scenic [ˈsiːnɪk] adj. 风景优美的；舞台的
『scene风景，场景（去e）+ic有…性质的→风景优美的；舞台的』

❶ [usually before noun] 风景优美的
having beautiful natural scenery
They took the scenic route back to the hotel.
他们选了一条景色优美的路线回旅馆。
This is an extremely scenic part of America.
这是美国风景非常秀丽的一个地区。

❷ [only before noun] 舞台布景的
scenic designs 布景设计

b. -tic 表示"有…性质的，属于…的，具有…的"

1. romantic [rəʊˈmæntɪk] adj. 浪漫的；爱情的
『romance浪漫；爱情（去ce）+tic有…性质的→浪漫的；爱情的』

2. dramatic [drəˈmætɪk] adj. 戏剧性的；巨大的
『drama戏剧+tic有…性质的→戏剧性的；巨大的』

❶（of a change, an event, etc. 变化、事情等）突然的；巨大的；令人吃惊的
sudden, very great and often surprising
The announcement had a dramatic effect on house prices.
这项公告对房屋价格产生了巨大的影响。
a dramatic increase/fall/change/improvement
暴涨/暴跌/巨变/巨大的改进

❷ 激动人心的；引人注目的；给人印象深刻的
exciting and impressive
They watched dramatic pictures of the police raid on TV.
他们在电视上看到了警察突击搜捕的激动人心的画面。

❸ 戏剧般的，夸张做作的
He flung out his arms in a dramatic gesture.
他夸张地张开双臂。

❹ 戏剧的；有关戏剧的
a local dramatic society 地方戏剧协会

3. kinetic [kɪˈnetɪk] adj. 运动的，运动引起的
『kine运动+tic属于…的→运动的；动力学的』

[usually before noun] (technical) 运动的；运动引起的
of or produced by movement
I add kinetic energy, and now I have a new speed which is higher. 我增加了动能，得到了一个更快的速度。

c. -etic表示"有…性质的，属于…的，具有…的"

1. energetic [ˌenəˈdʒetɪk] adj. 精力充沛的，充满活力的
『energy精力，能量（去y）+etic有…性质的→有精力的』

2. apologetic [əˌpɒləˈdʒetɪk] adj. 道歉的，愧疚的
『apology道歉，歉意（去y）+etic有…性质的→道歉的』

feeling or showing that you are sorry for doing sth wrong or for causing a problem
"Sorry," she said, with an apologetic smile.
"对不起，"她说，歉然一笑。
They were very apologetic about the trouble they'd caused.
他们对所惹的麻烦深感愧疚。

3. theoretic [ˌθɪəˈretɪk] adj. 理论上的
『theory理论（去y）+etic有…性质的→理论上的』

4. sympathetic [ˌsɪmpəˈθetɪk] adj. 同情的；赞同的
〈P245〉
『sympathy同情（去y）+etic有…性质的→同情的』

d. -atic 表示"有…性质的；…有性质的人"

1. fanatic [fəˈnætɪk] n. 狂热者，入迷者
『fan粉丝，入迷者+atic有…性质的人→狂热者』

❶（对某一活动、运动、生活方式）入迷者，痴狂者
Both Rod and Phil are football fanatics.
罗德和菲尔都是足球迷。

❷（政治、宗教等的）狂热分子
I am not a religious fanatic but I am a Christian.
我不是宗教狂热分子，但我是基督徒。

2. problematic [ˌprɒbləˈmætɪk] adj. 有问题的；有困难的
『problem问题+atic有…性质的→有问题的；有困难的』

Something that is problematic involves problems and difficulties.
Some places are more problematic than others for women traveling alone.
对那些独自旅行的女性来说，在有些地方遇到的问题会比其他地方更多。

3. systematic [ˌsɪstəˈmætɪk] adj. 系统的，有条理的
『system系统+atic有…性质的→系统的』

Something that is done in a systematic way is done according to a fixed plan, in a thorough and efficient way.
They went about their business in a systematic way.
他们按部就班地做生意。

② 构成名词，表示"人"

1. mimic [ˈmɪmɪk] vt. 模仿 n. 会模仿的人
『mim模仿+ic人→模仿者』

❶ 模仿（人的言行举止）；（尤指）做滑稽模仿
[VN] She's always mimicking the teachers.
她总喜欢模仿老师的言谈举止。

❷（外表或行为举止）像，似
[VN] The robot was programmed to mimic a series of human movements. 机器人可按程序设计模仿人的各种动作。

❸ [C] 会模仿的人（或动物）

2. sceptic [ˈskeptɪk] n. 惯持怀疑态度的人
（NAmE skeptic）
『scept怀疑+ic人→怀疑论者』

But he now has to convince sceptics that he has a serious plan.

但是他现在得让怀疑者相信他有一个严肃的计划。

▶**sceptical** [ˈskeptɪkl] adj. 怀疑的
（NAmE skeptical）

~ (about/of sth) 怀疑的
I am sceptical about his chances of winning.
我怀疑他取胜的可能性。
The public remain sceptical of these claims.
公众对这些说法仍持怀疑态度。

3. mechanic [məˈkænɪk] n.（尤指修理汽车的）机修工
『mechan(=machine)机器+ic人→修机器的人→机修工』

4. stoic [ˈstəʊɪk] n. 斯多葛派人（对痛苦或困难能默默承受或泰然处之）adj. 坚忍的，苦修的
『源自"斯多葛派"（Stoics）』

5. critic [ˈkrɪtɪk] n. 评论家；批评者〈P142〉
『crit判断+ic人→判断（别人的是非）的人→评论家』

③ 构成名词，表示"…学/术"

1. arithmetic [əˈrɪθmətɪk] n. 算术；算术运算
『arithm计算，数学+etic…术→算术』

2. logic n. 逻辑（学）
『log说话+ic…学→说话的学问→逻辑学』

▶**logical** [ˈlɒdʒɪkl] adj. 符合逻辑的；合乎情理的
Computer programming needs someone with a logical mind.
计算机编程需要擅长逻辑思维的人。
It was a logical conclusion from the child's point of view.
从小孩的观点来看这是个合乎情理的结论。

3. rhetoric [ˈretərɪk] n. 修辞学
『rhetor修辞学大师+ic…学→修辞学』

❶ [U] 修辞，修辞学

❷ [U] 花言巧语，华丽的辞藻，浮夸之词
speech or writing that is intended to influence people, but that is not completely honest or sincere
We'll get nothing from him but rhetoric and grief.
除了夸夸其谈和伤心难过之外，我们从他那什么也得不到。

▶**rhetorical** [rɪˈtɒrɪkl] adj. 反问的；修辞的；辞藻华丽的
"Don't you care what I do?" he asked, but it was a rhetorical question.
"我做什么，难道你不关心吗？"他问道，可那是个反问。
The present paper intends to make a rhetorical analysis of advertising texts.
本文试从西方修辞学的角度对广告文本进行分析。
Suddenly, the narrator speaks in his most rhetorically elevated mode.
突然，解说员开始用高昂煽情的语调解说起来。

④ 构成名词，表示"药"

1. anesthetic [ˌænɪsˈθetɪk] n. 麻醉药
『an无+esthet感觉+ic某种药→使人无感觉的药→麻醉药』

2. antibiotic [ˌæntibaɪˈɒtɪk] n. 抗生素 adj. 抗生素的
〈P119〉
『anti抗+bio生命；生物+tic有…性质的→抗生素的』

后缀39. -ic(al)构成形容词，表示"有…性质的；有关…的"，单词重音一般在其前一个音节上

1. botanical [bəˈtænɪkl] adj. 植物学的

『botany植物学（变y为i）+cal有关…的→有关植物学的→植物学的』

▶**botany** [ˈbɒtəni] n. 植物学

2. **methodical** [məˈθɒdɪkl] adj. 有条理的，有条不紊的
『method方法+ical有…性质的→（做事）具有"按照一定的方法"的性质→有条理的，有条不紊的』

If you describe someone as methodical, you mean that they do things carefully, thoroughly, and in order.
He always checked every detail in a methodical way.
他总是用有条不紊的方式检查每一个细节。
She's a very methodical person.
她是个很有条理的人。

▶**method** [ˈmeθəd] n. 方法；条理

❶ [C] 方法，办法
a planned way of doing something, especially one that a lot of people know about and use
Neill had considerable influence over modern teaching methods.
尼尔对现代教学方法有很大的影响。
Farmers are being encouraged to return to more traditional methods of farming.农民被鼓励回归更传统的耕作方式。

❷ [U] 条理，有条不紊
the quality of being well planned and organized
There's no method in the way they do their accounts.
他们的账目处理方式没有条理。

3. **typical** [ˈtɪpɪkl] adj. 典型的；有代表性的
『type种类，类型（去e）+ical有…性质的→有种类性质的→典型的』

❶ ~ (of sb/sth) 典型的；有代表性的
having the usual qualities or features of a particular type of person, thing or group
This is a typical example of Roman pottery.
这是一件典型的罗马陶器。
A typical working day for me begins at 7:30.
我的工作日一般在7:30开始。

❷ （表示批评或抱怨）果不其然的，不出所料的
It was typical of her to forget. 她这个人就是爱忘事。

小贴士 -ic和-ical两者，有时在意义上有别，有时则无。下面几组词是有差别的：

4. **economic** [ˌiːkəˈnɒmɪk] adj. 经济的
『econom经济+ic…的→经济的』

The pace of economic growth is picking up.
经济增长的步伐正在加快。
Education is central to a country's economic development.
教育对一个国家的经济发展至关重要。

▶**economical** [ˌiːkəˈnɒmɪkl] adj. 经济实惠的；节俭的

❶ 经济的，实惠的
providing good service or value in relation to the amount of time or money spent
It would be more economical to buy the bigger size.
买尺寸大点的更实惠。
Sometimes expensive drugs or other treatments can be economical in the long run.
有时昂贵的药物或其他治疗方法从长远来看可能是比较划算的。

❷ 节俭的，节约的
He was economical in all areas of his life.
他在生活的各个方面都精打细算。
He has to be economical, because he hasn't much money.
他非得节俭不可，因为他没多少钱。

▶**economy** [ɪˈkɒnəmi] n. 经济；经济体；节省
『eco环境；经济+nomy科学；法则→经济（学）』

❶ [C] 经济体
The United States has been the world's largest economy since 1871. 美国自1871年以来一直是世界上最大的经济体。

❷ [C] 经济；经济情况；经济结构（often the economy）
The economy is in recession. 经济处于衰退之中。
the world economy 世界经济
The Japanese economy grew at an annual rate of more than 10 per cent. 日本经济的年增长率超过10%。

❸ [C, U] 节约；节省；节俭
She writes with a great economy of words (= using only the necessary words). 她写作文字非常简练。

▶**economics** [ˌiːkəˈnɒmɪks] n. 经济学

5. **historic** [hɪˈstɒrɪk] adj. 历史上重要的，具有重大历史意义的
『history历史（去y）+ic有…性质的→具有作为历史（来记载）性质的→具有重大历史意义的』

important in history; likely to be thought of as important at some time in the future
It was an historic day, yet its passing was not marked by the slightest excitement.
那是具有历史意义的一天，但是一天过去了，也没有一丝的兴奋激动。

▶**historical** [hɪˈstɒrɪkl] adj. 历史的，历史上的
『history历史（去y）+ical有关…的→历史上发生的（也可以这样来记：后面的-al使我们想起all，all意为"所有的"，所有的事物和事情都要成为历史）』

Historical usually describes something that is connected with the past or with the study of history, or something that really happened in the past.
I have been doing some historical research.
我一直在进行史学研究。
You must place these events in their historical context.
你必须把这些事件同它们的历史背景联系起来看。

6. **mechanical** [məˈkænɪkl] adj. 机械的，机械学的
『mechan(=machine)机器+ical有关…的→机械的』

▶**mechanic** [məˈkænɪk] n. （尤指修理汽车的）机修工

▶**mechanics** [mɪˈkænɪks] n. 力学，机械学；运作方式
『mechan(=machine)机器+ics…学→机械学』

❶ [U] 力学；机械学
Mechanics is the part of physics that deals with the natural forces that act on moving or stationary objects.

❷ [C] (pl.) （过程、系统、动作等）运作方式；（具体的）方法，技巧
The mechanics of a process, system, or activity are the way in which it works or the way in which it is done.
The exact mechanics of how payment will be made will be decided later. 确切的付款方法以后再决定。

7. **theoretical** [ˌθɪəˈretɪkl] adj. 理论上的
『theory理论（变y为et）+ical…的→理论上的』

The first year provides students with a sound theoretical basis for later study.
第一年为学生以后的学习奠定坚实的理论基础。

后缀40. -ics 表名词，"…学，…术"

1. **physics** [ˈfɪzɪks] n. 物理学
   『phys有形；物质+ics…学→物理学』

2. **mathematics** [ˌmæθəˈmætɪks] n. 数学
   『mathemat(=science)理科+ics…学→数学』
   (also BrE informal) **maths**; (also NAmE informal) **math**
   ►**mathematical** [ˌmæθəˈmætɪkl] adj. 数学的；具有数学能力的
   a mathematical formula 数学公式
   children who display extraordinary mathematical ability
   显示出非凡的数学能力的儿童

3. **economics** [ˌiːkəˈnɒmɪks] n. 经济学
   『econom经济+ics…学→经济学』

4. **electronics** [ɪˌlekˈtrɒnɪks] n. 电子学
   『electron电子+ics…学→电子学』

5. **linguistics** [lɪŋˈgwɪstɪks] n. 语言学 〈P208〉
   『linguist语言学家+ics…学→语言学』

6. **athletics** [æθˈletɪks] n. (BrE) 田径运动（NAmE track and field）；(NAmE) 体育运动 〈P74〉
   『athlete运动员（去e）+ics…术→体育运动』

7. **mechanics** [mɪˈkænɪks] n. 力学，机械学；运作方式 〈P77〉
   『mechan(=machine)机器+ics…学→机械学』

8. **dynamics** [daɪˈnæmɪks] n. 动力学；驱动力 〈P157〉
   『dynam力量+ics…学→研究力量的学科→动力学』

9. **optics** [ˈɒptɪks] n. 光学 〈P238〉
   『opt视力+ics…学→光学』

后缀41. -id 常构成形容词，表示"…的"

1. **pallid** [ˈpælɪd] adj. （尤指因病）苍白的
   『pale苍白的（去e双写l）+id…的→苍白的』

2. **stupid** [ˈstjuːpɪd] adj. 头脑迟钝的，愚蠢的
   『stup笨，麻木+id…的→笨的』

3. **candid** [ˈkændɪd] adj. 坦率的，坦诚的
   『cand白，发光（candle蜡烛）+id…的→光明的→坦率的』

4. **frigid** [ˈfrɪdʒɪd] adj. 寒冷的，严寒的
   『frig冷，寒+id…的→寒冷的』
   A snowstorm hit the West today, bringing with it frigid temperatures. 暴风雪今天袭击了西部地区，导致气温骤降。

5. **staid** [steɪd] adj. 严肃的，古板的
   『sta(=stay)站+id…的→（呆板）站立的→呆板的』
   If you say that someone or something is staid, you mean that they are serious, dull, and rather old-fashioned.
   I always thought of him as a rather staid old gentleman.
   我一直以为他是个相当古板的绅士。

6. **fluid** [ˈfluːɪd] n. 流体 adj. 流畅的；不稳定的 〈P176〉
   『flu流动+id…的→流体』

7. **humid** [ˈhjuːmɪd] adj.（空气或气候）温暖潮湿的 〈P191〉
   『hum湿+id…的→潮湿的』

8. **florid** [ˈflɒrɪd] adj. （人脸）红润的；过分花哨的，过分修饰的 〈P175〉
   『flor花+id…的→（脸像）花一样（红）的；过分花哨的』

9. **valid** [ˈvælɪd] adj. 有效的；合理的 〈P344〉
   『val价值+id…的→有价值的→有效的，合理的』

10. **placid** [ˈplæsɪd] adj. （人或动物）温和的，平静的；（环境）平静的，宁静的，安静的 〈P255〉
    『plac使平静+id…的→安静的』

11. **morbid** [ˈmɔːbɪd] adj. 病态的，不正常的 〈P229〉
    『morb(=mort)死+id有…性质的→（总是想着）死的→病态的（也可谐音记忆"毛病的"→病态的）』

后缀42. -ie，-y 放在称呼或名词后，表昵称

1. **daddy** [ˈdædi] n.（尤作儿语）爸爸
   『dad爸爸（双写d）+y表昵称→爸爸』

2. **mummy** [ˈmʌmi] n.（儿语）妈妈
   『mum妈妈（双写m）+y表昵称→妈妈』

3. **birdie** [ˈbɜːdi] n. （儿语）小鸟
   『bird鸟+ie表昵称→小鸟』

4. **sweetie** [ˈswiːti] n.（用作称呼语）亲爱的；可爱的人
   『sweet亲爱的+ie表昵称→亲爱的』
   He's a real sweetie. 他的确招人喜欢。
   Yes, sweetie. I'm so happy. 当然了，亲爱的。我太高兴了。

5. **Johnnie** [ˈdʒɒni] n. 约翰尼 （John的昵称）
   『John约翰（双写n）+ie表昵称→约翰尼』

6. **Tommy** [ˈtɒmi] n. 汤米
   『Tom汤姆（双写m）+y表昵称→汤米』

后缀43. -ile 构成形容词，表示"易于…的"；构成名词，表示"物体"

① -ile 构成形容词，表示"易于…的"

1. **hostile** [ˈhɒstaɪl] adj. 敌意的；敌对的，不赞成的
   『host敌人+ile易于…的→易于当作敌人对待的→敌意的；敌对的』
   She was openly hostile towards her parents.
   她公然对抗她的父母。
   Their hostile looks show that I am unwelcome.
   他们怀有敌意的表情，显示出我不受欢迎。

2. **senile** [ˈsiːnaɪl] adj. 年老的；老糊涂的
   『sen老+ile易于…的→年老的』
   If old people become senile, they become confused, can no longer remember things, and are unable to look after themselves.
   She is suffering from senile dementia. 她患有老年痴呆症。

3. **agile** [ˈædʒaɪl] adj.（动作）敏捷的；（思维）机敏的 〈P111〉
   『ag做+ile易于…的→（动作）敏捷的；（思维）机敏的』

4. **facile** [ˈfæsaɪl] adj. 轻率做出的 〈P162〉
   『fac做，制作+ile易于…的→容易做的』

5. **versatile** [ˈvɜːsətaɪl] adj. （人）多面手的；（物）多用途的 〈P351〉
   『verse(=turn)转，改变（去e）+at+ile易于…的→改变（用途）容易的→（人）多面手的；（物）多用途的』

6. ductile ['dʌktaɪl] adj. （金属）可延展的 〈P156〉
『duct引导+ile易于…的→（金属）易于引导的→可延展的』

7. fragile 英 ['frædʒaɪl] 美 ['frædʒl] adj. 易碎的，易损的 〈P180〉
『frag破碎+ile易于…的→易破碎的』

8. fertile ['fɜːtaɪl] adj. 肥沃的；能生育的 〈P169〉
『fert(=fer)拿+ile易于…的→（土地）易于带来（收获）的→肥沃的』

9. servile ['sɜːvaɪl] adj. 奴性的，逢迎的 〈P297〉
『serve服务（去e）+ile易于…的→易于为别人服务的→奴性的』

② -ile 构成名词，表示"物体"

1. domicile ['dɒmɪsaɪl] n. （尤指正式或法律意义的）住处，住所 〈P152〉
『dom房屋+ic…的+ile物体→住所』

2. automobile ['ɔːtəməbiːl] n. 汽车 〈P226〉
『auto自己+mob移动+ile物体→自己（能）移动的物体→汽车』

3. projectile [prəˈdʒektaɪl] n. （武器发射的）投射物；枪弹；炮弹 〈P196〉
『pro向前+ject投射+ile物体→向前投射的物体→枪弹，炮弹』

4. missile 英 ['mɪsaɪl] 美 ['mɪsl] n. 导弹；发射物 〈P225〉
『miss(=send)发射+ile物体→发射出去的物体→导弹；发射物』

后缀44. -ine 构成形容词，表示"具有…性质的"；还可构成名词，表示"女人""药物"或抽象名词

① -ine 构成形容词，表示"具有…性质的"

1. canine ['keɪnaɪn] adj. 犬的；似犬的 n. （人或动物的）犬牙
『can犬+ine具有…性质的→犬的』
research into canine diseases 犬类疾病的研究
Canine teeth are for piercing and killing prey, and tearing flesh. 犬齿用来咬穿、咬死猎物，还可以撕肉。

2. crystalline ['krɪstəlaɪn] adj. 晶状的；清澈，晶莹的
『crystal水晶（双写l）+ine具有…性质的→晶状的；清澈的』
crystalline structure/rocks 晶体结构/结晶岩
a huge plain dotted with crystalline lakes
一个遍布着清澈湖泊的辽阔平原

3. elephantine [ˌelɪˈfæntaɪn] adj. 庞大的，笨重的
『elephant大象+ine具有…性质的→庞大的，笨重的』

② -ine 构成名词，表示"人或女人"

1. heroine ['herəʊɪn] n. 女英雄；女主人公；女偶像
『hero英雄；男主人公；男偶像+ine女人→女英雄；女主人公；女偶像』
同音词 heroin ['herəʊɪn] n. 海洛因

2. figurine [ˌfɪgəˈriːn] n. （人、动物的）小雕像
『figure人形，人影（去e）+ine人→小雕塑』
a small statue of a person or an animal used as a decorative object
She bought an exquisite china figurine.

她买了一尊小巧而精致的瓷塑像。

3. libertine ['lɪbətiːn] n. 放荡的男人，好色之徒
『liber自由+t+ine人→放任自由的人→浪荡子』

4. philistine ['fɪlɪstaɪn] n. 对文化艺术无知的人
『philist菲力斯人+ine人→对文化艺术无知的人』
Mr Prescott may be a business pragmatist, but he is not a philistine.
普雷斯科特也许是一个奉行实用主义的商人，但他却不是个俗人。

5. concubine ['kɒŋkjubaɪn] n. （旧时的）情妇；姜 〈P143〉
『con一起+cub躺+ine表女人→躺在一起的女人→情妇』

③ -ine 构成名词，表示"药物"或抽象名词

1. medicine ['medsn] n. 医学；药（尤指药水）
『medic治疗+ine抽象名词→医学』

2. routine [ruːˈtiːn] n. 常规 adj. 常规的
『route路（去e）+ine表抽象名词→常走的路线→常规』

3. famine ['fæmɪn] n. 饥荒
『fam饿+ine表抽象名词』
Thousands of refugees are trapped by war, drought and famine. 成千上万的难民陷于战争、旱灾和饥荒之中。
小贴士 famish ['fæmɪʃ] vt. 使挨饿
famished ['fæmɪʃt] adj. 很饿的

4. discipline ['dɪsəplɪn] n. 纪律；自制力 〈P53〉
『disciple门徒（去e）+ine表抽象名词→门徒要守纪→纪律』

5. doctrine ['dɒktrɪn] n. 教义；主义；学说 〈P152〉
『doctr(=doct)教，观点+ine表抽象名词→（宗教、政治或其他的）观点→教义；主义；学说』

后缀45. -ior 表示"较…的，属于…的"

1. junior ['dʒuːniə(r)] adj. 地位（或职位、级别）较低的
『jun年轻+ior较…的→年轻的→级别低的』
❶ adj. ~ (to sb) 地位（或职位、级别）较低的
I object to being told what to do by someone junior to me.
我反对下级告诉我该怎么做。
She is junior to me. 她职位比我低。
❷ junior high school (美)初级中学
❸ Junior (abbr. Jr) （尤用于美国，置于同名父子中儿子的姓名之后）小
"I have a Dream" is the famous speech of Martin Luther King Jr.
"我有一个梦想"是小马丁·路德·金的著名演说。
Neoconservatism has enormous influence on Regan and Bush Jr Administration in domestic and foreign policy.
新保守主义对里根时期和小布什政府时期的美国政府内政和外交政策有重大影响。
❹ [C] (NAmE) （四年制中学或大学中）三年级（学生）
I spent my junior year in France. 我三年级是在法国念的。

2. senior ['siːniə(r)] adj. 级别（或地位）高的
『sen年老+ior较…的→年老的，级别高的』
❶ adj. ~ (to sb) 级别（或地位）高的
a senior officer/manager/lecturer, etc.
高级军官/高级经理/高级讲师等
He is senior to me. 他的职位比我高。

❷ senior high school （美）高级中学

❸ Senior (abbr. Sr) （父子同名时，加在父亲的名字前）老，大

When George Bush Sr last ran for president in 1992, his eldest son had yet to hold elected office.
当老乔治·布什在1992年最后一次竞选总统时，他的大儿子还没有担任民选职务。

❹ [C] (NAmE) （四年制中学或大学中）四年级（学生）
Yes. I received the departmental scholarship in my senior year. 是的。我在四年级时获得了系级奖学金。

小贴士 大一学生 freshman；大二学生 sophomore ['sɒfəmɔː(r)]；大三学生 junior (student)；大四学生 senior (student)

▶ **seniority** [ˌsiːniˈɒrəti] n. 年长；级别高；资历

He has said he will fire editorial employees without regard to seniority.
他说过不管资历如何，任何编辑人员他都有可能解雇。

3. **inferior** [ɪnˈfɪəriə(r)] adj. 次的，比不上…的
『infer下面+ior较…的，属于…的→低下的，下等的』

❶ adj. ~ (to sb/sth) 次的；比不上…的
Modern music is often considered inferior to that of the past.
现代音乐常被认为不如过去。
to make sb feel inferior 使某人自惭形秽
an inferior officer 下级军官

❷ [C] 级别（或地位）低的人

4. **superior** [suːˈpɪəriə(r)] adj. 级别高的；更好的
『super上面+ior较…的，属于…的→上面的→级别高的』

❶ adj. ~ (to sb) （在级别、重要性或职位上）更高的
my superior officer 我的上级军官

❷ adj. ~ (to sb/sth) （在品质上）更好的；占优势；更胜一筹
This model is technically superior to its competitors.
这一款式在技术上超过了与之竞争的产品。
A few years ago it was virtually impossible to find superior quality coffee in local shops.
几年前在当地商店里几乎买不到优质咖啡。

❸ [C] 上级；上司

小贴士 在表示"比…"时，junior, senior, inferior, superior 这四个词要和to连用，而不是和than连用。

▶ **superiority** [suːˌpɪəriˈɒrəti] n. 优越性；优越感

the superiority of this operating system
这种操作系统的优越性
an air of superiority 优越感

5. **interior** [ɪnˈtɪəriə(r)] n.内部，里面 adj.内部的，里面的
『inter里面+ior较…的，属于…的→内部的』

❶ [C, usually sing.] 内部；里面
the interior of a building/a car 楼房/汽车的内部

❷ the interior [sing.] 内陆；内地
an expedition into the interior of Australia
深入澳大利亚腹地的探险

❸ the Interior [sing.] （国家的）内政，内务
the Department/Minister of the Interior 内政部/内政部长

❹ adj.（建筑物、车辆等）内部的
The interior walls were painted green. 内墙漆成了绿色。

6. **exterior** [ɪkˈstɪəriə(r)] n. 外部，外表 adj. 外部的
『exter外+ior较…的，属于…的→外部的』

❶ [C] （尤指建筑物的）外部，外观
The exterior of the house needs painting.
房子外墙需要油漆。

❷ [sing.] （人的）外貌，外表
Beneath his confident exterior, he was desperately nervous.
他表面上自信，内心极度紧张。

❸ adj. [usually before noun] 外面的；外部的
exterior walls/surfaces 外墙；外层表面

7. **anterior** [ænˈtɪəriə(r)] adj. （身体部位）前部的
『anter(=ante前面)+ior较…的，属于…的→较早的』

There are three knife wounds in the left anterior chest wall.
左前胸壁有三处刀伤。
This story is about people anterior to the flood.
这个故事是关于洪水时期以前的人们的。

8. **posterior** [pɒˈstɪəriə(r)] adj.（身体部位）后部的 n. 臀部，屁股
『post后，后面+er+ior较…的，属于…的→（在时间、次序上）较后的』

It's just that I have a rather sensitive posterior.
只不过我的臀部很敏感。
The posterior hypothalamus performs the function of defence against cold. 下丘脑后部执行着抵御寒冷的功能。

后缀46. -ise, -ize 构成动词，表示"使…成为"，名词形式为-isation, -ization。-ise 为英式英语，-ize 为美式英语

1. **modernize** ['mɒdənaɪz] v. 使现代化
『modern现代的+ize使…变成→使变成现代的』

The company is investing $9 million to modernize its factories. 这家公司要投资900万元将其工厂现代化。

▶ **modernization** [ˌmɒdənaɪˈzeɪʃn] n. 现代化；现代化的事物

the modernization of the telephone system
电话设备的现代化

2. **realize** ['riːəlaɪz] vt. 实现；意识到
『real真实的+ize使…变成→使变成真实的→实现』

▶ **realization** [ˌriːəlaɪˈzeɪʃn] n. 实现；认识

3. **civil** ['sɪvl] adj. 公民的；民事的；民用的；有礼貌的
『civ (=citizen) 公民+il表形容词→公民的；民用的』

❶ 国内的，国内人民间的
We cannot take sides in a civil war.
内战中我们不能支持任何一方。
Reports of civil unrest continue to come in from the northern provinces.
北部省份不断传出内乱的报道。

❷ 民事的（非刑事的）
a civil court 民事法庭

❸ 民用的（非军事的）
nuclear power for military and civil use军用和民用核能

❹ 有礼貌的；客气的
polite in a formal way but possibly not friendly
As visitors, the least we can do is be civil to the people in their own land.

作为来访者，我们最起码能做到的就是对当地人要彬彬有礼。

❺（权利）公民的，公民应有的
His courage in defending religious and civil rights inspired many outside the church.
他在捍卫宗教和公民权利时所表现出来的勇气鼓舞了许多教会之外的人。

❻ civil servants 公务员
The government has decided to increase salaries for all civil servants.
政府已决定给所有公务员加薪。

▶**civilize** ['sɪvəlaɪz] vt.教化；开化；使文明；使有教养
『civil有礼貌的，文明的+ize使…变成→使变得文明、有礼貌→教化，开化』

to educate and improve a person or a society; to make sb's behaviour or manners better
Schools will help to civilize the wild tribes there.
学校教育将有助于使那里的野蛮部落逐步开化。

▶**civilization** [ˌsɪvəlaɪˈzeɪʃn] n. 文明；文明社会

❶ [U] 文明，开化
a state of human society that is very developed and organized
The Victorians regarded the railways as bringing progress and civilization.
维多利亚时代的人认为铁路带来了进步和文明。

❷ [U, C]（特定时期和地区的）社会文明
a society, its culture and its way of life during a particular period of time or in a particular part of the world
the civilizations of ancient Greece and Rome
古希腊和古罗马的社会文明

❸ [U] 文明世界；文明社会
all the people in the world and the societies they live in, considered as a whole
Environmental damage threatens the whole of civilization.
环境的破坏威胁着整个文明世界。

❹ [U] (often humorous) 人类文明的生活
a place that offers you the comfortable way of life of a modern society
It's good to be back in civilization after two weeks in a tent!
在帐篷里住了两个星期后又回到人类文明的生活可真好呀！

▶**civilian** [səˈvɪliən] n. 平民，老百姓　adj.平民的
『civil公民+ian…的人→公民→平民』

In a military situation, a civilian is anyone who is not a member of the armed forces.

The safety of civilians caught up in the fighting must be guaranteed.
必须保证陷入战斗中的平民的人身安全。

The civilian population were suffering greatly at the hands of the security forces.
老百姓吃尽了安全部队的苦头。

4. **apologise** [əˈpɒlədʒaɪz] vi. 道歉，认错
『apology道歉+ize构成动词→道歉』

~ (to sb) (for sth)
You should apologise to her for blaming her wrongly.
是你错怪了她，你该给她赔个不是。

5. **industrialize** [ɪnˈdʌstriəlaɪz] v. 使工业化
『industrial工业的+ize使…成为→使成为工业的→使工业化』

[V] The southern part of the country was slow to industrialize.
这个国家的南部工业化进程缓慢。
[VN] Stalin's methods had industrialized the Russian economy.
斯大林采取的措施使俄国经济实现了工业化。

▶**industrialization** [ɪnˌdʌstriəlaɪˈzeɪʃn] n. 工业化

Industrialization and urbanization of China's modernization is the development of an irresistible trend.
工业化和城市化是中国现代化发展的不可阻挡的趋势。

6. **nationalize** ['næʃnəlaɪz] vt. 收归国有，使国有化
『national国家的+ize使…成为→使成为国家的→国有化』

The Obama administration says that while it wants tighter regulations, it has no plans to nationalize banks.
奥巴马政府表示，尽管它希望加强监管，但没有将银行国有化的计划。

▶**nationalization** [ˌnæʃnəlaɪˈzeɪʃn] n. 国有化

The issue of nationalization is no longer high on the agenda.
国有化问题不再是当务之急了。

后缀47. -ish 放在名词后构成形容词，表示"有…性质的"，多表贬义，还可构成动词，表示"使…"

① -ish 构成形容词，表示"有…性质的"

1. **bookish** ['bʊkɪʃ] adj. 书生气的；书呆子气的
『book书+ish有…性质的→书呆子气的』

Don't be so bookish and unrealistic. 不要书生气十足。

2. **childish** ['tʃaɪldɪʃ] adj. 幼稚的;孩子气的
『child孩子+ish有…性质的→孩子气的』

She's just being childish and immature.
她在耍小孩子脾气，真是任性。

3. **foolish** ['fuːlɪʃ] adj. 愚蠢的
『fool傻子+ish有…性质的→具有傻子性质的→愚蠢的』

4. **selfish** ['selfɪʃ] adj. 自私的
『self自己+ish有…性质的→只顾自己的→自私的』

5. **snobbish** ['snɒbɪʃ] adj. 势利的，自命不凡的
『snob势利小人（双写b）+ish有…性质的→势利的』

If you describe someone as snobbish, you disapprove of them because they are too proud of their social status, intelligence, or taste.

They had a snobbish dislike for their intellectual and social inferiors.
他们非常势利，不喜欢智力和社会地位不如自己的人。

▶**snob** [snɒb] n. 势利小人；自命不凡的人

❶ [C] 势利小人
a person who admires people in the higher social classes too much and has no respect for people in the lower social classes

❷ [C] 自命不凡的人
a person who thinks they are much better than other people because they are intelligent or like things that many people do not like

6. **boorish** ['bʊərɪʃ] adj. 粗野无礼的，无教养的

『boor粗野+ish有…性质的→粗野无理的，无教养的』

Boorish behaviour is rough, uneducated, and rude.
He disgusted many with his boorish behaviour.
他的粗野行为让很多人都讨厌他。

► **boor** [bʊə(r)] n. 粗野无礼的人；无教养的人

7. **modish** [ˈməʊdɪʃ] adj. 时髦的，流行的
『mode时髦（去e）+ish有…性质的→时髦的』

8. **fiendish** [ˈfiːndɪʃ] adj. 恶魔般的，凶残的
『fiend恶魔+ish有…性质的→恶魔般的』

► **fiend** [fiːnd] n. 恶魔；恶魔般的人

9. **sluggish** [ˈslʌgɪʃ] adj. 缓慢的，有气无力的
『slug懒汉（双写g）+ish有…性质的→缓慢的』

moving, reacting or working more slowly than normal and in a way that seems lazy

The economy remains sluggish. 经济的发展仍然非常缓慢。

10. **churlish** [ˈtʃɜːlɪʃ] adj. 不友好的，脾气坏的，粗鲁的
『churl粗鄙之人+ish有…性质的→不友好的，脾气坏的』

She would think him churlish if he refused.
他要是拒绝的话，她就会认为他不够友好。

11. **yellowish** [ˈjeləʊɪʃ] adj. 微黄色的
『yellow黄色+ish有…性质的→微黄色的』

② -ish 构成动词，表示"使…"

1. **impoverish** [ɪmˈpɒvərɪʃ] vt. 使贫穷；使贫瘠
『im使+pover贫穷（如poverty）+ish使…→使贫穷』

These changes are likely to impoverish single-parent families even further. 这些变革很可能使单亲家庭更加贫困。
Intensive cultivation has impoverished the soil.
集约耕作使土壤变得贫瘠。

2. **polish** [ˈpɒlɪʃ] v. 擦亮；改进 n. 上光剂；光泽
『pol光滑+ish使…→擦亮，抛光』

❶ [VN, V]（用擦亮剂等）擦，擦光，擦亮
Polish shoes regularly to protect the leather.
要经常擦鞋，以保护皮革。
He polished his glasses with a handkerchief.
他用手绢揩拭眼镜。

❷ [VN] 改善，改进
They just need to polish their technique.
他们只是需要改进一下技巧。
The statement was carefully polished and checked before release. 这项声明是经仔细润色检查后才发表的。
The hotel has polished up its act (= improved its service) since last year. 这家酒店自去年以来已经改善了服务水平。

❸ [U, C] 上光剂；光泽
furniture/floor/shoe/silver polish
家具上光漆/地板蜡/鞋油/银光剂
I give it a polish now and again. 我不时把它擦亮。

3. **admonish** [ədˈmɒnɪʃ] vt. 告诫，警告；力劝
『ad加强+mon提醒，警告（如monitor监视，监控）+ish使…→一再警告→告诫』

❶ 告诫，警告，责备
to tell sb firmly that you do not approve of sth that they have done
[VN] She was admonished for chewing gum in class.

她在课堂上嚼口香糖，受到了告诫。

❷ 力劝，忠告
to strongly advise sb to do sth
[VN to inf] Her teacher admonished her to work harder for her exams. 她的老师力劝她为了考试要更加努力。

4. **flourish** [ˈflʌrɪʃ] vi. 繁荣，昌盛；茁壮成长〈P175〉
『flour花+ish表动词→开花→繁荣；茁壮成长』

后缀48. -ism [izəm]，表示"主义，制度；行为"

① -ism表示"主义；制度"

1. **communism** [ˈkɒmjunɪzəm] n. 共产主义〈P230〉
► **communist** [ˈkɒmjənɪst] n. 共产主义者；共产党员

2. **socialism** [ˈsəʊʃəlɪzəm] n. 社会主义
► **socialist** [ˈsəʊʃəlɪst] n. 社会主义者

3. **capitalism** [ˈkæpɪtəlɪzəm] n. 资本主义（制度）
► **capitalist** [ˈkæpɪtəlɪst] n. 资本家;资本主义者

4. **Fascism** [ˈfæʃˌɪzəm] n. 法西斯主义
► **fascist** [ˈfæʃɪst] n. 法西斯分子

② -ism表示"主义；行为"

1. **extremism** [ɪkˈstriːmɪzəm] n. 极端主义
► **extremist** [ɪkˈstriːmɪst] n. 极端主义者，偏激的人

2. **terrorism** [ˈterərɪzəm] n. 恐怖主义
► **terrorist** [ˈterərɪst] n. 恐怖主义者，恐怖分子

3. **optimism** [ˈɒptɪmɪzəm] n. 乐观；乐观主义〈P238〉
► **optimist** [ˈɒptɪmɪst] n. 乐观主义者；乐天派

4. **pessimism** [ˈpesɪmɪzəm] n. 悲观；悲观主义
[U] ~ (about/over sth)
There is a mood of pessimism in the company about future job prospects. 公司中有一种对工作前景悲观的情绪。
► **pessimist** [ˈpesɪmɪst] n. 悲观主义者，悲观者
► **pessimistic** [ˌpesɪˈmɪstɪk] adj. 悲观主义的
~ (about sth)
They appeared surprisingly pessimistic about their chances of winning. 他们对胜利的可能性显得出奇地悲观。

5. **heroism** [ˈherəʊɪzəm] n. 英雄主义；英雄行为
The soldier's heroism in the fighting heightened my admiration.
战士们在战斗中的英雄行为增强了我对他们的崇敬。
► **heroic** [həˈrəʊɪk] adj. 英勇的；矢志不渝的
Rescuers made heroic efforts to save the crew.
救援人员不畏艰险努力营救全体船员。
► **heroics** n. [pl.] 英雄壮举；勇敢果断的行为
Thanks to Bateman's heroics in the second half, the team won 2-0. 由于贝特曼在下半场的英勇表现，球队以2:0获胜。
Cut it out, Perry. You've performed your heroics. It's all over now.
住手吧，佩里。你已经逞过英雄了。现在一切都结束了。

③ -ism表示"宗教"

1. **Buddhism** [ˈbʊdɪzəm] n. 佛教
► **Buddha** [ˈbʊdə] n. 佛陀；佛像

► **Buddhist** ['bʊdɪst] n. 佛教徒　adj. 佛教的

2. **Confucianism** [kən'fju:ʃənɪzm] n. 孔子思想，儒家思想

  ► **Confucian** [kən'fju:ʃən] adj. 孔子的，儒家的

  ► **Confucius** [kən'fju:ʃəs] n. 孔子

  ► **Confucius Institute** 孔子学院

3. **Islamism** ['ɪzləmɪzəm] n. 伊斯兰教义

  ► **Islamist** ['ɪzləmɪst] n. 伊斯兰主义者

  ► **Muslim** ['mʊzlɪm] n. 穆斯林　adj. 穆斯林的
  （美 ['mʌzləm, 'mʊz-, 'mʌs-, 'mʊs-]）

a person whose religion is Islam
Friday is a holiday in Muslim countries.
在穆斯林国家星期五是假日。
There are well over a million Muslims in Britain.
英国的穆斯林远远超过了一百万。

④ -sm表示"学术或学术流派"

1. **impressionism** [ɪm'preʃənɪzəm] n. 印象主义，印象派

2. **modernism** ['mɒdənɪzəm] n. 现代主义，现代派

⑤ -sm表示"行为，现象"

1. **tourism** ['tʊərɪzəm] n. 旅游业

2. **cannibalism** ['kænɪbəlɪzəm] n. 同类相食；食人肉

They were forced to practise cannibalism in order to survive.
为了活命，他们只好吃人肉。

  ► **cannibal** ['kænɪbl] n. 食人肉者

3. **plagiarism** ['pleɪdʒərɪzəm] n. 剽窃；剽窃作品

[U, C] an act of plagiarizing sth; sth that has been plagiarized
Now he's in real trouble. He's accused of plagiarism.
现在他是真遇到麻烦了。他被指控剽窃。
a text full of plagiarisms 满篇剽窃他人著作的文章

4. **barbarism** ['bɑ:bərɪzəm] n. 野蛮行为

5. **criticism** ['krɪtɪsɪzəm] n. 批评；评论 <P142>

后缀49. -ist 意为"…家，…者"，表示从事某种职业的人

1. **artist** ['ɑ:tɪst] n. 艺术家；画家；能手
『art艺术+ist…家→艺术家』

2. **activist** ['æktɪvɪst] n. 积极分子；激进分子
『active积极的（去e）+ist…者→积极分子；激进分子』

a person who works to achieve political or social change, especially as a member of an organization with particular aims
The police say they suspect the attack was carried out by animal rights activists.
警方说他们怀疑袭击是由动物权益保护的积极分子们发动的。

3. **journalist** ['dʒɜ:nəlɪst] n. 新闻工作者，新闻记者 <P198>
『journal报纸，杂志+ist…者→记者』

  ► **journal** ['dʒɜ:nl] n. 杂志；报纸；日志

4. **chemist** ['kemɪst] n. 化学家；药剂师
『chem化学+ist…家→化学家』

  ► **at the chemist's** 在药店

  ► **chemistry** ['kemɪstri] n.化学；化学成分或性质；吸引

❶ [U] 化学
a degree in chemistry 化学学位

❷ [U] 化学成分或性质
The patient's blood chemistry was monitored regularly.
那名患者的血液化学成分受到了定时的监测。

❸ [U]（互相之间的）吸引，亲密
If you say that there is chemistry between two people, you mean that it is obvious they are attracted to each other or like each other very much.
Trump also said that he and Kim have "good chemistry" together. 特朗普还说，他和金（正恩）有亲密的关系。
I can feel the chemistry between us.
我能感到我们之间那种亲密。

  ► **chemical** ['kemɪkl] adj. 化学的　n. 化学物质
The whole food chain is affected by the overuse of chemicals in agriculture.
整个食物链因农业生产过程过多使用化学品而受到影响。

5. **defeatist** [dɪ'fi:tɪst] n. 失败主义者　adj. 失败主义的
『defeat失败+ist…者→失败主义者』

someone who believes that they will not succeed
I don't approve of your defeatist attitude.
我不赞成你这种失败主义的态度。
Being defeatist will get us nowhere.
失败主义将令我们一事无成。

6. **dentist** ['dentɪst] n. 牙科医生<P148>
『dent牙齿+ist（从事某职业、研究的）人→牙科医生』

  ► **at the dentist's** 在牙科诊所

7. **florist** ['flɒrɪst] n. 花店店主，花商；种花人
『flor（=flower花）+ist表人→卖花的人→花商』

The same evening he went to a florist's.
那天晚上他去了一家花店。
The florist made up an attractive bouquet.
鲜花店店主做了一个吸引人的花束。

8. **novelist** ['nɒvəlɪst] n. 小说家
『novel小说+ist…家→小说家』

9. **pianist** ['pɪənɪst] n. 钢琴家
『piano钢琴（去o）+ist…家→钢琴家』

  ► **piano** [pi'ænəʊ] n. 钢琴

10. **scientist** ['saɪəntɪst] n. 科学家
『science科学（去ce）+t+ist…家→科学家』

11. **specialist** ['speʃəlɪst] n. 专家
『special专门的+ist…家→专家』

12. **typist** ['taɪpɪst] n. 打字员
『type打字（去e）+ist…者→打字员』

  ► **typewriter** ['taɪpraɪtə(r)] n. 打字机

13. **receptionist** [rɪ'sepʃənɪst] n. 接待员
『reception接待+ist…者→接待员』

后缀50. -ite 构成形容词或名词，表示"有…性质的，有…性质的人或物"；还可构成动词，表示"使…"

① -ite 构成形容词或名词，表示"有…性质的，有…性质的人或物"

1. favorite [ˈfeɪvərɪt] adj. 特别喜爱的 n. 特别喜爱的人或物
『favor喜爱+ite有…性质的→特别喜爱的』

2. opposite [ˈɒpəzɪt] adj. 对面的；相反的 adv. 对面 n. 对立面；反义词 prep. 在…对面〈P262〉
『op对着+pose放（去e）+ite有…性质的→放在（某物）的对立面的→对立的』

3. composite [ˈkɒmpəzɪt] n. 合成物，混合物 adj. 合成的，混合的〈P263〉
『com一起+pose放，放置（去e）+ite具有…性质的→合成物』

4. infinite [ˈɪnfɪnət] adj. 极大的，极度的；无限的〈P172〉
『in不+fine范围（去e）+ite有…性质的→没有范围的→无限的』

② -ite 构成名词，表示"人或物"

1. socialite [ˈsəʊʃəlaɪt] n. 社交名人
『social社交的+ite表人→社交名人』

a person who goes to a lot of fashionable parties and is often written about in the newspapers, etc.

2. granite [ˈgrænɪt] n. 花岗岩
『gran(=grain)颗粒，谷粒+ite表物→颗粒构成的石头→花岗岩』

③ -ite 构成动词，表示"使"

1. unite [juˈnaɪt] vt. 联合
『uni一个+(i)te使→使成为一个→联合』

2. ignite [ɪgˈnaɪt] v. （使）燃烧，点燃
『ign点火+ite使…→点燃』

[V] Gas ignites very easily. 汽油易燃。
[VN] Flames melted a lead pipe and ignited leaking gas.
火焰熔化了一段铅管，燃着了漏出来的煤气。

▶**ignition** [ɪgˈnɪʃn] n. 点火装置；点火

to turn the ignition on/off 打开/关上点火开关
The flames spread to all parts of the house within minutes of ignition.
着火后几分钟内火焰就蔓延到房子的各个部分。

3. expedite [ˈekspədaɪt] vt. 加快，加速〈P247〉
『ex出+ped脚+ite使…→把脚迈出去→加快』

后缀51. -itude 构成名词，表示"情况，性质，状态，事物"

1. altitude [ˈæltɪtjuːd] n.高度，海拔〈P112〉
『alt高+itude表状态→海拔』

2. latitude [ˈlætɪtjuːd] n. 纬度；回旋余地

『lat宽+itude表状态→距离很宽→纬度』
In the middle to high latitudes rainfall has risen steadily over the last 20-30 years.
在过去二三十年里，中高纬度地区的降雨量持续增加。
He would be given every latitude in forming a new government. 他将可以不受任何限制地组建新政府。

3. attitude [ˈætɪtjuːd] n. 态度，看法
『at(t)处于+itude表状态→（对于某事）处于某种状态→态度』

小贴士 注意上面这三个单词的拼写：attitude中的第一个 t 换为 l 便成了altitude（高度）；把altitude的前两个字母交换位置便成了latitude。

4. longitude [ˈlɒŋgɪtjuːd] n. 经度，经线
『long长的+itude表状态→经度』
Each point on the earth is specified by geographic latitude and longitude.
地球上每一点都可以用地理经度和纬度来确定。

5. gratitude [ˈgrætɪtjuːd] n. 感激，感谢
『grate感激（去e）+itude表状态→感激，感谢』

~ (to sb) (for sth)
I would like to express my gratitude to everyone for their hard work. 我要对所有辛勤劳动的人表示感谢。

▶**grateful** [ˈgreɪtfl] adj. 感谢的，感激的
~ (to sb) (for sth) | ~ (to do sth) | ~ (that…)
I am extremely grateful to all the teachers for their help.
我非常感谢所有老师的帮助。
I would be grateful if you could send the completed form back as soon as possible.
如您能尽快将表格填好寄回，我将不胜感激。

6. plenitude [ˈplenɪtjuːd] n. 完满；大量
『plen大量（如plenty）+itude表状态→大量；完满』

❶ [U] 完满
Plenitude is a feeling that an experience is satisfying because it is full or complete.
The music brought him a feeling of plenitude and freedom.
这音乐带给他一种完满和自由的感觉。

❷ [sing., U] 丰富，充足，大量
What is the use of a book about interior design without a plenitude of pictures in color?
要是没有大量的彩色图片，一本关于室内设计的书还有什么用途呢？

7. fortitude [ˈfɔːtɪtjuːd] n. 坚韧，刚毅〈P179〉
『fort(=strong)坚强的+itude表状态、性质→坚韧，刚毅』

8. solitude [ˈsɒlɪtjuːd] n. 独处，独居〈P304〉
『sol单独+itude表状态→独处，独居』

9. magnitude [ˈmægnɪtjuːd] n. 量级；巨大〈P213〉
『magn大+itude（去i）表性质、状态→巨大』

10. multitude [ˈmʌltɪtjuːd] n. 众多；大量；人群〈P23〉
『multi多种的+itude（去i）表状态、性质→众多，大量』

11. aptitude [ˈæptɪtjuːd] n. （适合做某事的）天资，天赋〈P114〉
『apt适合+itude表状态、性质→具有适合（做某事）性质→天资』

后缀52. -ity 用在形容词后构成名词，表示"具有某种性质"，单词重音在其前一个音节上

1. absurdity [əb'sɜːdətɪ] n. 荒谬；荒谬行为
『absurd荒谬的+ity表名词，具有某种性质→荒谬』

We all laughed at the absurdity in his reasoning.
我们都嘲笑他推理的荒谬。

2. activity [æk'tɪvətɪ] n. 活跃；活动
『active积极的（去e）+ity表名词，具有某种性质→活跃；活动』

❶ [U] 活动；热闹状况；活跃
a situation in which sth is happening or a lot of things are being done
The streets were noisy and full of activity.
街上熙熙攘攘，车水马龙。

❷ [C, usually pl.] （为兴趣、娱乐或达到一定目的而进行的）活动
The club provides a wide variety of activities including tennis, swimming and pingpong.
这家俱乐部的活动丰富多彩，诸如网球、游泳和乒乓球等。

3. creativity [ˌkriːeɪ'tɪvətɪ] n. 创造性，创造力
『creative 创造性的（去e）+ity表名词，具有某种性质→创造性，创造力』

4. density ['densətɪ] n. 稠密；密度；浓度
『dense稠密的，浓密的（去e）+ity表名词，具有某种性质→稠密；密度』

❶ [U] 密集，稠密；密度；浓度
the quality of being dense ; the degree to which sth is dense
population density 人口密度
low density forest 低密度森林

❷ [C, U] (physics 物理学中的) 密度
Mercury has a much greater density than water.
水银的密度比水大得多。

▶ **dense** [dens] adj. 密集的，稠密的；（雾、烟等）浓的
Where Bucharest now stands, there once was a large, dense forest. 布加勒斯特的所在地过去曾是一大片茂密的森林。
Java is a densely populated island. 爪哇是一个人口稠密的岛屿。
A dense column of smoke rose several miles into the air.
一股浓烟升到了几英里的高空。

▶ **condense** [kən'dens] v. （气体）凝结；（文章或讲话）精简；（使）浓缩
『con一起+dense稠密→浓缩到一起→凝结；精简；浓缩』

Steam condenses into water when it cools.
蒸汽冷却时凝结为水。
[VN] Condense the soup by boiling it for several minutes.
煮几分钟把汤熬浓。
The article was condensed into just two pages.
这篇文章被缩成两页。

5. electricity [ɪˌlek'trɪsətɪ] n. 电，电能
『electric电的+ity表名词→电，电能』

▶ **electric** [ɪ'lektrɪk] adj. 电的，电动的

6. familiarity [fəˌmɪlɪ'ærətɪ] n. 熟悉，通晓
『familiar熟悉的+ity表名词，具有某种性质→熟悉』

His familiarity with the language helped him enjoy his stay.

他通晓这种语言，所以逗留期间过得很惬意。

7. hospitality [ˌhɒspɪ'tælətɪ] n. 好客，殷勤
『hospit客人+al表形容词+ity表名词，具有某种性质→具有（把对方当作客人对待的）性质→好客』

[U] 好客，殷勤
Thank you for your kind hospitality.
感谢你的友好款待。

▶ **hospitable** [hɒ'spɪtəbl] adj. 好客的；（气候环境）适宜的

The local people are very hospitable to strangers.
当地人对外来客人十分友好热情。
Even in summer this place did not look exactly hospitable.
即使在夏天，这个地方看起来也不太舒适宜人。

比较 hospital ['hɒspɪtl] n. 医院

8. popularity [ˌpɒpju'lærətɪ] n. 受欢迎；流行
『popular流行的+ity表名词，具有某种性质→流行』

9. reality [rɪ'ælətɪ] n. 现实；事实
『real真实的+ity表名词，具有某种性质→事实，现实』

10. similarity [ˌsɪmə'lærətɪ] n. 相似性
『similar相似的+ity表名词，具有某种性质→相似性』

11. majority [mə'dʒɒrətɪ] n. 大部分，大多数 〈P214〉
『major主要的+ity表名词，具有某种性质→大部分』

12. minority [maɪ'nɒrətɪ] n. 少数；少数派 〈P21〉
『minor少数的+ity表名词，具有某种性质→少数』

13. equality [i'kwɒlətɪ] n. 平等 〈P158〉
『equal平等的+ity表名词，具有某种性质→平等』

▶ **inequality** [ˌɪnɪ'kwɒlətɪ] n. 不平等

后缀53. -ive 可以构成形容词和名词，构成的名词有的指人，有的指物

① -ive 构成形容词，表示"有…性质的"

1. creative [kri'eɪtɪv] adj. 创造（性）的；有创造力的
『create创造（去e）+ive有…性质的→有创造性的』

The course also features creative writing exercises and listening comprehension.
这门课程也包括创造性写作练习和听力理解。
He was one of the most creative and innovative engineers of his generation.
他是他那代人当中最富创造性与革新精神的工程师之一。

2. massive ['mæsɪv] adj. 巨大的，庞大的，厚重的；（疾病）非常严重的，十分危急的
『mass大块+ive有…性质的→大块的→巨大的，庞大的』

very large, heavy and solid; extremely large or serious
a massive rock 一块巨大的岩石
the massive walls of the castle 厚实坚固的城堡围墙
The explosion made a massive hole in the ground.
爆炸在地面留下了一个巨大的坑。
He died six weeks later of a massive heart attack.
六周后他因严重的心脏病发作去世。

▶ **mass** [mæs] n. 块，团；质量

❶ [C] ~ (of sth) 团；块；堆
a large amount of a substance that does not have a definite shape or form

The hill appeared as a black mass in the distance.
远远地看去，那座山是黑魆魆一片。
The sky was full of dark masses of clouds.
天空中乌云密布。

❷ [sing.] ~ of sth （聚成一体的）一团，一堆，一块
I struggled through the mass of people to the exit.
我在人群里挤来挤去，挤到了出口处。
The page was covered with a mass of figures.
纸上写满了密密麻麻的数字。

❸ masses (of sth) [pl.] (informal) 大量的东西（可以修饰可数名词也可以修饰不可数名词）
There were masses of people in the shops yesterday.
昨天商店里人如潮涌。
I've got masses of work to do. 我有一大堆的工作要做。

❹ the masses [pl.] 群众；平民百姓
His music is commercial. It is aimed at the masses.
他的音乐走商业化路线，针对的是一般大众。

❺ the mass of sth [sing.] 大多数；多数
The reforms are unpopular with the mass of teachers and parents. 大多数教师和家长并不赞成这些改革。

❻ [U] (物理学中的)质量
Astronomers know that Pluto and Triton have nearly the same size, mass, and density.
天文学家知道冥王星与海卫一拥有几乎相同的体积、质量与密度。

小贴士 物理中表示质量用的字母m就是mass的首字母。

❼ adj. [only before noun] 大批的；数量极多的
affecting or involving a large number of people or things
mass unemployment/production 大批失业；批量生产
weapons of mass destruction 大规模杀伤性武器

3. **active** [ˈæktɪv] adj. 积极的；活跃的；活动的
『act行动+ive有…性质的→活动的；活跃的』

❶ （身体）忙碌的，（思想）活跃的
Although he's nearly 80, he is still very active.
尽管快80岁了，他还是十分活跃。
Children raised like this must have a strong will, active mind and be full of creativity.
这样教育出来的孩子，一定会意志坚强，思维活跃，充满创造力。

❷ 积极（参与）的，主动的（与"消极的"相对）
involved in sth; making a determined effort and not leaving sth to happen by itself
She takes an active part in school life.
她积极参加学校活动。
Companies need to take active steps to increase exports.
各公司需要采取积极措施增加出口。

❸ 活动的
If you say that a person or animal is active in a particular place or at a particular time, you mean that they are performing their usual activities or performing a particular activity.
animals that are active only at night 仅在夜间活动的动物
The virus is still active in the blood.
这种病毒仍然在血液中起作用。
an active volcano (= likely to erupt) 活火山

❹ （语法）主动语态的 n. 主动语态

反义词 **passive** [ˈpæsɪv] adj. 消极的；被动的
『pass(=feeling)感情+ive表形容词→感情用事→被动的』

❶ 消极的，被动的
accepting what happens or what people do without trying to change anything or oppose them
He played a passive role in the relationship.
他在他们的关系中处于被动地位。
Watching television is a relatively passive activity.
看电视是一种相对被动的活动。

❷ 动语态的 n. 被动语态
passive voice 被动语态

4. **talkative** [ˈtɔːkətɪv] adj. 爱多说话的，多嘴的
『talk谈话+ative有…倾向（性质）的→有谈话倾向的→爱多说话的』
After downing three glasses, he became lively and talkative.
三杯酒入肚，他来了精神，话也多了。

② -ive 构成名词，表示"人"

1. **native** [ˈneɪtɪv] adj. 当地的 n. 当地人
『nate出生（去e）+ive表形容词或名词→当地出生的人；出生地的』

2. **representative** [ˌreprɪˈzentətɪv] n. 代表 adj. 有代表性的
『represent代表+ative表人→有代表性的人→代表』

3. **relative** [ˈrelətɪv] n. 亲属，亲戚
『relate相关（去e）+ive表人→（与某人）相关的人→亲属，亲戚』

4. **detective** [dɪˈtektɪv] n. 侦探 adj. 侦探的
『detect发觉；查明+ive表形容词或表人→侦探』

5. **captive** [ˈkæptɪv] n. 俘虏 adj. 被监禁的 <P122>
『capt拿，抓+ive表人→被抓住的人→俘虏』

6. **fugitive** [ˈfjuːdʒətɪv] n. 逃亡者 adj. 逃亡的；易逝的 <P181>
『fug逃离+it+ive表人→逃离（被逮捕的）人→逃亡者』

③ -ive构成名词，表示"物"或抽象名词

1. **explosive** [ɪkˈspləʊsɪv] n. 炸药
『explose爆炸（去e）+ive表物→爆炸物→炸药』

2. **additive** [ˈædətɪv] n. （尤指食品的）添加剂，添加物
『add加+it+ive表物→添加（到食品里的）东西→添加剂』
Strict safety tests are carried out on food additives.
对食品添加剂进行了严格的安全检测。

3. **adjective** [ˈædʒɪktɪv] n. 形容词 <P197>
『ad相当于to+ject投掷，扔+ive表名词→扔到名词前的词→形容词』

4. **archive** [ˈɑːkaɪv] n. 档案文件；档案馆；计算机档案文件压缩包 <P115>
『arch弓+ive表物→弓形的房子→档案馆』

5. **initiative** [ɪˈnɪʃətɪv] n. 倡议；主动性；主动权 <P195>
『initiate开始，发起（去e）+ive表性质→具有发起性质的→倡议；主动性；主动权』

6. **motive** [ˈməʊtɪv] n. 动机 <P225>
『mot移动+ive表名词→使（某人）行动起来（的原因）→动机』

后缀54. -let, -et 构成名词，表示"小"

1. booklet [ˈbʊklət] n. 小册子
『book书+let小→小册子』

A booklet is a small book that has a paper cover and that gives you information about something.

The contents of this booklet should be of use to all students.
这本小册子的内容应该会对所有的学生都有用处。
We bought a booklet about the castle from the tourist office.
我们从旅游办公室买了一本关于城堡的小册子。

2. leaflet [ˈliːflət] n. 传单，散页印刷品，小册子
『leaf树叶；一页纸+ let小→传单』

A printed sheet of paper or a few printed pages that are given free to advertise or give information about something.
Campaigners handed out leaflets on passive smoking.
活动人士派发了有关被动吸烟的宣传页。

3. pamphlet [ˈpæmflət] n. 小册子；手册
『pamph册子+let小→小册子』

A pamphlet is a very thin book, with a paper cover, which gives information about something.
Can I get a pamphlet for this museum?
能给我拿一份这个博物馆的小册子吗？

近义词 **brochure** [ˈbrəʊʃə(r)] n. （介绍产品或服务信息的）小册子

A brochure is a magazine or thin book with pictures that gives you information about a product or service.
The brochure offers a wide choice of hotels, apartments and holiday homes.
这本小册子提供了很多宾馆、公寓、度假屋供选择。

4. droplet [ˈdrɒplət] n. 小滴
『drop滴+let小→小滴』

We know that COVID-19 is spread primarily through droplet transmission. 我们知道COVID-19（新冠肺炎）主要通过飞沫传播。

5. tablet [ˈtæblət] n. 药片；匾，牌；平板电脑
『table桌子+(le)t小→（像）小的圆形的桌子；（像）小的方形的桌子→药片；匾，牌；平板电脑』

❶ 药片，片剂 （especially BrE，同义词 pill）
Take two tablets with water before meals.
每次两片，饭前用水冲服。

❷ （固定于墙上作纪念的）匾，牌（同义词 plaque）

a flat piece of stone that has words written on it, especially one that has been fixed to a wall in memory of an important person or event

(figurative) We can be very flexible—our entry requirements are not set in tablets of stone.
我们可以非常灵活——加入条件并非铁板钉钉。

❸ 平板电脑
The company has also expanded into smartphones and tablets.
这家公司也向智能手机和平板电脑市场吹响了进军的号角。

形近词 **tabloid** [ˈtæblɔɪd] n. 小报

通俗小报（文短图多，内容多为名人逸事，常被视为不太严肃）
The story made the front page in all the tabloids.
这件事成了所有小报的头版新闻。

6. piglet [ˈpɪglət] n. 猪仔，小猪
『pig猪+let小→小猪』

7. starlet [ˈstɑːlət] n. 小星星；未成名的年轻女演员
『star星星+let小→小星星』

8. bracelet [ˈbreɪslət] n. 手镯；手链；臂镯 〈P119〉
『brace手臂+let（佩戴的饰品）→（戴在）手腕上的饰品→手镯』

9. packet [ˈpækɪt] n. (BrE) 包装盒；包装袋
『pack包+et小→小包』

❶ [C] (BrE) 包装盒；包装袋（NAmE package）
Cook the rice according to instructions on the packet.
按照包装袋上的说明煮饭。
He had smoked half a packet of cigarettes.
他已经吸了半包香烟。

❷ （邮政）小件包裹

10. circlet [ˈsɜːklət] n. 小圈
『circle圆圈+(le)t小→小圈』

11. facet [ˈfæsɪt] n. 小平面；方面 〈P161〉
『face表面（去e）+et小→平面；（东西的）一面』

后缀55. -like 构成形容词，表示"像…一样"

1. dreamlike [ˈdriːmlaɪk] adj. 梦幻般的
『dream梦+like像…一样→像梦一样的→梦幻般的』

as if existing or happening in a dream
Her paintings have a naive, dreamlike quality.
她的画作带有质朴、空灵的韵味。

2. childlike [ˈtʃaɪldlaɪk] adj. 孩子般的
『child孩子+like像…一样→孩子般的』

childlike enthusiasm/simplicity/delight
孩子般的热情/淳朴/兴高采烈

后缀56. -ling 构成名词，表示"小（的东西，人或动物）"

1. duckling [ˈdʌklɪŋ] n. 小鸭，幼鸭
『duck鸭子+ling小→小鸭子』

2. gosling [ˈgɒzlɪŋ] n. 小鹅
『goose鹅（去o去e）+ling小→小鹅』

3. seedling [ˈsiːdlɪŋ] n. 幼苗，籽苗
『seed种子+ling小→由种子发出的小苗→幼苗』

A seedling is a young plant that has been grown from a seed.
Keep the soil moist. That way, the seedling will flourish.
保持土壤湿润，那样幼苗就能茁壮成长。

4. sapling [ˈsæplɪŋ] n. 幼树
『sap树液+ling小东西→小树苗』

A sapling needs pruning, a child discipline.
小树要砍，小孩要管。
newly planted saplings swaying gently in the spring breeze
随春风摇曳的新栽小树

5. sibling [ˈsɪblɪŋ] n. 兄；弟；姐；妹
『sib同胞家族成员+ling人或动物→兄弟或姐妹』

Your siblings are your brothers and sisters.
His siblings are mostly in their early twenties.
他的兄弟姐妹大多二十出头。

6. underling [ˈʌndəlɪŋ] n. 下手，下属

『under下面+ling人→位于手下的人→下手，下属』

a person with a lower rank or status
Every underling feared him. 所有的手下都怕他。

7. underling ['wi:klɪŋ] n. 瘦弱的人；性格软弱的人
『weak虚弱的+ling人→体弱的人』

a person who is not physically strong
The author characterized the central figure as a weakling.
作者把故事中的主人公描绘成一个软弱的人。

后缀57. -ly 可以构成形容词和副词

① -ly放在名词后，表示"…般的"

1. friendly ['frendli] adj. 友好的

2. brotherly ['brʌðəli] adj. 兄弟般的

He gave her a brotherly kiss on the cheek.
他像兄长一样吻了她的面颊。

3. motherly ['mʌðəli] adj. 慈母般的

It was an incredible display of motherly love and forgiveness.
那是慈母般关爱与宽容的了不起的表现。

4. fatherly ['fɑ:ðəli] adj. 父亲的；慈父般的

He keeps a fatherly eye on his players.
他像父亲一样照管着他的球员。

5. manly ['mænli] adj. 有男子气概的

I'm afraid his manly charms are starting to fade.
我担心他的男性魅力已经开始凋谢了。

② -ly 放在名词后，表示"有…性质的"

1. heavenly ['hevnli] adj. 天堂的；天堂般的，无比美好

Sichuan has always enjoyed the reputation of being a "Heavenly Land of Plenty".
四川素有"天府之国"的美称。

Heavenly music swelled from nowhere.
不知从何处响起天籁般的音乐。

2. worldly ['wɜ:ldli] adj. 尘世的；世故的；鄙俗的

❶ 尘世的
I think it is time you woke up and focused your thoughts on more worldly matters.
我认为是该你清醒过来把思想集中到更为现实的问题上的时候了。

❷ 世故的，老成练达的
At 15, he was more worldly than his older cousins who lived in the country.
他15岁就比他那些居住在乡村的表兄懂人情世故了。

❸ 名利的，鄙俗的
Today the media drive athletes to the view that the important thing is to gain worldly success.
现在，媒体使得运动员认为追逐逐利是很重要的。

▶ **unworldly** [ʌn'wɜ:ldli] adj. 超凡的，脱俗的

❶ 非尘世的；超凡的
It wasn't just that she was strikingly beautiful; there was an unworldly air about her.
不仅因为她美得惊人，而且她身上有一种不凡的气质。

❷ 不谙世故的
She was so young, so unworldly.

她太年轻，太不懂人情世故。

❸ 脱俗的，对钱财无兴趣的
Kitty's family was unworldly, unimpressed by power, or money. 基蒂一家清心寡欲，淡泊金钱与权力。

3. costly ['kɒstli] adj. 昂贵的，代价高的

Buying new furniture may prove too costly.
购买新家具可能会花太多钱。

Mining can be costly in terms of lives.
采矿有时会造成重大的生命损失。

4. cowardly ['kaʊədli] adj. 胆小的，懦弱的
『coward胆小鬼+ly有…性质的→胆小的』

I was too cowardly to complain. 我太胆小，不敢抱怨。

5. timely ['taɪmli] adj. 及时的，适时的

We are particularly grateful to him for his timely help.
我们特别感谢他的及时帮助。

A timely snow promises a good harvest.
瑞雪兆丰年。

6. homely ['həʊmli] adj. 家一般的；相貌平平的

❶ (BrE approving) 家一般的
（某地）家一般的舒适；（食物）家常的；
I wanted a homely room but I wanted it to look smart, too.
我想要一个像家一样舒适的房间，但也希望它看起来很漂亮。
homely cooking 家常烹调

❷ (NAmE disapproving) （外表）相貌平平的
The man was homely and overweight.
该男子其貌不扬，身材肥胖。

③ -ly放在表示时间的名词后，构成形容词、副词，表示多长时间一次的

1. daily ['deɪli] adj. 每日的；adv. 每日 n. 日报

The information is updated on a daily basis.
信息每天都更新。
The machines are inspected twice daily. 机器每日检查两次。
Copies of the local daily had been scattered on a table.
几份当地的日报散放在桌子上。

2. weekly ['wi:kli] adj. 一周一次的 adv. 每周 n. 周刊，周报

In addition to my weekly wage, I got a lot of tips.
除了每周的薪水外，我还能得到不少小费。
The group meets weekly. 这个小组每周见一次面。
Two of the four national daily papers are to become weeklies.
4份全国性日报中有两份将改为周报。

3. biweekly [baɪ'wi:kli] adj. 两周一次的 adv. 两周一次 n. 双周刊

4. monthly ['mʌnθli] adj. 每月的 adv. 每月 n. 月刊

5. hourly ['aʊəli] adj. 每小时的 adv. 每小时

6. yearly ['jɪəli] adj. 每年的 adv. 每年

④ -ly放在形容词后，表示"有…性质的"，但仍是形容词（个别兼作副词）

1. elderly ['eldəli] adj. 年纪大的，上了年纪的

❶ adj.（人）年纪较大的，上了年纪的（婉辞，与old同义）
used as a polite word for old
It occurs in elderly men, apparently as part of the ageing process.

这种情况出现在老年人当中，显然是衰老过程的一部分。

❷ the elderly [pl.] 老人，上了年纪的人
We should provide better care for the elderly.
我们应该为老年人提供更好照顾。

2. lonely [ˈləʊnli] adj. 孤独的，寂寞的；偏僻的
（lonelier, loneliest）

❶ 孤独的，寂寞的
She lives alone and often feels lonely.
她孑然一身，常感到寂寞。
I desperately needed something to occupy me during those long, lonely nights.
在那一个个漫长、孤单的夜晚，我极需找点事做。

❷ 偏僻的；荒凉的；人迹罕至的（只作定语）
It felt like the loneliest place in the world.
感觉这就像是天底下最荒凉的地方。

词义辨析 <P371第50>
孤独的；独自的 lone, alone, lonely, lonesome, solitary

3. deadly [ˈdedli] adj. 致命的（deadlier, deadliest）adv.极其，非常

❶ adj. 致命的
This is a potentially deadly disease.
这是一种潜在的致命疾病。
The police charged him with possession of a deadly weapon.
警察指控他持有致命武器。

❷ adj. 非常的 （complete）
A deadly silence followed her announcement.
她宣布此事后，一片死寂。

❸ adv. 极其，非常
completely or extremely
Broadcast news was accurate and reliable but deadly dull.
新闻广播准确可靠但却非常枯燥。
I thought she was joking but she was deadly serious.
我以为她在开玩笑，但她非常认真。

小贴士 dead作副词时，也有"非常地，完全地"之意
You're dead right! 你完全正确！
He's dead against the idea. 他坚决反对这个想法。
The instructions are dead easy to follow.
这些指令很容易执行。

4. lively [ˈlaɪvli] adj. 活泼的；热闹的；鲜艳的
（livelier, liveliest）

❶ （人）活泼的，精力充沛的，生气勃勃的
She had a sweet, lively personality. 她的性格可爱活泼。

❷ （事件、讨论等）热闹的，热烈的，激烈的
My teacher did what he could to make his class lively.
我的老师尽其所能使他的课堂生动。
The students were in the midst of a lively discussion when the teacher came in.
正当同学们热烈讨论的时候，老师进来了。

❸ 思维活跃的
Someone who has a lively mind is intelligent and interested in a lot of different things.
She was a very well educated girl with a lively mind, a girl with ambition.
她是个受过良好教育、思维敏捷、抱负远大的女孩子。

❹ （颜色）鲜艳的

a lively shade of pink 鲜艳的粉红色调

⑤ -ly放在形容词后，构成副词

一般直接加ly

1. extremely [ɪkˈstriːmli] adv. 极端地，非常
『extreme极端的+ly表副词→极端地』

2. politely [pəˈlaɪtli] adv. 有礼貌地
『polite有礼貌的+ly表副词→有礼貌地』

以-l结尾仍加ly

1. carefully [ˈkeəfəli] adv. 仔细地，小心谨慎地
『careful仔细的+ly表副词→仔细地』

2. especially [ɪˈspeʃəli] adv. 特别地，尤其地
『especial特别的+ly表副词→特别地』

以-le结尾去e加ly

1. gently [ˈdʒentli] adv. 轻轻地，温柔地
『gentle轻轻的（去e）+y→轻轻地』

2. possibly [ˈpɒsəbli] adv. 可能地
『possible可能的（去e）+y→可能地』

3. probably [ˈprɒbəbli] adv. 很可能地
『probable很可能的（去e）+y→很可能地』

以"辅音字母+y"结尾，变y为i加ly

1. healthily [ˈhelθɪli] adv. 健康地
『healthy健康的（变y为i）+ly表副词→健康地』

2. luckily [ˈlʌkɪli] adv. 幸运地
『lucky幸运的（变y为i）+ly表副词→幸运地』

以"元音字母+y"结尾，去e加ly

1. truly [ˈtruːli] adv. 真实地
『true真实的（去e）+ly表副词→真实地』

后缀58. -ment 可加在动词的后面，构成名词，表示"行为或结果"，也可表示具体的物

1. argument [ˈɑːɡjumənt] n. 争论，争吵；论据，论点
『argue争论；争吵（去e）+ment构成名词』

❶ [C, U] ~ (with sb) (about/over sth) 争论，争辩；争吵
We had an argument with the waiter about the bill.
我们和服务员就账单发生了争吵。
After some heated argument a decision was finally made.
激烈辩论以后终于作出了决定。

❷ [C] ~ (for/against sth) | ~ (that...) 论据，理由；论点
a reason or set of reasons that sb uses to show that sth is true or correct
There's a strong argument for lowering the price.
有充分理由要求降低价格。
His argument was that public spending must be reduced.
他的论点是公共开支必须减缩。

▶ argue [ˈɑːɡjuː] v. 争吵；辩论；认为

❶ [V] ~ (with sb) (about/over sth) 争吵，争执
to speak angrily to sb because you disagree with them
We're always arguing with each other about money.
我们总是为钱吵嘴。
The committee is concerned about players' behaviour, especially arguing with referees.
委员会很关注运动员的行为，特别是与裁判争吵的行为。

❷ [V] ~ (with sb) (about sth) 辩论，讨论

If you argue with someone about something, you discuss it with them, with each of you giving your different opinions.

He was arguing with the King about the need to maintain the cavalry at full strength.
他正和国王讨论保留骑兵全部力量的必要性。

❸ ~ that 主张，认为
If you argue that something is true, you state it and give the reasons why you think it is true.
His lawyers are arguing that he is unfit to stand trial.
他的律师正在提出理由说明他不适合出庭受审。

❹ ~ (for/against sth) | ~ (for/against doing sth) 争论；争辩
They argued for the right to strike.
他们据理力争罢工权利。
The report argues against tax increases.
报告提出理由反对提高税率。

❺ argue sb into/out of doing sth
说服（某人）做 / 不做（某事）
to persuade sb to do/not do sth by giving them reasons
They argued him into withdrawing his complaint.
他们说服他撤回了投诉。

词义辨析 <P371第53> 争辩 argue, debate, dispute

2. judg(e)ment ['dʒʌdʒmənt] n. 判断力；看法，判决
『judge判断（e可去可不去）+ment表名词→判断力；看法』
（BrE judgement; NAmE judgment）

❶ [U] 判断力
She showed a lack of judgement when she gave Mark the job.
她把这工作交给马克表明她缺乏判断力。
It's not something I can give you rules for; you'll have to use your judgement.
不是我把规则给你就行了，你得运用自己的判断力。

❷ [C, U] 看法，评价；判决
He refused to make a judgement about the situation.
他拒绝对形势作出评价。
Who am I to pass judgement on her behaviour?
我有什么资格对她的行为说三道四呢？
The judgment will be given tomorrow.
此案将于明日宣判。

▶judge [dʒʌdʒ] n. 法官；评委 v. 判断；评判

3. payment ['peɪmənt] n. 付款；款项
『pay付款+ment表名词→付款』

4. shipment ['ʃɪpmənt] n. 运输；运输的货物
『ship运输+ment表名词→运输；运输的货物』

❶ [U] 运输
The goods are ready for shipment. 货物备妥待运。
the illegal shipment of arms 非法的军火运输
shipment costs 运费

❷ [C] 运输的货物
A shipment is an amount of a particular kind of cargo that is sent to another place on a ship, train, aeroplane, or other vehicle.
arms shipments 运送的几批军火
a shipment of arms 运送的一批军火

5. pavement ['peɪvmənt] n. 人行道；（硬化的）路面
『pave铺路+ment行为或结果→人行道』

He was hurrying along the pavement. 他在人行道上疾行。

Two cars skidded on the icy pavement.
两辆汽车在结冰的路面上打滑。

▶pave [peɪv] vt. （用砖石）铺（地）
The avenue had never been paved, and deep mud made it impassable in winter.
这条大街从未铺过路面，冬天泥泞不堪，无法通行。
This agreement is expected to pave the way for a lasting peace. 人们期待这个协议将为持久和平铺平道路。

6. embankment [ɪm'bæŋkmənt] n. （公路和铁路）路堤；护坡；（河、海等的）堤，堤岸
『em使+bank岸+ment行为或结果→筑岸的结果→路堤；堤岸』

a wall of stone or earth made to keep water back or to carry a road or railway/railroad over low ground
We walked along the Thames embankment.
我们沿着泰晤士河的堤岸散步。

7. basement ['beɪsmənt] n. 地下室
base地基+ment表具体的物→地下室』

8. equipment [ɪ'kwɪpmənt] n. 设备；装备
『equip装备+ment表具体的物→设备；装备』

a useful piece of equipment for the kitchen
一件有用的厨房设备
0
这个摄影室的装备花费巨大。

▶equip [ɪ'kwɪp] vt. 装备；（尤指通过教育培训等）使具有能力
The centre is well equipped for canoeing and mountaineering.
本中心有齐全的划船和登山设备。
[VN] The course is designed to equip students for a career in nursing. 此课程旨在使学生能够胜任护理工作。

后缀59. -ness 常用在形容词后构成名词

1. kindness ['kaɪndnəs] n. 仁慈，友好；友好的行为
『kind友好的+ness表名词→友好，仁慈』

2. awareness [ə'weənəs] n. 察觉，意识
『aware意识到的+ness表名词→意识，察觉』

Fortunately, all the efforts made to promote/raise people's awareness of environment protection have paid off.
幸运的是，所有提高人们环保意识的努力都取得了成效。

3. illness ['ɪlnəs] n. 生病，不健康
『ill生病的+ness表名词→生病』

4. sickness ['sɪknəs] n. 生病；恶心
『sick生病的；恶心的+ness表名词→生病；恶心』

词义辨析 <P366第26>
疾病 illness, disease, disorder, infection, condition, bug, sickness

5. weakness ['wiːknəs] n. 弱点；缺点；喜爱
『weak虚弱的+ness表名词→虚弱；弱点』

❶ [U] 软弱；虚弱
lack of strength, power or determination
He thought that crying was a sign of weakness.
他认为哭是懦弱的表现。

❷ [C] （系统、性格等的）弱点，缺点，不足
It's important to know your own strengths and weaknesses.

了解自己的优缺点很重要。

❸ [C, usually sing.] ~ (for sb/sth) （对人或事物的）迷恋，无法抗拒 （可以看作❷的比喻引申义）
Stephen himself had a weakness for cats.
史蒂芬本人偏爱猫。

6. wilderness [ˈwɪldənəs] n. 荒野；（杂草丛生的）荒地
『wild荒凉的，荒芜的+er+ness表名词→荒野；荒地』

Their garden is a wilderness of grass and weeds.
他们的花园杂草丛生。

He stood on the lookout tower and gazed into the wilderness.
他站在瞭望塔上，向荒野里凝望。

后缀60. -o 构成名词，表示"音乐术语及乐器名称"，及"人、物、抽象名词"

① -o 构成名词，表示"音乐术语及乐器名称"

1. solo [ˈsəʊləʊ] adj. & adv. 独自进行的/地 n. 独奏；独唱；独舞 〈P304〉
『sol单独+o音乐术语及乐器名称→独奏（唱）』

2. tempo [ˈtempəʊ] n. （乐曲的）拍子，节奏；（事情发展的）节奏，速度 〈P326〉
『temp(=tempor)时间+o音乐术语及乐器名称→音乐进行时间（的快慢）→节拍』

3. trio [ˈtriːəʊ] n. 三人组；三重唱；三重奏 〈P41〉
『tri三+o音乐术语→三重奏，三重唱』

② -o 构成名词，表示"人或物"

1. virtuoso [ˌvɜːtʃʊˈəʊsəʊ] n. 大师 adj. 技艺精湛的
『virtuous有美德的（去u）+o人→有美德的人→大师』

❶ [C] 大师，（尤指）演奏家
A virtuoso is someone who is extremely good at something, especially at playing a musical instrument.
He is such a professional guitarist, a real virtuoso in guitar playing! 他是一个很专业的吉他手，一个真正的演奏家！

❷ adj. （演出或展示）杰出的，技艺精湛的
England's football fans were hoping for a virtuoso performance against Cameroon.
英格兰队的球迷期待着该队与喀麦隆队能够上演一场精彩对决。

小贴士 hero（英雄），tomato（西红柿），potato（土豆），这几个-o结尾的词在变复数时，要加es。一般称这几个词为"一人两菜"。

2. dynamo [ˈdaɪnəməʊ] n. 发电机；精力充沛的人〈P157〉
『dynam(=power)力量；电+o物→发电机』

3. fresco [ˈfreskəʊ] n. 湿壁画（墙壁灰泥未干时绘）；湿壁画技法
『fresc(=fresh)+o物→（趁墙上灰泥还）未干时画的画→湿壁画』

Painting in fresco is not a common technique these days.
用湿壁画技法作画现在已不常见了。
This fresco is typical of the painter's early manner.
这幅壁画是这个画家典型的早期风格。

4. memento [məˈmentəʊ] n. 纪念品
『mement (=moment)时刻+o物→记住那一时刻的物品→纪念品』

a thing that you keep or give to sb to remind you or them of a person or place （同义词 souvenir）
The photos will be a permanent memento of your wedding.
这些照片会成为你婚礼的永久纪念。

5. patio [ˈpætiəʊ] n. （房屋外面的）露台，平台
『pati(=open)开+o表物→（房外）开阔的（供坐人的）地方→露台，平台』

A patio is an area of flat blocks or concrete next to a house, where people can sit and relax or eat.
In the summer Jim and I have breakfast out on the patio.
夏天我和吉姆在平台上吃早饭。

6. tornado [tɔːˈneɪdəʊ] n. 龙卷风 〈P335〉
『torn转+ad+o物→龙卷风』

7. volcano [vɒlˈkeɪnəʊ] n. 火山
『volcan(=Vulcan)罗马神话中的火神+o物→火山』

③ -o 构成名词，表示"抽象名词"

1. lingo [ˈlɪŋgəʊ] n. 外国话；行话
『ling(=lingu)语言+o抽象名词→（尤指不会说或听不懂的）外国话；行话』

I don't speak the lingo. 我不会说这种语言。
baseball lingo 棒球术语

2. manifesto [ˌmænɪˈfestəʊ] n. （尤指政党或政府的）宣言，声明 〈P170〉
『manifest显示，表明+o抽象名词→表明（政党信仰）的东西→宣言，声明』

3. motto [ˈmɒtəʊ] n. 座右铭；格言；箴言
『mott(=mot)动+o抽象名词→行动之指南→座右铭』

A motto is a short sentence or phrase that expresses a rule for sensible behaviour, especially a way of behaving in a particular situation.
Our motto is "Plan for the worst and hope for the best".
我们的格言是："做最坏的打算，抱最大的希望"。

4. ratio [ˈreɪʃiəʊ] n. 比例，比率 〈P279〉
『rat估算+i+o抽象名词→估算（两个量）之间的关系→比例；也可以联想rate（比例，速率）来记忆』

后缀61. -ology [ˈɒlədʒɪ] (-logy)，构成名词，表示"…学"

1. microbiology [ˌmaɪkrəʊbaɪˈɒlədʒi] n. 微生物学
『micro小，微小+ biology生物学→微生物学』

2. archaeology [ˌɑːkiˈɒlədʒi] n. 考古学
『archae考古+ology…学→考古学』
（NAmE also archeology）

▶ **archaeologist** [ˌɑːkiˈɒlədʒɪst] n. 考古学家

3. ideology [ˌaɪdiˈɒlədʒi] n. 意识形态；思想体系
『ideo(=idea)思想，观点+logy…学→思想学（方面）→意识形态』

The ideology has great influence in the world.

这种思想体系在世界上有很大的影响。

China and Pakistan are states of completely different social system and ideology.

中国和巴基斯坦是社会制度和意识形态完全不同的两个国家。

4. physiology [ˌfizɪˈɒlədʒi] n. 生理学；生理机能
『physi生理；身体+ology学→生理学』

▶ **physiological** [ˌfizɪəˈlɒdʒɪk(ə)l] adj. 生理学的

5. meteorology [ˌmiːtiəˈrɒlədʒi] n. 气象学
『meteor流星+ology学→天象；气象』

▶ **meteorologist** [ˌmiːtiəˈrɒlədʒɪst] n. 气象学家

6. biology [baɪˈɒlədʒi] n. 生物学；生理 <P119>
『bio生命；生物+ logy…学→生物学』

7. geology [dʒiˈɒlədʒi] n. 地质学；（某地区的）地质 < P184>
『geo地，地球+logy…学→地质学』

8. ecology [iˈkɒlədʒi] n. 生态学；生态<P13>
『eco生态+logy…学→生态学』

9. theology [θiˈɒlədʒi] n. 神学；宗教学 <P333>
『theo神+logy…学→神学』

10. chronology [krəˈnɒlədʒi] n. 年代顺序；年表 <P131>
『chron时间+ology…学→年代学；年表』

11. pathology [pəˈθɒlədʒi] n. 病理学 <P245>
『path病+ology…学→研究病的（发展过程的）学科→病理学』

12. psychology [saɪˈkɒlədʒi] n. 心理学；心理特点 <P274>
『psycho心理，精神+ logy…学→心理学』

后缀62. -on 构成名词，指"人、物和一些物理学上的名词"

1. glutton [ˈglʌtn] n. 贪吃者；酷爱…的人
『glutt(=glut)吞吃+on人→贪吃者』

I can't control my eating. It's hard when people don't understand and call you a glutton.
我无法克制自己的食欲，当人们不理解而叫我贪吃鬼的时候心里别提有多难受了。
He was a glutton for hard work.
他是个吃苦耐劳的人。

2. felon [ˈfelən] n. 重罪犯
『来自拉丁文fello，意为恶棍』

▶ **felony** [ˈfeləni] n. 重罪

the act of committing a serious crime such as murder or rape ; a crime of this type
Everyone involved in that felony is charged with murder.
每个涉及重罪的人都被控谋杀。

3. patron [ˈpeɪtrən] n. 赞助人；代言人；主顾 <P246>
『patr父亲+on人→像父亲一样（关心对待）→赞助人』

4. baton [ˈbætɒn] n. 警棍；（乐队）指挥棒；接力棒
『bat打+on表物→打人的棒→警棍』

5. carton [ˈkɑːtn] n. 硬纸盒；硬纸箱；塑料盒
『cart(=card)纸片+on物→硬纸片做成的→硬纸盒』

A carton is a plastic or cardboard container in which food or drink is sold, or a large, strong cardboard box in which goods

are stored and transported.

a milk carton/a carton of milk 一盒牛奶
When the postal clerk delivers your order, check the carton before signing for it.
你订购的货物由邮政人员送达时，要先检查一下包装盒再签收。

6. automaton [ɔːˈtɒmətən] n. 不动脑筋机械行事的人；自动操作装置
『automat自动+on人或物→自动操作装置』

7. crayon [ˈkreɪən] n. 彩色铅笔（或粉笔、蜡笔）
『cray+on物→彩色铅笔』

He coloured the picture with crayon. 他用蜡笔给画上色。

8. electron [ɪˈlektrɒn] n. 电子
『electr电+on物质结构成分→电子』

9. neutron [ˈnjuːtrɒn] n. 中子
『neutr中间的+on物质结构成分→中子』

10. photon [ˈfəʊtɒn] n. 光子
『phot光+on物质结构成分→光子』

11. proton [ˈprəʊtɒn] n. 质子
『pro向前+t+on物质结构成分→质子』

后缀63. -or 放在动词后，表示动作的执行者

1. director [dəˈrektə(r)] n. 导演；主管，主任；董事
『direct指导+or表动作执行者→指导的人→导演；主管』

2. escalator [ˈeskəleɪtə(r)] n. 自动扶梯
『escalate逐步上升（去e）+or表动作执行者→自动扶梯』

▶ **escalate** [ˈeskəleɪt] v. 逐步扩大，不断恶化；升级

[V] The fighting escalated into a full-scale war.
这场交战逐步扩大为全面战争。
[V] Both unions and management fear the dispute could escalate. 工会和管理层都担心争端会恶化。
[VN] We do not want to escalate the war.
我们不想让战争升级。

▶ **de-escalate** [diːˈeskəleɪt] v. （使）逐步降级
『de表相反+escalate不断恶化→（使）逐步降级』

There are signs that the confrontation is beginning to de-escalate. 有迹象表明对抗局面开始缓和了。

3. elevator [ˈelɪveɪtə(r)] n. 电梯（BrE lift）<P205>
『elevate举起（去e）+or表动作执行者→电梯』

4. governor [ˈgʌvənə(r)] n. 州长；省长；总督
『govern通知；管理+or表动作执行者→管理者→州长』

▶ **governess** [ˈgʌvənəs] n. 女家庭教师

▶ **government** [ˈgʌvənmənt] n. 政府；政体

5. competitor [kəmˈpetɪtə(r)] n. 竞争者，对手；参赛者 <P252>
『compete竞争（去e）+it+or表动作执行者→参加竞争的人→竞争者；比赛者』

后缀64. -ory (-atory) 构成形容词，表示"有…性质的"；还可构成名词，表"场所，地点"，也可表示"物"

① -ory(-atory) 构成形容词，表示"有…性质的"

1. advisory [ədˈvaɪzəri] adj. 顾问的，提供咨询的
『advise建议（去e）+ory有…性质的→顾问的』

having the role of giving professional advice
Now my role is strictly advisory.
现在我的角色仅限于顾问。

2. contributory [kənˈtrɪbjətəri] adj. 促成的，导致的
『contribute贡献，促使（去e）+ory有…性质的→促成的』

Your stupidity was a contributory cause of the fire.
你的愚蠢是起火的原因。

3. preparatory [prɪˈpærətri] adj. 预备的，准备的
『prepare准备（去e）+atory有…性质的→准备的』

At least a year's preparatory work will be necessary before building can start.
在开始动工之前至少要做一年的准备工作。

4. explanatory [ɪkˈsplænətri] adj. 解释的，说明的
『explain解释（去i）+atory有…性质的→解释的，说明的』

These statements are accompanied by a series of explanatory notes. 这些陈述后面有一系列解释性说明。

▶ **explanation** [ˌekspləˈneɪʃn] n. 解释，说明

5. exploratory [ɪkˈsplɒrətri] adj. 探索的；探测的
『explore探索，探测（去e）+atory有…性质的→探索的；探测的』

Exploratory surgery revealed her liver cancer.
探查性的外科手术查出她患了肝癌。

6. obligatory 英[əˈblɪɡətri] 美 [əˈblɪɡətɔːri] adj. 强制性的；习惯性的
『oblige强迫（去e）+atory有…性质的→强制性的』

❶ （按照规定或法律）必须履行的，强制性的
Most women will be offered an ultrasound scan during pregnancy, although it's not obligatory.
大多数处于妊娠期的妇女将被建议接受超声检查，不过这不是强制性的。

❷ (often humorous) 习惯性的，随大流的
that you do because you always do it, or other people in the same situation always do it
His lips curved up in the obligatory smile, acknowledging the compliment.
他嘴边礼节性地挤出一个微笑，以示对称赞致谢。
In the mid 60s he took the almost obligatory trip to India.
六十年代中期，他也赶时髦约印度一游。

▶ **oblige** [əˈblaɪdʒ] v. （以法律、义务等）强迫；（根据要求或需要）帮忙

❶ [VN to inf] [usually passive] （以法律、义务等）强迫，迫使
Parents are obliged by law to send their children to school.
法律规定父母必须送子女入学。
I felt obliged to ask them to dinner. 我不得不请他们吃饭。

❷ ~ sb (by doing sth) | ~ sb (with sth) （根据要求或需要）帮忙，效劳
to help sb by doing what they ask or what you know they want
[VN] (formal) Would you oblige me with some information?
拜托您给我透露些消息好吗？
[V] Call me if you need any help—I'd be happy to oblige.
若有需要，尽管给我打电话。我很乐意帮忙。

❸ 感激不尽，不胜感激
Much obliged for your assistance. 对您的帮助我不胜感激。

I **would be obliged** if you could read it to us.
您若能把它读给大家听，我将不胜感激。

▶ **obligation** [ˌɒblɪˈɡeɪʃn] n. 责任，义务

the state of being forced to do sth because it is your duty, or because of a law, etc.; sth which you must do because you have promised, because of a law, etc.
She did not feel under any obligation to tell him the truth.
她觉得没有义务告诉他实情。
to fulfil your legal/professional/financial obligations
履行法律/职业/财务责任

② -ory(-atory) 构成名词，表示"场所，地点"

1. armory [ˈɑːməri] n. 武器库，军械库；法宝
『arm武器+ory表场所→放武器的场所→武器库』

Nuclear weapons will play a less prominent part in NATO's armory in the future.
今后核武器在北约武器装备中所起的作用将不那么显著。

2. factory [ˈfæktri] n. 工厂，制造厂
『fact做+or+y表场所→工厂』

3. dormitory [ˈdɔːmətri] n. （学校等的）宿舍，寝室
『dormit睡眠+ory表场所→宿舍，寝室』

▶ **dorm** [dɔːm] n. 同 dormitory

4. crematory [ˈkriːmətɔːri] n. 火葬场
『cremate焚烧（去e）+ory场所，地点→火葬场』
（=crematorium）

5. lavatory [ˈlævətri] n. (BrE) 卫生间；公共卫生间〈P201〉
『lav洗+atory表场所→卫生间』

6. observatory [əbˈzɜːvətri] n. 天文台〈P297〉
『observe观察（去e）+atory表场所→（天文学家）观察（星星的）地方→天文台』

7. purgatory [ˈpɜːɡətri] n. 炼狱；折磨；苦难〈P275〉
『purge纯的，干净的（去e）+atory表场所→（使灵魂）变纯洁的地方→炼狱』

8. laboratory [ləˈbɒrətri] n. 实验室；实验大楼〈P200〉
『labor劳动+atory场所→（实验人员的）工作场所→实验室』

9. depository [dɪˈpɒzɪtri] n. 仓库，储藏处，存放处〈P264〉
『de向下+posit放，放置+ory表场所→放东西的场所→仓库，储存处』

③ -ory(-atory) 构成名词，表示"物"

1. directory [dəˈrektəri] n. （通常按字母顺序排列的）通讯录，姓名住址录，公司名录；（计算机文件）目录
『direct指导，引导+ory物→电话目录』

2. incensory [ˈɪnsensəri] n. 香炉
『incense熏香（去e）+ory表物→香炉』

3. accessory [əkˈsesəri] n. 附件；（衣服的）配饰；从犯，帮凶 adj. 辅助的
『access达到，进入+ory表名词→可以到达某物的小东西→附件；配饰』

❶ [usually pl.] 附件，配件
an extra piece of equipment that is useful but not essential or that can be added to sth else as a decoration
an exclusive range of hand-made bedroom and bathroom accessories 一系列独家手工制作的卧室和浴室配件

❷ [usually pl.]（衣服的）配饰

a thing that you can wear or carry that matches your clothes, for example a belt or a bag

❸ [C] 帮凶；从犯

a person who helps sb to commit a crime or who knows about it and protects the person from the police

He was charged with being an accessory to murder.

他被控为谋杀罪的从犯。

❹ adj. 辅助的；非主要的

4. inventory [ˈɪnvəntri] n. 库存；清单〈P347〉

『in里面+vent来+ory表物→来到里面（商店、某处）的东西→库存；清单』

后缀65. -ot 构成名词，表示"…人"

1. idiot [ˈɪdiət] n. 蠢人，笨蛋，白痴

『idi个人，特殊+ot表人→特殊的个人→白痴』

2. bigot [ˈbɪɡət] n. 固执的人

『big大+ot人→自高自大（听不进意见）的人→固执的人』

a person who has strong, unreasonable beliefs and who thinks that anyone who does not have the same beliefs is wrong

A bigot is a stone-deaf orator.

一个执迷不悟的人是个全聋的演说家。

▶ **bigoted** [ˈbɪɡətɪd] adj. 顽固的

▶ **bigotry** [ˈbɪɡətri] n. 偏执；顽固

3. patriot [ˈpeɪtriət] n. 爱国者〈P246〉

『patri父亲，引申为"祖国"+ot表人→爱国者』

4. zealot [ˈzelət] n.（尤指宗教或政治的）狂热分子〈P360〉

『zeal热情+ot表示人→狂热分子』

后缀66. -ous (-eous, -ious, -uous, -tious, -acious, -ose)，构成形容词，表示"充满的；具有…性质的；有关…的"

① -ous 构成形容词，表示"充满的；…性质的；有关…的"

1. dangerous [ˈdeɪndʒərəs] adj. 危险的

『danger危险+ous充满的→危险的』

2. courageous [kəˈreɪdʒəs] adj. 英勇的，勇敢的

『courage勇气+ous充满的→有勇气的』

I hope people will be courageous enough to speak out against this injustice.

我希望人们能敢于大胆说出来，反对这种不公。

3. famous [ˈfeɪməs] adj. 著名的，出名的

『fame名气+ous充满的→有名气的』

4. humorous [ˈhjuːmərəs] adj. 幽默的;风趣的

『humor幽默+ous有…性质的→幽默的』

5. mountainous [ˈmaʊntənəs] adj. 多山的；山一般的，巨大的

『mountain山+ous充满的→多山的；山一般的』

Nowadays tractors are used even in remote mountainous regions. 现在连偏僻的山区也用上了拖拉机。

The plan is designed to reduce some of the company's mountainous debt. 该计划旨在减少公司堆积如山的债务。

The fishermen set off in mountainous seas.

渔夫们冒着汹涌的海浪出海了。

In the lighted doorway stood the mountainous figure of a woman. 一个身材高大的女人站在灯光明亮的门口。

6. adventurous [ədˈventʃərəs] adj. 有冒险精神的

『adventure冒险（去e）+ous充满的→有冒险精神的』

❶ （of a person）有冒险精神的，大胆开拓的

willing to take risks and try new ideas; enjoying being in new, exciting situations

For the more adventurous tourists, there are trips into the mountains with a local guide.

对更愿猎奇探险的旅游者，有本地向导带领进山游览。

Many teachers would like to be more adventurous and creative. 许多教师愿意更加进取，更富创造性。

❷ （指事物、方法、思想）新奇的

The menu contained traditional favourites as well as more adventurous dishes.

这份菜单有受欢迎的传统菜，也有较为新奇的菜肴。

7. nervous [ˈnɜːvəs] adj. 焦虑的，紧张的

『nerve神经（去e）+ous充满的→神经质的→紧张的』

▶ **nerve** [nɜːv] n. 神经；勇气

❶ [C] 神经

❷ [U] 勇气

It took a lot of nerve to take the company to court.

将这个公司告上法庭需要极大的勇气。

I don't know how you have the nerve to show your face after what you said!

真不知道你说了那些话以后怎么还有脸露面！

8. poisonous [ˈpɔɪzənəs] adj. 有毒的；有害的

『poison毒+ous充满的→有毒的』

9. virtuous [ˈvɜːtʃuəs] adj. 品行端正的；自命清高的

『virtue品行，美德（去e）+ous充满的→品行端正的』

❶ 品行端正的

behaving in a very good and moral way

a wise and virtuous man 博学多识的君子

She lived an entirely virtuous life. 她一生品行端正。

❷ (disapproving or humorous) 自命不凡的；自命清高的

claiming to behave better or have higher moral standards than other people

He was feeling virtuous because he had finished and they hadn't. 因为他完成了而他们没有，他自以为了不起。

▶ **virtue** [ˈvɜːtʃuː] n. 品行；美德；优点

❶ [U] 高尚品德

behaviour or attitudes that show high moral standards

He led a life of virtue. 他过着高尚的生活。

Virtue is not confined to the Christian world.

善行并不是仅限于基督教世界。

❷ [C] 美德；优秀品质

a particular good quality or habit

Patience is not one of her virtues, I'm afraid.

恐怕她没有耐性。

❸ [C, U] 优点；长处；用处

an attractive or useful quality

The plan has the virtue of simplicity.

这项计划的优点是简单。

They could see no virtue in discussing it further.

他们看不到再讨论下去有什么用处。

❹ **by/in virtue of sth** (formal) 凭借；因为

She got the job by virtue of her greater experience.

她由于经验较为丰富而得到了那份工作。

10. mysterious [mɪˈstɪəriəs] adj. 神秘的
『mystery神秘（变y为i）+ous充满的→神秘的』

▶**mystery** [ˈmɪstri] n. 神秘

11. industrious [ɪnˈdʌstriəs] adj. 勤奋的，勤劳的
『industry勤奋（变y为i）+ous充满的→勤奋的』

She was an industrious and willing worker.
她是个勤劳肯干的员工。

▶**industry** [ˈɪndəstri] n. 工业；行业；勤奋

❶ [U] 工业；生产制造
heavy/light industry 重/轻工业

❷ [C] 行业，产业
the catering/tourist, etc. industry 餐饮/旅游等行业

❸ [U] (formal) 勤奋，勤劳
We were impressed by their industry.
他们的勤奋给我们留下深刻印象。

▶**industrial** [ɪnˈdʌstriəl] adj. 工业的，产业的

industrial machinery and equipment 工业机械与设备

12. glorious [ˈɡlɔːriəs] adj. 荣耀的；壮丽的
『glory荣耀；壮丽（变y为i）+ous充满的→荣耀的；壮丽的』

❶ 光荣的，荣耀的
deserving or bringing great fame and success
a glorious victory 辉煌的胜利
a glorious chapter in our country's history
我国历史上光辉的一页

❷ 壮丽的；辉煌的
a glorious sunset 瑰丽的晚霞

▶**inglorious** [ɪnˈɡlɔːriəs] adj. 不光彩的
『in不+glorious光荣的→不光彩的』

The government played an inglorious role in the conflict.
政府在这场冲突中扮演了不光彩的角色。

▶**glory** [ˈɡlɔːri] n. 荣耀；壮丽

❶ [C, U] 荣誉，光荣；荣耀的事
I do all the work and he gets all the glory.
活儿都是我干，荣誉都是他得。
The temple is one of the glories of ancient Greece.
这座庙宇是古希腊的一大骄傲。

❷ [U] 壮丽；辉煌
The house has now been restored to its former glory.
这栋房子又恢复了它往日的辉煌。

13. envious [ˈenviəs] adj. 羡慕的；忌妒的
『envy羡慕；嫉妒（变y为i）+ous充满的→羡慕的；忌妒的』

~ (of sb/sth) 羡慕的；忌妒的
Everyone is so envious of her. 人人都那么羡慕她。
They were envious of his success. 他们忌妒他的成功。

▶**envy** [ˈenvi] n. & v. 羡慕；忌妒

❶ [U] ~ (of sb) | ~ (at/of sth) 羡慕；忌妒
He couldn't conceal his envy of me.
他掩饰不住对我的忌妒。
They looked with envy at her latest purchase.
他们艳羡地看着她最近买到的东西。
Her colleagues were green with envy.
她的同事都非常眼红。

❷ v. 羡慕；忌妒
[VNN] I envied him his good looks. 我羡慕他的英俊。
[VN -ing] I envy you having such a close family.
我羡慕你有这么一个亲密的家庭。
[VN] She has always envied my success.
她一直忌妒我的成功。

14. furious [ˈfjʊəriəs] adj. 暴怒的；激烈的
『fury狂怒（变y为i）+ous充满的→狂怒的』

❶ ~ (with sb) | ~ (at sth/sb) | ~ (that...) 狂怒的，暴怒的
She was absolutely furious at having been deceived.
她受了骗，怒不可遏。
He was furious with himself for letting things get so out of control.
他生自己的气，怪自己竟让事情搞得如此不可收拾。

❷ 激烈的；猛烈的
Furious is also used to describe something that is done with great energy, effort, speed, or violence.
a furious debate 激烈的辩论
She drove off at a furious pace. 她驾车飞驰而去。

▶**fury** [ˈfjʊəri] n. 狂怒；暴怒
He flew into a fury when I refused. 我拒绝，他就勃然大怒。
She screamed, her face distorted with fury and pain.
她尖叫着，脸部因狂怒和痛苦而扭曲。

② -eous 构成形容词，表示"充满的；…性质的；有关…的"

1. righteous [ˈraɪtʃəs] adj. 正当的，合理的；正派的，正义的
『right正确+eous充满的→正当的，正义的』

morally right and good
Righteous men are greater after their death than during their lifetime. 正人君子死后比生前更受崇敬。
The judges of Israel will pronounce true and righteous judgment. 以色列的法官们将依法做出公正的判决。

2. courteous [ˈkɜːtiəs] adj. 有礼貌的，恭敬的
『court宫廷+eous有…性质的→在宫廷中必须有礼貌→有礼貌的』

polite, especially in a way that shows respect
a courteous young man 一位彬彬有礼的年轻人
The hotel staff are friendly and courteous.
旅馆服务人员友好而有礼貌。

▶**court** [kɔːt] n. 法庭；宫廷；球场 v. 讨好；求爱

❶ [C, U] 法院，法庭；全体审判人员
the place where legal trials take place and where crimes, etc. are judged
the civil/criminal courts 民事/刑事法庭
Her lawyer made a statement outside the court.
她的律师在法庭外面发表了一份声明。
He knew that this would be his day in court — his last chance to explain why he acted as he did.
他知道这将是他出庭的日子，是他能够解释自己为何如此行事的最后机会。

the court 全体出庭人员，（尤指）全体审判人员
Please tell the court what happened.
请向法庭陈述事情的经过。

❷ [C, U] 王宫，宫廷；王室人员
the official place where kings and queens live

❸ [C]（网球等的）球场

He won after only 52 minutes on court.

他上场仅52分钟就赢得了胜利。

（the ball is）in your court （这球）下一步就看你的了

❹ [VN] 试图取悦，讨好

to try to please sb in order to get sth you want, especially the support of a person, an organization, etc.

Both candidates have spent the last month courting the media.

两位候选人在过去的一个月里都在取悦媒体。

❺ [VN]（向女子）求爱

if a man courts a woman, he spends time with her and tries to make her love him, so that they can get married

3. gaseous ['gæsiəs] adj. 气体的；气态的

『gas气体+eous有…性质的→气体的，气态的』

Freon exists both in liquid and gaseous states.

氟利昂有液态和气态两种形态。

4. piteous ['pɪtiəs] adj. 可怜的，令人怜悯的

『pity可怜（去y）+eous有…性质的，充满→可怜的』

Something that is piteous is so sad that you feel great pity for the person involved.

As they pass by, a piteous wailing is heard.

他们经过时，响起了令人哀怜的恸哭。

词义辨析 <P380第95> 可怜的 pitiful, piteous, pitiable

③ -ious 构成形容词，表示"充满的；…性质的；有关…的"

1. vicious ['vɪʃəs] adj. 凶残的；恶毒的

『vice恶行（去e）+ious充满→凶残的；恶毒的』

❶ 凶残的，凶恶的

A vicious person or a vicious blow is violent and cruel.

He was a cruel and vicious man.他是一个残忍凶狠的男人。

She had been viciously attacked with a hammer.

有人用锤子凶狠地攻击过她。

a vicious dog 恶犬

❷ 恶毒的，恶意的，不怀好意的

A vicious remark is cruel and intended to upset someone.

It is a deliberate, nasty and vicious attack on a young man's character.

这是对一个年轻人品格蓄意的、卑鄙的、恶毒的攻击。

▶ **vice** [vaɪs] n. 缺点；弱点 adj. 副的

❶ [U, C] 缺点；弱点

A vice is a habit which is regarded as a weakness in someone's character, but not usually as a serious fault.

His only vice is to get drunk on champagne after concluding a successful piece of business.

他唯一的缺点就是在成功做成一笔生意后会大喝香槟而醉。

❷ 前缀 vice

adj.（职务）副的

vice president 副总统

2. spacious ['speɪʃəs] adj. 宽敞的

『space空间（去e）+ious充满的→宽敞的』

The house has a spacious kitchen and dining area.

这座房子有一个宽敞的厨房和用餐区。

3. tedious ['tiːdiəs] adj. 枯燥的，乏味的

『ted厌倦+ious充满的→枯燥的，乏味的』

lasting or taking too long and not interesting

The journey soon became tedious.

那次旅行不久就变得乏味起来。

We had to listen to the tedious details of his operation.

我们不得不听他唠叨他那次行动烦琐的细节。

4. rebellious [rɪ'beljəs] adj. 反叛的；叛逆的 <P119>

『re往回+bell打斗+ious充满的→反抗的；难控制的』

④ -uous 构成形容词，表示"充满的；…性质的；有关…的"

1. sensuous ['senʃuəs] adj. 愉悦感官的；性感的 <P292>

『sense感觉（去e）+uous充满的→感觉的；愉悦感官的』

2. ingenuous [ɪn'dʒenjuəs] adj. 天真的；老实的 <P184>

『in里面+gen出生，产生+uous…性质的→（什么事情都是）发自内心的→天真的』

3. innocuous [ɪ'nɒkjuəs] adj. 无害的；无恶意的 <P233>

『in不，没有+noc伤害；毒+uous充满，具有→无害的；无恶意的』

⑤ -tious 构成形容词，表示"充满的；…性质的；有关…的"

1. nutritious [njuː'trɪʃəs] adj. 有营养的；营养丰富的 <P236>

『nutri滋养+tious充满的→充满营养的→营养丰富的』

2. cautious ['kɔːʃəs] adj. 小心的，谨慎的 <P32>

『cau小心+tious充满的→小心的，谨慎的（也可以看作caution变形容词时变tion为tious）』

3. infectious [ɪn'fekʃəs] adj. 传染性的，感染的 <P163>

『infect传染；感化+（t）ious…的→传染性的（也可以看作infection变形容词时变tion为tious）』

⑥ -acious 构成形容词，表示"充满的；…性质的；有关…的"

1. audacious [ɔː'deɪʃəs] adj. 敢于冒险的；大胆的

『aud(=bold)蛮勇+acious具有…的→具有蛮勇性质的→大胆的』

willing to take risks or to do sth shocking

Practice had hardened me, and I grew audacious to the last degree. 习惯使我的心硬化了，我胆大到了极点。

▶ **audacity** [ɔː'dæsəti] n. 鲁莽，大胆无礼

He had the audacity to say I was too fat.

他竟敢放肆地说我太肥胖。

小贴士

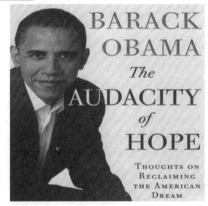

The Audacity of Hope: Thoughts on Reclaiming the American Dream 《无畏的希望：重拾美国梦》。作者美国前总统奥巴马通过讲述自己的亲身历程，盘点了美国近代政治，并试图探源激烈的党派偏见。

2. fallacious [fə'leɪʃəs] adj. 谬误的 <P165>

『fall错误+acious充满…的→错误的』

3. voracious [və'reɪʃəs] adj. 贪吃的；如饥似渴的 <P360>

『vore吃（去e）+acious充满…的→吃得多的→贪吃的』

4. vivacious [vɪˈveɪʃəs] adj. （尤指女子）可爱的；活泼的；动人的 <P356>
『vive活（去e）+acious充满…的→活泼的，可爱的』

5. loquacious [ləˈkweɪʃəs] adj. 话多的，喋喋不休的 <P211>
『loqu说话+acious充满…的→话多的』

6. tenacious [təˈneɪʃəs] adj. 不松手的；坚持的；坚毅的 <P325>
『ten(=hold)坚持；握住+acious有…性质的→坚持不松手的→顽强的』

⑦ -ose 构成形容词，表示"充满的；…性质的；有关…的"

1. grandiose [ˈɡrændiəʊs] adj. 华而不实的，浮夸的
『grand宏大的+i+ose充满的→浮夸的』

If you describe something as grandiose, you mean it is bigger or more elaborate than necessary.
Not one of Kim's grandiose plans has even begun.
金那些华而不实的计划甚至一个都还没有开始实施。
With a grandiose movement, he pointed out all the land belonged to him. 他用夸大的动作指出他所拥有的全部土地。
a grandiose opera house 华而不实的歌剧院

2. morose [məˈrəʊs] adj. 脾气不好的，闷闷不乐的
『mor(=mood)心情+ose充满的→多种心情的→闷闷不乐的』

unhappy, bad-tempered and not talking very much
She just sat there looking morose.
她就那样阴郁地坐在那儿。

3. verbose [vɜːˈbəʊs] adj. 冗长的，啰嗦的 <P348>
『verb词语+ose充满的→充满词语的→冗长的，啰嗦的』

4. bellicose [ˈbelɪkəʊs] adj. 好争辩的；好斗的 <P119>
『bellic(=bell)打斗+ose…性质的→好战的』

后缀67. -ple 构成形容词，表示"…倍的"

1. duple [ˈdjuːpl] adj. 双倍的；二重的
『du二+ple倍→双倍的』

与double词义相同，没有double常用

2. quadruple [ˈkwɒdrʊpl, kwɒˈdruːpl] adj. 四倍的；四方的；vt. 变为四倍
『quadru(=quadri)四+ple…倍→四倍的』

3. triple [ˈtrɪpl] adj. 三倍的 v. 成为三倍 <P41>
『tri三+ple倍→三倍的』

4. multiple [ˈmʌltɪpl] adj. 数量多的 n. 倍数 <P23>
『multi多的+ple倍→多倍的，数量多的』

后缀68. -proof 多加在名词后面，表示"防…的"

1. waterproof [ˈwɔːtəpruːf] adj. 防水的 n. 防水衣服
『water水+proof防…的→防水的』

❶ adj. 不透水的；防水的
waterproof clothing 防水衣
a waterproof camera 防水照相机

❷ [C, usually pl.] 防水衣物；雨衣
For staying dry you'll want nice lightweight waterproofs to wear over your leathers.
为了不被淋湿，你需要在皮衣外面套上一件轻便的防水服。

2. fireproof [ˈfaɪəpruːf] adj. 防火的
『fire火+proof防…的→防火的』

3. bulletproof [ˈbʊlɪtpruːf] adj. 防弹的
『bullet子弹+proof防…的→防弹的』

4. soundproof [ˈsaʊndpruːf] adj. 隔音的
『sound声音+proof防…的→隔音的』

5. airproof [ˈeəpruːf] adj. 密封的；气密的
『air空气+proof防…的→气密的』

后缀69. -ress 构成名词，表示"物品"

1. mattress [ˈmætrəs] n. 床垫
『mat垫子（双写t）+ress物→床垫』

2. buttress [ˈbʌtrəs] n. 扶墙；支墩 vt. 加强，支持
『butt树桩+ress物→用树桩支撑墙壁→扶墙；扶垛』

❶ [C] 扶墙；支墩
a stone or brick structure that supports a wall

❷ [VN] 加强（论点或制度）；支持（某人）
To buttress an argument, system, or person means to give them support and strength.
The sharp increase in crime seems to buttress the argument for more police officers on the street.
犯罪率急剧上升似乎肯定了街上增加巡警的论点。

3. fortress [ˈfɔːtrəs] n. 堡垒；防御阵地 <P179>
『fort坚固的+ress表物→堡垒』

后缀70. -ry 构成名词，表"行为；行业学科；（人或物）总称；场所"（参看-ary, -ery, -ory）

① -ry构成名词，表示"行为，状态，性质"

1. rivalry [ˈraɪvlri] n. 竞争；敌对
『rival对手+ry行为，状态，性质→竞争；敌对』

[C, U] Rivalry is competition or fighting between people, businesses, or organizations who are in the same area or want the same things.
There is a certain amount of friendly rivalry between the teams. 两队间有某种程度上的友好较量。

▶ **rival** [ˈraɪvl] n. 竞争对手 vt. 与…相匹敌
『riv河流+al人→河两岸争水的人→竞争者』

The Japanese are our biggest economic rivals.
日本人是我们最大的经济竞争对手。
Cassette recorders cannot rival the sound quality of CDs.
盒式磁带录音机的音质无法和CD相媲美。

2. mimicry [ˈmɪmɪkri] n. 模仿；模仿的技巧
『mimic模仿+ry行为→模仿』

One of his few strengths was his skill at mimicry.
他为数不多的强项之一就是善于模仿。

▶ **mimic** [ˈmɪmɪk] vt. 模仿 n. 模仿者
to copy the way sb speaks, moves, behaves, etc., especially in order to make other people laugh
He mimicked her southern accent.
他滑稽地模仿她的南方口音。

3. artistry [ˈɑːtɪstri] n. 艺术技巧
『artist艺术家+ry行为，状态，性质→艺术技巧』

He played the piece with effortless artistry.
他游刃有余地演奏了这首乐曲。

4. banditry ['bændɪtri] n. 土匪行为（或活动）

『bandit土匪+ry行为，状态，性质→土匪行为』

▶ **bandit** ['bændɪt] n. 土匪

② -ry构成名词，表示"行业，学科"

1. chemistry ['kemɪstri] n. 化学；吸引〈P83〉

『chemist化学家+ry行业，学科→化学』

2. husbandry ['hʌzbəndri] n. （尤指精心经营的）畜牧业，饲养业

『husband丈夫+ry行业，学科→丈夫所负责的（饲养）业→饲养业』

They depended on animal husbandry for their livelihood.
他们以畜牧业为生。

3. forestry ['fɒrɪstri] n. 林学，林业

『forest树林+ry行业，学科→林学，林业』

4. palmistry ['pɑːmɪstri] n. 手相术

『palm手掌+ist…者+ry行业，学科→从事看手相的人的行业→手相术』

I didn't know you did palmistry.
我不知道你会看手相。

③ -ry构成名词，表示"人或物的总称"

1. poetry ['pəʊətri] n. 诗歌（总称）；诗集

『poet诗人+ry表总称→诗歌（统称）』

[U] 诗集；诗歌
Since when have you been interested in poetry?
你从什么时候开始对诗歌感兴趣的？

▶ **poem** ['pəʊɪm] n. 诗歌

[C] 诗，韵文
This poem is typical of the Romantic period.
这首诗具有浪漫主义时期的特点。

▶ **poet** ['pəʊɪt] n. 诗人

[C] 诗人
He was a painter and poet. 他既是画家又是诗人。

2. peasantry ['pezntri] n. （总称）（一个地区或国家的）农民

『peasant农民+ry表总称→（一个地区或国家的）农民』

The Russian peasantry stood on the brink of disappearance.
俄罗斯农民濒临消亡。

▶ **peasant** ['peznt] n. （尤指昔日或贫穷国家的）农民

A peasant is a poor person of low social status who works on the land; used of people who live in countries where farming is still a common way of life.

3. citizenry ['sɪtɪzənri] n. （总称）市民；公民

『citizen公民+ry表总称→（总称）公民』

He used the medium of radio when he wanted to enlist public support or reassure the citizenry.
他利用广播媒介来获得公众支持或安定民心。

4. gentry ['dʒentri] n. 绅士阶层，上流社会人士

『gent绅士+ry表总称→绅士』

The gentry are people of high social status or high birth.
Most of the country estates were built by the landed gentry during the late 19th century.
乡间的大部分房子都是那些有土地的乡绅在19世纪后期修建的。

④ -ry构成名词，表示"行为，物，场所"

1. laundry ['lɔːndri] n. 洗的衣物；洗衣物；洗衣房

『launder洗涤（去er）+ry表行为，物，场所→洗衣；洗的衣服，洗衣房』

a pile of clean/dirty laundry　一堆干净的/脏的衣物
to do the laundry　洗衣服
He worked in the laundry at Oxford prison.
他在牛津监狱的洗衣房工作。

▶ **launder** ['lɔːndə(r)] vt. 洗熨（衣物）；洗（钱）

The House voted today to crack down on banks that launder drug money. 众议院今天投票决定打击为毒资洗钱的银行。
Some corrupt officials are adept at money laundering.
有些贪官是洗钱老手。

2. pantry ['pæntri] n. 食品储藏室，食品储藏柜

『pant(=pan)面包+ry表场所→面包所放的地方→食品储藏室』

3. foundry ['faʊndri] n. 铸造厂，玻璃厂

『found铸造+ry表场所→铸造厂』

4. quarry ['kwɒri] n. 采石场；追捕（猎）的对象

『quar 采石（=quarre "square stone"方形石头）+ry表场所→采石场』

5. treasury ['treʒəri] n. 宝库；（英、美等国的）财政部

『treasure财宝（去e）+(r)y表场所→放财宝的地方→宝库』

❶ the Treasury （英、美等国的）财政部

❷ [C]（城堡等中的）金银财宝库，宝库

后缀71. -ship 构成名词，表示"性质；技能；身份"

① -ship表示"性质"

1. friendship ['frendʃɪp] n. 友谊

『friend朋友+ship表示性质→友谊』

2. hardship ['hɑːdʃɪp] n. 艰难；困苦；拮据

『hard困难的+ship表示性质→困难』

Hardship is a situation in which your life is difficult or unpleasant, often because you do not have enough money.

Many poor households are experiencing real hardship.
很多贫穷家庭正经历严重的困难。

3. relationship [rɪ'leɪʃnʃɪp] n. 关系；联系

『relation关系，联系+ship表示性质→关系；联系』

4. scholarship ['skɒləʃɪp] n. 奖学金；学问，学术

『scholar学者+ship表示性质→学问』

❶ [C] 奖学金
She won a scholarship to study at Stanford.

她获得了奖学金，得以在斯坦福大学求学。

❷ [U] 学问，学术研究

Scholarship is serious academic study and the knowledge that is obtained from it.

I want to take advantage of your lifetime of scholarship.

我希望能够用到您一生的学识。

5. sportsmanship [ˈspɔːtsmənʃɪp] n. 运动员风范

『sportsman运动员+ship表示性质→具有运动员（公平竞争、尊重其他队员）性质→运动员风范，体育精神』

[U] 运动员风范，体育精神

Sportsmanship is behaviour and attitudes that show respect for the rules of a game and for the other players.

Even in the heat of a major sporting event, rivals can still show great sportsmanship with each other.

即使是在一个重大体育赛事的热度中，竞争对手仍然可以相互展示伟大的体育精神。

② -ship表示"技能；技术"

1. salesmanship [ˈseɪlzmənʃɪp] n. 推销术，销售技巧

『salesman销售员+ship表示技能，技术→销售技巧』

I was captured by his brilliant salesmanship.

我被他高明的推销技巧给征服了。

2. workmanship [ˈwɜːkmənʃɪp] n. 技艺，工艺

『workman工人，工匠+ship表示技能，技术→技艺，工艺』

[U] 手艺；技艺；工艺

the skill with which sb makes sth, especially when this affects the way it looks or works

Our buyers insist on high standards of workmanship and materials. 我们的买主对工艺和材料坚持要高标准。

③ -ship表示"身份；资格；职位"

1. citizenship [ˈsɪtɪzənʃɪp] n. 公民身份

『citizen公民+ship表示身份；资格→公民身份』

[U] 公民身份

After 15 years in the USA, he has finally decided to apply for American citizenship.

在美国生活了15年之后，他终于决定申请美国国籍。

2. membership [ˈmembəʃɪp] n. 会员身份；全体会员

『member会员+ship表示身份；资格→会员身份』

❶ [U] (BrE) ~ (of sth) (NAmE) ~ (in sth) 会员身份（资格）

The country has also been granted membership of the World Trade Organisation.

这个国家也被准予加入世界贸易组织。

❷ [C + sing./pl. v.] n. 全体会员

The membership has/have not yet voted.

会员还没有进行投票。

The club has a membership of more than 500.

俱乐部的会员人数超过了500名。

3. championship [ˈtʃæmpiənʃɪp] n. 冠军身份；锦标赛

『champion冠军+ship表示身份，资格→冠军身份；锦标赛』

❶ [C] 锦标赛，冠军赛

a competition to find the best player or team in a particular sport

The Open Golf Championship will be getting into its second day in a few hours.

再过几个小时，高尔夫公开锦标赛将进入第二天的比赛。

❷ [C. singular] 冠军头衔，冠军身份

He went on to take the championship.

他继而夺取冠军宝座。

They've held the championship for the past two years.

他们在过去的两年里一直保持着冠军地位。

▶ **champion** [ˈtʃæmpiən] n. 冠军；捍卫者，拥护者

❶ [C] 冠军

❷ [C] 支持者；拥护者；捍卫者

a person who fights for, or speaks in support of, a group of people or a belief

She was a champion of the poor all her life.

她终身都是穷苦人的卫士。

❸ [VN] 支持；拥护；捍卫

If you champion a person, a cause, or a principle, you support or defend them.

He has always championed the cause of gay rights.

他一直在为争取同性恋者的权利而斗争。

4. leadership [ˈliːdəʃɪp] n. 领导；领导地位

『leader领导+ship表示身份，资格→领导地位』

❶ [U] 领导；领导地位

The party thrived under his leadership.

这个党在他的领导下兴旺起来。

❷ [U] 领导才能

Strong leadership is needed to captain the team.

担任这个队的队长需要强有力的领导才能。

❸ [C + sing./pl. v.] 领导班子；领导层

The party leadership is/are divided.

这个党的领导阶层意见不合。

后缀72. -some 用在名词后，构成形容词，表示"充满…的，有…倾向的"

1. awesome [ˈɔːsəm] adj. 极好的；令人敬畏的

『awe敬畏+some充满…的，有…倾向的→令人敬畏的』

❶ (NAmE informal) 很好的（或极好玩的等）

very good, enjoyable, etc.

I just bought this awesome new CD!

我刚买了这张特棒的新CD！

Wow! That's totally awesome! 哇！真是棒极了！

小贴士 表示"好"的词

great, cool, fantastic, fabulous, terrific, brilliant, awesome, wonderful, incredible

❷ 令人敬畏的；让人惊叹的；使人畏怯的

An awesome person or thing is very impressive and often frightening.

They had an awesome task ahead.

他们就要有十分艰巨的任务。

The eruption of a volcano is awesome.

火山爆发的景象令人敬畏。

▶ **awe** [ɔː] n. 敬畏

❶ [U] 敬畏；惊叹

feelings of respect and slight fear; feelings of being very impressed by sth/sb

He speaks of her with awe. 他谈到她时肃然起敬。

She gazed in awe at the great stones.

她惊叹地盯着那些巨石。

❷ [VN] 使惊叹；使敬畏

She seemed awed by the presence of so many famous people.
见到这么多名人出席，似乎令她惊叹不已。

❸ **be/stand in awe of sb/sth** 对…敬畏

Caroline hardly dared talk in Alex's presence; she was so in awe of him.
卡罗琳在亚历克斯面前几乎不敢说话，她对他很是敬畏。

2. handsome [ˈhænsəm] adj. （男）英俊的；（女）健美的；数量大的
『hand手+some充满…的，有…倾向的→（大）手（大脚）的→英俊；数量大的』

❶ （of men 男子）英俊的

He was fantastically handsome — I just fell for him right away. 他帅极了——我一下子就爱上了他。

❷ （of women 女子）健美的

attractive, with large strong features rather than small delicate ones

And what sort of young lady is she? Is she handsome?
她是怎样的一位小姐？长得漂亮吗？

❸ （金额）相当大的，可观的

They will make a handsome profit on the property.
他们会从这片地产中赚取丰厚的利润。

3. tiresome [ˈtaɪəsəm] adj. 令人厌烦的；烦人的
『tire厌倦+some充满…的，有…倾向的→令人厌烦的』

making you feel annoyed (slightly angry) , bored or impatient
Buying a house can be a very tiresome business.
买房子会是件很麻烦的事。
The children were being very tiresome.
这些孩子非常讨人嫌。

小贴士 tiring 令人劳累的
It was a long, tiring day. 那是又长又累的一天。

4. troublesome [ˈtrʌblsəm] adj. 麻烦的；令人烦恼的
『trouble麻烦+some充满…的，有…倾向的→麻烦的』

causing trouble, pain, etc. over a long period of time
He needed surgery to cure a troublesome back injury.
他需要做手术来治好烦人的背伤。
The economy has become a troublesome issue for the Conservative Party.
经济状况已成为保守党的一大难题。

5. wearisome [ˈwɪərɪsəm] adj. 乏味的，令人厌倦的
『wear磨损，消耗+i+some充满…的，有…倾向的→消耗掉（热情）的→令人厌倦的』

that makes you feel very bored and tired
Simple repetitive tasks can be very wearisome.
简单的重复性工作会非常乏味。

6. lonesome [ˈləʊnsəm] adj. 孤独的，寂寞的；偏僻的
『lone独自的+some充满…的，有…倾向的→孤独的』
（常用于美语，与lonely同义）

I felt so lonesome after he left. 他离开后我感到非常孤单。
He was finding the river lonesome. 他发现这条河很偏僻。

词义辨析 <P371第50>
孤独的；独自的 lone, alone, lonely, lonesome, solitary

7. quarrelsome [ˈkwɒrəlsəm] adj. （人）爱争吵的
『quarrel争吵+some充满…的，有…倾向的→好争吵的』

He is bad-tempered and quarrelsome.

他脾气不好，爱跟人顶杠。

8. loathsome [ˈləʊðsəm] adj. 令人厌恶的，讨厌的
『loath不情愿的+some充满…的，具有…倾向的→讨厌的』

I think spiders are loathsome little creatures.
我认为蜘蛛是令人反感的小动物。

▶ **loath** [ləʊθ] adj. 不情愿的，不乐意的

not willing to do sth
He was loath to admit his mistake. 他不愿承认自己的错误。

▶ **loathe** [ləʊð] vt. 极不喜欢，厌恶

The two men loathe each other. 两个男人互相看不顺眼。
Whether you love or loathe their music, you can't deny their talent.
无论你是否喜欢他们的音乐，你都无法否认他们的才能。

▶ **oath** [əʊθ] n. （尤指对个人或国家的）誓言，誓约；（在法庭上承诺说实话的）誓言

He took an oath of loyalty to the government.
他宣誓效忠政府。
Before giving evidence, witnesses in court have to take the oath. 作证之前，证人必须当庭宣誓据实作证。

9. cumbersome [ˈkʌmbəsəm] adj. （物体）大而笨重的；（体制）缓慢复杂的；（词语）冗长的〈P145〉
『cumber障碍物+some充满…的，有…倾向的→大而笨重的』

后缀73. **-ster** 表示"…人"

1. gangster [ˈɡæŋstə(r)] n. 匪徒，歹徒
『gang黑帮，帮派+ster表人→帮派中的人→匪徒』

A gangster is a member of an organized group of violent criminals.
The gangster stabbed an innocent person to death.
歹徒刺死了一名无辜者。

▶ **gang** [ɡæŋ] n. 一帮，一伙

[C + sing./pl. v.]

❶ 一帮（罪犯）；一伙（闹事、斗殴的年轻人）

A four-man gang carried out the robbery.
这起抢劫是一个四人团伙所为。
He was attacked by a gang of youths.
他遭到一帮小混混的袭击。

❷ (informal) 一伙（经常聚在一起的朋友）

The whole gang will be there. 大伙儿都将在那儿。

2. youngster [ˈjʌŋstə(r)] n. 少年，年轻人，小孩子
『young年轻的+ster表人→年轻人』

a young person or a child
The camp is for youngsters aged 8 to 14.
这次夏令营是为8至14岁的少年儿童安排的。

3. spinster [ˈspɪnstə(r)] n. 未婚女人，老处女
『spin纺织+ster表人→（年龄大了还没有出嫁还在家里）纺织的女人→未婚女人，老处女』

小贴士 以前未婚的女性通常都在家纺线织布，过了适婚年龄还没结婚的女性被称为spinster。该词一般指中年或老年从来都未婚的女性。一般指处女要用virgin一词。

Maybe I am destined to be a sad old spinster.
或许我命中注定只是一个忧愁的老处女。

▶ **spin** [spɪn] v. 纺织；旋转

（spinning, spun, spun）

❶ [V, VN]（使）旋转
The plane was spinning out of control.
飞机失去控制，不停地旋转。
My head is spinning. 我觉得天旋地转。

❷ ~ (A into B) | ~ (B from A) 纺（线）；纺（纱）
[V] She sat by the window spinning. 她坐在窗前纺线。
spinning silk into thread 把蚕丝纺成线

4. pollster [ˈpəʊlstə(r)] n. 民意调查员
『poll民意调查+ster表人→民意调查员』

后缀74. -teen 用在数词后面，表示"十几"；-ty 用在数词后面，表示"几十"；-th 用在基数词后面，构成序数词

1. fourteen [ˌfɔːˈtiːn] num. 十四
『four四+teen表"十几"→十四』

▶ **forty** [ˈfɔːti] num. 四十
『four四（去u）+ty表"几十"→四十』

▶ **fourth** [fɔːθ] num. 第四
『four四+th表序数词→第四』

▶ **fortieth** [ˈfɔːtɪəθ] num. 第四十
『forty四十（ty变为tie）+th表序数词→第四十』

2. fifteen [ˌfɪfˈtiːn] num. 十五
『five五（变ve为f）+teen表"十几"→十五』

▶ **fifty** [ˈfɪfti] num. 五十
『five五（变ve为f）+ty表"几十"→五十』

▶ **fifth** [fɪfθ] num. 第五
『five五（变ve为f）+th表序数词→第五』

3. eighteen [ˌeɪˈtiːn] num. 十八
『eight八（去t）+teen表"十几"→十八』

▶ **eighty** [ˈeɪti] num. 八十
『eight八（去t）+ty表"几十"→八十』

▶ **eighth** [eɪtθ] num. 第八
『eight八（去t）+th表序数词→第八』

4. nineteen [ˌnaɪnˈtiːn] num. 十九
『nine九+teen表"十几"→十九』

▶ **ninety** [ˈnaɪnti] num. 九十
『nine九+ty表"几十"→九十』

▶ **ninth** [naɪnθ] num. 第九
『nine九（去e）+th表序数词→第九』

后缀75. -th 可用在形容词、动词后面构成名词

1. breadth [bredθ] n. 宽度；（知识、兴趣等的）广泛
『broad宽的（变oa为ea）+th表名词→宽度』

She estimated the breadth of the lake to be 500 meters.
她估计湖面大约有500米宽。
He was surprised at her breadth of reading.
他对于她的博览群书感到惊讶。

小贴士 bread 面包；broad 宽阔的；board 板；aboard 上车，上船；abroad 国外，海外

▶ **broad** [brɔːd] adj. 宽阔的；广泛的；概括的
broad shoulders 宽肩
a broad smile 咧嘴笑
a broad street 一条宽广的街道

(in) broad daylight 光天化日（之下）
The robbery occurred in broad daylight, in a crowded street.
抢劫就发生在光天化日之下的一条熙熙攘攘的街道上。

词义辨析 <P371第52> 宽的 wide, broad

2. width [wɪdθ] n. 宽度
『wide宽的（去e）+th表名词→宽度』
It's about 10 meters in width. 它宽约10米。

3. depth [depθ] n. 深度；深处
『deep深的（去一个e）+th表名词→深度』

❶ [C, U]（向下；向里）深度
What's the depth of the water here? 这儿的水有多深？
Water was found at a depth of 30 meters.
在30米深处找到了水。
The depth of the shelves is 30 centimeters.
书架的深度为30厘米。

❷ [U]（知识）渊博
We felt at home with her and were impressed with the depth of her knowledge.
我们与她在一起很自在，而她渊博的知识令我们叹服。

❸ [C, usually pl.] 最深处
She was in the depths of despair. 她处于绝望的深渊。
The ship vanished into the depths. 船消失在了大海深处。
Somewhere in the depths of the pine forest an identical sound reverberated. 从松林深处传来一声回响。

❹ in depth 全面地；深入地；详细地
I haven't looked at the report in depth yet.
我还没有细看这份报告。
We will discuss these three areas in depth.
我们将深入探讨这三个领域。

4. length [leŋθ] n. 长度
『long长的（变o为e）+th表名词→长度』

❶ [U, C] 长；长度
This room is twice the length of the kitchen.
这个房间的长度是厨房的两倍。
The river is 300 miles in length. 这条河长300英里。
The snake usually reaches a length of 100 cm.
蛇通常有100厘米长。

❷ [C]（绳、布、木头等的）一段，一节，一截
a length of rope/string/wire 一根绳子/细线/金属线

❸ at length 长时间地；详尽地
We have already discussed this matter at great length.
我们已经十分详尽地讨论了这个问题。

❹ go to any, some, great, etc. lengths (to do sth) 竭尽全力，不遗余力（做某事）
She goes to extraordinary lengths to keep her private life private. 她竭尽全力让自己的私生活不受干扰。

▶ **lengthy** [ˈleŋθi] adj.（事情或过程）漫长的；（报告、文章等）长篇大论的，冗长的
『length长度+y表形容词→冗长的』
This is not the place for a lengthy discussion.
这会儿不是讨论个没完的时候。
The book ends on a lengthy description of Hawaii.
这本书以对夏威夷的冗长描述为结尾。

5. strength [streŋθ] n. 力量；优点，长处
『strong强壮的，强烈的（o变为e）+th表名词→力量』

❶ [U]力量
He pushed against the rock with all his strength.
他用全力推那块石头。

❷ [C] 优点，长处
The ability to keep calm is one of her many strengths.
能够保持冷静是她的多项长处之一。

反义词 **weakness** [ˈwiːknəs] n. 弱点；喜爱〈P90〉

▶**strengthen** [ˈstreŋθn] vt. 加强；巩固

6. truth [truːθ] n. 真理；真相
『true真实的（去e）+th表名词→真相；真理』

7. warmth [wɔːmθ] n. 温暖，暖和；热情，热心
『warm温暖的，热心的+th表名词→温暖；热情』

8. youth [juːθ] n. 青年时期；青年
『young年轻的（去ng）+th表名词→青年时期；青年』
（youths 英[juːθs] 美[juːðz] n. 青少年）

❶ [U] 青年时期（尤指成年以前）
In my youth my ambition had been to be an inventor.
我年轻时的抱负是成为一个发明家。

❷ [U] 青春；朝气
She brings to the job a rare combination of youth and experience.
她很年轻，然而干这份工作已有经验，这是很难得的。

❸（新闻用语，尤指惹麻烦的）青年；小伙子
The fight was started by a gang of youths.
这场打斗是一伙少年挑起来的。

❹ the youth [pl.]（统称）青年；年轻人
He represents the opinions of the youth of today.
他代表着当今年轻人的看法。

9. stealth [stelθ] n. 秘密行动 adj. （飞机）隐形的
『steal偷+th表名词→秘密行动』

❶ [U]：秘密行动；不声张的活动
the fact of doing sth in a quiet or secret way
The government was accused of trying to introduce the tax by stealth. 有人指责政府想不事声张地开征这种税。

❷ adj. （飞机）隐形的
a stealth bomber 一架隐形轰炸机

▶**stealthily** [ˈstelθɪli] adv. 偷偷摸摸的；暗地里

A man stepped into the gas station stealthily.
一个男人偷偷地走进了加油站。

10. growth [grəʊθ] n. 生长；增长
『grow生长+th表名词→生长；增长』

11. death [deθ] n. 死亡
『dead死的（去d）+th表名词→死亡』

后缀76. -tion, -sion 用在动词的后面，构成名词
① -ide结尾的动词，名词形式为-sion，重音在其前一个音节上；形容词形式变为-sive

1. decide [dɪˈsaɪd] v. 决定

▶**decision** [dɪˈsɪʒn] n. 决定

▶**decisive** [dɪˈsaɪsɪv] adj. （事）决定性的；（人）果断的，有决断力的

They are ready to fight a decisive battle.
他们做好会战的准备。

He should give way to a younger, more decisive leader.
他应该让位于更年轻、更有决断力的领导者。

2. divide [dɪˈvaɪd] v. 分开；分配；除以

▶**division** [dɪˈvɪʒn] n. 分开；分歧；除法；部门；（军队）师

❶ [U, sing.] 分开；分隔；分配
a fair division of time and resources
时间和资源的合理分配
the division of the population into age groups
把人口分成不同的年龄组

❷ [U] 除（法）

小贴士 divide 除以；multiply 乘以
The children are already learning to multiply and divide.
孩子们已经开始学习乘法和除法了。
[VN] 2 multiplied by 4 is/equals/makes 8 (2×4 = 8) .
2乘以4等于8。
30 divided by 6 is 5 (30 ÷ 6 = 5) . 30除以6等于5。

❸ [C, U] ~ (in/within sth) | ~ (between A and B) 分歧，不和
There are deep divisions in the party over the war.
党内对于这场战争存在着严重的分歧。

❹ [C + sing./pl. v.] (abbr. Div.) （机构的）部门
the company's sales division 公司销售部

❺ [C + sing./pl. v.] (abbr. Div.) （军队）师

▶**divisive** [dɪˈvaɪsɪv] adj. 造成不和的，引起分歧的

causing people to be split into groups that disagree with or oppose each other
Abortion has always been a divisive issue.
人工流产一直是个引发争议的问题。

3. collide [kəˈlaɪd] vi. 相撞；碰撞
『col一起+lide滑→（两个运动的物体）滑到一起→相撞』

❶ [V] ~ (with sth/sb)
If two or more moving people or objects collide, they crash into one another. If a moving person or object collides with a person or object that is not moving, they crash into them.
The car and the van collided head-on in thick fog.
那辆小轿车和货车在浓雾中迎面相撞。
As he fell, his head collided with the table.
他跌倒时头部撞上了桌子。

❷ [V] ~ (with sb) (over sth)（人、意见等）严重不一致；冲突
They regularly collide over policy decisions.
他们经常在政策决策上发生冲突。

▶**collision** [kəˈlɪʒn] n. 碰撞；（意见、看法）的抵触

Stewart was injured in a collision with another player.
斯图尔特在与另一选手的相撞中受了伤。
In his work we see the collision of two different traditions.
在他的作品中我们看到两种不同传统的碰撞。

4. explode [ɪkˈspləʊd] v. 爆炸；爆发
『ex出+plode爆炸→（向外）爆炸→爆炸』

[V] Bombs were exploding all around the city.
城里到处都响起炸弹的爆炸声。
[VN] There was a huge bang as if someone had exploded a rocket outside.
突然一声巨响，仿佛有人在外面引爆了火箭似的。

▶**explosion** [ɪkˈspləʊʒn] n. 爆发；爆炸

►**explosive** [ɪkˈspləʊsɪv] adj. 易爆炸的 n. 爆炸物，炸药

The explosive device was timed to go off at the rush hour.
爆炸装置被设定在高峰时间引爆。

He made a loud, explosive noise of disgust.
他反感地爆发出一阵叫嚷。

The old man had an explosive temper. 那个老人脾气暴躁。

5. **expand** [ɪkˈspænd] v. 扩大；扩展
『ex向外+pand扩展→扩大，扩展』

❶ to become greater in size, number or importance; to make sth greater in size, number or importance
[V] Metals expand when they are heated. 金属受热会膨胀。
Student numbers are expanding rapidly.
学生人数在迅速增加。
There are no plans to expand the local airport.
目前尚无扩建地方机场的方案。

❷ 扩展，发展（业务）
If a business expands or is expanded , new branches are opened, it makes more money, etc.
[VN] We've expanded the business by opening two more stores. 我们增开了两个商店以扩展业务。
[V] an expanding economy 不断发展的经济

❸ [V] 细谈，详述
to talk more; to add details to what you are saying
I repeated the question and waited for her to expand.
我把问题重复了一遍，等着她详细回答。

►**expansion** [ɪkˈspænʃn] n. 扩大；扩张
a period of rapid economic expansion 经济迅猛发展期

►**expansive** [ɪkˈspænsɪv] adj. 广阔的；扩张的；健谈的
an expansive grassy play area 广阔的草地游乐场
He was becoming more expansive as he relaxed.
他放松的时候变得更加健谈。

反义词 **contract** [ˈkɒntrækt, kənˈtrækt] n. 合同 v. 签合同；收缩；感染〈P336〉
『con一起+tract拉→拉到一起；（把合同双方）拉到一起→合同；收缩』
（n. [ˈkɒntrækt]; v. [kənˈtrækt]）

6. **provide** [prəˈvaɪd] vt. 提供；规定〈P355〉
►**provision** [prəˈvɪʒn] n. 供应；条款

7. **conclude** [kənˈkluːd] v. 推断；得出结论〈P136〉
►**conclusion** [kənˈkluːʒn] n. 结论
►**conclusive** [kənˈkluːsɪv] adj. 确凿的；结论性的

8. **exclude** [ɪkˈskluːd] vt. 排除；不包括〈P137〉
►**exclusion** [ɪkˈskluːʒn] n. 排除
►**exclusive** [ɪkˈskluːsɪv] adj. 独有的；排外的；高档的

②以-t, -te结尾的动词，变名词时词尾变为-tion

1. **decorate** [ˈdekəreɪt] v. 装饰；粉刷
❶ [VN] ~ sth (with sth) 装饰；装潢
to make sth look more attractive by putting things on it
They decorated the room with flowers and balloons.
他们用花和气球装饰了房间。

❷ (especially BrE) 粉刷；油漆；糊墙纸
to put paint, wallpaper , etc. on the walls and ceilings of a room or house
The sitting room needs decorating. 客厅/起居室需要粉刷。

►**decoration** [ˌdekəˈreɪʃn] n. 装饰；装饰品
Christmas decorations 圣诞节装饰品

2. **donate** [dəʊˈneɪt] vt. 捐赠；献（血），捐（器官）
『don给予+ate表动词→捐赠』
[VN] ~ sth (to sb/sth)
❶ （尤指向慈善机构）捐赠，赠送
He donated thousands of pounds to charity.
他向慈善事业捐款数千英镑。
❷ 献（血）；捐献（器官）
All donated blood is tested for HIV and other infections.
对所有捐献的血都要进行艾滋病病毒和其他传染病病毒检测。

►**donor** [ˈdəʊnə(r)] n. 捐赠者
『don给予+or表动作执行者→捐赠者』

►**donation** [dəʊˈneɪʃn] n. 捐款；捐赠物
Charities appealed for donations of food and clothing for victims of the hurricane.
慈善机构呼吁为飓风的受害者们捐赠食品和衣物。

3. **devote** [dɪˈvəʊt] vt. 献身于，致力于；专用于
❶ devote yourself to sb/sth 献身于，致力于，专心于
She devoted herself to her career.
她全力倾注于自己的事业。
❷ devote sth to sth 把…用于
I could only devote two hours a day to the work.
我一天只能在这个工作上花两个小时。

►**devoted** [dɪˈvəʊtɪd] adj. 挚爱的；致力于；忠实的
❶ 深爱的，挚爱的
Someone who is devoted to a person，loves that person very much.
When you can drag him away from his work, he can also be a devoted father.
如果你能把他硬从工作中拉回来，他也会是个尽心尽责的父亲。
She was devoted to him, but she no longer loved him madly.
她一心一意地爱他，但是这份爱不再疯狂。

❷ be devoted to 热衷的，致力（于…）的
A period of time that is devoted to something is spent doing it in a determined way because you think it is important.
I have personally been devoted to this cause for many years.
多年来我个人一直一心扑在这项事业上。
The majority of her adult life was devoted to the relief of suffering. 她成年后的大部分时间都致力于减轻痛苦。
Considerable resources have been devoted to proving him a liar. 为了证明他是个骗子，已投入了相当多的人力和财力。

❸ 专用于…的
a major touring exhibition devoted to the work of disabled artists 致力于残疾人艺术家作品的一个重要巡回展

❹ 热心的，忠实的
strongly supporting someone or something because you admire or enjoy them
Thousands of devoted fans waited in the rain for the group to arrive. 数千名忠实粉丝在雨中等待着乐队的到来。

►**devotion** [dɪˈvəʊʃn] n. 关爱；奉献

❶ [U, sing.] 挚爱；关爱，关照
great love, care and support for sb/sth
His devotion to his wife and family is touching.
他对妻子和家人的关爱感人至深。

❷ [U, sing.] 奉献，献身；专心
the action of spending a lot of time or energy on sth
Her devotion to the job left her with very little free time.
她全身心投入工作，几乎没有闲暇。

▶**devotee** [ˌdevəˈtiː] n. （狂热的）爱好者；（某一宗教团体的）教徒
『devote献身于（去e）+ee被…的人→爱好者』

Mr Carpenter is obviously a devotee of Britten's music.
很显然，卡彭特先生是布里顿音乐的狂热爱好者。

③ 以-s或-se结尾的动词，变名词时词尾变为-sion

1. depression [dɪˈpreʃn] n. 抑郁；沮丧 ‹P269›
『depress使抑郁+ion表名词→抑郁；沮丧』

2. expression [ɪkˈspreʃn] n. 表达，表情 ‹P268›
『express表达+ion表名词→表达；表情』

④ 以-r或-re结尾的动词，变名词时词尾变为-ation

1. prepare [prɪˈpeə(r)] v. 做准备；做（饭）

❶ [VN] ~ sth/sb (for sb/sth) 使做好准备
The college prepares students for a career in business.
这个学院是培养商务人才的。
[VN] His doctor had told him to prepare himself for surgery.
他的医生已经告诉他做好动手术的准备。

❷ [VN] 做（饭）
to make food ready to be eaten
He was in the kitchen preparing lunch. 他在厨房做午饭。

❸ **prepare for** 为…做准备

▶**preparation** [ˌprepəˈreɪʃn] n. 准备

❶ [U] ~ (for sth) 准备
Careful preparation for the exam is essential.
认真准备考试十分必要。
The team has been training hard **in preparation for** the big game. 为备战这场重要比赛，队伍一直在严格训练。

❷ [C, usually pl.] ~ (for sth) | ~ (to do sth) 准备工作
The country is **making preparations for** war.
这个国家正在进行备战。
We made preparations to move to new offices.
我们已准备好要搬到新办公室。

▶**prepared** [prɪˈpeəd] adj. 准备好的；情愿的
I have to be well prepared for the game tomorrow.
我必须好好准备明天的比赛。
The police officer read out a prepared statement.
警方宣读了一份事先写好的声明。

2. consider [kənˈsɪdə(r)] vt. 考虑；认为

❶ ~ doing sth 考虑做某事
We're considering buying a new car.
我们在考虑买一辆新车。

❷ ~ sb/sth (as) sth | ~ sb/sth (to be) sth 把…看作…
This award is considered (to be /as) a great honour.
这项奖被视为极大的荣誉。
These workers are considered (to be /as) a high-risk group.
这些工人被视为高风险人群。

词义辨析 ‹P361第3› **认为，看作** consider, regard, view

❸ **all things considered** 考虑到所有情况
She's had a lot of problems since her husband died but she seems quite cheerful, all things considered.
自从丈夫死后，她面临很多困难，但总的来说她看上去情绪还是挺乐观的。

❹ [VN] 体谅，顾及
You should consider other people before you act.
你在行动之前应当考虑到别人。

▶**considerate** [kənˈsɪdərət] adj. 关心的，体贴的
『consider考虑+ate具有…性质的→具有考虑（别人）性质的→关心的，体贴的』

always thinking of other people's wishes and feelings; careful not to hurt or upset others
She is always polite and considerate towards her employees.
她对待雇员总是客客气气，关心体谅。

▶**considerable** [kənˈsɪdərəbl] adj. 相当大（或多）的
『consider考虑+able可以的→（大得）可以考虑的→相当大的』

adj. (formal) 相当多（或大、重要等）的
great in amount, size, importance, etc.
The project wasted a considerable amount of time and money.
那项工程耗费了相当多的时间和资金。
Damage to the building was considerable.
对这栋建筑物的损坏相当严重。

▶**consideration** [kənˌsɪdəˈreɪʃn] n. 考虑；考虑因素

❶ [U] (formal) 仔细考虑
the act of thinking carefully about sth
The proposals are currently under consideration (= being discussed). 那些提案目前正在审议中。
Careful consideration should be given to issues of health and safety. 健康与安全问题应该认真予以考虑。

❷ [C] （做计划或决定时）必须考虑的事（或因素、原因）
Time is another important consideration.
时间是另一个需要考虑的重要因素。

❸ [U] ~ (for sb/sth) （对他人的）周到考虑，体谅，顾及
They showed no consideration whatsoever for my feelings.
他们根本不体谅我的感情。

❹ **take sth into consideration** 考虑到
Everything taken into consideration, I'm sure I made the right decision.
把一切考虑在内，我确信我做了正确的决定。

后缀77. -ture, -ature, -iture, -ure 加在动词的后面构成名词，表结果、行为

1. mixture [ˈmɪkstʃə(r)] n. 混合物；混合
『mix混合+ture表结果→混合物』

2. failure [ˈfeɪljə(r)] n. 失败；不及格；失败的人或事
『fail失败+ure表行为→失败』

❶ [U] 失败；没做
She is still coming to terms with the failure of her marriage.
她还在努力适应婚姻失败的事实。
❷ [C] 失败的人（或事物）
The whole thing was a complete failure.
整个事情彻底失败了。
He was a failure as a teacher. 他当教师并不成功。

❸ [U, C] 故障；失灵

patients suffering from heart/kidney, etc. failure

心脏、肾等衰竭的病人

The cause of the crash was given as engine failure.

撞车事故的原因被认定是发动机故障。

▶ **fail** [feɪl] v. 不及格；失败；使失望；衰退，衰竭

❶ 不及格

[VN] He failed his driving test. 他驾驶执照考试没通过。

[V] What will you do if you fail?

如果你考试失败打算干什么？

❷ fail to do sth 未能（做到）；未做

I failed in my attempt to persuade her. 我未能说服她。

She failed to get into the art college. 她未能进入艺术学院。

❸ [VN] 使失望

When he lost his job, he felt he had failed his family.

他失去工作以后，感到辜负了他的家庭。

Words failed me to express how beautiful the scenery was.

风景如此之美，我已经无法用语言来表达。

❹（器官）衰竭；（机器部件）失灵；（健康、记忆、视力）衰退

The hospital said that his kidneys were failing.

医院说他的肾正在衰竭。

The patient's heart failed. 病人的心脏停止了跳动。

The brakes on my bike failed half way down the hill.

我骑自行车下山到中途刹车失灵了。

3. **gesture** [ˈdʒestʃə(r)] n. 手势，示意动作；姿态；表示

『gest(=carry)+ure表行为→带着（信息的）行为→手势』

❶ [C, U] 手势；姿势；示意动作

He made a rude gesture at the driver of the other car.

他向另外那辆汽车的司机做了个粗野的手势。

They communicated entirely by gesture.

他们完全用手势交流。

❷ [C]（表明感情或意图的）姿态；表示

They sent some flowers as a gesture of sympathy to the parents of the child.

他们送了一些花表示对孩子父母的同情。

It was a nice gesture to invite his wife too.

把他的妻子也请来是友好的表示。

❸ ~ (for/to sb) (to do sth) 用手势动作示意

[V] She gestured for them to come in. 她示意他们进来。

[V that] He gestured (to me) that it was time to go.

他示意（我）该走了。

4. **creature** [ˈkriːtʃə(r)] n. 生物；动物；人 〈P140〉

『create创造（去e）+ure表结果→（上帝）创造的东西→生物』

5. **departure** [dɪˈpɑːtʃə(r)] n. 离开；辞职 〈P243〉

『depart离开；离职+ure表行为→离开；辞职』

6. **signature** [ˈsɪɡnətʃə(r)] n. 签名；典型特征 〈P299〉

『sign标记，做标记+ature表行为或结果→做上（某人的）标记→签名』

7. **miniature** [ˈmɪnətʃə(r)] adj. 微型的 n. 缩微模型 〈P21〉

『mini小+ature行为，行为的结果→缩小之后的结果』

8. **expenditure** [ɪkˈspendɪtʃə(r)] n. 花费；消耗 〈P250〉

『expend花费+iture行为，行为的结果→消耗，支出』

小贴士 -ture在-s结尾的词根后变成-sure

1. **pressure** [ˈpreʃə(r)] n. 压力

『press压+ure表行为→压力』

2. **disclosure** [dɪsˈkləʊʒə(r)] n. 揭露，透露，公开；吐露的事 〈P136〉

『disclose揭露，吐露（去e）+ure表名词→揭露，吐露』

3. **closure** [ˈkləʊʒə(r)] n. 关停；封闭；宽慰 〈P136〉

『close关闭（去e）+ure表结果→关停；封闭』

4. **exposure** [ɪkˈspəʊʒə(r)] n. 暴露；揭露 〈P263〉

『expose暴露；揭露（去e）+ure表行为→暴露；揭露』

① -ty 构成名词，表性质或状态

1. **certainty** [ˈsɜːtnti] n. 确定性，确实性

『certain确定的+ty表名词→确定性』

2. **cruelty** [ˈkruːəlti] n. 残酷，残忍，残暴

『cruel残酷的+ty表名词→残酷』

3. **loyalty** [ˈlɔɪəlti] n. 忠诚，忠实

『loyal忠诚的+ ty表名词→忠诚』

They swore their loyalty to the king. 他们宣誓效忠国王。

▶ **loyal** [ˈlɔɪəl] adj. 忠诚的，忠心的

~ (to sb/sth) 忠诚的；忠实的

She has always remained loyal to her political principles.

她总是信守自己的政治原则。

4. **royalty** [ˈrɔɪəlti] n. 王室成员；版税；（发明、创意、矿区土地等的）使用费

『royal王室的+ty表名词→（因为土地是王室的，所以整个国家的人都要向王室缴租纳税，实际是缴的土地使用费）→（土地、财产等的）使用费』

❶ [U] 王室成员

We were treated like royalty. 我们受到了君王般的礼遇。

❷ [C, usually pl.]（作家、音乐家等通过自己作品所获得的）版税；（发明、创意、矿山、财产等的）使用费

I lived on about £3,000 a year from the royalties on my book.

我靠着写书得来的每年约3000英镑的版税生活。

The royalties enabled the inventor to re-establish himself in business. 专利使用费让这位发明家得以再次立足于商界。

▶ **royal** [ˈrɔɪəl] adj. 皇家的，王室的；庄严的，盛大的

the royal family 王室

the Royal Navy 皇家海军

We were given a royal welcome. 我们受到了盛大的欢迎。

5. **poverty** [ˈpɒvəti] n. 贫穷

『poor的名词形式』

6. **naivety** [nɑːˈiːvti] n. 天真

『naïve天真+ty表名词→天真』

▶ **naive** [naɪˈiːv] adj. 幼稚的；天真的

I can't believe you were so naive as to trust him!

真是难以相信你会幼稚到信任他！

Their approach to life is refreshingly naive.

他们对待生活的态度天真率直，令人耳目一新。

7. **subtlety** [ˈsʌtlti] n. 细微

『subtle微妙的+ty表名词→细微』

▶**subtle** [ˈsʌtl] adj. 微妙的，不明显的

Something that is subtle is not immediately obvious or noticeable.

subtle colours/flavours/smells, etc.

淡淡的色彩、味道、气味等

There are subtle differences between the two versions.

两个版本之间有一些细微的差异。

8. **novelty** [ˈnɒvlti] n. 新奇，新颖；新奇的人或事〈P237〉

『novel新颖的+ty表名词→新颖，新奇』

② -ety 构成名词，表示性质或状态

1. **gaiety** [ˈgeɪəti] n. 快乐，愉快

『gay快乐的（变y为i）+ety表名词→快乐，愉快』

The colourful flags added to the gaiety of the occasion.

彩旗增添了盛会的欢乐气氛。

2. **sobriety** [səˈbraɪəti] n. 未醉；清醒

『sober未醉的（去e加i）+ety表名词→未醉』

You had to get to Henry in those moments of sobriety.

你必须在亨利清醒的时刻同他打交道。

▶**sober** [ˈsəʊbə(r)] adj. 没喝醉的；严肃的，审慎的

❶ 没喝醉的

When Dad was sober he was a good father.

不喝醉的时候，父亲是一个好父亲。

❷ 严肃的，审慎的，头脑清醒的

A sober person is serious and thoughtful.

We are now far more sober and realistic.

我们现在清醒、现实多了。

3. **notoriety** [ˌnəʊtəˈraɪəti] n. 恶名；坏名声〈P236〉

『note知道（去e）+or表人+i+ety表状态→（因做坏事）让很多人知道→恶名；坏名声』

4. **propriety** [prəˈpraɪəti] n. 得体的举止；有分寸的行为〈P273〉

『proper合适的（去e加i）+ety表名词→得体的举止』

后缀79. -ule 构成名词，表示"小…"

1. **granule** [ˈɡrænjuːl] adj. 颗粒状物，微粒，细粒

『grain（去i）谷物；颗粒+ule小→小颗粒）』

instant coffee granules 速溶咖啡颗粒

2. **globule** [ˈɡlɒbjuːl] n. （液体或熔化了的固体的）小滴，小球体

『globe球体（去e）+ule小→小球体→小滴』

a globule of fat 一团脂肪

3. **nodule** [ˈnɒdjuːl] n. （植物或人身上的）节结，小瘤

『node节，瘤（去e）+ule小→节结，小瘤』

▶**node** [nəʊd] n. 茎节；（根或枝上的）瘤，节，结

后缀80. -ward(s) 表示"朝着"；构成副词时，-wards 为英式英语，-ward 为美式英语；构成形容词只用-ward；-ward 构成名词时只能作定语

1. **toward** [təˈwɔːd] prep. 向着；对于；接近

『to朝着+ward朝着→朝着，向着』

What's his attitude toward this business? Have you felt him out? 他对这事是什么态度？你摸底了吗？

He became violent and abusive toward Ben's mother.

他对本的妈妈动起粗来。

My feelings towards Susan have changed over the years.

这些年来我对苏珊的感情发生了变化。

小贴士 大部分情况下toward(s)是可以与介词to换用的。

2. **forward** [ˈfɔːwəd] adv. 向前地 adj. 向前的；未来的

v.转变

『fore前面（去e）+ward朝着→向前地/的』

❶ adv. 向前；进展；向将来

She leaned forward and kissed him on the cheek.

她倾身向前，吻了他的面颊。

We consider this agreement to be an important step forward.

我们认为，这项协定是向前迈出了重要的一步。

❷ adj. 向前的；未来的

The door opened, blocking his forward movement.

门开了，挡住他前进的路。

❸ [VN] 转寄，转投，转交

Applications should be forwarded through the secretary.

申请书应通过秘书转交。

3. **backward** [ˈbækwəd] adv. 向后地 adj. 落后的；向后的

『back后面+ward朝着→向后』

She felt that going back to live in her home town would be a backward step. 她觉得回到家乡生活就是没出息。

People still think of it as a backward country.

人们依旧认为这是一个落后的国家。

4. **inward** [ˈɪnwəd] adv. 向内地 adj. 内心的；向内的

『in里面+ward朝着→向内』

Her calm expression hid her inward panic.

她平静的外表掩盖了内心的恐慌。

an inward flow 向内流动

The door opens inwards. 门向里开。

5. **outward** [ˈaʊtwəd] adv. 向外地 adj. 外表的；向外的

『out外面+ward朝着→向外』

In spite of my outward calm I was very shaken.

我外表看似镇定，实则吓得不轻。

Tickets must be bought seven days in advance, with outward and return journey dates specified.

购票需提前7天，并确定往返日期。

Factories were spreading outwards from the old heart of the town. 工厂从旧城中心逐渐向外扩展。

6. **upward** [ˈʌpwəd] adv. 向上地 adj. 向上的；上升的

『up向上+ward朝着→向上』

She started once again on the steep upward climb.

她又开始沿着陡峭的山路往上爬。

A flight of steps led upwards to the front door.

一段台阶往上通向正门。

7. **downward** [ˈdaʊnwəd] adv. 向下地 adj. 向下的

『down向下+ward朝着→向下』

Downward movement is much faster than upward one.

向下移动比向上移动快得多。

She gazed downwards. 她朝下望去。

8. **homeward** [ˈhəʊmwəd] adv. 向家，向本国；adj. 向家的，向本国的

『home家+ward朝着→向家』

She is ready for her homeward journey.

她准备好踏上返家之程了。

They travelled happily homewards.
他们高高兴兴地往家赶。

9. northward ['nɔːθwəd] adv. 向北方；向北
『north北方+ward朝着→向北』

We were sailing northwards.
（当时）我们正在向北航行。

10. afterward ['ɑːftəwəd] adv. 以后，过后
『after在…之后+ward朝着→朝着…后面→之后，以后』

We went on to a nightclub afterward.
后来，我们去夜总会了。

Shortly afterwards, police arrested four suspects.
之后不久，警方逮捕了四名嫌犯。

11. leeward ['liːwəd] adj. & adv. 背风的（地）　n. 背风面
『lee背风处+ ward朝着→背风』

a harbour on the leeward side of the island
位于岛背风面的海港

▶**lee** [liː] n. 背风处；避风处

The sea started to ease as we came under Cuba's lee.
我们靠近古巴的背风海岸时风浪开始平息。

▶**windward** ['wɪndwəd] adj. & adv. 迎风的（地）　n. 迎风面

Gardens on the windward side of a hill receive more rain than those on the lee side.
山坡的花园迎风面比背风面的雨水多。

后缀81. -ware 构成名词，表示"某种物品"

1. hardware ['hɑːdweə(r)] n. （计算机）硬件；（家庭和园艺用的）五金制品；军事装备
『hard硬+ware物品→硬件；五金』

2. software ['sɒftweə(r)] n. 软件
『soft软的+ware物品→软件』

3. glassware ['glɑːsweə(r)] n. 玻璃器皿；玻璃制品
『glass玻璃+ware物品→玻璃制品』

4. warehouse ['weəhaʊs] n. 货仓，仓库
『ware物品+house房子→放物品的房子→仓库』

后缀82. -wise, -ways 构成形容词和副词，表示"方向；方式"

1. clockwise ['klɒkwaɪz] adj. 顺时针的　adv. 顺时针地
『clock时钟+wise表方向→按时钟运转的方向→顺时针方向』

Please turn the key in a clockwise direction.
请顺时针转动钥匙。

He told the children to start moving clockwise around the room.
他让孩子们开始按顺时针方向绕着房间走。

2. anticlockwise [ˌæntɪ'klɒkwaɪz] adj. 逆时针的　adv. 逆时针地
『anti表相反+clock时钟+wise表方向→按时钟运转的相反方向→逆时针方向』
（BrE anticlockwise　NAmE counterclockwise）

Turn the key anticlockwise/in an anticlockwise direction.
逆时针方向转动钥匙。

3. otherwise ['ʌðəwaɪz] adv. 否则，要不然
『other其他的+wise表方式→其他方式，其他情况→否则』

❶ adv./ conj. 否则，要不然
My parents lent me the money. Otherwise, I couldn't have afforded the trip.

我父母借钱给我了。否则，我可付不起这次旅费。

Shut the window, otherwise it'll get too cold in here.
把窗户关好，不然屋子里就太冷了。

❷ adv. 除此以外
There was some music playing upstairs. Otherwise the house was silent. 楼上有些音乐声。除此以外，房子里静悄悄的。

He was slightly bruised but otherwise unhurt.
他除了一点青肿之外没有受伤。

He was tired but otherwise in good health.
他累了，但身体健康。

❸ adv. 以其他方式
It is not permitted to sell or otherwise distribute copies of past examination papers.
不准出售或以其他方式散发过去的试卷副本。

You know what this is about. Why pretend otherwise (= that you do not)？
你明明知道这是怎么回事。为什么装作不知道？

❹ or otherwise 或其他情况；或相反
It was necessary to discover the truth or otherwise of these statements. 有必要查证这些说法的真实性或虚假性。

We insure against all damage, accidental or otherwise.
我们的保险包括一切意外或其他损失。

❺ adv. 与之不同地
Take approximately 60 mg up to four times a day, unless advised otherwise by a doctor.
每次服用大约60毫克，每天最多4次，除非另有医嘱。

I plan to wait here unless someone tells me otherwise.
我打算在这里等，除非有人让我别等了。

❻ adv. （后跟形容词或副词）原本
This spoiled an otherwise excellent piece of work.
这破坏了原本优秀的作品。

The decorations for the games have lent a splash of colour to an otherwise drab（单调乏味的）city.
为运动会所作的装扮给原本毫无生气的城市增添了一抹亮色。

4. likewise ['laɪkwaɪz] adv. 同样地，类似地
『like像+wise表方式→类似地』

He voted for the change and he expected his colleagues to do likewise. 他投票赞成变革并期望他的同事投同样的票。

Her second marriage was likewise unhappy.
她的第二次婚姻也不幸福。

"Let me know if you ever need any help." "Likewise."
"你要是需要帮助就告诉我。""你也一样。"

5. crosswise ['krɒswaɪz] adv. 对角横穿地

Cut the fabric crosswise. 把那块布沿对角剪开。

6. sideways ['saɪdweɪz] adv. 侧着地；平级（调动）地
『side侧边+ways表方向、方式→侧着地』

She sat sideways on the chair. 她侧坐在椅子上。
He looked sideways at her. 他斜着眼看她。
He has been moved sideways. 他平级调动工作了。

后缀83. -y 构成形容词和名称，表性质、状态或行为
① -y 用在名词后，构成形容词

1. foggy ['fɒgi] adj. 有雾的
『fog雾（双写g）+y…的→有雾的』

词义辨析 <P371第51> 雾 fog, mist, smog, haze

2. smoggy [ˈsmɒgi] adj. 烟雾弥漫的
『smog烟雾（双写g）+y…的→烟雾弥漫的』

▶ **smog** [smɒg] n. 烟雾 （smoke+fog）

smog是smoke和fog的合写形式，指烟与雾混合的空气污染物，尤见于城市。

词义辨析 <P371第51> 雾 fog, mist, smog, haze

misty [ˈmɪsti] adj. 多雾的；模糊的
『mist雾+y…的→多雾的；模糊的』

It's a bit misty this morning. 今晨有薄雾。
He paused, his eyes growing misty.
他停顿了一下，眼睛变得模糊起来。

▶ **mist** [mɪst] n. 迷雾；水汽

[U, C] 迷雾；水汽
a cloud of very small drops of water in the air just above the ground, that make it difficult to see
The hills were shrouded in mist.
群山被笼罩在薄雾之中。
We could just see the outline of the house through the mist.
透过薄雾，我们只能看到房子的轮廓。

词义辨析 <P371第51> 雾 fog, mist, smog, haze

showery [ˈʃaʊəri] adj. 阵雨的
『shower淋浴+y…的→像淋浴一样的→阵雨的』

▶ **shower** [ˈʃaʊə(r)] n. 阵雨；淋浴 v. 洒落；抛撒

❶ n. 阵雨；阵雪
We were caught in a heavy shower. 我们遇上一阵大雨。

❷ n. 淋浴；淋浴器；淋浴间
(especially BrE) to have a shower 洗淋浴
(especially NAmE) to take a shower 洗淋浴
a hotel room with bath and shower
配备有浴缸和淋浴间的旅馆客房
He's in the shower. 他在淋浴间冲澡。

❸ [V] （洗）淋浴
She showered and dressed and went downstairs.
她冲了澡，穿上衣服下楼去了。

❹ [V] ~ (down) on sb/sth | ~ down 洒落；纷纷降落
Volcanic ash showered down on the town after the eruption.
火山喷发后，小城落了一层火山灰。

❺ [VN] ~ sb with sth | ~ sth on sb 抛撒；大量地给
The bride and groom were showered with rice as they left the church. 新郎和新娘走出教堂时，人们朝他们抛撒大米。
He showered her with gifts. 他送给她许多礼物。

3. icy [ˈaɪsi] adj. 冰冷的；冰冻的
『ice冰（去e）+y…的→冰冷的；冰冻的』

4. spicy [ˈspaɪsi] adj. （食物）加有香料的；辛辣的
『spice香料（去e）+y…的→加有香料的』

Have you eaten too much spicy food?
你吃了太多的辛辣食物吗？

5. hairy [ˈheəri] adj. 多毛的
『hair头发；毛发+y…的→多毛的』

He was wearing shorts which showed his long, muscular
(['mʌskjələ(r)] 肌肉的，健壮的。musle的形容词), hairy
legs. 他穿着短裤，露出强壮多毛的长腿。

6. bloody [ˈblʌdi] adj. 血腥的；流血的
『blood血+y…的→血腥的；流血的』

Forty-three demonstrators were killed in bloody clashes
（[klæʃ] 冲突）.
43名示威者在流血冲突中丧生。
He was arrested last October still carrying a bloody knife.
去年10月他被捕时，身上还带着一把血迹斑斑的刀。

7. hilly [ˈhɪli] adj. 多丘陵的；多小山的
『hill小山，山岗+y…的→多丘陵的；多小山的』

The areas where the fighting is taking place are hilly and
densely（[ˈdenslɪ] adv. 密集地）wooded.
交战地区丘陵起伏，树木茂密。

8. bushy [ˈbʊʃi] adj. （毛发）浓密的；（枝叶）茂密的；灌木似的
『bush灌木+y…的→像灌木似的；浓密的』

a bushy beard/tail 密匝匝的胡子；毛茸茸的尾巴
bushy eyebrows 浓密的眉毛
Pinch out the tips of the young growths to make for compact, bushy plants.
掐掉幼株的芽尖以便让它们长得紧凑浓密，呈丛生状。

9. fiery [ˈfaɪəri] adj. 火一般的；暴躁的
『fire火（变re为r）+y…的→火一般的』

The sun was now sinking, a fiery ball of light in the west.
西边的太阳像一个发光的火球正在下沉。
fiery red hair 火红的头发
She has a fiery temper. 她脾气暴躁。

10. foxy [ˈfɒksi] adj. 狡猾的，奸诈的；（女子）性感的
『fox狐狸+y…的→狐狸般的』

No way! When someone says you are foxy, it means that they find you attractive.
不是！当有人说你像狐狸，是说你非常吸引人的意思。
You are too foxy to be my friend.
你不能成为我的朋友，因为你太狡猾了。

▶ **fox** [fɒks] n. 狐狸；狡猾的人；漂亮的女子

11. greedy [ˈgriːdi] adj. 贪婪的，贪心的
『greed贪婪，贪心+y…的→贪婪的』

12. guilty [ˈɡɪlti] adj. 有罪的；内疚的
『guilt有罪；内疚+y…的→有罪的；内疚的』

❶ ~ (about sth) 感到内疚的
I felt guilty about not visiting my parents more often.
我因没有常去看望父母而感到内疚。
John had a guilty look on his face.
约翰脸上显出惭愧的表情。

❷ ~ (of sth) 有罪责的
The jury found the defendant not guilty of the offence.
陪审团裁决被告无罪。

13. catchy [ˈkætʃi] adj. 悦耳易记的
『catch抓住+y…的→（音乐广告等）容易抓住人心的→悦耳好记的』

(of music or the words of an advertisement) pleasing and easily remembered
I would have to think up some more catchy names for these designs. 我不得不为这些设计想出一些更好的名称。

▶ **catch** [kætʃ] v. 接住；逮住；发现 n. 陷阱

❶ [C, usually sing.] 陷阱，隐藏的困难
A catch is a hidden problem or difficulty in a plan or an offer that seems surprisingly good.

All that money for two hours'work—what's the catch?
干了两小时的活就给那么些钱——这里面有什么鬼？

❷ **catch up on sth** 了解（已发生的事情）
We spent the evening catching up on each other's news.
我们那一晚上都一直在彼此通报情况。
I'll leave you two alone—I'm sure you've got a lot of catching up to do.
不再打扰你俩了——我相信你们要叙叙旧。

❸ **catch on (to sth)** 明白，意识到
It was a long time before the police caught on to what he was really doing.
过了很久，警察才明白他真正在做什么。
Wait a minute! I'm beginning to catch on.
等一下！我开始有点懂了。

❹ **catch on** 受欢迎；流行起来
He invented a new game, but it never really caught on.
他发明了一种新的游戏，但它从未真正流行起来。

14. smelly ['smeli] adj. 发出难闻气味的；有臭味的
『smell气味+y…的→有气味的→有臭味的』
He had extremely smelly feet. 他的脚奇臭无比。

▶ **smell** [smel] n. 气味 v. 闻；散发气味
❶ ~ **(of sth)** 有（或发出）…气味
The room smelled of lemons. 房间里有股柠檬的味道。
His breath smelt of garlic. 他呼出的气中有大蒜味。
❷ 散发异味；散发难闻的气味
to have an unpleasant smell
He hadn't washed for days and was beginning to smell.
他好久没洗澡了，身上都有味儿了。

15. silvery ['sɪlvəri] adj. 银色的
『silver银+y…的→银色的』
The bright moon climbed high in the sky, showering its silvery light on the ground. 明月高挂，银光泻地。

16. dreamy ['driːmi] adj. 出神的；梦幻般的；空想的
『dream梦+y…的→做梦般的→出神的；梦幻；空想的』
❶ 恍惚的；出神的
She had a dreamy look in her eyes.
她眼中流露出心不在焉的神情。
❷ 柔和的；梦幻（般）的
The film opens with a dreamy shot of a sunset.
电影的开始是一个梦幻般的太阳落山的镜头。
❸ 不切实际的；爱空想的
Paul was dreamy and not very practical.
保罗喜欢幻想，不太讲究实际。

17. handy ['hændi] adj. 易使用的；手边的；手巧的
『hand手+y…的→在手边的』
❶ 易使用的；容易做的
easy to use or to do
a handy little tool 好用的小工具
The book gives handy hints on looking after indoor plants.
这本书提供了一些关于如何照料室内花草的有用信息。
❷ 手边的；附近的
A thing or place that is handy is nearby and therefore easy to get or reach.
It would be good to have a pencil and paper handy.

最好在手边准备好纸和笔。
Always keep a first-aid kit handy. 跟前要常备急救箱。

❸ [not before noun] 手巧的，有手艺的
If you're handy with a needle you could brighten up your sweater with daisies.
如果你针线活做得好，可以在自己的毛衣上绣几朵雏菊做点缀。

❹ **come in handy** 派上用场
That key will come in handy if you lock yourself out.
要是你把自己锁在了屋外，那把钥匙就派上用场了。

近义词 **at hand** 在手边；即将来临
Having the right equipment at hand will be enormously helpful. 手头上有合适的设备将会帮上大忙。
The examination is near at hand. 考试临近了。

② -y 用在形容词后或名词后，构成名词

1. difficulty ['dɪfɪkəlti] n. 困难
『difficult困难的+ y表名词→困难』

2. honesty ['ɒnəsti] n. 正直，诚实
『honest诚实的+ y表名词→诚实』

3. jealousy ['dʒeləsi] n. 嫉妒；吃醋
『jealous嫉妒的+y表名词→嫉妒；吃醋』
They are consumed with jealousy at her success.
他们对她的成功充满了嫉妒。
Jealousy causes distress and painful emotions.
嫉妒会带来忧虑和痛苦。
Jealousy drives people to murder. 嫉妒驱使人们去杀人。

▶ **jealous** ['dʒeləs] adj. 嫉妒的；吃醋的
feeling angry or unhappy because sb you like or love is showing interest in sb else
❶ 吃醋的
He's only talking to her to make you jealous.
他跟她讲话就是为了让你吃醋。
❷ 嫉妒的
She's jealous of my success. 她嫉妒我的成功。

4. folly ['fɒli] n. 愚蠢，愚笨；愚蠢的想法或行为
『fool傻瓜（去o双写l）+y→愚蠢，愚笨』
Giving up a secure job seems to be the height of folly.
放弃一份安定的工作似乎愚蠢至极。

5. modesty ['mɒdəsti] n. 谦虚；小，少；端庄〈P226〉
『modest谦虚的+ y表名词→谦虚』

③ -y 用在动词或名词后构成名词，表行为

1. delivery [dɪ'lɪvəri] n. 传送，投递
『deliver投递+y表行为→传送，投递』
Please pay for goods on delivery (= when you receive them).
请货到付款。

▶ **deliver** [dɪ'lɪvə(r)] v. 递送；发表（讲话）
❶ ~ **(sth) (to sb/sth)** 递送，传送
[VN] Leaflets have been delivered to every household.
传单已发送到每家每户。
[V] We promise to deliver within 48 hours.
我们承诺在48小时内送到。
❷ 发表（讲话）
The president will deliver a speech about schools.

总统将就学校问题发表讲话。

❸ 接生（婴儿）

Her husband had to deliver the baby himself.

她丈夫不得不自己接生。

❹ [VN] be delivered of a baby 生孩子

She was delivered of a healthy boy.

她生下一个健康的男孩儿。

❺ ~ (on sth) 履行，兑现

[V] He has promised to finish the job by June and I am sure he will deliver.

他答应在六月底完成这项工作，我相信他会履行诺言。

[VN] If you can't deliver improved sales figures, you're fired.

如果你不能按照要求提高销售额，就会被解雇。

During the State Visit, we made a huge range of agreements that would bring us even closer together. This year will be about delivering on those things. （英前首相卡梅伦春节贺词）

在国事访问期间，我们达成了一系列协议，这将使我们两国关系更加紧密。今年将致力于实现这些目标。

2. discovery [dɪˈskʌvəri] n. 发现
『discover发现+y表行为→发现』

3. recovery [rɪˈkʌvəri] n. 痊愈；复苏；复得
『recover恢复+y表行为→恢复，痊愈』

4. injury [ˈɪndʒəri] n. 受伤；伤害
『injure受伤（去e）+y表行为→受伤；伤害』

5. mastery [ˈmɑːstəri] n. 精通；掌控
『master精通；控制+y表行为→精通；掌控』

❶ [U] 精通，掌握

If you show mastery of a particular skill or language, you show that you have learned or understood it completely and have no difficulty using it.

He doesn't have mastery of the basic rules of grammar.

他还没有完全掌握基本的语法规则。

❷ [U] 控制

Mastery is power or control over something.

Holland once competed with England for the mastery of the

high seas. 荷兰曾经同英国争夺公海的控制权。

▶**master** [ˈmɑːstə(r)] n. 主人；硕士 vt. 精通；控制

❶ [C] （旧时）男主人；（旧时）少爷；（宗教）师傅

❷ [C] 能手；（已故）著名画家

a master of disguise 精于伪装的人

an exhibition of work by the French master, Monet

法国著名画家莫奈的作品展

❸ master's (degree) 硕士学位；Master 硕士

He has a Master's in Business Administration.

他获得了工商管理硕士学位。

a Master of Arts/Science 文科/理科硕士

❹ ~ of sth 主宰；主人

She was no longer master of her own future.

她已无法把握自己的未来。

❺ [VN] 精通，掌握

to learn or understand sth completely

to master new skills/techniques 掌握新的技能/技术

❻ [VN] 控制，掌控（情绪、局势等）

She struggled hard to master her temper.

她竭力按住性子，不发脾气。

6. tyranny [ˈtɪrəni] n. 暴虐；暴君统治
『tyrant暴君（去t，双写n）+y表行为→暴虐；专横』

❶ [U, C] 暴虐；专横

The children had no protection against the tyranny of their father. 孩子们无法抵御其父的虐待。

❷ [U, C] 暴君统治；暴君统治的国家

The organization helps victims of domestic tyranny.

这个组织帮助那些家庭暴虐的受害者。

▶**tyrant** [ˈtaɪrənt] n. 专制统治者；暴君

Since 1804 the country has mostly been ruled by tyrants.

自1804 年以来，该国大部分时间都处于暴君的统治之下。

His boss is a complete tyrant.

他的老板是个不折不扣的暴君。

7. inquiry [ɪnˈkwaɪəri] n. 询问；调查〈P276〉
『inquire询问；调查（去e）+y表行为→询问』

第3讲　根据词根记单词

词根1. ag=do, act, lead，表示"做；行动；引导"

1. agent [ˈeɪdʒənt] n. 代理人；间谍；因素；作用剂
『ag做+ent表人或物→做某事的人或物→代理人；动因』

❶ [C] 代理人；经纪人；间谍

Our agent in New York deals with all US sales.

我们在纽约的代理商经办在整个美国的销售。

All these years he's been an agent for the East.

这些年来他一直是一位为东方国家效力的间谍。

❷ [C] 动力；因素；动因

If you refer to someone or something as the agent of a particular effect, you mean that they cause this effect.

In many societies, young men regard themselves as highly active, the agents of change, shapers of the world.

在许多社会中，年轻人将自己看成是高度活跃分子，是变革的推动者和世界的塑造者。

❸ [C]（化学）剂；作用剂

the bleaching agent in white flour 白面粉中的漂白剂

▶**agency** [ˈeɪdʒənsi] n. 代理机构；(especially NAmE)（政府的）专门机构

You can book at your local travel agency.

你可以在当地的旅行社订票。

小贴士 CIA（美国）中央情报局 the Central Intelligence Agency

▶**reagent** [riˈeɪdʒənt] n. 试剂
『re又，再+agent代理人→反复做（化学反应的）代理人→试剂』

a substance used to cause a chemical reaction, especially in order to find out if another substance is present

▶**counteragent** [ˌkaʊntəˈreɪdʒənt] n. 对抗力（者，物）；中和剂

2. agile [ˈædʒaɪl] adj. （动作）敏捷的；（思维）机敏的
『ag做+ile易于…的→（动作）敏捷的；（思维）机敏的』

At 20 years old he was not as agile as he is now.
20岁时他并不如现在这般敏捷。

She was quick-witted and had an extraordinarily agile mind.
她机智聪慧，思维极为敏捷。

▶**agility** [əˈdʒɪləti] n. （动作）敏捷；（思维）机敏

She blinked in surprise at his agility.
他敏捷的身手让她惊奇地直眨眼睛。

His intellect and mental agility have never been in doubt.
他的才智和机敏从未受到怀疑。

3. agitate [ˈædʒɪteɪt] vt. 煽动；鼓动
『ag做+it走+ate表动词→使（某物）从一个地方走到（另外一个地方）（再走回来）→摇动→（心）摇动→使不安→煽动，鼓动』

❶ [V] 煽动；鼓动；抗议

If people agitate for something, they protest or take part in political activity in order to get it.
The women who worked in these mills had begun to agitate for better conditions.
在这些工厂里做工的妇女们开始抗议要求改善工作条件。

❷ [VN] 搅动；摇动（液体）

If you agitate something, you shake it so that it moves about.
All you need to do is gently agitate the water with a finger or paintbrush. 你只需要用手指或刷子轻轻地搅动水。

❸ [VN] 使焦虑；使狂躁不安

If something agitates you, it worries you and makes you unable to think clearly or calmly.
The thought of them getting her possessions when she dies agitates her.
一想到他们可能会在她死后得到她的财产，她就心绪不安。

1. agony [ˈægəni] n. （精神或肉体的）极度的痛苦
『agon挣扎，斗争+y行为或结果→（因极度痛苦而）挣扎→极度的痛苦』

Jack collapsed in agony on the floor.
杰克十分痛苦地瘫倒在地板上。

It was agony not knowing where the children were.
孩子们下落不明真让人揪心。

▶**agonize** [ˈægənaɪz] vi. 焦虑不已；苦苦思索

[V] ~ (over/about sth)
to spend a long time thinking and worrying about a difficult situation or problem

I spent days agonizing over whether to take the job or not.
我用了好些天苦苦思考是否接受这个工作。

2. antagonize [ænˈtægənaɪz] vt. 惹恼；引起…的敌意（或反感）
『ant(=anti)意为against+agon斗争+ize使→使某人（和自己）斗争→惹恼』

If you antagonize someone, you make them feel angry or hostile towards you.

He didn't want to antagonize her. 他不想引起她的反感。

▶**antagonist** [ænˈtægənɪst] n. 对手；敌手

a person who strongly opposes sb/sth
Spassky had never previously lost to his antagonist.
斯帕斯基以往从未输给过他的对手。

3. protagonist [prəˈtægənɪst] n. （戏剧、电影、书的）主要人物；（比赛、斗争中的）主要人物；（政策、运动的）倡导者，拥护者
『pro向前+(t)agon斗争+ist人→（带领大家）向前斗争的人→主人公；主角；倡导者』

1. alter [ˈɔːltə(r)] v. （使）改变；修改（使衣服更合身）
❶ to become different; to make sb/sth different
[V] Prices did not alter significantly during 2004.
2004年期间，价格没有大的变化。
Nothing can alter the fact that we are to blame.
错在我们，这是无法改变的事实。

❷ [VN] 修改（使衣服更合身）
Can you alter this suit for me?
你可以为我修改这套衣服吗？

2. alternate [ˈɔːltəneɪt, ˈɔːltɜːnət] v. （使）交替 adj. 交替的；每隔一（天、周等）的
『altern(=change)改变+ate表动词或形容词→变来变去→交替』
（v. [ˈɔːltəneɪt]; adj. [ˈɔːltɜːnət]）

❶ v.（使）交替
[V] Her mood alternated between happiness and despair.
她一会儿高兴一会儿绝望。
[VN] Alternate cubes of meat and slices of red pepper.
交替放置肉丁和红辣椒片。

❷ adj. 交替的；每隔一（天、周等）的
Display compressed files and folders with alternate color.
使用交替的颜色显示压缩的文件和文件夹。
Lesley had agreed to Jim going skiing in alternate years.
莱斯莉已同意吉姆每隔一年去滑一次雪。

❸ (especially NAmE) =alternative adj. 供选择的

小贴士 交流电 alternating current (AC)
直流电 direct current (DC)
Either direct or alternating current may be used for driving electric trains. 直流电和交流电都可用来驱动电气火车。

电脑键盘上的"Alt"键是"Alternate"（交换，替换）的缩写，又名交替换档键、更改键、替换键，大多数情况下与其他键组合使用。

3. **alternative** [ɔːlˈtɜːnətɪv] n. 可供选择的事物 adj. 供选择的；可替代的；非传统的
『altern(=other; else)别的+ative表名词或形容词→可供选择的事物；供选择的』

❶ [C] 可供选择的事物
You can be paid in cash weekly or by cheque monthly; those are the two alternatives.
你的工资可以按周以现金支取，或按月以支票支取；二者可选其一。
We had no alternative but to fire Gibson.
我们别无他法，只有辞退吉布森。

❷ adj. [only before noun] 可替代的；非传统的，另类的
There were alternative methods of travel available.
还有其他可选的旅行方式。
alternative comedy/lifestyles/values
非传统喜剧/生活方式/价值观
alternative energy 可替代能源（指太阳能、风能、水能等）

4. **alias** [ˈeɪliəs] adv. 又名，化名 n. 化名，别名
『ali(=change)变化+as作为→名字变化为→化名』

❶ adv. （罪犯或演员等）又名；化名
Mick Clark, alias Sid Brown 米克·克拉克，又名锡德·布朗
Inspector Morse, alias John Thaw (= John Thaw plays the part of Inspector Morse) 检察官莫尔斯，由约翰·索扮演

❷ [C]（尤指罪犯所用的）化名；别名
Using an alias, he had rented a house in Fleet, Hampshire.
他用化名在汉普郡的舰队街租了间房子。

5. **alien** [ˈeɪliən] adj. 外国的；外星的；陌生的 n. 外国人；外星人
『ali(=other, else)其他的+en表性质→外国的；陌生的』

❶ adj. 外国的；异族的；外星的；陌生的
He said they were opposed to the presence of alien forces in the region. 他说他们反对外国军队驻扎在该地区。
In a world that had suddenly become alien and dangerous, he was her only security.
在一个突然变得陌生又危险的世界里，他是她唯一的守护神。
The idea is alien to our religion.
这种思想与我们的宗教不相容。

❷ [C] 外国人；外星人
Both women had hired illegal aliens for child care.
两个女人都曾雇过非法入境者照看孩子。
When an alien finally walked into the conference room everything changed.
最后一个外星人走进了会议室，一切才发生了改变。

▶**alienate** [ˈeɪliəneɪt] vt. 使疏远；使格格不入

The government cannot afford to alienate either group.
疏远两个团体中的任何一方都是政府承受不起的。
Very talented children may feel alienated from the others in their class.
天才出众的孩子可能觉得与班上的同学格格不入。

词根4. alti, alt=high，表示"高"

1. **altimeter** [ˈæltɪmiːtə(r)] n. 高度计
『alti高+meter仪表，仪器→测量高度的仪器→高度计』

2. **altitude** [ˈæltɪtjuːd] n. 高度；海拔
『alti高+tude表状态→海拔』

We are flying at an altitude of 6,000 meters.
我们的飞行高度是6000米。
Snow leopards live at high altitudes.
雪豹生活在海拔高的地区。

3. **altar** [ˈɔːltə(r)] n. 祭坛；圣坛
『alt高+ar表物→高出的东西→祭坛』

4. **alto** [ˈæltəʊ] n. 男高音；女低音
『alt高+o表人→男高音』

5. **exalt** [ɪgˈzɔːlt] vt. 颂扬，赞扬
『ex出+alt高→使高出→提升；赞扬』

However difficult she might have been, this book exalts her as both mother and muse.
尽管她可能很难相处，这本书还是对她给予了高度赞扬，称她既是母亲又是诗人。

小贴士 有的无人机的屏幕上在显示无人机飞行高度时就是用alt来表示"高度"的。

词根5. am, amor, amat=love，表示"爱，情爱"

1. **amiable** [ˈeɪmiəbl] adj. 和蔼可亲的；亲切友好的
『ami(=am)爱，情爱+able能够…的→值得爱的→友善的』

Someone who is amiable is friendly and pleasant to be with.
an amiable tone of voice 亲切的声调
Her parents seemed very amiable.
她的父母好像很和蔼可亲。

2. **amicable** [ˈæmɪkəbl] adj.（关系）友好的，和睦的
『amic(=am)爱，情爱+able能…的→友好的，和睦的』

When people have an amicable relationship, they are pleasant to each other and solve their problems without quarrelling. (done or achieved in a polite or friendly way and without arguing)
The meeting ended on reasonably amicable terms.
会议在较为友好的气氛中结束了。
An amicable settlement was reached. 已达成和解。
Our discussions were amicable and productive.
我们的讨论气氛非常友好并且富有成果。

3. **amity** [ˈæməti] n. 和睦；友好
『am爱，情爱+ity具备某种性质，状况→友好；和睦』

He wished to live in amity with his neighbour.
他希望与邻居和睦相处。

4. **amour** [əˈmʊə(r)] n.（尤指秘密的）恋情；风流韵事
『am爱，情爱+our→恋情』

An amour is a love affair, especially one which is kept secret.

5. **amorous** [ˈæmərəs] adj. 表示性爱的
『amor恋情+ous充满…的→充满恋情的→表示性爱的』

Mary rejected Tony's amorous advances.
玛丽拒绝了托尼的挑逗。

6. **amateur** [ˈæmətə(r)] n. 业余爱好者
『amat 爱，情爱+eur表人→爱…的人→业余爱好者』

The tournament is open to both amateurs and professionals.
这次锦标赛业余选手和职业选手均可参加。

词根6. ample=large，表示"大"

1. ample [ˈæmpl] adj. 充裕的；（身材）丰满的

❶ 大量的，充裕的

If there is an ample amount of something, there is enough of it and usually some extra.

There was ample time to get to the airport.
有足够的时间到达机场。

❷（身材）丰满的

▶ **amplify** [ˈæmplɪfaɪ] vt. 放大；增强

❶ [VN] 放大；增强（声音等）

❷ 增强，加强（效果等）

A funeral can amplify the feelings of regret and loss for the relatives. 葬礼会加深亲人的遗憾和失落感。

▶ **amplifier** [ˈæmplɪfaɪə(r)] n. 放大器；扩音器

▶ **amplitude** [ˈæmplɪtjuːd] n. （声波或电流信号的）振幅，强度

『ample大的（去e）+i+tude表名词→（声波或电流信号等）大的程度→振幅，强度』

[U, C]（physics 物）（声音、无线电波等的）振幅

In physics, the amplitude of a sound wave or electrical signal is its strength.

As we fall asleep the amplitude of brain waves slowly becomes greater.
进入睡眠状态时，我们的脑电波振幅慢慢变大。

词根7. angle，表示"角"，形容词为angular

1. angle [ˈæŋgl] n. 角；角度；立场

The photo was taken from an unusual angle.
这张照片是从不寻常的角度拍摄的。

You can look at the issue from many different angles.
你可以从很多不同的角度看这个问题。

2. triangle [ˈtraɪæŋgl] n. 三角形；三角形物体
『tri三+angle角→三个角→三角形』

(BrE) a right-angled triangle 直角三角形
(NAmE) a right triangle 直角三角形

Cut the sandwiches into triangles. 把三明治切成三角形。

▶ **triangular** [traɪˈæŋgjələ(r)] adj. 三角的，三角形的

3. rectangle [ˈrektæŋgl] n.长方形；矩形
『rect直，正+angle角→（四个角）都是直角→矩形』

What have we learned today? Rectangle and square.
今天我们学习了些什么？长方形和正方形。

▶ **rectangular** [rekˈtæŋgjələ(r)] adj. 长方形的；矩形的

词根8. ann(u), enn=year, one year，表示"年，一年"

1. annual [ˈænjuəl] adj. 每年的；一年的 n. 年刊；年报
『annu年，一年+ al…的→一年一度的』

❶ adj. 每年的；一年一次的
an annual meeting/event/report
年会；一年一度的大事；年度报告

❷ adj. 一年的
an annual income/subscription/budget
年收入；年度订阅费；年度预算

❸ [C] 年刊，年报；一年生植物
The football annual for 2001 kept his picture in it.
2001年的足球年刊上有他的照片。

2. annals [ˈænlz] n. 编年史；年鉴
『ann年，一年+al表人或物+s表复数→一年年的人和事物→编年史』

His deeds went down in the annals of British history.
他的事迹已载入英国史册。

3. anniversary [ˌænɪˈvɜːsəri] n. 周年纪念日
『ann年，一年+i+ vers转+ary物→一年转到一次的那天→周年纪念日』

on the anniversary of his wife's death
在他妻子去世的周年忌日
The society is celebrating its tenth anniversary this year.
这个协会今年将举办成立10周年庆典。

4. biannual [baɪˈænjuəl] adj. 一年两次的
『bi二+annu年，一年+al…的→一年两次的』

You will need to have a routine biannual examination.
你得接受一年两次的例行检查。

5. biennial [baɪˈeniəl] adj.（事件）两年一次的
『bi二+enn年+ial具有…的→两年（一次）的』

A biennial art show was held in the city in 1984，1986 and 1988.
1984年、1986年和1988年，在该市举行了每两年一次的艺术展览。

6. perennial [pəˈreniəl] adj. 长久的；（植物）多年生的 n. 多年生植物
『per (through)贯穿+enn年+ial…的→贯穿整年的→长久的』

❶ adj.（尤指问题或困难）永恒的；持续的
There's a perennial shortage of teachers with science qualifications.
有理科教学资格的老师一直都很短缺。

❷ adj.（植物）多年生的 n. 多年生植物
A perennial is a plant that lives indefinitely.
多年生植物是指能存活很多年的植物。

7. millennium [mɪˈleniəm] n. 一千年；千禧年
『mill千+enn年，一年+ium表名词→一千年』

How did you celebrate the millennium?
你们是如何欢庆千禧年的？
The Millennium Development Goals have cut poverty in half.
千年发展目标已经将贫穷减少了一半。

8. centenary 英 [senˈtiːnəri] 美 [senˈtenəri] adj. 一百周年的 n. 一百周年纪念

『cent百+en(= enn)年+ary…的，有…性质的→一百年的』
（also centennial NAmE, BrE）

The club will celebrate its centenary next year.
俱乐部明年要庆祝成立一百周年。

词根9. anim=life, mind, 表示"生命；内心"

1. animal [ˈænɪml] n. 动物
『anim生命+al表名词→动物』

2. animate [ˈænɪmeɪt, ˈænɪmət] vt. 使有活力 adj.有生命的
『anim(=life)生命，活力+ate表动词或形容词→使有活力；有生命的』
（v. [ˈænɪmeɪt]; adj. [ˈænɪmət]）

❶ [VN] 使具有活力
to make sth more lively or full of energy
A smile suddenly animated her face.
她嫣然一笑，立刻容光焕发。

❷ [usually passive] 把…制成动画片
How do you animate characters in the computer?
你怎样在电脑上给角色做动画？

❸ adj. 有生命的；活的
all aspects of the material world, animate and inanimate
物质世界的方方面面，包括有生命的和无生命的

▶ **animation** [ˌænɪˈmeɪʃn] n. 生气；活力；动画片制作
❶ [U] 生气；活力
His face was drained of all colour and animation.
他面如死灰。
❷ [C, U] 动画片；动画制作
This film is the first British animation sold to an American network. 这是第一部出售给美国电视网的英国动画片。

3. unanimous [juˈnænɪməs] adj. 一致同意的
『un（=uni）一个的+anim(mind)心思+ous充满→一个心思的→想法一致的→一致同意的』
Local people are unanimous in their opposition to the proposed new road. 当地居民一致反对拟建的新公路。
His proposal met with unanimous approval.
他的倡议得到了大家一致的赞同。

4. magnanimous [mæɡˈnænɪməs] adj. 宽宏的，大度的
『magn大+anim(mind)内心+ous充满→心胸大的→大度的』
If you are magnanimous, you behave kindly and generously towards someone, especially after defeating them or being treated badly by them.
I was prepared to be magnanimous, prepared to feel compassion for him.
我准备表现得宽宏大量，同情他的境遇。

5. equanimity [ˌekwəˈnɪməti] n. 镇静；沉着，冷静
『equ相等+anim内心+ity表名词→内心平静』
She accepted the prospect of her operation with equanimity.
她心情平静地接受了动手术的可能性。
▶ **equanimous** [ɪˈkwænɪməs] adj. 镇定的；安静的

6. animosity [ˌænɪˈmɒsəti] n. 敌意；怨恨，憎恶
『anim内心+osity多的状态→内心充满（怨恨）→敌意』
a strong feeling of opposition, anger or hatred
There's a long history of animosity between the two nations.
两国之间积怨已久。

词根10. anthrop= man, human being，表示"人，人类"

1. anthropology [ˌænθrəˈpɒlədʒi] n. 人类学
『anthrop人，人类+ology学→人类学』
▶ **anthropologist** [ˌænθrəˈpɒlədʒɪst] n. 人类学家

2. anthropomorphic [ˌænθrəpəˈmɔːfik] adj. 拟人化的
『anthrop人，人类+o+morph形状+ic…的→（赋予其他事物）人形的→拟人化的』
treating gods, animals or objects as if they had human qualities
The world of the gods is anthropomorphic, an imitative projection of ours.
神界是拟人化的，是模仿我们人类世界的一个投影。

3. philanthropy [fɪˈlænθrəpi] n. 慈善，捐助〈P254〉
『phil爱+anthrop人+y表行为→爱人类（所以给钱来帮助穷人）→慈善』

词根11. apt, ept=fit，表示"适合的"

1. apt [æpt] adj. 合适的
❶（话语、描述或选择）合适的，恰当的
The words of this report are as apt today as in 1929.
这份报告的措辞用在今天和用在1929年一样贴切。
❷ ~ to do sth 易于，倾向（指天生具有的做某事的倾向）
Babies are apt to put objects into their mouths.
婴儿爱把东西往嘴里塞。
This kind of apple is apt to go bad. 这种苹果容易坏。

▶ **aptitude** [ˈæptɪtjuːd] n.（适合做某事的）天资，天赋
『apt适合+itude表状态、性质→具有适合（做某事的）性质→天资』
[U, C] ~ (for sth) | ~ (for doing sth) 天生做某事的才能
She showed a natural aptitude for the work.
她表现出了做这工作的天赋。
His aptitude for dealing with children got him the job.
他善于和儿童打交道的本事使他得到了这份工作。

小贴士 an aptitude test 能力倾向测验
one designed to show whether sb has the natural ability for a particular job or course of education

2. adapt [əˈdæpt] v.（使）适应；改编
『ad(=to)到+apt适合的→使达到适合→使适应；改编』
❶ [VN] ~ sth (for sth) 使适应，使适合（新用途、新情况）
Most of these tools have been specially adapted for use by disabled people.
这些工具多数已经过特别改装，供残疾人使用。
❷ ~ (yourself) (to sth) 适应（新情况）
We have had to adapt quickly to the new system.
我们不得不迅速适应新制度。
It took him a while to adapt himself to his new surroundings.
他过了好一阵子才适应了新环境。
❸ [VN] ~ sth (for sth) (from sth) 改编；改写
Three of her novels have been adapted for television.
她的长篇小说中有三部已改编成电视剧。
▶ **adaptation** [ˌædæpˈteɪʃn] n. 适应；改编
▶ **adaptable** [əˈdæptəbl] adj. 可适应的；可改编的

3. adept [əˈdept] adj. 熟练的
『ad(=to)到+ept适合的→达到适合（做某事）→熟练的』

good at doing sth that is quite difficult

He's usually very adept at keeping his private life out of the media. 他通常很善于使自己的私生活避开媒体的关注。

4. inept [ɪˈnept] adj. 无能的；笨拙的

『in不+ept适合的→不适合（做某事的）→无能的』

If you say that someone is inept, you are criticizing them because they do something with a complete lack of skill.

He was inept and lacked the intelligence to govern.

他没有什么能力，缺乏管理才干。

▶ **ineptitude** [ɪˈneptɪtjuːd] n. 无能；笨拙

『inept无能，笨拙+itude表性质→无能，笨拙』

In the book she speaks of his "social ineptitude" and says he verbally abused her.

她在书中提到他"缺乏社交技能"，并且说他曾经对她出言不逊。

词根12. astro, aster=star，表示"星星"

1. astronomy [əˈstrɒnəmi] n. 天文学

『astro星星+nomy科学；法则→研究星星的科学法则→天文学』

2. astronaut [ˈæstrənɔːt] n. 宇航员 〈P232〉

『astro星星+naut船→驾驶飞船在星际航行的人→宇航员』

3. disaster [dɪˈzɑːstə(r)] n. 灾难，灾祸；彻底失败的人或事

『dis坏+aster星→星位不正，表示有灾难』

Thousands died in the disaster. 数千人在这场灾祸中丧生。

Disaster struck when the wheel came off.

车轮脱落，灾难就来了。

The play's first night was a total disaster.

这出戏头一晚就彻底演砸了。

▶ **disastrous** [dɪˈzɑːstrəs] adj. 灾难性的；极糟糕的

4. asterisk [ˈæstərɪsk] n. 星号 vt. 加星号于

『aster星星+isk→星号』

I've placed an asterisk next to the tasks I want you to do first.

我在要你首先完成的任务旁边标上了星号。

5. asteroid [ˈæstərɔɪd] n. 小行星

『aster星星+oid→小行星』

There is an asteroid on a collision course with the Earth.

有一颗小行星可能会与地球发生碰撞。

6. astral [ˈæstrəl] adj. 星的；多星的

『aster星星（去e）+al…的→星星的』

astral navigation 星际航行

astral light 星光

7. astrology [əˈstrɒlədʒi] n. 占星术；占星学

『aster星星（去e）+ology学→占星学』

词根13. arc(h)= bow，表示"拱形；弓，弓形"

1. arcade [ɑːˈkeɪd] n. 拱廊；室内（购物）商场

『arc拱形+ade某种材料的制成物→拱廊』

a covered passage between streets, with shops/stores on either side

I just told you. I went to the arcade.

我告诉你了，我上街去了。

2. arch [ɑːtʃ] n. 拱；拱形 v. 成弓形；拱起

❶ [C] 拱；拱门；拱形；拱形物

Go through the arch and follow the path.

穿过拱门沿小径往前走。

❷ [V, VN]成弓形；弓起（腰，眉毛等）

The cat arched its back and hissed.

猫弓起背发出嘶嘶声。

Tall trees arched over the path. 大树呈拱形遮阴了小道。

▶ **archer** [ˈɑːtʃə(r)] n. 弓箭手，射箭运动员

▶ **archway** [ˈɑːtʃweɪ] n. 拱门，拱道

3. archive [ˈɑːkaɪv] n. 档案文件；档案馆；计算机档案文件压缩包

『arch弓+ive表物→弓形的房子→档案馆』

I decided I would go to the archive the next day and look up the appropriate issue.

我决定第二天去档案馆查找对应的问题。

The importance of archives determines the significance of archive management.

档案的重要作用决定了档案管理工作的重要意义。

Select the files and folders to be added to the archive.

选择要添加存档的文件和文件夹。

One or more files in the archive are corrupted.

存档中的一个或多个文件已损坏。

4. architect [ˈɑːkɪtekt] n. 建筑师

『archi (=arch)弓+tect遮蔽→弓形遮蔽物的制造者→建筑师』

▶ **architecture** [ˈɑːkɪtektʃə(r)] n. 建筑学；建筑风格

『architect建筑师+ure与行为有关之物→建筑学；建筑』

❶ [U] 建筑学

He studied classical architecture and design in Rome.

他在罗马学习了古典建筑学和设计。

❷ [U] 建筑设计；建筑风格

The architecture is harmonious and no building is over five or six floors high.

这里的建筑风格和谐统一，没有哪座楼房高于五六层。

词根14. arch=ruler，表示"统治者"

1. monarch [ˈmɒnək] n. 君主，帝王

『mon单个，一个+arch统治者→一个人统治→君主』

a person who rules a country, for example a king or a queen

2. anarchic [əˈnɑːkɪk] adj. 无政府主义的；无秩序的

『an无+arch统治者+ic…的→无统治者的→无政府主义的』

If you describe someone or something as anarchic, you disapprove of them because they do not recognise or obey any rules or laws.

School violence is a behaviour that is anarchic and destructive to school's stability and studying circumstance.

校园暴力是一种无组织无纪律的破坏校园安定和学生学习环境的行径。

Tumor cells accumulate errors, become totally anarchic, and flout all the rules.

肿瘤细胞随着错误的累积，变得完全异常，违反了所有的自然规则。

▶ **anarchism** [ˈænəkɪzəm] n. 无政府主义

『an无+arch统治者+ism主义，行为→无政府主义』

He advocated anarchism as the answer to social problems.

他提倡以无政府主义来解决社会问题。

▶**anarchy** ['ænəki] n. 无政府状态；混乱；无法无天
『an无+arch统治+y表名词→无政府状态』

The overthrow of the military regime was followed by a period of anarchy.
军事统治政权被推翻以后，接着是一段时期的无政府状态。
There was complete anarchy in the classroom when their usual teacher was away. 任课老师不在时，班上一片混乱。

3. archbishop [ˌɑːtʃ'bɪʃəp] n. 大主教
『arch统治者+bishop主教→大主教』

a bishop of the highest rank, responsible for all the churches in a large area

4. hierarchy ['haɪərɑːki] n. 等级制度（尤指社会或组织）；统治集团；层次体系
『hier神+arch统治+y表名词→神统治（也是有等级制度的）→等级制度』

She's quite high up in the management hierarchy.
她位居管理层要职。
The hierarchy obtains more benefit.
统治集团得到更多的利益。
This can be a hierarchy of folders.
这可以是一个文件夹层次结构。

5. matriarch ['meɪtriɑːk] n. 女家长；女族长 〈P216〉
『matri母性，母亲+arch统治者→女家长』

6. patriarch ['peɪtriɑːk] n.（男性）家长；族长，酋长 〈P246〉
『patri父亲+arch统治者→家长；族长，酋长』

词根15. art=skill, joint, trick, 表示"技术；关节；诡计"

1. artisan [ˌɑːtɪ'zæn] n. 工匠；手艺人
『artis(=arti)技术+an精通…的人→精通某种技术之人→工匠』

a person who does skilled work, making things with their hands
The artisan can cut stones into various shapes.
这工匠能把石头雕成各种形状。

2. artifact/artefact ['ɑːtɪfækt] n. 手工制品；手工艺品
『arti/arte技术+fact做→用技术做出来的→工艺品』

an object that is made by a person, especially sth of historical or cultural interest

3. article ['ɑːtɪkl] n. 物品；冠词；文章；条款
『art技术+icle小→用技术做出的小东西→物品』

❶ [C] 物件，物品（尤指整套中的一件）
a particular item or separate thing, especially one of a set
articles of clothing 衣物
toilet articles such as soap and shampoo
肥皂和洗发剂之类的盥洗用品

❷ [C] 冠词；（报刊上的）文章；（协议、契约）条款
Article 10 of the European Convention guarantees free speech. 《欧洲公约》第10条保障言论自由。

4. artificial [ˌɑːtɪ'fɪʃl] adj. 人工的，人造的
『arti技术+fic做+ial…的→人工做出来的→人造的』

❶ 人造的（非自然生成的）
made or produced to copy sth natural; not real
an artificial limb/flower/sweetener/fertilizer
假肢；假花；人造甜味剂；化肥

artificial lighting/light 人工照明；人造光

❷ 人为的
the artificial barriers of race, class and gender
种族、阶级和性别的人为障碍

❸ 虚假的；假装的
artificial emotion 假装的情感

词义辨析 <P364第15>
假的，人造的 artificial, fake, false, synthetic, virtual

5. articulate [ɑː'tɪkjuleɪt, ɑː'tɪkjələt] v. 明确表达；清晰发音；用关节连接 adj. 善于表达的；口齿清楚的
『art关节+iculate+像关节一样（字字入扣）→咬字清楚』
（v. [ɑː'tɪkjuleɪt]; adj. [ɑː'tɪkjələt]）

❶ [VN] (formal) 明确表达；清楚说明
to express or explain your thoughts or feelings clearly in words
She struggled to articulate her thoughts.
她竭力表明她的想法。

❷ v. 清晰吐字；清晰发音
to speak, pronounce or play sth in a clear way
[V] He was too drunk to articulate properly.
他醉得连话都说不清楚。
[VN] Every note was carefully articulated.
每个音都唱得很认真，很清楚。

❸ adj. 善于表达的；口齿清楚的
All we could hear were loud sobs, but no articulate words.
我们听到的只是大声啜泣，没有清楚的话语。

❹ v. 用关节连接；与…合成整体
[VN] a robot with articulated limbs 关节型四肢机器人
[V] bones that articulate with others
与其他骨骼以关节相连的骨骼

词根16. audi, audit=hear, 表示"听"；au=ear, 表示"耳朵"

1. audible ['ɔːdəbl] adj. 听得见的
『audi听+(i)ble能…的→听得见的；可听的』

His voice was barely audible. 他的声音几乎听不见。

2. audience ['ɔːdiəns] n. 听众；观众
『audi听+ence表示名词→听的人→听众；观众』

[C+sing./pl. v.]
The audience was/were clapping for 10 minutes.
观众鼓掌了10分钟。

An audience of millions watched the wedding on TV.
几百万观众在电视上观看了婚礼。

3. audio ['ɔːdiəʊ] adj. 声音的，录音的

小贴士 记得电器上的音频插孔上写的什么吗？

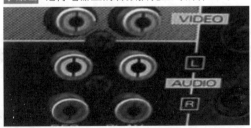

▶**video** ['vɪdiəʊ] n. 录像带；视频

4. auditorium [ˌɔːdɪ'tɔːriəm] n.（剧院或音乐厅的）观众席；会堂，礼堂，音乐厅

『audit听+orium地点，场所→听宣讲的地方→礼堂』

小贴士 如果觉得这个词难记，在写作要表达"礼堂"时可用lecture hall（演讲厅）来代替。

5. audition [ɔːˈdɪʃn] n. & v. 试音；试唱；试演

『audit听+(t)ion表示动作或事物→听听看是否合适→（对艺人的）面试（指试演、试唱等）』

I was auditioning for the part of a jealous girlfriend.
我试演一个喜欢吃醋的女友角色。
Apparently he made a mess of his audition.
看样子他把试镜搞砸了。

6. auditory [ˈɔːdətri] adj. 听觉的

『audit听+ory…的→听觉的』

So this is the time to begin providing auditory stimulation.
因此，这是开始提供听觉刺激的时候了。

7. aural [ˈɔːrəl] adj. 听觉的

『au耳朵+(r)al…的→耳朵的→听觉的；听的』

Aural means related to the sense of hearing.
He became famous as an inventor of astonishing visual and aural effects. 他因发明了神奇的视听效果而出名。

词根17. bar(r)=barrier，表示"栏，长条"，引申为"障碍"

1. bar [bɑː (r)] n. 长条；长棒 v. 封，堵；阻挡；阻止

❶ [C] 酒吧；吧台
We met at a bar called the Flamingo.
我们在一家名为"火烈鸟"的酒吧相遇。
It was so crowded I couldn't get to the bar.
人太多了，我无法挤到吧台那儿。

❷ [C]（专售某类饮食的）小吃店，小馆子
a sandwich bar 三明治店
a coffee bar 咖啡馆

❸ [C]（长方形）条；块
a bar of chocolate/soap 一条巧克力/肥皂

❹ [C] 长条；棒（木头或金属制成，常用作护栏）
He smashed the window with an iron bar.
他用铁棒敲碎了窗户。
All the ground floor windows were fitted with bars.
底层所有的窗户都装了铁栅。

❺ behind bars 被监禁；坐牢
The murderer is now safely behind bars.
杀人犯现在被关在监狱里，不会再造成危险了。

❻ [C, usually sing.] ~ (to sth) 障碍；羁绊
a thing that stops sb from doing sth
At that time being a woman was a bar to promotion in most professions.
那时在大多数职业中，身为女性就是晋升的障碍。

❼ [VN]（用铁条或木条）封，堵；阻挡；阻止
All the doors and windows were barred.
所有的门、窗都加上了铁条。
Two police officers were barring her exit.
两名警察挡着她的出路。

2. barricade [ˌbærɪˈkeɪd] n. 路障 vt. 设路障阻挡

『bar禁止，阻拦（双写r）+ic+ade表示动作或结果→路障；设路障阻挡』

❶ [C] 路障；街垒
A barricade is a line of vehicles or other objects placed across

a road or open space to stop people getting past, for example during street fighting or as a protest.
Large areas of the city have been closed off by barricades set up by the demonstrators.
城市中大片地区被示威者设立的路障封锁了。

❷ [VN] 设路障防护；阻挡
The rioters barricaded streets with piles of blazing tyres.
暴徒用一堆堆燃烧的轮胎在大街上筑起了路障。

❸ barricade yourself in/inside (sth) 躲在…里
to build a barricade in front of you in order to prevent anyone from coming in
He had barricaded himself in his room.
他把自己关在房间里。

3. barrier [ˈbæriə(r)] n. 关卡；栅栏；障碍

『bar栏；障碍（双写r）+i+er…的东西→由栏组成的具有阻拦性质的东西→关卡；栅栏；障碍』

❶ [C] 关卡；栅栏；分界线；屏障
Show your ticket at the barrier.
请在关卡处出示你的票。
crash barrier （高速公路中间的）防撞护栏
A severe storm, which destroyed a natural barrier between the house and the lake...
一场猛烈的暴风雨摧毁了房子和湖之间的一道天然屏障……
We have to build the wall or we have to build a barrier.
我们必须建这个隔离墙，或者我们必须建个栅栏。（特朗普答记者问）

barrier   wall

❷ [C] 障碍，阻碍；隔阂
Duties and taxes are the most obvious barrier to free trade.
关税和税收是自由贸易的最大壁垒。
There is no reason why love shouldn't cross the age barrier.
爱没有理由不能跨越年龄的阻碍。

❸ [C] 大关；界限
They are fearful that unemployment will soon break the barrier of three million.
他们担心失业人数很快将突破300万大关。

4. barrage [ˈbærɑːʒ] n. 弹幕；火力网；连珠炮似的（质问、抱怨等）

『bar阻拦；长条；一束光线（双写r）+age表示行为或行为的结果→（用连射的炮弹形成许多）光束般的长条来阻拦→弹幕；火力网』

❶ [C] 连续的炮火；弹幕；火力网
the continuous firing of a large number of guns in a particular direction, especially to protect soldiers while they are attacking or moving towards the enemy
The two fighters were driven off by a barrage of anti-aircraft fire. 两架战斗机被防空火力网逼退。

❷ [sing.] ~ (of sth) 接二连三的一大堆（质问或指责等）
He was faced with a barrage of angry questions from the floor. 他受到了与会者一连串愤怒的质询。

5. barrister ['bærɪstə(r)] n. （英格兰和威尔士地区有资格在高等法院出庭的）大律师

『bar禁止，阻拦（双写r）+ist表示人+er表示人→（在英国高等法庭上）阻止（出现冤假错案的）人』

6. barren ['bærən] adj. 贫瘠的，不毛的，荒芜的；不结果的，不育的

『bar棒，杆似…的→（草木似乎都是由）光杆组成的（枝叶不茂盛）→贫瘠的，荒芜的→不生育的，不结果的』

A barren landscape is dry and bare, and has very few plants and no trees.

He also wants to use the water to irrigate barren desert land.
他也想用这些水灌溉荒漠。

He prayed that his barren wife would one day have a child.
他祈祷自己不孕的妻子有朝一日能怀上宝宝。

词根18. ban= prohibit，表示"禁止"

1. ban [bæn] vt. 明令禁止 n. 禁令

Chemical weapons are banned internationally.
国际上禁止使用化学武器。

She's been banned from leaving Greece while the allegations are investigated.
在对那些指控进行调查期间，禁止她离开希腊。

There is to be a total ban on smoking in the office.
办公室将彻底禁止吸烟。

2. banish ['bænɪʃ] vt. 驱逐；消除

『ban禁止+ish使→禁止（在某地）→驱逐』

❶ [VN] 驱逐，流放

If someone or something is banished from a place or area of activity, they are sent away from it and prevented from entering it.

He was banished to Australia, where he died five years later.
他被流放到澳大利亚，五年后在那里去世。

The children were banished from the dining room.
孩子们被赶出餐厅。

❷ [VN] 消除，排除

If you banish something unpleasant, you get rid of it.

a public investment programme intended to banish the recession 旨在摆脱经济衰退的公共投资项目

He has now banished all thoughts of retirement.
他现在已经完全打消了退休的念头。

3. banal [bə'nɑ:l] adj. 平庸的，平淡无奇的

『ban禁止+al…的→禁止（平庸）的→平庸的』

very ordinary and containing nothing that is interesting or important

The lyrics are banal and the rhymes clumsy.
歌词平淡老套，押韵生硬蹩脚。

4. banister ['bænɪstə(r)] n. （楼梯的）栏杆，扶手

『ban禁止+ister表人或物→禁止（从楼梯上掉下去）的东西→栏杆』

（also bannister, BrE also banisters [pl.]）

I still remember sliding down the banisters.
我仍然记得从栏杆上滑下来的事。

词根19. bat=beat，表示"打，击"

1. batter ['bætə(r)] v. 连续猛击；殴打

『bat打（双写t）+er表反复→连续猛击』

[often passive] ~ at/on sth | ~ sb/sth 连续猛击；殴打

to hit sb/sth hard many times, especially in a way that causes serious damage

Somebody had battered her to death. 有人把她打死了。

Severe winds have been battering the north coast.
狂风一直在北海岸肆虐。

▶**battered** ['bætəd] adj. 破旧的，破烂的；受到重创的

He drove up in a battered old car.
他开着一辆又老又破的旧车。

Rockets and shells continued to hit the battered port.
火箭和炮弹继续袭击已遭受重创的港口。

小贴士 beat和batter都有用力反复打的意思，但batter更强调殴打致伤或造成破坏。

He had been badly battered around the head and face.
他被打得鼻青脸肿。

2. battle ['bætl] n. 战役，战斗

『bat打+tle→战役』

3. combat ['kɒmbæt] n. 战斗，搏斗；防止，打击

『com一起+bat打→搏斗，战斗』

❶ [U, C] 搏斗；打仗；战斗

fighting or a fight, especially during a time of war

He was killed in combat. 他在战斗中阵亡。

combat troops 作战部队

❷ [VN] 防止，打击

to stop sth unpleasant or harmful from happening or from getting worse

measures to combat crime/inflation/unemployment/disease
防止犯罪/通货膨胀/失业/疾病的措施

I'm proud to announce an additional $100M of existing funds to support China in combating the coronavirus.
我很自豪地宣布另外1亿美元的现有资金将用来支持中国对抗冠状病毒。（美国务卿蓬佩奥twitter）

词义辨析 <P379第92>

战争，战斗 war, battle, combat, fight

4. battery ['bætri] n. 电池；排炮

『bat（双写t）+er表反复+y表名词→反复打的东西→排炮→（排炮放在一起像电池组）电池』

to replace the batteries 更换电池

a rechargeable battery 充电电池

词根20. bell, bel=fight; fine，表示"打斗；美好"

1. rebel ['rebl , rɪ'bel] n. 造反者；叛逆者 v. 造反；反抗

『re往回+bel打斗→往回打斗→造反；叛逆』

❶ [C] 反政府者；反权威者；叛逆者

Armed rebels advanced towards the capital.
武装叛乱分子向首都推进。

I've always been the rebel of the family.
我在家里向来是个叛逆者。

❷ [V] 造反；反抗；背叛

He later rebelled against his strict religious upbringing.

他后来背叛了他所受的严格的宗教教育。
Most teenagers find something to rebel against.
大多数青少年都有反抗意识。

▶ **rebellious** [rɪˈbeljəs] adj. 反叛的；叛逆的
『re往回+bell打斗+ious充满的→反抗的；难以控制的』

rebellious teenagers　叛逆的青少年
rebellious cities/factions　叛乱的城市；反对派别
"I don't care!"　she said rebelliously.
"我不在乎!"　她桀骜不驯地说道。

▶ **rebellion** [rɪˈbeljən] n. 叛乱；反抗；叛逆
The army put down the rebellion. 军队镇压了叛乱。

2. bellicose [ˈbelɪkəʊs] adj. 好争辩的；好斗的
『bellic(=bell)打斗+ose…性质的→好战的』

having or showing a desire to argue or fight
His bellicose disposition alienated his friend.
他生性好斗，他的朋友们都疏远了他。

3. belligerent [bəˈlɪdʒərənt] adj.（人）好斗的，寻衅的
n. 交战双方
『bell打斗+i+ger带来+ent…的→带来战争的→寻衅的』

❶ adj.（人）好战的，寻衅的；交战的
A belligerent person is hostile and aggressive.
King Alfred turned it into a fortress against belligerent Danes.
阿尔弗列德国王将其修筑成堡垒，以抵御好战的丹麦人。
the belligerent countries/states/nations　交战各国

❷ [C] 交战国；交战双方
The belligerents were due, once again, to try to settle their differences. 交战双方应再一次设法解决分歧。

4. bellow [ˈbeləʊ] v.（公牛）吼叫；（对某人）大吼
『bell打斗+ow→打斗般地（吼叫）→（对某人）大吼』

to shout in a loud deep voice, especially because you are angry
[V] They bellowed at her to stop. 他们吼叫着让她停下。
[VN] The coach bellowed instructions from the sidelines.
教练在场边大声发号施令。

5. belle [bel] n. 美女；（某地）最美的女人
『bell美好+e→美女』

She was the belle of her Sunday School class.
在主日学校她是她们班的班花。

6. embellish [ɪmˈbelɪʃ] vt. 装饰；给（故事）润色
『em使…+bell美好+ish使…→使变得美好→装饰』

❶ [VN] 装饰，修饰
to make sth more beautiful by adding decorations to it
The stern was embellished with carvings in red and blue.
船尾饰有红色和蓝色的雕刻图案。

❷ [VN] 给（故事）润色
If you embellish a story, you make it more interesting by adding details which may be untrue.
I launched into the parable, embellishing the story with invented dialogue and extra details.
我开始讲那则寓言，并虚构了些对话，加了些细节对其进行润色。

词根21. bio, bi=life，表示"生命；人生"

1. biology [baɪˈɒlədʒi] n. 生物学；生理
『bio生命；生物+logy…学→生物学』

We dissected a frog in biology class.
我们在生物课上解剖了一只青蛙。
The biology of these diseases is terribly complicated.
这些疾病的机理极其复杂。

▶ **biologist** [baɪˈɒlədʒɪst] n. 生物学家

2. biochemistry [ˌbaɪəʊˈkemɪstri] n. 生物化学
『bio生命；生物+chemistry化学→生物化学』

3. antibiotic [ˌæntibaɪˈɒtɪk] n. 抗生素 adj. 抗生素的
『anti抗+bio生命；生物+tic有…性质的→抗生素的』

4. symbiosis [ˌsɪmbaɪˈəʊsɪs] n.（生物）共生关系；互惠互利关系
『sym共同+bio生活+sis表现象→共生』

The use of antibiotics disturbed the symbiosis between bacteria and fungi.
抗生素的使用，扰乱了细菌和真菌之间的共生关系。
Systemic symbiosis is the foundation for the development of electric vehicle industry.
系统性的互惠互利是实现电动汽车产业发展的基础。

5. biography [baɪˈɒɡrəfi] n. 传记；传记作品<P187>
『bio人生+graphy描述，呈现→描述呈现人生→传记』

词根22. brace=arm，表示"手臂"，引申为"支架；支撑"

1. brace [breɪs] n. 支架；大括号 vt. 加固，加强；做准备
『brace手臂；支架→牙箍；大括号；加固；支撑』

❶ [C] 箍子，夹子，支架；（儿童）牙箍
a device that holds things firmly together or holds and supports them in position
a neck brace (= worn to support the neck after an injury)
颈托

❷ braces (BrE) [pl.] 吊裤带　（NAmE suspenders）

❸ [C] 大括弧；大括号

小贴士 **bracket** [ˈbrækɪt] n. 括号
also **round bracket** (both BrE)
also **parenthesis** [pəˈrenθəsɪs] NAmE or formal

❹ [VN] (technical) 加强；加固
to make sth stronger or more solid by supporting it with sth
The roof was braced by lengths of timber.
屋顶用几根木头支撑固定住了。

❺ [VN] ~ sb/yourself (for sth)（为困难或坏事）做好准备
UN troops are braced for more violence.
联合国部队准备应付更多的暴行。
They are bracing themselves for a long legal battle.
他们在为漫长的法律诉讼作准备。

❻ [VN] 绷紧（身体）以顶住；绷紧（身体部位）做准备
They braced themselves against the wind.
他们顶着大风站稳。
He stood with his legs and shoulders braced, ready to lift the weights. 他绷紧腿和肩膀站着，准备举起杠铃。

2. bracelet [ˈbreɪslət] n. 手镯；手链；臂镯
『brace手臂+let（佩戴的饰品）→（戴在）手腕上的饰品→手镯』

3. embrace [ɪmˈbreɪs] n. & v. 拥抱；欣然接受
『em进入…之中+brace手臂；支架→进入手臂中→拥抱』

❶ 拥抱

[V] They embraced and promised to keep in touch.
他们互相拥抱，许诺将保持联系。
[VN] She embraced her son warmly.
她热情地拥抱儿子。
❷ [VN] (formal) 欣然接受，乐意采纳（思想、建议等）；信奉（宗教、信仰等）
to accept an idea, a proposal, a set of beliefs, etc., especially when it is done with enthusiasm
They'll be ready to embrace the new technology when it arrives.
他们随时准备迎接新技术的问世。
❸ [C, U] 拥抱；欣然接受
He held her in a warm embrace. 他热烈地拥抱着她。
There were tears and embraces as they said goodbye.
他们分别时又是流泪，又是拥抱。

词根23. cant, cent=sing, song, 表示"唱；歌"

1. chant [tʃɑ:nt] n. 反复唱（或喊）的话（或歌词） vt. 反复唱（或喊）
『chant(=cant)唱；歌→反复唱；反复唱的歌词』
❶ [C] 反复呼喊的话语；重复唱的歌词；反复吟咏的祷文
The crowd broke into chants of "Out! Out".
人群突然爆发出"下台！下台！"的反复呼喊声。
❷ 反复唱；反复呼喊
[VN] The crowd chanted their hero's name.
人群不断地呼唤着自己英雄的名字。
[V] A group of protesters, chanting and carrying placards, waited outside.
一群抗议者等候在外面，举着标语牌不停地喊着口号。

2. enchant [ɪn'tʃɑ:nt] vt. 使中魔法；使着迷，使陶醉
『en使进入…状态+chant唱→通过唱（咒语）使进入某种状态→使中魔法；使迷住』
King Arthur hid his treasures here and Merlin enchanted the cave so that nobody should ever find them.
亚瑟王将他的财宝藏在这里，墨林对洞穴施了魔法，这样永远不会有人找到那些财宝。
She enchanted you as she has so many others.
她迷住了你，就像她迷住了其他那么多人一样。

3. cant [kænt] n. （有关道德或宗教的）言不由衷的话；黑话，行话 倾斜 vt. 使倾斜
『cant（来自chant）唱；歌→（信教之人）所吟唱的祷词（不信也听不懂）→言不由衷的话；行话』
❶ [U] （有关道德或宗教的）言不由衷的话
If you refer to moral or religious statements as cant, you are criticizing them because you think the person making them does not really believe what they are saying.
There has been a great deal of politician's cant.
说了一大堆政客惯用的言不由衷的话。
❷ [U] 黑话，行话
special words used by a particular group of people such as thieves, lawyers or priests, often in order to keep things secret
❸ [C] 倾斜
The ship took on a dangerous cant to port.
船只出现向左舷的危险倾斜。

4. recant [rɪ'kænt] v. 公开放弃（信仰或意见）
『re返回+cant唱→又唱回来→公开放弃（信仰或意见）』

to say publicly that you no longer hold a set of beliefs that you had in the past
Prisoners were forced to publicly recant. 囚犯被迫公开认罪。
After the Reformation, many Catholics recanted to avoid punishment.
宗教改革运动后，许多天主教徒为了逃避惩罚而放弃了信仰。

5. incantation [ˌɪnkæn'teɪʃn] n. 咒语；念咒语
『in里面+cant唱+ation表行为或结果→在内心里吟唱的→咒语』

6. accent ['æksent] n. 口音；重音；着重点
『ac加强+cent唱→重点唱（某个地方）→重音；着重点；口音』
She spoke English with an accent. 她说英语带有口音。
In "today" the accent is on the second syllable.
"today"一词的重音在第二音节。
In all our products the accent is on quality.
我们的全部产品都强调质量。

▶ **accentuate** [ək'sentʃueɪt] vt. 强调；使突出
『accent重音；着重点+u+ate表动词→使…成为着重点→强调；突出』
His shaven head accentuates his large round face.
光头使他的大圆脸更加突出。
Well-off people will adopt fashions that conceal rather than accentuate their wealth.
富裕的人会采用隐藏而不是强调他们财富的时尚。

7. incentive [ɪn'sentɪv] n. 刺激；激励，奖励
『in里面+cent唱+ive表物→（教堂）里面在吟歌（激励你进去）→刺激；激励』或者：『in里面+cent一分钱+ive→里面有一分钱，干了某事就给你→刺激，激励』
[C，U] sth that encourages you to do sth
tax incentives to encourage savings 鼓励储蓄的税收措施
There is no incentive for people to save fuel.
没有使人们节约燃料的鼓励办法。

词根24. camp=field 表示"田野"

1. camp [kæmp] n. 营地，军营；阵营 v. 宿营
『camp(=field)田野→（度假）营地』
❶ [C, U] 度假村，度假营地；（旅行中临时的）营地；兵营
a place where people live temporarily in tents or temporary buildings
He spent two weeks at camp this summer.
他今年夏天在度假营玩了两个星期。
Let's return to camp. 咱们回营地吧。
❷ [C]（used in compounds 用于构成复合词）（为某一人群提供的）营地（如难民营、战俘营、军营等）
The suffering in the refugee camps is great.
难民营里的苦难是巨大的。
❸ [C] 阵营（指观点相同且与持不同观点者对立的集团）
They belong to different political camps.
他们属于不同的政治阵营。
❹ [V] 宿营；露营
I camped overnight in a field.
我在田野里露营过夜。
They go camping in France every year.
他们每年去法国野营。

2. campaign [kæmˈpeɪn] n. 活动，运动；战役 vi. 参加运动
『camp田野+aign→营地→战役』

❶ [C] ~ (against/for sth) 运动，活动（为社会、商业或政治目的而进行的一系列有计划的活动）
During his election campaign he promised to put the economy back on its feet.他在竞选时许诺将重振经济。
The advertising campaign is still in preparation.
广告宣传攻势仍在准备中。

❷ [C] 战役
a series of attacks and battles that are intended to achieve a particular military aim during a war
Alexander was free to go on with the Persian campaign.
亚历山大放手出征波斯。

❸ [V] ~ (for/against sb/sth) 参加运动；领导运动
We have campaigned against whaling for the last 15 years.
我们最近15年一直参加反对捕鲸的运动。
She is campaigning for an improved bus service.
她正在发起一项改进公共汽车运营服务的活动。

3. campus [ˈkæmpəs] n. （大学、学院的）校园；校区
『camp田野+us表名词→大学校园（像田野一样宽敞）』
（大学、学院的）校园；校区
the buildings of a university or college and the land around them
Private automobiles are not allowed on campus.
大学校园不许私人汽车入内。

词根25. cap(it), cip(it)=head，表示"头"

1. capital [ˈkæpɪtl] n. 首都；大写字母；资本，资金 adj. 大写的；可判死刑的
『capit(=head)+al表形容词或名词→首要的（城市）；（单词或句子的）首个（字母）；（财富的）源头；（罪可掉）头的→首都；大写字母（的）；资本；可判死刑的』

❶ [sing. U] 资本；资金；启动资金
a large amount of money that is invested or is used to start a business
to set up a business with a starting capital of £100,000
以10万英镑为启动资金创办一个企业
Companies are having difficulty in raising capital.
各公司融资困难。

make capital (out) of sth | capitalize on/upon sth
充分利用；从中获得好处
The rebels seem to be trying to capitalize on the public's discontent with the government.
叛乱分子似乎想要利用公众对政府的不满情绪。
The opposition parties are making political capital out of the government's problems.
各反对党都在利用政府存在的问题捞取政治资本。

❷ [sing. U] （借款或投资的）本金，本钱（与利息相对）
With a conventional repayment mortgage, the repayments consist of both capital and interest.
常规的按揭还款额既包含本金也包括利息。

❸ [C] 首都；（工商业活动的）中心
Cairo is the capital of Egypt. 开罗是埃及的首都。
(figurative) Paris, the fashion capital of the world
巴黎——世界时装之都

provincial capital 省会
Changsha is the provincial capital of Hunan.
湖南省的省会是长沙。

❹ [C] 大写字母
Please write in capitals/in capital letters.
请用大写字母书写。

with a capital A, B, etc. 真正地；名副其实地
He was romantic with a capital R. 他纯属浪漫派。
She's not feminist with a capital F. 她不是女权主义者。

小贴士 Caps Lock 是 Capitals Lock的简写，是大小写锁定键，键盘一个键位，为大小写切换之用。

❺ adj. 可判死刑的
Espionage is a capital offence in this country.
在这个国家，从事间谍活动是死罪。

▶ **capitalist** [ˈkæpɪtəlɪst] n. 资本家

▶ **capitalism** [ˈkæpɪtəlɪzəm] n. 资本主义（制度）

2. capitation [ˌkæpɪˈteɪʃn] n. 人头税；按人摊派的费用
『capit头+ation行为→按人头（收税收费）→人头税』

3. per capita [pə ˈkæpɪtə] adj. 每人的；人均的
『per每个+capit头+a→每个人头的→每人的』
They have the world's largest per capita income.
他们的人均收入居世界之首。
We are spending $5,000 per capita annually for education in this district.
我们每年为这个地区的教育支出人均5000美元（费用）。

4. capitulate [kəˈpɪtʃuleɪt] vi. 屈从；（有条件）投降
『capit(=head)标题+ul+ate表动词→以标题或章节（来起草投降条件）→（有条件）投降』
[V] ~ (to sb/sth) 投降；屈从
The town capitulated after a three-week siege.
这座城镇被围困三个星期后投降了。
They were finally forced to capitulate to the terrorists' demands. 他们最终被迫屈从于恐怖分子的要求。

5. recapitulate [ˌriːkəˈpɪtʃuleɪt] vi. 重述要点；简要回顾
『re返回+capit(=head)标题+ulate表动作→返回到标题上→重述要点』
[V] To recapitulate briefly, the three main points are these...
简要概括起来，主要有这样三点…
[VN] Let's just recapitulate the essential points.
我们再来回顾一下要点。

▶ **recap** [ˈriːkæp] v. 重述要点 n. 重述的要点
『recap=recapitulate或recapitulation』
[V] Let me just recap on what we've decided so far.
让我来概括一下到目前为止我们所作的决定吧。
Each report starts with a recap of how we did versus our projections.
每份报告的开头都扼要回顾了我们的表现和我们的预期目标。

6. decapitate [dɪˈkæpɪteɪt] vt. 杀头；斩首
『de去掉+capit头+ate使→杀头；斩首』

His decapitated body was found floating in a canal.
人们发现他被斩首的尸体漂浮在一条水渠里。

词根26. cap(t), cip, cup= take, hold, seize, 表示"拿，抓，握住"

1. captive [ˈkæptɪv] n. 俘虏；囚徒 adj. 被监禁的；被控制的
『capt拿，抓+ive表人→被抓住的人→俘虏』

They were taken captive by masked gunmen.
他们被蒙面的持枪歹徒劫持了。
Captors and Captives makes a significant contribution to regional history.
《捕获者和俘虏》一书对地区历史（的研究）作出了重要贡献。

►**captivate** [ˈkæptɪveɪt] v. 迷惑，吸引
『captive俘虏（去e）+ate使…→使…变成俘虏→被迷惑』

The children were captivated by her stories.
孩子们被她的故事迷住了。

2. capture [ˈkæptʃə(r)] v. 逮捕，捉拿
『capt拿，抓+ ure 表行为→抓住→逮捕』

❶ [VN]（尤指在战争中）俘虏，擒获；占领，夺取
The guerrillas shot down one aeroplane and captured the pilot.
游击队击落了一架飞机，并俘获了飞行员。
The city was captured in 1941. 这座城市于1941年被攻占。
❷ [VN] 吸引（注意力）；激发（想象）；赢得（喜爱）
The princess captured the hearts of the nation.
那位公主赢得了全体国民的心。
❸ [often passive] ~ sb/sth on film/ tape, etc. 拍摄；录制
The attack was captured on film by security cameras.
袭击事件已被保安摄像机拍摄下来。

3. captain n. 上尉；船长；机长；（运动队）队长
『capt拿，抓+ain表人→掌握（一群人）的人→首领』

►**captaincy** [ˈkæptənsi] n. 队长职位（或任期）

His captaincy of the team was ended by mild eye trouble.
他由于患轻度眼疾而不再担任队长一职。

4. caption [ˈkæpʃn] n.（图片、漫画）说明文字 v. 为（照片或漫画）添加说明文字
『cap拿，抓，握住+ tion表名词→抓住（图片的大意）→（图片、漫画的）说明文字』

He studied each photograph twice and read the caption intently.
他把每幅插图都看了两遍，又聚精会神地读了插图说明。
The photograph is captioned "People Power".
配图文字为"人民的力量"。

5. capacity [kəˈpæsəti] n. 容积；生产量；才能
『cap拿，抓，握住+ acity性质，状态，情况→抓住、容纳（事物）的能力→容积；才能』

❶ [U, C, usually sing.] 容量；容积；容纳能力
Each stadium had a seating capacity of about 50,000.
每个体育场均可容纳5万人左右。
They played to a capacity crowd (= one that filled all the space or seats). 他们给人山人海的观众表演。

小贴士 火车车厢里面的牌子：定员 capacity 118，表明这

节车厢能容纳118人。

❷ [sing., U] 生产量；生产能力
Bread factories are working at full capacity.
面包厂正在全力生产。
❸ [C, usually sing.] 职位；职责
Since 1928, Major Thomas has served the club in many capacities.
自1928年以来，托马斯少校担任过该俱乐部的多个职位。
❹ 领悟（或理解、办事）能力
the ability to understand or to do sth
The professor in his lecture went beyond the capacity of his audience. 这位教授的讲课超过了听众的接受能力。
He has a mind of great capacity. 他的理解能力极强。
Our capacity for giving care, love and attention is limited.
我们能够给予的关怀、关爱和关注是有限的。
❺ [C, U]（尤指车辆发动机的）容积，功率
an engine with a capacity of 1,600 ccs
一台功率为1.6升的发动机

词义辨析 <P370第46>
能力 capacity, capability, competence, ability

6. capable [ˈkeɪpəbl] adj. 有才能的；能胜任的
『cap拿，抓，握住+able可以的，能够的→能够胜任（hold）某个工作的→能胜任的』

❶ ~ of sth/of doing sth 有…能力的
having the ability or qualities necessary for doing sth
I'm perfectly **capable of** doing it myself, thank you.
谢谢，我完全有能力自己做。
❷ 足以胜任的
Someone who is capable has the skill or qualities necessary to do a particular thing well, or is able to do most things well.
She's a very capable teacher. 她是一位能力很强的教师。

►**incapable** [ɪnˈkeɪpəbl] adj. 无能力的；软弱无能的

❶ ~ of sth/of doing sth 没有能力（做某事）
not able to do sth
The children seem to be totally incapable of working by themselves. 孩子们好像完全不能独自做事。
❷ 不能克制自己的；不能自理的；什么事也做不好的
not able to control yourself or your affairs; not able to do anything well
He was found lying in the road, drunk and incapable.
他被发现躺在路上，烂醉如泥。
If people keep telling you you're incapable, you begin to lose confidence in yourself.
如果人们不断地对你说你无能，你就开始失去自信了。

►**capability** [ˌkeɪpəˈbɪləti] n. 能力；（国家）军事力量
Animals in the zoo have lost the capability to catch/of catching food for themselves.
动物园的动物已经丧失自己捕食的能力。

词义辨析 <P370第45>

有能力的；能够的 able, capable, competent

7. participate [pɑ:ˈtɪsɪpeɪt] v. 参加，参与

『part部分+i+cip (=take)拿+ate表动词→take part→参加』

[V] ~ (in sth) 参加；参与

to take part in or become involved in an activity

She didn't participate in the discussion. 她没有参加讨论。

We encourage students to participate fully in the running of the college. 我们鼓励学生全面参与学院的运作。

▶ **participant** [pɑ:ˈtɪsɪpənt] n. 参与者，参加者

▶ **participation** [pɑ:ˌtɪsɪˈpeɪʃn] n. 参与，参加

8. emancipate [ɪˈmænsɪpeɪt] vt. 解放，使不受束缚

『e出+man手+cip(=take)拿+ate表动词→把（被束缚的）手释放出来→解放』

[VN] [often passive] ~ sb (from sth)

解放；使不受（法律、政治或社会的）束缚

to free sb, especially from legal, political or social restrictions

Slaves were not emancipated until 1863 in the United States.

美国奴隶直到1863年才获得自由。

This new machine will emancipate us from the hard work.

这部新机器将把我们从繁重劳动中解放出来。

9. anticipate [ænˈtɪsɪpeɪt] v. 预料；预见；期盼

『anti(=ante前面)+cip(=take)拿+ate表动词→提前拿（采用）（某种想法）→预料』

❶ 预料；预期

to expect sth

[VN] We don't anticipate any major problems.

我们预料不会发生什么大问题。

[V that] We anticipate that sales will rise next year.

我们预料明年销售量将会增加。

❷ 预见

to see what might happen in the future and take action to prepare for it

[VN] We need someone who can anticipate and respond to changes in the fashion industry.

我们需要一个能预见时装业变化并做相应安排的人。

❸ 期盼；期望

to think with pleasure and excitement about sth that is going to happen

[VN] We eagerly anticipated the day we would leave school.

我们迫切地期盼着（毕业）离校的那一天。

▶ **anticipatory** [ænˌtɪsɪˈpeɪtəri] adj. 期待的；预期的

『anticipate预见（去ate）+atory有性质的→期待的』

10. incipient [ɪnˈsɪpiənt] adj. 刚开始的，早期的

『in里面+cip(=take)+ient…的→take in（进来）ient…的→开始的，初期的』

An incipient situation or quality is one that is starting to happen or develop.

That would cause a rise in inflation and choke off an incipient recovery.

这将导致通胀上升，并扼杀刚刚开始的复苏。

11. occupy [ˈɒkjupaɪ] vt. 占用；占领；忙于

『oc加强+ cup握住，拿下+ y表行为→占领；使用』

❶ [VN] 使用，占用（空间、面积、房间等）

The bed seemed to occupy most of the room.

床似乎占去了大半个屋子。

How much memory does the program occupy?

这个程序占用多少内存？

❷ [VN]占领；占据；侵占

Protesting students occupied the TV station.

抗议的学生占领了电视台。

U.S. forces now occupy a part of the country.

美国军队现在占领了该国的一部分。

❸ ~ sb/sth/yourself (in doing sth/with sb/sth)

使忙于（做某事）；忙着（做某事）

be occupied with sth 忙于做某事

She occupied herself with routine office tasks.

她忙于办公室的日常工作。

I had forgotten all about it because I had been so occupied with other things.

因为忙于其他事情，我把这件事忘得精光。

▶ **occupant** [ˈɒkjəpənt] n. 居住者；（房屋、建筑等的）使用者，（汽车等内的）乘坐者

『oc加强+ cup 拿，抓，握住+ ant人→占用者』

The previous occupants had left the house in a terrible mess.

以前的房客走后，房里凌乱不堪。

The car plunged into the river, killing all its occupants.

汽车掉进河中，车上所有乘客都死了。

▶ **occupancy** [ˈɒkjəpənsi] n. 占用，使用

Hotel occupancy has been as low as 40%.

酒店入住率最低达到40％。

▶ **occupation** [ˌɒkjuˈpeɪʃn] n. 职业；消遣；占有

❶ [C] 工作；职业

Please state your name, age and occupation below.

请在下面写明姓名、年龄和职业。

❷ [C] 消遣；业余活动

the way in which you spend your time, especially when you are not working

Her main occupation seems to be shopping.

逛商店购物似乎是她的主要消遣。

❸ [U] 侵占；占用

The areas under occupation contained major industrial areas.

被占领地区拥有主要的工业区。

The offices will be ready for occupation in June.

办公室将于六月交付使用。

12. 词义辨析 <P373第63>

职业，工作 career, profession, occupation, vocation**preoccupy** [priˈɒkjupaɪ] vt. 占据思想；使忧心忡忡

『pre事先+occupy占用→（心思）被事先占用（不能思考别的事情）→占据思想』

if sth is preoccupying you, you think or worry about it very often or all the time

That is the question starting to preoccupy Washington and Wall Street.

这是一个开始让华盛顿和华尔街伤透脑筋的问题。

He was too preoccupied with his own thoughts to notice anything wrong. 他只顾想着心事，没注意到有什么不对。

词根27. card, cord=heart，表示"心，心脏"

1. cardiac [ˈkɑ:diæk] adj. 心脏的；心脏病的

『card心+iac有…特征的；有…病的→心脏的；心脏病的』

cardiac disease/failure/surgery
心脏病；心力衰竭；心脏手术

2. electrocardiogram [ɪˌlektrəʊˈkɑːdiəʊɡræm] n.心电图
『electro电+cardi心，心脏+o+gram写，画→心电图』

3. cordial [ˈkɔːdiəl] adj. 友好的
『cord心，心脏+ial…的→用心的→友好的』

pleasant and friendly
He said the two countries had close and cordial relations.
他说两国之间有着密切友好的关系。

4. accord [əˈkɔːd] n. 一致；协议 vi. （与…）一致
『ac相当于to+cord心，心脏→心思一致→一致；协议』

❶ **in accord (with sth/sb)** (formal) 与…一致（或相符合）
This action would not be in accord with our policy.
这一行动不会符合我们的方针。

of your own accord 自愿地；主动地
without being asked, forced or helped
He came back of his own accord. 他自行回来了。
The symptoms will clear up of their own accord.
症状将会自行消失。

with one accord (BrE, formal) 全体一致；一致地

❷ [U]（国家、团体之间的正式）协定，协议，条约
The two sides signed a peace accord last July.
在刚过去的七月，双方签订了和平条约。

❸ [V] ~ (with sth) （与…）一致，符合，配合
These results accord closely with our predictions.
这些结果和我们的预测相当一致。

▶ **accordance** [əˈkɔːdns] n. 一致
We should make decisions in accordance with specific conditions.
我们应当根据具体情况做出决定。

5. concord [ˈkɒnkɔːd] n. 和谐，协调
『con共同+cord心→（相关各方）有共同的想法→协调』

Concord is a state of peaceful agreement.
They expressed the hope that he would pursue a neutral and balanced policy for the sake of national concord.
他们希望，为了国家的和谐，他会奉行中立、不偏不倚的政策。

6. discord [ˈdɪskɔːd] n. 不和；纷争
『dis不+ cord心→（相关各方）想法不一致→不和；纷争』

A note of discord surfaced during the proceedings.
事件进程中出现了不和的征象。
Don't fall into the enemy's trap of sowing discord among us.
不要中了敌人的反间计。

7. accordion [əˈkɔːdiən] n. 手风琴
『ac相当于to+cord心+ion表物→达到（手）心（一致）（才能一致）→手风琴』

词根28. carn(i)=flesh，表示"肉"

1. carnival [ˈkɑːnɪvl] n. 嘉年华；狂欢节
『carn肉+ival→（疯狂吃）肉的节日→狂欢节』

2. carnivore [ˈkɑːnɪvɔː(r)] n. 食肉动物；喜欢吃肉的人 <P360>
『carni肉+vore吃→吃肉（动物）→食肉动物』

3. carnage [ˈkɑːnɪdʒ] n. 大屠杀

『carn肉+age表行为→（把）切成肉的行为→大屠杀』
But CCTV footage seized by police, and seen by CNN, revealed a brutal afternoon of carnage.
但被警方抓获并被美国有线电视新闻网（CNN）看到的闭路电视录像显示，一个残酷的下午发生了大屠杀。

4. carnal [ˈkɑːnl] adj. 肉体的；肉欲的
『carn肉+al…的→肉体的；肉欲的』

Gluttong and drunkenness have been called carnal vices.
贪食和嗜酒被称为肉体上的罪恶。

5. incarnate [ɪnˈkɑːnət , ˈɪnkɑːneɪt] adj.（神灵）现身的；化身的 vt. 化身为；体现在
『in以…方式；使+carn肉+ate表动词或形容词→（使）以一种肉体的方式出现→化身为』

Why should God become incarnate as a male?
为什么上帝以男性之身显现呢？
She is evil incarnate. 她是邪恶的化身。
The god Vishnu was incarnated on earth as a king.
守护之神毗湿奴化身为下界的一位国王。
His ideals were incarnated in his music.
他的理想具体地体现在他的音乐中。

6. reincarnate [ˌriːɪnˈkɑːneɪt] v. 使投胎；转世
『re又+incarnate化身，现身→转世』

[VN] They believe humans are reincarnated in animal form.
他们相信人死后转生为动物。

7. carcass [ˈkɑːkəs] n. 动物死尸；（车辆、建筑等）残体
『carc(=carn)肉+ass→（动物死后变成的）肉→动物死尸』

The hunter knelt beside the animal carcass and commenced to skin it. 猎人跪在动物尸体旁边，开始剥皮。

词根29. cas, cata=fall，表示"落下；向下"

1. casual [ˈkæʒuəl] adj. 偶然的；漫不经心的
『cas落下+ual有…性质的→（偶然）落下的→偶然的』

❶ 偶然的，碰巧的
The exhibition is interesting to both the enthusiast and the casual visitor.
热心的爱好者和碰巧来参观的人都认为这个展览有意思。
The disease is not spread by casual contact.
此病不会通过偶然接触传染。

❷ 漫不经心的，不在乎的
It was just a casual remark—I wasn't really serious.
我只是随便说说——并不当真。
He tried to sound casual, but I knew he was worried.
他讲话时试图显得不在乎，但我知道他心里着急。

❸ （服装）休闲的；（场合）不正式的
I also bought some casual clothes for the weekend.
我还买了些周末穿的休闲装。
family parties and other casual occasions
家庭聚会和其他非正式场合

2. casualty [ˈkæʒuəlti] n. （战争或事故中的）伤员；遇难者；受害者
『casual偶然的+ty表名词→偶然中（受伤或死亡）→伤员；遇难者』

Both sides had suffered heavy casualties. 双方都伤亡惨重。

3. cascade [kæˈskeɪd] n. 小瀑布 v. 倾斜 <P48>
『casc(=cas)落下+ade表动作或动作的结果→小瀑布；倾斜』

4. catastrophe [kəˈtæstrəfi] n. 重大灾难

『cata落下+stro星星+phe(=phenomenon)现象→星星落下（引起大灾难的）现象→大灾难』

A catastrophe is an unexpected event that causes great suffering or damage.

From all points of view, war would be a catastrophe.

无论从哪方面说，战争都将是场灾难。

5. catalogue [ˈkætəlɒg] n. 目录，名录；一连串（坏事）v. 列入目录〈P210〉

『cata下面+logue说话→要说的话在下（后）面→目录』

6. catalyst [ˈkætəlɪst] n. 催化剂；引发变化的因素

『cata向下+lyst裂开；分解→（促进）向下分解→催化剂』

I very much hope that this case will prove to be a catalyst for change. 我非常希望这起事件能催生变革。

词根30. caval=horse，表示"马"

1. cavalcade [ˌkævlˈkeɪd] n. 骑兵队

『caval马+c+ade表行动的个人或团体→骑马的团体→骑兵队』

（参加典礼的）骑马队列，车队

a line of people on horses or in vehicles forming part of a ceremony

The great cavalcade was on the move.

伟大的骑兵正在前进。

2. cavalry [ˈkævlri] n. （旧时的）骑兵；装甲部队

『caval马+ry表总称→骑兵的总称』

[sing. + sing./pl. v.] （旧时的）骑兵；装甲兵

The cavalry scattered them and chased them off the field.

骑兵驱散了他们并把他们逐出了战场。

The cavalry were exercising on Salisbury Plain.

装甲部队在索尔兹伯里平原进行演习。

▶ **cavalryman** [ˈkævəlrɪmən] n. 骑兵

3. cavalier [ˌkævəˈlɪə(r)] n. <古>骑士；对女人彬彬有礼的绅士；对女人献殷勤的男子 adj. 不在乎的，漫不经心的

『caval马+i+er表示人→骑马的人→骑士』

[usually before noun] 漫不经心的；不在乎的

not caring enough about sth important or about the feelings of other people

The government takes a cavalier attitude to the problems of prison overcrowding.

政府对监狱拥挤不堪的问题不闻不问。

词根31. cave=hole，表示"洞"

1. cave [keɪv] n. 山洞；洞穴 v. （使）塌陷

『cave(=hole)→山洞』

a large hole in the side of a hill or under the ground

Another flash of lightning lit up the cave.

又一道闪电照亮了山洞。

The earthquake made the roadbed cave in.

地震后路基沉陷了。

cave in

（房顶、墙等）塌陷，坍塌；让步，屈从

The ceiling suddenly caved in on top of them.

天花板突然塌落在他们身上。

The President is unlikely to cave in to demands for a public inquiry. 总统未必会屈服而同意进行公开调查。

2. cavern [ˈkævən] n. 大洞穴，大山洞

『cave洞+(e)rn场所，地点→洞穴』

3. excavate [ˈekskəveɪt] vt. 发掘；挖掘

『ex出+cave洞（去e）+ate表动作→从洞中（挖）出来→挖掘』

❶ [VN] 发掘；挖出（古建筑或古物）

The site has been excavated by archaeologists.

这个遗址已被考古学家发掘出来。

❷ [VN] 挖掘；挖空（洞、隧道等）

They plan to excavate a large hole before putting in the foundations.他们计划打地基前先挖个大洞。

词根32. ceed, cess, cede=go，表示"行走，前进"，cess 为 ceed 的名词形式

1. succeed [səkˈsiːd] v. 成功；接替

『suc(=sub)下面+ceed走→走到（目标）下面；走到（前任）的下面→成功；接替』

❶ [V] 办到，做成

He succeeded in getting a place at art school.

他被艺术学校录取了。

You will have to work hard if you are to succeed.

要想有所作为，你必须苦干。

❷ [VN] 接替；继任；随后出现

Who succeeded Kennedy as President?

接替肯尼迪任总统的是谁？

Their early success was succeeded by a period of miserable failure.

他们起初获得成功，但随后有一段惨痛失败的时期。

▶ **success** [səkˈses] n. 成功；成功的人或事

❶ [U] ~ (in sth/in doing sth)

I didn't have much success in finding a job.

我找工作没什么结果。

Confidence is the key to success. 信心是成功的关键。

❷ [C] 成功的人（或事物）

The party was a big success. 这次聚会非常成功。

She wasn't a success as a teacher. 她教书没教出什么名堂。

▶ **successor** [səkˈsesə(r)] n. 接替者，继任者

『suc下面+cess走+or表人→来的下任→继任者』

Who's the likely successor to him as party leader?

谁较可能接替他担任党的领袖？

▶ **succession** [səkˈseʃn] n. 继任；一连串

She is now seventh in line of succession to the throne.

她目前是王位的第七顺位继承人。

She has won the award for the third year in succession.

这是她连续第三年获得此奖。

▶ **successive** [səkˈsesɪv] adj. 连续的；相继的

Jackson was the winner for a second successive year.

杰克逊已经是连续第二年获胜了。

▶ **predecessor** 英 [ˈpriːdəsesə(r)] 美 [ˈpredəsesər] n. 前任；前身

『pre前面+de离开+cess走+or表人→前面离开的人→前任』

The new president reversed many of the policies of his predecessor. 新任总统彻底改变了其前任的许多政策。

The car is some 40mm shorter than its predecessor.

这辆轿车比原先的车型短了约40毫米。

2. proceed [prəˈsiːd] v. 前进；继续进行

『pro向前+ceed行走，前进→向前走；继续做』

❶ **~ with sth** 继续做某事

We're not sure whether we still want to proceed with the sale.
我们不确定是否还要继续减价促销。

❷ **proceed to do sth** 接下来做（另外一件事情）

He outlined his plans and then proceeded to explain them in more detail.
他简单介绍了他的计划，接着又进行了较详细的解释。

❸ [V] （某事、活动或过程）继续进行（没有停止）

The ideas were not new. Their development had proceeded steadily since the war. 这些并不是什么新思想，自从战争开始就一直稳定地发展演变。

Work is proceeding slowly. 工作进展缓慢。

❹ [V + adv./prep.] (formal) （朝某个方向）前进，行进

Passengers for Rome should proceed to Gate 32 for boarding.
前往罗马的旅客，请到32号登机口登机。

词义辨析 <P361第4>

前进，进展 progress, advance, proceed

▶ **process** [ˈprəʊses, prəˈses] n. 过程；工艺 vt.加工，处理

『pro向前+cess行走，前进→向前走（的过程；方式）；使向前走→过程；工艺；处理』

（n. [ˈprəʊses]; vt. [ˈprəˈses]）

❶ [C] 过程，进程

I'm afraid getting things changed will be a slow process.
做任何改革恐怕都会是个缓慢的过程。

I was moving some furniture and I twisted my ankle in the process. 我在挪动家具时崴了脚。

❷ [C] 做事方法；工艺流程；工序

We are the only company in the world with this process.
对于这套工艺，我们是全球仅有的一家。

❸ [VN] 加工，处理

Most of the food we buy is processed in some way.
我们买的大部分食品都用某种方法加工过。

A computer is a fast and accurate symbol processing system. It can accept, store, process data and produce output results.
计算机是一种快速、精确的符号加工系统，它能接收、存储、处理数据并产生输出结果。

小贴士 processor 处理器

▶ **procedure** [prəˈsiːdʒə(r)] n. 程序；步骤；手续

『pro向前+cede行走，前进（去e）+ure表行为→向前进行（某事的步骤）→步骤；程序』

Making a complaint is quite a simple procedure.
申诉的手续相当简单。

The next day I repeated the procedure.
第二天我重复了这个程序。

The White House said there would be no change in procedure.
白宫说程序上不会发生变化。

▶ **proceeding** [prəˈsiːdɪŋ] n. 诉讼；事件；会议记录

『proceed向前进行+ing表行为或结果→诉讼；事件，活动』

❶ [C, usually pl.] ~ (against sb) (for sth) 诉讼；诉讼程序
to bring legal proceedings against sb 对某人提起法律诉讼

❷ proceedings （有组织的一系列）活动；事件

The proceedings of the enquiry will take place in private.
问讯将会秘密进行。

❸ proceedings （会议）记录

3. procession [prəˈseʃn] n. （人或车辆的）队列，行列；列队行进；游行

『pro向前+cess行走，前进+ion表名词→（一队人马或车队）向前走，列队行进』

A procession is a group of people who are walking, riding, or driving in a line as part of a public event.
Groups of unemployed people from all over the country marched in procession to the capital.
来自全国的失业群众列队向首都进发。

The three-mile procession snaked its way through the richest streets of the capital.
3英里长的游行队伍弯弯曲曲地穿过了首都最繁华的街道。

4. exceed [ɪkˈsiːd] vt. 超过

『ex出去+ceed走→走出（固定范围）→ 超出』

❶ [VN] 超过，超出（某数量、数字等）

Its research budget exceeds $700 million a year.
其研究预算每年超过7亿美元。

His achievements have exceeded expectations.
他的成就出乎预料。

❷ [VN] 超出，超越（限制、规定等）

She was exceeding the speed limit. 当时她超速驾驶。

▶ **exceedingly** [ɪkˈsiːdɪŋli] adv. 非常；极其

『exceeding过度的+ ly 表副词→过分地 』

(formal, becoming old-fashioned) 极其；非常；特别
extremely; very; very much

We had an exceedingly good lunch.
我们吃了一顿极为丰盛的午餐。

This was an exceedingly difficult decision to take.
做这个决定非常难。

词义辨析 <P368第34> **超出 exceed, surpass, excel**

▶ **excess** [ɪkˈses] n. 超过；超额；过量

『exceed的名词形式』

❶ [sing., U] ~ (of sth) 超过；过度；过分

Are you suffering from an excess of stress in your life?
你生活中的压力太大吗？

He started drinking to excess after losing his job.
他失业后便开始酗酒了。

❷ [C, U] 超过的量

We cover costs up to £600 and then you pay the excess.
我们最多支付600英镑的费用，超过的部分由你支付。

❸ adj. [only before noun] 超额的

Excess food is stored as fat. 多余的食物作为脂肪贮存起来。

▶ **excessive** [ɪkˈsesɪv] adj. 过多的，过度的

『excess的形容词形式』

They complained about the excessive noise coming from the upstairs flat. 他们抱怨楼上发出的噪声太大。

The amounts she borrowed were not excessive.
她借的数量没有超额。

5. access [ˈækses] n. 通道；机会；权力；途径 v. 进入；（电脑）存取

『ac相近于to+cess行走→可以走到某物前→有接近、利用某物的途径和机会』

注意 access作名词时是不可数名词，前面不能用不定冠词，常和介词to连用。

❶ [U] ~ (to sth) 通道；通路；进入途径
The only access to the farmhouse is across the fields.
去那农舍的唯一通路是穿过田野。

❷ [U] ~ (to sth) （使用或见到的）机会；权利；途径
Students must have access to good resources.
学生必须有机会使用好的资源。
You need a password to get access to the computer system.
你需要口令才能进入这个计算机系统。

❸ [VN] 存取，访问（计算机信息）；达到，进入
I can not access the file on your company because I have forgotten the code.
我无法访问你公司的文件，因为我把密码忘了。

▶ **accessible** [əkˈsesəbl] adj. 可以到达的；易懂的；（人）易接近的
『access 接触，接近+ible可…的，能…的→能接触到的，可接近的』
adj. ~ (to sb)

❶ 可到达的，可使用的
The remote desert area is accessible only by helicopter.
只有乘直升机才能进入那遥远的荒漠地区。
These documents are not accessible to the public.
公众无法看到这些文件。

❷ 容易理解的；易懂的
This book is easily accessible to the young reader.
这本书是年轻读者容易懂的。

❸ (of a person人) 易接近的；易相处的；易打交道的
Never had she seemed so accessible as now.
仿佛她从来没有像现在这样容易接近过。

6. recede [rɪˈsiːd] vi. 渐渐远去；逐渐减弱
『re向后+ cede行走，前进→后退』

❶ 逐渐远离；渐渐远去
to move gradually away from sb or away from a previous position
The sound of the truck receded into the distance.
卡车的声音渐渐在远处消失了。
She watched his receding figure.
她看着他的身影渐渐远去。

❷ （质量）下降;（问题或疾病等）逐渐减弱，好转
Just as I started to think that I was never going to get well, the illness began to recede.
正当我开始觉得自己永远也好不了了的时候，我的病开始好转了。
The pain was receding slightly. 疼痛正在一点一点地减弱。

❸ （前额的头发）脱落
His hair is beginning to recede from his forehead.
他的头发开始从前额往后秃了。

▶ **recession** [rɪˈseʃn] n. 经济衰退，经济萎缩
The recession caused sales to drop off.
经济不景气使销量下降。
There was a mild recession in the early 1950s.
20世纪50年代初期曾发生较轻微经济衰退。

7. recess [ˈriːses , rɪˈses] n. 休会期间；（墙上）凹处；幽深处
『re回+ cess行走，前进→走回去→休息；凹处』

❶ [C]（委员会、法庭或政府等的）休会期间，休息期间
The conference broke for a recess. 会议暂时休会。

The judge called a short recess. 法官宣布短暂休庭。

❷ [C]（墙上的）凹处，壁龛，壁橱
a recess for books 放书的壁橱

❸ [C, usually pl.] 隐蔽处；幽深处
He stared into the dark recesses of the room.
他盯着房间里黑暗的角落。
The doubt was still there, in the deep recesses of her mind.
在她的内心深处依然存有疑虑。

8. precede [prɪˈsiːd] v. 在…之前；走在…前面
『pre前；预先+cede走→走在（时间、某人）前面→先于』

❶ 在…之前发生（或出现）；先于
Industrial orders had already fallen in the preceding months.
工业订单在前几个月就已减少。
The earthquake was preceded by a loud roar and lasted 20 seconds. 地震前有一阵巨大的轰隆声，持续了20秒钟。

❷ [VN + adv./prep.] 走在…前面
She preceded him out of the room. 她先于他走出屋子。

▶ **precedent** [ˈpresɪdənt] n. 前例；先例
『precede在…之前+ent表名词→在前面的东西→前例』
The trial could set an important precedent for dealing with large numbers of similar cases.
这次审判能为处理大量类似案例开创重要的先例。
There is no precedent for a disaster of this scale.
这种规模的灾难是空前的。

小贴士 注意下面这两个词的读音：
president [ˈprezɪdənt] n. 总统；院长
precedent [ˈpresɪdənt] n. 前例；先例

▶ **unprecedented** [ʌnˈpresɪdentɪd] adj. 史无前例的
On the one hand, this gives us an unprecedented opportunity.
一方面，这给了我们一次前所未有的机会。

▶ **preceding** [prɪˈsiːdɪŋ] adj. 在…之前的
The dual leadership of the preceding three weeks was now over. 前三周的双重领导现在结束了。

9. antecedent [ˌæntɪˈsiːdnt] n. 先行词；祖先；前事 adj. 先前的
『ante前面+cede行走，前进+(e)nt表形容词或名词→走在前面→先行的；先行词』
It can be used as the antecedent of a relative clause.
它可被用作关系从句的先行词。
We shall first look briefly at the historical antecedents of this theory. 我们首先应大致看一下该理论在历史上的前身。
a Frenchman with Irish antecedents
祖先为爱尔兰人的法国人
There are always antecedent causes. 事情发生总会有前因。
The decision not to invite Joe was antecedent to his illness.
不邀请乔的决定是在他生病之前做出的。

10. intercede [ˌɪntəˈsiːd] vi. 向…说情；调解，斡旋
『inter在…之间+cede走→在两者之间走〔防止发生冲突〕→调停』
[V] ~ (with sb) (for/on behalf of sb)
to speak to sb in order to persuade them to show pity on sb else or to help settle an argument
They interceded with the authorities on behalf of the detainees. 他们为被拘留者向当局求情。

11. secede [sɪˈsiːd] v. 退出，脱离

『se分开，离开+cede走→走开→退出』

[V] ~ (from sth) (formal) (of a state, country, etc. 州、邦、国家等) 退出，脱离（组织等）

The Republic of Panama seceded from Colombia in 1903.
巴拿马共和国于1903年脱离哥伦比亚。

▶ **secession** [sɪˈseʃn] n. （从国家、大集团）退出，脱离，分离

Officials emphasized they were not establishing a separate government or seeking secession from Libya.
官员们强调，他们并没有另行成立一个政府，也没有寻求与利比亚分裂。

12. concede [kənˈsiːd] v. 不情愿地承认；（勉强）给予
『con一起+cede走→（承认自己错了才能）走到一起→不情愿地承认』

❶ ~ sth (to sb) | ~ sb sth
不情愿地承认（某事属实、合乎逻辑等）

[V (that)] He was forced to concede (that) there might be difficulties. 他被迫承认可能有困难。

[VN that] It must be conceded that different judges have different approaches to these cases.
必须承认不同的法官会采用不同的方法来判定这些案件。

❷ 承认（比赛、选举等失败）

[V] After losing this decisive battle, the general was forced to concede.
输掉了这场决定性的战役后，那位将军不得不承认失败。

She conceded even before all the votes had been counted.
她甚至在所有的票数都还没数出来之前就认输了。

[VN] He kept on arguing and wouldn't concede defeat.
他不停地争论，不肯认输。

❸ ~ sth (to sb) | ~ sb sth （勉强地）给予、让与、允许

A strike by some ten thousand bank employees has ended after the government conceded some of their demands.
政府答应了他们的一些要求后，大约有一万名银行员工参加的罢工结束了。

[VN] The President was obliged to concede power to the army. 总统被迫把权力让给军队。

▶ **concession** [kənˈseʃn] n. 让步；承认失败

❶ [C, U] 让步；妥协

The firm will be forced to make concessions if it wants to avoid a strike.
要想避免罢工，公司将不得不作出一些让步。

❷ [U] 承认失败

The former president's concession came even before all the votes had been counted.
前总统甚至在所有的选票都被统计出来之前就承认败选了。
a concession speech 败选演讲

▶ **concessive** [kənˈsesɪv] adj. 让步的

concessive adverbial clauses 让步状语从句

13. cede [siːd] vt. 割让（领土）；放弃（权力）
『cede行走，前进→（使）走开→割让』

Spain ceded the Philippines to the United States.
西班牙将菲律宾群岛割让给美国。

14. accede [əkˈsiːd] vi. 同意；（尤指君主）即位
『ac(=to)到+cede走→走到（王位；一起）→（尤指君主）即位；（从不同意到）同意』

~ (to sth) (formal)

❶ 同意（请求、建议等）（尤用于开始不同意）

to agree to a demand, proposal etc., especially after first disagreeing with it

He acceded to demands for his resignation.
他同意要他辞职的要求。

❷ （尤指君主）即位

to achieve a high position, especially to become king or queen

Queen Victoria acceded to the throne in 1837.
维多利亚女王于1837年即位。

▶ **accession** [ækˈseʃn] n. （尤指君主）即位

词义辨析 <P375第74>
同意 assent, consent, accede, approve

词根33. ceive, cep(t), cip=take, hold, seize，表示"拿，抓，握住"

1. receive [rɪˈsiːv] vt. 接收；接待
『re又，再+ceive(=take)拿→又拿→接收』

❶ [VN] ~ sth (from sb/sth) 接到，收到

❷ [VN] [often passive] ~ sb (with sth) | ~ sb (as sth) (formal)
接待；欢迎；招待

He was received as an honoured guest at the White House.
他在白宫受到贵宾的礼遇。

▶ **reception** [rɪˈsepʃn] n. 招待会；接待处

❶ [C] 招待会；欢迎会

A reception is a formal party which is given to welcome someone or to celebrate a special event.

At the reception they served smoked salmon.
招待会的餐桌上有熏制鲑鱼。

❷ [U] (especially BrE) 接待处；接待区

We arranged to meet in reception at 6:30.
我们约定6:30在接待处会面。

the reception desk服务台

▶ **receptionist** [rɪˈsepʃənɪst] n. 接待员

▶ **recipient** [rɪˈsɪpiənt] n. 接收者

The recipients of the prizes had their names printed in the paper. 获奖者的名字登在报上。

Now I have filled in the name and address of the recipient and of the sender.
现在，我已填好收款人和寄款人的姓名和地址。

▶ **receipt** [rɪˈsiːt] n. 收据，收条

Ask him to give you a receipt when you pay the bill.
你付账单时向他要一张收据。

▶ **receptacle** [rɪˈseptəkl] n. 容器
『re一再+cept拿+acle物→接收（东西）的物体→容器』

A receptacle is something you use to put or keep things in.

I took a pencil from the little receptacle I carried and tore a sheet from a small notebook.
我从随身携带的小容器里拿出一支铅笔，从一本小笔记本上撕下一张纸。

2. perceive [pəˈsiːv] vt. 注意到，察觉到；将…视为…
『per (through)通过+ceive抓，拿，握住→通过（某个细节）抓到（某种情况）→注意到，觉察到』

❶ 注意到，察觉，意识到（尤指不明显之物）

A key task is to get pupils to perceive for themselves the relationship between success and effort.
关键任务是让学生们自己认识到成功和努力之间的关系。
I perceived a change in his behaviour.
我注意到他举止有些改变。

❷ ~ sb/sth (as sth) 将…理解为；将…视为
This discovery was perceived as a major breakthrough.
这一发现被视为一项重大突破。

▶ **perception** [pəˈsepʃn] n. 知觉；看法；洞察力

❶ [U] 知觉；感知
visual perception 视觉

❷ [U] 洞察力；悟性
She showed great perception in her assessment of the family situation. 她对家庭状况的分析显示出敏锐的洞察力。

❸ [C] 看法，见解
There is a general public perception that standards in schools are falling. 公众普遍认为，学校的水平都在下降。
He is interested in how our perceptions of death affect the way we live.
他感兴趣的是我们对死亡的看法如何影响我们的生活。

▶ **perceptible** [pəˈseptəbl] adj. 可觉察的

▶ **perceptive** [pəˈseptɪv] adj. 有洞察力的，观察敏锐的；有悟性的

If you describe a person or their remarks or thoughts as perceptive, you think that they are good at noticing or realizing things, especially things that are not obvious.

a highly perceptive comment 见地高明的评论
It was very perceptive of you to notice that.
你能注意到此事，真够敏锐的。

词义辨析 <P361第1>
看 see, watch, observe, look, perceive

3. **conceive** [kənˈsiːv] v. 构想，想出；怀孕
『con共同，一起+ceive抓，拿→一起抓（主意、想法）→想出，构想』

❶ ~ (of) sth (as sth)
(formal) 想出（主意、计划等）；想象；构想；设想
to form an idea, a plan, etc. in your mind; to imagine sth
[VN] He conceived the idea of transforming the old power station into an arts centre.
他想出了一个把旧发电站改造为艺术中心的主意。
I cannot conceive what it must be like.
我想象不出它会是什么样子。
God is often conceived of as male.
上帝常常被想象为男性。

❷ 怀孕；怀（胎）
She is unable to conceive.她不能怀孕。

▶ **conception** [kənˈsepʃn] n. 构想，理解；怀孕

The plan was brilliant in its conception but failed because of lack of money.
尽管这计划构想绝妙，但终因资金不足而告流产。
He has no conception of how difficult life is if you're unemployed. 他不懂得如果你失业，生活会是怎样的艰难。
I do not think that he has any such conception.
我看他不至于有这种心思吧。

4. **deceive** [dɪˈsiːv] v. 欺骗，蒙骗

『de(=away)去掉，离开+ceive抓，拿，握住→（对你好目的是）拿走（你的东西）→欺骗』

to make sb believe sth that is not true
She deceived him into handing over all his savings.
她把他所有的积蓄都骗了出来。
Unless my eyes deceive me, that's his wife.
如果我没有看错的话，那是他的妻子。

▶ **deception** [dɪˈsepʃn] n. 欺骗；骗局

He was accused of obtaining property by deception.
他被指控骗取钱财。
The whole episode had been a cruel deception.
整个经历都是残酷的骗局。

▶ **deceptive** [dɪˈseptɪv] adj. 欺骗性的，误导的

Appearances can be deceptive. 外表可能是靠不住的。

5. **concept** [ˈkɒnsept] n. 概念，观念
『con一起+cept 拿，握住→把（同种类的事物）拿到一起（找出共同点）→概念』

指对某事物是什么、怎么做等的想法，通常指抽象概念。
She added that the concept of arranged marriages is misunderstood in the west.
她补充说，西方人对包办婚姻的概念有些误解。
Joe still has no concept of what it's like to be the sole parent.
乔对当单亲家长是什么滋味还没有任何概念。

6. **except** [ɪkˈsept] prep. & conj. 除…之外
『ex出，外面+cept拿，握住→把（某物）拿出去→除…之外』

We work every day except Sunday.
我们除星期天外每天都工作。
I didn't tell him anything except that I needed the money.
我什么都没告诉他，只是说我需要钱。

词义辨析 <P373第62> 除…之外 except, except for, apart from, aside from, besides

7. **accept** [əkˈsept] vt. 接受（建议、邀请等）
『ac相当于to+cept(=take)拿→拿过来→接受』

He asked me to marry him and I accepted.
他向我求婚，我答应了。
Please accept our sincere apologies.
请接受我们真诚的道歉。

8. **intercept** [ˌɪntəˈsept] v. 拦截
『inter在…之间+ cept(=take, hold, seize)抓，拿→在（路程间）被拿下→拦截』

to stop sb/sth that is going from one place to another from arriving
That secret message was intercepted by the spies.
那秘密消息被间谍中途拦截。
Gunmen intercepted him on his way to the airport.
持枪歹徒在他去机场的路上截击了他。

9. **inception** [ɪnˈsepʃn] n. （机构、组织等的）开端，创始
『in进入+cept(=take)拿+ion表名词→take in进来→开端』

The club has grown rapidly since its inception in 1990.
这个俱乐部自从1990年成立以来发展迅速。
Since its inception the company has produced 53 different aircraft designs.
该公司自成立以来已经完成了53种不同样式飞行器的设计。

10. susceptible [sə'septəbl] adj. 易受影响或伤害的；好动感情的

『sus下面+cept拿+ible能够的→能够（轻易地）被拿到下面的→易受影响的』

Young people are the most susceptible to advertisements.
年轻人最容易受广告的影响。

Walking with weights makes the shoulders very susceptible to injury. 负重行走时肩膀很容易受伤。

She was both charming and susceptible. 她迷人而多情。

11. precept ['pri:sept] n. （思想、行为的）准则，规范

『pre事先+cept拿→事先拿在心里的（准则）→准则』

A precept is a general rule that helps you to decide how you should behave in particular circumstances.

Example is better than precept. 言教不如身教。

The most fundamental of these precepts is that good is to be done and evil to be avoided.
这些箴规中最基本的规则就是行善避恶。

词根34. celebr=honor，表示"荣誉"

1. celebrate ['selɪbreɪt] v. 庆祝，祝贺

『celebr荣誉+ate使→使有荣誉→庆祝，祝贺』

The Society is celebrating its tenth anniversary this year.
这个协会今年将举办成立10周年庆典。

2. celebrity [sə'lebrəti] n. （尤指娱乐界的）名人，明星；名气

『celebr荣誉+ity具备某种性质→有荣誉的人→名人』

TV celebrities 电视名人

Joanna has finally made it to the first rank of celebrity after 25 years as an actress.
乔安娜当了25年演员后，终于跻身一线女明星之列。

词根35. celer=quick, speed，表示"快，速度"

1. accelerate [ək'seləreɪt] v. 加速，加快

『ac加强+celer快+ate使…→加速，加快』

[V] Inflation continues to accelerate. 通货膨胀不断加速。

[VN] Exposure to the sun can accelerate the ageing process.
暴露在日光下会加速衰老过程。

The runners accelerated smoothly around the bend.
赛跑运动员在转弯处顺畅地加速。

2. decelerate [ˌdi:'seləreɪt] v. 减速，减缓

『de表相反；减少+celer速度+ate使…→减速』

Inflation has decelerated remarkably over the past two years.
过去的两年里通货膨胀已经明显放缓。

the sensation of the train decelerating 列车正在减速的感觉

词根36. cens= judge，表示"审查；判断"

1. censor ['sensə(r)] n. （书籍、电影等的）审查员 vt. 审查、删减（书信或媒体）

『cens审查；判断+or表人→判断之人→审查员』

The report was cleared by the American military censors.
那篇报道得到美国军方审查官的批准。

The news reports had been heavily censored.
这些新闻报道已被大幅删减。

▶ **censorious** [sen'sɔ:riəs] adj. 挑剔的，吹毛求疵的

『censor审查+ious充满…的→挑剔的』

tending to criticize people or things a lot

His treatment of him is sympathetic rather than readily censorious. 他对他的态度是同情而并非一味批评。

2. censure ['senʃə(r)] vt. & n. 严厉批评

『cens审查；判断+ure表行为→审查（某人不合适的做法的）行为→严厉批评』

to criticize sb severely, and often publicly, because of sth they have done

He was censured for leaking information to the press.
他因泄露消息给新闻界而受到谴责。

I deserve neither such praise nor such censure.
这样的夸奖我不敢当，这样的责备我也不敢当。

3. census ['sensəs] n. 人口普查

『cens审查；判断+us表名词→判断（人口情况）→人口普查』

词根37. centr=center，表示"中心"

1. central ['sentrəl] adj. 中心的

『centr中心；中间+al…的→中心的』

2. centrifuge ['sentrɪfju:dʒ] n. 离心机 〈P181〉

『centr(i)中心+fug逃离+e→从中心逃离→离心机』

3. concentrate ['kɒnsntreɪt] v. 集中；专心 〈P7〉

『con一起+centr中心+ate表动词→一起在中心上→集中』

4. eccentric [ɪk'sentrɪk] adj. 古怪的；n. 古怪的人 〈P12〉

『ec(=e)出+centr中心+ic表形容词→偏离中心的→古怪的』

词根38. cert, cern, cret= be sure, separate，表示"确定；区别开"

1. ascertain [ˌæsə'teɪn] vt. 查明；弄清

『as(=to)达到+cert确定+ain→使达到确定的地步→查明』

[VN] It can be difficult to ascertain the facts.
可能难以查明事实真相。

[V that] I ascertained that the driver was not badly hurt.
我已查清，驾驶员伤势不重。

2. certainty ['sɜ:tnti] n. 确定；确定的事

『certain确定+ty表名词→确定』

Her return to the team now seems a certainty.
她的归队现在似乎已成定局。

I have told them with absolute certainty there'll be no change of policy. 我已经十分肯定地告诉他们，政策不会变。

3. certificate [sə'tɪfɪkət] n. 证书；结业证书，文凭

『cert确定+i+fic做+ate表动词或名词→制作的用来确定某事属实的文件』

❶ [C] 证明，证书

an official document that may be used to prove that the facts it states are true

a birth/marriage/death certificate 出生/结婚/死亡证明

❷ [C] 文凭；结业证书；合格证书

an official document proving that you have completed a course of study or passed an exam; a qualification obtained after a course of study or an exam

a Postgraduate Certificate in Education 教育学研究生文凭

4. certify ['sɜ:tɪfaɪ] vt. （尤指书面）证明，证实；颁发合格（或结业）证书

『cert确定+ify使…→通过证明使某事确定→证明；颁发证书』

[V (that)] He handed her a piece of paper certifying (that) she was in good health. 他递给她一份她的健康证明书。

The accounts were certified (as) correct by the finance department. 账目经财务部门证实无误。

They wanted to get certified as divers.
他们想拿到潜水员资格证。

5. certitude [ˈsɜ:tɪtjuːd] n. 确定；确定的事（=certainty）
『cert确定+i+tude表名词→确定；确定的事』

6. discern [dɪˈsɜ:n] vt. 觉察出；（依稀）分辨出
『dis分开+cern确定，区别开→区别开来→觉察出；分辨出』

❶ [VN] 觉察出
to know, recognise or understand sth, especially sth that is not obvious

It is possible to discern a number of different techniques in her work.
从她的作品中可以识别出许多不同的创作手法。
He discerned a certain coldness in their welcome.
他觉察到他们的欢迎有点冷淡。

❷ [VN] （依稀）分辨出
to see or hear sth, but not very clearly
We could just discern the house in the distance.
我们只能勉强分辨出远处的房子。

7. discrete [dɪˈskriːt] adj. 分离的；不相关的
『dis分开+crete区别开，分开→分开的→不相关的』

Discrete ideas or things are separate and distinct from each other.

Social structures are not discrete objects; they overlap and interweave. 社会结构之间不是离散的，他们相互重叠交织。

instruction manuals that break down jobs into scores of discrete steps 把工作分解成许多独立步骤的指导手册

同音词 **discreet** [dɪˈskriːt] adj. （言行）谨慎的

careful in what you say or do, in order to keep sth secret or to avoid causing embarrassment or difficulty for sb
He was always very discreet about his love affairs.
他对两性关系一贯谨小慎微。

▶ **discretion** [dɪˈskreʃn] n. 谨慎；自行决定权

This is confidential, but I know that I can rely on your discretion. 这是机密，不过我知道你靠得住。
How much to tell terminally ill patients is left to the discretion of the doctor.
晚期病人的病情让本人知道多少由医生自行决定。
There is no service charge and tipping is at your discretion.
不收服务费、给不给小费由你自行决定。

词根39. chron(o)=time，表示"时间"

1. chronic [ˈkrɒnɪk] adj. （疾病）慢性的；长期难解决的
『chron时间+ic…的→长期的；慢性的』

❶ （疾病、残疾）慢性的，长期的
10,000 deaths a year from chronic lung disease are attributable to smoking.
吸烟导致每年有1万人死于慢性肺病。

❷ （坏习惯）积习难改的；（问题）长期难以解决的
Anyone who does not believe that smoking is an addiction has never been a chronic smoker.
不相信抽烟能上瘾的人肯定不是老烟民。

One cause of the artist's suicide seems to have been chronic poverty. 那位艺术家自杀的一个原因似乎是长期贫困。

2. chronicle [ˈkrɒnɪkl] n. 编年史，大事年表 vt. 按事件发生顺序记载
『chron时间+icle小→按时间（记录事件）→编年史』

❶ [C] 编年（史）；大事年表
a written record of events in the order in which they happened
Her latest novel is a chronicle of life in a Devon village.
她的最近一部小说是德文郡一个小村庄的生活记事。

❷ [VN] (formal) 把…载入编年史；按事件发生顺序记载
Her achievements are chronicled in a new biography out this week. 她的成就已载入本周出版的一本新传记中。

3. chronology [krəˈnɒlədʒi] n. 年代顺序；年表
『chron时间+ology…学→年代学；年表』

He gave a detailed chronology of the main events of the last three days.
他详细按时间先后讲述了过去三天内发生的事件。
Chronology is the arrangement of facts and events in the order of time.
年表是按时间顺序排列的事实和事件。

4. synchronize [ˈsɪŋkrənaɪz] v. （使）时间同步
『syn同时+chron时间+ize使…→使时间同步→同时发生』

[V] The sound track did not synchronize with the action.
声迹与动作不同步。
[VN] Let's synchronize our watches. 我们对一下表吧。

词根40. cide=cut, kill，表示"切开，杀"

1. homicide [ˈhɒmɪsaɪd] n. （蓄意）杀人罪
『hom(= hum)人+i+cide→杀人；杀人罪』

[C, U] (especially NAmE, law) （蓄意）杀人罪
The police arrived at the scene of the homicide.
警方赶到了凶杀现场。
It was a clear case of homicide. 这显然是一宗杀人案。

同义词 **murder** [ˈmɜːdə(r)] n. 谋杀；凶杀

2. pesticide [ˈpestɪsaɪd] n. 杀虫剂，除害药物
『pest害虫+i+cide切；杀→杀虫剂』

[C, U]杀虫剂；除害药物
This pesticide is harmless to people. 这种农药对人体无害。

3. suicide [ˈsuːɪsaɪd] n. 自杀；自杀行为
『sui自己+ cide切；杀→自杀』

❶ [U, C]自杀
to commit suicide 自杀
attempted suicide 自杀未遂

❷ [U]自杀性行为；自毁；自取灭亡的行为
At the time there were people who thought he was committing professional suicide.
当时有人认为，他是在毁灭自己的职业。

4. insecticide [ɪnˈsektɪsaɪd] n. 杀虫剂
『insect昆虫+i+cide切；杀→杀虫剂』

词根41. cise=cut, kill，表示"切开；杀"

1. concise [kənˈsaɪs] adj. 简明的，简练的
『con一起+cise切→切掉（多余的）后再放到一起→简洁的，简练的』

giving only the information that is necessary and important, using few words

The explanation in this dictionary is concise and to the point. 这部词典里的释义简明扼要。

Whatever you are writing make sure you are clear, concise, and accurate. 无论写什么，一定要清晰、简练、准确。

牛津简明词典封面：

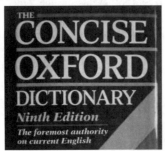

2. excise [ˈeksaɪz , ɪkˈsaɪz] n. 货物税，消费税；vt. 切除，删除

『ex出，出去+cise切→切出去→切除，删除』

Their very names needed to be excised from the history books. 他们的名字必须从历史书上删除掉。

Lebanon has cut fuel excise tax by over 1% of GDP. 黎巴嫩已对燃油消费税进行了削减，降幅超过GDP的1%。

Please excise the corn. I can stand the pain. 把这鸡眼切除了吧，再疼我也忍得住。

3. incise [ɪnˈsaɪz] vt. 雕，刻

『in里面+cise切→把（字、图案等）刻到里面→雕，刻』

[VN] ~ sth (in/on/onto sth)(formal) 雕，刻
to cut words, designs, etc. into a surface

After the surface is polished, a design is incised or painted. 表面磨光以后，刻入或画上图案。

▶ **incisive** [ɪnˈsaɪsɪv] adj.（表达、观点）尖锐的，深刻的
『in里面+cise切（去e）+ive表性质→（表达或观点）能切进去，入木三分→尖锐的，深刻的』

You use incisive to describe a person, their thoughts, or their speech when you approve of their ability to think and express their ideas clearly, briefly, and forcefully.

His incisive remarks made us see the problems in our plans. 他的话切中要害，使我们看到了计划中的一些问题。

She was always clear and incisive in practical suggestion. 她所提的切实可行的建议总是清晰而深刻。

4. precise [prɪˈsaɪs] adj. 准确的；确切的；精确的
『pre事先+cise切→事先按尺寸切好的（所以精确，准确）→准确的，精确的』

Can you give a more precise definition of the word? 你能给这个词下个更确切的定义吗？

He is able to tell the precise spot where each bullet must strike. 他能够估计每颗子弹的准确击中位置。

She is，to be precise，twenty years and two months old. 精确地说，她是20岁又两个月大。

You are a very precise person. 你是一个很严谨的人。

词根42. circ, cycle=ring, circle, 表示"圆，环"

1. bicycle [ˈbaɪsɪkl] n. 自行车 v. 骑自行车
『bi二+ cycle圆，环→两个轮子→自行车』

2. tricycle [ˈtraɪˌsɪkəl] n. 三轮车

『tri三+cycle圆，环→三个轮子→三轮车』

3. cycle [ˈsaɪkl] n. 自行车；循环 v. 骑自行车

❶ [C]自行车；摩托车 a bicycle or motorcycle
We went for a cycle ride on Sunday.
我们星期天骑自行车去兜风了。
a cycle route/track 自行车路线/车道

❷ [V , usually + adv./prep.] (especially BrE) 骑自行车
I usually cycle home through the park.
我通常骑自行车穿过公园回家。

❸ [C] 循环；周期
the cycle of the seasons 四季轮回

▶ **cyclist** [ˈsaɪklɪst] n. 骑自行车的人

4. recycle [ˌriːˈsaɪkl] vt. 回收利用；循环利用
『re (back)返回+cycle圆，环→再回到循环中→回收利用』

The objective would be to recycle 98 per cent of domestic waste. 目标是对98%的生活垃圾进行回收利用。

5. cyclone [ˈsaɪkləʊn] n. 旋风，龙卷风
『cycle圆，环 （去e）+one一→（龙卷风形状像）一个圆圈→旋风，龙卷风』

6. encyclopedia [ɪnˌsaɪkləˈpiːdiə] n. 百科全书
『en使…+cyclo(=cycle)圆，环+ped教育+ia→使（所有知识都进入）这个圈子→百科全书』

From wikipedia, the free encyclopedia.
转载自免费的维基百科全书。

The encyclopedia has twenty volumes.
这套百科全书有20卷。

7. circle [ˈsɜːkl] n. 圆形物；圆圈；圈子 v. 盘旋；圈起

❶ [C] 圆形物，圆片，圆块
Cut out two circles of paper. 剪出两个圆形纸片。

❷ [C] 圆圈，圆形
Draw a circle. 画一个圆圈。
She walked the horse round in a circle. 她牵着马兜圈子。
The children stood in a circle. 孩子们站成一圈。

❸ [C]（相同兴趣、职业等的人形成的）圈子，阶层，界
He has a small circle of friends. 他的朋友圈子很小。
They are new-comers to our circle.
他们是我们同行中新来的人。

❹ [V, VN]（尤指在空中）盘旋，环行，转圈
Seagulls circled around above his head.
海鸥在他的头顶上盘旋。

❺ [VN] 围绕…画圈；圈起来
Spelling mistakes are circled in red ink.
拼写错误都用红笔圈了出来。
This is the ring road that circles the city.
这是环绕市区的环路。

▶ **circular** [ˈsɜːkjələ(r)] adj. 圆形的；环形的
『circ圆，环+ular有…形状或性质的→圆形的』

The full moon has a circular shape. 满月时月亮是圆形的。
We have already worked out the conditions for a circular orbit. 我们已经算出了圆轨道的条件。

8. circulate [ˈsɜːkjəleɪt] v. 循环；（消息、故事等）传播
『circul(=circle圆，环 +ate表动词→使在圆形中（运转）→循环』

❶ （液体或气体）环流，循环

[V] The condition prevents the blood from circulating freely.
这种病阻碍了血液的循环畅通。

[VN] Cooled air is circulated throughout the building.
冷气在整座大楼循环。

❷ （消息、故事等）传播，流传，散布；传阅，传送

[V] Rumours began to circulate about his financial problems.
有关他财务困难的谣言开始流传开来。

[VN]The document will be circulated to all members.
这份文件将在所有成员中传阅。

9. circuit ['sɜːkɪt] n. 电路；环行

『circu(=circ)圆，环+ it走→走完一个环形→环行；电路』

❶ [C] 电路；线路

the complete path of wires and equipment along which an electric current flows

The current in all parts of the circuit is the same.
线路中各个部分的电流都相同。

❷ [C] （绕着某地的）环行，环游

The commanding officer made a circuit of the camp.
指挥官在营地巡视了一周。

10. circus ['sɜːkəs] n. 马戏团；马戏

『circ圆，环+ us表名词→圆形的地方→玩马戏时观众总是围成圆形→马戏，马戏团』

❶ [C] 马戏团

I'm going to be a clown in a circus when I grow up.
我打算长大后到马戏团当小丑。

❷ the circus [sing.] 马戏表演

We took the children to the circus.
我们带孩子去看了马戏表演。

词根43. cite= quote, call，表示"引用；唤起，激起"

1. recite [rɪ'saɪt] vt. （尤指对听众）背诵，吟诵；（口头）列举

『re返回+cite唤起→把（记在脑中的东西）唤回来→背诵』

[VN] Each child had to recite a poem to the class.
每个孩子都得在班上背诵一首诗。

[VN] She could recite a list of all the kings and queens.
她能一一说出所有的国王和王后的名字。

▶ **recital** [rɪ'saɪtl] n. 音乐演奏会；诗歌朗诵会；（口头）列举

I got the prize at poem recital. I'm the winner.
我在诗歌朗诵会上获奖了。我赢了。

2. excite [ɪk'saɪt] vt. 使激动，使兴奋

『ex出来+cite唤起，激起→把（兴奋）激出来→使激动』

3. incite [ɪn'saɪt] v. 煽动，鼓动

『in里面+cite唤起，激起→激起内心的（仇恨）→煽动』

~ sb (to sth) | ~ sth 煽动；鼓动

to encourage sb to do sth violent, illegal or unpleasant, especially by making them angry or excited

[VN] to incite crime/racial hatred/violence
教唆犯罪；煽动种族仇恨/暴力

They were accused of inciting the crowd to violence.
他们被控煽动群众暴乱。

4. cite [saɪt] vt. 援引（为例证）；传讯

『cite唤起→唤起（某事为证）；传唤（某人出庭）→援

引（为例证）；传讯』

❶ ~ sth (as sth) （尤指作为例证）引用，援引；提及

If you cite something, you quote it or mention it, especially as an example or proof of what you are saying.

He cited his heavy workload as the reason for his breakdown.
他说繁重的工作负荷是导致他累垮的原因。

❷ 传唤，传讯

If someone is cited, they are officially ordered to appear before a court.

She was cited in the divorce proceedings.
她在离婚诉讼中被传唤。

词根44. claim=cry out，shout，表示"叫，喊"

1. claim [kleɪm] v.& n. 声称；认领；索赔

『claim叫，喊→呼喊（说某事；要某物）→声称；认领』

❶ 宣称，声称

to say that sth is true although it has not been proved and other people may not believe it

[V to inf] I don't claim to be an expert. 我不敢自称为专家。

[VN] Scientists are claiming a major breakthrough in the fight against cancer.
科学家们宣称攻克癌症已有重大的突破。

[V (that)] He claimed that his motive for stealing was hunger.
他说他因为饿才去偷东西。

❷ [VN] 要求（拥有）；索要，认领；索赔，索款

to demand or ask for sth because you believe it is your legal right to own or to have it

Now they are returning to claim what was theirs.
如今他们回来索取本属于他们的东西。

Somebody has falsely claimed the watch.
有人冒领了那只手表。

They intend to claim for damages against the three doctors.
他们打算向那三位医生索要损害赔偿。

❸ [VN] （灾难、事故等）夺走，夺去（生命）

The car crash claimed three lives.
那次撞车事故导致三人死亡。

❹ [C] ~ (that...) 声明；宣称

The singer has denied the magazine's claim that she is leaving the band.
这名歌手已否认那家杂志有关她要离开乐队的说法。

❺ [C] ~ (on/to sth) 索要权；~ (for sth) 索赔，索款

They had no claim on the land. 他们无权索要那块土地。

Make sure your claims for expenses are submitted by the end of the month. 确定你的费用报销在月底以前提交。

❻ have a claim on sb 对某人有…的要求权
lay claim to sth 声称对…的拥有权

She'd no claims on him now. 现在他不欠她什么了。

Five Asian countries lay claim to the islands.
五个亚洲国家声称对那些岛屿拥有主权。

▶ **reclaim** [rɪ'kleɪm] vt. 收回；开垦

『re回来+ claim认领→认领回来→收回；开垦（荒地）』

❶ 要求归还（或恢复）；收回

If you reclaim something that you have lost or that has been taken away from you, you succeed in getting it back.

"I've come to reclaim my property," she announced to the desk clerk.

"我来要求归还我的房产，"她向接待人员宣布。

❷ ~ sth (from sth) 开垦（荒地）；开拓（耕地或建筑用地）
When people reclaim land, they make it suitable for a purpose such as farming or building.
The Netherlands has been reclaiming farmland from water.
荷兰人一直在围海造地。
Some reclaimed land can now be farmed again.
部分复垦的土地可以重新用于耕种。

▶ **disclaim** [dɪsˈkleɪm] vt. 公开否认；拒绝承认
『dis表相反+claim认领→否认，拒绝承认』

She disclaimed any knowledge of her husband's whereabouts.
她否认知道丈夫的下落。
The rebels disclaimed all responsibility for the explosion.
反叛分子否认对这次爆炸事件负有任何责任。

2. **acclaim** [əˈkleɪm] vt. & n. 称誉，赞扬
『ac加强+claim叫，喊→欢呼→称誉，赞扬』

❶ [VN] [usually passive] ~ sb/sth (as sth)
称誉某人/事物（为…）；给予高度评价

She has published six highly acclaimed novels.
她出版了六本备受赞誉的小说。
The work was acclaimed as a masterpiece.
该作品被誉为杰作。

❷ [U] 公开赞扬，称誉
Acclaim is public praise for someone or something.
The film met with considerable critical and public acclaim.
该影片受到了影评人和公众的高度评价。

▶ **acclamation** [ˌækləˈmeɪʃn] n. 欢呼，喝彩；口头表决

Acclamation is a noisy or enthusiastic expression of approval for someone or something.
The news was greeted with considerable popular acclamation.
消息赢得了相当普遍的欢呼。
He was elected chairman by acclamation.
他在拥立声中被选为主席。

3. **exclaim** [ɪkˈskleɪm] v. （由于强烈的情感或痛苦而）惊叫，呼喊
『ex出+claim叫，喊→叫喊；大声说出』

[V speech] "It isn't fair!," he exclaimed angrily.
"这不公平！"他气愤地喊道。
[V] She opened her eyes and exclaimed in delight at the scene. 她睁开眼睛，看到这情景，高兴地叫出声来。

▶ **exclamation** [ˌekskləˈmeɪʃn] n. 感叹；感叹语；感叹词
『exclaim惊叫（去i)+ation表名词→感叹』

He gave an exclamation of surprise. 他发出一声惊叹。

4. **proclaim** [prəˈkleɪm] vt. 宣告；明确表示；表明
『pro向前+ claim叫，喊→向前面大声讲话→宣布』

❶ 宣布；宣告
If people proclaim something, they formally make it known to the public.
[VN] The president proclaimed a state of emergency.
总统宣布了紧急状态。
[VN-N] He proclaimed himself emperor. 他自封为皇帝。
[V speech] "I think we have been heard today," he proclaimed.
"我想今天我们说的大家都听见了，"他明确地说。

❷ 成为标志；表明
to show sth clearly; to be a sign of sth

[VN] This building, more than any other, proclaims the character of the town.
这座建筑比任何其他建筑都能代表本城的特色。
[VN-N , VN to inf] His accent proclaimed him a Scot.
他的口音表明他是苏格兰人。

▶ **proclamation** [ˌprɒkləˈmeɪʃn] n. 宣言，公告，声明

There is a royal proclamation of the birth of the prince.
有一张王室的公告，宣告王子诞生了。

词义辨析 <P374第64> 宣布 declare, announce, proclaim

5. **declaim** [dɪˈkleɪm] v. （尤指在公众前）慷慨激昂地宣讲，慷慨陈词
『de向下+claim叫，喊→（好像站在讲台上）向下大喊→慷慨激昂地宣讲』

to speak loudly and with force about sth you feel strongly about, especially in public, or you speak dramatically, as if you were acting in a theatre.
He raised his right fist and declaimed: "Liar and cheat!"
他举起右拳高喊："骗子，骗子！"
He declaimed against the evils of alcohol.
他慷慨陈词，猛烈抨击酗酒的罪恶。

6. **clamor** [ˈklæmə(r)] n. 喧闹声；（表示抗议、要求等的）叫喊声
『claim叫，喊（去i)+or表情况→喧哗，吵闹』

❶ [U] 嘈杂声，喧闹声
The clamor of traffic gave me a headache.
交通噪声让我头痛。

❷ [C, U] （表示抗议、要求等的)叫喊声
After the bombing, there was a public clamor for vengence.
爆炸发生后，公众大声要求复仇。
The debate was interrupted by a clamor of opposition.
辩论被反对方的一声叫喊打断。

▶ **clamorous** [ˈklæmərəs] adj. 吵吵嚷嚷的，吵闹的
『clamor吵闹+ous表形容词→吵闹的』

He was deafened by the clamorous voices.
喧闹声震得他耳朵快要聋了。

词根45. clear, clar=clear，表示"清楚，明白"

1. **clear** [klɪə(r)] adj. 清楚的，明白的 vt. 清理；批准

❶ adj. （事）清晰易懂的；（人）清楚的，明白的
She gave me clear and precise directions.
她给了我清晰而准确的指示。
Are these instructions clear enough?
这些说明够清楚了吗？

❷ adj. 明显的；清晰的
His height gives him a clear advantage.
他的身高使他具有明显的优势。
It was quite clear to me that she was lying.
我十分清楚她在撒谎。

❸ adj. 头脑清醒敏锐的；问心无愧的
You'll need to keep a clear head for your interview.
你面试时需要保持清醒的头脑。
I could go away again with a clear conscience.
我可以问心无愧地再次离开。

❹ adj. （水）清澈的；（天空）晴朗无云的；（眼睛）明亮有神的
The water was so clear we could see the bottom of the lake.

湖水清澈见底。

On a clear day you can see France.

天气晴朗时你可以看见法国。

❺ adj. ~ (of sth) 畅通的；收拾干净的

The road was clear and I ran over.

路上没有东西挡着，我就跑了过来。

All exits must be kept clear of baggage.

所有出口必须保持通畅，不得堆放行李。

I always leave a clear desk at the end of the day.

每天工作结束时，我总是把桌上收拾干净不放任何东西。

❻ adj.~ of sth 摆脱掉（不愉快事物）的

They were still not clear of all suspicion.

他们仍未解除所有的嫌疑。

We are finally clear of debt. 我们终于偿清了债务。

❼ [VN] ~ A (of B) | ~ B (from/off A)

I cleared my desk of papers. 我清理好了写字台上的文件。

Clear all those papers off the desk.

把桌子上所有那些文件都拿走。

The streets had been cleared of snow.

街道上的积雪已被清除干净。

❽ [VN] ~ sb (of sth) 证明无罪（或无辜）

She was cleared of all charges against her.

对她的所有指控均已撤销。

❾ [VN] 批准；准许；得到许可

His appointment had been cleared by the board.

他的任命已由董事会批准。

The plane had been cleared for take-off.

飞机已得到起飞许可。

She hasn't been cleared by security.

她尚未获保安部门批准做机要工作。

▶ **clarify** [ˈklærəfaɪ] vt. 使清楚；澄清

『clear清楚的（去e加i）+fy使…变得→使变得清楚』

to make sth clearer or easier to understand

I hope this clarifies my position.

我希望这能阐明我的立场。

He issued a statement to clarify the situation.

他发表了一项声明以澄清情况。

▶ **clarification** [ˌklærəfɪˈkeɪʃn] n. 澄清，说明

▶ **clearance** [ˈklɪərəns] n. 清除；审查许可

❶ [C, U] 清除，清理

The UN pledged to help supervise the clearance of mines.

联合国承诺协助监督扫雷工作。

❷ [U, C]审查许可，审核批准

I'm waiting for clearance from headquarters.

我在等待总部的录用审查许可。

The pilot was waiting for clearance for take-off.

飞行员在等待起飞的许可。

▶ **clarity** [ˈklærəti] n. 清楚，清晰

『clear清楚的，清晰的（去e)+ity表名词→清楚，清晰』

The first thing to strike me was the amazing clarity of the water. 首先吸引我的是水的无比清澈。

He always put his point of view with clarity and with courage.

他总是清楚而勇敢地提出自己的观点。

2. clearing [ˈklɪərɪŋ] n.（林间）空地

『clear清理+ing名词后缀→把（树木）清除之后→空地』

A helicopter landed in a clearing in the dense jungle.

一架直升机降落在茂密丛林中的一片空地上。

3. declare [dɪˈkleə(r)] v. 宣布；宣称；申报

『de加强+clare(=clear)清楚→使清楚→宣布；宣称』

❶ 宣布，宣告

to say sth officially or publicly

[VN] The government has declared a state of emergency.

政府已宣布进入紧急状态。

[V that] The court declared that strike action was illegal.

法庭宣判罢工为非法。

❷ 表明，宣称，断言

to state sth firmly and clearly

[V that] He declared that he was in love with her.

他声称他已爱上她。

[VN] He declared his intention to become the best golfer in the world.

他表明自己想要成为世界上最好的高尔夫球选手。

❸ 申报（纳税品、收入等）

Do you have anything to declare? 你有什么要申报的吗？

词义辨析 <P374第64> 宣布 declare, announce, proclaim

▶ **declaration** [ˌdekləˈreɪʃn] n. 宣告；宣称；申报

词根46. cline=lean, slope，表示"倾斜，斜坡"

1. decline [dɪˈklaɪn] n.& vi. 减少；下降；衰落 v.谢绝

『de向下+cline倾斜→向下倾斜→下降；衰落』

❶ [C, usually sing., U] ~ (in sth) | ~ (of sth)（数量、价值、质量等）减少，下降；衰落，衰退

The company reported a small decline in its profits.

公司报告其利润略有减少。

An increase in cars has resulted in the decline of public transport. 汽车的增加导致了公共交通的减少。

Thankfully the smoking of cigarettes is **on the decline**.

令人欣慰的是，吸烟量在逐渐下降。

Libraries are an investment for the future and they should not be allowed to fall into decline.

图书馆是对未来的一项投资，不应任其日趋萎缩。

❷ [V] 减少；下降；衰弱；衰退

Support for the party continues to decline.

对该政党的支持继续下降。

The number of tourists to the resort declined by 10% last year.

去年到这个胜地旅游的人数减少了10%。

❸ (formal) 谢绝；婉言拒绝

[V] I offered to give them a lift but they declined.

我主动邀请他们搭车，但他们婉言谢绝了。

[V to inf] Their spokesman declined to comment on the allegations. 他们的发言人拒绝对这些指控加以评论。

2. incline [ɪnˈklaɪn , ˈɪnklaɪn] v. 倾向于；倾斜 n. 斜坡

『in里面+cline倾斜→内心里（向做某事）倾斜→倾向』

❶ ~ (sb) to/towards sth （使）倾向于，有…的趋势

[V] I incline to the view that we should take no action at this stage. 我倾向于认为我们在这个阶段不应采取行动。

[V to inf] The government is more effective than we incline to think. 政府的效率比我们所惯常以为的要高。

[VN] Lack of money inclines many young people towards crime. 缺钱使很多年轻人产生了犯罪倾向。

I **am inclined to** believe he is innocent.

我颇以为他是无辜的。

❷ ~ (sth) (to/towards sth) （使）倾斜
[V] The land inclined gently towards the shore.
地面缓缓向海岸倾斜。

3. recline [rɪˈklaɪn] v. 斜倚；斜躺；向后倾斜（座椅）
『re往回+ cline倾斜→往回斜过去→斜躺；倾斜』

❶ [V] ~ (against/in/on sth) (formal) 斜倚；斜躺；向后倚靠
He reclined comfortably on a sofa reading a newspaper.
他舒服地斜躺在沙发上看报。

❷ 向后倾斜（座椅）；（使）（座椅）椅背后仰
[V] Air France first-class seats recline almost like beds.
法国航空公司头等舱的座椅可以调低得几乎像床一样。
[VN] Ramesh had reclined his seat and was lying back smoking. 拉梅什把椅背调低，倚在上面吸烟。

词根47. clude, close=close，表示"关闭"

1. closure [ˈkləʊʒə(r)] n. 关停；封闭；宽慰
『close关闭（去e）+ure表结果→关停；封闭』

❶ [C, U]（医院、学校、工厂等）关停，倒闭
Almost three in four clinics say they face closure by the end of the year. 近四分之三的诊所说年底前要面临歇业。
This could mean the closure of thousands of small businesses which serve the community.
这可能意味着成千上万家服务社会的小企业将要倒闭。

❷ [C]（道路或边界的）封闭，封锁
notices on temporary road closure in Sha Tin
有关沙田区临时封路的最新通告

❸ [U] 解脱；宽慰
the feeling that a difficult or an unpleasant experience has come to an end or been dealt with in an acceptable way
The conviction of their son's murderer helped to give them a sense of closure.
谋杀儿子的凶手被判有罪，让他们得到了一些安慰。

2. disclose [dɪsˈkləʊz] vt. 揭露，透露，泄露
『dis表相反+ close关闭→揭发，泄露』

[VN] The spokesman refused to disclose details of the takeover to the press.
发言人拒绝向新闻界透露公司收购的详细情况。
[V that] The report discloses that human error was to blame for the accident. 报告披露这次事故是人为原因造成的。

▶**disclosure** [dɪsˈkləʊʒə(r)] n. 揭露，透露，公开；吐露的事
『disclose揭露，吐露（去e）+ure表名词→揭露，吐露』

Any public disclosure of this information would be very damaging to the company.
任何公开披露这些信息都会对公司造成极大的损害。
Winterbourne listened with interest to these disclosures.
温特伯恩聚精会神地听着这些新闻。

3. closet [ˈklɒzɪt] n. 贮藏室；壁橱
『close关闭 + et小（去e）→可开关的小东西→壁橱』

(especially NAmE) 贮藏室；壁橱（BrE cupboard or wardrobe）
a small room or a space in a wall with a door that reaches the floor, used for storing things
Pick up your garments and hang them in the closet.
把你的衣服收起来挂到衣柜里。
I don't have any skeleton in my closet. 我没有任何家丑。
Mrs Corney rose to get another cup and saucer from the

closet. 考尔尼太太起身从壁橱里取出另一副杯碟。
comes out of the closet 公开同性恋身份；出柜

4. enclose [ɪnˈkləʊz] vt. 围起来；随函（或包裹等）附上
『en使…成为+close关闭→使…成为关闭状→围起来』

❶ [usually passive] ~ sth (in/with sth)（用墙、篱笆等）把…围起来
The surrounding land was enclosed by an eight foot wire fence. 周围的土地围有8英尺高的铁丝栅栏。
She felt his arms enclose her. 她感到他搂住了她。

❷ ~sth (with sth) 附入；随函（或包裹等）附上
If you enclose something with a letter, you put it in the same envelope as the letter.
Please return the completed form, enclosing a recent photograph. 请将填好的表格寄回，并附上近照一张。
I enclose two tickets along with this letter.
我随信附上两张票。
Please enclose five dollars for postage and handling.
请内附五元邮费和手续费。

▶**enclosure** [ɪnˈkləʊʒə(r)] n. 圈地；圈用地；附件
a wildlife enclosure 野生动物围场
The letter said there was an enclosure, but they obviously forgot to put it in.
信上说有一附件，但他们显然忘记把它放进去了。

5. conclude [kənˈkluːd] v. 推断；结束；达成
『con一起+clude关闭→（把前面的内容）关闭到一起→推断；结束』

❶ ~ sth (from sth) | ~ (from sth) that… 推断出
He concluded from their remarks that they were not in favour of the plan. 他从他们的话语中推断出他们不赞同此计划。

❷ ~ (sth) (with sth) (formal) （使）结束，终止
He concluded by wishing everyone a safe trip home.
他讲话结束时祝愿大家回家一路平安。
The evening concluded with dinner and speeches.
这个夜晚在宴会和讲话中结束。

❸ [VN] ~ sth (with sb) 达成，订立，缔结（协定）
A trade agreement was concluded between the two countries.
两国之间签署了贸易协定。

▶**conclusion** [kənˈkluːʒn] n. 结论；结尾，结束
❶ [C] 结论；推论
I've come to the conclusion that he's not the right person for the job. 我断定他不适合做这项工作。
❷ [C, usually sing.] 结束；结果；结尾；结局
the end of sth such as a speech or a piece of writing
The conclusion of the book was disappointing.
这部书的结尾令人失望。
In conclusion, I wish this forum a brilliant success.
最后，我祝这个研讨会获得空前成功。
❸ in conclusion 总之，总而言之
You say "in conclusion" to indicate that what you are about to say is the last thing that you want to say.
In conclusion, walking is a cheap, safe, enjoyable and readily available form of exercise.
总而言之，步行是一种廉价、安全、愉快且容易获得的锻炼方式。

▶**conclusive** [kənˈkluːsɪv] adj. 确凿的；结论性的

Conclusive evidence shows that something is certainly true.
It's no use denying it; the evidence is conclusive.
证据确凿，不容狡赖。

6. include [ɪnˈkluːd] vt. 包括，包含
『in里面+ clude关→关在里面→包括』

❶ 包括；包含
if one thing includes another, it has the second thing as one of its parts
[VN] The tour included a visit to the Science Museum.
这次游览包括参观科学博物馆。
Does the price include tax? 这个价钱是否包括税款？
[V -ing] Your duties include typing letters and answering the telephone. 你的职责是打印信件和接电话。

❷ [VN] ~ sb/sth (as/in/on sth) 使成为…的一部分
to make sb/sth part of sth
You should include some examples in your essay.
你应该在文章里举一些例子。
Representatives from the country were included as observers at the conference.
这个国家的代表都被列为会议的观察员。

▶ **inclusive** [ɪnˈkluːsɪv] adj. 包括全部费用的；包容的

❶ from… to… inclusive (BrE) 首末项包括在内的
Training will commence on 5 October, running from Tuesday to Saturday inclusive.
培训将于10月5日开始，从星期二(含)到星期六(含)。

❷ 包容性强的；各种人都有的
The academy is far more inclusive now than it used to be.
该学会的包容性比过去强了很多。

❸ ~ (of sth) 包含全部费用；包括所提到的费用在内
The fully inclusive fare for the trip is £52.
这次旅行的全部费用是52英镑。
The rent is inclusive of water and heating.
租金包括水费和暖气费。

▶ **including** [ɪnˈkluːdɪŋ] prep. 包括…在内
Six people were killed in the riot, including a policeman.
暴乱中有六人死亡，包括一名警察。
Stars including Joan Collins are expected to attend.
包括琼·柯林斯在内的明星们，届时预计会参加。

7. exclude [ɪkˈskluːd] vt. 排除；不包括
『ex出去，外面+clude关闭→关在外面→不包括』

~ sth (from sth) 不包括；把…排除在外
Try excluding fat from your diet.
平时用餐时尽量避免含脂肪的食品。
Buses run every hour, Sundays excluded.
公共汽车每小时一班，星期天除外。
The police have excluded theft as a motive for the murder.
警方已排除这起谋杀案中的偷窃动机。

▶ **exclusive** [ɪkˈskluːsɪv] adj. 独有的；排外的；高档的
『exclude的形容词形式。"元音+de"结尾的动词，形容词形式以"元音+sive"结尾。如decide, decisive』

❶ 独有的；独家（报道）的
available or belonging only to particular people, and not shared
Our group will have exclusive use of a 60-foot boat.
我们小组将独用一条60英尺长的船。
His mother has told *The Times* about his death in an

exclusive interview (= not given to any other newspaper) .
他的母亲在接受《泰晤士报》的独家采访中谈到他的死亡。

❷ （团体、社团等）排外的；不愿接收新成员的
Why have we got this exclusive spirit?
为什么我们有这种排外的精神？

❸ ~ of sb/sth 不包括…的
The price is for accommodation only, exclusive of meals.
此价只包括住宿，饭费除外。

❹ 高档的；高级的；奢华的 （排斥一般人使用的）
He belongs to an exclusive club.
他参加的是一个上层人士俱乐部。
an exclusive hotel 高级旅馆

8. preclude [prɪˈkluːd] v. 使行不通；阻止，妨碍
『pre前；预先+clude关闭→事先关闭（做某事的可能性）→阻止』

~ sth | ~ sb from doing sth
to prevent sth from happening or sb from doing sth; to make sth impossible
[VN] Lack of time precludes any further discussion.
由于时间不足，不可能进行深入的讨论。
[VN -ing] His religious beliefs precluded him/his serving in the army. 他的宗教信仰不允许他服兵役。

9. seclude [sɪˈkluːd] vt. 与…隔绝；（使）隐居，独处
『se分开+clude关闭→关上（门与尘世）分开→使隔绝』

[VN] ~ yourself/sb (from sb/sth)
(formal) （使）与…隔离；（使）隐居，独处
She would seclude herself from the world forever.
她要永远摆脱这个世界。
The place was picturesque, secluded.
这地方风景如画，与世隔绝。

10. recluse [rɪˈkluːs] n. 隐居者；喜欢独处的人
『re回+cluse（=close）关闭→返回（家中）闭门不出→隐士』

After 1884 he lived the life of a recluse.
1884年后他过着隐居的生活。
The old recluse secluded himself from the outside world.
这位老隐士与外面的世界隔绝了。

词根48. cogn=know, 表示"知道"

1. recognise [ˈrekəgnaɪz] vt. 认出；承认；认可
『re又+cogn知道+ise表动词→认出』

❶ [VN] 认出
I recognised him as soon as he came in the room.
他一进屋我就认出了他。

❷ 承认；意识到
to admit or to be aware that sth exists or is true
[V wh-] Nobody recognised how urgent the situation was.
谁也没意识到形势有多么紧急。
[VN] They recognised the need to take the problem seriously.
他们认识到需要严肃对待这个问题。

❸ [VN] （formal）认可，承认
The UK has refused to recognise the new regime.
英国已拒绝承认这个新的政权。

❹ [VN] 赞赏，认可
The RAF recognised him as an outstandingly able engineer.
英国皇家空军认为他是一名非常能干的机械师。

2. cognition [kɒgˈnɪʃn] n. 认知，感知
『cogn知道+ition表名词→知道某事物→认知，感知』

Cognition is the mental process involved in knowing, learning, and understanding things.

▶ **cognitive** [ˈkɒɡnətɪv] adj. 认知的

As children grow older, their cognitive processes become sharper. 孩子们越长越大，他们的认知过程变得更为敏锐。

词根49. corp, corpor=body，表示"身体；团体"

1. corpse [kɔːps] n. 尸体，（尤指人的）死尸，尸首
『corp身体+se（谐音"死"）→人死后的身体→尸体』

He sat by the corpse all night, weeping in bitter earnest.
他整夜坐在尸体旁边，痛哭流涕。

2. corps [kɔː(r)] n. （陆军）特种部队；（美国）海军陆战队；军团；（从事某种特殊工作的）一组人，一群人
『corp身体；团体+s表复数→军队；团体』
（注意：其读音为[kɔː(r)]而不是[kɔːps]）
（pl. corps [C+sing./pl. v.]）

❶ （陆军）特种部队；（美国）海军陆战队

He was a soldier of marine corps.
他曾是海军陆战队里的一名士兵。

The corps are assembling near this town.
军团正在本城镇附近集结。

US officials say Washington may soon sanction a unit of Iran's Revolutionary Guard Corps.
美国官员说，华盛顿可能很快会制裁伊朗革命卫队的一个单位。

❷ （从事某种特殊工作的）一组人，一群人

A corps of doctors arrived to inoculate the recruits.
一队医生来给新兵打防疫针。

I had friends in the press corps.
我在记者团中有些朋友。

3. corporal [ˈkɔːpərəl] adj. 身体上的 n. 下士
『corpor身体+al表性质→身体上的』

Corporal punishment was banned by statute in 1987.
1987年通过的法令明文禁止体罚。

4. corpulent [ˈkɔːpjələnt] adj. 发福的，富态的（委婉说法，与fat同义）；肥胖的
『corp身体+ulent多…的→身体多肉的→肥胖的』

Sitting behind the window was a corpulent woman with a face of steel. 那窗口后面坐着一个面如镔铁的胖妇女。

5. corpuscle [ˈkɔːpʌsl] n. （红或白）血球，血细胞
『corp(=body)身体+uscle小→（血液内的）小球体→血球』

Deficiency of red corpuscles is caused by a lack of iron.
红细胞生成不足是由缺铁引起的。

6. corporation [ˌkɔːpəˈreɪʃn] n. 公司；法人
『corpor团体+ ate使→使成为团体→corporate（去e加ion构成名词）→变成团体后的事物→公司』

A changing world has put pressures on the corporation.
日新月异的世界使这家公司感到了压力。

词义辨析 <P369第38> 公司 company, corporation, firm

词义辨析 <P369第39>
公司（缩写）Inc., Corp., Ltd. 与 Co., Ltd.

▶ **corporate** [ˈkɔːpərət] adj. 公司的，法人的；共同的

『corpor团体+ ate有…性质的→共同的；团体的』

This established a strong corporate image.
这树立起了一种强有力的公司形象。

They no longer expect corporate profits to improve.
他们不再期待公司利润会增长。

corporate finance/planning/strategy 公司的财务/计划/战略

▶ **incorporate** [ɪnˈkɔːpəreɪt] vt. 合并，包含；成立公司
『in进入corpor团体+ate表动词→加入团体→合并』

❶ ~ sth (in/into/within sth) 合并，包含

Many of your suggestions have been incorporated in the plan.
你的很多建议都纳入计划中。

The new car design incorporates all the latest safety features.
新的汽车设计包括了所有最新的安全配备。

❷ [VN] 成立公司

The company was incorporated in 2002.
这家公司成立于2002年。

7. corporeal [kɔːˈpɔːriəl] adj. 有形的，实体的；身体的
『corpor身体；团体+eal…的，具有…性质的→有形体的』

that can be touched, physical rather than spiritual; of or for the body

All souls take corporeal forms, and when they fail they find places to hide.
所有灵魂都要有肉身，肉身坏掉之后它们就要找地方藏起来。

▶ **incorporeal** [ˌɪnkɔːˈpɔːriəl] adj. 无形体的，无形的
『in无+corporeal有形体的→无形体的』

They seemed to have the power to touch the incorporeal and see the invisible.
他们似乎有一种力量能触摸到无形的东西和看到不可见的东西。

词根50. cover=cover，表示"覆盖"

1. uncover [ʌnˈkʌvə(r)] vt. 揭开盖子；揭露，发现
『un表相反动作+ cover覆盖→揭开（隐藏的或被覆盖的）』

❶ [VN] 揭开…的盖子；除去…上的覆盖物
Uncover the pan and let the soup simmer.
揭开锅盖，让汤再慢火煨一下。

❷ [VN] 揭露，发现（隐秘之事）
Police have uncovered a plot to kidnap the President's son.
警方已侦破一起绑架总统之子的阴谋。

The son will uncover his father's guilt.
儿子将揭露父亲的罪行。

❸ [VN] 发现，发掘（地下埋藏之物）
Archaeologists have uncovered an 11,700-year-old hunting camp in Alaska.
考古学家在阿拉斯加发现了一个距今11700年的狩猎营地。

2. discover [dɪˈskʌvə(r)] vt. 发现
『dis表相反+ cover遮，盖→揭开→发现』

❶ [VN] （第一个）发现（某地、某物质等）
When someone discovers a new place, substance, scientific fact, or scientific technique, they are the first person to find it or become aware of it.
Cook is credited with discovering Hawaii.
人们把发现夏威夷的功劳归于库克。

Scientists around the world are working to discover a cure for AIDS. 全世界的科学家都在努力寻找治疗艾滋病的方法。

❷ [VN] [often passive] 发现（人才）
The singer was discovered while still at school.
这个歌唱家在上学的时候就受到赏识了。

❸（偶然）发现；找到（一直在寻找的某人或某物）
We discovered this beach while we were sailing around the island. 我们在围绕这个海岛航行时发现了这个海滩。

❹ 了解到；认识到；查明
to find out about sth; to find some information about sth
She discovered that they'd escaped. 她发现他们已经逃跑了。

词义辨析 <P366第25> 发现；查明 find out, find, discover

3. **recover** [rɪˈkʌvə(r)] v. 恢复（健康）；恢复（常态）
『re返回+cover覆盖→又覆盖回来→恢复；找到』

❶ [V] ~ (from sth) 恢复健康
He's still recovering from his operation.
手术后，他仍在恢复之中。

❷ [V] ~ (from sth)（从不愉快的经历中）恢复常态
It can take many years to recover from the death of a loved one. 从失去亲人的痛苦中恢复过来可能要花很多年。
The economy is at last beginning to recover.
经济终于开始复苏了。

❸ [VN] ~ sth (from sb/sth) 找回丢失或被偷的东西
The police eventually recovered the stolen paintings.
警方最终追回了失窃的油画。

❹ 恢复（意识、神志或身体状态）
[VN] It took her a few minutes to recover consciousness.
过了几分钟她才恢复知觉。

▶**recovery** [rɪˈkʌvəri] n. 恢复；复得

词根51. crat=ruler，表示"统治者"，cracy=rule，表示"统治或政体"

1. **democrat** [ˈdeməkræt] n. 民主主义者；民主党党员
『demo人民+crat统治者；权力→（想让）人们做统治者（的人）→民主主义者』

Congressman Tom Downey is a Democrat from New York.
国会议员汤姆·唐尼是来自纽约州的一名民主党人。
This is the time for democrats and not dictators.
现在需要的是民主主义者，而不是独裁者。

▶**democratic** [ˌdeməˈkrætɪk] adj. 民主的
『democrat民主主义者+ic有…性质的→民主的』

❶ 民主制度的，民主政体的
a democratic country 民主国家
a democratic system 民主制度

❷ 民主管理的；民主作风的
Education is the basis of a democratic society.
教育是民主社会的基础。
The country will hold democratic elections within a year.
该国将在一年之内举行民主选举。

▶**democracy** [dɪˈmɒkrəsi] n. 民主政体；民主国家；民主精神
『demo人民，人们+cracy政体→民主政体』

The new democracies face tough challenges.
这些新兴的民主国家面临着严峻挑战。
He has reaffirmed his faith in democracy.
他再次重申了自己的民主信仰。

2. **autocrat** [ˈɔːtəkræt] n. 独裁者；专横的人
『auto自己+crat统治者→自己做统治者（不听别人）→独裁者』

The nobles tried to limit the powers of the autocrat without success. 贵族企图限制专制君主的权力，但没有成功。
It seems to me that you talk like a great autocrat.
你说话活像个专制的暴君。

近义词 dictator 独裁者　tyrant 暴君，专制君主

▶**autocratic** [ˌɔːtəˈkrætɪk] adj. 独裁的；专制的
▶**autocracy** [ɔːˈtɒkrəsi] n. 独裁政体；专制制度

3. **bureaucrat** [ˈbjʊərəkræt] n. 官僚主义者；官僚
『bureau政府机构+crat统治者→官僚』

an official working in an organization or a government department, especially one who follows the rules of the department too strictly
The economy is still controlled by bureaucrats.
经济依然被官僚们所掌控。

▶**bureaucratic** [ˌbjʊərəˈkrætɪk] adj. 官僚的；官僚主义的
『bureaucrat官僚主义者+ic有…性质的→官僚的』

We must not put on bureaucratic airs.
我们不能摆官僚主义架子。

▶**bureaucracy** [bjʊəˈrɒkrəsi] n. 官僚主义；官僚作风；官僚体制；
『bureau政府机构+cracy统治或政体→官僚主义』

People usually complain about having to deal with too much bureaucracy. 人们经常抱怨不得不应付太多的繁文缛节。
Bureaucracy and corruption still exist to varying degrees in many sectors.
在不少环节上还不同程度存在官僚主义和腐败现象。

4. **theocratic** [ˌθiːəˈkrætɪk] adj. 神权政体的
『theo神+ crat统治者+ic有…性质的→神权政体的』

Iran implements theocratic political system and theocracy above all else.
伊朗实行的是政教合一、神权高于一切的政治体制。

▶**theocracy** [θiˈɒkrəsi] n. 神权政治；神权国
『theo神+cracy统治或政体→神权统治』

Israel, however, is not a theocracy and other religions are respected.
然而，以色列并不是一个神权国家，也尊重其他的宗教。

词根52. cred，creed=believe, trust，表示"相信，信任"

1. **credit** [ˈkredɪt] n. 赊购；赞扬；学分　vt. 存入金额；归功于
『cred相信，信任+it→信任；学分』

❶ [U] 赊购；赊欠
I have no cash on me. May I pay by credit card?
我没带现金。可以用信用卡付款吗？
We bought the dishwasher on credit .
我们赊购了一台洗碗机。
Your credit limit is now £2,000.
你的信用额度现在为2000英镑。

❷ [U] ~ (for sth) 赞扬，称赞；认可；功劳
He's a player who rarely seems to get the credit he deserves.
他这个选手好像很少得到应得的赞扬。

I can't take all the credit for the show's success—it was a team effort.
演出成功不是我一个人的功劳——这是集体努力的结果。

❸ [sing.] ~ to sb/sth 为…赢得荣誉的人/事物
She is a credit to the school. 她为学校赢得了荣誉。

❹ [C]（大学，以及美国中小学的）学分；学习单元
My math class is worth three credits.
我的数学课为三个学分。

❺ to sb's credit 值得赞扬的是
To his credit, Jack never told anyone exactly what had happened. 杰克对所发生的事守口如瓶，值得赞扬。

do sb credit / do credit to sb/sth 使值得赞扬（或表扬）
Your honesty does you great credit.
你的诚实值得大大表扬。

have sth to your credit 完成；取得
He's only 30, and he already has four novels to his credit.
他年仅30岁，却已著有四部小说。

❻ [VN] ~ A (with B) | ~ B (to A)
（给银行账户）存入金额；把…记入贷方
Your account has been credited with $50,000.
已把5万美元存入你的账户。
$50,000 has been credited to your account.
已把5万美元存入你的账户。

❼ [VN] [usually passive] ~ A with B | ~ B to A
认为是…的功劳；把…归于
The company is credited with inventing the industrial robot.
发明工业机器人是那家公司的功劳。
The invention of the industrial robot is credited to the company. 工业机器人的发明应归功于那家公司。

2. credible [ˈkredəbl] adj. 可信的；可靠的
『cred相信+ible可…的，能…的→可靠的，可信的』

❶ 可信的；可靠的
Baroness Thatcher's claims seem credible to many.
撒切尔夫人的主张在很多人看来是可信的。

❷ 有望成功的
Mr Robertson would be a credible candidate.
罗伯逊先生将是可能当选的候选人之一。
The challenge before the opposition is to offer credible alternative policies for the future.
摆在反对党面前的挑战是如何为未来发展提出其他可行性政策。

▶**incredible** [ɪnˈkredəbl] adj. 难以置信的；极好的；极大的
『in不+credible可信的→（好得、大得）难以置信的』

❶ 不能相信的；难以置信的
It seemed incredible that she had been there a week already.
真让人难以置信，她已经在那里待了一个星期了。

❷ (informal) 极好的；极大的，惊人的
The hotel was incredible. 这家旅馆棒极了。
We import an incredible amount of cheese from the Continent. 我们从欧洲大陆进口数量惊人的奶酪。

3. credence [ˈkriːdns] n. 可信性，真实性
『cred相信，信任+ ence表行为→相信』

They could give no credence to the findings of the survey.
他们不相信这次调查的结果。
All the people here refuse credence to the story.

这儿所有的人都不相信这个故事。

4. credentials [krəˈdenʃlz] n. [pl.] 资格，资历；资格证书
『cred相信，信任+ent表名词+ial …的→让人相信的东西→资格』

❶ ~ (as/for sth) 资格；资历
the qualities, training or experience that make you suitable to do sth
He has all the credentials for the job.
他做这项工作完全够格。

❷ 资格证书；证明书；证件
Someone's credentials are a letter or certificate that proves their identity or qualifications.
Britain's new ambassador to Lebanon has presented his credentials to the President.
英国驻黎巴嫩的新任大使已将国书递交给总统。

5. creed [kriːd] n. 信条；原则；纲领；信仰
『creed相信→相信的东西→信条；原则；信仰』

A creed is a set of beliefs, principles, or opinions that strongly influence the way people live or work.
What is his political creed? 他的政治信仰是什么？
The centre is open to all, no matter what race or creed.
该中心向所有人开放，不论种族和宗教信仰。

6. credulous [ˈkredjələs] adj. 轻信的；易受骗的
『cred相信，信任+ulous多…的→过分相信→轻信的』

Mary is so credulous that she may readily accept any excuse you make. 玛丽很轻信，你随便找个借口她都可以相信。

▶**incredulous** [ɪnˈkredjələs] adj. 不相信的；不轻信的；怀疑的
『in不+credulous轻信的→不轻信的』

If someone is incredulous, they are unable to believe something because it is very surprising or shocking.
"He made you do it？" Her voice was incredulous.
"他强迫你做的？" 她的语气里带着怀疑。

词根53. cre, crease=create, grow，表示"创造；增长"

1. create [kriˈeɪt] v. 创造；创作；创建
『cre创造+ate使…→产生→创造』

▶**creature** [ˈkriːtʃə(r)] n. 生物；动物；人
『create创造（去e）+ure表结果→（上帝）创造的东西→生物』

❶ （尤指不熟悉或想象中的）生物；动物
They have been visited by creatures from outer space.
有外星人拜访了他们。

❷ （置于形容词后）（具有某种特征的）人
He could not help having compassion for the poor creature.
他情不自禁地怜悯起那个可怜的人来。

2. recreation [ˌrekriˈeɪʃn] n. 消遣；休闲
『re返回+create创造（去e）+(t)ion表名词→创造（可理解为"工作"）后回来（做点别的事情消遣一下）→消遣』

❶ [U] 娱乐；消遣
the fact of people doing things for enjoyment, when they are not working
Saturday afternoon is for recreation and outings.
周六下午是休闲和外出游玩的时间。

❷ [C] (BrE) 消遣活动

a particular activity that sb does when they are not working
His recreations include golf, football and shooting.
他的娱乐活动包括打高尔夫球、踢足球和射击。

词义辨析 <P362第9>
娱乐 entertainment, amusement, recreation, pastime

3. crescent [ˈkresnt] n. 新月形
『cre增长+(e)scent开始出现…的→开始慢慢变大的（月亮）→新月』

❶ [C] 新月形，月牙形
The crescent moon had climbed high in the sky before she sent the others home.
一弯新月已经升到了天空，她才打发其他人回家。

❷[C]（常用于街道名称）　新月形街区
We live in a small house in a crescent.
我们住在一排新月形房屋中的一幢小房子里。

❸ [sing.] 新月（伊斯兰教的象征）
A glittering Islamic crescent tops the mosque.
新月形标志在清真寺顶端闪闪发光。

小贴士 在伊斯兰教中，新月代表一种新生力量，从新月到月圆，标志着伊斯兰教摧枯拉朽、战胜黑暗、功行圆满。

4. concrete [ˈkɒŋkriːt] n. 混泥土 adj. 确实的；有形的
『con一起+crete创造→（把石头、沙子、水泥）放到一起创造→混凝土→（混凝土看得见、摸得着）→确实的；有形的』

❶ [U] 混凝土
The posts have to be set in concrete.
这些柱子必须用混凝土固定。
a concrete floor 混凝土地面

set in concrete（计划或观点）固定的，不变的
As Mr Blunkett emphasised, nothing is yet set in concrete.
正如布伦基特先生所强调的，一切都还没有定下来。

❷ adj. 确实的（而非想象或猜测的）
based on facts, not on ideas or guesses
concrete evidence/proposals/proof
确凿的证据；具体的建议；确实的证明

❸ adj. 有形的，具体的
a concrete object is one that you can see and feel
It is easier to think in concrete terms rather than in the abstract. 结合具体的事物来思考要比抽象思考容易些。

反义词 **abstract** [ˈæbstrækt] adj. 抽象的 <P336>

❹ [VN] 用混凝土浇筑
He merely cleared and concreted the floors.
他只是把地面清理之后浇上了混凝土。

5. secrete [sɪˈkriːt] v. 分泌；藏，藏匿（小物件）
『se分开，离开+crete产生→产生后离开→分泌。也可与"secret [ˈsiːkrət]秘密的"联系记忆，看作是它的动词，分泌总是秘密地进行，藏匿也是秘密地进行』

❶ （身体或植物器官）分泌
The sweat glands secrete water. 汗腺分泌汗液。

❷ 隐藏，藏匿（小物件）
She secreted the gun in the kitchen cabinet.
她把枪藏在橱柜里。

6. decrease [dɪˈkriːs, ˈdiːkriːs] v. & n. 减少，减小，降低
『de向下+crease增长→向下增加→减少』
（v. [dɪˈkriːs]; n. [ˈdiːkriːs]）

❶ 减少；降低
[V] The number of new students decreased from 210 to 160 this year. 今年新生人数从210减少到160。
[V] The price of wheat has decreased by 15%.
小麦价格降低了15%。
[VN] People should decrease the amount of fat they eat.
人们应减少脂肪的摄入量。

❷ [C, U] 减少；降低
There has been a decrease in traffic accidents.
交通事故减少了。
The demand for tea is **on the decrease** each year.
茶叶的需求量逐年递减。

词义辨析 <P365第21> **减少 reduce, decrease**

7. increase [ɪnˈkriːs, ˈɪŋkriːs] v. & n.（使）增长；增多
『in使+crease增长→使增长→增加』
（v. [inˈkriːs]; n. [ˈɪŋkriːs]）

❶ 增长；（使）增长，增多
[V] The population has increased from 1.2 million to 1.8 million. 人口已从120万增加到了180万。
The rate of inflation increased by 2%.
通货膨胀率增长了2%。
[VN] We need to increase productivity.
我们需要提高生产力。

❷ [C, U] ~ (in sth) 增长，增多，增加
Crime is **on the increase**. 犯罪活动在不断增多。
He called for an increase of 1p on income tax.
他呼吁所得税提高1便士。
The clerk was given a promotion and an increase in salary.
那个职员升了职，加了薪。

词根54. crimin=crime; separate，表示"罪；区别"

1. criminal [ˈkrɪmɪnl] n. 罪犯，犯人
『crimin(=crime)犯罪+al表人→犯罪的人→罪犯』

2. incriminate [ɪnˈkrɪmɪneɪt] vt. 使负罪；连累
『in(=en)使+crimin犯罪+ate表动词→使负罪』

If something incriminates you, it suggests that you are responsible for something bad, especially a crime.
He claimed that the drugs had been planted to incriminate him. 他声称毒品是别人为了陷害他而故意种在那里的。
Police had reportedly searched his flat and found incriminating evidence.
据传闻，警方已经搜查了他的公寓并发现了他涉案的证据。

3. recrimination [rɪˌkrɪmɪˈneɪʃn] n. 反责，反诉
『re返回+crimin犯罪+ate表动词（去e）+ion表名词→反过来说别人有罪→反责，反诉』

an angry statement that sb makes accusing sb else of sth, especially in response to a similar statement from them
We spent the rest of the evening in mutual recrimination.

我们后来一晚上都在相互指责。

4. discriminate [dɪˈskrɪmɪneɪt] v. 区别，区分；歧视
『dis(=away)离开+crimin区分+ate表动词→区分开来→区别；歧视』

❶ ~ (between A and B) | ~ A from B 区别；区分
[V] The computer program was unable to discriminate between letters and numbers.
这计算机程序不能辨别字母与数字。
A number of features discriminate this species from others.
有许多特征使这一物种与其他物种区别开来。

❷ [V] ~ (against sb) | ~ (in favour of sb) 区别对待；歧视
It is illegal to discriminate on grounds of race, sex or religion.
因种族、性别或宗教信仰而有所歧视是非法的。
They believe the law discriminates against women.
他们认为该项法律歧视女性。

▶**discrimination** [dɪˌskrɪmɪˈneɪʃn] n. 区别；鉴别力；歧视

▶**discriminatory** [dɪˈskrɪmɪnətəri] adj. （法规、做法）不公平的，歧视的
discriminatory practices/rules/measures
不公正的做法/规定/措施

▶**indiscriminate** [ˌɪndɪˈskrɪmɪnət] adj. 不加区别的
『in不+discriminate区别→不加区别的』

If you describe an action as indiscriminate, you are critical of it because it does not involve any careful thought or choice.
The indiscriminate use of fertilisers is damaging to the environment. 乱用化肥会破坏环境。
The soldiers fired indiscriminately into the crowd.
士兵对着人群胡乱开枪。

词根55. crit, cris = judge，discern，表示"判断；分辨"

1. critic [ˈkrɪtɪk] n. 评论家；批评者
『crit判断+ic人→判断（别人是非）的人→评论家』

❶ [C] 评论家，评论员
a person who expresses opinions about the good and bad qualities of books, music, etc.
His work is highly thought of by the critics.
他的作品深受评论家推崇。

❷ [C] 批评者，反对者
a person who expresses disapproval of sb/sth and talks about their bad qualities, especially publicly
She is one of the ruling party's most outspoken critics.
她是最直言不讳地批评执政党的一个人。

▶**criticize** [ˈkrɪtɪsaɪz] vt. 批评，指责
『critic评论家，批评者+ize表动词→批评，指责』

~ sb/sth (for sth)
The government has been criticized for not taking the problem seriously.
政府因没有认真对待这个问题而受到指责。

▶**criticism** [ˈkrɪtɪsɪzəm] n. 批评；评论
『critic评论家，批评者+ ism表行为→批评；评论』

❶ [U, C] ~ (of sb/sth) | ~ (that…) 批评，责备，指责
There was widespread criticism of the government's handling of the disaster.
政府对灾难的处理方式遭到了普遍的批评。
I didn't mean it as a criticism. 我没有要责备的意思。

❷ [U] （尤指对书、音乐等的）评论文章，评论
She has published more than 20 books including novels, poetry and literary criticism.
她已出版了包括小说、诗歌和文学评论在内的20多部著作。

▶**critical** [ˈkrɪtɪkl] adj. 批评的；关键的；严重的；评判性的

❶ 批评的；评论的
The supervisor is always very critical. 主管总是很挑剔。
Tom's parents were highly critical of the school.
汤姆的父母对学校提出了强烈的批评。
The film met with considerable critical and public acclaim.
该影片受到了影评人和公众的高度评价。

❷ 评判性的，审慎的
A critical approach to something involves examining and judging it carefully.
Students are encouraged to develop critical thinking instead of accepting opinions without questioning them.
要鼓励学生培养判断力，而非不加质疑地接受各种观点。

❸ 关键的，至关紧要的
extremely important because a future situation will be affected by it
Your decision is critical to our future.
你的决定对我们的将来至关重要。
The incident happened at a critical point in the campaign.
该事件发生在竞选活动的关键时期。

❹ （局势）严重的；（病情）危急的
The German authorities are considering an airlift if the situation becomes critical.
如果局势变得危急，德国当局将考虑实施空运。
Ten of the injured are said to be in critical condition.
据说伤者中有10人情况危急。

词义辨析 <P363第12>
重要的，不可缺少的 essential, vital, crucial, critical, indispensable

2. criterion [kraɪˈtɪəriən] n. （评判）标准，准则
『crit判断+er表名词+ion表名词→做出判断的依据 →标准』

[C] （评判或作决定的）标准，准则，原则
The most important criterion for entry is that applicants must design and make their own work.
最重要的参赛标准是申请者必须设计并制作自己的作品。

▶**criteria** [kraɪˈtɪəriə] n. 标准；尺度 （criterion的复数形式）
What criteria are used for assessing a student's ability?
用什么标准来评定一个学生的能力？

3. crisis [ˈkraɪsɪs] n. 危机
『cris判断+is表情况→需要作出判断的时刻→危机时刻』

[C, U] 危机；危急关头
Natural disasters have obviously contributed to the continent's economic crisis.
很显然，自然灾害也是造成该大陆经济危机的原因之一。
a political/financial crisis 政治/金融危机

▶**crises** [ˈkraɪsiz] n. 危机（crisis的复数形式）

4. hypocrite [ˈhɪpəkrɪt] n. 伪君子，虚伪的人
『hypo下，低；次等+crite判断→（经）判断（实际水平）低于（所装出来的）人→伪君子』

a person who pretends to have moral standards or opinions that they do not actually have

The magazine wrongly suggested he was a liar and a hypocrite. 该杂志诬枉地暗示他撒谎，是伪君子。

▶**hypocritical** [ˌhɪpəˈkrɪtɪkl] adj. 虚伪的，伪善的
『hypocrite虚伪的人（去e）+ical构成形容词→虚伪的』

If you accuse someone of being hypocritical, you mean that they pretend to have qualities, beliefs, or feelings that they do not really have.

He would probably hate those hypocritical people.
而他最讨厌的人大概就是那些道貌岸然的人了吧

It would be hypocritical of me to have a church wedding when I don't believe in God.
我不信上帝却到教堂举行婚礼，那就是我的虚伪了。

▶**hypocrisy** [hɪˈpɒkrəsi] n. 伪善，虚伪

I challenged him on the hypocrisy of his political attitudes.
我就他虚伪的政治观点质问他。

词根56. cruc, crus, crux=cross，表示"十字形；交叉"

1. **crusade** [kruːˈseɪd] n. 十字军东征 n. & vi. 运动，斗争
『crus十字形；交叉+ ade表行动的个人或团体→十字军东征』

❶ n.（中世纪的）十字军东征

❷ n. & vi. ~ (for/against sth) | ~ (to do sth)
（长期坚定不移的）斗争，运动
Footballers launched an unprecedented crusade against racism on the terraces.
足球运动员们对阶梯看台上的种族歧视发起了一场空前的运动。

He headed the troops to crusade against the rebellion.
他率领军队讨伐叛乱。

2. **crucial** [ˈkruːʃl] adj. 至关重要的，关键性的
『cruc十字形；交叉+ial…的→在十字路口的→关键的』

~ (to/for sth) | ~ (that…) 至关重要的；关键性的
extremely important, because it will affect other things
Winning this contract is crucial to the success of the company.
赢得这份合同对这家公司的成败至关重要。

The next few weeks are going to be crucial.
接下来的几个星期是关键。

词义辨析 <P363第12>
重要的，不可缺少的　essential, vital, crucial, critical, indispensable

3. **crucify** [ˈkruːsɪfaɪ] vt. 钉在十字架上处死；严惩，折磨
『cruc十字形；交叉+ ify使…→使在十字架上→折磨』

❶ [VN] 把（某人）钉（或绑）在木十字架上处死
the day that Christ was crucified 耶稣受难日

❷ (informal) 严厉批评；严惩；折磨
The prime minister was crucified in the press for his handling of the affair.
首相因处理此事的方式而受到新闻界的严厉抨击。

4. **crux** [krʌks] n.（难题或问题的）关键，最难点，症结
『crux（crus 的变体）→十字路口→关键』

the most important or difficult part of a problem or an issue
He said the crux of the matter was economic policy.
他说问题的症结在于经济政策。

5. **cruciform** [ˈkruːsɪfɔːm] adj.（建筑等）十字形的
『cruc(i)十字形+ form形状→十字形的』

6. **cruise** [kruːz] n. & v. 乘船游览；巡航 v.（车、船或飞机）缓慢行进
『cru十字形+ise→做十字形航行→巡航』

❶ 乘船游览
[V] They cruised down the Nile. 他们乘船沿尼罗河游览。
[VN] We spent two weeks cruising the Bahamas.
我们花了两个星期乘船游览巴哈马群岛。

❷ [V]（汽车、飞机等）以平稳的速度行驶
a light aircraft cruising at 4,000 feet
一架在4000英尺高度巡航的轻型飞机

小贴士 大部分汽车有"定速巡航"这个功能。定速巡航系统（CRUISE CONTROL SYSTEM）　缩写为CCS，按司机要求的速度闭合开关之后，不用踩油门踏板就自动地保持车速，使车辆以固定的速度行驶。

❸ [V]（汽车等或驾驶员）（尤指查看或寻找时）慢速行驶，巡行
She cruised around the block looking for a parking space.
她绕着那个街区慢慢行驶，想找个停车的地方。

▶**cruiser** [ˈkruːzə(r)] n. 巡洋舰

▶**cruise missile** n. 巡航导弹

词根57. cub=lie down，表示"躺"

1. **incubate** [ˈɪŋkjubeɪt] v. 孵化；（病毒）潜伏；培养（细胞、细菌等）
『in里面+cub躺+ate使…→使躺在里面→孵化；孕育』

❶ [VN] 孵（卵）；孵化
The birds returned to their nests and continued to incubate the eggs. 鸟儿回到巢里继续孵卵。

❷ [V]（病毒）潜伏
The virus can incubate for up to ten days after the initial infection. 病毒在初次感染以后可以潜伏长达 10 天。

❸ [VN] 培养（细胞、细菌等）

▶**incubation** [ˌɪŋkjuˈbeɪʃn] n. 孵化；（传染病的）潜伏期；（细菌等的）繁殖

Most estimates of the incubation period for COVID-19 range from 1-14 days.
COVID-19（新冠肺炎）的潜伏期估计大多在1~14天之间。

2. **concubine** [ˈkɒŋkjubaɪn] n.（旧时的）情妇；妾
『con一起+cub躺+ine表女人→躺在一起的女人→情妇』

3. **cubicle** [ˈkjuːbɪkl] n.（大房间分隔出的）小房间，隔间
『cub躺+i+cle小→躺的小地方→小卧室→小房间，隔间。也可以这样记：cube立方（去e）+icle表物→类似立方形的东西→隔间』

a small room that is made by separating off part of a larger room, where you can have a shower or change your clothes
He made his way to the nearest toilet and locked himself in a cubicle.
他走到最近的卫生间，进了一个小隔间后把门反锁上。

词根58. cult=till, raise 表示"耕种；培养"

1. **cultivate** [ˈkʌltɪveɪt] vt. 耕作；培养
『cult耕种；培养+ ive有…性质的（去e）+ ate使…→耕作；培养』

❶ 耕作；种植

If you cultivate land or crops, you prepare land and grow crops on it.

[VN] The people cultivate mainly rice and beans.
这里的人们主要种植稻子和豆类。

[VN] The land around here has never been cultivated.
这一带的土地从未开垦过。

❷ 逐渐形成；培养（某种态度、形象或技能）

If you cultivate an attitude, image, or skill, you try hard to develop it and make it stronger or better.

[VN] He has written eight books and has cultivated the image of an elder statesman.

他已经写了8本书，树立起了其政界元老的形象。

[VN] One should cultivate good manners from childhood.
一个人要从小养成良好的举止。

❸ 结交（朋友）；建立（友谊）

[VN] He purposely tried to cultivate good relations with the press. 他特意设法与新闻界搞好关系。

2. culture [ˈkʌltʃə(r)] n. 文化
『cult耕种；培养+ure表行为→培养耕种的结果→文化』

3. cult [kʌlt] n. 狂热，崇拜；异教团体 adj. 作为偶像崇拜的
『cult耕种；培养→（精神世界的）培养（出来的）→狂热；教派』

❶ [usually sing.] ~ (of sth) 狂热，时尚，崇拜

[usually sing.] someone or something that has become very popular with a particular group of people

An extraordinary **personality cult** had been created around the leader.

在这位领导人的周围兴起了一场异乎寻常的**个人崇拜**。

Ludlam was responsible for making Ridiculous Theatre something of a cult.荒诞派戏剧的风靡要归功于勒德拉姆。

❷ adj. [only before noun] 作为偶像崇拜的

The singer has become a cult figure in America.
那位歌手在美国已成为人们狂热崇拜的偶像。

The cartoon has achieved cult status.
这部动画片达到了风靡一时的地步。

❸ n.（有极端宗教信仰的）异教团体

Their son ran away from home and joined a cult.
他们的儿子离家出走，加入了一个异教团体。

4. agriculture [ˈæɡrɪkʌltʃə(r)] n. 农业；农学；农艺
『agri田地+cult耕种；培养+ure行为有关→农业』

the science or practice of farming

The number of people employed in agriculture has fallen in the last decade. 过去十年，农业从业人数有所下降。

▶ **agricultural** [ˌæɡrɪˈkʌltʃərəl] adj. 农业的

小贴士
中国农业银行 Agricultural Bank of China 简写为 ABC

5. floriculture [ˈflɔːrɪkʌltʃə] n. 花卉栽培<P175>
『flor花+i+cult耕种；培养+ure行为有关→花卉栽培』

6. aquiculture [əkˈwɪkʌltʃər] n. 水产养殖
『aqui水+cult耕种；培养+ure行为有关→水产养殖』

7. mariculture [ˈmærɪkʌltʃə(r)] n. 海水养殖
『mari海洋+cult耕种；培养+ure行为有关→海水养殖』

8. horticulture [ˈhɔːtɪkʌltʃə(r)] n. 园艺
『horti花园+cult耕种；培养+ure行为有关→园艺；园艺学』

词根59. cumul(o)=heap，表示"堆积"

1. accumulate [əˈkjuːmjəleɪt] v. 积累；逐渐增加
『ac表加强+cumul堆积+ate表动词→不断堆积→积累』

to gradually get more and more of sth over a period of time

[VN] I seem to have accumulated a lot of books.
我好像已经收集了很多书。

[VN] By investing wisely she accumulated a fortune.
她投资精明，积累了一笔财富。

[VN] Debts began to accumulate. 债务开始增加。

2. cumulus [ˈkjuːmjələs] n. 积云
『cumul堆积+us表名词，用于科学术语→积云』

a type of thick white cloud

Around midday, the fog lifted and puffy cumulus clouds appeared across the sky.
中午前后雾散了，天空中出现了蓬松的积云。

▶ **cumuli** [ˈkjuːmjʊlaɪ] n. 积云（cumulus的复数形式）

3. cumulative [ˈkjuːmjələtɪv] adj. 积累的；渐增的
『cumul堆积+ative有…倾向（性质）的→积累的；渐增的』

If a series of events have a cumulative effect, each event makes the effect greater.

The benefits from eating fish are cumulative.
吃鱼的好处要长期才能显现。

词根60. cumb= lie down，表示"躺"

1. recumbent [rɪˈkʌmbənt] adj. [before noun] 躺着的
『re返回+cumb躺+ent表形容词→往回躺的→躺着的』

He looked down at the recumbent figure.
他低头看躺着的那个人。

2. incumbent [ɪnˈkʌmbənt] adj. 现任的；必须履行的 n. 现任者
『in里面+cumb躺+ent表形容词或名词→现在住在（官府）的人→现任者→必须履行义务→必须履行的』

Donald Trump is the weakest incumbent president in decades: If Democrats don't screw this up.
唐纳德·特朗普是数十年来最弱的现任总统：如果民主党不搞砸的话。（摘自英文媒体）

In general, incumbents have a 94 per cent chance of being reelected. 通常现任官员有 94% 的概率会再次当选。

It is incumbent upon all of us to make an extra effort.
我们所有人都必须加倍努力。

It's incumbent on you to advise your son before he leaves home. 你有责任在你儿子离家前给他忠告。

3. succumb [səˈkʌm] vi. 屈服，抵挡不住；死亡
『suc下面+cumb躺→（面对诱惑、攻击、疾病等）躺下去→屈从；死亡』

[V] ~ (to sth) 屈服；抵挡不住

to not be able to fight an attack, an illness, a temptation , etc.

The town succumbed after a short siege.
该城被围困不久即告失守。

His career was cut short when he succumbed to cancer.
他的事业随着他死于癌症而中断。

He finally succumbed to Lucy's charms and agreed to her request. 他最终为露西的魅力所倾倒，答应了她的请求。

词根61. cumber=barrier，表示"躺的东西"引申为"障碍物"

1. cumbersome [ˈkʌmbəsəm] adj. （物体）大而笨重的；（体制）缓慢复杂的；（词语）冗长的
『cumber障碍物+some充满…的，有…倾向的→大而笨重的』

Although the machine looks cumbersome, it is actually easy to use. 尽管这台机器看上去很笨重，操作起来却很容易。

They're making efforts to streamline their normally cumbersome bureaucracy.
他们正努力精简本来烦冗复杂的官僚体制。

His article is too cumbersome. 他的文章太冗长了。

2. encumber [ɪnˈkʌmbə(r)] vt. 阻塞；拖累
『en使+cumber障碍物→使成为障碍物→阻塞；拖累』

❶ [VN] 阻塞，塞满
If a place is encumbered with things, it contains so many of them that it is difficult to move freely there.

The police operation was encumbered by crowds of reporters.
警方的行动被成群的记者所妨碍。

❷ [VN] 拖累，妨碍
If you are encumbered by something, it prevents you from moving freely or doing what you want.

Lead weights and air cylinders encumbered the divers as they walked to the shore.
潜水员向海岸走去时，铅坠和氧气罐使他们步履维艰。

词根62. cur=care，表示"关心；照料"

1. curious [ˈkjʊəriəs] adj. 好奇的；不寻常的
『cur关心+i+ous…的→关心（不知道的事情）的→好奇的』

❶ 好奇的
They were very curious about the people who lived upstairs.
他们对住在楼上的人感到很好奇。

I was curious to find out what she had said.
我真想弄清楚她说了些什么。

❷ 不寻常的，难以理解的
It was a curious feeling, as though we were floating on air.
那是一种奇特的感觉，我们仿佛在空中飘浮。

It was curious that she didn't tell anyone.
她没有告诉任何人，这很反常。

▶ **curiosity** [ˌkjʊəriˈɒsəti] n. 好奇心；奇物，珍品
『curious好奇的（去u）+ity表性质、状态→好奇心』

Curiosity killed the cat. 好奇害死猫。

（used to tell sb not to ask questions or try to find out about things that do not concern them）
Children show curiosity about everything.
儿童对一切事物都显露出好奇心。

The museum is full of historical curiosities.
这座博物馆有许多珍奇历史文物。

2. secure [sɪˈkjʊə(r)] adj. 安心的；安全的 v. 获得；使安全
『se (away)分开+cure关心，忧虑→远离忧虑→安心的』

❶ adj. 安心的，不用忧虑的
At last they were able to feel secure about the future.

他们终于觉得不必为将来而担忧了。

She finished the match, secure in the knowledge that she was through to the next round.
她打完比赛，得知自己已进入下一轮，心里踏实了。

a secure job 一份稳定的工作

❷ adj. 安全的；坚固的；稳固的
Information must be stored so that it is secure from accidental deletion.
必须把资料保存起来，这样才不至于无意中删除。

Check that all windows and doors have been made as secure as possible. 看看是不是所有的门窗都关紧了。

It was difficult to maintain a secure foothold on the ice.
在冰上不容易站稳脚。

❸ [VN]（尤指经过努力）获得，取得，实现
The team managed to secure a place in the finals.
球队拼得了决赛的一席之地。

He secured himself a place at law school.
他取得了法学院的学籍。

❹ [VN] 使安全，加强保护
The windows were secured with locks and bars.
窗户已经插上栓，上了锁，都关好了。

❺ [VN] 缚牢，系紧
She secured the rope firmly to the back of the car.
她把绳子牢牢地拴在车后面。

▶ **security** [sɪˈkjʊərəti] n. 安全

❶ [U] 保安；安全
They are now under a great deal of pressure to tighten their airport security.
他们现在承受着加强机场安保措施的巨大压力。

national security 国家安全
the security forces/services 安全部队/机构

小贴士 ☞

the Security Council 安全理事会

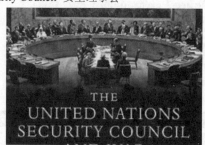

a security guard 一个保安

❷ [U] 安全感
He loves the security of a happy home life.
他喜欢幸福家庭生活所带来的安全感。

3. cure [kjʊə(r)] vt. 治愈 n. 药物；疗法
『cure=care关心；照料→治愈』

❶ ~ sb (of sth) 治愈，治好（病人或动物）

The doctors cured her of cancer. 医生治好了她的癌症。

❷ ~ (for sth) （特效）药；疗法

There is still no cure for a cold. 尚没有治疗感冒的特效药。

Punishment can never be an effective cure for acute social problems. 惩罚绝不是解决严重社会问题的有效办法。

▶ **curable** [ˈkjʊərəbl] adj. 可治愈的

4. accurate [ˈækjərət] adj. 精确的，准确的

『ac一再+cur关心+ate…的→一再关心→精确的；准确的』

Police have stressed that this is the most accurate description of the killer to date.

警方强调这是迄今对凶手最精确的描述。

The pilots, however, were not as accurate as they should be.

然而飞行员并不像他们该达到的水平那样精准。

▶ **accuracy** [ˈækjərəsi] n. 准确（性）；精确（程度）

『accurate准确的，精确的（去te）+cy表性质或状态→准确（性）；精确（程度）』

They questioned the accuracy of the information in the file.

他们怀疑档案中信息的正确性。

She hits the ball with great accuracy. 她击球十分准确。

5. curator [kjʊəˈreɪtə(r)] n. （博物馆或美术馆等的）馆长；负责人

『cur照看+ate表动词（去e）+or表人→负责照看（展品、珍藏品）的人→馆长』

6. procure [prəˈkjʊə(r)] v. 努力获得；设法取得

『pro向前+cure关心→向前关心（目标）→（设法）取得』

to obtain sth, especially with difficulty

[VN] She managed to procure a ticket for the concert.

她好不容易弄到一张音乐会入场券。

[VNN, VN] They procured us a copy of the report.

他们给我们弄到了一份报告。

7. manicure [ˈmænɪkjʊə(r)] n. & v. 修指甲；手部护理

『mani手+cure照料→手部护理』

8. pedicure [ˈpedɪkjʊə(r)] n. & v. 足部护理

『pedi脚+cure照料→足部护理』

I have a manicure and a pedicure every week.

我每周做一次手部护理和足部护理。

词根63. cur, curs, course, cour=run，表示"跑；发生"

① cur=run，表示"发生；流，跑"

1. occur [əˈkɜː(r)] vi. 发生；出现

『oc加强+cur发生→发生；出现』

❶ [V] (formal) 发生；出现（to happen）

When exactly did the incident occur?

这一事件究竟是什么时候发生的？

Something unexpected occurred.

发生了一件出乎意料的事。

❷ [V + adv./prep.] 存在于；出现在

to exist or be found somewhere

Sugar occurs naturally in fruit. 水果天然含糖分。

Misprints occur on every page. 每页都有印刷错误。

❸ occur to sb 想到，出现在头脑中

The idea occurred to him in a dream.

这个主意是他在梦中想到的。

It didn't occur to him that his wife was having an affair.

他没有想到自己的妻子有婚外情。

▶ **occurrence** [əˈkʌrəns] n. 事件；发生，出现

『occur发生；存在（双写r）+ence表行为或性质→发生；存在；发生或存在的事情』

The program counts the number of occurrences of any word, within the text.

这个程序可以统计任何单词在文本中出现的次数。

Complaints seemed to be an everyday occurrence.

似乎每天都有投诉。

词义辨析 <P370第47>

事件 accident, incident, event, occurrence

2. recur [rɪˈkɜː(r)] vi. 再发生；反复出现

『re又+cur发生→又发生→再发生；重现』

This theme recurs several times throughout the book.

这一主题在整部书里出现了好几次。

3. concur [kənˈkɜː(r)] vi. 同时发生；同意

『con一起+cur发生→（两件事；意见）一起发生→同时发生；同意』

❶ ~ (with sb) (in sth) | ~ (with sth) (formal) 同意；赞同

Historians have concurred with each other in this view.

历史学家在这个观点上已取得一致意见。

❷ 同时发生

Everything concurred to produce the desired effect.

所有的事凑合在一起产生了预期效果。

4. current [ˈkʌrənt] adj. 当前的 n. 水流；气流；电流

『cur(=run)流（双写r）+ent表名词或形容词→流动的→水流；电流；气流』

❶ adj. [only before noun] 现时发生的；当前的；现在的

happening now; of the present time

current prices 时价

your current employer 你现在的雇主

The current situation is very different to that in 1990.

当前的形势与1990年截然不同。

❷ adj. 通用的，流行的

Ideas and customs that are current are generally accepted and used by most people.

words that are no longer current 已不再通用的词

❸ [C] （河、湖或海的）水流，潮流；气流；电流

He swam to the shore against a strong current.

他逆着急流游向岸边。

Birds use warm air currents to help their flight.

鸟利用暖气流助飞。

A powerful electric current is passed through a piece of graphite. 给一块石墨通入强电流。

❹ [C] 思潮，潮流，趋向

Ministers are worried by this current of anti-government feeling. 部长们对这股反政府情绪感到担忧。

▶ **currency** [ˈkʌrənsi] n. 货币；通货；通用

❶ [C, U] 通货；货币

Would you like to change your foreign currency into Chinese money? 你想把你的外币换成人民币吗？

❷ [U] 通用，流行，流传

If a custom, idea, or word has currency, it is used and accepted by a lot of people at a particular time.

The term "post-industrial" now has wide currency.

"后工业化" 这个术语现已广为使用。

5. incur [ɪnˈkɜː(r)] vt. 遭受，招致
『in里面+cur跑→（不好的事情）跑进来→遭受，招致』

If you incur something unpleasant, it happens to you because of something you have done.
She had incurred the wrath of her father by marrying without his consent. 她未经父亲同意就结婚，使父亲震怒。

6. curriculum [kəˈrɪkjələm] n. （学校等的）全部课程
『cur(=run)运行（双写r）+i+culum小→（学校）运行的全部的（内容块）→全部课程』
（复数：curricula/curriculums）

Spanish is on/in the curriculum. 西班牙语已纳入课程内容。

▶ **curricular** [kəˈrɪkjələ(r)] adj. 课程的

近义词 **syllabus** [ˈsɪləbəs] n. 教学大纲

7. extracurriculum [ˌekstrəkəˈrɪkjʊləm] n. 业余课程 adj. 课外的
『extra以外+curriculum学校课程→学校课程以外（的课程）→业余课程』

▶ **extracurricular** [ˌekstrəkəˈrɪkjʊlə] adj. 课外的（学校课程以外的）

Each child had participated in extracurricular activities at school. 每个孩子都参加了学校的课外活动。

② curs=run，表示 "跑"

1. cursor [ˈkɜːsə(r)] n. （计算机荧光屏上的）光标
『curs跑+or表示人或者物→（在屏幕上）跑动的东西→光标』

The mouse moves the pointer or cursor on the computer screen. 鼠标移动电脑屏幕上的光标和指针。

2. cursive [ˈkɜːsɪv] adj. 练笔的；草书的 n. 草书体
『curs跑+ ive…的→像跑一样快地（写）→草书』

3. incursion [ɪnˈkɜːʃn] n. 突然入侵；侵入
『in里面+curs跑+ion表名词→（突然）跑到里面→突然入侵』

❶ [C] 突然入侵
a sudden attack on a place by foreign armies，etc.
The west dare not call the Russian incursion an act of aggression. 西方不敢将俄罗斯的入侵称为一种侵略行为。

❷ [C] 涌入，侵入，传入
the sudden appearance of sth in a particular area of activity that is either not expected or not wanted
Traditional crafts remain remarkably unchanged by the slow incursion of modern ways.
传统工艺继续保持原有的特色,没有因现代化手段的缓慢引入而改变。

4. excursion [ɪkˈskɜːʃn] n. 短途旅行；涉足，涉猎
『ex出+curs跑+ion表名词→跑出去（玩）→短途旅行』

❶ （尤指集体）远足，短途旅行
a short journey made for pleasure, especially one that has been organized for a group of people
They've gone on an excursion to York.
他们到约克旅游去了。

❷ ~into sth（formal）（短期的）涉足，涉猎
a short period of trying a new or different activity
After a brief excursion into drama, he concentrated on his

main interest, which was poetry.
他短暂涉猎过戏剧之后便把全部精力投入他的主要兴趣——诗歌中去了。

词义辨析 <P374第65>
旅行 **trip, journey, excursion, expedition, tour, travel, voyage**

5. precursor [priˈkɜːsə(r)] n. 先驱；前身
『pre前+curs跑+or表人→跑在前面的人→先驱』

A precursor of something is a similar thing that happened or existed before it, often something which led to the existence or development of that thing.
He said that the deal should not be seen as a precursor to a merger. 他说该笔交易不应该被看作是合并的前兆。
In this way, it's sort of a precursor to Apple's new GarageBand application.
这样，它成为苹果公司的新GarageBand应用程序的前身。

③ course，cour=run，表示 "跑"

1. course [kɔːs] n. 课程；一道菜；航线
『course跑→跑的（路线）→航线；过程』

❶ [C] ~ (in/on sth) （有关某学科的系列）课程，讲座
a series of lessons or lectures on a particular subject
to take/do a course in art and design
攻读美术与设计课程

❷ [U, C, usually sing.] （船或飞机的）航向，航线
The plane was on/off course (= going/not going in the right direction). 飞机航向正确/偏离。
He radioed the pilot to change course.
他用无线电通知飞行员改变航向。

❸ [C, usually sing.] 方针；行动方向
The president appears likely to change course on some key issues. 总统看起来可能要在某些重要问题上改变方针。

❹ [C] 一道菜
The main course was roast duck.主菜是烤鸭。

❺ **in course of sth** (formal) 在…的过程中
The new textbook is in course of preparation.
新的教科书正在准备之中。

in/over the course of… 在…期间；在…的时候
He's seen many changes in the course of his long life.
他在漫长的一生中目睹了许许多多的变化。

2. intercourse [ˈɪntəkɔːs] n. （人、国家等之间的）往来，交往
『inter在…之间+course跑→在二者之间跑→交流』

There was social intercourse between the old and the young.
老年人与年轻人之间有社会交往。

3. recourse [rɪˈkɔːs] n. 依赖，求助
『re回+course跑→跑回来（求助）→求助』

[U] (formal) 依靠；依赖；求助
the fact of having to, or being able to, use sth that can provide help in a difficult situation
Your only recourse is legal action.
你的唯一依靠就是诉诸法律。
She made a complete recovery without recourse to surgery.
她未做手术就完全恢复了健康。

4. discourse [ˈdɪskɔːs，dɪsˈkɔːs] n. 论文；演讲 vi. 高谈阔论

『dis不+course跑→不（往下）跑→不走过程→详细论述』
（n.[ˈdɪskɔːs]; vi. [dɪsˈkɔːs]）

❶ [C, U] (formal) 论文；演讲

a long and serious treatment or discussion of a subject in speech or writing

Gates responds with a lengthy discourse on deployment strategy. 盖茨以一篇有关部署策略的鸿篇大论予以回应。

❷ [V] discourse on/upon sth 高谈阔论

He discoursed for several hours on French and English prose.
他花了几个小时讲述法国和英国的散文。

5. **courier** [ˈkʊriə(r)] n.（递送包裹或重要文件的）信使 v. 快递

『cour跑+i+ er表人或物→跑着（送东西）的人→信使』

❶ [C]（递送包裹或文件的）信使，通讯员，快递公司

a person or company whose job is to take packages or important papers somewhere

We sent the documents by courier.
我们派了信使交送这些文件。

He worked as a motorcycle courier.
他的工作是骑摩托车送快递。

❷ [VN] 让快递员送；快递

I couriered it to Darren in New York.
我把它快递给纽约的达伦。

1. **custom** [ˈkʌstəm] n. 风俗；习惯

❶ [C, U] ~ (of doing sth) 风俗；习俗

an old/ancient custom 旧的/古老的习俗

It is the custom in that country for women to marry young.
女子早婚是那个国家的风俗。

❷ [sing.] (formal or literary)（个人的）习惯，习性

It was her custom to rise early. 早起是她的习惯。

As was his custom, he knocked three times.
他敲了三下，这是他的习惯。

2. **customer** [ˈkʌstəmə(r)] n. 顾客

『custom习惯+er表人→习惯（进商店的）人→顾客』

3. **customs** [ˈkʌstəmz] n. 海关；关税

『custom习惯+s（表复数）→关税（征关税是一种惯例）』

❶ [pl.] usually Customs （作主语时，北美英语使用单数动词，英国英语使用复数动词）

The Customs have seized large quantities of smuggled heroin.
海关查获了大量走私的海洛因。

❷（港口或机场的）海关

He walked through customs. 他步行通过海关。

❸ 关税；进口税

to pay customs on sth 为某物缴纳关税

4. **accustom** [əˈkʌstəm] v. 使习惯(于)；使适应

『ac相当于to+custom习惯→达到成为习惯→使习惯于』

❶ accustom yourself/sb to sth 使习惯于

It took a while for me to accustom myself to all the new rules and regulations here.
过了一段时间，我才习惯于这里的规章制度。

Shakespeare has accustomed us to a mixture of humor and tragedy in the same play.
莎士比亚让我们习惯于同一场戏目中的悲喜交错。

❷ be accustomed to (doing) sth. 习惯于

We were accustomed to working together.
我们习惯于一起工作。

He quickly became used to the dark. 他很快适应了黑暗。

小贴士 be accustomed to 后面一般跟动名词，也有跟动词原形的。be used to 和 be customed to 意思相同，口语中常用 be used to，但 be used to 后面跟动词作宾语时只能用其动名词形式。

1. **democrat** [ˈdeməkræt] n. 民主主义者；民主党党员 <P139>

『demo人民+crat统治者；权力→（想让）人们做统治者（的人）→民主主义者』

2. **endemic** [enˈdemɪk] adj.（疾病或问题在某地或某集体中）流行的，常见的

『en(=in)在…当中+dem人们+ ic…的→在（某类、某地）人们中间的→地方性的』

regularly found in a particular place or among a particular group of people and difficult to get rid of

Malaria is endemic in many hot countries.
疟疾是许多气候炎热国家的流行病。

Corruption is endemic in the system.
腐败在这种制度下普遍存在。

Polio was then endemic among children my age.
那时小儿麻痹症在我这个年纪的孩子中很常见。

3. **pandemic** [pænˈdemɪk] n.（全国或全球性）流行病

『pan全部+dem人们+ic…的→在广泛的（所有的）人群中的病→流行病』

A pandemic is an occurrence of a disease that affects many people over a very wide area.

They feared a new cholera pandemic.
他们担心新一轮的霍乱大流行。

The coronavirus spreading is now likely to become a pandemic that circles the globe.

冠状病毒的传播（导致其）现在可能成为一种全球性的流行病。

4. **epidemic** [ˌepɪˈdemɪk] n. 流行病

『epi(=upon)之上+dem人们+ic…的→在超过（某类、某地）人们之外的病→流行病』

❶（疾病的）流行，传播

A flu epidemic is sweeping through Moscow.
一场流感正席卷莫斯科。

The prospect is daunting. A pandemic—an ongoing epidemic on two or more continents—may well have global consequences.

前景令人望而生畏。大流行——在两个或多个大洲持续的流行病——很可能会造成全球性后果。

❷（坏事的）盛行，泛滥，猖獗

an epidemic of crime in the inner cities
市中心犯罪的流行

词义辨析 <P380第93>

流行病，传染病 endemic，epidemic, pandemic

1. **dentist** [ˈdentɪst] n. 牙科医生

『dent牙齿+ist（从事某职业、研究的）人→牙科医生』

2. denture [ˈdentʃə(r)] n.（一副）假牙
『dent牙齿+ure表物→假牙』

3. dent [dent] n. 凹痕，凹坑 vt. 使凹陷；损害
『dent牙齿→牙齿（在硬的表面）咬→凹痕，凹坑』

❶ [VN] 使凹陷
to make a hollow place in a hard surface, usually by hitting it
The back of the car was badly dented in the collision.
汽车尾部被撞后严重凹陷。

❷ [VN] 损害，伤害，挫伤（信心、名誉等）
to damage sb's confidence, reputation, etc.
It seemed that nothing could dent his confidence.
似乎任何事情都不会使他的信心受挫。

❸ [C] 凹痕，凹坑
a large dent in the car door 车门上的一大块凹陷
The commission had barely begun to make a dent in the problem. 委员会几乎还没有在这个问题上取得任何进展。

词根67. derm, dermat=skin，表示"皮肤"

1. dermal [ˈdɜːməl] adj. 皮肤的；真皮的
『derm皮肤+al…的→皮肤的』

2. epidermis [ˌepɪˈdɜːmɪs] n. 表皮
『epi在…上+derm皮肤+is性质，情况→表皮，外皮』

3. hypodermic [ˌhaɪpəˈdɜːmɪk] n. 皮下注射器 adj. 皮下注射的
『hypo下+derm皮肤+ic…的→皮下的→皮下注射的』

He held up a hypodermic to check the dosage.
他举起一个注射器查看剂量。
There is a risk of transmission of the virus between hypodermic users.
接受皮下注射者有相互传染病毒的可能。

词根68. dict, dic=say, assert，表示"说；断言"

1. predict [prɪˈdɪkt] vt. 预言
『pre (before)之前+dict说；断言→在（发生）之前说→预言』

Nobody could predict the outcome.
谁也无法预料结果如何。

▶ **prediction** [prɪˈdɪkʃn] n. 预言
Not many people agree with the government's prediction that the economy will improve.
没有多少人赞同政府认为经济将会有所改善的预测。

▶ **predictable** [prɪˈdɪktəbl] adj. 可预见的
The ending of the book was entirely predictable.
那本书的结局完全是可以预见的。

2. contradict [ˌkɒntrəˈdɪkt] v. 反驳；相矛盾
『contra相反+dict说；断言→说相反的话→相矛盾；反驳』

❶ [VN] 反驳，驳斥，批驳
All evening her husband contradicted everything she said.
整个晚上她说什么丈夫都反驳。
She dared not contradict him. 她不敢反驳他。

❷ [VN] 相矛盾
The two stories contradict each other.
这两种说法相互抵触。
Her version contradicted the Government's claim that they were shot after being challenged.
政府声称他们是在受到挑战后被开枪射杀，而她的说法

却与此相矛盾。

▶ **contradiction** [ˌkɒntrəˈdɪkʃn] n. 矛盾；反驳
▶ **contradictory** [ˌkɒntrəˈdɪktəri] adj. 矛盾的；反驳的
『contradict矛盾；反驳+ory有…性质的→矛盾的；反驳的』

We are faced with two apparently contradictory statements.
我们面前这两种说法显然是矛盾的。

3. addict [ˈædɪkt] n. 有瘾的人
『ad相当于to+dict说；断言→到达（不停地）说→上瘾』

❶ [C] 吸毒成瘾者
He's only 24 years old and a drug addict.
他只有 24 岁，却是个瘾君子。

❷ [C] 对…入迷的人
My nephew is a complete video game addict.
我侄子是个十足的电子游戏迷。

▶ **addicted** [əˈdɪktɪd] adj. 上瘾的；沉迷的
『动词 addict 的形容词形式』

be addicted to (doing) sth 沉溺于
I know a lot of people who are addicted to smoking.
我知道很多人吸烟上了瘾。
Many children are addicted to playing video games.
许多孩子迷上了玩电子游戏。

▶ **addictive** [əˈdɪktɪv] adj. 使成瘾的；易令人沉溺的
I find jogging very addictive.
我觉得慢跑锻炼很使人着迷。

4. dictate [dɪkˈteɪt , ˈdɪkteɪt] vt. 口述；发号施令；决定
『dict说；断言+ate表动词→说出来（让别人写或做）→口述；发号施令』

❶ ~ (sth) (to sb) 口述（让别人写）
to say words for sb else to write down
[VN] He dictated a letter to his secretary.
他向秘书口授信稿。

❷ ~ (sth) (to sb)（以令人不快的方式）指使，发号施令
to tell sb what to do, especially in an annoying way
[VN] They are in no position to dictate terms (= tell other people what to do). 他们没有资格发号施令。
[V wh-] What right do they have to dictate how we live our lives? 他们有什么权利强行规定我们该怎样生活？
She refused to be dictated to by anyone.
她不愿受任何人摆布。

❸ 决定，支配，影响
If one thing dictates another, the first thing causes or influences the second thing.
[VN] The film's budget dictated a tough schedule.
影片的预算决定了拍摄进度会很紧张。

▶ **dictator** [dɪkˈteɪtə(r)] n. 独裁者；发号施令者
『dictate发号施令（去e）+or表人→发号施令（让人做）的人→独裁者』

Their citizens are very thankful they are not governed by a dictator. 他们的公民十分庆幸没有受独裁者的统治。

▶ **dictatorship** [ˌdɪkˈteɪtəʃɪp] n. 独裁；独裁国家

5. indict [ɪnˈdaɪt] vt. 控告；起诉
『in里面+dict；断言→（在起诉书）里面说（有罪）→起诉』

[VN] [usually passive] ~ sb (for sth) | ~ sb (on charges/on a

charge of sth) (especially NAmE, law) 控告；起诉
to officially charge sb with a crime
The senator was indicted for murder.
那位参议员被控犯谋杀罪。
She was indicted on charges of corruption.
她被控贪腐，受到起诉。

6. edict [ˈiːdɪkt] n. 法令；命令；敕令
『e出+dict说→断言→说出（要求）→法令』

[U, C] (formal) 法令；命令；敕令
an official order or statement given by sb in authority
He issued an edict that none of his writings be destroyed.
他下令不得毁坏他的任何作品。
The emperor issued an edict forbidding doing trade with foreigners. 皇帝颁布了一项不得和外国人做生意的敕令。

7. diction [ˈdɪkʃn] n. 吐字；措辞
『dict说+ion表名词→说的方式或内容→吐字；措辞』

❶ [U] 吐字；发音方式
the way that sb pronounces words
His diction wasn't very good. 他的发音不是很清楚。
Clear diction is important. 吐字清晰非常重要。

❷ [U] (technical) 措辞；用语；用词
the choice and use of words in literature
His diction is rich and classical, and his imagery is striking and appropriate.
他的措辞丰富而古典，他的形象鲜明而得体。

8. dictionary [ˈdɪkʃənri] n. 词典，字典
『diction措辞+ary表物或场所→含有措辞的物→字典』

9. benediction [ˌbenɪˈdɪkʃn] n.（基督教的）祝福，祝祷
『bene善，好+diction措辞→好的措辞→祝福』

[C, U] (formal) （基督教的）祝福，祝祷
a Christian prayer of blessing
The minister pronounced the benediction.
牧师做了赐福祈祷。
She could only raise her hand in a gesture of benediction.
她只得举起手来做了一个祝福的手势。

10. malediction [mælə'dɪkʃən] n. 诅咒；咒骂
『male坏，恶+diction措辞→说坏话→诅咒』

a wish that something bad will happen to someone
Shakespeare's remains were guarded by a malediction.
莎士比亚的遗骨被咒语保护着。

11. jurisdiction [ˌdʒʊərɪsˈdɪkʃn] n. 司法权；管辖权；管辖区域『juris 发誓；法律+dict说，命令+ion表名词→（在）法律上有发言权→司法权；管辖权』

❶ [U] ~ (over sb/sth) | ~ (of sb/sth) (to do sth)
司法权；审判权；管辖权
The British police have no jurisdiction over foreign bank accounts. 外国银行账户不在英国警方的管辖权限之内。

❷ [C] 管辖区域；管辖范围
It hardly falls within the area under the police station's jurisdiction. 它几乎不在该派出所的辖区之内。

12. indicate [ˈɪndɪkeɪt] v. 表明；显示；象征；暗示
『in里面+ dic说：断言+ate表动词→（某个迹象）里面说出了（某个内容）→指示，表明』

❶ 表明；暗示

[VN] Record profits in the retail market indicate a boom in the economy.
零售市场上有史以来的最高利润显示出经济的突飞猛进。
[V that] Early results indicate that the government will be returned to power. 早期的结果预示这个政府将重新执政。
[VN] He indicated his willingness to cooperate.
他暗示愿意合作。

❷ 指示，指明
[VN] She took out a map and indicated the quickest route to us. 她拿出一张地图，给我们指出最快捷的路线。
[VN] He indicated left and then turned right. （NAmE signal）
他打出的是左转信号，然后却向右转了。

▶ **indicator** [ˈɪndɪkeɪtə(r)] n. 指示信号；指示器

▶ **indication** [ˌɪndɪ'keɪʃn] n. 表明；迹象；暗示
There is no indication that COVID-19 can be spread through food.
没有迹象表明COVID-19（新冠肺炎）可以通过食物传播。
There are clear indications that the economy is improving.
有明显的迹象显示经济已开始好转。

小贴士 用 sign 还是 indication？
indication 常常通过某人的说话表明，而 sign 通常为发生的事或某人所做的事。
Headaches may be a sign of stress. 头痛可能是紧张的迹象。
They gave no indication as to how the work should be done.
他们根本没说明这项工作该怎样做。

▶ **indicative** [ɪnˈdɪkətɪv] adj. 指示的；暗示的 n. 陈述语气
The result was indicative of a strong retail market.
结果表明零售业市场繁荣。

13. vindicate [ˈvɪndɪkeɪt] vt. 证明…正确；证明…无辜
『v胜利+indicate表明→表明胜利了→证明（某人某事）是正确的』

If a person or their decisions, actions, or ideas are vindicated, they are proved to be correct, after people have said that they were wrong.
New evidence emerged, vindicating him completely.
新证据出现了，证明他完全是无辜的。
The director said he had been vindicated by the experts' report. 主任说专家们的报告证明了他是正确的。
Ministers and officials are confident their decision will be vindicated.
部长们和官员们相信他们的决定会被证明是正确的。

14. predicate [ˈpredɪkət, ˈpredɪkeɪt] n. 谓语 vt. 阐明
『pre预先+dic说：断言+ate表动词→预先断言→阐明；断言』
（n. [ˈpredɪkət]; v. [ˈpredɪkeɪt]）

❶ 表明；阐明；断言
to state that sth is true
[V that] The article predicates that the market collapse was caused by weakness of the dollar.
这篇文章断言，市场的崩溃是美元疲软造成的。

❷ [VN] [usually passive] ~ sth on/upon sth
使基于；使以…为依据
if an action or event is predicated on a belief or situation, it is based on it or depends on it （A is predicated on B→由于B现象，A被断言→A以B为基础）

Democracy is predicated upon the rule of law.
民主是以法制为基础的。

❸ [C] 谓语

15. abdicate [ˈæbdɪkeɪt] v. 退位；放弃（职责）

『ab离开+dic说；断言+ate表动词→离开能断言的位置→退位；放弃（职责）』

❶ 退位；逊位

to give up the position of being king or queen
Yuan Shikai forced the emperor to abdicate and hand over power to him. 袁世凯逼迫皇帝逊位，把政权交给他。

❷ [VN] ~ responsibility 失（职）；放弃（职责）

to fail or refuse to perform a duty
The government cannot abdicate responsibility for national security. 政府不能放弃维护国家安全的责任。

16. dedicate [ˈdedɪkeɪt] vt. 奉献；题献词

『de向下+dic断言+ate表动词→（虽然艰难）断言还要向下（干）→努力献身』

❶ ~ yourself/sth to sth/to doing sth 把…奉献给（同义词devote）

She dedicates herself to her work. 她献身于自己的工作。
He dedicated his life to helping the poor.
他毕生致力于帮助穷人。

❷ ~ sth to sb （在书、音乐或作品的前部）题献词

This book is dedicated to my parents.
谨以此书献给我的父母。

❸ ~ sth (to sb/sth) 为（建筑、教堂等）举行落成典礼

A memorial stone was dedicated to those who were killed in the war. 为阵亡将士纪念碑举行了落成典礼。
The church is dedicated to St Mary of Bec.
该教堂供奉的是贝克的圣玛丽。

▶**dedication** [ˌdedɪˈkeɪʃn] n. 奉献；献词

His dedication to teaching gained the respect of his students.
他对教学的奉献得到了学生们尊敬。

▶**dedicated** [ˈdedɪkeɪtɪd] adj. 献身的；专用的

A few dedicated doctors have fought for years to enlighten the profession.
一些有献身精神的医生多年来一直努力指导业内同人。
He's quite dedicated to his students.
他对他的学生很投入。

17. interdict [ˌɪntəˈdɪkt] vt. 封锁，阻断 n. 禁令

『inter在…之间+dict说→在中途（拦住）说（不允许）→封锁，阻断』

❶ [VN] 封锁，阻断

If an armed force interdicts something or someone, they stop them and prevent them from moving. If they interdict a route, they block it or cut it off.
Troops could be ferried in to interdict drug shipments.
可以把军队渡运过来阻截毒品的装运。

❷ n.（官方的）禁令，强制令

An interdict is an official order that something must not be done or used.
The government has placed an interdict on fishing within territorial waters. 政府已禁止在领海内捕鱼。

18. verdict [ˈvɜːdɪkt] n.（陪审团或法官的）裁决，裁定；（经过思考或调查后的）意见，结论〈P348〉

『ver真实+ dict说；断言→说的真实的情况→裁决，裁定』

1. dignity [ˈdɪɡnəti] n. 尊严；尊贵

『dign配得上的；高贵的+ity表名词→（得到）配得上的（对待）；高贵→尊严；尊贵』

The terminally ill should be allowed to die with dignity.
应该允许垂危病人死得有尊严。
her extraordinary dignity and composure
她那种端庄沉着的非凡气质

▶**indignity** [ɪnˈdɪɡnəti] n. 侮辱；轻蔑

『in不+dignity尊严→使显得没有尊严→侮辱；轻蔑』

Later, he suffered the indignity of having to flee angry protesters.
后来，他不得不极不光彩地避开愤怒的抗议者溜走了。
Prisoners are spared the indignity of wearing uniforms.
囚犯们不必忍受身穿囚服的侮辱。

2. indignation [ˌɪndɪɡˈneɪʃn] n. 愤慨；义愤

『in不+dign配得上的；高贵的+ation表行为→受到了不公正对待→愤慨；义愤』

a feeling of anger and surprise caused by sth that you think is unfair or unreasonable
The rise in train fares has aroused public indignation.
火车票提价激起了公愤。
Joe quivered with indignation that Paul should speak to him like that. 乔认为保罗竟然那样对他说话，气得直发抖。

▶**indignant** [ɪnˈdɪɡnənt] adj. 愤慨的；义愤的

『in不+dign配得上的；高贵的+ant表形容词→受到了不般配（不公正）的对待→愤慨的；义愤的』

She was very indignant at the way she had been treated.
她对于自己受到的待遇大为光火。
They were indignant that they hadn't been invited.
他们因没有受到邀请而愤愤不平。

3. dignify [ˈdɪɡnɪfaɪ] vt. 使有尊严，使显贵；使显得堂皇

『dign配得上的；高贵的+ify使…→使有尊严』

The mayor was there to dignify the celebrations.
市长的光临为庆祝活动增了辉。
I'm not going to dignify his comments by reacting to them.
我才不会理睬他的评论以抬高其身价呢。

4. dignitary [ˈdɪɡnɪtəri] n.（政府或教会的）高官，显要

『dign高贵的+itary人→显贵，要人』

Each village has one or two important houses where the rich and powerful local dignitaries would have lived.
每个村庄都有一两栋重要的房子，有钱有势的当地政要都会住在那里。

1. docile [ˈdəʊsaɪl] adj. 温顺的；易控制的

『doc教+ile易…的→容易教的→温顺的』

A person or animal that is docile is quiet, not aggressive, and easily controlled.
They wanted a low-cost, docile workforce.
他们想要廉价的、听话的劳动力。
Circus monkeys are trained to be very docile and obedient.
马戏团的猴子被训练得服服帖帖的。

2. dogma [ˈdɒɡmə] n. 教条，信条，教义

『dog教；观点+ma→（自认为正确并要求别人也遵守的）观点→教条』

[U, C] a belief or set of beliefs held by a group or organization, which others are expected to accept without argument

He stands for freeing the country from the grip of dogma.
他主张将国家从教条的控制下解放出来。

3. doctrine [ˈdɒktrɪn] n. 教义；主义；学说
『doctr(=doct)教；观点+ine表抽象名词→（宗教、政治或其他的）观点→教义；主义；学说』

a belief or set of beliefs held and taught by a Church, a political party, etc.

The doctrine of surplus value is the cornerstone of Marx's economic theory. 剩余价值学说是马克思经济理论的基石。
They cling to the doctrine that high wages cause unemployment.
他们坚持认为高工资会导致失业（这一）信条。

▶ **doctrinaire** [ˌdɒktrɪˈneə(r)] adj. 空谈理论的，脱离实际的；教条主义的
『doctrin(e)教义；学说+aire…的→（盲目相信）某种学说或主义的→脱离实际的；教条主义的』

He is firm but not doctrinaire. 他很坚定但并不教条。
a doctrinaire communist 一位教条主义的共产主义者

词根71. dom(e)=house, 表示"房屋"

1. dome [dəʊm] n. 圆屋顶；半球形物，圆顶状物
『dome房屋→圆屋顶』

the dome of St Paul's Cathedral 圣保罗大教堂的穹顶

A band of gray hair encircled his bald dome.
他的秃头顶四周长着一圈灰白的头发。
the dome of the hill 山丘的圆顶

2. domestic [dəˈmestɪk] adj. 家的；家养的；国内的
『dom房屋+estic…的→房屋的→家的』

domestic appliances 家用电器
domestic chores 家务琐事
domestic service 家政服务
domestic cat 家猫
domestic affairs/politics 国内事务/政治

3. domicile [ˈdɒmɪsaɪl] n. （尤指正式或法律意义的）住处，住所
『dom房屋+ic…的+ile物体→住所』

name and domicile of the insurer 保险人名称和住所

词根72. domin=lord, 表示"主人"，引申为"控制"

1. dominate [ˈdɒmɪneɪt] v. 控制；在…中占首要地位
『domin控制+ate表动词→紧紧控制→统治』

❶ 支配；控制；左右；影响
to control or have a lot of influence over sb/sth, especially in an unpleasant way
[VN] As a child he was dominated by his father.
他小时候由父亲主宰一切。
He tended to dominate the conversation.
他往往左右着交谈的内容。
[V] She always says a lot in meetings, but she doesn't dominate.
她在会上总是滔滔不绝，但是她的话没有什么影响力。

❷ [VN] 在…中占首要地位
The train crash dominated the news.
火车相撞事故成了最重要的新闻。

❸ [VN] 在…中拥有最重要的位置；俯视；高耸于
The cathedral dominates the city. 大教堂俯视全城。

▶ **dominant** [ˈdɒmɪnənt] adj. 占支配地位的，显著的；（基因）显性的

The firm has achieved a dominant position in the world market. 这家公司在国际市场上占有举足轻重的地位。
The dominant feature of the room was the large fireplace.
这间屋子要数那个大壁炉最显眼了。

▶ **predominant** [prɪˈdɒmɪnənt] adj. 占主导地位的；占支配地位的

If something is predominant, it is more important or noticeable than anything else in a set of people or things.
Yellow is the predominant colour this spring in the fashion world. 黄色是今春时装界的流行颜色。

▶ **dominance** [ˈdɒmɪnəns] n. 支配；控制

Legislation is the only route to ending the car's dominance as a form of transport.
立法是终止汽车作为主导交通工具的唯一途径。

▶ **domination** [ˌdɒmɪˈneɪʃən] n. 控制；统治

2. domineering [ˌdɒmɪˈnɪərɪŋ] adj. 专横的，盛气凌人的
『domin控制+eer人+ing表形容词→具有控制人的性质的→专横的』

trying to control other people without considering their opinions or feelings
Emmanuel Macron had reportedly studied Donald Trump's style of domineering power-grabbing handshakes, apparently prepared to avoid being outdone by his counterpart.
据报道，埃曼纽尔·马克龙曾研究过唐纳德·特朗普霸气作风十足的握手风格，显然是为了避免被对手击败。

3. dominion [dəˈmɪniən] n. 控制，统治；领土，领地
『domin控制+ion表名词→控制；领土』

They truly believe they have dominion over us.
他们真的以为他们对我们有统治权。
The Republic is a dominion of the Brazilian people.
这个共和国是巴西人民的领土。

4. domain [dəˈmeɪn] n. 领土；领域；（计算机）域
『dom(=domin)控制+ain表物→控制的地方→领土；领域』

❶ [C] （尤指旧时个人、国家等所拥有或统治的）领土，领地，势力范围
The Spice Islands were within the Spanish domains.
香料群岛曾是西班牙的领地。

❷ [C] （尤指某人有控制力、责任或权利的）领域，范围
The care of older people is being placed firmly within the domain of the family.
照顾老人仍然被确认为是家庭范围的事。
Physics used to be very much a male domain.
物理学曾在很大程度上是男人的领域。
The state of their marriage has been put into the public domain. 他们的婚姻状况已公开。

❸ [C] （计算机）域
Is the domain name already registered or still available?
该域名已经被注册还是仍然可用？

词根73. don(e), dit, dow=give，表示"给予"

1. donate [dəʊˈneɪt] vt. 捐赠；献（血）；捐（器官）
『don给予+ate表动词→捐赠』

2. **condone** [kənˈdəʊn] vt. 容忍，纵容（不道德行为）
『con加强+done给予→给予（大度）→容忍』

[VN] Terrorism can never be condoned.
决不能容忍恐怖主义。

3. **endow** [ɪnˈdaʊ] vt. （向学校等机构）捐钱；使天生拥有；赋予，给予（品质等）
『en使+dow给予→使具有→捐赠；赋予』

❶ [VN] （向学校等机构）捐钱，捐赠
If someone endows an institution, scholarship, or project, they provide a large amount of money which will produce the income needed to pay for it.
Donna's parents plan to endow a scholarship fund in memory of their daughter.
唐娜的父母计划捐赠一笔奖学金以纪念他们的女儿。

❷ [VN] 赋予；使天生拥有
You say that someone is endowed with a particular desirable ability, characteristic, or possession when they have it by chance or by birth.
You are endowed with wealth, good health and a lively intellect. 你生来就拥有财富、健康和活跃的思维。

❸ [VN] 赋予，给予（品质等）
Herbs have been used for centuries to endow a whole range of foods with subtle flavours.
数个世纪以来，香草一直被用于给各种食物增添淡淡的香味。

4. **extradite** [ˈekstrədaɪt] vt. 引渡（嫌犯或罪犯）
『extra额外，向外+dite给予→（把罪犯）向外给予→引渡』

The British government attempted to extradite the suspects from Belgium. 英国政府试图从比利时引渡犯罪嫌疑人。

词根74. dox=opinion，表示"观点"

1. **orthodox** [ˈɔːθədɒks] adj. 正统的；正统教义的；东正教的
『ortho直，正+dox观点→正统观点的→正统的』

❶ 正统的，规范的，广为接受的
generally accepted or approved of；following generally accepted beliefs
orthodox medicine 传统医学
Most orthodox doctors however dismiss this as complete nonsense.
但大多数传统的医生认为此说法完全是胡说八道。

❷ 正统信仰的，正宗教义的
following closely the traditional beliefs and practices of a religion
an orthodox Jew 正统的犹太人

❸ Orthodox 东正教派的

▶ **orthodoxy** [ˈɔːθədɒksi] n. 正统观念；正统信仰
What was once a novel approach had become orthodoxy.
一度很新奇的做法如今已被广为接受。
As pope he won wide support for his strict orthodoxy.
作为教皇他严守正统教义，赢得了广泛的支持。

2. **heterodox** [ˈhetərədɒks] adj. 异端的，非正统的
『hetero其他的；不同+dox观点→异类观点的→异端邪说的』

Heterodox beliefs, opinions, or ideas are different from the accepted or official ones.
They left the country to avoid persecution for their heterodox views.
他们离开了这个国家以避免因非正统观点而引致的迫害。
But what exactly is heterodox economics?
但究竟什么是非正统经济学呢？

▶ **heterodoxy** [ˈhetərədɒksi] n. 异端；非正统
Despite his heterodoxy, faults, and weaknesses, Clare was a man with a conscience.
尽管克莱尔相信异端邪说，身上有种种缺点和弱点，他仍然是一个具有是非感的人。

3. **paradox** [ˈpærədɒks] n. 矛盾的人或事物；悖论
『para(=against)相对立+dox观点→相对立的观点→自相矛盾』

❶ [C] 矛盾的人（或事物、情况）
a person, thing or situation that has two opposite features and therefore seems strange
He was a paradox—a loner who loved to chat to strangers.
他真是个矛盾人物——生性孤僻却又喜欢和陌生人闲聊。
It is a curious paradox that professional comedians often have unhappy personal lives.
这真是个奇怪的矛盾现象，职业喜剧演员的私人生活往往并不快乐。

❷ [C, U] 悖论，似矛盾而（可能）正确的说法
"More haste, less speed" is a well-known paradox.
"欲速则不达"是人们熟知的隽语。

词根75. draw=pull，表示"拉"

1. **drawback** [ˈdrɔːbæk] n. 缺点，不利条件
『draw拉+back后面→向后拉→不利条件』

A drawback is an aspect of something or someone that makes them less acceptable than they would otherwise be.
He felt the apartment's only drawback was that it was too small. 他觉得这个公寓唯一的缺点就是太小了。
The main drawback of this cellphone is that its battery easily loses its charge.
这个手机的主要毛病在于它的电池不耐用。

2. **drawer** [drɔː(r)] n. 抽屉
『draw拉+er表物→（可以用手）拉出的东西→抽屉』
（注意：er没有发音）

3. **withdraw** [wɪðˈdrɔː] vt. 撤回；取（款）；退出〈P45〉
『with (back) 向后+draw拉→向后拉→撤回』

词根76. du(o), dub, dou(b)=two，表示"二，双"

1. **dubious** [ˈdjuːbiəs] adj. 可疑的，靠不住的；无把握的；不好的
『dub二+ious充满…的→两种（想法）的→不肯定的；也可以看作是doubt的形容词形式，去o和t加ious』

This claim seems to us to be rather dubious.
在我们看来这种说法靠不住。
My parents were dubious about it at first but we soon convinced them.
我父母起初对此心存疑虑，但是我们很快就让他们信服了。

2. **dual** [ˈdjuːəl] adj. 两部分的；双重的
『du二+al…的→两部分的；双重的』

He has a dual role as director and actor.
他兼任导演及演员的双重身份。
Rob may be entitled to dual nationality.
罗布或许能拥有双重国籍。

3. duel [ˈdjuːəl] n. 决斗；（双方的）争斗 vi. 进行决斗
『du二+el(=bell)斗→两个人的战斗→决斗』
to fight/win a duel 进行/赢得决斗
to challenge sb to a duel 要求与某人决斗
a verbal duel 舌战
[V] The two men duelled to the death.
这两个男人决斗至死。

4. duet [djuˈet] n. 二重奏；二重唱
『du二+et小→二人小型（演唱、演奏）→二重唱（奏）』

5. duplex [ˈdjuːpleks] n. 连栋式的两栋住宅；复式住宅
<P257>
『du二+plex重叠，折叠→（两层或两栋）重叠在一起→复式住宅』

6. duplicate [ˈdjuːplɪkeɪt, ˈdjuːplɪkət] vt. 复制 adj. 复制的 n. 复制品 <P260>
『du二，双+plic(=fold)折叠+ate表动词→折叠到一起形成两个完全相同的东西→复制』

词根77. duce, duct = lead, bring，表示"引导，带来"

1. produce [ˈprɒdjuːs, prəˈdjuːs] vt. 生产；制造；出示 n. 农产品
『pro向前+duce引导；带来→向前产出→生产』
(n. [ˈprɒdjuːs]; v. [prəˈdjuːs])

❶ [VN] 生产；制造（商品）
to make things to be sold, especially in large quantities
a factory that produces microchips 微芯片制造厂

❷ [VN] （运用技巧）制作，造出
to create sth, especially when skill is needed
She produced a delicious meal out of a few leftovers.
她利用几样剩下的东西烹制出一顿美味饭菜。

❸ [VN] 生产；生出；繁育（自然生产）
The region produces over 50% of the country's wheat.
这个地区出产全国50%以上的小麦。
Our cat produced kittens last week.
我家的猫上周生小猫咪了。
Her duty was to produce an heir to the throne.
她的任务就是生育王位继承人。

❹ [VN] ~ sth (from/out of sth) 出示；展现；提供
to show sth or make sth appear from somewhere
He produced a letter from his pocket.
他从口袋里掏出一封信来。
At the meeting the finance director produced the figures for the previous year.
会上，财务总监出示了上一年的数字。
They challenged him to produce evidence to support his allegations. 他们要他拿出证据证明自己的主张。

❺ [VN] 引起、导致、使产生（某种效果或结果）
to cause a particular result or effect
A phone call to the manager produced the result she wanted.
她给经理打了个电话便如愿以偿。
The drug produces a feeling of excitement.
这种药能使人产生兴奋的感觉。

❻ [VN] 栽培；培养（出人才）
He is the greatest athlete this country has ever produced.
他是这个国家培养的最了不起的运动员。

❼ [VN] 制作，拍摄（电影、戏剧等）
She produced a TV series about adopted children.
她拍了一部描写领养儿童的电视系列片。

❽ [U] 农产品
The shop sells only fresh local produce.
这家商店专售当地的新鲜农产品。

▶ **product** [ˈprɒdʌkt] n. 产品；产物
『pro向前+duct引导；带来→向前产出的东西→产品』

▶ **production** [prəˈdʌkʃn] n. 生产；产量；文艺作品
『produce生产（去e)+tion表名词→生产；产量』

❶ [U] 生产，制造，制作；出示
The new model will be in production by the end of the year.
新型号将于年底投产。
Discounts only on production of your student ID card.
须出示学生证方可打折。

❷ [U] 产量
a decline/an increase in production 产量的下降/增加

❸ [C, U] 电影、戏剧或广播节目；（戏剧的）排演；（电影、电视节目的）制作；（唱片的）灌制
During the film's production, the director wanted to shoot a riot scene but the filming was blocked.
在影片摄制期间，导演想拍摄一个暴乱场面，但被禁止了。
Some Chinese cartoon makers have already made changes to increase the success of their productions.
一些中国动漫制作人已经做了改变，以提高作品的成功率。

▶ **productive** [prəˈdʌktɪv] adj. 多产的；富有成效的
『produce生产（变duce为duct)+ive具有…性质的→具有产出性质的→多产的』
Training makes workers highly productive.
培训提高了工人们的生产力。
He was hopeful that the next round of talks would also be productive. 他希望下一轮会谈同样富有成效。
She is a very productive writer. 她是一个多产的作家。

▶ **productivity** [ˌprɒdʌkˈtɪvəti] n. 生产效率
『productive（去e)多产的+ity性质→多产性质→生产率』
The third-quarter results reflect continued improvements in productivity. 第三季度的结果表明生产率持续上升。

词义辨析 <P361第5>
产品，商品 product, production, produce, merchandise, goods, commodity

2. reduce [rɪˈdjuːs] vt. 减少；使陷入
『re (back)回+duce引导→返回引导→减少』

❶ [VN] ~ sth (from sth) (to sth) | ~ sth (by sth)
减少，缩小（尺寸、数量、价格等）
Costs have been reduced by 20% over the past year.
过去一年，各项费用已经减少了20%。
Giving up smoking reduces the risk of heart disease.
戒烟会减少得心脏病的风险。

❷ reduce sb/sth (from sth) to sth/to doing sth
[usually passive] 使陷入（更坏的）境地；使陷入窘境
She was reduced to tears by their criticisms.
他们的批评使她流下了眼泪。

They were reduced to begging in the streets.
他们沦落到沿街乞讨。
All the buildings in the town have been reduced to rubble.
城里所有的建筑都成了废墟。

▶**reduction** [rɪ'dʌkʃn] n. 减少，缩小
『reduce减少（去e）+tion表名词→减少，缩小』

There has been some reduction in unemployment.
失业人数有所减少。
They received a benefit in the form of a tax reduction.
他们获得了减税优惠。

3. induce [ɪn'dju:s] vt. 劝说；导致
『in里面+duce引导→引导到（做某事、某种状况）里面→劝说；导致』

❶ [VN to inf] (formal) 劝说；诱使
to persuade or influence sb to do sth
Nothing would induce me to take the job.
没有什么能诱使我接受这份工作。

❷ [VN] (formal) 引起；导致
to induce a state or condition means to cause it
Doctors said surgery could induce a heart attack.
医生们说手术有可能引起心脏病发作。

▶**induction** [ɪn'dʌkʃn] n. 归纳；归纳法
『in里面+duce引导（去e）+tion表名词→从（许多事例和个体）里面引导出来→归纳；归纳法』

4. deduce [dɪ'dju:s] vt. 推理，推断
『de向下+duce引导→向下引导→推理』

~ (sth) (from sth) (formal) 推论；推断；演绎
[V that] Can we deduce from your silence that you do not approve?
你保持沉默，我们是否可以据此推断出你不赞成？
[VN] We can deduce a lot from what people choose to buy.
从人们选购的东西可以作出多方面的推断。

同义词 infer [ɪn'fɜː(r)] v. 推理，推断　<P168>
『in里面+fer带来，拿来→从里面带出来→推理』

▶**deduction** [dɪ'dʌkʃn] n. 推论，推理；扣除，扣减
『deduce推理，推断（去e）+tion表名词→推理；推论』

❶ [U, C] 推理；推论
He arrived at the solution by a simple process of deduction.
他通过一番简单的推理得出了解决问题的方法。
If my deductions are correct, I can tell you who the killer was.
如果我的推论正确的话，我可以告诉你谁是凶手。

❷ [U, C] 扣除（额）；减去（数）
Net salary is gross salary minus tax and national insurance deduction. 净工资是工资总额减去税收和扣除国民保险。

5. deduct [dɪ'dʌkt] vt. （从总量中）扣除，减去
『de向下+duct引导→（从总量中把一部分）向下引导→扣除』

The cost of your uniform will be deducted from your wages.
制服费将从你的工资中扣除。
Ten points will be deducted for a wrong answer.
答错一题扣十分。

同义词 **subtract** [səb'trækt] vt. 减去　<P336>

▶**deduction** [dɪ'dʌkʃn] n. （看上一词条）

6. introduce [ˌɪntrə'dju:s] vt. 介绍；推出；引进
『intro进入+duce引导→引导进来→介绍；引入』

❶ ~ A (to B) | ~ A and B | ~ yourself (to sb) 把…介绍（给）
He introduced me to a Greek girl at the party.
他在聚会上介绍我认识了一位希腊姑娘。
Can I introduce myself? I'm Helen Robins.
我可以自我介绍一下吗？我叫海伦·罗宾斯。

❷ ~ sth (into/to sth) 推出；引进；引入
to bring a plan, system, or product into use for the first time
The company is introducing a new range of products this year.
公司今年将推出一系列新产品。
The new law was introduced in 1991.
这项新法律是于1991年开始实施的。

❸ introduce sb to sth / introduce sth to sb 介绍给；使了解
He introduced us to the delights of natural food.
他让我们认识到食用天然食物的乐趣。

▶**introduction** [ˌɪntrə'dʌkʃn] n. 介绍；推出，引进
『introduce介绍（去e）+tion构成名词→介绍』

▶**introductory** [ˌɪntrə'dʌktəri] adj.介绍的；初步的

7. seduce [sɪ'dju:s] vt. 引诱；诱奸
『se离开+duce引导→引开→引诱』

❶ ~ sb (into sth/into doing sth) 引诱，吸引，诱惑
If something seduces you, it is so attractive that it makes you do something that you would not otherwise do.
The promise of huge profits seduced him into parting with his money. 高额利润的许诺诱使他把钱出了手。
I was young and seduced by New York.
我很年轻，被纽约诱惑着。

❷ 诱奸
The professor was sacked for seducing female students.
这个教授因为诱奸女学生被解雇。

▶**seductive** [sɪ'dʌktɪv] adj. 迷人的；有吸引力的
『seduce引诱（e变t）+ive有…性质的→迷人的』

❶ 有吸引力的；令人神往的
The idea of retiring to the south of France is highly seductive.
退休后向法国南方去，这个主意令人心驰神往。

❷ 迷人的；性感的　(sexually attractive)
She used her most seductive voice.
她运用了自己最有魅力的嗓音。

8. conduct [kən'dʌkt, 'kɒndʌkt] v. 指挥；实施；引导
『con共同+duct引导→带来→引导共同做→指挥』
（v. [kən'dʌkt]; n. ['kɒndʌkt]）

❶ [VN]指挥（歌唱或音乐演奏）
Solti will continue to conduct here and abroad.
索尔蒂将继续在国内外担任指挥。

❷ [VN] 组织；安排；实施；执行
to organize and/or do a particular activity
to conduct an experiment/an inquiry/a survey
进行实验/询问/调查
I decided to conduct an experiment. 我决定进行一次实验。

❸ [VN + adv./prep.] 带领；引导；为（某人）导游
to lead or guide sb through or around a place
The guide conducted us around the ruins of the ancient city.
导游引导我们游览了古城遗迹。

❹ [VN + adv./prep.] ~ yourself (formal) 举止；表现
to behave in a particular way
He conducted himself far better than expected.
他表现得比预料的要好得多。

❺ [VN]（technical）（物质）传导（热或电等能量）
Copper conducts electricity well. 铜的导电性能好。

❻ [C] 经营方式，管理方法，实施办法
the way in which a business or an activity is organized and managed
There was growing criticism of the government's conduct of the war. 政府对战争的指挥方式受到越来越多的指责。

❼ [C] 行为，举止
指人在某个地方或某种情况下的表现，尤指在公开场合、工作岗位上的行为，常可与 behaviour 换用。
For Europeans, the law is a statement of basic principles of civilised conduct.
对于欧洲人来说，法律是对基本文明行为准则的表述。
Are you ashamed of your conduct?
你对自己的行为感到害臊吗？

▶ **conductor** [kən'dʌktə(r)] n. （乐队等）指挥；导体；（公交车）售票员，列车员

Who is the conductor of tonight's concert?
谁是今晚音乐会的指挥？
Wood is a poor conductor. 木头不是良好的导体。
The train conductor punched our tickets.
（列车）乘务员用剪票夹在我们的车票上打孔（验票）。

9. **abduct** [æb'dʌkt] v. 诱拐，劫持；绑架
『ab离开+duct引导→带离（到秘密的地方）→绑架』
take away to an undisclosed location against their will and usually in order to extract a ransom
His car was held up and he was abducted by four gunmen.
他的车遭遇拦劫，随后他被4名持枪歹徒劫持。

▶ **abduction** [æb'dʌkʃ(ə)n] n. 诱拐，劫持；绑架
The detective said there was a witness to the abduction.
侦探说有人目击了绑架。

词义辨析 <P374第66> 绑架；劫持 abduct, kidnap, hijack

10. **viaduct** ['vaɪədʌkt] n. 高架桥
『via路；走+ duct引导→引导（道路）经过（山谷河道等的桥）→高架桥』
a long high bridge, usually with arches , that carries a road or railway/railroad across a river or valley
An overhead road for cars or trains is called a viaduct.
建在头顶上供汽车和火车通过的叫高架桥。

▶ **via** ['vaɪə] prep. 经由（某地；某人）
We flew home via Dubai. 我们乘飞机经迪拜回国。
I heard about the sale via Jane.
我从简那里听说了这次减价。
The news programme came to us via satellite.
这新闻节目是通过卫星传送到我们这里来的。

11. **ductile** ['dʌktaɪl] adj. （金属）可延展的
『duct引导+ile易于…的→（金属）易于引导的→可延展的』

12. **aqueduct** ['ækwɪdʌkt] n. 渡槽，高架渠 〈P5〉
『aque(=aqua)水+duct引导→引导水→引水槽』

13. **ventiduct** ['ventɪdʌkt] n. 通风管道 〈P347〉
『vent风+i+duct引导→通风道』

词根78. dure，dur=last; hard，表示"持续；强硬"

1. **during** ['djʊərɪŋ] prep. 在…期间
『dure持续（去e）+ing→持续中→在…期间』
Please remain seated during the performance.
演出期间请不要站起来。
I only saw her once during my stay in Rome.
我在罗马逗留期间只见过她一次。

2. **durable** ['djʊərəbl] adj. 耐用的；持久的
『dure持续（去e）+able能够的→可以持续的→耐用的』
He bought himself a pair of durable trousers.
他给自己买了一条耐穿的裤子。

3. **duration** [dju'reɪʃn] n. 持续时间
『dure持续（去e）+ation表名词→持续期间』
The school was used as a hospital for the duration of the war.
战争期间这所学校被用作医院。

4. **endure** [ɪn'djʊə(r)] vt. 忍耐，容忍
『en使进入…状态+dure持续→使持续→忍耐』
❶ 忍耐；忍受
to experience and deal with sth that is painful or unpleasant, especially without complaining
[VN] They had to endure a long wait before the case came to trial. 在此案审理前他们只得忍受长时间的等待。
The pain was almost too great to endure.
痛苦得几乎难以忍受。

❷ [V] (formal) 持续；持久
If something endures, it continues to exist without any loss in quality or importance.
Somehow the language endures and continues to survive.
那种语言以某种方式保存下来，并继续存在下去。

▶ **endurance** [ɪn'djʊərəns] n. 耐力
Endurance is the ability to continue with an unpleasant or difficult situation, experience, or activity over a long period of time.
The exercise obviously will improve strength and endurance.
这种锻炼会明显改善体力，增加耐力。
The party turned out to be more of an endurance test than a pleasure.
这次聚会结果成了一次耐力测试，而不是一件乐事。

词义辨析 <P363第14>
忍受，遭受 bear, stand, endure, tolerate, put up with, sustain

5. **duress** [dju'res] n. 胁迫，强迫
『dur强硬+ess表名词→采用强硬手段→胁迫，强迫』
He signed the confession under duress.
他出于被迫在供状上签了字。

6. obdurate [ˈɒbdjərət] adj. 倔强的，执拗的
『ob(=agaist)反对+dur强硬+ate表形容词→强硬反对→倔强的』

refusing to change your mind or your actions in any way
Parts of the administration may be changing but others have been obdurate defenders of the status quo.
政府的一些部门可能正在作出改变，但是其他部门却执意维护现状。

词根79. dyn, dynam(o)= power 表示"力量"

1. dynamic [daɪˈnæmɪk] adj. 有活力的 n. 动力
『dynam力量+ic表形容词→有活力的』

❶ adj. 有活力的，有思想的
He seemed a dynamic and energetic leader.
他似乎是一个富有干劲、精力充沛的领导。
South Asia continues to be the most dynamic economic region in the world. 南亚仍然是世界上经济最活跃的地区。

❷ adj. （过程）动态的，不断发展变化的
a dynamic, evolving worldwide epidemic
不断发生变异、在世界范围内传播的流行病

❸ [C] 活力；驱动力
The dynamic of the market demands constant change and adjustment. 市场要有活力，需要不断地改变和调整。

❹ [C] (usu. pl.) 相互作用，驱动力
The dynamics of a situation or group of people are the opposing forces within it that cause it to change.
the dynamics of political change 政治变化的驱动力

▶ **dynamics** [daɪˈnæmɪks] n. 动力学；驱动力
『dynam力量+ics…学→研究力量的学科→动力学』

[U] 动力学；驱动力
His idea was to apply geometry to dynamics.
他的想法就是将几何学应用在力学上。
Scientists observe the same dynamics in fluids.
科学家们在液体中观察到了同样的驱动力。

2. dynamo [ˈdaɪnəməʊ] n. 发电机；精力充沛的人
『dynam(=power)力量；电+o物→发电机』

Myles is a human dynamo. 迈尔斯是个精力充沛的人。

3. dynamite [ˈdaɪnəmaɪt] n. 炸药
『dynam力量+ite表名词→力量非常大的东西→炸药』

4. dynasty 英 [ˈdɪnəsti] 美 [ˈdaɪnəsti] n. 朝代
『dyn力量+ast表人+y表名词→君主→朝代』

The Tang Dynasty was the golden age of classical Chinese poetry. 唐朝是中国古诗的极盛时期。

词根80. emper, imper=command, rule, 表示"命令；统治"

1. emperor [ˈempərə(r)] n. 皇帝；君主
『emper统治+or表人→统治的人→皇帝』

2. empress [ˈemprəs] n. 女皇；皇后
『emper统治(去r前的e)+ess表女性→统治的女性→女皇；皇后』

3. empire [ˈempaɪə(r)] n. 帝国
『empire(=emper)统治→帝国』

4. imperial [ɪmˈpɪəriəl] adj. 帝国的
『imper命令；统治+ ial具有…的→帝国的』

5. imperative [ɪmˈperətɪv] adj. 必须做的；祈使的 n. 必须做的事情
『imper命令+ative具有…性质的→必须做的；祈使的』

❶ adj. 因重要而必须做的
very important and needing immediate attention or action
It is absolutely imperative that we finish by next week.
我们的当务之急是必须于下周完成。
It is imperative to continue the treatment for at least two months. 必须继续治疗至少两个月。

❷ [C] 因重要而必须做的事情
The most important political imperative is to limit the number of US casualties.
现在的头等政治大事就是要控制美国人的伤亡数量。

❸ [only before noun] 表示命令的；祈使的
an imperative sentence 祈使句

6. imperious [ɪmˈpɪəriəs] adj. 专横的
『imper命令；统治+ious充满…的→专横的』

expecting people to obey you and treating them as if they are not as important as you
"Get it now," she demanded imperiously.
"现在就给我拿来，"她蛮横地要求。

词根81. empt, ample=take, procure, 表示"拿，获得"

1. exempt [ɪgˈzempt] adj. 免除的；豁免的 vt. 免除；豁免
『ex出来+empt拿→拿出来（不必履行）→免除，豁免』

❶ [not before noun] ~ (from sth) 免除（责任、付款等）的
if sb/sth is exempt from sth, they are not affected by it, do not have to do it, pay it, etc.
The interest on the money is exempt from tax.
这笔钱的利息免税。
Some students are exempt from certain exams.
有的学生可免除某些考试。
tax-exempt donations to charity 给慈善机构的免税捐款

❷ [VN] ~ sb/sth (from sth) (formal) 免除；豁免
to give or get sb's official permission not to do sth or not to pay sth they would normally have to do or pay
His bad eyesight exempted him from military service.
他因视力不好而免服兵役。
In 1983, charities were exempted from paying the tax.
1983年慈善团体均免付税款。

▶ **exemption** [ɪgˈzempʃn] n. 免除；豁免

She was given exemption from the final examination.
她已获准期末免试。

2. example [ɪgˈzɑːmpl] n. 举例子
『ex出来+ample拿→（从众多中）拿出来的一个→例子』

▶ **exemplify** [ɪgˈzemplɪfaɪ] vt. 举例说明；是…的典型
『exemple(=example)例子（去e+i）+fy使→使…成为例子→举例说明；是…的典型』

❶ [VN] 举例说明，例证
She exemplified each of the points she was making with an amusing anecdote.
她的每一个论点都用一个逸闻趣事来说明。

❷ [VN] 是…的典型
His food exemplifies Italian cooking at its best.
他的菜肴代表了意大利烹饪的最高峰。

▶ **exemplar** [ɪgˈzemplɑː(r)] n. 模范；典型

a person or thing that is a good or typical example of sth
It is an exemplar of a house of the period.
这是该时期房屋的典型。
They viewed their new building as an exemplar of taste.
他们认为他们的新大厦品位独特，可作为典范。

3. sample [ˈsɑːmpl] n. 样品，样本 vt. 品尝，体验
『s(=se)分开+ample拿→从一批中拿出来的→样品，样本』

❶ [C] （抽查的）样本；（用于化验的）取样；货样
The interviews were given to a random sample of students.
随机抽选出部分学生进行了采访。
Samples of the water contained pesticide.
水样中含有杀虫剂。
You'll receive samples of paint, curtains and upholstery.
你将收到涂料、窗帘、家具装饰的样品。

❷ [VN] 品尝；体验
We sampled a selection of different bottled waters.
我们品尝了一系列不同品牌的瓶装水。
the chance to sample a different way of life
体验不同生活方式的机会

4. peremptory [pəˈremptəri] adj. 强硬的；不容分辩的
『per彻底地+empt(=take)拿+ory有…性质的→彻底拿走（决定权）的→强硬的；不容分辩的』

With a brief, almost peremptory gesture he pointed to a chair.
他做了一个简单的手势，近乎霸道地指着椅子。

词根82. equ, equi=equal, even，表示"相等，平均"

1. equal [ˈiːkwəl] adj. 相等的；平等的；能胜任的 vt. 比得上
『equ相等+al…的→相等的；平等的』

❶ ~ (to sb/sth) （大小、数量、价值等）相等的
Investors can borrow an amount equal to the property's purchase price.
投资者可以获得与房产购买价格相等的借款额。

❷ 平等的；同等的
We will be justly demanding equal rights at work.
我们将要求享有工作中应得的平等权利。

❸ ~ to sth (formal) 能胜任的
I hope that he proves equal to the challenge.
我希望他最后能应付这一挑战。

❹（联系动词）（大小、数量、价值等）与…相等，等于
2x plus y equals 7. (2x+y=7)
A meter equals 39.38 inches. 1米等于39.38英寸。

❺ [VN] 比得上；敌得过
This achievement is unlikely ever to be equalled.
这一成就可能任何时候都没有能与之匹敌的。

▶ **equality** [iˈkwɒləti] n. 平等
Don't you believe in equality between men and women?
难道你不相信男女平等吗？

▶ **inequality** [ˌɪnɪˈkwɒləti] n. 不平等

2. equate [iˈkweɪt] vt. 使等同
『equ平等+ate使…→使平等』

[VN] ~ sth (with sth) 同等看待；使等同
It's a mistake to equate wealth with happiness.
将财富与幸福等同是错误的。
You equate home with safety, comfort, shelter, and protection.
你把家等同于安全、舒适、庇护和保护。

3. equation [ɪˈkweɪʒn] n. 等同；等式；方程式
『equate等同（去e）+ion表名词…→等同；等式』

❶ [C] (mathematics 数) 方程；方程式；等式

❷ [U, sing.] 相等；等同看待
The equation of wealth with happiness can be dangerous.
把财富与幸福等同起来可能是危险的。

4. equator [ɪˈkweɪtə(r)] n. 赤道
『equate等同（去e）+or人或物→（到地球两极距离）等同的地方→赤道』

Singapore is near the equator. 新加坡位于赤道附近。

5. equilibrium [ˌiːkwɪˈlɪbriəm] n. 平衡；平静
『equi等同的+libr自由+ium→（两个）自由（变化的力量达到）等同的→平衡』

❶ 平衡；均衡
a state of balance, especially between opposing forces or influences
We have achieved an equilibrium in the economy.
我们已在经济上达到平衡。
Some have found equilibrium between career challenges and family stability.
有些人找到了职业挑战和家庭稳定之间的平衡。

❷（心情、情绪）平静，安宁
I paused in the hall to take three deep breaths to restore my equilibrium.
我在大厅里停了一下，深吸了三口气以恢复平静。

6. adequate [ˈædɪkwət] adj. 足够的，合乎需要的
『ad相当于to+equ等同的+ate…的→达到（与需求）等同的→足够的，合乎需要的』

~ (for sth) | ~ (to do sth) 足够的；合格的；合乎需要的
enough in quantity, or good enough in quality, for a particular purpose or need
The room was small but adequate. 房间虽小但够用。
The space available is not adequate for our needs.
现有的空间不能满足我们的需要。

▶ **adequacy** [ˈædɪkwəsi] n. 足够，充分
Various standards have been developed around the world to evaluate nutritional adequacy.
世界各地都制定了各种标准来评估营养的充足性。

7. equivalent [ɪˈkwɪvələnt] adj. 等同的；对应的 n. 等同物；对应物 <P345>
『equi等同+val价值+ent具有…性质的→（价值）等同的』

8. equivocal [ɪˈkwɪvəkl] adj. 含糊其词的；难以理解的 <P357>
『equi等同+voc声音+al…的→（两种不同的）声音等同的→含糊其词的』

词根83. erg, ert=energy, work，表示"能量，活力；工作"

1. energy [ˈenədʒi] n. 精力；活力；能源
『en使+erg能量，活力+y表名词→使有活力的东西→精力；活力』

2. inert [ɪˈnɜːt] adj. 静止的；无生气的；（化）惰性的
『in不，无+ert能量，活力→静止的；无生气的』

He covered the inert body with a blanket.

他用毯子把那具一动不动的尸体盖上了。

The novel itself remains oddly inert.

小说本身异常平淡，了无生气。

▶ **inertia** [ɪˈnɜːʃə] n. 缺乏活力；惯性

『in不，无+ert能量，活力+ia表名词→没有能量（没有外加能量时，物体保持惯性）→缺乏活力；惯性』

❶ [U] 缺乏活力

If you have a feeling of inertia, you feel very lazy and unwilling to move or be active.

我好像无法摆脱这种无力的感觉。

❷ [U]（physics 物）惯性

Inertia carried the car to the pavement.

惯性使汽车驶到了人行道上。

▶ **inertial** [ɪˈnɜːʃl] adj. 惯性的

3. **exert** [ɪɡˈzɜːt] v. 施加（影响等）；竭力

『er出来+ert能量→使…的能量出来（影响）→施加（影响等）；竭力』

❶ 施加、运用（影响、压力、权威等）

to use power or influence to affect sb/sth

He exerted all his authority to make them accept the plan.

他利用他的所有权力让他们接受这个计划。

❷ ~ yourself 努力，竭力

to make a big physical or mental effort

In order to be successful he would have to exert himself.

他必须努力才能成功。

▶ **exertion** [ɪɡˈzɜːʃn] n. 施加，运用；尽力

Exertion of authority does not come easily to everyone.

行使权利并不是对每个人都是容易的。

He needed to relax after the exertions of a busy day at work.

他忙碌工作了一天后需要休息。

词根84. ev=age, lifetime 表示"年龄；时代；寿命"

1. **longevity** [lɒnˈdʒevəti] n. 长寿；持久

『long长的+ev年龄；寿命+ity表名词→长寿』

[U] (formal) 长寿；长命；持久

long life; the fact of lasting a long time

We wish you both health and longevity.

我们祝愿您二位健康长寿。

He prides himself on the longevity of the company.

他为公司悠久的历史而感到骄傲。

2. **primeval** [praɪˈmiːvl] adj. 远古的 〈P270〉

『prim最初的+ ev年龄；时代；寿命+ al…的→时间最早的→ 原始的』

3. **medieval** [ˌmediˈiːvl] adj. 中古的，中世纪的 〈P217〉

『medi中间+ev年龄；时代；寿命+ al…的→中世纪的』

词根85. err= wander, stray，表示"偏离，走失"

1. **err** [ɜː(r)] vi. 犯错误，出差错

『err偏离→偏离了正确的→犯错误』

[V] to make a mistake

To err is human. 是人都会犯错。

They may be wise to err on the side of caution.

他们小心谨慎也许是明智的。

▶ **error** [ˈerə(r)] n. 错误

No payments were made last week because of a computer error. 由于计算机出错，上周未付任何款项。

There are too many errors in your work. 你的工作失误太多。

2. **errant** [ˈerənt] adj. 行为不当的；出轨的

『err偏离+ant表形容词→行为偏离（可接受标准的）→行为不当的；出轨的』

Errant is used to describe someone whose actions are considered unacceptable or wrong by other people. For example, an errant husband is unfaithful to his wife.

They came straight up to me, like errant children, begging forgiveness.

他们径直走到我面前，像犯了错误的孩子乞求宽恕。

Usually his cases involved errant husbands and wandering wives.

通常他接的案子都涉及出轨的丈夫和离家出走的妻子。

3. **erroneous** [ɪˈrəʊniəs] adj. 错误的（认识、意见等）

『err偏离+on+eous…的→偏离（正确的）→错误的』

Beliefs, opinions, or methods that are erroneous are incorrect or only partly correct.

Some people have the erroneous notion that one can contract AIDS by giving blood.

一些人错误地认为献血会让人感染艾滋病。

They have arrived at some erroneous conclusions.

他们得出了一些错误的结论。

4. **erratic** [ɪˈrætɪk] adj. 不稳定的；难以预测的；无规律的

『err偏离+atic…的→偏离（预计）的→不稳定的；难以预测的』

❶ Something that is erratic does not follow a regular pattern, but happens at unexpected times or moves along in an irregular way.

Argentina's erratic inflation rate threatens to upset the plans.

阿根廷动荡不定的通货膨胀率可能会破坏那些计划。

Businessmen are displeased with erratic economic policy-making. 商界人士对变化无常的经济决策很是恼火。

5. **aberrant** [æˈberənt] adj. 异常的；违反常规的

『ab离开+err偏离+ant表形容词→偏离（正常社会规范的）→异常的；违反常规的』

Aberrant means unusual and not socially acceptable.

Ian's rages and aberrant behavior worsened.

伊恩的怒气越来越大，反常行为也恶化了。

词根86. fable, fabul, fess=speak，表示"讲，说"

1. **fable** [ˈfeɪbl] n. 寓言故事；谣传

『fable说，讲→讲的故事→寓言』

❶ [C, U] 寓言；寓言故事

Aesop's Fables《伊索寓言》

a land rich in fable 寓言之乡

❷ [C, U] 谣传；无稽之谈

You can describe a statement or explanation that is untrue but that many people believe as fable.

Is reincarnation fact or fable?

转世轮回是确有其事还是无稽之谈？

▶ **fabulous** [ˈfæbjələs] adj. 寓言中的；极好的；巨大的

fabulous beasts 传说中的野兽

a fabulous performance 精彩的表演

Jane is a fabulous cook. 简是个很棒的厨师。

Despite his fabulous wealth, he is very much a man of the people. 他虽然腰缠万贯，却非常亲民。

2. affable [ˈæfəbl] adj. 和蔼可亲的，平易近人的
『af相当于to+fable讲，说→可以走向前（随意讲话的）→和蔼的』

pleasant, friendly and easy to talk to
Mr Brooke is an extremely affable and approachable man.
布鲁克先生极为谦和，平易近人。

3. profess [prəˈfes] vt. 妄称；宣称
『pro向前，在前+ fess说→在前面说→宣称；妄称』

❶ 妄称；伪称；声称
to claim that sth is true or correct, especially when it is not
[VN] She still professes her innocence.
她仍然声称自己无辜。
[V to inf] I don't profess to be an expert in this subject.
我不敢自诩为这方面的专家。

❷ 宣称；公开表明
to state openly that you have a particular belief, feeling, etc.
[VN] He professed his admiration for their work.
他表示钦佩他们的工作。
[VN-ADJ] She professed herself satisfied with the progress so far. 她表示对目前为止的进度很满意。

同义词 **declare** [dɪˈkleə(r)] v. 宣布；宣称；申报〈P135〉
『de加强+clare(=clear)清楚→使清楚→宣布；宣称』

4. professor [prəˈfesə(r)] n. 教授
『pro在前+fess讲，说+or表人→在学生前面说话的人→教授』

5. profession [prəˈfeʃn] n. 职业，行业；职业界
『pro在前+fess讲，说+ion表名词→（听过）讲授（的职业）→（需要专门培训或接受过一定教育的）职业』

❶ [C] （需要专门技能，尤指需要较高教育水平的某一）行业，职业
a type of job that needs special training or skill, especially one that needs a high level of education
He was an electrician by profession. 他的职业是电工。
She was at the very top of her profession.
她是她那个行业中的佼佼者。

❷ the profession [sing.+ sing./pl. v.] （某）职业界；业内人士；同业；同行；同仁
all the people who work in a particular type of profession
The legal profession has/have always resisted change.
法律界向来抵制变革。

❸ the professions 职业界；专业界
the traditional jobs that need a high level of education and training, such as being a doctor or a lawyer
employment in industry and the professions
工业与专业中的就业

词义辨析〈P373第63〉
职业，工作 career, profession, occupation, vocation

6. professional [prəˈfeʃənl] adj. 职业的；专业的；n. 专业人士

❶ adj. 职业的；专业的；娴熟的
If it's a legal matter you need to seek professional advice.
如果这是法律问题，你需要进行专业咨询。
Most of the people on the course were professional women.

参加本课程的大多数人是职业女性。
He dealt with the problem in a highly professional way.
他处理这个问题非常专业。

❷ adj. 职业性的；非业余的
After he won the amateur championship he turned professional. 他获得业余赛冠军后就转为职业运动员了。

❸ [C] 职业人士；专业人士
My father wanted me to become a professional and have more stability.
我父亲想让我成为职业人士，这样能更稳定一些。
This was clearly a job for a real professional.
这显然是需要真正的专家才能担任的工作。

❹ [C] 职业运动员；（从事某活动的）专业人士（非业余）（also informal pro）
The professionals played football very well.
这些专业足球运动员踢得棒极了。

7. confess [kənˈfes] v. 坦白；忏悔；承认
『con一起+fess说→（警察或上帝）在一起时说→坦白；忏悔』

❶ ~ (to sth/to doing sth) 供认，坦白，承认（错误或罪行）
to admit, especially formally or to the police, that you have done sth wrong or illegal
[V] She confessed to the murder. 她供认犯了谋杀罪。
[V (that)] He confessed that he had stolen the money.
他承认他偷了那笔钱。

❷ （向上帝或神父）忏悔；告解（罪过）
You just go to the church and confess your sins.
你干脆去教堂忏悔自己的罪过吧。

❸ I confess. 我承认。
（用来对自己的过失等略表歉意）

▶ **confession** [kənˈfeʃn] n. 坦白；承认
After hours of questioning by police, she made a full confession.
经过警察数小时的审问，她才供认了全部罪行。
I've a confession to make—I lied about my age.
我有错要承认——我谎报了年龄。

词根87. fabric=make，表示"制作"

1. fabric [ˈfæbrɪk] n. 织物；（社会、建筑）结构
『fabric制作→制作（织物）→织物→结构』

❶ [U, C] 织物；布料
Glue the fabric around the window.
用胶水把布料粘在窗户周围。
The fabric is strong enough to withstand harsh processing.
这种织物非常结实，能经受粗加工。

❷ [sing.] the ~ (of sth) (formal) （社会、机构等的）结构
The whole fabric of society was changed by the war.
战争改变了整个社会的结构。

❸ [sing.] the ~ (of sth) （建筑物的）结构（如墙、地面、屋顶）
Condensation will eventually cause the fabric of the building to rot away. 冷凝作用将最终使建筑结构腐朽掉。

2. fabricate [ˈfæbrɪkeɪt] v. 编造（谎言）；制造
『fabric制作（织物）+ate表动词→编造（谎言）；（用某种材料）制造』

❶ [VN] 编造，捏造

to invent false information in order to trick people
The evidence was totally fabricated. 这个证据纯属伪造。

❷ [VN] 制造，制作
If something is fabricated from different materials or substances, it is made out of those materials or substances.
All the tools are fabricated from high quality steel.
所有工具均由精钢制成。

词根88. face, fic=face，表示"脸，表面"

1. facet ['fæsɪt] n. 小平面；方面
『face表面（去e）+et小→平面；（东西的）一面』

❶ （宝石的）小平面，琢面

❷ 部分；方面
a particular part or aspect of sth
Now let's look at another facet of the problem.
现在咱们看问题的另一面。

2. preface ['prefəs] n.（书的）前言，序言；作开场白
『pre前面+face面，脸→（书内容之前的）面→前言』

❶ [C]（书的）前言，序言

❷ ~ sth (with sth) 为…写序言
He prefaced the diaries with a short account of how they were discovered.
他在前言中简要叙述了日记发现的经过。

❸ ~ sth by/with sth | ~ sth by doing sth
(formal)作…的开场白
to say sth before you start making a speech, answering a question, etc.
I must preface my remarks with an apology.
讲话前，我必须先表示歉意。

3. surface ['sɜːfɪs] n. 表面；vi. 浮出水面
『sur上面+face表面→表面上面→表面』

❶ [C] 表面；表层
We'll need a flat surface to play the game on.
我们得有个平面才能玩这个游戏。
These plants float on the surface of the water.
这些植物漂浮在水面上。
It seems like a good idea on the surface but there are sure to be problems. 这主意乍一看不错，但肯定存在问题。

❷ [V] 浮出水面；重新出现
The ducks dived and surfaced again several meters away.
鸭子潜入水中，然后在几米开外钻出水面。
Doubts began to surface. 人们开始怀疑起来。

4. efface [ɪ'feɪs] vt. 抹去；擦掉
『ef出去+face表面→使从表面上出去→擦掉』

[VN] (formal) 抹去（记忆）；擦掉
Time alone will efface those unpleasant memories.
只有时间才能使人淡忘那些不愉快的记忆。

5. deface [dɪ'feɪs] vt. 损伤…的外貌（尤指乱涂、乱写）
『de去掉；取消；毁+face表面→把表面弄坏→损伤表面』

It's illegal to deface banknotes.
在钞票上乱涂乱画是违法的。
Chalk marks deface the wall of the house.
粉笔痕迹破坏墙壁的外观。

6. facetious [fə'siːʃəs] adj.（不分场合）乱开玩笑的
『face脸+tious…的→（不看对方）脸色（乱开玩笑）的→

乱开玩笑的』

The woman eyed him coldly. "Don't be facetious," she said.
妇人冷冷地看着他。她说道："别没正经了。"

7. superficial [,suːpə'fɪʃl] adj. 表面的；肤浅的 〈P39〉
『super上面+fic(=face)表面+ial…的→表面的』

词根89. fac, fact=make, do，表示"做，制作"

1. factory ['fæktri] n. 工厂，制造厂 〈P93〉
『fact做+ory表场所→工厂』

2. factor ['fæktə(r)] n. 因素
『fact做，制作+ or表人或物→（促使某事物）形成的东西→因素』

[C] 因素；要素
one of several things that cause or influence sth
The closure of the mine was the single most important factor in the town's decline.
矿山的关闭是这个镇衰落的唯一最重要的因素。
Luck is certainly one deciding factor.
运气当然是一个决定因素。

3. faction ['fækʃn] n. 派系；派系斗争
『fact做，制作+ ion表名词→（一帮人一起）做→派系』

❶ [C] 派系，派别，小集团
A peace agreement will be signed by the leaders of the country's warring factions.
该国各敌对派系领导人将签署和平协议。

❷ [U] 派系斗争；内讧

4. benefactor ['benɪfæktə(r)] n. 捐款人；赞助人
『bene善，好+ fact做+ or表人→做好事的人→行善者』

A benefactor is a person who helps a person or organization by giving them money.
In his old age he became a benefactor of the arts.
他晚年成了一个艺术赞助人。

5. manufacture [,mænju'fæktʃə(r)] v. & n. 大量生产
『manu手+fact做，制作+ure行为→用手做→制造』

❶ [VN]（用机器）大量生产，成批制造
Nike started as a small company manufacturing running shoes. 耐克最初是一家生产跑鞋的小公司。

❷ [U] 大量制造；批量生产
During World War Ⅱ, steel supplies were used in the manufacture of weapons.
在第二次世界大战期间，钢铁被用于制造武器。

❸ manufactures [pl.] (technical) 工业品
Agriculture is linked to industry through rural expenditure on manufactures .
农业与工业之间的联系是通过农村对制成品的消费来进行的。

❹ 虚构，捏造
If the media can manufacture stories like this, who are we supposed to believe?
如果媒体能制造这样的故事，我们应该相信谁？

▶**manufacturer** [,mænju'fæktʃərə(r)] n. 制造商
The contracts allow retailers to sell equipment at below the manufacturer's price.
这些合同允许零售商以低于制造商的价格出售设备。

6. facile ['fæsaɪl] adj. 轻率做出的

『fac做，制作+ile易于…的→容易做的』

（主张、建议）肤浅的，粗浅的，轻率的

produced without effort or careful thought

He proposed a facile solution to a complex problem.

他对一复杂问题提出了肤浅的解决办法。

That is only a facile answer. 那只是一个很肤浅的回答。

His writing lacks depth for being facile.

他的作品因轻易写出而缺少深度。

7. facility [fə'sɪləti] n. 设施；场所；功能；天资

『facile容易做出的（去e）+ity表名词→使（某活动）容易做出的（物质条件）→设施；功能；天资』

❶ facilities [pl.] 设施；设备

buildings, services, equipment, etc. that are provided for a particular purpose

What recreational facilities are now available?

现在有些什么娱乐设施？

Some people believe that the best way to improve public health is by increasing the number of sports facilities.

一些人认为，改善公共卫生的最好办法是增加体育设施的数量。

❷ [C] （供特定用途的）场所

a place, usually including buildings, used for a particular purpose or activity

The problem lies in getting patients to a medical facility as soon as possible. 问题在于要把病人尽快送至医院。

❸ [C] 附加服务；附加功能

a special feature of a machine, service, etc. that makes it possible to do sth extra

It is very useful to have an overdraft facility.

有透支功能用处很大。

It has no manual focus facility. 它没有手动调焦功能。

❹ [sing., U] ~ (for sth) 天资，才能，天赋

a natural ability to learn or do sth easily

He has a facility for designing beautiful clothes for women.

他有为妇女设计漂亮服装的能力。

8. facilitate [fə'sɪlɪteɪt] vt. 促进；促使

『facile容易做的（去e）+it+ate使…→使容易』

[VN] (formal) 促进；促使

to make an action or a process possible or easier

The new trade agreement should facilitate more rapid economic growth. 新贸易协定应当会加快经济发展。

The new airport will facilitate the development of tourism.

新机场将促进旅游业的发展。

9. factitious [fæk'tɪʃəs] adj. 虚假的；人为的

『fact做，制作+itious…的→做出来（使显得像真）的→虚假的；人为的』

not genuine but created deliberately and made to appear to be true

Extensive advertising can cause a factitious demand for an article. 大规模的广告宣传能引起对某一商品的反常需求。

10. faculty ['fæklti] n. 官能；能力；院系；院校全体教师

『fac做+ulty表名词→做某事所需的技能→官能』

❶ [C, usually pl.] 官能；天赋

any of the physical or mental abilities that a person is born with

the faculty of sight 视觉

She retained her mental faculties until the day she died.

她直到临终那天一直保持着思维和理解能力。

❷ [sing.] ~ of/for (doing) sth (formal) 才能；能力

a particular ability for doing sth

the faculty of understanding complex issues

理解复杂问题的能力

He had a faculty for seeing his own mistakes.

他具有看到自己错误的能力。

❸ [C] （高等院校的）系；院

the Faculty of Law 法学院

❹ [C, U] the faculty (NAmE) （某高等院校的）全体教师

The faculty agreed on a change in the requirements.

全体教师一致同意修改规定。

11. facsimile [fæk'sɪməli] n. 传真；复制本 〈P300〉

『fac做+simile相似，相同→做成相同的→传真；复制本』

词根90. fect=make, do，表示"做，制作"

1. affect [ə'fekt] v. 影响；感动；感染；假装

『af相当于to+fect做→做到…上→影响（某事、健康、情感、行为）→影响；感染、侵袭；感动；假装』

❶ [VN] [often passive] 影响

to produce a change in sb/sth

Your opinion will not affect my decision.

你的意见不会影响我的决定。

The south of the country was worst affected by the drought.

该国南方旱情最严重。

❷ [VN] [often passive] (of a disease 疾病) 侵袭；使感染

to attack sb or a part of the body; to make sb become ill/sick

The condition affects one in five women.

每五个妇女就有一个人患有这种病。

❸ [VN] [often passive] （感情上）深深打动；使悲伤（或怜悯等）

to make sb have strong feelings of sadness, pity, etc.

They were deeply affected by the news of her death.

她死亡的消息使他们唏嘘不已。

Rub the cream into the affected areas. 把乳膏揉进感染处。

❹ [VN] (formal, disapproving) 假装，佯装，装出…的样子

to use or wear sth that is intended to impress other people

I wish he wouldn't affect that ridiculous accent.

但愿他别故意装出那种可笑的腔调。

[VN] She affected a calmness she did not feel. 她强装镇静。

▶ **affectation** [ˌæfek'teɪʃn] n. 假装；做作；装模作样

He raised his eyebrows with an affectation of surprise (= pretending to be surprised).

他扬起双眉装出一副吃惊的样子。

2. affection [ə'fekʃn] n. 喜爱，钟爱；爱情

『affect影响+ion名词→影响（他人的）东西→爱』

❶ [U, sing.] ~ (for sb/sth) 喜爱；钟爱

the feeling of liking or loving sb/sth very much and caring about them

Children need lots of love and affection.

孩子需要多多疼爱和关怀。

He didn't show his wife any affection.

他没有向妻子表示一点爱。

I have a great affection for New York. 我很喜欢纽约。

❷ affections [pl.] (formal) 爱情
a person's feelings of love
Anne had two men trying to win her affections.
安妮有两个男人追求。

▶ **affectionate** [əˈfekʃənət] adj. 表示关爱的；表示爱的；充满深情的；满怀柔情的
『affection喜爱，钟爱+ate具有…性质的→表示爱的』
If you are affectionate, you show your love or fondness for another person in the way that you behave towards them.
She gave me a very long and affectionate hug.
她满怀深情地久久拥抱了我。
He looked affectionately at his niece.
他慈爱地看着他的侄女。

3. **effect** [ɪˈfekt] n. 效果，影响；v. 实施
『ef出来+fect做→所做的出了效果→影响』

❶ [C, U] ~ (on sb/sth) 影响，效应
hava a good/ bad/ great/ positive/ negative effect on sth
对某事有着好的/坏的/大的/积极的/消极的影响
It's a small reduction and will have no effect on domestic prices. 降幅太小，对国内价格不会产生影响。
The presence of humans can have a negative effect on wildlife.
人类的存在对野生动植物会有负面的影响。
to learn to distinguish between cause and effect
学会分清因果
the beneficial effects of exercise　锻炼的好处
green-house effect　温室效应
side effect　副作用

❷ [C, U] （艺术家或作家所要创造的）特定的效果
The stage lighting gives the effect of a moonlit scene.
舞台灯光产生出月下景色的效果。

❸ [VN] (formal) 使发生；使生效
Many parents lack confidence in their ability to effect change in their children's behaviour.
许多家长对他们改变孩子行为的能力缺乏信心。
The union between the two countries was effected three years ago. 两国合并是三年前实现的。

❹ **bring/put sth into effect** 实行，实施
The bill was put into effect last month.
该法案于上个月生效。

come into effect 生效；开始实施
The contract will come into effect upon signature.
此合同将在签字后生效。

take effect 见效；生效
The aspirins soon take effect. 阿司匹林很快见效。
The new law takes effect from tomorrow.
新法令明日起生效。

词义辨析 <P367第32>
结果 **effect, outcome, consequence, result, aftermath**
词义辨析 <P368第33> 影响 **effect, affect, influence**

▶ **effective** [ɪˈfektɪv] adj. 有效的；生效的
『effect效果+ive有…性质的→有效的；生效的』
Simple antibiotics are effective against this organism.
一般的抗生素能够有效对抗这种微生物。
The new rules will become effective in the next few days.
新规定将在几天后生效。

▶ **ineffectual** [ˌɪnɪˈfektʃuəl] adj. 不起作用的，徒劳无益的
『in不+effect效果+ual…的→没有效果的→不起作用的』
If someone or something is ineffectual, they fail to do what they are expected to do or are trying to do.
The mayor had become ineffectual in the struggle to clamp down on drugs. 市长打击毒品的努力未见成效。
近义词 **efficient** [ɪˈfɪʃnt] adj. 高效率的；高效能的
<P164>
『ef+fici做，制作+ent具有…性质的→具有（快速）做出来性质的→高效的』

4. **infect** [ɪnˈfekt] v. 传染；污染；感染（情感）
『in里面+fect做→（病毒、细菌，情感）进入到（另外一个）体内→传染；感染；污染』

❶ [VN]~ sb/sth (with sth) 传染，使感染；污染
to make a disease or an illness spread to a person, an animal or a plant
It is not possible to infect another person through kissing.
接吻不可能把这种病传染给他人。
people infected with HIV　染上艾滋病病毒的人
The birds infect the milk. 鸟污染了牛奶。

❷ 使感染（某种感情）；影响
to make sb share a particular feeling
She infected the children with her enthusiasm for music.
她对音乐的热爱感染了孩子们。

❸ 使感染（计算机病毒）
This virus infected thousands of computers within days.
这种病毒在短短几天内感染了数千台计算机。

▶ **infection** [ɪnˈfekʃn] n. 传染；感染

❶ [U] 传染；感染
The likelihood of infection is minimal. 感染的可能性极小。

❷ [C] （身体某部位的）感染；传染病
Ear infections are common in pre-school children.
耳部感染在学前儿童中很常见。
Daily new infections of COVID-19 continued a downward trend on Saturday.
COVID-19（新冠肺炎）的每日新感染人数在周六继续下降趋势。

词义辨析 <P366第26>
疾病 **illness, disease, disorder, infection, condition, bug, sickness**

▶ **infectious** [ɪnˈfekʃəs] adj. 传染性的，感染的（尤指通过呼吸）
『infect传染；感化+(t)ious…的→传染性的』
Flu is highly infectious. 流感的传染性很高。
I'm still infectious. 我还处在传染期。

词义辨析 <P379第91>
感染；传播 **infect, contract, transmit**

▶ **disinfectant** [ˌdɪsɪnˈfektənt] n. 消毒剂；杀菌剂
『dis不+infect感染，传染+ant剂→使不能感染（病毒）的药剂→消毒剂；杀菌剂』

5. **perfect** [ˈpɜːfɪkt, pəˈfekt] adj. 完美，极好的；十足的
vt. 使完美
『per彻底地+fect做→做得很彻底→完美的』
（adj. [ˈpɜːfɪkt]; v. [pəˈfekt]）

❶ adj. 完美的；极好的

The weather was perfect. 天气好极了。

He spoke perfect English. 他英语说得棒极了。

❷ adj. 十足的

She was a perfect fool. 她愚蠢至极。

❸ vt. 使完美；完善

As a musician, she has spent years perfecting her technique.
身为音乐家，她多年来不断在技艺上精益求精。

▶**perfection** [pə'fekʃn] n. 完善；完美

The fish was cooked to perfection. 这鱼烹得恰到好处。

His performance was perfection (= sth perfect).
他的演技真是炉火纯青。

They have been working on the perfection of the new model.
他们一直在努力完善新型号。

6. defect ['di:fekt , dɪ'fekt] n. 缺点，毛病；vt. 背叛
『de相当于away、off+fect做→离开去做→缺陷；背叛』
（n. ['di:fekt]; v. [dɪ'fekt]）

❶ 缺点；缺陷；毛病

He was born with a hearing defect.他患有先天性听力缺损。
A report has pointed out the defects of the present system.
一份报告指出了当前体制存在的毛病。

❷ [V] ~ (from sth) (to sth) 背叛；叛变；投敌

He tried to defect to the West last year.
去年他试图叛逃到西方。

7. confection [kən'fekʃn] n. （精美诱人的）甜点，甜食；
精工制作的物品（如建筑物或衣物）
『con一起+fect做+ion表名词→一起做成的精美的糖果物品等→甜点；精美物品』

Exquisite confection can be offered from night till early morning. 精美甜点可以从晚上一直提供至清晨。

词根91. fict, fice, fic(i), fig=make, do，表示"做，造，制作"

1. fiction ['fɪkʃn] n. 虚构；小说
『fict做，造+ion表名词→造出的（故事）→小说』

❶ [U] 小说

Immigrant tales have always been popular themes in fiction.
移民故事一直是小说中常见的主题。

❷ [C, U] 虚构的事；假想之物

The idea that the United States could harmoniously accommodate all was a fiction.
认为美国可以和谐地接纳所有人的想法是一个幻想。
Fiction and reality were increasingly blurred.
虚构和现实越来越难以区分了。

▶**fictitious** [fɪk'tɪʃəs] adj. 虚构的；虚假的
『fict做，造+itious有…性质的→造出来的→虚构的』

All the places and characters in my novel are fictitious.
我小说中的人物和地点纯属虚构。

2. figment ['fɪgmənt] n. 虚构的事物
『fig做，造+ment动作的结构→虚构的事物』

a figment of sb's imagination 凭空想象的事物
The attack wasn't just a figment of my imagination.
袭击可不是我凭空想象出来的。

3. efficient [ɪ'fɪʃnt] adj. 高效率的；高效能的
『ef出来+fici做，制作+ent具有…性质的→具有（快速）做出来性质的→高效的』

If something or someone is efficient, they are able to do tasks

successfully, without wasting time or energy.

An efficient transport system is critical to the long-term future of London.
高效的公共交通系统对伦敦的长远未来至关重要。
An efficient bulb may lighten the load of power stations.
一个节能灯泡也许就能减轻发电站的负荷。

近义词 **effective** [ɪ'fektɪv] adj. 有效的；生效的 <P163>
『effect效果+ive有…性质的→有效的；生效的』

▶**efficiency** [ɪ'fɪʃnsi] n. 效率；效能；功率

I was impressed by the efficiency with which she handled the crisis. 她应对危机效率之高给我留下了深刻的印象。
Defrost the fridge regularly so that it works at maximum efficiency. 定期给冰箱除霜，以使其发挥最高效率。

4. suffice [sə'faɪs] v. 充足，足够
『suf下+fice做→在下面（提前）做好→足够』

If you say that something will suffice, you mean it will be enough to achieve a purpose or to fulfil a need.

A cover letter should never exceed one page; often a far shorter letter will suffice.
附信不应超过一页，通常来说，一封相对非常简短的信就足够了。

suffice (it) to say (that)... 无须多说；只需说…就够了

Suffice it to say that afterwards we never met again.
简单地说，此后我们再也没有见过面。

▶**sufficient** [sə'fɪʃnt] adj. 足够的；充足的
『suffice满足（去e）+ient…的→足够的』

~ (to do sth) | ~ (for sth/sb) 足够的；充足的
These reasons are not sufficient to justify the ban.
这些理由不足以证明实施禁令有理。
Lighting levels should be sufficient for photography without flash.
光照亮度应达到不开闪光灯便可以清楚拍照的程度。

▶**sufficiency** [sə'fɪʃnsi] n. 足量；充足

5. deficient [dɪ'fɪʃnt] adj. 缺乏的；有缺点的
『de去掉+fici做+ent具有…性质的→（被）做去掉（一些）→不足；不够好』

❶ 缺乏的，缺少的，不足的

not having enough of sth, especially sth that is essential
The crops are suffering from deficient rain.
庄稼因雨量不足而遭受损害。
Blood tests can indicate if you're deficient in a number of key nutrients.
血液测试可以检测你是否在多个主要的营养方面摄取不足。

❷ 有缺点的；有缺陷的；不够好的

Someone or something that is deficient is not good enough for a particular purpose.
His theory is deficient in several respects.
他的理论在几个方面有缺陷。

▶**deficiency** [dɪ'fɪʃnsi] n. 缺乏，缺少；缺陷，不足

Vitamin deficiency in the diet can cause illness.
饮食中缺乏维生素可能导致疾病。

小贴士 AIDS stands for Acquired Immune Deficiency Syndrome. AIDS是获得性免疫缺损综合征的缩写。

6. proficient [prə'fɪʃnt] adj. 精通的；熟练的

『pro向前+ fici做+ent具有…性质的→向前（继续）做→做得多了就）熟练→熟练的』

~ (in/at sth) | ~ (in/at doing sth) 熟练的；娴熟的；精通的；训练有素的

able to do sth well because of training and practice

She's proficient in several languages. 她精通好几种语言。

▶ **proficiency** [prəˈfɪʃnsi] n. 熟练；精通

Evidence of basic proficiency in English is part of the admission requirement. 英语基本熟练是入学条件之一。

7. sacrifice [ˈsækrɪfaɪs] v. 牺牲 n. 牺牲；祭献

『sacri神圣+ fice做，制作→（甘愿）做神圣的事→牺牲』

❶ [VN] ~ sth (for sb/sth) 牺牲；献出

to give up sth that is important or valuable to you in order to get or do sth that seems more important for yourself or for another person

She sacrificed everything for her children.

她为子女牺牲了一切。

The designers have sacrificed speed for fuel economy.

设计者为节省燃料牺牲了速度。

❷ [VN , V] 以（人或动物）作祭献

to kill an animal or a person and offer it or them to a god, in order to please the god

The priest sacrificed a chicken. 祭司用一只鸡作祭品。

❸ [C, U] 牺牲，舍弃；祭献，祭祀

Her parents made sacrifices so that she could have a good education.

为了让她受良好的教育，她的父母作了很多牺牲。

They offered sacrifices to the gods. 他们向众神献上祭品。

8. beneficiary [ˌbenɪˈfɪʃəri] n. 受益人

『bene善，好+ fici(=fic)做+ary人→得到（做的）好处的人→受益者』

Please fill the name and address of the beneficiary.

请填上受益人的姓名和地址。

9. beneficent [bɪˈnefɪsnt] adj. 行善的；有益的

『bene善，好+fic做+ent…的→做好事的，有好处的→行善的；有益的』

A beneficent person or thing helps people or results in something good.

The demon as long as have a beneficent heart isn't a demon any more, but freak.

恶魔只要具有仁慈的心就不再是恶魔了，而是怪物。

It is a devastating or a beneficent force, just as we choose to make it.

它具有强大的破坏力或者造福力，只是取决于我们怎么去选择。

10. artificial [ˌɑːtɪˈfɪʃl] adj. 人工的，人造的 〈P116〉

『arti技术+fic做+ial…的→人工做出来的→人造的』

词根92. fall, false, fault= err，表示"错误"

1. fallacy [ˈfæləsi] n. 谬论；谬误推理

『fall错误+acy表名词→谬论』

A fallacy is an idea which many people believe to be true, but which is in fact false because it is based on incorrect information or reasoning.

It's a fallacy that the affluent give relatively more to charity than the less prosperous.

富人对慈善事业的捐助相对多于穷人，这是一种谬论。

▶ **fallacious** [fəˈleɪʃəs] adj. 谬误的

『fall错误+acious充满的→错误的』

If an idea, argument, or reason is fallacious, it is wrong because it is based on a fallacy.

Their main argument is fallacious. 他们的主要论点是错的。

2. fallible [ˈfæləbl] adj. 会犯错误的

『fall错误+ible能够的→会犯错的』

All human beings are fallible. 人人都难免犯错误。

▶ **infallible** [ɪnˈfæləbl] adj. 一贯正确的；绝对可靠的

『in不+fallible会犯错的→不会犯错的→一贯正确的』

Doctors are not infallible. 医生并非永不犯错。

an infallible method of memorizing things

一种绝对正确的记忆方法

3. false [fɔːls] adj. 错误的，不正确的

A whale is a fish. True or false? 鲸鱼是鱼。对还是错？

▶ **falsify** [ˈfɔːlsɪfaɪ] v. 篡改；伪造（文字记录、信息）

『false错误的（变e为i）+fy使→使…错误→篡改；伪造』

The charges against him include fraud, bribery, and falsifying business records.

对他的指控包括诈骗、行贿和伪造商业记录。

4. fault [fɔːlt] n. 过错；缺点；毛病，错误

It was his fault that we were late. 我们迟到责任在他。

He's proud of his children and blind to their faults.

他为孩子们感到自豪，对他们的缺点视而不见。

The book's virtues far outweigh its faults.

这本书优点远远大于缺点。

a major fault in the design 设计中的一个重大缺陷

She is generous **to a fault**. 她过分慷慨。

He could never accept that he had been **at fault**.

他怎么也无法承认是他的错。

I was disappointed whenever the cook **found fault with** my work. 每当厨师挑剔我干的活儿时，我都非常沮丧。

▶ **faulty** [ˈfɔːlti] adj. 不完美的；（设备）出故障的

Ask for a refund if the goods are faulty.

商品如有缺陷，可要求退款。

The money will be used to repair faulty equipment.

这笔钱将用来修理出故障的设备。

5. default [dɪˈfɔːlt] n. 违约；默认

『de离开+fault错误→因为离开（缺席）所形成的错误→违约；默认』

❶ [U, C] 违约（尤指未偿付债务）

failure to do sth that must be done by law, especially paying a debt.

The company is in default on the loan. 这家公司拖欠借款。

Mortgage defaults have risen in the last year.

按揭借款违约在近一年里呈上升趋势。

❷ [U, C, usually sing.] （计）默认；预置值

what happens or appears if you do not make any other choice or change

The default option is to save your work every five minutes.

默认设置为每五分钟存盘一次。

On this screen, 256 colours is the default.

这个显示屏的系统设定值是256色。

❸ by default 自动地（因可能阻止或改变结果之事未发生）

I would rather pay the individuals than let the money go to the State by default.

我宁愿把这些钱付给个人，也不愿它们因未作任何处置而自动地归国家所有。

Nagios offers pager and e-mail notifications by default.

在缺省情况下，网络监控提供了寻呼机和电子邮件通知方式。

词根93. feas=make, do, 表示"做，制作"

1. feasible [ˈfiːzəbl] adj. 可行的；可能的

『feas做，制作+ible可…的→能做的→可行的』

that is possible and likely to be achieved

It's just not feasible to manage the business on a part-time basis. 兼职管理业务是搞不好的。

词根94. femin=woman, 表示"女人"

1. feminist [ˈfemənɪst] n. 女权运动者

『femin女人+ist…者→女权运动者』

2. feminism [ˈfemənɪzəm] n. 女权主义；女权运动

『femin 女人 + ism …主义 → 争取女性权力 → 女权主义』

Feminism is simply another device to ensnare women.

女权主义只是使女性陷入圈套的另一种手段。

3. feminine [ˈfemənɪn] adj. 女人的；（词）阴性的

『femin女人+ine如…的→女人的』

❶ 女性的，女人的，女人味的

Feminine qualities and things relate to or are considered typical of women, in contrast to men.

That dress makes you look very feminine.

那件衣服你穿起来很有丽人风韵。

I've always been attracted to very feminine, delicate women.

我总是被十分娇柔纤弱的女子吸引。

❷ 阴性的

4. effeminate [ɪˈfemɪnət] adj. （男子）娘娘腔的，女人气的

『ef出，外+femin女人+ate有…性质的→（男子）表现出女人性质的→女人气的』

His voice was curiously high-pitched, reedy, almost effeminate. 他的嗓音出奇地高亢，刺耳，有些娘娘腔。

词根95. fend=strike，表示"打击"，名词形式为-fense, 形容词形式为-fensive

1. defend [dɪˈfend] vt. 防御；辩解；辩护

『de向下+fend打击→（站在城墙上）向下打击（敌人）→防御』

❶ ~ (sb/yourself/sth) (from/against sb/sth) 防御；保护；保卫

to protect sb/sth from attack

[VN] All our officers are trained to defend themselves against knife attacks.

我们所有的警察都接受过自卫训练，能够对付持刀袭击。

Troops have been sent to defend the borders.

已派出部队去守卫边疆。

❷ [VN] ~ sb/yourself/sth (from/against sb/sth) 辩解；辩白

to say or write sth in support of sb/sth that has been criticized

Politicians are skilled at defending themselves against their critics. 从政者都善于为自己辩解，反驳别人的批评。

❸ （为…）辩护；当辩护律师

to act as a lawyer for sb who has been charged with a crime

[VN] He has employed one of the UK's top lawyers to defend him. 他请了英国一位顶尖律师为他辩护。

▶**defence** [dɪˈfens] n. 防御；保护

（NAmE defense）

国防部 (BrE) the Ministry of Defence

(NAmE) the Department of Defense

国防部长 defense minister

▶**defensive** [dɪˈfensɪv] adj. 防御的；保护的

Troops took up a defensive position around the town.

部队在全城采取了守势。

Don't ask him about his plans—he just gets defensive.

别问他有什么计划——他老存有戒心。

on/onto the defensive 采取守势

Warnings of an enemy attack forced the troops onto the defensive.

敌军显示出进攻的迹象，部队不得不进入戒备状态。

▶**defendant** [dɪˈfendənt] n. 被告

『defend防御；辩解+ant表人→（为自己）辩解的人→被告』

反义词 **plaintiff** [ˈpleɪntɪf] n. 原告

2. offend [əˈfend] v. 得罪；冒犯

『of(=against)+fend 打击→打击（别人）→冒犯；得罪』

❶ 得罪，冒犯；令人不适

[VN] They'll be offended if you don't go to their wedding.

你若不参加他们的婚礼，他们会生气的。

[V] A TV interviewer must be careful not to offend.

电视采访者必须小心别得罪人。

[VN] The smell from the farm offended some people.

农场散发的气味让一些人闻了不舒服。

❷ [V] (formal) 犯罪

He started offending at the age of 16. 他16岁就开始犯法。

▶**offense** [əˈfens] n. 冒犯；违法行为

（NAmE offence）

❶ [U] 冒犯

I'm sure he meant no offense when he said that.

我相信他那么说并无冒犯的意思。

❷ [C] ~ (against sb/sth) 违法行为

He was not aware that he had committed an offense.

他没有意识到自己犯罪了。

▶**offensive** [əˈfensɪv] adj. 冒犯的；进攻性的 n. 进攻；攻势

❶ adj. ~ (to sb) 冒犯的，得罪人的；令人不适的

His comments were deeply offensive to a large number of single mothers. 他的评论严重触怒了众多的单身母亲。

an offensive smell 刺鼻的气味

❷ adj. [only before noun] 攻击性的；进攻性的

He was charged with carrying an offensive weapon.

他被指控携带攻击性武器。

❸ n. 进攻；攻势

a series of actions aimed at achieving something in a way that attracts a lot of attention

The government has launched a new offensive against crime.

政府发动了新的打击犯罪攻势。

❹ **on the offensive/ go on/to the offisive**
发动攻势；主动出击
The West African forces went on the offensive in response to attacks on them. 西非部队对袭击者展开全力还击。

3. fend [fend] v. 照料；挡开，避开
『fend打击→（为了自己）打击（攻击难题）→挡开』

❶ **fend for yourself** 照料自己
to take care of yourself without help from anyone else
His parents agreed to pay the rent for his apartment but otherwise left him to fend for himself.
他的父母同意替他付房租，其他的则让他自己解决。

❷ **fend sth/sb off** 挡开，避开（攻击）；回避（难题、批评等）
The police officer fended off the blows with his riot shield.
警察用防暴盾牌抵挡攻击。
She managed to fend off questions about new tax increases.
她设法避开了关于新增赋税的问题。

词根96. fer=bring, carry，表示"带来，拿来"

1. refer [rɪˈfɜː(r)] vt. 参考；参看；提及；指引
『re回；再+fer带来→回到（原出处）；再到（另一个地方）→查阅，参看；推荐，指引』
（注意：referred; referred; referring）

❶ **refer to sb/sth** 提到，谈及，说起
Her mother never referred to him again.
她的母亲再也没有提起过他。
I promised not to refer to the matter again.
我答应过再也不提这事了。

❷ **refer to sb or sth as** 称…为…
She always referred to Ben as "that nice man".
她总是称本为"那个大好人"。

❸ **(sth) refer to sb/sth** 描述；关系到
The star refers to items which are intended for the advanced learner. 标有星号的项目是给高阶学习者的。
The term "Arts" usually refers to humanities and social sciences. "Arts"一词通常指人文和社会科学。

❹ **refer to (a book, a dictionary)** 查阅、参考（书、字典等）
You may refer to your notes if you want.
如果需要，你可以查阅笔记。

❺ **refer sb to sb/sth** 将…送交给（以求获得帮助等）
to send someone to another person or place in order to get help, information, or advice
He could refer the matter to the high court.
他可以将此事交由高等法院裁决。
Now and then I referred a client to him.
我不时地介绍客户给他。
Mr Bryan also referred me to a book by the American journalist Anthony.
布赖恩先生还建议我参考美国记者安东尼的一本书。
The doctor referred me to a skin specialist.
医生让我去看皮肤专家。

▶**reference** [ˈrefrəns] n. 提到；参考；推荐信

❶ [C, U] ~ (to sb/sth) 说到（或写到）的事；提到
The book is full of references to growing up in India.
这本书谈到许多在印度怎样长大成人的事。
She made no reference to her illness but only to her future plans. 她没有提到她的病，只说了她未来的计划。

❷ [U] 参考；查询
I wrote down the name of the hotel for future reference (= because it might be useful in the future) .
我记下了这家酒店的名字，以后也许用得着。

❸ [C] 推荐人，介绍人（美语）；推荐信，介绍信
We will take up references after the interview.
我们在面试之后收推荐信。
My previous boss will act as a reference for me.
我的前任上司将做我的推荐人。

❹ **reference book** 参考书

▶**referee** [ˌrefəˈriː] n. 裁判员；推荐人
『refer参看+ ee被…的人→被参看的人→裁判；推荐人』

❶ [C] （某些体育比赛的）裁判，裁判员
He was sent off for arguing with the referee.
他因为和裁判发生争执而被罚出场。

❷ （求职等时的）推荐人(BrE)（美语中用reference）
Applicants should also send the names and addresses of two referees. 申请人还应提交两名裁判员的姓名和地址。

2. differ [ˈdɪfə(r)] vi. 不同；意见不同
『dif分开+fer带来，拿来→带向不同（的方向）→不同』

❶ A and B ~ (from each other) | A ~s from B
French differs from English in this respect.
在这方面法语不同于英语。
French and English differ in this respect.
在这方面法语和英语不同。

❷ ~ (with sb) (about/on/over sth) 意见不同
I have to differ with you on that.
在那点上我不能同意你的看法。

▶**difference** [ˈdɪfrəns] n. 差别；不同

▶**different** [ˈdɪfrənt] adj. 差别的；不同的

3. confer [kənˈfɜː(r)] v. 协商；授予
『con一起+fer带来，拿来→来到一起（协商）→协商；授予』
（注意：conferred; conferred; conferring）

❶ [V] ~ (with sb) (on/about sth) 商讨；协商；交换意见
to discuss sth with sb, in order to exchange opinions or get advice
He wanted to confer with his colleagues before reaching a decision. 他想与他的同事先商议一下再作出决定。

❷ [VN] ~ sth (on/upon sb)
授予（奖项、学位、荣誉或权利）
to give sb an award, a university degree or a particular honour or right
An honorary degree was conferred on him by Oxford University in 2001. 牛津大学于 2001 年授予他荣誉学位。

▶**conference** [ˈkɒnfərəns] n. 专题讨论会；正式商讨会
『confer协商+ence表行为→讨论会』

❶ （常持续数天的）专题讨论会，研讨会
She is attending a three-day conference on AIDS education.
她正在出席一个为期三天的有关艾滋病教育的会议。
The hotel is used for exhibitions, conferences and social events. 这家饭店用于举行展览、大型会议和社交活动。

❷ （正式）讨论会，商讨会
He had been in Beijing, attending the annual meeting of the Chinese People's Political Consultative Conference.

他曾在北京参加一年一度的中国人民政治协商会议（CPPCC）。

小贴士

press conference 新闻发布会

CPPCC: Chinese People's Political Consultative Conference 中国人民政治协商会议

4. infer [ɪnˈfɜː(r)] v. 推理，推断

『in里面+fer带来，拿来→从里面带出来→推理』

（注意：inferred; inferred; inferring）

~ sth (from sth) 推断；推论；推理

[VN] Much of the meaning must be inferred from the context. 大部分含义必须从上下文中推断。

[V that] It is reasonable to infer that the government knew about these deals. 有理由推想政府知悉这些交易。

▶**inference** [ˈɪnfərəns] n. 推理；推论

The clear inference is that the universe is expanding. 显然结论是宇宙在扩大。

It had an extremely tiny head and, by inference, a tiny brain. 它的头极小，由此推断其脑容量也非常小。

5. prefer [prɪˈfɜː(r)] vt. 更喜欢

『pre预先+fer带来，拿来→（在认真比较之前已经在心中把某一个）预先拿过来→更喜欢』

（注意：preferred; preferred; preferring）

❶ prefer A to B 与B相比，更喜欢A

I prefer coffee to tea. 与茶相比，我更喜欢咖啡。

I prefer going to the cinema to watching TV. 我更喜欢看电影而不是看电视。

❷ prefer to do sth 更愿做某事

The donor prefers to remain anonymous. 捐赠者希望不披露姓名。

I prefer not to think about it. 我不想考虑此事。

❸ prefer that （prefer后跟的宾语从句常用虚拟语气）

I would prefer that you did not mention my name. 我希望你不要说出我的名字。

▶**preference** [ˈprefrəns] n. 偏爱；偏爱的事物

It's a matter of personal preference. 那是个人的爱好问题。

The Pentagon will give preference to companies which do business electronically.

美国国防部将会优先考虑那些能够进行电子商务的公司。

I must say I have a strong preference for French movies. 我得说我对法国电影有强烈的偏爱。

6. defer [dɪˈfɜː(r)] v. 推迟；听从

『de向下+fer带来，拿来→往后带→延期； de向下+fer带来，拿来→（把自己）放到（别人的）下面→听从』

（注意：deferred; deferred; deferring）

❶ 推迟，拖延

If you defer an event or action, you arrange for it to happen at a later date, rather than immediately or at the previously planned time.

[VN] The department deferred the decision for six months. 这个部门推迟了六个月才作决定。

She had applied for deferred admission to college. 她已申请延期入学。

❷ 遵从，听从，顺从

If you defer to someone, you accept their opinion or do what they want you to do, even when you do not agree with it yourself, because you respect them or their authority.

Doctors are encouraged to defer to experts. 鼓励医生听从专家的意见。

词义辨析 <P365第22>

推迟，延期 delay, postpone, put off, defer, adjourn

7. ferry [ˈferi] n. 渡船 v. 摆渡

『fer带来+ry场地，地点→（把人从河一边）带到（另一边的）场所→渡船』

❶ 渡船

The ferry did not even have time to send out an SOS. 渡船甚至连发出紧急呼救信号的时间都没有。

They had recrossed the River Gambia by ferry. 他们乘渡船再次穿过冈比亚河。

❷ 摆渡

He offered to ferry us across the river in his boat. 他提出坐他的船把我们渡过河。

Every day, a plane arrives to ferry guests to and from Bird Island Lodge. 每天，都有一架飞机来鸟岛旅馆接送客人。

8. transfer [trænsˈfɜː(r)], ˈtrænsfɜː(r)] n. & v. 转移；调动

『trans 从…到…+fer (=carry) 运输→从一个地方到另一个地方→转移；调动』

（注意：v. [trænsˈfɜː(r)] n. [ˈtrænsfɜː]; transferred, transferred, transferring）

❶ ~ (sth/sb) (from…) (to…) （使）转移；（使）调动；转学；传染（疾病）；（运动员）转会；（旅途中的）中转

[V] The film studio is transferring to Hollywood. 这家电影制片厂正迁往好莱坞。

[VN] How can I transfer money from my bank account to his? 怎样才能把我账户上的钱转到他的账户上呢？

The patient was transferred to another hospital. 患者转送到了另一家医院。

[V] Children usually transfer to secondary school at 11 or 12. 儿童通常在11或12岁时升读中学。

This disease is rarely transferred from mother to baby. 这种疾病很少由母亲传给婴儿。

I was transferred to the book department. 我被调到图书部。

Passengers are transferred from the airport to the hotel by taxi. 旅客自机场改乘出租车到旅馆。

You can transfer data to a disk in a few seconds. 你可以在几秒钟内将数据转存到磁盘上。

❷ [U, C] 搬迁；转移；调动；变换

He has asked for a transfer to the company's Paris branch. 他要求调到公司的巴黎分部。

9. suffer v. 受苦；经受

『suf下+fer带来，拿来→带到下面（地狱）→受苦』

❶ [V] ~ (from sth) | ~ (for sth) （因疾病、痛苦、悲伤等）受苦，受难，受折磨

Many companies are suffering from a shortage of skilled staff.
许多公司苦于缺乏熟练员工。
He was eventually diagnosed as suffering from terminal cancer. 他最终被诊断为晚期癌症。
He made a rash decision and now he is suffering for it.
当初的草率决定现在让他吃苦头了。

❷ [VN] 遭受；蒙受

to experience sth unpleasant, such as injury, defeat or loss
The peace process has suffered a serious blow now.
现在和平进程遭到重创。
The party suffered a humiliating defeat in the general election.
该党在大选中惨败。

❸ [V] 变差；变糟

to become worse
His school work is suffering because of family problems.
由于家庭问题，他的学业日渐退步。

▶**suffering** [ˈsʌfərɪŋ] n. 疼痛；痛苦；折磨；苦难

[U，C] physical or mental pain
Death finally brought an end to her suffering.
死亡终于结束了她的痛苦。
This war has caused widespread human suffering.
这场战争给许许多多的人带来了苦难。
His many novels have portrayed the sufferings of his race.
他在很多小说中描述了他的种族所遭受的种种苦难。

10. fertile [ˈfɜːtaɪl] adj. 肥沃的；能生育的
『fert(=fer)拿+ile易于…的→（土地）易于带来（收获）的→肥沃的』

This leaves fertile soil unprotected and prone to erosion.
这会让肥沃的土壤暴露在外，使其容易受到侵蚀。
The treatment has been tested on healthy fertile women under the age of 35.
这个疗法已就35岁以下能生育的健康妇女进行了试验。

▶**fertilize** [ˈfɜːtəlaɪz] vt. 使受精；施肥于

Flowers are often fertilized by bees as they gather nectar.
花常在蜜蜂采蜜时受粉。
a fertilized egg 受精卵

▶**fertilizer** [ˈfɜːtəlaɪzə] n. 肥料

[C, U] 肥料
artificial/chemical fertilizers 人工/化学肥料

11. referendum [ˌrefəˈrendəm] n. 公民投票，全民公决
『refer参看+endum→参看（人民的意见）→全民公决』

A referendum showed beyond doubt that voters wanted independence. 全民公决无疑显示选民支持独立。

词根97. fest=feast，表示"节日"

1. festival [ˈfestɪvl] n. （音乐、电影等）节；节日
『fest节日+ival→节日』

2. festive [ˈfestɪv] adj. 充满节日气氛的；节日的
『fest节日+ive具有…性质的→节日的』

The town has a festive holiday atmosphere.
镇子上充盈着一种节日的喜庆气氛。
The factory was due to shut for the festive period.
节日期间工厂将关门。

▶**festivity** [feˈstɪvəti] n. 庆祝活动；欢庆，欢乐

The festivities included a huge display of fireworks.

庆祝活动包括盛大的焰火表演。
The wedding was an occasion of great festivity.
这个婚礼是喜庆盛事。

3. feast [fiːst] n. 盛宴；宗教的节日 v. 吃

❶ [C] 盛宴；宗教的节日
a wedding feast 婚筵
The Jewish feast of Passover began last night.
犹太人的宗教节日逾越节昨晚开始了。
the feast of Christmas 圣诞佳节

❷ [usually sing.] 大量使人欢快的事物（或活动）
The evening was a real feast for music lovers.
这个晚会真是让音乐爱好者大饱耳福。
This new series promises a feast of special effects and set designs. 这部新的系列剧将会是一场特效和舞美的盛宴。

❸ [V] ~ (on sth) 尽情地吃
They feasted well into the afternoon on mutton and corn stew.
他们吃玉米炖羊肉一直吃到下午。

❹ **feast your eyes (on sb/sth)** 尽情欣赏；大饱眼福
She stood feasting her eyes on the view.
她驻足凝神欣赏这片景色。

形近词 **fist** [fist] n. 拳头

feat [fiːt] n. 功绩，成就

something that is an impressive achievement, because it needs a lot of skill, strength etc. to do
The tunnel is a brilliant feat of engineering.
这条隧道是工程方面的光辉业绩。
That was no mean feat. 那是伟大的成就。
Man's first landing on the moon was a feat of great daring.
人类首次登月是一个勇敢的壮举。
The acrobat's feat took the audience's breath away.
杂技演员的惊险动作使观众为之咋舌。

词根98. fest=hostile，表示"仇恨的"

1. infest [ɪnˈfest] vt. 大量滋生；大批出没于
『in里面+fest仇恨的→里面许多令人仇恨的（物或人）→大量滋生；大批出没于』

❶ [VN] （昆虫、老鼠等）大量滋生
The kitchen was infested with ants. 厨房里到处是蚂蚁。

❷ [VN] （不喜欢或危险的人或物）大批出没于；遍布
Crime and drugs are infesting the inner cities.
市中心充斥着犯罪与毒品。

2. manifest [ˈmænɪfest] vt. 显露 adj. 显而易见的
『mani手+ fest仇恨→（因为）仇恨想（动手）打 →（情感）显而易见的；显露』

❶ [VN] 显示，显露
If you manifest a particular quality, feeling or illness, or if it manifests itself, it becomes visible or obvious.
He manifested a pleasing personality on stage.
在台上他表现出惹人喜爱的个性。
The symptoms of the disease manifested themselves ten days later. 十天后，这种病的症状显现出来。

❷ adj. 明显的，显而易见的
If you say that something is manifest, you mean that it is clearly true and that nobody would disagree with it if they saw it or considered it.
His nervousness was manifest to all those present.

所有在场的人都看出了他很紧张。

▶**manifestation** [ˌmænɪfeˈsteɪʃn] n. 显示；显现

New York is the ultimate manifestation of American values.
纽约是美国价值观的终极体现。

▶**manifesto** [ˌmænɪˈfestəʊ] n.（尤指政党或政府的）宣言，声明

『manifest显示，表明+o抽象名词→表明（政党信仰）的东西→宣言，声明』

a written statement in which a group of people, especially a political party, explain their beliefs and say what they will do if they win an election
The Tories are currently drawing up their election manifesto.
保守党人目前正在起草竞选宣言。

3. fester [ˈfestə(r)] vi. 恶化；化脓；（食物）腐烂
『fest仇恨+er反复→不好的东西不断加剧→恶化；腐烂』

❶ [V]（局势、问题或情感）恶化，激化，加剧
Resentments are starting to fester. 仇恨开始日益加深。

❷ [V]（伤口）化脓，溃烂；（食物）腐烂
The wound is festering, and gangrene has set in.
伤口在溃烂，已经生了坏疽。
The chops will fester and go to waste.
猪排会腐烂并给糟蹋掉。

词根99. fid=trust, faith，表示"相信；信念"

1. confident [ˈkɒnfɪdənt] adj. 自信的
『con加强+fid相信+ent具有…性质的→相信自己的→自信的』

I'm confident that you will get the job.
我肯定你能得到那份工作。
The team feels confident of winning.
这个队觉得有把握取胜。

▶**confidence** [ˈkɒnfɪdəns] n. 自信

2. confide [kənˈfaɪd] v.（向某人）吐露（隐私、秘密等）
『con加强+fide相信』

~ (sth) (to sb)
[VN] She confided all her secrets to her best friend.
她向她最要好的朋友倾吐了自己所有的秘密。
[V that] He confided to me that he had applied for another job. 他向我透露他已申请另一份工作。

▶**confidant** [ˈkɒnfɪdænt] n. 可吐露秘密的知己；密友
『confide透露（秘密）+ant表示人→可以向其吐露秘密的人→知己；密友』

I have only one confidant to whom I can tell my secrets.
我只有一个可以吐露秘密的知己。

3. confidential [ˌkɒnfɪˈdenʃl] adj. 机密的；保密的
『confident自信的+ial表形容词→自己才能知道的→机密的』

meant to be kept secret and not told to or shared with other people
She accused them of leaking confidential information about her private life. 她指责他们泄露其私生活的秘密。
"Look," he said in a confidential tone, "I want you to know that me and Joey are cops."
"听着，"他悄声说，"我想让你知道我和乔伊是警察。"

4. diffident [ˈdɪfɪdənt] adj. 缺乏自信的；羞怯的

『dif不+fid相信+ent具有…性质的→不相信（自己能力）的→缺乏自信的』

Someone who is diffident is rather shy and does not enjoy talking about themselves or being noticed by other people.
Helen was diffident and reserved. 海伦比较害羞内向。

5. fidelity [fɪˈdeləti] n. 忠诚，忠贞，忠心；准确，精确
『fid相信+el物+ity表名词→相信（某人某事）→忠贞；忠心（某人某事）』

❶ [U] 忠诚，忠实
I had to promise fidelity to the Queen. 我必须承诺效忠女王。
Kip was beginning to doubt Jessica's fidelity.
基普开始怀疑杰西卡的忠诚（夫妻间的忠诚）。

❷ [U] ~ (of sth) (to sth) (formal) 准确性；精确性
when you copy the detail and quality of an original, such as a picture, sound or story exactly （即忠诚于原来的程度）
The best ink-jet printers can reproduce photographs with amazing fidelity.
最好的喷墨打印机能以惊人的逼真度再现照片。

小贴士 Hi-Fi 高保真
Hi-Fi是英语High-Fidelity的缩写，翻译为"高保真"。其定义是：与原来的声音高度相似的重放声音。

6. infidel [ˈɪnfɪdəl] n. 异教徒
『in不+fid相信；信念+el表人→不信（宗教或某一宗教）的人→异教徒』

7. perfidy [ˈpɜːfədi] n. 背叛；背信弃义
『per假+fid相信；信念+y表名词→假装相信→不忠诚』

Perfidy is the action of betraying someone or behaving very badly towards someone.
He was quite certain now that she knew he was married and was angered at his perfidy.
他现在已可以断定，她已经得知他是有妇之夫，对于他的欺瞒行为非常生气。

▶**perfidious** [pəˈfɪdiəs] adj. 背叛的，不忠的

Their feet will trample on the dead bodies of their perfidious aggressors. 他们将从背信弃义的侵略者的尸体上踏过。

词根100. fine=boundary, end，表示"范围；结束"

1. confine [kənˈfaɪn] v. 限制；监禁 n. 范围
『con一起+fine范围→（使）在某个范围内→限制』

❶ ~ sb/sth to sth [often passive] 限制；限定
to keep sb/sth inside the limits of a particular activity, subject, area, etc.
The work will not be confined to the Glasgow area.
此项工作不会局限于格拉斯哥地区。
I will confine myself to looking at the period from 1900 to 1916.
我将把自己考察的范围限定在1900年至1916年这段时间以内。

❷ ~ sb/sth (in sth) [usually passive] 监禁；禁闭
to keep a person or an animal in a small or closed space
Keep the dog confined in a suitable travelling cage.

把狗关进适于旅行的笼子里。

❸ be confined to bed, a wheelchair, etc.
使离不开（或受困于床、轮椅等）
to have to stay in bed, in a wheelchair , etc.
She was confined to bed with the flu.
她因患流感卧病在床。
He was confined to a wheelchair after the accident.
经过那场事故后他就离不开轮椅了。

❹ confines [pl.] 范围；局限
The movie is set entirely within the confines of the abandoned factory.
电影的拍摄完全是在这个废弃的工厂厂区内进行的。
We must operate within the confines of the law.
我们必须在法律规定的范围内行事。

词义辨析 <P376第78> 限制 limit, confine, restrict

2. define [dɪˈfaɪn] vt.下定义；明确，界定
『de加强+fine范围→确定（单词词义；某事物）范围；→下定义；明确，界定』

❶ [VN] ~ sth (as sth)
解释（词语）的含义；给（词语）下定义
to say or explain what the meaning of a word or phrase is
The term "mental illness" is difficult to define.
"精神病"这个词很难下定义。

❷ 阐明；明确；界定
to describe or show sth accurately
[VN] We need to define the task ahead very clearly.
我们需要明确今后的任务。
[V wh-] It is difficult to define what makes him so popular.
很难解释清楚什么原因使他如此走红。

❸ [VN] 描出…的外形
to show clearly a line, shape or edge
The mountain was sharply defined against the sky.
那座山在天空的衬托下显得轮廓分明。

▶**definition** [ˌdefɪˈnɪʃn] n. 解释；定义；清晰度

❶ [C, U] 解释；定义；界定
To give a definition of a word is more difficult than to give an illustration of its use.
给一个词下定义要比举例说明它的用法困难得多。
The speakers criticised his new programme for lack of definition. 几位发言者批评他的新方案不够清楚明确。

❷ [U] 清晰度
（definition定义，界定→对图像的每一个细节界定都非常清楚，清晰度就高）
The definition of the digital TV pictures is excellent.
数字电视图像的清晰度很高。

小贴士 HD是英文"High Definition"的缩写形式，意思

是"高分辨率"， 通常把物理分辨率达到720p以上的格式称为高清。所谓全高清（Full HD），是指物理分辨率高达1920×1080的逐行扫描，即1080p高清。
UHD是Ultra High Definition的简写，意思是"超高清"。国际电信联盟(ITU)发布的"超高清UHD"标准的建议，将屏幕的物理分辨率达到3840×2160(4K×2K)及以上的显示称之为超高清，是普通Full HD（1920×1080）宽、高的各两倍，面积的四倍。

▶**definite** [ˈdefɪnət] adj. 明确的，清楚的；肯定的；清晰的
『define确定（去e）+ite表形容词→明确的，清楚的』

❶ 明确的，清楚的
Can you give me a definite answer by tomorrow?
你最晚明天能给我一个确定的答复吗？
They have very definite ideas on how to bring up children.
关于如何培养孩子，他们有非常明确的想法。
The look on her face was a definite sign that something was wrong. 一看她的神色就知道出事了。

❷ [not before noun] ~ (about sth) | ~ (that…)
(of a person 人) 肯定；有把握
I'm definite about this. 我对这点毫无疑问。

❸ 清晰的；分明的
Studying his face in the bathroom mirror he wished he had more definite features.
看着浴室镜子中的脸，他真希望自己的五官能够更分明一些。

▶**definitely** [ˈdefɪnətli] adv. 确定地；明确地
I definitely remember sending the letter.
我记得这封信肯定发出去了。
"Was it what you expected?" "Yes, definitely."
"那是你所期待的吗？" "当然是。"
The date of the move has not been definitely decided yet .
搬迁日期还未完全确定下来。

▶**indefinitely** [ɪnˈdefɪnətli] adv. 无限期地
『in不+definitely明确地，清楚地→不明确地→无限期地』
If a situation will continue indefinitely, it will continue for ever or until someone decides to change it or end it.
The visit has now been postponed indefinitely.
访问如今被无限期推迟。

▶**definitive** [dɪˈfɪnətɪv] adj. 明确的，最终的；最具权威的
『define明确，界定（变e为i）+tive具有…性质的→明确的；权威的』
No one has come up with a definitive answer as to why this should be so.
对于为什么应该是这样，还没有人想出最终确定的答案。
The definitive version of the text is ready to be published.
正式的文本很快就要发表了。
His *An Orkney Tapestry* is still the definitive book on the islands.
他的《奥克尼挂毯》一书仍是关于这些岛屿的最权威著作。

3. finite [ˈfaɪnaɪt] adj. 有限的；（语法）限定的
『fine范围（去e）+ite有…性质的→有范围的→有限的』
The world's resources are finite. 世界的资源是有限的。
These are the finite forms of a verb.
这些是一个动词的限定形式。

4. infinite [ˈɪnfɪnət] adj. 极大的，极度的；无限的
『in不+fine范围（去e）+ite有…性质的→没有范围的→无限的』

❶ 极大的，极度的，极多的
very great; impossible to measure
With infinite care, John shifted position.
约翰小心翼翼地挪动了位置。
Obviously, no company has infinite resources.
显然，没有哪个公司的资源是无限的。

❷ 无限的，无穷的
The universe seems infinite. 宇宙似乎是无限的。
The number of positive numbers is infinite.
正数的数量是无穷的。

5. infinitive [ɪnˈfɪnətɪv] n. （动词）不定式
『infinite无限的（去e）+ive表性质→不受人称和时态限制的→（动词）不定式』

6. refine [rɪˈfaɪn] vt. 提炼；改进
『re又+fine范围→又（缩小）范围→提炼；改进』

Oil is refined to remove naturally occurring impurities.
油经过提炼去除天然存在的杂质。
Surgical techniques are constantly being refined.
外科手术的技术不断得到完善。

▶**refinery** [rɪˈfaɪnəri] n. 精炼厂；提炼厂
『refine精炼，提炼+(e)ry表场所→精炼厂，提炼厂』

They have to put up with a giant oil refinery right on their doorstep. 他们不得不忍受就在家门口的巨型炼油厂。

7. affinity [əˈfɪnəti] n. 亲近；类似
『af相当于to+fin范围+ity表名词→属于同一范围的→类似；（因为位于同一范围故熟悉或类似，所以）亲近』

❶ [C, U] 类似；近似
If people or things have an affinity with each other, they are similar in some ways.
The two plots share certain obvious affinities.
这两个情节有某种明显的相似。
There is a close affinity between Italian and Spanish.
意大利语和西班牙语关系密切。

❷ [sing.] 喜好；喜爱
If you have an affinity with someone or something, you feel that you are similar to them or that you know and understand them very well.
Sam was born in the country and had a deep affinity with nature.
萨姆在乡下出生，特别喜爱大自然。
Trump seems to have developed an affinity for Kim as well.
特朗普似乎也对金（正恩）产生了喜爱。

8. final [ˈfaɪnl] adj. 最后的 n. 决赛
『fine结束（去e）+al…的→最后的；最终的』

❶ adj. [only before noun] 最终的；最后的
The referee blew the final whistle.
裁判吹响了终场的哨声。
No one could have predicted the final outcome.
谁也没有预想到最终结果会是这样。

❷ [C] 决赛
She reached the final of the 100m hurdles.
她取得了100米跨栏的决赛权。

小贴士 quarter-final 四分之一决赛 semi-final 半决赛

❸ [C] (NAmE) 期终考试 adj. 期末的
He failed two courses in the final exams.
期末考试他两门课没有通过。

小贴士 期中考试 midterm examination
My parents had a long talk with me after the midterm examination.
期中考试后我父母和我进行了长谈。

9. finish [ˈfɪnɪʃ] v. 完成，结束
『fine结束（去e）+i+sh使→使…结束→结束』

词根101. firm=firm，表示"坚固；坚定"

1. firm [fɜːm] n.商行 adj. 坚固的；坚定的

❶ [C] 商行；公司
a business or company
an engineering firm 工程公司
a firm of accountants 会计师事务所

❷ adj. 坚固的；坚硬的；结实的
fairly hard; not easy to press into a different shape
These peaches are still firm. 这些桃子还很硬。
Bake the cakes until they are firm to the touch.
把糕饼烤到摸来有硬感为止。

❸ adj. 牢固的；稳固的
strongly fixed in place
Stand the fish tank on a firm base.
把鱼缸放在牢固的基座上。
No building can stand without firm foundations, and neither can a marriage.
没有稳固的基础，建筑就不牢靠，婚姻也是如此。

❹ adj. (of sb's voice or hand movements 声音或手势) 强有力的；坚决的
"No," she repeated, her voice firmer this time.
"不，"她重复说，这次她的声音更坚定了。
Her handshake was cool and firm. 她握手镇定而有力。

❺ adj. 坚信的；坚决的
not likely to change
I have a firm belief that we should never shy away from difficult decisions.
我坚信我们不应该回避艰难的决定。

词义辨析 <P369第38>公司 company, corporation, firm

2. affirm [əˈfɜːm] vt. 肯定，确认；证实
『af相当于to+ firm坚定→使…达到坚定状态→肯定』

to state firmly or publicly that sth is true or that you support sth strongly
[V that] I can affirm that no one will lose their job.
我可以肯定，谁都不会丢掉工作。
[VN] Both sides affirmed their commitment to the ceasefire.
双方均申明答应停火。
Everything I had accomplished seemed to affirm that opinion.
我所取得的一切似乎都证明那个观点是对的。

反义词 **deny** [dɪˈnaɪ] vt. 否认；拒绝给予 <P51>

▶**affirmation** [ˌæfɜːˈmeɪʃ(ə)n] n. 肯定，确认；证实

▶**affirmative** [əˈfɜːmətɪv] adj. 肯定的

Haig was desperately eager for an affirmative answer.
黑格非常渴望得到一个肯定的回答。

反义词 **negative** [ˈnegətɪv] adj. 否定的 <P232>

3. confirm [kənˈfɜːm] v. 证实；确认

『con一起+firm坚定→一起坚定确认（某事）→证实；确认』

❶ （证据）证实，证明（情况属实）

New evidence has confirmed the first witness's story.

新的证据证实了第一个证人的说法。

To confirm my diagnosis I need to do some tests.

为了确认我的诊断，我需要做一些检查。

❷ （某人）证实，肯定，确认（某事）

Managers have so far refused to confirm or deny reports that up to 200 jobs are to go.

迄今为止，经理们拒绝证实或否认有多达200个工作岗位将被取消的报道。

❸ （正式）确认（预订、日期、安排等）

I am writing to confirm a booking for a single room for the night of 6 June.

我写信是为了确认6月6日晚上一间单人房的预订。

❹ 使确信（某种感觉）

The walk in the mountains confirmed his fear of heights.

在山里步行使他更加确信自己有恐高症。

▶**confirmation** [ˌkɒnfəˈmeɪʃn] n. 证实；确认

4. infirm [ɪnˈfɜːm] adj. 年老体弱的

『in不+firm坚固→（身体）不坚固的→病弱的』

A person who is infirm is weak or ill, and usually old.

I plan to settle there when I'm elderly and infirm.

我老了以后就到那里定居。

We are here to protect and assist the weak and infirm.

我们来这里保护、帮助年迈体弱者。

▶**infirmity** [ɪnˈfɜːməti] n.（长期的）体弱，生病

5. infirmary [ɪnˈfɜːməri] n.（常用于名称）医院；（学校、监狱等的）医务室

『infirm体弱的+ary表地点→体弱的人去的地方→医院』

词根102. fix=fix，表示"固定"

1. fix [fɪks] vt. 固定；修理；惩罚

❶ [VN] (especially BrE) 使固定；安装

to put sth firmly in a place so that it will not move

to fix a shelf to the wall　把搁架固定在墙上

to fix a post in the ground　把柱子固定在地上

❷ [VN] 修理；校正

to repair or correct sth

The car won't start—can you fix it?

这辆车发动不起来了——你能修理一下吗？

I've fixed the problem. 我已解决了这个问题。

❸ [VN] (informal) 惩罚；收拾

to punish sb who has harmed you and stop them doing you any more harm

Don't worry—I'll fix him.

别担忧——我会收拾他的。

2. prefix [ˈpriːfɪks] n. 前缀

『pre (before)之前+fix固定→固定在单词前面以改变其词义→前缀』

3. suffix [ˈsʌfɪks] n. 后缀（加在词尾，用以构成新词，如quickly中的-ly或sadness中的-ness）

『suf下+fix固定→固定在（单词）下面（末尾）→后缀』

词根103. flam, flagr= burn, blaze，表示"燃烧；火焰"

1. flame [fleɪm] n. 火焰；怒火 v. 燃烧；（脸因强烈情绪而）变红

❶ [C, U] 火焰，火舌；（怒）火

The flames were growing higher and higher.

火焰越来越高。

The building was in flames (= was burning) . 大楼失火了。

His writings fanned the flames of racism.

他的写作煽起了种族主义情绪。

a flame-red car　火红色的汽车

❷ [V, VN] 燃烧；（脸因强烈情绪而）变红

[V] The logs flamed on the hearth. 木柴在火炉里燃烧。

[V] Her cheeks flamed with rage. 她愤怒得两颊通红。

2. inflame [ɪnˈfleɪm] vt. 使愤怒；使（局势）恶化

『in(=en)使+flame怒火→使愤怒』

His comments have inflamed teachers all over the country.

他的评论激怒了全国教师。

The situation was further inflamed by the arrival of the security forces.　保安部队的到达使局势更加难以控制。

3. flammable [ˈflæməbl] adj. 易燃的；可燃的

『flame燃烧（去e双写m）+able能够的→易燃的；可燃的』

highly flammable liquids　高度易燃的液体

4. inflammation [ˌɪnfləˈmeɪʃn] n. 发炎；炎症

『in（使）+flame火焰；燃烧；变红（去e双写m）+ation表名词→使（皮肤或组织）变红→发炎；炎症』

[U, C] 发炎；炎症

a condition in which a part of the body becomes red, sore and swollen because of infection or injury

You have inflammation in your throat. 您的喉咙发炎了。

▶**inflammatory** [ɪnˈflæmətri] adj. 煽动性的；发炎的

She described his remarks as irresponsible, inflammatory and outrageous.

她称他的话不负责任、具煽动性且极端无礼。

5. flagrant [ˈfleɪɡrənt] adj. 公然的；罪恶昭彰的

『flagr燃烧+ant…的→（公然）使…燃烧的→公然的』

shocking because it is done in a very obvious way and shows no respect for people, laws, etc.

The judge called the decision "a flagrant violation of international law".

法官称这一决定是"对国际法的公然违背"。

He showed a flagrant disregard for anyone else's feelings.

他公然蔑视任何人的感情。

6. conflagration [ˌkɒnfləˈɡreɪʃn] n. 大火灾；大火

『con一起+flagr燃烧+ation表名词→（许多建筑）一起燃烧→大火灾』

Many people were burnt alive in the conflagration that happened in a multi-storeyed building.

在一幢多层建筑内发生的大火中，许多人被活活烧死。

词根104. flat(e)=blow，表示"吹"

1. inflate [ɪnˈfleɪt] v. 充气；鼓吹；抬高（物价）

『in里面+flate吹→把气吹到里面→充气；鼓吹』

[VN] Inflate your life jacket by pulling sharply on the cord.

猛拽绳扣使你的救生衣充气。

[V] The life jacket failed to inflate. 救生衣未能充气。

[VN] They inflated clients' medical treatment to defraud

insurance companies.
他们夸大客户的治疗情形以欺骗保险公司。
By this we can ruin their credit, and make their currency devaluate and inflate.
这样我们就可以摧毁他们的信用，使他们的货币贬值和通胀。

▶ **inflation** [ɪnˈfleɪʃn] n. 充气；通货膨胀

Wage increases must be in line with inflation.
工资的增长必须与通货膨胀率一致。
Inflation is currently running at 3%.
当前的通货膨胀率为3%。

2. deflate [dɪˈfleɪt] v. 放气；使泄气；通货紧缩
『de去掉+flate吹气→气吹出来→放气；泄气』

All the criticism had left her feeling totally deflated.
所有这些批评使她彻底失去了信心。
The Government decided to deflate. 政府决定紧缩通货。

▶ **deflation** [dɪˈfleɪʃn] n. 放气；泄气；通货紧缩

3. conflate [kənˈfleɪt] v. 合并；合成（描述或主意）
『con一起+flate吹→把气吹到一起→合并；合成』

Her letters conflate past and present.
在她的信中过去和现在融为一体。
Unfortunately the public conflated fiction with reality and made her into a saint.
不幸的是，公众把虚构和现实混为一谈，把她塑造成一个圣人。

▶ **conflation** [kənˈfleɪʃən] n. 合并

The story was a conflation of Greek myths.
这个故事是希腊神话的融合。

词根105. flect, flex=bend，表示"弯曲"

1. reflect [rɪˈflekt] v. 反射；反映；映出（影像）；反思
『re往回+flect弯曲→（光线）向回弯曲→反射』

❶ [VN] [usually passive] ~ sb/sth (in sth) 反映；映出（影像）
His face was reflected in the mirror. 他的脸映照在镜子里。

❷ [VN] 反射（声、光、热等）
When the sun's rays hit the earth, a lot of the heat is reflected back into space.
太阳光线照射到地球时，大量的热被反射回太空。

❸ [VN] 反映，显示，表达
Our newspaper aims to reflect the views of the local community. 我们的报纸旨在反映当地社区的意见。

❹ ~ (on/upon sth) 反思，认真思考
We must seriously reflect on the influence of violence on TV upon children.
我们必须仔细考虑电视中暴力行为对儿童的影响。
The manager demanded time to reflect on what to do.
经理要求给他时间考虑该做什么。

▶ **reflection** [rɪˈflekʃn] n. 影像；反射；反映；深思

Meg stared at her reflection in the bedroom mirror.
梅格注视着卧室中镜子里的自己。
The eyes of a hunting cat flashed green in reflection of the lights. 一只猎猫的眼睛在灯光的反射下闪着绿色的光。
Your clothes are often a reflection of your personality.
穿着常常反映出一个人的个性。
After days of reflection she decided to write back.
想了几天之后她决定回信。

▶ **reflective** [rɪˈflektɪv] adj. 反射的，反光的；反映…的；沉思的

On dark nights children should wear reflective clothing.
在漆黑的夜晚，儿童应该穿可以反光的衣服。
His abilities are not reflective of the team as a whole.
他的能力并不代表整个队的水平。
He gazed reflectively at his companion.
他盯着自己的同伴，若有所思。

2. deflect [dɪˈflekt] v. 使偏斜；转移；阻止
『de向下+flect弯曲→向下弯→偏斜』

❶ 使偏斜，使偏转
If you deflect something that is moving, you make it go in a slightly different direction, for example by hitting or blocking it.
[V] The ball deflected off Reid's body into the goal.
球打在里德身上反弹进了球门。
[VN] He raised his arm to try to deflect the blow.
他举起手臂试图挡开这一击。

❷ [VN] 转移；引开
to succeed in preventing sth from being directed towards you
All attempts to deflect attention from his private life have failed.
本想转移人们对他私生活的注意，但一切努力都失败了。
She sought to deflect criticism by blaming her family.
她责怪她的家人，想这样来转移对她的批评。

❸ [VN] ~ sb (from sth) 阻止（某人做已决定做的事）
The government will not be deflected from its commitments.
政府决不会因任何阻碍而放弃承诺。

▶ **deflection** [dɪˈflekʃn] n. 偏斜；偏转

The smallest deflection of the missile could bring disaster.
导弹有极微小的偏斜也可能酿出大祸。

3. flexible [ˈfleksəbl] adj. 易弯曲的；灵活的
『flex弯曲+ible可…的，能…的→易弯曲的；灵活的』

❶ 灵活的；易变通的；适应性强的
Something or someone that is flexible is able to change easily and adapt to different conditions and circumstances as they occur.
You need to be more flexible and imaginative in your approach. 你的方法必须更加灵活，更富有想象力。
Our plans need to be flexible enough to cater for the needs of everyone.
我们的计划必须能够变通，以满足每个人的需要。

❷ 可弯曲的；柔韧的
This flexible racquet offers lots of feel and control.
这款柔韧的网球拍可以提供很好的球感和控制感。

▶ **inflexible** [ɪnˈfleksəbl] adj. 不能弯曲的；死板的

He's completely inflexible on the subject.
他在这个问题上寸步不让。
Workers insisted the new system was too inflexible.
工人们坚持认为新制度太不灵活。

词根106. flict=strike，表示"打击"

1. conflict [ˈkɒnflɪkt] n. & v. 冲突
『con一起+flict打击→（两边）一起打斗→冲突→（从轻到重可以指）矛盾；争执；军事冲突』

❶ [C, U]矛盾，不一致

a situation in which there are opposing ideas, opinions, feelings or wishes; a situation in which it is difficult to choose

Many of these ideas appear to be in conflict with each other.

这些观念中有许多看上去似乎相互矛盾。

❷ [C, U] ~ (between A and B) | ~ (over sth) 冲突，争执，争论

a situation in which people, groups or countries are involved in a serious disagreement or argument

John often comes into conflict with his boss.

约翰经常和他的老板发生争执。

❸ [C, U]（军事）冲突

For years the region has been torn apart by armed conflicts.

多年来，该地区因武装冲突而四分五裂。

❹ [V] ~ (with sth) 冲突

These results conflict with earlier findings.

这些结果与早期的发现相矛盾。

2. afflict [əˈflɪkt] v. 折磨；使痛苦

『af相当于to+ flict打击→打到（…上）→折磨』

[VN] [often passive] (formal) 折磨；使痛苦

to affect sb/sth in an unpleasant or harmful way

About 40% of the country's population is afflicted with the disease. 全国40%左右的人口患有这种疾病。

Aid will be sent to the afflicted areas.

将向受灾地区提供援助。

I wish you would not afflict me with your constant complains.

我希望你不要总是抱怨，真让我心烦。

3. inflict [ɪnˈflɪkt] v. 使遭受打击；使吃苦头

『in使…；加以…+ flict打击→使受打击』

❶ [VN] ~ sth (on/upon sb/sth) 使遭受打击；使吃苦头

to make sb/sth suffer sth unpleasant

They inflicted a humiliating defeat on the home team.

他们使主队吃了一场很没面子的败仗。

They surveyed the damage inflicted by the storm.

他们察看了暴风雨造成的损失。

❷ inflict yourself/sb on sb 不请自来；打扰

to force sb to spend time with you, when they do not want to

Sorry to inflict myself on you again like this!

对不起，又这么打扰你了！

1. florist [ˈflɒrɪst] n. 花商；花店

『flor花+ist某种职业的人→卖花的人→花商』

I've ordered some flowers from the florist's.

我向花店订购了一些花。

2. floral [ˈflɔːrəl] adj. 绘有花的；有花卉图案的

『flor花+al…的→花的』

wallpaper with a floral design/pattern 有花卉图案的墙纸

a floral dress 有花卉图案的连衣裙

a floral arrangement/display 插花/花展

3. florid [ˈflɒrɪd] adj.（人脸）红润的；过分花哨的，过分修饰的

『flor花+id…的→（脸像）花一样（红）的；过分花哨的』

Jacobs was a stout, florid man.

雅各布斯身材结实，脸色红润。

Nobody likes this florid style with little content.

没有人喜欢这种缺乏内容的华丽风格。

4. floriculture [ˈflɔːrɪkʌltʃə] n. 花卉栽培

『flor花+i+cult耕种；培养+ure行为有关→花卉栽培』

5. flourish [ˈflʌrɪʃ] vi. 繁荣，昌盛；茁壮成长；挥舞

『flour花+ish表动词→开花→繁荣；茁壮成长』

❶ [V] 繁荣，昌盛，兴旺

to develop quickly and be successful or common

Few businesses are flourishing in the present economic climate. 在目前的经济气候下，很少有企业兴旺发达。

❷ [V] 茁壮成长；健康幸福

to grow well; to be healthy and happy

These plants flourish in a damp climate.

这些植物在潮湿的气候下长势茂盛。

❸ [VN]（为引起注意）挥舞

to wave sth around in a way that makes people look at it

He flourished the glass to emphasize the point.

他挥动手中的杯子来强调这一点。

1. fluent [ˈfluːənt] adj. 流利的，流畅的

『flu流动+ent表形容词→流动的→流利的』

She's fluent in Polish. 她的波兰语很流利。

He speaks fluent Italian. 他说一口流利的意大利语。

▶ **fluency** [ˈfluːənsi] n. 流利，流畅

『flu流动+ency表名词→流动→流利，流畅』

Fluency in French is required for this job.

这个工作要求法语熟练自如。

2. influence [ˈɪnfluəns] n. & vt. 影响

『in进来+flu流动+ence表行为→流入→影响』

❶ [U, C] ~ (on/upon sb/sth) 影响；作用

the effect that sb/sth has on the way a person thinks or behaves or on the way that sth works or develops

My mother has a great influence on me.

我母亲对我有深远的影响。

School life has a great influence on the formation of a child's character.

学校生活对小孩个性的形成有很大影响。

❷ [U] ~ (over sb/sth) 支配力；控制力；影响力

the power that sb/sth has to make sb/sth behave in a particular way

She could probably exert her influence with the manager and get you a job.

她很有可能对经理施展她的影响力，给你弄份工作。

He committed the crime under the influence of drugs.

他是在吸毒后犯罪的。

❸ [C] ~ (on sb/sth) 有影响的人（或事物）

a person or thing that affects the way a person behaves and thinks

Those friends are a bad influence on her.

那些朋友对她有负面的影响。

His first music teacher was a major influence in his life.

他的第一位音乐老师是他一生中对他影响非常大的人。

❹ [VN] 影响；支配

[VN] His writings have influenced the lives of millions.

他的作品影响了千百万人。

He is trying to improperly influence a witness.
他在试图误导证人。

词义辨析 <P368第33>影响 effect, affect, influence

►**influential** [ˌɪnfluˈenʃl] adj. （人或物）有影响力的
a highly influential book 十分有影响力的书
She is one of the most influential figures in local politics.
她是本地政坛举足轻重的人物。

3. **affluent** [ˈæfluənt] adj. 富裕的
『af相当于to+flu流+ent表形容词→达到富的（流油）→富裕的』
having a lot of money and a good standard of living
affluent Western countries 富裕的西方国家
a very affluent neighbourhood 富人区
affluent 2nd generation 富二代

►**affluence** [ˈæfluəns] n. 富裕，富足
For them, affluence was bought at the price of less freedom in their work environment.
对他们来说，富足是以减少在工作场所的自由为代价才获得的。

4. **confluent** [ˈkɒnfluənt] adj. （河流）汇合的
『con一起+flu流+ent表形容词→（河流）流到一起的→（河流）汇合的』

►**confluence** [ˈkɒnfluəns] n. （河流的）汇合处；（多个事情的）汇集
It wasn't long before we were facing the most dangerous part of the river, the confluence.
很快，我们来到河上最危险的一处，这是两条河交汇的地方。
Like most cases of extreme weather, its severity was due to an unusual confluence of events.
如同大多数极端天气状况一样，其剧烈程度是由于几种气象条件反常地汇集在一起造成的。

5. **effluent** [ˈefluənt] n. （工厂或污水处理厂排出的）废水，污水
『ef出+flu流动+ent表物→流出物』
The effluent from the factory was dumped into the river.
那家工厂的废水被排入河中。

6. **superfluous** [suːˈpɜːfluəs] adj. 过剩的；多余的
『super过多+flu流动+ous…的→过多流出来的→过剩的』
Something that is superfluous is unnecessary or is no longer needed.
She gave him a look that made words superfluous.
她看了他一眼，这已表明一切，无须多言了。
I rid myself of many superfluous belongings and habits that bothered me.
我把很多无用的物品都丢掉了，并且改掉了一些让我烦心的习惯。

7. **influenza** [ˌɪnfluˈenzə] n. （同flu）；流行性感冒
『in进入+ flu流动+ enza病→流行病→流行感冒』
Influenza usually breaks out in winter.
流感通常在冬天发生。

8. **flux** [flʌks] n. 变动，波动
『flu流动+x→（不停地）流动→不断变化』
[U] 不断的变动；不停的变化

continuous movement and change
Our society is in a state of flux. 我们的社会在不断演变。

9. **influx** [ˈɪnflʌks] n.（人、资金或事物的）涌入；流入
『in进入+flu流动+x→流入→涌入』
The country simply cannot absorb this influx of refugees.
这个国家实在不能接纳这么多涌入的难民。

10. **fluctuate** [ˈflʌktʃueɪt] vi. 波动
『flu流动+ctu+ate表动词→（在不同数值间）流动→波动』
[V] ~ (between A and B)
（大小、数量、质量等）波动；（在…之间）起伏不定
During the crisis, oil prices fluctuated between $20 and $40 a barrel. 在危机时期，每桶石油价格在20至40美元之间波动。
My mood seems to fluctuate from day to day.
我的情绪似乎天天在变。

►**fluctuation** [ˌflʌktʃuˈeɪʃn] n. 波动
The calculations do not take into account any fluctuation in the share price. 这些计算没有考虑到股价的波动。

11. **flush** [flʌʃ] v. & n. 脸红；冲
『flu流动+sh使→使流动→冲』
❶ (of a person or their face 人或脸) 发红；脸红
to become red, especially because you are embarrassed, angry or hot
[V] She flushed with anger. 她气得涨红了脸。
[V-ADJ] Sam felt her cheeks flush red.
萨姆感觉她满脸通红。
❷ [V , VN] 冲（抽水马桶）
She flushed the toilet and went back in the bedroom.
她冲完马桶回到卧室。
❸ [VN] 冲洗；冲走
Flush clean water through the pipe. 用净水冲洗管子。
They flushed the drugs down the toilet.
他们从马桶冲走了毒品。
❹ [C, usually sing.] 脸红；[sing.] 冲洗（抽水马桶）
A pink flush spread over his cheeks. 他满脸通红。
Give the toilet a flush. 冲抽水马桶。

词义辨析 <P366第27>脸红 blush, flush

12. **fluid** [ˈfluːɪd] n. 流体 adj. 流畅的；不稳定的
『flu流动+id…的→流体』
❶ [C, U] 液体；流体
The doctor told him to drink plenty of fluids.
医生要他多喝流质。
The cleaning fluid he was using had been very effective.
他用的清洗液很有效。
❷ adj. （动作、线条或设计）流畅优美的，优雅自然的
a loose, fluid style of dancing 灵活流畅的跳舞风格
❸ adj. （of a situation 形势）易变的；不稳定的
The situation is extremely fluid and it can be changing from day to day. 情况极不稳定，每天都有可能变化。

词根109. form= form；shape，表示"形成；形状，形式"

1. **transform** [trænsˈfɔːm] v. 改变；改观
『trans 从…到…+form形式→从一种形式转变到另一种形式→改变』
❶ [VN] ~ sth/sb (from sth) (into sth) 转换；改变；改造
to transform something into something else means to change

or convert it into that thing

They've transformed the old train station into a science museum. 他们把旧火车站改造成了科学博物馆。

The movie transformed her almost overnight from an unknown schoolgirl into a megastar.

这部电影几乎一夜之间把她从一个不知名的女学生变成了一个巨星。

❷ [VN] 改善，改观

to transform something or someone means to change them completely and suddenly so that they are much better or more attractive

Our younger generation are going to transform this country while at the same time being transformed themselves.

我们年轻一代要改变这个国家，同时也被改变。（杨澜演讲）

Rapid economic growth and develement has transformed the lives of people across China and lifted hundreds of millions out of poverty.

经济的快速增长和发展改变了中国人民的生活，使数亿人摆脱了贫困。（英国女王欢迎习主席演讲）

Whether Kong is changing his appearance or transforming his music, he is a pioneer in music today.

无论孔（祥东）是改变他的外表还是改变他的音乐，他都是当今音乐的先驱。（北师大版高中英语教材必修2）

▶**transformation** [ˌtrænsfəˈmeɪʃn] n. 变化，改变

But then we are also so fortunate enough to witness the transformation of the whole country.

但是我们也有幸见证了整个国家的变革。（杨澜演讲）

2. reform [rɪˈfɔːm] n. & vt. 改革
『re再+form形成→重新形成→改革』

❶ [VN] 改革（体制、组织、法律等）

to improve a system, an organization, a law, etc. by making changes to it

The law needs to be reformed. 法律需要进行改革。

He has displayed remarkable courage in his efforts to reform the party. 在政党改革中，他表现出了非凡的勇气。

❷ [U, C] 改革

The novel presents one aspect of the reform in the countryside. 这部小说反映了农村改革的一个侧面。

The government took another step on the road to political reform. 政府在实现政治改革的路上又迈进了一步。

Because of reform and opening up, China's industrial technology is advancing to ever higher levels.

由于改革开放，中国工业技术正向着越来越高的水平发展。

3. conform [kənˈfɔːm] vi. 顺从；遵守；相一致；相符合
『con共同+form形式→共同的形式→一致』

❶ ~ (to sth) 顺从，顺应（大多数人或社会）；随潮流

to behave and think in the same way as most other people in a group or society

There is considerable pressure on teenagers to conform.

年轻人被大力要求守规矩。

He refused to conform to the local customs.

他拒绝遵从当地的风俗习惯。

❷ ~ to/with sth 遵守，遵从，服从（规则、法律等）

to obey a rule, law, etc. （同义词 comply）

The building does not conform with safety regulations.

这座建筑物不符合安全条例。

You must conform to the school rules or leave the school.

你要么遵守校规，要么离开学校。

❸ ~ to sth 相一致；相符合

It did not conform to the usual stereotype of an industrial city.

这和一座常规的工业城市那种千篇一律的格局不一样。

4. formal [ˈfɔːml] adj. 正式的
『form形式+al表形容词→（重视）形式上的→正式的』

▶**informal** [ɪnˈfɔːml] adj. 非正式的

小贴士 **former** [ˈfɔːmə(r)] adj. 前面的

my former boss我的前老板

the former （二者中的）前者

tht latter （二者中的）后者

5. formation [fɔːˈmeɪʃn] n. 形成；形成物；队形，编队

❶ [U] 组成；形成

the formation of a new government 组成新政府

❷ [C] 组成物；形成物

rock formations 岩层

❸ [U, C] 编队；队形

He was flying in formation with seven other jets.

他和其他七架喷气机一起列队飞行。

6. uniform [ˈjuːnɪfɔːm] n. 制服 adj. 一致的；统一的
『uni一个的+form形式→（许多个体）一个形式→制服；统一的』

❶ [C, U] 制服；校服

Do you have to wear uniform? 你非得穿制服不可吗？

❷ adj.（同一物）始终如一的；（多个事物）相同的

not varying; the same in all parts and at all times

The windows in the house are all uniform.

房子里的窗户都是一样的。

The earth turns around at a uniform rate.

地球以相同的速度旋转。

7. perform [pəˈfɔːm] v. 表演，演出；做；表现（好或差）
『per自始至终+form形式→自始至终都是形式上→表演』

❶ [VN] 做；履行；执行（尤指复杂的任务或行动）

to do sth, such as a piece of work, task or duty

This operation has never been performed in this country.

这个国家从未做过这种手术。

A computer can perform many tasks at once.

电脑能同时做多项工作。

❷ 演出；表演

[VN] The play was first performed in 1987.

这个剧于1987年首次上演。

[V] I'm looking forward to seeing you perform.

我期待着看你演出。

❸ [V] ~ (well/badly/poorly) （人）表现良好/很差；（事物）运转良好/糟糕

to work or function well or badly

The engine seems to be performing well.

发动机似乎运转正常。

The company has been performing poorly over the past year.

这家公司过去一年业绩欠佳。

▶**performance** [pəˈfɔːməns] n. 演出；表现；执行

❶ [C] 表演，演出；演技

The performance starts at seven. 演出七点开始。

❷ [U, C] 表现；性能；业绩；工作情况

how well or badly you do sth; how well or badly sth works

He criticized the recent poor performance of the company.

他批评公司近期业绩不佳。

Are you satisfied with the performance of your new car?

你对你新车的性能满意吗？

❸ [U, sing.] (formal) 做；执行；履行

She has shown enthusiasm in the performance of her duties.

她在工作中表现出对工作的热忱。

8. inform [ɪnˈfɔːm] vt. 通知，告知

『in进入+form形式→按照某种形式（来告知信息）→通知』

~ sb (of/about sth) 通知；告知

[VN] Please inform us of any changes of address.

地址若有变动请随时通知我们。

[VN speech] "He's already left," she informed us.

"他已经走了，"她告诉我们说。

▶ **information** [ˌɪnfəˈmeɪʃn] n. 信息，消息

[U] ~ (on/about sb/sth)

For further information on the diet, write to us at this address.

欲知规定饮食的详情，请按这个地址给我们写信。

▶ **informative** [ɪnˈfɔːmətɪv] adj. 提供有用信息的

『inform通知+ative具有…性质的→具有通知性质的→提供有用信息的』

The talk was both informative and entertaining.

这次谈话既长见识又饶有趣味。

▶ **informed** [ɪnˈfɔːmd] adj. （人）有见识的；（决定）明智的

『inform告知（相关）信息+ed表被动→被告知过（相关）信息的→有见识的；明智的』

❶ （人）有见识的；了解情况的

Informed people know the company is shaky.

了解情况的人知道该公司状况不佳。

They are not fully informed about the changes.

他们不完全了解这些改变。

❷ （指决定、推测等）明智的，有见识的，有根据的

We are able to make more informed choices about how we use drugs. 我们能够更加明智地选择如何使用药物。

Here are some questions to ask your lender so that you can make informed decisions.

这里有一些问题要问你的贷方，使你能作出明智的决定。

9. deform [dɪˈfɔːm] v. 改变或损坏…的外形；使成畸形

『de去掉；取消；毁+form形状→把形状弄坏→损坏外形；使畸形』

to change or spoil the usual or natural shape of sth

The disease had deformed his spine. 疾病导致他脊柱变形。

The material begins to deform. 材料开始变形。

10. formula [ˈfɔːmjələ] n. 方案，秘诀；配方；计算式

『form形成+ula后缀→形成（某种想要结果的）方法→方案，秘诀；配方；计算式』

❶ [C] 方案，方法；秘诀

A formula is a plan that is invented in order to deal with a particular problem.

It is difficult to imagine how the North and South could ever agree on a formula to unify the divided peninsula.

很难想象南北双方如何就统一分裂半岛的方案达成一致。

There's no magic formula for a perfect marriage.

没有一个达到完美婚姻的神奇方法。

After he was officially pronounced the world's oldest man, he offered this simple formula for a long and happy life.

在他被正式宣布为世界上最长寿的人后，他给出了这样一个简单的快乐长寿的秘诀。

❷ [C] 配方

a list of the things that sth is made from, giving the amount of each substance to use

the secret formula for the blending of the whisky

调配威士忌的秘方

❸ [C] (mathematics 数) 公式；方程式；计算式

a series of letters, numbers or symbols that represent a rule or law

This formula is used to calculate the area of a circle.

这个公式用于计算圆的面积。

❹ [C] (chemistry 化) 分子式

CO is the formula for carbon monoxide.

CO是一氧化碳的分子式。

❺ [U, C] also formula milk 配方奶（母乳的替代品）

▶ **formulate** [ˈfɔːmjuleɪt] v. 构想；系统阐述

『formula方法，秘诀（去a）+ate表动词→想出、表达出（方法、秘诀）』

❶ [VN] 构想（方案、方法等）

Little by little, he formulated his plan for escape.

他一点一点地设计构思出了逃跑的方案。

❷ [VN] 明确表达；系统阐述

I was impressed by the way he could formulate his ideas.

他陈述观点的方式令我印象深刻。

词根110. fort=strong，表示"坚固的；坚强的；强项的"

1. comfort [ˈkʌmfət] n. 舒适；安慰；令人感到安慰的人（或事物）；舒适的设施 vt. 安慰

『com加强+fort坚强→使坚强→安慰』

❶ [U] 舒适，安逸；安慰

These tennis shoes are designed for comfort and performance.

这些网球鞋的设计穿起来舒服，易于发挥成绩。

I tried to offer a few words of comfort.

我试图说上几句安慰的话。

❷ [sing.] 令人感到安慰的人（或事物）

The children have been a great comfort to me through all of this.

在我经历这一切的日子里，孩子们一直是我巨大的安慰。

It's a comfort to know that she is safe.

知道她安然无恙是令人宽慰的事。

❸ [C, usually pl.] 舒适的设施（或条件）

She enjoys the material comforts married life has brought her.

她喜欢婚姻生活带给她的物质享受。

The hotel has all modern comforts/every modern comfort.

这家旅馆拥有各种现代化的舒适设施。

❹ [VN] 安慰

It comforted her to feel his arms around her.

感受到他的拥抱使她得到安慰。

2. fort [fɔːt] n. 要塞，堡垒；(NAmE) 兵营

『fort坚固的→要塞，堡垒』

a building or buildings built in order to defend an area against attack; a place where soldiers live and have their training

The old Dutch fort with its thick high walls looks virtually impregnable.

古老的荷兰城堡城墙又厚又高，看起来几乎固若金汤。

hold (down) the fort for sb 替人照料，代为负责

look after things for someone while they are somewhere else or are busy doing something else

His business partner is holding the fort while he is away.

他不在的时候，其生意伙伴代为负责。

3. fortress ['fɔ:trəs] n. 堡垒；防御阵地

『fort坚固的+ress表事物→堡垒』

A fortress is a castle or other large strong building, or a well-protected place, which is intended to be difficult for enemies to enter.

The low sun lit the fortress walls with yellow light.

低悬的太阳将黄灿灿的阳光泻在堡垒的墙壁上。

词义辨析 <P366第28> **要塞，堡垒 castle, fort, fortress**

4. fortify ['fɔ:tɪfaɪ] vt. 筑防于；加强，增强

『fort坚固的+i+fy…使→使坚固』

❶ [VN] 筑防于，设要塞于

to make a place more able to resist attack, especially by building high walls

British soldiers working to fortify an airbase in Bahrain

在巴林一空军基地筑防的英国士兵

❷ [VN] 加强，增强

to make sb/yourself feel stronger, braver, etc., to make a feeling or an attitude stronger

He fortified himself against the cold with a hot drink.

他喝了一杯热饮御寒。

The news merely fortified their determination.

这消息只是增强了他们的决心。

5. fortitude ['fɔ:tɪtju:d] n. 坚韧，刚毅

『fort坚强的+itude表状态、性质→坚韧，刚毅』

[U] (formal) （在巨大痛苦或困难面前表现出的）勇气，胆量，刚毅

He suffered a long series of illnesses with tremendous dignity and fortitude.

他凭借超乎常人的保持生命尊严的信念和顽强意志力忍受着各种病痛的折磨。

6. forte ['fɔ:teɪ] n. 专长，特长

『fort强项的+e→强项的→专长』

[sing.] 专长；特长

a thing that sb does particularly well

Languages were never my forte. 语言从来就不是我的强项。

词根111. **fortune=luck**，表示"运气"

1. fortune ['fɔ:tʃu:n] n. 运气；一大笔财富；命运

❶ [U] （尤指影响人生的）机会，运气

I have had the good fortune to work with some brilliant directors. 我有幸与一些卓越的主管人员共事。

❷ [C] 大笔的钱；巨款

That ring must be worth a fortune.

那枚戒指肯定值好多钱。

He went to Japan and soon made a big fortune.

他到了日本，不久便发了洋财。

❸ **seek your fortune** (literary) 外出寻找发财机会

to try to find a way to become rich, especially by going to another place

When he was twenty-two, he went to Vienna to seek his fortune. 当他22岁时，他去维也纳寻求发财的机会。**tell one's fortune** 算命

She playfully inspected Martin's hand and told his fortune.

她闹着玩，看马丁的手给他算命。

My wife went to see a fortune teller.

我老婆去见了个算命的。

2. fortunate ['fɔ:tʃənət] adj. 幸运的

『fortune运气（去e）+ate具有…性质的→具有运气性质的→幸运的』

▶ **unfortunate** [ʌnˈfɔ:tʃənət] adj. 不幸的

3. misfortune [ˌmɪsˈfɔ:tʃu:n] n. 不幸；不幸的事

『mis坏的+fortune运气→坏的运气→不幸』

❶ [U] 厄运；不幸

He had his full share of misfortune. 他吃尽了苦头。

❷ [C] 不幸的事

She bore her misfortunes bravely.

她勇敢地承受不幸的遭遇。

词根112. **found, fund=base**，表示"基础"

1. foundation [faʊnˈdeɪʃn] n. 地基；基础；基金会

『found基础；建立+ation表名词→基础→地基；基础』

❶ [C, usually pl.] 地基

The builders are now beginning to lay the foundations of the new school. 建筑工人正开始给新校舍打地基。

❷ [C, U] 根据；基础

Respect and friendship provide a solid foundation for marriage. 尊重和友爱是婚姻的牢固基础。

The rumour is totally without foundation (= not based on any facts). 这谣传毫无事实根据。

❸ [C] 基金会

The money will go to the San Francisco AIDS Foundation.

这笔钱将交给旧金山艾滋病基金会。

❹ [U] （机构或组织的）创建，创办

2. fund [fʌnd] n. 基金；资金 vt. 提供资金

『fund基础→（做某事的）基础→资金；基金』

❶ [C] 基金；专款

an amount of money that has been saved or has been made available for a particular purpose

Thank you for contributing generously to the scholarship fund. 谢谢你为奖学金基金慷慨捐款。

They collected donations for a fund to help military families.

他们为一个旨在帮助军人家属的基金筹集捐款。

❷ funds [pl.] 资金；现款

money that is available to be spent

The concert will raise funds for research into AIDS.

这场音乐将为艾滋病研究筹款。

The project has been cancelled because of lack of funds.

这个项目因缺乏资金已经撤销。

❸ [VN] 为…提供资金；拨款给

The Bush Foundation has funded a variety of faculty development programs.

布什基金会已经资助了许多教员发展项目。

3. fundamental [ˌfʌndəˈmentl] adj. 基本的，根本的

『fund基础+（a）+ment表名词+al表形容词→基础的，根本的』

❶ 基本的，根本的

There is a fundamental difference between the two points of view. 这两个观点有根本区别。

A fundamental change in the organization of health services was required.

公共医疗在组织上需要有一个根本性的变革。

❷ be fundamental to 基本的，不可缺的

He believes better relations with China are fundamental to the well-being of the area.

他相信和中国建立更加良好的关系对这一地区的繁荣发展至关重要。

❸ （研究）基础性的

Industry leaders want scientists to engage in fundamental research, not applied research.

行业领袖希望科学家从事基础性研究，而非应用性研究。

4. profound [prəˈfaʊnd] adj. 巨大的，深远的；深奥的

『pro向前+found基础→向前（影响）基础的→深远的』

❶ 深刻的；强烈的；巨大的

You use profound to emphasize that something is very great or intense.

My father's death had a profound effect on us all.

父亲的去世深深地影响了我们全家。

Science and technology have brought profound change to the mountain regions. 科学技术给山区带来了深刻变化。

❷ 深刻的；深奥的；知识渊博的

A profound idea, work, or person shows great intellectual depth and understanding.

This is a book full of profound, original and challenging insights. 这本书充满了深刻、原创和挑战性的见解。

The story, short as it is, contains a profound philosophy.

故事虽短，却蕴涵着深刻的哲理。

词根113. fract, frag=break, shatter, 表示"打碎；破碎"

1. fragment [ˈfræɡmənt , fræɡˈment] n. 碎片 v. （使）碎裂，破裂

『frag打碎；破碎+ment表行为或结果→碎片』

（n. [ˈfræɡmənt]; v. [fræɡˈment]）

❶ [C] 碎片；片段

Police found fragments of glass near the scene.

警方在现场附近发现了玻璃碎片。

The shattered vase lay in fragments on the floor.

打碎的花瓶在地上成了一堆碎片。

❷ [V , VN] （使）碎裂，破裂

The clouds fragmented and out came the sun.

乌云散开，太阳出来了。

2. fragile 英 [ˈfrædʒaɪl] 美 [ˈfrædʒl] adj. 易碎的，易损的

『frag破碎+ile易于…的→易破碎的』

❶ 易碎的，易坏的

fragile china/glass/bones 易碎的瓷器/玻璃制品/骨骼

❷ （形势、关系等）脆弱的；不牢固的

a fragile alliance/ceasefire/relationship

脆弱的联盟/停火/关系

The economy remains extremely fragile. 经济仍然极其脆弱。

❸ （身体）虚弱的

Her father is now 86 and in fragile health.

她的父亲现在86岁，身体虚弱。

❹ （外表）精致的，精巧的

The woman's fragile face broke into a smile.

那面孔秀丽的女子粲然一笑。

近义词 **frail** [freɪl] adj.（尤指老人）虚弱的

The old man is growing thin and frail. 那位老人日渐瘦弱。

She was still feeling a bit frail. 她仍然感觉身体有点虚弱。

3. suffrage [ˈsʌfrɪdʒ] n. 选举权，投票权

『suf下面+frag打碎+e→摔碎东西以庆祝（获得选举权）→选举权』

He was an advocate of universal suffrage as a basis for social equality. 他提倡普选权，认为这是社会公平的基础。

4. fraction [ˈfrækʃn] n. 小部分；分数

『fract打碎；破碎+ion表名词→把一个整体打碎后的其中的一小部分→小部分；分数』

❶ [C] 小部分；少量；一点儿

a small part or amount of sth

（如fraction与复数名词连用，则动词用复数）

Only a small fraction of a bank's total deposits will be withdrawn at any one time.

任何时候，一家银行的总存款只有少量会被提取。

She hesitated for a fraction of a second before responding.

她在回答之前犹豫了一下。

❷ [C] 分数

The students had a grasp of decimals, percentages and fractions. 学生们掌握了小数、百分数和分数。

5. fracture [ˈfræktʃə(r)] n. 骨折；断裂 v. 断裂；破裂

『fract打碎；破碎+ure表名词→（骨头）断裂→骨折；破裂』

You've fractured a rib, maybe more than one.

你的一根肋骨断了，可能不止一根。

What happened to your arm? Did you have a fracture?

你的胳膊怎么了？骨折了吗？

6. refract [rɪˈfrækt] vt. 使产生折射

『re返回+fract打碎；破碎→（光线）在返回时破碎了→折射』

Light is refracted when passed through a prism.

光通过棱镜时产生折射。

7. refractory [rɪˈfræktəri] adj. （人）不服管束的

『refract折射+ory有…性质的→宁折不弯的→不服管束的』

8. fractious [ˈfrækʃəs] adj. 暴躁的，易怒的

『fract打碎；破碎+ious充满…的→（火药一样）炸裂破碎的→暴躁的，易怒的』

(especially BrE) bad-tempered or easily upset, especially by small things

The relationship between Alibaba Chairman Jack Ma and former Yahoo Chief Executive Carol Bartz seemed fractious.

阿里巴巴集团主席马云和雅虎前首席执行长卡罗尔·巴茨之间的关系似乎充满了火药味。

词根114. front=face, 表示"面，面对"

1. confront [kənˈfrʌnt] v. （使）面对；对抗；对峙

『con相当于with+front面→和（困难、敌人等）面对面→面对；对抗』

❶ be confronted with 使面临（问题、任务或困难）

If you are confronted with a problem, task, or difficulty, you have to deal with it.

She was confronted with severe money problems.
她面临严峻的资金问题。

❷ [VN] 勇敢地面对；正视

We are learning how to confront death.
我们正在学习如何直面死亡。

❸ [VN] 与…对峙；与…对抗

She pushed her way through the mob and confronted him face to face. 她挤过骚动的人群，与他当面对峙。

▶ **confrontation** [ˌkɒnfrʌnˈteɪʃn] n. 对抗，对峙

She wanted to avoid another confrontation with her father.
她想避免和父亲再次发生冲突。

2. affront [əˈfrʌnt] n. & v. 侮辱；冒犯
『af相当于to+front面，脸→（打）到（某人的）脸上→侮辱；冒犯』

❶ [usually sing.] ~ (to sb/sth) 侮辱；冒犯

a remark or an action that insults or offends sb/sth

She has taken my enquiry as a personal affront.
她将我的询问当成了人身侮辱。

❷ [VN] [usually passive] (formal) 侮辱；冒犯

to insult or offend sb

He hoped they would not feel affronted if they were not invited. 他希望如果他们没有获得邀请也不要感到受辱。

3. effrontery [ɪˈfrʌntəri] n. 厚颜无耻
『ef出来+front面，脸+ery表行为→（不顾羞耻）把脸伸出去→厚颜无耻』

[U] behaviour that is confident and very rude, without any feeling of shame

He had the effrontery to suggest that she enjoyed being unhappy. 他无耻地大胆暗示她喜欢不快乐。

词根115. fug= flee, escape，表示"逃，逃离"

1. fugitive [ˈfjuːdʒɪtɪv] n. 逃亡者 adj. 逃亡的；易逝的
『fug逃离+it+ive表人→逃离（被逮捕的）人→逃亡者』

❶ [C] 逃亡者，逃犯

A fugitive is someone who is running away or hiding, usually in order to avoid being caught by the police.

Who knows what else he's done, but he's been a fugitive for years.
谁知道他还做了什么，但是他已经做了好几年的在逃犯了。
The fugitive leader was captured last night.
那个在逃的头目昨晚被捕了。

❷ adj. 短暂的；易逝的

(especially of thoughts or feelings) lasting for only a short time; temporary

a fugitive idea/thought 转瞬即逝的想法/思想

2. refuge [ˈrefjuːdʒ] n. 避难；避难所
『re又+ fug逃，逃离+e→又逃得远远的→避难』

❶ [U] ~ (from sb/sth) 庇护；避难；慰藉

A further 300 people have taken refuge in the US embassy.
又有300人在美国大使馆避难。
All too often, they get bored, and seek refuge in drink and drugs.
太多的时候，他们觉得无聊就在酒精和毒品中寻求慰藉。

❷ [C] ~ (from sb/sth) 避难所；庇护者

a place, person or thing that provides shelter or protection for sb/sth

He regarded the room as a refuge from the outside world.
他把这个屋子当作是逃避外界的避难所。

▶ **refugee** [ˌrefjuˈdʒiː] n. 避难者，难民
『refuge避难+(e)e表人→避难的人→难民』

a person who has been forced to leave their country or home, because there is a war or for political, religious or social reasons

They stay here a few hours before being sent to refugee camps, which are now almost full.
他们在这儿待了几个小时后被送往难民营，而那里现在几乎已经满员了。

3. centrifuge [ˈsentrɪfjuːdʒ] n. 离心机
『centr(i)中心+fug逃离+e→从中心逃离→离心机』

▶ **centrifugal** [ˌsentrɪˈfjuːgl] adj. 离心的

The juice is extracted by centrifugal force.
果汁是通过离心力提取的。

词根116. fum(e)=smoke，表示"烟"

1. fume [fjuːm] n. 烟，气体 vi. 冒烟；恼火
『fume烟；冒烟→怒火中烧→恼火』

❶ [V] ~ (at/over/about sb/sth) 大为生气，十分恼火
She sat in the car, silently fuming at the traffic jam.
她坐在车里，对交通堵塞感到十分恼火。
He was fuming with indignation. 他愤愤不平。

❷ [V] 冒烟；冒气

❸ n. fumes (pl.)（难闻且常为有害的）烟；气体
car exhaust fumes 汽车尾气

2. fumigate [ˈfjuːmɪgeɪt] vt.（为除菌、杀虫等用特殊化学药剂）烟熏，熏蒸
『fum烟+ig(=ag)做+ate使用烟（熏）→烟熏』

[VN] We had to fumigate the cellar to get rid of cockroaches.
我们不得不烟熏地下室来清除蟑螂。

3. perfume [ˈpɜːfjuːm] n. 香水；香味 vt. 抹香水；使香气弥漫
『per自始至终+fume（烟；气）→自始至终有香气→香水』

❶ [C，U] 香水；香味

We stock a wide range of perfumes.
我们备有各种各样的香水。
The perfume of the roses filled the room.
玫瑰的香味弥漫在房间里。

❷ [VN] 抹香水；使香气弥漫
She perfumed her bath with fragrant oils.
她沐浴时在浴缸内洒了些芳香油。
Flowers started to perfume the air.
花儿的香气开始弥漫在空气中。

词根117. fuse=pour，表示"流，泻"

1. confuse [kənˈfjuːz] v. 使困惑；混淆
『con共同+fuse流→（不同的液体）流到一起→混合到一起分不开→使困惑』

❶ [VN] 使糊涂；使迷惑
They confused me with conflicting accounts of what happened.

他们对发生的事所作的陈述自相矛盾，使我迷惑不解。

❷ ~ A and/with B （将…）混淆，混同

People often confuse me and my twin sister.
人们常常把我和我的孪生妹妹/姐姐搞错。

Be careful not to confuse quantity with quality.
注意不要把数量与质量混淆了。

▶ **confused** [kənˈfjuːzd] adj. 感到困惑的

People are confused about all the different labels on food these days.
人们如今被那些五花八门的食物标签搞得稀里糊涂。

▶ **confusing** [kənˈfjuːzɪŋ]] adj. 令人困惑的

The instructions on the box are very confusing.
盒子上的使用说明令人费解。

▶ **confusion** [kənˈfjuːʒn] n. 混淆；混乱；困惑

❶ [U, C] ~ (between A and B) 混淆；混同

To avoid confusion, please write the children's names clearly on all their school clothes.
为避免搞错，请在孩子所有的校服上写清楚他们的姓名。

❷ [U] 混乱局面；骚乱

Confusion is a situation in which everything is in disorder, especially because there are lots of things happening at the same time.

There was confusion when a man fired shots.
一个男子开了几枪，场面一片混乱。

❷ [U, C] ~ (about/over sth) | ~ (as to sth) 不确定；困惑

a state of not being certain about what is happening, what you should do, what sth means, etc.

There is some confusion about what the correct procedure should be. 对于应该采取什么正确步骤，还是有些不明确。

词义辨析 <P366第29>
混乱 disorder, chaos, confusion, mess

2. **refuse** [rɪˈfjuːz, ˈrefjuːs] v. 拒绝；回绝 n. 垃圾；废弃物
『re返回+fuse流→向回流→拒绝』
（v. [rɪˈfjuːz]; n. [ˈrefjuːs]）

❶ 拒绝；回绝

[V to inf] He flatly refused to discuss the matter.
他断然拒绝商讨这件事。

[VN] I politely refused their invitation.
我礼貌地回绝了他们的邀请。

❷ [U] 废弃物；垃圾（主要用于官方语言）

The District Council made a weekly collection of refuse.
区政务委员会每周收取一次垃圾。

▶ **refusal** [rɪˈfjuːzl] n. 拒绝

His refusal to discuss the matter is very annoying.
他拒绝商量这件事，令人很恼火。

a flat refusal 断然拒绝

词义辨析 <P374第67>
垃圾 rubbish, garbage, trash, refuse, litter, waste

3. **transfuse** [trænsˈfjuːz] v. 输血
『trans从…到…+fuse流→（让血）从…流到…→输血』

▶ **transfusion** [trænsˈfjuːʒn] n. 输血；（资金等）注入

She soon came to her senses after a blood transfusion.
输血后她很快就恢复了知觉。

The project badly needs a transfusion of cash.
这个项目急需追加现金投资。

4. **fuse** [fjuːz] n. 保险丝；导火索 v. 融合；熔断
『fuse流→（保险丝、金属）流动→（保险丝、金属）融化→保险丝；导火线；熔断』

❶ [C] 保险丝；熔断器

Check whether a fuse has blown.
检查一下保险丝是否熔断了。

❷ [C] 导火线；引信；雷管

He set the fuse to three minutes.
他把引信设定为三分钟。

I have a very short fuse and a violent temper.
我容易发怒，脾气暴躁。

❸ 融化；熔接，融合；熔断；安装保险丝

[VN] The two companies have been fused into a single organization. 两家公司合并成一个机构。

Is this plug fused? 这个插头有没有安装保险丝？

▶ **fusion** [ˈfjuːʒn] n. 融合；熔接

the fusion of copper and zinc to produce brass
铜与锌熔合成黄铜

The movie displayed a perfect fusion of image and sound.
这部电影展示了音响与影像的完美结合。

5. **profuse** [prəˈfjuːs] adj. 大量的，丰富的
『pro多+fuse流→多得流了出来→大量的，丰富的』

❶ 大量的（出汗、流血、呕吐等）

Profuse sweating, bleeding, or vomiting is sweating, bleeding, or vomiting large amounts.

There is usually trembling, faintness and palpitations, and there may be profuse sweating.
通常有颤抖、头晕和心悸，可能有大量出汗。

❷ 一再的（道歉或感谢）

If you offer profuse apologies or thanks, you apologise or thank someone a lot.

Then the policeman recognised me, breaking into profuse apologies. 然后这个警察认出了我，一个劲儿地给我道歉。

6. **diffuse** [dɪˈfjuːs, dɪˈfjuːz] v. 传播；扩散 adj. 分散的；弥漫的
『dif分开+fuse流→（光、气体、液体）扩散』
（adj. [dɪˈfjuːs]; v. [dɪˈfjuːz]）

❶ [V, VN] 传播，普及；使分散

The problem is how to diffuse power without creating anarchy. 问题在于如何将权力分散而不造成无政府状态。
Technologies diffuse rapidly. 技术普及非常快。

❷ [V, VN] （使气体或液体）扩散，弥漫，渗透

It allows nicotine to diffuse slowly and steadily into the bloodstream. 它能使尼古丁平稳缓慢地渗透到血液里。

❸ [VN] 使（光）漫射，使发散

The moon was fuller than the night before, but the light was diffused by cloud.
月亮比头一天晚上更圆，但因云层遮掩而月光朦胧。

❹ [VN] 宣泄，舒缓（尤指不良情绪）

The arrival of letters from the Pope did nothing to diffuse the tension. 教皇的来信并没有缓解紧张的气氛。

❺ adj. 分散的；弥漫的；不清楚的；啰嗦的

diffuse light 漫射光

a diffuse community 居住分散的社群

a diffuse style of writing 冗赘的文体

▶ **diffusion** [dɪˈfjuːʒən] n. 扩散；传播；漫射

7. refute [rɪˈfjuːt] vt. 驳斥；否认

『re返回+fute(=fuse)流→使流回去→驳斥；否认』

to prove that sth is wrong; to say that sth is not true or fair

It was the kind of rumour that it is impossible to refute.

这是那种让人根本无法批驳的谣言。

词根118. gam=marriage，表示"婚姻"

1. monogamy [məˈnɒgəmi] n. 一夫一妻（制）

『mono单个+gam婚姻+y性质，状态→一夫一妻制』

▶ **monogamous** [məˈnɒgəməs] adj. 一夫一妻的

2. polygamy [pəˈlɪgəmi] n. 一夫多妻（制）

『poly多+gam婚姻+y性质，状态→一夫多妻制』

▶ **polygamous** [pəˈlɪgəməs] adj. 多配偶（制）的；（尤指）一夫多妻的

3. bigamy [ˈbɪgəmi] n. 重婚罪

『bi二+gam婚姻+y性质，状态→（同时）两个婚姻→重婚罪』

▶ **bigamous** [ˈbɪgəməs] adj. 犯重婚罪的

词根119. gen, gener, geni=birth, produce，表示"出生；产生"

1. gene [dʒiːn] n. 基因

▶ **genetic** [dʒəˈnetɪk] adj. 基因的；遗传的

『gene基因+tic有…性质的→基因的；遗传的』

It's a genetic disease. 这是一种遗传性疾病。

▶ **genetics** [dʒəˈnetɪks] n. 遗传学

2. genome [ˈdʒiːnəʊm] n. 基因组；染色体组

『gen基因+ome→基因组；染色体组』

the complete set of genes in a cell or living thing

A genome contains all of the genetic information about an organism. 基因组包含了一种生物所有的基因信息。

3. generate [ˈdʒenəreɪt] vt. 产生，引起；发（电）

『gener产生+ate表动词→产生』

The company, New England Electric, burns coal to generate power. 新英格兰电力公司用煤发电。

▶ **generation** [ˌdʒenəˈreɪʃn] n. 一代（人）；一代（产品）

『gener出生，产生+ ation表名词，表结果→（同时期）产生的→一代』

My family have lived in this house for generations.

我家祖祖辈辈都住在这房子里。

a new generation of vehicle 新一代交通运输工具

小贴士 5G手机就是第5代手机。G代表generation。

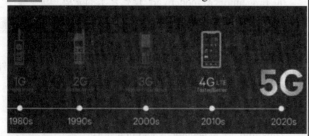

▶ **generator** [ˈdʒenəreɪtə(r)] n. 发电机

『gener产生+ ate表动词（去e）+or表物→能产生电的东西→发电机』

The factory's emergency generators were used during the power cut. 工厂应急发电机在停电期间用上了。

4. genetic [dʒəˈnetɪk] adj. 基因的；遗传的

『gene基因+tic有…性质的→基因的；遗传的』

5. heterogeneous [ˌhetərəˈdʒiːniəs] adj. 由不同成分组成的，成分混杂的

『hetero其他的，不同的+gen产生+eous充满…的→由不同成分组成的→成分混杂的』

consisting of many different kinds of people or things

a rather heterogeneous collection of studies from diverse origins 一组来源各异、内容丰富多样的研究组合

the heterogeneous population of the United States

由不同族裔组成的美国人口

6. homogeneous [ˌhɒməˈdʒiːniəs] adj. 由相同（或同类型）事物（或人）组成的

『homo相同的+gen产生+eous充满…的→由相同（成分）产生的→由相同事物或人组成的』

The unemployed are not a homogeneous group.

失业者不能一概而论。

Russia is ethnically relatively homogeneous.

俄罗斯是个民族成分相对单一的国家。

7. regenerate [rɪˈdʒenəreɪt] v. 使振兴，使复兴；再生

『re又，再+gener产生+ate表动词→使再产生→再生；使振兴』

❶ [VN] 使振兴；使复兴；发展壮大

to make an area, institution, etc. develop and grow strong again

The money will be used to regenerate the commercial heart of the town. 这笔钱将用来发展壮大市镇的商业中心。

❷ 再生；使再生

[V] Once destroyed, brain cells do not regenerate.

脑细胞一旦遭到破坏，就不能再生。

8. degenerate [dɪˈdʒenəreɪt , dɪˈdʒenərət] vi. 恶化；蜕变 adj. 堕落的；颓废的

『de向下+gener产生+ate表动词→变坏，变糟→恶化；颓废』

（v. [dɪˈdʒenəreɪt]; adj. [dɪˈdʒenərət]）

❶ [V] ~ (into sth) 恶化；蜕变；衰退

to become worse, for example by becoming lower in quality or weaker

The march degenerated into a riot. 示威游行变成了暴动。

Her health degenerated quickly. 她的健康状况迅速恶化。

❷ adj. 堕落的；颓废的

a degenerate popular culture 颓废的大众文化

9. generous [ˈdʒenərəs] adj. 慷慨的；丰富的；宽厚的

『gener产生+ous…的→能（不断）产生的→丰富的，（因此也）慷慨的→丰富的；慷慨的』

❶ ~ (with sth) （尤指在钱财上）慷慨的，大方的

It was generous of him to offer to pay for us both.

他主动为我们俩付钱，真是大方。

❷ 丰富的；充足的；大的

more than is necessary; large

The car has a generous amount of space.

这辆汽车的空间很大。

❸ 宽厚的；宽宏大量的

He was always generous in sharing his enormous knowledge.

他从不吝啬与人分享自己渊博的知识。

▶**generosity** [ˌdʒenəˈrɑːsəti] n. 慷慨，大方；宽宏大量

10. genius [ˈdʒiːniəs] n. 天才；天赋
『geni出生+us表名词→天生（就有才）→天才』

❶ [U] 天才；天资；天赋
a statesman of genius 天才的政治家

❷ [C] 天才人物
He's a genius at organizing people.
他是人员组织方面的天才。

❸ [sing.] ~ for sth/for doing sth （特别的）才能，本领
He had a genius for making people feel at home.
他有一种能够使人感觉轻松自在的本领。

11. ingenious [ɪnˈdʒiːniəs] adj.（人）心灵手巧的；（物）新颖巧妙的
『in里面+geni产生+ous有…性质的→里面有产生（新主意）性质的→心灵手巧的；新颖巧妙的』

❶（人）心灵手巧的
having a lot of clever new ideas and good at inventing things
an ingenious cook 心灵手巧的厨师
She is an ingenious girl. 她是位很灵巧的姑娘。

❷（物体、计划、思想）新颖巧妙的
very suitable for a particular purpose and resulting from clever new ideas
ingenious ways of saving energy 节约能源的巧妙方法
This mousetrap is an ingenious device.
这个捕鼠器是一件巧妙的装置。

12. genuine [ˈdʒenjuɪn] adj.（物）真正的，非伪造的；（人）诚实可靠的；（感情）真挚的，真实的
『genu(=gen)产生+ine里面→（从本质或内心）产生的→真正的；真诚的』

❶ 真正的，非伪造的
Is the painting a genuine Picasso?
这幅画是毕加索的真迹吗？

同义词 **authentic** [ɔːˈθentɪk] adj. 真正的；真品的

❷ 真挚的；真诚的；真实的
Genuine refers to things such as emotions that are real and not pretended.
She is very caring and very genuine.
她非常体贴，非常诚实可靠。
There was genuine joy in this room.
房间里充满了真正的快乐。
He made a genuine attempt to improve conditions.
他真心实意地努力改善环境。

13. ingenuous [ɪnˈdʒenjuəs] adj. 天真的；老实的
『in里面+gen出生，产生+uous…性质的→（什么事情都是）发自内心的→天真的』

(formal, sometimes disapproving) 单纯的；天真的
honest, innocent and willing to trust people
You're too ingenuous. 你太天真了。
an ingenuous smile 纯真的微笑
It is ingenuous to suppose that money did not play a part in his decision.
如果以为他的决定没有金钱的因素，那就太天真了。

小贴士 ingenious和ingenuous这两个单词的词义不好记，也容易混。可以按下面的办法。ingenious含有读音[ˈdʒiːniəs]（genius天才）的读音，ingenious可以联想为"里面有天

才的"，所以词义为"（人）心灵手巧的；（物）新颖巧妙的"。ingenuous中含有genuine（真正的；真诚的）一词中的字母组合"genuine"，ingenuous可以联想为"（一个人）里面都是真诚的，没有一点假的"，故词义为"天真的，老实的"。

14. indigenous [ɪnˈdɪdʒənəs] adj. 当地的；土生土长的
『indi(=in)+gen出生+ous…的→当地出生的→土生土长的』

the country's indigenous population 该国的本土人口
The kangaroo is indigenous to Australia.
袋鼠原产于澳大利亚。

15. congenital [kənˈdʒenɪtl] adj.（疾病）先天的；生性的（only before noun）
『con一起+geni出生+t+al…的→出生时一起来的→先天的』

When John was 17, he died of congenital heart disease.
约翰17岁时死于先天性心脏病。
He was a congenital liar and usually in debt.
他生性爱说谎，而且经常债务缠身。

16. genial [ˈdʒiːniəl] adj. 友好的，亲切的
『geni出生+al…的→出生就有的（人之初，性本善）→出生就友善的→友好的，亲切的』

He was a warm-hearted friend and genial host.
他是个热心的朋友，也是友善待客的主人。

17. congenial [kənˈdʒiːniəl] adj. 情趣相投的，合得来的
『con一起+genial亲切的→亲切的人在一起→合得来的』

pleasant to spend time with because their interests and character are similar to your own
She and he were congenial companion in youth.
他和她青梅竹马，志趣相投。

18. progeny [ˈprɒdʒəni] n. 子孙；幼崽；幼苗
『pro向前+gen出生+y表名词→向前出生的→子孙；幼崽；幼苗』

He was surrounded by his numerous progeny.
众多的子孙簇拥着他。

19. progenitor [prəʊˈdʒenɪtə(r)] n.（人或动、植物等的）祖先，祖代；创始人
『pro向前+gen出生+it+or做某个动作的人或物→做向前出生这个动作的人或物→（人或动、植物等）祖先，祖代』

He was the progenitor of a family of distinguished actors.
他是一个著名演艺世家的先辈。
the progenitors of modern art 现代艺术的先驱

词根120. ge(o)=earth，表示"地；地球"

1. geography [dʒiˈɒɡrəfi] n. 地理（学）；地貌，地形
『geo地；地球+graph写；画+y性质，状态→画地球的外形→地理（学）；地形』

We're familiar with the geography of New England.
我们熟悉新英格兰的地形。
They find joy in geography and in history.
他们在地理和历史中找到了乐趣。

2. geology [dʒiˈɒlədʒi] n. 地质学；（某地区的）地质
『geo地，地球+logy…学→地质学』

▶**geologist** [dʒiˈɒlədʒɪst] n. 地质学家

3. geometry [dʒiˈɒmətri] n. 几何（学）；几何图形

『geo地；地球+ metry测量→测量地面→几何学』

Arithmetic, algebra, geometry and trigonometry are branches of mathematics. 算术、代数、几何和三角是数学的分科。

4. geopolitics [ˌdʒiːəʊˈpɒlətɪks] n. 地缘政治

『geo地；地球+politics政治→地缘政治』

Geopolitics has a big impact on economic risks.
地缘政治对经济风险有很大的影响。

▶ **geopolitical** [ˌdʒiːəʊpəˈlɪtɪkl] adj. 地缘政治学的

Hungary and Poland have suffered before because of their unfortunate geopolitical position on the European map.
匈牙利和波兰因其在欧洲地图上的极为不利的地缘政治位置而备受磨难。

词根121. gon=angle，表示"角"

1. pentagon [ˈpentəgən] n. 五边形；五角形；五角大楼（指美国国防部）

『penta五+ gon角→五角形，也指美国五角大楼』

The Pentagon will give preference to companies which do business electronically.
美国国防部将会优先考虑那些能够进行电子商务的公司。

2. diagonal [daɪˈægənl] n. 对角线 adj. 对角线的

『dia穿过；两者之间+gon角+al表物→穿过两个对角（的线）→对角线』

Draw a diagonal line to divide the square into two triangles.
画一条对角线，把正方形分成两个三角形。

词根122. grace, grat(e), gree=pleasing，表示"令人高兴的"

1. grace [greɪs] n. （动作）优雅；（举止）文雅；恩宠 v. 为……增色；使优美

『grace令人高兴的→（动作优雅、举止文雅）令人高兴→优美；文雅』

❶ [U] 优美；优雅

an attractive quality of movement that is smooth, elegant and controlled

She moves with the natural grace of a ballerina.
她的动作具有芭蕾舞演员自然优雅的丰姿。

❷ [U] 文雅；高雅

a quality of behaviour that is polite and pleasant and deserves respect

He conducted himself with grace and dignity throughout the trial. 在整个审讯过程中他表现得文雅而有尊严。
He did not even have the grace to apologise.
他甚至连一个道歉都没有。

❸ graces [pl.] (especially BrE) 风度；体面

The graces are the ways of behaving and doing things which are considered polite and well-mannered.

She didn't fit in and she had few social graces.
她不适合这种场合，对社交礼仪所知甚少。

❹ [VN] 为…增色；使…生辉

He went to the beautiful old Welsh dresser that graced this homely room.
他走到为这间舒适的房间增色不少的漂亮的旧威尔士碗橱前。
He had been invited to grace a function at the evening college.
他应邀为这所夜校的活动捧场。

❺ [U] （上帝的）恩宠，恩典

It was only by the grace of God that no one died.
承蒙上帝保佑才无人死亡。

▶ **graceful** [ˈgreɪsfl] adj. （动作）优美的；（物品）雅致的；（尤指困境中举止）得体有风度的

The dancers were all tall and graceful.
这些舞蹈演员都个子高高的，动作十分优雅。
the graceful curves of the hills 连绵起伏的山峦美景
His father had always taught him to be graceful in defeat.
他父亲总是教导他输了也要有风度。

2. gracious [ˈgreɪʃəs] adj. （尤指对社会地位较低者）和蔼的，慈祥的，宽厚的；仁慈的（女王；上帝）

『grace令人高兴的，文雅（去e）+ious充满…的→（地位高的人所表现出）文雅的→仁慈的；宽厚的』

She is a lovely and gracious woman.
她是位可爱又亲切的女人。
her gracious Majesty the Queen 仁慈的女王陛下
a gracious act of God 上帝的慈悲

3. agreeable [əˈgriːəbl] adj. 宜人的；（人）讨人喜欢的；同意的

『a处于某种状态+gree令人高兴的+able能够的→能够令人高兴的→宜人的；讨人喜欢的』

We spent a most agreeable day together.
我们在一起度过了非常愉快的一天。
He seemed extremely agreeable. 他似乎特别招人喜欢。
The deal must be agreeable to both sides.
交易必须是双方都可以接受的。

4. gratify [ˈgrætɪfaɪ] vt. 使高兴；满足（愿望等）

『grat令人高兴的+ify使…→使（人、愿望等）高兴的→使高兴；满足（愿望）』

[VN to inf] It gratified him to think that it was all his work.
他想到这都是他的工作成果，感到十分欣慰。
[VN] I was gratified by their invitation.
收到他们的邀请，我感到很高兴。
He only gave his consent in order to gratify her wishes.
他只是为满足她的愿望才同意的。

5. grateful [ˈgreɪtfl] adj. 感谢的，感激的

『grate令人高兴的+ful充满…的→（因某事对某人）充满高兴的→感谢的』

I am extremely grateful to all the teachers for their help.
我非常感谢所有老师的帮助。
I would be grateful if you could send the completed form back as soon as possible. 如果您能尽快将表格填好寄回，我将不胜感激。

▶ **gratitude** [ˈgrætɪtjuːd] n. 感激；感谢

I would like to express my gratitude to everyone for their hard work. 我要对所有辛勤劳动的人表示感谢。

6. gratuity [grəˈtjuːəti] n. 赏钱，报酬；(BrE) 退职金

『grat令人高兴的+u+ity表名词→令人高兴的东西→报酬』

The porter expects a gratuity. 行李员想要小费。

▶ **gratuitous** [grəˈtjuːɪtəs] adj. 无缘无故的；不必要的

『grat令人高兴的+u+itous→只是为了使人高兴（但却没有实际意义）→不必要的』

（gratuity赏钱，去y加ous→gratuitous）

done without any good reason or purpose and often having harmful effects

There's too much crime and gratuitous violence on TV.
电视里充斥着犯罪和无端的暴力。

7. ingratiate [ɪnˈɡreɪʃieɪt] vt. 讨好，巴结
『in使+grat令人高兴的+i+ate表动词→使自己变得令别人高兴→变得讨好，巴结』

to do things in order to make sb like you, especially sb who will be useful to you

The first part of his plan was to ingratiate himself with the members of the committee.
他的计划的第一步是拉拢委员会的成员。

词根123. grade=step, grade，表示"度；步；级"

1. centigrade [ˈsentɪɡreɪd] adj.摄氏度的
『centi百+grade度；级→百分之一度的→摄氏度』

The temperature dropped to minus ten degrees centigrade.
温度降到了摄氏零下10度。

小贴士 摄氏度和华氏度
在标准大气压下，冰水混合物的温度为0℃，水的沸点为100℃，中间划分为100等份，每等份为1℃，用符号"℃"表示，单位是℃。在标准大气压下，冰的熔点为32°F，水的沸点为212°F，中间有180等份，每等份为华氏1度。华氏温标，符号为F，单位为°F。
华氏℉（Fahrenheit [ˈfærənhaɪt]）=℃×9/5+32
摄氏℃（Celsius [ˈselsiəs] or Centigrade）=5/9×(℉-32)

It will be a mild night, around nine degrees Celsius.
晚间天气温和，温度约9摄氏度。

Highest temperatures 11° Celsius, that's 52° Fahrenheit.
最高温度11摄氏度，即52华氏度。

By mid-morning, the temperature was already above 100 degrees Fahrenheit.
到早上10点钟，温度已经超过100华氏度了。

2. gradual [ˈɡrædʒuəl] adj. 逐渐的；逐步的
『grade级(去e)+ual有…性质的→有级别性质的→逐渐的』

Losing weight is a slow, gradual process.
减肥是一个缓慢而渐进的过程。

3. degrade [dɪˈɡreɪd] vt. 降低（身份）质量）；降解
『de向下+grade级→到下级→降级』

❶ [VN] 降低…的身份；侮辱…的人格
This poster is offensive and degrades women.
这张海报冒失无礼，有辱女性尊严。
You degrade yourself when you tell a lie.
你撒谎时就贬低了自己。

❷ [VN] (technical) 降低，削弱（尤指质量）
to make sth become worse, especially in quality
However, this will also degrade database performance.
然而，这种方式也会降低数据库性能。

❸（使物质）降解
[VN] This substance degrades rapidly in the soil.
这种物质在土壤里会迅速降解。

4. downgrade [ˌdaʊnˈɡreɪd] vt. 使降职；使降级
『down向下+grade级→降到下一级→降级；降职』

She's been downgraded from principal to vice-principal.
她已从校长降职为副校长。
The boy's condition has been downgraded from critical to serious. 男孩已脱离生命危险，但病情仍很严重。

5. upgrade [ˌʌpˈɡreɪd , ˈʌpɡreɪd] n. & v. 升级
『up向上+grade级→向上升级→升级』
（v. [ʌpˈɡreɪd]; n. [ˈʌpɡreɪd]）

❶ [VN] 使（机器、计算机系统等）升级；提高
Helicopters have been upgraded and modernized.
直升机已经更新换代，装配了现代化设备。
I have to upgrade my computer; it is out of date.
我要升级我的电脑，它太过时了。

❷ [VN] 晋升；提升；提拔
He was upgraded to security guard. 他被提升为保安。

❸ [VN] 提高（设施、服务等的）档次
You can upgrade from self-catering accommodation to a hotel. 您可以将自理膳食旅店升级为酒店。

词根124. graph, gram=write，表示"写；画图"

1. photograph [ˈfəʊtəɡrɑːf] n. 照片，相片
『photo光+graph写；画→用光画出的东西→相片』

▶ **photo** [ˈfəʊtəʊ] n. 照片 （同photograph，复数photos）

2. graph [ɡrɑːf] n. 图表；曲线图
a planned drawing, consisting of a line or lines, showing how two or more sets of numbers are related to each other
The graph shows how house prices have risen since the 1980s.
此图表明了自20世纪80年代以来房价上涨的情况。

3. graphic [ˈɡræfɪk] n. 图表，图画 adj. 绘图的，图画的；形象的，具体的
『graph写；画+ic表形容词→绘图的』

❶ [C] 图表，图形，图画（尤指电脑或书籍、报纸上的）
Graphics are drawings and pictures that are composed using simple lines and sometimes strong colours.
The articles are noticeably shorter with strong headlines and graphics.
这些文章明显短了许多，并且配上了醒目的标题和图表。
The Agriculture Department today released a new graphic to replace the old symbol.
农业部今天发布了一个新图标以取代旧标志。

❷ adj. 绘画的；绘图的；图像的
Graphic means concerned with drawing or pictures, especially in publishing, industry, or computing.
She asked her son, a graphic designer, to create letterheads and stationery.
她请做平面设计师的儿子设计了信头和信笺。

❸ adj. （对令人不快之事的描述）形象的，具体的，活灵活现的
a graphic account/description of a battle
对战斗的生动叙述/描述
He kept telling us about his operation, in the most graphic detail.
他不停地向我们绘声绘色地讲述他动手术的详细情况。

小贴士 在看视频时，血腥场面的前面常有这样的提示：

Warning: contains graphic content, viewer discretion advised

警告：包含有令人不适的内容，建议观众谨慎观看

▶ **graphics** [ˈɡræfiks] n. 制图学；绘画；平面设计

[U] Graphics is the activity of drawing or making pictures, especially in publishing, industry, or computing.

a computer manufacturer which specialises in graphics
专注于图形设计的计算机制造商

词义辨析 <P365第23>
表格 **diagram, chart, table, graph, graphic**

4. **autograph** [ˈɔːtəɡrɑːf] n. 亲笔签名；v. 签名
『auto自己+graph写；画→自己写的字→亲笔签名』

Could I have your autograph? 我能请你签个名吗？
The whole team has autographed a football, which will be used as a prize. 全体队员在一个足球上签了名，用作奖品。

5. **telegraph** [ˈtelɪɡrɑːf] n. 电报 <P40>
『tele (far off) 远处（引申为"电"）+graph写；画→从远处传来的写的东西→电报』

6. **telegram** [ˈtelɪɡræm] n. 电报 <P40>
『tele (far off) 远处（引申为"电"）+gram写；画→从远处传来的写的东西→电报』

7. **diagram** [ˈdaɪəɡræm] n. 图表；示意图；图解
『dia穿过；两者之间+gram写；画→交叉着画→图表』

a simple drawing using lines to explain where sth is, how sth works, etc.

词义辨析 <P365第23>
表格 **diagram, chart, table, graph, graphic**

8. **program** [ˈprəʊɡræm] n. 程序 vt. 编写程序
『pro向前+gram写；画→写的要发生的东西→计划；提纲』

9. **epigram** [ˈepɪɡræm] n. 诙谐短诗；警句；隽语
『epi在+gram写→（因为智慧幽默）在（人们之间流传）的写出的话→警句；隽语』

a short poem or phrase that expresses an idea in a clever or amusing way

"I can resist everything except temptation" is a very interesting epigram.
"除了诱惑我什么都能够抵制"是句非常有趣的隽语。

10. **epigraph** [ˈepɪɡrɑːf] n. （建筑物或雕塑的）刻文，铭文；（书籍卷首或章节前的）引言，题词
『epi在+graph写→在（建筑物、雕塑、书上）写的字』

This article consists one epigraph and the other six chapters.
本文由引言和六个章篇构成。

词根125. **graphy=write**，表示"描述，呈现"，重音在其前面一个音节上

1. **photography** [fəˈtɒɡrəfi] n. 照相术，摄影
『photo光+graphy描述，呈现→用光呈现（事物）→摄影』

Her hobbies include hiking and photography.
她的业余爱好包括徒步旅行和摄影。

2. **calligraphy** [kəˈlɪɡrəfi] n. 书法作品；书法艺术
『calli美丽+graphy描述，呈现→用（字）来呈现美→书法』

Her calligraphy was the clearest I'd ever seen.
她的书法是我见过的字迹最工整的。

8. **topography** [təˈpɒɡrəfi] n. 地形，地貌；地形学
『top顶，上部+o+graphy描述，呈现→（地面）上部所呈现的状态→地形』

The topography of the river's basin has changed significantly since the floods.
该河流域的地形自洪水以来发生了显著变化。

3. **biography** [baɪˈɒɡrəfi] n. 传记；传记作品
『bio人生+graphy描述，呈现→描述呈现人生→传记』

After reading a biography of Lincoln he was able to tell many stories about the President.
他读了林肯的传记后，能讲出许多关于这位总统的故事。

4. **autobiography** [ˌɔːtəbaɪˈɒɡrəfi] n. 自传；自传文学
『auto自己+bio人生+graphy描述，呈现→描述呈现自己的人生→自传』

5. **geography** [dʒiˈɒɡrəfi] n. 地理（学）；地貌，地形 <P184>
『geo地；地球+graphy写；画+y性质，状态→画地球的外形→地理（学）；地形』

词根126. **grav(e), griev(e), grief=heavy**，表示"重"

1. **grave** [ɡreɪv, ɡrɑːv] n. 坟墓 adj. 严重的；严肃的
『grave重→（死人抬着很）重→坟墓→严重的；严肃的』

❶ [C] 坟墓
We visited Grandma's grave. 我们给祖母扫了墓。
There were flowers on the grave. 坟上有些花。

the grave 死亡
Is there life beyond the grave? 人死后有来生吗？

turn in his/her grave 九泉之下不得安宁

from the cradle to the grave 从生到死

dig your own grave 自取灭亡

have one foot in the grave 大去之期不远

❷ adj.（形势）严重的；（人）严肃的
very serious and important, giving you a reason to feel worried; serious in manner, as if sth sad, important or worrying has just happened

The police have expressed grave concern about the missing child's safety. 警方对失踪孩子的安全深表关注。
The consequences will be very grave if nothing is done.
如果不采取任何措施后果将会是非常严重的。
He looked very grave as he entered the room.
他进屋时表情非常严肃。

▶ **aggravate** [ˈæɡrəveɪt] vt. 使严重；（尤指故意）使恼火
『ag(=to)到+grave严重；严肃（去e）+ate使…→使（形势）严重；使（人）严肃→使严重；使恼火』

Pollution can aggravate asthma. 污染会使哮喘加重。
Military intervention will only aggravate the conflict even further. 军事介入只会使冲突加剧。
What aggravates you most about this country?
这个国家的哪一点让你最恼火？

▶ **aggravation** [ˌæɡrəˈveɪʃn] n. 恶化；挑衅

At first, it was an aggravation, but then it turned into a certain passion. 最初，（我认为）这是个挑衅，但后来，这变成了一种热情（我也喜欢上了）。（乔丹在科比葬礼上的祷词）

▶ **gravity** [ˈɡrævəti] n. 重力；严重性；严肃
『grave重；严重的；严肃的（去e）+ity表名词→重力；严重性；严肃』

Arrows would continue to fly forward forever in a straight line were it not for gravity, which brings them down to earth.
要不是重力使箭落向地面，它们将永远以直线往前飞行。

They deserve punishment which matches the gravity of their crime. 应当根据罪行的严重性来惩治他们。

They were asked to behave with the gravity that was appropriate in a court of law.
他们被要求在法庭上表现出应有的严肃态度。

2. gravitate [ˈɡrævɪteɪt] vi. 被吸引到
『grave重力（去e）+it走+ate表动词→受重力（引力）作用而向…走→被吸引』

If you gravitate towards a particular place, thing, or activity, you are attracted by it and go to it or get involved in it.
Many young people gravitate to the cities in search of work.
许多年轻人被吸引到城里找工作。

▶ **gravitation** [ˌɡrævɪˈteɪʃn] n. 引力

Newton's law of gravitation refers to the force between two particles. 牛顿的万有引力定律指的是两个质点之间的力。

3. grieve [ɡriːv] v. （尤指因某人的去世而）悲伤；使悲伤
『grieve重→（死人抬着很）重→死人→悲伤』

❶ ~ (for/over sb/sth) （尤指因某人的去世而）悲伤，悲痛
to feel very sad, especially because sb has died
[V] They are still grieving for their dead child.
他们还在为死去的孩子伤心。
[VN] She grieved the death of her husband.
她为丈夫的去世而悲伤。

❷ [VN] 使难过，使悲伤
If you are grieved by something, it makes you unhappy or upset.
He was deeply grieved by the sufferings of the common people. 百姓的困苦使他痛心不已。

▶ **grief** [ɡriːf] n.（尤指因某人的去世而）悲伤；伤心事
She was overcome with grief when her husband died.
丈夫去世时她悲痛欲绝。
It was a grief to them that they had no children.
没有孩子是他们的一块心病。

come to grief 失败；受伤
So many marriages have come to grief over lack of money.
许多婚姻都因缺钱而以失败告终。

▶ **grievous** [ˈɡriːvəs] adj. 极其严重的；极痛苦的
『grieve悲伤（去e）+ous充满→充满悲伤的→极其严重的；极痛苦的』

❶ 极其严重的
If you describe something such as a loss as grievous, you mean that it is extremely serious or worrying in its effects.
Their loss would be a grievous blow to our engineering industries.
失去它们将会是对我们工程行业的一个沉重打击。

❷ 剧烈的，极痛苦的
A grievous injury to your body is one that causes you great pain and suffering.
He survived in spite of suffering grievous injuries.
尽管身受重伤，他还是活下来了。

4. grievance [ˈɡriːvəns] n. 委屈；抱怨，牢骚
『grieve悲伤（去e）+ance表名词→（因受到不公平待遇而感到）悲伤→委屈；抱怨，牢骚』

something that you think is unfair and that you complain or protest about

Parents were invited to air their grievances at the meeting.
家长们应邀在会上诉说他们的苦衷。
He had been nursing a grievance against his boss for months.
他几个月来一直对老板心怀不满。

词根127. greg=group, flock; collect 组，群；聚集

1. congregate [ˈkɒŋɡrɪɡeɪt] vi. 聚集，集合
『con一起+greg群；聚集+ate表动词→聚集，集合』

Young people often congregate in the main square in the evenings. 年轻人傍晚时经常聚集在大广场上。

▶ **congregation** [ˌkɒŋɡrɪˈɡeɪʃn] n.（教堂的）会众

The congregation stood to sing the hymn.
会众站起来唱圣歌。

2. segregate [ˈseɡrɪɡeɪt] vt.（种族、宗教、性别等）隔离，分开
『se分开+greg群；聚集+ate表动词→分开聚集→隔离』

a culture in which women are segregated from men
妇女受到隔离歧视的文化
a racially segregated community 实行种族隔离的社会
Police segregated the two rival camps of protesters.
警察把两个敌对阵营的抗议人群隔离开来。

反义词 **integrate** [ˈɪntɪɡreɪt] v. 合并，整合；融入（群体）〈P193〉

▶ **segregation** [ˌseɡrɪˈɡeɪʃn] n. 隔离

The Supreme Court unanimously ruled that racial segregation in schools was unconstitutional.
最高法院一致裁定学校实行种族隔离措施违反宪法。

3. aggregate [ˈæɡrɪɡət , ˈæɡrɪɡeɪt] n. 合计 adj. 总数的 vt. 总计
『ag相当于to+greg群；聚集+ate表动词或形容词→聚集到一起→合计；总数的』
（n. & adj. [ˈæɡrɪɡət]; vt. [ˈæɡrɪɡeɪt]）

The world economic aggregate is increasing year by year.
全球经济总量逐年增长。
aggregate demand/investment/turnover 总需求/投资/成交量
an aggregate win over their rivals 以总分战胜他们的对手

4. gregarious [ɡrɪˈɡeəriəs] adj. （人）爱交际的，合群的；（鸟、动物）群居的
『greg群；聚集+arious…的→爱群体的→群居的』

She is such a gregarious and outgoing person.
她很外向，喜欢交朋结友。
Snow geese are very gregarious birds. 雪雁是群居性鸟类。

5. egregious [ɪˈɡriːdʒiəs] adj. 极糟的，极坏的
『e出+greg群；聚集+ious充满…的→超出正常群体的→极坏的』

In a few cases, such egregious online behavior has led to their dismissal from medical school.
在少数情况下，这种恶劣的网络行为导致他们被医学院开除。

词根128. gress=go, walk，表示"行走"

1. progress [ˈprəʊɡres] n. & v. 进步；前进
『pro (forward)前+gress (walk)走→向前走→前进；进步』
（n. 英[ˈprəʊɡres], 美[ˈprɑːɡres]; vi. [prəˈɡres]）

❶ [U] 进步，进展
make great/rapid/stead/good progress in

取得大的/迅速的/平稳的/良好的进展

❷ [U] 前进；行进

She watched his slow progress down the steep slope.
她望着他慢慢走下陡坡。

❸ [V] 进步；改进

The course allows students to progress at their own speed.
本课程允许学生按各自的速度学习。

❹ [+ adv./prep.] (formal) 前进；行进

The line of traffic progressed slowly through the town.
车流缓慢地穿过城镇。

词义辨析 <P361第4>

前进，进展 progress, advance, proceed

2. **aggressive** [əˈgresɪv] adj. 有闯劲的；进攻性的
　『ag相当于to+gress走+ive有…性质的→（憋足劲）向（目标）走过去→有闯劲的；具有进攻性的』

❶ 有闯劲的；积极进取的

He is respected as a very aggressive and competitive executive.
他是一位锐意进取、竞争意识很强的主管，颇受尊敬。

❷ 好斗的；具有攻击性的

He gets aggressive when he's drunk.
他喝醉了就喜欢寻衅滋事。

These fish are very aggressive. 这些鱼极具攻击性。

▶ **aggression** [əˈgreʃn] n. 侵略；进攻性

❶ [U] 好斗情绪；攻击性

The research shows that computer games may cause aggression. 研究显示，电脑游戏可能引起好斗情绪。

❷ [C, U] 侵略；挑衅

None of these soldiers want to die in a war of aggression.
这些士兵没有一个愿意为侵略战争卖命。

3. **congress** [ˈkɒŋgres] n. （美）国会；议会
　『con一起+gress行走→走到一起（商量国家大事）→国会』

Congress（美国及其他一些国家的）国会，议会

the name of the group of people who are elected to make laws, in the US consisting of the Senate(参议院) and the House of Representatives(众议院)

Congress will vote on the proposals tomorrow.
国会明天将对提案进行投票表决。

4. **digress** [daɪˈgres] v. 离题，偏离主题
　『di分开，离开+gress走→离开（话题）→离题』

To make this clear, I must digress.
要把这一点说清楚，我必须离题说几句。

▶ **digression** [daɪˈgreʃn] n. 离题

[C, U] After several digressions, he finally got to the point.
说了几句题外话后，他终于言归正传。

词根129. habit=dwell，表示"居住"

1. **habitat** [ˈhæbɪtæt] n. 栖息地
　『habit居住+at地方→（动植物）居住地，栖息地』

[C, U] （动植物的）生活环境，栖息地

The panda's natural habitat is the bamboo forest.
大熊猫的天然栖息地是竹林。

2. **inhabit** [ɪnˈhæbɪt] vt. 居住在
　『in里面+habit居住→在…里面居住→居住于』

They inhabit the tropical forests. 他们居住在热带森林中。

The valley is inhabited by the Dani tribe.
山谷里居住着达尼部落。

词义辨析 <P376第76>

居住　reside, inhabit, dwell, live, settle, stay

▶ **inhabitant** [ɪnˈhæbɪtənt] n. （某地）居民；栖息动物
　『inhabit在…居住+ant人→在某地居住的人』

We will try to give cheap electric energy and heat to every inhabitant of the world.
我们努力向全世界每位居民提供廉价的电能和热能。

Cairo has only thirteen square centimeters of green space for each inhabitant. 开罗居民的人均绿地面积仅13平方厘米。

3. **habitable** [ˈhæbɪtəbl] adj. 适合居住的
　『habit居住+able能够→可以居住的』

The house should be habitable by the new year.
房子到新年时应该就可以住进去了。

4. **cohabit** [kəʊˈhæbɪt] vi. （无婚姻关系）同居
　『co一起+habit居住→居住在一起→同居』

Most couples today cohabit before they marry.
现在，大多数人在结婚前都已经同居。

词根130. hale= breathe，表示"呼吸"

1. **inhale** [ɪnˈheɪl] v. 吸气；吸入
　『in里面+hale呼吸→吸到里面→吸气』

to take air, smoke, gas, etc. into your lungs as you breathe

[V] She closed her eyes and inhaled deeply.
她合上双眼，深深吸了一口气。

He inhaled deeply on another cigarette.
他又点了一根烟深深地吸了一口。

[VN] Local residents needed hospital treatment after inhaling fumes from the fire.
当地居民吸入了大火的浓烟，需要入院治疗。

2. **exhale** [eksˈheɪl] v. 呼气；呼出（肺中的烟等）
　『ex出来+hale呼吸→呼出了→呼气』

[V] He sat back and exhaled deeply. 他仰坐着深深地呼气。

[VN] She exhaled the smoke through her nose.
她从鼻子里喷出烟雾。

3. **hale** [heɪl] adj. （尤指老人）健壮的；矍铄的
　『hale呼吸→（老人剧烈运动后能）呼吸（自如）→健壮的』

hale and hearty （尤指老年人）健壮的；硬朗的
especially of an old person strong and healthy

The old man is still hale and hearty. 老人的身体还挺硬朗。

词根131. hibit=hold，表示"拿；使停下"

1. **exhibit** [ɪgˈzɪbɪt] v. 展出；显示 n. 展品；物证
　『ex出+hibit拿→拿出去（让别人看）→展览』

❶ ~ (sth) (at/in…) 展览；展出

[VN] They will be exhibiting their new designs at the trade fairs. 他们将在商品交易会上展出他们新的设计。

[V] By 1936 she was exhibiting at the Royal Academy.
到1936年她已在皇家艺术学院展出作品。

❷ [VN] (formal) 表现，显示出（感情、品质或能力）

The patient exhibited signs of fatigue and memory loss.
病人表现出疲劳和记忆力丧失的迹象。

❸ [C] 展品；（在法庭上出示的）物证，证据

Shona showed me round the exhibits.
肖纳带我参观了展品。

The first exhibit was a knife which the prosecution claimed was the murder weapon.
当庭出示的第一件物证就是控方称为杀人凶器的一把刀。

❹ (NAmE) 展览 （BrE exhibition）
The new exhibit will tour a dozen US cities next year.
这批新展品明年将在美国十二个城市巡回展出。

▶**exhibition** [ˌeksɪˈbɪʃn] n. 展览；展览会

❶ [C] 展览会
The opening of the exhibition has been postponed.
展览会开幕的日期延迟了。

❷ [U] ~ of sth 展览；展出
She refused to allow the exhibition of her husband's work.
她拒不允许展出她丈夫的作品。

❸ [sing.] an ~ of sth 展示，显示
He responded in champion's style by treating the fans to an exhibition of power and speed.
他向崇拜者展示了他的力量和速度，表现得颇有冠军风范。

2. prohibit [prəˈhɪbɪt] vt. 禁止；阻止
『pro向前+ hibit(=hold)使停下→被制止向前→禁止；阻止』

~ sth | ~ sb from doing sth (formal)
❶ （尤指以法令）禁止
Soviet citizens were prohibited from travelling abroad.
苏联时代的公民被禁止出国旅游。
同义词 forbid [fəˈbɪd] vt. 禁止；阻止

❷ 阻止；使不可能
to make sth impossible to do
The high cost of equipment prohibits many people from taking up this sport.
昂贵的装备令许多人对这项运动望而却步。
同义词 prevent [prɪˈvent] vt. 阻止；挡住

▶**prohibition** [ˌprəʊɪˈbɪʃn] n. 禁止；禁令
We consistently stood for the complete prohibition and thorough destruction of nuclear weapons.
我们一贯主张核武器的全面禁止和彻底销毁。

▶**prohibitive** [prəˈhɪbətɪv] adj. （以法令）禁止的；贵得买不起的
The cost of private treatment can be prohibitive.
自费治疗的费用高得让人望而却步。

词义辨析 <P375第68> 禁止 **forbid, ban, bar, prohibit**

3. inhibit [ɪnˈhɪbɪt] vt. 阻碍，抑制；使拘束
『in里面+hibit(=hold)使停下→从里面阻止（做某事）→妨碍某事物发展→阻碍；使拘束』

❶ 抑制；阻碍
If something inhibits an event or process, it prevents it or slows it down.
Wine or sugary drinks inhibit digestion.
葡萄酒或含糖饮料抑制消化。
A lack of oxygen may inhibit brain development in the unborn child. 缺氧可能阻碍胎儿的大脑发育。

❷ inhibit sb from doing sth 使拘束紧张而不能做某事
to make sb nervous or embarrassed so that they are unable to do sth

The managing director's presence inhibited them from airing their problems.
总经理的在场使他们不便畅谈他们的问题。

词根132. her=heir，表示"继承人"

1. heir [eə(r)] n. 继承人；传人

~ (to sth) | ~ (of sb)
a person who has the legal right to receive sb's property, money or title when that person dies
He had no title and was not the heir to a great estate.
他没有爵位，也不是巨额财产的继承人。

▶**heiress** [ˈeəres] n. 女继承人
『heir继承人+ess表女性→女继承人 』
We have just heard of his marriage to an heiress.
我们刚刚听说他与一位女继承人结了婚。

2. inherit [ɪnˈherɪt] v. 继承（财产、某种状况、遗传特征等）；经遗传获得
『in里面+her继承人+it(=go)走→（财产）走到继承人里面→继承』

❶ [V,VN] 继承（金钱、财产等）
[VN] She inherited a fortune from her father.
她从她父亲那里继承了一笔财富。

❷ [VN] （从前人、前任等）接过；得到
The government inherited an impossible situation from its predecessors.
这届政府从前任那里接过了一个非常棘手的烂摊子。

❸ [VN] 经遗传获得（特征、特质等）
We inherit from our parents many of our physical characteristics.
我们的许多身体特征都是从父母那里遗传而来的。

▶**inheritance** [ɪnˈherɪtəns] n. 遗产；继承物；遗传特征
She spent all her inheritance in a year.
她在一年之内用完了所有继承的遗产。
The title passes by inheritance to the eldest son.
这一头衔按世袭传给长子。
the situation that was Truman's inheritance as President
杜鲁门继任总统时面临的（上届政府所传下来的）状况
Physical characteristics are determined by genetic inheritance.
身体的特征取决于基因遗传。

▶**inheritor** [ɪnˈherɪtə(r)] n. 后继者；继承人

3. heritage [ˈherɪtɪdʒ] n. 遗产；传统
『her继承人+ it(=go)走+age集合名词，总称→继承的东西的总称→遗产』

[U] 遗产（指国家或社会长期形成的历史、传统和特色）
It is a marvelous mountain area, now on the UNESCO World Cultural and Natural Heritage List.
这是个奇妙的山区，已被联合国教科文组织列入世界文化遗产和自然遗产名录。
We are proud of our heritage and our culture.
我们以中国的传统和中华文化而自豪。
The historic building is as much part of our heritage as the paintings.
这座历史建筑和这些画一样，都是留给我们的文化遗产的一部分。

近义词 **legacy** [ˈlegəsi] n. 遗产；（事件或历史的）遗留
You could make a real difference to someone's life by

leaving them a generous legacy.
慷慨留下您的遗产，改写他人的人生。
We both recognise that this is history's legacy.
我们都承认这是历史遗留问题。

4. heredity [hə'redəti] n. 遗传；遗传特征
『her继承人+ed表被动+ity表名词→（生物特征）被传给继承人→遗传』

[U] 遗传（过程）；遗传特征
Heredity is not a factor in causing the cancer.
这种癌症和遗传无关。

▶ **hereditary** [hə'redɪtri] adj. （生物学中）遗传的；（头衔职位）世袭的

Is this disease hereditary? 这种病遗传吗？

词义辨析 <P372第59>
遗产；遗传 inheritance, heritage, legacy; heredity

词根133. her(e), hes=stick，表示"黏附"

1. adhere [əd'hɪə(r)] vi. 黏附；支持；遵守
『ad相当于to+here黏附→黏附到』

[V] ~ (to sth) (formal)

❶ 黏附；附着
to stick firmly to sth
Once in the bloodstream, the bacteria adhere to the surface of the red cells. 细菌一进入血液里，就附着在红细胞表面上。

❷ 支持，拥护（观点或信仰）；遵守（规定或协议）
He urged them to adhere to the values of Islam which defend the dignity of man.
他鼓励他们坚守伊斯兰教维护人类尊严的价值观。
All members of the association adhere to a strict code of practice. 协会的所有成员都遵守一套严格的行为规范。
Berlin police said that most protesters were not adhering to social distancing or wearing masks.
柏林警方说大多数抗议者没有遵守社交距离或戴口罩。

▶ **adherent** [əd'hɪərənt] n. （政党、思想的）拥护者；追随者；信徒 adj. 黏的
『adhere支持，拥护+(e)nt表示人或形容词→支持者；拥护者；黏的』

This idea is gaining adherents.
这种观念正在赢得更多的拥护者。
The skin can become adherent to the underlying tissues.
皮肤能和下层组织粘连。

▶ **adherence** [əd'hɪərəns] n. 遵守；遵循；依附

The teacher demanded **adherence to** the rules.
老师要求（学生们）遵守纪律。

2. cohere [kəʊ'hɪə(r)] vi. 连贯
『co一起+here黏附→（句子、论证、人等）黏附在一起→连贯』

[V] ~ (with sth) (formal)
This view does not cohere with their other beliefs.
这个观点与他们的其他看法不一致。
The various elements of the novel fail to cohere.
这部小说的各部分之间缺乏连贯性。

▶ **coherent** [kəʊ'hɪərənt] adj. 合乎逻辑的，有条理的；一致的，连贯的

He's so calm when he answers questions in interviews. I wish I could be that coherent.
他在面试中回答问题时非常从容镇静。我希望自己也能那样条理清晰。
He has failed to work out a coherent strategy for modernising the service.
他未能制订出一条连贯的策略来实现服务的现代化。

▶ **coherence** [kəʊ'hɪərəns] n. 连贯性；条理性

The points you make are fine, but the whole essay lacks coherence. 你提出的论点很好，但整篇文章缺乏呼应连贯。
To get policy and strategy right, we need organization-wide coherence.
要使政策和战略正确发挥作用，我们需要全组织范围内的一致性。

3. inherent [ɪn'hɪərənt] adj. 固有的；内在的
『in里面+here黏附→黏附在里面，去不掉的+(e)nt表示人或形容词→固有的』

that is a basic or permanent part of sb/sth and that cannot be removed
Stress is an inherent part of dieting. 节食必定会带来压力。
The desire for freedom is inherent in us all.
对自由的渴望是我们所有人的天性。

4. adhesion [əd'hi:ʒn] n. 黏附（力），黏着（力）
『ad相当于to+hes黏附+ion表名词→黏附（某物的能力）→黏附（力），黏着（力）』

Better driving equipment will improve track adhesion in slippery conditions.
较好的驾驶设备能够提升在湿滑路面上的抓地力。

▶ **adhesive** [əd'hi:sɪv] adj. 黏附的 n. 黏合剂
『ad相当于to+hes黏附+ive表形容词或表物→黏附的；黏合剂』

adhesive tape 胶带
Glue the mirror in with a strong adhesive.
用强力胶将镜子固定到位。

5. cohesion [kəʊ'hi:ʒn] n. 团结；凝聚力
『co一起+hes黏合+ion表名词→（人心）黏合在一起→团结；凝聚力』

If there is cohesion within a society, organization, or group, the different members fit together well and form a united whole.
By 1990, it was clear that the cohesion of the armed forces was rapidly breaking down.
显然，到1990年时，武装部队的凝聚力正迅速瓦解。

▶ **cohesive** [kəʊ'hi:sɪv] adj. 团结的；有凝聚力的
『co一起+hes黏合+ive有…性质的→（成员能）黏合到一起的→团结的』

The members of the group remained remarkably cohesive.
这个团体的成员始终十分团结。

词根134. hum(e)=earth, ground; moist，表示"土，地；潮湿的"

1. humid ['hju:mɪd] adj. （空气或气候）温暖潮湿的
『hum湿+id…的→潮湿的』

Overweight and sweating in the humid weather, she stamped from room to room.
她很胖，在潮湿的天气里浑身大汗，（烦躁地）在各个房间之间走来走去。

It was a hot, humid summer day. 这是个炎热潮湿的夏日。

▶ **humidity** [hjuːˈmɪdəti] n. 湿度；湿热

These plants need heat and humidity to grow well.
这些植物在高温潮湿的环境中才能生长得旺盛。
The humidity is relatively low. 湿度相对较低。

▶ **humidifier** [hjuːˈmɪdɪfaɪə(r)] n. 加湿器

2. **posthumous** [ˈpɒstjʊməs] adj. 死后的；遗腹的，死后出生的；作者死后出版的
『post (after)之后+hum土+ous…的→在入土之后的→死后的』

occurring or coming into existence after a person's death
I was a posthumous child. 我是个遗腹子。
He received a posthumous award for bravery.
他表现勇敢，死后受到了嘉奖。

3. **humble** [ˈhʌmbl] adj. 谦逊的；地位低下的 vt. 使卑微
『hum土，地+ ble→（在土地上干活的人）身份低的→把自己身份放得很低的→谦恭的』

❶ adj. 谦逊的；虚心的
showing you do not think that you are as important as other people
Be humble enough to learn from your mistakes.
要虚心地从自己的错误中学习。

❷ adj. 愚（见）的；拙（见）的
In my humble opinion , you were in the wrong.
依拙见，你错了。

❸ adj. （人）地位低下的；（物）不起眼的
having a low rank or social position; (of a thing) not large or special in any way
He started his career as a humble fisherman.
他第一份职业是一名地位卑贱的渔夫。
The company has worked its way up from humble beginnings to become the market leader.
公司已从创业期的微不足道发展成了市场的主导者。

❹ [VN] 使感到卑微
Ted's words humbled me. 特德的话让我感到自惭。
He was humbled by her generosity.
她的大度使他觉得自己渺小。

❺ [VN] [usually passive] 轻松打败（尤指强大的对手）
The world champion was humbled last night in three rounds.
这位世界冠军昨晚三个回合就被轻松击败。

4. **humiliate** [hjuːˈmɪlieɪt] v. 羞辱
『hum土，地（地位低下的）+i +liate 使…→使地位低下→羞辱』

[VN] 羞辱；使丧失尊严
I didn't want to humiliate her in front of her colleagues.
我不想当着她同事们的面令她难堪。
The Conservatives have suffered a humiliating defeat.
保守党人遭受了一次颜面尽失的失败。

▶ **humiliation** [hjuːˌmɪliˈeɪʃn] n. 羞辱；丢脸的事

5. **exhume** [eksˈhjuːm] vt. 挖出，发掘出
『ex出去+ hume土→出土→挖出』

[VN] [usually passive] (formal) （为检查死因）掘出（尸首）
His remains have been exhumed from a cemetery in Queens, New York City.
他的遗体被从纽约市皇后区的墓地里挖了出来。

词根135. hum(e), hom=man，表示"人"

1. **human** [ˈhjuːmən] adj. 人的，人类的；人本性的；有人情味的 n. 人，人类
『hum人+an表形容或副词→人的；人』

Human remains were found inside the house.
在房子里发现了尸体。
human beings 人，人类
It's only human to want the best for your children.
为自己的孩子谋求最好的条件是人之常情。
He's really very human when you get to know him.
你若了解他，就知道他确实很有人情味。
Dogs can hear much better than humans.
狗的听觉比人灵敏得多。

▶ **humanity** [hjuːˈmænəti] n. 人，人类；人性（而不是动物或机器）；人道，仁慈

crimes against humanity 危害人类罪
The story was used to emphasize the humanity of Jesus.
人们用这个故事来强调耶稣人性（而不是神）的一面。
The judge was praised for his courage and humanity.
法官的勇气和人道受到称赞。
(the) humanities 人文科学

▶ **inhuman** [ɪnˈhjuːmən] adj. 不人道的，野蛮的；非人的，怪异的
『in不，非+human人的；有人情味的→不人道的；非人的』

The detainees are often held in cruel and inhuman conditions.
被拘留者的关押环境常常恶劣严酷且很不人道。
inhuman shrieks that chilled my heart
让我心惊胆寒的尖叫声

2. **humane** [hjuːˈmeɪn] adj. 人道的，仁爱的，博爱的
『hum人+ane表形容词→人道的，仁爱的』

showing kindness towards people and animals by making sure that they do not suffer more than is necessary
Prisoners of war should receive humane treatment.
战俘应受到人道待遇。
Their aim is for a more just and humane society.
他们的目标是建立一个更加公正、博爱的社会。

3. **humanitarian** [hjuːˌmænɪˈteəriən] adj. 人道主义的 n. 人道主义者
『human人+it+arian…的；…人→人道主义的；人道主义者』

[usually before noun] concerned with reducing suffering and improving the conditions that people live in
They are calling for the release of the hostages on humanitarian grounds.
他们站在人道主义立场要求释放人质。

4. **homicide** [ˈhɒmɪsaɪd] n. （蓄意）杀人罪<P131>
『hom(= hum)人+i+cide杀→杀人；杀人罪』

词根136. hydr, hydr(o)=water，表示"水"

1. **dehydrate** [ˌdiːhaɪˈdreɪt] v. 为保存使（食物）脱水；（使）（身体）脱水
『de去+hydr水+ate表动词→使脱水』

Normally specimens have to be dehydrated.
标本通常需要经过干燥处理。
Dehydrated meals, soups and sauces contain a lot of salt.
脱水后的饭菜、汤和调味料中含有很多盐分。

Drink lots of water to avoid becoming dehydrated.
大量喝水以免发生虚脱。

2. carbohydrate [ˌkɑːbəʊˈhaɪdreɪt] n. 碳水化合物
『carbo碳+hydr水+ate表总称→碳水化合物』

Food is made up of carbohydrates, proteins and fats.
食物由碳水化合物、蛋白质和脂肪构成。

3. hydrate [haɪˈdreɪt, ˈhaɪdreɪt] n. 水合物 vt. 给（皮肤）补水
『hydr水+ate表总称或动词→水合物；使水合』

After-sun products will cool and hydrate your skin.
晒后护肤品会清凉肌肤并为其补水。

4. hydrant [ˈhaɪdrənt] n. 消防栓，消防龙头
『hydr水+ant表名词→消防栓』

5. hydroelectric [ˌhaɪdrəʊɪˈlektrɪk] adj. 使用水力发电的
『hydro水+electric电的→使用水力发电的』

6. hydropower [ˈhaɪdrəʊˌpaʊə] n. 水力发电
『hydro水的+power电→水力发电』

If we had listened to them, this hydropower station would never have been built.
当初要是依了他们的主张，今天就不可能有这个水电站。

7. anhydrous [ænˈhaɪdrəs] adj. 无水的（尤指结晶水）
『an无+hydr水+ous…的→无水的』

8. hydrogen [ˈhaɪdrədʒən] n. 氢气；氢
『hydro水+gen生成→由水生成的→氢』

Water is a compound containing the elements hydrogen and oxygen. 水是含有氢元素和氧元素的化合物。

词根137. integr=whole，表示"整体"

1. integrate [ˈɪntɪgreɪt] v. 合并，整合；融入（群体）
『integr整体+ate使→使成为一个整体→整合；融合』

❶ [VN]~ (A) (into/with B) | ~ A and B 合并，整合；融合
to combine two or more things in order to become more effective

[VN] The aim, said the minister, was to integrate Britain both politically and economically **into** the European Community.
部长说，目的是使英国在政治和经济上融入欧洲共同体。

[VN]The idea with young children is to integrate learning **with** play.
孩子们的想法是把学习和游戏结合起来。

❷ ~ (sb) (into/with sth) 融入（群体）
[V] They have not made any effort to integrate with the local community. 他们完全没有尝试融入本地社区。
[VN] The policy is to integrate children with special needs into ordinary schools.
这项政策旨在使有特殊需要的儿童融入普通学校。

反义词 **segregate** [ˈsegrɪgeɪt] vt. （种族、宗教、性别等）隔离，分开 〈P188〉

▶**integrated** [ˈɪntɪgreɪtɪd] adj. 综合的；整合的；融合的
an integrated transport system 综合联运体系
He thinks we are living in a fully integrated, supportive society.
他认为我们生活在一个完全和谐、相互扶持的社会里。
We believe that pupils of integrated schools will have more tolerant attitudes.

我们相信在综合学校就读的学生会有更宽容的态度。

▶**integrated circuit** [ˌɪntɪgreɪtɪd ˈsɜːkɪt] n. 集成电路

▶**integration** [ˌɪntɪˈgreɪʃn] n. 整合；融合

The aim is to promote closer economic integration.
目的是进一步促进经济一体化。
racial integration in schools 学校中的种族融合

▶**disintegrate** [dɪsˈɪntɪgreɪt] vi. 解体；瓦解
『dis表相反+integrate整合；融入→解体；瓦解』

The plane disintegrated as it fell into the sea.
飞机坠入大海时解体了。
During October 1918 the Austro-Hungarian Empire began to disintegrate. 在1918年10月间，奥匈帝国开始瓦解。

2. integral [ˈɪntɪgrəl] adj. 构成整体所必需的
『integr整体+al…的→整体中（一部分）的→构成整体所必需的』

Music is an integral part of the school's curriculum.
音乐是这所学校课程中基本的一环。

3. integrity [ɪnˈtegrəti] n. 诚实正直；完整
『integr整体+ity表名词→完整→完整（人格）→诚实正直』

I have always regarded him as a man of integrity.
我一直认为他诚实正直。
We support its independence, territorial integrity and sovereignty. 我们支持它的独立、领土和主权完整。

词根138. isle, isol, insul=island，表示"岛"

1. isle [aɪl] n.（常用于诗歌和名称中）岛

the British Isles 英伦列岛

▶**island** [ˈaɪlənd] n. 岛
『isle（去e）+(l)and陆地→岛』

2. isolate [ˈaɪsəleɪt] vt. 隔离；孤立；分离
『isol岛+ate使→使…像岛一样（存在）→隔离；孤立』

❶ [VN]（使）隔离；孤立
Patients with the disease should be isolated.
这种病的患者应予以隔离。
This decision will isolate the country from the rest of Europe.
这一决定会使国家从欧洲其他地方中孤立出来。

❷ 将…剔出；分离
We can use genetic engineering techniques to isolate the gene that is responsible.
我们可以使用基因工程技术把相关基因分离出来。

▶**isolation** [ˌaɪsəˈleɪʃn] n. 隔离；孤立

3. peninsula [pəˈnɪnsjələ] n. 半岛
『pen近似，几乎+insul岛+a→近似像岛一样→半岛』

The boat was anchored off the northern coast of the peninsula.
这艘船停泊在离该半岛北部海岸不远的地方。

▶**peninsular** [pəˈnɪnsjələ(r)] adj. 半岛的

4. insulate [ˈɪnsjuleɪt] vt. 使隔热；使隔音；使绝缘；使不受影响
『insul岛屿+ate表动词→像岛屿般与世隔绝→隔离』

❶ [VN]~ sth (from/against sth) 使隔热；使隔音；使绝缘
Home owners are being encouraged to insulate their homes to save energy. 当局鼓励房主给住房加隔热装置以节约能源。
Is there any way we can insulate our home from the noise?
有什么办法可以使我们的住宅隔音吗？

❷ [VN]~ sb/sth from/against sth 使免除（不愉快的经历）；使免受（不良影响）

They have found a way to insulate themselves against the cost of inflation.
他们找到了使自己免受通货膨胀影响的办法。

▶ **insulation** [ˌɪnsjuˈleɪʃn] n. 隔热，隔音，绝缘；隔热材料

▶ **insulator** [ˈɪnsjuleɪtə(r)] n. 隔热（或绝缘、隔音等的）材料（或装置）

Fat is an excellent insulator against the cold.
脂肪是极好的抵御寒冷的绝热体。

5. insular [ˈɪnsjələ(r)] adj. 海岛的；保守的，思想狭隘的
『insul岛+ar…的→海岛的→像海岛上的人一样不与外界接触的→保守的，思想狭隘的』

If you say that someone is insular, you are being critical of them because they are unwilling to meet new people or to consider new ideas.

We have suddenly become an insular people, unconcerned with the underdeveloped countries.
我们突然变成了一个与世隔绝的民族，对于不发达国家漠不关心了。

词根139. it=go，表示"行走"

1. exit [ˈeksɪt] n. 出口；退场 v. 出去；退出
『ex出+it行走→走出去（的地方）→出口；退出』

❶[C] 出口

He picked up the case and walked towards the exit.
他提起箱子，向出口走去。

He made a quick exit to avoid meeting her.
他迅速离去以避免见到她。

❷出去；退出

[V] The bullet entered her back and exited through her chest.
子弹从她背部穿胸而过。

[VN] As the actors exited the stage the lights went on.
演员们退场时灯光便亮了起来。

2. transit [ˈtrænzɪt] n. 运输；中转；过境 v. 穿过；经过
『trans从…到…+ it走→从…走到…→运输』

❶ [U] 运输

The cost includes transit. 成本中包括运费。

During their talks, the two presidents discussed the transit of goods between the two countries.
会谈中，两位总统讨论了两国间货物运输的问题。

An insurance policy will cover the risk of damage to goods in transit.
保险单将承保在途货物损坏的风险。

❷ [U，C] 中转；过境
a transit visa 过境签证

❸ [U] (NAmE) 交通运输系统 （BrE transport system）
the city's mass/public transit system
城市的公共交通运输系统

3. transition [trænˈzɪʃn] n. 过渡；转变
『trans从…到…+ it走+ion表名词→从（一种状态）到（另一种状态）的过程→过渡；转变』

[U，C] ~ (from sth) (to sth) | ~ (between A and B)
the process or a period of changing from one state or condition to another

We need to ensure a smooth transition between the old system and the new one.
我们得确保新旧制度间的平稳过渡。

In the past this process of transition has often proven difficult.
过去这一过渡过程常常很艰难。

4. transient [ˈtrænziənt] adj. 转瞬即逝的；流动的 n. 暂住某地的人
『trans从…到…+it走（去t）+ent表形容词→从…走到…→转瞬即逝的；流动的』

❶ adj. 短暂的，转瞬即逝的
Transient is used to describe a situation that lasts only a short time or is constantly changing.
the transient nature of speech 言语的即逝性
the transient nature of high fashion 最新时尚的瞬息万变性

❷ [C] (especially NAmE) 暂住某地的人；流动短工
a hotel for transients 为过路客人开设的旅馆

5. transitory [ˈtrænzətri] adj. 短暂的，转瞬即逝的
『trans从…到…+it走+ory有…性质的→短暂的』

continuing for only a short time
Most teenage romances are transitory.
绝大多数十几岁少年的恋情转瞬即逝。

6. circuit [ˈsɜːkɪt] n. 环行；电路
『circu环形+it走→走一个环形→环行；电路』

❶ （绕着某地的）环行，环游
The earth takes a year to make a circuit of the sun.
地球绕太阳运行一周需要一年的时间。
She made a slow circuit of the room.
她绕着房间缓缓地走了一圈。

❷ 电路，线路
an electrical circuit 电路
Any attempts to cut through the cabling will break the electrical circuit. 只要一割断电缆，电路就中断。

7. initial [ɪˈnɪʃl] adj. 最初的 n.（名字的）首字母
『in进入+ it行走+ial…的→（最早）走进的→开始的』

My initial reaction was to decline the offer.
我最初的反应是要婉言谢绝这个提议。
At present, China is still on the initial stage of socialism.
现在，中国仍然处在社会主义的初级阶段。
John Fitzgerald Kennedy was often known by his initials JFK.
人们常以姓名的首字母JFK称约翰·菲茨杰拉德·肯尼迪。

8. initiate [ɪˈnɪʃieɪt，ɪˈnɪʃiət] vt. 开始；发起；使初步了解
『in进入+ it行走+i+ate表动词→使…进入→开始；创始』
（v. [ɪˈnɪʃieɪt]；n. [ɪˈnɪʃiət]）

❶ (formal) 开始；发起；创始
to make sth begin
The government has initiated a programme of economic reform. 政府已开始实施经济改革方案。
They wanted to initiate a discussion on economics.
他们想启动一次经济学讨论。

❷ ~ sb (into sth) 使初步了解；使开始尝试
to explain sth to sb and/or make them experience it for the first time
Many of them had been initiated into drug use at an early age.
他们中有很多人在早年就被教会了吸毒。

He initiated her into the study of other cultures.
他将她领进了研究其他文化的大门。

9. initiative [ɪˈnɪʃətɪv] n. 倡议；主动性；主动权
『initiate开始；发起（去e）+ive表性质→具有发起性质的→倡议；主动性；主动权』

❶ [C] 倡议；新方案
a new plan for dealing with a particular problem or for achieving a particular purpose
I am proud to be a co-founder of this important initiative.
能成为这一重要倡议的共同创办者，我很自豪。

❷ [U] 主动性；自发性
the ability to decide and act on your own without waiting for sb to tell you what to do
You won't get much help. You'll have to use your initiative.
你不会得到多少帮助。你得自己想办法。

❸ the initiative 主动权
In a fight or contest, if you have the initiative, you are in a better position than your opponents to decide what to do next.
We have the initiative; we intend to keep it.
我们拥有主动权；我们不打算放弃它。

小贴士　一带一路（倡议）　Belt and Road Initiative

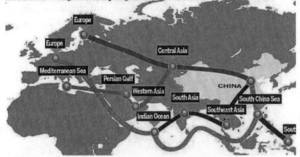

Routes of the China-proposed Belt and Road Initiative

Though proposed by China, the Belt and Road Initiative is a common aspiration of all countries along their routes.
"一带一路"倡议虽然是中国提出的，但却是沿线各国的共同愿望。

词根140. ject=throw, cast，表示"投掷，扔"

1. reject [rɪˈdʒekt, ˈriːdʒekt] vt. 拒绝；不录用；排斥；不关心 n. 次品；不合格者
『re (back)向回+ ject投掷→扔回去→拒绝』
(v. [rɪˈdʒekt]; n. [ˈriːdʒekt])

❶ [VN] 拒绝接受，不予考虑（要求、建议、决议等）
The proposal was firmly rejected. 这项提议被断然否决。

❷ [VN] 不录用（求职者）
Please reject the following candidates. 请排除以下候选人。
I've been rejected by all the universities I applied to.
所有我申请的大学都没有录取我。

❸ [VN] (of the body 身体) 排斥，排异（移植的器官）
It was feared his body was rejecting a kidney he received in a transplant four years ago.
令人担心的是，他的身体可能对4年前移植的肾产生了排斥反应。

❹ [VN]不够关心；冷漠对待
to fail to give a person or an animal enough care or affection
When her husband left home she felt rejected and useless.
丈夫离家后，她觉得遭到了抛弃而且无能为力。

You make friends with people and then make unreasonable demands so that they reject you.
你和别人交朋友，然后提出无理要求，结果被别人拒绝。

❺ [C] 次品；不合格者
someone or something that is not accepted because they have not reached the necessary standard
It's so cheap because it's a reject.
这非常便宜，因为它是次品。
The players were all rejects from other teams.
这些队员都是从其他队淘汰下来的。

2. inject [ɪnˈdʒekt] vt. 注射；注资
『in向内+ject投掷，扔→（把注射器针头）向（皮肉）里面投→注射』

❶ ~ A (into B) | ~ B (with A)（给…）注射（药物等）
His son was injected with strong drugs.
他儿子被注射了烈性麻醉药。
Chemicals are injected into the fruit to reduce decay.
水果注入了化学药品以防腐坏。
The fruit is injected with chemicals to reduce decay.
水果注入了化学药品以防腐坏。

❷ [VN] 注入（某种特性）
She kept trying to inject a little fun into their relationship.
她一直在设法为他们的关系增添一些乐趣。

❸ [VN] 注入（资金）
They are refusing to inject any more capital into the industry.
他们拒绝对这一产业投入更多的资金。

▶ **injection** [ɪnˈdʒekʃn] n. 注射；注资
They gave me an injection to help me sleep.
他们给我打了一针帮助我入睡。

3. project [ˈprɒdʒekt , prəˈdʒekt] n. 工程；课题 vt. 投射；预测；（使）展现
『pro向前+ject投掷→向前投掷→投射；展现』
(n. [ˈprɒdʒekt]; v. [prəˈdʒekt])

❶ [C] 项目；工程；计划；规划
Money will also go into local development projects in Vietnam. 钱也会用于越南的地方发展项目当中。

❷ [C] （学生的）课题，研究项目
Students complete projects for a personal tutor, working at home at their own pace.
学生完成做私人家教的课题，在家里按自己的步调工作。

❸ [VN] 投射；放映
The team tried projecting the maps with two different projectors onto the same screen.
这个小组想用两台不同的投影仪把这些地图投射到同一个屏幕上。

❹（使）呈现；（使）表现；（使）展现
They sought advice on how to project a more positive image of their company.
他们就如何加强树立公司的良好形象征询意见。

❺ [usually passive] 预测
The unemployment rate has been projected to fall.
据预测失业率将下降。

▶ **projector** [prəˈdʒektə(r)] n. 投影仪；放映机；幻灯机

▶**projectile** [prəˈdʒektaɪl] n. （武器发射的）投射物；枪弹；炮弹

『pro向前+ject投射+ile物体→向前投射的物体→枪弹，炮弹』

In confrontations, police sprayed Mace at protesters who got too close and they threw projectiles at police officers in response.
在对抗中，警察向离得太近并向他们投掷东西的抗议者喷洒了梅斯催泪气体。

▶**projection** [prəˈdʒekʃn] n. 预测；投射；突起物

While new projections show New Brunswick is doing remarkably well in terms of COVID-19 numbers, projection authors are warning that it's far too soon to go back to normal.
虽然新的预测显示，新不伦瑞克在COVID-19（新冠肺炎）的数据方面做得非常好，但预测者警告说，要恢复正常还为时过早。

tiny projections on the cell 细胞上的小尖突出物

4. subject [ˈsʌbdʒɪkt] n. 学科；主题 adj. 需服从的

『sub (under)下面+ject投掷，扔→扔到下面→（把精力扔到）话题、主题、实验的对象、表现的对象（下面）→学科；主题』

❶ [C] 学科；科目；课程
Biology is my favourite subject. 生物是我最喜欢的学科。

❷ [C] 主题，话题
I wish you'd change the subject (= talk about sth else).
我希望你换个话题。

❸ [C] 主语

❹ [C] 接受试验者；实验对象
We need male subjects between the ages of 18 and 25 for the experiment. 我们需要18至25岁之间的男性来接受试验。

❺ [C] 表现对象；绘画（或拍摄）题材
Focus the camera on the subject.
把相机的焦距调到被拍对象上。
Classical landscapes were a popular subject with many 18th century painters.
古典风景画是18世纪许多画家所喜欢用的题材。

❻ [C] （尤指君主制国家的）国民，臣民

❼ adj. be subject to 可能受…影响的；易遭受…的
All train times are subject to change in bad weather conditions.
在恶劣的天气状况下，所有列车时刻都常有变动。

❽ adj. be subject to 受…支配；服从于
All building firms are subject to tight controls.
所有建筑公司都受到严格的控制。

▶**subjective** [səbˈdʒektɪv] adj. 主观的
反义词 **objective** [əbˈdʒektɪv] adj. 客观的 〈P196〉

5. object [ˈɒbdʒɪkt, əbˈdʒekt] vi. 反对 vt. 提出…作为反对的理由 n. 物体；目标；宾语；客体；对象
『ob对着+ject投掷→向…扔东西→反对』
（n. [ˈɒbdʒɪkt]; v. [əbˈdʒekt]）

❶ vi. object to 反对
[V] ~ (to sb/sth) | ~ (to doing sth/to sb doing sth)
I really object to being charged for parking.
我非常反对收停车费。
Many local people object to the building of the new airport.
许多当地的居民反对兴建新机场。

❷ [V that] 提出…作为反对的理由
He objected that the police had arrested him without sufficient evidence.
他抗辩说警察没有充分的证据就逮捕了他。

❸ [C] 物体；物品；东西
Glass and plastic objects lined the shelves.
架子上排列着玻璃和塑料制品。

小贴士 UFO 不明飞行物 Unidentified Flying Object

❹ [C] 情感或反应的对象
She had become an object of desire for him.
她成了他追求的对象。
The band is currently the object of much media attention.
乐队现在成了媒体关注的对象。

❺ [C] 目的；目标
The object of what someone is doing is their aim or purpose.
The object of the exercise is to raise money for the charity.
那样做旨在筹集善款。

❻ （grammar语法）宾语

▶**objection** [əbˈdʒekʃn] n. 反对；反对的理由
I have no objection to him coming to stay.
我不反对他来小住。
The main objection to the plan was that it would cost too much. 反对这个计划的主要理由是费用过高。

▶**objective** [əbˈdʒektɪv] n. 目标 adj. 客观的
『object目的；物体+ive具有…的→目标；客观的』

❶ [C] 目标
You must set realistic aims and objectives for yourself.
你必须给自己确定切实可行的目的和目标。
The main objective of this meeting is to give more information on our plans.
这次会议的主要目的是进一步介绍我们的计划。

❷ adj. 客观的
I find it difficult to be objective where he's concerned.
只要涉及他，我就难以做到保持客观。

词义辨析 <P369第42> 反对 oppose, object, protest
词义辨析 <P369第43>
目标，目的 object, purpose, aim, goal, target, objective

6. eject [iˈdʒekt] v. 弹出；喷出；驱逐
『e出来+ject投掷，扔→投掷出来→弹出；喷出；驱逐』

❶ [V] （通常指飞行员从即将坠毁的飞机中）弹射出来
The pilot ejected from the plane and escaped injury.
飞行员从飞机中弹出，安然无恙。

❷ [V] 喷出；弹出
to suddenly send something out
Used cartridges are ejected from the gun after firing.
空弹壳在射击后从枪里弹出。
Two engines cut out and the plane started to eject fuel as it lost height.

两台发动机熄火，飞机失去高度后开始喷射燃料。

❸ [VN] ~ sb (from sth) (formal) 驱逐；逐出；赶出
Police ejected a number of violent protesters from the hall.
警察将一些暴力抗议者赶出了会议厅。

7. conjecture [kənˈdʒektʃə(r)] n. & v. 猜测；推测
『con共同+ject投掷，扔+ure行为，行为的结果→把（已知的不同方面的情况）放到一起（想出未知的情况）→猜测，推测』

❶ [C, U] 猜测；推测
The truth of his conjecture was confirmed by the newspaper report. 新闻报道证明了他的推测果然不假。
What was going through the killer's mind is a matter for conjecture.
凶手作案时心里是怎样想的，这是个猜测。

❷ 猜测；推测
[VN] She conjectured the existence of a completely new species. 她推测有一个全新物种存在。
[V that] He conjectured that the population might double in ten years. 他推测人口在十年后可能会增加一倍。

8. adjective [ˈædʒɪktɪv] n. 形容词
『ad相当于to+ject投掷，扔+ive表名词→扔到名词前的词→形容词』

9. abject [ˈæbdʒekt] adj. 凄惨的；自卑的
『ab离开+ject投掷，扔→被扔掉的→被抛弃的→凄惨的；自卑的』

[usually before noun] (formal)

❶ 凄惨的，糟透的
You use abject to emphasize that a situation or quality is extremely bad.
Both of them died in abject poverty.
他们两人都于穷困潦倒中死去。

❷ 自卑的，怯懦的
If you describe someone as abject, you think they have no courage or respect for themselves.
He sounded abject and eager to please.
他低声下气，急于讨好别人。

10. interject [ˌɪntəˈdʒekt] v. 插话
『inter在…之间+ject投掷，扔→（在别人说话）中间投进（自己的话）→插话』

[V speech] "You're wrong," interjected Susan.
"你错了，"苏珊插嘴说。

▶ **interjection** [ˌɪntəˈdʒekʃn] n. 感叹词；感叹语

小贴士 单词后面标明词性的interj.就是interjection的简写形式。有的地方简写为int.。

11. trajectory [trəˈdʒektəri] n. 轨道；轨迹
『tra(=trans从…到)+ject投掷，扔+ory表物→（把某物）从一个地方扔到另外一个地方的轨迹→轨道；轨迹』

a missile's trajectory 导弹的弹道
My career seemed to be on a downward trajectory.
我的事业似乎在走下坡路。
The trajectory and current extent of COVID-19 are unclear and hard to predict.
COVID-19（新冠肺炎）的轨迹和目前的范围尚不清楚，也很难预测。

词根141. judg(e), judic(e)=judge，表示"判断"

1. judge [dʒʌdʒ] n. 法官；评委 v. 判断；评判

❶ n. 法官；（竞赛）评委；鉴定人
The judge sentenced him to five years in prison.
法官判他五年监禁。
the panel of judges at the flower show 花展评判小组
She's a good judge of character. 她很善于鉴定别人的性格。

❷ v. 判断，认为
[V] As far as I can judge, all of them are to blame.
依我看，他们都应承担责任。
[V] Judging by her last letter, they are having a wonderful time. 从她上封信看，他们过得非常愉快。
[V] To judge from what he said, he was very disappointed.
从他的话判断，他非常失望。
[VN] The tour was judged (to have been) a great success.
这次巡回演出被认为是大获成功。

❸ v. 裁判，评判，担任裁判
[VN] She was asked to judge the essay competition.
她被邀请担任散文比赛的评委。

❹ v. 批评、指责、评判（某人）
to give your opinion about sb, especially when you disapprove of them
[VN] What gives you the right to judge other people?
你有什么权利对别人评头论足？

2. prejudice [ˈpredʒudɪs] n. 偏见
『pre之前+judice判断→事先已经判断好→偏见』

[U, C] ~ (against sb/sth)
There is little prejudice against workers from other EU states.
对来自其他欧盟国家的劳工可说并无偏见。

3. judicious [dʒuˈdɪʃəs] adj. 明智的；有见地的
『judice判断（变e为i）+ous充满…的→充满判断的→明智的』

If you describe an action or decision as judicious, you approve of it because you think that it shows good judgment and sense.
Our leaders made a judicious decision for our company's future. 我们公司的领导为我们公司做出了明智的抉择。

▶ **injudicious** [ˌɪndʒuˈdɪʃəs] adj. 不明智的
He thought it would be injudicious to question her.
他认为质问她是不明智的。

4. judiciary [dʒuˈdɪʃəri] n. 司法部；司法系统
『judice判断（变e为i）+ary表人、物或场所→判断（法律是否被遵守的）部门→司法部；司法系统』

The three branches of government in the USA are the legislative, the executive, and the judiciary.
美国政府的三个分支分别是立法部门、行政部门和司法部门。

5. judicial [dʒuˈdɪʃl] adj. 法庭的；审判的；司法的
『judice判断（变e为i）+al…的→法庭的；审判的；司法的』

[usually before noun]
connected with a court, a judge or legal judgement
Hearing the case in an open court is only one part of the judicial process. 公开审理这一案件只是司法程序的一部分。

词根142. junct, join=join，表示"结合，连接"

1. conjunction [kənˈdʒʌŋkʃn] n. 连词；联合，一起
『con一起+junct(=join)结合，连接→（句子成分：不同事件，不同的部门）结合到一起→连词；联合，一起』

❶ [C] (grammar 语法) 连词，连接词（如and、but、or）常简写作conj.

❷ [C] 联合，结合，一起
The conjunction of low inflation and low unemployment came as a very pleasant surprise.
低通货膨胀与低失业率的同时出现是一大惊喜。
The police are working in conjunction with tax officers on the investigation. 警方正和税务官员协同进行调查。

2. junction [ˈdʒʌŋkʃn] n. 交叉路口；交汇处
『junct结合，连接+ion表名词→接合点；汇合处』

❶ (especially BrE) (NAmE usually intersection) 交叉路口
It was near the junction of City Road and Old Street.
那是在城市路与老街的交叉路口附近。
Come off the motorway at junction 6.
在6号交叉路口驶离高速公路。

❷ （电缆的）主接点；（河流的）汇合处
a telephone junction box 电话分线盒

同义词 **intersection** [ˌɪntəˈsekʃn] n. 十字路口；交叉 <P291>
『inter相互之间+sect切割+(t)ion表行为或结果→十字路口』

3. juncture [ˈdʒʌŋktʃə(r)] n. 特定时刻；关头
『junct结合，连接+ure表名词→连接（一个过程并且可能对事情发展有很大影响的）时刻→特定时刻』

a particular point or stage in an activity or a series of events
The battle had reached a crucial juncture.
战斗已到了关键时刻。
At this juncture, I would like to make an important announcement. 此时此刻我要宣布一项重要的事情。

4. adjunct [ˈædʒʌŋkt] n. 附加语；附属物
『ad相当于to+junct结合，连接→被连接到另外一个更大更重要的主体上的东西→附属物』

❶ [C] (grammar 语法) 附加语；修饰成分
In "She went home yesterday" and "He ran away in a panic", "yesterday" and "in a panic" are adjuncts.
在"She went home yesterday"和"He ran away in a panic"两句中，"yesterday"和"in a panic"是修饰成分。

❷ [C] 附属物，附件
a thing that is added or attached to sth larger or more important
The memory expansion cards are useful adjuncts to the computer. 内存扩充卡是计算机很有用的附件。
Physical therapy is an important adjunct to drug treatments.
物理疗法是戒毒治疗中的一种重要辅助性疗法。
An adjunct professor is also a limited or part-time position, to do research or teach classes.
兼职教授也是有限的或兼职的职位，或者做研究，或者授课。

5. injunction [ɪnˈdʒʌŋkʃn] n.（法院）强制令；命令，指令
『in不+junct结合，连接+ion表名词→不让连接→强制令』

❶ [C]（法院）强制令
He took out a court injunction against the newspaper demanding the return of the document.
他取得了法院强制令，要求报社归还那份文件。

❷ [C] 命令，指令
We hear endless injunctions to build a sense of community among staff.
我们听到上面没完没了地讲要在员工中培养一种集体归属感。

6. subjunctive [səbˈdʒʌŋktɪv] n. 虚拟语气
『sub下面+junct结合，连接+ive表名词或形容词→在下面（也就是在心中）（把句意与语境）连接到一起（才能理解句子的真正含义）→虚拟语气』

7. adjoin [əˈdʒɔɪn] v. 紧挨；邻接；毗连
『ad相当于to+join连接→…连接到…→（…）紧挨，相连』

If one room, place, or object adjoins another, they are next to each other.
Fields adjoined the garden and there were no neighbours.
田园相连，四下无邻。
They stayed in adjoining rooms. 他们住的房间紧挨着。

▶ **adjacent** [əˈdʒeɪsnt] adj. 毗连的
The planes landed on adjacent runways.
这些飞机在毗连的跑道上降落。
Our farm land was adjacent to the river.
我们的农田在河边。

8. joint [dʒɔɪnt] adj. 联合的，共同的 n. 关节

❶ adj. [only before noun] 联合的；共同的
involving two or more people together
The report was a joint effort (= we worked on it together).
这个报告是大家共同努力的结果。
They were joint owners of the house.
他们共同拥有这栋房子。
Chinese marines arrived in Thailand this week to join a joint military drill with Thai troops.
本周中国海军抵达泰国与泰方军队进行联合军事演习。

❷ [C] 关节
Her joints ache if she exercises. 她一运动关节就疼。

词根143. journ=day，表示"日期"

1. journal [ˈdʒɜːnl] n. 日志；日记；杂志；报纸
『journ日期+al表物→日报，报纸；杂志』

❶ 日志；日记
a written record of the things you do, see, etc. every day
He kept a journal of his travels across Asia.
他把自己的亚洲之行记录下来了。

❷（某学科或专业的）报纸；刊物，杂志
the British Medical Journal 《英国医学杂志》

❸（用于报纸名）…报
the Wall Street Journal 《华尔街日报》

▶ **journalist** [ˈdʒɜːnəlɪst] n. 新闻记者；新闻工作者
『journal报纸；杂志+ist从事某职业的人→记者』

2. adjourn [əˈdʒɜːn] v. 休庭；休会
『ad相当于to+journ日期→（暂停会议或审判然后）到（另一个）时间或日期（再进行）→休庭；休会』

[V] The court adjourned for lunch. 午餐时间法庭休庭。
[VN] The trial has been adjourned until next week.
审判延期至下周。

词义辨析 <P365第22>
推迟，延期 delay, postpone, put off, defer, adjourn

词根144. jure, juris=swear; law 发誓；法律

1. jury [ˈdʒʊəri] n. 陪审团
『jure发誓；法律（去e）+y表总称→发过誓（要公正）的人→陪审团』

▶**juror** [ˈdʒʊərə(r)] n. 陪审团成员

2. abjure [əbˈdʒʊə(r)] vt. 公开保证放弃
『ab离开+jure发誓→发誓离开（某种信仰或生活方式）→公开保证放弃』

If you abjure something such as a belief or way of life, you state publicly that you will give it up or that you reject it.
The conqueror tried to make the natives abjure their religion.
征服者试着让当地人宣誓放弃他们的宗教。
Second, I am not stating that the US should abjure action forever. 其次，我没有说美国应当永远放弃采取行动。

3. conjure [ˈkʌndʒə(r)] vt. 变戏法，变魔术；使…变戏法般出现（或消失）
『con一起+jure发誓→（魔术师面对观众）发誓（自己身边没有某物但转眼间某物却突然出现在眼前）→变戏法』

If you conjure something out of nothing, you make it appear as if by magic.
That smell always conjures up memories of holidays in France.
那种气味总是令人勾起在法国度假那段日子的回忆。
Thirteen years ago she found herself having to conjure a career from thin air.
13年前，她认识到自己得白手起家创造出一番事业来。

4. perjure [ˈpɜːdʒə(r)] vt. 作伪证；发假誓
『per害，假+jure发誓→发假誓→作伪证』

If someone perjures themselves in a court of law, they lie, even though they have promised to tell the truth.
Witnesses lied and perjured themselves. 证人撒谎作伪证。
She would rather perjure herself than admit to her sins.
她宁愿在法庭上撒谎也不愿承认她的罪行。

▶**perjury** [ˈpɜːdʒəri] n. 伪证

This witness has committed perjury and no reliance can be placed on her evidence.
这名证人作了伪证，她的证词不可信。

5. jurisdiction [ˌdʒʊərɪsˈdɪkʃn] n. 司法权；管辖权 <P150>
『juris发誓；法律+dict说，命令+ion表名词→（在）法律上有发言权→司法权；管辖权』

词根145. just=right，表示"正确；刚好"

1. adjust [əˈdʒʌst] vt. & vi.（改变…以）适应；调整
『ad到+just正确→使达到正确→调整』

❶ [VN] ~ sth (to sth)调整；调节
Watch out for sharp bends and adjust your speed accordingly.
当心急转弯并相应调整车速。
This button is for adjusting the volume.
这个按钮是调节音量的。

❷ ~ (to sth/to doing sth) | ~ (yourself to sth) 适应；习惯
It took her a while to adjust to living alone.
她过了一段时间才适应独自生活。
After a while his eyes adjusted to the dark.

过了一会儿他的眼睛习惯了黑暗。
You'll quickly adjust yourself to student life.
你将很快适应学生生活。

2. justify [ˈdʒʌstɪfaɪ] v. 证明（决定、行为或想法）正当
『just正确+ify使…→使…正确→证明』

No argument can justify a war.
任何理由都不能为战争开脱。
We'll always justify our actions with noble sounding theories.
我们总会用听起来非常高尚的理论为我们的行动辩护。
Do the ends justify the means?
只要目的正当就可以不择手段吗？

▶**justification** [ˌdʒʌstɪfɪˈkeɪʃn] n. 正当理由

I can see no possible justification for any further tax increases.
我看不出还能提出什么理由来进一步加税了。

3. justice [ˈdʒʌstɪs] n. 公平；合理；司法制度

❶ [U] 公平；合理
They are demanding equal rights and justice.
他们要求平等的权利和公平的待遇。
Who can deny the justice of their cause?
谁能否认他们的追求是合理的呢？

❷ [U] 司法制度
The European Court of Justice 欧洲法院
Many in Toronto's black community feel that the justice system does not treat them fairly.
多伦多的黑人社区中有很多人觉得司法制度对待他们有失公正。

❸ **bring sb to justice** （将某人）绳之以法，缉拿归案
They demanded that those responsible be brought to justice.
他们要求将责任人缉拿归案。

do justice to sb/sth; do sb/sth justice 恰当处理；逼真再现
It is impossible here to do justice to the complex history of the Legion.
在这里不可能完整地论述古罗马军团复杂的历史。
The photograph I had seen didn't do her justice.
我看到的那张照片把她拍得走样了。

▶**injustice** [ɪnˈdʒʌstɪs] n. 不公正
『in不+ justice公正→不公正』

[U, C] 不公正
They'll continue to fight injustice.
他们将继续与不公平现象作斗争。
The report exposes the injustices of the system.
报告揭露了这个制度的种种不公正。
We may have been doing him an injustice. This work is good.
我们可能冤枉他了。这工作干得不错。

词根146. juven=young，表示"年轻，年少"

1. juvenile [ˈdʒuːvənaɪl] adj. 青少年的；幼稚的 n. 青少年
『juven年轻+ile属于…的，易于…的→青少年的』

❶ [only before noun](formal or law) 少年的；未成年的
juvenile crime/employment 少年犯罪；童工的雇佣
juvenile offenders 少年犯

❷ (disapproving) 幼稚的；不成熟的；孩子气的
juvenile behaviour 幼稚的行为
Don't be so juvenile! 别那么孩子气！

❸ [C] (formal or law) 青少年
The number of juveniles in the general population has fallen

by a fifth in the past 10 years.
总人口中青少年所占比例在过去10年中下降了1/5。

2. rejuvenate [rɪ'dʒuːvəneɪt] vt. 使年轻；使更有活力
『re返回+juven年轻+ate使→使重新年轻→使年轻；使更有活力』

Shelley was advised that the Italian climate would rejuvenate him.
有人建议雪莱去意大利，那里的天气会使他恢复活力。

词根147. labor=work，表示"劳动"

1. laboratory [lə'bɒrətri] n. 实验室；实验大楼
『labor劳动+atory场所→（实验人员的）工作场所→实验室』

常简写作lab。

2. elaborate [ɪ'læbərət , ɪ'læbəreɪt] adj. 详尽的；精心制作的 v. 详细说明；精心制作
『e出+labor劳动+ate表动词→劳动超出正常（的时间或强度）→详细说明；精心制作』
（adj. [ɪ'læbərət]; v. [ɪ'læbəreɪt]）

❶ adj. [usually before noun] 复杂的；详尽的；精心制作的
very complicated and detailed; carefully prepared and organized
She had prepared a very elaborate meal.
她做了一顿精美的饭菜。
He is known for his elaborate costumes.
他以着装精致而闻名。

❷ 精心制作；详细说明
[VN] The inventor spent months in elaborating his plans for a new engine.
这位发明家花费了几个月的时间精心绘制了一种新发动机的平面图。
[V] A spokesman declined to elaborate on a statement released late yesterday.
发言人拒绝对昨天晚些时候发表的声明详加说明。

3. collaborate [kə'læbəreɪt] vi. 合作，协作
『col共同+labor劳动+ate表动词→一起工作→合作』
We have collaborated on many projects over the years.
这些年来我们合作搞了许多项目。

词根148. lapse=slip，表示"滑；溜走"

1. collapse [kə'læps] v. 崩溃；倒塌；折叠；（尤指工作劳累后）坐下；晕倒
『col共同+lapse滑；溜走→一起滑落→倒塌』

❶ [V] （建筑物突然）倒塌，坍塌
The roof collapsed under the weight of snow.
房顶在雪的重压下突然坍塌下来。

❷ [V] （尤指因病重而）倒下；晕倒
to fall down (and usually become unconscious), especially because you are very ill/sick
He collapsed in the street and died two hours later.
他晕倒在大街上，两小时后便去世了。

❸ [V] (informal) （尤指工作劳累后）坐下；躺下放松
to sit or lie down and relax, especially after working hard
When I get home I like to collapse on the sofa and listen to music. 回到家时，我喜欢躺在沙发上听音乐。

❹ [V] 突然失败；崩溃；瓦解

to fail suddenly or completely
All opposition to the plan has collapsed.
所有反对此计划的力量均已消除。

❺ [V] （突然）降价；贬值；暴跌
Share prices collapsed after news of poor trading figures.
在交易数额不佳的消息公布后，股票价格暴跌。

❻ [V] [VN]折叠；套缩；可折叠（或套缩）
[V] The table collapses for easy storage.
这桌子可折叠起来方便存放。

▶ **collapsible** [kə'læpsəbl] adj. （家具）可折叠的
a collapsible chair/boat/bicycle 折叠式椅子/小船/自行车

2. elapse [ɪ'læps] vi. （时间）消逝，流逝
『e出去+lapse滑；溜走→（时间）溜走→流逝』

Forty-eight hours have elapsed since his arrest.
从他被捕至今已经过去48小时了。

3. lapse [læps] n. 疏忽；间隔时间；失足 vi. 期满；衰退；陷入；背弃
『lapse滑；溜走→（注意力）溜走；（时间）溜走；（精力、活力）溜走→疏忽；间隔时间；衰退；陷入』

❶ [C] （一时的）疏忽，大意，开小差
a small mistake, especially one that is caused by forgetting sth or by being careless
A momentary lapse in the final set cost her the match.
她最后一盘稍有失误，输掉了整场比赛。

❷ [C] （两件事发生的）间隔时间
After a lapse of six months we met up again.
相隔六个月之后我们又相遇了。

❸ [C] 行为失检；（平时表现不错的人一时的）失足
an example or period of bad behaviour from sb who normally behaves well

❹ [V] （合同、协议等）期满终止
She had allowed her membership to lapse.
她的会员资格期满终止，没有再续。

❺ [V] 衰退，衰弱；（逐渐）陷入
His concentration lapsed after a few minutes.
几分钟后他的注意力就下降了。
to lapse into unconsciousness/a coma
逐渐失去知觉/陷入昏迷状态
She lapsed into silence again. 她又陷入了沉默。
He soon lapsed back into his old ways.
他很快又犯老毛病了。

❻ [V] ~ (from sth) 背弃，放弃（宗教信仰）
He lapsed from Judaism when he was a student.
他当学生时就放弃了犹太教。

4. relapse ['riːlæps , rɪ'læps] n. & vi. 旧病复发；重新陷入
『re返回+ lapse滑；溜走→滑回到（原来状态）→旧病复发』
（n. ['riːlæps]; vi. [rɪ'læps] ）

❶ [V] ~ (into sth) 旧病复发；重新陷入
He relapsed into his old bad habits. 他重染恶习。
In 90 per cent of cases the patient will relapse within six months. 90%的病人在6个月内会再次发病。

❷ [C, U] 旧病复发；重新陷入
a risk of relapse 旧病复发的危险
a relapse into the nationalism of the nineteenth century

倒退回19世纪的民族主义

1. bilateral [ˌbaɪˈlætərəl] adj. 双边的，双方的
『bi二+later边+al…的→双边的』

This is the basis on which our bilateral relations can and should continue to develop.
这是我们两国关系能够并且应该继续发展的基础。

2. lateral [ˈlætərəl] adj. 侧面的；横向的 n. 舌侧音
『later侧面+al…的→侧面的』

McKinnon estimated the lateral movement of the bridge to be between four and six inches.
麦金农估计大桥的侧向移动介于4至6英寸之间。

3. unilateral [ˌjuːnɪˈlætrəl] adj. 单边的；单方的
『uni一个的+later边+al…的→单边的』

They were forced to take unilateral action.
他们被迫采取单方面行动。

▶**unilateralism** [ˌjuːnɪˈlætrəlɪzəm] n. 单边主义

American diplomacy is shifting towards unilateralism, bringing about strong impact on international relations.
美国外交向强化单边主义调整，对国际关系的影响和冲击最大。

4. multilateral [ˌmʌltiˈlætərəl] adj. 多边（国）的
『multi多种的+later边+al…的→多边的，多方面的』

Many want to abandon the multilateral trade talks in Geneva.
很多国家想退出在日内瓦举行的多边贸易会谈。

▶**multilateralism** [ˌmʌltiˈlætərəlɪzəm] n. 多边主义

We all need peace, multilateralism and dialogue, instead of war, unilateralism, and confrontation.
要和平不要战争、要多边不要单边、要对话不要对抗是我们的共识。

5. equilateral [ˌiːkwɪˈlætərəl] adj. 等边的
『equi相等+later边+al…的→等边的』

Its outline roughly forms an equilateral triangle.
它的轮廓大致形成一个等边三角形。

6. collateral [kəˈlætərəl] n. 抵押物；担保品 adj. 附属的，附带的；并行的
『col共同，一起+later边+al…的→边挨着边的→并列的→（和某个主要事件）并列→（贷款和抵押物是）并列（近似等同关系）→附带的；抵押物』

❶ [U] (finance) 抵押物；担保品
Many people use personal assets as collateral for small business loans.
很多人把个人财产用作小额商业贷款的抵押品。

❷ adj. 附属的；附带的；并行的
The government denied that there had been any collateral damage.
政府否认空袭期间有任何附带性的破坏（即对平民或建筑物的损害）。

The pattern of commom governance includes two collateral mechanisms: the board of directors and supervisory committee.
共同治理模式包括两个并行的机制：董事会和监事会。

1. lavish [ˈlævɪʃ] adj. 铺张的，奢侈的；慷慨的 vt. 浪费；慷慨给予
『lav洗+ish表动词→（花钱、赞扬）如水→铺张的；慷慨的』

❶ [VN] lavish sth on/upon sb/sth 浪费；非常（或过分）慷慨地给予
If you lavish money, affection, or praise on someone or something, you spend a lot of money on them
Prince Sadruddin lavished praise on Britain's contributions to world diplomacy.
萨德鲁丁王子大力赞扬英国对世界外交做出的贡献。

❷ adj. 铺张的；奢侈的；盛大的
If you describe something as lavish, you mean that it is very elaborate and impressive and a lot of money has been spent on it.
lavish gifts/costumes/celebrations
丰厚的礼品；昂贵的服装；规模盛大的庆典
They lived a very lavish lifestyle.
他们过着挥霍无度的生活。
Critics attack his lavish spending and flamboyant style.
评论家抨击他大肆挥霍、恣意张扬的作风。

❸ adj. ~ (with/in sth) 慷慨的，大方的
He was lavish in his praise for her paintings.
他大力赞扬她的绘画。

2. lavatory [ˈlævətri] n. (BrE) 卫生间；公共卫生间
『lav洗+atory表场所→卫生间』

3. dilute [daɪˈluːt] vt. 稀释；冲淡 adj. 稀释过的
『di分开+lute冲洗→冲洗使分开→稀释；冲淡』

❶ [VN] 稀释，冲淡（液体）；使降低效果
The paint can be diluted with water to make a lighter shade.
这颜料可用水稀释以使色度淡一些。
Large classes dilute the quality of education that children receive. 大班上课会降低孩子所受教育的质量。

❷ adj. 稀释过的（＝diluted）
a dilute solution of bleach 经稀释的漂白剂

4. deluge [ˈdeljuːdʒ] n. 暴雨；大量涌来的事物 vt. （暴雨）袭击；使涌现
『de离开+luge(=luv)冲洗→被冲走→暴雨』

❶ [usually sing.] 暴雨，大雨；大量涌来的事物
About a dozen homes were damaged in the deluge.
在这场暴雨中大约有十几家房屋被毁。
A deluge of manuscripts began to arrive in the post.
大量的手稿开始通过邮递涌来。

❷ [VN] （暴雨）袭击；使涌现
At least 150 people are believed to have died after two days of torrential rain deluged the capital.
连续两天的滂沱大雨致使首都积水成灾，据信至少已有150人死亡。
During 1933, Papen's office was deluged with complaints.
1933年间，大量的投诉信涌进了巴本的办公室。

1. elect [ɪˈlekt] vt. 选举 adj. 候任的
『e出来+lect选择→（把某一职务的人）选择出来→选举』

❶ ~ sb (to sth) | ~ sb (as) sth 选举；推选
The people of the Philippines have voted to elect a new president.
菲律宾人民已投票选举出了一位新总统。

❷ adj. （用于名词后）当选而尚未就职的，候任的
the president elect 候任总统

词义辨析 <P367第31>**挑选 choose, elect, select, pick, opt**

2. elector [ɪˈlektə(r)] n. 选民
『elect选举+or表人→（参加）选举的人→选民』

3. electorate [ɪˈlektərət] n. （某国或某地区）全体选民
『elect选举+or做某动作的人+ate表总称→全体选民』

[C + sing./pl. v.]
He has the backing of almost a quarter of the electorate.
他得到了几乎1/4选民的支持。

4. select [sɪˈlekt] vt. 选拔；挑选 adj. 精选的；优等的
『se (apart)分开+lect选择→分开选→选择』

❶ [VN] 选拔

to choose sb/sth from a group of people or things, usually according to a system

[VN] He hasn't been selected for the team.
他未能入选进队。
All our hotels have been carefully selected for the excellent value they provide.
我们住的旅馆都是精心挑选的，最为合算。

❷ [VN] （在计算机屏幕上）选定；（从菜单中）选择
Select the text you want to format by holding down the left button on your mouse.
按住鼠标左键选取你想要格式化的文本。

❸ adj. 精选的；优等的；只为富人（或上层人士）而设的

Only a select few have been invited to the wedding.
婚礼只邀请了几个至亲好友参加。
They live in a very select area.
他们住在一个上层人士住宅区。

词义辨析 <P367第31>**挑选 choose, elect, select, pick, opt**

5. collect [kəˈlekt] v. 收集；收藏；接走；聚积；募捐
『col共同+lect选择；收集→选择后放在一起→收集』

❶ [VN] ~ sth (from sb/sth) 收集；采集
to collect data/evidence/information 收集数据/证据/信息
Samples were collected from over 200 patients.
已从200多名病人取样。

❷ [VN] 收藏
to collect stamps/postcards, etc. 集邮/收集明信片等

❸ [V] 聚集，集合，汇集
A crowd began to collect in front of the embassy.
人群开始聚集在大使馆的前面。
Dirt had collected in the corners of the room.
房间的角落里积满了灰尘。

❹ [VN] ~ sb/sth (from…) 领取；收走；接走
（常用在英国英语中，美国英语通常用pick up）
(BrE) She's gone to collect her son from school.
她到学校接她儿子去了。
The package is waiting to be collected.
这包裹在等人领取。

❺ ~ (sth) (for sth) 募捐；募集
[V] We're collecting for local charities.
我们正在为当地慈善机构募捐。
[VN] We collected over £300 for the appeal.
我们为此呼吁募集了 300 多英镑。

❻ collect yourself （尽力）镇定下来，敛神专注
I'm fine—I just need a minute to collect myself.
我没事——只是需要稍稍镇定一下。

小贴士 表示镇静的词，参看compose <P262>
词义辨析 <P365第20> **聚集；收集 collect, gather**

6. collective [kəˈlektɪv] adj. 集体的；总体的
『collect收集+ive…的→集中到一起→集体的』

It was a collective decision. 这是集体的决定。
Their collective volume wasn't very large.
他们的总量不是太大。
Social science is a collective name, covering a series of individual sciences.
社会科学是一个统称，涵盖一系列的独立学科。

7. recollect [ˌrekəˈlekt] v.（努力）记起，想起
『re (back)+collect收集→（把过去的记忆）一点一点地收集回来→（努力）回忆起』

（不用于进行时）(rather formal) 记起，回忆起
to remember sth, especially by making an effort to remember it
[VN] She could no longer recollect the details of the letter.
她想不起那封信的细节了。
[V wh-] I don't recollect what he said.
我不记得他说过什么。
[VN -ing] I recollect him/his saying that it was dangerous.
我记得他说那很危险。

▶**recollection** [ˌrekəˈlekʃn] n. 回忆；记起
To the best of my recollection (=if I remember correctly) I was not present at that meeting.
如果我没记错的话，我没有出席那次会议。
You have no recollection of the incident?
你一点都不记得那次事故了吗？

词义辨析 <P362第7> **记起 remember, memorise, recall, recollect**

8. neglect [nɪˈglekt] vt. 忽视；疏忽 n. 忽视
『neg否认，拒绝+lect选择→没能选择→忽视；疏忽』

❶ [VN] 疏于照顾
to fail to take care of sb/sth
She denies neglecting her baby.
她不承认没有照看好她的孩子。
The buildings had been neglected for years.
这些大楼多年来一直无人看管。

❷ [VN] 忽视
She has neglected her studies. 她忽视了自己的学习。

❸ [V to inf] (formal) 疏忽
You neglected to mention the name of your previous employer. 你遗漏了你前雇主的名字。

❹ [U] ~ (of sth/sb) 忽视
The buildings are crumbling from years of neglect.
由于多年无人维修，这些建筑物行将倒塌。

词义辨析 <P373 第 60>

忽视，无视 ignore, neglect, disregard

▶ **negligence** [ˈneɡlɪdʒəns] n. 疏忽；失职

『neg否认，拒绝+lig选择+ence表名词→没能选择→疏忽；失职』

[U] (formal or law) 疏忽；失职；失误；过失

the failure to give sb/sth enough care or attention

The accident was caused by negligence on the part of the driver. 事故是由于司机的过失造成的。

The doctor was sued for medical negligence.
这名医生因为引致医疗事故而被起诉。

▶ **negligent** [ˈneɡlɪdʒənt] adj. 疏忽的，玩忽职守的；（人）放松的，随便的

The jury determined that the airline was negligent in training and supervising the crew.
陪审团裁定航空公司在对全体机组人员的培训和管理问题上存在疏漏。

He waved his hand in a negligent gesture.
他漫不经心地挥了挥手。

9. negligible [ˈneɡlɪdʒəbl] adj. 微不足道的；不值一提的

『neg否认，拒绝+lig选择+ible可…的→可以不选择的→可以忽视的→微不足道的』

of very little importance or size and not worth considering

The pay that the soldiers received was negligible.
士兵拿到的军饷少得可怜。

10. eligible [ˈelɪdʒəbl] adj. 有资格的；合适的

『e出+lig选择+ible可…的→可选择的→有资格的』

❶ ~ (for sth) | ~ (to do sth)有资格的；合格的；具备条件的
Only those over 70 are eligible for the special payment.
只有70岁以上的人才有资格领取这项专款。

When are you eligible to vote in your country?
在你们国家多大才有资格投票选举呢？

❷ （作为结婚对象）合适的，中意的
Stephen was regarded as an eligible bachelor.
斯蒂芬被认为是一个可以考虑（作为结婚对象）的单身汉。

11. elegant [ˈelɪɡənt] adj. （人或物）优美的；（文字、想法、计划等）简练的；巧妙的

『e出来+leg选择+ant…的→（从众多中）选出来的→优美的；简练的』

❶ （人或物）优美的，雅致的
If you describe a person or thing as elegant, you mean that they are pleasing and graceful in appearance or style.

Patricia looked beautiful and elegant as always.
帕特里夏一如既往地美丽优雅。

❷ （文字、想法、计划等）简洁的，简练的；巧妙的
If you describe a piece of writing, an idea, or a plan as elegant, you mean that it is simple, clear, and clever.

an elegant solution to the problem
解决这个问题的简要方法

▶ **elegance** [ˈelɪɡəns] n. 优美，高雅

Everyone admired her elegance and her beauty.
人人都羡慕她的优雅和美丽。

12. intellect [ˈɪntəlekt] n. 智力；高智力；高智力的人

『intel(=inter)在…之间+lect选择→从（一堆人中）选出的（人才）→智者』

❶ [U, C] （尤指高等的）智力，思维逻辑领悟力；智力

The intellect is not the most important thing in life.
才智不是生活中最重要的东西。

Her intellect is famed far and wide.
她的非凡才智闻名遐迩。

❷ [C] 智力高的人；才智超群的人
My boss isn't a great intellect. 我的老板才智并不出众。

▶ **intellectual** [ˌɪntəˈlektʃuəl] adj. 智力的；高智力的 n. 知识分子；脑力劳动者

『intellect智慧；智者+ ual有…性质的→智力的,高智力的』

❶ [usually before noun] 智力的；脑力的
High levels of lead could damage the intellectual development of children.
铅含量过高会损害儿童的智力发展。

❷ (of a person) 有才智的；智力发达的
She's very intellectual. 她很聪慧。

❸ [C] 知识分子；脑力劳动者
She was a fiery, brilliant and unyielding intellectual and politician.
她是个充满激情、才华卓越、毫不妥协的知识分子和政治家。

▶ **intellectual property** 知识财产；知识产权

It involves all the fields from trade, investment to intellectual property protection.
它涉及贸易、投资和知识产权保护等广泛领域.

13. intelligent [ɪnˈtelɪdʒənt] adj. 聪明的；有灵性的；智能的

『intel(=inter)在…之间+lig选择+ent表形容词→具有从（一堆人中）选出的（人才的）品质→聪明的』

❶ 聪颖的；有才智的；有灵性的
A person or animal that is intelligent has the ability to think, understand, and learn things quickly and well.

Susan's a very bright and intelligent woman who knows her own mind. 苏珊是个非常聪明、有主见的女子。

❷ 能思维的；智能的
Finally, the paper forecasts the development tendency of artificial intelligence and intelligent control.
最后，该文章展望人工智能和智能控制的发展趋势。

▶ **intelligence** [ɪnˈtelɪdʒəns] n. 智力，才智，智慧；（尤指关于敌对国家的）情报，情报人员

❶ [U] 智力，才智，智慧
a person of high/average/low intelligence
智力高的/一般的/低下的人

He didn't even have the intelligence to call for an ambulance.
他连呼叫救护车的头脑都没有。

❷ [U] 情报；情报人员
She first moved into the intelligence services 22 years ago.
22年前她初次进入情报部门。

小贴士 CIA（美国）中央情报局 Central Intelligence Agency

AI 人工智能 Artificial Intelligence

IQ 智商 Intelligence Quotient

词义辨析 <P375第69>

高智力的，聪明的 intelligent, intellectual

▶ **intelligible** [ɪnˈtelɪdʒəbl] adj. 容易理解的

His lecture was readily intelligible to all the students.

他的讲课学生们都能轻松地听懂。

14. elite [eɪˈliːt] n. 精英，杰出人物 adj. 精英的
『e出+lite(=lect)选择→从（许多中）选择出来的→精英』

[C+sing./pl. v.] 精英，杰出人物

a group of people in a society, etc. who are powerful and have a lot of influence, because they are rich, intelligent, etc.
Public opinion is influenced by the small elite who control the media. 舆论为少数控制着新闻媒介的上层人士所左右。
In these countries, only the elite can afford an education for their children.
在这些国家里，只有上层人士才供得起子女上学。

---

1. lecture [ˈlektʃə(r)] n. & v. 讲课；演讲；训斥
『lect说，讲+ure表名词→讲课；演讲』

❶ [C]（通常指大学里的）讲座，讲课；演讲
to deliver/give a lecture to first-year students
给一年级学生讲课
a lecture room/hall 演讲室/厅

❷ [C]（冗长的）训斥，说教
a long angry talk that sb gives to one person or a group of people because they have done sth wrong
I know I should stop smoking—don't give me a lecture.
我知道我该戒烟——别再教训我了。

❸ [V] ~ (in/on sth)（大学里）讲课；演讲
She lectures in Russian literature. 她讲授俄罗斯文学。
She then invited him to Atlanta to lecture on the history of art.
她于是邀请他去亚特兰大讲授艺术史。

❹ [VN] ~ sb (about/on sth) 训斥
He's always lecturing me about the way I dress.
他总是对我的衣着指手画脚。

▶**lecturer** [ˈlektʃərə(r)] n. 讲课者；演讲者

2. dialect [ˈdaɪəlekt] n. 方言
『dia二者之间+lect讲，读→在一部分人之间说→方言』

They began to speak rapidly in dialect.
他们开始快速地说起地方话来。

3. legible [ˈledʒəbl] adj.（手写或印刷文字）清晰可读的
『leg读，讲+ible能够的→（清晰）可读的』

The signature was still legible. 签名仍清晰可辨。

▶**illegible** [ɪˈledʒəbl] adj. 字迹模糊的；难以辨认的

4. legend [ˈledʒənd] n. 传说；传奇故事；传奇人物
『leg说，讲+end表名词→（听人们）讲的→传说』

❶ [C, U] 传说；传奇故事
the legend of Robin Hood 罗宾汉的传奇故事
Legend has it that the lake was formed by the tears of a god.
据传说这个湖是一位神仙的眼泪积聚而成的。

❷ [C]（尤指某领域中的）传奇人物
She was a legend in her own lifetime.
她在世的时候就是一个传奇人物。

▶**legendary** [ˈledʒəndri] adj. 传奇的；极其著名的

Her patience and tact are legendary.
她的耐心与策略是出了名的。

5. allege [əˈledʒ] vt.（未给出证据的）声称，宣称

『al相当于to+lege说，讲→说到（某事）→声称』

to state sth as a fact but without giving proof
[VN that] It is alleged that he mistreated the prisoners.
据称他虐待犯人。
The accused is alleged to have killed a man.
被告据称谋杀了一名男子。

▶**alleged** [əˈledʒd] adj. 声称的，宣称的

They have begun a hunger strike in protest at the alleged beating. 他们开始绝食以抗议有人所宣称的殴打行为。

▶**allegation** [ˌæləˈgeɪʃn] n.（无证据的）说法；指控

a public statement that is made without giving proof, accusing sb of doing sth that is wrong or illegal
The company has denied the allegations.
公司否认了这些指控。

---

1. legal [ˈliːgl] adj. 法律的
『leg法律+al…的→法律的』

2. legislate [ˈledʒɪsleɪt] vi. 制定法律，立法
『leg法律+i+slate计划，安排→制定法律』

The government will legislate against discrimination in the workplace. 政府将制定法律，在工作场所禁止歧视。
They promised to legislate to protect people's right to privacy.
他们承诺立法保护公民的隐私权。

▶**legislation** [ˌledʒɪsˈleɪʃn] n. 立法；法律

New legislation on the sale of drugs will be introduced next year. 有关药物销售的新法规将于明年出台。
Legislation will be difficult and will take time.
立法既费力又耗时。

▶**legislature** [ˈledʒɪsleɪtʃə(r)] n. 立法机关；议会

These rules may have the same effect as a law passed by the legislature.
这些规章可能和立法机关通过的法律具有同等效力。

▶**legislative** [ˈledʒɪslətɪv] adj. 立法的

a legislative process/council 立法过程/委员会

3. legitimate [lɪˈdʒɪtɪmət] adj. 合法的；合理的；合法婚姻所生的
『leg法律+it走+i+mate配偶，伴侣→走过法律程序的伴侣→合法的』

❶ 合法的；法律认可的
the legitimate government of the country
这个国家的合法政府
Is his business strictly legitimate?
他的生意是否绝对合法？

❷ 正当的，合情合理的
That's a perfectly legitimate fear.
怀有这种恐惧完全在情理之中。

❸ 合法婚姻所生的
We only married in order that the child should be legitimate.
我们结婚纯粹是为了给孩子一个合法身份。

▶**legitimacy** [lɪˈdʒɪtɪməsi] n. 合法（性）；合理

The opposition parties do not recognise the political legitimacy of his government.
反对党不承认他的政府在政治上的合法性。

词根154. leg=appoint, send，表示"任命；派遣"

1. delegate [ˈdelɪgət , ˈdelɪgeɪt] n. 代表；　v. 委派
『de离开+leg任命；派遣+ate表动词→把（人或事）派遣走→委派』

❶ [C] 代表；会议代表
The conference was attended by delegates from 56 countries.
此次会议有来自56个国家的代表出席。

❷ [VN] 委派
The job had to be delegated to an assistant.
这工作得交给助手负责。
I've been delegated to organize the Christmas party.
我被选派来组织圣诞聚会。

▶**delegation** [ˌdelɪˈgeɪʃn] n. 代表团；委派
The delegation has concluded its visit to China.
代表团结束了对中国的访问。

2. relegate [ˈrelɪgeɪt] vt. 使贬职，使降级
『re返回+leg任命+ate表动词→（把某人）任命回去→降级，降职』

She was then relegated to the role of assistant.
随后她被降级做助手了。
He relegated the incident to the back of his mind.
他将这个事件抛到了脑后。

词根155. lev=raise, lighten，表示"提高，举起；变轻"

1. lever [ˈliːvə(r)] n. 杠杆；操作杆；施压手段
『lev举起，提高+er表物→举起（重）的东西→杠杆』

❶ [C]（操作机械的）杆，柄，把手
Pull the lever towards you to adjust the speed.
把操纵杆向你身体一侧拉动以调节速度。

❷ [C] 杠杆

❸ [C]（用作施加压力等的）手段，方法
The threat of sanctions is our most powerful lever for peace.
实施制裁的威胁是我们争取和平最有力的施压手段。

▶**leverage** [ˈliːvərɪdʒ] n. 杠杆作用；影响力
『lever杠杆+age表行为或结果→杠杆作用』

❶ [U]（能够操控形势的）影响力，手段，优势
His function as a Mayor affords him the leverage to get things done through attending committee meetings.
他的市长身份使他有能力通过出席委员会会议来达成一些事情。

❷ [U] 杠杆力；杠杆作用
The spade and fork have longer shafts, providing better leverage. 锹和耙的手柄较长，可发挥较好的杠杆作用。

2. elevate [ˈelɪveɪt] vt. 举起，升高；提拔
『e出+lev举起+ate表动词→举出→举起』

❶ ~ sb/sth (to sth) | ~ sth (into sth)
(formal) 提拔（到不应有的位置）
He elevated many of his friends to powerful positions within the government.
他将许多朋友都提拔到政府部门的要职上。

❷ (technical or formal) 举起；抬起；使升高
It is important that the injured leg should be elevated.
将受伤的腿抬高是很重要的。
Smoking often elevates blood pressure.
抽烟常常使血压升高。

▶**elevator** [ˈelɪveɪtə(r)] n. 电梯　（BrE lift）
词义辨析 <P375第70> 电梯 lift, elevator, escalator

3. alleviate [əˈliːvieɪt] vt. 减轻，缓解（痛苦等）
『al相当于to+lev举起；变轻+i+ate表动词→使达到轻的状态→减轻』

If you alleviate pain, suffering, or an unpleasant condition, you make it less intense or severe.
Nowadays, a great deal can be done to alleviate back pain.
如今，减轻背部疼痛可以有许多方法。
The drug will alleviate her suffering.
这药可以减轻她的痛苦。

4. relieve [rɪˈliːv] vt. 减轻；解脱；接替；解围
『re一再+lieve(=lev)提高，举起，变轻→使（不愉快的情况）变轻→减轻；解脱；接替；解围』

❶ [VN] 解除，减轻，缓和（不快、痛苦、不愉快的事）
to relieve anxiety/guilt/stress 消除焦虑/内疚；缓解压力
Being able to tell the truth at last seemed to relieve her.
能够最后讲出真话似乎使她感到轻松。
efforts to relieve poverty 缓解贫困的努力
to relieve traffic congestion 缓解交通拥堵
We played cards to relieve the boredom of the long wait.
长时间等待实在无聊，我们就打扑克来解闷儿。

❷ [VN] 使（从…中）解脱出来
A porter relieved her of the three large cases.
一个行李搬运工替她扛了3个大包。
A part-time bookkeeper will relieve you of the burden of chasing unpaid invoices and paying bills.
雇一个兼职簿记员将使你摆脱追讨未付单据和支付账单的负担。

❸ [VN] 接替，给…换班；解除（或免除）…的职务
At seven o'clock the night nurse came in to relieve her.
7点钟的时候夜班护士来接她的班。
The officer involved was relieved of his duties because he had violated strict guidelines.
那名相关的官员被免除了职务，因为他违反了要求严格的规章制度。

❹ [VN] 解围；排便
The offensive began several days ago as an attempt to relieve the town. 进攻于几天前开始，试图解放这个城镇。
It is not difficult to train your dog to relieve itself on command. 训练你的狗按指令大小便并非难事。

▶**relief** [rɪˈliːf] n.（不快过后的）宽慰，轻松；（焦虑、痛苦等的）减轻；救济，救援物品；换班者；解围

We all breathed a sigh of relief when he left.
他走了以后，我们大家都如释重负地松了口气。
modern methods of pain relief 消除疼痛的新办法
a relief agency/organization/worker 救助机构/组织/工作者
The next crew relief comes on duty at 9 o'clock.
下一批换班的员工9点钟接班。

5. levee [ˈlevi] n. 防洪堤；（河边乘客上下船的）码头
『lev提高+ee与…有关的物→（河岸）升高（以防洪）→防洪堤』

Engineers are blowing up that levee in order to let water from the Ohio River flow into the Mississippi.
工程兵部队炸毁堤坝是为了让俄亥俄河中的水流入密西西比河。

6. levy [ˈlevi] vt. 征收；征（税）n. 征收额；税款

『lev提高+y表行为→提高（政府收入）的行为→征税』

A new tax was levied on consumers of luxury goods.
对奢侈品消费者征收了新税。

They imposed a 5% levy on alcohol.
他们对酒精征收5%的税。

7. levity [ˈlevəti] n. 轻佻；轻浮

『lev提高，变轻+ity表性质→轻浮』

Levity is behaviour that shows a tendency to treat serious matters in a non-serious way.

His remarks injected a note of levity into the proceedings.
他的话将一丝轻率带入了议事过程中。

It's about how "levity" can transform the workplace.
这是关于"轻佻"如何改变办公场所（的书）。

词根156. liber=free, weight, consider，表示"自由；考虑"

1. liberal [ˈlibərəl] adj. 开明的；自由的；大方的 n. 开明的人；自由党成员

『liber自由+al表形容词或人→开明的；自由的；开明的人』

❶ adj.（人）开明的

willing to understand and respect other people's behaviour, opinions, etc., especially when they are different from your own; believing people should be able to choose how they behave

liberal attitudes/views/opinions 开明的态度/观点/意见

❷ adj.（政治经济上）自由的，开明的；支持（社会、政治或宗教）变革的

liberal theories 自由主义的理论

a liberal politician 支持改革的政治家

❸ Liberal 自由党的

❹ adj. 慷慨的，大方的

She is very liberal with her money. 她用钱很大方。

❺ [C] 开明的人；支持变革的人

2. liberate [ˈlibəreɪt] vt. 解放；使自由

『liber自由+ate使→使自由→解放』

The city was liberated by the advancing army.
军队向前挺进，解放了那座城市。

Writing poetry liberated her from the routine of everyday life.
写诗使她从日常生活的例行公事中解脱出来。

▶ **PLA** People's Liberation Army 人民解放军

3. liberty [ˈlibəti] n. 自由

『liber自由+ty表名词→自由』

❶ [U] 自由（自己选择生活方式而不受政府及权威限制）

the fight for justice and liberty 争取正义和自由的斗争

❷ [U] 自由（不受关押或奴役的状态）

He had to endure six months' loss of liberty.
他得忍受六个月失去自由之苦。

❸ **at liberty to do sth** 获准做某事

You are at liberty to say what you like. 你尽可畅所欲言。

take the liberty of doing sth 擅自；冒昧

I took the liberty of going into Assunta's wardrobe.
阿孙塔的衣橱敞着，我便擅自在里面翻了一下。

4. libertine [ˈlibəti:n] n. 放荡的男人

『liber自由+tine→放荡的人』

a person, usually a man, who leads an immoral life and is interested in pleasure, especially sexual pleasure

5. deliberate [dɪˈlibərət , dɪˈlibəreɪt] vi. 慎重考虑 adj. 故意的；从容的

『de加强+liber考虑+ate表动词或形容词→慎重考虑→（经过深思熟虑后的行为）故意的；从容的』

❶ adj. 故意的

The speech was a deliberate attempt to embarrass the government. 这一发言蓄意使政府难堪。

❷ adj. 从容的，不慌不忙的

done slowly and carefully

She spoke in a slow and deliberate way.
她说话慢条斯理不慌不忙。

❸ [V] 慎重考虑

to think very carefully about sth, usually before making a decision

[V] The jury deliberated for five days before finding him guilty. 陪审团认真讨论了五天才裁定他有罪。

词根157. lic=allure，表示"引诱"

1. delicious [dɪˈliʃəs] adj. 美味的，可口的

『de加强+lic引诱+ious充满…的→（食物）引诱的→美味的，可口的』

2. delicate [ˈdelikət] adj. 精美的；易损的；需要精心处理的；娇弱的；（色）柔和的，（味）清淡的

『de加强+lic引诱+ate表形容词→（物）引诱人的→精美的』

❶ 娇美的；精美的；雅致的；纤细的

small and having a beautiful shape or appearance

She had delicate hands. 她有一双纤细的手。

❷（颜色）柔和的；（味道）清淡可口的；（气味）清香的

Something that is delicate has a colour, taste, or smell which is pleasant and not strong or intense.

a delicate fragrance/flavour 清新的芳香；鲜美的味道

❸（物）娇贵易碎的；（人）柔弱的

easily damaged or broken; not strong and easily becoming ill/sick

delicate china teacups 易碎的瓷茶杯

Babies have very delicate skin. 婴儿的皮肤非常娇嫩。

the delicate ecological balance of the rainforest
热带雨林极易被破坏的生态平衡

a delicate child/constitution 纤弱的孩子/体质

❹ 微妙的；棘手的；需要小心处理的

（problems, situations, matter）that need/needs to be dealt with carefully and sensitively in order to avoid upsetting things or offending people

a delicate problem 棘手的问题

The delicate surgical operation took five hours.
这精细的外科手术花了五个小时。

❺ 精细的；精密的

made or formed in a very careful and detailed way

the delicate mechanisms of a clock 钟的精密机件

3. delicacy [ˈdelikəsi] n. 精美；娇贵；棘手；佳肴

『delicious和delicate共同的名词形式』

❶ [U] 精美；娇贵；棘手

There is a matter of some delicacy which I would like to discuss. 有件有点儿棘手的事我想要商量一下。

Both countries are behaving with rare delicacy.
两个国家都表现出少有的谨慎。

❷ [C] 佳肴
a type of food considered to be very special in a particular place
local delicacies 当地的美味佳肴

4. elicit [iˈlɪsɪt] vt. 引出；探出；诱出
『e出来+lic引诱+it→诱出』

to get information or a reaction from sb, often with difficulty
I could elicit no response from him.
我从他那里得不到任何回应。

词根158. limin, lim=threshold，表示"门槛"，引申为"限制"

1. limit [ˈlɪmɪt] n. & vt. 限制

There is a limit to the amount of pain we can bear.
我们能忍受的疼痛是有限的。
Violent crime is not limited to big cities.
暴力犯罪并不局限于大城市。

▶ **limitation** [ˌlɪmɪˈteɪʃn] n. 限制；局限

❶ [U] 限制；控制
the act or process of limiting or controlling sb/sth
They would resist any limitation of their powers.
他们会抵制对他们权力的任何限制。

❷ [C] ~ (on sth) 起限制作用的规则（或事实、条件）
a rule, fact or condition that limits sth
Disability is a physical limitation on your life.
残疾在身体方面限制了你的生活。

❸ [C, usually pl.] 局限；限度
a limit on what sb/sth can do or how good they or it can be
This technique is useful but it has its limitations.
这种技术实用，但也有局限性。
I realized how possible it was to overcome your limitations, to achieve well beyond what you believe yourself capable of.
我意识到，要超越自己的局限、取得超乎自己想象的成就是完全有可能的。

2. delimit [diˈlɪmɪt] vt. 定…的界限，界定
『de表加强+limit限制→定…的界限』

We need to delimit the scope of our discussion.
我们需要限定讨论的范围。

3. eliminate [iˈlɪmɪneɪt] vt. 排除；除掉
『e出+limin限制+ate表动词→限制在外→消除』

❶ [VN] ~ sth/sb (from sth) 排除；清除；消除
Credit cards eliminate the need to carry a lot of cash.
有了信用卡就用不着携带很多现金。
The police have eliminated two suspects from their investigation. 警方通过调查已经排除了两名犯罪嫌疑人。

❷ [VN] (formal) 消灭，干掉（尤指敌人或对手）
Most of the regime's left-wing opponents were eliminated.
这个政权的左翼反对派多数已被除掉。

4. preliminary [prɪˈlɪmɪnəri] adj. 预备的；初步的 n. 准备工作，初步行动；预赛，初赛
『pre事先+limin门槛+ary…的→入门前的→初步的,预备的』

❶ adj. ~ (to sth) 预备性的；初步的；开始的
happening before a more important action or event

After a few preliminary remarks he announced the winners.
说了几句开场白之后，他即宣布优胜者名单。
preliminary results/findings/enquiries 初步结果/发现/调查
the preliminary rounds of the contest 预赛

❷ [C] 准备工作；初步行动
A preliminary is something that you do at the beginning of an activity, often as a form of preparation.
A physical examination is a preliminary to joining the army.
体格检查是参军的初步准备。

❸ [C] 预赛；初赛；初试
The winner of each preliminary goes through to the final.
每场初赛的获胜者进入决赛。

5. subliminal [ˌsʌbˈlɪmɪnl] adj. 下意识的，潜意识的
『sub下面+limin限制+al…的→限制在（意识）下面的→下意识的』

affecting your mind even though you are not aware of it
Colour has a profound, though often subliminal influence on our senses and moods.
颜色会极大地影响我们的感官和情绪，尽管这种影响通常是潜意识的。

词根159. line=line,表示"直线，线条"

1. underline [ˌʌndəˈlaɪn] vt. 在…下画线；强调，凸显
『under下面+line线条→在下面画线；强调』

Underline the following that apply to you.
在符合自身情况的项下画线。
Her question underlined how little she understood him.
她的问题表明她多么不了解他。

2. outline [ˈaʊtlaɪn] v. 概述；显示…的轮廓 n. 概述；轮廓线
『out外面+line线→轮廓；概述』

[VN] We outlined our proposals to the committee.
我们向委员会概述了我们的提案。
This is a brief outline of the event. 这就是事件的简要情况。

3. linear [ˈlɪniə(r)] adj. （发展或运动）沿直线的；利用线条的
『line直线+ar…的→直线的』

Students do not always progress in a linear fashion.
学生不会总是顺着一条直线进步。
If you try this example, you might notice that the motion is not linear.
如果试着运行这个例子，你会注意到这种运动不是线性的。

4. lineage [ˈlɪniɪdʒ] n. 宗系；血统
『line直线+age表名词→族谱构成的直线→血统』

They can trace their lineage directly back to the 18th century.
他们的世系可以直接追溯到18世纪。

5. liner [ˈlaɪnə(r)] n. 班机；邮轮
『line直线，线+(e)r表人或物→沿线路在海上航行的客轮』

It became impractical to make a business trip by ocean liner.
乘坐远洋班轮进行商务旅行变得不合时宜了。

6. delineate [dɪˈlɪnieɪt] vt. （详细地）描述；勾画
『de强调+line直线，线条+ate表动词→用线条勾画→描述；勾画』

to describe, draw or explain sth in detail
Our objectives need to be precisely delineated.

我们的目标需详细解释清楚。
The ship's route is clearly delineated on the map.
这条船的航线清楚地标在地图上。

1. lingual [ˈlɪŋgwəl] adj. 语言的；舌的
『lingu语言；舌→语言的；舌的』

2. monolingual [ˌmɒnəˈlɪŋgwəl] adj. 单语的
『mono单个+ lingu语言+al…的→单语的』

Research by Australian universities has shown that a monolingual country often performs worse in international trade and diplomacy.
澳大利亚大学的研究表明，单语国家通常在国际贸易和外交中表现不佳。

3. bilingual [ˌbaɪˈlɪŋgwəl] adj. 双语的
『bi二，两+lingu语言+al…的→双语种的』

Many parents oppose bilingual education in schools.
很多家长反对学校实行双语教学。
He is bilingual in an Asian language and English.
他会说一门亚洲语言和一门英语。

4. trilingual [traɪˈlɪŋgwəl] adj. 使用三种语言的
『tri三+ lingu语言+al…的→使用三种语言的』

5. multilingual [ˌmʌltiˈlɪŋgwəl] adj. 使用多种语言的
『multi多+ lingu语言+al…的→使用多种语言的』

multilingual translators/communities/societies
多语翻译者/社群/社会

6. linguist [ˈlɪŋgwɪst] n. 语言学家
『lingu语言+ist学家→语言学家』

▶ **linguistics** [lɪŋˈgwɪstɪks] n. 语言学
『linguist语言学家+ics…学→语言学』

▶ **linguistic** [lɪŋˈgwɪstɪk] adj. 语言的，语言学的

connected with language or the scientific study of language
linguistic and cultural barriers 语言和文化上的障碍
a child's innate linguistic ability 儿童的先天语言能力
new developments in linguistic theory 语言学理论的新发展

1. delinquent [dɪˈlɪŋkwənt] adj. （通常指青少年）有违法倾向的；拖欠债务的 n. 少年犯
『de加强+linqu离开+ent具有…性质的→一再离开（正道）→有过失的；有违法倾向的』

❶ adj. （通常指青少年）有违法倾向的；屡犯轻罪的
delinquent teenagers 不良青少年

❷ adj. 拖欠债务的；到期未还的
a delinquent borrower 欠债未还的借款人
a delinquent loan 逾期未还的贷款

❸ [U] 不良青少年；少年犯
a nine-year-old delinquent 9岁的少年犯

▶ **delinquency** [dɪˈlɪŋkwənsi] n. （尤指青少年的）违法行为；逾期未还债务（或未缴税款）

2. relinquish [rɪˈlɪŋkwɪʃ] vt. （不情愿地）放弃（权力或希望等）
『re返回+linguish(=leave)离开→离开返回→放弃』

He does not intend to relinquish power.
他没有打算放弃权力。

They had relinquished all hope that she was alive.
他们已经完全不指望她还活着了。

3. ellipse [ɪˈlɪps] n. 椭圆；椭圆形
『el出来+lipse离开→（圆的对应边）偏离（圆心）→椭圆；也可这样记：el出来+lips嘴唇+e→嘴唇噘出来（微张时的形状）→椭圆形』

The Earth orbits in an ellipse. 地球轨道呈椭圆形。

4. eclipse [ɪˈklɪps] n. 日食；月食 vt. 使黯然失色
『ec出去+lipse离开→（太阳或月亮的一部分）离开不见了→日食，月食；也可这样记：e(c)出去+clip剪+se→（太阳或月亮的一部分像是被）剪掉→日食；月食』

❶ [C] 日食；月食
an eclipse of the sun/moon 日食；月食
a total/partial eclipse 日全食；日偏食

❷ [VN] 使黯然失色；使相形见绌；盖过
If one thing is eclipsed by a second thing that is bigger, newer, or more important than it, the first thing is no longer noticed because the second thing gets all the attention.
Though a talented player, he was completely eclipsed by his brother.
他虽是一个天才运动员，但与他兄弟相比就黯然失色了。

▶ **clip** [klɪp] n. 回形针，夹子；（电影）片段 vt. 夹住；修剪

❶ [C] 回形针，夹子；（电影）片段
She took the clip out of her hair. 她把发夹取了下来。
Here is a clip from her latest movie.
这是她最新电影的片段。

❷ [VN] 夹住；修剪
Clip the pages together. 把这些散页夹在一起。
to clip a hedge 修剪树篱
He clipped off a length of wire. 他剪掉了一段金属线。

1. liquid [ˈlɪkwɪd] n. 液体 adj. 液体的，液态的；易变为现金的
『liqu液体+id…的→液体的→流动的→易变现的』

❶ [U, C] 液体
She poured the dark brown liquid down the sink.
她把深棕色的液体倒进了污水池。

❷ adj. 液体的；液态的
liquid soap 肥皂液
liquid nitrogen 液态氮

❸ adj. 易变为现金的
liquid assets 流动资产

▶ **liquidity** [lɪˈkwɪdəti] n. 资产流动性，资产变现能力

the state of owning things of value that can easily be exchanged for cash
The company maintains a high degree of liquidity.
公司保持着很高的资产折现度。

▶ **liquidate** [ˈlɪkwɪdeɪt] v. 破产清算；变卖；清除
『liquid易变现的+ate表动词→把（资产）变现→清算』

❶ [V, VN] （破产）清算；变卖
to close a business and sell everything it owns in order to pay debts
A unanimous vote was taken to liquidate the company.
全体投票一致通过停业清理公司。

The company went into liquidation. 公司进入了清盘阶段。
to liquidate assets 变卖资产

❷ [VN] 消灭；摧毁；清除

If someone in a position of power liquidates people who are causing problems, they get rid of them, usually by killing them.

They have not hesitated in the past to liquidate their rivals.
过去他们曾毫不犹豫地铲除对手。

2. liquor [ˈlɪkə(r)] n. (NAmE) 烈性酒；(BrE)含酒精饮料
『liqu液体+or表物→液体的东西→烈性酒』

词根163. liter=letter，表示"文字，字母"

1. literature [ˈlɪtrətʃə(r)] n. 文学作品；文献，资料
『liter文字，字母+ature与行为有关之物→文学』

❶ [U] 文学；文学作品
Dickens' novels have enriched English literature.
狄更斯的小说丰富了英国文学。

❷ [U]（某一学科的）文献资料
I've read all the available literature on keeping rabbits.
我阅读了我能找到的养兔的全部资料。

❸ [U] 印刷的宣传品
I am sending you literature from two other companies that provide a similar service.
我把另外两家提供类似服务的公司的宣传资料发给你。

2. literary [ˈlɪtərəri] adj. 文学的
『liter文字，字母+ary…的→文学的』

Her literary criticism focuses on the way great literature suggests ideas.
她的文学批评集中关注的是伟大的文学作品表达思想的方式。

3. literal [ˈlɪtərəl] adj. 字面上的；直译的
『liter文字，字母+al…的→文字上的→字面上的』

❶ 字面上的
I am not referring to "small" people in the literal sense of the word. 我指的不是字面意义上的"小"人。

❷ 逐字的；直译的
A literal translation of the name Tapies is "walls".
Tapies这个名字直译过来是"墙"。

❸ 言辞刻板的；听话不听音的
Dennis is a very literal person. 丹尼斯是个听话不听音的人。

❹ 确确实实的；完完全全的
He was saying no more than the literal truth.
他说的全是不折不扣的事实。

▶ **literally** [ˈlɪtərəli] adv. 直译地；确确实实地
Every part of you will literally scream—my time has come.
你身体的每一部分将会真正地尖叫出来——我的时刻已经到来！
It literally changed the way I see things.
这真正地改变了我看待事物的方式。
The word "volk" translates literally as "folk".
"volk"这个单词直译过来为"folk"（人们）。

4. literate [ˈlɪtərət] adj. 有读写能力的；有文化的
『liter文字，字母+ate具有…的→有读写能力的』

❶ 有读写能力的
Over one-quarter of the adult population are not fully literate.

1/4以上的成年人不具备完全的读写能力。

❷ 受过良好教育的；（尤指）有文化修养的
intelligent and well-educated, especially about literature and the arts
Scientists should be literate and articulate as well as able to handle figures.
科学家除了能处理数字，还应该具有文学素养且善于表达。

❸ 通晓（某方面知识）的
Head teachers need to be financially literate.
校长需要通晓财政。

▶ **literacy** [ˈlɪtərəsi] n. 有读写能力；通晓某方面知识
『literate有续写能力的，识字的（去te）+cy表性质或状态→识字，有文化』

Literacy is an essential foundation for development and prosperity. 识字是发展和繁荣必不可少的基础。
Political selection is more dependent on sophistry and less on economic literacy.
政治选举更多地取决于诡辩的能力，而不在于是否懂经济。

5. illiterate [ɪˈlɪtərət] adj. 文盲的；n. 目不识丁者
『il不+ liter文字，字母+ate表形容词→不识字的，文盲的』

❶ adj. 文盲的；行文拙劣的
A large percentage of the population is illiterate.
文盲人口占有相当高的比例。

❷ adj.（对某学科）了解不多的，外行的
Many senior managers are technologically illiterate.
许多高级经理都对技术知之甚少。

❸ n. 文盲（指人）
I was an illiterate in the old society, but now I can read.
我这个旧社会的文盲，如今也认字了。

▶ **illiteracy** [ɪˈlɪtərəsi] n. 文盲；无知
Poverty and illiteracy go together with high birth rates.
贫困、文盲与高出生率密切相关。

6. obliterate [əˈblɪtəreɪt] vt. 毁掉；覆盖；清除
『ob反对，否定+liter文字，字母+ate使→去掉文字→擦掉』

The building was completely obliterated by the bomb.
炸弹把那座建筑物彻底摧毁了。
The snow had obliterated their footprints.
白雪覆盖了他们的足迹。
Everything that happened that night was obliterated from his memory. 那天夜里发生的一切都从他的记忆中消失了。

词根164. lith(o)=stone，表示"石头"

1. lithosphere [ˈlɪθəsfɪə(r)] n. 岩石圈，岩石层
『litho石头+sphere范围，领域→岩石圈』

2. megalith [ˈmeɡəlɪθ] n. （尤指古代用于祭祀的）巨石
『mega巨大+lith石头→巨石』

3. Neolithic [ˌniːəˈlɪθɪk] adj. 新石器时代的
『neo新的+lith石的+ic…的→新石器时代的』

4. palaeolithic [ˌpæliəˈlɪθɪk] adj. 旧石器时代的
『palaeo旧的+lith石的+ic…的→旧石器时代的』

词根165. loc=place，表示"地方"

1. local [ˈləʊkl] adj. 地方的，当地的 n. 当地人
『loc地方+al…的→地方的』

A local man was accused of the murder.

有一本地人被指控为这起谋杀案的凶手。
The locals are very friendly. 当地人很友好。

▶ **locality** [ləʊˈkæləti] n. （所处或提及的）地区

people living in the locality of the power station
居住在发电站周围地区的人
There is no airport in the locality. 这个地区没有飞机场。

2. locate [ləʊˈkeɪt] vt. 确定…的位置；使坐落于
『loc地方+ate表动词→（使到）某个地方；（确定）位置→使坐落于；确定位置』

❶ [VN] 找出…的准确位置
The mechanic located the fault immediately.
机修工立即找到了出故障的地方。
Rescue planes are trying to locate the missing sailors.
救援飞机正在努力查明失踪水手的下落。

❷ [VN] 把…安置在（或建造于）
They located their headquarters in Swindon.
他们把总部设在了斯温登。

▶ **located** [ləʊˈkeɪtɪd] adj. 位于；坐落在
The house is located next to the river. 房屋位于河附近。

▶ **location** [ləʊˈkeɪʃn] n. 位置，地方
The first thing he looked at was his office's location.
他首先看的是自己办公室的位置。

3. allocate [ˈæləkeɪt] vt. 分配；分派；划拨
『al相当于to+ loc地方+ate表动词→（正式把某物）划拨到某个地方→分配；划拨』

~ sth (for sth) | ~ sth (to sb/sth) | ~ (sb/sth) sth
to give sth officially to sb/sth for a particular purpose
[VN] They intend to allocate more places to mature students this year. 今年他们打算给成人学生提供更多的名额。
A large sum has been allocated for buying new books for the library. 已划拨了一大笔款项给图书馆购买新书。

▶ **allocation** [ˌæləˈkeɪʃn] n. 分配的东西；划拨的款项
How much CPU and memory allocation is required?
需要分配多少CPU和内存资源？

词义辨析 <P364第19> **分发 allocate, allot, distribute**

4. locomotive [ˌləʊkəˈməʊtɪv] n. 机车；火车头
『loc(o)地方+mot动+ive表物→从一个地方跑到另一个地方的东西→火车头』

Steam locomotives pumped out clouds of white smoke.
蒸汽机车喷出一团团白烟。

5. dislocate [ˈdɪsləkeɪt] vt. 使脱臼；扰乱；使混乱
『dis离开+loc位置+ate表动词→使离开位置→使脱臼；扰乱』

❶ 使（骨头）脱位；使脱臼
He dislocated his shoulder in the accident.
他在事故中肩膀脱臼了。

❷ 扰乱；使混乱；使运转不正常
It would help to end illiteracy and disease, but it would also dislocate a traditional way of life.
这将有助于消除文盲和疾病，但也会扰乱传统的生活方式。
The strike at the financial nerve centre was designed to dislocate the economy.
在金融活动中心地区的罢工是为了扰乱经济秩序。

词根166. logue, loqu, log=speak，表示"说话"

① logue=speak，表示"说话"

1. dialogue [ˈdaɪəlɒg] n. 对话，对白
『dia穿过；两者之间+logue说话→两人对讲→对话』

2. prologue [ˈprəʊlɒg] n. 序言；序幕；开场白
『pro向前，在前+logue说话→说在前面的（话）→前言』
a speech, etc. at the beginning of a play, book, or film/movie that introduces it
The prologue to the novel is written in the form of a newspaper account.
这本小说的序言是以报纸报道的形式写的。
This was a prologue to today's bloodless revolution.
这拉开了当今不流血革命的序幕。

3. epilogue [ˈepilɒg] n. （书、电影等）收场白，后记
『epi在…后面+logue说话→在（故事结束后）说的话→收场白，后记』
An epilogue is a passage or speech which is added to the end of a book or play as a conclusion.
Narrator: [epilogue] And so, all ended well for both Horton and Who's, and for all in the jungle, even kangaroos.
旁白：于是，霍顿和无名氏们都平安无事了，整个丛林，甚至袋鼠也都一团和气。

4. monologue [ˈmɒnəlɒg] n. 长篇大论；独白，独角戏
『mono单个，一个+ logue说话→一个人说→独白』

❶ [C, U] 独角戏；（戏剧、电影等的）独白

❷ [C] 长篇大论，滔滔不绝的讲话
a long speech by one person during a conversation that stops other people from speaking or expressing an opinion
He went into a long monologue about life in America.
他开始滔滔不绝地谈起美国的生活。

5. catalogue [ˈkætəlɒg] n. 目录，名录；一连串（坏事）
v. 列入目录
『cata下面+logue说话→要说的话在下（后）面→目录』

❶ [C] 目录；目录簿；名录
a complete list of items, for example of things that people can look at or buy
the world's biggest seed catalogue
世界上内容最丰富的种子目录
Look in the catalogue to see whether the library has this book.
查看目录，看看图书馆里是否有这本书。

❷ [C] （尤指坏事）一连串，一系列
His story is a catalogue of misfortune.
他的故事充满着接二连三的不幸。

❸ [VN] 列入目录；列举，历数（尤指一连串坏事）
The Royal Greenwich Observatory was founded to observe and catalogue the stars.
当初创立皇家格林尼治天文台就是为了观察星体并对其进行编目。
Speaker after speaker lined up to catalogue a series of failures under his leadership.
发言者一个接一个，历数在他的领导下遭遇的一次次失败。

② loqu=speak，表示"说话"

1. colloquial [kəˈləʊkwiəl] adj. 口语的
『col一起+loqu说话+ial表形容词→（语言）一起说话性质的→口语的』

English slang is a new kind of youth language which is more colloquial and abbreviated.
英语俚语是一种年轻人喜欢使用的非正式的、更简短的语言类型。

2. loquacious [ləˈkweɪʃəs] adj. 话多的，喋喋不休的
『loqu说话+acious充满…的→话多的』

Kennedy had become almost as loquacious as Joe.
肯尼迪变得和乔一样唠叨了。

3. eloquent [ˈeləkwənt] adj. 能言善辩的；表达生动的
『e出来+loqu说话+ent表形容词→能（把要表达的流利、生动地）说出来的→能言善辩的』

I heard him make a very eloquent speech at that dinner.
在那次晚宴上，我听到他作了一番非常有说服力的陈词。
He was eloquent about his love of books.
说起对书的喜爱他就会停不住嘴。

4. soliloquy [səˈlɪləkwi] n. 独白（的台词）；独白
『sol单独的+i+ loqu说话+y表名词→一个人说→独白』

Hamlet's soliloquy is probably the most famous in English drama. 哈姆雷特的独白在英国戏剧中大概是最出名的了。

③ log=speak，表示"说话"

1. analogy [əˈnælədʒi] n. 类比，类似
『ana类似+log说话+y表名词→说类似的→类比，类似』

If you make or draw an analogy between two things, you show that they are similar in some way.

The teacher drew an analogy between the human heart and a pump. 老师打了个比喻，把人的心脏比作水泵。
It is sometimes easier to illustrate an abstract concept by analogy with something concrete.
有时通过与某种具体事物的类比，更容易说明某个抽象的概念。

▶**analogous** [əˈnæləgəs] adj. 类似的

Sleep has often been thought of as being in some way analogous to death.
人们常常认为睡眠在某种意义上来说类似死亡。

▶**analogue** [ˈænəlɒg] n. 相似物 adj. （电子处理方法）模拟的；（钟、表）指针式的

❶ [C] 相似物，类似物
If one thing is an analogue of another, it is similar in some way.
No model can ever be a perfect analogue of nature itself.
任何模型都无法完全模拟自然本身。

❷ adj.（电子处理方法）模拟的
The analogue signals from the video tape are converted into digital code. 该录像带中的模拟信号被转换成数字代码。

❸ （钟、表）指针式的（BrE also analog）

2. eulogy [ˈjuːlədʒi] n. 颂词，颂文；悼词
『eu好+log说话+y表名词→说好话→颂辞；悼词』

Mr Garth gave a long eulogy about their achievements in the research. 加思先生对他们的研究成果大大地颂扬了一番。
Joe will deliver the eulogy and then we can leave.
乔会发表一篇悼词，然后我们就可以离开了。

词根167. lude=play，表示"表演；演奏"

1. prelude [ˈpreljuːd] n. 序曲；前奏

『pre前+lude演奏→在（长短音乐）前面演奏的→序曲』
The curtain rises toward the end of the prelude.
序曲将近结束时帷幕升起来了。
Most unions see privatisation as an inevitable prelude to job losses. 大多数工会认为私有化是失业的前奏。

2. interlude [ˈɪntəluːd] n. 幕间休息；间歇；插入的事件
『inter在…之间+lude表演→在前后两场表演中间的时间→幕间休息；间歇』

An interlude is a short period of time when an activity or situation stops and something else happens.
Apart from a brief interlude of peace, the war lasted nine years. 除了一段短暂的和平，那场战争持续了九年。
After this interlude, the band started up again.
幕间休息之后，乐队又开始演奏了。

3. delude [dɪˈluːd] vt. 欺骗；哄骗
『de下面+lude表演→在下面（暗地里偷偷地）表演（欺骗你相信）→欺骗；哄骗』

~ sb/yourself (into doing sth) 欺骗；哄骗
to make sb believe sth that is not true
[VN] Don't be deluded into thinking that we are out of danger yet. 不要误以为我们已脱离危险。
The President was deluding himself if he thought he was safe from such action.
总统如果认为这样的行为不会威胁到他，那他就是在自欺欺人。

▶**delusion** [dɪˈluːʒn] n. 错觉；幻觉；妄想

I was under the delusion that he intended to marry me.
我误认为他要娶我。
This was not optimism；it was delusion.
这不是乐观，这是妄想。
the delusions of the mentally ill 精神病患者的妄想

词义辨析 <P380第94> 幻想 fantasy, illusion, delusion

4. collude [kəˈluːd] vi. 共谋，勾结，串通
『col一起+lude表演→一起表演（暗地里做坏事）→共谋，勾结，串通』

They colluded with terrorists to overthrow the government.
他们与恐怖分子密谋推翻政府。

▶**collusion** [kəˈluːʒn] n. 共谋，勾结，串通

The police were corrupt and were operating in collusion with the drug dealers. 警察腐败，与那伙毒品贩子内外勾结。

5. allude [əˈluːd] vi. 间接提到；暗指，影射
『al相当于to+lude表演，演戏→对…演戏→不直截了当→暗指；间接提到』

Don't allude to his father's death when you meet him.
当你和他见面时，不要提到他父亲的死。

▶**allusion** [əˈluːʒn] n. 间接提到，暗指，影射；典故

His statement was seen as an allusion to the recent drug-related killings.
他的声明被视为暗指最近与毒品有关的多起凶杀案。
Her poetry is full of obscure literary allusion.
她的诗随处可见晦涩的文学典故。

6. elude [iˈluːd] vt. （尤指机敏地）避开，逃避；想不起
『e出去+lude表演→表演诡计（逃）出去→（机敏地）避开』

The two men managed to elude the police for six weeks.

这两个男人想方设法逃避警方追捕达六个星期。

He was extremely tired but sleep eluded him.
他累极了，却睡不着。

Finally he remembered the tiny detail that had eluded him the night before. 他终于想起了前一天晚上想不起来的细节。

▶**elusive** [i'lu:sɪv] adj. 像躲避似的（难以得到的；难以描述的；想不起来的；难以实现的）

In London late-night taxis are elusive and far from cheap.
在伦敦，深夜时难以打到出租车，而且车费非常贵。

Happiness, which had been so elusive in Henry's life, still evaded him.
亨利生活中过去一直难以捕捉的幸福仍然与他无缘。

But why does creativity remain so elusive?
不过，为什么创意还是这么可遇不可求？

7. illusion [ɪ'lu:ʒn] n. 幻想；假象
『illude的名词形式。il里面+lusion表演→（某想法）在内心里面表演（在实际中实现的可能性不大）→幻想』

❶ [C, U] 错误的想法或观念；幻想
An illusion is a false idea or belief.

She's under the illusion that (= believes wrongly that) she'll get the job. 她存有幻想，认为她会得到那份工作。

He could no longer distinguish between illusion and reality.
他再也分不清幻想与现实之间的区别了。

❷ [C] 假象
Floor-to-ceiling windows can give the illusion of extra height.
从地板直抵天花板的窗子会给人高出实际距离的幻觉。

词义辨析 <P380第94> 幻想 **fantasy, illusion, delusion**

8. ludicrous ['lu:dɪkrəs] adj. 愚蠢的；荒唐的；可笑的
『ludicr(= lud)玩；表演+ous…的→（某事有点像）演戏似的（严重脱离现实）→荒唐的；可笑的』

If you describe something as ludicrous, you are emphasizing that you think it is foolish, unreasonable, or unsuitable.

It was ludicrous to suggest that the visit could be kept secret.
认为此次访问能够保密是可笑的。

I find it ludicrous that nothing has been done to protect passengers from fire.
乘客没有受到任何防火保护，这让我觉得十分荒唐。

词根168. **lumin, luster, luc, lun**=light, shine，表示"光，照亮（指柔光，光泽）"

小贴士 lumen ['lu:mɪn] n. 流明 （光通量单位）。lumin的读音与lumen（流明）相同，这可以帮助我们记忆lumin表示"光，照亮"这一词义。

另外，按照英语中的思维方式：有光了，就能看见事物，就知道是什么情况；没有光线了，就什么都看不见了，就什么情况就不知道了。如：
keep sb in the dark 瞒着某人
throw/shed light on 使明白，使理解；阐明
in the light of 鉴于，考虑到
本组词中，有些单词词义的理解，要用到这点知识。

① lumin=light, shine，表示"光，照"

1. luminous ['lu:mɪnəs] adj. 夜光的；发光的；鲜亮的
『lumin光+ous充满→（夜间）充满光的→夜光的；发光的』

luminous paint 发光漆
luminous hands on a clock 钟的夜光指针
staring with huge luminous eyes 用亮晶晶的大眼睛盯着

2. luminary ['lu:mɪnəri] n. 专家，权威
『lumin光+ary表示人→能够像光一样给别人指明方向的人→专家，权威』

The lunch was attended by 38 luminaries from various walks.
来自各行各业的38位权威人士出席了午餐会。

3. illuminate [ɪ'lu:mɪneɪt] vt. 照亮；阐明，解释
『il(=en)使+lumin光+ate表动词→使…有光→照亮』

❶ 照明，照亮，照射 to shine light on sth
Floodlights illuminated the stadium. 泛光灯照亮了体育场。
The earth is illuminated by the sun. 太阳照亮地球。

❷ 阐明，解释
to make sth clearer or easier to understand
This text illuminates the philosopher's early thinking.
这篇课文解释了这位哲学家的早期思想。
They use games and drawings to illuminate their subject.
他们用游戏和图画来阐明他们的主题。

▶**illuminating** [ɪ'lu:mɪneɪtɪŋ] adj. 有启发性的
This is an illuminating analysis. 这是很有启发的分析。
What is conveyed in the picture is both positive and illuminating. 图片传递的内容是积极的和富有启发性的。

② luster=light, shine，表示"光，照"

1. luster ['lʌstə] n. （物体表面的）光泽；光彩，荣耀
The chair has a metallic luster. 这把椅子有金属光泽。
But in the past few months, JPMorgan and its CEO seem to have lost their luster.
但过去几个月，摩根大通及其首席执行官似乎失去了光彩。

▶**lustrous** ['lʌstrəs] adj. 有光泽的；闪亮的；光亮的
I also have noticed some new hair has grown back and is more lustrous and young looking.
我也注意到我的头发开始长回来了，看起来更加亮泽也更年轻了。

2. illustrate ['ɪləstreɪt] vt. 给…加插图；（用示例、图画等）说明；表明
『il(=in)进入+luster光（去e）+ate表动词→让光亮照进（模糊的事物）内部→使明白→说明』

❶ [VN] [usually passive] ~ sth (with sth) 加插图于
to use pictures, photographs, diagrams, etc. in a book, etc.
She went on to art school and is now illustrating a book.
她后来读了艺术学校，现在正在为一本书配插图。

❷ （用示例、图画等）说明，解释
to make the meaning of sth clearer by using examples, pictures, etc.
[VN] To illustrate my point , let me tell you a little story.
为了说明我的观点，让我来给你们讲个小故事。

❸ 表明…真实；显示…存在
[VN] The incident illustrates the need for better security measures. 这次事件说明了加强安全措施的必要。

▶**illustration** [,ɪlə'streɪʃn] n. 插图；图解；实例
She looked like a princess in a nineteenth-century illustration.
她看起来像19世纪插图读物中的公主。
The delay is a perfect illustration of why we need a new computer system.
这次延误是个很好的例证，说明了为什么我们需要新的计算机系统。

► **illustrative** [ˈɪləstrətɪv] adj. 说明性的

3. illustrious [ɪˈlʌstriəs] adj. 著名的；杰出的；卓越的
『il(=in)里面+luster光（去e）+i+ous充满→充满光泽的→光彩的；杰出的』

The composer was one of many illustrious visitors to the town. 那位作曲家是许多造访过这个城市的杰出人物之一。

③ luc=light, shine, 表示"光，照"

1. translucent [trænsˈluːsnt] adj. 半透明的
『trans从…到…+luc光，光泽+ent表形容词→柔光从一侧到另一侧→半透明的』

The building is roofed entirely with translucent corrugated plastic. 这座建筑完全用半透明波纹塑料封顶。
She had fair hair, blue eyes and translucent skin.
她金发碧眼，皮肤透亮。

近义词 **transparent** [trænsˈpærənt] adj. 透明的；清澈的；易识破的；显而易见的 ＜P242＞

2. lucid [ˈluːsɪd] adj. 表达清楚的；（人病后）清醒的
『luc光+id表形容词→有光就能看到一切，就能明白一切的→清楚的，明白的』

❶ 表达清楚的；易懂的
a lucid account of the history of mankind
对人类历史的清楚记述

❷（病后或糊涂过后）清醒的，思路清晰的
He wasn't very lucid, and he didn't quite know where he was.
他神志不是很清醒，不太知道自己在哪里。

③ lun=light, shine, 表示"光，照"

1. lunar [ˈluːnə(r)] adj. 月亮的，月球的；阴历的；农历的
『lun光，照+ar…的→发光的→（月亮）发光的→月亮的；阴历的』

The beginning of the solar and lunar years coincided every 13 years. 太阳年和太阴年的起始时间每13年重合一次。
It's to celebrate the lunar calendar's New Year.
它是为了庆祝中国农历的新年。

► **lunatic** [ˈluːnətɪk] n. 精神错乱者 adj. 疯狂的
『lun月亮（Luna原指罗马神话中的月亮女神）+atic有…性质的→（古时候人们认为精神病与月的盈亏有关）受月亮影响的→精神错乱』

❶ n. 精神错乱者；狂人
a person who does crazy things that are often dangerous
This lunatic in a white van pulled out right in front of me!
这个疯子开着一辆白色货车直接冲到了我前面！

❷ adj. 疯狂的；荒唐可笑的；极其愚蠢的
crazy, ridiculous or extremely stupid
Officers will crack down on lunatic motorists who speed or drive too close to the car in front.
警察将会严厉打击超速或是紧贴前车行驶的疯狂司机。

词根169. magn=great, 表示"大"

1. magnify [ˈmæɡnɪfaɪ] vt. 放大；增强；夸大
『magn大+ify使…→放大；夸大』

❶ [VN] 放大
This version of the Digges telescope magnifies images 11 times. 这种型号的迪格斯望远镜可将图像放大11倍。

❷ 扩大；增强

to make sth bigger, louder or stronger
The dry summer has magnified the problem of water shortages. 干燥的夏季加剧了缺水的问题。

❸ [VN]夸大；夸张
They do not grasp the broad situation and spend their time magnifying ridiculous details.
他们不去把握大局，而是在细枝末节上花费时间大做文章。

小贴士 放大镜 magnifying glass

2. magnificent [mæɡˈnɪfɪsnt] adj. 壮丽的；宏伟的
『magnify放大（变y为i）+cent表形容词→很大的→宏伟的；壮丽的』

extremely attractive and impressive; deserving praise
The Taj Mahal is a magnificent building.
泰姬陵是一座宏伟的建筑。
She looked magnificent in her wedding dress.
她穿着婚纱，看上去漂亮极了。

► **magnificence** [mæɡˈnɪfɪsns] n. 宏伟；壮丽
『magnify放大（变y为i）+cence表名词→变得很大→宏伟；壮丽』

We were all impressed with the magnificence of Russia's Winter Palace.
气势宏伟的俄国冬宫给我们留下了深刻的印象。

3. magnitude [ˈmæɡnɪtjuːd] n. 量级；巨大
『magn大+itude（去i）表性质、状态→巨大』

❶ [U] (formal) 巨大；重大；重要性
We did not realize the magnitude of the problem.
我们没有意识到这个问题的重要性。
Ministers underestimated the magnitude of the task confronting them.
部长们低估了他们所面临的任务的艰巨性。

❷ [U, C] 星等（指星的亮度）；震级；（爆炸的）强度；量级
The San Francisco earthquake of 1906 had a magnitude of 8.3. 1906年旧金山地震的震级为8.3级。
The country's debt this year will be of the same order of magnitude as it was last year.
这个国家今年的债务规模和去年相同。

4. magnate [ˈmæɡneɪt] n. 巨头；大亨
『magn大+ate表人→巨头；大亨』

A magnate is someone who has earned a lot of money from a particular business or industry.
They've linked her with various men, including magnate Donald Trump.
他们把她与不同的男人扯上关系，包括大亨唐纳德·特朗普。
The press magnate decided on a merger with another company to expand his empire.
那位报业巨头决定与另一家公司合并，以扩展他的企业王国。

5. magnanimous [mæɡˈnænɪməs] adj. 宽宏的，大度的 ＜P114＞
『magn大+anim(mind)内心+ous充满→心胸大的→大度的』

词根170. main, man=stay, 表示"停留；逗留"

1. remain [rɪˈmeɪn] vi. 仍然是；剩余 n. 残余（物）；遗迹；遗体
『re又+main停留→又停留在这里→仍然是；残余（物）』

❶ V-LINK 仍然是，仍然保持

The three men remained silent. 这三个人保持着沉默。

The fact remains that inflation is unacceptably high.
事实是通货膨胀率仍高得离谱。

Major questions remain to be answered about his work.
关于他工作的许多重要问题仍然悬而未决。

❷ [V, usually + adv./prep.] 仍然留在某处

The plane remained on the ground. 飞机仍未起飞。

❸ [V] 剩余；遗留；继续存在

Very little of the house remained after the fire.
火灾之后，这座房子所剩无几。

❹ remains 残余（物）；遗迹；遗体

They were tidying up the remains of their picnic.
他们正在收拾野餐后剩下的东西。

The unrecognizable remains of a man had been found.
一具无法辨认的男性尸体被发现了。

There are Roman remains all around us.
我们周围都是古罗马的遗迹。

►remaining [rɪˈmeɪnɪŋ] adj. 剩下的，剩余的

The remaining twenty patients were transferred to another hospital. 其余的20名病人被转到了另一家医院。

►remainder [rɪˈmeɪndə(r)] n. 剩余的（人或物）；余数

I kept some of his books and gave away the remainder.
我保留了一些他的书，其余的都送人了。

Only 5.9 per cent of the area is now covered in trees. Most of the remainder is farmland.
这个地区的树木覆盖率只有5.9%。其他多数地方都是农田。

Divide 2 into 7, and the answer is 3, remainder 1.
7除以2，商3余1。

►remnant [ˈremnənt] n. 残余部分，剩余部分；布头
『remain剩下（去ai）+ant表名词→剩余部分』

❶ [usually pl.] 残余部分；剩余部分

a part of sth that is left after the other parts have been used, removed, destroyed, etc.

After twenty-four hours of fighting, the remnants of the force were fleeing.
战斗持续了24个小时后，该部队残部正在逃离。

❷ [C] 布头

A remnant is a small piece of cloth that is left over when most of the cloth has been sold. Shops usually sell remnants cheaply.

2. maintain [meɪnˈteɪn] vt. 维持；维修，保养 〈P324〉
『main逗留+tain保持→保持停留状态→维持；保养』

3. permanent [ˈpɜːmənənt] adj. 永久的，长久的 〈P30〉
『per自始至终+man停留+ent表形容词→始终停留的→永久的』

4. immanent [ˈɪmənənt] adj. 内在的，固有的；无所不在的
『im里面+man停留+ent有…性质的→停留在内部的→内在的→内在的东西无所不在→无所不在的』

present as a natural part of sth; present everywhere

He believes that beauty is not something imposing, but something immanent.他认为美丽不是外在的而是内在的。

God is immanent in the world. 上帝无所不在。

词根171. maj=great，表示"大；伟大"

1. major [ˈmeɪdʒə(r)] adj. 主要的 n. 专业课；专业课学生
『maj大；伟大+ or表情况→较大的；主要的』

❶ adj. 主要的；重要的

There were calls for major changes to the welfare system.
有人要求对福利制度进行重大改革。

❷ [C] 专业课；专业课学生

Her major is French. 她的专业课是法语。

She's a French major. 她是法语专业的学生。

❸ major in sth 主修

She majored in History at Stanford. 她在斯坦福主修历史。

►majority [məˈdʒɒrəti] n. 大部分；大多数

[sing. + sing./pl. v.] ~ (of sb/sth) 大部分；大多数

The majority was/were in favour of banning smoking.
大多数人支持禁烟。

2. majesty [ˈmædʒəsti] n. 壮观，庄严；陛下
『maj大；伟大+esty→壮观；庄严』

❶ 壮观；庄严；雄伟

The majesty of the occasion thrilled us all.
那庄严的场面使我们每个人都激动不已。

❷ 陛下（对国王或王后的尊称）

I quite agree, Your Majesty. 我十分赞成，陛下。

3. majestic [məˈdʒestɪk] adj. 雄伟的；威严的；壮观的
『majesty壮观；庄严（去y）+ic表形容词→威严的；壮观的』

The majestic manners of the new queen produced a striking effect on her subjects.
新女王的王者风范给她的臣民留下了很深的印象。

词根172. mand=order，表示"命令"

1. command [kəˈmɑːnd] n. & v. 命令；掌控
『com和…一起+mand命令→和命令在一起→指挥；掌控』

❶ [C] 命令

Begin when I give the command. 我发出命令时开始。

You must obey the captain's commands.
你必须服从船长的命令。

❷ [U] 控制，管辖，指挥

He has 1,200 men under his command. 他掌管着1200人。

For the first time in years, she felt in command of her life.
多少年来第一次，她觉得生活掌握在自己的手里。

❸ [U, sing.] ~ (of sth)（尤指对语言的）掌握，运用能力

Applicants will be expected to have (a) good command of English. 申请人必须精通英语。

❹ [C] 兵团；指挥部，司令部

There would continue to be a joint command of US and Saudi forces operating within Saudi borders.
美国军队和沙特军队共同组成的联合部队将继续在沙特阿拉伯境内实施军事行动。

He had authorisation from the military command to retaliate.
他得到军事指挥部授权，准备反击。

❺ 命令

[VN to inf] He commanded his men to retreat.
他命令手下撤退。

❻ 指挥，统率（陆军、海军等）

[VN] The troops were commanded by General Haig.
这些部队由黑格将军统率。

❼ [VN] 应得，值得

to deserve and get sth because of the special qualities you have

She was able to command the respect of the class.
她赢得了全班的尊敬。
The headlines commanded her attention.
那些标题引起了她的注意。

2. demand [dɪˈmɑ:nd] n. & v. 要求；需要
『de加强+mand命令→（坚决）要求；需要』

❶ [C] ~ (for sth/that...) （坚决的）要求；所需之物
There have been demands for services from tenants up there.
那里的房客要求提供服务。
Feed the baby **on demand**. 宝宝需要就喂食。

❷ demands [pl.] ~ (of sth) | ~ (on sb)
（尤指困难、使人劳累、令人烦恼等的）要求
the demands of children/work
孩子烦人的事；工作中累人的事
Flying makes enormous demands on pilots.
驾驶飞机对飞行员要求很高。

❸ [U, C] ~ (for sth/sb) （顾客的）需求，需要
to meet the demand for a product 满足对某产品的需求
There's an increased demand for organic produce these days.
目前对有机农产品有更大的需求。
Good secretaries are always **in demand**.
优秀的秘书总是很抢手。

❹ 强烈要求
[VN] She demanded an immediate explanation.
她强烈要求立即作出解释。
[V that] The UN has demanded that all troops be withdrawn.
联合国已要求撤出所有部队。

❺ [VN] 需要
This sport demands both speed and strength.
这项运动既需要速度也需要体力。

▶ **demanding** [dɪˈmɑ:ndɪŋ] adj. （工作）要求高的；（人）要求苛刻的

He found he could no longer cope with his demanding job.
他发现自己已无力应对那份劳神费力的工作了。
Her boss was very demanding but appreciative of Christina's talents.
克里斯蒂娜的老板非常苛刻，但同时也很欣赏她的才华。

3. mandate [ˈmændeɪt] n. 授权；政府任期 v. 授权；强制执行
『mand命令+ate表动词→命令→强制执行』

❶ (especially NAmE) 强制执行
to order sb to behave, do sth or vote in a particular way
The proposed initiative would mandate a reduction of carbon dioxide of 40%.
方案将强制规定将二氧化碳排放量减少40%。

❷ [VN to inf] 授权
The assembly was mandated to draft a constitution.
大会被授权起草一份章程。

❸ [C] 授权；授权书
The election victory gave the party a clear mandate to continue its programme of reform.
选举获胜使这个政党拥有了明确的继续推行改革的权力。
The bank had no mandate to honour the cheque.

银行没有得到指令来承兑这张支票。

❹ （政府的）任期
The presidential mandate is limited to two terms of four years each. 总统的任期不得超过两届，每届四年。

▶ **mandatory** [ˈmændətəri] adj. 强制性的；法定的
『mand命令+atory有…性质的→强制性的；法定的』
required by law
It is mandatory for blood banks to test all donated blood for the virus. 血库必须检查所有捐献的血是否含有这种病毒。
The offence carries a mandatory life sentence.
这种罪行依照法律要判无期徒刑。

词根173. mar(i), marine=sea，表示"海洋，海的"

1. marine [məˈri:n] adj. 海洋的；海运的 n. 海军陆战队士兵

❶ adj. 海洋的，海生的，海产的
connected with the sea and the creatures and plants that live there
The sinking of the tanker has made aspects of marine pollution particularly topical.
油轮的沉没使得海洋污染的方方面面都成为眼下大家尤为关注的热点话题。

❷ adj. 海船的，海运的，海事的
connected with ships or trade at sea
Marine insurance is governed by a strict series of rules and regulations.
关于海险有一系列严格的规章制度对其作了规定。

❸ [C] 海军陆战队士兵
The marine held it tightly in his fist.
那个海军陆战队士兵把它紧握在手掌心里。

2. submarine [ˌsʌbməˈri:n] adj. 水下的 n. 潜艇
『sub下面+marine海的→在海下面的→海下的；潜艇』

❶ [C] 潜艇（亦使用缩略形式sub）
The submarine at last emerged. 那艘潜艇终于浮出了水面。

❷ adj. 水下的
Submarine earthquakes often happen in ocean.
海洋中经常发生海底地震。

3. maritime [ˈmærɪtaɪm] adj. 海的；海事的；海运的
『mari海洋+time→海的』
maritime 可以指与海洋间接相关的
the largest maritime museum of its kind
同类中最大的海洋博物馆
Shanghai Maritime Univeristy 上海海事大学

4. mariculture [ˈmærɪkʌltʃə(r)] n. 海水养殖 〈P144〉
『mari海洋+cult耕种；培养+ure行为有关→海水养殖』

词根174. mark=sign，表示"标记；符号"

1. remark [rɪˈmɑ:k] n. & vi. 评述；评论
『re (again)一再+mark标记→反复做标记→评论』

❶ ~ (on/upon sth/sb) | ~ (how...) 评论；评述
to say or write a comment about sth/sb
"It's much colder than yesterday," he remarked casually.
"今天比昨天冷多了，"他漫不经心地说。
She remarked how tired I was looking.
她说我看上去显得特别累。

❷ [C] 评论；意见

something that you say or write which expresses an opinion, a thought, etc. about sb/sth

He made a number of rude remarks about the food.
关于这里的食物他说了许多无礼的评论。
What exactly did you mean by that last remark?
你最后那句话究竟是什么意思？

▶ **remarkable** [rɪˈmɑːkəbl] adj. 非凡的，引人注目的

『re (again)一再+mark标记+able可以→可以一再做标记的→值得注意的；不平常的』

~ (for sth) 非凡的，引人注目的
unusual or surprising in a way that causes people to take notice

She was a truly remarkable woman.
她是一位真正非同凡响的女人。
The area is remarkable for its scenery.
这一地区以其优美的景色而引人瞩目。

词义辨析 <P362第6>
评论 remark, comment, note, observe

2. **bookmark** [ˈbʊkmɑːk] n. 书签
『book书+mark记号；符号→书签』

3. **landmark** [ˈlændmɑːk] n. 地标；里程碑
『land地+mark记号；符号→地上的标志→里程碑』

❶ [C] 地标
A landmark is a building or feature which is easily noticed and can be used to judge your position or the position of other buildings or features.
The Times Square in New York City is a famous landmark.
纽约市的时代广场是一个著名的地标。

❷ [C] 里程碑
The ceasefire was seen as a major landmark in the fight against terrorism.
停火协定被看作是与恐怖主义斗争的重要里程碑。

4. **trademark** [ˈtreɪdmɑːk] n. 商标；（人行为衣着）特征
『trade贸易+ mark记号；符号→商标』

People have now come to know the importance of trademark.
人们现在逐步认识到了商标的重要性。

近义词 **brand** [brænd] n. 品牌 vt. 加污名于

[C] Which brand of toothpaste do you use?
你用什么牌子的牙膏？
[VN-N] The newspapers branded her a hypocrite.
报章指她是伪君子。

5. **hallmark** [ˈhɔːlmɑːk] n. 特征，标志；（金、银）印记
『hall大厅+ mark记号；符号→大厅的标记→标志，特征』

❶ [C] 特征；特点
a feature or quality that is typical of sb/sth
Police said the explosion bore all the hallmarks of a terrorist attack. 警方称这次爆炸具有恐怖分子袭击的所有特征。

❷ （金、银等制品上标明纯度、产地、制造者的）印记

6. **demarcate** [ˈdiːmɑːkeɪt] vt. 标出界线或界限
『de加强+marc(mark)标记+ate表动词→做（界线或界限）标记→标出界线或界限』

A special UN commission was formed to demarcate the border. 联合国成立了一个特别委员会来划定边界。
Plots of land have been demarcated by barbed wire.

一块块土地都用带刺的铁丝网圈了起来。
Responsibilities within the department are clearly demarcated.
该部门内的职责划分明确。

▶ **demarcation** [ˌdiːmɑːˈkeɪʃn] n. 界线；界限

It was hard to draw clear lines of demarcation between work and leisure. 在工作和闲暇之间很难划出明确的界限。
Talks were continuing about the demarcation of the border between the two countries.
关于两国之间边界划定问题的谈判仍在继续。

词根175. matern, matr(i)=mother，表示"母性，母亲"（参看词根"patern, patr(i)"）

1. **maternal** [məˈtɜːnl] adj. 母亲的，母性的，母系的
『matern母亲+al…的→母亲的，母性的，母系的』

❶ 母亲般慈爱的
having feelings that are typical of a caring mother towards a child
maternal love 母爱
She didn't have any maternal instincts.
她没有一点做母亲的天性。

❷ 母亲的
Maternal is used to describe things that relate to the mother of a baby.
Maternal smoking can damage the unborn child.
母亲吸烟会对胎儿造成不良影响。
Maternal age affects the baby's survival rate.
母亲的年龄影响婴儿的成活率。

❸ 母系的
my maternal grandfather 我的外祖父

▶ **maternity** [məˈtɜːnəti] n. 母亲身份；怀孕
『matern母性，母亲+ity具备某种性质，状况→母性』

maternity clothes 孕妇装
a maternity ward/hospital 产科病房；妇产医院

2. **matriarch** [ˈmeɪtriɑːk] n. 女家长；女族长
『matri母性，母亲+arch统治者→女家长』

▶ **matriarchy** [ˈmeɪtriɑːki] n. 母权制，母系社会

3. **matrimony** [ˈmætrɪməni] n. 结婚；婚姻
『matri母性，母亲+mony表行为或结果→结婚后会成为母亲→婚姻』

[U] marriage; the state of being married
There were times when matrimony itself seemed to him to be a gamble not worth the taking.
在他看来，有时婚姻本身就是一场赌博，不值得去赌。
Do you take this woman to be your lawful wedded wife to live together in the holy estate matrimony?
你愿意让这个女人成为你的合法妻子，与你共同生活在圣洁的婚姻中吗？

4. **matrix** [ˈmeɪtrɪks] n. （人或社会成长和发展的）环境；矩阵
『matri母性，母亲+x→母体，子宫→（人或社会成长和发展的）环境；矩阵』

❶ [C] （人或社会成长和发展的）环境
the formal social, political, etc. situation from which a society or person grows and develops
the matrix of their culture 他们文明的摇篮

❷ [C] （数学中）矩阵

词根176. med=heal，表示"治疗"

1. medicine 英 [ˈmedsn] 美 [ˈmedɪsn] n. 医学；药 （尤指药水）
『med治疗+ic+ine表名词→治疗（病）的东西→药』

❶ [U] 医学
the study and treatment of diseases and injuries
advances in modern medicine 现代医学的发展
to study/practise medicine 学医；行医

❷ [U, C] 药，（尤指）药水
Did you take your medicine? 你吃过药了吗？

小贴士 pill [pɪl] n. 药丸　tablet [ˈtæblət] n. 药片；平板电脑

2. medic [ˈmedɪk] n. (BrE) 医科学生；医生 (NAmE) （尤指军队中的）救护人员
『med治疗+ic表人→治疗的人→医科学生』

3. medication [ˌmedɪˈkeɪʃn] n. 药；药物
『med治疗+ic+ate表动词（去e）+ion表名词→药物（medicate v. "用药物治疗"的名词形式）』

Are you currently taking any medication?
你在服用什么药吗？
Many flu medications are available without a prescription.
许多流感药不用处方就可以买到。

4. remedy [ˈremədi] n. 解决办法；治疗方法；药品 vt. 补救，纠正
『re又，再+med治疗+y表名词→治疗』

❶ [C]（问题的）解决方法，解决良方
A remedy is a successful way of dealing with a problem.
There is no simple remedy for unemployment.
失业问题没有简单的解决办法。
There are a number of possible remedies to this problem.
这个问题有许多可能采取的解决办法。

❷ [C] 药品；治疗方法
a herbal remedy 草药疗法
an excellent home remedy for sore throats
治疗咽喉疼痛的极佳的家庭疗法

❸ [VN] 纠正，补救，矫正
A great deal has been done internally to remedy the situation.
已经做了很多内部工作对这种情形进行补救。

词根177. med(i), mid=middle，表示"中间"

1. immediate [ɪˈmiːdiət] adj. 即刻的；直接的
『im无+medi中间+ate表形容词→无中间过程的→直接的』

2. medium [ˈmiːdiəm] adj. 中等的；n. 媒介
『med(=middle)中间的+ium部分→中间部分→中等的；媒介』
（pl. media）

❶ adj. [usually before noun] (abbr. M) 中等的；中号的
a man of medium height/build 中等身材的人
There are three sizes—small, medium and large.
有三种尺寸——小号、中号和大号。
Choose medium to large tomatoes. 选取中到大个的西红柿。

❷ [C]（传播信息的）媒介，手段，方法
Television is the modern medium of communication.
电视是现代传媒。
the medium of radio/television 广播/电视媒介

the media [U + sing./pl. v.] 媒体

The trial was fully reported in the media.
媒体对这次审判进行了全面报道。
The media was/were accused of influencing the final decision.
人们指责媒体左右了终审判决。

❸ [C] 媒介（手段；工具；方法）
Video is a good medium for learning a foreign language.
录像是一种学习外语的好方法。
English is the medium of instruction. 用英语进行教学。
Watercolour is his favourite medium.
水彩画是他最喜欢的表现方式。
Blood is the medium in which oxygen is carried to all parts of the body. 血液是将氧气输送到人体各个部位的媒介。

❹ (biology 生物学) 介质；培养基；环境
a substance that sth exists or grows in or that it travels through
The bacteria were growing in a sugar medium.
细菌在糖基中生长。

3. median [ˈmiːdiən] adj. 中间的；中位数的
『med中间+ian表形容词→中间的→位置上处于正中间的』
the median age/price 中年；中等价位
a median point/line 中点/线

4. medieval [ˌmediˈiːvl] adj. 中古的，中世纪的
『medi中间+ev年龄；时代；寿命+ al…的→中世纪的』
This is a valuable medieval manuscript.
这是一本有价值的中世纪手抄本。

5. midday [ˌmɪdˈdeɪ] n. 正午
『mid中间+ day一天→一天的正中时间→正午』
The train arrives at midday. 列车正午到达。

6. midnight [ˈmɪdnaɪt] n. 午夜
『mid中间+night夜晚→午夜』

7. midst [mɪdst] n. 中间
『mid中间+st→中间』

❶ in the midst of sth/of doing sth
当某事发生时；正在做某事时
She discovered it in the midst of sorting out her father's things. 她在整理父亲的东西时发现了它。
We are in the midst of one of the worst recessions for many, many years.
我们正处在多年来最严重的一次经济衰退之中。

❷ in one's midst | in the mist of 在…当中
Many were surprised to see him exposed like this in the midst of a large crowd.
许多人看到他像这样暴露在一大群人中间都非常吃惊。
There is a traitor in our midst. 我们中间有个叛徒。

词义辨析 <P372第55>
中心，中间 center, core, middle, midst

8. mediate [ˈmiːdieɪt] v. 调停，调解，斡旋；促成
『medi中间+ate表动词→位于（矛盾双方的）中间→调停，调解』
The Secretary-General was asked to mediate in the dispute.
有人请秘书长来调解这次纷争。
An independent body was brought in to mediate between staff and management.
由一个独立机构介入，在劳资之间进行调解。

► **mediator** [ˈmiːdieɪtə(r)] n. 调停者，斡旋者

9. intermediate [ˌɪntəˈmiːdiət] adj. 中间的；中等的
『inter在…之间+medi中间+ate表形容词→中间的』

❶ （两地、两物、两种状态等）之间的，中间的
Liquid crystals are considered to be intermediate between liquid and solid. 液晶被认为介于液态和固态之间。

❷ （水平）中级的，中等的
an intermediate skier/student, etc.
中等程度的滑雪者/学生等
an intermediate coursebook 中级课本

10. intermediary [ˌɪntəˈmiːdiəri] n. 中间人，调解人
『inter在…之间+medi中间+ary表人→在（矛盾双方）中间（调解）的人→中间人，调解人』

All talks have so far been conducted through an intermediary.
到目前为止所有的谈判都是通过调停人进行的。

词根178. memor, mem=memory，表示"记忆"

1. memory [ˈmeməri] n. 记忆力；记忆；对死者的记忆
『memor记忆；记+y表结果→记忆；记忆力』

❶ [C, U] ~ (for sth) 记忆力；记性
I have a bad memory for names. 我不善于记名字。
He suffered loss of memory for weeks after the accident.
事故之后他有几个星期失去记忆。

❷ [U] 记忆所及的时期；回忆所及的范围
There hasn't been peace in the country in/within my memory.
在我的记忆里，这个国家从没太平过。

❸ [C] 回忆；记忆
I have vivid memories of my grandparents.
我依然清楚地记得我的祖父母。

❹ [U] (formal) 对死者的记忆
Her memory lives on (= we still remember her) .
我们永远怀念她。
He founded the charity **in memory of** his late wife.
他创办了这一慈善事业以纪念他已故的妻子。

2. memorise [ˈmeməraɪz] vt. 记住
『memory记忆（去y）+ize使→变成→使变成记忆→记住』

Whenever he has a bit of spare time, he uses it to memorise English words. 他一有空闲时间就背英文单词。

词义辨析 <P362第7>
记起 remember, memorise, recall, recollect

3. remember [rɪˈmembə(r)] v. 想起；记住
『re返回+member (=memor)记忆；记→返回到记忆中→想起；记住』

❶ remember doing sth 记着过去曾经做过的某事
I remember posting the letter. 我记得把信寄出去了。

❷ remember to do sth 记着要做某事
I remember to post the letter.
我没有忘记要寄信。

4. memorial [məˈmɔːriəl] n. 纪念碑（章、堂）adj. 纪念的
『memor记忆；记+ ial …的→纪念的』

❶ [C] 纪念碑（章、像、堂、仪式等）
Building a memorial to Columbus has been his lifelong dream. 为哥伦布建一座纪念碑是他一生的梦想。
The museum will serve as a memorial to the millions who

passed through Ellis Island.
这个博物馆将用来纪念经过埃利斯岛的数百万人。

❷ （对逝者）纪念的；悼念的；追思的
A memorial service is being held for her at St Paul's Church.
她的追悼会正在圣保罗教堂举行。

小贴士 Memorial Day 阵亡将士纪念日
（美国假日，通常为5月的最后一个星期一）

5. commemorate [kəˈmeməreɪt] vt. 纪念
『com一起，共同+ memor记忆+ ate表动词→纪念』

[VN] （用…）纪念；作为…的纪念
A series of movies will be shown to commemorate the 30th anniversary of his death.
为纪念他逝世30周年，有一系列的电影要上映。

10. memoir [ˈmemwɑː(r)] n. 回忆录，传记
『mem记忆+oir→记忆（某人）事件的书或文章→传记』

A memoir is a book or article that you write about someone who you have known well.
He has just published a memoir in honour of his captain.
他刚刚出版了一本传记来纪念他的队长。

11. memorandum [ˌmeməˈrændəm] n. 备忘录；建议书；报告
『memor记忆+andum→（帮助）记的东西→备忘录』
（pl. memoranda）

❶ [C] （外交）备忘录；协议备忘录
The three countries have signed a memorandum pledging to work together.
这三个国家签署了一份备忘录，承诺共同努力。
Nevertheless, we will, of course, require your assistance in drafting the non-financial section of the memorandum.
不过，我们当然会要求你协助起草备忘录的非财务部分。

❷ [C] (=memo) （公司或组织内部的）公务便条；备忘录
a short written report prepared specially for a person or group of people which contains information about a particular matter
I sent him a memo reminding him about the meeting.
我给他发了一份备忘录，提醒他开会的事。
I have sent out a memo to all staff, reminding them of the procedure for taking sick leave.
我已经给全体员工发了一份备忘录，提醒他们请病假的程序。

► **memo** [ˈmeməʊ] n. 备忘录（also formal memorandum）

词根179. merge, merse=sink，表示"沉，没"

1. emerge [iˈmɜːdʒ] vi. 浮现
『e出来+merge沉没→从沉没中露出了→浮现』

❶ [V] ~ (from sth) （从隐蔽处或暗处）出现，浮现
to come out of a dark, confined or hidden place
The swimmer emerged from the lake.
游泳者从湖水中浮了出来。
She finally emerged from her room at noon.
中午，她终于从屋里出来了。

❷ （of facts, ideas, etc. 事实、意见等）暴露；露出真相
[V] No new evidence emerged during the investigation.
调查过程中未发现新证据。

❸ [V] ~ (as sth) 露头；显现；显露
to start to exist；to appear or become known

After the elections opposition groups began to emerge.
经过选举，反对派开始露头。
He emerged as a key figure in the campaign.
他已初露头角，成为这次运动的主要人物。

▶ **emergence** [ɪˈmɜːdʒəns] n. 出现；兴起
『emerge出现（去e）+ence表名词→出现』
The emergence and spread of new diseases is one example.
新疾病的出现和传播是一个例子。

▶ **emergent** [ɪˈmɜːdʒənt] adj. 新兴的；处于发展初期的
『emerge出现（去e）+ent表形容词→刚出现的』
Bioengineering is an emergent branch of learning.
生物工程是一门新兴的学科。
emergent market countries 新兴市场国家

▶ **emergency** [ɪˈmɜːdʒənsi] n. [C, U] 突发事件；紧急情况
『emerge出现（去e）+ency表行为→（突然）出现→突发事件』
The government has declared a state of emergency following the earthquake. 地震发生后政府已宣布进入紧急状态。
This door should only be used in an emergency.
这道门只能在紧急情况下使用。

小贴士 美国报警电话是911。

2. **submerge** [səbˈmɜːdʒ] v. 淹没，沉没；沉浸；掩盖
『sub (under)下面+merge 下沉→沉下去→淹没』

❶ （使）潜入水中，没入水中，浸没，淹没
[V] The submarine had had time to submerge before the warship could approach.
潜水艇没等军舰靠近就及时潜入水下了。
[VN] The fields had been submerged by floodwater.
农田被洪水淹没了。

❷ submerge oneself in 沉浸于，陷入，埋头于
to become very involved in something so that you do not think about anything else
He submerges himself in the world of his imagination.
他沉浸在自己想象的世界中。
She wanted to submerge herself in her writing.
她想埋头于写作中。

❸ [VN] 掩盖（思想、感情等）
if something （ideas, feelings, opinions, etc.） is submerged, it becomes hidden so that people do not notice it or think about it
Doubts that had been submerged in her mind suddenly resurfaced. 她心里早已湮灭的疑团突然又浮现出来。

3. **immerse** [ɪˈmɜːs] v. 浸没；沉浸
『im进入+merse沉，没→沉进去→沉浸』

❶ ~ sb/sth (in sth) 使浸没于
Caution: to Prevent Electric Shock Do Not Immerse in Water.
注意：不可浸没在水中，以防触电。

❷ ~ yourself/sb in sth （使）深陷于，沉浸在
She immersed herself in her work. 她埋头工作。
Clare and Phil were immersed in conversation in the corner.

克莱尔和菲尔在角落里深谈。

小贴士 submerge强调"潜入，没入"而immerse强调"沉浸，浸泡"。

4. **merge** [mɜːdʒ] v. 合并；融入
『merge沉没→A和B沉没到一起→合并』

❶ ~ (with/into) sth | ~ A with B | ~ A and B (together) （使）合并，结合，并入
His department will merge with mine.
他的部门将和我的合并。
The villages expanded and merged into one large town.
这些村庄扩大了并且结合成了一个大集镇。

❷ [V] 融入；渐渐消失在某物中
The hills merged into the dark sky behind them.
山峦渐渐隐入他们背后漆黑的夜空之中。

▶ **merger** [ˈmɜːdʒə(r)] n. （机构或企业的）合并，归并
Both companies were keen on a merger.
两家公司都很想合并。

词根180. meter, meas, mens(e)=measure，表示"计量；测量"

1. **metric** [ˈmetrɪk] adj. 公制的
『meter测量（去e）+ic…的→（有关）测量的→公制的』
These screws are metric. 这些螺丝钉是用公制尺码制造的。
metric units/measurements/sizes 公制单位/尺寸/大小

小贴士 公制亦称"米制""米突制"。1858年《中法通商章程》签订后传入中国的一种国际度量衡制度。公制单位在早期有两个重要的发展原则：第一项是要十进位以便计算。现代公制包括以下的基本单位：长度单位——米（m）；时间单位——秒（sec）；质量单位——千克（kg）。

2. **barometer** [bəˈrɒmɪtə(r)] n. 气压计；晴雨表
『baro(=bar)重+meter计量→气压计』
an instrument for measuring air pressure to show when the weather will change
The barometer is falling. 气压在下降。
In past presidential elections, Missouri has been a barometer of the rest of the country.
在过去的总统选举中，密苏里州一直是该国其他州的晴雨表。

3. **geometry** [dʒiˈɒmətri] n. 几何学；几何形状
『geo地，地球+metry（=meter）测量→测量地面→几何学（也可以利用谐音记忆。[dʒiˈɒ]谐音为"几何"。』

4. **perimeter** [pəˈrɪmɪtə(r)] n. （土地的）外缘；周长
『peri周围的+meter测量→周长；（土地）外缘』

❶ （土地的）外缘，边缘
the outside edge of an area of land
Guards patrol the perimeter of the estate.
保安人员在庄园四周巡逻。
a perimeter fence/track/wall 围绕四周的栅栏/小径/墙

❷ 周长（circumference只指圆的周长）

5. **voltmeter** [ˈvəʊltmiːtə(r)] n. 电压表
『volt电压+meter测量→测量电压的仪器→电压表』

6. **symmetry** [ˈsɪmətri] n. 对称；相仿
『sym相同的+meter测量（去e）+y构成名词→（两边）测量相同的→对称；相仿』

❶ [U] 对称

I loved the house because it had perfect symmetry.
我喜欢这所房子，因为它非常对称。

❷ [U] 相似，相仿，相等

There's a certain symmetry in the careers of the two brothers.
这两兄弟的职业生涯有一定相似性。

The superpowers pledged to maintain symmetry in their arms shipments.
超级大国承诺在武器运输方面要保持数量均衡。

▶**symmetrical** [sɪˈmetrɪkl] adj.对称的

7. thermometer [θəˈmɒmɪtə(r)] n. 温度计<P333>
『therm热+o+meter计量；测量→温度计』

8. diameter [daɪˈæmɪtə(r)] n. 直径<P10>
『dia穿过；两者之间+ meter测量→穿过（圆心）测量→直径』

9. measure [ˈmeʒə(r)] v. 测量；量度 为 n. 措施；量
『meas计量；测量+ure表行为或结果→测量；量度』

❶ 测量；估量

[VN] A ship's speed is measured in knots. 船速以节测量。
[VN] It is difficult to measure the success of the campaign at this stage. 在现阶段还难以估量这场运动的成败。

❷ linking verb（指尺寸、长短、数量等）量度为

The main bedroom measures 12ft by 15ft.
主卧室宽12英尺，长15英尺。

❸ [C] ~ (to do sth) 措施；方法

We must take preventive measures to reduce crime in the area. 我们必须采取预防措施来减少这个地区的犯罪。

❹ [sing.] （一定的）量，程度

A measure of technical knowledge is desirable in this job.
做这项工作最好多懂一些技术知识。

❺ [C] 判断；衡量

Is this test a good measure of reading comprehension?
这种测试是判断阅读理解力的好方法吗？

10. immense [ɪˈmens] adj. 极大的，巨大的
『im不+mense计量；测量→（大得）不能测量的→极大的』

There is still an immense amount of work to be done.
还有非常非常多的工作没有做。
The benefits are immense. 效益是极大的。

11. dimension [daɪˈmenʃn] n. 维度；规模；方面
『di离开+mens计量；测量+ion表名词→测量离开（某一点的距离）→维度』

❶ 维（构成空间的因素）；尺寸

We measured the dimensions of the kitchen.
我们测量了厨房的大小。

❷ [usually pl.] 规模；程度；范围

the size and extent of a situation or a problem
a problem of considerable dimensions
一个涉及面相当广的问题

❸ 方面；侧面

an aspect, or way of looking at or thinking about sth
There is a political dimension to the accusations.
这些指控含有政治方面的因素。

小贴士 3D是英文"3 Dimensions"的缩写，中文是指三维，即长、宽、高。

词根181. merc(e), merch=trade，表示"交易；商业"

1. commerce [ˈkɒmɜːs] n. [U] 商业；贸易
『com共同+merce交易→（双方）一起进行交易→商业』

Commerce in the urban districts has been carried on smoothly since winter set in.
自从冬季来临后，市区的商业一直在顺利开展着。

Ministry of Commerce 商务部

2. commercial [kəˈmɜːʃl] adj. 商业的 n.（电台或电视播放的）广告
『commerce商业（去e）+ial表形容词→商业的』

❶ adj. 商业的

Their more recent music is far too commercial.
他们最近的音乐过分商业化了。
It is an agricultural market and a commercial center.
它是一个农业市场和商业中心。

❷ [C]（电台或电视播放的）广告

The government has launched a campaign of television commercials and leaflets.
政府通过电视广告和传单的形式发起了宣传活动。

3. merchant [ˈmɜːtʃənt] n. 商人
『merch商业；交易+ ant表人→商人』

4. merchandise [ˈmɜːtʃəndaɪs , ˈmɜːtʃəndaɪz] n. [U]商品
『merch商业；交易+andise→商品』

Retailers can return defective merchandise.
零售商可以退回有缺陷的商品。

词义辨析 <P361第5>

产品，商品 product, production, produce, merchandise, goods, commodity

---

词根182. milit=soldier；fight，表示"士兵；战斗"

1. military [ˈmɪlətri] adj. 军事的，军队的 n. 军队
『milit士兵；战斗+ary…的→军队的』

❶ adj. 军队的，军事的

Military action may become necessary.
也许有必要采取军事行动。

❷ the military [sing. + sing./pl. v.] 军队

The military was/were called in to deal with the riot.
已调来军队平息暴乱。

▶**militarize** [ˈmɪlɪtəraɪz] vt. 军事化

a militarized zone 军事化地区

▶**demilitarize** [ˌdiːˈmɪlɪtəraɪz] 从…撤军；使非军事化
『de去掉+military军队（去y）+ize表动词→去掉军队→使非军事化』

He said the UN had made remarkable progress in demilitarizing the region.
他说联合国在促使该地区非军事化的进程中已经取得了显著进展。

2. militant [ˈmɪlɪtənt] adj. 激进的；好战的 n. 激进分子
『milit士兵；战斗+ant表形容词或人→好战的；激进分子』

❶ adj. 激进的；好战的

We were accused of being militant left-wingers.
我们被人指责是好战的左翼分子。

❷ n. 激进分子

The militants might still find some new excuse to call a strike.

那些激进分子也许还会找到新的理由举行罢工。

3. militia [mə'lɪʃə] n. 民兵组织；国民卫队
『milit士兵+ia总称→（像）士兵（一样作战的）人→民兵』
[sing. + sing./pl. v.] 民兵组织；国民卫队
a group of people who are not professional soldiers but who have had military training and can act as an army
The troops will not attempt to disarm the warring militias.
部队并不打算解除战斗中的民兵武装。

词根183. migr=remove，表示"迁移"

1. migrate [maɪ'ɡreɪt] vi. 迁徙；移居
『migr迁移+ate表动词→迁徙；移居』

❶ [V]（鸟类、动物等）（随季节变化）迁徙
Swallows migrate south in winter.
燕子在冬天迁徙到南方。

❷ [V]（许多人）移居，迁移（尤指到外地寻找工作或暂住）
to move from one town, country, etc. to go and live and/or work in another
People migrate to cities like Jakarta in search of work.
人们为找工作而迁移到雅加达这类城市里。

▶ **migrant** ['maɪɡrənt] n. 流动工人；候鸟；迁徙动物

❶（尤指为寻找工作而迁移的）移居者；流动工人
The theme of the play is the life of migrant workers.
这个剧本以民工生活为题材。

❷ 候鸟；迁徙动物
The area was an important resting place for many types of migrant birds. 这个地区是多种候鸟的重要栖息地。

小贴士 民工 migrant workers

▶ **migration** [maɪ'ɡreɪʃn] n. [U, C] 迁徙；移居
Swallows begin their migration south in autumn.
燕子在秋季开始向南方迁移。

2. emigrate ['emɪɡreɪt] vi. 移居国外
『e出，外+migr迁移+ate表动词→移居国外』
[V] ~ (from...) (to...) 移居国外；移民
He emigrated to Belgium. 他移民到了比利时。

▶ **emigrant** ['emɪɡrənt] n. 移居外国的人
They are emigrant labourers. 他们是移居他国的劳工。
He is a British emigrant to Australia.
他是个移居澳大利亚的英国人。

▶ **emigration** [ˌemɪ'ɡreɪʃn] n. 移民出境
The government tried to control the population through restriction on emigration.
政府试图通过限制移民来控制人口。

3. immigrate ['ɪmɪɡreɪt] vi. 移民入境
『im向内；进入+migr迁移+ate表动词→迁移进入境内→移民入境』
[V] ~ (to...) (from...)（从外地）移居
He immigrated from Ulster in 1848.
他1848年从阿尔斯特移民到这里。

▶ **immigrant** ['ɪmɪɡrənt] n. 外来移民
『im向内；进入+migr迁移+ant表人→外来移民』
North Africans make up the largest and poorest immigrant group in the country.

北非人构成了该国最大也是最贫困的移民群。

▶ **immigration** [ˌɪmɪ'ɡreɪʃn] n. 移民入境
Between 1966 and 1996 the UK actually lost more people through emigration than it gained through immigration.
事实上，从1966年到1996年，移居海外的英国人比进入英国的移民更多。

词根184. min=project，表示"伸出，突出"

1. eminent ['emɪnənt] adj.（某专业中）卓越的，著名的
『e出+min伸出，突出+ent表形容词→突出的，杰出的』
He is one of the three eminent professors in the college.
他是这所大学三名杰出教授之一。

▶ **eminence** ['emɪnəns] n. 卓越，显赫
Beveridge was a man of great eminence.
贝弗里奇是个非常有名的人。

2. prominent ['prɒmɪnənt] adj. 重要的；显眼的；突出的
『pro向前+min伸出，突出+ent具有…性质的→向前突出→杰出的』

❶ 重要的；有名的
conspicuous in position or importance
The most prominent poets of the Victorian period had all but faded from the scene.
维多利亚时期最显赫的诗人差不多已全部湮没无声了。
He played a prominent part in the campaign.
他在这次运动中发挥了重要作用。

❷ 显眼的
The church tower was a prominent feature in the landscape.
教堂的尖塔曾经是此地景观的重要特色。
The story was given a prominent position on the front page.
这则报道刊登在头版的显著位置。

❸ 突出的，凸现的
a prominent nose 高鼻子
prominent cheekbones 突出的颧骨

▶ **prominence** ['prɒmɪnəns] n. 杰出，著名
If someone or something is in a position of prominence, they are well-known and important.
He came to prominence during the World Cup in Italy.
他在意大利的世界杯赛中声名鹊起。

3. imminent ['ɪmɪnənt] adj.（尤指不愉快的事）临近的，即将发生的；逼近的
『im进来+min伸出+ent具有…性质的→（已经）伸进来的→临近的；逼近的』
If you say that something is imminent, especially something unpleasant, you mean it is almost certain to happen very soon.
The system is in imminent danger of collapse.
这个体制面临着崩溃的危险。
An announcement about his resignation is imminent.
马上就要宣布他的辞职。

▶ **imminence** ['ɪmɪnəns] n. 临近，逼近
The imminence of war was on everyone's mind.
每个人都感受到了战争的迫近。

词根185. mir(e)=wonder；look，表示"惊奇；看"

1. mirror ['mɪrə(r)] n. 镜子
『mir看（双写r）+or表器物 →能看见（自己的）器物→镜子』

2. admire [əd'maɪə(r)] v. 钦佩；欣赏

『ad(=to)到+mire惊奇；看→达到惊奇这个地步；惊奇地看→钦佩；看』

❶ ~ sb/sth (for sth) | ~ sb (for doing sth) 钦佩，仰慕

I really admire your enthusiasm. 我确实钦佩你的热情。

The school is widely admired for its excellent teaching.

这所学校教学优秀，远近称誉。

❷ 欣赏，用钦佩的眼光看

We took time to stop and admire the view.

我们特意驻足欣赏风景。

▶ **admiration** [ˌædməˈreɪʃn] n. 钦佩；羡慕

Meg's eyes widened in admiration.

梅格羡慕地睁大了双眼。

3. miracle ['mɪrəkl] n. 奇迹

『mire(=wonder)惊奇（去e）+acle表名词→令人惊奇的事情→奇迹』

❶ [sing.] (informal) 奇迹；不平凡的事

a lucky thing that happens that you did not expect or think was possible

It's a miracle (that) nobody was killed in the crash.

撞车事故中竟然没有一人丧生，这真是奇迹。

It would take a miracle to make this business profitable.

让这个公司赢利简直是天方夜谭。

❷ [C] 圣迹；神迹

an act or event that does not follow the laws of nature and is believed to be caused by God

Do you believe in miracles? 你相信神迹吗？

▶ **miraculous** [mɪˈrækjələs] adj. 奇迹般的；不可思议的

She's made a miraculous recovery.

她奇迹般地康复了。

4. mirage ['mɪrɑːʒ] n. 海市蜃楼；妄想

『mire惊奇；看（去e）+age表名词→让人惊奇的景象→海市蜃楼』

The girl was a mirage, cast up by his troubled mind.

那个女孩是他的幻觉，是他那忧郁不安的头脑妄想出来的。

词根186. miss, mit=send, cast，表示"送，放出"，名词形式为-mission，形容词形式为-missive

1. transmit [trænsˈmɪt] vt. 传送；输送；发射；传染

『trans从…到+mit送→从一个地方发送到另一个地方→传送；传染』

❶ [VN] ~ (sth) (from…) (to…) 发射；播送

The ceremony was transmitted live by satellite to over fifty countries.

典礼通过卫星向50多个国家进行了实况转播。

❷ [VN] 传播，传染（疾病）

Can stray cats transmit COVID-19?

流浪猫能传染COVID-19（新冠肺炎）吗？

Altogether 131 domestically transmitted COVID-19 cases were reported on the Chinese mainland in April.

4月份，中国大陆共报告131例国内传播的COVID-19（新冠肺炎）病例。

词义辨析 <P379第91>

感染；传播 infect, contract, transmit

▶ **transmission** [trænzˈmɪʃn] n. 发射；传染；（汽车）变速器

The car was fitted with automatic transmission.

这辆车装配了自动变速器。

The experiment successfully reduced the female Asian Tiger Mosquito population—the main source of bites and disease transmission — by up to 94%.

这项实验成功地将雌性亚洲虎蚊的数量减少了94%——虎蚊是叮咬和传播疾病的主要来源。

小贴士 AT, MT, AMT

AT：Automatic Transmission 自动挡

MT：Manual Transmission 手动挡

AMT：手自一体。简单地说就是自动化的MT，自动离合手动变速器。

2. submit [səbˈmɪt] v. 呈递；屈从

『sub(under)下面+mit(send)送→从下面送→呈递；屈从』（submitted, submitted, submitting）

❶ [VN] ~ sth (to sb/sth) 提交，呈递（文件、建议等）

to give a document, proposal, etc. to sb in authority so that they can study or consider it

Completed projects must be submitted by 10 March.

完成的方案必须在3月10日前提交上来。

The draft outline (of the plan) is now submitted to you for review. 这个（计划的）纲要草案已发给你们，请审议。

❷ ~ (yourself) (to sb/sth) 顺从；屈服，被迫接受

to accept the authority, control or greater strength of sb/sth; to agree to sth because of this

She refused to submit to threats. 她面对威胁，拒不低头。

He submitted himself to a search by the guards.

他接受卫兵搜查。

They did not submit to the enemy. 他们没有向敌人屈服。

同义词组 give in to sb/sth 向…屈服

▶ **submission** [səbˈmɪʃn] n. 屈服；递交

When is the final date for the submission of proposals?

呈交提案的最后日期是什么时候？

The army intends to take the city or simply starve it into submission.

军队打算占领该城市或干脆截断其粮食补给迫使其投降。

▶ **submissive** [səbˈmɪsɪv] adj. 唯命是从的，顺从的

She followed him like a submissive child.

她对他百依百顺，像个听话的孩子。

3. admit [ədˈmɪt] v. 承认；准许进入；录取；收治

『ad相当于to+mit→送到（学校、医院、公园等）→录取；收治；准许进入』

❶ ~ (to sth/to doing sth) | ~ (to sb) (that…) （常指勉强）承认

to agree, often unwillingly, that sth is true

[V] She admits to being strict with her children.

她承认对自己的孩子很严厉。

Don't be afraid to admit to your mistakes. 不要怕认错。

[VN] He admitted all his mistakes. 他承认了全部错误。

I couldn't admit to my parents that I was finding the course difficult. 我无法向父母实话实说，我觉得这门课程很难。

[V] She admitted to having stolen the car.

她供认偷了那辆轿车。

He refused to admit to the other charges.

他拒不承认其他指控。

❷ [VN] ~ sb/sth (to/into sth) 准许…进入（某处）

Each ticket admits one adult. 每张票只准许一位成人入场。

The narrow windows admit little light into the room.
窗户狭窄，只有少量光线可以照进房间。
You will not be admitted to the theatre after the performance has started. 演出开始后不许进入剧场。

❸ [VN] ~ sb (to/into sth) 准许加入；招生，录取
The society admits all US citizens over 21.
凡21岁以上的美国公民均可加入该社团。
My hope is that I can be admitted to a key university.
我的希望是我能被重点大学录取。

❹ 接受（入院）；收治
Two crash victims were admitted to the local hospital.
两位车祸受害者已送进当地医院。

▶**admission** [ədˈmɪʃn] n. 承认；准许进入；录取；住院；入场费

The minister's resignation was an admission that she had lied.
这位部长辞职等于承认她自己撒过谎。
Last admissions to the park are at 4 p.m.
公园最晚的入园时间是下午4点。
She failed to gain admission to the university of her choice.
她未获自己选择的大学录取。
Hospital admission is not necessary in most cases.
大多数情况下，病人无须住院。
What's the admission? 门票多少钱？

4. commit [kəˈmɪt] v. 做（错事）；承诺；送；调配
『com共同，一起+ mit送→把…一起送到→把（人）一起送到医院、监狱；把（时间、资源等）调配到；把（自己或者某人）送到（不得不做某事的境地）→送；调配；承诺』

❶ [VN] 做（错的或非法的事）
to commit murder/suicide, etc. 谋杀、自杀等

❷ ~ sb/yourself (to sth/to doing sth)
[often passive] 承诺，保证；忠于
If you commit yourself to something, you say that you will definitely do it. If you commit yourself to someone, you decide that you want to have a long-term relationship with them.
The President is committed to reforming health care.
总统承诺要改革卫生保健制度。
Once we have committed to this course of action there is no going back.
一旦我们承诺采取这一行动，就没有回头路了。

❸ [VN] 明确表态
If you do not want to commit yourself on something, you do not want to say what you really think about it or what you are going to do.
It isn't their diplomatic style to commit themselves on such a delicate issue.
对这样一个微妙的问题明确表态并非他们的外交风格。

❹ [VN] [often passive] ~ sb to sth
（下令）把（某人）送进（医院或监狱等）
If someone is committed to a hospital, prison, or other institution, they are officially sent there for a period of time.
She was committed to a psychiatric hospital.
她被送进了精神病院。

❺ [VN] 拨出；调配（时间、资金、资源等）
If you commit money or resources to something, you decide to use them for a particular purpose.

They called on Western nations to commit more money to the poorest nations.
他们呼吁西方国家向极端贫困国家投入更多的钱。
The council has committed large amounts of money to housing projects. 市政会在住宅项目上投入了大量资金。

▶**committed** [kəˈmɪtɪd] adj. 尽心尽力的；坚信的；坚定的
『commit承诺，致力于（双写t）+ed表被动→尽心尽力的；坚信的；坚定的』

loyal and willing to give your time and energy to something that you believe in

They are committed socialists. 他们是坚定的社会主义者。
When we rebuild our business, we'd like to find committed employees among fresh graduates.
当我们重整公司业务的时候，我们希望在应届毕业生中找到忠诚的员工。
They are committed to staff development.
他们致力于员工的发展。

▶**commitment** [kəˈmɪtmənt] n. 承诺；奉献，投入

❶ [C, U] ~ (to sb/sth) | ~ to do sth 承诺
She doesn't want to make a big emotional commitment to Steve at the moment.
她不想在此刻对史蒂夫在感情上作出重大的承诺。
We made a commitment to keep working together.
我们承诺继续合作。

❷ [C] 承诺的事；不得不做的事
Will the job fit in with your family commitments?
这个工作能和你的家庭义务相融合吗？

❷ [U] ~ (to sb/sth) （对工作或某活动）献身；奉献，投入
A career as an actor requires one hundred per cent commitment. 干演员这一行需要百分之百的投入。

5. permit [pəˈmɪt , ˈpɜːmɪt] v. 允许 n. 许可证
『per(=through)自始至终；穿过+mit(send)送→（可以）送过去→允许』
（v. [pəˈmɪt]; n.[ˈpɜːmɪt]）

❶ permit doing sth. | permit sb to do sth允许；准许
The prison authorities permit visiting only once a month.
监狱当局每月只允许探监一次。
Visitors are not permitted to take photographs.
参观者请勿拍照。
I'll come tomorrow, weather permitting.
天气许可的话，我明天过来。

❷ [C] 许可证，特许证（尤指有限期的）
The majority of foreign nationals working here have work permits. 大多数在这里工作的外国人都有工作许可证。

▶**permission** [pəˈmɪʃn] n. 许可；许可证

❶ [U] 准许，许可
The school has been refused permission to expand.
学校扩充未得到许可。

❷ [C, usually pl.]书面许可
an official written statement allowing sb to do sth
The publisher is responsible for obtaining the necessary permissions to reproduce illustrations.
出版者负责取得准予复制插图的必要许可。

6. emit [iˈmɪt] vt. 放出（光、热、声音、气等）
『e出+mit送，放出→放出（光、热、声音、气等）』

[VN] (formal) 发出，射出，散发（光、热、声音、气等）

The metal container began to emit a clicking sound.

金属容器开始发出咔嗒咔嗒的声音。

The new device emits a powerful circular column of light.

新设备发出明亮的圆形光柱。

The greenhouse gas that we emit have reached its peak at this time. 此时此刻，我们制造的温室气体已经到达了顶峰。

▶**emission** [iˈmɪʃn] n. 排放；排放物

Your second question is about our position on greenhouse gas emission.

你提的第二个问题，是关于我们对温室气体排放的态度。

Under the new rules, some factories will cut emissions by as much as 90 percent.

按照新规定，一些工厂的减排量要多达90%。

7. intermittent [ˌɪntəˈmɪtənt] adj. 间歇的；断断续续的

『inter在…之间+mit送，放出（双写t）+ent表形容词→在（每隔一段时间）之间发出的→间歇的；断断续续的』

After three hours of intermittent rain, the game was abandoned. 3个小时断断续续的降雨之后，比赛取消了。

8. mission [ˈmɪʃn] n. 传教；传教使团；使团；使命

『mission是mit的动词形式，意为send→送（到海外传教）→传教；传教士；传教区→使团；使命』

❶ 传教；传教使团；传教区

They say God spoke to them and told them to go on a mission to the poorest country in the Western Hemisphere.

他们说上帝让他们去西半球最贫困的国家传播教义。

a Catholic mission in Africa 在非洲的天主教传教活动

I reside at the mission at St Michael's.

我住在圣·米歇尔教堂的传道会里。

❷ 使团；使命

A UN fact-finding mission is on its way to the region.

联合国调查团正在前往该地区的途中。

His function is vital to the accomplishment of the agency's mission. 要完成该机构的使命，他的作用至关重要。

❸ [C] 使命；天职

particular work that you feel it is your duty to do

Her mission in life was to work with the homeless.

她以帮助无家可归者为己任。

❹ [C] 军事行动；太空飞行任务

You know perfectly well I can't be blamed for the failure of that mission. 你很清楚那次任务的失败不该怪我。

The mission for the crew of the space shuttle Endeavour is essentially over.

"奋进号"航天飞机上全体机组人员的任务基本上已经完成了。

9. missionary [ˈmɪʃənri] n. 传教士

『mission传教，布道+ary从事…的人→从事传教的人→传教士』

An American missionary was released today after more than two months of captivity.

一位美国传教士在被关押两个多月后于今天获释。

missionary zeal=with great enthusiasm 极大的热忱

She had a kind of **missionary zeal** about bringing culture to the masses. 她对于向大众传播文化有着满腔的热忱。

10. commission [kəˈmɪʃn] n. 委员会；佣金；委托 vt. 委托

『com共同，一起+mission任务→带有具体任务的人们；完成销售任务随着而来的；让某人和具体任务在一起→委员会；佣金；委托』

❶ [C] （通常为政府管控或调查某事的）委员会

(BrE) The government has set up a commission of inquiry into the disturbances at the prison.

政府成立了一个委员会来调查监狱骚乱事件。

a commission on human rights 人权委员会

❷ [U, C] 佣金；回扣

an amount of money that is paid to sb for selling goods and which increases with the amount of goods that are sold

You get a 10% commission on everything you sell.

你可从你售出的每件商品中获得10%的佣金。

❸ [U] （银行等的）手续费

1% commission is charged for cashing traveller's cheques.

兑现旅行支票收取1%的手续费。

❹ [VN] 正式委托

She has been commissioned to write a new national anthem.

她已接受谱写新国歌的委托。

The Ministry of Agriculture commissioned a study into low-input farming. 农业部委托对低投入耕作进行研究。

❺ [U, C] 委托；委托之事

He approached John Wexley with a commission to write the screenplay of the film.

他找到约翰·韦克斯利，委托他创作这部电影的剧本。

11. emissary [ˈemɪsəri] n. 特使，密使

『e出去+miss送+ary表人→（一个国家政府）派出去的人→特使，密使』

An emissary is a representative sent by one government or leader to another.

12. committee [kəˈmɪti] n. 委员会

『commit（委托）双写t+ee被…者→被委托给的人→委员会』

『com共同，一起+ mit送（双写t）+ee被…者→（被人们）一起送去（负责处理某事物）的一群人→委员会』

[C + sing./pl. v.] 委员会

A committee is a group of people who meet to make decisions or plans for a larger group or organization that they represent.

The committee has/have decided to close the restaurant.

委员会已决定关闭这家餐馆。

13. dismiss [dɪsˈmɪs] v. 解雇；解散

『dis离开+miss送，放出→把（人）送走→解雇；解散』

❶ ~ sb (from sth) 解雇；免职；开除

She claims she was unfairly dismissed from her post.

她声称自己被无理免职。

❷ ~ sb (from sth) 把（某人）打发走；解散

At 12 o'clock the class was dismissed. 12点下课了。

I dismissed him from my mind. 我不再想他了。

Two more witnesses were called, heard and dismissed.

又有两个目击者被传唤，提供证言后获准退席。

❸ ~ sb/sth (as sth) 不予理睬

to decide that sb/sth is not important and not worth thinking or talking about

I think we can safely dismiss their objections.

我认为我们对他们的异议完全可以不予理会。

He dismissed the opinion polls as worthless.
他认为民意测验毫无用处而不予考虑。

词义辨析 <P365第24>

解雇 **dismiss, fire, lay off, remove, sack**

14. missile 英 [ˈmɪsaɪl] 美 [ˈmɪsl] n. 导弹；发射物
『miss(=send)发射+ile物体→发射出去的物体→导弹；发射物』

The authorities offered to stop firing missiles if the rebels agreed to stop attacking civilian targets.
当局表示，如果叛乱分子答应停止攻击平民目标，就不再发射导弹。
The football supporters began throwing missiles, one of which hit the referee.
足球迷们开始扔东西，其中还砸到了裁判一次。

15. omit [əˈmɪt] vt. 忽略；遗漏
『o(=ob=away)离开+mit送→送走了→忽略；遗漏』

❶ [VN] 忽略；遗漏
to not include sth/sb, either deliberately or because you have forgotten it/them
If you are a student, you can omit questions 16-18.
学生可以免做16至18题。
People were surprised that Smith was omitted from the team.
人们感到惊讶，史密斯竟未列入该队。

❷ [V to inf] 未（做）；没有（做）
to not do or fail to do sth
His new girlfriend had omitted to tell him she was married.
他的新女友未把自己已婚的事实告诉他。

▶ **omission** [əˈmɪʃn] n. 省略；遗漏
The play was shortened by the omission of two scenes.
此剧删减了两场戏。
There were a number of errors and omissions in the article.
这篇文章中有多处错误和疏漏。

词根187. mot(e), mob=move，表示"动，移动"

① mot=move，表示"动，移动"

1. motion [ˈməʊʃn] n. 移动；动议 v. & n. 示意
『mot动+ion动作或状态→运动』

❶ [U, sing.] 运动；移动；动
Rub the cream in with a circular motion.
转着圈将乳霜揉进去。

❷ [C], [V, VN] （以头或手）做动作，示意
At a single motion of his hand, the room fell silent.
他手一挥，屋子里便安静了下来。
He motioned for us to follow him. 他示意我们跟他走。

❸ [C] 动议；提议
a formal proposal that is discussed and voted on at a meeting
The motion was adopted/carried by six votes to one.
这项提议以六比一的票数通过。

▶ **motionless** [ˈməʊʃnləs] adj. 一动不动的；静止的
He stood there motionless. 他一动不动地站在那儿。

2. commotion [kəˈməʊʃn] n. （突然发生的）喧闹；骚乱，骚动
『com共同，一起+motion移动→（许多人）一起移动→骚动』
He heard a commotion outside. 他听见外面一阵骚动。

3. emotion [ɪˈməʊʃn] n. 强烈的情感；激情；情绪
『e出来+motion移动→（内心强烈的情感不停地）移动、冲动而表现出来的→强烈的情感；激情』

An emotion is a feeling such as happiness, love, fear, anger, or hatred, which can be caused by the situation that you are in or the people you are with.
Her voice trembled with emotion.
她的声音因情绪激动而颤抖。
He lost control of his emotions. 他情绪失去了控制。
The decision was based on emotion rather than rational thought.
这个决定不是基于理性的思考而是基于感情做出的。

▶ **emotional** [ɪˈməʊʃənl] adj. 情感（上）的；感情冲动的
『emotion情感+al…的→感情（上）的』

Mothers are often the ones who provide emotional support for the family. 母亲通常是家庭的情感支柱。
He tends to get emotional on these occasions.
他在这些场合往往容易动感情。
He is a very emotional man. 他是个很情绪化的人。

4. promote [prəˈməʊt] vt. 促进；促销；提升
『pro向前+mote移动→使向前移动→促进；促销；提拔』

❶ [VN] 促进；增进；推动
You don't have to sacrifice environmental protection to promote economic growth.
你不必为了促进经济增长而牺牲环境保护。

❷ ~ sth (as sth) 促销；推销
The meeting discussed how to promote this latest product.
这次会议讨论了如何开展这种新产品的推销工作。

❸ ~ sb (from sth) (to sth) 提升；晋升
She worked hard and was soon promoted.
她工作勤奋，不久就得到提升了。

5. demote [ˌdiːˈməʊt] vt. 使降职；使（球队）降级
『de向下+mote移动→向下动→降级』

[VN] [often passive] ~ sb (from sth) (to sth)
使降级，使降职，使降低地位（常作为惩罚）
He was demoted to the rank of ordinary soldier.
他被降为普通士兵。
The club was demoted at the end of last season.
上个赛季末该俱乐部被降级了。

6. motive [ˈməʊtɪv] n. 动机
『mot移动+ive表名词→使（某人）行动起来（的原因）→动机』

~ (for sth) 动机
a reason for doing sth
Police have ruled out robbery as a motive for the killing.
警方已排除因抢劫而杀人的可能。

▶ **motivate** [ˈməʊtɪveɪt] vt. 使有动机做…；激发，激励
『motive动机（去e）+ate使→使有（做某事的）动机』

He is motivated entirely by self-interest.
他做事完全出于私利。
She's very good at motivating her students.
她非常擅长激励她的学生。
The plan is designed to motivate employees to work more efficiently. 这个计划旨在促使员工更加卓有成效地工作。

▶ **motivation** [ˌməʊtɪˈveɪʃn] n. 动力；诱因

Unless you are trying to lose weight to please yourself, it's going to be tough to keep your motivation level high.
除非减肥是为了悦已，否则很难保持积极性。
Most people said that pay was their main motivation for working. 大多数人说赚取报酬是他们工作的主要动机。

7. locomotive [ˌləʊkəˈməʊtɪv] n. 火车头
『loco地方+mot动+ive表物→从一个地方跑到另一个地方的东西→火车头』

② mob=move，表示"动，移动"

1. mobile [ˈməʊbaɪl] adj. 移动的
『mob移动+ile容易的→容易移动的』

手机 mobile phone; cell phone
中国移动 China Mobile

2. automobile [ˈɔːtəməbiːl] n. 汽车（也常写作**auto**）
『auto自己+mob移动+ile物体→自己（能）移动的物体→汽车』

Japanese auto makers suspended marketing and closed plants.
日本汽车生产商暂停了营销活动，并关闭了工厂。
You must obtain a new automobile license when your old one expires. 当旧的汽车牌照满期，你得领取新的。

3. mobilize [ˈməʊbəlaɪz] vt. 动员；调动
『mob(le)移动（去e）+ize使…→（为了某目的）使（人员、军队、物资）动起来→动员；调动』

The unions mobilized thousands of workers in a protest against the cuts.
各级工会组织了数千名工人抗议削减工资。
The troops were ordered to mobilize. 部队接到了动员令。
They were unable to mobilize the resources they needed.
他们无法调用他们需要的资源。

4. mob [mɒb] n. 暴民，暴徒
『mob移动→通过迅速移动聚到一起之人→暴民，暴徒』

[C, sing. + sing./pl. v.] 人群；（尤指）暴民
The mob was/were preparing to storm the building.
暴民准备猛攻大楼。

词根188. mod=mode, manner，表示"方式，模式；风度"

1. mode [məʊd] n. 方式；模式
❶ [C]（生活、行为或做事的）方式；模式（多因习惯、传统或习俗而形成）
They have a relaxed mode of life that suits them well.
他们的轻松的生活方式很适合他们。
He switched automatically into interview mode.
他自动切换到访谈模式。
They have different modes of thought.
他们有不同的思维方式。
The holidays mode begins. 假期模式开启。

❷ [C, U]（设备的）模式，工作状态
Switch the camera into the automatic mode.
将照相机调到自动拍摄状态。

▶**modal** [ˈməʊdl] n. 情态动词
『mod方式，模式+al表名词→用来表示以某个动作的词→情态动词』

2. modest [ˈmɒdɪst] adj. 谦虚的；不大的；（女子）端庄的
『mod方式，模式+est最→最好的方式→谦虚的；端庄的』

❶ 谦虚的；谦逊的
She's very modest about her success.
她对自己的成功非常谦虚。

❷ 些许的；不太大，不太贵，不太重要的
not very large, expensive, important, etc.
He charged a relatively modest fee. 他收取的费用不算高。
The research was carried out on a modest scale.
这个研究项目开展的规模不算太大。

❸ （of people, especially women, or their clothes 人，尤指妇女或其衣着）庄重的；朴素的；不性感的
shy about showing much of the body; not intended to attract attention, especially in a sexual way
Asian women are more modest and shy, yet they tend to have an inner force.
亚洲女性表现得更为端庄腼腆，却往往外柔内刚。

▶**modesty** [ˈmɒdəsti] n. 谦虚；小，少；端庄
『modest谦虚的+ y表名词→谦虚』

❶ [U] 谦虚；谦逊
His modesty does him credit, for the food he produces speaks for itself.
他的谦逊值得称赞，因为他做的食物本身就说明了这一点。
❷ [U]（地方）小，（数量等）少，有限
You can refer to the modesty of something such as a place or amount when it is fairly small.
The modesty of the town itself comes as something of a surprise. 这座城市本身就小得让人惊讶。
❸ [U]（尤指女性的）端庄，庄重

3. model [ˈmɒdl] n. 模型；模范；型号；模特儿
『mod方式，模式+el表物或人→其他都按这种方式进行的→模型；范例；模范』

❶ （依照实物按比例制成的）模型
The architect had produced a scale model of the proposed shopping complex.
建筑师为提议建设的购物中心做了一个比例模型。
I had made a model aeroplane. 我做了一架模型飞机。

❷ 范例，样板
something such as a system that can be copied by other people
The nation's constitution provided a model that other countries followed. 这个国家的宪法成了别国仿效的范例。

❸ 模范；典型
a person or thing that is considered an excellent example of sth
However, to be a model student is by no means an easy thing.
然而，做模范学生却不容易。

role model 榜样，楷模
someone that you try to copy because they have qualities you would like to have
My elder brother has always been a role model for me.
我的哥哥总是我的行为榜样。

❹ （机器等的）型号
The latest models will be on display at the motor show.
最新的车型将会在这次汽车展上展出。

❺ （时装）模特儿；（绘画或雕塑的）模特儿

4. moderate [ˈmɒdərət] adj. 适度的；温和的；合理的　vt. 主持（讨论、辩论等）

『mod方式，模式+er+ate表动词→使（辩论）以某种方式（进行，不至于出现太过分的情况）→主持（讨论、辩论等）→适度的，温和的』

❶ adj. 适度的；中等的

not very large or very small, very hot or very cold, very fast or very slow, etc.

Even moderate amounts of the drug can be fatal.
这种药的用量即使不很大也会致命。

students of moderate ability　能力一般的学生

❷ adj. （政治上）温和的；不偏激的

having or showing opinions, especially about politics, that are not extreme

He was an easygoing man of very moderate views.
他是一个有着温和观点，性情随和的人。

❸ adj. 合理的；有节制的

staying within limits that are considered to be reasonable by most people

a moderate drinker　不过多饮酒的人
moderate wage demands　合理的工资要求

❹ 缓和；使适中

[V] By evening the wind had moderated slightly.
到黄昏时，风稍稍减弱了。

[VN] We agreed to moderate our original demands.
我们同意降低我们原先的要求。

❺ [VN] 主持（讨论、辩论等）

The television debate was moderated by a law professor.
这场电视辩论由一位法学教授主持。

5. modify [ˈmɒdɪfaɪ] vt. 调整，改进；修饰

『mode模式，方式（变e为i）+fy使→使成为（更合适）的方式→调整；修饰』

❶ [VN] 调整，调节，改进（同义词 adapt）

to change sth slightly, especially in order to make it more suitable for a particular purpose

The software we use has been modified for us.
我们使用的软件已按我们的需要作过修改。

Patients are taught how to modify their diet.
病人获得有关如何调节自己饮食的指导。

❷ [VN] (语法) 修饰

In "walk slowly", the adverb "slowly" modifies the verb "walk". 在"walk slowly"中，副词"slowly"修饰动词"walk"。

▶ **modifier** [ˈmɒdɪfaɪə(r)] n. 修饰语

▶ **modification** [ˌmɒdɪfɪˈkeɪʃn] n. 调整；改进

Considerable modification of the existing system is needed.
需要对现有的系统进行相当大的改进。

6. accommodate [əˈkɒmədeɪt] v. 向…提供住处；容纳；使适应

『ac相当于to+com共同+mod方式+ate表动词→使方式相同→与…符合→适合…的要求』

❶ [VN] 为（某人）提供住宿（或膳宿、座位等）

The hotel can accommodate up to 500 guests.
这家旅馆可供500位旅客住宿。

❷ [VN]（有足够的空间）容纳，接纳

The school was not big enough to accommodate all the

children. 这所学校不够大，容不下所有的孩子。

❸ [VN] 顾及；考虑到

Our proposal tries to accommodate the special needs of minority groups.
我们的提案尽量照顾到少数群体的特殊需要。

❹ ~ to sth | ~ sth/yourself to sth 顺应，适应（新情况）

I needed to accommodate (myself) to the new schedule.
我需要适应新的时间表。

▶ **accommodation** [əˌkɒməˈdeɪʃn] n.住处；适应

『accommodate 的名词形式』

[U or pl.] 住处；住所

（在英国英语中是不可数名词，在美国英语中常用复数形式，哪怕只指一个房间）

Can I find accommodations at your hotel for the night?
你们旅馆有房间让我过夜吗？（美国英语）

The price for the trip doesn't include accommodation.
旅行的价格不包括住宿。（英国英语）

7. module [ˈmɒdjuːl] n. 模块；组件，部件

『mod方式，模式+ule表名词→能够以某种模式运转的东西→模块；组件』

❶ [C]（教材的）单元；模块

These courses cover a twelve-week period and are organised into three four-week modules.
这些课程要上12周，分为3个单元，每单元4周。

Module 2　Unit1
There's Chinese dancing.

❷ [C]（机器的）组件，部件；（计算机的）模块，程序块；（航天器的）分离舱

A module is a part of a machine, especially a computer, which performs a particular function.

In the user administration module, you can delete users as administration authority.
管理员管理用户模块，可对用户进行删除操作。

8. modulate [ˈmɒdjuleɪt] vt. 调节，调整（声音电波等）

『mod方式，模式+ul+ate表动词→使方式（发生改变）→调节，调整』

❶ [VN] 改变，调节（嗓音、声音或乐曲等）

The speaker had a really noble voice which he could modulate with great skill.
这位演说者有副相当好的嗓子，他能很有技巧地调节它。

"Who's this?" asked a well-modulated voice.
一个优美的声音问道："谁呀？"

At this point the players have to modulate from E to G.
这时演奏者必须由E调转到G调。

❷ [VN] 调节，调整

To modulate an activity or process means to alter it so that it is more suitable for a particular situation.

innovating industrial policies to modulate the industrial structure　创新产业政策推进产业结构调整

9. commodious [kəˈməʊdiəs] adj. 宽敞的

『com共同+mod方式，模式+ious…的→大家都有（地方以相同的模式生活）的→宽敞的』

A commodious room or house is large and has a lot of space.
The halls and stairways are commodious.
大厅和楼梯都很宽敞。

10. commodity [kəˈmɒdəti] n. 商品
『com共同+mod方式，模式+ity具备某种性质→有共同模式的东西→商品』

(economics) 商品
a product or a raw material that can be bought and sold
rice, flour and other basic commodities
稻米、面粉和其他基本商品
Crude oil is the world's most important commodity.
原油是世界上最重要的商品。

词义辨析 <P361第5>
产品，商品 product, production, produce, merchandise, goods, commodity

词根189. monstr=show，表示"显示，演示"

1. demonstrate [ˈdemənstreɪt] v. 证明，说明，表明；演示；游行示威
『de(=fully)表强调+monstr显示，演示+ate表动词→说明；演示』

❶ 证明，证实，说明，表明
to show sth clearly by giving proof or evidence
[V that] These results demonstrate convincingly that our campaign is working.
这些结果有力地证明，我们的运动正在发挥作用。
[VN to inf] The theories were demonstrated to be false.
这些理论已被证明是错误的。
[V wh-] His sudden departure had demonstrated how unreliable he was. 他突然离去，这说明他是多么不可靠。
We want to demonstrate our commitment to human rights.
我们想表明我们对人权的信念。

❷ ~ sth (to sb) 示范，演示
to show and explain how sth works or how to do sth
[VN] Her job involves demonstrating new educational software. 她的工作包括演示新的教学软件。

❸ [V] ~ (against sth) | ~ (in favour/support of sth)
集会示威；游行示威
They are demonstrating in favour of free higher education.
他们举行示威游行，要求实行免费高等教育。

▶**demonstration** [ˌdemənˈstreɪʃn] n. 证明，表明；演示；游行示威

▶**demonstrator** [ˈdemənstreɪtə(r)] n. 演示者；示威者

▶**demonstrative** [dɪˈmɒnstrətɪv] adj. 感情外露的 n. 指示代词

❶ adj. 感情外露的
Someone who is demonstrative shows affection freely and openly.
Some people are more demonstrative than others.
有些人更容易流露感情。

❷ [C] 指示代词
In grammar, the words "this", "that", "these", and "those" are sometimes called demonstratives.
在语法中，"this" "that" "these"和"those"有时被称

为指示代词。

2. remonstrate [ˈremənstreɪt] vi. 抗议；反对；抱怨
『re返回+monstr显示+ate表动词→反过来（向对方）显示）→抗议』

~ (with sb) (about sth)
If you remonstrate with someone, you protest to them about something you do not approve of or agree with, and you try to get it changed or stopped.
He remonstrated with the referee. 他向裁判抗议。
They remonstrated with the official about the decision.
他们就这一决定向这位官员提出了抗议。

▶**remonstrance** [rɪˈmɒnstrəns] n. 抗议；抱怨

词根190. morph=form，表示"形状"

1. morphology [mɔːˈfɒlədʒi] n. 形态学；构词法

The morphology of something is its form and structure. In linguistics, morphology refers to the way words are constructed with stems, prefixes, and suffixes.
The morphology of the region indicates that it has been uplifted recently.
这个地区的地形表明，它最近一直在上升。
They usually differ markedly in morphology.
它们在形态学上是有明显不同的。

2. amorphous [əˈmɔːfəs] adj. 无固定形状（或结构）的
『a无+morph形状+ous…的→无形状的』

A dark, strangely amorphous shadow filled the room.
一团形状怪异的黑影笼罩了整个房间。

词根191. mors(e)=bite，表示"咬"

1. morsel [ˈmɔːsl] n. 一点点，一小份（尤指食物）
『mors咬+el小→咬一小口→一点点（食物）』

The hungry children did not leave a morsel of food on their plates. 饿了的孩子们没有在盘子里留下一点食物的碎屑。

2. remorse [rɪˈmɔːs] n. 懊悔，自责
『re返回+morse咬→（因懊悔想）反过来咬自己→懊悔』

the feeling of being extremely sorry for sth wrong or bad that you have done
I felt guilty and full of remorse. 我感到内疚，并且非常懊悔。
He was filled with remorse for not believing her.
他因为没有相信她而懊悔不已。

▶**remorseful** [rɪˈmɔːsfl] adj. 懊悔的，悔恨的
He was genuinely remorseful. 他真的感到懊悔。

词根192. mort=death，表示"死"

1. mortal [ˈmɔːtl] adj. 不能永生的；致命的 n. 凡人
『mort死+al…的→死的；致命的→（早晚要）死的→凡人』

❶ adj. 不能永生的；终将死亡的
We are all mortal. 我们都总有一死。

❷ adj. 致命的
The police were defending themselves and others against mortal danger. 警察在保护自己和他人免遭致命危险。

❸ n. 凡人
Such things are not for mere mortals like ourselves.
这种事不会落在我们这样的凡夫俗子身上。

▶**mortality** [mɔːˈtæləti] n. 生命的有限；死亡数量；死亡

❶ [U] 生命的有限

After her mother's death, she became acutely aware of her own mortality.

她母亲去世后，她开始强烈意识到自己的生命是有限的。

❷ [U] 死亡数量；死亡率

Yet even with similar populations of infected patients as, for example, France, Spain and the US, the German COVID-19 mortality rate is about 0.4%.

然而，即使与法国、西班牙和美国的感染者群体相比，德国COVID-19（新冠肺炎）的死亡率也只有0.4%。

❸ [C] 死亡

So far, there have already been over 150,000 mortalities from COVID-19.

到目前为止，已经有超过15万人死于COVID-19（新冠肺炎）。

▶ **immortal** [ɪˈmɔːtl] adj. 不死的；流芳百世的

『im不+mortal死→不朽的』

❶ 长生的；永世的

The soul is immortal. 灵魂不灭。

❷ （人、物、语句）著名的，流芳百世的

Someone or something that is immortal is famous and likely to be remembered for a long time.

Maybe my work is not immortal, but it will live for a while.

也许我的作品不能流芳百世，但它能流传一阵子。

I keep remembering Hannah Pakula's immortal line: "Hollywood is no place for a woman over forty with a library card."

我一直谨记汉娜·帕库拉的名言："好莱坞不是年过40手拿图书证的女人待的地方。"

2. **mortuary** [ˈmɔːtʃəri] n. 太平间；停尸房

『mortu(= mort)死+ary场地→放死尸的地方→停尸室』

3. **mortify** [ˈmɔːtɪfaɪ] vt. 使难堪；使羞愧

『mort死+ ify使…→使人想死→使受辱』

Jane mortified her family by leaving her husband.

简离开丈夫的做法使她的家庭蒙羞。

▶ **mortified** [ˈmɔːtɪfaɪd] adj. 感到羞愧的

He felt mortified for his mistake.

他因为他的错误感到耻辱。

▶ **mortifying** [ˈmɔːtɪfaɪɪŋ] adj.令人羞愧的；令人窘迫的

There were some mortifying setbacks.

有了一些令人难堪的挫折。

▶ **mortification** [ˌmɔːtɪfɪˈkeɪʃn] n. 屈辱感；窘迫感

To my mortification, my manuscript was rejected.

使我感到窘迫的是，我的稿件被退了回来。

4. **morbid** [ˈmɔːbɪd] adj. 病态的，不正常的

『morb(=mort)死+id有…性质的→（总是想着）死的→病态的（也可谐音记忆"毛病的"→病态的）』

having or expressing a strong interest in sad or unpleasant things, especially disease or death

He had a morbid fascination with blood.

他对血有着一种病态的喜好。

The teen had a morbid fascination with violence.

这名青少年对暴力有着病态的迷恋。

5. **postmortem** [ˌpəʊstˈmɔːtəm] n. 尸检；事后反思

『post后+mort死+em→死后（进行的）→尸检』

Police said a postmortem examination would be carried out today. 警方说今天可能会进行验尸。

The postmortem on the presidential campaign is under way.

正在对总统竞选活动进行反思。

6. **mortgage** [ˈmɔːɡɪdʒ] n. & v. 按揭贷款；抵押贷款

『mort死+gage抵押物→生死存亡之时用房子作为抵押物换来了钱→按揭贷款』

❶ [C] 按揭（由银行等提供房产抵押借款）；按揭贷款

I am a family man with a mortgage.

我是个有家室的男人，还有笔按揭款要偿付。

The bank refused to accept any mortgage on land.

银行拒绝接受任何土地抵押。

❷ [VN] 抵押贷款

He had to mortgage his house to pay his legal costs.

他不得不把房子抵押出去来付诉讼费。

词根193. mount=ascend，表示"登上；山"

1. **mount** [maʊnt] n. 山 v. 登上；骑上；逐步增加

❶ Mount 山；山峰

在现代英语里仅用于地名，可缩写作Mt

Mount Kilimanjaro 乞力马扎罗山

Mt Tai 泰山

❷ [VN] (formal) 登上，爬上（台阶、平台）

She slowly mounted the steps. 她慢慢地爬上台阶。

He mounted the platform and addressed the crowd.

他登上讲台对人群发表演说。

❸ [VN] 骑上，跨上（马、自行车等）

He mounted his horse and rode away. 他骑上马走了。

❹ [V] 逐步增加

Pressure is mounting on the government to change the law.

迫使政府修改法律的压力不断增加。

The death toll continues to mount. 死亡人数持续增加。

▶ **dismount** [dɪsˈmaʊnt] vi. 下（马、自行车、摩托车）

词义辨析 <P375第71> 山 mount, mountain, hill

2. **surmount** [səˈmaʊnt] vt. 克服（困难）；置于顶端

『sur (over) 上面+mount山→（攀登或放置于）山的上面→克服（困难）；置于顶端』

❶ [VN] 克服（困难）

She was well aware of the difficulties that had to be surmounted. 她很清楚必须克服哪些困难。

❷ [usually passive] 处于（某物）上面

The island is surmounted by a huge black castle.

岛的最高处耸立着一座巨大的黑色城堡。

▶ **insurmountable** [ˌɪnsəˈmaʊntəbl] adj. 难以克服的

3. **paramount** [ˈpærəmaʊnt] adj. 最重要的；权力最大的

『para (over) 超过+mount山→超过山顶的→最重要的』

This matter is of paramount importance. 此事至关重要。

The child's welfare must be seen as paramount.

必须把儿童福利摆在首位。

小贴士 下面这个图标我们可能很熟悉吧？派拉蒙影业公司（英文名称：Paramount Pictures, Inc.）。

它出品了《阿甘正传》《泰坦尼克号》《碟中谍》《变形金刚》《怪物史莱克3》《忍者神龟》《星际旅行》等多部电影，高质量的影片和遍布全美的连锁影院，使其一直坐在好莱坞霸主的宝座上。

词根194. mun(e)=public, 表示"公共的"

1. communist [ˈkɒmjənɪst] n. 共产主义者
『com共同+mun公共+ist者→（支持）共同拥有公共财产的人→共产主义者』

▶ **communism** [ˈkɒmjunɪzəm] n. 共产主义
『com共同+mun公共+ism主义→支持共同拥有公共财产的主义→共产主义』

▶ **CCP** （abbr. Chinese Communist Party ）中国共产党
The 17th conference of CCP puts forward a system reform to deepen administration, build service type government.
党的十七大提出了要深化行政管理体制改革，建设服务型政府。

2. commune [ˈkɒmjuːn, kəˈmjuːn] n. 群居团体，公社
v. 与（自然等）融为一体
『com共同+mune公共→共同拥有公共的东西（的群体）；（和自然等）共同拥有一切→群居团体；与（自然等）融为一体』
（n. [ˈkɒmjuːn]; v. [kəˈmjuːn]）

❶ [C] 群居团体；公社
A commune is a group of people who live together and share everything.
Mack lived in a commune. 麦克生活在一个群居团体里。

❷ [V] 与（动物、精灵或大自然）交流；与…融为一体
to share your emotions and feelings with sb/sth without speaking
He spent much of this time communing with nature.
他这个时期的许多时间都沉浸在大自然中。

形近词 **commute** [kəˈmjuːt] v. & n. 通勤〈P231〉
『com一起+mute交换→（和别人一起）换乘→通勤』

▶ **communal** [kəˈmjuːnl] adj. 公共的；群体的
『commune群居社团（去e)+al…的→公共的；群体的』

❶ （尤指居住在一起的人）共有的，共用的
shared by, or for the use of, a number of people, especially people who live together
a communal kitchen/garden, etc. 共用的厨房/花园等

❷ （集体中）不同群体的
involving different groups of people in a community
communal violence between religious groups
不同教派之间的暴力冲突
He said that communal carnage was ripping the country apart.
他说种族间的相互残杀正在让这个国家走向分裂。

3. community [kəˈmjuːnəti] n. 社区；（国际）社会；社团，团体
『com共同+mun公共+ity表名词→共同拥有一些共同（特征）的团体→社区；社团』

❶ [sing.] 社区；社会
all the people who live in a particular area, country, etc. when talked about as a group
The local community was shocked by the murders.
当地社会对这些谋杀案感到震惊。
the international community 国际社会
good community relations with the police
社区与警方之间的良好关系

❷ [C+sing./pl. v.] 团体；社团；界
a group of people who share the same religion, race, job, etc.
the Polish community in London 在伦敦的波兰侨民团体
the farming community 农业界

❸ [U] 共享；共有
the feeling of sharing things and belonging to a group in the place where you live
There is a strong sense of community in this town.
这个镇上有一种强烈的社区意识。
community spirit 团体精神

4. communicate [kəˈmjuːnɪkeɪt] v. 交流；传达；沟通
『com共同+mun公共+i+cate使→使（信息、意见等）成为说话双方公共的东西→交流』

❶ ~ (with sb)（与某人）交流（信息或意见等）；沟通
to exchange information, news, ideas, etc. with sb
[V] We only communicate by email. 我们只是互通电子邮件。
They communicated in sign language. 他们用手语沟通。

❷ 传达，传递（想法、感情、思想等）
[VN] He was eager to communicate his ideas to the group.
他急于把他的想法传达给小组。

❸ [V] ~ (with sb) 沟通
to have a good relationship because you are able to understand and talk about your own and other people's thoughts, feelings, etc.
The novel is about a family who can't communicate with each other.
这部小说写的是成员彼此无法沟通的一个家庭。

▶ **communication** [kəˌmjuːnɪˈkeɪʃn] n. 交流；通讯，交通；信息

❶ [U] 表达；交流
Speech is the fastest method of communication between people.
说话是人与人之间交流最快捷的方法。
All channels of communication need to be kept open.
所有沟通渠道都得保持畅通无阻。

❷ [U] also communications [pl.] 通信
methods of sending information, especially telephones, radio, computers, etc. or roads and railways
a communications satellite 通信卫星
The new airport will improve communications between the islands. 新机场将改善岛屿间的交通联系。

❸ [C] (formal) 信息
The ambassador has brought with him a communication from the President. 大使带来了总统的口信。

5. immune [ɪˈmjuːn] adj. 有免疫力的；不受影响的；免除
『im不+mune公共→不会受公共的敌人（疫情）影响的→有免疫力的』

This blood test will show whether or not you're immune to the disease.
这个血检会显示你是否对这种疾病具有免疫力。
You'll eventually become immune to criticism.
你终究会变得不在乎批评了。
No one should be immune from prosecution.
任何人都不应免于被起诉。

▶**immunity** [ɪˈmjuːnəti] n. 免疫力；免除

The vaccine provides longer immunity against flu.
这种疫苗对流感的免疫效力时间较长。
The spies were all granted immunity from prosecution.
这些间谍都获得免予公诉。

▶**immunize** [ˈɪmjunaɪz] vt. （尤指注射疫苗）使免疫

We should require that every student is immunized against hepatitis B. 我们应要求每个学生都注射乙肝疫苗。

6. municipal [mjuːˈnɪsɪpl] adj. 市政的；地方政府的

associated with or belonging to a city or town that has its own local government

The municipal authorities gave the go-ahead for the march.
市政当局批准了这次游行。
He works in the municipal government. 他在市政府工作。

▶**municipality** [mjuːˌnɪsɪˈpæləti] n. 自治市，自治区；市政当局

A railway, connecting Lanzhou and the Chongqing Municipality, is under construction.
一条连接兰州和重庆市的铁路正在修建之中。
The municipality of Hangzhou has awarded him the permanent residence for his notable contribution to the city.
为表彰他的特殊贡献，杭州市政府授予他永久居留权。

词根195. mute=change，表示"改变；交换"

1. mutate [mjuːˈteɪt] v.（使）变异，突变；变化
『mute改变（去e）+ate表动词→（基因）改变→变异』

❶ （使）变异，突变
[V] the ability of the virus to mutate into new forms
病毒变异成新菌株的能力
So it likely took decades for RaTG13-like viruses to mutate into 2019-nCoV.
因此，类似RaTG13的病毒可能需要数十年才能变异为2019-nCoV。
[VN] mutated genes 发生变异的基因

❷ [V] 转变；转换
to change into a new form
Overnight, the gossip begins to mutate into headlines.
一夜之间，传闻变成了报纸的头条新闻。

▶**mutation** [mjuːˈteɪʃn] n. 变异；改变

2. commute [kəˈmjuːt] v. & n. 通勤
『com一起+mute交换→（和别人一起）换乘→通勤』

❶ 上下班往返，通勤
to travel regularly by bus, train, car, etc. between your place of work and your home
[V] She commutes from Oxford to London every day.
她每天上下班往返于牛津与伦敦之间。
[V] I live within commuting distance of Dublin.
我住在离都柏林上下班可乘公交车往返的地方。

❷ [C] 上下班路程
a two-hour commute into downtown Washington
去华盛顿中心区两小时的上下班路程
I have only a short commute to work. 我上班的路程很近。

▶**commuter** [kəˈmjuːtə(r)] n. 通勤者

3. mutable [ˈmjuːtəbl] adj. 可变的，会变的
『mute改变（去e）+able能够的→会变的』

And, too, because a man must know in his bones that his true spirit was as mutable as ivory or clay.
还有，因为一个人必须从骨子里知道，他真正的灵魂就像象牙或黏土一样易变。

▶**immutable** [ɪˈmjuːtəbl] adj. 不可改变的，永恒不变的
Something that is immutable will never change or cannot be changed.
the eternal and immutable principles of right and wrong
永恒不变的对错法则

4. mutual [ˈmjuːtʃuəl] adj. 相互的；共同的
『mute改变（去e）+ual表形容词→（双方一起）改变→相互的 』

❶ 相互的，彼此的
The East and the West can work together for their mutual benefit and progress.
东西方可以为彼此共同的利益和发展而合作。
A meeting would take place at a mutually convenient time.
会议拟在双方都方便的时候召开。

❷ [only before noun] 共有的，共同的
They do, however, share a mutual interest in design.
不过他们确实都对设计感兴趣。
We met at the home of a mutual friend.
我们在彼此都认识的朋友家中会面。

5. transmute [trænzˈmjuːt] v. （使）变形，（使）变化
『trans从…到…+mute变→从一种事物变到另一种事物→变化』

She ceased to think, as anger transmuted into passion.
当怒火转化为激情，她停止了思考。
It was once thought that lead could be transmuted into gold.
有人曾经认为铅可以变成黄金。

6. mutiny [ˈmjuːtəni] n. & vi. （尤指士兵或船员）哗变，暴动
『mute改变（去e）+in+y表名词→（士兵或船员）改变（对自己上级的态度，不再服从）→哗变，暴动』

Discontent among the ship's crew finally led to the outbreak of mutiny. 船员的不满情绪最终酿成了暴乱。
Units stationed around the capital mutinied because they had received no pay for nine months.
驻扎在首府周边的部队因9个月没有领到军饷而哗变。

▶**mutinous** [ˈmjuːtənəs] adj. 反叛的；不驯服的
『mutiny反叛（去y）+ous充满→充满反叛精神的→反叛的』

If someone is mutinous, they are strongly dissatisfied with a person in authority and are likely to stop obeying them.
mutinous workers 桀骜不驯的工人
a mutinous expression 反抗的神色

词根196. nate=born，表示"出生；天生"

1. native [ˈneɪtɪv] adj. 当地的 n. 当地人
『nate出生（去e）+ive表形容词或名词→出生地的；当地出生的人』

2. innate [ɪˈneɪt] adj. 天生的，先天的，与生俱来的
『in里面+nate出生→出生时从里面带出来的→天生的』

Americans have an innate sense of fairness.
美国人有一种天生的公平观。
There are three innate items: love, jealousy and fear.
有三件东西是与生俱来的：爱、嫉妒和恐惧。

3. postnatal [ˌpəʊstˈneɪtl] adj. 产后的
『post之后+nate出生（去e）+al…的→出生后的→产后的』

We got health advice and learnt about postnatal care.
我们得到了健康建议，并了解了产后护理。
She suffered from postnatal depression at the start and it lasted a couple of years.
她一开始就患有产后抑郁症，并持续了几年。

4. prenatal [ˌpriːˈneɪtl] adj. 孕期的，产前的
『pre之前+ nate出生（去e）+al…的→出生之前的→产前的』
（NAmE antenatal）

I'd met her briefly in a prenatal class.
我曾经在一次产前辅导课上和她有过一面之缘。

5. antenatal [ˌæntiˈneɪtl] adj. 产前的
『ante前，在前+nate出生（去e）+al…的→产前的』
（BrE）（also prenatal NAmE, BrE）

6. neonate [ˈniːəʊneɪt] n.（指出生不足四周的）新生儿
『neo新+nate出生→新生儿』

Jaundice is a common condition in neonates up to four weeks old. 黄疸是4周大的新生儿的常见情况。

7. nature [ˈneɪtʃə(r)] n. 自然；本性
『nate出生（去e）+ure表名词→出生就有的→本性』

It's not in his nature to be unkind. 他天生不会刻薄。
She is very sensitive by nature. 她生性很敏感。

▶ **natural** [ˈnætʃrəl] adj. 天生的；与生俱来的

It's only natural to worry about your children.
为孩子操心是很自然的。
He's a natural leader. 他天生是个领袖。

8. renaissance [rɪˈneɪsns] n. 文艺复兴
『re又，再+naiss(=nate)出生+ance表名词→（文艺）再出生→文艺复兴』

词根197. naus, naut, nav=ship，表示"船"

1. nausea [ˈnɔːziə] n. 恶心；作呕；反胃
『naus船+ea(=ia病)→坐船不舒服→晕船→作呕』

[U] the feeling that you have when you want to vomit , for example because you are ill/sick or are disgusted by sth
A wave of nausea swept over her. 她觉得一阵恶心。
Nausea and vomiting are common symptoms.
恶心呕吐是常见的症状。

▶ **nauseate** [ˈnɔːzieɪt] vt. 使恶心；使厌烦
『nausea恶心+(a)te使→使恶心』

I was nauseated by the violence in the movie.
影片中的暴力场面让我感到恶心。

▶ **nauseating** [ˈnɔːzieɪtɪŋ] adj.令人厌恶的，令人恶心的

a nauseating smell 令人作呕的气味
his nauseating behavior 他那令人厌恶的行为

▶ **nauseous** [ˈnɔːziəs] adj. 恶心的，想呕吐的
『nausea恶心（去a）+ous充满→恶心的，想呕吐的』

If the patient is poorly nourished, the drugs make them feel nauseous. 如果患者进食欠佳，药物会让他们感觉作呕。

2. astronaut [ˈæstrənɔːt] n. 宇航员
『astro星星+naut船→驾驶飞船在星际航行的人→宇航员』

3. nautical [ˈnɔːtɪkl] adj. 航海的

『naut船+ical…的→与船（航海）有关的→航海的』
nautical terms 航海术语
a nautical chart of the region you sail
你航行途经地区的航海图

4. navy [ˈneɪvi] n. 海军；海军蓝
『nav船+y表人→开船的人→海军』

[C + sing./pl. v.] 海军；海军部队

The navy is/are considering buying six new warships.
海军正在考虑购买六艘新战舰。
He's joined the navy/the Navy. 他加入了海军。

▶ **naval** [ˈneɪvl] adj. 海军的
『nav船+al…的→海军的』

a naval base/officer/battle 海军基地/军官；海战

5. navigate [ˈnævɪgeɪt] v. 航行；导航；成功应对（困境）
『nav船+ig(=drive)驾驶+ate表动词→驾船走→航海；导航』

❶ [VN] 航行
The river became too narrow and shallow to navigate.
河道变得又窄又浅，无法航行。

❷ 导航；确定位置和路线
[V] I'll drive, and you can navigate. 我开车，你引路。
[VN] How do you navigate your way through a forest?
你怎么才能设法走出森林？

❸ [VN] 成功应对（困境）
to find the right way to deal with a difficult or complicated situation
We next had to navigate a complex network of committees.
我们下一步必须设法使各级委员会予以通过。

▶ **navigator** [ˈnævɪgeɪtə(r)] n. （飞机或船只的）领航员，导航员

▶ **navigation** [ˌnævɪˈgeɪʃn] n. 导航；领航；航行
navigation systems 导航系统

词根198. neg=deny，表示"否认，拒绝"

1. negate [nɪˈgeɪt] vt. 否认；使失效
『neg否认，拒绝+ ate表动词→否认；取消』

He angrily negate that he had stolen those documents.
他愤怒地否认他偷了那些文件。

▶ **negation** [nɪˈgeɪʃn] n. 对立面；否定

This political system was the negation of democracy.
这种政治制度是对民主的否定。
She shook her head in negation. 她摇头表示拒绝。

▶ **negative** [ˈnegətɪv] adj. 否定的；阴性的；阴极的；消极的
『negate否认（去e）+ive表形容词→否定的』

❶ 否定的
His response was negative. 他的回答是否定的。

❷ (abbr. neg.) 结果为阴性的
Her pregnancy test was negative. 她的孕检呈阴性。

❸ (technical) 负极的；阴极的
the negative terminal of a battery 电池的负极

❹ 消极的；负面的；缺乏热情的
Scientists have a fairly negative attitude to the theory.
科学家对这个理论的态度是相当消极的。
The crisis had a negative effect on trade.

这次危机对贸易产生了很坏的影响。

反义词 positive [ˈpɒzətɪv] adj. 肯定的；阳性的；正极的；积极的

2. neglect [nɪˈglekt] vt. 忽视；疏忽 n. 忽视 <P202>
『neg否认，拒绝+lect选择→没能选择→忽视；疏忽』

3. negligence [ˈneglɪdʒəns] n. 疏忽；失职 <P203>
『neg否认，拒绝+lig选择+ence表名词→没能选择→疏忽；失职』

4. negligible [ˈneglɪdʒəbl] adj. 微不足道的；不值一提的 <P203>
『neg否认，拒绝+lig选择+ible可…的→可以不选择的→可以忽视的→微不足道的』

5. renegade [ˈrenɪgeɪd] n. 变节者，背叛者
『re又，再+neg否认+ade→一再否认自己信仰的人』

A renegade is a person who abandons the religious, political, or philosophical beliefs that he or she used to have, and accepts opposing or different beliefs.

The makeshift police training centre was built in the aftermath of the worst attack against the British military by a renegade member of the Afghan security forces.
临时警察训练中心是在阿富汗安全部队一名叛变成员对英国军队发动最严重袭击后建造的。

词根199. neur =nerve，表示"神经"

1. neural [ˈnjʊərəl] adj. 神经的，神经系统的
『neur神经+al表形容词→神经的』

They have identified a protein that stops new neural connections forming in adult brains.
他们发现了一种阻止成年大脑新神经连接形成的蛋白质。

2. neuron [ˈnjʊərɒn] n. 神经元
『neur神经+on表物→神经元』

Information is transferred along each neuron by means of an electrical impulse. 信息在电脉冲作用下经神经元传递。

3. neurology [njʊəˈrɒlədʒi] n. 神经学；神经病学
『neur神经+ology学科→神经学』

词根200. neutr(o)= middle; neither，表示"中间；两者都不"

1. neutral [ˈnjuːtrəl] adj. 中立的 n. 中立方；空挡

❶ adj. 中立的
Journalists are supposed to be politically neutral.
新闻工作者在政治上应持中立态度。
I didn't take my father's or my mother's side; I tried to remain neutral.
我既不支持父亲也不袒护母亲；我尽力做到不偏不倚。

❷ adj.（声音或表情）平淡的；（颜色）淡素的
"So you told her?" he said in a neutral tone of voice.
"那么你告诉她了？"他平静地说。
At the horizon the land mass becomes a continuous pale neutral grey. 陆地在地平线处变成了一片浅灰。

❸ [C] 中立方
It was a good game to watch for the neutrals.
对中立方来说，这是一场精彩的比赛。

❹ [U]（汽车排挡）空挡
Graham put the van in neutral and jumped out into the road.
格雷厄姆把货车挂到空挡，自己跳到马路上。

小贴士 "排挡"，参看 reverse <P350>

▶**neutralize** [ˈnjuːtrəlaɪz] vt. 使中和；使无法正常工作
『neutral中立的+ize使→使中立』

The intruder smashed a window to get in and then neutralized the alarm system.
闯入者打碎了一扇窗户进来，然后破坏了警报系统。
Bombardment intended to destroy or neutralize enemy weapons. 轰炸意在破坏或压制敌人的武器。

2. neutron [ˈnjuːtrɒn] n. 中子
『neutr中间的+on物质结构成分→中子』

词根201. noc(u), nox=hurt; poison，表示"伤害；毒"

1. innocent [ˈɪnəsnt] adj. 清白的；无辜的；天真的
『in无+noc伤害；毒+ent具有…性质的→单纯无害人之心的→无害的；天真的』

❶ 清白的
If someone is innocent, they did not commit a crime which they have been accused of.
The police knew from day one that I was innocent.
警方一开始就知道我是无辜的。

❷ 无辜（受害）的
Innocent people are those who are not involved in a crime or conflict, but are injured or killed as a result of it.
All those wounded were innocent victims.
所有伤者都是无辜的受害人。

❸ 无恶意的；无冒犯之意的
not intended to cause harm or upset sb
It was a perfectly innocent remark.
那是一句毫无冒犯之意的话。

❹ 天真的，幼稚的；不谙世故的
If someone is innocent, they have no experience or knowledge of the more complex or unpleasant aspects of life.
They seemed so young and innocent.
他们看起来如此少不更事。

▶**innocence** [ˈɪnəsns] n. 清白；无辜；单纯
『in无+noc伤害；毒+ence表名词→没有伤害的→清白；无辜；单纯』

This new evidence will prove their innocence.
这一新的证据将证明他们的清白。
Children lose their innocence as they grow older.
儿童随着年龄的增长而失去其天真。

2. obnoxious [əbˈnɒkʃəs] adj. 令人讨厌的；使人反感的
『ob对+nox伤害；毒+ious充满→对人有伤害（毒害）的→令人讨厌的』

extremely unpleasant, especially in a way that offends people
The people at my table were so obnoxious that I simply had to change my seat. 我那桌的人如此讨厌，我只好换了座位。

3. innocuous [ɪˈnɒkjuəs] adj. 无害的；无恶意的
『in不，没有+noc伤害；毒+uous充满，具有→无害的；无恶意的』

Something that is innocuous is not at all harmful or offensive.
Both mushrooms look innocuous but are in fact deadly.
这两种蘑菇看起来似乎都无害，实际上却是致命的。
Even seemingly innocuous words are offensive in certain contexts.
甚至看似毫无恶意的言辞在某些语境下也具有冒犯性。

4. inoculate [ɪˈnɒkjuleɪt] vt. 打预防针，接种

『i(=in)进入+noc伤害；毒+u+late使→使毒进入体内（引起免疫反应的）→接种（疫苗）』

A corps of doctors arrived to inoculate the recruits.
一队医生来给新兵打防疫针。

词根202. nomin=name，表示"名称，名字"

1. nominal ['nɒmɪnl] adj. 名义上的；象征性的
『nomin名称，名字+al…的→名义上的』

❶ 名义上的；有名无实的
being sth in name only, and not in reality
He remained in nominal control of the business for another ten years. 他名义上又掌管了这家公司十年。

❷ （价格或款项）微不足道的，象征性的
We only pay a nominal rent. 我们只象征性地付一点租金。

2. nominee [ˌnɒmɪ'ni:] n. 被提名者；候选人
『nomin名称，名字+ ee被…者→被提名者』

a presidential nominee 总统候选人
an Oscar nominee 奥斯卡提名人

3. nominate ['nɒmɪneɪt] vt. 提名；任命；指定

❶ ~ sb (for/as sth) 提名；推荐
She has been nominated for the presidency.
她已经获得了董事长职位的提名。

❷ ~ sb (to/as sth) 任命；指派
She was nominated to speak on our behalf.
她被指派代表我们发言。

❸ ~ sth (as sth) 挑选，指定（时间、日期、名称等）
1 December has been nominated as the day of the election.
12月1日被指定为选举日。

▶**nomination** [ˌnɒmɪ'neɪʃn] n. 提名；任命；指定

3. ignominy ['ɪgnəmɪni] n. 公开的耻辱，不名誉
『ig(=in)不+nomin名称，名字+y表名词→不名誉』

public shame and loss of honour （同义词 disgrace）
They suffered the ignominy of defeat.
他们蒙受了失败的耻辱。

▶**ignominious** [ˌɪgnə'mɪniəs] adj. 耻辱的，不光彩的

He made one mistake and his career came to an ignominious end. 他犯了一个错误，他的事业就很不体面地结束了。

4. denominate [dɪ'nɒmɪneɪt] v. 以（某种货币）为单位；将…命名为
『de使…+nomin名称，名字+ate使…→使有名字→给…命名』

The loan was denominated in US dollars.
这笔贷款是以美元计算的。

So after that, I decided to use this word to denominate and start my band. 因此在那之后我决定用这个词命名乐队。

▶**denominator** [dɪ'nɒmɪneɪtə(r)] n. 分母

▶**denomination** [dɪˌnɒmɪ'neɪʃn] n. （基督教）教派，宗派；（尤指钱的）面额，面值

Christians of all denominations attended the conference.
基督教所有教派的人都出席了这次会议。

coins and banknotes of various denominations
各种面额的硬币和纸币

词根203. nom(y)=science, laws "科学；法则"

1. autonomy [ɔ:'tɒnəmi] n. 自治；自主权
『auto自己+nomy法则→按自己的法则办事→自治；自主权』

Activists stepped up their demands for local autonomy last month. 上个月激进分子对地方自治的呼声更高了。
Each of the area managers enjoys considerable autonomy in the running of his own area.
每个区域经理在他们各自负责的地区的运营上都享有高度的自主权。

▶**autonomous** [ɔ:'tɒnəməs] adj. 自治的；有自治权的

an autonomous republic/state/province 自治共和国/州/省
autonomous vehicle 自动驾驶汽车

2. economy [ɪ'kɒnəmi] n. 经济；经济体；节省〈P77〉
『eco环境；经济+nomy科学；法则→经济（学）』

3. astronomy [ə'strɒnəmi] n. 天文学〈P115〉
『astro星星+nomy科学；法则→研究星星的科学法则→天文学』

4. antinomy [æn'tɪnəmi] n. 自相矛盾
『anti反对，相反+nomy法则→法则相反→自相矛盾』

The third antinomy is the government leading shortage and the higher school.

其三，是政府引导不足与高校盲目扩招的矛盾。

5. agronomy [ə'grɒnəmi] n. 农学；作物栽培学
『agro(=agri)田地+nomy科学→研究田地的科学→农学』

词根204. norm=rule; norm，表示"规则，规范；正常"

1. normal ['nɔ:ml] adj. 正常的 n. 常态；通常标准
『norm正常+ al…的→正常的』

❶ adj. 典型的；正常的；一般的
Her temperature is normal. 她的体温正常。
It's normal to feel tired after such a long trip.
这样长途旅行之后感到疲劳是正常的。

❷ [U] 常态；通常标准；一般水平
Things soon returned to normal. 情况很快恢复了正常。
Rainfall has been above normal this July.
今年7月的降雨量在标准以上。

▶**normality** [nɔ:'mæləti] n. 常态，正常状态
（**normalcy** ['nɔ:məlsi] especially in NAmE）

They are hoping for a return to normality now that the war is over. （既然）战争结束了，他们希望一切都恢复常态。
Can China return to normalcy while keeping the coronavirus in check? 中国能在控制冠状病毒的同时恢复正常吗？

2. enormous [ɪ'nɔ:məs] adj. 巨大的，庞大的，极大的
『e超出+norm正常+ous表形容词→超出正常的→巨大的』

an enormous house/dog 巨大的房子；大狗
enormous interest 浓厚的兴趣
The problems facing the President are enormous.
总统面临的问题是巨大的。

▶**enormity** [ɪ'nɔ:məti] n. 巨大；严重性

the enormity of the task 任务的艰巨性

词义辨析 〈P367第30〉
巨大的 huge, enormous, giant, gigantic, immense, vast

3. abnormal [æb'nɔ:ml] adj. 反常的
『ab离开+normal正常的→离开正常的→不正常的』

different, esp in an undesirable way, from what is normal, ordinary or expected

abnormal weather conditions, behaviour 反常的天气/行为

abnormally large feet 异常巨大的脚

They thought his behaviour was abnormal.
他们认为他行为反常。

4. norm [nɔːm] n. 常态；规范；定额，定量

❶ [sing.] 常态；正常行为

Families of six or seven are the norm in Borough Park.
在伯勒公园住宅区六口或七口之家十分普遍。

If cheating becomes the norm, then we are in big trouble.
如果欺骗成了常态，那我们就麻烦大了。

❷ norms [pl.] 规范；行为标准

Understanding an organization means understanding its culture, values, norms, and principles.

了解一个组织意味着了解其文化、价值观、规范和原则。

❸ [C] 标准；定额；定量

These questions primarily involve labor norm, production management, incentive system.

这些问题主要涉及劳动定额、生产管理、激励制度等方面。

词根205. note=know；mark，表示"知道；标记"

1. notice [ˈnəʊtɪs] v. 注意 n. 通知

『note知道（去e）+ice表行为→知道；使知道→注意；通知』

2. note [nəʊt] n. 笔记；便条；纸钞；注解 vt. 注意；特别指出

『note知道；标记→请注意，指出；笔记，注释』

❶ [C] 笔记；记录（听讲或读书等时的记录常用notes）

Please make a note of the dates. 请记下日期。

Can I borrow your lecture notes?
我可以借你的讲稿看看吗？

❷ [C] 短笺；便条

She left a note for Ben on the kitchen table.
她在厨房的餐桌上给本留了个便条。

❸ [C] 注释；批注

See note 3, page 259. 见259页注释3。

❹ [C] 纸币 （美语中用bill）

❺ [VN] 请注意；请留意

Please note (that) the office will be closed on Monday.
请注意办事处星期一将关闭。

❻ [VN] 指出；特别提到

The report notes that export and import volumes picked up in leading economies.

报告特别指出经济大国的进出口量攀升。

▶**annotate** [ˈænəteɪt] vt. 给…作注解（或评注）

『an相当于to+note注解（去e）+ate表动词→给…作注解』

[VN] 加注

to add notes to a book or text, giving explanations or comments

Historians annotate, check and interpret the diary selections.
历史学家对日记选篇进行加注、查考以及阐释。

▶**annotation** [ˌænəˈteɪʃn] n. 注解；评注

It will be published with annotations and index.
这本书出版时将附有注释和索引。

3. notable [ˈnəʊtəbl] adj. 重要的；显著的

『note标记（去e）+able可以的→可以加标记的→显著的』

His eyes are his most notable feature.
他的双眼是他最明显的特征。

The proposed new structure is notable not only for its height, but for its shape.
拟建的新建筑令人瞩目，不仅是因其高度，也因其外形。

4. notify [ˈnəʊtɪfaɪ] vt. （正式）通报；通知

『note知道（去e）+ify使…→使…知道→通知』

~ sb (of sth) | ~ sth to sb （正式）通报；通知

to formally or officially tell sb about sth

（告诉朋友某事一般不能用notify，因为notify常用于正式场合。）

The police must be notified of the date of the demonstration.
必须向警方报告游行示威的日期。

▶**notification** [ˌnəʊtɪfɪˈkeɪʃn] n. 通知

You should receive (a) notification of our decision in the next week. 关于我们的决定，下周你会接到通知。

5. denote [dɪˈnəʊt] vt. 预示；（符号等）表示；意指

『de强调+note标记→是…的标记→预示；表示』

❶ 预示；是…的征兆

A very high temperature often denotes a serious illness.
高烧通常意味着严重的疾病。

❷ （符号等）表示；（某一词）意指

The red triangle denotes danger. 红色三角形表示危险。

Here "family" denotes mother, father and children.
此处的"family"指母亲、父亲和孩子。

6. connote [kəˈnəʊt] v. （词或名字）隐含；暗示

『con一起+note标记→（实际含义）和标记在一起→隐含』

If a word or name connotes something, it makes you think of a particular idea or quality.

The term "organization" often connotes a sense of neatness.
"organization"这个词常让人想到整洁。

The adjectives used in the poem all connote death and destruction.
诗中所用的形容词全都隐含着死亡和毁灭之意。

▶**connotation** [ˌkɒnəˈteɪʃn] n. 含义，隐含意义

The word "professional" has connotations of skill and excellence.
"professional"这个词隐含着技艺和专长的意思。

7. notion [ˈnəʊʃn] n. 观念；看法

『note知道（去e）+ion表名词→自己所知道的（关于某事的情况）→观念；看法』

A notion is an idea or belief about something.

I have to reject the notion that greed can be a good thing.
我不能接受那种认为贪欲也可以是件好事的观点。

Their relationship turned the standard notion of marriage on its head. 他们的关系完全颠覆了传统的婚姻观念。

8. notorious [nəʊˈtɔːriəs] adj. 臭名昭著的

『note知道（去e）+or表人+ious多…的→（因做坏事）让很多人知道→臭名昭彰的』

~ (for sth/for doing sth) | ~ (as sth)
声名狼藉的；臭名昭著的

The bar has become notorious as a meeting-place for drug dealers.

这家酒吧作为毒品贩子接头的场所已变得声名狼藉。

▶ **notoriety** [ˌnəʊtəˈraɪəti] n. 恶名；坏名声

『note知道（去e）+or表人+i+ety表状态→（因做坏事）让很多人知道→恶名；坏名声』

She achieved notoriety for her affair with the senator.
她因为和参议员的风流韵事而声名狼藉。

词根206. nounce =speak，表示"讲话，说出"

1. announce [əˈnaʊns] vt. 通知；宣告（决定、计划等）；宣称（某个事实）

『an相当于to+ nounce讲，说→向…讲→通知，宣告』

❶ （尤指通过广播）通知
[V that] They announced that the flight would be delayed.
广播通知，该航班将晚点。

❷ ~ (sth) (to sb) 宣布，宣告（决定、计划等）
The government yesterday announced to the media plans to create a million new jobs.
政府在昨天向媒体宣布了创造一百万个新工作岗位的计划。

❸ [VN] 声称；宣称
to say sth in a loud and/or serious way
She announced that she'd given up smoking.
她宣称她已戒烟。

▶ **announcement** [əˈnaʊnsmənt] n. 公告；宣告

词义辨析 <P374第64> 宣布 declare, announce, proclaim

2. pronounce [prəˈnaʊns] vt. 发音；正式宣布
『pro向前+ nounce讲，说→向前讲话→宣告』

Very few people can pronounce my name correctly.
很少有人能把我的名字念正确。
I now pronounce you man and wife. 现在正式宣布你们结为夫妻。

▶ **pronunciation** [prəˌnʌnsiˈeɪʃn] n. 发音；读音

3. denounce [dɪˈnaʊns] vt. 痛斥；检举
『de毁+nounce讲，说→说诋毁的话→痛斥』

❶ [VN] 谴责；痛斥
If you denounce a person or an action, you criticize them severely and publicly because you feel strongly that they are wrong or evil.
She publicly denounced the government's handling of the crisis. 她公开谴责政府处理这场危机的方式。

❷ [VN] 告发，检举
She denounced him to the police. 她向警察检举了他。

4. renounce [rɪˈnaʊns] vt. 放弃（信仰、行为、头衔等）
『re返回，又+nounce讲，说→又说→（原来努力争取，现在）又说（不要了）→放弃』

❶ [VN] 宣布放弃，抛弃（信仰或行为方式）
After a period of imprisonment she renounced terrorism.
在被囚禁一段时间之后，她宣布放弃恐怖主义。

❷ 正式放弃（要求、官阶或头衔）
He renounced his claim to the French throne.
他正式放弃对法国王位的继承权。
She renounced her citizenship.
她放弃了她的公民身份。

词根207. nour, nur, nutri=nourish，表示"滋养"

1. nourish [ˈnʌrɪʃ] vt. 给…提供营养，滋养；培养，助长

『nour滋养+ish做…→养育，哺育』

❶ 给…提供营养；滋养
The food she eats nourishes both her and the baby.
她吃的食物给她和婴儿提供了营养。
All the children were well nourished and in good physical condition. 所有这些孩子都营养良好，身体健康。

❷ 培养，助长（情绪、观点等）
Journalists on the whole don't create public opinion. They can help to nourish it.
大体说来记者不制造舆论。他们会助长舆论。
By investing in education, we nourish the talents of our children. 我们通过教育投资，培养孩子们的才能。

▶ **nourishment** [ˈnʌrɪʃmənt] n. 营养；营养品

Can plants obtain adequate nourishment from such poor soil?
土壤这样贫瘠，植物能获得足够的养分吗？

2. nutrition [njuˈtrɪʃn] n. 营养（作用）；滋养（过程）
『nutri滋养+tion表动作或过程→营养；滋养』

Nutrition is the process of taking food into the body and absorbing the nutrients in those foods.
She's a professor of nutrition at Columbia University.
她是哥伦比亚大学的营养学教授。
Nutrition and exercise are essential to fitness and health.
营养和锻炼对身体健康至关重要。

▶ **nutritionist** [njuˈtrɪʃənɪst] n. 营养学家

3. malnutrition [ˌmælnjuˈtrɪʃn] n. 营养不良
『mal坏+nutrition营养；滋养→营养不良』

Infections are more likely in those suffering from malnutrition. 营养不良的人更有可能被传染。

4. nutrient [ˈnjuːtriənt] n. 营养素；营养物
『nutri滋养+ent表物→营养素；营养物』

a substance that is needed to keep a living thing alive and to help it to grow
Plants draw minerals and other nutrients from the soil.
植物从土壤中吸取矿物质和其他养分。

5. nutritious [njuˈtrɪʃəs] adj. 有营养的；营养丰富的
『nutri滋养+tious充满的→充满营养的→营养丰富的』

very good for you; containing many of the substances which help the body to grow
It is always important to choose enjoyable, nutritious foods.
选择好吃的、营养价值高的食物总是很重要。

6. nurture [ˈnɜːtʃə(r)] vt. & n. 养育；培养
『nur滋养+ture表动作→养育；培养』

to care for and protect sb/sth while they are growing and developing
As a record company director, his job is to nurture young talent. 作为唱片公司董事，他的工作是培养年轻人才。
These delicate plants need careful nurturing.
这些幼嫩的植物需要精心培育。
It's important to nurture a good working relationship.
维持良好的工作关系非常重要。
She had always nurtured great ambitions for her son.
她总是培养儿子树立远大抱负。
Which do you believe has the strongest influence on how children develop—nature or nurture?
你认为哪一个对孩子的成长有最大的影响——先天遗传

还是后天培养？

词根208. nov=new，表示"新的"

1. novel ['nɒvl] n. 小说 adj. 新颖的，新奇的
『nov新的+el表物→小说；novel小说（有新颖、新奇的故事情节的小说才会受欢迎）→新颖的，新奇的』

Novel things are new and different from anything that has been done, experienced, or made before.

In consequence, many novel features presented themselves.
结果许多新奇的特点出现了。
I hope I am full of novel ideas.
我希望我满脑子都是新奇的想法。

小贴士 引起2019年的新冠肺炎的病毒nCoV-2019（novel corona virous-2019），"新"就是用的novel，表示"与以前所不同的"。

▶ **novelty** ['nɒvlti] n. 新奇，新颖；新奇的人或事

It was fun working there at first but the novelty soon wore off.
开始时在那里工作很有趣，但这股新鲜劲很快就过去了。
Electric-powered cars are still something of a novelty.
电动汽车仍然是一种新鲜玩意儿。

2. novice ['nɒvɪs] n. 新手，初学者
『nov新的+ice表人→新手』

I'm a complete novice at skiing. 滑雪我完全是个新手。
As a novice writer, this is something I'm interested in.
作为初涉写作的人，我对此很感兴趣。

3. renovate ['renəveɪt] vt. 修复，改造，翻新
『re又，再+nov新的+ate使…→使…再成为新的→翻新』

to repair and improve something, especially a building
The couple spent thousands renovating the house.
这对夫妇花了数千元来翻新房子。

▶ **renovation** [ˌrenə'veɪʃ(ə)n] n. 修复，改造，翻新

After renovation and reconstruction the old port has changed beyond recognition. 经过改建，旧港口面貌焕然一新。

4. innovate ['ɪnəveɪt] v. 革新，创新
『in里面+nov新的+ate使…→使新的东西进入里面→革新，创新』

to introduce new things, ideas, or ways of doing sth
[V] We must constantly adapt and innovate to ensure success in a growing market.
我们必须不时地适应并创新，以确保在不断扩大的市场中取得成功。
We are alway trying our best to improve and innovate products. 我们一直在努力不断改进和创新我们的产品。

▶ **innovation** [ˌɪnə'veɪʃn] n.革新，创新

We must encourage innovation if the company is to remain competitive. 如果公司要具有竞争力，我们必须鼓励创新。

▶ **innovative** ['ɪnəveɪtɪv] adj. 革新的，创新的；有创新精神的

Japanese companies have been pumping out plenty of innovative products.
日本公司一直在生产大量富有创意的产品。
He was one of the most creative and innovative engineers of his generation.
他是他那代人当中最富创造性与革新精神的工程师之一。

词根209. numer=number；count，表示"数；计数"

1. numerous ['njuːmərəs] adj. 数不清的，很多的
『numer数字+ous有…的，多…的→很多的』

existing in large numbers
He has been late on numerous occasions.
他已经迟到过无数次了。
The advantages of this system are too numerous to mention.
这套系统的好处不胜枚举。

2. enumerate [ɪ'njuːməreɪt] vt. 列举，枚举
『e出来+numer数字+ate表动词→列举』

I enumerate the work that will have to be done.
我列举了必须得做的一些工作。
The names of items are too numerous to enumerate.
名目繁多，不胜枚举。

3. innumerable [ɪ'njuːmərəbl] adj. 多得数不清的
『in不+numer数字，数+able能够的→数字多，不能数清→多得数不清的』

He has invented innumerable excuses, told endless lies.
他编造了数不清的借口，撒了无数的谎。

4. numerate ['njuːmərət] adj. 识数的，有计算能力的
『numer数字+ate具有…性质的→具有识数和运算性质的→识数的，有计算能力的』

Your children should be literate and numerate.
你的孩子应该会识字算数。

▶ **numeracy** ['njuːmərəsi] n. 识数，计算能力

Six months later John had developed literacy and numeracy skills, plus confidence.
6个月后，约翰已经渐渐能够识字和算数，也有了自信。

形近词 **literate** ['lɪtərət] adj. 有读写能力的；有文化的 <P209>

5. supernumerary [ˌsuːpə'njuːmərəri] adj. 多余的；编外的 n. 多余的人员；编外的人员
『super过多+ numer数字+ary表性质或表人→多出的那些；多出的那些人』

It also raised the supernumerary city sanitation workers the basic wage. 它还提高了编外环卫工人的基本工资。

6. numerical [nuː'merɪkl] adj. 数字的，数值的
『numer数字+ical…的→数字的』

numerical data 数字数据
The results are expressed in descending numerical order.
结果按数字降序列出。

词根210. onym=name，表示"名称，名字"

1. anonymous [ə'nɒnɪməs] adj. 匿名的，无名的（没有特色的）
『an无+onym名称，名字+ous…的→没有名称的→匿名的』

The money was donated by a local businessman who wishes to remain anonymous.
这笔款子是当地一位不愿透露姓名的企业家捐赠的。
It's nice to stay in a home rather than in an anonymous holiday villa.
待在家里比待在单调乏味的度假别墅里要惬意得多。

▶ **anonymity** [ˌænə'nɪməti] n. 匿名

2. homonym ['hɒmənɪm] n. 同形（同音）异义词
『homo相同的+(o)nym名字→名字相同（但意义不同）的词→同音异义词』

"No" and "know" are homonyms. "no" 和 "know" 是同音异义词。
"Bow" (= bend at the waist) and "bow" (=weapon) are also homonyms. "bow"（鞠躬）和 "bow"（弓）是同形异义词。

3. synonym ['sɪnənɪm] n. 同义词
『syn共同+onym名称，名字→（不同的单词所指的内容）相同→同义词』

The words "small" and "little" are synonyms.
单词 "small" 和 "little" 是同义词。

▶**synonymous** [sɪˈnɒnɪməs] adj. 同义的；等同的

In politics, power and popularity are not synonymous.
在政治上，权力和声望并非相依而存。
Wealth is not necessarily synonymous with happiness.
财富未必等同于幸福。

4. antonym ['æntənɪm] n. 反义词
『ant相反+onym名称，名字→名称相对→反义词』

Give out the synonym and antonym of this word.
给出这个词的同义词和反义词。

5. pseudonym ['su:dənɪm] n. 假名；笔名
『pseud假，伪+onym名字→假名；笔名』

Both plays were published under the pseudonym of Philip Dayre. 两个剧本都是以菲利普·戴尔的笔名出版的。

6. acronym ['ækrənɪm] n. 首字母缩略词
『acro顶点，高点+(o)nym名字→顶点（也就是每个单词的第一个字母）构成的名字→首字母缩略词』

Could you tell me what this acronym stands for?
你能告诉我这个缩写代表什么吗？

词根211. opt=choose，表示"选择"

1. opt [ɒpt] v. 选择

to choose to take or not to take a particular course of action
After graduating she opted for a career in music.
毕业后她选择了从事音乐工作。
Many workers opted to leave their jobs rather than take a pay cut. 许多工人宁可下岗也不接受减薪。

▶**option** ['ɒpʃn] n. 选择；选修课；选项

❶ [C, U] ~ (of doing sth) | ~ (to do sth) 可选择的事物；选择，选择权
As I see it, we have two options.
据我看，我们有两种选择。
Going to college was not an option for me.
上大学不是我可以选择的道路。

❷ [C] 选修课
The course offers options in design and computing.
这一学程开了设计和计算机技术的选修科目。

❸ [C] (computing 计) 选项
Choose the "Cut" option from the Edit menu.
从编辑选单上选"剪切"项。

▶**optional** ['ɒpʃənl] adj. 可选择的；选修的

Certain courses are compulsory, and others are optional.
某些课程是必修的，其他是选修的。
Our attendance at graduation is optional.
我们的毕业典礼可以自愿参加。

词义辨析 <P367第31> 挑选 choose, elect, select, pick, opt

2. adopt [əˈdɒpt] vt. 采纳；收养

『ad相当于to+opt选择→选择到→采纳；收养』

❶ ~ sb (as sth) 收养
Having no children of their own they decided to adopt an orphan. 他们因没有亲生儿女，所以决定领养一个孤儿。
He is their adopted son. 他是他们的养子。

❷ 采纳；采取；采用
adopt a name/a custom/an idea/a style of dress
取名；随俗；采纳一意见；采用一服装式样
The council is expected to adopt the new policy at its next meeting. 委员会有望在下次会议上通过这项新政策。

▶**adoption** [əˈdɒpʃn] n. 收养；采纳

▶**adoptive** [əˈdɒptɪv] adj. 收养的
his adoptive parents 他的养父母

词根212. op, opt=eye, sight，表示"眼睛；视力"

1. myopia [maɪˈəʊpiə] n. 近视
『my近+op视力+ia某种病→近视』

Maybe you have got myopia, or you are just too tired. 也许你已经近视了，或者你只是太累了。

▶**myopic** [maɪˈɒpɪk] adj. 近视的；目光短浅的

The Government still has a myopic attitude to spending.
政府在开支问题上仍然目光短浅。

2. hyperopia [ˌhaɪpəˈrəʊpiə] n. 远视
『hyper超过+op视力+ia某种病→超过正常视力→远视』

▶**hyperopic** [ˌhaɪpəˈrɒpɪk] adj. 远视的

3. optic ['ɒptɪk] adj. 眼的；视觉的
『opt眼睛；视力+ic…的→眼的；视觉的』

[usually before noun]（technical 术语）眼的；视觉的
connected with the eye or the sense of sight
The reason for this is that the optic nerve is a part of the brain.
这其中的原因在于视神经是大脑的一部分。

▶**optical** ['ɒptɪkl] adj. 视力的；视觉的；光的；光学的

Optical devices, processes, and effects involve or relate to vision, light, or images.
These optical fibres may be used for new sorts of telephony.
这些光纤可能被用于新型电话通信系统。
Telescopes and microscopes are optical instruments.
望远镜和显微镜是光学仪器。

4. optics ['ɒptɪks] n. 光学
『opt视力+ics…学→光学』

词根213. optim=best，表示"最好，最佳"

1. optimism ['ɒptɪmɪzəm] n. 乐观；乐观主义
『optim最好，最佳+ism主义→乐观主义』

[U] ~ (about/for sth)
There are very real grounds for optimism.
的确有理由可以乐观。
The Indian Prime Minister has expressed optimism about India's future relations with the USA.
印度总理对未来的印美关系表示乐观。

▶**optimist** ['ɒptɪmɪst] n. 乐观主义者；乐天派

▶**optimistic** [ˌɒptɪˈmɪstɪk] adj. 乐观的，乐观主义的
~ (about sth) | ~ (that…)
She's not very optimistic about the outcome of the talks.
她对会谈的结果不太乐观。

2. optimum [ˈɒptɪməm] adj. 最佳的，最适宜的
『optim最佳，最好+um表场所→最佳的』

The optimum or optimal level or state of something is the best level or state that it could achieve.

The hot sun enables the grapes to reach optimum ripeness.
炙热的阳光使葡萄能够达到最佳成熟状态。

Do you know the optimum temperature for the growth of plants? 你知道庄稼生长的最佳温度吗？

3. optimal [ˈɒptɪməl] adj. 最优的；最佳的（=optimum）
『optim最佳，最好+al…的→最佳的』

This gives optimal performance at the expense of structure and flexibility. 这以结构及灵活性为代价换来了最佳性能。

4. optimize [ˈɒptɪmaɪz] vt. 使…最优化；充分利用
『optim最佳，最好+ize使→使…最佳』

Doctors are concentrating on understanding the disease better, and on optimizing the treatment.
医生正致力于更好地了解这种疾病，并使治疗方法尽可能完善。

We need to optimize our use of the existing technology.
我们需要优化现有技术的使用。

1. oral [ˈɔːrəl] adj. 口头的；口腔的，用口的 n. 口试
『or嘴+al表形容词→口头的；口腔的，用口的』

a test of both oral and written French 法语口试和笔试
good oral hygiene 良好的口腔卫生
He failed the oral. 他口试不及格。

2. oration [ɔːˈreɪʃn] n. 演说，致辞（尤指作为仪式的一部分）
『or说，讲+ate表动词（去e）+ion表名词→演说，致辞』

He asked for no funeral oration.他不要人在葬礼上宣读悼词。

3. orator [ˈɒrətə(r)] n. 讲演者；善于演说的人
『or说，讲+ate表动词（去e）+or表人→演讲者』

He was so eloquent that he cut down the finest orator.
他能言善辩，胜过最好的演说家。

4. oratory [ˈɒrətri] n. 演讲术；（私人）祈祷室
『orator演讲者+y表名词→演讲术』

5. oracle [ˈɒrəkl] n. 先知，预言者；神谕
『or嘴；说+acle表物→（神）说出的东西→神谕』

❶（古希腊的）传神谕者，神使

In ancient Greece, an oracle was a priest or priestess who made statements about future events or about the truth.

This advice must have come from the oracle. It is difficult to understand. 这个忠告一定是来自先知。（因为）它难以理解。

❷（古希腊常有隐含意义的）神谕，神示

a prophecy, often obscure or allegorical, revealed through the medium of a priest or priestess at the shrine of a god

And if the oracle was right, the grateful sent even more gifts.
如果神谕对了，感恩的人会送更多的礼物。

❸ [usually sing.] 权威，智囊；神预言

a person or book that gives valuable advice or information; a statement believed to be infallible and authoritative

My sister's the oracle on investment matters.

我姐姐是个万无一失的投资顾问。

▶ **oracular** [əˈrækjələ(r)] adj. 神谕般的；天书般的

But with all my oracular powers, I do not yet know the truth about her. 尽管我有神谕般的能力，我还是不知道她的真相。

1. ordinal [ˈɔːdɪnl] n. 序数词 adj. 序数的
『ordin顺序+al…的→按顺序的→序数词；序数的』

小贴士 **cardinal** [ˈkɑːdɪnl] n. 基数词

2. coordinate [kəʊˈɔːdɪneɪt , kəʊˈɔːdɪnət] vt. 使协调 n.坐标
『co共同+ordin顺序；秩序+ate表动词或名词→使（不同的事物）有共同的顺序或秩序→协调』
（n. [kəʊˈɔːdɪnət]; v. [kəʊˈɔːdɪneɪt]）

❶ [VN] 使协调

They appointed a new manager to coordinate the work of the team. 为协调这个队的工作，他们任用了一位新经理。

We need to develop a coordinated approach to the problem.
我们需要拿出解决这一问题的协调一致的办法。

❷ [C] 坐标

Can you give me your coordinates?
您能告诉我您的坐标吗？

3. subordinate [səˈbɔːdɪnət , səˈbɔːdɪneɪt] adj. 从属的；次要的 n. 下属 vt. 使处于次要位置
『sub下面+ordin顺序+ate表形容词或动词→顺序在下面的→从属的；下属』

❶ adj. 从属的，下级的；次要的

In many societies women are subordinate to men.
在许多社会中，妇女都从属于男人。

It was an art in which words were subordinate to images.
这是一种形象胜于语言的艺术。

❷ [C] 下级，下属

Haig tended not to seek guidance from subordinates.
黑格不愿向下属请教。

❸ [VN] 使处于次要位置

He was both willing and able to subordinate all else to this aim.
为了这个目标他愿意并能够把其他一切都放在次要位置。

4. insubordinate [ˌɪnsəˈbɔːdɪnət] adj. 不顺从的
『in不+subordinate从属的→不（把自己放在）从属位置的→不顺从的』

The old school headteacher remembered him as an insubordinate child. 老校长记得他是一个不听话的孩子。

5. inordinate [ɪnˈɔːdɪnət] adj. 过度的，过分的
『in无+ordin秩序+ate有…性质的→无秩序的→（因为过多、过度而）显得无秩序的→过度的，过分的』

far more than is usual or expected

They spend an inordinate amount of time talking.
他们花在说上的时间太多了。

6. ordinance [ˈɔːdɪnəns] n. 条理；法令；法规
『ordin秩序+ance表名词→使有秩序的东西→法规，条理』

Marriages in Hong Kong are governed by the Marriage Ordinance and the Marriage Reform Ordinance.
香港的婚姻，受《婚姻条例》和《婚姻改革条例》所规限。

词根216. ori, orig=rise, begin，表示"升起；开始"

1. origin [ˈɒrɪdʒɪn] n. 起源；出身 （also origins）
『orig开始+in…素→（生命）开始→起源』

If it's possible, track the rumour back to its origin.
如果可能，应追查谣言的源头。
Thomas has not forgotten his humble origins.
托马斯没有忘记自己卑微的出身。

2. originate [əˈrɪdʒɪneɪt] vi. 起源，发源
『origin起源+ate表动词→起源于』

The disease is thought to have originated in the tropics.
这种疾病据说起源于热带地区。

3. original [əˈrɪdʒənl] adj. 起初的；原创的；原作的 n. 原件；原著
『origin起源+al表名词或形容词→原件；起源的』

❶ adj. [only before noun] 原来的；起初的；最早的
The room still has many of its original features.
房间还保留着当初的许多特点。
I think you should go back to your original plan.
我认为你应该回头执行你原来的计划。

❷ adj. 首创的；独创的
That's not a very original suggestion.
那个建议没什么新意。

❸ adj. [usually before noun] 原作的；真迹的
The original manuscript has been lost. 原稿已经遗失。

❹ [C] 原件；正本；原稿；原作
This painting is a copy; the original is in Madrid.
这幅画是复制品，原画在马德里。

❺ in the original 用原著的语言；未经翻译
I studied Italian so that I would be able to read Dante in the original. 我学习意大利语以便能读但丁的原著。

4. aboriginal [ˌæbəˈrɪdʒənl] adj. 土著的 n. （尤指澳大利亚的）土著居民
『ab+origin起源+al表人或形容词→起源的（人）→土著居民；土著的』

▶ **aborigine** [ˌæbəˈrɪdʒəni] n. 原住民

5. orient [ˈɔːrient] vt. 确定方向；使熟悉；以…为（发展、研究等）方向 n. 东方
『ori升起；开始+ ent具有…性质的→（太阳）升起的地方→东方→方向→确定方向』

Orient [ˈɔːriənt]) n. 东方

（BrE）**Orientate** [ˈɔːriənteit] n. 东方

❶ ~ yourself 确定方位
The mountaineers found it hard to orient themselves in the fog. 登山者发现在大雾中很难辨认方向。

❷ ~ yourself 熟悉；适应
When you orient yourself to a new situation or course of action, you learn about it and prepare to deal with it.
It took him some time to orient himself in his new school.
他经过了一段时间才熟悉新学校的环境。

❸ [usually passive] ~ sb/sth (to/towards sb/sth)以…为方向
Our students are oriented towards science subjects.
我们教的学生都是理科方向的。
We run a commercially oriented operation.
我们经营一个商业性的企业。

Neither of them is politically oriented.
他俩都无意涉足政治。

▶ **-oriented** (US) **-orientated**(UK) 以…为导向的

She wants to turn the company into a **profit**-orientated organization. 她想把公司变成一个以利润为导向的组织。
The whole group became more child-orientated.
整个小组更重视儿童问题了。

▶ **orientation** [ˌɔːriənˈteiʃn] n. 方向；培训

We employ people without regard to their political or sexual orientation. 我们雇用的人不考虑他们的政治或性取向。
They give their new employees a day or two of perfunctory orientation. 他们对新员工进行了一两天例行公事的培训。

6. oriental [ˌɔːriˈentl] adj. 东方（尤指中国和日本）的；东方人的
『orient东方+al…的→东方的』

Many Westerners are very interested in the oriental cultures and customs. 许多西方人对东方文化和习俗很感兴趣。

词根217. orn=embellish, equip，表示"装饰；配备"

1. ornament [ˈɔːnəmənt, ˈɔːnəment] n. 装饰品；首饰
『orn装饰+a+ment表名词→装饰品』

❶ [C]（家中或花园里的）装饰物，装饰品，点缀品
An ornament is an attractive object that you display in your home or in your garden.
a shelf containing a few photographs and ornaments
摆放着几张照片和些许装饰品的架子

❷ [C] 首饰，饰物
Pieces of jewellery are sometimes referred to as ornaments.
I guessed he was the chief because he wore more gold ornaments than the others.
我估计他是酋长，因为他戴的金饰最多。

❸ [U]（建筑或家具的）装饰物，装饰图案；装饰
The clock is simply for ornament; it doesn't work any more.
这只时钟纯属摆设，它再也不走了。
walls of glass overlaid with ornament 贴满装饰物的玻璃墙

❹ [C] (NAmE) ~ to sth 为…增添光彩的人（或事物）
The building is an ornament to the city.
这座建筑物为整个城市增色不少。

2. adorn [əˈdɔːn] vt. 装饰，装扮
『ad相当于to+orn装饰→起装饰作用→装饰，装扮』

[VN] [often passive] ~ sth/sb (with sth) (formal) 装饰；装扮
to make sth/sb look more attractive by decorating it or them with sth
The walls were adorned with paintings. 墙上装饰了绘画。
The children adorned themselves with flowers.
孩子们佩戴着鲜花。
Gold rings adorned his fingers. 他的手指上戴着几枚金戒指。

▶ **adornment** [əˈdɔːnmənt] n. 装饰物；装饰，装扮

It was a building without any adornment or decoration.
这是一幢没有任何装潢或粉饰的大楼。
Cosmetics are used for adornment. 化妆品是用来装扮的。

小贴士 ornament 和 adornment 的区别
They are very different.

Ornaments are items with memories, or just look pretty that are hung onto Christmas trees to decorate them. Look up Christmas ornaments online for examples.

Adornments are anything that is added to something else to make it look prettier. It doesn't necessarily have to be a Christmas tree. For example, an adornment can be a shell glued to a picture frame to make it look prettier.

3. ornate [ɔːˈneɪt] adj. 装饰华丽的

『orn装饰+ate表形容词→装饰过的→装饰华丽的』

covered with a lot of decoration, especially when this involves very small or complicated designs

An ornate building, piece of furniture, or object is decorated with complicated patterns or shapes.

That style of architecture is too ornate for my taste.
那种建筑风格对我来说太华丽了。

Then suddenly he saw a church in front of him, with a great ornate silver door.
突然，他看见前面有一座教堂，有一扇华丽的银色大门。

词根218. omni=all; knowing all，表示"全部；全知"

1. omnipresent [ˌɒmnɪˈpreznt] adj. 无所不在的

『omni全部+present出现的→全部地方都出现的→无所不在的』

The sound of sirens was an omnipresent background noise in New York. 在纽约，警报声是无处不在的背景噪声。

2. omnivore [ˈɒmnɪvɔː(r)] n. 杂食动物；杂食的人

『omni全部+vore吃→杂食（动物或人）』

▶**omnivorous** [ɒmˈnɪvərəs] adj. 杂食的；兴趣广泛的

Brown bears are omnivorous, eating anything that they can get their paws on. 棕熊是杂食性动物，抓到什么吃什么。
As a child, Coleridge developed omnivorous reading habits.
柯尔律治从孩提时期便养成了广泛阅读的习惯。

3. omnibus [ˈɒmnɪbəs] n. 公共汽车；（书）汇编；（广播、电视）综合节目

『omni全部+bus公共汽车→全部人都可以坐的公共汽车→公共汽车』

4. omnipotent [ɒmˈnɪpətənt] adj. 万能的，全能的〈P267〉

『omni全部+pot力量+ent表形容词→万能的』

5. omniscient [ɒmˈnɪsiənt] adj. 无所不知的〈P288〉

『omni全部+sci知道+ ent具有…性质的→全知道→ 无所不知的』

词根219. ortho=straight, right，表示"直，正"

1. orthodontist [ˌɔːθəˈdɒntɪst] n. 正牙医生

『ortho直，正+dont牙齿+ist从事某职业的人→正牙医生』

2. orthop(a)edic [ˌɔːθəˈpiːdɪk] adj. （关节和脊柱）矫形的，矫形外科的

『ortho直，正+ped儿童+ic…的→原指对畸形儿童的整形→整形外科的』

3. orthography [ɔːˈθɒɡrəfi] n. （文字的）拼写体系，拼写法

『ortho直，正+graph写+y表名词→正统的写法→拼写』

[U] the system of spelling in a language

In dictionaries, words are listed according to their orthography.
在词典中，单词是按照拼写顺序排列的。

The writing was, in reality, charming, and the orthography irreproachable. 那一手字的确很漂亮，拼写也无可挑剔。

▶**orthographic** [ˌɔːθəˈɡræfɪk] adj. 拼写的

This type of orthographic normalization is not supported.

这种拼字规范化不受支持。

4. orthodox [ˈɔːθədɒks] adj. 正统的；正统教义的；东正教的〈P153〉

『ortho直，正+dox观点→正统观点的→正统的』

词根220. pact=fastened，表示"紧的"

1. compact [kəmˈpækt, ˈkɒmpækt] v. 压实，压紧 adj. 小型的；（人）矮小结实的

『com一起+pact紧的→压到一起的→压实，压紧』

（v. [kəmˈpækt]; adj. [ˈkɒmpækt]）

❶ adj. 小型的；袖珍的
a compact camera 袖珍照相机
The kitchen was compact but well equipped.
这间厨房虽然空间小但设备齐全。

❷ adj. （人）矮小结实的，矮壮的
He was compact, probably no taller than me.
他矮小壮实，可能并不比我高。

❸ [VN] 把…压实（或压紧）
The Smith boy was compacting the trash.
史密斯家的男孩在把垃圾压紧。

小贴士 CD 光盘，激光唱片，光碟（全写为 compact disc）

2. impact [ˈɪmpækt, ɪmˈpækt] n. & v. 撞击；影响

『im进去+pact紧的→（撞击时物体）紧缩并进去→撞击；影响』

（n. [ˈɪmpækt]; v. [ɪmˈpækt]）

❶ [C, usually sing., U] 冲击，撞击；巨大影响
The bomb explodes on impact (= when it hits something).
炸弹受到撞击就爆炸。
They say they expect the meeting to have a marked impact on the future of the country.
他们称，他们预期会议对国家的未来会产生显著影响。

❷ [V, VN] ~ (on/upon/with) sth 冲击，撞击；影响
Her father's death impacted greatly on her childhood years.
父亲去世对她的童年造成巨大影响。

3. pact [pækt] n. 条约；协议；公约

『pact紧的→把双方向一处拉紧的→对双方都有约束的→条约，协议（再如"contract 合同"：con一起，tract拉）』

~ (between A and B) | ~ (with sb) (to do sth)
条约；协议；公约

A pact is a formal agreement between two or more people, organizations, or governments to do a particular thing or to help each other.

Last month he signed a new non-aggression pact with Germany. 上个月，他与德国签订了新的互不侵犯条约。

词根221. par(e)=equal，表示"平等，相等"

1. compare [kəmˈpeə(r)] vt. 比较；比作

『com一起+pare相等→放在一起，看是否相等→比较』

❶ compare A with B 把 A 与 B 作比较
The police compared the suspect's fingerprints with those found at the crime scene. 警察把犯罪嫌疑人的指纹和在犯罪现场发现的指纹作了比较。

Compared to/with our small flat, Bill's house seemed like a palace.

与我们的小公寓相比，比尔的房子像个宫殿。

❷ compare A to B 把 A 比作 B

The poet compares his lover's tongue to a razor blade.
该诗人把他爱人的舌头比作刀片。

People have compared me to Elizabeth Taylor.
人们把我比作伊丽莎白·泰勒。

▶ **comparable** [ˈkɒmpərəbl] adj. 类似的；可比较的

A comparable house in the south of the city would cost twice as much.

一栋类似的房子位于城市南部就是两倍的价钱。

▶ **comparative** [kəmˈpærətɪv] adj. 相对的；比较级的

The company is a comparative newcomer to the software market. 就软件市场来说，这家公司相对而言就是新手了。

▶ **comparison** [kəmˈpærɪsn] n. 比较

By comparison, expenditure on education increased last year.
相比之下，去年教育经费增加了。

2. parity [ˈpærəti] n. （尤指薪金或地位）平等

『par相等+ity表性质或状态→相等』

Prison officers are demanding pay parity with the police force. 狱警正要求与警察同工同酬。

3. disparity [dɪˈspærəti] n. （尤指因不公正对待引起的）不同，不等，差异

『dis不+par相等+ity表性质或状态→不等，差异』

The increasing income distribution disparity between residents is a striking problem in China's current economic development.
居民之间收入分配差距的不断扩大，是当前中国经济发展中的突出问题。

近义词 **discrepancy** [dɪsˈkrepənsi] n. 差异，不一致

a difference between two or more things that should be the same

There was considerable discrepancy between the two accounts of the battle. 两份关于那次战役的报道大有出入。

小贴士 disparity 和 discrepancy 的区别

Discrepancy is sometimes wrongly used where *disparity* is meant. A *discrepancy* exists between things which ought to be the same; it can be small but is usually significant. A *disparity* is a large difference between measurable things such as age, rank, or wages.

4. disparate [ˈdɪspərət] adj. 完全不同的；由不同人或事物组成的

『dis不+par相等+ate表形容词→不同的』

The nine republics are immensely disparate in size, culture and wealth.
这 9 个共和国在面积、文化和财富上迥然不同。

a disparate group of individuals 三教九流的一帮人

5. disparage [dɪˈspærɪdʒ] vt. 贬低；轻视

『dis不+par相等，平等+age表行为→不平等地（看待、对待）→贬低；轻视』

If you disparage someone or something, you speak about them in a way which shows that you do not have a good opinion of them.

People used to disparage a comet as "a disaster star".
过去人们贬称彗星为"扫帚星"。

词根222. parent=come in sight，表示"看见"

1. transparent [trænsˈpærənt] adj. 透明的；清澈的；易识破的；显而易见的

『trans从…到…+parent看见（如：apparent明显的）→从一边到另一边能看见的→透明的』

❶ （玻璃、塑料等）透明的

The insect's wings are almost transparent.
这昆虫的翅膀几乎是透明的。

Pure water is transparent. 纯净的水是透明的。

❷ 易懂的，一目了然的；（借口、谎言等）易识破的

If a situation, system, or activity is transparent, it is easily understood or recognised.

We need a transparent financial system.
我们需要一个透明的财务系统。

a transparent attempt to buy votes 收买选票的明显企图

a transparent effort by officials to blame foreigners
官员指摘外国人的明显企图

▶ **transparency** [trænsˈpærənsi] n. 透明；易懂

小贴士 注意读音 parent [ˈpeərənt] n. 父（母）亲

2. apparent [əˈpærənt] adj. 明显的，显而易见的

『ap相当于to+parent看见→可以看到的→明显的』

❶ [not usually before noun] ~ (from sth) (that…) | ~ (to sb) (that…) 显而易见的

It was apparent from her face that she was really upset.
从面容上一眼就可以看出她确实心绪烦乱。

Their devotion was apparent. 他们的忠诚显而易见。

It soon became apparent to everyone that he couldn't sing.
很快大家都明白他不会唱歌。

❷ [usually before noun]貌似的，表面上的

that seems to be real or true but may not be

My parents were concerned at my apparent lack of enthusiasm for school.
我看起来对上学不感兴趣，使父母担心。

3. apparition [ˌæpəˈrɪʃn] n. 幻影；鬼魂；幽灵

『ap相当于to+par看见+ition由行为产生的事物→看到的凭空出现的事物→幽灵』

An apparition is someone you see or think you see but who is not really there as a physical being.

The patient recognised one of the women as the apparition she had seen. 病人认出其中一个女人是她曾见过的幽灵。

词根223. part=divide；part，表示"分开；部分"

① part表示"分开"

1. part [pɑːt] v. 离开；分开

We parted at the airport. 我们在机场分手了。

The puppies were parted from their mother at birth.
小狗崽儿一出生就和它们的妈妈分开了。

The elevator doors parted and out stepped the President.
电梯门打开了，总统从里面步出。

2. partition [pɑːˈtɪʃn] n. 隔断 v. 区分；隔开

『part 分开+ition 表行为或结果→分成各个部分（的东西）→分隔；隔断』

❶ [C] 隔断；隔板墙

a glass partition 玻璃隔板；partition walls 隔断墙

❷ [VN] 隔开

Bedrooms have again been created by partitioning a single larger room.
通过将一间大屋用隔断断开的方法再隔出了几间卧室。

3. depart [dɪˈpɑːt] v. 离开（某地）；离职；去世

『de(=off, away)离开+part分开→分开并离去→离开』

❶ ~ (for...) (from...) 离开，出发

[V] Flights for Rome depart from Terminal 3.
飞往罗马的班机从 3 号航站楼出发。

[VN] (NAmE) The train departed Amritsar at 6:15 p.m.
火车在下午 6 点 15 分离开了阿姆利则。

❷ [V, VN] 离职

Lipton is planning to depart (from) the company he founded.
利普顿打算离开他创立的那家公司。

❸ [V, VN] 去世

He departed this world with a sense of having fulfilled his destiny.
他带着一种已完成使命的满足感离开了这个世界。

▶ **departure** [dɪˈpɑːtʃə(r)] n. 离开；辞职

『depart离开；离职+ure表行为→离开；辞职』

❶ [U, C] 启程，出发，动身

His sudden departure threw the office into chaos.
他的突然离去使这个部门陷入一片混乱。

Flights should be confirmed 48 hours before departure.
航班应在起飞前48小时予以确认。

❷ [U, C] 辞职，离职

He refused to discuss his departure from the government.
他拒绝讨论他离开政府的事。

❸ [C]（在特定时间）离开的飞机（或火车等）

There are several departures for New York every day.
每天都有几趟去纽约的航班。

the departure lounge/time/gate
候机（或车）室；离站时间；登机（或上车）口

4. department [dɪˈpɑːtmənt] n. 部；司；局；处；系

『de(=off, away)离开+part分开+ment表结果→（各个相互）分开的部门→部；系』

He moved to the sales department. 他转到了销售部。

5. apart [əˈpɑːt] adv.（指空间或时间）相隔，相距

『a处于某种状态+part分开→处于分开状态→相隔，相距』

The two houses stood 500 meters apart.
两座房子相距 500 米。

Their birthdays are only three days apart.
他们的生日仅隔三日。

We had to take the engine apart. 我们不得不卸下引擎。

6. apartment [əˈpɑːtmənt] n. 公寓

『apart相隔+ment表名词→（相邻的两个）相隔→公寓』

公寓: apartment (US); flat (UK)

7. compartment [kəmˈpɑːtmənt] n.（火车）分隔间；（供储物的）格，隔层

『com共同，一起+part分开+ment表结果→被分隔开，多个连在一起→分隔间；（储物）格，隔层』

All the seat in the compartment is reserved.
隔间里所有的座位都被预订了。

The car's attendant showed me to my compartment.
这节车厢的服务员领我到我的包厢。

I put a bottle of champagne in the freezer compartment.
我把一瓶香槟放进冷冻室。

The batteries are safely enclosed in a watertight compartment.
电池被安全地密封在一个防水的隔间里。

② part表示"部分"

1. partial [ˈpɑːʃl] adj. 部分的；偏爱的；偏心的

『part部分+ial部分的→部分的；特别喜欢某一部分或某一个的→部分的；偏爱的；偏心的』

❶ 部分的；不完全的

It was only a partial solution to the problem.
那只是部分地解决了这个问题。

❷ 偏爱的；偏袒的，偏心的

He's partial to sporty women with blue eyes.
他喜欢爱运动的蓝眼睛女子。

I might be accused of being partial. 可能会有人骂我偏心。

▶ **impartial** [ɪmˈpɑːʃl] adj. 公正的；中立的

『im不+partial偏袒的→不偏袒的→中立的』

As an impartial observer my analysis is supposed to be objective. 作为中立的观察员,我的分析应该是客观的。

A free, fair and impartial investigation is under way, he said.
他说，一个自由、公平、公正的调查正在进行中。

2. impart [ɪmˈpɑːt] vt. 传授；告知；把（某性质）赋予

『im进入+part部分→使一部分（知识、消息；性质）进入到…→传授，告知；把（某性质）赋予』

The ability to impart knowledge and command respect is the essential qualification for teachers.
具备传授知识并赢得尊敬的能力是对教师的基本要求。

The spice imparts an Eastern flavour to the dish.
这种调味品会给菜肴添加一种东方风味。

3. particle [ˈpɑːtɪkl] n. 颗粒；微粒；离子

『part部分+ icle小→很小的部分→颗粒；微粒』

4. partner [ˈpɑːtnə(r)] n. 配偶；伙伴

『partn(=part)部分+er表人→（同是某个活动、生意、家庭等）一部分的人→配偶；伙伴；搭档』

❶ [C] 配偶；性伴侣

Come to the New Year disco and bring your partner!
携伴来参加新年迪斯科舞会吧！

❷ [C] 合伙人

He's a partner in a Chicago law firm.
他是芝加哥一家律师事务所的合伙人。

❸ [C] 搭档

Talk about it with your partner. 和你的同伴一起讨论它。

5. participate [pɑːˈtɪsɪpeɪt] v. 参加，参与〈P123〉

『part部分+i+cip (=take)拿+ate表动词→take part→参加』

词根224. pass(e)=pass through，表示"通过"

1. passage [ˈpæsɪdʒ] n. 章节；通道；通过，经过

『pass通过+age表动作或行为→通道；通过』

❶ [C] 章节；段落；乐段

a short section from a book, piece of music, etc.

Read the following passage and answer the questions below.
阅读下面这段文章并回答后面的问题。

❷ [C] 通道；过道

Harry stepped into the passage and closed the door behind him. 哈里走进过道，随手关上了门。

blocked nasal passages 鼻腔堵塞

❸ [U] 通过；经过

Germany had not requested Franco's consent for the passage of troops through Spain.

德国没有征求佛朗哥的同意便让军队通过了西班牙。
It's been 200 years since the passage of the *Bill of Rights*.
《权利法案》通过已经 200 年了。
an asset that increases in value with the passage of time
价值与日俱增的资产

2. compass [ˈkʌmpəs] n. 指南针，罗盘；圆规
『com一起+pass通过→（去遥远陌生的地方），和（指南针）一起（才能）通过→指南针→（指南针和罗盘一般是圆形的）→圆规』

注意：a pair of compasses 一副圆规

3. surpass [səˈpɑːs] vt. 超过，胜过
『sur在上面+ pass通过→经过某人并且到了他的上面→超过』

to do or be better than sb/sth
[VN] He hopes one day to surpass the world record.
他希望有一天能刷新世界纪录。
Its success has surpassed all expectations.
它所取得的成功远远超出了预期。

4. trespass [ˈtrespəs] v. 擅自进入
『tres(= trans)从…到…+pass通过→从外面到里面→侵入』

~ (on sth) 擅自进入，非法侵入（他人的土地或建筑物）
They were trespassing on private property.
他们擅自闯入私人房屋。

5. passport [ˈpɑːspɔːt] n. 护照
『pass通过+ port港口→通过港口的凭证→护照』

6. impasse [ˈɪmpæs] n. 绝境；僵局；死胡同
『im不+passe走；通过→不能通过→死路』

a difficult situation in which no progress can be made because the people involved cannot agree what to do
Negotiations have reached an impasse. 谈判已陷入僵局。

7. bypass [ˈbaɪpɑːs] n. 旁路，旁道 vt. 绕过，避开
『by旁边+pass通过→从旁边通过→旁路；绕过』

A new bypass around the city is being built.
一条新的绕城环线正在建设当中。
A new road now bypasses the town. 一条新路绕城镇而过。

8. pastime [ˈpɑːstaɪm] n. 消遣，休闲活动
『pas(=pass)通过+time时间→让时间通过→打发时间→消遣，休闲活动』

[C] something that you enjoy doing when you are not working
His favourite pastime is golf. 他最喜欢的消遣是打高尔夫。
词义辨析 <P362第9>
娱乐 entertainment, amusement, recreation, pastime

词根225. pass=feeling，表示"感情"

1. passion [ˈpæʃn] n. 激情，酷爱；热恋
『pass(=feeling)感情+ion表名词→强烈感情→激情』

❶ [C, U] 强烈情感；激情
a very strong feeling of love, hatred, anger, enthusiasm, etc.
He spoke with great passion. 他发表了热情洋溢的讲话。
He's a man of violent passions. 他是个性情暴烈的人。

❷ [C] ~ (for sth) 酷爱；热衷的爱好（或活动等）
a very strong feeling of liking sth; a hobby, an activity, etc. that you like very much

The English have a passion for gardens. 英国人酷爱花园。
Music is a passion with him. 他对音乐情有独钟。

❸ [U] ~ (for sb) 强烈的爱（尤指两性间的）
His passion for her made him blind to everything else.
他钟情于她，达到了不顾一切的地步。

▶**passionate** [ˈpæʃənət] adj. 热诚的；感情强烈的
『passion强烈感情+ate具有…性质的→感情强烈的』

❶ 热诚的；狂热的
having or showing strong feelings of enthusiasm for sth or belief in sth
He is very passionate about the project.
他对那个项目非常热心。
He brought to the job not just considerable experience but passionate enthusiasm.
他不仅给这一工作带来了不少经验，而且倾注了极大的热情。

❷ 强烈感情的（热恋的；怒不可遏的）
having or showing strong feelings of sexual love or of anger, etc.
He was passionately in love with her. 他热恋着她。
I am passionately opposed to the death penalty.
我坚决反对死刑。

2. compassion [kəmˈpæʃn] n. 怜悯，同情；侧隐之心
『com共同+passion强烈情感→有共同的感情→同情』

a strong feeling of sympathy for people who are suffering and a desire to help them
He could not help having compassion for the poor creature.
他情不自禁地怜悯起那个可怜的人来。
Elderly people need time and compassion from their physicians.
老年人需要医生多花时间，还需要他们的关爱。

▶**compassionate** [kəmˈpæʃənət] adj. 有同情心的
『compassion同情→ate表形容词→同情的』

These charities depend on the compassionate feelings and generosity of the general public.
这些慈善团体依赖于公众的怜悯之心和慷慨解囊。

3. passive [ˈpæsɪv] adj. 消极的；被动的 〈P86〉
『pass(=feeling)感情+ive表形容词→感情用事→被动的』

词根226. pathy=feeling, 表示"感情"，形容词形式为 pathetic

1. sympathy [ˈsɪmpəθi] n. 同情；赞同
『sym相同+pathy感情→感情相同→同情；赞同』

❶ [U, C, usually pl.] 同情
I have a lot of sympathy for her; she had to bring up the children on her own.
我很同情她；她必须自己抚养孩子。
Our heartfelt sympathy goes out to the victims of the war.
我们对战争的受害者表示由衷的同情。

❷ [U, C, usually pl.] 赞同，支持
the act of showing support for or approval of an idea, a cause, an organization, etc.
I have some sympathy with this point of view.
我比较同意这个观点。
Several hundred workers struck in sympathy with their colleagues. 几百名工人罢工以声援他们的同事。

❸ [U] 意气相投；志同道合
There was no personal sympathy between them.

他们个人之间全无相投之处。

▶ **sympathetic** [ˌsɪmpəˈθetɪk] adj. 同情的；赞同的
『sympathy同情（去y）+etic有…性质的→同情的』

❶ ~ (to/towards sb) 同情的；有同情心的；表示同情的
I did not feel at all sympathetic towards Kate.
我对凯特一点也不同情。

❷ ~ (to/towards sb/sth) 赞同的；支持的
Russian newspapers are largely sympathetic to the president.
俄罗斯报章大都支持总统。

She met people in London who were sympathetic to the Indian freedom struggle.
她在伦敦结识了一些支持印度独立运动的人。

▶ **sympathise** [ˈsɪmpəθaɪz] vi. 同情；支持
『sympathy同情（去y）+ise表动词→同情』

❶ ~ (with sb/sth) 同情
I find it very hard to sympathise with him.
我觉得很难去同情他。

❷ ~ with sb/sth 赞同；支持
He has never really sympathised with the aims of animal rights activists.
他从来没有真正赞同过动物权利保护者的目标。

2. **antipathy** [ænˈtɪpəθi] n. 厌恶；反感
『anti反对+pathy感情→反对的感情→反感』

[U, C, usually sing.] ~ (between A and B) | ~ (to/toward(s) sb/sth)　(formal) 厌恶；反感
He showed a strong antipathy to this place.
他对这个地方表示了强烈的反感。

▶ **antipathetic** [ˌæntɪpəˈθetɪk] adj. 厌恶的，反感的

3. **apathy** [ˈæpəθi] n. 冷漠，淡漠，无兴趣
『a无+pathy感情→冷漠』

[U] 冷漠；淡漠
the feeling of not being interested in or enthusiastic about anything
There is widespread apathy among the electorate.
选民普遍态度冷淡。

▶ **apathetic** [ˌæpəˈθetɪk] adj. 冷漠的；无兴趣的

Even the most apathetic students are beginning to sit up and listen. 连最不感兴趣的学生都开始坐直了听讲。

4. **empathy** [ˈempəθi] n. 同感，共鸣，同情
『em使…进入…状态+pathy情感→使（自己）进入（别人的）情感状态→同感，共情』

[U] ~ (with sb/sth) | ~ (for sb/sth) 同感，共鸣，同情
Empathy is the ability to share another person's feelings and emotions as if they were your own.
Having begun my life in a children's home I have great empathy with the little ones.
由于从小生活在儿童福利院，我对小家伙们产生了强烈的共鸣。

▶ **empathetic** [ˌempəˈθetɪk] adj. 移情的；有同感的

There's another reason nice people take on too much work: They are overly empathetic.
善良的人承担太多的工作还有一个原因：他们过于善解人意了。

▶ **empathize** [ˈempəθaɪz] v. 有同感，产生共鸣

I clearly empathize with the people who live in those neighborhoods. 我非常同情生活在那些地方的人们。

5. **compatible** [kəmˈpætəbl] adj. 相容的；合得来的
『com共同，一起+pat(=pathy)感情+ible能…的→感情相同的→合得来的；相容的』

❶ 兼容的，可共存的
The new system will be compatible with existing equipment.
新的系统将与现有的设备相互兼容。
Are measures to protect the environment compatible with economic growth?
保护环境的措施与经济的增长协调吗？

❷ （因志趣等相投而）关系好的，和睦相处的
Mildred and I are very compatible. She's interested in the things that interest me.
我和米尔德丽德很合得来。我感兴趣的东西她也感兴趣。

▶ **incompatible** [ˌɪnkəmˈpætəbl] adj. 不相容的；合不来的
The hours of the job are incompatible with family life.
这份工作的上班时间和家庭生活有冲突。

词根227. path=suffering；illness，表示"痛苦；病"

1. **pathology** [pəˈθɒlədʒi] n. 病理学
『path病+ology…学→研究病的（发展过程）学科→病理学』

2. **psychopath** [ˈsaɪkəpæθ] n. 精神病患者
『psycho精神+path病→患有精神病→精神病人』

a person suffering from a serious mental illness that causes them to behave in a violent way towards other people

▶ **psycho** [ˈsaɪkəʊ] n. 精神病患者（psychopath的非正式形式）

3. **neuropathy** [ˌnjʊəˈrɒpəθi] n. 神经系统疾病
『neuro神经+path病+y表名词→神经系统疾病』

4. **pathogen** [ˈpæθədʒən] n. 病原体
『path病+o+gen产生→使产生病的（生物）→病原体』

This deprives the pathogen of its hosts and stops the infection in its tracks.
这就剥夺了病原体的宿主，并阻断了感染的进程。

5. **pathetic** [pəˈθetɪk] adj. 可怜的；令人怜悯的；悲惨的
『path痛苦+etic表形容词→痛苦的→可怜的』

If you describe someone or something as pathetic, you mean that they make you feel impatient or angry, often because they are weak or not very good.
The starving children were a pathetic sight.
饥饿的儿童看起来是一幅凄惨的景象。
You're a pathetic loser, right?
你是个悲哀的失败者，对吗？

词根228. patern, patr(i)=father，表示"父亲"，引申为"祖国"（参看词根"matern, matr(i)"）

1. **paternal** [pəˈtɜːnl] adj. 父亲的；父亲般的；父系的
『patern父亲+al…的→父亲的；父亲般的；父系的』

He gave me a piece of paternal advice.
他给了我慈父般的忠告。
He smiled paternally at them. 他像慈父一样对他们微笑着。
my paternal grandmother 我的祖母

▶ **paternalism** [pəˈtɜːnəlɪzəm] n. 家长式管理

『paternal父亲般的+ism…主义；行为→家长式管理』

Paternalism means taking all the decisions for the people you govern, employ, or are responsible for, so that they cannot or do not have to make their own decisions.

The government should be guided by the criteria of efficiency and not state paternalism.
政府应该以效率为准则，而不是国家家长制。

2. paternity [pə'tɜ:nəti] n. 父亲的身份（或地位）
『patern父亲+ity具备某种性质，状况→父亲的身份；父系』

He refused to admit paternity of the child.
他拒不承认是那孩子的父亲。

Paternity leave is unlikely to be for longer than two weeks.
父亲亲子（陪产）假不太可能超过两周。

But she agreed to a paternity test. 但她同意做亲子鉴定。

3. patriarch ['peɪtriɑ:k] n. （男性）家长；族长，酋长
『patri父亲+arch统治者→家长；族长，酋长』

Joseph Kennedy, the clan's patriarch, communicated with Bobby in a series of notes.
宗族族长约瑟夫·肯尼迪通过一系列便笺和博比交流。

▶ **patriarchy** ['peɪtriɑ:ki] n. 父权制；父系社会

▶ **patriarchal** [,peɪtri'ɑ:kl] adj. 族长制的；父权制的

4. patrimony ['pætrɪməni] n. 祖传财产；（国家的）文物，遗产
『patri父亲+mony表行为或结果→父亲留下的物品→遗产』

5. patriot ['peɪtriət] n. 爱国者
『patri父亲，引申为"祖国"+ot表人→爱国者』

As a boy he was a fanatical patriot.
年少时，他是个狂热的爱国者。

▶ **patriotic** [,pætri'ɒtɪk] adj. 爱国的

patriotic songs 爱国歌曲
Woosnam is fiercely patriotic. 伍斯纳姆非常爱国。

▶ **patriotism** ['pætriətɪzəm] n. 爱国主义；爱国精神
『patriot爱国者+ism表主义→爱国主义』

He was a country boy who had joined the army out of a sense of patriotism and adventure.
他是个乡下小伙儿，参军是出于爱国之心和冒险精神。

6. compatriot [kəm'pætriət] n. 同胞，同国人
『com共同+patri祖国+ot表人→同一个祖国→同胞』

My dear compatriot, it is time that we did something for our country. 亲爱的同胞们，为国效劳的时候到了。

7. expatriate [,eks'pætriət] n. 侨民 adj. 移居国外的 vt. 驱逐
『ex出+patri国家+ate表动词、名词、形容词→侨民；居住在国外的；驱逐』

Expatriate candidates are also welcomed.
我们也欢迎海外的应聘者。

I am a senior expatriate manager in a privately held Asian company. 我是一家亚洲私人企业的高级外籍经理。

The new leaders expatriated the ruling family.
新的领导人把原统治家族驱逐到了国外。

8. repatriate [,ri:'pætrieɪt] vt. 遣送回国
『re回+patri祖国+ate使…→使回到祖国→遣返回国』

❶ [VN] 遣送回国

It was not the policy of the government to repatriate genuine refugees. 遣返真正的难民回国并非政府的政策。

❷ [VN] 把（海外利润）调回国内

Foreign investors are to be allowed to repatriate profits over one billion rupees.
外国投资者将被允许调回超过10亿卢比的利润。

▶ **repatriation** [,ri:pætri'eɪʃən] n. 遣返回国

9. patron ['peɪtrən] n. 赞助人；代言人；主顾
『patr父亲+on人→像父亲一样（关心对待）→赞助人』

❶ 赞助人，资助人

A patron is a person who supports and gives money to artists, writers, or musicians.

Catherine the Great was a patron of the arts and sciences.
凯瑟琳大帝资助发展艺术和科学研究。

❷ 代言人，名义赞助人

The patron of a charity, group, or campaign is an important person who allows his or her name to be used for publicity.

Fiona and Alastair have become patrons of the National Missing Person's Helpline.
菲奥娜和阿拉斯泰尔已经成为国家失踪人口服务热线的代言人。

❸ （酒吧、旅馆等的）主顾，顾客

He spent the night at the Savoy: like so many of its patrons, he could not resist the exclusively English cooking.
他在萨沃伊过了夜：和许多顾客一样，他无法抗拒精美的英式菜肴。

▶ **patronage** ['pætrənɪdʒ] n. 赞助；惠顾
『patron赞助人+age表名词→赞助』

The event was under the patronage of the Prince of Wales.
这项活动受到威尔士亲王的赞助。

Though it was not yet noon, there was considerable patronage.
虽然时间未到中午，店中已有许多顾客惠顾。

▶ **patronize** ['pætrənaɪz] vt. 资助；惠顾；屈尊俯就

❶ [VN] 资助；惠顾

She patronizes many contemporary British artists.
她赞助许多英国当代艺术家。

The club is patronized by students and locals alike.
学生和当地居民都经常去那个俱乐部。

❷ [VN] 对…摆出屈尊俯就的样子

If someone patronizes you, they speak or behave towards you in a way which seems friendly, but which shows that they think they are superior to you in some way.

Don't you patronize me!
别在我面前摆出一副屈尊俯就的样子！

▶ **patronizing** ['pætrənaɪzɪŋ] adj. 自认为高人一等的

I was only trying to explain; I didn't want to sound patronizing.

我只是想解释一下而已，我绝无自诩清高之意。

词根229. ped(e)=foot，表示"脚"

1. pedestrian [pə'destriən] n. 行人
『ped脚+estrian…的人→用脚走路的人→行人』

Pedestrian accidents are down by 5%.
行人受伤事故下降了5%。

2. expedition [,ekspə'dɪʃn] n. 远征；探险

『ex出+ped脚+ition表行为→走出去（到远方）→远征』

❶ [C] 远征；探险
an organized journey with a particular purpose, especially to find out about a place that is not well known
They have gone on an expedition to the Antarctica.
他们到南极洲探险去了。

❷ [C] 远征队；探险队
Three members of the Everest expedition were killed.
三名珠穆朗玛峰探险队员遇难。

▶ expeditionary [ˌekspəˈdɪʃənri] adj. 远征的
词义辨析 <P374第65>
旅行 trip, journey, excursion, expedition, tour, travel, voyage

3. pedal [ˈpedl] n. （自行车等的）脚镫子；（钢琴的）踏板 v. 骑自行车；踩踏板
『ped脚+al…的→用脚蹬的→脚蹬，踏板；踩踏板』

❶ [C]（自行车等的）脚镫子；（钢琴的）踏板
I couldn't reach the pedals on her bike.
我骑她的车够不到脚镫子。

❷ 骑自行车；踩踏板
[V] He jumped on his bike and pedalled off.
他跳上自行车就骑走了。
[VN] She had been pedalling her exercise bike all morning.
她整个上午都在蹬健身车。

4. pedlar [ˈpedlə(r)] n. （旧时的）流动小贩
『ped脚+lar表人→用脚走来走去（卖东西的人）→流动小贩』

5. pedestal [ˈpedɪstl] n.（柱子或雕塑等的）底座，基座
『ped脚+e+stal安装→安装放东西的基座』

I replaced the vase carefully on its pedestal.
我小心地把花瓶放回基座上。

to put/place sb on a pedestal （盲目）崇拜某人
to admire sb so much that you do not see their faults
Since childhood, I put my own parents on a pedestal. I felt they could do no wrong.
从童年起，我就把自己的父母当作偶像崇拜，觉得他们做的一切都是对的。

6. centipede [ˈsentɪpiːd] n. 蜈蚣
『centi百+pede脚→百脚之虫→蜈蚣』

7. impede [ɪmˈpiːd] v. 阻碍；阻止
『im不+pede脚→使脚不能向前走→阻碍；阻止』

[VN] [often passive] (formal) 阻碍；阻止
to delay or stop the progress of sth
Work on the building was impeded by severe weather.
楼房的施工因天气恶劣而停了下来。

▶ impediment [ɪmˈpedɪmənt] n. 障碍；口吃

❶ [C] ~ (to sth) 妨碍；阻碍；障碍物
Something that is an impediment to a person or thing makes their movement, development, or progress difficult.
He was satisfied there was no legal impediment to the marriage.
这一婚姻没有任何司法上的障碍，他对此很满意。

❷ [C] 口吃；结巴；语言障碍

8. expedient [ɪkˈspiːdiənt] n. 权宜之计，应急办法 adj. 权宜之计的

『ex出+ped脚+ient…的→先跨出去（解燃眉之急的）→权宜之计』

❶ [C] 权宜之计；应急办法
an action that is useful or necessary for a particular purpose, but not always fair or right
The disease was controlled by the simple expedient of not allowing anyone to leave the city.
通过禁止任何人出城的简单应急办法使疾病得到了控制。

❷ adj. 有利的；方便的；权宜之计的
useful or necessary for a particular purpose, but not always fair or right
The government has clearly decided that a cut in interest rates would be politically expedient.
政府显然认定降息是政治上的权宜之计。

9. expedite [ˈekspədaɪt] vt. 加快，加速
『ex出+ped脚+ite使…→把脚迈出去→加快』

[VN] (formal) 加快，加速
to make a process happen more quickly
We have developed rapid order processing to expedite deliveries to customers.
我们已创造了快速处理订单的方法以便迅速将货物送达顾客。

词根230. pel=drive, push，表示"驱动，推"，名词形式为-pulse，形容词形式为-pulsive

1. compel [kəmˈpel] v. 强迫；迫使
『com加强+pel驱动，推→加强推→强迫』

If a situation, a rule, or a person compels you to do something, they force you to do it.
[VN to inf] The law can compel fathers to make regular payments for their children.
这项法律可强制父亲定期支付子女的费用。
I feel compelled to write and tell you how much I enjoyed your book. 我觉得必须写信告诉你我是多么欣赏你的书。
[VN] Last year ill health compelled his retirement.
去年他因身体不好被迫退休了。
He spoke with an authority that compelled the attention of the whole crowd.
他用权威的口气讲话，引起了整个人群的注意。

▶ compulsory [kəmˈpʌlsəri] adj. （因法律或规则而）必须做的，强制的，强迫的

It is compulsory for all motorcyclists to wear helmets.
所有骑摩托车的人都必须戴头盔，这是强制性的。
English is a compulsory subject at this level.
英语在这一级别是必修科目。
反义词 voluntary [ˈvɒləntri] adj. 自愿的

▶ compulsion [kəmˈpʌlʃn] n. 强迫；冲动

❶ [U, C] 强迫；强制
You are under no compulsion to pay immediately.
没有人强迫你立刻付款。
There are no compulsions on students to attend classes.
没有强求学生上课。

❷ [C] 强烈欲望，冲动
a strong desire to do sth, especially sth that is wrong, silly or dangerous
He felt a great compulsion to tell her everything.
他感到一阵强烈的冲动，想要把一切都告诉她。

▶ **compulsive** [kəmˈpʌlsɪv] adj. 难以抑制的；引人入胜的

❶ 难以抑制的

He was a compulsive gambler and often heavily in debt.
他嗜赌成癖，常常债台高筑。

❷ （书或电视节目等）吸引人的，有趣的，引人入胜的

These chilling heroines make Hart's books compulsive reading.
这些令人毛骨悚然的女主人公使哈特的书读起来让人爱不释手。

2. expel [ɪkˈspel] vt. 开除；驱逐；排出
『ex出去+ pel驱动，推→推出去→开除』

[VN] ~ sb/sth (from sth) 开除；驱逐

She was expelled from school at 15.
她15岁时被学校开除了。

Foreign journalists are being expelled.
外国记者被驱逐出境。

to expel air from the lungs 用力呼出肺里的气

▶ **expulsion** [ɪkˈspʌlʃn] n. 开除；驱逐；排出

The headteacher threatened the three girls with expulsion.
校长威胁要开除这三名女学生。

These events led to the expulsion of senior diplomats from the country. 这些事件导致一些高级外交官被驱逐出境。

3. impel [ɪmˈpel] vt. 促使；驱使；迫使
『im里面+pel驱动，推→从里面驱动→驱使』

~ sb (to sth) 促使；驱策；迫使

if an idea or feeling impels you to do sth, you feel as if you are forced to do it

She was in such a mess I felt impelled to offer her services.
她一团糟，我觉得有必要帮助她。

▶ **impulse** [ˈɪmpʌls] n. 冲动

[C, usually sing., U] ~ (to do sth) 冲动；心血来潮

a sudden strong wish or need to do sth, without stopping to think about the results

He had a sudden impulse to stand up and sing.
他突然心血来潮，想站起来歌唱。

I resisted the impulse to laugh.
我强忍着没有笑出来。

▶ **impulsive** [ɪmˈpʌlsɪv] adj. 易冲动的

You're so impulsive! 你太冲动了！

He has an impulsive nature. 他生性冲动。

4. propel [prəˈpel] vt. 推动；驱使
『pro向前+pel推动→向前推→推进』

❶ [VN] 推动；驱动

to move, drive or push sth forward or in a particular direction

He succeeded in propelling the ball across the line.
他成功地把球带过线。

❷ [VN] 驱使

If something propels you into a particular activity, it causes you to do it.

He is propelled by both guilt and the need to avenge his father. 他受到内疚感和为父报仇之心的双重驱使。

▶ **propulsion** [prəˈpʌlʃn] n. 推动力；驱使

▶ **propeller** [prəˈpelə(r)] n. 螺旋桨（飞机或轮船的推进器）

▶ **propellant** [prəˈpelənt] n. 推进剂

5. repel [rɪˈpel] vt. 击退；使厌恶 v. （磁极、电荷之间）排斥
『re返回+pel驱动，推→推回去→击退』

❶ [VN] (formal) 击退；驱逐

They have fifty thousand troops along the border ready to repel any attack.
他们有5万人的部队驻扎在边境，随时准备击退任何进攻。

❷ [V, VN] （磁极、电荷之间）排斥

Like poles repel, unlike poles attract. 同极相斥，异极相吸。

❸ [VN] 使厌恶，使讨厌

I was repelled by the smell. 这种气味让我恶心。

▶ **repulsion** [rɪˈpʌlʃn] n. 厌恶感；排斥力

▶ **repulsive** [rɪˈpʌlsɪv] adj. 令人厌恶的；引起排斥的

What a repulsive man! 这个人真讨厌！

6. dispel [dɪˈspel] v. 驱散；消除
『dis离开+pel驱动；推→推开→驱散』

[VN] 驱散；消除（尤指感觉或信仰）

to make sth, especially a feeling or belief, go away or disappear

His speech dispelled any fears about his health.
他的发言消除了人们对他身体健康的担心。

7. pulse [pʌls] n. 脉搏；脉冲 v. 搏动
『pulse驱动，推→向前推动时产生脉冲、搏动→脉冲；搏动』

❶ [usually sing.] 脉搏；脉率

The doctor took/felt my pulse.
医生给我量了脉搏/把了脉。

Fear sent her pulse racing (= made it beat very quickly) .
她吓得脉搏急速跳动。

❷ [C] （音乐的）拍子，节奏；脉冲

An electrical pulse in a wire travels close to the speed of light.
电线里的电脉冲以接近光速传输。

❸ [usually sing.] 意向；心态

He claims to have his finger on the pulse of the industry.
他声称该对行业了如指掌。

One may feel the social, economic, and political pulse of the state.
任何人都可以感觉到这个国家的社会、经济和政治的脉搏。

❹ [V, VN] （有节奏地）跳动，搏动；测脉搏，把脉

His temples pulsed a little, threatening a headache.
他的太阳穴跳了一会儿，像是头痛要发作了。

词根231. pen, pun=penalty, 表示"处罚"

1. penal [ˈpiːnl] adj. 惩罚的；刑罚的
『pen处罚+al…的→惩罚的；刑罚的』

[usually before noun] 惩罚的；刑罚的

connected with or used for punishment, especially by law

penal reforms 刑罚改革

the penal system 刑罚制度

▶ **penalize** [ˈpiːnəlaɪz] vt. 惩罚；处罚

You will be penalized for poor spelling.
你拼写不好将会受到处罚。

Some of the players may, on occasion, break the rules and be penalized. 这些选手中有些偶尔可能会违规而受罚。

▶ **penalty** [ˈpenəlti] n. 惩罚；处罚

『penal刑罚的+ty表名词→惩罚』

❶ [C] 刑罚；处罚

A penalty is a punishment that someone is given for doing something which is against a law or rule.

One of those arrested could face the death penalty.
被捕的那些人中有一人可能被判死刑。

❷ [C] 罚球；点球

2. penance ['penəns] n. 赎罪

『pen处罚+ance表名词→（因做错事而）惩罚自己的行为』

[C, U] 补赎；悔罪；忏悔

If you do penance for something wrong that you have done, you do something that you find unpleasant to show that you are sorry.

Yeah. I'm doing penance for forgetting her birthday last week.
是啊。我是在为上星期忘了她生日而赎罪。

He believed the death of his child was penance for his sins.
他认为孩子的死是对他罪过的惩罚。

3. penitent ['penɪtənt] adj. 忏悔的，后悔的，愧疚的

『penit(=pen)惩罚+ent具有…性质的→因受惩罚而后悔→后悔的』

feeling or showing that you are sorry for having done sth wrong

It was hard to be angry with him when he looked so penitent.
当他看起来如此懊悔时，很难对他发火。

▶**penitence** ['penɪtəns] n. 后悔，愧疚

The thief expressed penitence for all his past actions.
那盗贼对他犯过的一切罪恶表示忏悔。

▶**penitentiary** [ˌpenɪ'tenʃəri] n. 监狱

『penitent后悔的，忏悔的+i+ary表地点→让（犯罪的人）忏悔的地方→监狱』

4. repent [rɪ'pent] v. 后悔

『re又+pent(=pen)惩罚→（因为做错的事情）反复惩罚自己→后悔』

to feel and show that you are sorry for sth bad or wrong that you have done

[V] God welcomes the sinner who repents.
上帝欢迎悔过的罪人。

She had repented of what she had done.
她对自己所做的事深感懊悔。

[VN] He came to repent his hasty decision.
他开始后悔自己的草率决定。

▶**repentant** [rɪ'pentənt] adj. 后悔的，表示悔改的

He was feeling guilty and depressed, repentant and scared.
他感到内疚、沮丧、后悔和害怕。

▶**repentance** [rɪ'pentəns] n. 后悔，悔过

He shows no sign of repentance. 他没有丝毫悔悟的表示。

5. punish ['pʌnɪʃ] vt. 处罚，惩罚

『pun处罚+ish使…→处罚，惩罚』

▶**punishment** ['pʌnɪʃmənt] n. 处罚，惩罚

6. punitive ['pjuːnətɪv] adj. 惩罚性的

『pun处罚+i+tive有…性质的→惩罚性的』

There are calls for more punitive measures against people who drink and drive.
有人呼吁对酒后驾车的人采取更具处罚性的措施。

7. impunity [ɪm'pjuːnəti] n. 不受惩处

『im不+pun惩罚+ity具备某种性质，状况→不受惩罚』

This year's International Women's Day is devoted to ending impunity for violence against women and girls.
今年的国际妇女节致力于终止对妇女和女孩施暴而不受惩罚的现象。

One cannot commit crimes with impunity.
一个人不能犯了罪不受惩罚。

词根232. pend=hang，表示"悬挂"

1. depend [dɪ'pend] vi. 取决于

『de向下+pend悬挂→（某事是否成功）悬挂在…上→取决于』

2. append [ə'pend] vt.（在文章后面）附加，增补

『ap相当于to+pend悬挂→（使）悬挂到…下面→附加』

It was a relief that his real name hadn't been appended to the manuscript.
令人庆幸的是，手稿未落上他的真实姓名。

3. appendix [ə'pendɪks] n. 阑尾；（书、文件的）附录

『ap相当于to+pend悬挂+ix→挂在（书、文件的）后面的；挂在（大肠的）下面的→附录；阑尾』

He had to have his appendix out (= removed).
他不得不切除了阑尾。

4. appendage [ə'pendɪdʒ] n. 附加物，附属物

『append附加，增补+age行为或行为的结果→附加物』

The house of Commons must not be only an appendage of the executive. 下议院不能只是行政机构的附属。

5. pendant ['pendənt] n. （项链上的）垂饰，饰坠

『pend悬挂+ant表物→悬挂在（项链）下面的→垂饰』

6. pending ['pendɪŋ] adj. 待决的；待定的；待处理的

『pend悬挂+ing表正在进行→（事情）正悬在那里→待决的；待处理的』

Nine cases are still pending. 尚有九宗案件待决。

7. impending [ɪm'pendɪŋ] adj. 即将发生的

『im(=in)进来+pending悬着的→悬在那里就要进来的→即将发生的』

[only before noun] that is going to happen very soon

On the morning of the expedition I awoke with a feeling of impending disaster.
出发远征的那个早上，我醒来就有一种灾难即将来临的感觉。

his impending retirement 他即将到来的退休

8. suspend [sə'spend] vt. 悬挂；暂停，暂缓

『sus下+pend悬挂→挂在下面→悬吊，引申为停止』

❶ [VN] 悬挂

A lamp was suspended from the ceiling.
一盏吊灯悬在天花板上。

❷ [VN] 暂停；暂缓；暂时停职

Production has been suspended while safety checks are carried out. 在进行安全检查期间生产暂停。

The introduction of the new system has been suspended until next year. 新制度推迟到明年再行实施。

The police officer was suspended while the complaint was investigated. 投诉调查期间，这位警员被暂停职务。

▶**suspension** [sə'spenʃn] n. 悬挂；暂停

These events have led to the suspension of talks.
这些事件导致谈判延期。

suspension bridge 悬索桥；吊桥

▶**suspense** [sə'spens] n.（对即将发生的事等的）担心；焦虑；兴奋；悬念

Don't keep us in suspense. Tell us what happened!
别让我们心老悬着了。告诉我们出了什么事！
I couldn't bear the suspense a moment longer.
这样提心吊胆，我一刻也受不了了。

9. perpendicular [ˌpɜːpən'dɪkjələ(r)] adj. 垂直的，成直角的 n. 垂直线（或位置、方向）
『per(=thoroughly)完全地+pend悬挂+icular有…性质的→完全悬挂在那里的→垂直的』

❶ adj. 垂直的，成直角的
Are the lines perpendicular to each other?
这些直线相互垂直吗？
The staircase was almost perpendicular (= very steep).
楼梯几乎成垂直的了。

❷ the perpendicular 垂直线（或位置、方向）
The wall is a little out of the perpendicular.
墙壁有点倾斜。

10. pendulum ['pendjələm] n. 钟摆
『pend悬挂+ulum表物→悬摆着的东西→钟摆』

The pendulum stopped swinging. 钟摆停止了摆动。

词根233. pend, pense= weigh; pay，表示"称重量；花费，支付"

1. expend [ɪk'spend] vt. 花费
『ex出+pend花费，支付→花费出去』

较正式用词，通常指为某一专门目的而花费大量金钱、时间或精力。
She expended all her efforts on the care of home and children.
她把所有精力都花在料理家务和照顾孩子上。

▶**expense** [ɪk'spens] n. 费用；代价

❶ [U] 费用
the money that you spend on sth
The garden was transformed at great expense.
花园改建花了一大笔费用。
He's arranged everything, no expense spared.
他不惜代价把一切安排得井井有条。
The results are well worth the expense.
有这些结果花的钱很值。

❷ [C, usually sing.] 花钱的东西
Running a car is a big expense. 养一辆车开销很大。

❸ expenses [pl.] 开支；花费；费用
money that you spend when you are doing your job, that your employer will pay back to you
living/household/medical/legal, etc. expenses
生活费用；家庭开支；医疗、律师等费用
The payments he gets barely cover his expenses.
他几乎入不敷出。

❹ at sb's expense/ at the expense of 由某人付钱；以…为代价
We were taken out for a meal at the company's expense.
公司出钱请我们外出就餐。
He built up the business at the expense of his health.

他以自己的健康为代价逐步建立起这家公司。
I think he's having fun at our expense.
我想他在拿我们寻开心。

▶**expensive** [ɪk'spensɪv] adj. 昂贵的
『expense费用（去e）+ive具有…性质的→昂贵的』

▶**expenditure** [ɪk'spendɪtʃə(r)] n. 花费；消耗
『expend花费+iture行为，行为的结果→消耗；支出』

Policies of tax reduction must lead to reduced public expenditure. 减税政策必然导致公共支出的削减。
This study represents a major expenditure of time and effort.
这项研究意味着要耗费大量的时间和精力。

2. dispense [dɪ'spens] vt. 分发；提供；配（药）
『dis分散+pense称重量→称出不同的重量分发出去→分发；配（药）』

❶ [VN] ~ sth (to sb) 分发；施与（提供服务）
to give out things, especially products, services or amounts of money, to people
The organization dispenses free health care to the poor.
这个机构为穷人提供免费医疗。
The charity has been given a large sum of money to dispense as it sees fit.
这个慈善机构获得一大笔钱，可自行适时分配。

❷ [VN]（机器自动）提供（货物等）
For two weeks, the cash machine was unable to dispense money. 该自动取款机已有两个星期不能提供现金。
The machine dispenses a range of drinks and snacks.
这台机器发售各种饮料和零食。

❸ [VN] 配（药）
Doctors confine themselves to prescribing rather than dispensing. 医生仅仅是开处方而不配药。

❹ dispense with 不需要，不再用
to stop using sb/sth because you no longer need them or it
I think we can dispense with the formalities.
我想我们就免去客套吧。
It's so warm today that I can dispense with an overcoat.
今天非常暖和，我不穿大衣也行。

▶**dispensary** [dɪ'spensəri] n. 药房，配药处
『dispense配药（去e）+ary场地→配药的地方→药房，配药处』

Yes, you do have the flu. Take this prescription to the dispensary for your medicine.
对，您的确得了流感，拿这张药方到药房配药。

3. dispensable [dɪ'spensəbl] adj. 非必要的，可有可无的
『dispense分发（去e）+able可以的→可以分发出去的→非必要的，可有可无的』

All those people in the middle are dispensable.
所有那些立场骑墙的人都可要可不要。
Don't buy anything that's dispensable.
可有可无的东西不要买。

▶**indispensable** [ˌɪndɪ'spensəbl] adj. 不可或缺的
『in不+dispensable可有可无的→不是可有可无的→不可或缺的』

Cars have become an indispensable part of our lives.
汽车已成了我们生活中必不可少的一部分。

词义辨析 <P363第12>
重要的，不可缺少的 essential, vital, crucial, critical,

indispensable

4. pension [ˈpenʃn] n. 养老金，退休金，抚恤金
『pense(=pay)支付，花费（去e）+ion表名词→支付（用来养老和生活的）钱→养老金』

an amount of money paid regularly by a government or company to sb who is considered to be too old or too ill/sick to work

His company has the best pension scheme in the industry.
他所在公司有本行业最好的养老金制度。

He did have pension money coming to him when the factory shut down. 工厂倒闭的时候，他的确拿到了养老金。

5. compensate [ˈkɒmpenseɪt] v. 赔偿，补偿
『com共同+pense(=pay)支付，花费（去e）+ate表动词→（因遭受损失）共同支付→赔偿，补偿』

❶ [V] ~ (for sth) 补偿；弥补
to provide sth good to balance or reduce the bad effects of damage, loss, etc.

Nothing can compensate for the loss of a loved one.
失去心爱的人是无法补偿的。

❷ [VN] ~ sb (for sth) 给（某人）赔偿（或赔款）
to pay sb money because they have suffered some damage, loss, injury, etc.

Her lawyers say she should be compensated for the suffering she had been caused.
她的律师说她应该为所遭受的痛苦得到赔偿。

▶ **compensatory** [ˌkɒmpenˈseɪtəri] adj. 赔偿性的

He received a compensatory payment of $ 20,000.
他获得了2万美元的赔偿金。

▶ **compensation** [ˌkɒmpenˈseɪʃn] n. 补偿；补偿金

6. propensity [prəˈpensəti] n. （行为方面的）倾向；习性
『pro向前+pense(=weigh)重量（去e）+ity表名词→重量偏向前→倾向』

~ (for sth) | ~ (for doing sth) | ~ (to do sth)
a tendency to a particular kind of behavior

Mr Bint has a propensity to put off decisions to the last minute. 宾特先生习惯拖到最后时刻才作决定。

7. pensive [ˈpensɪv] adj. 沉思的，忧伤的
『pense重量（去e）+ive表形容词→称重量→掂量→沉思的』

thinking deeply about sth, especially because you are sad or worried

You may remember the way each scene ended with someone looking pensive or significant.
你或许还记得，每一场的结尾要么是某人作沉思状，要么是某人故作深沉。

词根234. per(i), pir=try，表示"尝试"

1. experiment [ɪkˈsperɪmənt] n. & v. 实验
『ex出来+ peri尝试+ment表名词→（通过）尝试（让结果）出来→实验』

2. experience [ɪkˈspɪəriəns] n. 经验 v. 经历，体验
『ex出+peri尝试+ence表行为或结果→（通过）尝试出来的东西→经验』

3. empirical [ɪmˈpɪrɪkl] adj. 以实验或经验为依据的
『em(=in)在+pir尝试+ical…的→在尝试中（得出的）→以实验或经验为依据的』

Emirical evidence or study relies on practical experience rather than theories.

There is no empirical evidence to support his thesis.
他的论文缺乏实验证据的支持。

▶ **empiricism** [ɪmˈpɪrɪsɪzəm] n. 实证论；经验论
『empiric实证者+ism主义或学派→实证论；经验主义』

[U] the use of experiments or experience as the basis for your ideas; the belief in these methods

The opposite of empiricism is rationalism.
经验论的对立面是唯理论。

4. peril [ˈperəl] n. 严重危险；危害
『per尝试+il→尝试→危险』

❶ [U] 严重危险
serious danger

The country's economy is now in grave peril.
现在，这个国家的经济陷入了严重危机。

ignore it at your peril 无视该问题要自担风险

❷ [C, usually pl.] ~ (of sth) 危害；险情
the fact of sth being dangerous or harmful

a warning about the perils of drug abuse
对吸毒之害的警告

▶ **perilous** [ˈperələs] adj. 非常危险的
『peril严重危险+ous充满→非常危险的』

The road grew even steeper and more perilous.
道路变得越来越陡峭，越来越凶险。

小贴士 **perish** [ˈperɪʃ] v. 惨死；毁灭；老化
『per(=away)+ish使→使离开→惨死；毁灭；老化』

❶ [V] （人或动物）惨死，暴死
to die, especially in a sudden violent way

A family of four perished in the fire.
一家四口死于火灾之中。

❷ [V] 毁灭；丧失
If something perishes, it comes to an end or is destroyed for ever.

Buddhism had to adapt to the new world or perish.
佛教必须适应新时代，否则将会消亡。

❸ [V , VN] （物质或材料）老化，腐烂，脆裂
Even the best quality rubber will perish with age.
就是质量最佳的橡胶也会因老化而腐烂。

▶ **perishable** [ˈperɪʃəbl] adj. 易腐烂的，易变质的

Raw eggs are highly perishable and must be chilled before and after cooking. 生鸡蛋非常容易变质，烹制前后必须冷藏。

词根235. pet(e)=seek, strive，表示"寻求；力争"

1. compete [kəmˈpiːt] vi. 竞争；参加比赛
『com共同+pete寻求；力争→共同追求（一个目标）→竞争』

❶ ~ (with/against sb) (for sth) 竞争；对抗
[V] Several companies are competing for the contract.
为得到那项合同，几家公司正在竞争。

We can't compete with them on price.
我们在价格上无法与他们竞争。

❷ [V] ~ (in sth) (against sb)
He's hoping to compete in the London marathon.
他期盼着参加伦敦马拉松比赛。

► **competent** ['kɒmpɪtənt] adj. 足以胜任的，称职的
『compete竞争（去e）+ent具有…性质的→具有（能够）去竞争性质的→胜任的』

~ (to do sth) 足以胜任的；有能力的；称职的
Make sure the firm is competent to carry out the work.
要确保这家公司有能力完成这项工作。
He's very competent in his work.
他非常胜任自己的工作。

► **competence** ['kɒmpɪtəns] n. 能力；胜任

He stood out in terms of competence from all his fellows.
他在能力上远远胜过其他同事。

词义辨析 <P370第45> 有能力的；能够的 able, capable, competent

► **incompetent** [ɪnˈkɒmpɪtənt] adj. 无能力的；不胜任的
『in不+competent胜任的→不胜任的，无能力的』

Lazy and incompetent police officers are letting the public down. 懒惰兼无能的警官令公众失望。

► **competition** [ˌkɒmpəˈtɪʃn] n. 竞争；比赛

❶ [U] 竞争
We are in competition with four other companies for the contract. 我们在与其他四家公司竞争这项合同。

❷ [C] 比赛
The outcome of the competition is not known yet.
比赛结果还不清楚。

❸ the competition [sing. + sing./pl. v.] 竞争者；对手
We'll be able to assess the competition at the conference.
我们可以在会上对竞争对手进行估量。

► **competitor** [kəmˈpetɪtə(r)] n. 竞争者，对手；参赛者
『compete竞争（去e）+it+or表动作执行者→参加竞争的人→竞争者；比赛者』

The bank isn't performing as well as some of its competitors.
这家银行表现得不如几家竞争对手出色。
Over 200 competitors entered the race.
200多名选手参加了赛跑。

► **competitive** [kəmˈpetətɪv] adj. 竞争的；有竞争力的；好竞争的
『compete竞争（变e为it）+ive有…倾向（性质）的→有竞争力的』

❶ 竞争的
Graduates have to fight for jobs in a highly competitive market.
毕业生不得不在竞争激烈的市场上奋力争取找到工作。

❷ ~ (with sb/sth) 有竞争力的
as good as or better than others
We need to work harder to remain competitive with other companies.
我们必须更加努力工作以保持对其他公司具有竞争力。
a shop selling clothes at competitive prices
在服装价格上有竞争力的商店

❸ 好竞争的；好胜的
A competitive person is eager to be more successful than other people.
He has always been ambitious and fiercely competitive.
他一直都雄心勃勃，而且极其好胜。

2. **impetus** ['ɪmpɪtəs] n. 推动，促进，推动力
『im里面+pet追求+us表名词→使内部（有）追求（的动力）→推动』

Something that gives a process impetus or an impetus makes it happen or progress more quickly.
His articles provided the main impetus for change.
他的那些文章是促进变革的主要推动力。
The president's plan gave fresh impetus to industry.
总统的计划进一步推动了工业的发展。

► **impetuous** [ɪmˈpetʃuəs] adj. 鲁莽的，冲动的，轻率的
『impetus推动力（去s）+ous充满…的→（内心）充满推动力的→冲动的』

He was young and impetuous. 他年轻，易于冲动。

3. **petition** [pəˈtɪʃn] n. 请愿书；申诉书 v. 请愿，请求
『pet寻求+ition行为→寻求（某事得到妥善解决）→请愿』

❶ [C] ~ (against/for sth) 请愿书
We recently presented the government with a petition signed by 4,500 people.
最近我们向政府递交了有4500人签名的请愿书。

❷ [C] 申诉书；申请书
A petition is a formal request made to a court of law for some legal action to be taken.
His lawyers filed a petition for all charges to be dropped.
他的律师提请撤销所有指控。

❸ 请愿；请求
to make a formal request to sb in authority, especially by sending them a petition
[V] Local residents have successfully petitioned against the siting of a prison in their area.
当地居民反对在他们所在地区内兴建监狱的请愿成功了。
[VN to inf] Parents petitioned the school to review its admission policy. 家长请愿恳求学校修订招生政策。

4. **perpetual** [pəˈpetʃuəl] adj. 持续的；没完没了的
『per自始至终+pet寻求；追求+ual有…性质的→一追到底→永久的』

❶ 不间断的；持续的；长久的
A perpetual feeling, state, or quality is one that never ends or changes.
The rest of the world struggles on with its perpetual problems, poverty and debt.
世界上其他国家仍在苦苦与永恒的贫困和债务问题作斗争。

❷ 无尽无休的；没完没了的
A perpetual act, situation, or state is one that happens again and again and so seems never to end.
I thought her perpetual complaints were going to prove too much for me. 我想我再也受不了她无休无止的抱怨了。

► **perpetuate** [pəˈpetʃueɪt] vt. 使永久化，使持续
『per自始至终+pet追求+u+ate使→自始至终追求（某种不好的情况）→使持续』

[VN] 使（尤指不好的情况、制度、信仰等）继续，延长
We must not perpetuate the religious divisions of the past.
我们绝对不能让过去的宗教分裂继续下去。

5. **appetite** ['æpɪtaɪt] n. 食欲，胃口；强烈欲望
『ap加强+pet寻求+ite表物→一再追求→欲望』

❶ [U, C, usually sing.] 食欲；胃口
He suffered from headaches and loss of appetite.
他患有头痛和食欲不振。
The walk gave me a good appetite. 散步使我胃口大开。

❷ [C] ~ (for sth) 强烈欲望

a strong desire for sth

The public have an insatiable appetite for scandal.
公众对丑事总是喜闻乐道。

▶ **appetizer** [ˈæpɪtaɪzə(r)] n. （餐前的）开胃品

I would like a cucumber salad for an appetizer.
我要一份黄瓜沙拉作开胃菜。

▶ **appetizing** [ˈæpɪtaɪzɪŋ] adj. 开胃的，引起食欲的

The sounds and smells that came from the open kitchen door were appetizing.
从敞着门的厨房飘进来的声音和气味让人发馋。

词根236. petr, petro=stone，表示"石头，岩石"

1. petroleum [pəˈtrəʊliəm] n. 石油，原油
『petr石+ole油+um表名词→石油』

▶ **petrol** [ˈpetrəl] n. 汽油

词义辨析 <P380第96>
汽油，石油　petroleum, gas, gasoline

2. petrify [ˈpetrɪfaɪ] vt. 使吓呆；（使）石化
『petr石头+ify使…→（因为害怕）使（人变得像）石头一样（不能动、不能思考）→使吓呆』

❶ [VN] 使吓呆

If you are petrified, you are extremely frightened, perhaps so frightened that you cannot think or move.

Prison petrifies me and I don't want to go there.
监狱太可怕了，我不想去那里。

I found the climb absolutely petrifying.
我觉得这次爬山太吓人了。

I've always been petrified of being alone.
我总是害怕单独相处。

❷ [V , VN] （使）石化

A petrified plant or animal has died and has gradually turned into stone.
石化的植物或动物（指）已经死亡并逐渐变成了石头。

词根237. phan, fan=appearace，表示"出现"

1. fantasy [ˈfæntəsi] n. 幻想，想象；想象产物；幻想作品
『fan出现+tasy→（凭空）出现的→幻想，想象』

❶ [C] 憧憬，幻想

A fantasy is a pleasant situation or event that you think about and that you want to happen, especially one that is unlikely to happen.

I used to have fantasies about living in Paris with an artist.
我曾经幻想过和一个艺术家住在巴黎。

Everyone's fantasy is that one day they will win the National Lottery. 每个人的幻想是有一天他们会赢得全国彩票。

❷ [C] 想象产物；幻想作品

a product of your imagination

The film is more of an ironic fantasy than a horror story.
这部影片与其说是恐怖片，不如说是带有讽刺意味的奇幻片。

I saw you smiling at me. Was it real or just my fantasy?
我看到你对我微笑。那是真的还是只是我的幻想？

❸ [U] 幻想，想象

the act of imagining things; a person's imagination

Children use fantasy to explore worrying aspects of real life.
孩子们用幻想来探索现实生活中令人不安的各种事情。

Enough of fantasy, the workaday world awaited him.
天马行空地幻想一番之后，等待他的是平淡无奇的现实生活。

▶ **fantastic** [fænˈtæstɪk] adj. 极好的；很大的；怪诞的
『fantasy幻想（去y）+tic有…性质的→幻想般的→极好的；怪诞的』

❶ (informal) 极好的；了不起的

extremely good; excellent

You've got the job? Fantastic! 你得到那工作了？太好了！
The meal is fantastic. 这饭太好吃了。

❷ (informal) 很大的；大得难以置信的

very large; larger than you expected

The car costs a fantastic amount of money.
这轿车的价格贵得吓人。

❸ [usually before noun] 奇异的，奇妙的，荒诞的

You describe something as fantastic or fantastical when it seems strange and wonderful or unlikely.

fantastic dreams of forests and jungles
关于森林和热带丛林的怪梦

2. phantom [ˈfæntəm] n. 幽灵 adj. 幻觉的；虚假的
『phan出现+tom→（凭空）出现的→幽灵；幻觉的』

❶ [C] 幽灵

They vanished down the stairs like two phantoms.
他们像两个幽灵似的消失在了楼下。

❷ adj. 幻觉的，幻象的

You use phantom to describe something which you think you experience but which is not real.

She was always taking days off for what her colleagues considered phantom illnesses.
她总是请病假，同事们认为她所说的病纯属无中生有。

❸ adj. 虚假骗人的

Because few investors have the courage to dismiss a phantom bid as a phantom.
因为很少有投资者有勇气把虚标当作虚标。

❹ adj.（尤指罪犯）身份不明的

victims of alleged "phantom" withdrawals from high-street cash machines
据称被人从商业大街的取款机上冒取现金的受害者

3. diaphanous [daɪˈæfənəs] adj.（布料）轻柔细密的，半透明的
『dia穿过+phan出现+ous…的→透过（薄的布料）显示出来的→半透明的』

(of cloth) so light and fine that you can almost see through it
She wore a diaphanous garment. 她穿了件薄如轻纱的衣裳。

词根238. phobia=fear, dislike，表示"恐惧；厌恶"，其形容词形式为phobic

1. phobia [ˈfəʊbiə] n. 恐怖；（构成名词）对…的恐惧症
『phobe恐惧症患者（去e）+ia某种病→恐惧症』

A phobia is a very strong irrational fear or hatred of something.

The man had a phobia about flying. 这人害怕坐飞机。

I've been thinking about your public bathroom phobia.
我一直在想你的公共厕所恐惧症。

They keep asking why I'm so nervous, but I do suffer from social phobia and anxiety disorders.
他们一直问我为什么这么紧张，可我真的患有社交恐惧症和焦虑症。

▶**phobic** [ˈfəʊbɪk] adj. 恐惧症的 n. 恐惧症患者

In Victorian times people were phobic about getting on trains. They weren't used to it.
在维多利亚时代，人们对坐火车怕得要命。他们对此还不习惯。

Social phobics quake at the thought of meeting strangers.
患有社交恐惧症的人一想到要见陌生人就发抖。

▶**-phobe** [fəʊb] n. 恐惧或憎恶者

2. xenophobia [ˌzenəˈfəʊbiə] n. 仇外，惧外（对外国人的厌恶或惧怕）

『xenophobe仇外者，惧外者（去e）+ia表名词→仇外，惧外』

[U] (disapproving) a strong feeling of dislike or fear of people from other countries

a campaign against racism and xenophobia
反对种族主义和仇外情绪的运动

▶**xenophobic** [ˌzenəˈfəʊbɪk] adj. 仇外的，惧外的

Xenophobic nationalism is on the rise in some West European countries.
西欧一些国家的仇外民族主义有所抬头。

▶**xenophobe** [ˈzenəfəʊb] n. 仇外者；惧外者

He was attacked as a racist, xenophobe, and neo nazi.
他被攻击是种族主义、排外和新纳粹。

3. acrophobia [ˌækrəˈfəʊbiə] n. 恐高症

『acro顶点，高点+phob恐惧；厌恶+ia 某种病→恐高症』

Well, I have acrophobia. I have a chronic fear of flying.
嗯，我有恐高症。我有一种长期的对坐飞机的恐惧感。

4. claustrophobia [ˌklɔːstrəˈfəʊbiə] n. 幽闭恐怖（症）

『claustro(=close)封闭+ phobia恐惧；厌恶→幽闭恐怖（症）』

5. homophobia [ˌhəʊməˈfəʊbiə] n. 同性恋憎恶症

『homo相同；同性恋+phobia厌恶→同性恋憎恶症』

▶**homophobic** [ˌhəʊməˈfəʊbɪk] adj. 同性恋憎恶症的

▶**homophobe** [ˈhɒməfəʊb] n. 憎恶同性恋的人

词根239. phone=sound，表示"声音"

1. telephone [ˈtelɪfəʊn] n. 电话 v. 打电话
『tele远处+phone声音→从远处传来的声音→电话』

2. symphony [ˈsɪmfəni] n. 交响乐
『sym同时+phone声音（去e）+y构成名词→同时奏出的美妙的声音→交响乐』

3. microphone [ˈmaɪkrəfəʊn] n. 话筒；麦克风
『micro小+phone声音→使小声音变大的东西→麦克风』

4. phonetics [fəˈnetɪks] n. 语音学
『phone声音+tics…学→语音学』

5. cacophony [kəˈkɒfəni] n. 刺耳的嘈杂声
『caco不良，坏+ phone声音（去e）+y表名词→不好的声音→刺耳的嘈杂声』

Much of it takes place in pitch darkness to a cacophony of industrial noise. 大部分发生在漆黑的工业噪声中。

6. megaphone [ˈmegəfəʊn] n. 扩音器，喇叭筒 ＜P22＞
『mega巨大+phone声音→让声音变大→扩音器』

词根240. pheme, phet=speech，表示"讲话"

1. blaspheme [blæsˈfiːm] v. 亵渎（上帝或神明）
『blas毁坏+pheme讲话→毁坏神的话→亵渎』

to speak about God or the holy things of a particular religion in an offensive way; to swear using the names of God or holy things

▶**blasphemous** [ˈblæsfəməs] adj. 亵渎神明（或宗教）的

You can describe someone who shows disrespect for God or a religion as blasphemous. You can also describe what they are saying or doing as blasphemous.

She was accused of being blasphemous. 她被控亵渎神明。

▶**blasphemy** [ˈblæsfəmi] n. 亵渎上帝，亵渎神明
『blaspheme亵渎（去e）+y表行为→亵渎神明』

He was found guilty of blasphemy and sentenced to three years in jail. 他被判犯有亵渎神明罪，刑期3年。

2. euphemism [ˈjuːfəmɪzəm] n. 委婉语，委婉说法
『eu好的+pheme讲话（去e）+ism学术或行为→讲好（听）的话语→委婉语』

"Pass away" is a euphemism for "die".
"去世"是"死"的委婉语。

3. prophet [ˈprɒfɪt] n. （宗教）先知；预言者
『pro向前+phet说→说向前（将要发生的事）的人→先知；预言者』

The faithful revered him then as a prophet.
那时，信徒们尊他为先知。

▶**prophecy** [ˈprɒfəsi] n. 预言；预言能力

He's the innocent prophet who is martyred for his prophecy.
他是个无辜的先知，因他的预言而殉教。

▶**prophesy** [ˈprɒfəsaɪ] vt. 预言

He prophesied that within five years his opponent would either be dead or in prison.
他预言五年内他的对手要么死要么坐牢。

词根241. phil(o)=love，表示"爱"

1. philanthropy [fɪˈlænθrəpi] n. 慈善，捐助
『phil爱+anthrop人+y表行为→爱人类（所以捐钱来帮助穷人）→慈善』

[U] the practice of helping the poor and those in need, especially by giving money

We do both business and philanthropy.
我们做生意和慈善事业。

▶**philanthropist** [fɪˈlænθrəpɪst] n. 慈善家

▶**philanthropic** [ˌfɪlənˈθrɒpɪk] n. 慈善的

Some of the best services for the ageing are sponsored by philanthropic organizations.
一些一流老龄服务机构是由慈善组织资助的。

2. philosophy [fəˈlɒsəfi] n. 哲学；哲学思想 ＜P306＞
『philo爱+soph智慧，聪明+y表名词→爱智慧（研究哲学需要高智慧的人）→哲学』

词根242. pil(e)=heap，表示"堆积"

1. pile [paɪl] n. 堆；摞；垛；沓 vt. 堆放；摞起；叠放

He arranged the documents in neat piles.
他把文件一摞摞码得整整齐齐。

piles of dirty washing 成堆待洗的脏衣物

She piled the boxes one on top of the other.

她把盒子一个个地摞起来。

2. stockpile [ˈstɒkpaɪl] n. 囤聚的物资　vt. 大量储备
『stock库存+pile堆积→囤聚的物资』

Some state officials said that help from the federal stockpile didn't always match their needs.
一些州政府官员说，联邦储备的帮助并不总是符合他们的需要。

3. compile [kəmˈpaɪl] vt. 汇编；编制；编纂
『com一起+pile堆积→（把内容）堆放到一起→汇编』

When you compile something such as a report, book, or programme, you produce it by collecting and putting together many pieces of information.

We are trying to compile a list of suitable people for the job.
我们在努力编制一份适合做这项工作的人员名单。
The album was compiled from live recordings from last year's tour.
这张专辑由去年巡回演出的实况录音汇编而成。

词根243. pict=paint, picture，表示"描画"

1. picture [ˈpɪktʃə(r)] n. 图画　vt. 想象
『pict描画+ure表示行为或结果→图画』

❶ [C] 图画；相片

❷ the big picture (especially NAmE) 整个局面，大局
Right now forget the details and take a look at the big picture.
现在别管细节问题，先通观全局。

❸ [VN] 想象
I can still picture the house I grew up in.
我还能回忆起我童年时住的那座房子。

2. picturesque [ˌpɪktʃəˈresk] adj. 风景如画的；（语言）生动形象的
『picture图画+（e）sque像…的→像图画的→风景如画的』

He painted the picturesque fishing village in the bay.
他画了海湾里一个风景如画的渔村。

3. depict [dɪˈpɪkt] vt. 画；描写，描述
『de向下+ pict画，描绘→描述，描绘』

❶ [VN] 画
The artist had depicted her lying on a bed.
画家画了她躺在床上的画像。

❷ [VN] 描写，描述，刻画
The cartoons vividly depict the current celebration of western and Chinese festivals in China.
这些漫画生动描述了当前中国庆祝西方和中国节日的现状。

▶ **depiction** [dɪˈpɪkʃn] n. 描述；描画

词根244. plac=calm, soothe; please 表示"使平静，安慰；取悦，使满意"

1. placate [pləˈkeɪt] vt. 安抚；平息（怒气）
『plac使平静；安慰+ate使…→使…平静→安慰』

to make sb feel less angry about sth
The concessions did little to placate the students.
让步根本未能平息学生的愤怒。

2. implacable [ɪmˈplækəbl] adj. 不能安抚的，毫不妥协的
『im不+plac使平静，安慰+able能…的→难以安慰的』

If you say that someone is implacable, you mean that they have very strong feelings of hostility or disapproval which

nobody can change.
The move has won the implacable opposition of many economists. 此举遭到了许多经济学家的坚决反对。

3. placid [ˈplæsɪd] adj. （人或动物）温和的，平静的；（环境）平静的，宁静的，安静的
『plac使平静+id…的→安静的』

A placid person or animal is calm and does not easily become excited, angry, or upset. A placid place, area of water, or life is calm and peaceful.
Marcus remained placid in the face of her outburst.
马库斯面对她的发作保持平静。
the placid waters of Lake Erie 伊利湖宁静的湖水
Until the thunders of the siege began, he had never known anything but a happy, placid, quiet life.
在围城的炮声打响以前，他一直过的是愉快平稳而宁静的生活。

4. placebo [pləˈsiːbəʊ] n. （用于测试新药效力的）无效对照剂；（用以安慰想象自己得病的人的）安慰剂
『plac使平静，安慰+ebo→让人平静（的东西）→安慰剂』

5. complacent [kəmˈpleɪsnt] adj. 自满的，自鸣得意的
『com加强+plac取悦，使满意+ent具有…性质的→（自己）非常满意→自满的』

too satisfied with yourself or with a situation, so that you do not feel that any change is necessary
We cannot afford to be complacent about our health.
对于健康我们不能掉以轻心。

▶ **complacency** [kəmˈpleɪsnsi] n. 自满，自鸣得意

词根245. plast=form，表示"形成，塑成"

1. plastic [ˈplæstɪk] n. 塑料；信用卡　adj. 塑料的；可塑的；做作的
『plast形成，塑成+ic表名词或形容词→塑成的东西→塑料』

❶ [U] 塑料；信用卡
The pipes should be made of plastic.
这些管子应该是用塑料制成的。
a sheet of clear plastic 一片透明的塑料
Do they take plastic? 他们收信用卡吗？

❷ adj. 塑料（制）的；可塑的（easily formed into different shapes）；做作的，虚伪的
a plastic bag/cup/toy 塑料袋/杯/玩具
Clay is a plastic substance. 黏土是可塑物质。
plastic surgery 整形手术
TV game show hosts with their banal remarks and plastic smiles 语言陈腐、笑容刻板的电视竞赛节目主持人

2. plaster [ˈplɑːstə(r)] n. 灰泥；熟石膏；膏药　vt. 涂灰泥于；在…上大量粘贴（海报，画等）；（给自己）涂上，抹上
『plast形成，塑成+er表物→塑成的东西→灰泥，熟石膏→黏稠物质→涂抹；涂抹（后再粘贴）→涂灰泥；粘贴』

❶ [U] （石灰、沙、水混合后做成的）灰泥；熟石膏；膏药
an old house with crumbling plaster and a leaking roof
一栋灰泥剥落、屋顶漏水的老房子
a plaster bust of Julius Caesar 一尊朱利叶斯·凯撒的半身石膏像
(BrE) She broke her leg a month ago and it's still in plaster.
她一个月前腿骨骨折，至今仍打着石膏。（美国英语用 in a cast）

❷ [VN] 涂灰泥于；在…上大量粘贴（海报，画等）；（给自己）涂上，抹上

The ceiling he had just plastered fell in and knocked him off his ladder.
他刚抹上灰泥的天花板塌了，把他从梯子上砸了下来。

They plastered the city with posters condemning her election.
他们在城里到处张贴谴责她当选的海报。

She plastered herself from head to toe in high factor sun lotion. 她给自己从头到脚都抹上了强效防晒露。

词根246. plat(e)=flat，表示"平坦"

1. plate [pleɪt] n. 盘子；车牌号
『plate平坦→盘子（盘子底是平的）』

2. plateau [ˈplætəu] n. 高原
『plat平的，平坦的+eau表名词→平坦地→高原』

3. platform [ˈplætfɔːm] n. 站台；讲台；平台

❶ [C]（火车站的）站台；月台
The train was about to leave and I was not even on the platform. 火车就快开了，可我还没到站台。

❷ [C] 讲台，舞台
Nick finished what he was saying and jumped down from the platform. 尼克讲完后，从讲台上跳了下来。

❸ [C]（公开发表意见或表达愿望的）机会，论坛

❹ [C] 平台
They found a spot on a rocky platform where they could pitch their tents.
他们在一块岩石平台上找到了一个可以搭帐篷的地方。

4. platitude [ˈplætɪtjuːd] n. 陈词滥调；套话
『plat平+itude情况→用词平平，毫无新意→陈词滥调』

A platitude is a statement which is considered meaningless and boring because it has been made many times before in similar situations.

Why couldn't he say something original instead of spouting the same old platitudes?
他为什么就不能讲些有新意的话，而不是喋喋不休地老生常谈呢？

词根247. plaud, plaus(e)=clap hands，表示"鼓掌"

1. applaud [əˈplɔːd] v. 鼓掌；称赞，赞许
『ap加强+plaud鼓掌→鼓掌；称赞』

to show your approval of sb/sth by clapping your hands
to express praise for sb/sth because you approve of them or it
[V] He started to applaud and the others joined in.
他开始鼓掌，其他人也跟着鼓起掌来。
[VN] They rose to applaud the speaker.
他们起立向演讲者鼓掌。
[VN] She was applauded as she came on stage.
她上台时人们向她鼓掌。

▶ **applause** [əˈplɔːz] n. 鼓掌；喝彩
Give her a big round of applause! 为她热烈鼓掌！
The audience broke into rapturous applause.
听众中爆发出一片欢呼喝彩声。

2. plausible [ˈplɔːzəbl] adj.（解释或说法）似乎真实的，貌似合理的；（人）花言巧语的，貌似可信的
『plaus鼓掌+ible可以→可以（为之）鼓掌的→似乎真实的，貌似可信的』

❶（解释或说法）似乎真实的，貌似合理的
An explanation or statement that is plausible seems likely to be true or valid.
A more plausible explanation would seem to be that people are fed up with the Conservative government.
更加合理的解释似乎是，人们已经厌倦了保守党政府。

❷（人）貌似可信的，花言巧语的
If you say that someone is plausible, you mean that they seem to be telling the truth and to be sincere and honest.
He was so plausible that he conned everybody.
他那么会花言巧语，以至于骗过了所有的人。

词根248. plete, ple, pli, plen=fill; full，表示"充满；满的"
① plete, ple=fill; full，表示"充满；满的"

1. complete [kəmˈpliːt] adj. 完全的 vt. 完成
『com加强+plete充满；满的→完成；完全的』

2. complement [ˈkɒmplɪment, ˈkɒmplɪmənt] v. 补充；补足；使完美 n. 补充物；补足物
『com一起+ple充满；满的+ment表名词→放到一起使更完美→补足，使完美』
（n. [ˈkɒmplɪmənt]; v. [ˈkɒmplɪment]）

❶ [VN] 补充，补足，使完美
to add to sth in a way that improves it or makes it more attractive
The excellent menu is complemented by a good wine list.
佳肴佐以美酒，可称完美无缺。
The team needs players who complement each other.
球队需要能够相互取长补短的队员。

❷ [C] ~ (to sth) 补充物；补足物
The green wallpaper is the perfect complement to the old pine of the dresser.
绿色的墙纸完美地衬托出衣橱那年代久远的松木。

❸ [C] 补语（平时我们所说的"表语"）

▶ **complementary** [ˌkɒmplɪˈmentri] adj. 互补的
The school's approach must be complementary to that of the parents. 学校与家长的教育方法必须相辅相成。

3. deplete [dɪˈpliːt] vt.（大量）减少，消耗
『de表相反+plete充满；满的→减少，消耗』
to reduce sth by a large amount so that there is not enough left
Food supplies were severely depleted. 食物供应已严重不足。
They fired in long bursts, which depleted their ammunition.
他们长时间开火，耗尽了弹药。

▶ **depletion** [dɪˈpliːʃn] n. 减少；耗尽

4. replete [rɪˈpliːt] adj. 充满的，充足的；很饱的，饱食的
『re又，再+plete满的→又满了→充满的，充足的』
The harbor was replete with boats. 港口里满是船只。
History is replete with examples of populations out of control.
历史上人口失控的例子比比皆是。

5. implement [ˈɪmplɪment, ˈɪmplɪmənt] vt. 贯彻，实施 n. 工具
『im使…+ple满的；填满+ment表名词→使填满→实现』
（n. [ˈɪmplɪmənt]; v. [ˈɪmplɪment]）

❶ [VN] 贯彻，实施
to make sth that has been officially decided start to happen or be used

to implement changes/decisions/policies/reforms
实行变革；执行决议 / 政策；实施改革
The government promised to implement a new system to control financial loan institutions.
政府许诺实施新的制度来控制金融贷款机构。

❷ [C] 工具；器具；（常指）简单的户外用具
a tool or an instrument, often one that is quite simple and that is used outdoors
agricultural implements 农具

6. supplement [ˈsʌplɪmənt , ˈsʌplɪment] vt. 增补 n. 补品；增刊；附加费用
『sup下面+ple满的；填满+ment表名词→从下面增加以填满→补充』
（n. [ˈsʌmplɪmənt]; v. [ˈsʌmplɪment]）

❶ [C]（报章杂志）增刊，副刊；（书）附录，补编
the supplement to the *Oxford English Dictionary*
《牛津英语词典》补编
the Sunday colour supplements 星期日彩色增刊

❷ [C] 补品；附加费用；额外补助
a multiple vitamin and mineral supplement
含复合维生素和矿物质的补充剂
Safety deposit boxes are available at a supplement.
有贵重物品保管箱可供使用，费用另计。

❸ [VN] 增补；补充
people doing extra jobs outside their regular jobs to supplement their incomes
除了正常的工作外还要额外兼职以贴补收入的人

▶ **supplementary** [ˌsʌplɪˈmentri] adj. 增补性的
Supplementary oxygen is rarely needed in pressurized aircrafts. 密封的飞机内很少需要补充氧气。

② pli=fill; full，表示"充满；满的"

1. compliment [ˈkɒmplɪmənt,ˈkɒmplɪmənt] n. & v. 恭维，赞美，奉承
『com一起+pli充满；满的+ment表名词→（说）使对方充满（快乐的话）→恭维』
（n. [kɒmplɪmənt]; v. [ˈkɒmplɪment]）

You can do no harm by paying a woman compliments.
对女人说些恭维话没有坏处。
They complimented me on the way I looked each time they saw me. 每次见到我，他们都称赞我的外貌。
My compliments to the chef. 向厨师致意。

▶ **complimentary** [ˌkɒmplɪˈmentri] adj. 赞扬的；（座位、票或书）免费赠送的

We often get complimentary remarks regarding the cleanliness of our patio.
我们经常听人称赞我们的露台非常干净。
He had complimentary tickets to take his wife to see the movie. 他有几张赠票，可以带妻子去看电影。

小贴士 complement与compliment读音完全相同，但拼写不同，前一词字母"l"后面是字母"e"，后一词字母"l"后面是字母"i"。complement很容易使我们想起complete"完成（剩余部分）"一词，它的词义也与complete词义相近，是"补充；使完美"之意。而compliment中间的特征字母"i"形状像人的简笔画，与人相处之道是要学会恭维别人，因此compliment意为"恭维，赞美"。

2. accomplish [əˈkʌmplɪʃ] vt. 完成

『ac（=to）+com一起+pli充满，满的+(i)sh使→使…达到圆满→完成』
If you accomplish something, you succeed in doing it.
If we'd all work together, I think we could accomplish our goal. 只要大家齐心协力，我想我们就能实现目标。

③ plen=fill; full，表示"充满；满的"

1. plenty [ˈplenti] n. 充足，大量
『plen充满；满的+ty表名词→充足，大量』
There was still plenty of time to take Jill out for pizza.
还有充裕的时间带吉尔出去吃披萨。

▶ **plentiful** [ˈplentɪfl] adj. 充足的，大量的
『plenty充足（变y为i）+ful充满的→充足的，大量的』
Fish are plentiful in the lake. 这个湖里鱼很多。

2. plenary [ˈpliːnəri] adj.（会议）全体参加的 n. 全会
『plen充满；满的+ary表形容词→（开会时人）满的→（会议）全体参加的』
The programme was approved at a plenary session of the Central Committee last week.
这个方案在上周的中央委员会全体会议上获得了通过。

3. replenish [rɪˈplenɪʃ] vt. 补充；重新装满
『re又，再+plen充满；满的+ish使→重新装满』
to replenish food and water supplies 补充食物和水
Allow me to replenish your glass. 让我再给您斟满。

词根249. plex= fold，表示"重叠，折叠"

1. complex [ˈkɒmpleks] adj. 复杂的；（句子）复合的 n. 综合大楼，综合建筑群
『com一起+ plex重叠，折叠→（许多不同的组成部分）折叠到一起→复杂的』

❶ adj. 复杂的；难懂的；费解的
made of many different things or parts that are connected; difficult to understand
The students work in groups on complex problems.
学生们分组研究复杂的问题。

❷ adj.（句子）复合的

❸ [C] 综合建筑群；综合大楼
A complex is a group of buildings designed for a particular purpose, or one large building divided into several smaller areas.
The complex opens to the public tomorrow.
这幢综合大楼将于明天对公众开放。
They form a graceful architectural complex of ancient temples. 它们构成了优美的古庙建筑群。

▶ **complexity** [kəmˈpleksəti] n. 复杂性
I was astonished by the size and complexity of the problem.
这个问题的复杂性和涉及面之广使我感到惊讶。

词义辨析 <P375第72>
复杂的 complicated, complex, intricate, sophisticated

2. duplex [ˈdjuːpleks] n. 连栋式的两栋住宅；复式住宅
『du二+plex重叠，折叠→（两层或两栋）重叠在一起→复式住宅』
a building divided into two separate homes；a flat/apartment with rooms on two floors

小贴士 **compound** 指的是有院子的房子 <P265>

3. perplex [pə'pleks] vt. 使迷惑；使复杂化

『per (thoroughly)彻底地+plex折叠→彻底地折叠在一起（使看不清）→使迷惑；使复杂化』

[usually passive] 迷惑；使困惑
This problem is hard enough to perplex even the teacher.
这个问题确实很难，连老师都迷惑不解。

▶ **perplexed** [pə'plekst] adj. 困惑的，迷惑不解的

She is perplexed about what to do for her daughter.
她不知道该为女儿做些什么。

▶ **perplexing** [pə'pleksɪŋ] adj. 令人困惑的

It took years to understand many perplexing diseases.
许多疑难病症要耗时数年才能搞明白。

词根250. ploy, ploit=use, 表示"使用"

1. employ [ɪm'plɔɪ] vt. 雇用；运用

『em使+ploy用→使用→雇用；运用』

❶ [VN] 雇用
How many people does the company employ?
这个公司雇用了多少人？

❷ [VN] 运用
to use a particular object, method, skill, etc. in order to achieve something

He criticized the repressive methods employed by the country's government.
他指责了这个国家政府采取的镇压手段。

❸ be employed in doing sth 从事于，忙于（做某事）
She was employed in making a list of all the jobs to be done.
她忙着把要做的所有工作列一个清单。

❹ in sb's employ/in the employ of sb
(formal) 替某人工作；为某人所雇

▶ **employer** [ɪm'plɔɪə(r)] n. 雇主，老板
『employ雇用+er做某动作的人→雇主』

▶ **employee** [ɪm'plɔɪiː] n. 雇工，雇员
『employ雇用+ee被…的人→被雇的人→雇工，雇员』

2. ploy [plɔɪ] n. 计谋；手段

『ploy使用→（为使自己获得优势）使用（的手段）→计谋；手段』

A ploy is a way of behaving that someone plans carefully and secretly in order to gain an advantage for themselves.

Christmas should be a time of excitement and wonder, not a cynical marketing ploy.
圣诞节应该是兴奋和美妙的时刻，而不该是一种肆无忌惮的营销策略。

Using the Welsh name was a clever marketing ploy.
用威尔士这个名字是个聪明的营销策略。

3. deploy [dɪ'plɔɪ] vt. 部署，调度（军队或武器）

『de加强+ploy使用→使用（部队或武器）→部署，调度』

2,000 troops were deployed in the area.
那个地区部署了2000人的部队。

At least 5,000 missiles were deployed along the border.
沿边境至少部署了5000枚导弹。

4. exploit [ɪk'splɔɪt, 'eksplɔɪt] vt. 利用（…为自己谋利），剥削 n. 英勇或有趣的行为

『ex出来+ploit使用→（把某人或某物的用处）拿出来供自己使用→利用；剥削』

❶ [VN] 压榨，剥削
What is being done to stop employers from exploiting young people? 目前有什么措施制止雇主剥削年轻人呢？

❷ [VN] (disapproving) 利用（…为自己谋利）
to treat a person or situation as an opportunity to gain an advantage for yourself

He exploited his father's name to get himself a job.
他利用他父亲的名声为自己找到一份工作。

She realized that her youth and inexperience were being exploited. 她意识到自己的年轻和缺乏经验正受人利用。

❸ [VN] 充分利用
If you exploit something, you use it well, and achieve something or gain an advantage from it.

You'll need a good aerial to exploit the radio's performance.
你需要弄个好天线来发挥广播的性能。

❹ [VN] 开采，开发
I think we're being very short sighted in not exploiting our own coal. 我认为不开采我们自己的煤是非常短视的做法。

❺ [usually pl.] 英勇（或激动人心、有趣）的行为
His wartime exploits were later made into a film.
他在战争中的英勇行为后来被改编成一部电影。

词根251. ply=fold, 表示"重叠，折叠"

1. apply [ə'plaɪ] vt. 申请；应用；适用；涂，敷

『ap相当于to+ply折叠→（把申请信）折叠到一起（后送到用人单位）→申请』

❶ ~ (to sb/sth) (for sth) （通常以书面形式）申请，请求
Students apply to a particular college for admission.
学生们申请上特定的大学。

❷ [VN] ~ sth (to sth) 使用；应用
The new technology was applied to farming.
这项新技术已应用于农业。

You can apply the same rules to your work environment.
你可以把同样的规则运用到工作环境。

❸ ~ (to sb/sth) 适用；适合
If something such as a rule or a remark applies to a person or in a situation, it is relevant to the person or the situation.

The convention does not apply to us.
这条惯例对我们不适用。

But because the study did not involve men, you can't say the results apply to them.
但是因为这项研究并没有包括男士，对于他们，这项结果并不适合。

❹ [VN] ~ yourself (to sth/to doing sth)
使（自己）全神贯注于；专心致志于
If you apply yourself to something or apply your mind to something, you concentrate hard on doing it or on thinking about it.

We applied our minds to finding a solution to our problem.
我们绞尽脑汁寻求解决问题的办法。

It's difficult to apply oneself to a boring task.
很难专心致志地干一件枯燥无味的事。

❺ [VN] ~ sth (to sth) 涂；敷
to put or spread sth such as paint, cream, etc. onto a surface
Apply the cream sparingly to your face and neck.
把乳霜薄薄地抹在脸和脖子上。

▶ **applicant** ['æplɪkənt] n. 申请人

▶**application** [ˌæplɪ'keɪʃn] n. 申请；应用；应用程序

His application for membership of the organisation was rejected. 他想要加入该组织的申请遭到了拒绝。

The invention would have wide application/a wide range of applications in industry.

这项发明会在工业中得到广泛应用。

小贴士 手机上的app就是application（应用程序）的简写形式。

2. multiply ['mʌltɪplaɪ] v. 乘；成倍增加；繁殖〈P23〉

『multi多的+ply折叠→折叠多次→成倍增加；乘』

3. ply [plaɪ] n. （毛线、绳子、木板等的计量单位）股，层

v. （船、飞机或车辆）定期往返于

『ply(=fold)折叠→线多次折叠成绳；木板多层折叠成胶合板；（船、飞机或车辆）定期往返的路线也是一种重叠→股；定期往返于』

Eighteen boats plied the 1,000 miles of river along a trading route. 18艘船沿着贸易航线往返于1000英里长的河面上。

four-ply knitting yarn 四股毛线

4. plywood ['plaɪwʊd] n. 胶合板

『ply重叠，折叠+wood木材→木材重叠→胶合板』

5. pliable ['plaɪəbl] adj. 易弯曲的，柔韧的；（人）易受影响的

『ply(fold)折叠（变y为i）+able可…的，能…的→易折叠的→易弯的→易受影响的』

As your baby grows bigger, his bones become less pliable.

随着宝宝的成长，其骨骼的柔韧性会降低。

He'd always thought of her as pliable.

他一向认为她耳软心活。

6. comply [kəm'plaɪ] vi. 服从；遵守（要求、规则等）

『com共同，一起+ply折叠，重叠→（所做的）同（要求、规则等）重叠到一起→服从；遵守』

[V] ~ (with sth) 遵从；服从

to obey a rule, an order, etc.

The commander said that the army would comply with the ceasefire. 指挥官说军队会遵守停火协议。

The factory was closed for failing to comply with government safety regulations.

工厂由于未能遵守政府的安全条例而被关闭了。

▶**compliant** [kəm'plaɪənt] adj. 顺从的，百依百顺的

She was much naughtier than her compliant brother.

她哥哥很听话，她却调皮得多。

▶**compliance** [kəm'plaɪəns] n. 服从；顺从

The company says it is in full compliance with US labor laws.

这家公司说自己严格遵守美国的各项劳工法。

7. imply [ɪm'plaɪ] v. 暗示；意味着

『im(=in)里面+ply折叠→折叠在里面→暗示；意味着』

❶ 暗指，暗示

to suggest that sth is true or that you feel or think sth, without

saying so directly

[V (that)] Are you implying (that) I am wrong?

你的意思是不是说我错了？

[VN] I disliked the implied criticism in his voice.

我讨厌他暗中批评的口吻。

❷ 意味着

to make it seem likely that sth is true or exists

[V (that)] The survey implies (that) more people are moving house than was thought.

调查显示，准备搬家的人口比想象的要多。

[VN] The fact that she was here implies a degree of interest.

她到场就说明了她有一定程度的兴趣。

▶**implication** [ˌɪmplɪ'keɪʃn] n. 暗示；可能引发的后果

❶ 暗示，含义

The implication was obvious: vote for us or it will be very embarrassing for you.

弦外之音很明显：投票给我们，否则你会非常难堪。

❷ 可能引发的后果（某种现象所意味着的东西）

The low level of current investment has serious implications for future economic growth.

当前低迷的投资水平会对未来的经济增长产生严重影响。

小贴士 （implication既是imply又是implicate的名词形式）

词根252. plic=fold，表示"重叠；折叠"

1. implicate ['ɪmplɪkeɪt] vt. 牵扯，牵连

『im里面+plic(=fold)折叠+ate表动词→（某人）也被折叠到（某个不好的事情）里面→牵扯，牵连』

~ sb (in sth) 牵涉，牵连（某人）

to show or suggest that sb is involved in sth bad or criminal

He tried to avoid saying anything that would implicate him further. 他尽力避免说出任何会进一步牵连他的事情。

He was obliged to resign when one of his own aides was implicated in a financial scandal.

当他自己的一位助手牵涉进一起金融丑闻时，他被迫辞职。

▶**implication** [ˌɪmplɪ'keɪʃn] n. 牵连，牵涉

He resigned after his implication in a sex scandal.

他在涉及一件性丑闻之后辞职了。

小贴士 （implication既是imply又是implicate的名词形式）

▶**implicit** [ɪm'plɪsɪt] adj. 含蓄的；固有的；完全的（相信）

『im里面+plic(=fold)折叠+it表形容词→折叠在里面→（真实意图）折叠在（语言）里面；（某一品质）折叠在（某人某物）里面；（对某事的信任）折叠在（本性）里面→含蓄的；固有的；完全的，绝对的』

❶ ~ (in sth) 含蓄的；不直接言明的

Implicit in his speech was the assumption that they were guilty. 他话语中的言外之意是设定他们有罪。

The doctor gave an implicit answer.

医生给了一个含蓄的回答。

❷ 内含的，固有的

If a quality or element is implicit in something, it is involved in it or is shown by it.

The ability to listen is implicit in the teacher's role.

教师的角色包含了懂得倾听。

❸ 完全的，无疑问的，绝对的

If you say that someone has an implicit belief or faith in something, you mean that they have complete faith in it and

259

no doubts at all.

She had the implicit trust of her staff.
她得到了全体职员的绝对信任。

2. explicate [ˈeksplɪkeɪt] v. 详细解释；详细分析（想法或文学作品）

『ex外面+ plic(=fold)折叠+ate表动词→把折叠在（作品、想法）里面的东西弄出来→详细解释』

Informal activities that help the student define, explicate and test his values.
有助于学生界定、阐明、检验其价值观的一些非正式活动。

It will explicate the historical and societal contexts from which modern schooling system and its policies are generated.
它将讲解现代教育制度及其相关政策产生的历史及社会背景。

▶ **explicable** [ɪkˈsplɪkəbl] adj. 可解释的

His behaviour is explicable only in terms of his origins.
他的行为只能根据他的出身才解释得通。

▶ **explicit** [ɪkˈsplɪsɪt] adj. 明确的；清晰的；直言的

『ex外面+plic(=fold)折叠+it表形容词→（折叠在语言里面的东西）放在外面的→明确的；清晰的；直言的』

He gave me very explicit directions on how to get there.
他清楚地向我说明了去那儿的路线。

She made some very explicit references to my personal life.
她毫不隐讳地谈到了我的私生活。

3. complicate [ˈkɒmplɪkeɪt] vt. 使复杂化

『com一起+plic折叠；重叠+ate表动词→（许多）折叠在一起（导致理不出头绪）→使复杂化』

[VN] 使复杂化
to make sth more difficult to do, understand or deal with

I do not wish to complicate the task more than is necessary.
我不想使这项任务不必要地复杂化。

To complicate matters further, there will be no transport available till 8 o'clock.
使事情更难办的是8点钟之前不会有交通工具。

▶ **complicated** [ˈkɒmplɪkeɪtɪd] adj. 复杂的

The instructions look very complicated.
这说明书看起来很难懂。

It's all very complicated—but I'll try and explain.
尽管这一切都很难理解，但我会尽力解释。

近义词 **intricate** [ˈɪntrɪkət] adj. 错综复杂的

『in里面+tric(=trick)诡计+ate表性质→里面复杂得不容易看透→错综复杂的』

having a lot of small parts or details that are arranged in a complicated way and are therefore sometimes difficult to understand, solve or produce

The watch mechanism is extremely intricate and very difficult to repair. 手表的机械装置非常复杂，很难修理。
Police officers uncovered an intricate web of deceit.
警察发现了一个错综复杂的骗局。

词义辨析 <P375第72>
复杂的 complicated, complex, intricate, sophisticated

4. duplicate [ˈdjuːplɪkeɪt, ˈdjuːplɪkət] vt. 复制 adj. 复制的 n. 复制品

『du二，双+plic(=fold)折叠+ate表动词→折叠到一起形成两个完全相同的东西→复制』

（vt. [ˈdjuːplɪkeɪt]; n. & adj. [ˈdjuːplɪkət]）

❶ [VN] 复制，复印，重写；重做
a duplicated form 复制的表格

She found Ned alone in the photocopy room, duplicating some articles.
她发现内德一个人在复印室里复印一些文章。

His task will be to duplicate his success overseas here at home.
他在海外取得了成功，现在的任务就是要在国内再创辉煌。

There's no point in duplicating work already done.
重复别人已经做过的工作毫无意义。

❷ adj. [only before noun] 完全一样的；复制的；副本的
a duplicate invoice 发票副本

He let himself in with a duplicate key.
他用一把复制的钥匙打开门进去。

❸ [C] 完全一样的东西；复制品；副本
Is this a duplicate or the original? 这是副本还是正本？

▶ **duplication** [ˌdjuːplɪˈkeɪʃn] n. （不必要的）重复

This can reduce the duplication of investment, time, and labor. 这能减少资金投入、时间和劳动的重复。

▶ **duplicity** [djuːˈplɪsəti] n. 欺骗，奸诈（行为）

『du二，双+plic(=fold)折叠+ity表名词→（明里一套暗里一套）双重性质→欺骗』

[U] dishonest behaviour that is intended to make sb believe sth which is not true

That sounds like honesty rather than duplicity.
听起来像是诚实而不是口是心非。

5. replicate [ˈreplɪkeɪt] vt. 复制，重做（实验、研究等）；（分子）复制

『re又，再+plic(=fold)折叠+ate表动词→又折叠一次→又生成一个与前面完全相同的东西→重做』

❶ [VN] (formal) 复制，重做（实验、研究等）
If you replicate someone's experiment, work, or research, you do it yourself in exactly the same way.

Subsequent experiments failed to replicate these findings.
后来的实验没有得出同样的结果。

❷ [V, VN]（分子）复制
If a molecule replicates, it divides into smaller molecules which are exact copies of itself.

Cells can reproduce but only molecules can replicate.
细胞可以再生，但是只有分子可以复制。

▶ **replica** [ˈreplɪkə] n. （建筑、枪、艺术品等的）复制品，仿制品；酷似的人

A replica of something such as a statue, building, or weapon is an accurate copy of it.

It was a replica gun, for display only.
那是一把仿真枪，仅供展示。

This is an exact replica of the original ship.
这件是和原船一模一样的复制品。

Tina as a child was a replica of her mother.
蒂娜小的时候和她妈妈简直一模一样。

6. supplicant [ˈsʌplɪkənt] n. （尤指向神灵或有权势者）恳求者，哀求者，祈求者

『sup下面+plic(=fold)折叠+ant表示人→（人腿）向下折叠→跪下；俯首跪拜→恳求者，哀求者』

In the otherwise empty church, a solitary supplicant knelt before the altar.

空荡荡的教堂里，只有一个孤独的祈求者正跪在圣坛前。

▶ **supplication** [ˌsʌplɪˈkeɪʃn] n. 恳求，哀求，祈求

He raised his arms in a gesture of supplication.
他举起双手祈求。

词根253. plor(e)= cry, weep，表示"喊，哭"

1. implore [ɪmˈplɔː(r)] v. 恳求；哀求
『im里面+plore喊，哭→内心在哭喊→哀求』

to ask sb to do sth in an anxious way because you want or need it very much
[VN to inf] She implored him to stay. 她恳求他留下。
[V speech] "Help me," he implored.
"救救我吧，"他哀求道。

2. deplore [dɪˈplɔː(r)] vt. 强烈反对；公开谴责
『de加强+plore喊，哭→使劲哭喊→强烈反对』

Like everyone else, I deplore and condemn this killing.
我同所有人一样强烈谴责这桩凶杀案。

▶ **deplorable** [dɪˈplɔːrəbl] adj. 令人震惊的，愤慨的

very bad and unacceptable, often in a way that shocks people
They were living in the most deplorable conditions.
他们生活在最糟糕的环境里。

词根254. polis=state, city，表示"国家；城市"，其形容词形式为-politan

1. cosmopolis [kɒzˈmɒpəlɪs] n. 国际大都市（由来自许多不同国家的人居住的大城市）
『cosmo世界+polis城市→国际化大都市』

▶ **cosmopolitan** [ˌkɒzməˈpɒlɪtən] adj. 国际化大都市的

❶（城市）国际化大都市的
A cosmopolitan place or society is full of people from many different countries and cultures.
London has always been a cosmopolitan city.
伦敦一直是一个国际化的城市。

❷（人）国际化大都市的
Someone who is cosmopolitan has had a lot of contact with people and things from many different countries and as a result is very open to different ideas and ways of doing things.
The family are rich, and extremely sophisticated and cosmopolitan.
这个家庭很富有，而且见多识广，有国际化视野。

2. metropolis [məˈtrɒpəlɪs] n. 大都市
『metro大都市的+polis城市→大城市』

A metropolis is the largest, busiest, and most important city in a country or region.
Shenzhen exploded into a metropolis.
深圳迅速发展成为一个大都市。

▶ **metropolitan** [ˌmetrəˈpɒlɪtən] adj. 大都市的；大都市人的 n. 大都市人

It would be a mistake, in my opinion, for you to turn yourself into a metropolitan person.
在我看来，你把自己变成一个都市人是错误的。

词根255. pone=put, place，表示"放，放置"

1. opponent [əˈpəʊnənt] n. 对手；反对者
『op(=against)+pone放置（去e)+ent表人→位于对立面→对手』

❶ [C]（政治上或体育竞赛中的）对手

His forceful arguments silenced his opponent.
他论辩有力，把对方说得哑口无言。
He downed his opponent with three blows.
他三拳击倒了对手。

❷ [C]（观点、政策等的）反对者
He became an outspoken opponent of the old Soviet system.
他成为旧苏联体制直言不讳的抨击者。

2. proponent [prəˈpəʊnənt] n. 倡导者；支持者；拥护者
『propone提议（去e)+ent表示人→倡导者，支持者』

You are a big proponent of electronic records.
你是电子记录的忠实拥护者。

3. component [kəmˈpəʊnənt] n. 组成部分
『com共同+pone放，放置（去e)+ent表形容词或名词→共同放到一起→组成部分；成分』

the components of a machine 机器部件
the car component industry 汽车零部件制造业

词义辨析 <P370第48>
组成部分 element, component, ingredient

4. postpone [pəˈspəʊn] n. 延迟；延期
『post (behind)之后+pone放置→向后面放→延迟』

We'll have to postpone the meeting until next week.
我们将不得不把会议推迟到下周举行。
It was an unpopular decision to postpone building the new hospital. 延迟兴建新医院的决定是不得人心的。

词义辨析 <P365第22>
推迟，延期 delay, postpone, put off, defer, adjourn

5. exponent [ɪkˈspəʊnənt] n. 倡导者；指数，幂
『ex出+pone放置（去e)+ent表人或名词→被放置出来（到上面位置的数字）→指数，幂』

▶ **exponential** [ˌekspəˈnenʃl] adj. 指数的；越来越快的
Since then, the spread of COVID-19 has increased exponentially, with the World Health Organization declaring a pandemic on 11 March.
此后，COVID-19（新冠肺炎）的传播呈指数级增长，世界卫生组织于3月11日宣布大流行。

词根256. pose, posit, pound=put, place，表示"放，放置"
① pose=put, place，表示"放，放置"

1. pose [pəʊz] v. 摆姿势；造成（威胁、问题）n. 姿势
『pose放置→把自己按一定姿势放置；放置（威胁等）→摆姿势；造成（威胁、问题等）』

❶ [V] ~ (for sb/sth)（为图像、摄影）摆好姿势
The delegates posed for a group photograph.
代表们摆好姿势准备拍集体照。

❷ [VN] 造成（威胁、问题等）
to pose a threat/challenge/danger/risk
构成威胁/挑战/危险/风险
The task poses no special problems.
这项任务不会造成特别的问题。

❸ [C]（为图像、拍照等摆的）姿势
He adopted a relaxed pose for the camera.
他摆了个悠闲的姿势拍照。

2. posture [ˈpɒstʃə(r)] n. 姿势；姿态 vi. 故作姿态
『post(=pose)摆姿势+ure表名词→姿势；姿态』

❶ [U, C] （坐立的）姿势

Good posture is essential when working at the computer.
用电脑工作时良好的姿势极其重要。

Back pains can be the result of bad posture.
腰背疼可能是不良姿势造成的。

❷ [C, usually sing.] 姿态，态度

your attitude to a particular situation or the way in which you deal with it

The government has adopted an aggressive posture on immigration. 政府对移民入境采取了强硬的态度。

❸ [V] 故作姿态，装模作样

You can say that someone is posturing when you disapprove of their behaviour because you think they are trying to give a particular impression in order to deceive people.

She says the President may just be posturing.
她说总统也许只是在做样子而已。

3. impostor ['ɪmpɒstə] n. 冒名顶替者

『im里面+post(=pose)摆姿势+or人→摆姿势（使自己像别的）人→冒名顶替者』

If he allowed this conversation to go on much longer she was bound to find out that he was an impostor.
如果他让这次谈话继续下去，她一定会发现他是个骗子。

4. position [pə'zɪʃn] n. 位置；职位 vt. 使处于某个位置

『pose放置（变e为i）+tion表行为或结果→位置』

She quickly positioned herself behind the desk.
她迅速在桌子后面就位。

5. oppose [ə'pəʊz] vt. 反对

『op对着+pose放→放在（某物）的对立面→反对』

He threw all those that opposed him into prison.
他把所有反对他的人都投进了监狱。

I would oppose **changing** the law.
我将反对改变这个法规。

▶**opposed** [ə'pəʊzd] adj. 强烈反对的；截然不同的

be opposed to 反对（to是介词）

She remained bitterly opposed to the idea of moving abroad.
她仍然强烈反对移居国外。

Our views are diametrically opposed on this issue.
在这个问题上，我们的观点大相径庭。

词义辨析 <P369第42> **反对 oppose, object, protest**

6. opposite ['ɒpəzɪt] adj. 对面的；相反的 adv. 对面 n. 对立面；反义词 prep. 在…对面

『op对着+pose放（去e）+ite有…性质的→放在（某物）的对立面的→对立的』

❶ adj. 对面的，另一边；相反的

We live further down on the opposite side of the road.
我们住在马路对面再远一点的地方。

He sat down in the chair opposite.
他在对面的椅子上坐了下来。

She tried calming him down but it seemed to be having the opposite effect. 她试着让他平静下来，却似乎火上浇油了。

❷ adv. 对面

There's a newly married couple living opposite.
有一对新婚夫妇住在马路对面。

❸ prep. 在…对面

I sat opposite him during the meal.
席间我坐在他的对面。

❹ n. 对立的人（或物）；反义词

What is the opposite of heavy? 重的反义词是什么？

I thought she would be small and blonde but she's the complete opposite.
我原以为她是一位身材娇小的金发女郎，但是恰恰相反。

7. compose [kəm'pəʊz] vt. 组成；作曲；使镇静

『com一起+pose放置→把多个（组成部分、音符、各种心思感官）放置在一起→组成；作曲；使镇静）』

❶ [VN] （不用于进行时） 组成，构成

Ten men compose the committee. 委员会由十人组成。

The committee is composed mainly of lawyers.
委员会主要由律师组成。

❷ [VN 作曲，创作（音乐）

[VN] Mozart composed his last opera shortly before he died.
莫扎特在创作出他最后一部歌剧后不久便去世了。

❸ [VN] [no passive] (formal) 使镇静；使平静

I was so confused that I could hardly compose my thoughts.
我心烦意乱，难以镇定思绪。

▶**composed** [kəm'pəʊzd] adj. 镇定的，沉着的

If someone is composed, they are calm and able to control their feelings.

Laura was very calm and composed. 劳拉十分冷静沉着。

▶**composure** [kəm'pəʊʒə(r)] n. 沉着，镇静，镇定

For a minute he looked uncertain, and then recovered his composure.
有一小会儿他看上去有些迟疑不定，之后又恢复了镇定。

小贴士 英语中表示"振作起精神"大多与"（把部件）放到一起"有关。人在失意时就像一部机器各个部件支离破碎，不能正常运转。只有把各个部件拼凑到一起，才能正常运转。

I'm fine—I just need a minute to collect myself.
我没事，只是需要稍稍镇定一下。

The fire was a blow, but we were determined to pick up the pieces and get the business back on its feet.
这场火灾是一次打击，但我们决心收拾残局，使生意恢复元气。

Pull yourself together. I'm sure everything will turn out fine.
你要振作起来，我相信一切都会变好的。

This will give you time to compose yourself and relax a little.
这让你有时间镇定下来，放松一下。

▶**decompose** [ˌdi:kəm'pəʊz] v. 腐烂；（使）分解
『de相反+compose组成→分解』

词义辨析 <P375第73>
由…组成 make up, consist of, compose, constitute, comprise

8. composition [ˌkɒmpə'zɪʃn] n. 构成；创作；（音乐、艺术、诗歌的）作品；作文

『compose的名词形式』

Scientists study the composition of the soil.
科学家们研究土壤的构成。

These plays are arranged in their order of composition.
这些剧作是按照其创作的先后顺序安排的。

Mozart's compositions are undoubtedly amongst the world's greatest.

莫扎特的作品无疑位居世界最伟大的作品之列。

The teacher singled out one composition for class discussion.

教师挑选出一篇作文来供课堂上讨论。

9. composite [ˈkɒmpəzɪt] n. 合成物，混合物 adj. 合成的，混合的

『com一起+pose放，放置（去e）+ite具有…性质的→合成物』

(something) made up of different parts or materials

The document was a composite of information from various sources. 这份文件是不同来源信息的综合。

Spain is a composite of diverse traditions and people.

西班牙是一个汇集了多种传统和民族的国家。

小贴士　上海证交所综合指数

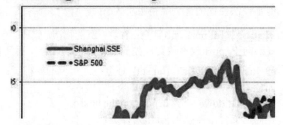

Shanghai SSE Composite Index

10. expose [ɪkˈspəʊz] vt. 揭露；露出；使接触

『ex出来+pose放置→放出来→暴露』

❶ [VN] 暴露；露出

He smiled suddenly, exposing a set of amazingly white teeth.

他突然一笑，露出一口雪白的牙齿。

Do not expose babies to strong sunlight.

不要让婴孩受到强烈的阳光照射。

❷ [VN] 揭露；揭穿

She was exposed as a liar and a fraud.

她说谎和欺骗的面目被揭穿了。

He threatened to expose the racism that existed within the police force.

他扬言要把警察内部存在的种族歧视公之于众。

❸ ~ sb to sth 使接触；使体验

to let sb find out about sth by giving them experience of it or showing them what it is like

We want to expose the kids to as much art and culture as possible.

我们想让孩子们受到尽可能多的艺术和文化熏陶。

▶ **exposure** [ɪkˈspəʊʒə(r)] n. 暴露；揭露；接触，体验

Long exposure to noisy surroundings may result in some physical and mental problems.

长久暴露于嘈杂的环境中会引起一些身体的和心理的问题。

Daniel's early exposure to motor racing did not excite his interest.

丹尼尔早期与摩托车赛的接触并没有激发他的兴趣。

11. propose [prəˈpəʊz] vt. 提议，建议；求婚

『pro向前+pose放→（把建议）放到别人前面（供考虑）→提议』

❶ 提议；建议

to suggest a plan, an idea, etc. for people to think about and decide on

[VN] The government proposed changes to the voting system.

政府建议修改表决制度。

[V -ing] He proposed changing the name of the company.

他建议更改公司的名称。

[V that] She proposed that the book be banned.

她提议查禁这本书。

❷ ~ (sth) (to sb) 求婚　to ask sb to marry you

She proposed to me! 她向我求婚了！

小贴士　"求婚""订婚"和"结婚"都和介词to连用。

He is engaged to a pretty girl.他跟一个漂亮的姑娘定亲了。

He was married to a daughter of a farmer.

他与一个农民的女儿结婚了。

❸ [VN] ~ sth | ~ sb (for/as sth) 提名，提出…供表决

to suggest sth at a formal meeting and ask people to vote on it

I propose Tom Ellis for chairman.

我提名汤姆·埃利斯做主席。

▶ **proposal** [prəˈpəʊzl] n. 建议；提议；求婚

The President is to put forward new proposals for resolving the country's constitutional crisis.

总统将提出解决国家宪法危机的新议案。

12. impose [ɪmˈpəʊz] v. 强加

『im里面+pose放置→（强行把某物）放置到…上』

❶ [VN] 强制实行；强加

A new tax was imposed on fuel.

当局开始对燃油征收一项新税。

❷ [VN] 把（观点、愿望等）强加于人

She didn't want to impose her values on her family.

她并不想勉强家人接受自己的价值观。

❸ [VN] 打扰；勉强

I didn't want to impose myself on my married friends.

我不想打扰自己已婚的朋友。

▶ **imposing** [ɪmˈpəʊzɪŋ] adj. 壮观的；使人印象深刻的

『impose强加（去e）+ing表形容词→（因为大、壮观等使人不得不留下深刻印象，好像这种印象是）强加（给自己）的→使人印象深刻的』

impressive to look at; making a strong impression

It was his size which took one's breath away—his size and his imposing presence.

是他的身材让人屏住了呼吸——他的身材和他的威严。

13. suppose [səˈpəʊz] v. 猜想；假定

『sup下面+pose放，放置→把（想法）放置在暗地里（没说出来）→猜想』

❶ [VN]（根据所知）认为，推断，料想

Getting a visa isn't as simple as you might suppose.

办签证不像你想的那么容易。

❷ 假定；假设

[V (that)] Suppose flights are fully booked on that day—which other day could we go?

假定那天的航班都订满了——我们还可以在哪天走呢？

❸（婉转表达）我看，要我说，要不

used to make a statement, request or suggestion less direct or less strong

[V] "Can I borrow the car?" "I suppose so (= Yes, but I'm not happy about it) ." "我能借这辆车吗？" "应该可以吧（但我其实不想借）。"

[V (that)] Suppose we take a later train?

要不我们坐晚一点的火车？

[VN] I get a bit uptight these days. Hormones, I suppose.

这些天我有点焦躁。我看是荷尔蒙在作怪。

❹ be supposed to do （按规定、习惯、安排等）应当，应

I thought we were supposed to be paid today.
我以为我们今天会领到薪水。

小贴士 使用动词 suppose 加 that 从句表达否定的意见或看法时，通常否定 suppose 而非 that 从句中的动词。例如，通常说 "I don't suppose he ever saw it."（我认为他从没见过），而不说 "I suppose he didn't ever saw it."。同样的句型也适用于其他含义相近的动词，如 believe, consider 和 think。

14. depose [dɪˈpəʊz] v. 罢免，废黜（统治者或政治领导人）
『de离开+pose放置→使离开（职位）→罢免』

Mr Ben Bella was deposed in a coup in 1965.
本·贝拉先生在1965年的一次政变中被罢免。

▶ **deposition** [ˌdepəˈzɪʃn] n. 罢免，免职

Your name has appeared in deposition records.
你的名字出现在了免职名单上。

He lived a poor life after his deposition.
他被免职后过着贫穷的生活。

15. dispose [dɪˈspəʊz] vi. 处理
『dis离开+pose放置→把（不想要的）放置开→处理掉』

dispose of sb/sth 处理掉

❶ 去掉；清除；销毁（不想要的东西）
to get rid of sb/sth that you do not want or cannot keep

They have no way to dispose of the hazardous waste they produce. 他们没有办法处理掉他们产生的有害废料。

❷ 解决，处理（任务、问题等）
You did us a great favour by disposing of that problem.
你解决了那个问题，可算是帮了我们一个大忙。

❸ 打败；杀死
It took her a mere 20 minutes to dispose of her opponent.
她仅用了20分钟就击败了对手。

They had hired an assassin to dispose of him.
他们已雇了刺客来除掉他。

▶ **disposal** [dɪˈspəʊzl] n. 处理

at sb's disposal 任某人处理；由某人自行支配

He will have a car at his disposal for the whole month.
他将有一辆汽车归他使用一个月。

If I can be of service, I am at your disposal.
如果我可以效劳的话，敬请吩咐。

▶ **disposable** [dɪˈspəʊzəbl] adj. 一次性的；可任意处理的

He shaved himself with a disposable razor.
他用一次性刀片刮脸。

Gerald had little disposable income.
杰拉尔德的可支配收入很少。

16. interpose [ˌɪntəˈpəʊz] vt. 插进（问题或话语）；插入
『inter在…之间+pose放，置→插入』

"He rang me just now," she interposed.
"他刚刚给我打过电话，"她插嘴说。

Police had to interpose themselves between the two rival groups. 警方不得不对这两个对立团体进行干预。

② posit=put，place，表示"放，放置"

1. proposition [ˌprɒpəˈzɪʃn] n. 观点；命题；建议；提议
『pro向前+posit放置+ion表名词→放到前面（供别人考虑

的东西）命题；建议；提议』

❶ [C] 见解；观点；命题
a statement that consists of a carefully considered opinion or judgment

Most people accept the proposition that we have a duty to protect endangered animals.
大多数人接受我们有责任保护濒危动物的主张。

The theory is founded on two basic propositions.
这一理论建立在两个基本观点之上。

❷ [C] 建议；提议；提案
an idea or a plan of action that is suggested, especially in business

I'd like to put a business proposition to you.
我想向您提个业务上的建议。

He was trying to make it look like an attractive proposition.
他正设法使他的计划显得吸引人。

2. deposit [dɪˈpɒzɪt] n. 订金；存款；沉淀物 v. 放置；存款
『de向下+posit放，放置→先放下去的钱→订金；存款』

❶ [usually sing.] a ~ (on sth) 订金；（租赁的）押金；保证金
We've put down a 5% deposit on the house.
我们已支付了房款的5%作为订金。

It is common to ask for the equivalent of a month's rent as a deposit. 索要相当于一个月的房租作押金是很常见的。

❷ [C] 存款
Deposits can be made at any branch.
在任何一家分行都可以存钱。

❸ [C] 沉淀物，沉积物
There is too much deposit in a bottle of wine.
一瓶酒里有太多的沉淀物。

❹ [VN] 放下；存款；沉淀；付订金

3. depository [dɪˈpɒzɪtri] n. 仓库，储藏处，存放处
『de向下+posit放，放置+ory表场所→放东西的场所→仓库，储存处』

A depository is a place where objects can be stored safely.
They have 2,500 tons of paper stored in their depository.
他们有2500吨纸存放在仓库里。

4. repository [rɪˈpɒzətri] n. 仓库，贮藏室；博学者
『re返回+posit放+ory表场所→可以把（物品、知识）放回的地方→仓库；博学者』

a place where sth is stored in large quantities; a person or book that is full of information

A church in Moscow became a repository for police files.
莫斯科的一座教堂成了警方存放档案的地点。

My father is a repository of family history.
我的父亲对家族史无所不知。

5. exposition [ˌekspəˈzɪʃn] n. 解释，说明；交易会，博览会
『ex出来+posit放置+ion表名词→把（深奥的理论、要卖的商品）放出来→解释；博览会』

❶ [C] 阐述，解释，说明
An exposition of an idea or theory is a detailed explanation or account of it.

This is a clear exposition of the theory of evolution.
这是对进化论的清晰阐述。

❷ [C] 商品交易会；产品博览会

小贴士 exposition也常简写作：**expo** ['ekspəʊ]

6. disposition [ˌdɪspə'zɪʃn] n. 性格，性情；倾向，意向
『dis离开+posit放置+ion表示名词→把（东西）分开放置（这是他的倾向，也反映了他的性格）→性格；倾向』

❶ [C, usually sing.] 性格；性情
the natural qualities of a person's character
The rides are unsuitable for people of a nervous disposition.
骑马（或乘坐）这一活动不适合天性易紧张的人。

❷ [C, usually sing.] ~ to/towards sth | ~ to do sth (formal)
倾向；意向
a tendency or willingness to behave in a particular way
Neither side shows the slightest disposition to compromise.
双方都没有丝毫妥协的倾向。

7. appositive [ə'pɒzɪtɪv] adj. 同位的 n. 同位语
『ap(=to)到+posit放置+ive表形容词或名词→（把一名词）放到（另一名词后面，以解释说明前面名词）→同位的，同位语』

subject, predicate, object, objective complement, attribute, adverbial modifier, predicative, appositive
主语，谓语，宾语，宾语补足语，定语，状语，表语，同位语

▶ **apposition** [ˌæpə'zɪʃn] n. 同位

In the phrase "Paris, the capital of France", "the capital of France" is in apposition to "Paris".
在短语"巴黎，法国的首都"中，"法国的首都"是"巴黎"的同位语。

8. symposium [sɪm'pəʊziəm] n. 专题讨论会
『sym共同+pose放（去e）+ium场所，地点→共同放在一起（讨论）的场所→专题讨论会』

He had been taking part in an international symposium on population.
他那时正参加一个有关人口问题的国际研讨会。

③ pound=put, place，表示"放，放置"

1. compound ['kɒmpaʊnd , kəm'paʊnd] n. 混合物，化合物；院子 adj. 复合的 v. 混合；使加重
『com一起+pound放，放置→都放到一起→混合物,化合物』
（n. & adj. ['kɒmpaʊnd]; v. [kəm'paʊnd]）

❶ [C] 复合物；混合物；化合物；复合词
Honey is basically a compound of water, two types of sugar, vitamins and enzymes.
蜂蜜基本上是水、两种糖、维生素和酶的混合物。
Organic compounds contain carbon in their molecules.
有机化合物的分子中含有碳。

❷ [C] 有围栏（或围墙）的场地
an area surrounded by a fence or wall in which a factory or other group of buildings stands
Al-Baghdadi was killed in a late-night US-led airstrike in a compound near the village of Barisha in northwestern Syria on Oct. 26, 2019.
巴格达迪于2019年10月26日深夜在叙利亚西北部巴里沙村附近的一处大院中被美国领导的空袭炸死。

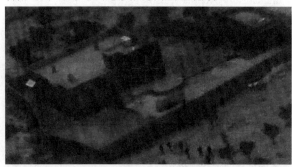

❸ adj. 复合的
a compound adjective, such as fair-skinned
复合形容词，如fair-skinned
A compound sentence contains two or more clauses.
复合句包含两个或多个从句。
compound interest 复合利率

❹ [VN] 混合；使加重
The problems were compounded by severe food shortages.
严重的食物短缺使问题进一步恶化。
Most tyres are made of rubber compounded with other chemicals and materials.
大多数轮胎是由橡胶与其他化学物质和材料复合而成的。

2. impound [ɪm'paʊnd] vt. （由警察、法庭等）暂时没收；扣押
『im里面+ pound 放，放置→（警察）把（被扣押的物品）放到（院子）里面→扣押』

The car was impounded by the police after the accident.
那辆车在发生车祸之后被警察扣留了。

词根257. port=part; divide，表示"部分；分开"

1. portion ['pɔːʃn] n. 部分 vt. 分成若干部分
『port部分；分开+ion表名词→分成若干部分』

❶ [C] 部分；（食物的）一份，一客
Only a small portion of the budget is spent on books.
购书只占预算的一小部分。
She cut the cake into six small portions.
她把蛋糕切成了六小份。

❷ [VN] ~ sth (out) 把…分成若干份
We'll have to portion the money out among/between the six of us. 我们得把钱分给我们六个人。

2. apportion [ə'pɔːʃn] vt. 分配；分摊；分派
『ap相当于to+portion分成若干部分→分成若干份给他人→分配；分派』

[VN] ~ sth (among/between/to sb) 分配；分摊；分派
They apportioned the land among members of the family.
他们把土地分给了家中各人。
The programme gives the facts but does not apportion blame.
这个节目只摆出事实，并不评论谁是谁非。

3. proportion [prə'pɔːʃn] n. 部分；比例
『pro向前+portion部分→向前的部分（与所有的部分）→

部分；比例』

❶ [C + sing./pl. v.] 部分；份额
Water covers a large proportion of the earth's surface.
水覆盖了地球表面的大部分。

❷ [U] ~ (of sth to sth) 比例
The proportion of men to women in the college has changed dramatically over the years.
近年来，这个学院的男女学生比例出现了明显变化。

The proportion of small cars on America's roads is increasing.
美国公路上小汽车的比例在逐渐增加。

A high proportion of five-year-olds have teeth in poor condition. 五岁儿童牙齿不健康的比例高。

❸ [U, C, usually pl.] 正确的比例；均衡；匀称
The head is out of proportion with the body.
头部和身体不成比例。

an impressive building with fine proportions
比例协调的雄伟建筑物

They earn salaries **out of all proportion to** their ability.
他们挣的工资与其能力不相称。

❹ proportions （通常指极其巨大的事物的）大小，尺寸；规模，程度
a food shortage that could soon reach crisis proportions
可能会很快达到危机程度的粮食短缺

COVID-19 is a pandemic of historic proportions.
COVID-19（新冠肺炎）是一种历史性的传染病。

In the tropics plants grow to huge proportions.
在热带地区，植物会长得非常高大。

▶ **proportional** [prə'pɔːʃnl] adj. 成比例的

His pay is proportional to the amount of work he does.
他的工资和工作量相称。

Salary is proportional to years of experience.
薪金视资历而定。

词根258. port=carry; port，表示"运输；港口"

1. **export** vt. [ɪk'spɔːt, 'ekspɔːt] vt. & n. 出口
『ex出去+port港口→（货物）出港→出口』
（vt. [ɪk'spɔːt]; n. ['ekspɔːt]）

❶ [VN] ~ (sth) (to sb) 出口
90% of the engines are exported to Europe.
90%的发动机都出口到欧洲。

❷ [VN] 传播，输出（思想或活动）
American pop music has been exported around the world.
美国流行音乐已传播到世界各地。

❸ [U, C] 出口，输出；出口产品，输出品
Then the fruit is packaged for export.
然后水果便包装出口。

the country's major exports 该国的主要出口产品

2. **import** ['ɪmpɔːt , ɪm'pɔːt] n. 进口；进口商品 vt.进口<P18>
『im进入+port港口→从港口进来→进口』

3. **transport** ['trænspɔːt] n. & vt. 运输〈P41〉
『trans从…到…+port港口→从一个港口到另一个港口→运输』

4. **passport** ['pɑːspɔːt] n. 护照
『pass通过+ port港口→通过港口（的凭证）→护照』

5. **deport** [dɪ'pɔːt] vt. 驱逐出境
『de离开+port港口→使（某人）离开港口→驱逐出境』

She praised the government's decision not to deport the migrants. 她称赞政府不驱逐这些移民的决定。

6. **porter** ['pɔːtə(r)] n. （尤指火车站、机场或旅馆的）行李员；搬运工
『port运输+er表人→搬运（货物）的人→搬运工』

7. **portable** ['pɔːtəbl] adj. 便携式的；手提的
『port运输+able可以，能够→可以拿来拿去的→便携的』

8. **portly** ['pɔːtli] adj. （尤指男性）肥胖的，过胖的
『port运输+ly表形容词→（经常）运送（货物的）→肥胖的』

9. **portfolio** [pɔːt'fəʊliəʊ] n. 文件夹，公事包；图画作品集；组合
『port运输+folio古时纸张很大的书→可以拿来拿去的（里面是图画的）书→图画作品集→像大纸张的图画作品集一样可以拿来拿去的东西→公文夹；组合』

❶ [C] 文件夹；公事包

❷ [C] （参赛或应聘用的）画作选辑

❸ [C] 有价证券组合；投资组合
Short-term securities can also be held as part of an investment portfolio.
投资组合里也可以包括短期有价证券。

❹ [C] 产品组合；系列设计
The company has continued to invest heavily in a strong portfolio of products.
公司继续在强大的产品组合上投入大笔资金。

10. **purport** [pə'pɔːt] vt. 自称，标榜
『pur向前+port拿→（把自己要说的）向前拿出来（不管别人信不信）→自称，标榜』

[V to inf] (formal) to claim to be sth or to have done sth, when this may not be true
Such books purport to be works of history, yet they are rarely written by historians.
这些书号称是历史著作，但它们很少由历史学家撰写。

词根259. pot=drink; power，本义为"罐子"，引申为"喝"，再引申为"力量"（可能是喝了魔法药水）

1. **potion** ['pəʊʃn] n. 药水，魔水
『pot喝；力量+ion表名词→喝了有力量→药水，魔水』

A potion is a drink that contains medicine, poison, or something that is supposed to have magic powers.
So it's a magic potion? 那么，这是个神药？

2. **potent** ['pəʊtnt] adj. 很有效的，强有力的
『pot力量+ent表形容词→强有力的』

Something that is potent is very effective and powerful.
The drug is extremely potent, but causes unpleasant side effects. 这种药药效极强，但会产生令人不快的副作用。
Their most potent weapon was the Exocet missile.
飞鱼导弹是他们最有攻击力的武器。

▶ **potence** ['pəʊtəns] n. 力量，效力

The drug has lost its potence by being exposed to moisture.
这药因受潮失去了效力。

3. impotent [ˈɪmpətənt] adj. 无能为力的
『im不+pot力量+ent表形容词→无能为力的』

having no power to change things or to influence a situation
Without the chairman's support, the committee is impotent.
没有主席的支持，委员会是无能为力的。

▶ **impotence** [ˈɪmpətəns] n. 无能力

In the midst of his feelings of impotence, a comforting thought arrived.
正在他觉得很无奈的时候，一个令人欣慰的想法冒了出来。

4. omnipotent [ɒmˈnɪpətənt] adj. 万能的，全能的
『omni全部+pot力量+ent表形容词→万能的』

Someone or something that is omnipotent has complete power over things or people.
Doug lived in the shadow of his seemingly omnipotent father.
道格生活在他那看似权威至高无上的父亲的阴影里。
You are not the God, and no one expect you to be omnipotent.
你不是上帝，没有人期望你无所不能。

▶ **omnipotence** [ɒmˈnɪpətəns] n. 全能

She knows Omnipotence has heard her prayer.
她知道全能的神已听见祈祷。

5. potential [pəˈtenʃl] adj. 潜在的 n. 潜力；可能
『potent强有力的+ial表形容词或名词→潜力』

First we need to identify actual and potential problems.
首先，我们需要弄清实际的问题和潜在的问题。
The European marketplace offers excellent potential for increasing sales. 欧洲市场带来了扩销的大好机遇。
All children should be encouraged to realize their full potential. 应当鼓励所有的儿童充分发挥他们的潜能。

词根260. prece, praise=price，表示"价格；价值"

1. precious [ˈpreʃəs] adj. 珍贵的，宝贵的
『prece价值（去e加i）+ous充满的→充满价值的→宝贵的』

Her family's support is particularly precious to Josie.
家庭的支持对乔茜来说尤为可贵。

2. appreciate [əˈpriːʃieɪt] v. 感激；欣赏；意识到；增值
『ap(=fully)表加强+prece价值（去e加i）+ate表动词→完全知道…的价值→感激；理解；赏识』

❶ 感激，感谢；欢迎
to be grateful for sth that sb has done; to welcome sth
[VN] Your support is greatly appreciated.
十分感谢你的支持。
[VN] I would appreciate it if you paid in cash.
假如你支付现金的话，我会不胜感激。
[VN -ing] We would appreciate you letting us know of any problems. 如有任何问题，请告诉我们。

❷ 理解；意识到
to understand that sth is true
[V wh-] I don't think you appreciate how expensive it will be.
我想你不了解它会有多昂贵。
[V that] We didn't fully appreciate that he was seriously ill.
我们没有充分认识到他的病情很严重。

❸ [VN] 欣赏，赏识
to recognise the good qualities of sb/sth

You can't really appreciate foreign literature in translation.
看翻译作品不能真正欣赏到外国文学原著的美妙之处。
Her family doesn't appreciate her. 她的家人不重视她。

❹ [V] 增值，升值
to increase in value over a period of time
Their investments have appreciated over the years.
他们的投资这些年来已经增值。

▶ **appreciative** [əˈpriːʃətɪv] adj. 感激的；欣赏的，赞赏的（showing pleasure or enjoyment）
『appreciate感激；欣赏（去e）+ive…性质的→感激的；欣赏的』

We have been very appreciative of their support.
我们对他们的支持一直心存感激。
There is a murmur of appreciative laughter.
（传来）一阵赞赏的低笑声。

3. depreciate [dɪˈpriːʃieɪt] v.（货币等）贬值，跌价；折旧
『de向下+prece价值；价格（去e加i）+ate表动词→价值、价格降低→贬值，跌价』

If something such as a currency depreciates or if something depreciates it, it loses some of its original value.
New cars start to depreciate as soon as they are on the road.
新车一上路就开始贬值。
Shares continued to depreciate on the stock markets today.
今日股市股价继续下跌。
Countries may also find their currency is depreciating in foreign markets.
一些国家也可能会发现本国货币正在国外市场上贬值。
The bank depreciates PCs over a period of five years.
这家银行把个人计算机分五年折旧。

4. praise [preɪz] n. & v. 表扬，赞美
『praise(=price)价格；价值→（认可某人的）价值→表扬』

His teachers are full of praise for the progress he's making.
老师们对他的进步赞不绝口。
She wrote poems in praise of freedom. 她写诗讴歌自由。

5. appraise [əˈpreɪz] vt. 评估；估量
『ap(=to)+praise价值→（注意力集中）到价值上→评估』

If you appraise something or someone, you consider them carefully and form an opinion about them.
She stepped back to appraise her workmanship.
她后退一步，鉴赏她作品的艺术性。
His eyes coolly appraised the young woman before him.
他双眼冷静地打量着面前的年轻女子。
Managers must appraise all staff.
经理必须对全体员工作出评价。

▶ **appraisal** [əˈpreɪzl] n. 评价，评估，估量；考核

What is needed in such cases is a calm appraisal of the situation. 此类情况下需要对形势有一个冷静的评估。
Staff problems should be addressed through training and appraisals. 职员问题应该通过培训和考核评定来解决。

词根261. prehend, prehens=seize，表示"抓"

1. apprehend [ˌæprɪˈhend] vt. 逮捕，拘押；理解，明白
『ap(=to)+prehend抓→（人；要义）被抓住→逮捕；理解』

Police have not apprehended her killer.
警察还未抓获谋杀她的凶手。
Only now can I begin to apprehend the power of these forces.
直到现在我才真正了解这些队伍的力量。

▶ **apprehension** [ˌæprɪˈhenʃn] n. 忧虑，担心；逮捕；理解
『ap(=to)+prehend抓(去d加s)+ion表名词→逮捕→（因为害怕被逮捕）忧虑→忧虑』

❶ [U, C] 忧虑，担心
worry or fear that sth unpleasant may happen
There is growing apprehension that fighting will begin again.
人们愈来愈担心会重开战火。

❷ [U] 逮捕；理解
The apprehension of the drug dealers means that the streets of New York will be a little safer now.
贩毒者的被拘捕意味着纽约街头现在可以稍微太平些了。

▶ **apprehensive** [ˌæprɪˈhensɪv] adj. 忧虑的，担心的
worried or frightened that sth unpleasant may happen
You have no reason to be apprehensive of the future.
你没有理由忧虑未来。

2. comprehend [ˌkɒmprɪˈhend] v. 理解
『com一起+prehend抓→（把要点）抓到一起→理解』
（常用于否定句）to understand sth fully
[VN] The infinite distances of space are too great for the human mind to comprehend.
太空的无垠距离遥遥远得让人类的大脑无法理解。
[V wh-] She could not comprehend how someone would risk people's lives in that way.
她不明白怎么会有人竟拿人们的生命那样去冒险。

▶ **comprehension** [ˌkɒmprɪˈhenʃn] n. 理解；（语言学习中的）理解练习（或训练）
His behaviour was completely beyond comprehension.
他的举止完全令人费解。
listening comprehension 听力练习
reading comprehension 阅读理解练习

▶ **comprehensive** [ˌkɒmprɪˈhensɪv] adj. 全面的，详尽的，综合性的 n. （英）综合中学
Something that is comprehensive includes everything that is needed or relevant.
The Rough Guide to Nepal is a comprehensive guide to the region.
《尼泊尔概况》是一本全面介绍该地区的旅游指南。
All the products are labelled with comprehensive instructions.
所有产品均标有详尽的使用说明。

3. reprehensible [ˌreprɪˈhensəbl] adj. 不道德的，应受指责的
『re又，再+prehens抓+ible可以…的→（坏得）可以反复抓起来的→不道德的，应受指责的』
If you think that a type of behaviour or an idea is very bad and morally wrong, you can say that it is reprehensible.
Mr Cramer said the violence by anti-government protestors was reprehensible.
克拉默先生说反政府示威者的暴力活动应该受到谴责。

词根262. press=press, force 挤压；逼迫

1. express [ɪkˈspres] v.表达；快递邮寄 adj. 特快的 adv. 使用快递服务 n. 特快列车
『ex出+press挤压→把（思想）挤出来→表达』

❶ 表达
主要指通过语言、表情、动作等表达想法、感情等。
[VN] Teenagers often have difficulty expressing themselves.
十来岁的孩子在表达思想方面常常有困难。

❷ (NAmE) 快递邮寄（或发送）

[VN] As soon as I receive payment I will express the book to you. 我一收到款就把书用快递给你寄去。
I'd like to send this express, please. 劳驾，我要寄快递。

❸ adj. 特快的（火车，客车等）；用快递寄送的；提供快递服务的
an express bus/coach/train
特快公共汽车/长途汽车/列车
express delivery services 快递服务
an air express company 航空快递公司

❹ adv. 使用快递服务

❺ n. 特快列车
[C] the 8:27 express to Edinburgh
8:27开往爱丁堡的特快列车

▶ **expression** [ɪkˈspreʃn] n. 表达；表情；词语或短语
『express 表达 + ion 表名词 → 表达；表情』

❶ [U, C] 表示；表达；表露
Expressions of sympathy flooded in from all over the country.
同情之意潮水般地从全国各地涌来。
Freedom of expression (=Freedom to say what you think) is a basic human right. 言论自由是基本的人权。

❷ [C] 表情；神色
There was a worried expression on her face.
她脸上流露出担心的神色。
The expression in her eyes told me something was wrong.
她的眼神告诉我出事了。

❸ [C] 词语；措辞；表达方式
She spoke in a quiet voice but used remarkably coarse expressions.
她说话声音很小，但是用了些特别粗俗的字眼儿。

▶ **expressive** [ɪkˈspresɪv] adj. 有表现力的；表达

❶ 有表现力的
She has wonderfully expressive eyes.
她有一双极富表现力的眼睛。
the expressive power of his music
他的音乐的表现力

❷ [not before noun] ~ of sth (formal) 表现；表达；表示
Every word and gesture is expressive of the artist's sincerity.
这位艺术家的真诚从一言一行中表现出来。

2. impress [ɪmˈpres] v. 使留下深刻印象
『im里面+press压→压进（脑子）里面→留下深刻印象』

❶ ~ sb (with sth/sb) 使钦佩；使敬仰；留下深刻的好印象
if a person or thing impresses you, you feel admiration for them or it
He impressed her with his sincerity. 他的真诚打动了她。
I'm very impressed with the new airport.
新机场给我留下了很深的印象。

❷ [VN] ~ sth on/upon sb 使铭记，使注意到；使留下印象
He impressed on us the need for immediate action.
他让我们认识到立刻采取行动的必要。
What he said that day was deeply impressed on my memory.
他那天说的话深深地印在我的脑海里。

▶ **impression** [ɪmˈpreʃn] n. 印象

❶ ~ (of sb/sth) | ~ (that…) 印象
She gives the impression of being very busy.
她给人的印象是特别忙。
My first impression of him was favourable.
他给我的第一印象不错。

❷ make/leave a good/bad/deep impression (on sb)
给某人留下好的/坏的/深的印象
His trip to India made a strong impression on him.
他的印度之行对他的触动很大。

▶**impressive** [ɪmˈpresɪv] adj. 令人赞叹的；令人敬佩的
『impress留下深刻印象+ive具有…性质的→具有给人留下深刻好印象的性质的→令人敬佩的』

It is an impressive achievement. 那是一项不起的成就。

▶**impressionism** [ɪmˈpreʃənɪzəm] n. 印象主义；印象派

▶**impressionist** [ɪmˈpreʃənɪst] n. 印象派画家

3. **depress** [dɪˈpres] vt. 使抑郁；使减少
『de向下+press压→（感到心情）向下压→使抑郁』

❶ [VN] 使抑郁，使沮丧，使消沉
Wet weather always depresses me.
阴雨天总使我心情抑郁。
I must admit the state of the country depresses me.
我必须承认国家的现状让我倍感沮丧。

❷ 使（工资、价格）降低，减少；使萧条，使不景气
The stronger US dollar depressed sales.
美元走强导致销售额下降。
The recession has depressed the housing market.
经济衰退导致住房市场不景气。

▶**depressed** [dɪˈprest] adj. 抑郁的；沮丧的

❶ 抑郁的；沮丧的；意志消沉的
very sad and without hope
She felt very depressed about the future. 她感到前途无望。

❷ 不景气的；萧条的
The pressure of putting food on the table in this depressed economy is overwhelming.
在经济萧条的情况下要养活一家，压力真的够大。

▶**depression** [dɪˈpreʃn] n. 抑郁；沮丧；萧条；洼地
『depress使抑郁+ion表名词→抑郁；沮丧』

❶ [U] 抑郁症；精神忧郁
She suffered from severe depression after losing her job.
她失业后患了严重的抑郁症。

❷ [U, C] 抑郁；沮丧；消沉
There was a feeling of gloom and depression in the office when the news of the job cuts was announced.
裁员消息宣布时办公室里一片忧郁和沮丧的气氛。

❸ [C, U] 萧条期；经济衰退；不景气
The country was in the grip of (an) economic depression.
当时国家处于经济萧条期。
the Great Depression of the 1930s
20世纪30年代的经济大萧条

❹ [C] (formal) 洼地；凹地；坑
Rainwater collects in shallow depressions on the ground.
雨水积在地上的浅坑里。

4. **suppress** [səˈpres] vt. 镇压；抑制
『sup(=sub)下面+press压→被压到下面→镇压；抑制』

❶ [VN] （政府、统治者等）镇压；（武力）平定；压制
He was prepared to suppress rebellion by shooting down protesters. 他准备开枪射击抗议者以镇压叛乱。

❷ [VN] 封锁（消息）；禁止（发表）；查禁
to prevent sth from being published or made known
The police were accused of suppressing vital evidence.
警方被指隐瞒关键证据。

❸ [VN] 抑制（身体的某种情感反应）
She was unable to suppress her anger. 她按捺不住怒火。

❹ [VN] 抑制，阻止（进程或活动）
These drugs should suppress your appetite.
这些药会抑制你的食欲。

词义辨析 <P380第97> 压制，克制 suppress, repress

5. **repress** [rɪˈpres] vt. 抑制，克制；压制，限制（自由）
『re返回+press压→（把感情、微笑等）压回去→克制，抑制；压制』

❶ [VN] 抑制，克制
If you repress a feeling, you make a deliberate effort not to show or have this feeling. If you repress a smile, sigh, or moan, you try hard not to smile, sigh, or moan.
People who repress their emotions risk having nightmares.
压抑情绪的人容易做噩梦。
He repressed a smile. 他忍住了笑。

❷ [VN] 压制，限制（自由）
If a section of society is repressed, their freedom is restricted by the people who have authority over them.
Turkish Kurds have been repressed for decades by the Ankara government.
土耳其的库尔德人已经被安卡拉政府压制了几十年。

词义辨析 <P380第97> 压制，克制 suppress, repress

6. **oppress** [əˈpres] vt. 压迫；使压抑
『op(=against)对着+press压→对着压→压迫』

❶ [VN] 压迫，压制
These people often are oppressed by the governments of the countries they find themselves in.
这些人经常受到所在国政府的压迫。

❷ [VN] 使心情沉重，使压抑
to make sb only able to think about sad or worrying things
The gloomy atmosphere in the office oppressed her.
办公室的低沉气氛使她感到郁闷。

▶**oppression** [əˈpreʃn] n. 压迫

▶**oppressive** [əˈpresɪv] adj. 压迫的；（环境）令人窒息的

7. **compress** [kəmˈpres , ˈkɒmpres] v. 压缩；精简 n. 敷布
『com一起+press压→压到一起→压缩；精简』
（v. [kəmˈpres]; n. [ˈkɒmpres]）

❶ ~ (sth) (into sth) （被）压紧，压缩
to press or squeeze sth together or into a smaller space
[VN] compressed air/gas 压缩空气/气体
[V] Her lips compressed into a thin line.
她的双唇抿成了一道缝。

❷ [VN] ~ sth (into sth) 精简；浓缩；压缩
The main arguments were compressed into one chapter.

主要的论证被压缩进了一个章。

The four debates will be compressed into an unprecedentedly short eight-day period.

这4场辩论将被压缩到前所未有的短短8天时间。

❸ [C]（医）敷布

词根263. prim(e), prin, prem=first; chief，表示"最初的；首先的；主要的"

① prim(e)=first; chief，表示"最初的；首先的；主要的"

1. prime [praɪm] adj. 首要的；主要的 n. 盛年；鼎盛时期

❶ adj. [only before noun] 首要的；主要的

My prime concern is to protect my property.

我最关心的是保护自己的财产。

Winning is not the prime objective in this sport.

获胜不是这项体育运动的主要目的。

prime minister 首相

The building is a prime example of 1960s architecture.

这座大楼是20世纪60年代的典型建筑。

❷ [sing.] 盛年；鼎盛时期

She won prizes every year when she was in her prime.

她鼎盛时期时每年都获奖。

2. primary ['praɪməri] adj. 主要的；最初的

『prim首先的；主要的；最初的+ary表形容词→首先的；最初的；主要的』

❶ [usually before noun] 主要的；最重要的

The primary aim of this course is to improve your spoken English. 这门课的主要目的是提高你的英语会话能力。

❷ [usually before noun] 最初的；小学教育的

The disease is still in its primary stage.

这病尚处于初始阶段。

primary school 小学

小贴士 小学 primary school; elementary school

3. primitive ['prɪmətɪv] adj. 原始的；落后的

『prim最初的+ itive有…性质的→原始的』

The conditions are primitive by any standards.

无论用什么标准来衡量，其条件都很简陋。

Primitive humans needed to be able to react like this to escape from dangerous animals.

原始人必须能作出这样的反应才能逃离危险的动物。

4. primate ['praɪmeɪt] n. 灵长类；灵长类动物

『prim最初的+(m) ate同伴→（我们）最初的同伴→灵长类』

Today the human brain is three times the size of our primate ancestors.

如今人类大脑是我们祖先灵长类动物大小的三倍。

5. primeval [praɪ'mi:vl] adj. 远古的

『prim最初的+ ev年龄；时代；寿命+ al…的→时间最早的→原始的』

from the earliest period of the history of the world, very ancient

In the vast primeval forest, there are many rare birds and unusual animals. 在大片的原始森林中，有很多珍禽异兽。

6. prior ['praɪə(r)] adj. 先前的；优先的

『pri(=prim)首先的；最初的+or表状态→最初（都存在的）→在前的；优先的』

❶ [only before noun] 事先的；在前的

happening or existing before sth else or before a particular time

This information must not be disclosed without prior written consent. 未事先征得书面许可，此消息不得泄露。

Please give us prior notice if you need an evening meal.

如果您需要用晚餐，请预先通知我们。

❷ [only before noun] 优先的

Mothers with young children have a prior claim on funds.

有年幼子女的母亲有优先索取资金的权利。

❸ **prior to** (formal) 在…之前

Prior to his Japan trip, he went to New York.

在去日本之前，他去了纽约。

It is important to enrich the soil prior to planting.

在种植前给土壤增肥很重要。

▶ **priority** [praɪ'ɒrəti] n. 优先事项；优先

『prior在前的；优先的+ity表名词→优先』

❶ [C] 优先事项；最重要的事；首要事情

Our first priority is to improve standards.

我们的头等大事是提高水平。

Financial security was high on his list of priorities.

在他的心目中，金融安全是十分重要的一环。

❷ [U] ~ (over sth) 优先；优先权

The search for a new vaccine will take priority over all other medical research.

研制新的疫苗将排在其他一切医学研究之前。

② prin=first; chief，表示"最初的；首先的；主要的"

1. principle ['prɪnsəpl] n. 准则；原则，原理

『prin主要的+cip抓+le做某种动作时所使用的东西 →握住主要（原则）→原则』

❶ [C, usually pl., U] 道德原则；行为准则

I refuse to lie about it; it's against my principles.

我绝不为此事撒谎；那是违背我的原则的。

❷ [C] 法则；原则；原理

a law, a rule or a theory that sth is based on

The principle behind it is very simple.

其中的原理十分简单。

These people lack all understanding of scientific principles.

这些人对科学原理一窍不通。

❸ **in principle** 理论上；大体上，基本上

Even assuming this to be in principle possible, it will not be achieved soon.

即使假定这在理论上行得通，它也不可能于短期内实现。

They have agreed to the proposal in principle but we still have to negotiate the terms.

他们已基本同意了这项提议，但我们还得磋商各项条款。

2. principal ['prɪnsəpl] adj. 最主要的 n. 校长

『prin第一+ cip抓+ al表形容词或名词→最重要的；（学校）最重要的（领导）→最重要的；校长』

❶ [only before noun] 最重要的；主要的

Principal means first in order of importance.

New roads will link the principal cities of the area.

新建道路将连通这个地区的主要城市。

The low salary is her principal reason for leaving the job.

工资太低是她辞去那工作的最重要的原因。

❷ [C]（中小学）校长；（英国）大学校长

③ prem=first；chief，表示"最初的；首先的；主要的"

1. premier 英[ˈpremiə(r)] 美 [prɪˈmɪr] adj. 最好的，最重要的 n. 总理；首相

『prem(=first; chief)+i+er表人或物→第一的，主要的→最好的，最重要的；总理（最重要的部长）』

❶ adj. 最好的；最重要的

Premier is used to describe something that is considered to be the best or most important thing of a particular type.

one of the country's premier chefs 国家名厨之一

❷ [C] 总理；首相

Chinese Premier Li Keqiang will pay an official visit to Brazil, Colombia, Peru and Chile from May 18 to 26. 中国总理李克强将于5月18日至26日对巴西、哥伦比亚、秘鲁和智利进行正式访问。

2. premiere 英[ˈpremieə(r)] 美[prɪˈmɪr] n. & v.（电影、戏剧的）首映

『prem(=first)+imere→第一次（演出）→首映 』

The movie will have its premiere in July. 这部电影将于7月间首映。

His new movie premieres in New York this week. 他的新电影本周在纽约首映。

3. premium [ˈpriːmiəm] n. 保险费；附加费 adj. 优质的

『prem(=first)+ium表名词→先付一点（后面得到更多）→保险费；附加费（premium最初词义为prize，付保险费有可能得到理赔，付额外费用会得到更多更优质的服务，at a premium表示"溢价"，都可看作是一种奖赏）』

❶ [C] 保险费

an amount of money that you pay once or regularly for an insurance policy

a monthly premium of £6.25 每月6.25英镑的保险费

❷ [C] 额外费用，附加费

an extra payment added to the basic rate

You have to pay a high premium for express delivery. 快递须付高额的附加费。

❸ adj. 优质的，高端的

Premium goods are of a higher than usual quality and are often expensive.

高档商品的质量比一般商品高，而且往往很贵。

❹ **at a premium** 稀少的，难得的；溢价，以高价（买进或售出）

Space is at a premium in a one-bedroomed apartment. 单居室公寓的空间是很有限的。

The shares are selling at a premium. 这种股票以高于面值的价格出售。

词根264. prise=seize，表示"抓"

1. surprise [səˈpraɪz] n. & v. 吃惊

『sur上面+prise抓→（突然有人）从上面抓（你）你惊不惊→吃惊』

2. comprise [kəmˈpraɪz] vt. 包括；由…组成

『com一起+prise抓→抓到一起（组成一个整体）→包括；由…组成』

❶ 包括；由…组成

The collection comprises 327 paintings. 这部画册收有327幅画。

The committee is comprised of representatives from both the public and private sectors.

委员会由公共和私人部门的双方代表组成。

❷ 是（某事物的）组成部分

Older people comprise a large proportion of those living in poverty. 在那些生活贫困的人中，老年人占有很大的比例。

词义辨析 <P375第73>

由…组成 **make up, consist of, compose, constitute, comprise**

3. enterprise [ˈentəpraɪz] n. 企业；企业经营；事业，项目；事业心，进取心

『enter进入+prise抓→进入（到这个事情，就要用心）抓取→事业心，进取心』

❶ [C]（常指小型）企业，公司

There are plenty of small industrial enterprises. 有许多小型工业企业。

❷ [C]（新的、困难的或重要的）事业，项目，计划

Her latest enterprise (= plan) is to climb Mount Everest. 她最近的计划是攀登珠穆朗玛峰。

❸ [U] 创业；企业经营

Enterprise is the activity of managing companies and businesses and starting new ones.

He is still involved in voluntary work promoting local enterprise. 他仍在从事促进当地企业发展的志愿者工作。

enterprise culture 企业文化

free enterprise 自由企业（体制）

❹ [U] 事业心；进取心；创业精神

eagerness to do something new and clever, despite any risks

We need someone with enterprise and imagination to design a marketing strategy.

我们需要一个有进取心和想象力的人来设计营销策略。

词根265. prive=individual，表示"个人的"

1. private [ˈpraɪvət] adj. 私有的；个人的

『prive个人（去e）+ate表形容词→个人的，私有的』

The sign said, "Private property. Keep out." 标牌上写着："私人领地，禁止进入。"

They were sharing a private joke. 他们讲着外人听不懂的笑话。

private banks/companies/schools 私营银行/公司；私立学校

▶ **privacy** [ˈprɪvəsi] n. 隐私

the state of being alone and not watched or disturbed by other people

She was longing for some peace and privacy. 她渴望过清静的私人生活。

2. deprive [dɪˈpraɪv] vt. 剥夺

『de去掉，离开+prive个人→使离开某个人→剥夺』

deprive sb/sth of sth 剥夺

They were imprisoned and deprived of their basic rights. 他们遭到监禁并被剥夺了基本权利。

3. privilege [ˈprɪvəlɪdʒ] n. 特权；荣幸 v. 特殊对待

『prive个人（去e）+i+leg法律+e→法律上只属于某个人（或某些人的）→特权』

❶ [C]（某人或某团体独享的）特权，优惠

Education should be a universal right and not a privilege. 教育应当是全民的权利而非某部分人特别享有的。

You can enjoy all the benefits and privileges of club

membership. 你可以享受俱乐部成员的一切福利和优惠。

❷ [U]（常指因财富、社会地位而享有的）特权，优惠

Pironi was the son of privilege and wealth, and it showed.
皮罗尼出身于有钱有势的豪门，这看得出来。

❸ [sing.] 荣幸

something that you are proud and lucky to have the opportunity to do　（极少数人因为幸运才有机会享有的特权，所以称为"privilege"）

I hope to have the privilege of working with them again.
但愿有幸与他们再度合作。

It was a great privilege to hear her sing.
听她唱歌真是三生有幸。

❹ [VN] 特殊对待；给予…特权

We want to privilege them because without the top graduate students, we can't remain a top university.
我们希望给予这些最顶尖的研究生特别照顾，因为没有他们，我们就无法继续处于一流大学之列。

▶ **privileged** [ˈprɪvəlɪdʒd] adj. 有特权的；荣幸的

Those in authority were in a privileged position.
有地位者自有特权。

In those days, only a privileged few had the vote.
在那个时代，只有少数特权人物才享有选举权。

I am privileged to have worked with her so often.
我很荣幸能经常和她一起工作。

So I am privileged to have the opportunity to share ideas about US-China relations in the modern era of globalization with you.
所以，能够有机会与诸位就当今全球化时代的美中关系交换意见，我深感荣幸。

▶ **underprivileged** [ˌʌndəˈprɪvəlɪdʒd] adj. 贫困的；弱势的

Underprivileged people have less money and fewer possessions and opportunities than other people in their society.（underprivileged是poor的委婉说法）

government plans to make more jobs available to the underprivileged
旨在为贫困人口创造更多就业机会的政府计划

词根266. proach=become near，表示"接近，靠近"

1. approach [əˈprəʊtʃ] v. 接近；着手处理 n. 方法

❶ （在距离或时间上）靠近，接近

[V] We heard the sound of an approaching car/a car approaching. 我们听见一辆汽车驶近的声音。

❷ 与…接洽；找…商量

If you approach someone about something, you speak to them about it for the first time, often making an offer or request.

[VN] When Chappel approached me about the job, my first reaction was of disbelief.
当查普尔为这份工作找我商量时，我的第一反应是不相信。

❸ [VN] 着手处理；对付

to start dealing with a problem, task, etc. in a particular way

What's the best way of approaching this problem?
什么是处理这个问题的最佳方式？

❹ [C] ~ (to sth) 方法，手段

Your approach to a task, problem, or situation is the way you deal with it or think about it.

We will be exploring different approaches to gathering

information. 我们将探索收集信息的不同方法。

2. reproach [rɪˈprəʊtʃ] n. 责备，批评；没面子
『re又+proach接近→又走上来（责备）→责备』

❶ [U, C] 责备，批评；责备批评的话语

His voice was full of reproach.
他的话里充满了责备的语气。

He listened to his wife's bitter reproaches.
他听了妻子严厉的责备。

❷ [U, C] 没面子；没面子的事

Her actions brought reproach upon herself.
她的举动使她很丢面子。

Such living conditions are a reproach to our society.
这样的生活条件是我们这个社会的耻辱。

词根267. probe, prove=test, examine，表示"测试，检验；仔细检查"

1. probe [prəʊb] v. 盘问，调查；探查 n. 详细调查；太空探测器，医用探针
『probe仔细察看→仔细查看（某事；伤口；太空）→盘问，调查；探查；太空探测器』

❶ ~ (into sth) 盘问，追问，调查

to ask questions in order to find out secrets or hidden information about sb/sth

[V] He didn't like the media probing into his past.
他不愿意媒体追问他的过去。

[VN] a TV programme that probed government scandals in the 1990s 追查20世纪90年代政府丑闻的电视节目

小贴士　中央电视台的"新闻调查"译作"News Probe"

❷ [VN] （用细长工具）探查，查看

The doctor probed the wound for signs of infection.
医生检查伤口是否有感染的迹象。

Searchlights probed the night sky. 探照灯扫视着夜空。

❸ [C] 探究；详尽调查

a police probe into the financial affairs of the company
警方对这家公司财务进行的详细调查

❹ [C] 太空探测器；（医生用的）探针

2. probate [ˈprəʊbeɪt] n. & v. 遗嘱检验；遗嘱认证
『probe仔细查看（去e）+ate表动词→仔细查看（遗嘱）是否有效→遗嘱检验』

Probate cases can go on for two years or more.
遗嘱认证案可能要持续两年或者更长时间。

3. probation [prəˈbeɪʃn] n. 缓刑期；试用期
『probe仔细查看（去e）+ation表名词→仔细查看（是否真正悔改、是否称职）→缓刑期；试用期』

❶ [U] 缓刑期

a system that allows a person who has committed a crime not to go to prison if they behave well and if they see an official regularly for a fixed period of time

The prisoner was put on probation. 犯人已获缓刑。

He was given two years' probation. 他被判缓刑两年。

❷ [U] 试用期，见习期

a time of training and testing when you start a new job to see if you are suitable for the work

After a further four-month extension of her probation period, she was sacked. 在又试用了4个月后，她被开除了。

4. reprobate [ˈreprəbeɪt] n. 堕落的人；不道德的人

『re又，再+probe仔细查看（去e）+ate表名词→反复被仔细查看的人→堕落的人』

a person who behaves in a way that society thinks is immoral

The reprobate and Satan will suffer eternal punishment in hell. 堕落的人和撒旦会在地狱受到永恒的刑罚。

词根268. proper=private，表示"私人的"，引申为"恰当的"

1. proper [ˈprɒpə(r)] adj. 合适的，适当的，得体的

『proper私人的→适合某个人的→合适的，得体的』

Two out of five people lack a proper job.

每五人中有两人没有正当的工作。

The Supreme Court will ensure that the proper procedures have been followed.

最高法院将确保程序的履行合乎规范。

In those days it was not thought entirely proper for a woman to be on the stage.

那个时候，女性登台表演被认为不太得体。

▶ **improper** [ɪmˈprɒpə(r)] adj. 不合适的

▶ **propriety** [prəˈpraɪəti] n. 得体的举止；有分寸的行为

『proper合适的（去e加i）+ety表名词→得体的举止』

[U] moral and social behaviour that is considered to be correct and acceptable

Nobody questioned the propriety of her being there alone.

没人认为她只身出现在那里不得体。

China has always been known as a land of propriety and righteousness. 中国从来以礼仪之邦著称。

2. property [ˈprɒpəti] n. 财产；房地产；特性

『proper私人的+ty表名词→属于私人的财产；属于某类物品（而不是别的类）的特征；财产；特性』

❶ [U] 所有物，财产，财物

a thing or things that are owned by sb

This building is government property.

这座大楼是政府的财产。

Be careful not to damage other people's property.

小心别损及别人的财物。

intellectual property 知识产权

public property 公共财产；公众人物

lost property 失物；失物招领处 （NAmE, lost and found）

❷ [U] 不动产，房地产

land and buildings

The price of property has risen enormously.

房地产的价格大幅上升了。

❸ [C] 房屋及院落

There are a lot of empty properties in the area.

这个地区有大量的闲置房地产。

❹ [C, usually pl.] (formal) 性质；特性

a quality or characteristic that sth has

Compare the physical properties of the two substances.

比较一下这两种物质的物理特性。

a plant with medicinal properties 药用植物

词义辨析 <P378第87>

特性 quality, attribute, characteristic, trait, feature, peculiarity, property

▶ **proprietor** [prəˈpraɪətə(r)] n. 业主，所有人

『proper私人的（去e再加iet）+or表人→业主，所有人』

The proprietor of a hotel, shop, newspaper, or other business is the person who owns it.

newspaper proprietors 报业老板

the proprietor of a local restaurant 一家当地餐馆的老板

▶ **proprietary** [prəˈpraɪətri] adj. 专利的；专卖的

『proper私人的（去e再加iet）+ary…的→属于某人或某公司的→专利的』

made and sold by a particular company and protected by a registered trademark

a proprietary medicine 专卖药品

proprietary brands 专利品牌

a proprietary name 专利名称

3. appropriate [əˈprəʊpriət, əˈprəʊprieɪt] adj. 合适的 vt. 盗用，挪用；拨出（专款）

『ap(=to)+proper合适的；私人的（去e）+i+ate表形容词或动词→合适的；使成为个人的→合适的；盗用，侵占』

（adj. [əˈprəʊpriət]; vt. [əˈprəʊprieɪt]）

❶ ~ (for/to sth) 合适的，恰当的

suitable, acceptable or correct for the particular circumstances

Now that the problem has been identified, appropriate action can be taken.

现在既已找出问题的症结，即可采取适当行动。

Jeans are not appropriate for a formal party.

正式聚会上穿牛仔裤不合适。

❷ [VN] 盗用，挪用，占用，侵吞

to take sth, sb's ideas, etc. for your own use, especially illegally or without permission

He was accused of appropriating club funds.

他被控盗用俱乐部资金。

Some of the opposition party's policies have been appropriated by the government.

反对党的一些政策已被政府挪用。

❸ [VN] 拨出（专款）

If a government or organization appropriates an amount of money for a particular purpose, it reserves it for that purpose.

Five million dollars has been appropriated for research into the disease. 已拨款五百万元用于这种疾病的研究。

4. expropriate [eksˈprəʊprieɪt] vt. 征收，征用（私人财产）

『ex出去+proper私人的（去e）+i+ate表动词→使私人的（财产）出去（成为国家的）→征用』

If a government or other authority expropriates someone's property, they take it away from them for public use.

In our country, it's inevitable to expropriate rural lands in the process of industrialization and the urbanization.

我国工业化和城市化过程中不可避免要征用农村大量的土地。

词根269. proxim=near, close，表示"接近，靠近"

1. approximate [əˈprɒksɪmət, əˈprɒksɪmeɪt] adj. 大约的，近似的 vt. 近似；接近

『ap(=to)+proxim接近+ate表动词或形容词→近似的；接近』（adj. [əˈprɒksɪmət]; v. [əˈprɒksɪmeɪt]）

❶ adj. 大约的；近似的

almost correct or accurate, but not completely so

The cost given is only approximate. 所列成本仅系约计。

❷ 近似；接近

to be similar or close to sth in nature, quality, amount, etc., but not exactly the same

[V] His story approximates to the facts that we already know.
他的陈述和我们已掌握的事实接近。

[VN] The animals were reared in conditions which approximated the wild as closely as possible.
这些动物是在尽可能接近自然的环境下饲养的。

2. proximity [prɒkˈsɪməti] n.（时间或空间）接近，邻近

『proxim接近+ity表名词→接近，邻近』

The proximity of the college to London makes it very popular.
这所学院因靠近伦敦而备受欢迎。

词根270. psych(o)=mind, spirit，表示"心理，精神"

1. psychology [saɪˈkɒlədʒi] n. 心理学；心理特点

『psycho心理，精神+logy…学→心理学』

He obtained his doctorate in Social Psychology.
他获得了社会心理学博士学位。

a fascination with the psychology of murderers
对杀人犯心理的着迷

▶ **psychologist** [saɪˈkɒlədʒɪst] n. 心理学家

2. psychopath [ˈsaɪkəpæθ] n. 精神病患者

『psycho精神+path痛苦；病→患有精神病→精神病人』

a person suffering from a serious mental illness that causes them to behave in a violent way towards other people

▶ **psycho** [ˈsaɪkəʊ] n. 精神病患者

A psycho is someone who has serious mental problems and who may act in a violent way without feeling sorry for what they have done. (an informal and offensive word for psychopath or psychopathic)

Some psycho picked her up, and killed her.
有个变态搭上了她，然后把她杀了。

3. psyche [ˈsaɪki] n. 精神，心灵，内心

『psych精神+e→心智，心灵』

In psychology, your psyche is your mind and your deepest feelings and attitudes.

She knew, at some deep level of her psyche, that what she was doing was wrong.
在她内心深处，她知道自己当时正在做错误的事。

▶ **psychic** [ˈsaɪkɪk] adj. 通灵的；心灵的

4. psychiatry [saɪˈkaɪətri] n. 精神病学

『psych心理，精神+iatry治疗→精神病学』

the study and treatment of mental illness

▶ **psychiatrist** [saɪˈkaɪətrɪst] n. 精神病学家，精神科医生

『psychiatry精神病学（去y)+ist从事某职业的人→精神科医生』

词根271. punct, pung= point；prick，表示"点；刺"

① punct=prick，表示"刺"

1. puncture [ˈpʌŋktʃə(r)] n. 小洞，扎孔 v. 使泄气

❶ [C] (BrE)（轮胎上刺破的）小孔，小洞

I had a puncture on the way and arrived late.
我在路上扎破了轮胎，所以迟到了。

❷ [C]（皮肤上的）扎孔，刺伤

An instrument called a trocar makes a puncture in the abdominal wall.
一种叫做套管针的工具在腹壁上刺了一个孔。

❸ 扎孔，刺破；使泄气

[VN] She was taken to the hospital with broken ribs and a punctured lung. 她肋骨骨折、肺部穿孔，被送往医院。

[V] One of the front tyres had punctured.
一个前轮被扎破了。

[VN] His enthusiasm for fishing had been punctured by the sight of what he might catch.
看到只能钓到这种东西，他钓鱼的热情受到了打击。

2. compunction [kəmˈpʌŋkʃn] n. 内疚，愧疚

『com一起+punct刺+ion表名词→（因为做错事感觉像许多针）一起刺（心）→内疚，愧疚』

[C, U] a guilty feeling about doing sth

She felt no compunction about leaving her job.
她对自己的辞职一点儿也不感到懊悔。

He had lied to her without compunction.
他向她撒了谎却毫无愧疚。

▶ **compunctious** [kəmˈpʌŋkʃəs] adj. 惭愧的，内疚的

He is deeply compunctious for his outburst.
他为自己的大发雷霆深感懊悔。

3. acupuncture [ˈækjupʌŋktʃə(r)] n. 针刺疗法；针灸

『acu尖，锐利+punct刺+ure表行为→用尖（针）刺→针灸』

4. punch [pʌntʃ] vt. 拳打；打孔 n. 拳打；打孔机

『punch(=punct)刺→打孔』

❶ [VN] ~ sth (in/through sth) 打孔

The machine punches a row of holes in the metal sheet.
机器在金属薄板上冲出一排孔。

punch in/out (NAmE) 上下班打卡，刷计时卡

❷ [VN] ~ sb/sth (in/on sth) 拳打；以拳痛击

He was kicked and punched as he lay on the ground.
他倒在地上，被拳打脚踢。

She punched him on the nose.
她一拳打中了他的鼻子。

❸ [VN] 按（键）；压（按钮）

I punched the button to summon the elevator.
我按钮叫电梯。

He punched in the security code. 他输入了密码。

He picked up the telephone and punched out his friend's number. 他拿起电话，拨打朋友的电话号码。

❹ [C] 重拳击打；打孔机

Hill threw a punch at the police officer.
希尔对警察挥了一拳。

❺ [U] 潘趣酒

a hot or cold drink made by mixing water, fruit juice, spices, and usually wine or another alcoholic drink

② punct=point，表示"点"

1. punctual [ˈpʌŋktʃuəl] adj. 按时的，准时的
『punct点+ual有…性质的→（按时间）点的→准时的』

She has been reliable and punctual. 她一直可靠守时。

▶ **punctuality** [ˌpʌŋktʃuˈælɪti] n. 准时，守时

I'll have to have a word with them about punctuality.
我必须和他们谈一谈守时的问题。

2. punctuate [ˈpʌŋktʃueɪt] v. 加标点；不时打断
『punct点+u+ate表动词→（给句子加）点→加标点→（给某人说的话）加上标点→不时打断』

The children have not yet learned to punctuate correctly.
这些孩子尚未学会正确使用标点符号。
Her speech was punctuated by bursts of applause.
她的讲演不时被阵阵掌声打断。

▶ **punctuation** [ˌpʌŋktʃuˈeɪʃn] n. 标点符号；标点用法

He was known for his poor grammar and punctuation.
他不通语法和乱用标点是出了名的。
Jessica scanned the lines, none of which had any punctuation.
杰西卡飞快地扫了一眼这几行，没有任何一行加了标点。

3. punctilious [pʌŋkˈtɪliəs] adj. 一丝不苟的
『punct点+il+ious…的→（做事细致到一个个小）点的→一丝不苟的』

very careful to behave correctly or to perform your duties exactly as you should
He was punctilious about being ready and waiting in the entrance hall exactly on time.
他一丝不苟地作好准备并准时地在门厅等候。

③ pung(相当于 punct)=prick，表示"刺"

1. pungent [ˈpʌndʒənt] adj. （味道或气味）刺激性的；（语言）一针见血的
『pung刺+ent表形容词→（气味、语言等）像刺人的一样→（味道或气味）刺激性的；（语言）一针见血的』

❶ 味道（或气味）强烈的；刺激性的
the pungent smell of burning rubber 烧橡胶的刺鼻气味
The pungent, choking smell of sulphur filled the air.
空气中弥漫着刺鼻呛人的硫黄气味。

❷ 一语道破的，一针见血的
If you describe what someone has said or written as pungent, you approve of it because it has a direct and powerful effect and often criticizes something very cleverly.
He enjoyed the play's shrewd and pungent social analysis.
他喜欢剧中尖锐机敏、一针见血的社会分析。

▶ **pungency** [ˈpʌndʒənsɪ] n. （气味等的）刺激性；（语言）辛辣，尖刻

2. expunge [ɪkˈspʌndʒ] vt. 抹去，除去，删去
『ex出去+punge刺→把（有害的内容）刺掉→抹去，除去』

to remove or get rid of sth, such as a name, piece of information or a memory, from a book or list, or from your mind, because it causes problems or bad feelings
Details of his criminal activities were expunged from the file.
他犯罪活动的详细情况已从档案中删去。
The revolutionaries expunged domestic opposition.
革命者肃清了国内敌对势力。

词根272. pure, purge=pure, clearn，表示"纯的，干净的"

1. pure [pjʊə(r)] adj. 纯的；纯净的；纯粹的 〈P72〉

2. puritan [ˈpjʊərɪtən] n. 清教徒
『pure纯净的（去e加i）+tan表示人→纯粹信教的人→清教徒』

3. impurity [ɪmˈpjʊərəti] n. 杂质；不纯
『im不+pure纯净的（去e）+ity表名词→不纯净』

A filter will remove most impurities found in water.
过滤器会滤掉水中的大部分杂质。

4. purge [pɜːdʒ] vt. 清洗（异己）；清除 n.（对异己的）清洗，清除
『purge纯的，干净的→使纯净，使干净→清洗；清除』

❶ ~ sth (of sb) | ~ sb (from sth)
清除，清洗（组织中的异己分子）
His first act as leader was to purge the party of extremists.
他当上领导的第一件事就是清除党内的极端分子。
He purged extremists from the party.
他把极端分子清除出党。

❷ ~ yourself/sb/sth (of sth) | ~ sth (from sth) 清除；消除
He closed his eyes and lay still, trying to purge his mind of anxiety. 他闭上眼睛躺着不动，试图消除内心的焦虑。
Nothing could purge the guilt from her mind.
她内心的愧疚是无法消除的。

❸ [C]（对异己的）清洗，清除
His own father died during Stalin's purges.
他自己的父亲在斯大林发动清洗运动期间去世。

5. expurgate [ˈekspɜːgeɪt] vt. 删去，删除（著作中有所冒犯或令人震惊之处）
『ex出去+purge纯的，干净的（去e）+ate表动词→使（有冒犯的地方）出去从而变纯净→删去，删除』

He heavily expurgated the work in its second edition.
在第二版中，他对书中内容进行了大幅删减。

6. purgatory [ˈpɜːgətri] n. 炼狱；折磨；苦难
『purge纯的，干净的（去e）+atory表场所→（使灵魂）变纯洁的地方→炼狱』

Purgatory is the place where Roman Catholics believe the spirits of dead people are sent to suffer for their sins before they go to heaven.
Prayers were said for souls in purgatory.
祷告词是为炼狱中的灵魂念的。
Every step of the last three miles was purgatory.
最后3英里时每一步都像是受罪。

词根273. pute=think，表示"认为，思考，相信"

1. compute [kəmˈpjuːt] vt. 计算，估算
『com一起+pute思考→（把几个数放到）一起思考→计算』

▶ **computer** [kəmˈpjuːtə(r)] n. 计算机，电脑

2. dispute [dɪˈspjuːt] n. 争端；争论 v. 争执；争论；质疑
『dis不+pute认为→不（这样）认为→争端，质疑』

❶ [C, U] 争端；争论
a dispute between the two countries about the border
两国间的边界争端
The cause of the accident was still in dispute (= being argued about). 事故的原因仍在争议之中。

❷ 争执；争论

[VN] disputed territory 有争议的领土

[VN] The issue remains hotly disputed.
这个问题至今仍在激烈地辩论中。

❸ 质疑，表示异议

[VN] The family wanted to dispute the will.
家属想对遗嘱提出质疑。

3. reputation [ˌrepjuˈteɪʃn] n. 名誉，名声
『re又，再+pute思考（去e）+ation表名词→反复思考的是（怕影响自己的名声）→名声』

I'm aware of Mark's reputation for being late.
我知道马克迟到是出了名的。

to have a good/bad reputation 有好/坏名声

▶ **repute** [rɪˈpjuːt] n. 名誉，名声

She is a writer of international repute.
她是一位享有国际声誉的作家。

He was a writer of repute. 他曾经是一位颇有名望的作家。

词义辨析 <P380第98>
名声 fame, renown, repute, reputation

4. impute [ɪmˈpjuːt] vt. 归咎于，归罪于
『im(=in)里面+pute认为→内心认为（是某人的错）→归咎于』

It is grossly unfair to impute blame to the United Nations.
把责任归咎于联合国极其不公。

I impute his failure to laziness. 我把他的失败归咎于懒惰。

5. deputy [ˈdepjuti] n. 副职，副手
『de向下+pute思考（去e）+y表名词→（主管不在时又有任务要完成）向下考虑→副职，副手』

A deputy is the second most important person in an organization such as a business or government department. Someone's deputy often acts on their behalf when they are not there.

The deputy airport manager said there was no apparent explanation for the crash.
机场副经理说那次飞机失事没有明显的原因。

词根274. quest=seek, obtain，表示"寻求；获得"

1. request [rɪˈkwest] v. & n.（正式或礼貌地/的）要求，请求
『re又，再+quest寻求→一再寻求某事→要求，请求』

❶ [C] ~ (for sth) | ~ (that...)（正式或礼貌的）要求，请求
They made a request for further aid.
他们要求再给一些帮助。

He was there at the request of his manager.
他按照经理的要求到了那里。

My request was granted. 我的要求得到了满足。

❷（正式或礼貌地）请求，要求

[VN] You can request a free copy of the leaflet.
你可以索要一份免费的宣传单。

[V that] She requested that no one be told of her decision until the next meeting.
她要求下次开会前不要向任何人透露她的决定。

2. quest [kwest] n.（长期艰难的）追求，探索，寻找
『quest(=seek, obtain)→追求，探索』

a long search for something that is difficult to find, or an attempt to achieve something difficult

Nothing will stop them in their quest for truth.
没有什么能阻止他们追求真理。

Industries are still engaged in a quest for increased productivity. 各行业仍在寻求提高生产率。

3. inquest [ˈɪnkwest] n.（死因）调查；（失败）原因调查
『in里面+quest寻求；获得→深入里面寻求（死亡、失败原因）→（死因）调查；（失败）原因调查』

An inquest was held to discover the cause of death.
对死亡原因进行了调查。

An inquest was held on the team's poor performance.
对该队在比赛中的差劲表现进行了检讨。

4. conquest [ˈkɒnkwest] n. 征服，占领；征服的土地
『con一起+quest寻求；获得→征服』

He had led the conquest of southern Poland in 1939.
1939年，他指挥了攻占波兰南部的行动。

▶ **conquer** [ˈkɒŋkə(r)] vt. 征服；克服

❶ [VN] 占领，征服
The Normans conquered England in 1066.
诺曼人于1066年征服了英格兰。

❷ [VN] 克服，攻克
I was certain that love was quite enough to conquer our differences. 我相信爱足以克服我们的种种差异。

5. query [ˈkwɪəri] n. 疑问；问号
『que(=quest)寻求+ry表行为→疑问；问号』

❶ [C] 询问；疑问；问号
Our assistants will be happy to answer your queries.
我们的助理很乐意回答诸位的问题。

If you have a query about your insurance policy, contact our helpline. 若对保险单有疑问，请拨打我们的咨询热线。

You have forgotten to put a query at the end of the sentence.
你忘了在句尾加个问号。

❷ 询问；疑虑

[V speech] "Who will be leading the team?" queried Simon.
"由谁当队长呢？"西蒙问道。

[VN] I'm not in a position to query their decision.
我无权怀疑他们的决定。

词根275. quire, quis=seek, obtain，表示"寻求；获得"

1. inquire/enquire [ɪnˈkwaɪə(r)] v. 询问；调查
『in里面+ quire寻求；获得→深入询问→询问；调查』

❶ 询问，打听
to ask sb for some information

[V] I called the station to enquire about train times.
我打电话到车站询问火车时刻。

[VN] He enquired her name. 他打听她的姓名。

❷ enquire into sth 调查
Inspectors were appointed to inquire into the affairs of the company. 督查员受委派调查该公司的事务。

▶ **inquiry/ enquiry** 英 [ɪnˈkwaɪəri] 美 [ˈɪnkwəri] n. 询问；调查
『inquire询问；调查（去e）+y表行为→询问；调查』

He made some inquiries and discovered she had gone to the Continent. 他打听了一番，发现她已经去了欧洲大陆。

Two men were helping police with their inquiries last night.
两名男子昨晚接受了警方盘问。

▶ **inquisitive** [ɪnˈkwɪzətɪv] adj. 过分打听他人私事的；好探问的；过于好奇的

Don't be so inquisitive. It's none of your business!
别这么追根问底的。这与你无关！

2. require [rɪˈkwaɪə(r)] vt. 需要；要求
『re又，再+quire寻求；获得→一再要获得→需要；要求』

❶ 需要
to need sth; to depend on sb/sth

[VN] These pets require a lot of care and attention.
这些宠物需要悉心照顾。

[V that] The situation required that he be present.
这种情形需要他在场。

[V -ing] Lentils do not require soaking before cooking.
小扁豆在烹饪前不必浸泡。

❷ [often passive] ~ sth (of sb) （尤指根据法规规定）要求
The wearing of seat belts is required by law.
法律规定必须系安全带。

Several students failed to reach the required standard.
有几名学生没有达到规定的标准。

Then he'll know exactly what's required of him.
到那时他就会确切地知道对他的要求是什么了。

▶ **requirement** [rɪˈkwaɪəmənt] n. 必需品；要求

Our immediate requirement is extra staff.
我们亟须增加人手。

Its products met all legal requirements.
它的产品符合所有的法律要求。

▶ **requisite** [ˈrekwɪzɪt] adj. 必须的 n. 必需品

She lacks the requisite experience for the job.
她缺少做这份工作所必需的经验。

A good book is a requisite for long journeys.
一本好书是长途旅行的必需品。

3. exquisite [ɪkˈskwɪzɪt] adj. 精美的，精致的；剧烈的；极度的
『ex出来+quis寻求+ite有…性质的→（努力）寻求出来的→精美的，精致的』

❶ 精美的；精致的
extremely beautiful or carefully made

The Indians brought in exquisite beadwork to sell.
印度人带了精美的珠饰来卖。

❷ 剧烈的，极度的
Exquisite is used to emphasize that a feeling or quality is very great or intense.

The room was decorated in exquisite taste.
这个房间装饰得很高雅。

The words issuing from her lips gave exquisite pleasure as they flowed over him.
听到从她嘴里说出来的话，他感到极大的快乐。

4. acquire [əˈkwaɪə(r)] vt. 获得；购得；（后天）获得
『ac相当于to+quire寻求；获得→寻求到→获得』

❶ 获得；购得
If you acquire something, you buy or obtain it for yourself, or someone gives it to you.

[VN] He acquired the firm in 1978.
他在1978年收购了这家公司。

[VN] Manning hoped to acquire valuable works of art as cheaply as possible.
曼宁希望以尽可能低的价格获得有价值的艺术品。

❷ 获得（技能）；养成（习惯）

If you acquire something such as a skill or a habit, you learn it, or develop it through your daily life or experience.

He spent years acquiring his skills as a surgeon.
他花了好几年时间来学习外科医生的技能。

He acquired a good knowledge of Chinese.
他学得了丰富的汉语知识。

❸ **an acquired taste** 后天养成的爱好
a thing that you do not like much at first but gradually learn to like

Living alone is an acquired taste. 独处是一种修得的境界。

小贴士 AIDS stands for Acquired Immune Deficiency Syndrome. "爱滋病"代表着获得性免疫缺损综合征。

▶ **acquisition** [ˌækwɪˈzɪʃn] n. 获得；购得

❶ [U] （知识、技能等的）获得，习得
He devotes his time to the acquisition of knowledge.
他把时间都花在求知上。

❷ [C] 购得物
They have made acquisitions in several EU countries.
他们在几个欧盟国家购买了一些产业。

▶ **acquisitive** [əˈkwɪzətɪv] adj. 渴求获取财物的

词根276. quit=free; release，表示"自由；释放"

1. quit [kwɪt] v. 辞职；停止（做某事）；离开（某地）
『quit自由→（辞职后）自由→辞职』

[V] If I don't get more money I'll quit. 不给我加薪我就辞职。
[VN -ing] I've quit smoking. 我戒了烟。
[VN] We decided it was time to quit the city.
当时我们决定，该离开城市生活了。

2. acquit [əˈkwɪt] vt. 宣判…无罪；表现好（或坏等）
『ac(=to)+quit自由；释放→（无罪）使自由→宣判无罪』

The jury acquitted him of murder.
陪审团宣告他谋杀罪不成立。

The Senate has voted to acquit President Trump on both articles of impeachment.
参议院投票通过了特朗普总统在两项弹劾条款上的无罪判决。

He acquitted himself brilliantly in the exams.
他在考试中表现出色。

▶ **acquittal** [əˈkwɪtl] n. 无罪判决

The jury voted for acquittal. 陪审团表决赞成判定无罪。

词根277. rase(raze), rade=scrape 表示"刮，擦"

1. erase [ɪˈreɪz] vt. 擦除；抹去
『e出去+rase擦，刮→擦去，抹去』

❶ [VN] 擦掉，抹掉（笔迹等）；抹去，清洗（磁带上的录音或存储器中的信息）
He had erased the wrong word. 他擦去了写错的字。
Parts of the recording have been erased. 部分录音已被抹掉。

❷ [VN] 抹去（想法或感受）
She tried to erase the memory of that evening.
她试图忘却那天晚上的事。

All doubts were suddenly erased from his mind.
他心中所有的疑虑突然烟消云散了。

▶ **eraser** [ɪˈreɪzə(r)] n. 橡皮擦；黑板擦

2. raze [reɪz] vt. 将…夷为平地
『raze擦，刮→（把建筑，城镇等）从地面上刮去→夷为平地』

The village was razed to the ground.
这座村庄被夷为平地。

▶ **razor** [ˈreɪzə(r)] n. 剃须刀；刮脸刀
『raze刮（去e）+or表物→刮（胡须、汗毛）的东西→剃须刀；刮脸刀』

3. abrade [əˈbreɪd] vt. 磨损；擦伤（皮肤）
『ab离开+rade擦，刮→（皮肤被）擦→擦伤』

My skin was abraded and very tender.
我擦破皮了，很疼。

▶ **abrasion** [əˈbreɪʒn] n. （皮肤）擦伤；（表皮）磨损

He suffered cuts and abrasions to the face.
他的脸上有许多划伤和擦伤。
Diamonds have extreme resistance to abrasion.
钻石极抗磨损。

▶ **abrasive** [əˈbreɪsɪv] adj. （人）态度、方式粗鲁伤人的；（物）粗糙的，有研磨性质的 n. 磨料，磨蚀剂

His abrasive manner has won him an unenviable notoriety.
他生硬粗暴的态度让他声名狼藉。
She had abrasions to her wrists where the abrasive rope had scraped her.
她的手腕有多处擦伤，那是被粗糙的绳索刮伤的。
Avoid abrasives, which can damage the tiles.
避免使用磨蚀剂，以免损坏瓷砖。

词根278. rad(ic)=root，表示"根"

1. eradicate [ɪˈrædɪkeɪt] vt. 根除（不好的东西）
『e出来+radic根+ate表动词→（连）根拔出来→根除』

Polio has been virtually eradicated in Brazil.
在巴西脊髓灰质炎实际上已经根除。
We are determined to eradicate racism from our sport.
我们决心要杜绝体育竞技活动中的种族歧视现象。

▶ **eradicable** [ɪˈrædɪkəbl] adj. 可根除的

2. radical [ˈrædɪkl] adj. 根本的；激进的 n. 激进分子
『radic根+al表形容词→（从）根上（都改变）的→根本的；激进的』

[usually before noun]
❶ adj. 根本的，彻底的；全新的
concerning the most basic and important parts of sth; thorough and complete
Radical changes are needed to health systems' design and to training for healthcare workers.
需要对卫生系统的设计和卫生保健工作者的培训进行根本的变革。
The new methods are radically different from the old.
新的方法迥然不同于旧的方法。
a radical solution to the problem 解决问题的根本方法

❷ adj. 激进的；极端的
in favour of thorough and complete political or social change
Radical feminism is currently the fashionable topic among the chattering classes.
激进的女权主义是时下聒噪阶层热议的话题。

❸ [C] 激进分子
He established his reputation as a radical.
他建立了作为激进分子的名声。

词根279. radi(o)=ray，表示"光线"，引申为"辐射；放射"

1. radio [ˈreɪdiəʊ] n. 无线电；收音机
『radi辐射+o→以电磁辐射形式来发射接收信号→无线电；收音机』

2. radium [ˈreɪdiəm] n. 镭
『radi辐射（引申为放射）+um表物质→放射性物质→镭』

3. radius [ˈreɪdiəs] n. 半径；半径范围
『radi辐射+us表名词→（从圆心向周围）辐射的东西（或范围）→半径；半径范围』

He indicated a semicircle with a radius of about thirty miles.
他标示出一个半径大约为30英里的半圆形。
Nigel has searched for work in a ten-mile radius around his home. 奈杰尔一直在他家周围10英里的范围内找工作。

4. radial [ˈreɪdiəl] adj. 放射状的 n. 辐射式轮胎
『radi辐射+al…的→放射的，辐射的』

5. radiate [ˈreɪdieɪt] v. 辐射；发散；散发着
『radi辐射+ate表动词→（光、热、情感等向外）辐射→辐射；发散；散发着』

❶ （热、光、能量）辐射；（路等从中心向外）发散
[V] Heat radiates from the stove. 炉子的热向外散发。
[V] From here, contaminated air radiates out to the open countryside. 被污染的空气从这里扩散到开阔的乡村地区。
The pain started in my stomach and radiated all over my body. 我的疼痛从腹部开始扩散到全身。

❷ 流露，散发（情感、品质）
[VN] He radiated self-confidence and optimism.
他显得自信乐观。

▶ **radiant** [ˈreɪdiənt] adj. （人）容光焕发的；光芒四射的；辐射的

The bride looked radiant. 新娘看上去满面春风。
She was radiant with health. 她身体健康，容光焕发。
The sun was radiant in a clear blue sky.
湛蓝的天空阳光灿烂。
The earth would be a frozen ball if it were not for the radiant heat of the sun.
如果没有太阳辐射的热量，地球将是一个冰封的球体。

▶ **radiance** [ˈreɪdiəns] n. 容光焕发；光辉

There was about her a new radiance. 她焕发出新的神采。
The dim bulb of the bedside lamp cast a soft radiance over his face. 床头灯朦胧的光柔和地投射在他脸上。

▶ **radiator** [ˈreɪdieɪtə(r)] n. 散热器；暖气片；（汽车等的）水箱，冷却器
『radiate辐射（去e）+or表人或物→向外辐射（热量）的东西→散热器；暖气片』

Wade placed his chilled hands on the radiator and warmed them. 韦德把冰凉的双手放在暖气片上取暖。

6. radioactive [ˌreɪdiəʊˈæktɪv] adj. 放射性的
『radio辐射；放射+active活动的→放射性的』

The government has been storing radioactive waste at Fernald for 50 years.
政府在弗纳德存放放射性废料已达50年之久。

7. radiology [ˌreɪdiˈɒlədʒi] n. 放射学
『radi放射+ology学科→放射学』

8. radiotherapy [ˌreɪdiəʊˈθerəpi] n. 放射疗法

『radio放射+therapy治疗→放射疗法』

Surgery and radiotherapy should be combined.
手术和放射治疗必须相结合。

词根280. rap(t), rav=seize, snatch，表示"抓，夺；攫取"

1. rape [reɪp] vt. 强奸 n. 强奸罪
『rape抓→通过暴力手段来实施犯罪→强奸』

▶ **rapist** [ˈreɪpɪst] n. 强奸犯

2. rapacious [rəˈpeɪʃəs] adj. 贪婪的，自私的
『rap抓，攫取+acious…的→抓，攫取（钱财）的→贪婪的』

If you describe a person or their behaviour as rapacious, you disapprove of their greedy or selfish behaviour.
Rapacious soldiers looted the houses in the defeated city.
贪婪的士兵洗劫了被打败的城市。

▶ **rapacity** [rəˈpæsəti] n. 贪婪，贪得无厌

3. raptor [ˈræptə(r)] n. 猛禽
『rapt抓+or表物→抓（地上小动物）的（鸟类）→猛禽』

4. rapt [ræpt] adj. 全神贯注的
『rapt抓→（一个人所有的注意力都被）抓去的→全神贯注的』

If someone watches or listens with rapt attention, they are extremely interested or fascinated.
She listened to the speaker with rapt attention.
她全神贯注地听演讲者讲话。

5. rapture [ˈræptʃə(r)] n. 狂喜，欣喜若狂
『rapt抓+ure表行为→抓到了（自己非常想要的东西）→狂喜』

[U] Rapture is a feeling of extreme happiness or pleasure.
The children gazed at her in rapture.
孩子们欣喜若狂地看着她。
The critics went into raptures about her performance.
评论家们对她的表演赞不绝口。

▶ **rapturous** [ˈræptʃərəs] adj. 兴高采烈的；狂喜的
『rapture狂喜（去e）+ous充满→狂喜的』

The students gave him a rapturous welcome.
学生们欢天喜欢地迎接他。

6. raven [ˈreɪvn] n. 渡鸦 adj. （头发）乌黑的；发亮的
『rav抓，夺+en一种喜欢以"抓夺"来觅食的鸟→渡鸦』

The one I seek has raven hair and lips red as rubies.
我要找的那个人，有乌黑的秀发，红宝石般的嘴唇。

7. ravage [ˈrævɪdʒ] vt. 毁坏，摧毁，搞垮
『rav抓，夺+age表名词→你争我夺（结果造成严重破坏）→毁坏，搞垮』

A town, country, or economy that has been ravaged is one that has been damaged so much that it is almost completely destroyed.

For two decades the country has been ravaged by civil war and foreign intervention.
20年来，这个国家一直被内战外侵所蹂躏。

词根281. rat(e)=calculate, reckon; reason，表示"计算，估算"，
引申为"理由"

1. ration [ˈræʃn] n. 定量，配给量 vt. 配给，定量供应
『rat估算+ion表名词→（在物资匮乏时通过）估算（后分给每个人的量）→定量，配给量』

The meat ration was down to one pound per person per week.
肉的配给量降到了每人每周一磅。
Staples such as bread, rice and tea are already being rationed.
面包、大米和茶叶等日常必需品已实行配给。

2. ratio [ˈreɪʃiəʊ] n. 比例，比率
『rat估算+i+o抽象名词→估算（两个量）之间的关系→比例；也可以联想rate（比例，速率）来记忆』

A ratio is a relationship between two things when it is expressed in numbers or amounts. For example, if there are ten boys and thirty girls in a room, the ratio of boys to girls is 1:3, or one to three.
What is the ratio of men to women in the department?
这个部门的男女比例是多少？
The school has a very high teacher-student ratio.
这所学校的师生比例很高。

3. rational [ˈræʃnəl] adj. 理性的，理智的
『ration(=reason)理由+al…的→（行为、主意等）建立在理由之上的→理性的，理智的』

based on reason rather than emotions
There is no rational explanation for his actions.
对他的所作所为无法作出合理的解释。
No rational person would ever behave like that.
有头脑的人都不会这样做。
She argued her case calmly and rationally.
她冷静而又理智地为她的情况辩解。

▶ **irrational** [ɪˈræʃənl] adj. 不合逻辑的，没有道理的

▶ **rationalist** [ˈræʃnəlɪst] n. 理性主义者，唯理论者

▶ **rationalism** [ˈræʃnəlɪzəm] n. 理性主义；唯理论

4. rationale [ˌræʃəˈnɑːl] n. 基本原理；根本原因
『rat理由+ion表名词+ale→（某个行为或决定的）理由基础→基本原理；根本原因』

the principles or reasons which explain a particular decision, course of action, belief, etc.
However, the rationale for such initiatives is not, of course, solely economic.
然而，这种提议的根据当然并不仅仅是经济方面的。

5. ratify [ˈrætɪfaɪ] v. 正式批准，使正式生效
『rat理由+ify使…→使（协议等）成为（可以为自己行为辩解的）理由→正式批准（协议等）』

to make an agreement officially valid by voting for or signing it
The treaty was ratified by all the member states.
这个条约得到了所有成员国的批准。

词根282. rect=straight, right，表示"直的；正确的"

1. erect [ɪˈrekt] adj. 竖直的 v. 竖立；建立
『e出来+rect直的→使直立（上端露）出来→树立；竖直』

❶ (formal) 垂直的；竖直的

Stand with your arms by your side and your head erect.
手放两边，昂首站立。

❷ [VN] 竖立，搭起；建立
Police had to erect barriers to keep crowds back.
警察得设立路障来阻截人群。
The church was erected in 1582. 此教堂建于1582年。

2. rectify [ˈrektɪfaɪ] vt. 矫正，纠正；改正
『rect正确的；直的+ify使…→使…正确→改正，纠正』
to put right sth that is wrong
We must take steps to rectify the situation.
我们一定要采取措施整顿局面。
The damage will be easily rectifiable.
所受损坏很容易修复。

3. rectitude [ˈrektɪtjuːd] n. 公正；正直；诚实
『rect正确的；直的+ itude表状态→正直；正确』
the quality of thinking or behaving in a correct and honest way
The governor has the rectitude of his motives in policy reforming. 在这次改革中，这位地方长官的动机纯正。

4. rectum [ˈrektəm] n. 直肠
『rect直的+um表名词→直的（内脏器官）→直肠』

▶**rectal** [ˈrektəl] adj. 直肠的

5. rector [ˈrektə(r)] n. （圣公会的）教区牧师；（英国一些大学的）校长
『rect正确的+or表名词→（使人行为）正确的人→教区教师；校长』

6. rectangle [ˈrektæŋgl] n.长方形；矩形〈P113〉
『rect直，正+angle角→（四个角）都是直角→矩形』

词根283. reg=king, 表示"国王"，有时引申为"统治"

1. regal [ˈriːgl] adj. 王者的；豪华的
『reg国王+al具有…性质的→王者的；豪华的』
If you describe something as regal, you mean that it is suitable for a king or queen, because it is very impressive or beautiful.
He sat with such regal dignity.
他端坐在那里，浑身透着王者的威严。
He thought he looked really regal in it.
他觉得穿上它真的很高贵。

2. regent [ˈriːdʒənt] n. 摄政者；摄政王
『reg国王+ent表人→（代替）国王（管理国家的）人→摄政者』
A regent is a person who rules a country when the king or queen is unable to rule, for example because they are too young or too ill.
The regent carried out an advanced system in his country.
摄政者在他的国家推行了一套先进的制度。

▶**regency** [ˈriːdʒənsi] n. 摄政期，摄政

3. regicide [ˈredʒɪsaɪd] n. 弑君（罪）；弑君者
『reg国王+i+cide杀→杀国王→弑君』
He had become czar through regicide.
他通过弑君登上了沙皇宝座。
Some of the regicides were sentenced to death.
一些弑君者被判处死刑。

4. regime [reɪˈʒiːm] n. （尤指未通过公正选举的）政权，政体；管理体制
『reg统治+ime→（近似于国王的那种）统治、管理方式或体系→政权；管理体制』

❶ [C]（尤指未通过公正选举的）政权，政体
a method or system of government, especially one that has not been elected in a fair way
US and other Western intelligence reports say the Assad regime was responsible.
美国和其他西方情报机构称，阿萨德政权（叙利亚政府）应对此负责。

❷ [C] 管理体制
A regime is the way that something such as an institution, company, or economy is run, especially when it involves tough or severe action.
Our tax regime is one of the most favourable in Europe.
我们的税收管理体制是欧洲最受欢迎的税收体制之一。

5. region [ˈriːdʒən] n. 地区，地带；行政区域
『reg统治+ion表名词→（某种特征）占统治地位的地方→（具有某种特征的）地方，区域』

❶ [C]（通常界限不明的）地区，区域，地方
A region is a large area of land that is different from other areas of land, for example because it is one of the different parts of a country with its own customs and characteristics, or because it has a particular geographical feature.
the Arctic/tropical/desert, etc. regions
北极、热带、沙漠等地区
one of the most densely populated regions of North America
北美人口最为稠密的地区之一

❷ [C] 行政区
one of the areas that a country is divided into, that has its own customs and/or its own government
The Hong Kong Special Administrative Region was sworn in by the Central People's Government.
中央人民政府主持了中华人民共和国香港特别行政区的成立和宣誓仪式。

词义辨析 <P380第99>
地区 zone, area, district, region, stretch, belt

6. regiment [ˈredʒɪmənt] n. （军队的）团；一大群
『reg统治+i+ment表名词→统治者所依赖的工具→军（团）』
The task of their regiment was to pin down one of the flanks of the invading army. 他们团的任务是牵制侵略军的侧翼。

7. realm [relm] n. 领域；场所；王国
『reg国王；统治（去e)+alm→国王统治（的范围）→王国』

❶ [C] 领域；场所
an area of activity, interest, or knowledge
in the realm of literature 在文学领域内
At the end of the speech he seemed to be moving into the realms of fantasy. 讲话的最后，他似乎进入了虚幻的境地。
A successful outcome is not beyond the realms of possibility.
最后取得成功并非没有可能。

❷ [C] 王国
a country ruled by a king or queen
The king maintained order within the bounds of his realm.
国王在其王国的疆界之内维持着秩序。

词根284. rend(er)=give，表示"给"

1. surrender [səˈrendə(r)] v. 投降；（被迫）交出

『sur (above) 在上面+render给→（被迫把武器）交给上面→投降；交出』

❶ ~ (yourself) (to sb) 投降

The rebel soldiers were forced to surrender. 叛军被迫投降。

❷ [VN] ~ sth/sb (to sb) （被迫）放弃，交出

They surrendered their guns to the police.
他们向警察交出了枪。

2. render [ˈrendə(r)] vt. 给予；提交；作出；呈现；使变得

『render给→给予（帮助）；提交；给出（判决等）；呈现』

❶ ~ sth (to sb/sth) | ~ (sb) sth 给予（帮助），提供（服务）

[VN] He had a chance to render some service to his country.
他有了一个为国服务的机会。

❷ [VN] (formal) 递交，提交

to present sth, especially when it is done officially

The committee was asked to render a report on the housing situation. 要求委员会提交一份有关住房情况的报告。

❸ [VN]（法庭或权力部门）作出（判决、决定或回应）

The board had been slow to render its verdict.
董事会迟迟未能作出决定。

❹ [VN] 表达；呈现；表演；翻译

to express or present something in a particular way

The artist has rendered the stormy sea in dark greens and browns. 画家用了深绿色和棕色来表现波涛汹涌的大海。

He stood up and rendered a beautiful version of "Summertime". 他站起来表演了一段优美的《夏日时光》。

The Italian phrase can be rendered as "I did my best".
这个意大利语短语可以译为"我尽力了"。

❺ [VN-ADJ] (formal) 使变得，使处于某状态（=make）

It contained so many errors as to render it worthless.
它错误太多，所以毫无用处。

3. rendition [renˈdɪʃn] n. （剧本、诗歌或音乐作品的）演出，表演，演绎

『rend给+ition表行为→给出→呈现→表演』

She lifted her voice during her rendition of the classic opera song. 表演古典歌剧时，她提高了嗓门放声歌唱。

词根285. rept=creep，表示"爬"

1. reptile [ˈreptaɪl] n. 爬行动物

『rept爬+ile表示物→爬行动物』

The sea turtle is the largest reptile in the aquarium.
海龟是现今海洋世界中躯体最大的爬行动物。

2. surreptitious [ˌsʌrəpˈtɪʃəs] adj. 秘密的；鬼鬼祟祟的

『sur下+rept爬+itious有…性质的→在下面爬（以防被看见）的→鬼鬼祟祟的』

done secretly or quickly, in the hope that other people will not notice

She sneaked a surreptitious glance at her watch.
她偷偷看了一眼手表。

His surreptitious behaviour naturally aroused suspicion.
他那鬼鬼祟祟的行为自然引起了旁人的怀疑。

词根286. rid(e), ris=laugh，表示"嘲笑"

1. ridicule [ˈrɪdɪkjuːl] n. & v. 嘲笑，奚落，讥讽

『rid笑+icule→嘲笑』

❶ [VN] 嘲笑；奚落；讥笑

If you ridicule someone or ridicule their ideas or beliefs, you make fun of them in an unkind way.

I admired her all the more for allowing them to ridicule her and never striking back.
她能听任他们嘲笑却从不还击，这让我更加敬佩她。

❷ [U] 嘲笑；奚落；讥笑

If someone or something is an object of ridicule or is held up to ridicule, someone makes fun of them in an unkind way.

She is an object of ridicule in the tabloid newspapers.
她是小报讥笑讽刺的对象。

▶ **ridiculous** [rɪˈdɪkjələs] adj. 愚蠢的，荒谬的，荒唐的

very silly or unreasonable

I look ridiculous in this hat. 我戴这顶帽子看上去很可笑。

It is ridiculous to suggest we are having a romance.
暗示我们正在谈恋爱的说法真是太荒谬了。

2. deride [dɪˈraɪd] vt. 嘲笑，愚弄，揶揄

『de下面+ride嘲笑→在下面嘲笑→嘲笑』

[VN] [often passive] ~ sb/sth (as sth) 嘲笑，愚弄，揶揄

to treat sb/sth as ridiculous and not worth considering seriously

His views were derided as old-fashioned.
他的观点被当作旧思想受到嘲弄。

Opposition MPs derided the Government's response to the crisis. 反对党议员嘲弄政府针对危机做出的反应。

▶ **derisive** [dɪˈraɪsɪv] adj. 嘲笑的

『-ide的形容词形式是-isive，名词形式是-ision』

She gave a short, derisive laugh. 她讥讽地笑了笑。

▶ **derision** [dɪˈrɪʒn] n. 嘲笑，取笑，奚落

『-ide的形容词形式是-isive，名词形式是-ision』

Her speech was greeted with howls of derision.
她的演讲受到阵阵嘲笑。

3. risible [ˈrɪzəbl] adj. 可笑的，滑稽的

『ris嘲笑+ible可以的，能够的→可以被嘲笑的→可笑的』

deserving to be laughed at rather than taken seriously

The notion that they should be pushed aside is risible.
应该把它们推到一边的想法可笑至极。

词根287. rode=bite，表示"咬"，形容词形式为-rosive，名词形式为-rosion

1. erode [ɪˈrəʊd] v. 侵蚀，腐蚀；逐渐毁坏

『e出去+rode咬→（一口一口）咬掉，流走→侵蚀，腐蚀』

❶ 侵蚀；腐蚀；风化

to gradually destroy the surface of sth through the action of wind, rain, etc.; to be gradually destroyed in this way

[VN] The cliff face has been steadily eroded by the sea.
峭壁表面逐渐被海水侵蚀。

[V] The rocks have eroded away over time.
这些岩石随着时间的推移逐渐风化了。

❷ （权威、权利、信心等）逐渐丧失、毁坏

to gradually destroy sth or make it weaker over a period of time; to be destroyed or made weaker in this way

[VN] Her confidence has been slowly eroded by repeated failures. 她的自信心因屡屡失败慢慢消磨掉了。

▶ **erosion** [ɪˈrəʊʒn] n. 侵蚀，腐蚀；（权威、权利、信心等的）逐渐丧失

Tree-planting helps to conserve water and prevent soil erosion. 植树有助于涵养水源，防止水土流失。

The president was facing a very significant erosion of public support. 总统面临着公众支持大幅度下降的局面。

▶ **erosive** [ɪˈrəʊsɪv] adj. 侵蚀性的

They're the most powerful erosive force on our planet. 它们是地球上最强大、最有侵蚀性的力量。

2. **corrode** [kəˈrəʊd] v. （化学）腐蚀，侵蚀
『cor一起+rode咬→（物质被酸等）咬掉，一起流走→侵蚀，腐蚀』

to destroy sth slowly, especially by chemical action; to be destroyed in this way

[VN] Acid corrodes metal. 酸腐蚀金属。

He warns that corruption is corroding Russia.
他警告说腐败正在侵蚀俄罗斯。

▶ **corrosion** [kəˈrəʊʒn] n. 腐蚀，侵蚀

▶ **corrosive** [kəˈrəʊsɪv] adj. 腐蚀性的，侵蚀性的

3. **rodent** [ˈrəʊdnt] n. 啮齿动物
『rode咬（去e）+ent表名词→咬东西的动物→啮齿动物』

词根288. rog=ask，表示"要求；询问"

1. **arrogant** [ˈærəgənt] adj. 傲慢的，自大的
『ar加强+rog要求+ant…的→无理要求（别人）的→傲慢的』

behaving in a proud, unpleasant way, showing little thought for other people

I thought him conceited and arrogant.
我认为他既自负又傲慢。

▶ **arrogance** [ˈærəgəns] n. 傲慢，自大

At times the arrogance of those in power is quite blatant.
有时那些当权者颇为傲慢嚣张。

2. **abrogate** [ˈæbrəgeɪt] vt. 废除，废止（法律、协议等）
『ab去掉+rog要求+ate表动词→要求去掉（法律、协议等）』

If someone in a position of authority abrogates something such as a law, agreement, or practice, they put an end to it.

The next prime minister could abrogate the treaty.
下一任首相可能会废除这个条约。

a proposal to abrogate temporarily the right to strike
暂时取消罢工权的提议

▶ **abrogation** [ˌæbrəˈgeɪʃn] n. 取消，废除

China regrets the abrogation of the Anti-Ballistic Missile Treaty. 中国对《反弹道导弹条约》的废除感到遗憾。

3. **derogatory** [dɪˈrɒgətri] adj. 贬低的；贬义的
『de向下+rog要求+atory有…性质的→（评价别人时）要求（向下，即向"坏处"）的→贬低的』

He refused to withdraw derogatory remarks made about his boss. 他拒绝收回那些贬损老板的话。

4. **interrogate** [ɪnˈterəgeɪt] vt. 讯问；审问；盘问
『inter在…之间+rog要求+ate表动词→在讯问期间要求（说出真相）→讯问；审问；盘问』

to ask sb a lot of questions over a long period of time, especially in an aggressive way

He was interrogated by the police for over 12 hours.

他被警察审问了12个多小时。

▶ **interrogation** [ɪnˌterəˈgeɪʃn] n. 讯问；审问；盘问

She hated her parents' endless interrogations about where she'd been. 她讨厌她的父母没完没了地盘问她去哪里了。

5. **prerogative** [prɪˈrɒgətɪv] n. 特权，优先权
『pre前+rog要求+ative有…性质的→（可以在一般人）之前要求（某种权力的）→特权』

a right or advantage belonging to a particular person or group because of their importance or social position

In many countries education is still the prerogative of the rich.
在许多国家接受教育仍然是富人的特权。

6. **rogue** [rəʊg] n. 捣蛋鬼；无赖，流氓 adj. 非同寻常的；流氓的（程序）；行为失常的
『rog要求+ue→（无理）要求别人的人→无赖，流氓』

❶ [C] 捣蛋鬼，小淘气，小坏蛋

If a man behaves in a way that you do not approve of but you still like him, you can refer to him as a rogue.

He's a bit of a rogue, but very charming.
他好捣蛋，但却很讨人喜欢。

❷ [C] (old-fashioned) 无赖，流氓，恶棍
a man who is dishonest and immoral

The rogue swore against the young man, saying he was a thief. 那个流氓诬赖那个年轻人，说他是小偷。

❸ adj. 非同寻常的，有破坏性的

A rogue element is someone or something that behaves differently from others of its kind, often causing damage.

Computer systems throughout the country are being affected by a series of mysterious rogue programs, known as viruses.
全国的计算机系统都感染了一系列诡异的被称为病毒的流氓程序。

7. **surrogate** [ˈsʌrəgət] adj. 替代的，代用的
『sur下面+rog要求+ate表形容词→要求下面的（替代）→替代的，代用的』

used to describe a person or thing that takes the place of, or is used instead of, sb/sth else

She saw him as a sort of surrogate father.
在她心目中，他仿佛是能替代父亲角色的人。

词根289. rot=wheel；turn，表示"轮子；旋转"

1. **rotate** [rəʊˈteɪt] v. 旋转，转动；轮值，轮换
『rot轮子；旋转+ate表示动词→旋转，转动』

❶ ~ (about/around sth) （使）旋转，转动

[V] Stay well away from the helicopter when its blades start to rotate. 直升机的螺旋桨开始转动时，尽量离远点儿。

[VN] Rotate the wheel through 180 degrees.
将方向盘转动180度。

The earth rotates itself and around the sun.
地球在自转的同时绕太阳公转。

❷ （工作或人员）轮值，轮换

[V] The EU presidency rotates among the members.
欧盟主席一职由其成员国轮流担任。

[VN] We rotate the night shift so no one has to do it all the time. 我们轮流值夜班，这样就不会有人总是夜班了。

▶ **rotating** [rəʊˈteɪtɪŋ] adj. 轮流的；转动的

China has once again become the rotating president of the Security Council after one year.

这是时隔一年后,中国再次成为安理会轮值主席国。

▶ **rotation** [rəʊˈteɪʃn] n. 旋转;轮值

▶ **rotary** [ˈrəʊtəri] adj. 旋转的;转动的

2. rotund [rəʊˈtʌnd] adj. 胖乎乎的,圆胖的

『rot轮子;旋转+und溢出→人肥胖得像轮子一样→圆胖的』

A rotund, smiling, red-faced gentleman appeared.
一位身材圆胖、面带笑容、满脸通红的先生出现了。

词根290. rupt=break,表示"破,断裂"

1. interrupt [ˌɪntəˈrʌpt] v. 插嘴;使暂停

『inter在…之间+rupt断裂→在(讲话)中间打断→插嘴』

❶ ~ (sb/sth) (with sth) 插嘴;打扰;打岔

to say or do sth that makes sb stop what they are saying or doing

[V] Sorry to interrupt, but there's someone to see you.
对不起打扰一下,有人要见你。

❷ [VN] 使暂停;使中断

The game was interrupted several times by rain.
比赛因下雨中断了几次。

▶ **interruption** [ˌɪntəˈrʌpʃən] n. 打断;中断

2. erupt [ɪˈrʌpt] v. (火山)喷发;爆发

『e出+ rupt破,断裂→破裂而喷出→爆发』

❶ (火山)喷发;(岩浆、烟等)喷出

[V] The volcano could erupt at any time.
这座火山随时可能爆发。

[VN] An immense volume of rocks and molten lava was erupted. 大量岩石和熔岩喷发出来。

❷ [V] 爆发

My father just erupted into fury. 我父亲勃然大怒。

Violence erupted outside the embassy gates.
大使馆门外突然发生了暴乱。

▶ **eruption** [ɪˈrʌpʃ(ə)n] n. 爆发

3. bankrupt [ˈbæŋkrʌpt] adj. 破产的,倒闭的 vt. 使破产

『bank银行+rupt破,断裂→银行倒闭→破产的』

❶ adj. 破产的,倒闭的

They went bankrupt in 1993. 他们于1993年破产。

The company was declared bankrupt in the High Court.
那家公司经高等法院宣告破产。

❷ [VN] 使破产,使倒闭

The move to the market nearly bankrupted the firm and its director. 入市几乎使公司及其董事破产。

▶ **bankruptcy** [ˈbæŋkrʌptsi] n. 破产

4. corrupt [kəˈrʌpt] adj. 贪污的;腐败的 v.使腐化;使堕落

『cor一起+rupt破,断裂→(行贿人和受贿人)一起使(制度)破裂→贪污的;腐败的』

❶ adj. (人)贪污的,受贿的,营私舞弊的

(of people) willing to use their power to do dishonest or illegal things in return for money or to get an advantage

The protesters say the government is corrupt and inefficient.
抗议者称政府腐败无能。

❷ of behaviour (行为) 不诚实的;不道德的

dishonest or immoral

corrupt practices 营私舞弊

❸ [VN] 使腐化;使堕落

to have a bad effect on sb and make them behave in an immoral or dishonest way

He was corrupted by power and ambition.
权力与野心使他腐化堕落。

▶ **corruption** [kəˈrʌpʃn] n. 腐败;贪污;贿赂;受贿

The President faces 54 charges of corruption and tax evasion.
总统面临54项腐败和逃税的指控。

5. abrupt [əˈbrʌpt] adj. 突然的;(言行)粗鲁、莽撞的

『ab离去+rupt破,断裂→(突然)断开离开(常规的反应或思路)→突然的;粗鲁的』

❶ 突然的;意外的

sudden and unexpected, often in an unpleasant way

The man's abrupt appearance almost spoiled the party.
那个男人的突然出现几乎搅浑了这场晚会。

Here the river takes an abrupt bend to the west.
这条河在这里急转向西流去。

❷ (言语、行为)粗鲁的,莽撞的,唐突的;生硬的

speaking or acting in a way that seems unfriendly and rude; not taking time to say more than is necessary

She was offended by his abrupt manner.
他的粗鲁无礼的举止触怒了她。

6. disrupt [dɪsˈrʌpt] vt. 扰乱,打乱

『dis离开+rupt破,断裂→断开(使不能正常进行)→扰乱』

to make it difficult for sth to continue in the normal way

Demonstrators succeeded in disrupting the meeting.
示威者成功地扰乱了会议。

Bus services will be disrupted tomorrow because of the bridge closure. 明日公共汽车将因大桥停止通行而受影响。

▶ **disruption** [dɪsˈrʌpʃn] n. 扰乱;打乱

The strike is expected to cause delays and disruption to flights from Britain.
预计罢工将导致英国航班的延误和中断。

▶ **disruptive** [dɪsˈrʌptɪv] adj. 引起混乱的,扰乱性的

Alcohol can produce violent, disruptive behavior.
酒精会引发暴力和破坏性的行为。

7. rupture [ˈrʌptʃə(r)] n. & v. (体内组织、管道容器、关系等)破裂

『rupt破,断裂+ure表行为或结果→破裂』

❶ [C, U] (体内组织等的)断裂,破裂;疝气

the rupture of a blood vessel 血管破裂

I nearly gave myself a rupture lifting that pile of books.
提那一大堆书差点儿让我得了疝气。

❷ [C, U] (管道、容器等)破裂

ruptures of oil and water pipelines 石油和输水管道的爆裂

❸ [C, U] (关系)破裂

The incidents have not yet caused a major rupture in the political ties between countries.
这些事件目前尚未造成国家之间政治关系的严重破裂。

❹ [V, VN] (体内组织、管道容器、关系等)破裂

His stomach might rupture from all the acid.
他的胃可能因为这些酸液而穿孔。

He ruptured himself playing football.
他踢足球引发了疝气。

Certain truck gasoline tanks can rupture and burn in a collision. 某些卡车的油箱在碰撞时可能发生爆裂并起火。

The incident ruptures a recent and fragile ceasefire.
这次事件使最近达成的不堪一击的停火协议破裂。

词根291. sacr(i), sanct=holy，表示"神圣"

① sacr(i)=holy，表示"神圣"

1. sacred [ˈseɪkrɪd] adj. 上帝的，神的；神圣不可侵犯的
『sacr神圣+ed表形容词→神圣的』

❶ 上帝的；神圣的
connected with God or a god; considered to be holy
a sacred image/shrine/temple 圣像/地/殿
Cows are sacred to Hindus. 印度教徒把牛奉为圣物。

❷ 神圣不可侵犯的
Human life must always be sacred.
人的生命在任何时候都必须得到尊重。
For journalists nothing is sacred.
在记者眼里，没有什么是不可冒犯的。

2. sacrifice [ˈsækrɪfaɪs] n. & v. 牺牲；献祭
『sacri神圣+fice做→做神圣的事情→牺牲；献祭』

❶ [C, U] 牺牲，舍弃；祭祀；祭品
Her parents made sacrifices so that she could have a good education.
为了让她受到良好的教育，她的父母作了很多牺牲。
They offered sacrifices to the gods. 他们向众神献上祭品。

❷ [VN] 牺牲，奉献；献祭
The designers have sacrificed speed for fuel economy.
设计者为节省燃料牺牲了速度。
She sacrificed everything for her children.
她为子女牺牲了一切。
The priest sacrificed a chicken. 祭司用一只鸡作祭品。

3. sacrilege [ˈsækrəlɪdʒ] n. （对圣物或圣地的）亵渎
『sacri神圣+lege拿走→盗走圣物→亵渎』

Stealing from a place of worship was regarded as sacrilege.
从礼拜场所偷东西是对神灵的亵渎。
It is a sacrilege to offend democracy.
违反民主是冒天下之大不韪。

▶**sacrilegious** [ˌsækrəˈlɪdʒəs] adj. 亵渎神圣的

4. sacrosanct [ˈsækrəʊsæŋkt] adj. 神圣不可侵犯的
『sacr神圣+o+sanct神圣→比神圣更神圣→神圣不可侵犯或改变的』

If you describe something as sacrosanct, you consider it to be special and are unwilling to see it criticized or changed.
Freedom of the press is sacrosanct.
新闻自由是神圣不可侵犯的。

5. sacrament [ˈsækrəmənt] n. 圣事，圣礼；圣餐
『sacr神圣+a+ment表行为或事物→圣事，圣礼』

an important religious ceremony such as marriage, baptism or communion, or the bread and wine that are eaten and drunk during the service of communion
When the priest does the sacrament of confession we are completely forgiven.
当牧师举行告解圣事时，我们全然获得饶恕。

6. consecrate [ˈkɒnsɪkreɪt] vt. 祝圣；奉为神圣
『con一起+secr(=sacr)神圣+ate使→一起（举行仪式）使（教堂等）圣化→祝圣』

When a building, place, or object is consecrated, it is officially declared to be holy. When a person is consecrated, they are officially declared to be a bishop.
The church was consecrated in 1834.
这座教堂于1834年祝圣。

7. desecrate [ˈdesɪkreɪt] vt. 亵渎（圣物或圣地）
『de坏+secr(=sacr)神圣+ate使→使神圣（的品质）受到破坏→亵渎』

If someone desecrates something which is considered to be holy or very special, they deliberately damage or insult it.
She shouldn't have desecrated the picture of a religious leader.
她不该亵渎宗教领袖的画像。

② sanct=holy，表示"神圣"

1. sanction [ˈsæŋkʃn] n. & vt. 制裁；处罚；批准
『sanct神圣+ion表名词→神圣（给的权力）→制裁；处罚；批准』

❶ [C, usually pl.] ~ (against sb) （对某国的）制裁
an official order that limits trade, contact, etc. with a particular country, in order to make it do sth, such as obeying international law
Trade sanctions were imposed against any country that refused to sign the agreement.
凡拒签该协议的国家均受到贸易制裁。
The economic sanctions have been lifted.
经济制裁业已取消。

❷ [C] 处罚
A sanction is a severe course of action which is intended to make people obey instructions, customs, or laws.
As an ultimate sanction, they can sell their shares.
作为最终的处罚，他们可以出售他们的股份。

❸ [U] (formal)许可，批准
official permission or approval for an action or a change
These changes will require the sanction of the court.
这些变更须经法院认可。

❹ [VN] 制裁；处罚；批准
their failure to sanction Japan for butchering whales in violation of international conservation treaties
对日本违反国际保护条约残杀鲸鱼的行为他们未能进行制裁
The government refused to sanction a further cut in interest rates. 政府拒绝批准进一步降低利率。

2. sanctify [ˈsæŋktɪfaɪ] vt. 使神圣化；批准；认可
『sanct神圣+ify使…→使…神圣化（神圣化了的东西人们自然会认可）→使神圣化；批准；认可』

❶ [VN] 使神圣化
to make sth holy
From the mountains, from the plains, from far-off villages, they came to be sanctified by seeing or touching him.
从山上，从平原，从远方的村庄，他们通过看或摸他而成为圣洁。

❷ [VN] 批准，认可
to make something seem morally right or acceptable or to give something official approval
These arbitrary customs have been sanctified over a long time.
长期以来，这些武断的习俗已经得到了认可。
This was a practice sanctified by tradition.
这是一种合乎传统的做法。

3. sanctuary [ˈsæŋktʃuəri] n. 避难所；禁猎区；圣所
『sanctu(=sanct)神圣+ary场所，地点→圣地；避难所』

❶ [C] 鸟兽保护区；禁猎区
a bird/wildlife sanctuary 鸟类/野生动物保护区

❷ [C, usually sing.] 避难所，庇护所
a safe place, especially one where people who are being chased or attacked can stay and be protected
The church became a sanctuary for the refugees.
教堂成为这些难民的庇护所。

❸ [C] 圣所，圣殿

4. sanctity [ˈsæŋktəti] n. 神圣
『sanct神圣+ity表名词→神圣』

If you talk about the sanctity of something, you mean that it is very important and must be treated with respect.
We must safeguard the uniformity and sanctity of the legal system and prevent or overcome local and departmental protectionism.
我们必须维护法制的统一和神圣，防止或克服地方和部门保护主义。
He believed in Christian values and the sanctity of marriage.
他信仰基督教教义和婚姻的圣洁。

5. sanctimonious [ˌsæŋktɪˈməʊniəs] adj. 故作清高的
『sanct神圣+i+monious更→觉得比别人神圣（高尚）→故作清高的，虚伪的』

giving the impression that you feel you are better and more moral than other people
You sanctimonious little hypocrite!
你这个道貌岸然的伪君子！

词根292. sal, sult=leap，表示"跳"

1. result [rɪˈzʌlt] n. & vi. 结果
『re回来+sult跳→（动作后）跳回来的东西→结果』

result in 导致…的结果
These policies resulted in many elderly people suffering hardship. 这些政策使得许多老人饱受困苦。

result from 由…引起
Many hair problems result from what you eat.
很多头发问题都是由饮食引起的。

▶ **resultant** [rɪˈzʌltənt] adj. 因而发生的
At least a quarter of a million people have died in the fighting and the resultant famines.
至少25万人死于这场战斗和由此引发的饥荒。

2. insult [ɪnˈsʌlt, ˈɪnsʌlt] n. & vt. 谩骂；侮辱
『in使+sult跳→（因为侮辱，使别人想）跳起来→侮辱』

to say or do sth that offends sb
I have never been so insulted in my life!
我一生中从未被如此侮辱过！
The crowd were shouting insults at the police.
人群大声辱骂着警察。

3. exult [ɪgˈzʌlt] vi. 欢欣鼓舞；兴高采烈
『ex出来+ult(=sult)跳→（听说喜讯后高兴得）跳出来→兴高采烈』

~ (at/in sth) 欢欣鼓舞；兴高采烈；喜形于色
to feel and show that you are very excited and happy because of sth that has happened
[V] He leaned back, exulting at the success of his plan.
他向后一靠，为自己计划成功而得意扬扬。

[V speech] "We won!" she exulted.
"我们赢了！"她欣喜若狂道。

4. desultory [ˈdesəltri] adj. 无条理的，漫不经心的
『de向下+sult跳+ory有…性质的→跳下来→（走错路）跳下来（继续漫不经心地走）→无条理的，漫不经心的』

without a clear plan or purpose and showing little effort or interest
He broke into a desultory chat with me over his business affairs. 他突然开始和我漫无边际地谈起他的生意来了。

5. assault [əˈsɔːlt] n. （军队）猛攻；抨击；人身攻击或性侵 adj. 攻击性的（武器） vt. 袭击（某人）
『as(=to) +sault(=sult)跳→向…跳去→进攻』

语气比 assail 强，指突然发起猛烈进攻或近身暴力攻击；也可以指严厉批评某人的观念、计划等。
An assault on the capital was launched in the early hours of the morning. 凌晨时分向首都发起了攻击。
The paper's assault on the president was totally unjustified.
这份报纸对总统的攻击纯属无稽之谈。
Both men were charged with assault.
两人均被控侵犯他人身体罪。
A significant number of indecent assaults on women go unreported. 很大数量的猥亵妇女罪没有举报。
We have seen a dramatic rise of assault weapons being seized in Mexico.
我们看到在墨西哥被缴获的攻击性武器的数量显著增加。
He has been charged with assaulting a police officer.
他被控袭击警察。

6. assail [əˈseɪl] vt. 攻击；抨击；困扰
『as(=to) +sail(=sal)跳→向…跳去→进攻』

❶ [VN] 攻击；抨击
to attack sb violently, either physically or with words
He was assailed with fierce blows to the head.
他的头部遭到猛烈殴打。
The proposal was assailed by the opposition party.
提案遭到反对党的抨击。

❷ [VN] 困扰
to be assailed by worries/doubts/fears
为焦虑/疑虑/担心所困扰

▶ **assailant** [əˈseɪlənt] n. 行凶者，攻击者

7. salient [ˈseɪliənt] adj. 最重要的，显著的
『sal跳+i+ent具有…性质的→跳出来的→最显著的，最重要的』

The salient points or facts of a situation are the most important ones.
She pointed out the salient features of the new design.
她指出新设计的几个显著特征。
He summarized the salient points. 他对要点作了归纳。

词根293. sal(i)=salt，表示"盐"

1. saline [ˈseɪlaɪn] adj. 盐的；含盐的；咸的 n. 盐水
『sal盐+ine…的→含盐的』

Wash the lenses in saline solution. 用盐溶液清洗镜片。

▶ **salinity** [səˈlɪnəti] n. 盐浓度，盐分
They are monitoring ocean currents, salinity and other factors.
他们正在监测洋流、盐度和其他因素。

2. salty ['sɔ:ltɪ] adj. 咸的
『salt盐+y…的→咸的』

3. desalinate [,di:'sælə,neɪt] vt. 去除盐分；淡化海水
『de去掉+saline含盐的（去e）+ate表动词→去掉所含盐分』
（与desalinize、desalt的词义相同）

To make fresh water, more cities are burning fuel to desalinate seawater, but that helps push up the price of oil.
为了制造淡水，更多的城市正在消耗燃料以淡化海水，但这会推高油价。

4. salary ['sæləri] n. 薪金，薪水（尤指按月发放的）
『sal盐+ary表物→古罗马发盐给士兵作为薪饷→薪金』

词根294. sane=healthy，表示"健康的"

1. sane [seɪn] adj. 神志正常的；理智的
『sane健康的→神志正常的；理智的』

❶神志正常的，精神健全的
having a normal healthy mind; not mentally ill
No sane person would do that.
没有一个神志正常的人会做那样的事。
Being able to get out of the city at the weekend keeps me sane. 要不是能出城过周末，我简直快憋疯了。

❷ 明智的，理智的，合乎情理的
sensible and reasonable
After all, there is no sane alternative.
毕竟，我们没有另外一种明智的选择。

▶**sanity** ['sænəti] n. 神志正常，精神健全；理智
His behaviour was so strange that I began to doubt his sanity.
他行为怪异，我有点怀疑他是否神智正常。

2. insane [ɪn'seɪn] adj. 精神错乱的；疯狂的；愚蠢的
『in不+ sane心智健全的→精神错乱的』

The prisoners were slowly going insane.
囚犯正慢慢地变得精神错乱起来。
I must have been insane to agree to the idea.
我肯定是犯傻了，居然同意了这个想法。

▶**insanity** [ɪn'sænəti] n. 精神错乱，精神失常；愚蠢

3. sanitary ['sænətri] adj. 卫生的
『sane健康的（去e）+it+ary表形容词→健康的→卫生的』

❶ [only before noun] 卫生的；环境卫生的；公共卫生的
connected with keeping places clean and healthy to live in, especially by removing human waste
Overcrowding and poor sanitary conditions led to disease in the refugee camps.
过度拥挤和恶劣的卫生状况导致难民营中出现疾病。
The hut had no cooking or sanitary facilities.
这间茅屋里没有厨具和卫生设施。

▶**sanitary towel** (US **sanitary napkin**；Australia **sanitary pad**) 卫生巾

▶**sanitary fittings** (US：**bathroom fittings**) 卫浴产品，卫生设备

❷ （地方）卫生的，干净的
clean; not likely to cause health problems
It's not the most sanitary place one could swim.
这个游泳的地方不太卫生。
The new houses were more sanitary than the old ones had been. 新房子比老房子卫生。

4. sanitation [,sænɪ'teɪʃn] n. 卫生设备；卫生设施体系
『sane健康的（去e）+it+ation表名词→与健康有关的设备→卫生设备，卫生设施体系』

Sanitation is the process of keeping places clean and healthy, especially by providing a sewage system and a clean water supply.
Many illnesses are the result of inadequate sanitation.
许多疾病都来源于不健全的卫生设施。

近义词 **hygiene** ['haɪdʒi:n] n. 卫生
『可以谐音记忆，与"干净"读音相近』

[U] 卫生
the practice of keeping yourself and your living and working areas clean in order to prevent illness and disease
Be extra careful about personal hygiene.
要非常注意个人卫生。

▶**hygienic** [haɪ'dʒi:nɪk] adj. 卫生的
Food must be prepared in hygienic conditions.
食物必须在卫生的环境中制作。

5. sanatorium [,sænə'tɔ:riəm] n. 疗养院
『sanat(=sane)健康+orium地点，场所→（让人重获）健康的场所→疗养院』
（NAmE also sanitarium）

I had tuberculosis and was told I'd be in the sanatorium for two years. 我得了肺结核，被告知要在疗养院待两年。

词根295. sat(i), satis, satur=enough, full，表示"足够；充满"

1. sate [seɪt] vt. 满足（欲望）
『sat（=enough）足够+e→满足（欲望）』
to satisfy a desire

2. satiate ['seɪʃieɪt] vt. 使充分满足
『sati足够+ate使…→使充分满足』

[VN] [usually passive] (formal) 满足
to give sb so much of sth that they do not feel they want any more
The Edinburgh International Festival offers enough choice to satiate most appetites.
爱丁堡国际艺术节提供了足够的选择来满足大多数人的胃口。

▶**insatiable** [ɪn'seɪʃəbl] adj. 无法满足的；贪得无厌的
『in不+sati足够+able能够→不能达到足够的→无法满足的』

If someone has an insatiable desire for something, they want as much of it as they can possibly get.
The public has an insatiable appetite for stories about the famous. 公众对名人有着难以满足的好奇心。

3. satiety [sə'taɪəti] n. 饱足，餍足；满足
『sati足够+ety表状态→饱足；满足』

[U] (formal or technical) 饱足；满足
the state or feeling of being completely full of food, or of having had enough of sth
He stretched in the double luxury of fatigue and satiety, his consciousness drifting.
他在极度疲乏和饱足中舒展身体，渐入梦乡。

4. satisfy ['sætɪsfaɪ] vt. 满足
『satis充满+fy使…的→使充满的→满足』

5. saturate ['sætʃəreɪt] vt. 使湿透；使饱和

『satur足够，充满→ate使→使充满，使饱和（水在衣服里面饱和，意即"湿透"）』

The continuous rain had saturated the soil.
连绵不断的雨水浸透了土壤。

In the last days before the vote, both sides are saturating the airwaves.
选举前最后几天，竞选双方占用了所有的广播电台和电视台。

As the market was saturated with goods and the economy became more balanced, inflation went down.
随着市场上商品饱和，经济趋于平衡，通货膨胀就减弱了。

▶ **saturation** [ˌsætʃəˈreɪʃn] n. 饱和；饱和度

Reforms have led to the saturation of the market with goods.
改革导致市场上商品饱和。

词根296. sav(e), salv(e)=save，表示"救助，拯救"

1. savior [ˈseɪvjə(r)] n. 救世主；拯救者
『sav救助+i+or表人→拯救者』

a person who rescues you from harm or danger

Then a saviour appeared in the form of a man called Arthur Grogan.
接着，一个叫亚瑟·格罗根的人以救世主的身份出现了。

2. salve [sælv] vt. 使良心得到宽慰 n. 药膏
『salve拯救→拯救（良心、疼痛）→使宽慰；药膏』

❶ [VN] ~ your conscience 使良心得到宽慰；减轻内疚感
to do sth that makes you feel less guilty

He gives them a little money to salve his conscience.
他给了他们一些钱以宽慰自己的良心。

❷ [U, C]（治愈伤痛的）药膏；软膏

He could feel the nurse's hands smearing salve on his back again. 他感觉到护士的手又在往他背上擦药膏。

3. salvage [ˈsælvɪdʒ] n.（对财物的）抢救；抢救出的财物 vt. 打捞，营救（船只、财物等）；挽回（局面）
『salv拯救+age表行为→拯救（正在遭受损失的）东西→抢救（财物、船只等）；挽回（局面）』

❶ [U]（对财物等的）抢救；抢救出的财物
the salvage of the wrecked tanker 对失事油轮的打捞
an exhibition of the salvage from the wreck

沉船打捞物品展览

❷ [VN] 打捞，营救（失事船舶等）；抢救（失事船舶、火灾等中的财物）

The wreck was salvaged by a team from the RAF.
失事船只被英国皇家空军救援小组打捞起来。

We only managed to salvage two paintings from the fire.
我们只从火灾中抢救出两幅画。

❸ [VN] 挽救，挽回（局面、尊严、名声等）

He wondered what he could do to salvage the situation.
他不知道怎样才能挽回这个局面。

What can I do to salvage my reputation?
我怎样才能挽回我的名声呢？

4. salvation [sælˈveɪʃn] n. 拯救；拯救者，救世主
『salv拯救+ation表名词→拯救；拯救者』

They were praying for the salvation of the world.
他们在为拯救世界而祷告。

The country's salvation lies in forcing through democratic reforms. 拯救国家的希望在于强制推行民主改革。

I consider books my salvation. 我视书本为救星。

5. salutary [ˈsæljətri] adj. 有益的（尽管往往让人不愉快）
『salut(=salv)拯救+ary表形容词→拯救的，使向好的方面发展的→有益的』

having a good effect on sb/sth, though often seeming unpleasant

It was a salutary experience to be in the minority.
敌众我寡时倒是可以磨炼人。

The accident was a salutary reminder of the dangers of climbing.
这次事故提醒人们注意登山的种种危险，倒也不无益处。

词根297. scend=climb，表示"爬，攀"，名词形式为-scent

1. ascend [əˈsend] v. 上升；升高；登高
『a相当于to+ scend 爬，攀→攀到→登高；上升』

[V] The path started to ascend more steeply.
小径开始陡峭而上。

Mist ascended from the valley. 薄雾从山谷升起。

The air became colder as we ascended.
我们越往上攀登，空气就越冷。

The results, ranked in ascending order, are as follows.
结果按由低到高的顺序排列如下。

Her heart was thumping as she ascended the stairs.
她上楼梯时，心怦怦跳个不停。

▶ **ascent** [əˈsent] n. 上升；升高；登高

The cart began its gradual ascent up the hill.
运货马车开始缓缓上山。

At the other side of the valley was a steep ascent to the top of the hill. 山谷的那边是直达山顶的陡坡。

2. descend [dɪˈsend] v. 降临；下来
『de向下+scend爬，攀→向下爬→下来』

[V] The plane began to descend. 飞机开始降落。

[VN] She descended the stairs slowly.
她缓慢地走下楼梯。

Darkness has now descended and the moon and stars shine hazily in the clear sky.
夜幕降临，晴朗的天空里月影婆娑，星光朦胧。

An uneasy calm descended on the area.
一种令人不安的平静笼罩了该地区。

▶ **descent** [dɪˈsent] n. 下降；下倾；斜坡；血统，出身

All the contributors were of African descent.
所有的撰稿人都是非裔人士。

▶ **descendant** [dɪˈsendənt] n. 后裔，后代；派生物
『descend下来+ant表示人→（从前代）传下来的人→后代』

Many of them are descendants of the original settlers.
他们中许多人都是早期移民的后裔。

His design was a descendant of a 1956 device.
他的设计是从一个1956年的装置衍生而来的。

3. condescend [ˌkɒndɪˈsend] vi. 屈尊，俯就；（对某人）表现出优越感
『con一起+descend下降→（高贵的人）放下架子（和地位低的人）一起→屈尊』

❶ [V to inf] (often disapproving) 屈尊；俯就
If someone condescends to do something, they agree to do it, but in a way which shows that they think they are better than other people and should not have to do it.

We had to wait almost an hour before he condescended to see us. 我们等了几乎一小时他才屈尊来见我们。

❷ [V] ~ to sb （对某人）表现出优越感

to behave towards sb as though you are more important and more intelligent than they are

When giving a talk, be careful not to condescend to your audience.

发表讲话时，注意别对听众表现出高人一等的样子。

▶ **condescending** [ˌkɒndɪˈsendɪŋ] adj. 表现出优越感的；居高临下的

I'm fed up with your money and your whole condescending attitude. 我讨厌你的钱，也受够了你居高临下的态度。

4. **transcend** [trænˈsend] v. 超出，超越（通常的界限）

『tran横过，越过+scend爬→爬越（障碍）→超越』

The best films are those which transcend national or cultural barriers. 最好的电影是那些超越国家或文化障碍的电影。

The underlying message of the film is that love transcends everything else. 这部电影隐含的信息是爱超越了一切。

词根298. sci=know，表示"知道"

1. **science** [ˈsaɪəns] n. 科学

『sci知道+ence状态，行为→知道知识→科学（知识）』

2. **conscience** [ˈkɒnʃəns] n. 良心，良知；内疚

『con一起+science科学，知识→和科学知识在一起→知道是正确还是错误→良心，良知』

❶ [C, U] 良心；良知

the part of your mind that tells you whether your actions are right or wrong

to have a clear/guilty conscience (= to feel that you have done right/wrong) 问心无愧/有愧

❷ [U, C] 内疚；愧疚

a guilty feeling about sth you have done or failed to do

She was seized by a sudden pang of conscience.

她突然感到一阵内疚。

I'll write and apologise. I've had it **on my conscience** for weeks.

我要写信赔礼道歉。几个星期以来我都为此良心不安。

Her **conscience pricked her** as she lied to her sister.

她对姐姐撒谎时良心上感到很不安。

3. **conscious** [ˈkɒnʃəs] adj. 有意识的；注意到的；刻意的

『con一起+sci知道+ous…的→和知道的在一起→有意识的；注意到的』

❶ [not before noun] ~ of (doing) sth | ~ that 意识到；注意到

aware of sth; noticing sth

She's very conscious of the problems involved.

她完全意识到了所涉及的问题。

❷ 神志清醒的；有知觉的；有意识的

able to use your senses and mental powers to understand what is happening

A patient who is not fully conscious should never be left alone. 神志并非完全清醒的病人必须时刻有人照料。

❸ （决定、行动等）有意的，刻意的

A conscious decision or action is made or done deliberately with you giving your full attention to it.

I don't think we ever made a conscious decision to have a big family. 我觉得我们没有刻意地决定要生很多孩子。

environmentally conscious 有环保意识的

They have become increasingly health-conscious.

他们的健康意识越来越强。

▶ **unconscious** [ʌnˈkɒnʃəs] adj. 未注意到的；昏迷的；无意的

He himself seemed totally unconscious of his failure.

他本人似乎对自己的失败全然不知。

By the time ambulancemen arrived he was unconscious.

救护人员到达时他已经不省人事了。

We are breathing, but it is unconscious breathing.

我们有在呼吸，但这是无意识呼吸。

4. **subconscious** [ˌsʌbˈkɒnʃəs] adj. 下意识的 n. 潜意识

『sub下面+ conscious有意识的→下意识的』

Subconsciously, he blames himself for the accident.

他下意识地把事故归咎于自己。

And they do this on a subconscious level.

他们在潜意识层面上这样做。

Because my subconscious feels that someone else is creating this world. 因为我的潜意识感觉到这世界是别人创造的。

5. **conscientious** [ˌkɒnʃiˈenʃəs] adj. 认真的，一丝不苟的

『con全部+sci知道+entious…的→完全知道（自己职责的）→有责任心的→一丝不苟的』

taking care to do things carefully and correctly

We are generally very conscientious about our work.

我们普遍对工作都非常认真。

a conscientious student/teacher/worker

勤勉认真的学生；一丝不苟的老师；认真负责的工人

6. **omniscient** [ɒmˈnɪsiənt] adj. 无所不知的

『omni全部+sci知道+ ent具有…性质的→全知道→ 无所不知的』

No one is omniscient; we're all ignorant about something.

没有人是无所不知的，对于某些事情，我们都很无知。

▶ **omniscience** [ɒmˈnɪsiəns] n. 无所不知

7. **prescience** [ˈpresiəns] n. 预知，先见之明

『pre前，事先+sci知道+ence表名词→预知』

apparent knowledge of things before they happen or come into being

Experience has shown the wisdom of his prescience.

历史经验证明了他的先见之明。

▶ **prescient** [ˈpresiənt] adj. 预知的，先觉的

We can now see how prescient a move it really was.

时至今日，我们知道这一步是多么有先见之明。

词根299. scope=watch; mirror，表示"观察；镜"

1. **telescope** [ˈtelɪskəʊp] n. 望远镜

『tele远处+scope镜→观察远处用的镜→望远镜』

▶ **scope** [skəʊp] n. 机会，能力；（涉及的）范围

❶ [U]（话题、组织、活动、书等所涉及的）范围

the range of things that a subject, an organization, an activity, etc. deals with

This subject lies beyond the scope of our investigation.

这一问题超出了我们的考察范围。

These issues were outside the scope of the article.

这些问题不属本文论述范围。

❷ [U] ~ (for sth) | ~ (for sb) (to do sth) 机会，施展余地

If there is scope for a particular kind of behaviour or activity, people have the opportunity to behave in this way or do that activity.

There's still plenty of scope for improvement.
还有很大的改进余地。

The extra money will give us the scope to improve our facilities.
有了这笔额外资金，我们就能把设备加以改进了。

First try to do something that is within your scope.
你先试着做一件自己力所能及的事。

▶ **cope** [kəʊp] vi. （成功地）对付，处理

[V] ~ (with sth) （成功地）对付，处理

I got to the stage where I wasn't coping any more.
到了这个阶段，我已经无法应付了。

He wasn't able to cope with the stresses and strains of the job.
对付这项工作的紧张与压力，他无能为力。

Desert plants are adapted to cope with extreme heat.
沙漠植物适于耐酷热。

2. **microscope** [ˈmaɪkrəskəʊp] n. 显微镜
『micro微小+scope镜→观察微小东西的镜→显微镜』

3. **periscope** [ˈperɪskəʊp] n. 潜望镜
『peri周围+scope镜→（伸出水面）观察四周情况的镜→潜望镜』

词根300. scribe, script=write, 表示"写"，名词形式为-script, -scription

1. **describe** [dɪˈskraɪb] v. 描述；形容
『de向下+ scribe写→（把具体情况）写下来→描写』

~ sb/sth (to/for sb) | ~ sb/sth (as sth) 描述；形容
[VN] Can you describe him to me?
你能向我描述一下他的样子吗？

The man was described as tall and dark, and aged about 20.
据描述这男人高个子，深色皮肤，年龄在20岁左右。

▶ **description** [dɪˈskrɪpʃn] n. 描述，形容

Police have issued a description of the gunman.
警方发布通告，描述了持枪歹徒的特征。

▶ **descriptive** [dɪˈskrɪptɪv] adj. 描写的；说明的

The term I used was meant to be purely descriptive.
我所用的措辞是纯叙述性的（并非作出判断）。

2. **prescribe** [prɪˈskraɪb] vt. 开药方；规定，指定
『pre预先+scribe写→（抓药之前要）预先写（处方）；预先写（规则）→开处方；（法律、规则）指定』

❶ ~ (sb) sth (for sth) 给…开（药），开处方
He may be able to prescribe you something for that cough.
他也许能给你开一些咳嗽药。

❷ （人、法律、规则）规定，指定
What punishment does the law prescribe for this crime?
法律规定是怎样惩罚这种罪行的？

Do not prescribe to me what I am go to do.
不要规定我做什么事。

▶ **prescription** [prɪˈskrɪpʃn] n. 处方

3. **subscribe** [səbˈskraɪb] vi. 订购；订阅；捐款
『sub下面+scribe写→在（单子）下面写上（名字）→订阅；认购』

❶ [V] ~ (to sth) 定期订购（或订阅等）

to pay an amount of money regularly in order to receive or use sth

We subscribe to several sports channels (= on TV).
我们付费收看好几个体育频道。

Which journals does the library subscribe to?
图书馆订有哪些报刊？

❷ [V] ~ (to sth) 定期交纳（会员费）；定期捐款
I subscribe to a few favourite charities.
我定期向几个喜欢的慈善机构捐款。

▶ **subscription** [səbˈskrɪpʃn] n. 订购，订阅；定期捐款

4. **inscribe** [ɪnˈskraɪb] vt. 刻写；题写
『in里面+ scribe写→把（词语、名字等）写到（石头、金属、书）里面→刻写；题写』

[VN] ~ A (on/in B) | ~ B (with A) 在…上写（词语、名字等）；题；刻
His name was inscribed on the trophy.
他的名字刻在奖杯上。

She signed the book and inscribed the words "with grateful thanks" on it. 她在书上签了名，并题词"谨致深切的感谢"。

▶ **inscription** [ɪnˈskrɪpʃn] n. 刻印文字；题词

The inscription reads: "To Emma, with love from Harry."
题赠写着："献给爱玛，爱你的哈里。"

The inscription of the monument has worn away over a long period of time. 年深月久，碑文已经磨损了。

5. **transcribe** [trænˈskraɪb] vt. 笔录；转写；用音标标音
『trans从…到+ scribe写→从一种形式写为另一种形式→笔录；转写』

❶ 笔录；转写
to record thoughts, speech or data in a written form, or in a different written form from the original
Clerks transcribe everything that is said in court.
书记员把在法庭上所有的话都记录在案。

How many official documents have been transcribed into Braille for blind people?
有多少官方文件已经转写成盲文供盲人阅读？

❷ ~ sth (for sth) 改编（乐曲，以适合其他乐器或声部）
a piano piece transcribed for the guitar
为吉他改编的钢琴曲

❸ 用音标标音

▶ **transcription** [trænˈskrɪpʃn] n. 笔录；转写；（乐曲的）改编

6. **circumscribe** [ˈsɜːkəmskraɪb] vt. 限制，约束（自由、权利、权力等）；画…的外接圆
『circum环绕，周围+scribe写→环绕着写一圈→画外接圆→限制，约束』

The army evidently fears that, under him, its activities would be severely circumscribed.
军方显然担心在他的领导下，军队活动将受到严重制约。

7. **ascribe** [əˈskraɪb] vt. 把…归于…
『a相当于to+scribe写→把…写到（某人身上）→把…归于』

ascribe sth to sb 把…归于…

❶ 认为…是（某人）所写、所说
This play is usually ascribed to Shakespeare.
通常认为这部剧是莎士比亚所写。

He mistakenly ascribes the expression "survival of the fittest" to Charles Darwin.

他错误地认为"适者生存"是查尔斯·达尔文说的。

❷ 把…归因于

He ascribed his failure to bad luck.

他认为自己的失败是运气不好。

❸ 认为…具有…特征

We do not ascribe a superior wisdom to the government or the state. 我们并不认为政府或国家有超凡的智慧。

8. script [skrɪpt] n. 剧本，广播稿；（计算机）脚本 v. 写剧本

『script写→写出来（供演出、执行命令的）东西→剧本，广播稿；（计算机）脚本』

❶ （戏剧、电影）剧本；（广播、电视节目）广播稿

Jenny's writing a film script. 珍妮在写一个电影剧本。

Losing was not in the script. 没想到会输。

❷ [U, C] （计算机）脚本（程序）

a series of instructions for a computer

The bug was caused by an error in the script.

这个故障是由脚本程序出错造成的。

❸ [VN] 写剧本，写广播稿；撰稿

James Cameron scripted and directed both films.

詹姆斯·卡梅隆为这两部电影编剧并执导。

9. postscript [ˈpəʊstskrɪpt] n. （信末签名后的）附言；（正文后的）补充说明

『post (after)之后+script写→（在稿子之后）又写上去的内容→附言』

❶ [C] (abbr. PS)（加于信末的）附言，又及

A brief, handwritten postscript lay beneath his signature.

在他的签名下，有一句简短的手写附言。

She mentioned in the postscript to her letter that the parcel had arrive. 她在信末附笔中说包裹已寄到。

❷ [C] （加在故事、记述、声明末尾的）附言，补充说明；补编

Finally, in the postscript part, I will discuss the relativity of the Franz Kafka's experience and us.

最后，在后记部分中，我将论述卡夫卡作品的经验与我们的相关性。

10. conscript [kənˈskrɪpt, ˈkɒnskrɪpt] vt. 征（兵）；n. 应征入伍者

『con一起，共同+script写→（征兵的与应征的）一起写（征兵合同）→征（兵）』

（v. [kənˈskrɪpt]; n. [ˈkɒnskrɪpt]）

He was conscripted into the army in 1939.

他于1939年应征入伍。

One young conscript rose with a message of thanks, his voice choked with emotion.

一个年轻的新兵起立致谢，激动得声音哽咽。

11. manuscript [ˈmænjuskrɪpt] n. 手稿，原稿

『manu手+script写→手写的→手稿；原稿』

I read her poems in manuscript. 我读过她的诗作的手稿。

12. scripture [ˈskrɪptʃə(r)] n.《圣经》；（某宗教的）圣典，经文，经典

『script写+ure与行为有关之物→经文；文稿』

Scripture, also the Scriptures [pl.] 《圣经》

Hindu scriptures 印度教经文

13. scribble [ˈskrɪbl] v. 草草记下；胡写胡画 n. 潦草的文字；胡写乱画的东西

『scribb(= scribe)写+le表反复，连续→乱写』

❶ ~ (sth) | ~ sth down

草草记下，匆匆书写（尤指因时间仓促）

She scribbled down her phone number and pushed it into his hand. 她匆匆写下自己的电话号码，塞进他手里。

❷ [V, usually + adv./prep.] 胡写；乱画

to draw marks that do not mean anything

Someone had scribbled all over the table in crayon.

不知谁用蜡笔胡写乱画，桌面上都涂满了。

❸ [U, sing.] 潦草的文字；[C, usually pl.] 胡写乱画的东西

How do you expect me to read this scribble?

这种写得歪歪扭扭的东西，让我怎么看？

The page was covered with a mass of scribbles.

那页纸上净是胡写乱画的东西。

词根301. sect, seg=cut, divide，表示"切割；划分"

1. insect [ˈɪnsekt] n. 昆虫

『in以某种方式存在+sect切，割→以类似被切割成一节一节的形式存在（的生物）→昆虫』

The traveller's face was covered with insect bites.

旅行者满脸都是被虫子叮咬的疙瘩。

2. section [ˈsekʃn] n. 部分；部门；截面图；切片

『sect切割；划分+(t)ion表行为或结果→（一个整体分割成的）部分；截面图』

❶ [C] 部分；地段；区域；部门；阶层；（文件的）节，章

any of the parts into which sth is divided

That section of the road is still closed. 那段公路依旧封闭。

the sports section of the newspaper 报纸的体育版

She was standing with a book in her hands near the "English literature" section.

她手里拿着一本书站在"英国文学"区附近。

Passengers are allowed to smoke only in the smoking section.

乘客只能在吸烟区吸烟。

He's the director of the finance section. 他是财务处处长。

These issues will be discussed more fully in the next section.

这些问题将在下一节中有更充分的讨论。

an issue that will affect large sections of the population

涉及人口中广大阶层的问题

The furniture they ordered was transported to them in sections. 他们订购的家具是分装运送的。

❷ [C] 断面图，剖面图，截面图；切片

For some buildings a vertical section is more informative than a plan.

有些建筑的立面图能比平面图提供更多的信息。

Each section is mounted on a slide and examined under the microscope. 每个切片都放在显微镜下检查。

3. sector [ˈsektə(r)] n. （经济的）部门，行业，领域

『sect切割；划分+or表物→（经济领域）分割成的部分』

❶ [C]（经济的）部门，行业，领域

A particular sector of a country's economy is the part connected with that specified type of industry.

In the financial sector, banks and insurance companies have both lost a lot of money.

在金融领域，银行和保险公司都损失惨重。

The new government's policy is to transfer state industries from the public sector to the private sector.

新政府的政策是将国有工业从公共部门转移到私营部门。

The proportion of service sector jobs within the economy has grown. 服务业就业在经济中的比重有所上升。

As the industrial sector grew, more and more of the population moved to the cities.

随着工业部门的发展，越来越多的人口迁往城市。

❷ [C]（尤指军事管制的）区域，地带

Officers were going to retake sectors of the city.

军官们打算重新夺回该市的（防御）区域。

4. intersect [ˌɪntəˈsekt] v. 相交，交叉；横穿

『inter相互之间+sect切割→相互切割→交叉』

❶ [V, VN]（of lines, roads, etc. 线、道路等）相交；交叉

The lines intersect at right angles. 线条垂直相交。

The path intersected with a busy road.

小路与一条繁忙的大路相交。

❷ [VN] [usually passive] ~ sth (with sth) 横穿；贯穿；横断

to divide an area by crossing it

The city is intersected by three main waterways.

该城市由三条主要水路贯穿。

5. intersection [ˌɪntəˈsekʃn] n. 十字路口；交叉

『inter相互之间+sect切割+(t)ion表行为或结果→十字路口』

Traffic lights have been placed at all major intersections.

所有重要的交叉路口都安装了交通信号灯。

6. bisect [baɪˈsekt] v. 对半分，二等分

『bi二，两+ sect切割→一分为二→二等分』

The main street bisects the town from end to end.

这条主干道把整个小镇一分为二。

7. dissect [dɪˈsekt] vt. 解剖；剖析，仔细研究

『dis(=away, off)离开，分开+sect切割；划分→（把一个整体）切割开成一个个部分（进行研究）→解剖；剖析』

❶ [VN] 解剖（人或动植物）

to cut up a dead person, animal or plant in order to study it

In biology classes at school we used to dissect rats.

在学校的生物课上，我们常解剖老鼠。

❷ [VN] 剖析；仔细研究；详细评论

to study sth closely and/or discuss it in great detail

Her latest novel was dissected by the critics.

评论家对她最近出版的一部小说作了详细剖析。

▶ **dissection** [dɪˈsekʃən] n. 解剖；剖析，仔细研究

The novel is really a dissection of nationalism.

这部小说实际上是对民族主义的剖析。

8. sectarian [sekˈteəriən] adj.（宗教）教派的，派性的

『sect分割+ary表示具有某种性质（去y）+ian表性质或人→（宗教中）具有分割性质的（一群人）→派性的』

He was the fifth person to be killed in sectarian violence.

他是宗派暴力中的第5个罹难者。

9. segment [ˈsegmənt , segˈment] n. 部分 vt. 分割

『seg分割+ment表行为或结果→部分』

❶ [C] 部分，片段；（柑橘、柠檬等的）瓣

Lines divided the area into segments.

这一地区用线条分成了若干部分。

She cleaned a small segment of the painting.

她把画上的一小部分擦干净了。

❷ [VN] 分割；划分

Market researchers often segment the population on the basis of age and social class.

市场研究人员常常按年龄和社会阶层划分人口。

词根302. semin, semen=seed，表示"种子"

1. seminal [ˈsemɪnl] adj.（对以后的发展）影响深远的

『semin种子+al表性质→具有种子性质的→（对以后的发展）影响深远的』

The reforms have been a seminal event in the history of the NHS.

这些改革已成为（英国）国民医疗服务体系历史上影响深远的一件大事。

小贴士 sesame [ˈsesəmi] n. 芝麻

2. seminary [ˈsemɪnəri] n. 神学院

『semin种子+ary表场所→培养（宗教）种子（priests, ministers, or rabbis）的地方→神学院』

▶ **seminar** [ˈsemɪnɑː(r)] n. 研讨会；研讨课

❶ [C]（大学教师带领学生作专题讨论的）研讨课

Teaching is by lectures and seminars.

教学形式为讲座和研讨课。

❷ [C] 专题讨论会

A seminar is a meeting where a group of people discuss a problem or topic.

While it will be fun, the seminar also promises to be most instructive.

这次研讨会不仅会有趣，而且也会颇具启发意义。

3. disseminate [dɪˈsemɪneɪt] vt. 散布，传播（信息、知识等）

『dis(=away)+semin种子+ate使→使种子（知识、信息等就像种子，能生根发芽）离开（到不同的地方）→传播』

to spread information, knowledge, etc. so that it reaches many people

It took years to disseminate information about aids in Africa.

在非洲传播有关艾滋病方面的知识耗时数年。

词根303. sen=old，表示"老；年老"

1. senior [ˈsiːniə(r)] adj. 级别（或地位）高的〈P79〉

『sen年老+ior较…的→年老的；级别高的』

2. senile [ˈsiːnaɪl] adj. 年老的；老糊涂的〈P78〉

『sen老+ile易于…的→年老的』

3. senate [ˈsenət] n. 参议院

『sen老+ate表职位→资格老的人组成的团体→参议院』

The Senate is expected to pass the bill shortly.

预计参议院不久就会通过此议案。

▶ **senator** [ˈsenətə(r)] n. 参议员

He has served as a Democratic senator for Texas since 2000.

自2000年以来，他一直是得克萨斯州的民主党参议员。

词根304. sense=feel, feeling，表示"感觉；意义"

1. sense [sens] n. 感觉官能；意义；意识到 v. 感觉；觉察到

『sense感觉到→感觉官能；意识到』

❶ [C] 感觉官能（即视、听、嗅、味、触五觉）

She stared at him again, unable to believe the evidence of her senses. 她再度盯着他看，无法相信自己的眼睛和耳朵。

❷ 感觉到，觉察到，意识到

[VN] Sensing danger, they started to run.

他们感到有危险，撒腿就跑。

[V (that)] Lisa sensed that he did not believe her.

莉萨意识到他不相信她。

❸ [C] 感觉到，意识到；判断力，理解力

Suddenly you got this sense that people were drawing themselves away from each other.

突然间你就有这样一种感觉：人们正在彼此疏远。

He has a very good sense of direction (= finds the way to a place easily). 他的方向感很强。

❹ [C] 意义；含义

The word "love" is used in different senses by different people. "爱"这个字不同的人用来表示不同的意思。

❺ there is no sense in doing sth 做某事没有意义

There's no sense in (= it is not sensible) worrying about it now. 现在大可不必为那件事忧虑。

in a sense 从某种意义上来说

In a sense, both were right. 从某种意义上来说，两者都对。

make sense 可以理解，讲得通；（行为方式）有道理，合乎情理

This sentence doesn't make sense. 这个句子不通。

doesn't make sense/makes no sense 没道理，不合乎情理

It makes sense to buy the most up-to-date version.

买最新的版本是明智的。

Who would send me all these flowers? It makes no sense.

谁会给我送这么多花呢？真不可思议。

It doesn't make any sense to grow economic plants in such a poor country.

在如此贫困的国家种植经济作物是毫无意义的。

make sense of 弄懂，理解

I can't make sense of this poem, but perhaps I will if I read it again.

我弄不懂这首诗的意义，但再读一遍或许我就能读懂了。

come to one's senses/ be brought to one's senses 恢复理智
lose one's senses/ take leave of one's senses 失去理智

They looked at me as if I had taken leave of my senses.

他们看着我，就像我已经失去了理智。

He waited for Dora to come to her senses and return.

他盼着多拉冷静下来后回来。

If she threatens to leave, it should bring him to his senses.

假如她威胁着要走，说不定他会清醒过来。

2. nonsense [ˈnɒnsns] n. 胡扯；愚蠢行为；无意义内容

『non不，非+ sense意义→无意义（的话）→废话』

❶ [U] 谬论；胡扯

Reports that he has resigned are nonsense.

有关他已经辞职的报道是无稽之谈。

You're talking nonsense! 你在胡说八道！

❷ [U] 愚蠢的行为，不可接受的行为

The new teacher won't stand for any nonsense.

这位新教师不会容忍任何无礼行为。

❸ [U] 毫无意义的话或文章

a book of children's nonsense poems 一本儿童打油诗集

Most of the translation he did for me was complete nonsense.

他给我做的大多数译文完全不知所云。

3. sensor [ˈsensə(r)] n. 传感器，感应器

『sense感觉（去e）+or表物→用来感觉（光、声音、气味、远近等的）设备→感应器』

If you buy a drier, look for one with a sensor which switches off when clothes are dry.

你若要买烘干机，找一台带感应器的，可以在衣服干的时候自动断电。

4. sensible [ˈsensəbl] adj. 明智的，合理的；意识到的

『sense感觉（去e）+ible能够的→能感觉到的→合理的』

❶ （人及行为）明智的；理智的；合理的

I think the sensible thing would be to take a taxi home.

我想还是坐出租车回去的好。

She was a sensible girl and did not panic.

她是一个理智的女孩，没有惊慌失措。

❷ 意识到的，可以感觉到的

He did not appear to be sensible of the difficulties that lay ahead. 他似乎对前面的困难并不了解。

There's been a sensible rise in temperature recently.

最近气温明显上升。

5. senseless [ˈsensləs] adj. 无意义的；失去知觉的；不明智的，愚蠢的

『sense感觉；意义+less无→失去知觉的；没有意义的』

His death was a senseless waste of life.

他白浪费了性命，死得毫无意义。

He was beaten senseless. 他被打昏了。

He said it would be senseless to educate a generation for unemployment.

他说为了失业问题教育一代人是毫无意义的。

6. sensitive [ˈsensətɪv] adj. 体贴的；敏感的

『sense感觉（变e为i）+tive具有…性质的→具有容易感觉到性质的→敏感的』

❶ 体贴的，善解人意的

aware of and able to understand other people and their feelings

She is very sensitive to other people's feelings.

她很能体谅他人的感情。

❷ ~ (to sth) 敏感的（过敏的；灵敏的；易怒的；艺术感觉好的）

reacting quickly or more than usual to sth

My teeth are very sensitive to cold food.

我的牙齿对冷的食物很敏感。

The stock exchange is very sensitive to political change.

证券市场对政局变化非常敏感。

a sensitive instrument 灵敏的仪器

Health care is a politically sensitive issue.

医疗卫生是政界的一个敏感问题。

She's very sensitive to criticism. 她一听批评就急。

an actor's sensitive reading of the poem

演员对那首诗富有表现力的朗诵

7. sensuous [ˈsenʃuəs] adj. 愉悦感官的；性感的

『sense感觉（去e）+uous充满的→感觉的；愉悦感官的』

I'm drawn to the poetic, sensuous qualities of her paintings.
我喜欢她的画中那种充满诗意、赏心悦目的特性。
his full sensuous lips 他的丰满性感的嘴唇

8. sensation [senˈseɪʃn] n. 感觉；轰动
『sense感觉（去e）+ation表名词→（身体上的）感觉→感觉，知觉』

❶ [C] （身体上的）感觉，知觉
a feeling that you get when sth affects your body
I had a sensation of falling, as if in a dream.
我有一种坠落的感觉，像在梦中似的。

❷ [U] 感觉能力，知觉能力
She seemed to have lost all sensation in her arms.
她的两条胳膊好像完全失去知觉了。

❸ [C, usually sing.] （莫名其妙的）感觉；总体印象
a general feeling or impression that is difficult to explain; an experience or a memory
He had the eerie sensation of being watched.
他不安地感到有人在监视他。
When I arrived, I had the sensation that she had been expecting me. 我到那儿后，感觉到她一直在等着我。

❹ [C, usually sing., U] 轰动；引起轰动的人（或事物）
News of his arrest caused a sensation.
他被捕的消息引起了轰动。
The band became a sensation overnight.
一夜之间，这支乐队名声大振。

▶ **sensational** [senˈseɪʃənl] adj. 轰动性的；极好的；哗众取宠的

The world champions suffered a sensational defeat.
世界冠军遭遇惨败。
Her voice is sensational. 她的嗓音非常动听。
sensational tabloid newspaper reports 哗众取宠的小报报道

9. consensus [kənˈsensəs] n. 一致的意见，共识
『con共同+sense感觉（去e）+us表名词→感觉相同→一致的意见』

[sing., U] ~ (among sb) | ~ (about sth) | ~ (that…)共识
an opinion that all members of a group agree with
There is a general consensus among teachers about the need for greater security in schools.
教师们对必须加强学校的安保有普遍的共识。

词根305. sent=feel, feeling, 表示"感觉"

1. assent [əˈsent] n. 同意 vi. 同意
『as相当于to+sent感觉→达到同种感觉→同意』

❶ [U] ~ (to sth) (formal) 同意；赞成
official agreement to or approval of sth
The director has given her assent to the proposals.
负责人已表示同意提案。

❷ [V] ~ (to sth) (formal) 同意，赞成（要求、想法或建议）
to agree to a request, an idea or a suggestion
[V] Nobody would assent to the terms they proposed.
谁也不会同意他们提出的条件。

词义辨析 <P375第74>
同意 assent, consent, accede, approve

2. consent [kənˈsent] n. 同意 vi. 同意

『con共同+sent感觉→同感→同意』

❶ [U] ~ (to sth) 同意；准许；允许
permission to do sth, especially given by sb in authority
He is charged with taking a car without the owner's consent.
他因未征得车主的同意自行开走车而受到指控。
Children under 16 cannot give consent to medical treatment.
16岁以下的儿童不得自行同意接受治疗。

❷ ~ (to sth) 同意；准许；允许
He finally consented to go. 他最终同意去了。
He reluctantly consented to his daughter's marriage.
他勉强同意了女儿的婚事。

词义辨析 <P375第74>
同意 assent, consent, accede, approve

3. dissent [dɪˈsent] n. （与官方的）不同意见，异议 vi. 持异议
『dis分离+ sent感觉→感觉有分歧→持不同意见』

❶ [U] （与官方的）不同意见，异议
He is the toughest military ruler yet and has responded harshly to any dissent.
他是迄今最强硬的军事统治者，对任何异议都一律进行打压。
Political dissent would no longer be tolerated.
政见不和将不再被容忍。

❷ [V] ~ (from sth)不同意，持异议（尤指与多数人或权威人士支持的观点、决定相左）
I dissent altogether from such an unwise idea.
我完全不同意这样愚昧的见解。

4. sentiment [ˈsentɪmənt] n. 情绪，态度；伤感
『sent感觉+i+ ment表名词→感觉→情绪；伤感』

❶ [C, U] 态度，情绪；看法（日常多用feeling）
A sentiment that people have is an attitude which is based on their thoughts and feelings.
He was more in touch with public sentiment than many of his critics. 他比许多批评者更能接触公众情绪。
Public sentiment rapidly turned anti-American.
公众情绪迅速转变，开始反对美国。
I must agree with the sentiments expressed by John Prescott.
我不得不对约翰·普雷斯科特的见解表示赞同。

❷ [U] (sometimes disapproving) （失之过度或不恰当的）伤感，柔情，哀伤
Sentiment is feelings such as pity or love, especially for things in the past, and may be considered exaggerated and foolish.
Laura kept that letter out of sentiment.
劳拉因无法释怀而一直保留着那封信。
There is no room for sentiment in business.
在生意场上不能感情用事。

▶ **sentimental** [ˌsentɪˈmentl] adj. 多愁善感的；伤感的

I don't like opera. It's so sentimental.
我不喜欢歌剧。太感伤了。
My mum loves sentimental songs that can make her cry.
我母亲喜欢能让她哭的伤感歌曲。

5. presentiment [prɪˈzentɪmənt] n. 预感；（尤指）不祥之感
『pre预先+sent感觉+i+ ment表名词→预感』

I had a presentiment that he represented a danger to me.

我预感他会给我带来危险。

6. resent [rɪˈzent] v. 怨恨；气愤

『re返回+sent感情→（自己被不公正对待的这种）情感回应→怨恨』

to feel bitter or angry about sth, especially because you feel it is unfair

[VN] I deeply resented her criticism.
我对她的批评感到非常气愤。

[V -ing] He bitterly resents being treated like a child.
他十分厌恶被别人当孩子对待。

[VN -ing] She resented him making all the decisions.
她讨厌什么事都要听他的。

▶ **resentment** [rɪˈzentmənt] n. 怨恨；愤恨

She could not conceal the deep resentment she felt at the way she had been treated.
受到那样的待遇，她无法掩藏内心强烈的愤恨。

词根306. sequ, secute=follow，表示"跟随"

1. consequence [ˈkɒnsɪkwəns] n. 结果；后果

『con一起+sequ跟随+ence表名词→跟随着（某事）一起来的→结果；后果』

[C] ~ (for sb/sth) 结果；后果

This decision could have serious consequences for the industry. 这项决定可能对该行业造成严重后果。

These pilots must now face the consequences of their actions and be brought to trial.
这些飞行员现在必须为自己的行为承担后果并接受审判。

As a consequence, most patients seek treatment too late, and both the direct and indirect costs are considerable.
因此，大多数患者就医太晚，直接和间接费用相当高。

词义辨析 <P367第32>

结果 effect, outcome, consequence, result, aftermath

▶ **consequent** [ˈkɒnsɪkwənt] adj. 随之发生的，作为结果的

The warming of the Earth and the consequent climatic changes affect us all.
地球变暖以及随之而来的气候变化影响着我们所有人。

My car broke down and **consequently** I was late.
我的汽车坏了，所以我迟到了。

▶ **consequential** [ˌkɒnsɪˈkwenʃl] adj. 随之而来的；重要的，有重要意义的

❶ 随之而来的（同 consequent）

retirement and the consequential reduction in income
退休与随之而来的收入减少

❷ 重要的；有重要意义的

The report discusses a number of consequential matters that are yet to be decided.
这份报告讨论了许多有待决定的重大问题。

2. subsequent [ˈsʌbsɪkwənt] adj. 随后的，之后的

『sub下面+sequ跟随+ent表形容词→下面跟随的→随后的』

Subsequent events confirmed our doubts.
后来发生的事证实了我们的怀疑。

Developments on this issue will be dealt with in a subsequent report. 这个问题的发展将在以后的报道中予以说明。

3. sequence [ˈsiːkwəns] n. 一系列；次序 v. 按顺序排列

『sequ跟随+ence表名词→（一个）跟随（一个）→一系列；次序』

❶ [C] 一系列；一连串

He described the sequence of events leading up to the robbery. 他描述了抢劫案发生前的一系列有关情况。

❷ [C, U] 顺序；次序

The tasks had to be performed in a particular sequence.
这些任务必须按一定次序去执行。

❸ [V] 按顺序排列

The human genome has now been sequenced.
人体基因组的序列现已测定。

▶ **sequential** [sɪˈkwenʃl] adj. 按顺序的，序列的

4. consecutive [kənˈsekjətɪv] adj. 连续不断的

『con一起+secute跟随（去e）+ive…的→（一个）跟随（一个）一起→连续不断的』

[usually before noun] 连续不断的

following one after another in a series, without interruption

She was absent for nine consecutive days.
她一连缺席了九天。

America won the championship for the fourth consecutive year. 美国连续四年获得了冠军。

5. persecute [ˈpɜːsɪkjuːt] vt. （因种族、宗教或政治信仰）迫害；骚扰

『per自始至终+ secute跟随→自始至终跟在后面（坏你的事）→迫害』

Throughout history, people have been persecuted for their religious beliefs.
人们因宗教信仰而受迫害的情况贯穿了整个历史。

Why are the media persecuting him like this?
新闻媒体为什么总这样揪住他不放？

6. prosecute [ˈprɒsɪkjuːt] vt. 起诉；控告

『pro向前，在前+secute跟随→跟随（事情发展）向前 →起诉；控告』

~ (sb) (for sth/doing sth) 起诉；控告

If the authorities prosecute someone, they charge them with a crime and put them on trial.

The police have decided not to prosecute because the evidence is not strong enough.
由于证据不足，警方已决定不起诉。

▶ **prosecution** [ˌprɒsɪˈkjuːʃn] n. 起诉，诉讼

❶ [U, C] （被）起诉，检举，告发

Yesterday the head of government called for the prosecution of those responsible for the deaths.
昨天，政府首脑呼吁起诉那些该为这些人的死负责的人。

❷ the prosecution [sing. + sing./pl. v.] 原告，控方（包括原告和原告律师等）

The prosecution has/have failed to prove its/their case.
控方未能证明所控属实。

词根307. sert=join, insert，表示"加入；插入"

1. insert [ɪnˈsɜːt, ˈɪnsɜːt] vt. 插入 n. 插入物

『in里面+sert插入→插入到里面→插入』

（v. [ɪnˈsɜːt]; n. [ˈɪnsɜːt]）

❶ [VN] 插入；嵌入

to put sth into sth else or between two things

Insert coins into the slot and press for a ticket.
把硬币放进投币口，按钮取票。

He took a small key from his pocket and slowly inserted it into the lock.
他从口袋里掏出一把小钥匙，慢慢地插到锁眼里。

Position the cursor where you want to insert a word.
把光标移到你想插入字词的地方。

Later, he inserted another paragraph into his will.
后来他在他的遗嘱中又加了一段。

❷ [C] 插入物；（书报中插入的）活页广告
These inserts fit inside any style of shoe.
这些鞋垫适合任何式样的鞋。

小贴士 电脑键盘上写有Insert（有的只写作Ins）的键是"插入"键。如果你在word上输入文字时，发现输入新的文字，后面原来的文字没有了，这是Insert键启用的缘故，按一下Insert键停用它即可。

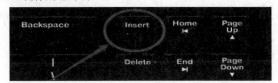

2. concert ['kɒnsət] n. 音乐会，演奏会；一起，共同
『con一起+cert(=sert)加入→加入一起（听音乐，做某事）→音乐会；共同』
in concert 共同（做某事）
He wants to act in concert with other nations.
他想和其他国家采取一致行动。

▶**concerted** [kən'sɜːtɪd] adj. 联合的；竭力的
❶ 联合的，同心协力的
A concerted action is done by several people or groups working together.
Why has there not been concerted action to address this?
为什么没有采取一致行动来解决这一问题？

❷ **make a concerted effort** 竭力的，尽力的
She has begun to make a concerted effort to find a job.
她开始尽全力寻找工作。

3. assert [ə'sɜːt] vt. 断言；坚定主张；表现坚定
『as相当于to+sert插入→（强行把自己的观点）插入到别人身上（使别人相信或承认）→断言；坚定主张』
❶ 明确肯定，断言
to state clearly and firmly that sth is true
[V that] She continued to assert that she was innocent.
她仍然坚称自己无辜。
[VN] She continued to assert her innocence.
她仍然坚称自己无辜。

❷ **assert yourself** 坚持（自己）的主张；表现坚定
If you assert yourself, you speak and act in a forceful way, so that people take notice of you.
He's speaking up and asserting himself confidently.
他明确表态，信心十足地阐述自己的观点。

❸ [VN] 坚定维护自己的权利（或权威）
to make other people recognise your right or authority to do sth, by behaving firmly and confidently
I was determined to assert my authority from the beginning.
我决心一开始就维护我的权威。
The republics began asserting their right to govern themselves. 各加盟共和国开始要求获得自治权。

❹ [VN] ~ itself 生效；起作用
to start to have an effect
Then your true nature asserted itself.
然后你们的真实本性显露了。

▶**assertion** [ə'sɜːʃn] n. 断言；坚决主张，坚持维护
Do you have any evidence to support your assertions?
你的断言是否有真凭实据？
The demonstration was an assertion of the right to peaceful protest. 这次示威游行是使用和平抗议权。

▶**assertive** [ə'sɜːtɪv] adj. 坚定自信的；坚决主张的
They begin to mute their voices, not be as assertive.
他们开始压低嗓门，不再那么肯定了。

▶**reassert** [ˌriːə'sɜːt] vt. 重申；坚持
She found it necessary to reassert her position.
她觉得有必要重申她的立场。

词根308. serve=serve，keep，表示"服务；保持"

1. reserve [rɪ'zɜːv] vt. 预订；保留（权利）　n. 保护区
『re又，再+serve服务→（先保留着，以后）再服务→预订；re又，再+serve保留→保留住（以后）再用→预订』
❶ [VN] ~ sth (for sb/sth) 预订（座位、席位、房间等）
I'd like to reserve a table for three for eight o'clock.
我想预订八点钟供三人用餐的桌位。
I've reserved a room in the name of Jones.
我以琼斯的名字预订了一个房间。
I'd prefer to reserve (my) judgement until I know all the facts.
在了解全部事实之前我保留（我的）意见。

❷ [VN] 拥有，保持，保留（某种权利）
The management reserves the right to refuse admission.
管理部门有权拒绝接收。
（law）All rights reserved. 版权所有。

❸ [C, usually pl.] 储备（量）；储藏（量）
large oil and gas reserves 大量的石油和天然气贮藏量
He discovered unexpected reserves of strength.
他出乎意料地发现还有体力。
reserve funds 储备金

❹ [C]（动植物）保护区；自然保护区(NAmE also **preserve**)
a wildlife reserve 野生动植物保护区

❺ [C] 替补队员；后备部队
He ended up as a reserve, but still qualified for a team gold medal. 他最后成了替补队员，但仍有资格获得团体金牌。
the army reserve(s) 预备役部队

▶**reservation** [ˌrezə'veɪʃn] n. 预订；保留意见
❶ [C] 预订；预约
I'll call the restaurant and make a reservation.
我要给饭店打个电话预订座位。
❷ [C, U] 保留意见
I have serious reservations about his ability to do the job.
我非常怀疑他有没有能力胜任这项工作。

▶**reserved** [rɪ'zɜːvd] adj. 内向的，矜持的
slow or unwilling to show feelings or express opinions
He was unemotional, quite quiet, and reserved.
他感情淡漠，沉默寡言，性格内敛。

词义辨析 <P374第75> 保护 reserve, preserve, conserve

2. reservoir ['rezəvwɑː(r)] n.水库；（大量的）储备,储藏

『reserve保留（去e）+oir表名词→（把水）保留在那里→水库』

A large quantity of water is stored in the reservoir.
水库存了大量的水。

The masses have a vast reservoir of enthusiasm.
群众蕴藏了极大的积极性。

3. preserve [prɪˈzɜ:v] vt. 保护，保存 n. 专门领域，保护区
『pre事先+serve服务→在服务之前（要使其不受破坏）→保护，保存；pre之前+serve（相当于keep）保持→用之前，使其保持（良好状态）→保护；保存』

❶ [VN] 保护（某种特质、物品、食物、生物）不受破坏
He was anxious to preserve his reputation.
他急于维护自己的名声。

Efforts to preserve the peace have failed.
维护和平的努力失败了。

a perfectly preserved 14th century house
保存完好的14世纪房屋

Study on Non-Refrigeration Technology to Preserve Fresh Meat 鲜肉非冷藏保鲜技术研究

Wax polish preserves wood and leather.
上光蜡可保护木材和皮革。

The society was set up to preserve endangered species from extinction. 成立这个协会是为了保护濒危物种不致灭绝。

We should preserve our environment.
我们应该保护我们的环境。

❷ [C] (NAmE) 保护区（同义词 reserve）

▶ **preservation** [ˌprezəˈveɪʃn] n. 保护，维护

the act of keeping sth in its original state or in good condition
building preservation 建筑保护
wood preservation 木材保存

There is great public concern about some of the chemicals used in food preservation.
公众对一些用于食品保存的化学物质非常关注。

She belongs to the Association for the Preservation of Civil War Sites. 她属于内战遗址保护协会。

▶ **preservative** [prɪˈzɜ:vətɪv] n. 防腐剂，保护剂

The juice contains no artificial preservatives.
这种果汁不含人工防腐剂。

词义辨析 <P374第75> 保护 reserve, preserve, conserve

4. conserve [kənˈsɜ:v] vt. 节省；保护
『con一起，共同+serve服务→（和我们享受）服务一起（的是，我们要节约，不浪费资源）→节约；保护（资源等）；con一起+serve保持，保留→（在使用的同时要注意）保留→节省；保护』

❶ [VN] 节省；节约

to use as little of sth as possible so that it lasts a long time
To conserve electricity, we are cutting down on our central heating. 为了节约用电，我们正在减少集中供暖。

I'm not being lazy—I'm just conserving my energy/strength for later.
我不是懒惰——我只是在为以后保存我的能量/力量。

❷ 保护（自然资源等）

to prevent land, water, or other natural resources from being damaged or destroyed
Such information is helpful for developing countries to manage, maintain and conserve their resources.

这些信息对于发展中国家管理、维护和保护它们的资源有一定的帮助。

New laws to conserve wildlife in the area have been published. 保护该地区野生动物的新法律已经颁布。

▶ **conservation** [ˌkɒnsəˈveɪʃn] n. 保护；节约

the protection of the natural environment

[U]（对自然环境、水土的）保护；节约
Conservation programs cannot function without local support.
没有地方的支持，保护项目就无法运作。

词义辨析 <P374第75> 保护 reserve, preserve, conserve

5. servant [ˈsɜ:vənt] n. 仆人
『serve服务（去e）+ant人→服务的人→仆人』

6. service [ˈsɜ:vɪs] n. & vt. 服务
『serve服务（去e）+ice性质，行为，情况→服务』

❶ [C] 服务
The government aims to improve public services, especially education. 政府致力于改善公共服务事业，尤其是教育。
Our main concern is to provide quality customer service.
我们最关心的是为顾客提供优质服务。

at the service of sb/ at sb's service 随时可供使用或帮助
If you need anything, I am at your service.
您要是需要什么，请尽管吩咐。

be of service (to sb) (formal)（对某人）有用，有帮助
Can I be of service to anyone? 有谁需要我帮忙吗？

❷ [VN] 提供服务
Our jobs may be different but we all serve the people.
我们职务不同，但都是为人民服务。

❸ [C] 兵役
After a year's military service, he went to California.
一年的军队服役后，他去了加利福尼亚。

❹ [C] 宗教礼仪，礼拜仪式
After the hour-long service, his body was taken to a cemetery in the south of the city.
在长达一小时的悼念仪式结束后，他的遗体被送到了城南的一所公墓。

❺ **services/ service station/ service area**
（高速路上的）服务站 (US：rest area)

They had to pull up, possibly go to a motorway services or somewhere like that.
他们不得不停车，可能得去高速公路服务站之类的地方。

7. observe [əbˈzɜ:v] vt. 观察；评论；遵守；庆祝（节日）
『ob (agaist) 对着+serve保持→保持对着的状态→观察』

❶ 看到；注意到；观察到
to see or notice sb/sth
observe sb do/doing sth 注意到某人做某事
[VN inf] The police observed a man enter the bank.
警察注意到一个男人走进了银行。
[VN -ing] They observed him entering the bank.

他们看见他走进银行。

❷ 观察

to watch sb/sth carefully, especially to learn more about them

[VN] I felt he was observing everything I did.
我觉得他正在注视着我做的每一件事。

[VN] The patients were observed over a period of several months. 这些病人被观察了数月之久。

❸ 说话；评论

to make a remark

[V that] She observed that it was getting late.
她说天色晚了。

❹ [VN] 遵守（规则、法律等）

We cannot always observe the traditions handed down to us from the past. 我们不能永远遵守过去传下来的传统。

❺ [VN] (formal) 庆祝（节日、生日等）

Do they observe Christmas?
他们过不过圣诞节？

词义辨析 <P362第6>
评论 remark, comment, note, observe

词义辨析 <P361第1>
看 see, watch, observe, look, perceive

▶ **observatory** [əbˈzɜːvətri] n. 天文台
『observe观察（去e）+atory表场所→（天文学家）观察（星星的）地方→天文台』

▶ **observance** [əbˈzɜːvəns] n. 遵守（法律、习俗）；庆祝（节日）

8. **conservative** [kənˈsɜːvətɪv] adj. 保守的，守旧的，（英国）保守党的
『con一起+serve保持（去e）+ative表性质→保持的→保守的』

Her style of dress was never conservative.
她的服装式样一点儿也不保守。

Conservative members/supporters 保守党的党员/支持者

At a conservative estimate , he'll be earning £50,000.
保守估计，他会赚到5万英镑。

9. **servitude** [ˈsɜːvɪtjuːd] n. 奴役；任人差遣
『serve服务（去e）+itude表状况→为别人服务的状况→奴役；任人差遣』

The essay exhorts women to cast off their servitude to husbands and priests.
该文劝告女性不要再对丈夫和牧师低三下四。

10. **servile** [ˈsɜːvaɪl] adj. 奴性的，逢迎的
『serve服务（去e）+ile易于…的→易于为别人服务的→奴性的』

wanting too much to please sb and obey them

They said she had a servile attitude to her employer.
他们说她对她的老板阿谀逢迎。

11. **subservient** [səbˈsɜːviənt] adj. 屈从的，恭顺的；次要的
『sub下面+ serve服务（去e）+ient…的→甘心在下面为别人服务的→屈从的，恭顺的』

too willing to obey other people; less important than sth else

The press was accused of being subservient to the government. 有人指责新闻界一味迎合政府的旨意。

The needs of individuals were subservient to those of the group as a whole. 个人的需求需服从于集体的需求。

词根309. sid(e), sed(e)=sit，表示"坐"

1. **preside** [prɪˈzaɪd] vi. 主持（会议、仪式等）
『pre前面+side坐→坐在前面→主持（会议）』

[V] ~ (at/over sth) 主持（会议、仪式等）

They asked if I would preside at/over the committee meeting.
他们问我是否会主持委员会会议。

2. **president** [ˈprezɪdənt] n. 总统；总裁；校长
『preside主持+(e)nt表人→主持（会议、工作）的人→总统；总裁』

▶ **presidency** [ˈprezɪdənsi] n. 总统（总裁、主席）职位或任期

He was a White House official during the Bush presidency.
他是布什任总统时的白宫官员。

Britain will support him as a candidate for the presidency of the organisation. 英国会支持他竞选这个组织的主席职位。

3. **reside** [rɪˈzaɪd] vi. 居住，定居
『re又，再+ side坐→又重新坐（在某地）→居住（于某地）』

[V + adv./prep.] (formal) 居住在；定居于

to live in a particular place

He returned to Britain in 1939, having resided abroad for many years.
他在国外居住多年以后，于1939年回到了英国。

词义辨析 <P376第76>
居住 reside, inhabit, dwell, live, settle, stay

▶ **resident** [ˈrezɪdənt] n. 居民
『reside居住，定居+(e)nt表人→居住（在某地的）的人』

More than 10 percent of Munich residents live below the poverty line. 超过10%的慕尼黑居民生活在贫困线以下。

▶ **residence** [ˈrezɪdəns] n. 住处，住宅

▶ **residential** [ˌrezɪˈdenʃl] adj. 住宅的
『resident居民+ial表形容词→住宅的，居住的』

They live in a good residential district.
他们居住在一个很好的住宅区。

4. **subside** [səbˈsaɪd] vi. 下沉；下降；减弱
『sub下+side坐→向下坐→下沉』

❶ （地面、建筑物）下沉，沉降
Does that mean the whole house is subsiding?
那意味着整个房子正在下陷吗？

❷ （水位）回落，（尤指洪水）减退，消退
Local officials say the flood waters have subsided.
当地官员称洪水已经退去了。

❸ （感情、斗争、噪声等）减弱，平息
Violence has subsided following two days of riots.
两天的暴乱过后，暴力事件开始平息。
The pain had subsided during the night.
晚间疼痛已经减轻了。
She waited nervously for his anger to subside.
她提心吊胆地等他的怒气平息下来。

5. **subsidy** [ˈsʌbsədi] n. 补贴；补助金
『sub向下+sid坐+y表行为或结果→（使钱）向下坐→使钱下沉到（农民或生产者手中以降低生产或服务的成本）→补贴』

[C, U] 补贴；补助金

money that is paid by a government or an organization to reduce the costs of services or of producing goods so that their prices can be kept low

agricultural subsidies 农业补贴

to reduce the level of subsidy 降低补贴标准

6. subsidiary [səbˈsɪdiəri] adj. 辅助的，次要的 n. 附属公司，子公司

『sub向下+sid坐+i+ary表性质或场所→坐在下面（一级）的→次要的；子公司』

❶ ~ (to sth) 辅助的，次要的

This is only a subsidiary subject in the course of our study.

这只是我们学习课程里的一个辅助科目。

❷ 附属公司；子公司

It set up a wholly owned subsidiary in Australia last year.

它去年在澳大利亚设立了一家全资子公司。

One of our subsidiary companies was a security company.

我们的子公司中有一家保安公司。

7. assiduous [əˈsɪdjuəs] adj. 兢兢业业的，勤勤恳恳的

『as处于某种状态+sid坐+uous…的→（经常）处于坐着（工作或学习）状态的→兢兢业业的』

working very hard and taking great care that everything is done as well as it can be

They planned their careers and worked assiduously to see them achieved.

他们规划了自己的事业，并且勤奋工作以实现目标。

8. dissident [ˈdɪsɪdənt] n. 持不同政见者 adj. 持不同政见的

『dis不；分开+sid坐+ent表性质或人→（与当局者）分开坐的（人）→持不同意见的』

She was suspected of having links with a dissident group.

她被怀疑与一个持不同政见的政治团体有关联。

The dissident was cast out from his country.

这位持不同政见者被驱逐出境。

9. insidious [ɪnˈsɪdiəs] adj. 潜伏的；隐袭的；阴险的

『in里面+sid坐+ious…的→坐在里面（暗中破坏的）→阴险的』

Something that is insidious is unpleasant or dangerous and develops gradually without being noticed.

Discouragement is the most dangerous feeling there is, because it is the most insidious.

沮丧是最危险的感觉，因为它最阴险。

The changes are insidious, and will not produce a noticeable effect for 15 to 20 years.

变化是悄然发生的,15 到 20 年间不会产生明显影响。

10. sedate [sɪˈdeɪt] vt. 给…服镇静剂 adj. 镇静的，泰然的；不苟言笑的

『sed坐+ate使…→使（狂躁的人）坐下来→使镇静』

❶ adj.（人）庄重的，不苟言笑的；宁静的

If you describe someone or something as sedate, you mean that they are quiet and rather dignified, though perhaps a bit dull.

She took them to visit her sedate, elderly cousins.

她带他们去拜访她那些不苟言笑的表兄表姐们。

a sedate country town 宁静的乡间小镇

❷ at a sedate pace 以不慌不忙的/从容的步伐

slow, calm and relaxed

We set off again at a more sedate pace.

我们重新上路了，步调更加从容。

❸ [VN] 给…服镇静剂

Most of the patients are heavily sedated.

多数病人服了大剂量镇静药。

▶**sedative** [ˈsedətɪv] n. 镇静剂

The effects of the sedative have gone off.

镇静剂的作用消失了。

11. sediment [ˈsedɪmənt] n. 沉淀物，沉积物

『sed坐+i+ment表名词→坐下来的东西→沉淀物,沉积物』

Many organisms that die in the sea are soon buried by sediment.

海洋里死亡的许多生物会很快被沉淀物掩埋。

12. supersede [ˌsuːpəˈsiːd] v. 取代，替代（已非最佳选择或已过时的事物）

『super上面+sede坐→坐到…上面→取代』

We must supersede old machines by/with new ones.

我们必须以新机器取代旧机器。

13. residue [ˈrezɪdjuː] n. 残余物，遗留物，残渣

『re返回+sid坐+ue表物→（使用后）又坐回来的东西→残余物，遗留物，残渣』

a small amount of sth that remains at the end of a process

pesticide residues in fruit and vegetables

残留在水果和蔬菜中的杀虫剂

Always using the same shampoo means that a residue can build up on the hair.

总是用同一种洗发水就意味着某种残留物会在头发上越积越多。

14. sedentary [ˈsedntri] adj.（工作等）需要久坐的；（人）惯于久坐的；（人）定居的，（动物、鸟）不迁徙的

『sed坐+ent具有…性质的+ary…的→坐着的；久坐的』

a sedentary job/occupation/lifestyle

倾向于久坐的工作/职业/生活方式

He became increasingly sedentary in later life.

到晚年，他变得越来越不爱动了。

Rhinos are largely sedentary animals.

大致说来，犀牛是一种定栖动物。

词根310. sight=vision，表示"视力；视野"

1. sight [saɪt] n. 视力；看见；视野；景象

❶ [U] 视力；视觉 （the ability to see）

She has very good sight. 她的视力很好。

The disease has affected her sight. 这种病影响了她的视力。

short-sighted (UK) / near-sighted (US)

近视的；目光短浅的

My husband is extremely long-sighted while I am very short-sighted. 我丈夫深度远视，而我则严重近视。

He's being very short-sighted about this.

在这件事上他的目光非常短浅。

❷ [U] ~ of sb/sth 看见

I have been known to faint at the sight of blood.

大家都知道，我看到血就会晕倒。

She caught sight of a car in the distance.

她看见远处有一辆汽车。

It was love **at first sight** (= we fell in love the first time we saw each other). 我们一见钟情。

❸ [U] 视力范围；视野

the area or distance within which sb can see or sth can be seen

She never lets her daughter out of her sight.
她从来不让女儿走出她的视线范围。

Get out of my sight! (= Go away!) 滚开！

out of sight, out of mind (saying) 眼不见，心不想

❹ [C] 看见（或看得见）的事物；景象；情景

The bird is now a rare sight in this country.
如今在这个国家，这种鸟已罕见了。

The museum attempts to recreate the sights and sounds of wartime Britain. 博物馆试图再现战时英国的情景。

❺ sights [pl.] 名胜；风景

the interesting places, especially in a town or city, that are often visited by tourists

We're going to Paris for the weekend to see the sights.
我们打算去巴黎过周末，参观那里的名胜。

2. sightseeing [ˈsaɪtsiːɪŋ] n. & v. 观光，游览
『sight风景+see看+ing表名词→观光』

Let's go sightseeing in Shanghai sometime.
咱们哪天到上海逛逛去吧。

Did you have a chance to do any sightseeing?
你有没有出去游览的机会？

3. insight [ˈɪnsaɪt] n. 洞察力；深刻见解
『in里面+sight视野，景象+（看到）里面的景象（的能力）→洞察力；深刻见解』

❶ [U] (approving) 洞察力；领悟

the ability to see and understand the truth about people or situations

He was a man with considerable insight.
他是个富有洞察力的人。

❷ [C, U] ~ (into sth) 深刻见解

These texts give the reader an insight into the Chinese mind.
这些文章使读者对中国人的思维有了深层次的认识。

词根311. sign=mark，表示"记号，标记，信号"

1. signal [ˈsɪɡnəl] n. 信号；暗号 v. 发信号；标志
『sign信号+al表物→信号』

He signalled to the waiter for the bill. 他示意服务员结账。
This announcement signalled a clear change of policy.
这个声明显示政策有明显的改变。
When I give the signal, run! 我一发信号，你就跑！
Kurdish leaders saw the visit as an important signal of support.
库尔德领导人将这次访问视作一种表示支持的重要信号。

2. resign [rɪˈzaɪn] v. 辞职
『re又，再+sign记号；签字→（入职时在劳务合同上签字）再签字（走人）→辞职』

❶ 辞职
[V] He resigned as manager after eight years.
八年后，他辞去了经理的职务。
[VN] My father resigned his directorship last year.
我父亲去年辞去了董事的职位。

❷ **resign oneself to** 屈从

If you resign yourself to an unpleasant situation or fact, you accept it because you realize that you cannot change it.
She was not a woman to resign herself to fate.
她不是一个愿意屈从于命运的女子。

▶ **resignation** [ˌrezɪɡˈneɪʃn] n. 辞职；辞职信

There were calls for her resignation from the board of directors. 有人要求她辞去董事会中的职务。
We haven't received his resignation yet.
我们还没有收到他的辞呈。

3. assign [əˈsaɪn] vt. 布置（工作、任务）；指定；指派
『as表示to+sign标记→（把某任务）标记给（某人）布置；指派』

❶ ~ sth (to sb) | ~ (sb) sth 分派，布置（工作、任务等）
to give sb sth that they can use, or some work or responsibility
[VN] The two large classrooms have been assigned to us.
这两间大教室分配给了我们。
The teacher assigned a different task to each of the children.
老师给每个儿童布置的作业都不相同。

❷ ~ sb (to sth/as sth) 指定；指派
to provide a person for a particular task or position
[VN] They've assigned their best man to the job.
他们指派了最优秀的人担任这项工作。
[VN to inf] British forces have been assigned to help with peacekeeping. 英国军队被派遣协助维持和平。

▶ **assignment** [əˈsaɪnmənt] n. 工作，任务；分派，布置

❶ [C, U] （分派的）工作，任务
You will need to complete three written assignments per semester. 你每学期要完成三个书面作业。

❷ [U] （工作等的）分派，布置
Task assignment is the selection of a person or group that will be responsible for a task.
任务分配就是对负责一项任务的人员或组的选择。

4. signature [ˈsɪɡnətʃə(r)] n. 签名；典型特征
『sign标记，做标记+ature表行为或结果→做上（某人的）标记→签名』

❶ [C, U] 签名；署名
He was attacked for having put his signature to the deal.
他因在协议上签了字而受到攻击。
Two copies of the contract will be sent to you for signature.
合同一式两份，将送交您签署。

❷ [C, usually sing.] 明显特征
Nobody suggests it is first-rate music, but the whole world recognises it as Vienna's signature tune.
也许没有人说它是一流的音乐，但全世界都认为它是带有鲜明维也纳特征的乐曲。

5. signify [ˈsɪɡnɪfaɪ] v. 表示，表明
『sign标志+ify使…→使成为…的标志』

to be a sign of sth
[VN] This decision signified a radical change in their policies.
这个决定表明了他们的政策发生了根本的变化。
[V that] This mark signifies that the products conform to an approved standard.
这个标志说明这些产品符合指定的标准。
[VN] She signified her approval with a smile.
她笑了笑表示赞同。

[V that] He nodded to signify that he agreed.
他点头表示同意。

▶ **significant** [sɪɡˈnɪfɪkənt] adj. 有重要意义的；明显的
『sign记号，标志+i+ficant…的→具有标志意义的→有重大意义的』

❶ 有重大意义的；有影响的
having an important effect or influence, especially on what will happen in the future

The result is highly significant for the future of the province.
这一结果对该省未来发展具有重要意义。

It is significant that the writers of the report were all men.
报告的作者都是男性，这是很有意义的。

❷ 显著的，明显的
large enough to be noticeable or have noticeable effects

A significant part of Japan's wealth is invested in the West.
日本财富的很大一部分投资于欧美地区。

The number of MPs now supporting him had increased significantly. 现在支持他的议员人数显著增加。

❸ 别有含义的；意味深长的
a significant look, smile, etc. has a special meaning that is not known to everyone

Mrs Bycraft gave Rose a significant glance.
拜克拉夫特夫人意味深长地瞥了罗丝一眼。

▶ **significance** [sɪɡˈnɪfɪkəns] n. 重要意义

the importance of sth, especially when this has an effect on what happens in the future

The new drug has great significance for the treatment of the disease. 这种新药对于这种病的治疗有重大的意义。

6. **designate** [ˈdezɪɡneɪt] vt. 指派；指定；标示 adj. （已当选或委任）尚未就职的
『design设计+ate表动词→按设计，某人干某职业→指派，委任』

❶ [VN] ~ sb (as) sth 选定，指派，委任（某人任某职）
Thompson has been designated (as/to be) team captain.
汤普森被任命为队长。

She has been designated to organise the meeting.
她被指定组织这次会议。

❷ [VN] ~ sth (as) sth 指定为
This floor has been designated a no-smoking area.
这一楼层已定为无烟区。

Some of the rooms were designated as offices.
其中一些房间被指定用作办公室。

Trump designates Iran's Revolutionary Guards a foreign terrorist Group.
特朗普指认伊朗革命卫队为外国恐怖组织。

❸ [VN] 标示为，把…定名为
It is occasionally necessary to use a number system to designate the position of each ligand.
有时需要用一种编号系统来标明各配体的位置。

❹ adj. [ˈdezɪɡnət] （已当选或委任）尚未就职的[after noun]
Japan's Prime Minister-designate is completing his Cabinet today. 日本的当选首相今日将完成组阁。

7. **consign** [kənˈsaɪn] vt. （为摆脱或除掉而）把…送到…；把…置于（不愉快的境地）
『con一起+sign签字，标志→一起签字后（把…送到…）→把…送到…』

❶ ~ sb/sth to sth （为摆脱或除掉而）把…送到…
to put sb/sth somewhere in order to get rid of them/it
I consigned her letter to the waste basket.
我把她的信丢进了废纸篓。

What I didn't want was to see my mother consigned to an old people's home.
我不愿意看到我母亲被送进养老院。

❷ ~ sb/sth to sth 把…置于（不愉快的境地）
The decision to close the factory has consigned 6,000 people to the scrap heap.
关闭那家工厂的决定使6000人遭到了遗弃。

A car accident consigned him to a wheelchair for the rest of his life. 一次车祸使他落得在轮椅上度过余生。

8. **signet** [ˈsɪɡnət] n. 图章，印 vt. 盖印章于
『sign签字，标志+et小→起签字作用的小标志→图章，印』

The order was sealed with the king's signet.
这一命令是用国王的印记加封的。

9. **ensign** [ˈensən] n.（表明国籍的）舰旗，商船旗
『en使…+sign记号→成为舰船的记号→舰旗，商船旗』

10. **insignia** [ɪnˈsɪɡniə] n. （常指军队的）徽章，标志
『in里面+sign标志+ia表名词→里面是（身份或组织的）标志→徽章，标志』

the royal insignia 皇家的徽章
His uniform bore the insignia of a captain.
他的制服上有上尉徽章。

词根312. simil, simul, semble=alike, same，表示"相类似，一样"

① simil, simul=alike, same，表示"相类似，一样"

1. **similar** [ˈsɪmələ(r)] adj. 相似的
『simil相似+ar表形容词→类似的』

▶ **similarity** [ˌsɪməˈlærəti] n. 相似性；类似性

2. **assimilate** [əˈsɪməleɪt] v. （使）同化，（使）融入；理解，学习，吸收
『as相当于to+simil相似，相同+ate使…→使（某人）达到（与别人）相同；使（别人的主意、技术）与自己的相同→（使）同化，（使）融入；学习，吸收』

❶ ~ (sb) (into/to sth) （使）同化
[V] New arrivals find it hard to assimilate.
新来者感到难以融入当地社会。

[VN] Immigrants have been successfully assimilated into the community. 外来移民顺利地融入当地社会。

❷ 理解；吸收；学习
If you assimilate new ideas, techniques, or information, you learn them or adopt them.
The board will need time to assimilate the information.
董事会需要时间来吃透这些信息。

We should assimilate the good things in ancient Chinese culture, as well as in foreign cultures.
对中国古代的文化，我们要吸收其中有益的东西，同样，对外国的也应如此。

3. **simile** [ˈsɪməli] n. 明喻；明喻的运用
『simil相似+e→像…一样→明喻』

4. **facsimile** [fækˈsɪməli] n. 传真；复制本
『fac做+simil相同+e→做成相同的→传真；复制本』

❶ [C] 复制品，仿制品，摹本
A facsimile of something is an copy or imitation of it.
a facsimile edition 摹本版

❷ [C, U] (formal) = fax 传真；传真机
Can I send a facsimile to Japan? 我能发个传真到日本吗？
Yes I can use a facsimile machine skillfully.
是的，我能熟练地使用传真机。

5. simulate [ˈsɪmjuleɪt] vt. 装出；仿制；模拟
『simul相似，相同+ate表动词→使相同→仿制；模拟』

[VN] 装出（某种表情、动作）；模仿（某种物质、物品、声音）；模拟（某种环境）

I tried to simulate surprise at the news.
听到这个消息后，我竭力装出一副吃惊的样子。
The wood had been painted to simulate stone.
木头被漆成了石头的样子。
Some driving teachers use computers to simulate different road conditions for learners to practise on.
一些驾驶老师用电脑模拟不同的路况，供学习者练习。

▶ **simulation** [ˌsɪmjuˈleɪʃn] n. 模拟；假装

a computer simulation of how the planet functions
行星活动方式的计算机模拟

形近词 **stimulate** [ˈstɪmjuleɪt] v. 刺激；激发 <P315>

6. simultaneous [ˌsɪmlˈteɪniəs] adj. 同时发生或进行的
『simul相似，相同+t+aneous有…特征的→（发生时间）相同的→同时发生的』

There were several simultaneous attacks by the rebels.
反叛者同时发动了几起攻击。
simultaneous translation/interpreting 同声传译/口译

② semble=alike, same，表示"相类似，一样"

1. resemble [rɪˈzembl] vt. 看起来像；像
『re又，再+semble相似，相同→像』

[VN] [no passive]（不用于进行时）看起来像；显得像；像
to look like or be similar to another person or thing
She closely resembles her sister. 她和她姐姐很像。
The plant resembles grass in appearance.
这种植物的外形像草。

▶ **resemblance** [rɪˈzembləns] n. 相似；相像

The movie bears little resemblance to the original novel.
电影和原著相去甚远。

2. dissemble [dɪˈsembl] v. 掩盖，掩饰（真实感情意图）
『dis不+semble相同，相似→使不像→掩盖，掩饰』

[V] She was a very honest person who was incapable of dissembling. 她是一个非常诚实的人，不会伪装。
She tried to dissemble her anger with a smile on her face.
她试着用微笑掩饰她的愤怒。

3. assemble [əˈsembl] v. 集合，聚集；组装
『as相当于to+semble相似，相同→使相似或相同的（到一起）→聚集，集合』

❶ 聚集，集合；收集
to come together as a group; to bring people or things together as a group
[V] All the students were asked to assemble in the main hall.
全体学生获通知到大礼堂集合。

[VN] The manager has assembled a world-class team.
经理已聚集了一个世界一流的班子。

❷ [VN] 装配；组装
The shelves are easy to assemble. 搁架容易装配。

▶ **assembly** [əˈsembli] n. 议会；集会；组装

❶ [C] 立法机构；会议；议会
a group of people who have been elected to meet together regularly and make decisions or laws for a particular region or country
Power has been handed over to provincial and regional assemblies. 权力已移交给省和地区议会。
the California Assembly 加利福尼亚州众议院
the UN General Assembly 联合国大会

❷ [U, C] 集会；（统称）集会者
the meeting together of a group of people for a particular purpose; a group of people who meet together for a particular purpose
They were fighting for freedom of speech and freedom of assembly. 他们为言论自由和集会自由而斗争。
He was to address a public assembly on the issue.
他要对公众集会发表演说谈论这个问题。

❸ [C, U]（全校师生的）晨会，朝会

❹ [U] 装配，组装
a car assembly plant 汽车装配厂

词根313. sinu=bend，表示"弯曲"

1. sinuous [ˈsɪnjuəs] adj. 弯曲有致的
『sinu弯曲+ous充满…的→弯曲的』

turning while moving, in an elegant way; having many curves
I drove along sinuous mountain roads.
我行驶在蜿蜒的山路上。
a sinuous movement 婀娜多姿的动作

2. insinuate [ɪnˈsɪnjueɪt] vt. 暗示；巧妙地取得
『in里面+sinu弯曲+ate表动词→弯弯曲曲地进入到某事里面→巧妙完成某事→暗示；巧妙地取得』

❶ 暗示，旁敲侧击地指出（不快的事）
to suggest indirectly that sth unpleasant is true
[V that] The article insinuated that he was having an affair with his friend's wife.
文章含沙射影地点出他和朋友的妻子有染。
[VN] What are you trying to insinuate?
你拐弯抹角想说什么？

❷ [VN] ~ yourself into sth 钻营，活动
to manage very cleverly, and perhaps dishonestly, to get into a situation
He gradually insinuated himself into her life.
他处心积虑，终于一步步走进了她的生活。

词根314. sist=stand，表示"站立；坚持"

1. insist [ɪnˈsɪst] v. 坚决要求；坚持说
『in里面+sist站立；坚持→站立，坚持（某个立场）→坚决要求；坚持说』

❶ 坚决要求（后面宾语从句要用虚拟语气）
He insists that she (should) come. 他执意要她来。
She insisted on his/him wearing a suit. 她坚持要他穿西装。

❷ 坚持说（后面宾语从句要用陈述语气）
He insisted on his innocence. 他坚持说他是无辜的。

He insisted (that) he was innocent. 他坚持说他是无辜的。

2. consist [kənˈsɪst] vi. 由…组成；在于
『con一起+sist站立→站到一起→由…组成』

❶ **consist of sth** 由…组成（或构成）
The committee consists of ten members.
委员会由10人组成。

❷ **consist in sth** (formal) 存在于；在于
Our team's repeated failures consist in the discouragement of the coach. 我们球队一再失利，原因在于教练的气馁。
The beauty of the city consists in its magnificent buildings.
这座城市的美就在于它那些宏伟的建筑。

词义辨析 <P375第73>
由…组成 make up, consist of, compose, constitute, comprise

3. consistent [kənˈsɪstənt] adj. 前后一致的；不矛盾的
『con一起+sist站立+ent表性质→（始终）站到一起的→前后一致的；不矛盾的』

❶ (approving) 一贯的，一致的，始终如一的
She's not very consistent in the way she treats her children.
她对待孩子反复无常。
It's something I have consistently denied.
那是我自始至终否认的事。
These are clear consistent policies which we are putting into place. 这些就是我们正在付诸实施的政策，不但清楚而且前后一致。

❷ （观点等）一致的，吻合的，不矛盾
The results are entirely consistent with our earlier research.
这些结果与我们早些时候的研究完全吻合。

▶**consistency** [kənˈsɪstənsi] n. 一致性；连贯性
There are checks to ensure consistency between interviewers.
有一些检查以确保面试官之间的一致性。

4. resist [rɪˈzɪst] vt. 抵制；抵抗；抵挡（诱惑）
『re反复+sist站→反复站起来（表示抗议）→抵抗』

❶ 抵抗，抵制；反对
If you resist something such as a change, you refuse to accept it and try to prevent it.
[VN] They are determined to resist pressure to change the law. 他们决心顶住要求改革法律的压力。
[V -ing] The bank strongly resisted **cutting** interest rates.
银行强烈反对降低利率。

❷ 反抗；回击；抵抗
to fight back when attacked; to use force to stop sth from happening
[VN] She was charged with resisting arrest.
她被控拒捕。

❸ **can't resist sth/ doing sth** 抵挡不住（诱惑）
[VN] I finished the cake. I couldn't resist it.
我忍不住诱惑，把整块蛋糕都吃了。
[V -ing] He couldn't resist **showing** off his new car.
他忍不住炫耀起了他的新车。

▶**resistance** [rɪˈzɪstəns] n. 抵制；抵抗；阻力；电阻
As with all new ideas it met with resistance.
和所有的新观念一样，它受到了抵制。
the War of Resistance Against Japan 抗日战争
We increase the length of the wire, thus increasing its resistance. 我们增加导线的长度，从而增加了导线的电阻。

小贴士 物理中电阻符号"R"就是resistance的首字母

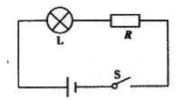

▶**resistant** [rɪˈzɪstənt] adj. 抵抗的；抵制的
Some people are very resistant to the idea of exercise.
有些人十分反对锻炼。

5. irresistible [ˌɪrɪˈzɪstəbl] adj. 不可抗拒的；诱人的
『ir不+resist抵抗+ible可…的→不可抗拒的』

❶ 不可遏止的；无法抵制的
I felt an irresistible urge to laugh. 我禁不住想笑出来。

❷ ~ (to sb) 极诱人的
It proved an irresistible temptation to Hall to go back.
事实证明回去对霍尔是个不可抗拒的诱惑。

6. assist [əˈsɪst] vt. 帮助，协助
『as相当于to+sist站立→站立到（旁边）→帮助』

~ (sb) (in/with sth) | ~ (sb) (in doing sth)
[VN] We'll do all we can to assist you. 我们要尽量帮助你。
We will assist you in finding somewhere to live.
我们将帮你找个住的地方。
Julia was assisting him to prepare his speech.
朱莉娅正在帮他准备演讲稿。
The family decided to assist me with my chores.
全家人决定帮助我做家务。

▶**assistant** [əˈsɪstənt] n. 助手 adj. 助理的

▶**assistance** [əˈsɪstəns] n. 帮助；援助
~ (with sth) | ~ (in doing sth/to do sth)
Can I be of any assistance? 我能帮上忙吗？
Despite his cries, no one came to his assistance.
尽管他喊叫，却没有人来帮助他。
She offered me practical assistance with my research.
她给我的研究提供了实实在在的援助。
The company provides advice and assistance in finding work.
公司提供咨询并帮助找工作。

7. persist [pəˈsɪst] vi. 执意；坚持；持续存在
『per (through)自始至终+sist站立；坚持→始终坚持→执意坚持』

❶ ~ (in sth/in doing sth) | ~ (with sth)
顽强地坚持；执意做
to continue to do sth despite difficulties or opposition, in a way that can seem unreasonable
Why do you persist in blaming yourself for what happened?
你何必为已发生的事没完没了地自责？

❷ 持续存在
If something undesirable persists, it continues to exist.
If the symptoms persist, consult your doctor.
如果症状持续存在，就得去看医生。

▶**persistence** [pəˈsɪstəns] n. 坚持不懈；持续
It was her sheer persistence that wore them down in the end.
最终把他们拖垮的纯粹是她的不屈不挠。

▶**persistent** [pəˈsɪstənt] adj. 执着的；持续的

8. subsist [səbˈsɪst] vi. （勉强）生存

『sub下面+sist站立；坚持→持续在（必须是生活标准）下面→勉强生存』

~ (on sth) （尤指靠有限的食物或钱）维持生活，度日

to manage to stay alive, especially with limited food or money

Old people often subsist on very small incomes.

老人往往靠十分微薄的收入艰难度日。

▶ **subsistence** [səbˈsɪstəns] n. 勉强维持生活

Many families are living below the level of subsistence.

许多家庭难以度日。

词根315. soci=companion，表示"同伴"，引申为"社会"

1. social [ˈsəʊʃl] adj. 社会的；社交的；群居的

『soci社会；同伴+al表形容词→社会的；社交的』

❶ [only before noun] 社会的；社会上的

a call for social and economic change

呼吁社会和经济变革

❷ [only before noun] 社交的；交际的

Team sports help to develop a child's social skills.

集体体育运动有助于培养孩子的交际能力。

❸ [only before noun] (technical) 群居的

These endangered gentle giants are highly social animals.

这些濒临灭绝的、性情温顺的大型动物属于高度群居的动物。

2. society [səˈsaɪəti] n. 社会；社团

『soci社会+ ety表性质→社会』

❶ [U] 社会（视作一个有组织的大群体）

They carried out research into the roles of men and women in today's society.

他们就男人和女人在当今社会中所扮演的角色展开研究。

❷ [C, U] 社会（共同遵守一定习俗、法律等的特定群体）

Can Britain ever be a classless society?

英国能否有朝一日成为一个无阶级社会？

They were discussing the problems of Western society.

当时他们正在讨论西方社会的问题。

❸ [C] (abbr. Soc.) (especially in names 尤用于名称) 社团；协会；学会

a group of people who join together for a particular purpose

The society often arranges poetry readings and musical evenings. 该社团经常安排诗歌朗诵和音乐晚会。

3. socialism [ˈsəʊʃəlɪzəm] n. 社会主义

『social社会的+ism主义→社会主义』

4. sociable [ˈsəʊʃəbl] adj. （人）好交际的

『soci社会；交际+able能够…的→能够交际的→社交的；好交际的』

enjoying spending time with other people

She's a sociable child who'll talk to anyone.

她是个合群的孩子，跟谁都有话说。

I'm not feeling very sociable this evening.

今晚我不大想跟人应酬。

5. associate [əˈsəʊʃieɪt] vt. 联系；联想 adj. 副的

『as相当于to+soci社会；同伴+ate使…→使达到伴随状态→联系；联想』

❶ [VN] ~ sb/sth (with sb/sth) （在心中）联想；联系

to make a connection between people or things in your mind

People always associate Hangzhou with the West Lake.

提起杭州，人们就联想到西湖。

I always associate the smell of baking with my childhood.

一闻到烘烤食物的味道我就想起了童年。

❷ ~ with sb 交往；（尤指）混在一起

to spend time with sb, especially a person or people that sb else does not approve of

I don't like you associating with those people.

我不喜欢你和那些人混在一起。

❸ adj. (often in titles 常用于头衔) 非正式的；准的；副的

associate membership 非正式会员身份

associate member/director/editor 准会员；副导演/主编

associate professor 副教授

▶ **association** [əˌsəʊʃiˈeɪʃn] n. 联想；协会；社团

『associate的名词形式』

❶ [C, usually pl.] 联想；联系

an idea or a memory that is suggested by sb/sth; a mental connection between ideas

The seaside had all sorts of pleasant associations with childhood holidays for me.

海滨使我联想起童年假期的各种愉快情景。

❷ [C + sing./pl. v.] 协会；社团；联盟

Do you belong to any professional or trade associations?

你参加了专业学会或行业协会没有？

the Football Association 足球协会

小贴士

FIFA 国际足联 (from French)；国际足球联合会

(Fédération Internationale de Football Association)

NBA （美国）全国篮球协会

(National Basketball Association)

❸ [C, usually pl.] 联想；联系

He has a shelf full of things, each of which has associations for him.

他的一个搁架上摆满了东西，每一样都能勾起他许多回忆。

词根316. sol(e)=sun; alone，表示"太阳；单独的"

① sol(e)=sun，表示"太阳"

1. solar [ˈsəʊlə(r)] adj. 太阳的；太阳能的

『sol太阳+ar…的→太阳的』

A total solar eclipse is due to take place some time tomorrow.

明天某个时刻会发生日全食。

2. parasol [ˈpærəsɒl] n. 太阳伞；（海滩上、餐馆外等处的）大遮阳伞

『para (=against)防避+sol太阳→防避太阳→太阳伞』

[C] 太阳伞；（海滩上、餐馆外等处的）大遮阳伞

A parasol is an object like an umbrella that provides shade from the sun.

In summer when you stroll on the boardwalk in the noonday sun, it is advisable to take along a parasol.

在夏季，当你在正午的太阳下漫步于（常在海滨）用木板铺成的小道上时，撑一把太阳伞是明智的。

3. solace [ˈsɒləs] n. 安慰，慰藉；给以安慰的人（或事物）

『sol太阳+ace表名词→（在悲伤时得到）阳光→安慰』

Solace is a feeling of comfort that makes you feel less sad. If something is a solace to you, it makes you feel less sad.

I found solace in writing when my father died three years ago.
我父亲三年前去世的时候，我从写作中找到了安慰。

She found the companionship of Marcia a solace.
她觉得马西娅的陪伴是莫大的安慰。

4. console [kənˈsəʊl] v. 安慰，抚慰，慰藉

『con一起+sole太阳→（悲伤时）和太阳在一起→感到心里暖暖的→安慰，慰藉』

~ sb/yourself (with sth)

to give comfort or sympathy to sb who is unhappy or disappointed

[VN] Nothing could console him when his wife died.
他妻子去世后，什么事情也不能使他感到宽慰。

She put a consoling arm around his shoulders.
她搂住他肩膀以示安慰。

Console yourself with the thought that you did your best.
你可以安慰自己的是你已经尽了最大的努力。

② sol(e)=alone，表示"单独的"

1. sole [səʊl] adj. 仅有的，唯一的；独占的 n. 脚掌；鞋底；袜底

『sole单独的→仅有的，唯一的；独占的』

❶ adj. [only before noun] 仅有的，唯一的

My sole reason for coming here was to see you.
我到这儿唯一的原因就是来看你。

This is the sole means of access to the building.
这是这栋建筑物唯一的入口。

❷ adj. [only before noun] 独占的，专有的

belonging to one person or group; not shared

Many women are left as the sole providers in families after their husband has died.
许多女人在丈夫去世之后只好独自供养一家人。

She has sole responsibility for the project.
那个项目由她一人负责。

❸ [C] 脚掌；鞋底；袜底

The hot sand burned the soles of their feet.
灼热的沙地使他们的脚掌感到火辣辣的。

shoes with rubber soles 橡胶底的鞋子

2. solo [ˈsəʊləʊ] adj. & adv. 独自进行的/地 n. 独奏；独唱；独舞

『sol单独的+o音乐术语及乐器名称→独奏（唱）』

❶ adj. & adv. 独自进行的/地；独唱的/地，独奏的/地

He had just completed his final solo album.
他刚刚录完了他的最后一张独唱专辑。

Mrs Obama won't be the first American first lady to travel solo to China.
奥巴马夫人并非美国唯一的单独访华的第一夫人。

❷ n. 独奏；独唱；独舞

The original version featured a guitar solo.
吉他独奏是原版的特色。

3. solitary [ˈsɒlətri] adj. 独居的，独处的；独自的；孤单的，孤零零的

『sol单独的+it走+ary表形容词→单独行动的→独自的』

❶ （人或动物）（惯于或喜欢）独处的，独居的

He was a solitary child. 他是一个孤僻的孩子。

Tigers are solitary animals. 虎是独居动物。

❷ [usually before noun] （行动）独自的，单独的

His evenings were spent in solitary drinking.
他晚上的时间都是靠独自喝闷酒打发。

❸ 单个的，孤单的，孤零零的

alone, with no other people or things around

A solitary light burned dimly in the hall.
大厅里点着一盏孤灯，发出昏暗的光。

▶ **solitude** [ˈsɒlɪtjuːd] n. 独处，独居

『sol单独的+itude表状态→独处，独居』

[U] （尤指平静愉快的）独居，独处

the state of being alone, especially when you find this pleasant

He enjoyed his moments of solitude before the pressures of the day began.
他喜欢在白天的压力到来之前享受独处的时光。

4. desolate [ˈdesələt，ˈdesəleɪt] adj. 荒凉的；孤独忧伤的 vt. 使悲伤绝望

『de表加强+sol单独的+ate有…性质的→单独（没有别的人或物）→荒凉的 』

（adj. [ˈdesələt]; v. [ˈdesəleɪt]）

❶ adj. （地方）荒无人烟的；荒凉的

empty and without people, making you feel sad or frightened

We saw few houses in the desolate valley.
在这荒凉的山谷里，我们很少见到房子。

❷ adj. （人）孤独忧伤的

If someone is desolate, they feel very sad, alone, and without hope.

He was desolate without her. 没有她，他感到孤独而凄凉。

❸ [VN] 使悲伤绝望

to make sb feel sad and without hope

She had been desolated by the death of her friend.
朋友的去世使她感到十分悲伤。

5. soliloquy [səˈlɪləkwi] n. 独白（的台词）；独白 <P211>

『sol单独的+i+ loqu说话+y表名词→一个人说→独白』

词根317. solve=loosen，表示"松开"，引申为"解决；溶解"

1. resolve [rɪˈzɒlv] v. 解决；决定；决心；分解

『re又，再+solve解决→解决；决定』

❶ [VN] 解决（问题或困难）

to find an acceptable solution to a problem or difficulty

to resolve an issue/a dispute/a conflict/a crisis
解决问题/争端/冲突/危机

❷ ~ (on sth/on doing sth) 决心，决定

to make a firm decision to do sth

She resolved to report the matter to the hospital's nursing manager. 她决定把这件事汇报给医院的护士长。

❸ （委员会、会议等）表决，决定

to reach a decision by means of a formal vote

[V that] It was resolved that the matter be referred to a higher authority. 经过表决决定把这件事提交给上级主管部门。

[V to inf] The Supreme Council resolved to resume control over the national press.

最高理事会决定重新接管对国家新闻机构的控制。

❹ resolve into sth/resolve sth into sth（使）分解为

to resolve a complex argument into its basic elements 把一个复杂的论点分解成几个基本要点

❺ [U] ~ (to do sth) 决心（同resolution）

The difficulties in her way merely strengthened her resolve. 她所遇到的困难只是让她更加坚定。

► **resolution** [ˌrezə'luːʃn] n. 决议；决心；清晰度

❶ [C] 决议，正式决定

The UN resolution required Iraq to surrender any weapons of mass destruction.

联合国决议要求伊拉克交出全部大规模杀伤性武器。

❷ [C] ~ (to do sth) 决心，决定

As my New Year's resolution, I made a decision to change my life and be healthy.

正如我的新年决心，我决定改变我的生活，（使我）变得健康。

❸ [U] 坚定，坚决，有决心（同resolve ❺）

the quality of being resolute or determined

The reforms owe a great deal to the resolution of one man. 这些改革主要归功于一个人的坚定决心。

❹ [U, sing.] 清晰度，分辨率

（resolve有"分解"之意。把图像分解成一个个像素，图片像素的多少就是它的分辨率。）

Now this machine gives us such high resolution that we can see very small specks of calcium.

现在这台机器可以呈现很高的分辨率，我们可以看见非常小的钙微粒。

小贴士　分辨率（resolution）

分辨率常用来表示屏幕和图像的清晰度。通常情况下，图像的分辨率越高，所包含的像素就越多，图像就越清晰。通常，"分辨率"被表示成每一个方向上的像素数量，比如640×480等。

► **resolute** ['rezəluːt] adj. 坚决的，有决心的

having or showing great determination

He became even more resolute in his opposition to the plan. 他更加坚决地反对这个计划。

词义辨析 <P381第100> 决定 decide, determine, resolve

2. **absolve** [əb'zɒlv] vt. 宣告…无罪；判定…无责

『ab离开+solve松开；解决→松开（让其）离开（不再受罪名束缚）→宣告无罪；判定无责』

[VN] ~ sb (from/of sth)

to state formally that sb is not guilty or responsible for sth

The court absolved him of all responsibility for the accident. 法院宣告他对该事故不负任何责任。

► **absolution** [ˌæbsə'luːʃn] n. 赦罪

She felt as if his words had granted her absolution. 她感觉他的那番话好似给她下了道赦令。

► **absolute** ['æbsəluːt] adj. 完的，全部的，绝对的

『ab离开+solut (=loosen)松开+e→完全自由→完全的，全部的』

a class for absolute beginners　零起点班

absolute confidence/trust/silence/truth

充满信心；绝对信任；万籁俱寂；绝对真实

You're absolutely right.　你完全正确。

3. **solve** [sɒlv] vt. 解决（问题）；解答

『slove松开→使（难解的问题）松开，松散→解答』

Attempts are being made to solve the problem of waste disposal. 正在想办法解决废物处理的问题。

to solve an equation/a puzzle/a riddle

解方程；解难题；解谜

► **solution** [sə'luːʃn] n. 解决办法；答案；溶解；溶液

『slove松开→使（难解的问题、固体）松开，松散→解答；溶解→（再变为名词）solution』

❶ [C] ~ (to sth) 解决办法；答案

Do you have a better solution? 你有更好的解决办法吗？

The solution to last week's quiz is on page 81.

上星期测验的答案在第81页。

❷ [C, U] 溶液；溶解

Vitamins in solution are more affected than those in solid foods.

溶液中的维生素比固体食物中的维生素受到的影响更大。

► **soluble** ['sɒljəbl] adj. 可溶的；可解决的

Glucose is soluble in water. 葡萄糖可溶于水。

Someone would have found the answer by now if the problem were soluble.

如果那个问题是可以解决的，到现在应该有人已经找到了答案。

► **solute** ['sɒljuːt] n. 溶质，溶解物

► **solvent** ['sɒlvənt] n. 溶剂 adj. 有偿付能力的

『solve解决（问题）+(e)nt构成形容词→（有钱就能）解决问题→有钱的→有偿付能力的』

They're going to have to show that the company is now solvent. 他们必须证明公司目前具备偿还能力。

► **solvency** ['sɒlvənsi] n. 偿还能力

► **insolvent** [in'sɒlvənt] adj. 无偿还能力的

4. **dissolve** [dɪ'zɒlv] v. 溶解；解散；消散

『dis(=away)离开+solve松开→松开，离开→溶解；解散；消散』

❶ [V, VN]（使）溶解

Salt dissolves in water. 盐溶于水。

Dissolve the tablet in water. 把药片溶于水中。

❷ [VN] 解除（婚姻关系）；终止（商业协议）；解散（议会、团体或机构）

The marriage was dissolved in 1976.

这段婚姻于1976年结束。

The present assembly will be dissolved on April 30th.

现在的议会将于4月30日解散。

❸ [V, VN]（使）消失，消散

[V] When the ambulance had gone, the crowd dissolved.

救护车离开后人群便散开了。

[VN] His calm response dissolved her anger.

他平静的回答化解了她的怒气。

▶ **dissolution** [ˌdɪsəˈluːʃn] n. （婚姻关系的）解除；（商业协议的）终止；（议会的）解散；解体

He stayed on until the dissolution of the firm in 1948.
他一直待到1948年公司解散。

▶ **dissolvable** [dɪˈzɒlvəbl] adj. 可溶解的

▶ **dissolute** [ˈdɪsəluːt] adj. 放荡的，道德沦丧的
『dissolve溶解；消失→（在诱惑面前道德底线）溶解消失→放荡，道德沦丧→（变为形容词）dissolute→放荡的』
enjoying immoral activities and not caring about behaving in a morally acceptable way
His dissolute life is inconsistent with his Puritan upbringing.
他的放荡生活和他的清教徒教养相悖。

词根318. somn(i), somno=sleep，表示"睡眠"

1. insomnia [ɪnˈsɒmniə] n. 失眠（症）
『in不+somn睡眠+ia某种病→睡不着觉的病→失眠症』

Too much caffeine can cause anxiety, depression, and insomnia. 过量的咖啡因会导致焦虑、抑郁和失眠。

▶ **insomnious** [ɪnˈsɒmnɪəs] adj. 患失眠症的
Among 911 subjects with insomnious symptom, 212 cases were diagnosed as chronic insomnia.
在有失眠症状的911例受试者中，212例被诊断为慢性失眠。

▶ **insomniac** [ɪnˈsɒmnɪæk] n. 失眠患者

2. somnolent [ˈsɒmnələnt] adj. 睡意蒙眬的，昏昏欲睡的
『somnol(=somno)睡眠+ent…的→昏昏欲睡的』

❶ 昏昏欲睡的
If you are somnolent, you feel sleepy.
The sedative makes people very somnolent.
这种镇静剂会让人瞌睡。

❷ 静寂的，沉寂的
If a place is somnolent, it is very peaceful and quiet.
All the order he saw beneath him—the streets, the parked cars, this somnolent London square—had a transient quality.
他所看到的一切秩序——街道、停着的汽车、这个沉睡的伦敦广场——都是短暂的。

词根319. son=sound，表示"声音"

1. sonic [ˈsɒnɪk] adj. 声音的；声速的
『son声音+ic…的→声音的』

He activated the door with the miniature sonic transmitter.
他用微型声波发射器开启了门。

2. supersonic [ˌsuːpəˈsɒnɪk] adj. 超声速的
『supper超过的+sonic声速的→超过声速的→超声速的』

a supersonic aircraft 超声速飞机

3. ultrasonic [ˌʌltrəˈsɒnɪk] adj. 超声的
『ultra (beyond) 超出+sonic声音的→超声波的』

He measured the speed at which ultrasonic waves travel along the bone. 他测出了超声波穿过骨头的速度。

4. resonate [ˈrezəneɪt] vi. 回响，回荡；共鸣

❶ ~ (with sth) 回响；回荡
His voice resonated in the empty church.
他的声音在空荡荡的教堂里回荡。
The noise of the bell resonated through the building.
钟声在大楼里回荡。

❷ ~ (with sb/sth) 使产生联想；引起共鸣

These issues resonated with the voters.
这些问题引起了投票者的共鸣。

▶ **resonant** [ˈrezənənt] adj. 响亮的；共鸣的
a deep resonant voice 深沉而响亮的声音

▶ **resonance** [ˈrezənəns] n. 洪亮；共鸣

5. consonant [ˈkɒnsənənt] n. 辅音，辅音字母
『con共同+son声音+ant…的→（口腔的不同部分）一起（形成阻塞）发出的声音→辅音』

词根320. soph=wisdom, wise，表示"智慧，聪明"

1. philosophy [fəˈlɒsəfi] n. 哲学；哲学思想；人生哲学
『philo爱+soph智慧，聪明+y表名词→爱智慧（研究哲学需要高智慧的人）→哲学』

❶ [U] 哲学
He studied philosophy and psychology at Cambridge.
他在剑桥大学学习哲学和心理学。

❷ [C] 哲学体系，哲学理论
the philosophies of Socrates, Plato, and Aristotle
苏格拉底、柏拉图和亚里士多德的哲学思想

❸ [C] 人生哲学，人生信条
a set of beliefs or an attitude to life that guides sb's behavior
Her philosophy of life is to take every opportunity that presents itself.
她的处世态度是不放过任何呈现眼前的机会。

▶ **philosopher** [fəˈlɒsəfə(r)] n. 哲学家；善于思考的人

▶ **philosophic(al)** [ˌfɪləˈsɒfɪk(l)] adj. 哲学的；处乱不惊的，达观的
He was philosophical about losing and said that he'd be back next year to try again.
他对失败处之泰然，声称来年将再来一试身手。

小贴士 PhD (also **D Phil**) 是doctor of philosophy的缩写，译为"哲学博士"。通常是学历架构中最高级的学衔。拥有人一般在大学本科（学士）及/或研究院（硕士）毕业后，再进行相当年数的研修后，撰写毕业论文并通过答辩，方能获得哲学博士学位。哲学博士的拥有人并不一定修读"哲学"。从西方学术史看，科学是哲学的衍生物。

2. sophist [ˈsɒfist] n. （古希腊的）哲学教师；诡辩家
『soph智慧+ist人→智慧之人→哲学教师；诡辩家』

▶ **sophistry** [ˈsɒfistri] n. 诡辩；诡辩术
Political selection is more dependent on sophistry and less on economic literacy.
政治选举更多地取决于诡辩的能力，而不在于是否懂经济。

3. sophisticate [səˈfɪstɪkeɪt] n. 老于世故的人；见多识广的人
『sophist博学之人；诡辩家+icate→（见多识广才）善于诡辩→见多识广之人』
A sophisticate is someone who knows about culture, fashion, and other matters that are considered socially important.
You are a sophisticate. 你是见过世面的人。

▶ **sophisticated** [səˈfɪstɪkeɪtɪd] adj. （人）见过世面的；精明老练的；（机器设备等）高端的，先进的

❶ （人）见多识广的，老练的，见过世面的
having a lot of experience of the world and knowing about fashion, culture and other things that people think are socially important

❷ （机器、装置等）高端的，先进的，复杂的
A sophisticated machine, device, or method is more advanced or complex than others.

Honeybees use one of the most sophisticated communication systems of any insect.
蜜蜂之间所用的交流方式是昆虫中最为复杂的方式之一。

❸ （人）精明老练的，会处事的
A sophisticated person is intelligent and knows a lot, so that they are able to understand complicated situations.

These people are very sophisticated observers of the foreign policy scene. 这些人是观察外交政策领域动向的行家里手。

词义辨析 <P375第72>
复杂的 complicated, complex, intricate, sophisticated

4. **sophomore** [ˈsɒfəmɔː(r)] n. 大二（或高二）学生
『sopho(=soph)智慧+more更→更有智慧→大二学生比大一学生懂得更多→大学二年级学生』

词根321. sort=kind，表示"种类"

1. **assorted** [əˈsɔːtɪd] adj. 各种各样的，混杂的，什锦的
『as(=to)+sort分类+ed表形容词→可以被分成不同种类的→各种各样的，混杂的』

The meat is served with salad or assorted vegetables.
端上的肉配有色拉或什锦蔬菜。

2. **consort** [kənˈsɔːt] v. 厮混；鬼混
『con一起+sort种类→相同种类的人在一起→厮混』

[V] ~ with sb (formal) 厮混；鬼混
to spend time with sb that other people do not approve of
He regularly consorted with known drug-dealers.
他经常与几个臭名昭著的毒贩鬼混。

3. **consortium** [kənˈsɔːtiəm] n. 联合企业
『con一起+sort种类+ium表名词→（不同）种类的（企业）联合到一起（来完成某项工程）→联合企业』

a group of people, countries, companies, etc. who are working together on a particular project
The consortium includes some of the biggest building contractors in Britain.
该联合企业包括英国最大的一些建筑承包商。

词根322. spect, spic, specul= look, see，表示"看"

1. **inspect** [ɪnˈspekt] vt. 查看；视察
『in里面+spect看→进到里面查看（是否正常；要求是否被落实）→查看；视察』

❶ ~ sth/sb (for sth) 检查；查看
to look closely at sth/sb, especially to check that everything is as it should be
The plants are regularly inspected for disease.
对这些植物定期做病害检查。
Make sure you inspect the goods before signing for them.
要确保在签收货物之前进行检验。

❷ [VN] 视察
to officially visit a school, factory, etc. in order to check that rules are being obeyed and that standards are acceptable
Some government leaders came to inspect our school yesterday. 一些政府领导人昨天来视察了我们的学校。

2. **prospect** [ˈprɒspekt] n. 希望；前景；前途
『pro向前+spect看→向前看→前景』

❶ [U, sing.] 可能性；希望
the possibility that sth will happen
There is no immediate prospect of peace.
短期内没有和平的可能。

❷ [sing.] ~ (of sth/of doing sth) 前景；要发生的事
an idea of what might or will happen in the future
The prospect of becoming a father filled him with alarm.
一想到将为人父他就满怀忧思。

❸ [pl.] ~ (for/of sth) （工作或事业）成功的机会；前途
the chances of being successful, especially in a job or career
At 25 he was an unemployed musician with no prospects.
25岁的他是个没有工作、前途渺茫的乐师。

▶ **prospective** [prəˈspektɪv] adj. 预期的
The story should act as a warning to other prospective buyers.
这篇报道应该对其他潜在的购买者起到警示作用。

3. **perspective** [pəˈspektɪv] n. 观点，看法，视角
『per (through)穿过+spect看+ive…的→（从某个地方）穿过（时空）来看→视角』

❶ [C] ~ (on sth) 观点，看法，视角
Try to see the issue **from a different perspective**.
试以不同的角度看待这件事。
He says the death of his father 18 months ago has given him a new perspective on life.
他说18个月前父亲的去世让他对人生有了新的认识。

from/in one's perspective 在某人看来
In my perspective, the plan is far from perfect.
在我看来，这个计划还很不完善。

小贴士 "在我看来"的表达方法：
in/from my perspective, in my opinion, in my view, in my point of view, personally, as far as I'm concerned...

❷ [U] 透视法
We learnt how to draw buildings in perspective.
我们学习如何用透视法画建筑物。

▶ **perspicacious** [ˌpɜːspɪˈkeɪʃəs] adj. 敏锐的；有洞察力的；精辟的
『per(through)穿过+spic看+acious有…性质的→看透的→有洞察力的』

It was very perspicacious of you to find the cause of the trouble so quickly.
你真是心明眼亮，问题的原因这么快就找出来了。

4. **expect** [ɪkˈspekt] vt. 预料；期待；期望；认为
『ex出，向外+pect(=spect)看→向外看→翘首以待→期待』

❶ 预料；预期；期待
to think or believe that sth will happen or that sb will do sth
[VN] We are expecting a rise in food prices this month.
我们预计这个月食物价格会上涨。
Don't expect sympathy from me! 休想得到我的同情！
[VN to inf] I didn't expect him to become a successful writer.
我没想到他会成为一个成功的作家。

❷ （常用于进行时）等待；期待；盼望
to be waiting for sb/sth to arrive, as this has been arranged
[VN] Are you expecting visitors? 你在等客人吗？
[VN] I am expecting several important letters but nothing has arrived. 我正在等几封重要的信件，可是一封都没到。

❸ ~ sth (of/from sb) 要求；指望；期望
to demand that sb will do sth because it is their duty or

responsibility

[VN] Her parents expected too much of her.
她的父母对她的期望太高。

Are you clear what is expected of you?
你清楚大家对你的期望吗？

He's still getting over his illness, so don't expect too much from him. 他仍处于康复期，所以不要对他期望过高。

❹ (informal, especially BrE) (不用于进行时) 猜想；认为；料想

[V] "Will you be late？" "I expect so."
"你会迟到吗？" "我想会的。"

"Are you going out tonight？" "I don't expect so."
"你今晚要出去吗？" "我想不会吧。"

▶ **expectation** [ˌekspekˈteɪʃn] n. 预料；期望

❶ [U, C] ~ (of sth) | ~ (that…) 预料；预期
There was a general expectation that he would win.
（人们）普遍认为他会获胜。

The expectation is that property prices will rise.
预计地产价格会上涨。

Contrary to expectations, interest rates did not rise.
出乎意料的是利率并未上涨。

❷ [C, usually pl.] 期望；指望
a strong belief about the way sth should happen or how sb should behave

Some parents have unrealistic expectations of their children.
有的父母对孩子的指望不切实际。

Only in this way can we **live up to their expectations** and take better care of our aged parents in the future.
只有这样我们才能达到他们的期望，未来更好地照料我们的父母亲。

5. **respect** [rɪˈspekt] n. 尊重，尊敬；方面 vt. 尊重；尊敬
『re再，又+spect看→一再看（望某人）→尊敬』

❶ [U, sing.] ~ (for sb/sth) 尊敬；尊重
I have the greatest respect for your brother.
我非常尊敬你的哥哥。

He has no respect for her feelings. 他根本不尊重她的感受。

Everyone has a right to be treated with respect.
人人有权受到尊重。

❷ [C] （事物的）方面，细节
In this respect we are very fortunate.
在这方面，我们是很幸运的。

There was one respect, however, in which they differed.
然而，他们在一点上有分歧。

in respect of sth (UK) /with respect to sth 关于；就…而言
The two groups were similar with respect to income and status. 这两组在收入和地位方面是相似的。

I have a problem in respect of the writing style.
关于写作风格上我有一个问题。

with respect/ with all due respect 恕我直言
(formal) （通常在表示强烈不同意之前说）
With all due respect, the figures simply do not support you on this. 恕我直言，这些数字根本不能支持你的观点。

❸ [VN] ~ sb/sth (for sth) 尊敬；尊重；仰慕
She had always been honest with me, and I respect her for that. 她一直对我很诚实，我非常敬重她这一点。

She promised to respect our wishes.
她保证尊重我们的愿望。

小贴士 with respect to, in respect of, with regard to, in regard to都可表示"关于；就…而言"。regard和respect都有"尊重"之意。

▶ **respectful** [rɪˈspektfl] adj. 表示敬意的；恭敬的
『respect尊敬+ful充满…的→充满敬意的→恭敬的』

The onlookers stood at a respectful distance.
旁观者站在一定的距离之外，以示尊敬。

We were brought up to be respectful of authority.
我们从小就学会了尊重权威。

▶ **respected** [rɪˈspektɪd] adj. 受尊敬的；受敬重的
『respect尊敬+ed表被动→被人尊敬的→受尊敬的』

She is a well respected member of the international community. 她在国际社会中非常受人敬重。

▶ **respectable** [rɪˈspektəbl] adj. 体面的；值得尊敬的
『respect尊敬+able可以的→可以尊敬的→值得尊敬的』

At last I have something respectable to wear!
我终于可以穿上体面的衣服了！

I have to prove myself as a respectable, balanced person.
我必须证明自己是个正派、稳重的人。

6. **respective** [rɪˈspektɪv] adj. （只用在名词前）各自的，分别的
『re再；又+spect看+ive有…性质→再看看（各自的）→各自的』

Steve and I were at very different stages in our respective careers.
史蒂夫和我在各自的职业生涯中处于迥然不同的阶段。

The error and warning messages are shown in red and yellow, respectively. 错误和警告消息分别以红色和黄色显示。

7. **irrespective** [ˌɪrɪˈspektɪv] adj. 不管，不顾
『ir不+respect尊重+ive有…性质的→不尊重…→不管』

Everyone, irrespective of means or occupation, shall have an equal opportunity.
每个人，不论其财富或职业，都应有平等的机会。

8. **aspect** [ˈæspekt] n. 方面；层面
『a一个+spect看→看到的一个（方面）→方面；层面』

The book aims to cover all aspects of city life.
这本书旨在涵盖城市生活的各个方面。

She felt she had looked at the problem from every aspect.
她觉得她已从各个角度考虑了这个问题。

小贴士 "在这方面"的表达方法：
in this aspect, in this respect, in this regard...

9. **spectator** [spekˈteɪtə(r)] n. （尤指体育比赛的）观看者，观众
『spect看+ator表人→观看的人→观众』

Thirty thousand spectators watched the final game.
3万名观众观看了决赛。

10. **spectacle** [ˈspektəkl] n. 眼镜；奇观
『spect看+acle表物或抽象概念→看的东西；看到的（好东西）→眼镜；奇观』

❶ [C] spectacles [pl.] (formal) = glasses
a pair of spectacles 一副眼镜
a spectacle case 眼镜盒
He looked at me over the tops of his spectacles.
他从眼镜框的上方看了看我。

❷ [C, U] 精彩的表演；壮观的场面
The carnival parade was a magnificent spectacle.
狂欢节游行场面热烈，蔚为大观。
It was a spectacle not to be missed.
这是个不容错过的奇观。

❸ [sing.] 奇特的现象；出人意料的情况
I remember the sad spectacle of her standing in her wedding dress, covered in mud.
我记得她穿着婚纱、满身泥污站在那儿的凄惨样。

▶ **spectacular** [spek'tækjələ(r)] adj. 壮观的；令人惊叹的
Something that is spectacular is very impressive or dramatic.
spectacular scenery 壮丽的景色
It was a spectacular achievement on their part.
这是他们取得的一项了不起的成就。

11. suspect [sə'spekt，'sʌspekt] v. 怀疑 n. 犯罪嫌疑人 adj. 可疑的
『sus(=sub)下面+(s)pect看→从下面看→怀疑』
（v. [sə'spekt]; n. & adj. ['sʌspekt]）

❶ 疑有，觉得（尤指坏事可能属实或发生）
I began to suspect (that) they were trying to get rid of me.
我开始觉察出，他们试图摆脱我。

❷ [VN] 怀疑；感觉有问题；不信任
I suspected her motives in offering to help.
她主动要帮忙，我怀疑她的动机。

❸ [VN] ~ sb (of sth/of doing sth) 怀疑（某人有罪）
He resigned after being suspected of theft.
他被怀疑有偷窃行为，随后就辞职了。

❹ [C] 犯罪嫌疑人，可疑对象
Police have arrested a suspect in a series of killings.
警方逮捕了一系列凶杀案中的犯罪嫌疑人。

❺ adj. 可疑的；可能有危险的
a suspect package 可疑包裹

▶ **suspicious** [sə'spɪʃəs] adj. 怀疑的；令人怀疑的

▶ **suspicion** [sə'spɪʃn] n. 怀疑

词义辨析 <P376第77> **怀疑 doubt, suspect**

12. retrospect ['retrəspekt] n. 回顾，回想
『retro往回+spect看→回顾，回想』

in retrospect 回顾；回想；追溯往事
thinking about a past event or situation, often with a different opinion of it from the one you had at the time
In retrospect, I think that I was wrong.
回首往事，我觉得当时我错了。
The decision seems extremely odd, in retrospect.
回想起来，这个决定显得极其荒谬。

13. circumspect ['sɜ:kəmspekt] adj. 小心谨慎的
『circum环绕，周围+spect看→看周围→小心谨慎的』
thinking very carefully about sth before doing it, because there may be risks involved
The banks should have been more circumspect in their dealings. 那些银行在交易中本该更加谨慎的。

14. spectrum ['spektrəm] n. 光谱；波谱；系列，范围
『spect看+rum→看到的（系列的光波、波长）→光谱；波谱；系列』
（复数形式为spectra ['spektrə]）

A spectrum is a range of a particular type of thing.
She'd seen his moods range across the emotional spectrum.
她见识过他的情绪波动有多大。

15. despise [dɪ'spaɪz] v. 鄙视，蔑视，看不起
『de向下+spise(=spic)看→向下看(look down upon)→蔑视』
She despised gossip in any form.
她对任何形式的流言蜚语都嗤之以鼻。
He despised himself for being so cowardly.
他为自己如此怯懦而自惭形秽。

▶ **despicable** [dɪ'spɪkəbl] adj. 可鄙的
『de向下+spic看+able可…的→可以向下看的→可鄙的』
The Minister said the bombing was a despicable crime.
部长说这次爆炸是一起卑劣的罪行。

16. conspicuous [kən'spɪkjuəs] adj. 显眼的，引人注目的
『con一起+spic看+uous…的→（因显眼而被别人）一起看了又看的→显眼的』
Mary's red hair always made her conspicuous at school.
玛丽的红头发在学校里总是很惹眼。
I felt very conspicuous in my new car.
坐在我的新车里，我感到十分惹人注目。

17. auspicious [ɔ:'spɪʃəs] adj. 吉利的，吉祥的
『au(=av鸟)+spic看+ious…的→看见鸟（如喜鹊）的→吉利的』
showing signs that sth is likely to be successful in the future
His career as a playwright had an auspicious start.
他的剧作家生涯有了一个好的开头。

18. speculate ['spekjuleɪt] v. 思索；投机；推测
『specul看+ate表动词→看→看的过程在思索，思索的目的是盈利→思索；投机』

❶ ~ (about/on sth) 推测；猜测；推断
to form an opinion about sth without knowing all the details or facts
[V] We all speculated about the reasons for her resignation.
我们大家都推测过她辞职的原因。
[V wh-] It is useless to speculate why he did it.
对他为什么这么做妄加猜测毫无用处。

❷ [V] ~ (in/on sth) 投机；做投机买卖
to buy goods, property, shares, etc., hoping to make a profit when you sell them, but with the risk of losing money
He likes to speculate on the stock market. 他喜欢炒股。

词根323. **spec(i)=look，表示"外观；看起来"**

1. specious ['spi:ʃəs] adj. 似是而非的，貌似有理的
『spec看+ious…的→看起来（正确的）→似是而非的』
Something that is specious seems to exist or be true, but is not real or true.
It is unlikely that the Duke was convinced by such specious arguments. 公爵不太可能相信这种似是而非的论点。

2. species ['spi:ʃi:z] n. 物种
『speci看+es表复数→看起来相同的许多东西→物种』

3. specimen ['spesɪmən] n. 标本；样品；（化验）尿样、血样等
『speci看+men表实物名词→用来看（以掌握同类情况）的东西→标本；样品』
200,000 specimens of fungus are kept at the Komarov

Botanical Institute.
有20万份菌类标本被保存在科马罗夫植物研究所。
Job applicants have to submit a specimen of handwriting.
求职者必须提交一份笔迹样本。
He refused to provide a specimen. 他拒绝提供血样。

4. specific [spəˈsɪfɪk] adj. 具体的；特定的；特有的
『speci看+fic…的→看到的某一个→具体的；特定的』

I asked him to be more specific. 我要求他说得更具体些。
The money was collected for a specific purpose.

这笔钱是为一个特定用途而收的。
a belief that is specific to this part of Africa
非洲这一地区特有的信仰

▶ **specify** [ˈspesɪfaɪ] vt. 具体指定；具体说明

[VN] Remember to specify your size when ordering clothes.
订购服装时记着要详细说明你要的号码。
[V wh-] The contract clearly specifies who can operate the machinery. 合同明确规定谁可以操作机器。

▶ **specification** [ˌspesɪfɪˈkeɪʃn] n. 规格；具体要求

The house has been built exactly to our specifications.
房子完全是按照我们的工程设计书建造的。

5. special [ˈspeʃl] adj. 特别的；专门的
『speci看+al…的→看起来很特别的→特别的』

There is something special about this place.
这个地方有几分特别。
These teachers need special training.
这些教师需要专门的培训。

▶ **specialize** [ˈspeʃəlaɪz] vt. 专门研究（或从事）

He specialized in criminal law. 他专攻刑法。

▶ **specialist** [ˈspeʃəlɪst] n. （专注于某方面的）专家

You need some specialist advice. 你需要咨询专业人士。

▶ **speciality** [ˌspeʃiˈæləti] n. 专长；特产；特色菜
（NAmE，**specialty**）

My father was a historian of repute. His speciality was the history of Germany.
我父亲是一名颇有名气的历史学家，他专门研究德国历史。
Rhineland dishes are a speciality of the restaurant.
莱茵兰菜是这家饭店的特色菜。

词根324. sperse, sparse=scatter，表示"散开"

1. disperse [dɪˈspɜːs] v.（使）分散，散开；疏散；驱散
『dis(=away) +(s)perse散开→散开后离去→分散，散开』

[V] The fog began to disperse. 雾开始散了。
The crowd dispersed quickly. 人群很快便散开了。
[VN] Police dispersed the protesters with tear gas.
警察用催泪弹驱散了抗议者。
The oil appeared to be dispersing. 油好像在扩散。

▶ **dispersal** [dɪˈspɜːsl] n. 分散；疏散；散布

The police ordered the dispersal of the crowds gathered round the building.
警方命令聚集在建筑物四周的人群散开。

▶ **dispersion** [dɪˈspɜːʃn] n. 分散；散开；散布

2. intersperse [ˌɪntəˈspɜːs] vt. 散布，点缀
『inter在…之间+sperse散开→分散在…当中→散布，点缀』

[VN] to put sth in sth else or among or between other things

Lectures will be interspersed with practical demonstrations.
讲课中将不时插入实际示范。

3. sparse [spɑːs] adj. 稀少的，稀疏的，零落的
『sparse散开→不多的东西在一定范围内散开的→稀疏的』

only present in small amounts or numbers and often spread over a large area
Vegetation becomes sparse higher up the mountains.
山上越高的地方植物越稀少。

词根325. sper=hope，表示"希望"

1. desperate [ˈdespərət] adj.（因绝望而）不惜冒险的
『de无+sper希望+ate…的→因没有希望而（不惜冒险的）』

❶（因绝望而）孤注一掷的，铤而走险的，拼命的
The prisoners grew increasingly desperate.
犯人因绝望而越来越胆大妄为。
His increasing financial difficulties forced him to take desperate measures.
不断增加的经济困难迫使他采取了铤而走险的办法。

❷ 极需要的，渴望的
I was absolutely desperate to see her.
我极想见到她。

2. despair [dɪˈspeə(r)] n. & vi. 绝望
『de无+spair(=sper)希望→没有希望→绝望』

She uttered a cry of despair. 她发出了绝望的叫声。
He gave up the struggle in despair. 他绝望地放弃了斗争。
They'd almost despaired of ever having children.
他们对生孩子几乎不抱任何希望了。
I despair of him; he can't keep a job for more than six months.
我对他绝望了，他做任何工作都超不过半年。

3. prosper [ˈprɒspə(r)] vi. 兴旺；繁荣；成功
『pro向前+sper希望→向前（发展有）希望→兴旺；成功』

If people or businesses prosper, they are successful and do well.
The high street banks continue to prosper.
商业街上的银行仍旧一派繁荣景象。
His teams have always prospered in cup competitions.
他的队伍在杯赛上总是成绩不俗。
He may have to become more conformist if he is to prosper again. 要想再现辉煌，他可能得更多地依习惯办事。

▶ **prosperity** [prɒˈsperəti] n. 兴旺；繁荣；成功

Prosperity is a condition in which a person or community is doing well financially.
Our future prosperity depends on economic growth.
我们未来的繁荣昌盛依赖经济的发展。
The country is enjoying a period of peace and prosperity.
国家正值国泰民安、繁荣昌盛的时期。

▶ **prosperous** [ˈprɒspərəs] adj. 繁荣的，兴旺的

The place looks more prosperous than ever.
这地方显得空前繁荣。

词根326. spire=breathe，表示"呼吸"

1. inspire [ɪnˈspaɪə(r)] vt. 激励；给人灵感
『in进入+spire呼吸→吸进（新鲜空气）（顿时来了灵感）→激励；给人灵感』

❶ ~ sb (to sth) 激励；鼓舞

to give sb the desire, confidence or enthusiasm to do sth well

By visiting schools, the actors hope to inspire children to put on their own productions.

演员希望通过访问学校鼓励孩子们演出自己的作品。

Our challenge is to motivate those voters and inspire them to join our cause.

我们面临的挑战是如何调动那些选民的积极性并鼓励他们加入我们的事业。

❷ [VN] [usually passive] 启发，给人灵感

to give sb the idea for sth, especially sth artistic or that shows imagination

The sea inspired many of the artist's later paintings.

大海激发了这位艺术家后来的许多绘画灵感。

a piece of music inspired by dolphin sounds

以海豚的声音为灵感的音乐

❸ 作为…的灵感来源；是…的原型

If a book, work of art, or action is inspired by something, that thing is the source of the idea for it.

The book was inspired by a real person, namely Tamara de Treaux. 那本书的灵感源于一个真实人物塔玛拉·德特罗。

❹ [VN] 激起，唤起（某种感情或反应）

The car's performance quickly inspires confidence.

该汽车的性能会很快唤起驾驶者的信心。

▶ **inspiring** [ɪnˈspaɪərɪŋ] adj. 鼓舞人心的

She was one of the most inspiring people I've ever met.

她是我见过的最能鼓舞人心的人之一。

▶ **inspiration** [ˌɪnspəˈreɪʃn] n. 灵感

❶ [U] ~ (to do sth) | ~ (for sth) 灵感

Dreams can be a rich source of inspiration for an artist.

梦境可以成为艺术家灵感的丰富源泉。

Both poets drew their inspiration from the countryside.

两位诗人都是从乡村得到他们的灵感。

❷ [C, usually sing.] ~ (for sth) 启发灵感的人或事物

India's myths and songs are the inspiration for her books.

印度的神话与歌曲是她那些书的灵感来源。

❸ [C, usually sing.] ~ (to/for sb) 鼓舞人心的人（或事物）

Her charity work is an inspiration to us all.

她的慈善工作激励着我们大家。

Powell's unusual journey to high office is an inspiration to millions.

鲍威尔升任高官的不寻常历程对数以百万计的人都是一个激励。

❹ [C, usually sing., U] （突然想到的）好主意，妙计

He had an inspiration: he'd give her a dog for her birthday.

他突然想到一个好主意，他要送她一条狗作为生日礼物。

2. conspire [kənˈspaɪə(r)] vi. 密谋，阴谋；共同导致（不良后果）

❶ [V] ~ (with sb) (against sb) | ~ (together) 密谋；阴谋

to secretly plan with other people to do sth illegal or harmful

They were accused of conspiring against the king.

他们被指控阴谋反对国王。

She admitted conspiring with her lover to murder her husband. 她承认与情夫密谋杀害亲夫。

❷ ~ against sb/sth | ~ to do sth

（of events 事件） 似乎共同导致（不良后果）

Circumstances had conspired against them.

各种情况都对他们不利。

Falling demand and high interest rates have conspired to produce a big drop in profits.

需求下降和高利率共同导致利润大幅下降。

▶ **conspiracy** [kənˈspɪrəsi] n. 密谋；阴谋

They were charged with conspiracy to murder.

他们被指控密谋策划谋杀。

3. aspire [əˈspaɪə(r)] vi. 渴望；有志于

『a相当于to+spire呼吸→吸口气（攒劲为了）达到（某一目的）→渴望；有志于』

~(to sth) 渴望（成就）；有志（成为）

to have a strong desire to achieve or to become sth

[V] She aspired to a scientific career.

她有志于科学事业。

[V to inf] He aspired to be their next leader.

他渴望成为他们的下一届领导人。

▶ **aspiration** [ˌæspəˈreɪʃn] n. 抱负；志向

[C, usually pl., U] ~ (for sth) | ~ (to do sth) 渴望；抱负；志向

a strong desire to have or do sth

He has never had any aspiration to earn a lot of money.

他从未企求赚很多钱。

I've never had any political aspirations.

我从来没有任何政治抱负。

4. respire [rɪˈspaɪə(r)] vi. 呼吸

『re又，再+spire呼吸→反复呼吸→呼吸』

These patients are told to blink their eyes and to respire through their noses.

这些患者被告之要眨眼，并由鼻孔呼吸。

▶ **respiration** [ˌrespəˈreɪʃn] n. 呼吸

She was given artificial respiration and cardiac massage.

有人给她做了人工呼吸和心脏按压。

▶ **respiratory** [rəˈspɪrətri, ˈrespərətɔːri] adj. 呼吸的

If you smoke then the whole respiratory system is constantly under attack. 如果抽烟，整个呼吸系统就会一直受到损害。

小贴士 SARS 严重急性呼吸综合征；非典型肺炎 Severe Acute Respiratory Syndrome

5. expire [ɪkˈspaɪə(r)] vi. 到期；死亡

『ex出去+(s)pire呼吸→呼出去了，没了呼吸→死亡』

❶ [V] (of a document, an agreement, etc. 文件、协议等) （因到期而）失效，终止

When does your driving licence expire?

你的驾照什么时候到期？

His term of office expires at the end of June.

他的任期6月底届满。

❷ [V] 断气，死亡

6. perspire [pəˈspaɪə(r)] vi. 出汗，流汗

『per穿过+spire呼吸→（汗）穿过（毛孔）呼吸→出汗』

The victim will perspire heavily, vomit blood, and collapse within an hour.

中毒者大量出汗、吐血，一小时内就会倒地。

7. transpire [trænˈspaɪə(r)] vi. 透露，为人所知

『trans从…到…+(s)pire呼吸→透气（透露的信息）传出来为人所知→透露』

If it transpires that something has happened, this previously secret or unknown fact becomes known.

It transpired that the gang had had a contact inside the bank.
据报这伙歹徒在银行里有内应。

This story, as it later transpired, was untrue.
后来得知，此事纯属凭空假造。

8. spire ['spaɪə(r)] n. （教堂等顶部的）尖塔，尖顶
『spire呼吸→肺→胸腔周围的肋骨的形状→螺旋形→尖塔』

The church spire was struck by lightning.
教堂的尖顶遭到了雷击。

▶ **spiral** ['spaɪrəl] n. 螺旋形 adj. 螺旋形的 v. 螺旋式上升（或下降）

❶ [C] 螺旋形；螺旋形上升或下降

The birds circled in a slow spiral above the house.
鸟儿在房子上空缓缓盘旋。

the destructive spiral of violence in the inner cities
市中心日益严重的暴力行为

the upward/downward spiral of sales
日渐上升/下降的销售额

❷ adj. 螺旋形的

A snail's shell is spiral in form. 蜗牛壳呈螺旋形。

❸ [V] 螺旋式上升（或下降）

Production costs began to spiral. 生产成本开始急速上升。

The plane spiralled down to the ground. 飞机盘旋降落。

The COVID-19 crisis is spiraling out of control.
COVID-19（新冠肺炎）危机（引发的灾难）正在失控。

词根327. st, stance, stant, stat, sta, stead, stin=stand，表示"站"

① st, stance, stant=stand，表示"站"

1. stable ['steɪbl] adj. 稳定的，牢固的 n. 赛马
『st站+able能够的→能够站立的→稳定的，牢固的』

❶ 稳定的，稳固的，牢固的

firmly fixed; not likely to move, change or fail

This ladder doesn't seem very stable. 这架梯子好像不太稳。

a stable relationship 稳定的关系

The patient's condition is stable. 患者病情稳定。

❷ [C] 赛马

There have been just three winners from his stable this season.
这个赛季他的马只有三匹获胜。

▶ **stability** [stə'bɪləti] n. 稳定性；稳固性

I am confident that we can restore peace, stability and respect for the rule of law.
我相信我们能恢复和平、稳定和对法治的尊重。

2. obstacle ['ɒbstəkl] n. 障碍（物）
『ob逆+st站+acle表物→逆向站的东西→障碍』

❶ ~ (to sth/to doing sth) 障碍；阻碍；绊脚石

A lack of qualifications can be a major obstacle to finding a job. 资历不足可能成为谋职的主要障碍。

❷ 障碍物

Most competition cars will only roll over if they hit an obstacle. 大多数赛车只有在撞上障碍物才会翻车。

词义辨析 <P372第56>

障碍 obstacle, barrier, obstruction, bar

3. distance ['dɪstəns] n. 距离；间距 <P55>
『dis(=away)离开+(s)tance站→（两地）相离而站→距离』

▶ **distant** ['dɪstənt] adj. 遥远的

4. instant ['ɪnstənt] adj. 立刻的；速溶的 n. 片刻
『in里面+stant站→（立即）站到里面→立刻的；速溶的』

Mr Porter's book was an instant hit.
波特先生的书一经推出便大受欢迎。

instant coffee 速溶咖啡

I'll be back in an instant. 我马上就来。

▶ **instantaneous** [ˌɪnstən'teɪniəs] adj. 立即的，立刻的

Death was instantaneous because both bullets hit the heart.
因为两颗子弹都击中了心脏，所以死亡是瞬间发生的。

5. instance ['ɪnstəns] n. 例子，事例
『in里面+stance站→站在（那一群）里面→例子』

a particular example or case of sth

The report highlights a number of instances of injustice.
这篇报道重点列举了一些不公正的实例。

There are a number of improvements; for instance, both mouse buttons can now be used.
许多地方有了改进，例如，鼠标的左右键都可以使用了。

6. circumstance ['sɜːkəmstəns] n. 环境；境遇
『circum环绕，周围+ stance站→置身在其中→环境；状况』

[C, usually pl.] 条件；环境；状况

the conditions and facts that are connected with and affect a situation, an event or an action

The company reserves the right to cancel this agreement in certain circumstances.
本公司保留在一定条件下取消这项协议的权利。

in/under the circumstances 在这种情况下

Under the circumstances, it seemed better not to tell him about the accident.
在这种情况下，不告诉他这次事故似乎更好。

in/under no circumstances 决不；无论如何都不

Under no circumstances should you lend Paul any money.
你无论如何都不能借钱给保罗。

7. constant ['kɒnstənt] adj. 不断的，一直的；恒定的 <P56>
『con强调+stant站→一直站（在那里）→不断的；恒定的』

8. substance ['sʌbstəns] n. 物质；实质 <P37>
『sub下面+stance (stand)站→站在（表面）下面→实质』

② stat, sta=stand，表示"站"

1. static ['stætɪk] adj. 静止的，不变化的 n. 静电
『stat站+ic…的→站着（不动）的→静止的』

not moving, changing or developing

Prices on the stock market, which have been static, are now rising again. 股市价格一直停滞不动，现在又在上涨了。

a static population level 稳定的人口水平

My hair gets full of static when I brush it.
我梳头时头发就有好多静电。

2. stationary ['steɪʃənri] adj. 不动的，静止的
『stat站+ion表名词+ary有…性质的→站着的→静止的』

Something that is stationary is not moving.

Stationary cars in traffic jams cause a great deal of pollution.
交通堵塞中静止不动的汽车产生了大量污染。

形近词 **stationery** ['steɪʃənri] n. 文具；信纸

[U] Stationery is paper, envelopes, and other materials or equipment used for writing.

You can buy ready-printed forms for wills at stationery shops.
你可以在文具店买到已印好的遗嘱单。
Stationery can be imprinted with your message or logo.
可以把你的信息或标志印在信纸上。

3. statue [ˈstætʃuː] n. 雕塑，雕像
『stat站+ue→（大小通常等于或大于真人或实物）的雕像站在那里→雕塑，雕像』

4. stature [ˈstætʃə(r)] n. 身高，个子；地位，声望
『stat站+ure表状态→站立时的状态→身高→地位，声望』

It's more than his physical stature that makes him remarkable.
让他与众不同的不仅仅是他的身高。
The orchestra has grown in stature.
这支管弦乐队的声望有所提高。

5. status [ˈsteɪtəs] n. 地位；状况
『stat站+us表名词→（人在社会上）站的位置；（事情在发展中）的位置→地位；状况』

❶ （法律上的或社会上的）身份地位；上层地位
They were granted refugee status. 他们获得了难民身份。
Women are only asking to be given equal status with men.
女性只是要求得到和男性平等的地位。
The job brings with it status and a high income.
担任这一职务既有显贵的地位又有丰厚的收入。

❷ [U] （进展的）状况，情形
the situation at a particular time during a process
What is the current status of our application for funds?
我们申请资金目前进展状况如何？

▶ **status quo** [ˌsteɪtəs ˈkwəʊ] n. 现状；状况
The status quo is the state of affairs that exists at a particular time, especially in contrast to a different possible state of affairs.
Furthermore, this study brings forward some education measures that associated with the status quo.
此外，研究进一步提出了相关的教育措施。
We must not return to the status quo. 我们绝不能恢复原状。

6. statute [ˈstætʃuːt] n. 成文法；法规
『stat站+ute→已经站立起来成形的法律→成文法；法规』
A statute is a rule or law which has been made by a government or other organization and formally written down.
Corporal punishment was banned by statute in 1987.
1987年通过的法令明文禁止体罚。
Under the statutes of the university they had no power to dismiss him. 按大学的规章制度，校方无权开除他。

7. stamina [ˈstæmɪnə] n. 耐力，持久力
『sta站+mina→长久站所需要的力→耐力，持久力』
the physical or mental strength that enables you to do sth difficult for long periods of time
It takes a lot of stamina to run a marathon.
跑马拉松需要很大的耐力。
Hillary Clinton does not have the "look" or the "stamina" to be president, Donald Trump said.
唐纳德·特朗普说，希拉里·克林顿没有当总统的"容貌"和"耐力"。

8. stagnant [ˈstæɡnənt] adj. （水或空气）不流动而污浊的；（经济或社会）停滞不前的
『stagn(=sta)站+ant…的→站立不动的→停滞不前的』

He is seeking advice on how to revive the stagnant economy.
他正在就如何振兴低迷的经济征求意见。
The stagnant water was a breeding ground for disease.
污浊的死水是疾病的滋生地。

③ stead, stin=stand，表示"站"

1. instead [ɪnˈsted] adv. 代替
『in里面+stead站→（一事）站到（另一事）里面→代替』
He didn't reply. Instead, he turned on his heel and left the room. 他没有回答，反而转身离开了房间。

2. homestead [ˈhəʊmsted] n. 家宅；农庄
『home家+stead站→家所站立的地方→（包括周围土地和附属房屋的）家宅』

3. steadfast [ˈstedfɑːst] adj. 坚定的
『stead站+fast牢固的→立场牢固的→坚定的』
not changing in your attitudes or aims
He remained steadfast in his determination to bring the killers to justice. 他要将杀人凶手绳之以法的决心一直没有动摇。

4. obstinate [ˈɒbstɪnət] adj.（人）固执的；（事、物）顽固的
『ob逆+stin站+ate有…性质的→（和要求）反着站→顽固的』
He can be very obstinate when he wants to be!
他的犟劲儿一上来，简直执拗得要命！
the obstinate problem of unemployment
失业这个棘手的问题
an obstinate stain 除不掉的斑渍

词根328. stall=place，表示"放"

1. install [ɪnˈstɔːl] vt. 安装；正式任命；安顿
『in里面+stall放→把（机器、软件、人）放到里面（使其正常运转）→安装；正式任命；安顿』

❶ [VN] 安装（家具）；安装（电脑程序）
He's getting a phone installed tomorrow. 他明天要装电话。
I'll need some help installing the software.
我需要帮助安装这个软件。

❷ [VN] 使就职；任命
If someone is installed in a new job or important position, they are officially given the job or position, often in a special ceremony.
A new Catholic bishop was installed in Galway yesterday.
昨天在戈尔韦任命了一位新的天主教主教。

❸ 安顿，安置
If you install yourself in a particular place, you settle there and make yourself comfortable.
Before her husband's death she had installed herself in a modern villa.
丈夫去世之前她已经在一所现代化别墅里安顿下来了。

▶ **installation** [ˌɪnstəˈleɪʃn] n. 安装；安装的设备；就职，就职仪式；（军事）设施
installation costs 安装费
a heating installation 供暖装置
the installation of the new vice chancellor 新任副校长就职
a military installation 军事设施

2. installment [ɪnˈstɔːlmənt] n. 分期付款；（丛书杂志等的）一部，一期
『in里面+stall放+ment表名词→把（钱、故事等分批）放

进去→分期付款；（丛书杂志等的）一部，一期』

I shall soon pay the last installment of my debt.
不久我将付清我的最后一期债款。

We agreed to pay for the car by/in installments.
我们同意分期付款买车。

The novel has been serialized for radio in five installments.
这部小说已分五期在广播连载。

3. forestall [fɔːˈstɔːl] vt. 预先阻止
『fore前面+stall放→（把障碍物）放到前面→预先阻止』

Try to anticipate what your child will do and forestall problems.
尽量预见你的孩子会干什么，并预先阻止问题发生。

4. stall [stɔːl] n. 摊位；马厩；前排座位 v.（车）熄火；故意拖延
『stall放→放（货物、牛马、听的人）的地方→摊位；马厩；前排座位；stall放→（车行驶中突然）放到那里了→（发动机）熄火；拖延』

❶ [C] 货摊，摊位，售货亭（尤指集市上的）

❷ [C] 牲畜栏；马厩；牛棚

❸ the stalls（戏院、音乐厅、教堂内）正厅前排座位

❹（车辆或发动机的）熄火；（飞机）失速

[V] The car stalled and refused to start again.
汽车熄火打不着了。

❺ 故意拖延（以赢得时间）

[V] They are still stalling on the deal.
他们仍在拖时间，而不急于达成协议。

[VN] See if you can stall her while I finish searching her office. 你看能不能拖住她，我好把她的办公室搜查完。

词根329. stell=star，表示"星星"

1. stellar [ˈstelə(r)] adj. 星的，恒星的；优秀的，出色的
『stell星星+ar…的→星星的；优秀的』

A stellar wind streams outward from the star.
那颗恒星不断吹出恒星风。

a stellar performance 精彩的演出

2. interstellar [ˌɪntəˈstelə(r)] adj. 星际的
『inter在…之间+stell星星+ar…的→星际的』

These elements become part of the interstellar gas and dust.
这些元素成了星际气体和星际尘埃的一部分。

3. constellation [ˌkɒnstəˈleɪʃn] n. 星座；一群，一组（相似的事物）
『con一起+stell星星+ation表名词→（许多）星星聚在一起→星座；一群，一组』

The largest gallery contains at its centre a constellation of photographs called My Wishes.
最大的画廊在中心位置展出了一组名为《我的心愿》的摄影作品。

词根330. still=small drop，表示"小水滴"

1. instill [ɪnˈstɪl] vt. 逐渐灌输
『in里面+still小水滴→像小水滴一样滴进去→逐渐灌输』

to instill confidence/discipline/fear into sb
逐步使某人树立信心/守纪律/产生恐惧

2. distill [dɪˈstɪl] v. 蒸馏；提炼，浓缩
『di离开，分开+still小水滴→（水加热后形成蒸汽，蒸汽再

凝结成水珠）滴下来→蒸馏』

❶ [VN] 蒸馏

to make a liquid stronger or purer by heating it until it changes to a gas and then cooling it so that it changes back into a liquid

Some strong alcoholic drinks such as whisky are made by distilling.
一些烈性酒精饮料，如威士忌，是由蒸馏制成的。

❷ [VN] 提炼，浓缩

to get the essential meaning or ideas from thoughts, information, experiences, etc.

Over 80 hours of footage have been distilled **into** these 40 minutes. 超过80小时的录像被浓缩成40分钟。

The notes I made on my travels were distilled into a book.
我的旅行笔记精选汇编成了一本书。

词根331. sting, stinct, stig, stimul=stick，表示"棍子"，引申为prick，表示"刺；戳"

1. sting [stɪŋ] v. 刺；蜇；叮；激怒；使不安
『sting刺，戳→刺；蜇；叮』
（stung, stung）

❶（昆虫或植物）刺；蜇；叮
[VN] I was stung on the arm by a wasp.
我的胳膊被黄蜂蜇了一下。

❷（使）感觉刺痛，感觉灼痛
[V] My eyes were stinging from the smoke.烟熏得我眼睛疼。

[VN] Tears stung her eyes. 她流泪流得眼睛疼。

❸ [VN] ~ sb (to/into sth) | ~ sb (into doing sth)
激怒；使不安

He was stung by their criticism. 他们的批评使他心烦意乱。
Their cruel remarks stung her into action.
他们伤人的话激怒了她，使她不得不采取行动。

▶**stingy** [ˈstɪndʒi] adj. 小气的；吝啬的
『sting叮；刺+y表形容词→（花钱时心里）像被刺了一样的→小气的；吝啬的』

2. extinct [ɪkˈstɪŋkt] adj. 灭绝的；消亡的
『ex出+(s)tinct刺；戳→戳出去（杀死猎物）→灭绝的』

❶ 灭绝的，绝种的
It is 250 years since the wolf became extinct in Britain.
狼在英国已经灭绝250年了。

❷（某种类型的人、工作或生活方式）绝迹的；消亡的
Servants are now almost extinct in modern society.
在现代社会里奴仆已近乎不复存在。

❸（火山）不再活跃的；死的

▶**extinction** [ɪkˈstɪŋkʃn] n.（植物、动物、生活方式等的）灭绝，绝种，消亡

An operation is beginning to try to save a species of crocodile from extinction.
一项努力拯救一个鳄鱼物种、使其免于灭绝的行动已经开始。

▶**extinguish** [ɪkˈstɪŋgwɪʃ] vt. 扑灭（火），熄灭（灯）；使（希望、想法）破灭
『extinct灭绝（变ct为gu）+ish使→使（火、希望等）熄灭』

Firefighters tried to extinguish the flames.
消防队员奋力救火。

(formal) All lights had been extinguished.
所有灯光都熄灭了。

The message extinguished her hopes of Richard's return.
那条消息使她对理查德归来的希望彻底破灭了。

▶ **extinguisher** [ɪkˈstɪŋgwɪʃə(r)] n. 灭火器

3. **distinct** [dɪˈstɪŋkt] adj. 清楚的；确定无疑的；有区别的
『dis(=away)离开+(s)tinct刺，戳→在（猎物）离开时（一定要看清楚，确定无疑时再）戳→清楚的；确定无疑的』

❶ 清楚的，清晰的，明显的
If something is distinct, you can hear, see, or taste it clearly.
There was a distinct smell of gas. 有一股明显的煤气味。
His voice was quiet but every word was distinct.
他说话声音不大，但吐字清晰。

❷ [only before noun] 确定无疑的，确实的，确切的
used to emphasize that you think an idea or situation definitely exists and is important
Being tall gave Tony a distinct advantage.
托尼个子高是个明显的优势。
I had the distinct impression I was being watched.
我确实感到有人在监视我。

❸ ~ (from sth) 截然不同的；有区别的；不同种类的
clearly different or of a different kind
The results of the survey fell into two distinct groups.
调查结果分为截然不同的两组。
The two concepts are quite distinct from each other.
这两个概念相互是有明显区别的。

▶ **distinctive** [dɪˈstɪŋktɪv] adj. 独特的，有特色的
『distinct清楚的，有区别的+ive有…特征的→具有（与别的）区别开的特征的→独特的』

When Miles Davis died, jazz was robbed of its most distinctive voice.
随着迈尔斯·戴维斯的去世，爵士乐界失去了其最与众不同的声音。
Cooking with the lid on gives the food that distinctive smoky flavour.
盖上盖子烹饪会让这种食物有一种熏制般的独特风味。

▶ **distinction** [dɪˈstɪŋkʃn] n. 区分；特质；优秀

❶ [C, U] 区分，区别
The new law makes no distinction between adults and children. 这项新法律对成人和孩子同等对待。
There are obvious distinctions between the two wine-making areas. 两个酿酒地区之间有着显著的差别。

❷ [sing.] 特质，特点
the quality of being sth that is special
She had the distinction of being the first woman to fly the Atlantic. 她不同凡响，是第一个飞越大西洋的女子。

❸ [U] 优秀；杰出；卓越
the quality of being excellent or important
a writer of distinction 一位优秀作家

▶ **distinguish** [dɪˈstɪŋgwɪʃ] vt. 区别；使出众
『distinct清楚；有区别的（变ct为gu）+ish使→使…区别开来→区别』

❶ ~ (between) A and B | ~ A from B 区分，辨别，分清
to recognise the difference between two people or things
[V] At what age are children able to distinguish between right and wrong? 儿童到什么年龄才能明辨是非？

[VN] It was hard to distinguish one twin from the other.
很难分辨出一对孪生儿谁是谁。

❷ ~ A (from B) （特质或特征）使有别于
There is something about music that distinguishes it from all other art forms.
音乐的某种特质使其有别于所有其他艺术形式。

❸ [VN] 看清；认出；听出
to be able to see or hear sth
I could not distinguish her words, but she sounded agitated.
我听不清她说的话，但听得出她很紧张不安。

❹ [VN] ~ yourself (as sth) 使出众，使著名
She has already distinguished herself as an athlete.
作为运动员她已享有盛名。

▶ **distinguished** [dɪˈstɪŋgwɪʃt] adj. 卓越的，杰出的；尊贵的

He was one of Australia's most distinguished artists, renowned for his portraits, landscapes and nudes.
他是澳大利亚最为杰出的艺术家之一，以肖像画、风景画和裸体画而闻名。
In particular, I would like to welcome our distinguished guests and delegates from overseas.
我特别要欢迎来自海外的嘉宾和代表。

4. **instinct** [ˈɪnstɪŋkt] n. 本能，天性；直觉
『in里面，内心+stinct刺；戳→内心里（知道怎样戳是）本能；直觉→本能；直觉』

His first instinct was to run away. 他的本能反应就是逃跑。
Even at school, he showed he had an instinct for business.早在求学时期他就表现出经商的天赋。
Her instincts had been right. 她当时的直觉是对的。

▶ **instinctive** [ɪnˈstɪŋktɪv] adj. 本能的；天生的；直觉的
She's an instinctive player. 她是个天生的运动员。
My instinctive reaction was to deny everything.
我的本能反应是否认一切。

5. **instigate** [ˈɪnstɪgeɪt] vt. 煽动，唆使，鼓动
『in里面+stig刺，戳+ate表动词→在里面戳（使人做坏事）→煽动，唆使，鼓动』

to cause sth bad to happen
They were accused of instigating racial violence.
他们被控煽动种族暴力。

6. **stigma** [ˈstɪgmə] n. 耻辱，羞耻
『stig刺，戳+ma→（做了蠢事，感觉别人在）戳→耻辱』

If something has a stigma attached to it, people think it is something to be ashamed of.
There is no longer any stigma attached to being divorced.
离婚不再是什么丢脸的事。

▶ **stigmatize** [ˈstɪgmətaɪz] vt. 侮辱，污蔑
They are often stigmatized by the rest of society as lazy and dirty. 他们经常被社会中的其他人污蔑为懒惰和肮脏。

7. **stimulate** [ˈstɪmjuleɪt] v. 刺激；激发
『stimul刺激+ate表动词→刺激；激发』

[VN] Parents should give children books that stimulate them.
父母应给孩子能启发他们的书。
America's priority is rightly to stimulate its economy.
美国的首要任务自然是刺激经济。

形近词 **simulate** [ˈsɪmjuleɪt] vt. 装出；模仿；模拟
<P301>

▶ **stimulant** [ˈstɪmjələnt] n. 兴奋剂；引起兴奋的药物
『stimul刺激+ant剂→兴奋剂』

词根332. stitute, stit=set up; place，表示"建立；放"

1. constitute [ˈkɒnstɪtjuːt] v. 构成，组成；成立
『con一起+stitute放→（把多个部分）放在一起（构成一个整体）→组成；构成；成立』

❶ linking verb [V-N] （不用于进行时）是；被算作；被视为
If something constitutes a particular thing, it can be regarded as being that thing.
Does such an activity constitute a criminal offence?
难道这样的活动也算刑事犯罪吗？

❷ linking verb [V-N] （不用于进行时）组成；构成
to be the parts that together form sth
Female workers constitute the majority of the labour force.
女性雇员占劳动力的多数。

❸ [VN] [usually passive] （合法或正式地）成立，设立
to form a group legally or officially
The committee was constituted in 1974 by an Act of Parliament. 该委员会是根据议会法案于1974年设立的。

词义辨析 <P375第73>
由…组成 **make up, consist of, compose, constitute, comprise**

▶ **constitution** [ˌkɒnstɪˈtjuːʃn] n. 宪法；组成
『constitute设立；组成（去e)+ion表名词→设立的（法律文件）；组成→宪法；组成』
The king was forced to adopt a new constitution which reduced his powers. 国王被迫采用了削弱其权力的新宪法。

2. institute [ˈɪnstɪtjuːt] n. （教育、专业等）机构 vt. 制定（体系、政策等）
『in使+stitute建立→建立机构→（教育、专业等）机构』

❶ [C] （教育、专业等）机构；机构建筑
a research institute 研究所
institutes of higher education 高等学校
the National Cancer Institute 国家癌症研究所

❷ [VN] (formal) 建立，制定（体系、政策等）；开始；实行
to introduce a system, policy, etc. or start a process
We will institute a number of measures to better safeguard the public. 我们将实施一系列措施来更好地保障公众安全。

▶ **institution** [ˌɪnstɪˈtjuːʃn] n.（大学、银行、慈善、福利等规模大的）公共机构；（由来已久的）风俗习惯；制度

❶ [C]（大学、教会、银行等）（大型）机构
An institution is a large important organization such as a university, church, or bank.
For this example, the partners are the customer and the financial institution.
对于这个示例来说，伙伴是客户和金融机构。

❷ [C] 慈善机构；社会福利机构
a place or building where people are sent to be cared for, especially a hospital or prison
We want this to be like a home, not an institution.
我们希望这里像个家，而不像收容所。

young offenders' institution 少年犯收容所
Larry has been in an institution since he was four.
拉里从4岁起就一直生活在孤儿院。

❸ [C] （由来已久的）风俗习惯，制度
a custom or system that has existed for a long time among a particular group of people
I believe in the institution of marriage. 我相信婚姻制度。
The institution of slavery was once widespread.
奴隶制度曾经很普遍。

❹ [U] 建立；设立；制定
the act of starting or introducing sth such as a system or a law
the institution of new safety procedures 新安全规程的制定

3. substitute [ˈsʌbstɪtjuːt] v. 替代 n. 替代者，替代品
『sub下+stitute放→（把A）放到（B的）下面（来作为B）→代替』

❶ ~ A (for B) | ~ B (with/by A) | ~ for sb/sth 用A替代B
[VN] You can substitute water for milk in the recipe.
你可以在食谱中以水代替牛奶。
[V] If you cannot go yourself, try to find someone to substitute for you. 你要是自己不能去，可以找个人来代替。
[VN] Margarine can be substituted for butter in this recipe.
做这道菜可以用人造黄油代替黄油。
Butter can be substituted with margarine in this recipe.
做这道菜可以用人造黄油代替黄油。

❷ [C] ~ (for sb/sth) 代替者
Paul's father only saw him as a substitute for his dead brother.
保罗的父亲只是把他当作他死去的哥哥来看待。

❸ [C] 替补（运动员）
词义辨析 <P363第11> 替代 **replace, substitute**

4. destitute [ˈdestɪtjuːt] adj. 贫困的，贫穷的，赤贫的
『de离开+stitute放→被放到（不得不）离开（家乡这种状态）→因贫穷到一无所有而不得不背井离乡→贫穷的』
without money, food and the other things necessary for life
When he died, his family was left completely destitute.
他死时家里一贫如洗。

5. prostitute [ˈprɒstɪtjuːt] n. 妓女，卖淫者
『pro在前+stitute放→（站）在（路）前的女人→妓女』

6. superstition [ˌsuːpəˈstɪʃn] n. 迷信；迷信观念
『super上+stit站+ion行为，由行为产生的事物→站在上面的（人）→（地位高的人容易）迷信→迷信』

▶ **superstitious** [ˌsuːpəˈstɪʃəs] adj. 迷信的 <P38>
『super上面+stit(set up) 建立+ious…的→上层的人（喜欢把自己的决定）建立在（迷信之上）→迷信的』

词根333. strain=tighten，表示"拉紧"

1. strain [streɪn] n. 拉力；压力；拉伤；种类 v. 竭力；拉伤
『strain拉紧→（物体、负荷、精神、肌肉）拉紧→拉力；压力；拉伤』

❶ [U, C] 压力；拉力；张力；应力
the pressure that is put on sth when a physical force stretches, pushes, or pulls it
The rope broke under the strain. 绳子拉断了。
You should try not to place too much strain on muscles and joints. 你要尽量不让肌肉和关节太吃力。
The ground here cannot take the strain of a large building.

这块地承受不住大型建筑的压力。

❷ [U, C] 压力，负担，重负；（精神上的）压力，重负；带来压力的因素

The prison service is already under considerable strain.
监狱系统已经承受了巨大的压力。

She was tired and under great strain. 她身心疲惫，压力很大。

COVID-19 has placed a huge strain on the resources of the country's hospitals.
COVID-19（新冠肺炎）对该国医院的资源造成了巨大压力。

❸ [U, C]（肌肉的）扭伤，拉伤，劳损

Avoid muscle strain by warming up with slow jogging.
先慢跑热热身，免得拉伤肌肉。

❹ [C]（动、植物的）系，品种；（疾病的）类型

Every year new strains of influenza develop.
每年都有新的流感病毒出现。

❺ ~ (sth) (for sth) | ~ (sth) (to do sth) 尽力；竭力；使劲
[VN to inf] I strained my ears (= listened very hard) to catch what they were saying. 我竖起耳朵去听他们在说些什么。
[VN] Necks were strained for a glimpse of the stranger.
大家伸长了脖子想看一看这个陌生人。
She strained against the ropes that held her.
她使劲挣了挣拴着她的绳子。

❻ [VN] 过度使用；使不堪承受
The sudden influx of visitors is straining hotels in the town to the limit. 游客突然涌入，城里的旅馆全都爆满。
His constant complaints were straining our patience.
他没完没了的抱怨让我们忍无可忍。

❼ [VN] 损伤；拉伤；扭伤
He strained his back during a practice session.
他在一次锻炼中拉伤了背部。

2. constrain [kənˈstreɪn] vt. 限制；迫使
『con一起+strain拉紧→（各种因素）一起拉紧（使不能做某事或不得不做某事）→限制；迫使』

❶ [VN to inf] [usually passive] 强迫，迫使
to force sb to do sth or behave in a particular way
to force someone to do something that they do not want to do
The evidence was so compelling that he felt constrained to accept it. 证据是那样的令人折服，他觉得不得不接受。

❷ [VN] [often passive] ~ sb (from doing sth) 限制，约束
to limit someone's freedom to do what they want
Research has been constrained by a lack of funds.
研究工作因经费不足而受限制。
Criticism tends to undermine and constrain the artist's creativity. 批评往往会削弱和限制艺术家的创造力。

▶**constraint** [kənˈstreɪnt] n. 限制，约束
[C] (often pl.) 限制，约束
something that limits your freedom to do what you want
Their decision to abandon the trip was made because of financial constraints.
他们决定放弃这次出游是因为财力有限。
An American military presence has further served as a **constraint on** Iran's nuclear program.
美国的军事存在进一步限制了伊朗的核计划。

词义辨析 <P377第79>
限制 **limit, restriction, constraint, restraint**

3. restrain [rɪˈstreɪn] vt. 制止；克制；控制
『re回来+strain拉紧→（有想做某事的冲动，思想上或行动上赶紧）拉回来→制止；克制』

❶ ~ sb/sth (from sth/from doing sth)（尤指用武力）制止，阻止，管制（某人的行动或自由）
to stop sb/sth from doing sth, especially by using physical force
The prisoner had to be restrained by the police.
警察只能强行控制住囚犯。
He placed a restraining hand on her arm.
他拉住她的胳膊制止她。

❷ ~ yourself (from sth/from doing sth) 约束（自己）；控制（自己）；克制
to stop yourself from feeling an emotion or doing sth that you would like to do
John managed to restrain his anger.
约翰努力压制住自己的怒气。
She had to restrain herself from crying out in pain.
她只得忍住疼痛，不哭出来。

近义词 **refrain** [rɪˈfreɪn] vi. 克制，节制
[V] ~ (from sth/from doing sth)
to stop yourself from doing sth, especially sth that you want to do
Please refrain from smoking. 请勿吸烟。
He has refrained from criticizing the government in public.
他克制住了自己，没有在公开场合批评政府。

词义辨析 <P377第80> 克制 **restrain, refrain**

❸ 抑制；控制 （keep under control）
to stop sth that is growing or increasing from becoming too large
The government is taking steps to restrain inflation.
政府正在采取措施控制通货膨胀。
Some say there is a need to restrain public spending.
有些人认为需要控制公共支出。

▶**restraint** [rɪˈstreɪnt] n. （武力）制止；克制；控制，控制措施

the physical restraint of prisoners 对囚犯的人身限制
He exercised considerable restraint in ignoring the insults.
他表现出极大的克制，没去理会种种侮辱。
The government has imposed export restraints on some products. 政府对一些产品实行了出口控制。

词义辨析 <P377第79>
限制 **limit, restriction, constraint, restraint**

词根334. strict, string=tighten，表示"拉紧"

1. restrict [rɪˈstrɪkt] vt. 限制，限定；妨碍，束缚
『re又，再+ strict拉紧→一再拉紧→限制』

~ sth (to sth) 限制，限定（数量、范围、规模等）
Speed is restricted to 30 mph in towns.
在城里车速不得超过每小时30英里。
Having small children tends to restrict your freedom.
有年幼的孩子往往会限制你的自由。
The hospital may restrict bookings to people living locally.
这家医院可能会限定只有当地居民才能预约。
The long skirt restricted her movements.
长裙妨碍了她的行动。

▶**restriction** [rɪˈstrɪkʃn] n. 限制，约束

▶**restrictive** [rɪ'strɪktɪv] adj. 限制性的；约束的

词义辨析 <P376第78> **限制 limit, confine, restrict**

词义辨析 <P377第79>

限制 limit, restriction, constraint, restraint

2. constrict [kən'strɪkt] v. 收紧；束缚

『con一起+strict拉紧→拉紧到一起→收紧；束缚』

❶ （使）（身体部位，尤指喉咙）收紧，收缩

[V] Her throat constricted and she swallowed hard.
她喉咙发紧，使劲地咽了一下唾沫。

[VN] a drug that constricts the blood vessels
收缩血管的药

❷ [VN] 限制，束缚，约束

If something constricts you, it limits your actions so that you cannot do what you want to do.

She objects to the tests the Government's advisers have devised because they constrict her teaching style.
她反对政府顾问设计的考试，因为这些考试限制了她的教学风格。

▶**constriction** [kən'strɪkʃn] n. 收缩；束缚

3. stringent ['strɪndʒənt] adj. （法律、规章等）严格的；（财政状况）紧缩的

『string拉紧+ent…的→拉紧的→严格的；紧缩的』

He announced that there would be more stringent controls on the possession of weapons.
他宣布将对武器的持有实行更严格的控制。

the government's stringent economic policies
政府严格的经济政策

▶**stringency** ['strɪndʒənsi] n. 财政紧缩

Bankers say financial stringency constitutes a serious threat to the country.
银行家们表示，财政紧缩对国家构成了严重的威胁。

▶**string** [strɪŋ] n. 细绳；一串，一系列；弦 vt. 系；串（strung, strung）

❶ [U, C] 细绳；一根细绳

a piece/length of string 一根/一段细绳

The key is hanging on a string by the door.
钥匙拴在门边的带子上。

❷ [C] 一串；一系列；字符串

a string of pearls 一串珍珠

a string of attacks 一系列袭击事件

❸ [C] （乐器的）弦；the stings 弦乐器组

The opening theme is taken up by the strings.
开始的主旋律由弦乐器演奏。

❹ [VN] 系；扎；串起来

Flags were strung out along the route. 沿途悬挂着旗子。

She had strung the shells on a silver chain.
她把贝壳串在一条银链子上。

词根335. struct=build，表示"建立，建造"

1. construct [kən'strʌkt] vt. 建筑，建造

『con一起+ struct建造，建立→建造到一起→建筑，建造』

▶**construction** [kən'strʌkʃn] n. 建筑，建造

Our new offices are still under construction.
我们的新办公楼尚在修建中。

▶**constructive** [kən'strʌktɪv] adj. 建设性的

having a useful and helpful effect rather than being negative or with no purpose

The government is encouraging all parties to play a constructive role in the reform process.
政府鼓励所有的政党在改革过程中发挥建设性的作用。

After their meeting, both men described the talks as frank, friendly and constructive.
会面之后，两位男士均表示此次会谈坦率、友好且富有建设性。

2. destruction [dɪ'strʌkʃn] n. 破坏

『de相反+struct建设+ion表名词→破坏』

the act of destroying sth; the process of being destroyed

weapons of mass destruction 大规模杀伤性武器

There is worldwide concern about the destruction of the rainforests. 全世界都在关注热带雨林遭到破坏的问题。

▶**destructive** [dɪ'strʌktɪv] adj. 破坏性的

Tanks are heavy on fuel and destructive to roads.
坦克要耗费大量的燃料，而且会破坏道路。

He was unable to contain his own destructive feelings.
他无法抑制自己消极的情绪。

3. instruct [ɪn'strʌkt] vt. 指示；传授（技能等）

『in里面+struct建造→把（指示、知识）建筑到里面（内心里）→指示；传授』

❶ (formal) 指示；命令；吩咐

to tell sb to do sth, especially in a formal or official way

[VN] She arrived at 10 o'clock as instructed.
她依照指示于10点钟到达。

[V that] He instructed that a wall be built around the city.
他下令在城的周围筑一道城墙。

❷ [VN] ~ sb (in sth) (formal) 教授，传授（技能等）

to teach sb sth, especially a practical skill

He instructed family members in nursing techniques.
他教授家人护理技巧。

▶**instructor** [ɪn'strʌktə(r)] n. 教练，指导者；（美国英语亦指）教师，大学讲师

His sailing instructor fell overboard and drowned during a lesson. 他的航海教练在一次训练课时从船上失足跌入水中，溺水身亡。

▶**instruction** [ɪn'strʌkʃn] n. 说明；指令；教授

❶ instructions [pl.] 用法说明；操作指南

detailed information on how to do or use sth

Follow the instructions on the packet carefully.
请仔细按照包装上的说明操作。

Always read the instructions before you start.
使用前务请阅读操作说明。

小贴士 direction作"用法说明，操作指南"（Directions are instructions that tell you what to do, how to do something, or how to get somewhere.）解时，也常用复数形式。

I should know by now not to throw away the directions until we've finished cooking.
现在我知道了不该在完成烹饪之前就扔掉说明。

Let's stop and ask for directions. 我们停下来问问路吧。

❷ [C, usually pl.] 指示；命令；吩咐

something that sb tells you to do

Two lawyers were told not to leave the building but no reason for this instruction was given. 两名律师被告知不得

离开大楼，但对这一命令并没有提供任何理由。
I'm under instructions to keep my speech short.
我接到指示讲话要简短。

❸ [U] ~ (in sth) (formal) 教授；教导；传授
the act of teaching sth to sb
About 110 schools use English as the medium of instruction.
约有110所学校用英语授课。

4. obstruct [əbˈstrʌkt] vt. 阻挡，阻塞；妨碍；阻挠
『ob(=against)对着+struct建造→对着（通道）建造→阻塞』

❶ [VN] 阻挡；阻塞；遮断
to block a road, an entrance, a passage, etc. so that sb/sth cannot get through, see past, etc.
You can't park here, you're obstructing my driveway.
你不能在这里停车，你挡住了我家的车道。
The pillar obstructed our view of the stage.
柱子挡着，我们看不见舞台。

❷ [VN] （故意）妨碍，阻挠，阻碍（进展或进程）
to prevent sb/sth from doing sth or making progress, especially when this is done deliberately
The authorities are obstructing a United Nations investigation.
当局正在阻挠联合国的调查。

▶ **obstruction** [əbˈstrʌkʃn] n. 障碍物；阻挠
US lawmakers charge Trump with abuse of office and obstruction of the congressional impeachment inquiry.
美国国会议员指控特朗普滥用职权、阻挠国会弹劾调查。

词义辨析 <P372第56>
障碍 obstacle, barrier, obstruction, bar

5. structure [ˈstrʌktʃə(r)] n. 结构，构造；结构体
『struct建造，建立+ure表结果→结构；构造』

❶ [U, C] 结构；构造
the structure of the building　建筑物的结构
changes in the social and economic structure of society
社会和经济结构的变化

❷ [C] 结构体；（尤指）建筑物
The house was a handsome four-story brick structure.
这房子是一幢造型美观的四层砖砌建筑物。

6. superstructure [ˈsuːpəstrʌktʃə(r)] n. 上层建筑
『super上面的+structure结构→上层的结构→上层建筑』

So this problem involves the superstructure, our system, and policies.
这个问题涉及上层建筑、我们的制度和政策。

7. infrastructure [ˈɪnfrəstrʌktʃə(r)] n. 基础设施
『infra (below) 以下+structure结构体→基础设施』

The infrastructure, from hotels to transport, is old and decrepit. 从酒店到交通，所有的基础设施都已陈旧失修。

词根336. sum=add up，表示"总；加"

1. sum [sʌm] n. 总和 v. 总结；概括

To sum up, there are three main ways of tackling the problem.
概括起来说，这一问题主要有三种解决办法。
Large sums of money were lost. 损失了大笔钱财。

2. summary [ˈsʌməri] n. 总结；概括 <P60>
『sum总；加（双写m）+ary表物→总结；概括』

3. summit [ˈsʌmɪt] n. 山顶；峰会

『sum总；加（双写m）+it表名词→总数→最高→山顶；峰会』

We reached the summit at noon. 中午时分我们抵达峰顶。
The Group of Seven major industrial countries concluded its annual summit today.
由主要工业国家组成的七国集团今天结束了其年度峰会。

4. consummate [kənˈsʌmət，ˈkɒnsəmeɪt] adj. 技艺高超的 vt. 使完整；使完美

❶ adj. 技艺高超的
He acted the part with consummate skill.
他以精湛的演技饰演了这一角色。

❷ [VN] 使完整；使完美

词根337. sume, sumpt=take，表示"拿，取"

1. consume [kənˈsjuːm] vt. 消耗；消费
『con一起+sume拿，取→把…一起拿来（消费掉）→消耗；消费』

❶ [VN] 消耗，耗费（燃料、能量、时间等）
The electricity industry consumes large amounts of fossil fuels. 电力工业消耗大量的矿物燃料。

❷ [VN] 吃；喝；饮；消费
Before he died he had consumed a large quantity of alcohol.
他死亡前喝了大量的酒。

▶ **consumption** [kənˈsʌmpʃn] n. （能量或材料的）消耗；吃，喝；肺结核（一种消耗性疾病，同 tuberculosis）
The laws have led to a reduction in fuel consumption in the US. 这些法律已经使美国燃料消耗量有所减少。
Most of the wine was unfit for human consumption.
这些酒中大部分都不适于人类饮用。

▶ **consumer** [kənˈsjuːmə(r)] n. 消费者，顾客，用户
A consumer is a person who buys things or uses services.
Nowadays, many consumers prefer to shop on the Internet.
如今，许多消费者更愿意在网上购物。

词义辨析 <P377第81> 顾客 client, consumer, customer

2. sumptuous [ˈsʌmptʃuəs] adj. 华贵的，豪华的，奢华的
『sumpt拿，取+uous多…的→拿得多的→花销大的→奢华的』
very expensive and looking very impressive
She produces elegant wedding gowns in a variety of sumptuous fabrics. 她用各种华贵的布料制作高雅的婚纱。

3. assume [əˈsjuːm] vt. 假定，认为；取得（权力）；呈现，显露
『as相当于to+sume拿，取→拿（采用）到（某种想法；某个职位或责任；某种外观或特征）；认为；就职；呈现』

❶ [VN] 假定；猜想；认为
to think or accept that sth is true but without having proof of it
[V (that)] It is reasonable to assume (that) the economy will continue to improve. 认为经济将继续好转是有道理的。
Let us assume for a moment that the plan succeeds.
让我们暂时假设计划成功了。
She would, he assumed, be home at the usual time.
他认为，她会在通常时间回到家的。

❷ [VN] 承担（责任）；就职；取得（权力）
Mr Cross will assume the role of Chief Executive with a team

of four directors.
克劳斯先生将出任由4名董事组成的团队的首席执行官。
Rebel forces have assumed control of the capital.
反叛武装力量已控制了首都。

❸ [VN] (formal) 呈现（外观、样子）；显露（特征）
to begin to have a particular quality or appearance

In the story the god assumes the form of an eagle.
在这个故事中神以鹰的形象出现。

▶ **assumption** [əˈsʌmpʃn] n. 假定，假设；（权力的）取得，（责任的）承担

His assumption proved to be wrong.
他的设想证明是错误的。

词义辨析 <P377第82>
推测，假定 assume, presume, suppose

4. **resume** [rɪˈzjuːm] v. 重新开始;继续；恢复（职位）
『re又，再+sume拿，取→继续；恢复（职位）』

❶ 重新开始；（中断后）继续
if you resume an activity, or if it resumes, it begins again or continues after an interruption

[V] The noise resumed, louder than before.
噪声再起，比先前更大。
[V -ing] He got back in the car and resumed driving.
他回到车上，继续开车。

❷ [VN] ~ your seat/place/position 恢复席位/地位/职位
"I changed my mind," Blanche said, resuming her seat.
"我改变主意了，"布兰奇说着回到她的座位上。

❸ résumé (US) (=CV) 履历，简历

▶ **resumption** [rɪˈzʌmpʃn] n. 重新开始；继续；恢复

5. **presume** [prɪˈzjuːm] vt. 假定，认为
『pre之前，预先+sume(=take) 拿，取→之前采取；采取之前→采取（某种想法）之前（事先分析考虑过）；（发现有罪）之前，（对嫌疑人）采取（视为无罪的态度）；（在别人同意）之前采取（某种行为）→（考虑后的）假定，认为；假定（无罪）』

❶ 假设，假定，认为
to suppose that sth is true, although you do not have actual proof

They are very expensive, I presume?
我想这些东西很贵吧？
"Is he still abroad?" "I presume so."
"他还在国外吗？" "我想是吧。"
I presume they're not coming, since they haven't replied to the invitation.
鉴于他们还没有回复邀请，我认为他们不会来了。
I presume from your pronunciation and intonation that you are a foreigner.
按你说话的语音语调，我推测你是个外国人。

❷ presume to do 冒昧；擅自；妄行
I know my place and I wouldn't presume to tell an expert how to do his job.
我知道该怎样做，我不会冒昧地去指挥一个行家的工作。
Do not presume to know what I am thinking or feeling.
不要认为自己知道我的想法和感觉。

❸ （法律上）假定，认为（无罪）
to accept that sth is true until it is shown not to be true, especially in court

In English law, a person is presumed innocent until proved guilty.
英国法律规定，一个人被证明有罪前假定为无罪。

▶ **presumption** [prɪˈzʌmpʃn] n. 推测，假定；擅自，冒昧

❶ [C] 推测，假定，可能的事
There is a general presumption that the doctor knows best.
一般人都以为医生最了解情况。

❷ [U] (formal) 非分的行为
They were angered by his presumption.
他们对他的放肆行为感到非常愤怒。

▶ **presumably** [prɪˈzjuːməbli] adv. 据推测；很可能
used to say that you think that sth is probably true

You'll be taking the car, presumably?
想必您是要买这辆汽车了？
I couldn't concentrate, presumably because I was so tired.
我的精神集中不起来，大概是太累了吧。

词义辨析 <P377第82>
推测，假定 assume, presume, suppose

词根338. surg(e)=rise，表示"升起"

1. **surge** [sɜːdʒ] vi. & n. 涌动；激增

❶ [V] （水、风、人群等）涌，涌动
to move quickly and with force in a particular direction

The gates opened and the crowd surged forward.
大门打开了，人群向前涌去。
Flood waters surged into their homes.
洪水涌进了他们的房子。

❷ [V] （感情、感觉）突袭，涌动，突发
Relief surged through her. 她顿觉宽慰。
Nausea surged in him and he retched violently.
他突然觉得恶心，猛烈地干呕起来。

❸ [V] 急剧上升；飞涨；激增
If something surges, it increases suddenly and greatly, after being steady or developing only slowly.

Share prices surged. 股价猛涨。
The COVID-19 cases surged in South Asia on Friday as India reported the record high of 26,506 new cases during the past 24 hours.
周五，南亚的COVID-19（新冠肺炎）病例激增，印度报告过去24小时新增病例26506例，创历史新高。

❹ [C] （强烈感情的）突发；（数量的）急剧上升；（风、水等的）奔涌，汹涌
She felt a sudden surge of anger. 她突然感觉怒火中烧。
We are having trouble keeping up with the recent surge in demand. 对于近来出现的需求猛增，我们难以应对。
An electrical surge damaged the computer's disk drive.
电浪涌损坏了计算机的磁盘驱动器。

2. **upsurge** [ˈʌpsɜːdʒ] n. 急剧上升；飙升
『up向上+surge激增→急剧上升』

an upsurge in violent crime 暴力犯罪的猛增

3. **resurgence** [rɪˈsɜːdʒəns] n. 复苏，复兴
『re返回+surg升起+ence表名词→重新升起→复苏，复兴』

[sing., U] 复苏，复兴
the return and growth of an activity that had stopped

Police say drugs traffickers are behind the resurgence of

violence. 警方说毒贩是暴力活动重新抬头的罪魁祸首。

▶ **resurgent** [rɪˈsɜːdʒənt] adj. 重新兴起的；复苏的

That could harm exports and growth in the resurgent eurozone.

这可能会危害到正在复苏的欧元区的出口和增长。

4. insurgent [ɪnˈsɜːdʒənt] n. 叛乱者 adj. 叛乱的

『in里面+surg升起；涌起+ent表人或形容词→（国内突然）涌起的→叛乱者』

[usually pl.] (formal) 起义者；叛乱者；造反者

a person fighting against the government or armed forces of their own country

By early yesterday, the insurgents had taken control of the country's main military air base.

到昨天清晨为止,叛乱者已经控制了该国的主要空军基地。

▶ **insurgency** [ɪnˈsɜːdʒənsi] n. 起义；叛乱；造反

词根339. sure，表示"确定，确信"

1. assure [əˈʃʊə(r)] vt. 使确信；向…保证

『as相当于to+sure确信→使达到确信的地步→使确信』

❶ ~ sb (of sth) 使确信；向…保证

We assured him of our support.

我们向他保证给予支持。

You think I did it deliberately, but I assure you (that) I did not. 你认为我是故意的，但我向你保证不是的。

❷ rest assured (that…) （强调所言确凿无误）尽管放心

You may rest assured that we will do all we can to find him.

你就放心吧，我们会千方百计找到他。

▶ **assurance** [əˈʃʊərəns] n. 保证，确保；（人寿）保险

He would like an assurance that other forces will not move into the territory that his forces vacate.

他想确保其他势力不会在他的军队撤离后进入这个地区。

词义辨析 <P364第18>

保证 assure, guarantee, promise, swear

2. reassure [ˌriːəˈʃʊə(r)] v. 使安心，使消除疑虑

『re又，再+assure使确信→又使确信→使安心』

to say or do sth that makes sb less frightened or worried

The doctor reassured him that there was nothing seriously wrong. 医生安慰他说，没什么严重的病。

▶ **reassuring** [ˌriːəˈʃʊərɪŋ] adj. 令人放心的

The mother smiled and gave him a reassuring hug.

母亲笑了笑，给了儿子一个安慰的拥抱。

3. insure [ɪnˈʃʊə(r)] vt. 投保；给…保险

『in使+sure确定的→使（发展、前途）确定→投保』

~ (yourself/sth) (against/for sth) 投保；给…保险

The painting is insured for $1 million.

这幅油画投了一百万美元的保险。

Luckily he had insured himself against long-term illness.

幸运的是，他为自己投保了长期病险。

▶ **insurance** [ɪnˈʃʊərəns] n. 保险；保险业；保费

life/car/travel/household, etc. insurance

人寿/汽车/旅行/家庭等保险

He works in insurance. 他在保险业工作。

to pay insurance on your house 交住房保险金

When her husband died, she received £50,000 in insurance.

她丈夫去世，她得到了一笔5万英镑的保险金。

insurance policy 保险单

Check that your insurance policy covers breakages and damage during removals.

查看一下你的保险单，看其是否对搬运过程中的破损和毁坏进行赔偿。

4. ensure [ɪnˈʃʊə(r)] vt. 确保；保证 <P15>

『en使进入…状态+sure确信→使确信→保证』

（also **insure** especially in NAmE）

词根340. tact, tag , tig, tach, tack, ting, tang=touch，表示"接触"

1. contact [ˈkɒntækt] n. 联系，联络 v. 联系，联络

『con一起+tact接触→接触到一起→联络』

❶ [U] ~ (with sb) | ~ (between A and B)

（尤指经常的）联系，联络

I don't have much contact with my uncle.

我和叔叔甚少联系。

Have you **kept in contact with** any of your friends from college? 你和你大学里的朋友还保持联系吗？

She's **lost contact with** (= no longer sees or writes to) her son.

她和儿子失去了联系。

❷ [VN] 联系，联络（如用电话或信件）

I've been trying to contact you all day.

我整天一直在设法与你联系。

2. intact [ɪnˈtækt] adj. 完好无损的

『in不+tact接触→没接触→没碰到的→完好无损的』

[not usually before noun] 完好无损的

Most of the house remains intact even after two hundred years. 虽然过了两百年，这房子的大部分还保持完好。

He emerged from the trial with his reputation intact.

他受审获释，名誉丝毫未受损害。

3. contagious [kənˈteɪdʒəs] adj. （疾病）接触传染的

『con一起+tag接触+ious…的→接触到一起（就会得病的）→接触传染的』

Scarlet fever is highly contagious.

猩红热的接触传染性很强。

(figurative) His enthusiasm was contagious.

他的热情富有感染力。

▶ **contagion** [kənˈteɪdʒən] n. 接触传染；接触性传染病

4. contiguous [kənˈtɪɡjuəs] adj. 相接的；相邻的

『con一起+tig接触+uous有…性质的→有接触在一起性质的→相邻的；相接的』

touching or next to sth

The countries are contiguous. 这些国家互相接壤。

5. tact [tækt] n. （言谈举止的）老练，得体

『tact接触→（与人）接触（的技巧）→老练，得体』

[U] （处事、言谈等的）老练，圆通，得体，乖巧

the ability to deal with difficult or embarrassing situations carefully and without doing or saying anything that will annoy or upset other people

Settling the dispute required great tact and diplomacy.

解决这个争端需要十分老练和娴熟的外交手腕。

She is not exactly known for her tact.

她并不以策略见称。

▶ **tactful** [ˈtæktfl adj. 得体的；不得罪人的

I tried to find a tactful way of telling her the truth.
我设法找一个妥善的办法，把实情告诉她。

▶ **tactless** [ˈtæktləs] adj. 得罪人的；不圆通的

6. tactile [ˈtæktaɪl] adj. 触觉的；手感好的
『tact接触+ile表形容词→触觉的』

visual and tactile communication 视觉和触觉交流
tactile fabric (= pleasant to touch) 手感好的织物
He's a very tactile man (= he enjoys touching people).
他这个人很喜欢触碰别人身体。

7. tactic [ˈtæktɪk] n. 策略，手段
『tact接触+ic(s)学问→接触（别人的）学问→策略』

❶ [C, usually pl.] 策略；手段；招数
the particular method you use to achieve sth
They tried all kinds of tactics to get us to go.
他们施尽所有的招数想让我们离开。
Confrontation is not always the best tactic.
对抗并非总是上策。

❷ tactics [pl.] 战术；兵法

▶ **tactical** [ˈtæktɪkl] adj. 策略上的，战术上的

8. attach [əˈtætʃ] vt. & vi. 附上；贴上；系上
『at相当于to+tach接触→使…接触到…→系上；附上』

❶ 缚上；系上；贴上；附加
We attach labels to things before we file them away.
存档前，我们先贴上标签。
For further information, please contact us on the attached form. 欲了解更多信息，请通过所附表格联系我们。
He said they would attach conditions to the handover of the base. 他说他们将对基地的移交附加一些条件。

❷ [VN] ~ importance, significance, value, weight, etc. (to sth) 认为有重要性、有意义、有价值、有分量等；重视
I attach great importance to reading. 我非常重视阅读。
The authorities attached much significance to his visit.
当局非常重视他的访问。

❸ [VN]（计算机中）附上，粘贴（附件）

▶ **attached** [əˈtætʃt] adj. 附加的；依恋的
Please complete the attached application form.
请填写所附申请表。
We've grown very attached to this house.
我们变得非常喜欢这座房子。

▶ **attachment** [əˈtætʃmənt] n. 依恋，爱慕；附件
As a teenager she formed a strong attachment to one of her teachers. 少女时代的她曾迷上了自己的一个老师。
When you send an e-mail you can also send a sound or graphic file as an attachment.
在发送电子邮件时，你也可以附上一份声音或图片文件。

9. detach [dɪˈtætʃ] v. 拆卸
『de去掉；离开+tach接触→使不接触→拆开』

~ (sth) (from sth) 拆卸；（使）分开，脱离
Detach the coupon and return it as soon as possible.
将赠券撕下后尽快寄回。
She detached herself from his embrace. 她挣脱了他的拥抱。

反义词 **attach** [əˈtætʃ] vt. & vi. 附上；贴上；系上

10. tack [tæk] n. 大头钉 vt. 用大头钉钉

『tack接触→使接触→用大头钉钉住（使接触）』

The carpet was tacked to the floor.
地毯是被钉在地板上的。

11. contingent [kənˈtɪndʒənt] n. 分遣队；代表团 adj. 取决于，视情况而定的
『con一起+ting接触+ent…的→（两件事）接触在一起的→两件事相联系的→后发生的事取决于前面发生的事的→取决于』

❶ [C + sing./pl. v.]（警察、军队的）分遣队，小分队
The army has been strengthened by a large contingent of foreign soldiers.
大批外国士兵增强了军队的力量。

❷ 代表团，代表队
a group of people at a meeting or an event who have sth in common, especially the place they come from, that is not shared by other people at the event
A strong contingent of local residents were there to block the proposal.
由当地居民组成的强大的代表团在那里阻止通过这项提案。

❸ adj. ~ (on/upon sth) (formal) 依情况而定的，取决于
Acceptance on the course is contingent on your examination results.
是否接受这门课程取决于你的考试成绩。

▶ **contingency** [kənˈtɪndʒənsi] n. 可能发生的事
We must consider all possible contingencies.
我们必须考虑一切可能发生的事。

12. tangible [ˈtændʒəbl] adj. 有形的；可以注意到的
『tang接触+ible可以的→可以接触到的→有形的』

❶ **tangible assets/properties** 有形资产/财产
tangible properties or tangible assets are real things that a company has, such as buildings or equipment

❷ 清晰可见的，可感知的
If something is tangible, it is clear enough or definite enough to be easily seen, felt, or noticed
There should be some tangible evidence that the economy is starting to recover. 应该有明显迹象表明经济开始复苏了。
The tension between them was almost tangible.
他们之间的紧张关系几乎让人都感觉得出来。

▶ **intangible** [ɪnˈtændʒəbl] adj. 无形的
『in不，无+tangible有形的→无形的』

❶ 无形的（资产）
that does not exist as a physical thing but is still valuable
intangible assets/property 无形资产/财产
intangible cultural heritage 非物质文化遗产

❷ 无形的，不易捉摸的，难以确定的
not able to be touched or measured, and difficult to describe or explain
She has that intangible quality that a player must possess to be a champion.
她有一种无形的品质，一个运动员要想成为冠军必须具备这种品质。

13. tangent [ˈtændʒənt] n. 切线；正切
『tang接触+ent表名词→切线；正切』

fly/go off at a tangent 突然转换话题；突然改变行动

词根341. tail= cut，表示"剪，割"

1. tailor [ˈteɪlə(r)] n. （男装）裁缝 vt. 按需定制
『tail剪+or人→剪（布做衣服）的人→裁缝』

to make or adapt sth for a particular purpose, a particular person, etc.

[VN] Special programmes of study are tailored to the needs of specific groups. 制订特殊课程，以满足特定群体的需要。

2. detail [ˈdiːteɪl] n. 细节 vt. 详细介绍
『de加强+tail剪→不断剪→详细介绍』

This issue will be discussed in more detail in the next chapter.
这个问题将在下一章详细论述。

Tell me the main points now; leave the details till later.
现在把要点告诉我，细节留到以后再说。

The brochure details all the hotels in the area and their facilities. 这本小册子详细介绍了当地所有旅馆及其设施。

3. retail [ˈriːteɪl , rɪˈteɪl] n. 零售 v. 零售
『re又，再+tail剪→剪（成很多份）再（卖）→零售』
（n. [ˈriːteɪl]; v. [rɪˈteɪl]）

The recommended retail price is £9.99.
建议零售价为9.99英镑。

The firm manufactures and retails its own range of sportswear. 公司生产并零售自己的运动服装系列。

The book retails at £14.95. 这本书的零售价为14.95英镑。

4. curtail [kɜːˈteɪl] vt. 缩短，减缩
『cur短的+tail剪→被剪短的→缩短，减缩』

If you curtail something, you reduce or limit it.

Spending on books has been severely curtailed.
购书开支已被大大削减。

The lecture was curtailed by the fire alarm going off.
那次讲座被突然鸣响的火警中断了。

▶ **curt** [kɜːt] adj. 唐突无礼的

appearing rude because very few words are used, or because sth is done in a very quick way
a curt reply 唐突无礼的答复
a curt nod 草草的点头

5. entail [ɪnˈteɪl] vt. 牵涉；势必造成
『en使+tail尾巴→把B绑在A的尾巴上→拉动A后B必然会动→牵涉；势必造成』

If one thing entails another, it involves it or causes it.
[VN] The job entails a lot of hard work.
这工作需要十分艰苦的努力。

Such a decision would entail a huge political risk.
这样的决定势必带来巨大的政治风险。

词根342. tain, ten=hold，表示"拿住；保持"

1. attain [əˈteɪn] vt. & vi. 达到，获得
『at相当于to+tain拿住→（经过努力）拿到→（经过努力）获得』

[VN] （通常经过努力）获得，得到

Most of our students attained five "A" grades in their exams.
我们多数学生的考试成绩是五个优。

Still greater efforts are needed before we can attain our goal.
我们必须百尺竿头，更进一步，才能达到目的。

词义辨析 <P377第83> 获得 acquire, attain, obtain, gain

2. obtain [əbˈteɪn] vt. 得到，获得；实现

『ob对着+tain拿住→得到』

To obtain something means to get it or achieve it.

Evans was trying to obtain a false passport and other documents. 埃文斯正试图取得一本假护照和其他证件。

Only with mass direct action will we obtain such change.
只有采取大规模直接行动，我们才会取得这样的改变。

词义辨析 <P377第83>
获得 acquire, attain, obtain, gain

3. contain [kənˈteɪn] vt. 装有，含有；控制，遏制
『con一起+tain(=hold) 使保持→使（某些物品或内容）保持一起（在…里面）→装有；控制』

❶ [VN] 装有；含有
The bag contained a Christmas card.
这个包里装着一张圣诞卡。

This drink doesn't contain any alcohol.
这种饮料不含任何酒精。

❷ [VN] 控制，克制，抑制（感情）
She was unable to contain her excitement.
她无法抑制内心的激动。

❸ [VN] 控制，遏制（发展）
More than a hundred firemen are still trying to contain the fire at the plant.
上百名消防队员仍在试图控制工厂的火势。

Simultaneously, it wants Washington to do more to contain China. 同时，它希望华盛顿采取更多手段遏制中国。

▶ **container** [kənˈteɪnə(r)] n. 容器；货柜；集装箱

▶ **content** [ˈkɒntent] n. 内容，内容物 adj. 满足的
[kənˈtent] vt. 使满足

❶ contents [pl.] 所容纳之物，所含之物
He tipped the contents of the bag onto the table.
他把提包里的东西倒在桌子上。

Fire has caused severe damage to the contents of the building.
大火导致那栋大楼里的东西严重损毁。

❷ contents [pl.] （书的）目录，目次
a contents page 目录页

❸ [sing.] （书、讲话、节目、课程等的）内容
She is reluctant to discuss the content of the play.
她不愿意谈该剧的内容。

Previous students have had nothing but praise for the course content and staff.
往届学生对课程内容与教员全是赞扬之词。

❹ adj. 满足的
I am content to admire the mountains from below.
我满足于从山脚下观赏山景。

He had to be content with third place. 他只好屈居第三名。

❺ [VN] 满足，满意
Martina contented herself with a bowl of soup.
马丁娜喝了一碗汤就心满意足了。

词义辨析 <P378第84> 满足的 content与contented

4. detain [dɪˈteɪn] vt. 扣留，阻留，耽搁
『de向下+tain(=hold)拿住；保持→（持续）控制住（某人）→扣留』

❶ [VN] 扣留
When people such as the police detain someone, they keep them in a place under their control.

One man has been detained for questioning.

一个男人被拘留审问。

❷ [VN] 阻留，耽搁

To detain someone means to delay them, for example by talking to them.

Thank you. We won't detain you any further.
非常感谢。我们就不再耽搁您的时间了。

▶**detainee** [ˌdiːteɪˈniː] n. （因其政治观点或活动而)被拘留者，被扣押者
『detain扣留+ee被…的人→被扣留的人』

▶**detention** [dɪˈtenʃn] n. 拘留，扣押，监禁；（惩罚顽皮学童的）放学后留校

During the time of detention the detainee's food costs shall be paid by himself.
在拘留期间，被拘留人的伙食费由自己负担。

The teacher kept the boys in detention after school.
老师将这些男生课后留堂。

5. sustain [səˈsteɪn] v. 维持；保持
『sus(=sub)下面+tain保持，坚持→在下面保持着→维持；保持』

❶ [VN] 维持（生命、生存）

Which planets can sustain life?
哪些行星可以维持生命的存在？

❷ [VN] 保持；使持续

to make sth continue for some time without becoming less

She managed to sustain everyone's interest until the end of her speech. 她使每个人兴趣盎然，一直听她把话讲完。

a period of sustained economic growth
经济持续增长的时期

A cup of coffee isn't enough to sustain you until lunchtime.
一杯咖啡不足以维持你到午餐时间。

❸ [VN] 遭受

to experience sth bad

to sustain damage/an injury/a defeat
遭受损失；受伤；遭到失败

Several companies have sustained heavy financial losses due to the unfair competition.
好几家公司都因不正当竞争而遭受了严重的经济损失。

▶**sustainable** [səˈsteɪnəbl] adj. 可持续的
sustainable economic growth 经济的可持续增长

词义辨析 <P363第14>

忍受，遭受 bear, stand, endure, tolerate, put up with, sustain

▶**sustenance** [ˈsʌstənəns] n. 食物；营养

Sustenance is food or drink which a person, animal, or plant needs to remain alive and healthy.

There's not much sustenance in a bowl of soup.
一碗汤没多少营养。

6. maintain [meɪnˈteɪn] vt. 维持；维修，保养
『main逗留+tain保持→保持停留状态→维持；保养』

❶ [VN] 维持；保持

to make sth continue at the same level, standard, etc.

The two countries have always maintained close relations.
这两个国家一直保持着密切关系。

It is important to maintain a constant temperature inside the greenhouse. 保持温室内恒温是很重要的。

❷ [VN] 维修；保养

to keep a building, a machine, etc. in good condition by checking or repairing it regularly

The house is large and difficult to maintain.
房子很大，难以养护。

▶**maintenance** [ˈmeɪntənəns] n. 维持；维护

the maintenance of international peace 维护世界和平

The school pays for heating and the maintenance of the buildings. 学校负担这些大楼的供热和维修费用。

car maintenance 汽车保养

7. retain [rɪˈteɪn] vt. 保留；保持；保存
『re又，再+tain保持→一再保持→保留；保持；保存』

To retain something means to continue to have that thing.

The interior of the shop still retains a nineteenth-century atmosphere.
这家商店的内部装修仍然保留着19世纪的风格。

He struggled to retain control of the situation.
他曾努力保持对局势的控制。

a soil that retains moisture 保持水分的土壤

She has a good memory and finds it easy to retain facts.
她记忆力好，很容易记住事情。

▶**retention** [rɪˈtenʃn] n. 保留；保持；记性

❶ [U] 保持；维持；保留

the action of keeping sth rather than losing it or stopping it

The company needs to improve its training and retention of staff. 公司需要改进对员工的培训和留用工作。

❷ [U] （液体、热量等的）保持

❸ [U] 记忆力；记性

Visual material aids the retention of information.
直观材料有助于加强记忆。

8. pertain [pəˈteɪn] vi. 相关
『per自始至终+tain保持→始终保持（关系）→相关』

pertain to sth/sb (formal) 与…相关；关于

I would much rather that you asked Mrs Zuckerman any questions pertaining to herself.
我宁愿你问楚克尔曼夫人的是与她本人相关的问题。

▶**pertinent** [ˈpɜːtɪnənt] adj. 有关的；相宜的
『pertain相关（去a)+ent表形容词→相关的』

appropriate to a particular situation; Something that is pertinent is relevant to a particular subject.

Please keep your comments pertinent to the topic under discussion. 请勿发表与讨论主题无关的言论。

She had asked some pertinent questions.
她问了一些相关的问题。

▶**impertinent** [ɪmˈpɜːtɪnənt] adj. 不敬的；无礼的
『im不+pertinent相关的；相宜的→不相宜的；无礼的』

rude and not showing respect for sb who is older or more important

Would it be impertinent to ask where exactly you were?
能冒昧问一下您所在的确切位置吗？

You are being impertinent, child. 你太无礼了，孩子。

9. abstain [əbˈsteɪn] vi. 戒除，节制；（投票时）弃权
『abs离开+tain(=hold)坚持住，把得住→（面对诱惑）把持得住，离开了→戒除；abs离开+tain(=hold)握着→握着（选票）离开→（投票时）弃权』

❶ （投票时）弃权

Three Conservative MPs abstained in the vote.

三名保守党议员投了弃权票。

❷ 戒；戒除

to decide not to do or have sth, especially sth you like or enjoy, because it is bad for your health or considered morally wrong

to abstain from alcohol/sex/drugs 戒酒；禁欲；戒毒

▶ **abstention** [əbˈstenʃn] n. 弃权（不投票）；戒除

▶ **abstinence** [ˈæbstɪnəns] n. 戒绝；节制；禁欲

『abstain戒绝；节制（去a）+ence表名词→戒绝；节制』

Abstinence is the practice of abstaining from something such as alcoholic drink or sex, often for health or religious reasons. Complete abstinence from alcohol is the single most important treatment for alcoholic hepatitis.

完全戒酒是治疗酒精性肝炎最重要的治疗方法。

10. entertain [ˌentəˈteɪn] v. 招待；娱乐；心存

『enter进来+tain(=hold)拿住，保持→（客人）一进来（就通过招待、娱乐等方式）保持住（留住）→招待；娱乐』

❶ （尤指在自己家中）招待，款待

to invite people to eat or drink with you as your guests, especially in your home

[V] The job involves a lot of entertaining.

这项工作需要经常招待客人。

[VN] Barbecues are a favourite way of entertaining friends.

烧烤是最受人喜爱的待客方式。

❷ ~ (sb) (with sth) 使有兴趣；使快乐；娱乐

to interest and amuse sb in order to please them

[VN] He entertained us for hours with his stories and jokes.

他既讲故事又说笑话，把我们逗得乐了好几个小时。

[V] The aim of the series is both to entertain and inform.

这个系列节目旨在集娱乐和知识为一体。

❸ [VN] 心存，考虑，怀有（主意、建议等）

If you entertain an idea or suggestion, you allow yourself to consider it as possible or as worth thinking about seriously.

I feel how foolish I am to entertain doubts.

我竟然心存怀疑，真是太愚蠢了。

I wouldn't entertain the idea of such an unsociable job.

我不会考虑从事这种不跟人打交道的工作。

▶ **entertaining** [ˌentəˈteɪnɪŋ] adj. 有趣的；娱乐的；使人愉快的

To generate new money the sport needs to be more entertaining.

要想创造更多的收入，这项体育活动需要更具趣味性。

This is a surprisingly entertaining film.

这部电影的娱乐性十足，让人意想不到。

▶ **entertainment** [ˌentəˈteɪnmənt] n. 娱乐节目；娱乐活动

❶ [U, C] 娱乐片；文娱节目；表演会；娱乐活动

films/movies, music, etc. used to entertain people; an example of this

radio, television and other forms of entertainment

广播、电视和其他形式的娱乐活动

Local entertainments are listed in the newspaper.

本地的娱乐活动刊登在报纸上。

❷ [U] 招待，款待

词义辨析 <P362第9>

娱乐 entertainment, amusement, recreation, pastime

11. tenacious [təˈneɪʃəs] adj. 不松手的；坚持的；坚毅的

『ten(=hold)坚持；握住+acious有…性质的→坚持不松手的→顽强的』

❶ 不松手的；坚持的

that does not stop holding sth or give up sth easily; determined

She's a tenacious woman. She never gives up.

她是个坚毅的人，从不放弃。

The party has kept its tenacious hold on power for more than twenty years. 这个政党已牢牢掌握政权20多年。

❷ （观点、信念）根深蒂固的

▶ **tenacity** [təˈnæsəti] n. 坚韧，坚毅

Talent, hard work and sheer tenacity are all crucial to career success.

事业要成功，天赋、勤奋和顽强的意志都至关重要。

12. tenure [ˈtenjə(r)] n. 任期；（尤指大学教师的）终身职位

『ten(=hold)持有+ure表行为或结果→持有（某职位的时间）→任期』

❶ [U] （尤指重要政治职务的）任期，任职

He did nothing noteworthy during his tenure.

他在任职期间毫无建树。

❷ [U] （尤指大学教师的）终身职位；长期聘用

It's still extremely difficult to get tenure.

要取得终身职位仍然极其困难。

13. tenant [ˈtenənt] n. 房客；租户；佃户

『ten持有+ant人→持有（居住权、种地权）的人→租户；佃户』

The decorating was done by a previous tenant.

装修是前一位房客搞的。

▶ **tenancy** [ˈtenənsi] n. （房屋、土地等的）租用；租用期限

a three-month tenancy 三个月的租期

a tenancy agreement 租赁协议

词根343. techn=art, skill，表示"技艺，技术"

1. technology [tekˈnɒlədʒi] n. 科技

『techn技艺，技术+ology…术，…学→科技』

Technology refers to methods, systems, and devices which are the result of scientific knowledge being used for practical purposes.

Technology is changing fast. 科技日新月异。

2. technique [tekˈniːk] n. 技巧，方法；技术，技能

『techn技艺，技术+ique→技巧，方法』

❶ [C] 技巧，方法

A technique is a particular method of doing an activity, usually a method that involves practical skills.

The artist combines different techniques in the same painting.

这位艺术家在同一幅画中把不同的画法结合在一起。

❷ [U, sing.] （艺术、体育等方面的）技术，技能

Her technique has improved a lot over the past season.

在过去的一个赛季里，她的技术大有长进。

3. technician [tekˈnɪʃn] n. 技术员，技师；（艺术、体育等的）技巧精湛者

『techn技艺，技术+ic+ian表人→（熟悉）掌握某种技术的』

人→技术员』

❶ [C] 技术员，技师

a person whose job is keeping a particular type of equipment or machinery in good condition

a laboratory technician 实验室技术员

❷ [C] （艺术、体育等的）技巧精湛者

词根344. temper=restrain; moderate，表示"克制；适度"

1. temper [ˈtempə(r)] n.（坏）脾气 v. 使缓和

『temper克制→（脾气需要）克制→脾气』

❶ [C, usually sing., U] 脾气

a violent/short/quick, etc. temper 烈性子、暴脾气、急性子

He must learn to control his temper. 他得学会捺住性子。

She broke the plates in a fit of temper.

她一气之下把盘子摔碎了。

lose/keep your temper (with sb) 发脾气；忍住怒火

She lost her temper with a customer and shouted at him.

她对一位顾客发了脾气，冲着人家大喊大叫。

I struggle to keep my temper with the kids when they misbehave. 孩子们淘气时，我强捺住性子不发脾气。

❷ **good-/bad-tempered** 脾气好/坏

❸ [VN] 调节，使缓和，使温和

To temper something means to make it less extreme.

He had to learn to temper his enthusiasm.

他必须学会克制自己的热情。

Justice must be tempered with mercy. 法外尚需施恩。

2. temperate [ˈtempərət] adj.（气候）温和的；（行为）有节制的，温和的

『temper克制+ate表性质→（冷热、行为）有克制的→（气候）温和的；（行为）有节制的』

❶ （气候）温和的；（地区）温带的

The Nile Valley keeps a temperate climate throughout the year. 尼罗河流域一年四季气候温和。

Asia extends across the frigid, temperate and tropical zones.

亚洲地跨寒、温、热三带。

❷ （行为）温和的，有节制的

behaving in a calm and controlled way

He is a temperate man, and never drinks too much.

他是一个有节制的人，从不过量饮酒。

▶**temperance** [ˈtempərəns] n. 戒酒；节制

A person who shows temperance has a strong mind and does not eat too much, drink too much, or do too much of anything.

3. temperament [ˈtemprəmənt] n. 性情，秉性；易冲动

『temper克制+a+ment表名词→（一个人遇事）克制（的状况）→性情，秉性』

❶ [C, U] （人或动物的）性情，性格，禀性

His impulsive temperament regularly got him into difficulties.

他容易冲动，经常因此惹麻烦。

The Republican front-runner is trying to calm the nerves of those who fear he doesn't have the experience or the temperament to be president.

这位共和党领先者试图安抚那些担心他（特朗普）没有足够的经验或魄力来担任总统的人的情绪。

❷ [U] 易冲动；（性情）暴躁

Mark does have a habit of allowing his temperament to get

the better of him. 马克的确经常由着自己的性子来。

词根345. tempor=time，表示"时间"

1. temporary [ˈtemprəri] adj. 暂时的，临时的

『tempor时间+ary表形容词→有时间性的→临时的』

I'm looking for some temporary work.

我在找某个临时工作。

They had to move into temporary accommodation.

他们不得不搬进临时住所。

反义词 **permanent** [ˈpɜːmənənt] adj. 永久的〈P30〉

2. contemporary [kənˈtemprəri] adj. 同时代的；当代的 n. 同代人

『con共同+tempor时间+ary表示人→同时间的人→同代人』

❶ adj. 当代的；现代的

Only the names are ancient; the characters are modern and contemporary.

只有姓名是古代的；人物都是现代的、摩登的。

❷ adj. ~ (with sb/sth) 属同时期的；同一时代的

We have no contemporary account of the battle (= written near the time that it happened) .

我们没有当时人们对这一战役的记载。

❸ n. 同代人；同辈人；同龄人

Like most of my contemporaries, I grew up in a vastly different world.

和大多数同辈人一样，我生长在一个截然不同的世界。

3. temporal [ˈtempərəl] adj. 世间的，世俗的；时间的；太阳穴的

『tempor时间+al…性质的→（人有生死，固有）时间性质的→世俗的；时间的』

❶ (formal) 世间的；世俗的

connected with the real physical world, not spiritual matters

Although spiritual leader of millions of people, the Pope has no temporal power.

教皇虽是数百万人的精神领袖，但没有丝毫的世俗权力。

❷ (formal) 时间的

a universe which has spatial and temporal dimensions

有时空维度的宇宙

❸ 太阳穴的

小贴士 **temple** [ˈtempl] n. 寺院；太阳穴

4. tempo [ˈtempəʊ] n. （乐曲的）拍子，节奏；（事情发展的）节奏，速度

『temp(=tempor)时间+o音乐术语及乐器名称→音乐进行时间（的快慢）→节拍』

It's a difficult piece, with numerous changes of tempo.

这支曲子节奏变化多，难度很大。

the increasing tempo of life in Western society

西方社会日益加速的生活节奏

5. tempest [ˈtempɪst] n. 大风暴，暴风雨；风波，风暴

『temp(tempor)时间+est→短时间内天气骤变→暴风雨』

Torrential rain and a howling tempest cut a swathe of destruction across the country.

狂风暴雨横扫全国，所到之处，一片狼藉。

I hadn't foreseen the tempest my request would cause.

我没有料到我的请求会掀起这么大一场风波。

▶**tempestuous** [temˈpestʃuəs] adj. （关系）紧张的；

（局势）动荡不定的；风暴引起的，风暴的

If something such as a relationship or time is tempestuous, it is full of strong emotions

For years, the couple's tempestuous relationship made the headlines.
好多年，那对夫妻跌宕起伏的关系总是登上报纸头条。
Their ship was sailing dangerously in the tempestuous sea.
他们的船在浪急风高的海上危险地航行着。

6. extemporize [ɪkˈstempəraɪz] v. 即席发言；即兴表演
『ex出来+tempor时间+ize表动词→（演讲、表演）即时出来的→即席发言；即兴表演』

Because he had lost his notes, the lecturer had to extemporize.
因为演讲人丢了稿子，只好即席发言。

▶ **extemporaneous** [eksˈtempəˈreɪnɪəs] adj. （讲话或做事）毫无准备的；即席的

近义词 **improvise** [ˈɪmprəvaɪz] vt. 临时拼凑；即时创作

词根346. tempt=tempt; scorn，表示"引诱；鄙视"

1. tempt [tempt] vt. 引诱；劝诱
❶ 引诱；诱惑
to attract sb or make sb want to do or have sth, even if they know it is wrong
[VN] I was tempted by the dessert menu.
甜食菜单馋得我垂涎欲滴。
[VN to inf] I was tempted to take the day off.
我动了心，想那一天休假。
❷ 劝诱，鼓动
to persuade or try to persuade sb to do sth that you want them to do, for example by offering them sth
[VN] How can we tempt young people into engineering?
我们怎样才能吸引年轻人学习工程学呢？

▶ **tempting** [ˈtemptɪŋ] adj. 诱人的
It was a tempting offer. 这是个诱人的提议。
That cake looks very tempting. 那蛋糕的样子让人嘴馋。

▶ **temptation** [tempˈteɪʃn] n. 诱惑；煽诱人的事物
I couldn't resist the temptation to open the letter.
我抵制不住好奇心把信打开了。
An expensive bicycle is a temptation to thieves.
高档自行车对窃贼是个诱惑。

2. attempt [əˈtempt] n. & v. 企图；试图；尝试
『at相当于to+tempt引诱→引诱去（做某事）→尝试；企图』

❶ [C, U] ~ (to do sth) | ~ (at sth/at doing sth) 企图；试图
an act of trying to do sth, especially sth difficult, often with no success
Two factories were closed in an attempt to cut costs.
为削减费用，关闭了两家工厂。
They made no attempt to escape. 他们没有企图逃跑。

❷ an attempt on sb's life 杀人企图
Someone has made an attempt on the President's life.
有人企图刺杀总统。

❸ an attempt on a record （运动员创造纪录的）尝试，冲击
Everything is almost ready for me to make another attempt on the record.
一切几乎都已准备就绪，就等我向纪录发起再一次冲击了。

❹ vt. 尝试；试图
to make an effort or try to do sth, especially sth difficult
[V to inf] I will attempt to answer all your questions.
我将努力回答你的全部问题。
[VN] The prisoners attempted an escape, but failed.
囚犯企图逃跑，但失败了。

3. contempt [kənˈtempt] n. 鄙视；蔑视
『con一起+tempt鄙视→鄙视；蔑视』

❶ [U, sing.] ~ (for sb/sth) 蔑视，鄙视；不顾
the feeling that sb/sth is without value and deserves no respect at all
She looked at him with contempt. 她轻蔑地看着他。
I shall treat that suggestion with the contempt it deserves.
我对那项建议当然会不屑一顾。
The firefighters showed a contempt for their own safety.
那些消防队员已把他们自己的安全置之度外。

❷ = contempt of court 藐视法庭
He could be jailed for two years for contempt.
他由于藐视法庭可能被监禁两年。

▶ **contemptible** [kənˈtemptəbl] adj. 可轻蔑的，可鄙的
I think it's contemptible the way he's behaved toward her.
我认为他对她的态度是可耻的。

▶ **contemptuous** [kənˈtemptʃuəs] adj. 鄙视的，表示轻蔑的
『contempt鄙视+uous…性质的→瞧不起人的→鄙视的』
She gave him a contemptuous look. 她鄙夷地看了他一眼。
He was contemptuous of everything I did.
他对我所做的一切都不屑一顾。

词根347. tend, tent，tense=stretch，表示"伸展"；名词形式为-tention；形容词形式为-tensive

1. extend [ɪkˈstend] v. 延长；扩大；扩展
『ex向外+tend伸展→延长；扩大；扩展』

❶ [VN] 延长；扩大；扩展
make longer/larger/wider
to extend a fence/road/house 扩建护栏/公路/房子
The show has been extended for another six weeks.
展览会又延长了六周。
The company plans to extend its operations into Europe.
公司打算将业务扩展到欧洲。

❷ [V+adv./prep.] （范围）扩大；（距离）延伸；（时间）延续
His willingness to help did not extend beyond making a few phone calls. 他的乐意帮助只不过限于打几个电话罢了。
Our land extends as far as the river.
我们的土地一直延伸到河边。

❸ [VN] 提供；给予
to offer or give sth to sb
I'm sure you will join me in extending a very warm welcome to our visitors.
我相信你们会和我一起向我们的客人表示热烈欢迎。
Is it OK to extend an invitation by phone?
利用电话邀请是否可行？

❹ [VN] [often passive] 使竭尽全力
to make sb/sth use all their effort, abilities, supplies, etc.
Jim didn't really have to extend himself in the exam.
吉姆大可不必为这次考试那么拼命。

Hospitals were already fully extended because of the epidemic. 这场流行病已使各医院以最大负荷运转。

▶ **extension** [ɪk'stenʃn] n. 扩大，延伸；扩建部分

❶ [U, C] ~ (of sth) 扩大；延伸
the extension of new technology into developing countries
新技术向发展中国家的传播
The extension of the subway will take several months.
扩建地铁需用几个月时间。
a planned two-storey extension to the hospital
计划在医院增建一栋两层的楼
He's been granted an extension of the contract for another year. 他的合同获得延期一年。

❷ [C] (abbr. ext.) 电话分机号码
What's your extension number? 你的分机号码是多少？
Can I have extension 4332 please? 请接4332号分机。

❸ [C] 文件的扩展名

▶ **extensive** [ɪk'stensɪv] adj. 广阔的，广大的；广泛的

Extensive repair work is being carried out.
大规模的修缮工作正在进行。
Extensive research has been done into this disease.
对这种疾病已进行了广泛研究。

▶ **extent** [ɪk'stent] n. 程度，限度；大小，范围

It is difficult to assess the full extent of the damage.
损失情况难以全面估计。
I was amazed at the extent of his knowledge.
他知识之渊博令我惊奇。
You can't see the full extent of the beach from here.
从这儿看不到海滩全貌。

to... extent 到…程度；在…程度上
To a certain extent, we are all responsible for this tragic situation. 我们都在一定程度上对这悲惨的局面负有责任。
To some extent what she argues is true.
她的论证在某种程度上是符合事实的。

2. distend [dɪ'stend] v.（使）膨胀，（使）肿胀
『dis(=away)+tend伸展→（向各个方向）分散伸展→膨胀』
（使）膨胀，（使）肿胀
If a part of your body is distended, or if it distends, it becomes swollen and unnaturally large.
starving children with huge distended bellies
鼓着浮肿肚子的饥饿儿童

▶ **distension** [dɪ'stenʃn] n. （身体）膨胀，肿胀

[U] distension of the stomach 胃胀

3. tentacle ['tentəkl] n. 触须，触角；束缚
『tent伸展+acle物→伸展出去探的东西→触角』

❶ （章鱼等的）触须，触手，触角
(figurative) Tentacles of fear closed around her body.
恐惧的阴影笼罩着她。

❷ tentacles [pl.] (usually disapproving) （大的地方、组织或系统难以避免的）影响，束缚，约束
Free speech is being gradually eroded year after year by new tentacles of government control.
言论自由正在一年又一年逐渐被政府不断施加的影响力所削弱。

4. contend [kən'tend] v. 认为；竞争；处理（问题）
『con一起+tend伸展→一起（都要）伸展（个人观点）→

认为；竞争』

❶ （尤指在争论中）声称，主张，认为
to say that sth is true, especially in an argument
[V that] I would contend that the minister's thinking is flawed on this point. 我倒认为部长的想法在这一点上有漏洞。

❷ [V] ~ (for sth) 竞争；争夺
to compete against sb in order to gain sth
Three armed groups were contending for power.
三个武装集团在争夺权力。

❸ contend with sth （不得不）处理问题，对付困境
to have to deal with a problem or difficult situation
Nurses often have to contend with violent or drunken patients.
护士经常不得不对付粗暴的或喝醉酒的病人。

5. attend [ə'tend] v. 出席，参加；注意；照料
『at(=to)+tend伸展→（人或注意力）伸展到（某地或某事）→参加；注意；照料』

❶ 出席、参加（会议、婚礼、葬礼）；去（学校、教堂）
to be present at an event; to go regularly to a place
[VN] The meeting was attended by 90% of shareholders.
90%的股东出席了会议。
to attend a wedding/funeral 参加婚礼/葬礼
Our children attend the same school.
我们的孩子上同一所学校。
How many people attend church every Sunday?
每个星期天有多少人去教堂？

❷ [V] ~ (to sb/sth) (formal) 注意；专心
She hadn't been attending during the lesson.
上课时她一直不专心。
（pay attention to "注意"。attention是attend的名词形式。）

❸ [VN] (formal) 随同；陪同
to be with sb and help them
The President was attended by several members of his staff.
总统有几名幕僚随从。

❹ **attend to sb/sth** 处理；对付；照料
to deal with sb/sth; to take care of sb/sth
I have some urgent business to attend to.
我有一些急事要处理。
A nurse attended to his needs constantly.
有一位护士经常照料他的需要。

▶ **attendance** [ə'tendəns] n. 出席；出席人数

Attendance at these lectures is not compulsory.
这些讲座不是硬性规定要参加的。
There was an attendance of 42 at the meeting.
有42人参加了会议。

▶ **attentive** [ə'tentɪv] adj. 注意的，专心的；关心的，体贴的

He questioned Chrissie, and listened attentively to what she told him. 他询问了克里茜，并仔细聆听她所说的话。
At society parties he is attentive to his wife.
在社交聚会上，他对妻子体贴周到。

▶ **attendant** [ə'tendənt] n. 服务员，侍者；随从

She was interrupted by the entrance of an attendant.
服务员进来，打断了她的话。

6. tend [tend] v. 往往会；倾向
『tend伸展→（向某种情况）伸展→倾向；往往会』

tend to do sth 往往会；倾向

to be likely to do sth or to happen in a particular way because this is what often or usually happens

Women tend to live longer than men. 女人往往比男人长寿。

When I'm tired, I tend to make mistakes. 我累了就容易出错。

▶ **tendency** ['tendənsi] n. 倾向；趋势

I have a tendency to talk too much when I'm nervous.
我紧张时总爱唠叨。

There is a growing tendency among employers to hire casual staff. 雇主雇用临时职员有增加的趋势。

7. intend [ɪn'tend] v. 打算；意图

『in里面，内心+tend伸展→内心（向…）伸展→打算；意图』

❶ [V to inf] 打算；计划；想要

Where do you intend to go this summer?
今年夏天你准备到哪儿去？

❷ be intended to/for 拟用于；意图

This money is intended for the development of the tourist industry. 这笔钱准备用于旅游业的开发。

This book is intended for the general reader rather than the student. 这本书面向一般读者而非学生。

▶ **intention** [ɪn'tenʃn] n. 打算；意图

He has announced his intention to retire.
他已经宣布他打算退休。

▶ **intent** [ɪn'tent] adj. 专心的；决心的　n. 意图

❶ adj. ~ on/upon sth | ~ on/upon doing sth
(formal) 决心做（尤指伤害他人的事）

The rebels are obviously intent on keeping up the pressure.
叛乱分子显然决心继续施压。

They were intent on murder. 他们存心谋杀。

❷ adj. 专心的，专注的

If someone does something in an intent way, they pay great attention to what they are doing.

She looked from one intent face to another.
她看着一张张专注的面孔。

He listened intently, then slammed down the phone.
他专心地听着，然后砰地挂了电话。

❸ [U] ~ (to do sth) (formal or law) 意图，目的

The act had a specific intent, to protect freed slaves from white mobs.
这项法案有明确的目的，即保护被解放的奴隶免受白人暴民的伤害。

Evidence in a criminal trial concerns the intent, motive, means, and opportunity to commit a crime.
刑事审判中的证据关系到犯罪的目的、动机、手段和机会等。

词义辨析 <P378第85> **目的，意图 intention与intent**

▶ **superintend** [ˌsuːpərɪn'tend] vt. 主管，监管

『super上面，上层+intend打算，意图→作为上级来打算（事情怎样做）→监管』

▶ **superintendent** [ˌsuːpərɪn'tendənt] n. 主管人，负责人；监管人

8. tense [tens] adj. 紧张的　n. 时态

『tense伸展→有拉力的→紧张的』

❶ adj. （人、局势、气氛、肌肉等）紧张的

He's a very tense person. 他是个神经非常紧张的人。

I spent a tense few weeks waiting for the results of the tests.
等候测试结果的这几个星期里我寝食不安。

The atmosphere in the meeting was getting more and more tense. 会议的气氛越来越紧张。

A massage will relax those tense muscles.
按摩会使紧张的肌肉松弛。

❷ n. 时态

▶ **tension** ['tenʃn] n. 紧张；冲突；张力

❶ [U] （人、局势、气氛等）紧张

The tension between the two countries is likely to remain.
那两个国家间的紧张局面可能会持续下去。

She has done her best to keep calm but finds herself trembling with tension and indecision.
她尽力保持镇定，可还是由于紧张、犹豫不决而抖个不停。

❷ [C, U]（势力、观点、影响之间的）冲突，分歧

There is often a tension between the aims of the company and the wishes of the employees.
公司的目标和雇员的愿望之间经常存在矛盾。

❸ [U] 拉紧程度；拉力；张力

Adjust the string tension of your tennis racket to suit your style of playing. 调节网球拍的网张力以适合你的打法。

9. intense [ɪn'tens] adj. 强烈的；激烈的；极度的

『in里面+tense伸展→里面都伸展了→强烈的，激烈的』

Intense is used to describe something that is very great or extreme in strength or degree.

He was sweating from the intense heat.
高温酷热让他大汗淋漓。

The battle for third place was intense.
第三名的争夺紧张激烈。

The pain was so intense that I couldn't sleep.
疼痛如此剧烈以至于我睡不着觉。

I felt so self-conscious under Luke's mother's intense gaze.
在卢克母亲强烈的注视下，我感到极不自在。

▶ **intensity** [ɪn'tensəti] n. 强烈，剧烈；烈度

Speech is made up of sound waves that vary in frequency and intensity. 语音是由不同频率和强度的声波组成的。

The most visible sign of the intensity of the crisis is unemployment.
危机严重程度的最显著迹象就是失业。

▶ **intensify** [ɪn'tensɪfaɪ] v. （使）加强，增强

[V] Violence intensified during the night.
在夜间暴力活动加剧了。

[VN] The opposition leader has intensified his attacks on the government. 反对派领袖加强了对政府的攻击。

10. intensive [ɪn'tensɪv] adj. 密集的；加强的；集中的

『intense强烈的（去e）+ive具有…性质的→加强的；密集的；集中的』

❶ 短时间内集中紧张进行的；密集的；加强的

Intensive activity involves concentrating a lot of effort or people on one particular task in order to try to achieve a great deal in a short time.

an intensive language course 强化语言课程

two weeks of intensive training 两周的强化训练

intensive diplomatic negotiations 密集的外交谈判

❷ **intensive farming** 集约（精耕）农业

intensive reading 精读

In English study, intensive reading must be combined with extensive reading.

在英语学习中，精读必须与泛读结合起来。

小贴士 ICU (Intensive Care Unit) 重症监护室

11. pretend [prɪˈtend] v. 假装

『pre事先+tend伸展→事先伸展过→假装』

[V (that)] He pretended to his family that everything was fine.

他对家人佯称一切都好。

[V to inf] He pretended not to notice. 他假装没注意。

▶ **pretentious** [prɪˈtenʃəs] adj. 炫耀的，虚夸的

He's so pretentious! 瞧他那副自命不凡的样儿！

His response was full of pretentious nonsense.

他的答复是一派荒谬的虚夸之词。

词根348. tenu=thin，表示"细，薄"

1. tenuous [ˈtenjuəs] adj. 微弱的，缥缈的；纤细的，薄的

『tenu细，薄+ous…的→微弱的；纤细的』

so weak or uncertain that it hardly exists; extremely thin and easily broken

a tenuous hold on life 命若游丝

His links with the organization turned out to be, at best, tenuous.

最后证实他与这个组织的关系不过是不即不离罢了。

2. attenuate [əˈtenjueɪt] vt. 使减弱，使降低效力

『at相当于to+tenu细，薄+ate使…→使变薄→使减弱』

The drug attenuates the effects of the virus.

这药能减轻病毒的危害。

You could never eliminate risk, but preparation and training could attenuate it.

风险不可能完全消除，但可以通过防范和培训来降低。

词根349. term, termin=limit, boundary，表示"界限"

1. term [tɜːm] n. 学期，期限；术语；条款 v. 把…称为

『term界限→（时间、概念、合同协议的）界限范围→学期，期限；术语；条款』

❶ [C, U] 学期（尤用于英国，学校一年分三个学期）

the spring/summer/autumn/fall term 春季/夏季/秋季学期

（NAmE semester，一年两个学期）

❷ [C] 期；期限；任期

a long term of imprisonment 长期监禁

His life had reached its natural term. 他已终其天年。

❸ [C] 术语，措辞

a technical/legal/scientific, etc. term

技术、法律、科学等术语

❹ [VN-N] [often passive] (formal) 把…称为

At his age, he can hardly be termed a young man.

到了这个年纪，他称不上是年轻人了。

❺ terms（协议、条约等的）条款，条件

These terms were favourable to India.

这些条款对印度有利。

❻ **in terms of/ in … terms** 谈及；就…而言；在…方面

What does this mean in terms of cost?

这在成本上意味着什么？

The operation was considered a success in military terms.

就军事角度看，这次行动是成功的。

The video explains in simple terms how the new tax works.

录像用简单易懂的语言解释了新税法。

in the long/short/medium term 长/短/中期内

Such a development seems unlikely, at least in the short term.

这样的发展看来可能性不大，至少短期之内如此。

come to terms with 勉强接受；向…让步，对…妥协

If you come to terms with something difficult or unpleasant, you learn to accept and deal with it.

She had come to terms with the fact that her husband would always be crippled.

她只能接受丈夫将终身残疾这个现实。

on good/friendly terms with sb 和某人关系好

Madeleine is on good terms with Sarah.

马德琳和萨拉相处很好。

2. terminal [ˈtɜːmɪnl] n. 终点站；（电脑）终端 adj. （疾病）晚期的

『termin界限+al…的→（交通线、网线、电路、疾病）到达界限（尽头）的地方→终点站；（电脑）终端；（电路）端子；（疾病）晚期的』

❶ [C]（公共汽车、火车、船、货运的）终点站

a railway/bus/ferry terminal

铁路/公共汽车终点站；渡船码头

❷ [C] 终端，终端机；（电路的）端子，接线头

Carl sits at a computer terminal 40 hours a week.

卡尔每周在电脑终端前坐 40 个小时。

the positive terminal of the battery 蓄电池的阳极

❸ adj.（疾病）不治的，晚期的；（病人）患绝症的，晚期的，病危的

But when the 86-year-old man was diagnosed with terminal cancer, it appeared his dream would never come true.

但当这个86岁的老人被诊断为癌症晚期的时候，看起来他的梦想没有办法实现了。

3. terminate [ˈtɜːmɪneɪt] v.（使）停止；到达终点

『termin界限+ate表动词→到达界限→结束，停止』

❶ （使）停止，结束，终止

[V] Your contract of employment terminates in December.

你的聘约12月到期。

[VN] The agreement was terminated immediately.

那项协议立即被终止了。

to terminate a pregnancy (= to perform or have an abortion)

终止妊娠（堕胎）

❷ （火车、公共汽车）到达终点

This train will terminate at Taunton.

这列火车的终点站是汤顿。

▶ **termination** [ˌtɜːmɪˈneɪʃn] n. 结束；终止

4. interminable [ɪnˈtɜːmɪnəbl] adj. 冗长的，没完没了的

『in没有+termin界限+able可以…的→没有界限的→冗长的』

an interminable speech/wait/discussion
无休止的讲话/等待/讨论

5. exterminate [ɪkˈstɜːmɪneɪt] v. 灭绝，根除
『ex出+termin界限+ate使…→使超出界限→灭绝』

A huge effort was made to exterminate the rats.
灭鼠花了大力气。

They have a real fear that they'll be exterminated in the ongoing civil war.
他们十分害怕自己会在持续的内战中被彻底消灭。

<u>词根350.</u> terr(i)=earth，表示"土地"

1. territory [ˈterətri] n. 领土；地盘；领域
『terri土地+tory场所→地的范围→领地』

❶ [C, U] 领土；版图；领地
They have refused to allow UN troops to be stationed in their territory. 他们拒不允许联合国部队驻扎在他们的国土上。

❷ [C, U] （个人、群体、动物的）领地；地盘；管区
Mating blackbirds will defend their territory against intruders.
乌鸫交配时会保护自己的地盘，不允许外来者侵入。

❸ [U] （知识）领域，范围
This type of work is uncharted territory for us.
我们从未涉足这类工作。
Legal problems are Andy's territory.
法律问题由安迪负责处理。

2. terrace [ˈterəs] n. 梯田；排屋；平台
『terr土地+(f)ace平面→土地组成的（窄长）（一个或多个相连的）平面→平台，阳台；梯田』

❶ [C] 梯田，阶地

❷ [C] 排屋（指相互连接、式样相似的房屋）

❸ [C] （尤指房屋或餐馆外的）露天平台，阳台
a flat, hard area, especially outside a house or restaurant, where you can sit, eat and enjoy the sun
All rooms have a balcony or terrace.
所有的房间都有阳台或露台。
There is an inviting restaurant with an outdoor terrace.
有一家诱人的带露天阳台的餐厅。

3. terrain [təˈreɪn] n. 地形；地势；地带
『terr土地+ain表事物→地形；地带』

[C, U] 地形；地势；地带
used to refer to an area of land when you are mentioning its natural features, for example, if it is rough, flat, etc.
difficult/rough/mountainous, etc. terrain
难以通过的地带、崎岖不平的地形、多山的地形等

<u>词义辨析</u> <P378第86>
乡村，地貌 country, countryside, landscape, terrain

4. Mediterranean [ˌmedɪtəˈreɪniən] adj. 地中海的
『medi中间+terr土地+anean有…性质的→被陆地包围的一片海洋的→地中海的』

5. inter [ɪnˈtɜː(r)] vt. 埋葬（遗体）
『in里面+terr土地（去r）→使（遗体）入到土里面→埋葬（遗体）』

▶**interment** [ɪnˈtɜːmənt] n. 埋葬；安葬

Nowadays, great changes have taken place in regard to funerals and interment.
现在，殡葬方式有了很大改变。

6. subterranean [ˌsʌbtəˈreɪniən] adj. 地下的
『sub下面+terr土地+anean有…性质的→地下的』

All the buildings are connected with subterranean tunnels.
所有的楼房都与地下隧道相连。

<u>词根351.</u> terr=frighten，表示"恐吓；使害怕"

1. terror [ˈterə(r)] n. 恐怖事物；恐惧；恐怖活动
『terr恐吓；使害怕+or表人或物→引起恐怖的人或物→恐怖活动』

❶ [C] 可怕的人；恐怖的事；可怕的情况
The terrors of the night were past.
夜间那些恐怖的事情都已经成为过去。
These street gangs have become the terror of the neighbourhood.
这些街头少年团伙使得周围邻里谈之色变。

❷ [U, sing.] 惊恐；恐惧；惊骇
a feeling of extreme fear
Her eyes were wild with terror. 她的眼睛里充满了恐惧。
People fled from the explosion in terror.
人们惊恐地逃离了爆炸现场。

❸ （尤指有政治目的的）恐怖活动
The bomb attack on the capital could signal the start of a pre-election terror campaign.
对首都的炸弹袭击可能标志着选举前的恐怖活动开始了。

▶**terrorism** [ˈterərɪzəm] n. 恐怖主义
▶**terrorist** [ˈterərɪst] n. 恐怖分子

2. terrible [ˈterəbl] adj. 可怕的；非常讨厌的
『terr恐吓；使害怕+ible可以，能够→能够使人害怕的→可怕的』

3. terrific [təˈrɪfɪk] adj. 极好的；很多的，很大的
『terr使害怕+ific的→（好的、大的、多的）可怕的→极好的；很多的，很大的』

What a terrific idea! 多么好的主意！
He did a terrific amount of fundraising.
他做了大量的筹款工作。

4. deter [dɪˈtɜː(r)] vt. 阻止；威慑；使不敢
『de离开+terr使害怕，恐吓（去r）→使其因为害怕而离开→威慑』

~ sb (from sth/from doing sth) 威慑；使不敢
to make sb decide not to do sth or continue doing sth, especially by making them understand the difficulties and unpleasant results of their actions
The high price of the service could deter people from seeking advice. 这么高的服务费可能使咨询者望而却步。

▶**deterrent** [dɪˈterənt] n. 威慑因素 adj. 威慑的
『deter威慑（双写r）+ent表形容词或名词→威慑的；威慑因素』

~ (to sb/sth) 威慑因素；遏制力
a thing that makes sb less likely to do sth (= that deters them)
Hopefully his punishment will act as a deterrent to others.
对他的惩罚但愿能起到杀一儆百的作用。
There's no credible alternative to the nuclear deterrent.
没有可以取代核威慑力量的可靠办法。
Their missiles are viewed as a defensive and deterrent force.
他们的导弹被视为一种防御和威慑力量。

▶**deterrence** [dɪˈterəns] n. 威慑，遏制

『deter威慑（双写r）+ence表名词→威慑』

Militarily, our basic defense strategy is deterrence.
在军事上，我们的基本防御战略是威慑。

词根352. test(i)=test, witness，表示"测试；证明"

1. protest [ˈprəʊtest , prəˈtest] n. & v. 抗议
『pro在前面+test证明→在前面证明（反对某事）→抗议』
（n. [ˈprəʊtest]; v. [prəˈtest]）

The director resigned in protest at the decision.
主任辞职以示抗议这项决定。
Students took to the streets to protest against the decision.
学生们走上街头，抗议这项决定。

▶ **Protestant** [ˈprɒtɪstənt] n. 新教教徒 adj. 新教教徒的

2. contest [ˈkɒntest , kənˈtest] n. 竞赛，比赛 vt. 争取赢得；提出异议
『con一起+test证明→一起向（评委）证明自己（行）→竞赛
（n. [ˈkɒntest]; v. [kənˈtest]）

❶ [C] 比赛，竞赛
a singing contest 歌咏比赛
a talent contest 才艺比赛
to enter/win/lose a contest 参加/赢得竞赛；竞赛失败

❷ [C] （控制权或权力的）争夺，竞争
a contest for the leadership of the party 争夺政党的领导权

❸ [VN] 争取赢得（比赛、选举等）
Three candidates contested the leadership.
有三位候选人角逐领导权。
a hotly/fiercely/keenly contested game
竞争十分激烈的比赛

❹ [VN] 就…提出异议
to contest a will 对遗嘱提出质疑

▶ **contestant** [kənˈtestənt] n. 比赛者，参赛者

3. testify [ˈtestɪfaɪ] v. （尤指出庭）作证，证实
『testi证明+fy使…→作证明→作证』

~ (against/for sb) | ~ (to/about sth) （尤指出庭）作证
To make a statement that sth happened or that sth is true, especially as a witness in court. If one thing testifies to another, it supports the belief that the second thing is true.
[V] John Bolton won't testify against Trump, and neither will anyone else at least not in the senate.
约翰·博尔顿不会指证特朗普，其他人也不会，至少不会在参议院。
[V] Recent excavations testify to the presence of cultivated inhabitants on the hill during the Arthurian period.
最近几次发掘证实了亚瑟王时期这座山上有农耕人口存在过。

4. testimony [ˈtestɪməni] n. 证明；证词，口供
『testi证明+mony表名词→能够作为证据的东西→证明；证词，口供』

❶ [U, sing.] ~ (to sth) 证据；证明
a thing that shows that sth else exists or is true
The pyramids are an eloquent testimony to the ancient Egyptians' engineering skills.
金字塔是古埃及人非凡工程技术的证明。

❷ [C, U] 证词；口供
Can I refuse to give testimony? 我能拒绝作证吗？

5. detest [dɪˈtest] v. 厌恶，憎恨，讨厌
『de毁坏+test证明→（因为憎恨）向坏处证明→厌恶，憎恶，讨厌』

to hate sb/sth very much
They detested each other on sight.
他们互相看着就不顺眼。

▶ **detestable** [dɪˈtestəbl] adj. 可憎的
『detest憎恶+able可以→可憎的』

All terrorist crime is detestable, whoever the victims.
无论受害者是谁，一切恐怖主义罪行都是可憎的。

6. attest [əˈtest] v. 证实，证明（某事属实）
『at相当于to+test证明→对某事的证明→证实，证明』

To attest something or attest to something means to say, show, or prove that it is true.
Police records attest to his long history of violence.
警方记录证明他有长期从事暴力活动的前科。

词根353. text=weave，表示"编织"

1. context [ˈkɒntekst] n. 语境；上下文
『con一起+text编织→编织在一起（来理解）→语境』

❶ [C, U] 上下文；语境
You should be able to guess the meaning of the word from the context. 你应该能从上下文猜出这个词的含义。

❷ [C, U] （事情发生的）背景，环境
His decision can only be understood in context.
只有了解来龙去脉才能明白他的决定。

2. pretext [ˈpriːtekst] n. 借口；托词
『pre预先+text编织→预先编好的→借口』

a false reason that you give for doing sth, usually sth bad, in order to hide the real reason; an excuse
He left the party early on the pretext of having work to do.
他借口有事要处理，早早离开了聚会。

3. textile [ˈtekstaɪl] n. 纺织品
『text编织+ile物品→编织出的物品→纺织品』

❶ [C] 纺织品
He was assigned into the textile factory after education.
毕业后他被分配到纺织厂。

❷ textiles [pl.] 纺织业
Another 75,000 jobs will be lost in textiles and clothing.
纺织和服装业又要失去75000个工作岗位。

4. texture [ˈtekstʃə(r)] n. 质地；结构
『text编织+ure表结果→编织的结果→质地；结构』

[C, U] 质地；手感
the way a surface, substance or piece of cloth feels when you touch it, for example how rough, smooth, hard or soft it is
She uses a variety of different colours and textures in her wall hangings. 她悬挂的帷幔色彩和质地多姿多彩。
Each brick also varies slightly in tone, texture and size.
每块砖在色调、质地与大小上也都略有不同。

词根354. the(o)=god，表示"神"

1. theism [ˈθiːɪzəm] n. 有神论
『the神+ism主义，学术流派→有神论』

2. atheism [ˈeɪθiɪzəm] n. 无神论
『a无+ the神+ism主义，学术流派→无神论』

3. theology [θiˈɒlədʒi] n. 神学；宗教学

『theo神+logy…学→神学』

4. pantheism [ˈpænθiɪzəm] n. 泛神论（认为神存在于万事万物）

『pan全部+the神+ism主义→泛神论』

5. theocracy [θiˈɒkrəsi] n. 神权政治；神权国〈P139〉

『theo神+cracy统治或政体→神权统治』

词根355. thes, thet=place, put 表示"放置"

1. thesis [ˈθiːsɪs] n. 毕业论文，学位论文；命题，论题

『thes放+is表名词→（事先）放好的（研究主题）→论文；命题，论题』

（pl. theses [ˈθiːsiːz]）

He was awarded his PhD for a thesis on industrial robots.
他凭一篇研究工业机器人的论文获得博士学位。
This thesis does not stand up to close inspection.
这个命题经不起仔细推敲。

2. antithesis [ænˈtɪθəsɪs] n. 对立（面）；对照，对比

『anti相反+thes放+is表名词→放在相反位置上（的东西）→对立（面）』

This is not democratic. It is the antithesis of democracy.
这不是民主。这是民主的对立面。

▶ **antithetical** [ˌæntɪˈθetɪkl] adj. 相反的，对立的

This attitude is antithetical to my beliefs.
这种态度与我的信仰背道而驰。

3. synthesis [ˈsɪnθəsɪs] n. 综合；合成

『syn同时+thes放+is表名词→同时放到一起→综合；合成』

❶ [U, C] ~ (of sth) 综合；综合体
A synthesis of different ideas or styles is a mixture or combination of these ideas or styles.
His novels are a rich synthesis of Balkan history and mythology.
他的小说融合了大量巴尔干半岛的历史和神话故事。
the synthesis of art with everyday life
艺术与日常生活的结合

❷ （物质在动植物体内的）合成；（人工的）合成；（用电子手段对声音、音乐或语音的）合成
protein synthesis 蛋白质合成
the synthesis of penicillin 青霉素的合成
speech synthesis software 语音合成软件

▶ **synthetic** [sɪnˈθetɪk] adj. 合成的，人造的

Boots made from synthetic materials can usually be washed in a machine. 合成材料制成的靴子通常可以机洗。

词义辨析 〈P364第15〉

假的，人造的 artificial, fake, false, synthetic, virtual

▶ **synthesize** [ˈsɪnθəsaɪz] vt. 合成

A vitamin is a chemical compound that cannot be synthesized by the human body. 维生素是一种人体无法合成的化合物。

4. hypothesis [haɪˈpɒθəsɪs] n. 假说；假设

『hypo下+thes放置+is表情况→放在下面（还不能作为正式理论）→假说』

A hypothesis is an idea which is suggested as a possible explanation for a particular situation or condition, but which

---

has not yet been proved to be correct.
Work will now begin to test the hypothesis in rats.
现在将开始在老鼠身上验证该假设。

▶ **hypothetical** [ˌhaɪpəˈθetɪkl] adj. 假设的，假定的

a hypothetical question/situation/example
假设的问题/情况/例子

▶ **hypothesize** [haɪˈpɒθəsaɪz] vt. 假设，假定

5. parenthesis [pəˈrenθəsɪs] n. 圆括号；插入语

『par旁边+en使+thes放+is表名词→使放在旁边（不是重点）→插入语；括号（插入语常放在括号里面）』

Irregular forms are given in parentheses.
不规则形式标注在括号内。
In parenthesis, I'd say that there were two aspects to writing you must never lose sight of.
插一句，关于写作，我认为有两个方面你绝不能忽视。

▶ **parenthetical** [ˌpærənˈθetɪkl] adj. 作为插入语的；补充说明的

『par旁边+en使+thet放置+ical…的→使放在旁边（不是重点）的→作为插入语的；补充说明的』

Fox was making a long parenthetical remark about his travels on the border of the country.
福克斯正在插入一大段题外话，讲他在该国边境游历的故事。

词根356. therm=heat，表示"热"

1. thermos [ˈθɜːməs] n. 热水瓶

『therm热+os表物→（使开水保持）热（的）物品→热水瓶』

She poured hot water from the thermos.
她从热水瓶倒出热水。

2. thermal [ˈθɜːml] adj. 热的，热量的；保暖的

『therm热+al…的→热的，热量的』

thermal energy 热能
thermal springs 温泉

3. geothermal [ˌdʒiːəʊˈθɜːml] adj. 地热的

『geo地+therm热+al…的→地热的』

Increasing use will be made of geothermal and solar energy for heating and cooling.
将更多地利用地热与太阳能取暖和制冷。

4. thermometer [θəˈmɒmɪtə(r)] n. 温度计

『therm热+o+meter计量；测量→温度计』

The nurse shook the thermometer and put it under my armpit.
护士甩了甩体温计，然后放到了我的腋下。

5. hypothermia [ˌhaɪpəˈθɜːmiə] n. 体温过低

『hypo低+therm热（引申为温度）+ia表疾病→体温低于（正常值的）病→体温过低』

Hypothermia can be mild, moderate or severe.
低体温有轻微、中度和重度之分。
Some India soldiers perished from wounds and hypothermia.
一些印度士兵死于受伤和低温。

词根357. tim=fear，表示"害怕"

1. timid [ˈtɪmɪd] adj. 胆小的，缺乏自信的；犹豫不决的

『tim害怕+id…的→胆怯的』

The little girl is as timid as a hare, shy in the presence of

strangers. 这小姑娘胆小如兔，在陌生人面前怕羞。
They've been rather timid in the changes they've made.
他们对所进行的变革一直小心翼翼。

▶ **timidity** [tɪ'mɪdətɪ] n. 胆小

2. intimidate [ɪn'tɪmɪdeɪt] vt. 恐吓，威胁
『in使+timid胆小的，害怕的+ate使→使害怕→恐吓，威胁』

[VN] ~ sb (into sth/into doing sth)
They were accused of intimidating people into voting for them. 他们被控胁迫选民投他们的票。
She refused to be intimidated by their threats.
她没有被他们的威胁吓倒。

词根358. tir(e)=draw, 表示"拉"

1. attire [ə'taɪə(r)] n. 衣服
『at相当于to+tire拉→拉到（身上的）→衣服』

[U] (formal) 服装，衣服
In those crowded streets her attire did not rate a second glance. 在那些拥挤的街道上，她的穿着并未引起注意。

2. tirade [taɪ'reɪd] n. （批评或指责性的）长篇激烈讲话
『tir拉+ade动作的结果→把（话）拉长→长篇演说』

She launched into a tirade of abuse against politicians.
她发表了长篇演说，愤怒地谴责政客。

词根359. tom=cut, 表示"切割"

1. atom ['ætəm] n. 原子
『a不+tom切割→不能再切割的小东西→原子』

▶ **atomic** [ə'tɒmɪk] adj. 原子的

2. anatomy [ə'nætəmɪ] n. 解剖；人体解剖；（动植物的）结构；剖析
『ana在旁边；类似+tom切割+y表行为→切开→解剖』

the anatomy of the horse 马的身体构造
an anatomy of the current recession 对当前经济衰退的剖析

3. epitome [ɪ'pɪtəmɪ] n. 典型，典范
『epi在+tom切割+e→（把典型特征）切割之后放在一起→典型，典范』

If you say that a person or thing is the epitome of something, you are emphasizing that they are the best possible example of a particular type of person or thing.
Maureen was the epitome of sophistication.
莫琳是个典型的老油条。

▶ **epitomize** [ɪ'pɪtəmaɪz] vt. 成为…的典型

The fighting qualities of the team are epitomized by the captain. 这个队的战斗精神从队长身上体现出来。
These movies seem to epitomize the 1950s.
这些影片似乎就是20世纪50年代的缩影。

词根360. tort, tors=twist; wrench, 表示"扭曲；猛扭，猛拉；使痛苦"

1. contort [kən'tɔːt] v. （使）扭曲，走样
『con一起+tort扭曲→扭曲，走样』

If someone's face or body contorts or is contorted, it moves into an unnatural and unattractive shape or position.
His face contorts as he screams out the lyrics.
当他吼出这些歌词的时候，脸都扭曲了。

2. contortionist [kən'tɔːʃənɪst] n. 柔体杂技演员

『con一起+tort扭曲+ion表名词+ist人→（身体）一起扭曲的人→柔体杂技演员』

3. distort [dɪ'stɔːt] vt. 使变形，使失真；歪曲，扭曲
『dis(=away)+tort扭曲→离开就变形了→扭曲；变形』

❶ [VN] 使变形；扭曲；使失真
If something you can see or hear is distorted or distorts, its appearance or sound is changed so that it seems unclear.
A painter may exaggerate or distort shapes and forms.
画家可能会对线条和形状进行夸大或扭曲。
The loudspeaker seemed to distort his voice.
他的声音从喇叭里传出来好像失真了。

❷ [VN] 歪曲；扭曲
If you distort a statement, fact, or idea, you report or represent it in an untrue way.
The media distorts reality; it categorises people as all good or all bad.
媒体会歪曲事实，将人说得不是完美无缺就是一无是处。

▶ **distortion** [dɪ'stɔːʃn] n. 变形，失真；扭曲，歪曲
Audio signals can be transmitted along cables without distortion. 声音信号可以通过电缆传送而不失真。

4. extort [ɪk'stɔːt] vt. 敲诈，勒索；强取，逼取
『ex出来+tort扭曲；猛扭→（用力）把（某物）猛扭出来』

❶ [VN] 敲诈，勒索
If someone extorts money from you, they get it from you using force, threats, or other unfair or illegal means.
Corrupt government officials were extorting money from him.
腐败的政府官员向他敲诈钱财。

❷ [VN] 强取，逼取
If someone extorts something from you, they get it from you with difficulty or by using unfair means.
Some magistrates have abused their powers of arrest to extort confessions. 有些地方执法官滥用逮捕权进行逼供。

▶ **extortion** [ɪk'stɔːʃn] n. 敲诈，勒索
He has been charged with extortion and abusing his powers.
他被控敲诈勒索和滥用职权。

5. torsion ['tɔːʃn] n. （物体等一端固定的）扭转
『tors扭转+ion表名词→扭转』

6. tortuous ['tɔːtʃuəs] adj. （道路、河流等）弯弯曲曲的；（过程）迂回复杂的
『tort扭曲+uous有…性质的→弯弯曲曲的』

The only road access is a tortuous mountain route.
唯一的陆路通道是一条蜿蜒的山道。
The parties must now go through the tortuous process of picking their candidates.
各政党现在必须经历挑选候选人的曲折过程。

7. retort [rɪ'tɔːt] vt. & n. 反驳，回嘴
『re返回+tort扭曲→（把别人说的话）扭曲后返回→反驳』

"Don't be ridiculous!" Pat retorted angrily.
"别荒唐了！"帕特生气地回答道。
His sharp retort clearly made an impact.
他尖锐的反驳显然起了作用。

8. torment ['tɔːment , tɔː'ment] n. （尤指精神上的）折磨，痛苦 vt. 使备受折磨；使痛苦；戏弄
『tor(= tort)使痛苦+ment表名词→使痛苦；折磨』

（n. [ˈtɔːment]; vt. [tɔːˈment]）

❶ [U, C]（尤指精神上的）折磨，痛苦；苦难之源
extreme suffering, especially mental suffering; a person or thing that causes this
She suffered years of mental torment after her son's death.
儿子去世后，她多年悲痛欲绝。
The flies were a terrible torment. 苍蝇一度肆虐。

❷ [VN] 使备受折磨，使痛苦
If something torments you, it causes you extreme mental suffering.
At times the memories returned to torment her.
有时，她再度想起往事，又会痛苦万分。

❸ [VN] 戏弄，捉弄
If you torment a person or animal, you annoy them in a playful, rather cruel way for your own amusement.
My older brother and sister used to torment me by singing it to me. 哥哥姐姐以前常唱那首歌来戏弄我。

9. torture [ˈtɔːtʃə(r)] n. & vt. 拷打，拷问，折磨，（使）痛苦
『tort痛苦+ure表名词或动词→拷打；（使）痛苦』

❶ [U, C] 拷打；拷问
the act of causing sb severe pain in order to punish them or make them say or do sth
Many of the refugees have suffered torture.
许多难民都遭受过拷打。
His confessions were made under torture. 他被屈打成招。

❷ [U, C]（精神上或肉体上的）折磨，痛苦
mental or physical suffering; sth that causes this
The interview was sheer torture from start to finish.
这次面试从头至尾使人备受煎熬。

❸ [VN] 拷打，拷问；折磨，使痛苦
French police are convinced that she was tortured and killed.
法国警方确信她是被拷打致死的。
He would not torture her further by trying to argue with her.
他不愿与她争辩而令她更痛苦。

词根361. tour, tourn, torn=turn，表示"转，环绕"

1. tour [tʊə(r)] n. 旅游；参观；巡回比赛（或演出等）
『tour转→（在多地或某个地方、某个建筑）转来转去（目的是看）→旅游；参观；（在多地）转来转去（演出或比赛）→巡回比赛或演出』

❶ ~ (of/round/around sth)（在多地间）旅游
a journey made for pleasure during which several different towns, countries, etc. are visited
a coach tour of northern France
乘长途汽车在法国北部旅游

❷ 参观（某地、某个建筑等）
an act of walking around a town, building, etc. in order to visit it
We were given a guided tour (= by sb who knows about the place) of the palace. 我们由导游带领参观游览了那座宫殿。

❸ 巡回比赛（或演出等）；巡视
The band is currently on a nine-day tour of France.
这支乐队目前正在法国进行9天的巡回演出。

▶**tourist** [ˈtʊərɪst] n. 旅游者；观光者

▶**tourism** [ˈtʊərɪzəm] n. 旅游业

2. tournament [ˈtʊənəmənt] n. 锦标赛
『tourn转+a+ment表名词→转着轮流比赛→锦标赛』
A tournament is a sports competition in which players who win a match continue to play further matches in the competition until just one person or team is left.

3. detour [ˈdiːtʊə(r)] n. & v. 绕道
『de离开+ tour转→转身离开（原来的路线）→绕路』

❶ [C] 绕道，绕路，迂回
a longer route that you take in order to avoid a problem or to visit a place
It's well worth making a detour to see the village.
绕道去参观一下这村子很是值得。

❷ [V] (NAmE) ~ (to…) 绕道，绕行
The President detoured to Chicago for a special meeting.
总统绕道去了芝加哥参加一个特别会议。

4. contour [ˈkɒntʊə(r)] n. 外形，轮廓；等高线
『con一起+tour转→（把描画外形的线）一起转→轮廓』

❶ [C] 外形；轮廓
the outer edges of sth; the outline of its shape or form
The road follows the natural contours of the coastline.
这条路沿着海岸线的自然轮廓延伸。

❷ [C]（地图上表示相同海拔各点的）等高线

5. tornado [tɔːˈneɪdəʊ] n. 龙卷风
『torn转+ad+o物→龙卷风』

词根362. tox=poison，表示"毒"

1. toxin [ˈtɒksɪn] n. 毒素（尤指生物体自然产生的毒物）
『tox毒+in…素→毒素』
Experts have linked this condition to a build-up of toxins in the body. 专家已把这一病症与体内毒素的积累联系起来。

2. toxic [ˈtɒksɪk] adj. 有毒的
『tox毒+ic…的→有毒的』
toxic chemicals/fumes/gases/substances
有毒的化学品/烟雾/气体/物质

3. intoxicated [ɪnˈtɒksɪkeɪtɪd] adj. 醉酒的；陶醉的
『in处于…当中+toxic有毒的+ate使+(e)d表状态→（因酒精或好事）使处于中毒状态→醉酒的；陶醉的』
He was arrested for DWI (= driving while intoxicated).
他因酒醉驾驶而被拘捕。
They seem to have become intoxicated by their success.
他们似乎陶醉在成功的喜悦中。

词根363. tract =draw，表示"拉，拖"

1. tractor [ˈtræktə(r)] n. 拖拉机；牵引机
『tract拉，拖+or表动作执行者→用来拖拉的东西→拖拉机』

2. tractable [ˈtræktəbl] adj. 易处理的；易驾驭的
『tract拉+able可…的，能…的→能够拉（回来）→易处理的』

If you say that a person, problem, or device is tractable, you mean that they can be easily controlled or dealt with.

He could easily manage his tractable and worshipping younger brother.
他能轻而易举地管住听话并且崇拜自己的弟弟。

▶**intractable** [ɪn'træktəbl] adj. （人）难驾驭的；（事情）难处理的

『in不+tractable易处理的；易驾驭的→难处理的；难驾驭的』

The economy still faces intractable problems.
经济仍然面临着一些棘手的问题。

3. **distract** [dɪ'strækt] vt. 使分心
『dis离开+tract拉→把（心）拉开→分心』

You're distracting me from my work.
你使我不能专心工作。
Don't talk to her—she's very easily distracted.
不要和她讲话——她的注意力很容易分散。

▶**distraction** [dɪ'strækʃn] n. 分散注意力（的事）
I find it hard to work at home because there are too many distractions.
我发觉在家里工作很难，因为使人分心的事太多。

▶**distracting** [dɪ'stræktɪŋ] adj. 令人分心的

4. **contract** ['kɒntrækt, kən'trækt] n. 合同 v. 签合同；收缩；感染
『con一起+tract拉→拉到一起；（把合同双方）拉到一起→合同；收缩』
（n. ['kɒntrækt]; v. [kən'trækt]）

❶ [C] ~ (with sb) | ~ (between A and B) | ~ (for sth/to do sth)
合同；合约；契约
These clauses form part of the contract between buyer and seller. 这些条款构成买卖双方所签合同的一部分。
Under the terms of the contract the job should have been finished yesterday.
根据合同的条款，这项工作本应于昨天完成。

❷ 签合同
[V] She has contracted to work 20 hours a week.
她已签订每周工作20小时的合同。
[V] You can contract with us to deliver your cargo.
你可以跟我们签订送货合同。
[VN to inf] The player is contracted to play until August.
这位选手签约参加比赛到8月份。

❸ [V] （使）收缩，缩小
a contracting market 萎缩的市场
The heart muscles contract to expel the blood.
心脏肌肉收缩以挤压出血液。

❹ [VN] (medical) 感染（疾病）；得（病）
to contract AIDS/a virus/a disease 感染艾滋病/病毒/疾病
It is unknown where she contracted the coronavirus.
不知道她在哪里感染了冠状病毒。

词义辨析 <P379第91>
感染；传播 infect, contract, transmit

5. **abstract** ['æbstrækt] adj. 抽象的 v. 提取；抽取 n. 摘要
『abs去掉，离去+tract拉→将（许多具体的事物中相同的部分）拉出来→抽象的』
❶ adj. 抽象的（与个别情况相对）；纯理论的

The research shows that preschool children are capable of thinking in abstract terms.
研究表明，学龄前儿童具有抽象思维的能力。
We may talk of beautiful things but beauty itself is abstract.
我们尽可谈论美的事物，但美本身却是抽象的。

❷ [VN] 提取；抽取
She abstracted the main points from the argument.
她把论证概括成要点。

❸[C] （文献等的）摘要，概要

6. **attract** [ə'trækt] v. 吸引；诱惑
『at相当于to+tract拉→拉到→吸引』

~ sb (to sb/sth) 吸引；使喜爱
I had always been attracted by the idea of working abroad.
我总是向往去国外工作。
The exhibition has attracted thousands of visitors.
展览吸引了成千上万的参观者。

▶**attractive** [ə'træktɪv] adj. 迷人的，有魅力的

▶**attraction** [ə'trækʃn] n. 有吸引力的地方（或事物）；吸引力
The walled city is an important tourist attraction.
这座由城墙围绕的城市是个重要的旅游胜地。
This attraction was too much for him.
这诱惑对他太大了。

7. **detract** [dɪ'trækt] v. 诋毁，贬低，损减
『de向下+tract拉→（把…）向下拉→毁损』

If one thing detracts from another, it makes it seem less good or impressive.
The publicity could detract from our election campaign.
这些宣传报道可能会有损我们的竞选活动。

8. **subtract** [səb'trækt] vt. 减去
『sub下面+tract拉→（在竖式减法中，把减数从被减数中）拉下来→减去』

6 subtracted from 9 is 3.　9减6等于3。

小贴士 plus和minus表示"加、减"时是介词；multiply和divide表示"乘、除"时是动词。

9. **extract** ['ekstrækt , ɪk'strækt] vt. 提取；摘录；拔出 n. 摘录
『ex出+tract拉→拉出来→提取；拔出；摘录』
（n. ['ekstrækt]; v. [ɪk'strækt]）

❶ [VN] 提取；提炼
to extract essential oils from plants 从植物中提取精油

❷ [VN] 摘录
This article is extracted from his new book.
本文选自他的新书。

❸ [VN] （用力）取出，拔出
The dentist may decide that the wisdom teeth need to be extracted. 牙医可能会认为智齿需要拔掉。

❹ n. 摘录；提取物
The following extract is taken from her new novel.
下面一段摘自她的新小说。
face cream containing natural plant extracts
含有天然植物提取物的面霜

10. **protract** [prə'trækt] vt. <贬>延长，拖延（某事物）
『pro向前+tract拖，拉→（时间上）向前拖拉→延长』

Let's not protract the debate any further.
我们不要再继续争论下去了。

11. retract [rɪ'trækt] v. 收回，撤回；缩回
『re返回+tract拉→拉回来→收回，撤回；缩回』

❶ [V, VN] 收回，撤回（所说的话或写的东西）
They tried to persuade me to retract my words.
他们试图说服我收回我的话。

❷ [V, VN] 缩回，缩入
Tigers retract their claws. 老虎平时是将爪子收起来的。

词根364. treat=handle，表示"处理"

1. retreat [rɪ'triːt] n. & v. 撤退；退缩
『re返回+treat处理→返回处理→撤退；退缩』

❶ [V] 撤退
to move away from a place or an enemy because you are in danger or because you have been defeated
The army was forced to retreat after suffering heavy losses.
部队因伤亡惨重被迫撤退。
We retreated back down the mountain.
我们从山上撤了下来。

❷ [V] 退缩，改变主意
to change your mind about sth because of criticism or because a situation has become too difficult
The government had retreated from its pledge to reduce class sizes. 政府已经改变了缩小班级规模的承诺。

❸ [V] 隐退，逃避
to escape to a place that is quieter or safer
Bored with the conversation, she retreated to her bedroom.
她厌倦了这样的交谈，躲进了自己的卧室。
I believe people should live in houses that allow them to retreat from the harsh realities of life.
我认为人们所居住的房子应该能让他们远离残酷的现实生活。

❹ [V] 离开，后退
He watched her retreating figure.
他看着她的身影渐渐远去。
The flood waters slowly retreated. 洪水慢慢地消退。
"I've already got a job," I said quickly, and retreated from the room.
"我已经有了一份工作，"我马上说道，并从房间里退了出来。

❺ [C, U] 撤退；退缩；改变主意；隐退，逃避
The army was in full retreat (= retreating very quickly).
部队全线撤退。
The Senator made an embarrassing retreat from his earlier position. 这位参议员很尴尬地改变了他早先的立场。
Is watching television a retreat from reality?
看电视是对现实的一种逃避吗？

❻ [C] 僻静处，隐居处
a quiet, private place that you go to in order to get away from your usual life
a country retreat 乡间幽静的住所

2. treaty ['triːti] n. （国家之间的）条约，协定
『treat处理+y表名词→处理（纷争的）文件→条约』
to draw up/sign/ratify a treaty 起草/签署/正式批准条约

3. entreat [ɪn'triːt] vt. 恳求；乞求

『en使+treat处理→使（某人）来处理（某事）』
to ask sb to do sth in a serious and often emotional way
[VN] Please help me, I entreat you. 请帮帮我吧，求你了。
[VN to inf] She entreated him not to go. 她恳求他不要走。

▶ **entreaty** [ɪn'triːti] n. 恳求；乞求

词根365. trem=quiver，表示"颤抖"

1. tremble ['trembl] vi. & n. 颤抖；颤动
『trem颤抖+ble可以的→可以颤抖的→颤抖』
My legs were trembling with fear. 我吓得双腿直发抖。
He felt the earth tremble under him.
他感到大地在脚下颤动。

2. tremor ['tremə(r)] n. 轻微地震；（由于寒冷或恐惧等引起的身体某一部分）颤抖，战栗，哆嗦；（在某一人群中引起的）震动，波动
『trem颤抖+or表情况→颤抖，哆嗦』
The tremor was centered just south of San Francisco and was felt as far as 200 miles away.
震中位于旧金山南部，在200英里外也有震感。
There was a slight tremor in his voice.
他的声音略微有点儿颤抖。
News of 160 redundancies had sent tremors through the community.
将会裁员160人的消息在该团体中引起了震动。

3. tremulous ['tremjələs] adj. （因紧张）颤抖的
『trem颤抖+ul+ous充满…的→颤抖的』
In a tremulous voice she whispered: "Who are you people?"
她用颤抖的声音低声说："你们是谁？"

4. tremendous [trə'mendəs] adj. 巨大的；极好的
『trem颤抖+end+ous…的→（大得）让人震颤的→巨大的』
A tremendous amount of work has gone into the project.
大量的工作已投入到这项工程。
It was a tremendous experience. 这是个了不起的经历。

词根366. tribute=give，表示"给予"

1. contribute [kən'trɪbjuːt] v. 捐献；贡献；撰稿
『con一起+tribute给予→（和别人）一起给→贡献』

❶ ~ (sth) (to/towards sth) 捐献，捐赠（尤指款或物）
to give sth, especially money or goods, to help sb/sth
[VN] We contributed £5,000 to the earthquake fund.
我们向地震基金捐赠了5000英镑。
[V] Would you like to contribute to our collection?
你愿意给我们的募捐捐款吗？

❷ [V] ~ (to sth) 促使，是…的原因之一
to be one of the causes of sth
Medical negligence was said to have contributed to her death.
据说医务人员的玩忽职守是她死亡的原因之一。

❸ contribute to（为…）作贡献
The three sons also contribute to the family business.
这3个儿子也为家族事业作出了贡献。
This book contributes little to our understanding of the subject. 此书对我们了解这门学科助益甚少。

❹ ~ (sth) (to sth) （为报纸、杂志、电台或电视节目）撰稿
[VN] She contributed a number of articles to the magazine.
她给这家杂志撰写了一些稿件。

► **contribution** [ˌkɒntrɪˈbjuːʃn] n. 捐款；贡献；稿件

❶ [C] 捐款；捐资

All contributions will be gratefully received.
我们对所有捐资表示感谢。

to make a contribution to charity 给慈善事业捐款

❷ [C, usually sing.] 贡献；促成作用

These measures would make a valuable contribution towards reducing industrial accidents.
这些措施将会对减少工伤事故起重要的作用。

❸ [C] 稿件

All contributions for the May issue must be received by Friday.
所有要在5月这一期发表的稿件必须在星期五以前寄到。

❹ [U] 捐赠；捐助；（尤指）捐款

We rely entirely on voluntary contribution.
我们全靠自愿捐赠。

2. **attribute** [əˈtrɪbjuːt, ˈætrɪbjuːt] vt.把…归因于 n.属性
『at相当于to+tribute给予→把（原因）给…→归因于』
（v. [əˈtrɪbjuːt]；n. [ˈætrɪbjuːt]）

❶ ~ sth to sth 把…归因于

She attributes her success to hard work and a little luck.
她把她的成功归因于工作努力和一点运气。

❷ ~ sth to sth 认为（文章、艺术品或评论）出自

This play is usually attributed to Shakespeare.
人们通常认为这出戏剧是莎士比亚所写。

❸ [C]（人或物的）品质，特征

Patience is one of the most important attributes in a teacher.
耐心是教师最重要的品质之一。

词义辨析 <P378第87>

特性 quality, attribute, characteristic, trait, feature, peculiarity, property

3. **distribute** [dɪˈstrɪbjuːt] vt. 分发；分销；使散开
『dis离开+tribute给予→（分别）给出去→分配；分散』

~ sth (to/among sb/sth)

❶ 分发；分配

to give things to a large number of people; to share sth between a number of people

The organization distributed food to the earthquake victims.
这个机构向地震灾民分发了食品。

❷ 分销

Who distributes our products in the UK?
谁在英国经销我们的产品？

❸ [often passive] 使散开；使分布；分散

Make sure that your weight is evenly distributed.
注意让你的重量分布均匀。

词义辨析 <P364第19> **分发 allocate, allot, distribute**

4. **retribution** [ˌretrɪˈbjuːʃn] n. 惩罚；报应
『re回+tribute给予（去e）+ion表名词→给回去→报应；惩罚』

[U] ~ (for sth) (formal) 严惩；惩罚；报应
severe punishment for sth seriously wrong that sb has done

People are seeking retribution for the latest terrorist outrages.
人们在设法对恐怖分子最近的暴行进行严惩。

5. **tribute** [ˈtrɪbjuːt] n. 悼念；致敬，赞扬；体现

『tribute给予→给予（敬意、赞美、怀念）→赞扬；悼念』

❶ [U, C] ~ (to sb) 悼念；致敬，赞扬

A tribute is something that you say, do, or make to show your admiration and respect for someone.

At her funeral her oldest friend paid tribute to her life and work.
在葬礼上，与她相识最久的老朋友对她的一生和工作给予了高度的赞扬。

He paid tribute to the organising committee.
他向组委会致敬。

❷ [sing.] ~ to sth/sb （良好效果或影响的）体现，显示
showing the good effects or influence of sth/sb

His recovery is a tribute to the doctors' skill.
他的康复充分显示了各位医生高超的医术。

6. **tributary** [ˈtrɪbjətri] n. 支流 adj. 支流的
『tribute给予（去e）+ary…的→给（大河水）的→支流的』

The Missouri River is the chief tributary of the Mississippi.
密苏里河是密西西比河的主要支流。

词根367. trude=push，表示"推"，名词形式为-trusion

1. **intrude** [ɪnˈtruːd] vi. 闯入，侵入；打扰
『in里面+trude推→推着进去→闯入；打扰』

❶ ~ (into/on/upon sb/sth) 闯入；侵入
to go or be somewhere where you are not wanted or are not supposed to be

The press has been blamed for intruding into people's personal lives in an unacceptable way.
媒体因以令人难以容忍的方式侵扰人们的私生活而受到指责。

I'm sorry to intrude, but I need to talk to someone.
对不起打扰了，不过我有话要找人谈。

❷ ~ (on/into/upon sth) 干扰，扰乱

I don't want to intrude on your meeting.
我不想打扰你们的会议。

► **intruder** [ɪnˈtruːdə(r)] n. 闯入者，侵入者

The police warned the intruder off. 警察警告闯入者离开。

► **intrusion** [ɪnˈtruːʒn] n. 闯入，侵入；干扰，影响

She apologised for the intrusion but said she had an urgent message. 她对径自闯进来表示道歉，但说她有紧急消息。
They claim the noise from the new airport is an intrusion on their lives.
他们声称新机场的噪声侵扰了他们的生活。
This was another example of press intrusion into the affairs of the royals. 这是新闻界侵扰王室成员私事的又一实例。

► **intrusive** [ɪnˈtruːsɪv] adj. 侵扰的，烦扰的

affecting someone or something in an annoying, disturbing and unwanted way

The constant presence of the media was very intrusive.
媒体一直在场十分令人讨厌。

2. **protrude** [prəˈtruːd] vi. 突出；伸出
『pro向前+trude推→向前推→突出，伸出』

[V] ~ (from sth) (formal) 突出；伸出；鼓出
to stick out from a place or a surface

He hung his coat on a nail protruding from the wall.
他把上衣挂在凸出墙面的一根钉子上。

► **protrusion** [prəˈtruːʒn] n. 突出物，凸起

a protrusion on the rock face　岩石表面的突起部分

3. extrude [ɪkˈstruːd] v.（被）挤压出
『ex出去+trude推→（在挤压中）被推出→（被）挤压出』

[VN] Lava is extruded from the volcano.
熔岩从火山中喷出。

[VN] These crystals are then embedded in a plastic, and the plastic is extruded as a wire.
然后将这些晶体嵌入塑料中，再把塑料挤压成线。

4. abstruse [əbˈstruːs] adj. 难解的，深奥的
『abs(=away)+truse(=trude)推→（尽力理解某事却被）推开→深奥的，难解的』

unnecessarily complicated and difficult to understand
The involved and abstruse passage makes several interpretations possible.
这段艰涩的文字可以作出好几种解释。

词根368. tut(e), tuit=protect or guard, guide or teach，表示"保护；指导，教育"

1. tutor [ˈtjuːtə(r)] n. 家庭教师；导师 vt. 教授，指导
『tut指导，教育+or人→家庭教师』

❶ [C] 家庭教师，私人教师
His parents employed a tutor to teach him mathematics.
他的父母雇了一位家庭教师教他数学。

❷ [C]（英）大学导师；（美）大学助教

❸ [VN] 教授，指导
The old man was tutoring her in the stringed instruments.
那个老人在教她弹弦乐器。

▶ **tutorial** [tjuːˈtɔːriəl] adj. 导师的，辅导的 n. 辅导课；教程

Students may decide to seek tutorial guidance.
学生可以决定寻求导师指导。
The methods of study include lectures, tutorials, case studies and practical sessions.
学习方法包括讲座、辅导、个案研究与实践课程。
I hope you found this tutorial fun and useful.
我希望您发现本教程的乐趣和益处。

2. tuition [tjuˈɪʃn] n.（尤指对个人或小组的）教学；（大学）学费
『tuit指导，教育+ion表名词→教学；学费』

She received private tuition in French. 她由私人教授法语。
He economized on food and clothing to save for his tuition.
他省吃俭用积攒学费。

3. intuition [ˌɪntjuˈɪʃn] n. 直觉力；（一种）直觉
『in里面+tuit指导+ion表名词→是内心指导下知道的（不是分析外部情况而知道的）→直觉』

Her intuition was telling her that something was wrong.
她的直觉告诉她一定出了什么问题。
I had an intuition that I would find you.
我有一种直觉，我能找到你们。

▶ **intuitive** [ɪnˈtjuːɪtɪv] adj. 直觉的

4. tutelage [ˈtjuːtəlɪdʒ] n. 教导，指导
『tutel(=tut)指导，教育+age表行为→教导，指导』

If one person, group, or country does something under the tutelage of another, they do it while they are being taught or

guided by them.
He made good progress under her tutelage.
他在她的指导下进步很大。

5. astute [əˈstjuːt] adj. 精明的，敏锐的
『as表加强+tute教育→受过专门教育的→精明的，敏锐的』

very clever and quick at seeing what to do in a particular situation, especially how to get an advantage
It was an astute move to sell the shares then.
那时出售股份是精明之举。
He is an extremely astute political tactician.
他是个极其精明的政治谋略家。

同义词 **shrewd** [ʃruːd] adj. 精明的，敏锐的

A shrewd person is able to understand and judge a situation quickly and to use this understanding to their own advantage.
She's a shrewd businesswoman. 她是个精明的女商人。
A shrewd man knows what he can say and what he can't.
一个精明的人懂得什么能说，什么不能说。

词根369. turb=stir，表示"搅动"

1. disturb [dɪˈstɜːb] vt. 打扰，扰乱，搅乱
『dis分散；离开+turb搅动→搅动使（心思、物品）离开→打扰；搅乱』

❶ [VN] 打扰；干扰；妨碍
to interrupt sb when they are trying to work, sleep, etc.
I'm sorry to disturb you, but can I talk to you for a moment?
对不起，打扰你一下，我能跟你谈一会儿吗？
If you get up early, try not to disturb everyone else.
如果你起得早，尽量不要打扰别人。

❷ [VN] 搅乱，弄乱，搞乱
to move sth or change its position
Don't disturb the papers on my desk.
别把我写字台上的文件弄乱了。

❸ [VN] 使焦虑，使不安，使烦恼
to make sb worry
The letter shocked and disturbed me.
这封信使我感到震惊和不安。

▶ **disturbing** [dɪˈstɜːbɪŋ] adj. 令人不安的

a disturbing piece of news　一则令人不安的消息

▶ **disturbance** [dɪˈstɜːbəns] n. 干扰；骚乱；（身体或心理上的）失调，紊乱

The building work is creating constant noise, dust and disturbance. 建筑施工不断制造噪声、灰尘和干扰。
He was charged with causing a disturbance after the game.
他被指控在比赛结束后制造骚乱。
emotional disturbance　情绪失常

2. perturb [pəˈtɜːb] vt. 使焦虑；使不安
『per彻底地+turb搅动→（心思）被彻底搅动了→使焦虑；使不安』

to make sb worried or anxious
Her sudden appearance did not seem to perturb him in the least. 她的突然出现似乎一点也没有令他不安。

3. turbine [ˈtɜːbaɪn] n. 涡轮机，汽轮机
『turb搅动+ine表名词→搅动（空气或水）的设备→涡轮机，汽轮机』

4. turmoil [ˈtɜːmɔɪl] n. 动乱，骚乱
『turm(=turb)搅动+oil→混乱』

[U, sing.] 动乱；骚动

Turmoil is a state of confusion, disorder, uncertainty, or great anxiety.

Her marriage was in turmoil. 她的婚姻一团糟。

The period since the revolution has been one of political turmoil. 革命爆发后就陷入了政治动乱期。

5. turbulent [ˈtɜːbjələnt] adj. 动荡的，动乱的；汹涌的
『turb搅动+ulent多…的→多搅动的→动荡的；汹涌的』

❶ 动荡的，动乱的
A turbulent time, place, or relationship is one in which there is a lot of change, confusion, and disorder.

The present international situation remains tense and turbulent. 当前的国际局势依然紧张动荡。

Those were turbulent years. 那是多事的年头。

❷ (of air or water 空气或水) 汹涌的；猛烈的；湍动的
The aircraft is designed to withstand turbulent conditions.
这架飞机是为经受猛烈的气流而设计的。

I had to have a boat that could handle turbulent seas.
我必须有一艘能经得起狂风骇浪的船。

▶**turbulence** [ˈtɜːbjələns] n. 动乱；湍流，涡流

❶ 骚乱；动乱；混乱
It was a time of change and turbulence.
这是风云变幻、动荡不安的一个时期。

❷ （空气或水）湍流，涡流
We experienced severe turbulence during the flight.
我们在飞行中遇到了强烈的气流。

6. turbid [ˈtɜːbɪd] adj. 浑浊的，污浊不清的
『turb搅动+id有…性质的→搅动的→浑浊的』

(formal) (of liquid 液体) 浑浊的；污浊不清的
full of mud, dirt, etc. so that you cannot see through it

The pure water is clean; but when mud or sand is poured into water, it becomes turbid.
水纯则清，但当泥浆或沙子倒进水里，水就浑浊了。

词根370. twin(e)=twine，表示"缠绕"

1. twine [twaɪn] n. （两股或多股的）线，绳 v. 缠绕

Have you got some twine to tie this box up?
你有没有绳子来把这些箱子捆好？

[V] ivy twining around a tree trunk 缠绕在树干上的藤蔓

[VN] She twined her arms around my neck.
她用双臂搂着我的脖子。

2. entwine [ɪnˈtwaɪn] vt. 缠绕；与…密切相关
『en使+twine缠绕→缠绕；与…密切相关』

They strolled through the park, with arms entwined.
他们挽着胳膊漫步穿过公园。

Her destiny was entwined with his.
她与他的命运紧密相连。

3. intertwine [ˌɪntəˈtwaɪn] v. 缠绕，缠结；密切联系
『inter在…之间+twine缠绕→相互缠绕→缠绕；密切联系』

Trees, undergrowth and creepers intertwined, blocking our way. 树木、灌木与藤蔓植物盘根错节，挡住了我们去路。
Their destinies are intertwined. 他们的命运交织在一起。

词根371. und=overflow, wave，表示"溢出；波动"

1. inundate [ˈɪnʌndeɪt] vt. 淹没；使应接不暇
『in里面+und溢出+ate表动词→溢出（流）进来→淹没』

❶ [VN] 淹没，泛滥（同义词 flood）
Their neighborhood is being inundated by the rising waters of the Colorado River.
他们的街区正被科罗拉多河上涨的河水淹没。

❷ [VN] （信件、要求、请求等）使应接不暇
Her office was inundated with requests for tickets.
她所在的售票处收到铺天盖地的购票请求。

2. abundant [əˈbʌndənt] adj. 大量的，丰盛的，充裕的
『ab加强+und溢出+ant…的→溢出来的→丰富的』

We have abundant evidence to prove his guilt.
我们有充分的证据证明他有罪。

▶**abundance** [əˈbʌndəns] n. 大量，丰盛，充裕

The area has an abundance of wildlife.
这片地区有丰富的野生动植物。

3. undulate [ˈʌndjuleɪt] vi. 起伏，波动，荡漾；摇曳
『und波动+ul+ate表动词→波动』

to go or move gently up and down like waves
The countryside undulates pleasantly. 原野起伏，景色宜人。
I love the gently undulating hills of the Dales.
我喜欢达莱斯起伏的小山。

4. redundant [rɪˈdʌndənt] adj. 多余的；被裁减的
『red(=re)返回+und溢出+ant…的→（因过多）溢出而返回→多余的』

My husband was made redundant late last year.
我丈夫去年年底被裁员了。

Changes in technology may mean that once-valued skills are now redundant.
技术上的革新可能意味着曾经被重视的技术现在已变得多余。

词根372. up=up, over，表示"向上"

1. uphold [ʌpˈhəʊld] vt. 支持，维护（法律、正义等）；维持（原判）
『up向上+hold坚持→使…处于向上的状态→支持；维持』

❶ [VN] 支持，维护（正义等）
We have a duty to uphold the law. 维护法律是我们的责任。

❷ [VN] 维持，坚持（原判）
The appeal court uphold the sentence. 上诉法庭维持了判决。

2. upheaval [ʌpˈhiːvl] n. 剧变；激变；动乱，动荡
『up向上+heave举起（去e）+al表名词→（地震地壳）向上隆起→剧变→激变；动乱』

a big change that causes a lot of confusion, worry and problems

Wherever there is political upheaval, invariably there are refugees. 哪里有政治动乱，哪里就一定有难民。

Some would like to go out, but dread the upheaval it causes their family.
有些人想出去，但害怕这会给他们的家庭带来剧变。

3. upgrade [ˌʌpˈgreɪd, ˈʌpgreɪd] n. & vt. 升级；提高
『up向上+grade级别→使级别向上→升级；提高』
（n. [ˈʌpgreɪd]; v. [ˌʌpˈgreɪd]）

You can upgrade from self-catering accommodation to a hotel. 您可以将自理膳食旅店升级为酒店。

Medical facilities are being reorganized and upgraded.
正在对医疗设施进行重组和升级。

4. upbraid [ʌpˈbreɪd] vt. 训斥，责骂
『up向上+braid辫子→提起小辫子→训斥，责骂』

If you upbraid someone, you tell them that they have done something wrong and criticize them for doing it.
His mother summoned him, upbraided him, wept and prayed.
他母亲把他叫到跟前训斥了一番，又哭哭啼啼地祷告。

5. upright [ˈʌpraɪt] adj. （人）直立的；（物）立式的，竖直的；（人）正直的
『up向上+right刚好→直立的；正直的』

She sat upright in bed. 她挺直地坐在床上。
Gradually raise your body into an upright position.
慢慢起身，成直立状态。
Keep the bottle upright. 保持瓶子直立。
an upright freezer 立式冰柜
a very upright, trustworthy man 一个非常正直可靠的人

词根373. urb=city，表示"城市"

1. urban [ˈɜːbən] adj. 城市的，都市的，城镇的
『urb城市+an…的→城市的』

[usually before noun] 城市的；都市的；城镇的
connected with a town or city
School crime and violence cuts across urban, rural and suburban areas.
城市、乡村和郊区都出现了校园犯罪和校园暴力现象。

反义词 rural [ˈrʊərəl] adj. 乡下的

▶ **urbanize** [ˈɜːbənaɪz] v. 城市化
For China to modernize its economy, it must further industrialize, and urbanize.
为了实现经济现代化，中国必须扩大工业化和城市化。

2. urbane [ɜːˈbeɪn] adj. 温文儒雅的；从容不迫的
『urb城市+ane…的，有…性质的→有都市（人）性质的→文雅的，从容的』

(of a man) good at knowing what to say and how to behave in social situations; appearing relaxed and confident
She describes him as urbane and charming.
她说他文雅而迷人。

3. suburb [ˈsʌbɜːb] n. 郊区
『sub下面+urb城市→在城市下面→郊区』

❶ [C] suburb of a city 城市的一个郊区
Anna was born in 1923 in Ardwick, a suburb of Manchester.
安娜1923年生于曼彻斯特郊区的阿德维克。

❷ the suburbs 城郊住宅区
His family lived in the suburbs. 他家住在城郊。

▶ **suburban** [səˈbɜːbən] adj. 郊区的
But it's another story in urban and suburban areas.
但在市区和城市郊区却是另一番情况。

词根374. ut, util=use，表示"用"

1. utilize [ˈjuːtəlaɪz] vt. 使用，利用
『util用+ize使→使用，利用』

to use sth, especially for a practical purpose
The Romans were the first to utilize concrete as a building material. 罗马人首先使用混凝土作建筑材料。

The resources at our disposal could have been better utilized.
我们所掌握的资源本来可以利用得更好，获得更高的效益。

2. utility [juːˈtɪləti] n. 公用事业；实用，有用
『util用+ity表性质、状况→公用事业；有用』

❶ [C] (especially NAmE) 公用事业
a service provided for the public, for example an electricity, water or gas supply
Does your rent include utilities?
你的房租包括水电费吗？
public utilities such as gas, electricity and phones
煤气、电和电话等公共设施

❷ [U] (formal) 实用，有用
the quality of being useful (=usefulness)
Belief in the utility of higher education is shared by students nationwide. 全国的学生都相信高等教育是有用的。

3. utensil [juːˈtensl] n. （家庭）用具，器皿，家什
『ut用+ensil表物品→用的物品→用具』

a tool that is used in the house
cooking/kitchen utensils 炊具；厨房用具
The best carving utensil is a long, sharp, flexible knife.
最好的雕刻工具是锋利而灵活的长刻刀。

4. utilitarian [ˌjuːtɪlɪˈteəriən] adj. 实用的；实用主义的 n. 实用主义者
『util用+it+arian…的；…者→以实用为主的→实用主义的；实用主义者』

designed to be useful and practical rather than attractive
Bruce's office is a corner one, utilitarian and unglamorous.
布鲁斯的办公室在角落里，实用而普通。

词根375. vac, vacu, van, vain, void=empty，表示"空"

1. vacant [ˈveɪkənt] adj. 空的；空闲的；空缺的；失神的
『vac空+ant表形容词→空的；空闲的』

❶ （座位、旅馆房间、房屋等）空着的，未被占用的
The seat next to him was vacant. 他旁边的座位空着。
In every major city there are more vacant buildings than there are homeless people.
各大城市里空置的楼房都比无家可归的人多。

❷ （职位）空缺的
The post of chairman has been vacant for some time.
主席之位已经空缺一段时间了。

❸ （神情）茫然的，失神的
She had a kind of vacant look on her face.
她脸上有种茫然的神情。

▶ **vacancy** [ˈveɪkənsi] n.（旅馆等的）空房；（职位的）空缺

I am afraid we have no vacancy at this time.
恐怕我们现在没有空房间了。
Most vacancies are at senior level, requiring appropriate qualifications.
大多数空缺属于高层职位，要求具备相应的资历。

2. vacate [vəˈkeɪt] vt. 腾出（空间）；辞去（职位）
『vac空+ate表动词→使成为空的→腾出；辞去』

Guests are requested to vacate their rooms by noon on the day of departure.
房客务请在离开之日的中午以前腾出房间。
We have to vacate these offices by December 31st.

我们必须在12月31日前辞职。

3. vacation [vəˈkeɪʃn] n. 假期，休假
『vacate腾出（去e）+ion构成名词→空出来（不用上学、不用上班的）一段时间→假期』

4. vacuum [ˈvækjuəm] n. 真空；空白；空虚 vt. 用吸尘器打扫
『vacu空+um表名词→空虚；真空』

❶ [C] 真空
vacuum-packed foods 真空包装的食品
a vacuum cleaner 真空吸尘器

❷ [usually sing.] 真空状态；空白
a situation in which sb/sth is missing or lacking
His resignation has created a vacuum which cannot easily be filled. 他的引退造成了难以填补的空白。

❸ [VN] （用真空吸尘器）打扫
I vacuumed the carpets today.
今天我用吸尘器清洁了地毯。

5. vacuous [ˈvækjuəs] adj. 思想贫乏的，无知的；空洞的
『vac空+uous充满…的→（人或评论）空的→无知的；空洞的』

If you describe a person or their comments as vacuous, you are critical of them because they lack intelligent thought or ideas.
Sure, he delivered a vacuous inaugural speech.
当然，他发表了一篇空洞的就职演说。

6. evacuate [ɪˈvækjueɪt] vt. 疏散；撤离
『e出+vacu空+ate使…→使出去而使（某地）变成空的→撤离；疏散』

[VN] （把人从危险的地方）疏散，转移，撤离
Police evacuated nearby buildings.
警方已将附近大楼（的居民）疏散。
Children were evacuated from London to escape the bombing.
为躲避轰炸，孩子们都撤离了伦敦。
Employees were urged to evacuate their offices immediately.
已敦促各雇员立即从办公室撤出。

▶**evacuation** [ɪˌvækjuˈeɪʃn] n. 疏散；撤离

7. vanish [ˈvænɪʃ] vi. 突然消失；不复存在
『van空+ish使…→使变成空的→消失』

❶ （莫名其妙地）突然消失
to disappear suddenly and/or in a way that you cannot explain
The magician vanished in a puff of smoke.
魔术师在一股烟雾中突然不见了。
My glasses seem to have vanished.
我的眼镜似乎不翼而飞了。

❷ 不复存在；消亡；绝迹
to stop existing
All hopes of a peaceful settlement had now vanished.
和平解决的全部希望现已化为泡影。
By the 1930s, the wolf had vanished from the American West.
到了20世纪30年代，狼已经从美国西部消失了。

词义辨析 <P379第88>
消失 vanish, disappear, evaporate

8. vain [veɪn] adj. 徒劳的；自负的
『vain空→徒劳的；自负的』

❶ 徒劳的
that does not produce the result you want
She closed her eyes tightly in a vain attempt to hold back the tears. 她紧闭双眼，却无法忍住眼泪。
I knocked loudly in the vain hope that someone might answer.
我敲门敲得很响，希望有人应声，却是徒然。

❷ 自负的；自视过高的
too proud of your own appearance, abilities or achievements
She's too vain to wear glasses. 她太爱虚荣，不肯戴眼镜。

❸ in vain 枉费心机，徒劳
They tried in vain to persuade her to go.
他们极力劝说她去，但枉费了一番口舌。
All our efforts were in vain.
我们的所有努力都付诸东流了。

▶**vanity** [ˈvænəti] n. 虚荣；自负
『vain虚荣的（去i）+ity表名词→虚荣；自负』

[U] 自负；自大；虚荣
too much pride in yourself, so that you are always thinking about yourself and your appearance
With my usual vanity, I thought he might be falling in love with me.
由于我一贯的虚荣心作祟，我以为他可能爱上了我。
Her refusal to cooperate with him was a wound to his vanity.
她拒绝与他合作是对他虚荣心的伤害。

9. void [vɔɪd] n. 空间；空白；空虚 adj. 缺乏

❶ [C] 空间；空白；空虚
a large empty space
Below him was nothing but a black void.
他下面只是一片漆黑。
The void left by his mother's death was never filled.
他母亲死后留下的空虚感永远没能填补上。

❷ adj. ~ of sth　(formal) 缺乏；没有
He rose, his face void of emotion as he walked towards the door. 他站起来，面无表情地朝门口走去。

▶**avoid** [əˈvɔɪd] vt. 避开，避免
『a处于某种状态+void空白；缺乏，没有→（使）处于没有…的状态→避开，避免』

[VN] 避免；防止
They narrowly avoided defeat. 他们险些儿被打败。

小贴士 [V -ing] avoid后面跟动名词作宾语
You should avoid mentioning his divorce.
你应该避免提及他离婚的事。
They built a wall to avoid soil being washed away.
他们建了一堵墙防止土壤流失。

词义辨析 <P379第89> 躲避，回避 avoid, evade, elude

10. devoid [dɪˈvɔɪd] adj. 完全没有；缺乏
『de加强+void空→空的→缺乏』

If you say that someone or something is devoid of a quality or thing, you are emphasizing that they have none of it.
I have never looked on a face that was so devoid of feeling.
我从来没有见过一张如此面无表情的脸。
The letter was devoid of warmth and feeling.
这封信既无热情又无感情。

11. evanescent [ˌevəˈnesnt] adj. (literary) 瞬息即逝的；迅速遗忘的
『e出去+van空+escent变得→刚出现就变空了→瞬息即逝的』

disappearing quickly from sight or memory

All was unstable; quivering as leaves, evanescent as lightning.
一切都是不稳定的，都像树叶似的颤动翻转，像闪电似的倏忽明灭。

► **evanescence** [ˌevəˈnesns] n. 逐渐消失

词根376. vade=go，表示"走"，名词形式为-vasion

1. invade [ɪnˈveɪd] v. 侵略；侵入；侵犯
『in里面+vade走→走进（别人的领域）→入侵』

❶ 侵略；侵犯
to enter a country, town, etc. using military force in order to take control of it
[V] Troops invaded on August 9th that year.
军队是在那年的8月9日入侵的。
[VN] When did the Romans invade Britain?
古罗马人是何时侵略英国的？

❷ [VN]（尤指造成损害或混乱地）涌入；侵袭
Demonstrators invaded the government buildings.
大批示威者闯进了政府办公大楼。

❸ [VN] 侵扰；干扰
to affect sth in an unpleasant or annoying way
Do the press have the right to invade her privacy in this way?
新闻界有权以这种方式干扰她的私生活吗？

► **invasion** [ɪnˈveɪʒn] n. 侵略；侵入；侵犯

► **invasive** [ɪnˈveɪsɪv] adj. 侵入的；侵袭的
spreading very quickly and difficult to stop
They found invasive cancer during a routine examination.
他们在常规体检中发现了扩散性的癌变。

2. evade [ɪˈveɪd] vt. 躲避；回避；逃避
『e出去+vade走→（见某人遇某事时）走开→逃避』

❶ 躲避（某人）；回避（某事）；逃避（法律、责任）
[VN] For two weeks they evaded the press.
他们有两周一直对记者避而不见。
He managed to evade capture. 他设法逃脱了抓捕。
[VN] Come on, don't you think you're evading the issue?
得了吧，你不认为你是在回避这个问题吗？
She is trying to evade all responsibility for her behaviour.
她在试图逃避应为自己的行为承担的所有责任。

❷ [VN] (formal) 想不出；不发生
The answer evaded him (= he could not think of it).
他答不上来。
Happiness still evaded him. 幸福仍旧与他无缘。

► **evasion** [ɪˈveɪʒn] n. 躲避；回避；逃避
His behaviour was an evasion of his responsibilities as a father. 他的行为是逃避为父之责。
She's been charged with tax evasion. 她被控逃税。

► **evasive** [ɪˈveɪsɪv] adj. 回避的；避而不谈的；含糊其词的
He was evasive about the circumstances of his first meeting with Stanley Dean.
他避而不谈他和斯坦利·迪安第一次会面的情况。

词义辨析 <P379第89> 躲避，回避 avoid, evade, elude

3. pervade [pəˈveɪd] vt. 弥漫，渗透
『per贯穿，完全+vade走→走到所有地方→弥漫』
to spread through and be noticeable in every part of sth

a pervading mood of fear 普遍的恐惧情绪
the sadness that pervades most of her novels
充斥她大部分小说的悲怆情绪
The entire house was pervaded by a sour smell.
整栋房子都充满了酸味。

► **pervasive** [pəˈveɪsɪv] adj. 遍布的，弥漫的
A sense of social change is pervasive in her novels.
她的小说里充斥着社会变化的意识。

词根377. vag=wander; uncertain，表示"漫无目的；不确定"

1. vague [veɪg] adj. 模糊的，不清楚的
『vag漫无目的地（想，说）+ue→模糊的』
to have a vague impression/memory/recollection of sth
对某事印象/记忆模糊
They had only a vague idea where the place was.
他们只是大概知道那个地方的位置。
The politicians made vague promises about tax cuts.
政界人物的减税承诺言辞含混。
In the darkness they could see the vague outline of a church.
他们在黑暗中能看到一座教堂的朦胧轮廓。

2. vagabond [ˈvæɡəbɒnd] n. 流浪汉；无业游民；漂泊者
『vag漫无目的地（走）+a+bond倾向于…的→倾向于漫无目的地走（的人）→流浪汉』
(old-fashioned, disapproving)
a person who has no home or job and who travels from place to place

3. vagrant [ˈveɪɡrənt] n. 流浪汉，漂泊者，乞丐
『vag漫无目的（地走）+r+ant表人→流浪汉』
(formal or law) 无业游民；流浪者；（尤指）乞丐
a person who has no home or job, especially one who begs from people

4. extravagant [ɪkˈstrævəɡənt] adj. 挥霍的，奢侈的；过分的
『extra额外的+vag漫无目的+ant表形容词→漫无目的（花销、做、说）多了→挥霍的；过分的』

❶ 挥霍的；铺张浪费的；奢侈的
spending a lot more money or using a lot more of sth than you can afford or than is necessary
I felt very extravagant spending £100 on a dress.
我觉得花100英镑买一条连衣裙太奢侈了。
Residents were warned not to be extravagant with water, in view of the low rainfall this year.
鉴于今年降雨量少，居民被告诫不得浪费用水。

❷ （想法或言行）离谱的，不切实际的；过分的
He made extravagant claims on his son's behalf.
他代儿子提出了过分的要求。
He will pay for his extravagant behavior.
他将为他放肆的行为付出代价。

► **extravagance** [ɪkˈstrævəɡəns] n. 挥霍；奢侈品
Why waste money on such extravagances?
为什么把钱浪费在这些奢侈品上呢？
His extravagance drained all his fortune.
他的挥霍无度耗尽了他所有的财富。

► **extravaganza** [ɪkˌstrævəˈɡænzə] n. 铺张华丽的娱乐表演
An extravaganza is a very elaborate and expensive show or

performance.

词根378. vail, val(ue)=strong; of value，表示"强壮；有价值"

① vail, val(ue)=value，表示"价值"

1. avail [əˈveɪl] n. 效用，帮助 vt. 利用
『a表所处状态+vail价值→有价值→有帮助』

❶ **to little/no avail** (formal) 没有什么效果；不成功
The doctors tried everything to keep him alive but to no avail.
医生千方百计想使他活下来，但无济于事。

❷ **of little/no avail** (formal) 没有什么用处；没有用
Your ability to argue is of little avail if the facts are wrong.
如果论据是错的，你的辩才也就没有什么用了。

❸ **avail yourself of sth** (formal) 利用（尤指机会、提议等）
Guests are encouraged to avail themselves of the full range of hotel facilities. 旅馆鼓励旅客充分利用各种设施。

▶**available** [əˈveɪlɔbl] adj. 可得到的；有空的

❶ (of things 东西) 可获得的；可购得的；可找到的
that you can get, buy or find
Tickets are available free of charge from the school.
学校有免费票。
Further information is available on request. 详情备索。
This was the only room available. 这是唯一可用的房间。

❷ (of a person 人) 有空的
free to see or talk to people
Will she be available this afternoon? 今天下午她有空吗？

2. valid [ˈvælɪd] adj. 有效的；合理的
『val价值+id…的→有价值的→有效的；合理的』

❶ （法律上）有效的；（正式）认可的
They have a valid claim to compensation.
他们有要求赔偿的合法权利。
a valid passport 有效的护照

❷ 有根据的，正当的，合理的
A valid argument, comment, or idea is based on sensible reasoning.
They put forward many valid reasons for not exporting.
他们提出了很多不出口的正当理由。

❸ (computing) 有效的；系统认可的
a valid password 有效密码

▶**validate** [ˈvælɪdeɪt] vt. 确证，确认；认可

❶ [VN] 证实，确证，确认
To validate something such as a claim or statement means to prove or confirm that it is true or correct.
This discovery seems to validate the claims of popular astrology. 这个发现似乎能印证流行占星术的一些说法。

❷ [VN] 证明…有价值；认可
To validate a person, state, or system means to prove or confirm that they are valuable or worthwhile.
She is looking for an image that validates her.
她在寻求一种能够证明自己价值的形象。

▶**validity** [vəˈlɪdəti] n. 有效性；正当性

Some people, of course, denied the validity of any such claim.
当然，一些人否定了此类说法的合理性。

▶**invalid** [ɪnˈvælɪd, ˈɪnvəlɪd] adj. 无效的；站不住脚的 n. 病弱者
『in不+valid有效的；正当的→无效的；站不住脚的』

（adj. [ɪnˈvælɪd]; n. [ˈɪnvəlɪd]）

❶ adj. 无效的；（论据、结论）站不住脚的
The trial was stopped and the results declared invalid.
审判被中止,判决结果被宣布无效。
an invalid argument 站不住脚的论点

❷ [C] 病弱者；久病衰弱者
An invalid is someone who needs to be cared for because they have an illness or disability.
I hate being treated as an invalid.
我讨厌被人当作伤病号对待。

3. valuable [ˈvæljuɔbl] adj. 有价值的；贵重的，值钱的
『value价值；珍视（去e）+able可以的→可以珍视的→有价值的；贵重的』
（以"元音字母+e"结尾的单词，加后缀时，要去e。如：truly, argument, arguable, arguing, valuable, valuing, 但valueless不去e。另外judgement为英式拼写，judgment为美式拼写）

❶ 有价值的
The book provides valuable information on recent trends.
此书就近来的发展趋势提供了宝贵的信息。

❷ 值钱的，贵重的
Luckily, nothing valuable was stolen.
幸运的是，没有贵重物品失窃。

▶**invaluable** [ɪnˈvæljuɔbl] adj. 难以估价的，极宝贵的
『in不+value价值；估价+able能够的→不能估价的→极其宝贵的』

The research should prove invaluable in the study of children's language.
这项调查对于儿童语言的研究将极有价值。

▶**valueless** [ˈvæljuːləs] adj. 无价值的；不值钱的
『value价值+less没有的→没有价值的→无价值的』

His suggestion is valueless. 他的建议毫无价值。
The necklace is valueless. 这项链不值钱。

▶**priceless** [ˈpraɪsləs] adj. 无价的；极珍贵的
『price价钱+less无，没有+没有价钱的→难以计算其价值的→极珍贵的；无价的』

They are priceless, unique and irreplaceable.
它们是独一无二、不可替代的无价之宝。

▶**value** [ˈvælju:] n. 价值 vt. 重视；估价

❶ [U, C] （商品）价值
Sports cars tend to hold their value well.
跑车往往很能保值。
The winner will receive a prize to the value of £1,000.
获胜者将得到价值为1000英镑的奖品。

❷ [U] (especially BrE) （与价格相比的）值，划算程度
In most cases it is certainly good value for money.
在许多情况下，价钱还是很合算的。
Larger sizes give the best value for money.
较大尺寸的最划算。

❸ [U] 用途，积极作用
The value of regular exercise should not be underestimated.
经常锻炼的好处不应低估。

❹ values [pl.] 价值观（是非标准，生活准则）
The young have a completely different set of values and expectations. 年轻人有一整套截然不同的价值观和期望。

❺ [VN] 重视，珍视

I really value him as a friend. 我真的把他视为好朋友。

❻ [VN] [usually passive] ~ sth (at sth) 估价，定价
The property has been valued at over $2 million.
这处房地产估价为200多万美元。

4. equivalent [ɪˈkwɪvələnt] adj. 等同的；对应的　n. 等同物；对应词
『equi等同+val价值+ent具有…性质的→（价值）等同的』

❶ adj. ~ (to sth) 等同的，相同的
Eight kilometers is roughly equivalent to five miles.
八公里约等于五英里。

❷ n. 等同物；等值物；对应词
This word has no satisfactory equivalent in English.
这个词在英语中没有令人满意的对应词。

▶**equivalence** [ɪˈkwɪvələns] n. （用途、功能、尺寸、价值等）相等；对等；相同

5. evaluate [ɪˈvæljueɪt] v. 估价；评估
『e出来+value价值（去e）+ate表动词→使价值出来→估价』

to form an opinion of the amount, value or quality of sth after thinking about it carefully

[VN] Our research attempts to evaluate the effectiveness of the different drugs.
我们的研究试图对不同药物的疗效进行评估。

[V wh-] We need to evaluate how well the policy is working.
我们需要对这一政策产生的效果作出评价。

6. devaluation [ˌdiːvæljʊˈeɪʃən] n.（货币）贬值
『de向下+value价值（去e）+ation表名词→使价值向下→贬值』

② vail, val(ue)=strong，表示"强壮"

1. prevail [prɪˈveɪl] v. 盛行；占上风
『pre事先+vail强壮→事先强壮的→盛行；占上风』

❶ ~ (in/among sth) 普遍存在；盛行；流行
to exist or be very common at a particular time or in a particular place
We were horrified at the conditions prevailing in local prisons. 地方监狱的普遍状况让我们震惊。
Those beliefs still prevail among certain social groups.
这些信念在某些社会群体中仍很盛行。

❷ ~ (against/over sth) 占上风，占优势；获胜
Justice will prevail over tyranny. 正义必将战胜暴虐。
Fortunately, common sense prevailed. 幸而理智占了上风。
He appears to have the votes he needs to prevail.
他似乎已经获得了取胜所需的选票。

❸ prevail on/upon sb to do sth 劝说
to persuade sb to do sth
I'm sure he could be prevailed upon to give a talk.
我相信能说服他来做一次报告。
We must, each of us, prevail upon our congressman to act.
我们每一个人都必须说服我们各自的国会议员采取行动。

▶**prevailing** [prɪˈveɪlɪŋ] adj. 盛行的；普遍的
The prevailing view seems to be that they will find her guilty.
一般人的看法似乎认为她会被判有罪。

▶**prevalent** [ˈprevələnt] adj. 流行的，盛行的
that exists or is very common at a particular time or in a particular place

These prejudices are particularly prevalent among people living in the North. 这些偏见在北方人中尤为常见。

2. valiant [ˈvæliənt] adj. 勇敢的；坚决的
『vali(=val)强壮+ant…的→勇敢的』

A valiant action is very brave and determined, though it may lead to failure or defeat.

Despite valiant efforts by the finance minister, inflation rose to 36%.
尽管财政部部长采取了一系列果决措施，通货膨胀率还是涨到了36%。

3. valour [ˈvælə(r)] n.（尤指战争中的）英勇，勇气
『val强壮+our表名词→因为强壮所以勇敢→英勇』

He was himself decorated for valour in the war.
他本人因在战争中的英勇表现而获得了勋章。

4. convalescent [ˌkɒnvəˈlesnt] adj. 正在康复的；康复期的　n. 恢复期的病人
『con加强+val强壮+escent变得→（开始）变强壮→正在康复的』

In spring this convalescent hospital is a good place, with singing birds and fragrant flowers.
春天，这个疗养院是个充满了鸟语花香的好地方。
He was transferred to a convalescent clinic.
他被转到了康复诊所。
I treated him as a convalescent, not as a sick man.
我把他当作正在康复的人，而不是病人。

▶**convalescence** [ˌkɒnvəˈlesns] n. 康复期
Another apparent sign of convalescence is more ambiguous.
另一个恢复的表面信号更为模糊。

词根379. vary=vary, change，表示"变化"

1. vary [ˈveəri] v.（大小、形状）相异；变化
The quality of the students' work varies considerably.
学生作业的质量甚是参差不齐。
The menu varies with the season. 菜单随季节而变动。

▶**various** [ˈveəriəs] adj. 各种各样的
『vary变化（变y为i）+ous充满…的→各种各样的』
Tents come in various shapes and sizes.
帐篷有各种各样的形状和大小。

▶**varied** [ˈveərid] adj. 各种各样的，不同的
『vary变化（变y为i）+ed表形容词→各种各样的』
It is essential that your diet is varied and balanced.
关键是你的饮食要多样化，并保持均衡。

▶**variety** [vəˈraɪəti] n. 不同种类
There is a wide variety of patterns to choose from.
有种类繁多的图案可供选择。

▶**variation** [ˌveəriˈeɪʃn] n. 变化，变动；变化形式
The dial records very slight variations in pressure.
该刻度盘能显示很微小的压力变化。
Currency exchange rates are always subject to variation.
货币的兑换率始终波动。
This soup is a spicy variation on a traditional favourite.
这种汤是在一种受欢迎的传统汤羹中加了香料。

2. variable [ˈveəriəbl] adj. 多变的，易变的；可更改的　n. 变量，可变因素

『vary变化（变y为i）+able能够…的→可改变的』

variable temperatures 变化不定的气温

The drill has variable speed control. 这钻机有变速控制。

With so many variables, it is difficult to calculate the cost. 有这么多的可变因素，很难计算出成本。

▶**invariable** [ɪnˈveəriəbl] adj. 不变的；始终如一的

『in不+variable多变的→不变的』

It was his invariable custom to have one whisky before his supper. 晚饭前喝杯威士忌，这是他一直以来的习惯。

3. variance [ˈveəriəns] n. 变化幅度；差额

『vary变化（变y为i）+ ance状态，性质→变化幅度』

[U, C] (formal) 变化幅度；差额

the amount by which sth changes or is different from sth else

I could detect subtle variances in fragrance as we strolled through the garden. 当我们漫步花园时，我能察觉到香味的细微变化。

at variance (with sb/sth) 看法不一；矛盾

These conclusions are totally at variance with the evidence. 这些结论与证据完全相悖。

词根380. ven(e), vent=come，表示"来"

1. convene [kənˈviːn] v. 召集，召开（正式会议）

『con一起+vene来→来到一起→召开（正式会议）』

❶ [VN] 召集，召开（正式会议）

to convene a meeting 召开会议

A Board of Inquiry was convened immediately after the accident. 事故后调查委员会立即召开了会议。

❷ [V] （为正式会议而）聚集，集合

The committee will convene at 11:30 am next Thursday. 委员会将在下星期四上午11:30开会。

2. advent [ˈædvent] n. （重要事件、人物、发明等）出现；到来

『ad（=to）+vent来→（重要事件、人物、发明等）到来』

Deptford had come alive with the advent of the new priest at St Paul's.
圣保罗教堂新牧师的到来使德特福德变得生机勃勃。

Advent [U] 将临节，（基督教）降临节（圣诞节前的四个星期左右）

3. adventure [ədˈventʃə(r)] n. 冒险；冒险经历

『ad(=to)+vent来+ure表行为→来到（危险的）地方→冒险』

an unusual, exciting or dangerous experience, journey or series of events

4. venture [ˈventʃə(r)] n. 风险项目 v. 冒险

『vent来+ure行为，行为的结果→来到（有风险的地方）→冒险』

❶ [C] 风险项目（或活动）；冒险事业

A venture is a project or activity which is new, exciting, and difficult because it involves the risk of failure.

A disastrous business venture lost him thousands of dollars.
一个彻底失败的经营项目使他损失严重。

❷ [V, V to inf] 敢于（去某处）；冒险（做某事）

They ventured nervously into the water.
他们紧张地硬着头皮下水。

"Don't ask," he said, whenever Ginny ventured to raise the subject.
每当金尼鼓起勇气提起这个话题时，他就说"不要问"。

He enjoyed little success when he ventured into business.
他冒险涉足商界后几乎没有取得什么成功。

❸ [VN] ~ sth (on sth) 冒着（失去贵重或重要东西的）危险

It was wrong to venture his financial security on such a risky deal.
他牺牲自己的财务安全去做风险这么大的交易是错误的。

Nothing ventured, nothing gained. 不敢冒险就一事无成。

❹ 小心地说，谨慎地做

to say or do sth in a careful way, especially because it might upset or offend sb

[VN] She hardly dared to venture an opinion.
她几乎不敢亮明观点。

[V to inf] I ventured to suggest that she might have made a mistake. 我小心地提醒说她可能出了差错。

5. intervene [ˌɪntəˈviːn] v. 介入；插嘴

『inter之间+vene来→来到两者之间→介入』

❶ [V] ~ (in sth) 出面；介入

to become involved in a situation in order to improve or help it

She might have been killed if the neighbours hadn't intervened. 要不是邻居介入，她可能会没命了。

❷ 插嘴；打断（别人的话）

[V speech] "But," she intervened, "what about the others?"
"但是，"她插嘴说，"其他的怎么办呢？"

❸ [V] 阻碍；阻挠；干扰

They were planning to get married and then the war intervened. 他们正准备结婚，不巧却因爆发战事而受阻。

6. contravene [ˌkɒntrəˈviːn] v. 违犯，违反（法律或规则）

『contra相反+vene来→向相反的方向来→违反』

The company was found guilty of contravening safety regulations. 那家公司被判违反了安全条例。

▶**contravention** [ˌkɒntrəˈvenʃən] n. 违反；触犯

This was a clear contravention of the rules.
这明显违反了规则。

7. convention [kənˈvenʃn] n. 常规；大会；公约

『con一起+vent来+ion表名词→来到一起（开大会、签公约）（这是常规做法）→常规；大会；公约』

❶ [C, U] 习俗；常规；惯例

the way in which sth is done that most people in a society expect and consider to be polite or the right way to do it

social conventions 社会习俗

By convention the deputy leader was always a woman.
按惯例，这一领导职务的副职总是由女性担任。

❷ [C] （某职业、政党等成员的）大会，集会

a large meeting of the members of a profession, a political party, etc.

the Democratic Party Convention (= to elect a candidate for president) 民主党大会（选举总统候选人）

❸ [C] （国家或首脑间的）公约，协定，协议

an official agreement between countries or leaders

the Geneva Convention 日内瓦公约

the United Nations Convention on the Rights of the Child
联合国儿童权利公约

► **conventional** [kənˈvenʃənl] adj. 常规的；依照惯例的；传统的

conventional weapons 常规武器（非核武器）
conventional methods/approaches 传统方法/途径
She's very conventional in her views. 她的观点很守旧。

8. convent [ˈkɒnvənt] n. 女修道院
『con一起+vent来→一起来到（女修道院）→女修道院』

9. revenue [ˈrevənjuː] n. 财政收入；收益
『re回+ven来+ue→回来的东西→收入』

[U] also revenues [pl.] （公司、组织的）收入，收益；（政府的）财政收入，税收
Revenue is money that a company, organization, or government receives from people.
The revenue from tourism is the biggest single item in the country's invisible earnings.
旅游业收入是该国无形收益当中最大的一项。
The state does not collect enough revenue to cover its expenditure. 该国政府入不敷出。

10. avenue [ˈævənjuː] n. （城镇的）大街；林荫道（尤指通往大住宅的）
『a+ven来+ue→大街』

❶ 用于街名 (abbr. Ave.) (abbr. Av.) （城镇的）大街
a hotel on Fifth Avenue 第五大街上的一家旅馆

❷ (BrE) 林荫道（尤指通往大住宅的）

11. inventory [ˈɪnvəntri] n. 库存；清单
『in里面+vent来+ory表物→来到里面（商店、某处）的东西→库存；清单』

❶ [C, U] (NAmE) （商店的）存货，库存
The inventory will be disposed of over the next twelve weeks.
在未来的12个星期中将进行清仓处理。

❷ 详细目录，清单
An inventory is a written list of all the objects in a particular place.
Before starting, he made an inventory of everything that was to stay. 开始之前,他把所有要留下的东西列了详细的清单。

12. circumvent [ˌsɜːkəmˈvent] vt. 规避（规则或限制）；绕过；躲避（障碍或危险）
『circum环绕+vent来→绕过（规则、障碍或危险）』

They found a way of circumventing the law.
他们找到了规避法律的途径。
They opened an office abroad in order to circumvent the tax laws. 他们在外国开设了一个办事处，以避开税法。
You've somehow managed to circumvent my security.
你用某种方式突破了我的安全系统。

词根381. vent=wind，表示"风，通风"

1. vent [vent] （空气、气体、液体的）出口，进口，漏孔
『vent通风→通风孔，排气口→（空气、气体、液体的）出口，进口』

❶ [C] 通风孔，排气口
air/heating vents 通气/热风孔
Quite a lot of steam escaped from the vent at the front of the machine. 大量蒸汽从机器前部的排风口冒了出来。

❷ [VN][C] 发泄，宣泄（情感）
She telephoned her best friend to vent her frustration.
她给最要好的朋友打电话倾诉自己的沮丧。
She gave vent to her anger and jealousy.
她宣泄了自己的愤怒和嫉妒。

2. ventilate [ˈventɪleɪt] vt. 使通风；表达（感情）
『vent通风+il+ate表动词→使通风』

Ventilate the room properly when paint stripping.
当油漆开始剥落时，要给房间适当通风。

► **ventilation** [ˌventɪˈleɪʃən] n. 通风
Make sure that there is adequate ventilation in the room before using the paint. 在使用油漆前确保室内通风充足。

► **ventilator** [ˈventɪleɪtə(r)] n. 通风设备；呼吸器
Hospitals across the US are in urgent need of ventilators as the number of COVID-19 patients rapidly escalates.
随着COVID-19（新冠肺炎）患者数量的迅速增加，美国各地的医院急需呼吸机。

3. ventiduct [ˈventɪdʌkt] n. 通风管道
『vent风+i+duct引导→通风道』

词根382. venge=punish，表示"惩罚"，引申为"报仇"

1. vengeance [ˈvendʒəns] n. 报仇，复仇
『venge报仇+ance表名词→报仇』

[U] ~ (on/upon sb)
He swore vengeance on his child's killer.
他发誓要找杀害他孩子的凶手报仇。

with a vengeance 努力地；激烈地
to a greater degree than is expected or usual
It began to rain again with a vengeance. 又开始下起了大雨。

2. vengeful [ˈvendʒfl] adj. 心存报复的
『venge报仇+ful充满…的→心存报复的』

He was stabbed to death by his vengeful wife.
他被图谋报复的妻子拿刀捅死了。

3. revenge [rɪˈvendʒ] n. & vt. 报仇
『re又，再+venge报仇→报仇』

❶ [U] 报仇；雪耻
He swore to take (his) revenge on his political enemies.
他发誓要报复他的政敌。
She is seeking revenge for the murder of her husband.
丈夫遭到谋杀，她在寻找机会报仇。
The bombing was in revenge for the assassination.
爆炸事件是对暗杀行为的报复。
The team wanted to get revenge for their defeat earlier in the season. 球队想要为这个赛季早先的失败雪耻。

❷ [VN] revenge yourself on sb/be revenged on sb 报复某人
She vowed to be revenged on them all.
她发誓一定要报复他们所有的人。
The Sunday Mercury accused her of trying to revenge herself on her former lover.
《星期日水星报》指责她企图报复她以前的情人。

4. avenge [əˈvendʒ] vt. 报（某事）之仇；报复（某人）
『a加强+venge报仇→报仇』

[VN] ~ sth | ~ yourself on sb
He promised to avenge his father's murder.
他发誓要报杀父之仇。
She was determined to avenge herself on the man who had betrayed her. 她决心向那个负心男人报仇。

词义辨析 <P381第101> 报仇，报复 revenge, avenge

词根383. ver(i)=true，表示"真实的；真实"

1. very [ˈveri] adj. 正是的（起强调作用）
『veri（变i为y）真实的→正是的』

Those were her very words. 这些都是她的原话。
It happens at the very beginning of the book.
这事发生在书的一开头。
The very thought of drink made him feel sick.
他一想到酒就觉得恶心。

▶**verity** [ˈverəti] n. 真理；客观事实

an important principle or fact that is always true
Yet, surely, the eternal verities of any game still apply.
然而，毫无疑问，任何游戏的永恒真理仍然适用。

2. verify [ˈverɪfaɪ] vt. 核实；证实
『veri真实的+fy使→使…（确实）真实→证实』

[VN] We have no way of verifying his story.
我们无法核实他所说的情况。
[VN] Her version of events was verified by neighbours.
她对这些事件的说法已得到邻居的证实。

▶**verification** [ˌverɪfɪˈkeɪʃən] n. 核实；证实

3. veritable [ˈverɪtəbl] adj. 名副其实的，不折不扣的
『veri真实的+t+able可以→真实可以（证实）的→名副其实的』

This book is a veritable storehouse of information.
这本书是名副其实的信息宝库。
It was not easy to work in the shed; in winter it was a veritable ice-box.
在这木棚里工作是很不容易的，这木棚冬天是个名副其实的冰箱。

4. verdict [ˈvɜːdɪkt] n. （陪审团或法官的）裁决，裁定；（经过思考或调查后的）意见，结论
『ver真实+dict说；断言→说的真实的情况→裁决，裁定』

The jury returned a unanimous guilty verdict.
陪审团一致作出了有罪裁决。
The doctor's verdict was that he was entirely healthy.
医生的结论是他完全健康。

5. aver [əˈvɜː(r)] vt. 断言，坚称
『a强调+ver真实→坚持（说）某事是真实的』

[V that] She averred that she had never seen the man before.
她斩钉截铁地说以前从未见过这个男人。

6. veracity [vəˈræsəti] n. 真实；诚实
『ver真实+acity表性质→真实；诚实』

[U] the quality of being true; the habit of telling the truth
They questioned the veracity of her story.
他们质疑她所述事情的真实性。
He was shocked to find his veracity questioned.
发现自己的诚信受到了质疑，他很震惊。

词根384. verb(i)=word; verb，表示"词语；动词"

1. adverb [ˈædvɜːb] n. 副词
『ad(=to)+verb动词→修饰动词的→副词』

▶**adverbial** [ædˈvɜːbiəl] adj. 副词的；状语的
adverbial clause 状语从句

2. verbose [vɜːˈbəʊs] adj. 冗长的，啰嗦的
『verb词语+ose多→多词语的→冗长的，啰嗦的』

His writing is difficult and often verbose.
他的文章很晦涩，而且往往篇幅冗长。

▶**verbosity** [vɜːˈbɒsəti] n. 冗长，赘述

3. verbal [ˈvɜːbl] adj. 文字的；口头的；动词的
『verb词语；动词+al…的→文字的；口头的；动词的』

The job applicant must have good verbal skills.
应聘这份工作的人必须具有良好的语言表达技能。
a verbal agreement/warning 口头协议/警告
a verbal noun 动名词

▶**verbalize** [ˈvɜːbəlaɪz] vt. 用语言表达

He's a real genius but he has difficulty verbalizing his ideas.
他确实是个天才，可是难以用语言表达他的思想。

4. proverb [ˈprɒvɜːb] n. 谚语，格言
『pro赞同+verb词语→被赞同的词语→格言』

An old Arab proverb says, "The enemy of my enemy is my friend."
一句古老的阿拉伯谚语说："敌人的敌人就是我的朋友。"

▶**proverbial** [prəˈvɜːbiəl] adj. 常说的，出自谚语的；众所周知的

The limousine sped off down the road in the proverbial cloud of dust. 豪华轿车沿公路飞驰而去，那真是卷起一路风尘。
His mastery of the French language was proverbial.
他对法语的精通是众所周知的。

词根385. verge=turn，表示"转"

1. verge [vɜːdʒ] n. （路边）绿地；接近于
『verge转→即将变化→接近于』

❶ [C] (BrE)（道路的）植草边沿（美语用shoulder）

❷ on/to the verge of sth/of doing sth 接近于
He was on the verge of tears. 他差点儿哭了出来。
They are on the verge of signing a new contract.
他们即将签订一份新的合同。
Many species have been shot to the verge of extinction.
很多物种已经濒临灭绝。

2. converge [kənˈvɜːdʒ] vi. 汇集；会合；趋同
『con一起+verge转→转到一起→汇集；会合』

Thousands of supporters converged on London for the rally.
成千上万的支持者从四面八方汇聚伦敦举行集会。
There was a signpost where the two paths converged.
两条小路的相交处有一路标。
Speeches delivered by Mr Dewar and Mr Wallace indicated their views were converging.
杜瓦先生和华莱士先生发表的讲话表明他们的观点越来越接近了。

3. diverge [daɪˈvɜːdʒ] v. 分叉；分歧；偏离
『di(=away)离开+verge转→转开→分叉；分歧；偏离』

We went through school and college together, but then our paths diverged.
我们从小学到大学一直在一起，但后来就分道扬镳了。
Opinions diverge greatly on this issue.
在这个问题上意见分歧很大。

词根386. vers(e), vert=turn，表示"转"

1. verse [vɜːs] n. 诗；韵文

『verse转→（一句一）转（即：另起一行）；（一段一）转（即：另起一段）→韵文；诗节』

❶ [U] 诗；韵文

Most of the play is written in verse, but some of it is in prose.
这剧本大部分是用韵文写的，不过有一些是用散文。

❷ [C] 诗节；歌曲的段落

a hymn with six verses　一首六节赞美诗

2. versus ['vɜːsəs] prep. （比赛中）与…对阵；（不同想法、选择等）与…相比，与…相对

『vers(=turn)转：轮流到+us→轮流到（A与B对阵）→与…对阵』

It is France versus Brazil in the final.
决赛是法国队对巴西队。

It was the promise of better job opportunities versus the inconvenience of moving away and leaving her friends.
那是她承诺的就业前景与搬走并远离朋友的不便之间的矛盾。

3. version ['vɜːʃn] n. 说法；版本

『vers转+ion表名词→从一种形式转化来的另一种形式→版本；说法』

the film version of *War and Peace*
《战争与和平》的电影版

She gave us her version of what had happened that day.
她向我们描述了她认为那天发生的事情。

the latest version of the software package
软件包的最新版本

4. adverse ['ædvɜːs] adj. 不利的，有害的

『ad相当于to+verse转→转到（相反的地方）→不利的』

[usually before noun] 不利的；有害的；反面的

negative and unpleasant; not likely to produce a good result

Lack of money will have an adverse effect on our research programme. 缺少资金将对我们的研究方案有不利影响。

They have attracted strong adverse criticism.
他们已招致强烈非难。

▶ **adversity** [əd'vɜːsəti] n. 困境；逆境

He overcame many personal adversities.
他克服了多次个人不幸。

He showed courage in adversity. 他在逆境中表现出了勇气。

▶ **adversary** ['ædvəsəri] n. （辩论或战斗中的）敌手，对手

『ad相当于to+vers转+ary表人→转到（自己对面的）人→对手』

His political adversaries were creating a certain amount of trouble for him. 他的政敌正在给他制造一些麻烦。

You are my adversary, but you are not my enemy, because your resistance gives me strength.
你是我的对手，但不是我的敌人，因为你的对抗给了我力量。

同义词 **opponent** [ə'pəunənt] n. 对手；反对者〈P261〉

5. avert [ə'vɜːt] vt. 避免；阻止；转移（目光等）

『a(=away)离开+vert转→（从不好的事上）转开→避开』

❶ [VN] 防止，避免（危险、坏事）

to prevent sth bad or dangerous from happening

A disaster was narrowly averted. 及时防止了一场灾难。

He did his best to avert suspicion. 他尽量避嫌。

❷ [VN] ~ your eyes, gaze, face (from sth)
转移眼睛/目光；背过脸

to turn your eyes, etc. away from sth that you do not want to see

She averted her eyes from the terrible scene in front of her.
她背过脸，不去看面前可怕的场面。

▶ **aversion** [ə'vɜːʃn] n. 厌恶；憎恶

『avert避开（坏事或危险）（去t）+sion表名词→避开的原因→厌恶；憎恶』

[C, U] ~ (to sb/sth) 厌恶；憎恶

a strong feeling of not liking sb/sth

He had an aversion to getting up early. 他十分讨厌早起。

▶ **averse** [ə'vɜːs] adj. 不喜欢；不想做

He was averse to any change. 他反对任何改变。

6. convert [kən'vɜːt , 'kɒnvɜːt] v. 转换；改变（信仰）n. 皈依者

『con一起+vert转→（所有一起）转变→转换；改变』

（n. ['kɒnvɜːt]; v. [kən'vɜːt]）

❶ ~ (sth) (from sth) (into/to sth) （使）转变，转换，转化

to change or make sth change from one form, purpose, system, etc. to another

[VN] The hotel is going to be converted into a nursing home.
那家旅馆将被改建成疗养院。

What rate will I get if I convert my dollars into euros?
如果我把美元兑换成欧元，汇率是多少？

[V] a sofa that converts into a bed 可改作床用的沙发

❷ ~ (sb) (from sth) (to sth)
（使）改变（宗教或信仰）；（使）皈依，归附

He converted from Christianity to Islam.
他由基督教改信伊斯兰教。

❸ ~ (sb) (from sb) (to sth) （使）改变（观点、习惯等）

[V] I've converted to organic food. 我改吃有机食品了。

[VN] I didn't use to like opera but my husband has converted me. 我过去不喜欢歌剧，但我丈夫改变了我。

▶ **convertible** [kən'vɜːtəbl] adj. 可改变的；可转换的

a convertible sofa (= one that can be used as a bed) 沙发床
The bonds are convertible into ordinary shares.
债券可兑换为普通股。

▶ **conversion** [kən'vɜːʃn] n. 转变，转换；皈依

7. converse [kən'vɜːs , 'kɒnvɜːs] vi. 交谈 n. 相反的情况

『con一起+verse转→（一起）转着（即：轮流着）（说）→交谈；交谈时已经不一致时可能会说相反的话→相反的情况』

（v. [kən'vɜːs]; n. ['kɒnvɜːs]）

❶ [V] ~ (with sb) (formal) 交谈；谈话

Luke sat directly behind the pilot and conversed with him.
卢克就坐在飞行员后面，并且和他说着话。

❷ the converse 相反的事物（陈述，话，言论）

He says she is satisfied, but I believe the converse to be true: she is very dissatisfied.
他说她已心满意足了，不过我认为实际情况相反：她很不满意。

▶ **conservation** [ˌkɒnvə'seɪʃn] n. 交谈；谈话

I had a long conversation with her the other day.

前几天我与她作了一次长谈。

词义辨析 <P379第90> 相反 inverse, reverse, converse

8. invert [ɪnˈvɜːt] v. （使）倒转，颠倒，倒置

『in里面+vert转→使（里面的水上下）翻转→倒置』

[VN] (formal) （使）倒转，颠倒，倒置

to change the normal position of sth, especially by turning it upside down or by arranging it in the opposite order

Place a plate over the cake tin and invert it.

在蛋糕烤模上盖一个盘子，然后将其翻倒过来。

▶ **inversion** [ɪnˈvɜːʃn] n. 倒置；颠倒

the inversion of normal word order 正常词序的倒装

an inversion of the truth 颠倒是非

▶ **inverse** [ˌɪnˈvɜːs] adj.（数量、位置）相反的，反向的

A person's wealth is often in inverse proportion to their happiness. 一个人的财富常常与他的幸福成反比。

It's the inverse transformation. 这是一个逆变换。

词义辨析 <P379第90> 相反 inverse, reverse, converse

9. revert [rɪˈvɜːt] vi. 回到，恢复到；归还

『re返回+vert(=turn)转→return→恢复到；归还』

❶ **revert to sth** 回复；恢复

to return to a former state; to start doing sth again that you used to do in the past

After her divorce she reverted to her maiden name.

离婚以后，她重新用起娘家的姓氏。

This means that groups sizes for overnights stays at campsite revert to pre-COVID-19 limits.

这意味着在营地过夜的团队人数将恢复到新冠肺炎疫前的限制。

Try not to revert to your old eating habits.

尽量不要恢复你过去的饮食习惯。

❷ **revert to sb/sth** (law) (of property, rights, etc. 财产、权利等) 归还；归属

▶ **reversion** [rɪˈvɜːʃn] n. 回复，回归；归还

the reversion of Hong Kong to China 香港回归中国

a reversion to traditional farming methods
传统耕作方法的回归

▶ **irreversible** [ˌɪrɪˈvɜːsəbl] adj. 不可逆转的

『ir不+re向回，返回+vers转+ible能够的→不可逆转的』

She could suffer irreversible brain damage if she is not treated within seven days.

如果她在7天之内没有得到治疗，她的大脑有可能遭受不可逆转的损伤。

South Africa was going through a period of irreversible change. 南非正在经历一场不可逆转的变革。

10. reverse [rɪˈvɜːs] v. 倒车；颠倒 n. 相反；背面；倒车 adj. 相反的；背面的

『re向回，返回+verse(=turn)转→向回转，向相反的方向转→倒车；颠倒；背面』

❶ (especially BrE) (US back) （使）倒退行驶；倒车

[VN] Now reverse the car. 现在倒车。

She reversed into a parking space. 她将车倒着开进停车位。

❷ [VN] 使反转；使次序颠倒；逆转

Writing is reversed in a mirror. 镜子里的字是反的。

You should reverse the order of these pages.

你该把这几页的顺序颠倒过来。

The government has failed to reverse the economic decline.
政府未能扭转经济滑坡的趋势。

It felt as if we had reversed our roles of parent and child.
感觉就像我们父母和孩子交换了角色。

The Court of Appeal reversed the decision.
上诉法庭撤销了这项裁决。

❸ the reverse [sing.] 相反的情况（或事物）；背面；反面

Although I expected to enjoy living in the country, in fact the reverse is true.

尽管我原以为会喜欢乡村生活，但实际情况正好相反。

In the south, the reverse applies. 在南方，情况相反。

the reverse of a coin, piece of paper 硬币、纸的背面

❹ [U] also reverse gear 倒挡

Put the car in/into reverse. 把汽车挂上倒挡。

❺ **in reverse** 反向；相反

The secret number is my phone number in reverse.

这个密码是我的电话号码的逆序排列。

go/put sth into reverse （使）出现逆转

In 2022 economic growth went into reverse.

2022年，经济增长发生了逆转。

❻ adj. 相反的；背面的；反向的

The winners were announced in reverse order.

获胜者是按逆序宣布的。

Iron the garment on the reverse side. 这件衣服要从反面熨。

小贴士 vice versa [ˌvaɪs ˈvɜːsə] adv. 反之亦然

汽车自动挡上的几个字母表示什么：

"P" —Parking 泊车挡	"R" —Reverse 倒车挡
"N" —Neutral gear 空挡	"D" —Drive 前进挡
"S" —Sport 运动模式	

词义辨析 <P379第90> 相反 inverse, reverse, converse

11. pervert [pəˈvɜːt , ˈpɜːvɜːt] v. 使走样；使堕落 n. 性变态者

『per坏+vert转→使向坏处转变→使走样；使堕落』

（v. [pəˈvɜːt]; n. [ˈpɜːvɜːt]）

❶ [VN] 败坏；使走样

to change a system, process, etc. in a bad way so that it is not what it used to be or what it should be

Some scientific discoveries have been perverted to create weapons of destruction.

某些科学发明被滥用来生产毁灭性武器。

❷ [VN] 使堕落；腐蚀；侵害

Some people believe that television can pervert the minds of children. 有些人认为，电视能腐蚀儿童的心灵。

❸ [C] 性变态者

12. divert [daɪˈvɜːt] vt. 绕道；改变（资金）用途；使分心

『di分开+vert(=turn)转→（从一个）分开转入（另一个）

→绕道；改变；分心』

[VN] ~ sb/sth (from sth) (to sth)

❶ （使）绕道，转向 （NAmE detour）
Northbound traffic will have to be diverted onto minor roads.
北行车辆将不得不绕次要道路行驶。

❷ 改变（资金、材料）的用途
The government is trying to divert more public funds from west to east.
政府正试图将更多的公共基金从西部转到东部。

❸ 转移（某人）的注意力；使分心
to take sb's thoughts or attention away from sth
The war diverted people's attention away from the economic situation. 战争把民众的注意力从经济状况上移开了。

同义词 **distract** [dɪˈstrækt] vt. 使分心 〈P336〉
『dis离开+tract拉→把（心）拉开→分心』

▶ **diversion** [daɪˈvɜːʃn] n. 改道；转移注意力的事物；消遣，娱乐

a river diversion project 河流改道工程
We made a short diversion to go and look at the castle.
我们绕了一小段路去参观城堡。
A smoke bomb created a diversion while the robbery took place. 劫案发生时，一枚烟幕弹转移了人们的视线。
The party will make a pleasant diversion.
晚会会是一个很不错的消遣。

13. diverse [daɪˈvɜːs] adj. 不同的；多种多样的
『di分开+verse(=turn)转，变→变得分开→不同的，多种多样的』

very different from each other and of various kinds
people from diverse cultures 不同文化背景的人
My interests are very diverse. 我的兴趣非常广泛。

▶ **diversify** [daɪˈvɜːsɪfaɪ] vt. （使）多样化
『diverse多样的（去e加i）+fy使…化→使多样化』

Manufacturers have been encouraged to diversify.
制造商们被鼓励要做到（产品）多样化。
The culture has been diversified with the arrival of immigrants.
随着外来移民的到来，这里的文化变得多元化了。

▶ **diversity** [daɪˈvɜːsəti] n. 多样性；多样化

the cultural diversity of British society
英国社会文化的多元性
Two of our greatest strengths are diversity and community.
我们最大的两个优势是多样性和团体精神。

▶ **diversification** [daɪˌvɜːsɪfɪˈkeɪʃn] n. 多样化

These strange diversifications could have damaged or even sunk the entire company.
这些陌生的新增业务可能会破坏甚至是葬送整个公司。

14. transverse [ˈtrænzvɜːs] adj. 横向的
『trans从…到…+verse转→（可以）从一边转到另一边的→横向的』

A transverse bar joins the two posts.
一根横杆连接着两根立柱。

15. vertical [ˈvɜːtɪkl] adj. 竖的，垂直的 n. 垂直位置
『vert转+ical…的→转（90度角所构成）的→垂直的』

❶ adj. 垂直的

The cliff was almost vertical. 那悬崖几乎是垂直的。

❷ the vertical 垂直位置
The wall is several degrees off the vertical.
这堵墙倾斜了有好几度。

16. versatile [ˈvɜːsətaɪl] adj.（人）多面手的；（物）多用途的
『verse(=turn)转，改变（去e）+at+ile易于…的→改变（用途）容易的→（人）多面手的；（物）多用途的』

❶ （人） 多才多艺的；有多种技能的；多面手的
He's a versatile actor who has played a wide variety of parts.
他是个多才多艺的演员，扮演过各种各样的角色。

❷ （机器、工具、材料等）多用途的
Never before has computing been so versatile.
计算机的用途从没像现在这么广泛过。

17. introvert [ˈɪntrəvɜːt] n. 内向的人
『intro向内+vert转→（注意力）转向内心的→内向的人』

You think you're an extrovert or an introvert?
你认为你是个性外向的人还是个性内向的人？

18. extrovert [ˈekstrəvɜːt] n. 性格外向者
『extro向外+vert转→（注意力）转向外部的→外向的人』

19. controversy [ˈkɒntrəvɜːsi] n. 争论，争议
『contro相反+verse转（去e)+y表行为→（观点）相反的人轮流（说）→争论』

Controversy is a lot of discussion and argument about something, often involving strong feelings of anger or disapproval.
The proposed cuts have caused considerable controversy.
削减开支的提议引起了诸多争议。

▶ **controversial** [ˌkɒntrəˈvɜːʃl] adj. 引起争论的；有争议的

Immigration is a controversial issue in many countries.
在很多国家，移民都是一个颇有争议的问题。

词根387. vest=clothes，表示"衣服"

1. vest [vest] n. 背心（NAmE undershirt）；坎肩（BrE waistcoat）vt. 赋予（权力或责任）

He's wearing a bulletproof vest.
他穿着防弹背心。
And now, by the power vested in me by god，I pronounce you husband and wife.
现在，我以上帝的名义，宣布你们结为夫妇。

2. invest [ɪnˈvest] vt. 投资；投入（时间和精力等）
『in里面+vest衣服→（把）衣服里面的钱（拿出来）→投资』

❶ 投资（到股票、房地产等以赚取更多的钱）
[V] Now is a good time to invest in the property market.
现在是对房地产市场投资的好时机。
[VN] He invested his life savings in his daughter's business.
他把一生的积蓄投资到了女儿的企业。

❷ 投入（资金）
to spend money on sth in order to make it better or more successful
[V] The government has invested heavily in public transport.
政府已对公共交通投入了大量资金。
[VN] In his time managing the club he has invested millions

on new players.
他在管理俱乐部期间投入了几百万元培养新球员。

❸ 投入（时间、精力等）

I would rather invest time in Rebecca than in the kitchen.
我宁愿把时间花在丽贝卡身上也不愿花在厨房里。

▶ **investment** [ɪnˈvestmənt] n. 投资；投资物；值得买的东西；投入

This country needs investment in education.
这个国家需要对教育进行投资。
We bought the house as an investment.
我们买这所房子作为投资。

3. **divest** [daɪˈvest] vt. 使脱衣；处理掉；摆脱
『di离开+vest衣服→使衣服离开→使脱衣』

He divested himself of his jacket. 他脱去了短上衣。
The company is divesting itself of some of its assets.
该公司正在剥离部分资产。

词根388. vi(a), voy, vi=way, 表示"路"，引申为"走"
① via=way, 表示"路"，引申为"走"

1. **via** [ˈvaɪə] prep. 经由；凭借
『via路；走→取道于→经由；凭借』

We flew home via Dubai. 我们乘飞机经迪拜回国。
I heard about the sale via Jane.
我从简那里听说了这次大减价。
The news programme came to us via satellite.
新闻节目是通过卫星传送到我们这里来的。

2. **viable** [ˈvaɪəbl] adj. 切实可行的
『vi(a)走+able→可以走的→切实可行的』

There is no viable alternative. 没有可行的替代方案。

3. **trivia** [ˈtrɪviə] n. 琐事
『tri三+via路→（过去容易发生琐事的）三岔路口→琐事』

We spent the whole evening discussing domestic trivia.
我们整个晚上都在谈论家庭琐事。

▶ **trivial** [ˈtrɪviəl] adj. 不重要的，微不足道的
『trivia琐事+(a)l…的→不重要的』

The director tried to wave aside these issues as trivial details that could be settled later.
主管认为这是些细枝末节的小事，可以以后再解决。

4. **viaduct** [ˈvaɪədʌkt] n. 高架桥〈P156〉
『via路；走+ duct引导→引导（道路）经过（山谷河道等的）桥）→高架桥』

② voy=way, 表示"路"，引申为"走"

1. **voyage** [ˈvɔɪdʒ] n. 航行；航天 vi. 航行
『voy走+age表行为→航行；航天』

2. **convoy** [ˈkɒnvɔɪ] n. 车队；舰队 vt. 护送；护航
『con一起+voy走→护送；护航』

They were injured when a parked car exploded as their convoy passed by.
车队经过时，一辆停放着的汽车爆炸了，他们受了伤。
He ordered the combined fleet to convoy troops to Naples.
他命令联合舰队将军队护送到那不勒斯。

3. **envoy** [ˈenvɔɪ] n. 使者；（谈判等的）代表
『en使+voy走→使走到（另外一方）人→使者；代表』

The President's envoy set off on another diplomatic trip.
总统的使节开始了又一次外交之旅。

③ vi=way, 表示"路"，引申为"走"

1. **previous** [ˈpriːviəs] adj. 先前的
『pre之前+vi路；走+ous表形容词→之前走了的→先前的』

2. **deviate** [ˈdiːvieɪt] vi. 偏离，背离
『de离开+vi路；走+ate表动词→偏离』

The bus had to deviate from its usual route because of a road closure. 因为道路封闭，公共汽车只得绕道而行。
He never deviated from his original plan.
他从未偏离自己最初的计划。

▶ **deviant** [ˈdiːviənt] adj. 不正常的 n. 偏常者
『de离开+vi路；走+ant…的；人→离开正常方向的（人）→不正常的；偏常者』

different from what most people consider to be normal and acceptable

Teenagers' deviant behaviour has become a serious social problem. 青少年偏差行为已经成为一个严重的社会问题。
Are you a deviant or something? 你是有点变态还是什么？

▶ **devious** [ˈdiːviəs] adj. 不诚实的，欺诈的；（路线或道路）曲折的，迂回的
『de离开+vi 路；走+ous充满→总是离开（正常）道路或方法的→（人或行为）奸诈的；（路线或道路）曲折的』

Newman was devious, prepared to say one thing in print and another in private. 纽曼阴险得很，明里一套，暗里一套。
He followed a devious route. 他走了一条迂回路线。

3. **obviate** [ˈɒbvieɪt] vt. 消除；排除
『ob(=against)对着+vi路；走+ate表动词→对着走过去→消除；排除』

He destroyed the letter to obviate any suspicion that might fall on him.
他销毁了那封信，以消除可能给他招来的任何怀疑。
Improved public transportation would obviate the need for everyone to have their own car.
公共交通的改善消除了每个人都要有车的必要性。

词根389. vict, vince=conquer, overcome, 表示"征服；克服"

1. **victor** [ˈvɪktə(r)] n. 胜利者，获胜者
『vict征服；克服+or表人→胜利者』

▶ **victory** [ˈvɪktəri] n. 胜利

2. **convict** [kənˈvɪkt, ˈkɒnvɪkt] vt. 宣判有罪 n. 囚犯
『con一起+vict征服→（陪审团）一起征服（嫌犯）（嫌犯认罪）→宣判有罪』
（vt. [kənˈvɪkt]; n. [ˈkɒnvɪkt]）

He was convicted of fraud. 他被判犯有诈骗罪。
We think he is an escaped convict.
我们想他可能是个逃跑的罪犯。

小贴士 convict作动词时反义词是acquit；convict非正式文体常简写作con。

3. **evict** [ɪˈvɪkt] vt. 赶出，逐出
『e出去+vict征服→征服（某人）让其出去→赶出，逐出』

to force sb to leave a house or land, especially when you have the legal right to do so

A number of tenants have been evicted for not paying the

rent. 许多房客因不付房租被赶了出来。

4. convince [kənˈvɪns] vt. 使相信

『con一起+vince征服→一起征服（某人）→使相信』

[VN] You'll need to convince them of your enthusiasm for the job. 你要使他们相信你殷切希望得到这份工作。

5. evince [ɪˈvɪns] vt. 表明；显示

『e出来+vince征服→征服后出来→表明；显示』

to show clearly that you have a feeling or quality

The new president has so far evinced no such sense of direction. 新总统到目前尚未表现出对未来发展的判断力。

He evinced a strong desire to be reconciled with his family. 他表现出与家人和好的强烈愿望。

6. invincible [ɪnˈvɪnsəbl] adj. 不可战胜的；不能改变的

『in不+vince征服（去e）+ible可…的→不可征服的→不可战胜的；不能改变的』

The team seemed invincible. 这个队似乎战无不胜。

He also had an invincible faith in the medicinal virtues of garlic. 他同时也对大蒜的医学功效深信不疑。

词根390. view=see，表示"看"

1. preview [ˈpriːvjuː] n. & vt. 预演；预先评论

『pre事先+view看→预演；预先评述』

❶ [C] 预演；预映；预展

A preview is an opportunity to see something such as a film, exhibition, or invention before it is open or available to the public.

He had gone to see the preview of a play.

他去看了一场戏剧的预演了。

❷ [C]（报刊上有关电影电视节目等的）预先评述，预告

a description in a newspaper or a magazine that tells you about a film/movie, a television programme, etc. before it is shown to the public.

Turn to page 12 for a preview of next week's programmes.

下周节目预告请见第12页。

❸ [VN]为（影视节目）写预评

The exhibition was previewed in last week's issue.

本刊上周对展览作了预评。

❹ [VN] (especially NAmE) 概述；扼要介绍

The professor previewed the course for us.

教授为我们扼要介绍了这门课程。

2. review [rɪˈvjuː] n. & vt. 评论；审查；复习

『re又+view看→再看→复习；审查』

❶ [C, U] （对书籍、戏剧、电影等的）评价，评论

He submitted his latest novel for review.

他提交了自己的最新小说供评论。

❷ [U, C] 审议；审查（以进行必要的修改）

an examination of sth, with the intention of changing it if necessary

The terms of the contract are under review.

合同条文正在审议。

The president ordered a review of US economic aid to Jordan.

总统下令对美国向约旦提供的经济援助进行审查。

❸ [C] 报告；汇报

a report on a subject or on a series of events

a review of customer complaints 有关消费者投诉的汇报

to publish a review of recent cancer research

发表有关最近癌症研究的报告

❹ [C] (NAmE) （尤指为准备考试的）温习课，复习课

a lesson in which you look again at sth you have studied, especially in order to prepare for an exam

Let's set aside an hour a day for review purpose.

我们每天留出一小时用于复习吧！

❺ [VN] 写（关于书籍、戏剧、电影等的）评论；评介

The play was reviewed in the national newspapers.

全国性报纸都对这部戏剧作了评论。

❻ [VN] 审视；细查

to carefully examine or consider sth again, especially so that you can decide if it is necessary to make changes

to review the evidence 复查证据

The government will review the situation later in the year.

政府将在今年晚些时候对形势重新加以研究。

❼ [VN] （为备考）复习，温习

Reviewing for exams gives you a chance to bring together all the individual parts of the course.

考前复习让你有机会把一门课程所有零碎的知识都融会贯通。

3. overview [ˈəʊvəvjuː] n. 概述，纵览

『over过去+view看→看过去→概述，纵览』

An overview of a situation is a general understanding or description of it as a whole.

The central section of the book is a historical overview of drug use. 该书的核心部分对毒品的使用作了历史概述。

4. interview [ˈɪntəvjuː] v. & n. 面试；采访

『inter相互+view看→面对面相互看→面试；采访』

❶ [VN, V] ~ sb (for a job, etc.) 对（某人）进行面试

We interviewed ten people for the job.

我们为这份工作面试了10人。

The website gives you tips on interviewing for colleges.

这个网站为你提供大学面试的窍门。

❷ [VN] ~ sb (about sth)记者采访

The Prime Minister declined to be interviewed.

首相婉拒了采访。

❸ [C] 面试；采访

He has an interview next week for the manager's job.

他下周要接受一个经理职位的面试。

Yesterday, in an interview on German television, the minister denied the reports.

昨天，在德国电视台的采访中，部长否认了那些报道。

▶ **interviewer** [ˈɪntəvjuːə(r)] n. 主持面试者；采访者

▶ **interviewee** [ˌɪntəvjuːˈiː] n. 参加面试者；被采访者

5. viewpoint [ˈvjuːpɔɪnt] n. （看事情或问题的）角度

『view看+point观点→从某个观点看（事情）→角度』

The novel is shown from the girl's viewpoint.

这部小说是从这个女孩的视角来叙述的。

The artist has painted the scene from various viewpoints.

那位画家从各种角度把这一景色画了下来。

6. point of view 看法，简介；角度

Try to look at this from my point of view.

试着从我的角度来看这件事。

Thanks for your point of view, John.

约翰，感谢你发表见解。

7. view [vjuː] n. 看法；视野；风景 vt. 把…视为

❶ [C] ~ (about/on sth) （个人的）看法
His views on the subject were well known.
他对这个问题的看法众所周知。
In my view it was a waste of time. 依我看，这是浪费时间。

❷ [U, sing.] 视野，视域
The lake soon came into view. 那湖很快映入眼帘。
The sun disappeared from view. 太阳看不见了。

❸ [C] （从某处看到的）景色，风景
The view from the top of the tower was spectacular.
从塔顶远眺景色蔚为壮观。

❹ [VN] 把…视为
When the car was first built, the design was viewed as highly original. 这种车刚造出时，其设计被认为是独具匠心。

词根391. vis(e), vid(e)=see，表示"看"，名词形式为 vision
① vis(e)=see，表示"看"

1. visible ['vɪzəbl] adj. 看得见的；能注意到的
『vis看+ible可…的→可见的』

Most stars are not visible to the naked eye.
大多数星星肉眼看不见。
He showed no visible sign of emotion. 他丝毫不露声色。

2. visual ['vɪʒuəl] adj. 视力的；视觉的
『vis看+ual表形容词→看见的→视觉的』

❶ adj. 视力的；视觉的
of or connected with seeing or sight
I have a very good visual memory. 我过目不忘。
the visual arts 视觉艺术
The building makes a tremendous visual impact.
这栋建筑物给人极其深刻的视觉印象。

❷ [C] 视觉资料（指说明性的图片、影片等）
He used striking visuals to get his point across.
他用醒目的视觉资料解释他的观点。

▶ **visualize** ['vɪʒuəlaɪz] vt. 使形象化；想象

~ sth (as sth) 使形象化；想象；构思；设想
to form a picture of sb/sth in your mind
[VN] Try to visualize him as an old man.
尽量设想他是一位老人。
[V wh-] I can't visualize what this room looked like before it was decorated.
我想象不出这个房间在装修之前是什么样子。

3. vision ['vɪʒn] n. 视力，视野；愿景，想象；幻觉
『vis看+ion表名词→看（的能力或结果）→视力；视野』

❶ [U] 视力；视野
the ability to see; the area that you can see from a particular position
to have good/poor/normal vision 视力好/差/正常
The couple moved outside her field of vision.
这对夫妇离开了她的视野。

❷ [C] 想象；愿景
an idea or a picture in your imagination
He had a vision of a world in which there would be no wars.
他幻想有一个没有战争的世界。
I appreciate their support and their commitment to the vision

of the World Bank.
我赞赏他们对世界银行的愿景的支持与承诺。

❸ [C] 幻觉，幻象，梦幻
a dream or similar experience, especially of a religious kind
He had a vision of Cheryl, slumped on a plastic chair in the waiting-room.
他想象谢里尔瘫坐在候诊室的一把塑料椅子上。

▶ **visionary** ['vɪʒənri] adj. 有远见卓识的；幻觉的 n. 有远见的人

❶ adj. 有远见卓识的，有眼力的；梦幻的，神示的
a visionary leader 有远见卓识的领袖
Many are hailing Rendell's ideas as visionary.
许多人都称赞伦德尔的想法很有远见。

❷ [C] 有远见的人
The world has lost a visionary.
世界失去了一位有远见的人。

▶ **envision** [ɪn'vɪʒn] v. 展望；想象
『en使成为…状态+vision愿景→展望』

to imagine what a situation will be like in the future, especially a situation you intend to work towards
They envision an equal society, free of poverty and disease.
他们向往一个没有贫穷和疾病的平等社会。

▶ **envisage** [ɪn'vɪzɪdʒ] v. 设想；展望
『en使+vis看+age表行为→使看到将来→设想；展望』

(especially BrE) (NAmE usually envision)

4. revise [rɪ'vaɪz] vt. 修订，修正；复习
『re (again)又+vise看→再看→修订；复习』

❶ [VN] 修改，修订（书刊、估算、计划、政策等）
a revised edition of a textbook 课本的修订版
I'll prepare a revised estimate for you.
我将为你准备一份经过修正的评估报告。
The government may need to revise its policy in the light of this report. 政府可能需要根据这份报告改变其政策。

❷ [VN] 修正（想法）
He soon came to revise his opinion of the profession.
他很快就改变了对这个职业的看法。
I can see I will have to revise my opinions of his abilities now. 我明白我现在不得不改变对他的能力的看法了。

❸ (BrE) 复习 （NAmE review）
to prepare for an exam by looking again at work that you have done
[V] I spent the weekend revising for my exam.
我花了整个周末复习备考。
[VN] I'm revising Geography today. 我今天复习地理。

▶ **revision** [rɪ'vɪʒn] n. 修订；复习

5. supervise ['suːpəvaɪz] vt. 监督；管理
『super在上面+vise看→在上面看着→监管』

to be in charge of sb/sth and make sure that everything is done correctly, safely, etc.
She supervised the children playing near the pool.
她照料着在水池附近玩的几个孩子。
One of his jobs was supervising the dining room.
他的工作之一是管理餐厅。

▶ **supervision** [ˌsjuːpə'vɪʒn] n. 监督；管理
The plan calls for a ceasefire and UN supervision of the country.

该计划要求双方停火并由联合国对该国进行监督。

6. improvise [ˈɪmprəvaɪz] v. 临时凑成；即兴创作

『im不+pro向前+vise看→事先没有向前看→事先没有准备→临时凑成；即兴创作』

[VN] We improvised some shelves out of planks of wood and bricks. 我们用木板和砖头临时搭了些架子。

[V] I asked her what the piece was and she said, "Oh, I'm just improvising."

我问她那一段是什么音乐，她说："噢，我只是即兴弹的。"

② vid(e)=see，表示"看"

1. evident [ˈevɪdənt] adj. 清楚的，明显的

『e出+vid看+ent具有…性质的→看出来了的→明显的』

▶ **evidence** [ˈevɪdəns] n. 证据，证明

2. provide [prəˈvaɪd] vt. 提供；规定

『pro向前+vide看→提前看好→提供』

❶ [VN] ~ sb (with sth) | ~ sth (for sb) 提供

We are here to provide a service for the public.
我们来这里是为公众服务。

We are here to provide the public with a service.
我们来这里是为公众服务。

❷ [V that] (formal) （of a law or rule）规定

to state that sth will or must happen

The treaty provides that, by the end of the century, the United States must have removed its bases.
条约规定，到本世纪末，美国必须撤除其基地。

▶ **provision** [prəˈvɪʒn] n. 供应；条款

❶ [U, C, usually sing.] 提供；供应品

The government is responsible for the provision of health care. 政府负责提供医疗服务。

❷ [U, C] ~ for sb/sth （为将来做的）准备

You should make provision for things going wrong.
你要采取措施，以防不测。

❸ [pl.] （尤指旅途中的）饮食供应

On board were enough provisions for two weeks.
船上有足够两周吃的食物。

❹ [C] （法律文件的）规定，条款

Under the provisions of the lease, the tenant is responsible for repairs. 按契约规定，房客负责房屋维修。

小贴士 supply sb with sth | supply sth to sb

They were arrested for supplying counterfeit medicine to street vendors. 他们因向街头小贩提供假药而被捕。

Cows supply us with milk. 母牛供给我们牛奶。

▶ **provided** [prəˈvaɪdɪd] conj. 如果，假如

Provided (that) you have the money in your account, you can withdraw up to £100 a day.
只要你账户存款足够，每天最多可提取100英镑。

▶ **providing** [prəˈvaɪdɪŋ] conj. 如果，假如 （=provided）

3. provident [ˈprɒvɪdənt] adj. 精打细算的；未雨绸缪的

『pro向前+vid看+ent具有…性质的→能够为未来考虑的→精打细算的』

careful in planning for the future, especially by saving money

Provident men lay aside money for their families.
深谋远虑的人为家庭贮蓄钱财。

▶ **improvident** [ɪmˈprɒvɪdənt] adj. 不顾将来的；不节俭的

---

4. providential [ˌprɒvɪˈdenʃl] adj. 天缘巧合的

『pro向前+vid看+ent…的+ial表性质→好像预先看到似的→天缘巧合的』

lucky because it happens at the right time, but without being planned

Their departure just before the floods was providential.
他们恰在发洪水之前离开，走得真是时候。

词根392. vid(e), vis(e)=separate，表示"分开"

1. divide [dɪˈvaɪd] vt. 分开；分配；除以 ＜P102＞

『di分开，离开+vide分开→分开；分配』

2. individual [ˌɪndɪˈvɪdʒuəl] adj. 个别的，单独的 n. 个人

『in不+divide分开（去e）+ual…的→不能再分开的→个人的』

There are 96 pieces and they are worth, individually and collectively, a lot of money.
共有 96 件，它们无论单独一件还是放在一起，都值很多钱。

The competition is open to both teams and individuals.
团队和个人均可参加比赛。

3. dividend [ˈdɪvɪdend] n. 红利；股息

『divide分开（去e）+end表抽象名词→（公司）分给（持股人）的→红利；股息』

an amount of the profits that a company pays to people who own shares in the company

The first quarter dividend has been increased by nearly 4 per cent. 第一季度的股息增长了近 4%。

Exercising regularly will **pay dividends** in the end.
经常运动最终会对身体大有好处的。

4. devise [dɪˈvaɪz] vt. 发明；设计；想出

『de加强+vise分开→（新办法是）彻底分开→发明；想出』

to invent sth new or a new way of doing sth

A new system has been devised to control traffic in the city.
控制城市交通的新系统已经设计出来。

▶ **device** [dɪˈvaɪs] n. 装置，设备；手段

a water-saving device 节水装置

Sending advertising by email is very successful as a marketing device.
作为一种营销手段，用电子邮件发送广告是非常成功的。

词根393. vil(e)=base，表示"卑劣"

1. vile [vaɪl] adj. 糟透的；邪恶的

❶ 糟透的，极坏的

extremely unpleasant or bad

The weather was really vile most of the time.
天气大部分时间都糟糕得很。

He was in a vile mood. 他的心情坏极了。

❷ 邪恶的

morally bad

the vile practice of taking hostages 扣押人质的卑劣行径

2. villain [ˈvɪlən] n. 恶棍，坏蛋；（小说、电影或戏剧中的）主要反面人物

『vill(=vile)卑劣+ain人→卑劣的人→恶棍，坏蛋』

A villain is someone who deliberately harms other people or breaks the law in order to get what he or she wants.

He often plays the part of the villain. 他经常扮演反面人物。

3. devil [ˈdevl] n. 魔鬼

『de加强+vil卑劣→卑劣到极点→魔鬼；也可看作是lived
反过来写：上辈子活着的时候与正常人相反，死了做魔鬼』

4. evil [ˈiːvl] adj. 恶毒的，邪恶的；讨厌的 n. 邪恶；害处

『e加强+vil卑劣→十分卑劣→邪恶的；也可看作是live反
过来写：与正常人活法相反的人是邪恶的』

His boss is an evil man. 他的老板是个坏人。

an evil smell 难闻的气味

You cannot pretend there's no evil in the world.
你不能睁着眼睛瞎说世界上没有罪恶。

the evils of drugs/alcohol 毒品/酒的害处

People voted for him as **the lesser of two evils**.
人们投票支持他只不过是两害相权取其轻罢了。

5. revile [rɪˈvaɪl] vt. 憎恶；斥责

『re一再+vile卑劣→一再（说某人）卑劣→憎恶』

If someone or something is reviled, people hate them
intensely or show their hatred of them.

He was just as feared and reviled as his tyrannical parents.
他和他专横残暴的父母一样为人惧怕和憎恨。

词根394. vive, vit(e), vig=life, live, 表示"生命；活"

1. vivid [ˈvɪvɪd] adj. 生动的，逼真的；明亮的

『vive生命（去e）+id…的→有生命似的→生动的』

❶ （记忆、描述、想象等）生动的，逼真的，清晰的

He gave a vivid account of his life as a fighter pilot.
他生动地描述了他那战斗机飞行员的生活。

I vividly remember the day we first met.
我对我们第一次相见的那天记忆犹新。

On Wednesday night I had a very vivid dream which really
upset me.
周三晚上，我做了个十分逼真的梦，让我很不安。

❷ （色彩）明亮的，鲜艳的

She was wearing a vivid pink skirt.
她穿着一条色彩鲜艳的粉红色裙子。

2. survive [səˈvaɪv] v. 幸存；比…长寿

『sur (over) 过来+vive活→活过来→幸存』

❶ [V] ~ (from sth) | ~ (on sth) | ~ (as sth) 幸存；留存

Of the six people injured in the crash, only two survived.
这次撞车事故受伤的六人中只有两人活了下来。

Some strange customs have survived from earlier times.
有些奇怪的风俗是从早年留存下来的。

I can't survive on £40 a week.
一星期40英镑，我无法维持生活。

❷ [VN]幸存；幸免于难；艰难度过

The company managed to survive the crisis.
公司设法渡过了危机。

Many birds didn't survive the severe winter.
很多鸟死于这次严冬。

❸ [VN] 比…活（或存在）的时间长

She survived her husband by ten years.
丈夫死后她又活了10年。

▶ **survival** [səˈvaɪvl] n. 幸存；幸存物

His only chance of survival was a heart transplant.
只有进行心脏移植，他才有望活下去。

the survival of the fittest 适者生存

3. revive [rɪˈvaɪv] v.（使）苏醒；复苏；复活

『re又，再+vive活→（使）又活了→苏醒；复苏』

❶ （使）苏醒；复活；复苏

[V] The flowers soon revived in water.
这些花浇了水很快就活过来了。

The economy is beginning to revive. 经济开始复苏。

[VN] The paramedics couldn't revive her.
医护人员无法使她苏醒。

❷ [VN] 重新使用；重新上演；重新做

This 1930s musical is being revived at the National Theatre.
这部20世纪30年代的音乐剧正在国家剧院重新上演。

▶ **revival** [rɪˈvaɪvl] n. 振兴，复苏；再流行，重演

Jazz is enjoying a revival. 爵士音乐再度盛行。

an economic revival 经济复苏

4. vivacious [vɪˈveɪʃəs] adj. （尤指女子）可爱的；活泼
的；动人的

『vive活（去e）+acious充满…的→活泼的，可爱的』

having a lively, attractive personality

He had three pretty, vivacious daughters.
他有三个活泼漂亮的女儿。

5. convivial [kənˈvɪviəl] adj. （气氛或性格）欢快友好的

『con一起+vive活（去e）+ial表形容词→在一起很活泼快
乐→（气氛或性格）欢快友好的』

cheerful and friendly in atmosphere or character

a convivial evening/atmosphere 欢乐的夜晚/气氛

6. vital [ˈvaɪtl] adj. 极其重要的；充满活力的

『vit生命+al…的→有生命的；生死攸关的→有活力的，
重要的』

❶ ~ (for/to sth) 必不可少的；对…极重要的

necessary or essential in order for sth to succeed or exist

Reading is of vital importance in language learning.
阅读在语言学习中至关重要。

The police play a vital role in our society.
警察在我们的社会中起着极其重要的作用。

❷ [only before noun] 生命的；维持生命所必需的

connected with or necessary for staying alive

the vital organs (= the brain, heart, lungs, etc.) 重要脏器

❸ 充满活力的；生气勃勃的

They are both very vital people and a good match.
他俩都很有活力，十分般配。

▶ **vitality** [vaɪˈtæləti] n. 生命力；活力；热情

Mr Li said China's reforms had brought vitality to its
economy. 李先生说中国的改革给其经济注入了活力。

词义辨析 <P363第12>

**重要的，不可缺少的 essential, vital, crucial, critical,
indispensable**

7. revitalize [ˌriːˈvaɪtəlaɪz] vt. 使复兴；使恢复活力（或健
康）

『re又，再+vital充满活力的+ize使→使再充满活力→使复
兴』

To revitalize something that has lost its activity or its health
means to make it active or healthy again.

We need to revitalize human nutritional research.
我们需要振兴人类营养学研究。

We should develop community health services and revitalize
urban primary health care.

我们应该发展社区卫生服务，振兴城市初级卫生保健。

8. vitamin [ˈvɪtəmɪn] n. 维生素，维他命
『vit生命+amin→维持生命营养元素→维他命 （也就是"维生素"）（vitamin过去音译作"维他命"）』

9. vigor [ˈvɪgə] n. 精力；活力；热情
『vig活+or表物→使充满活力的东西→精力；活力』
Vigour is physical or mental energy and enthusiasm.
He worked with renewed vigour and determination.
他以新的活力和决心工作着。

▶ **vigorous** [ˈvɪgərəs] adj. 充满活力的
❶ （人）活跃的，积极的；（活动）热烈的
A vigorous person does things with great energy and enthusiasm. A vigorous campaign or activity is done with great energy and enthusiasm.
Sir Robert was a strong and vigorous politician.
罗伯特爵士是位坚定而又活跃的政治家。
They will take vigorous action to recover the debts.
他们将积极讨回债款。
❷ （体育活动）剧烈的，强度大的，强劲的；（人）精力旺盛的，充满活力的
Very vigorous exercise can increase the risk of heart attacks.
运动太过剧烈会增大心脏病发作的风险。
He was a vigorous, handsome young man.
他是个精力充沛、年轻帅气的小伙子。

10. invigorate [ɪnˈvɪgəreɪt] vt. 使有活力
『in(=en)使+vigor活力+ate表动词→使有活力』
❶ [VN] 使生气勃勃；使精神焕发
The cold water invigorated him. 冷水让他起了精神。
They felt refreshed and invigorated after the walk.
散步之后他们感到精神焕发。
❷ [VN] 激发活力；振兴
To invigorate a situation or a process means to make it more efficient or more effective.
They are looking into ways of invigorating the department.
他们正在寻找激发这个部门活力的方法。

11. vigil [ˈvɪdʒɪl] n. 守夜
『vig(=life, live)生命；活+il→（处于）有活力、有生机状态→没休息→守夜』
[C] 守夜（祈祷）；（夜间的）静默抗议
a period of time when people stay awake, especially at night, in order to watch a sick person, say prayers, protest, etc.
Mourners are to stage a candlelit vigil in Liverpool.
哀悼者准备在利物浦举行一次烛光祈祷。

▶ **vigilant** [ˈvɪdʒɪlənt] adj. 警觉的；警惕的
『vigil守夜（不休息）+ant表形容词→警觉的；警惕的』
very careful to notice any signs of danger or trouble
（同义词：alert, watchful）
A pilot must remain vigilant at all times.
飞行员必须随时保持警惕。

▶ **vigilance** [ˈvɪdʒɪləns] n. 警觉；警惕
『vigil守夜（不休息）+ance表名词→警觉；警惕』
She stressed the need for constant vigilance.
她强调必须时常保持警惕。

1. advocate [ˈædvəkeɪt, ˈædvəkət] v. 提倡；拥护 n. 提倡者，拥护者
『ad相当于to+voc叫喊；声音+ate表动词或表人→向（众人）喊（呼吁支持或参与）→提倡；拥护者』
（v. [ˈædvəkeɪt]; n. [ˈædvəkət]）
❶ 拥护；支持；提倡
to support sth publicly
[VN] The group does not advocate the use of violence.
该团体不支持使用暴力。
[V-ing] Many experts advocate rewarding your child for good behaviour.
很多专家主张对小孩的良好表现加以奖励。
[V that] The report advocated that all buildings be fitted with smoke detectors.
报告主张所有的建筑物都应安装烟火探测器。
❷ [C] 拥护者；支持者；提倡者
He was a strong advocate of free market policies and a multi-party system.
他是自由市场政策和多党派制度的坚决拥护者。

▶ **advocacy** [ˈædvəkəsi] n. 提倡，拥护
I support your advocacy of free trade.
我支持你自由贸易的主张。
CMHA accomplishes this mission through advocacy, education, research and service.
CMHA通过宣传、教育、科研和服务来完成这一使命。

2. equivocal [ɪˈkwɪvəkl] adj. 含糊其词的；难以理解的
『equi等同+voc声音+al…的→（两种不同的）声音等同的→含糊其词的』
❶ 含糊其词的，模棱两可的
If you are equivocal, you are deliberately vague in what you say, because you want to avoid speaking the truth or making a decision.
Many were equivocal about the idea.
很多人对这一观点都含糊其词。
❷ （常因自相矛盾而）难以理解的
difficult to understand or explain clearly or easily
The experiments produced equivocal results.
这些实验产生的结果难以理解。

▶ **equivocate** [ɪˈkwɪvəkeɪt] v. （故意）含糊其词
He had asked her once again about her finances. And again she had equivocated.
他又一次询问她的财务状况，她再次含糊其词。

3. provoke [prəˈvəʊk] vt. 激起，引起；挑衅，激怒
『pro向前+voke喊→向前面喊→激起，引起；挑衅，激怒』
[VN] The announcement provoked a storm of protest.
这个声明激起了抗议的风潮。
[VN] The article was intended to provoke discussion.
这篇文章旨在引发讨论。
[VN] He started beating me when I was about fifteen but I didn't do anything to provoke him.
在我快15岁时他开始打我，可我并没有任何招惹他的举动。

▶ **provocative** [prəˈvɒkətɪv] adj. 挑衅的，煽动性的；挑逗的
His provocative language provoked Peter.
他挑衅的话语激怒了彼得。

4. invoke [ɪnˈvəʊk] vt. 援引；（向神）求助
『in里面+voke喊→里面喊了（某个法律条款）来证明；内心喊了（某个神）来帮助→援引；求助』

❶ [VN] 援引，援用（法律、规则等作为行动理由）；提及，援引（某人、某理论、实例等作为支持）
The judge invoked an international law that protects refugees.
法官援引了一项保护难民的国际法。

She invoked several eminent scholars to back up her argument. 她援引了几位赫赫有名的学者来支持她的论点。

❷ [VN] 向（某人）请求帮助，（尤指）祈求神助
The great magicians of old always invoked their gods with sacrifice. 旧时一些有名的巫师经常以祭品祈求他们所供奉神灵的助佑。

5. revoke [rɪˈvəʊk] vt. 取消，废除，使无效
『re回+voke喊→喊回（原来的许可、法律、协议等）→取消』

When people in authority revoke something such as a licence, a law, or an agreement, they cancel it.
Only the owner of the current database can grant or revoke this permission.
只有当前数据库的所有者才能授予或废除这一权限。

▶ **irrevocable** [ɪˈrevəkəbl] adj. 无法改变的；不可更改的
It may well be worth waiting for better times before making any irrevocable commitment.
最好等到更合适的时候再作出不能反悔的承诺。

6. evoke [ɪˈvəʊk] vt. 引起；唤起（感情、记忆或形象）
『e出来+voke喊→喊出（感情、记忆或形象）→唤起』

The music evoked memories of her youth.
这乐曲勾起了她对青年时代的回忆。
His case is unlikely to evoke public sympathy.
他的情况不大可能引起公众的同情。

7. vocation [vəʊˈkeɪʃn] n. 使命，天职；（适合自己的）职业
『voc喊+ation表名词→（感到某个职业在）召唤→使命』

❶ [C]（认为特别适合自己的）工作，职业
You missed your vocation—you should have been an actor.
你入错行了，你本该当演员。

❷ [C, U] 使命，天职
the feeling that the purpose of your life is to do a particular type of work, especially because it allows you to help other people
She is a doctor with a strong sense of vocation.
她是一位具有强烈使命感的医生。

He was quite young when he decided he had a religious vocation. 当他决定从事宗教职业时，他还很年轻。

▶ **avocation** [ˌævəʊˈkeɪʃn] n. 业余爱好；副业
『a非+vocation职业→不是职业→业余爱好；副业』

Your avocation is a job or activity that you do because you are interested in it, rather than to earn your living.

8. vocal [ˈvəʊkl] adj. 嗓音的；直言不讳的 n. 声乐部分
『voc(=voice)声音+al…的→嗓音的；声乐部分』

the vocal organs (= the tongue, lips, etc.) 发声器官
He has been very vocal in his criticism of the government's policy. 他对政府政策的批评一直是直言不讳。

9. vociferous [vəˈsɪfərəs] adj.（表达观点时）大声的，激昂的

『voci(=voc)声音+fer带来，运送+ous…的→想把声音（观点）传出去的→激昂的』
expressing your opinions or feelings in a loud and confident way
He was a vociferous opponent of Conservatism.
他高声反对保守主义。

词根396. volunt, vol =wish, will，表示"意愿；意志"

1. volunteer [ˌvɒlənˈtɪə(r)] n. 志愿者；自告奋勇者
『volunt意愿+eer从事某种工作的人→自愿去做某种工作的人→志愿者』

❶ n. 义务工作者；志愿者
Schools need volunteers to help children to read.
学校需要义务工作者帮助儿童阅读。

❷ n. 自告奋勇者；主动做某事的人
Are there any volunteers to help clear up?
有自愿帮助清扫的人吗？

❸ n. 志愿兵
a person who chooses to join the armed forces without being forced to join

❹ vt. 自告奋勇；主动要求
Aunt Mary volunteered to clean up the kitchen.
玛丽阿姨主动要求清扫厨房。

2. voluntary [ˈvɒləntri] adj. 自愿的；无偿的
『volunt意愿+ary有…性质的→自愿的』

❶ 自愿的，主动的
Attendance on the course is purely voluntary.
听这门课纯粹是自愿的。

❷ 无偿的，义务性的，志愿性的
I do some voluntary work at the local hospital.
我在当地医院从事一些义务性工作。
Some local authorities and voluntary organizations also run workshops for disabled people.
一些当地机构和志愿组织也为残疾人举办了一些讲习班。

▶ **involuntary** [ɪnˈvɒləntri] adj. 不由自主的，不自觉的；非自愿的；强迫的

Another surge of pain in my ankle caused me to give an involuntary shudder.
脚踝突然又一阵疼痛，痛得我直哆嗦。

They argued that legalising voluntary euthanasia would eventually lead to involuntary euthanasia.
他们争论说，使自愿安乐死合法化最终会导致非自愿的安乐死。

3. volition [vəˈlɪʃn] n. 自愿选择，自行决定
『vol意愿+ition行为，状态→（出于自己的）意愿→自愿选择，自行决定』

They left entirely of their own volition.
他们完全是自愿离开的。

4. benevolent [bəˈnevələnt] adj.（当权者）仁慈的；乐善好施的
『bene好+vol意愿+ent具有…性质的→意愿是好的→仁慈的；乐善好施的』

The company has proved to be a most benevolent employer.
事实证明，这家公司是非常好的雇主。
the Army Benevolent Fund 陆军慈善基金

▶ **benevolence** [bəˈnevələns] n. 仁爱；善行

5. malevolent [məˈlevələnt] adj. 恶意的
『male坏+vol意愿+ent具有…性质的→坏意→恶意的』

There was malevolent criticism of government policies.
有人对政府的政策进行恶意的批评。

▶ **malevolence** [məˈlevələns] n. 恶意

词根397. volve, vol, volt =roll，turn，表示"卷，转"

1. involve [ɪnˈvɒlv] vt. 参加；涉及
『in里面+volve卷→卷入到（某事）里面→参加；涉及』

❶ [VN] ~ sb (in sth/in doing sth) （使）参加，加入
to make sb take part in sth
We want to involve as many people as possible in the celebrations. 我们希望参加庆典的人越多越好。
Parents should involve themselves in their child's education.
父母应当参与孩子的教育。
She has been involved in the war against organised crime.
她参与了打击有组织犯罪的斗争。

❷ 需要；包含；涉及
[VN] Many of the crimes involved drugs.
许多罪案都与毒品有关。
[V -ing] The test will involve answering questions about a photograph. 考试将包括回答一些关于一张照片的问题。
[VN -ing] The job involves me travelling all over the country.
这份工作需要我在全国各地跑。
If there was a cover-up, it involved people at the very highest levels of government.
如果有隐情，那就涉及政府部门最高层的人物。

▶ **involvement** [ɪnˈvɒlvmənt] n. 参加；涉及

2. evolve [iˈvɒlv] v. 进化；逐渐发展
『e出+volve卷，转→（随着时间的年轮）转出来→进化』

❶ （动植物等）进化
[V] The three species evolved from a single ancestor.
这三种生物从同一祖先进化而来。
[VN] The dolphin has evolved a highly developed jaw.
海豚已经进化形成高度发达的下颌。

❷ ~ (sth) (from sth) (into sth)
（使）逐渐形成，逐步发展，逐渐演变
[V] The idea evolved from a drawing I discovered in the attic.
这种想法是从我在阁楼里发现的一幅画中得到启发的。
The company has evolved into a major chemical manufacturer. 这家公司已逐步发展成一家大型化工厂。

▶ **evolution** [ˌiːvəˈluːʃn] n. 进化；发展
Darwin's theory of evolution 达尔文进化论
But the Internet has brought about a new evolution in languages. 但互联网带来了语言的新发展。

▶ **evolutionary** [ˌiːvəˈluːʃənri] adj. 进化的；逐渐的
evolutionary theory 进化论
evolutionary change 逐渐演变

3. revolve [rɪˈvɒlv] vi. 旋转；环绕
『re又，再+volve转→一再转→旋转；环绕』

❶ [V] 旋转；环绕
to go in a circle around a central point
The fan revolved slowly. 电扇缓慢地转动着。
The earth revolves around the sun. 地球绕太阳公转。

❷ [V] 以…为中心
His whole life revolves around surfing.
他一生都在做与冲浪相关的事。
She thinks that the world revolves around her.
她以为整个世界都以她为中心。

▶ **revolver** [rɪˈvɒlvə(r)] n. 左轮手枪

▶ **revolution** [ˌrevəˈluːʃn] n. 旋转
the revolution of the earth around the sun
地球环绕太阳的公转

4. devolve [dɪˈvɒlv] v.（使）（权力、职责等）下放；转交（遗产）
『de向下+volve转→向下转交→下放；转交』

We have made a conscious effort to devolve responsibility.
我们已有意识地下放职责。
A large portion of this cost devolves upon the patient.
这笔费用的很大一部分落在病人身上。

5. revolution [ˌrevəˈluːʃn] n. 革命；大变革
『re返回+volution转(volve的名词形式)→反转过来（对抗自己的政府）→革命』

❶ [C, U] 革命
the outbreak of the French Revolution in 1789
1789年法国大革命的爆发

❷ [C] ~ (in sth) 巨变；大变革
A revolution in information technology is taking place.
信息技术正在发生巨变。

▶ **revolutionary** [ˌrevəˈluːʃənəri] adj. 革命的；大变革的 n. 革命者；(支持)改革者
a revolutionary leader 革命领袖
a revolutionary idea 革命性的想法
socialist revolutionaries 社会主义革命者

6. revolt [rɪˈvəʊlt] n. 反抗；叛乱 v. 反抗；令人厌恶
『re返回+volt转→反转过来（对抗当权者）→反抗；叛乱』

❶ [C, U] （尤指针对政府的）反抗；违抗；叛乱
The army quickly crushed the revolt. 军队很快镇压了叛乱。

❷ [V] ~ (against sb/sth) 反抗，反叛（当权者）；违抗
Finally the people revolted against the military dictatorship.
人民最终起来反抗军事独裁。
Teenagers often revolt against parental discipline.
青少年常常不遵从父母的条条框框。

❸ [VN] 使惊骇；令人厌恶
to make you feel horror or disgust
The way he ate his food revolted me.
他吃饭的样子让我感到恶心。

7. volume [ˈvɒljuːm] n. 体积，容积；音量；（书）一卷
『vol 卷，转+ume→装订成卷→卷，册』

❶ [U, C] 体积；容积；容量
How do you measure the volume of a gas?
你如何计量气体的体积？

jars of different volumes 不同容量的罐子

小贴士 表示体积和容量的"V"就是volume的首字母。

❷ [U, C] 量；额
the amount of sth

New roads are being built to cope with the increased volume of traffic. 正在修建新的道路以应付增加的交通量。

Sales volumes fell 0.2% in June.
六月份的销售额下降了0.2%。

❸ [U] 音量；响度
to turn the volume up/down 把音量调大 / 小

❹ [C] (abbr. vol.) （成套书籍中的）一卷，一册
an encyclopedia in 20 volumes 一套20卷的百科全书

❺ [C] (formal) 书
a library of over 50,000 volumes 藏书5万多册的图书馆

8. **voluble** [ˈvɒljʊbl] adj. 健谈的，滔滔不绝的
『vol卷，转+u+ble（相当于able）能够的→（舌头）能够轻松卷起的→口齿伶俐的→健谈的』

If you say that someone is voluble, you mean that they talk a lot with great energy and enthusiasm.

Evelyn was very voluble on the subject of women's rights.
伊夫林谈起女权这个话题口若悬河。

词根398. vore=eat，表示"吃"

1. **voracious** [vəˈreɪʃəs] adj. 贪吃的；如饥似渴的
『vore吃（去e）+acious充满…的→吃得多的→贪吃的』

They must take a break from their voracious consumption.
他们那种贪婪的消费必须止步了。

Joseph Smith was a voracious book collector.
约瑟夫·史密斯是个如饥似渴的藏书家。

2. **carnivore** [ˈkɑːnɪvɔː(r)] n. 食肉动物；喜欢吃肉的人
『carni肉+vore吃→吃肉（动物）→食肉动物』

This is a vegetarian dish that carnivores love.
这是一道肉食主义者爱吃的素菜。

▶ **carnivorous** [kɑːˈnɪvərəs] adj. 食肉的

3. **herbivore** [ˈhɜːbɪvɔː(r)] n. 食草动物
『herb草+i+vore吃→吃草（动物）→食草动物』

▶ **herbivorous** [hɜːˈbɪvərəs] adj. 食草的

4. **insectivore** [ɪnˈsektɪvɔː(r)] n. 食虫动物
『insect昆虫+i+vore吃→吃虫（动物）→食虫动物』

▶ **insectivorous** [ˌɪnsekˈtɪvərəs] adj. 食虫动物的

5. **omnivore** [ˈɒmnɪvɔː(r)] n. 杂食动物；杂食的人 ⟨P241⟩
『omni全部+vore吃→杂食（动物或人）』

6. **devour** [dɪˈvaʊə(r)] vt. （因饿）狼吞虎咽；如饥似渴地读或看；吞没
『de去掉+vour(=vore)吃→（一口气）吃完→狼吞虎咽』

A medium-sized dog will devour at least one can of food per day. 中型犬每天至少要吃掉一罐狗粮。

She began devouring newspapers when she was only 12.
年仅12岁时，她就开始如饥似渴地阅读报纸。

词根399. zeal=ardor，表示"热情"

1. **zeal** [ziːl] n. 热情；激情

[U, C] ~ (for/in sth) (formal) 热情；激情
great energy or enthusiasm connected with sth that you feel strongly about
her missionary/reforming/religious/political zeal
她的传教士般的/改革/宗教/政治热情

▶ **zealous** [ˈzeləs] adj. 热情的，热烈的，充满激情的
『zeal热情+ous充满→充满热情的』

She was a zealous worker for charitable bodies.
她对慈善事业充满热忱。

2. **zealot** [ˈzelət] n. （尤指宗教或政治的）狂热分子
『zeal热情+ot表示人→狂热分子』

If you describe someone as a zealot, you think that their views and actions are very extreme, especially in following a particular political or religious belief.

He was forceful, but by no means a zealot.
他个性坚定，但绝不是什么狂热分子。

第二部分　同义词辨析

1. 看 see, watch, observe, look, perceive

see 看见，看到，观看
侧重看的结果；也指眼睛看得见或观看比赛、电视节目等。
He looked but **saw** nothing. 他看了看，但什么也没有看见。
Did you see that programme last night?
你昨晚看那个节目了吗？

watch 注视，观看
指在一段时间内关注某人或某事。
watch television 看电视
Next time you visit the zoo, watch the tigers carefully.
下次你们参观动物园，要仔细观察老虎。

observe 观察（到），观看
指注意到某事物，或为了了解某人、某事而对其进行仔细观察。
The far side of the moon is difficult for us to observe.
我们难以观察到月亮的另一面。

look 看
侧重短暂的看的动作，但并不一定能看见，有时用来唤起别人的注意。
Look at the blackboard. 看黑板。
She covered her eyes, afraid to look. 她蒙上眼睛，不敢看。

perceive 察觉，注意到；看待
指发现或意识到难以发现的某事
I perceived a change in his behaviour.
我发觉他的行为有些变化。

2. 小心的 cautious, careful

cautious 小心谨慎的
指人因担心某事危险或不明智而缓慢行事或小心谨慎。
（反义词为 rash）
On this account we should be more cautious on this voyage.
因此，我们应该在这次航行中格外小心谨慎。

careful 仔细的
指人并非担心害怕，但为确保万无一失而做事小心仔细。
（反义词为 careless）

3. 认为，看作 consider, regard, view

consider 与 regard 两词词义相同，但用于不同的句型和结构。

consider 必须与补语或从句连用，可用 consider sb/sth to be sth 或 consider sb/sth as sth，不过 to be 或 as 常常省略不用：
He considers himself (to be/as) an expert.
他认为自己是专家。
This award is considered (to be) a great honour.
这个奖被认为是极大的荣誉。
These workers are considered (as) a high-risk group.
这些工人被认为是一个高危人群。
用 consider that sb/sth is sth 亦可，that 同样可以省略。
The Home Secretary will release prisoners only if he considers (that) it is safe to do so.
内政大臣只有在他认为这样做是安全的情况下才会释放囚犯。

regard 可用的句型和结构较少，最常用的结构是 regard sb/sth as sth，但 as 不可省略：
We always regard him as a friend, but he showed his colours in the current emergency.
我们一贯把他看作朋友，但在当前的紧急关头中，他原形毕露了。

view 与 regard、consider 意义相同，但较不常用，也较非正式。主要结构有 view sb/sth as sb/sth（把…视为…）（as 不能省略）和 view sb/sth with sth（以…眼光看待…）。
First-generation Americans view the United States as a land of golden opportunity.
第一代美国人认为美国是一个充满了机遇的国度。
She viewed him with suspicion.
她以怀疑的目光看待他。

4. 前进，进展 progress, advance, proceed

progress 进展，进步
指发展、提高，也指工作或计划继续进行。
He progressed to running the company within just two years.
他仅用了两年时间就晋升到公司的管理层。
Work on the bridge progressed quickly.
大桥的施工进展迅速。

advance 前进，进展
尤指士兵向前行进，也指科学技术发展进步。
The soldiers were advancing towards the village nearby.
士兵们正向附近的村庄挺进。
Our understanding of the HIV virus has advanced considerably.
我们对艾滋病病毒的了解有了很大进展。

proceed 前进
指向某一方向移动，也可指继续做某事。
Passengers for Atlanta should proceed to Gate 5.
前往亚特兰大的旅客请到 5 号登机口。
The government has decided to proceed with the election.
政府决定继续进行选举。

5. 产品，商品 product, production, produce, merchandise, goods, commodity

product 产品，制品
主要指工厂里大批量制造的产品，通常用于出售。
Where are the finished products assembled?
成品是在哪里组装的？

production （电影、戏剧或广播节目的）上映，上演，播出，制作
a groundbreaking new production 一部开创性的新作品
a new production of *King Lear* 新制作的《李尔王》

produce 农产品
不可数名词，指生产出来用于出售的农产品。
Fresh local produce is usually cheap and delicious.
新鲜的本地农产品通常味美价廉。

goods 商品（只用复数形式）
泛指用于出售的货品。
Leather goods are very popular in that country.
皮革类制品在那个国家很受欢迎。

merchandise 商品，货品 （不可数名词）

指商品、货品、相关商品、指定商品。
official Olympic merchandise
奥林匹克运动会官方指定商品
A range of official Snoopy merchandise is on sale in the visitors' centre.
一系列正版的史努比商品在游客中心出售。

强调商品制作的原料或用途 goods：
leather/household goods 皮革商品；家庭用品
如果不太强调商品本身，而更强调品牌或买卖则用 merchandise。
Did they inspect the merchandise after its arrival?
货到之后他们检查过吗？

commodity（经）商品
尤指国家间贸易的商品或原材料。
The country's most valuable commodities include tin and diamonds. 这个国家最有价值的商品包括锡和钻石。

6. 评论 remark, comment, note, observe

remark 评述，评论
remark on sth 或者 make a remark about sth，经常指比较随意地评论，说出所思所见。
Visitors remark on how well the children look.
来访者说孩子们看上去很好。
Critics remarked that the play was not original.
评论家指出这部戏剧缺乏创意。

comment 评论
comment on a situation 或者 make a comment on a situation，指就某事发表自己的观点。
Mr Cook has not commented on these reports.
库克先生还没有对这些报告作出评论。

observe 说起，评论
指说出或写出所注意到的内容（observe 本身有 "观察" 之意）。
She observed that it was getting late. 她说天色晚了。

comment 比较正式，既可以是官方的也可以是个人的；但 remark 总是非官方的，说话者可能未经深思熟虑的。
remark on 或 observe 表示谈论或评论注意到的事物。我们可以说 refuse to comment，但不能说 refuse to remark 或 refuse to observe。

note 注意
指特别提到或指出。
It must be noted, however, that not all British and American officers carried out orders.
然而，一定要注意不是所有的英国和美国军官都执行了命令。

7. 记起 remember, memorise, recall, recollect

remember 想起；记住
普通用词，指记得（做过）某事时，通常后接名词、动名词、that 从句；指记得要做某事时，通常后接动词不定式。
He still remembers the days when he worked in the country.
他依然会想起在乡下劳动的日子。
I remember returning the book to you.
我记得这本书已经还给你了。
Remember to take your key. 别忘了拿钥匙。

memorise 记住，熟记，背熟
指将所有细节都牢牢记住或背熟。
The professor had his students memorise a short poem of

Yeats. 教授让他的学生背熟一首叶芝的短诗。
It is important to memorise these regulations.
记住这些规则很重要。

recall 回想，回忆起
指记起发生在过去的事情。
Can you recall who gave that document to you?
你能记起谁给你的那份文件吗？
She didn't recall having dined with him.
她想不起来曾经和他一起吃过饭。

recollect （努力）想起
较正式用词，指力图想起有些许印象的事。
As far as he can recollect, that tall man was not there when the party began.
据他回忆，聚会开始时那个高个男子不在场。

8. 小吃，点心 snack, refreshment

snack 小吃，点心
指正餐以外的小吃、零食。
Don't have too many snacks, or you may get fat.
别吃太多零食，你会变胖的。

refreshment 茶点，点心
通常用复数，指会议、聚会、体育赛事等期间提供的点心和饮料。
Light refreshments will be served at the back of the hall.
会堂后面将供应简单的茶点。

9. 娱乐 entertainment, amusement, recreation, pastime

entertainment 电影、电视剧、表演等娱乐项目或活动
各类以娱悦大众为目的的综艺及影视节目就属于 "entertainment 娱乐节目"。而 "entertainment industry" 指的是 "娱乐行业"。我们也常把 "演艺人员" 称作 "entertainer"。
To watch entertainment news, click here to "subscribe" to this channel. 观看娱乐新闻，点击此处订阅此频道。

amusement 文娱活动，游戏
包含这个单词的常用搭配有 "amusement park 露天游乐园，主题公园"；它还可以泛指 "被逗笑的，感到有趣的一种状态"。
I'll sing a little song later, for your amusement.
待会儿我献唱一曲，就为了博您一乐。
Last night we went to the amusement park.
昨天晚上，我们去了游乐园。
Her chief amusement is enjoying music.
她的主要消遣是欣赏音乐。

recreation 休闲活动
在工作之外的闲暇时间内用来放松身心的活动，这个单词多用来指各类体育运动。
Her only form of recreation seems to be shopping.
她唯一的消遣好像就是购物。
His favourite recreations include golf and fishing.
他最喜欢的消遣活动包括打高尔夫球和钓鱼。

pastime 娱乐活动
pastime 听起来没有 recreation 那么积极。顾名思义，"pastime" 指用来 "pass time 消磨时间" 的娱乐活动或爱好，比如打扑克牌、钓鱼等。
Hunting used to be one of the royals' favourite pastimes.
打猎曾经是最受皇室喜爱的消遣方式之一。

10. 地铁 subway, underground, tube, metro

在英国英语中城市的地铁系统通常称为 underground（常作 the Underground），在北美英语中为 subway。说英国英语的人指美国城市的地铁亦用 subway，而指其他欧洲国家的地铁则用 metro。伦敦的地铁通常称为 the Tube。

11. 替代 replace, substitute

replace 取代，更换
泛指任何简单的"代替、取代"，尤其是指取代陈旧的、用坏的、丢失的东西或不能再发挥作用的人，带有长期地、永久地代替的含义。也可指取代、替换某人的工作。
Who will replace Sam on the team?
谁将接替队里的萨姆？
Three of the bulbs have to be replaced.
其中 3 个灯泡必须得换下来。
They replaced the wooden chairs with plastic ones.
他们用塑料椅子来代替木头椅子。

substitute 替代，替换
往往带有只是暂时代替的意思，可以指某人因故不在时由他人来代行其职，或用某物来替代某一个通常情况下使用的东西。
The chef said you could substitute ketchup for the vinegar.
主厨说过你可以用番茄酱代醋。
Who substituted for Susan when she was out sick?
苏珊生病没上班时，谁暂时接替了她的工作？
After 20 minutes on the field he had to be substituted.
上场 20 分钟后他不得不被替换下来。

在搭配上，"replace A with B"表示"用 B 来替代 A"，而"substitute A for B"则表示"用 A 来代替 B"。
（小窍门：从构词上看 sub-表示"下面"，stitute 表示"放"，substitute 表示"把…放到下面"；而 for 表示"作为；为了"。substitute A for B 表示"把 A 放到（B 位置的）下面来代替 B，因此表示的是"用 A 来代替 B"。

12. 重要的，不可缺少的 essential, vital, crucial, critical, indispensable

essential 必要的，重要的，基本的
语气较强，强调极其重要、必不可少的，暗含某物如缺少某部分，则失去其本质特征的意味。
Water and food are essential to life.
水和食物对生命是必不可少的。
Experience is essential for this job.
对于这个工作，经验是非常重要的。

vital 极其重要的
vital 和 essential 在词义上无实质区别，只是在语气上稍有不同：essential 用以说明事实或表明权威意见，vital 本身有"维持生命所必需的，生死攸关的"之意，所以它表示"重要，不可缺少时"含有"对某事感到忧虑或需要使人相信某事正确或重要等"。vital 较少用于否定句。
The police play a vital role in our society.
警察在我们的社会中起着极其重要的作用。
It was vital to show that he was not afraid.
最重要的是要表现出他毫无畏惧。

crucial 决定性的，关键的
构词上，cruc 相当于 cross，表示"十字路口"，因此，crucial 指处于某一重要转折点的，强调某事物非常重要，是其他事物依赖的对象。
It is crucial that we get this right.
我们把这个问题弄明白是极其重要的。

Negotiations are now at a crucial stage.
目前，谈判正处于关键阶段。

critical 极其重要的，关键的
Your decision is critical to our future.
你的决定对我们的将来至关重要。
critical 和 crucial 在意义上无实质区别，只是有时在语境上稍有区别。critical 常用于商业或科学的技术问题，crucial 常用于可能引起焦虑或其他情感方面的问题。

indispensable 必需的，不可缺少的
Cars have become an indispensable part of our lives.
汽车已成了我们生活中不可缺少的一部分。

13. 物质 material, matter, stuff, substance

material 材料，原料；素材
尤指木材、石头、金属、塑料等用于制作某物的原材料；也可指文学创作的素材。
He is now collecting material for a biography.
他正在为写一部传记收集素材。
As a building material, wood is not sturdy enough.
作为一种建筑材料，木材不够结实。

matter 物质
一切有形物质的总称，既指构成宇宙万物的物质，也指哲学上与意识相对的物质。
The entire universe is made up of different kinds of matter.
整个宇宙是由各种物质构成的。

stuff 东西，物品
多用于日常口语，可指各种叫不出名称的物质、材料、物体等；有时指无关紧要的东西，含轻视意味。
Put all the stuff into the box and seal it tightly with sticky tape. 把所有的东西都放进盒子里，再用胶带封好。

substance 物质
通常指有某种特性的固体、液体或气体物质。
Soil consists of various chemical substances.
土壤由各种化学物质组成。
Water, ice and steam are the same substance in different forms. 水、冰和蒸汽是形态不同的同一物质。

14. 忍受，遭受 bear, stand, endure, tolerate, put up with, sustain

bear, stand, endure 作"忍受"讲时，后面可以跟动词不定式作宾语，也可以跟动名词作宾语，而 tolerate 后面只能跟动名词作宾语。它们在表示"承受困难和不快，容忍"时，有时可以互换。

bear 和 **stand** 作"忍受"解时，可以换用，通常用于疑问句和否定句中，主要指对某人、某种困难情况的忍受或承受。
She cannot stand/bear her husband coming home late all the time. 她不能容忍丈夫老是晚回家。
She couldn't bear/stand to see others suffer.
她不忍看见别人受苦。

bear 还可指承受困难或不愉快的情形而没有抱怨，多强调忍受者的勇敢和坚毅。
A strong man will bear hardship without complaining.
一个坚强的人会忍受困苦而不抱怨。
She bore all her suffering with incredible patience.
她以难以置信的耐心忍受着所有的痛苦。

stand 还可作"经受"解，常与 could 或 can 连用，指足够好或结实而没有被影响或损坏。

These are plants that can't stand the cold well.
这些植物经受不住寒冷的考验。
Modern plastics can stand very high and very low temperatures.
新型塑料能耐极高温和极低温。

endure 忍受，忍耐
强调长期性，主要指对灾难、困难、疼痛等长时间忍受而不抱怨。
It takes patience to endure hardship. 忍受苦难需要忍耐力。
She longs for a love that can endure all things.
她渴望一份能经受住一切考验的爱情。

tolerate 忍受，容忍
指以克制的态度容忍令人反感或厌恶的事物，含默认、宽容之意。
He won't tolerate anyone questioning his decisions.
他不会容忍任何人质疑他的决定。
For years the workers have had to tolerate low wages and terrible working conditions.
多年来，工人们不得不忍受低工资和恶劣的工作环境。
The school won't tolerate cheating on exams.
学校不容许考试作弊。

put up with 与 tolerate 意思相近，有"不计较，将就"之意，多用于口语。可与其他词互换。
I can't put up with her another day—she never stops complaining. 她整天抱怨，我一天也不能忍受了。

bear 和 stand 主要指对饥寒、疼痛、不幸、损失、困难等的忍受和承受；endure 主要指对重大灾祸和困难的长时间忍受；tolerate 主要指容忍和自己的愿望相反的事；put up with 指某些不愉快的或有轻微伤害的事情。

sustain 遭受，经受
指受到损害、创伤或金钱方面的损失。
Two soldiers from his squad sustained serious injuries.
他队中的两名士兵受了重伤。

15. 假的，人造的 artificial, fake, false, synthetic, virtual

artificial 人工的、人造的
artificial flowers 假花
He was given an artificial heart. 他得到了一颗人造心脏。

synthetic 合成，人造的
synthetic fabrics 合成纤维织物

fake 伪造的，冒充的，用以骗人的
a fake passport 假护照
美国前总统特朗普说媒体报道"假新闻"，用的就是"fake news"。

false 假的，人造的（尤用于牙齿、睫毛和胡须）
false teeth 假牙；a false beard 假胡子

virtual 虚拟的
a virtual tour of the garden 虚拟花园之旅

16. 电报 telegraph, telegram
telegraph 电报
不可数名词，强调电报的通信方式或电报业务。
These islands are connected by telegraph.
这些岛屿用电报联系。
The telegraph between the two regions has been cut.
这两个地区之间的电报业务已经中断。

telegram 电报，电文

指通过电报系统发出的信息，强调具体的一份份电报。
This telegram must be sent at once.
这封电报必须立即发出。
He received an urgent telegram from his father.
他收到了他父亲的一封加急电报。

17. 翻译 translate, interpret

translate 翻译
主要指笔译，主语通常是人，也可以指某种翻译软件。
Are you going to translate the novel?
你打算翻译这部小说吗？
These poems don't translate easily.
这些诗不好翻译。

Interpret 翻译
主要指口译，包括交替传译和同声传译。
He only spoke German so someone had to interpret for him.
他只会说德语，所以得有人给他翻译。

18. 保证 assure, guarantee, promise, swear

assure 向…保证，使确信
指用言语承诺某事一定会发生或一定是真实的，以消除他人的疑虑或担心。
I can assure you that you'll have a good time here.
我可以向你保证，你在这里会很快乐的。
We assured the tourists of an enjoyable holiday.
我们使游客确信准能过一个愉快的假期。

guarantee 保证，担保
指以口头或书面形式作保证、担保、承诺，含若违背则予以补偿之意。
He gave me a guarantee that it would never happen again.
他向我保证这种事情绝不会再发生。
They are demanding certain guarantees before they sign the treaty. 他们要求得到某些保证后才签署条约。

promise 保证，答应
指保证一定会做某事或提供某物，或某事一定会发生，侧重于自己的主观意向，用言语使人感到放心。
He promised to return the money to me. 他保证把钱还给我。
He promised her that he would marry her. 他保证要娶她。

swear 起誓保证；发誓，保证
指以发誓的形式作出保证，或强调自己所说的是真话。
I never touched his wallet, I swear!
我绝没有碰过他的钱包，我发誓！
He swore never to gamble again.
他发誓再也不赌博了。

19. 分发 allocate, allot, distribute

allocate 分配，配给
指（为特定用途而）把…拨给，把…拨出；把（物资、资金）划归。
Two million dollars was allocated for disaster relief.
已经拨出200万美元用于救灾。

allot 分配；分给
尤指将特定的时间、金钱、空间等分给某人或某事，可后接双宾语。
You should allot 3 hours a day for revision.
你应该每天抽出3个小时复习。
Everyone who works for the corporation has been allotted 50 shares. 该公司的每位员工分到50股股票。

distribute 分配，散布；散发，分发

将某物分成若干部分后分发给若干人。

Food and water have been distributed among the refugees.

已经向难民分发了食物和水。

Do you know the man distributing leaflets to passers-by?

你认识那名向路人派发传单的男子吗？

20. 聚集；收集 collect, gather

指人聚集时，gather侧重于围绕某个中心而聚集；而collect指人在某一处集中或逐渐聚集成群。

The boys and girls gathered for a picnic.

男生和女生集合起来去野餐。

A crowd was starting to collect around the spot of the accident.

人群开始聚集在事故现场。

collect和gather均可指收集资料、情报或证据。将分散在附近的东西、财物或文件收拢用gather；从不同的人或分散的地方收集样品用collect。

to collect/gather data/evidence/information

收集数据/证据/信息

I waited while he gathered up his papers.

他整理文件时我就在一旁等待。

Detectives have spent months gathering evidence.

侦探花了数月时间搜集证据。

We've been collecting data from various sources.

我们一直从各种渠道收集资料。

Two young girls were collecting firewood.

两个小女孩正在拾柴火。

21. 减少 reduce, decrease

reduce 和 decrease 均可以表示事物在数量、强度和程度方面变小，都可以作为及物和不及物动词来使用。但当一个句子中有宾语的时候，我们则更多地使用 reduce，而句子中没有宾语的时候，则使用 decrease。也可以说，reduce 强调主观人为的减少，decrease强调客观上的减少。

Therefore we've had to reduce our spending.

因此，我们不得不减少开支。

Our company's profits decreased in 2018.

我们公司的利润2018年下降了。

另一个区别是，reduce 可以描述人或事陷入了更差、更糟糕的境地。

She was reduced to a nervous wreck after the accident.

那场意外之后，她陷入了精神紧张不安的状态。

22. 推迟，延期 delay, postpone, put off, defer, adjourn

delay、postpone 和 put off 都可以表示"推迟"，后面有动词时都必须跟动词作宾语，但是，delay 常表示带有不可控因素，而且略有"不情愿"的感觉，而 postpone 则是主动去推迟。put off 和 postpone 的意思和用法更加相似，但它是一个口语表达，经常出现在日常生活对话中。例如，在表达"我们决定把我们的假期推迟到下个月"时：

We have decided to **delay** our holiday until next month.

表示可能是因为碰到了问题，被迫推迟，比如，可能是突然被安排到国外工作，或者预订好的酒店出了问题等，不得不推迟。

We have decided to **postpone** our holiday until next month.

表示并不是因为有意外或者由不定因素导致而需要延期，可能就是"我"觉得下个月度假更好。

We have decided to **put off** our holiday until next month.

这样表达更口语化一些。

另外，delay 还可表示"耽误，耽搁"，而 postpone 则没有这个意思；delay 还可以用作名词，而 postpone 只能作动词。

I was delayed by heavy traffic this morning.

今天早上，因为交通堵塞，我迟到了。

There's been a delay in the school's production of *Beauty and the Beast*. 学校组织的话剧《美女和野兽》演出时间延期了。

defer 推迟，延期

较正式用词，多指故意拖延。

Hand in your proposal as soon as possible—you have deferred too long.

尽快提交你的议案——你拖延得太久了。

adjourn 休（会），休（庭），延期

指会议休会、法庭休庭或审判延期。

The meeting is adjourned for an unknown reason.

会议莫名其妙地休会了。

It was almost 10 o'clock when the court adjourned.

法庭休庭的时候差不多已经10点了。

23. 表格 diagram, chart, table, graph, graphic

table 一般指类似 excel 中的表格。一张 table 中所包含的事项和数据是以若干纵列、若干横行的样式呈现的。

The teacher created a table that shows the final marks of all the students in the class.

老师做了一张显示这个班级所有学生期末分数的表格。

diagram 简易示意图。通常用来描述"某个过程或结构"。比如，注明机器运转过程的原理图，建筑或机器等实际事物的平面图、分解示意图等。

Follow the instructions in the diagram, and you will learn how to operate the machine correctly.

按照这张原理图上的用法说明操作，你就会正确地使用这台机器了。

chart 和 **graph** 这两个词都可以泛指用直线或曲线显示信息和数据的图表、示意图，所以在使用的时候大家会把它们当成同义词替换使用。

但是，**graph** 多用来强调两个变量的数值在变化中所体现的数学关系，或用于对比，饼图、条形图、曲线图都可以叫做 graph。一张 graph 上可能会出现 x 轴和 y 轴，但 graph 的涵义更为抽象，主要用于说明各种事物之间存在的函数关系。

chart 主要与坐标有关，在海事上都用这个。而如果拿一个画板，简单地用坐标图描述营收变化与成本或时间的关系等，一般也用 chart。另外，chart 还可以指"天文图、气象图、航海图"。

The crew used a naval chart to navigate their way across the sea. 船员们凭借航海图在海上确定航向。

graphic 图形，图片。词义较广，指用于出版、工业或计算机领域等目的而设计出的pictures、drawings等。

总而言之，在日常生活中，chart 是相对简单的说法，graph 更专业些，diagram 侧重于具体事物，table 侧重于数据表格，graphic 侧重于图形图片。

24. 解雇 dismiss, fire, lay off, remove, sack

dismiss 开除，解雇

指正式解除某人的职务，常可与fire、sack换用。

Employees can be dismissed/fired/sacked for playing computer games at work.

员工上班时间玩电脑游戏会遭到解雇。

fire [口] 解雇，开除

指强行解除某人的职务，常可与 sack 换用。

He has just been fired/sacked for being late.
他刚刚因为迟到被解雇。

lay off 解雇，下岗

指因为没有工作可做而解雇员工。

Millions of workers were laid off during the economic crisis.
经济危机期间，数百万工人被解雇。

remove 开除，罢免

指免除某人的职务，尤指罢免身居要职者。

The committee removed the corrupt official.
委员会罢免了那名腐败的官员。

Congress has the right to remove the President from office.
国会有权罢黜总统。

sack 开除，解雇

指解除某人的职务，非正式用语。

He was sacked from the job, although he did nothing wrong.
他没做错事却被解雇了。

25. 发现；查明 find out, find, discover

find out, find, discover 都可以用于描述获知事实情况：

We found out that she was wrong. 我们发现她错了。
The young child finds that noise attracts attention.
小孩子发现吵闹能吸引注意力。
He discovered the whole school knew about it.
他发现整个学校都知道这件事了。

discover 比 **find** 稍正式，并常用于谈论科学研究和正式的调查。例如，可以用于表示发现治疗某种疾病的方法，还可以指偶然间的发现。

This well-known flower was discovered in 1903.
这种著名的花是1903年发现的。

找不到某物用 cannot find somthing, dicover和 find out 则无此用法。如：

I'm lost — I can't find the bridge.
我迷路了——我找不到那座桥了。

find out 可以指弄清很容易就发现的事实, 但 discover 和 find 则无此用法。

I found out the train times. 我查到了列车时刻表。

26. 疾病 illness, disease, disorder, infection, condition, bug, sickness

illness和**sickness** 常可通用，它们主要用于表示生病的时间或因病(disease)导致的不健康状态等。

He can't come because of illness. 他因病不能来。
He died after a long illness. 他死之前病了很久。

sickness最常用于与工作和保险有关的语境中，通常与pay、leave、absence和insurance等词连用。

I recommend you get insurance against sickness and unemployment. 我建议你办个疾病和失业保险。

Disease 疾病

通常指具体的"疾病"(可数)。

Most diseases could be wiped out. 多数疾病是可以消灭的。
有时指疾病的总称（不可数），即通称的"疾病"。
Rats spread disease. 老鼠传播疾病。
Cleanliness helps prevent disease. 清洁有助于预防疾病。

disease指较严重的身体疾病，尤其影响身体器官的疾病。
illness指重病或小病均可，也可指精神上的疾病。
~~heart/kidney/liver illness~~
~~mental disease~~
另，disease不指患病期：
~~She died after a long disease.~~

disorder 失调，紊乱

a mental disorder 精神障碍

infection 指由细菌或病毒引起的身体某部位的感染或传染疾病。

a throat infection 喉部感染

condition 指因不可治愈而长期患有的疾病。

a heart condition 心脏病

bug 本义指"小虫""细菌"，作"疾病"讲时指轻微的传染病、小病。

a flu bug 流感

27. 脸红 blush, flush

blush 脸红

指因内心害羞、惭愧、窘困等而脸红。

She blushed with shame. 她羞愧得脸都红了。
He blushed at the praise. 他听到表扬脸突然红了。

flush 脸红

指因喜悦、生气、尴尬、发烧等而脸红。

The girl flushed with fever. 那个女孩因发烧而脸通红。
He flushed with excitement. 他兴奋得脸都红了。
She flushed with anger. 她气得涨红了脸。
Sam felt her cheeks flush red.
萨姆感觉她脸颊涨得通红。

28. 要塞，堡垒 castle, fort, fortress

castle 城堡
指古代为了防御敌人进攻而修建的庞大而坚固的建筑物。
Visitors to the castle are asked not to take photographs.
来城堡参观者不得拍照。

fort 要塞，堡垒
指在重要之地修建的建筑物或建筑群，常围有高墙，用于屯兵守卫。
There are many forts on the coastline. 海岸线上有许多要塞。

fortress 要塞，堡垒
指比 fort 大的堡垒，用于防御。
Our soldiers took over the fortress.
我们的士兵占领了那个要塞。

29. 混乱 disorder, chaos, confusion, mess

disorder 混乱，杂乱
指杂乱无章、混乱无序的状态。
The books on the desk are in disorder. 桌子上的书很凌乱。
The whole plan was thrown into disorder.
整个计划被搞得乱七八糟。

chaos 混乱
语气极强，指绝对的、令人无能为力或感到绝望的混乱状态。
The seaside towns were in a state of **chaos** after the hurricane had struck them.
飓风袭击后，这些海边城镇处于一片混乱状态。
After the failure of electricity supplies, the city was

completely **in chaos**.
电力供应中断后，这个城市完全陷于混乱之中。

mess 混乱，杂乱
普通用词，指不整齐或无秩序的状态。也可指思想、工作、生活等的秩序被打乱的状态。mess 前常用不定冠词"a"。in a mess 是固定短语。
The house is a complete mess after the party.
聚会之后房子里一片狼藉。
The kitchen was left in an awful mess.
厨房被弄得凌乱不堪。
My life is a mess. 我的生活一团糟。

confusion 混乱
从构词上来讲，con-表示"一起"，-fuse表示"流"，confuse "混淆"，指不同的东西流到一起分辨不开。
There was a confusion of cries and yells in the village as the enemy started to attack.
敌人开始进攻时，村子里哭喊声交织在一起，乱作一团。

30. 巨大的 huge, enormous, giant, gigantic, immense, vast

huge 巨大的，庞大的
含义很广，指体积、数量、程度方面极大的，但通常不用于重量。
The road was blocked by a huge rock.
道路被一块巨石堵住了。
The play was a huge success.
该剧获得巨大成功。

enormous 巨大的，庞大的
指尺寸或数量巨大的。
She has bought an enormous house.
她买了一幢大房子。
He saved up an enormous amount of money for his daughter.
他为女儿存了一大笔钱。

giant 巨大的，庞大的
只作定语，指比其他同类事物大的。（n. 巨人；巨兽）
They found a giant tortoise. 他们发现了一只巨龟。
He is a manager of a giant electronics company.
他是一家特大型电子公司的经理。

gigantic 巨大的，庞大的
指规格、数量或程度巨大的，含超出常规或预想之意。
This is the most gigantic pizza I've ever seen.
这是我见过的最大披萨了。
The gigantic task of reconstruction awaits them.
重建的艰巨任务等着他们去完成。

immense 巨大的，广大的，无限的
指体积、数量或程度等超过一般标准的。
It's almost impossible to find him in the immense ocean.
在无边无际的海洋中要找到他几乎是不可能的。
The value of the helicopter is immense. It can hardly be measured. 这架直升机的价值是巨大的，很难估量。

vast 巨大的，广阔的，浩瀚的
多指空间、面积、范围巨大的。
The vast plain stretches for 800 miles.
那片辽阔的平原绵延800英里。
The Pacific Ocean is a vast expanse of water.
太平洋是一片浩瀚的水域。

31. 挑选 choose, elect, select, pick, opt

elect 选举
指按照一定的规章或法律，用投票等方式进行的认真而慎重的选择。
Americans elect a president every four years.
美国人每四年选一次总统。

Choose、select 和 **pick** 表示一般意义的"选择"时，若不严格区分，三者可换用。如：
He chose/ picked/ selected a dictionary for his son.
他为他儿子买了本字典。

但严格说来，三者仍有差别：**choose**是一般性用语，指按照个人的认识或判断来进行选择；**pick** 与 **choose** 的用法很接近，但**pick**适于口语用法，它既可以表示随意的选择，也可以表示仔细的、慎重的选择；而 **select** 则指在广泛的范围内，经过慎重考虑，认真仔细选择，并往往有选出好的或适合的，去掉差的或不适合的，其淘汰意味较浓。如：
Choose/ Pick me a good one, please. 请给我选一个好的。
We must select some for seeds. 我们必须选一些作种子。

另外，在两者中选择或后跟不定式时通常用choose。
He chose death before dishonour. 他宁死不屈。
I chose not to go with them. 我决定不同他们一起去。

opt 选择
指选择是否采取某种行动。
After a lot of thought, I opted against buying a motorbike.
经过反复考虑，我决定不买摩托车。

32. 结果 effect, outcome, consequence, result, aftermath

effect 影响；结果
指对人/事产生的效应、影响、结果。
Her criticisms had the effect of discouraging him completely.
她的批评使他完全丧失了信心。

result （直接的）结果
常指引起的直接后果，常用于事情过去之后的结果。
She died as a result of her injuries. 她由于受伤而死亡。
This book is the result of 25 years of research.
这本书是25年研究的结晶。

outcome （某一行动及过程的）结果
较常指某一过程完结时的结果，原因和结果之间的关系已不太明显，常用于谈及行动或过程可能会产生的结果。
We are waiting to hear the final outcome of the negotiations.
我们在等待谈判的最终结果。
We are confident of a successful outcome.
我们相信会有圆满的结果。

consequence （不好的）后果
consequence最常用以指可能产生的负面结果，常与disastrous（灾难性的）、fatal（致命的）、harmful、negative、serious、tragic、unfortunate等词连用。即使没有形容词修饰，consequence也常含负面结果之意。
This decision could have serious consequences for the industry.
这项决定可能会对该行业产生严重后果。

aftermath 后果，余殃
强调灾难（如风暴、地震、战争等）留下的后果。
Life became even harder in the aftermath of the war.
战争过后生活变得更加艰难。
Measures were taken to prevent the disease in the aftermath of the earthquake. 已采取措施预防地震后引发疫病。

33. 影响 effect, affect, influence

effect 影响，结果

除作名词外，还可作动词，罕见且正式，意为"实现，产生"。

The French Revolution effected great changes in the law.
法国大革命给法律带来了很大的变化。

affect 影响

affect是effect的动词形式，affect sth = have an effect on sb/sth。

Does television affect children's behaviour?
电视对孩子的行为有影响吗？

Does television have an effect on children's behaviour?
电视对孩子的行为有影响吗？

affect 通常由物作主语，多产生消极作用。

The food is for the areas affected by the flood.
食物是为受洪水影响的地区准备的。

Drugs affect health. 毒品影响健康。

influence 通常指潜移默化地起作用。

What influenced him to take up teaching?
是什么影响他去从事教学工作？

She can influence his decision.
她能影响他的决定。

34. 超出 exceed, surpass, excel

exceed 超出

指超越职权范围、法律规定等，或超出数量、程度、大小等。

Tom was exceeding the speed limit.
汤姆当时在超速行驶。

Working hours must not exceed 8 hours a day.
工作时间每天不得超过8小时。

surpass 优于，超过

指在技能、成就等方面超越同类。

He surpassed me in mathematics. 他数学比我强。

China will surpass Japan in economy.
中国将在经济上超过日本。

excel 优于，超过

通常指在成就、学识等方面胜过他人，不用进行时。其形容词是 excellent （优秀的）。

She excels in dancing. 她在舞蹈方面出类拔萃。

35. 偶遇；遭遇 encounter, meet with, run across, run into, come across

come across和**run across**可以换用，指偶然遇见某人，偶然发现某物。

I ran/came across him in the cafeteria. 我在食堂碰见他了。

She ran/came across an old diary while clearing out her drawer.
她在清理抽屉的时候发现了一本旧日记本。

run into sb指偶然遇见某人，**run into sth**指遭遇不好的事情。**run into**还可表示"撞上"。

His company ran into financial difficulties.
他的公司陷入了经济困境。

Guess who I ran into this morning!
猜猜今天早上我碰见了谁！

I had to brake suddenly, and the car behind ran into me.
我不得不突然刹车，后面的车撞到了我。

encounter 尤指遇到困难、问题或他人的反对，也指偶遇某人。

The new manager encountered some difficulties in his first week. 新来的经理在第一周遇到了一些困难。

When did you first encounter him?
你第一次遇到他是在什么时候？

meet sb 可以指偶然遇到，也可以指通过安排遇到。

[VN] Guess who I met in town today.
猜我在城里碰见什么人了。

[VN] We're meeting them outside the theatre at 7.
我们7点钟在剧院外面和他们会合。

meet with sb 一般指正式会面。

They are meeting with Russian leader to try to end the crisis.
他们正在与俄罗斯领导人会面，试图结束这场危机。

meet sth和**meet with sth**都可指遭遇不愉快的事情。

Others have met similar problems.
其他人遇到过同样的问题。

She met with an accident yesterday. 她昨天遇到一起事故。

Now I meet with fewer difficulties in my work.
现在我工作中困难少些了。

meet 和 **meet with** 后面都可以表示遇到某种结果或反应，可以是好的也可以是坏的。

They finally came to a decision that has met (with) general approval. 他们最终做出了一项得到普遍认可的决定。

Her proposal met (with) resistance from the Left.
她的提议遭到了左翼的抵制。

总之，偶然遇到某人可以用come across, run across, run into, encounter, meet；遭遇到不愉快的事情可用 encounter, run into, meet, meet with；偶然发现某物可用 come across, run across。

36. 害怕 fright, fear, alarm, afraid

fear 的含义较 **fright** 广泛。对总是使人害怕的事物和对未来可能发生的事情感到担忧均可用 fear，但不能用 fright。

~~I have a fright of spiders.~~ 我害怕蜘蛛。

~~his fright of what might happen~~ 他对可能发生的事情的恐惧

fright 指对刚刚发生或正在发生的事情的反应。

She cried out in fright. 她吓得大声叫喊。

alarm 惊慌，恐慌

指对可能将要发生的不好的事情的恐慌。

The doctor said there was no cause for alarm.
医生说不必惊慌。

afraid 只能作形容词，指害怕、担心不幸的事可能发生。

There's nothing to be afraid of.
没有什么要害怕的。

Aren't you afraid (that) you'll fall?
你不怕会跌倒吗？

37. 惊吓 frighten, scare, alarm

frighten 使惊吓、使惊恐
常指突如其来地。

He brought out a gun and frightened them off.
他掏出一把枪，把他们吓跑了。

scare 指使害怕、使恐惧

They managed to scare the bears away.
他们设法把那些熊吓跑了。

frighten和scare均为通用词，意思非常相似，用任何一个均可，scare较frighten稍非正式。

Stop it! You're frightening/scaring me!

停下！你吓了我一跳！

alarm 使害怕，使担心

它的主语通常为事物、事件或形势而非人，用于形容不好的事情或危险将要发生时的心情，多为忧虑而非真的害怕。

It alarms me that nobody takes this problem seriously.
谁都不认真对待这个问题，这使我非常担心。

They should not be too alarmed by the press reports.
对于新闻报道他们不应过于担心。

38. 公司 company, corporation, firm

company 公司
多指生产、销售产品或服务的公司。

He works for a bus company.
他在一家公共汽车公司工作。

This computer company was formed in 2004.
这家计算机公司成立于2004年。

corporation （大）公司，企业集团
多指综合型大公司，也指在其他地区或国家拥有分公司的大集团。

It takes brains to run a multinational corporation.
管理跨国公司需要有头脑。

firm 公司，商行，事务所
尤指小型公司或商行。

He has set up an electronics firm of his own.
他自己开了一家电子公司。

Kim is with a firm of accountants in Birmingham.
金在伯明翰的一家会计师事务所工作。

39. 公司（缩写）Inc., Corp., Ltd. 与 Co., Ltd.

Inc. 是incorporated的缩写，用于公司名称后，表示"组成公司的，股份有限的"。如：
Bishop Computer Services, Inc.

Co., Ltd. 是英文 Company Limited 的简写，意思是"有限责任公司"。"Co"后面的"."是英文中表示词语短缩省略的符号，所以"Ltd"的后面也应该有一个"."。而"Co." 后面的","则是用来区分前后两个词的分离号。

Corp., Ltd 是Corporation Limited 的简写，意思是"股份有限公司"。

现在的公司基本上都是有限公司，指公司以其全部资产对公司的债务承担责任。而个体企业负债时，在企业资产抵完后，还需要用企业主个人的资产去承担。

40. 交换 interchange, exchange, switch, trade

interchange 侧重指交流思想、信息或交换位置等。
As a manager, he often interchanges ideas with his workers.
作为经理，他经常与员工交换意见。

The thief interchanged the diamonds with some pieces of glass.
小偷用几片玻璃替换了钻石。

exchange 通常指互相交换同类东西。
Mary exchanged coats with Lucy.
玛丽与露西交换了外套。

Both sides exchanged their opinions on the issue at the meeting.
在会上，双方就此问题交换了意见。

switch 多用于口语，常可与 exchange 换用，但侧重于调换之意。
Our glasses have been switched/exchanged——this is mine.

咱俩的玻璃杯对调了——这个是我的。
switch更多的时候表示"切换"。
He switched automatically into interview mode.
他自动切换到访谈模式。

Then he switched sides and turned against his former allies.
然后他转而反对他的前盟友。

trade 尤指买卖货物，也可表示交换物品。
She traded her books for his CDs. 她用书换他的光盘。

41. 错误 mistake, error

mistake和error都可指用词或数字上的错误（口误、笔误），error为mistake的正式用语。

It's a common mistake among learners of English.
这是学英语的人常犯的错误。

I think you have made an error in calculating the total.
我想你在计算总数时出了差错。

42. 反对 oppose, object, protest

oppose 反对，阻碍
不赞同某一政策、计划等，含抵制或阻挠之意，多指反对一些较重大的事，隐含其正当性。

The committee opposed changing the regulations.
委员会反对改变规则。

There was a major campaign to oppose the building of a nuclear reactor.
有一项重大的运动反对建造核反应堆。

The King killed anyone who opposed him.
这个国王处了任何反对他的人。

object 反对，不赞成
指不喜欢或不赞同某事，语气比oppose弱。

If nobody objects, we'll postpone the meeting till next week.
如果没有人反对，我们就把会议推迟到下周。

I object to paying that much for milk.
我反对为牛奶付那么多钱。

小贴士 object是不及物动词，反对某事常用object to sth, object to doing sth.
在表示"不反对…"时，习惯上用 have no objection to，而不用 do not object to。
I have no objection to your plan.
我不反对你的计划。

protest ~ (about/against/at sth) 抗议
通常指人们聚集在一起，以言语、行为等公开表示不满或异议，也可指个人不认同某事或对某事心有不满。

Students took to the streets to protest against the decision.
学生们走上街头，抗议这项决定。

43. 目标，目的 object, purpose, aim, goal, target, objective

object 目的
指某一计划、行为或活动的目的，通常用单数。

The parents first wanted to know what the object of this game was. 家长们首先想知道这项游戏的目的是什么。

purpose 目的
普通用词，指经过考虑而要做某事的意图，通常用单数。

He came to New York with the purpose of doing business.
他来纽约是为了做生意。

aim 目标，目的
强调希望做成某事的具体意图，多指短期目标。

The main aim of this course is to improve your oral English.
这一课程的主要目标是提高你的口语。

The campaign with the aim of helping the victims of crime has received worldwide attention.
这场旨在帮助罪案受害者的运动在全球范围内得到了关注。

goal 目标，目的

多指想要通过一段时间的努力而在未来实现某事的意图。
Did they reach their goal of expanding the company's market share? 他们实现扩大公司市场份额的目标了吗？

target 目标

多用于数量、时间、财务等方面，表示想要达到的具体目标。
financial targets 财务指标

objective 目标

尤用于商业或政治方面，侧重指人所想要实现的目标。
He has to achieve certain objectives before the end of his presidency. 他在总统任期结束之前必须实现某些目标。

44. 残疾的 disabled, handicapped

disabled 是最广为接受的用语，指残疾人或伤残人。
handicapped 稍有些过时，现在许多人认为该词含冒犯意。现在人们喜欢用 disability 而非 handicap。disabled people 比 the disabled 更为人所接受，原因是听起来较人性化。

45. 有能力的；能够的 able, capable, competent

able 指某人聪明能干，有多才多艺的概括涵义；**capable** 仅指具有应付某一特指工作要求的能力。
She is an able teacher. 她是个能干的教师。
The doctor seems very capable. 医生似乎很能干。
He is capable of running a mile in a minute.
他能在一分钟内跑完一英里。
The workers are perfectly capable of running the organization themselves. 工人们完全有能力自己管理这个组织。

capable 除表示"有能力的"外，还可用以表示"有可能的"涵义，able 则没有这个用法。
The situation is capable of improvement.
此情况有可能好转。
She's capable of becoming a successful musician.
她能够成为一位成功的音乐家。
He is capable of anything. 他什么事都能干。

able 的反义词是 unable；capable 的反义词是 incapable。另一点值得注意的是，able 的名词是 ability，词义是"能力"（the power to do）；capable 的名词是 capability 或 capacity，capability 词义是"具有从事某事的能力"，capacity 词义是"容纳能力"或"受容力"。

competent 意为"胜任的，有能力的"，指受过专业训练的，但不是指超群的能力。
A doctor should be competent to treat many diseases.
医生应该能治多种疾病。

46. 能 力 capacity, capability, competence, ability

ability 是指人（或其他智慧型生命体）运用脑力或体力完成特定任务的能力（侧重于能还是不能）。这种能力是与生俱来的。

capability 是指实现特定目标或任务所必须具备的技能或资质（不局限于人，更侧重能把事情做好或达到目的，多数情况下指机器、工具、武器等"非人"力量所具备的能力）。也就是说它表示的意思更接近于汉语中的"实力"（因为储备而构成的"克敌制胜"的能力），因为"实力"是摆在那里，故能把事情做成功，如军事实力、核打击能力、排污能力、抗压能力，等等。这种"实力"是可以通过努力来提高的。

capacity 侧重容纳能力或吞吐能力。如某个广场能容纳多少人，某个港口和车站能容纳多大的吞吐量，某个工厂的日产能有多大，等等。

competence 是指按质按量完成既定任务或交付产品的能力，也就是"胜任工作"的能力，它更强调"胜任"而不是"有没有能力"。

I have the ability to run. 我有跑步的能力。
（"跑步"是与生俱来的能力）
I have the capacity to run a 100 m race in 18 seconds.
我有能力在 18 秒内跑完 100 米赛跑。
（自己目前的最大能力也许就是这样了）
I have the capability to improve my capacity through training to 15 seconds.
我有通过训练把我的最好成绩提高到 15 秒这个能力。
（这种"实力"是可以提高的。）
As a runner I am incompetent as I cannot compete successfully.
作为一名运动员，我不能胜任，因为我无法成功竞争。
（incompetent 不能胜任）

47. 事件 accident, incident, event, occurrence

accident 事故；意外事件

指导致某人受伤或某物受损的事故，也可指并非有意造成的意外事件。
A traffic accident occurred this morning.
今天早上发生了一起交通事故。
I'm sorry about knocking over your coffee cup—it was an accident. 我很抱歉打翻了你的咖啡杯——这是个意外。

incident 可指不寻常、不愉快的小事件，也可指严重的、重要的或暴力的事件。

Apart from the incident in Las Vegas our vacation was completely trouble-free.
除了拉斯维加斯的那次事故外，我们的假期完全没有麻烦。
The fans were well behaved, and the game was played without incident. 球迷们表现得很好，比赛进行得很顺利。

event 尤指重要的事件或大事，也常指体育赛事。
The discovery of X-rays was a big event in the history of physics. X射线的发现是物理学史上的重大事件。
Getting married was one of the major events in his life.
结婚是他一生中的大事之一。
The 800 meters is the fourth event of the afternoon.
800米赛是下午的第四项比赛。

occurrence 事件

occur本身有"出现"的意思，所以以occurrence比较中性，指生活中发生的一般的或偶然的事件。
Extreme weather is a rare occurrence in that country.
那个国家不常出现极端天气。

48. 组成部分 element, component, ingredient

element 基本部分，要素

尤指一整套系统、计划、作品等中最基本或最重要的部分或特征。
They are advanced elements in the organization.
他们是该组织中的先进分子。
Speed is an important element of the athletic event.
速度是这一体育项目的要素。

component 组成部分，成分
指一个整体的组成部分，多用于机器、机械系统等。
There are many components to the machine.
这台机器有许多部件。
This system consists of various components.
该系统由各种部件组成。

ingredient 成分，原料
指混合物的成分，尤指烹饪原料。
This skin cream contains only natural ingredients.
这种护肤霜只含天然成分。
Flour and sugar are the most important ingredients in baking bread. 面粉和糖是烤面包最重要的原料。

49. 照料 take care of, look after, care for

照看小孩、老人、病人或物品可用 **take care of** 也可用 **look after**，英国英语尤用 look after。
We've asked my mother to take care of/look after the kids while we're away.
我们已请我母亲在我们外出时照看孩子。
You can borrow my camera if you promise to take care of/look after it.
只要你答应把我的相机保管好就可以借去用。

在较正式用语中，照看或照顾某人亦可用 care for。
She does some voluntary work, caring for the elderly.
她干一些照顾老人的义务工作。

但 care for 更常用于表示喜欢：
I don't really care for spicy food.
我其实不喜欢吃辛辣食物。

50. 孤独的；独自的 lone, alone, lonely, lonesome, solitary

lone 孤零零的，独自的
可用于修饰人或事物，只作定语。
He lives a lone life in the country.
他孤身一人在乡下生活。
A lone gull flew across the sky.
一只孤单的海鸥从天空飞过。

alone 单独的；独自地
作形容词时，指独自一人的，只作表语。
He feels lonely when he is alone.
他一个人的时候，就感到孤独。
I don't like going out alone at night.
我不喜欢夜晚单独外出。

lonely 孤独的，寂寞的；荒凉的
指感到寂寞的或在孤单中度过的；也指地方人迹罕至的，此时，只作定语。
He has so few friends that his life is very lonely.
他的朋友很少，因此生活很孤单。
We found a lonely road.
我们发现了一条偏僻的道路。

lonesome [美]孤寂的；荒凉的
与 lonely 基本同义，常可换用。
She felt lonesome/lonely without children.
没有孩子，她一个人感到很寂寞。
It is a lonesome/lonely spot near the canyon.
那是靠近峡谷的一个人烟稀少的地方。

solitary 独自的，孤单的；喜欢独处的
指单独做某事的或无其他人、事物等相伴的；形容人、动物等时可指生性孤僻的，通常作定语。

She led a solitary life. 她过着独居生活。
Pandas are solitary creatures. 熊猫是喜欢独处的动物。

51. 雾 fog, mist, smog, haze

haze 霾，薄雾；烟雾
指由烟、灰尘或轻微水蒸气引起的雾气，通常在天气炎热时出现。
There is haze today because the wind has carried smoke from the steel plant.
风把钢铁厂的烟吹过来了，所有今天有雾霾。

fog 雾
主要指近地面空气冷却使水汽凝结而形成的雾，能见度较低。
You can lose your way in thick fog. 在大雾中你会迷路的。

mist 雾霭，薄雾
指由小水滴构成的轻雾，即雾霭。
The hills were covered in mist. 群山笼罩在雾霭中。

smog 烟雾
该词由 smoke 和 fog 合成，通常指工业区里烟和雾的混合物，多见于重工业城市。
Black smog reduced visibility to about thirty yards.
黑色烟雾使能见度降到大约 30 码。

52. 宽的 wide, broad

形容道路、河流、峡谷等宽时，broad 常可与 wide 换用，但更强调面积的宽广；形容肩、背、胸等宽时，都应用 broad，而不用 wide。
The river is 30 meters broad/wide. 这条河有 30 米宽。
The broad/wide avenue has 6 traffic lanes.
那条宽阔的大街有 6 条车道。
The Pacific Ocean is very broad/wide. 太平洋非常宽阔。
He was of medium height, but had very broad shoulders.
他中等身材，但肩膀很宽。

wide 和 broad 均可修饰 range；但 variety 常用 wide 修饰。
a wide/broad range of products 各种各样的产品
a wide variety of products 琳琅满目的商品

另外，broad 还可表示"大概、粗略、不详细"，wide 无此义。
All of us are in broad agreement on this matter.
我们大家就此事基本达成一致意见。

53. 争辩 argue, debate, dispute

argue 争辩；争论
指为自己或自己一方的看法或立场辩护，侧重说理、论证和说服。
He argued that she should not go. 他争辩说她不该去。
She argued against delaying the meeting.
她据理反对推迟开会。

debate 讨论；辩论
指持不同意见的双方或多方进行正式或公开的论辩，旨在得出结论或找出解决办法。
I debated the plan with Mr Green.
我与格林先生就该项计划展开辩论。
The UN members were debating the situation in the Middle East. 联合国成员正在就中东局势展开辩论。

dispute 争辩；争执
较正式用语，侧重指激烈地争辩，常隐含"各持己见"或"争论不休"的意味，尤指就某物的归属问题进行争辩。
The union is in dispute with management over working hours.

工会与资方在工时问题上发生纠纷。

54. 要求 demand, require, insist, expect

demand 强烈要求，坚决要求
She demanded an immediate explanation.
她要求立即作出解释。

require 要求
指要求做（某事）、达到（某水平），尤指根据法规或规定。
All candidates will be required to take a short test.
所有候选者都要参加一个小测验。

expect 期望；要求
指尤因义务或责任而要求某人做某事。
Sex education is also expected to help check the spread of AIDS. 人们还希望性教育有助于控制艾滋病的蔓延。

insist 坚持要求
I didn't want to go but he insisted.
我并不想去，但他非要我去。

55. 中心，中间 center, core, middle, midst

center 中心；集中点
指空间、地域或物体的中心点，也可指学术、商业等活动的中心。
There is a huge oak table in the center of the meeting room.
会议室中央有一张巨大的橡木桌子。
Beijing is the political and cultural center of China.
北京是中国的政治和文化中心。

core 核心
指某物体的中心部分或某事物最重要的部分。
Remove the cores, and thinly slice the apples.
去除果核，把苹果切成薄片。
The core of their appeal is freedom of speech.
他们呼求的核心是言论自由。
We should respect each other's core interests and major concerns.
我们要尊重彼此的核心利益和重大关切。

middle 中间，中央，中部
指空间、时间或事件的中间部分。
He came back home in the middle of the night.
他半夜才回家。

midst 中间
较正式用语，指位于某地的中部或者处于一群人、一堆物品中间，也可指在某事的进行过程中。
We found him in the midst of a group of his usual friends.
我们在他的一群老朋友中找到了他。
In the midst of my work I snatched an hour's rest.
我在工作的间隙休息了一个钟头。

56. 障碍 obstacle, barrier, obstruction, bar

obstacle 障碍（物）
指在达到目的或前行的过程中必须消除或绕过的障碍（物），可以是具体的或抽象的东西。
Terrorism is an obstacle to peace. 恐怖主义是和平的障碍。
His car hit an obstacle yesterday in the competition.
昨天他的车在比赛中撞上了障碍物。

barrier 障碍，壁垒
多指产生阻碍或限制作用的政策、法律、问题等。
The removal of trade barriers means a lot to that country.
贸易壁垒的消除对那个国家而言意义重大。

obstruction 障碍物，阻塞物
There may be an obstruction in the drainpipe.
排水管里可能有阻塞物。
Remove the vehicle that is causing the obstruction.
把造成阻塞的车辆挪走。

bar 障碍；阻碍；妨碍
bar 作名词有"条，棒"之意，作动词时可指用木条、铁条等闩门，由此义可以引申为"阻拦，阻挡"。名词意思为"障碍，阻碍"，指做某事的障碍，通常指抽象之物。
They have decided to set a bar to competition.
他们已决定要设置障碍以阻止竞争。
At that time being a woman was a bar to promotion in this profession.
那时在这一职业中，身为女性便是晋升的障碍。

57. 边界 border, boundary, frontier

border 边界；边境
多指靠近两国或两地区分界线的区域。
Two years later, he was sent to the border between China and Myanmar. 两年以后，他被派到了中缅边界。
a national park on the border between Kenya and Tanzania
位于肯尼亚和坦桑尼亚边界的国家公园

boundary 边境线；分界线
侧重指某区域最外的界线，常和领土有关，也指地图上正式标定的、双方认可的边界或较小行政单位间的界线。
They marked the boundaries of the basketball court.
他们标出了篮球场的边界。
The river forms the boundary between my land and his.
这条河构成了我这块地和他那块地之间的分界线。

frontier [英] 边界；边境
指两国接壤的前沿地区，多有军队驻防。
Soldiers guard the frontier against invasion.
士兵们守卫边境，以防止入侵。

58. 约束，束缚 bind, bound

bind 捆绑；联合；约束
She was bound to a chair. 她被捆在一把椅子上。

Organizations such as schools and clubs bind a community together. 诸如学校、俱乐部等机构使社区成为一个整体。

You are bound by the contract to pay before the end of the month. 按照合同规定，你必须在月底前付款。

bound 形成边界
The field was bounded on the left by a wood.
那片地左边依傍着一片树林。

59. 遗产；遗传 inheritance, heritage, legacy; heredity

heritage 遗产
指国家、社会等长期形成的历史、传统和特色，涵盖文化、语言、建筑等多个方面。
People are gradually realizing the importance of preserving national heritage.
人们正逐渐意识到保护民族遗产的重要性。

inheritance 继承物，遗产
指从逝者那里继承得到的钱财等，也指从上辈遗传下来的遗传特征。
He feared losing his inheritance to his elder brother.
他担心他继承的遗产会被哥哥夺走。
The title passes by inheritance to the eldest son.

这一头衔按世袭传给长子。
Physical characteristics are determined by genetic inheritance.
身体的特征取决于基因遗传。

inherit 继承；经遗传获得
She inherited a fortune from her father.
她从她父亲那里继承了一大笔财富。
He has inherited his mother's patience.
这种耐心是母亲遗传给他的。

legacy 遗产；遗留
指从逝者那里继承得到的钱财等，也指历史（如文化、传统、战争等）的遗留影响或问题。
He received a small legacy from his grandfather.
他从祖父那里继承了一小笔遗产。
Future generations will be left with a legacy of pollution and destruction. 留给子孙后代的将是环境的污染与破坏。

heredity 遗传（过程）；遗传特征
Heredity is not a factor in causing the cancer.
这种癌症和遗传无关。

hereditary 遗传性的；世袭的
a hereditary illness/disease/problem 遗传的疾病/问题
a hereditary title 世袭的头衔

60. 忽视，无视 ignore, neglect, disregard

neglect 忽视，忽略
指未能妥善照顾某人或给予某事足够的关注，也指未履行职责、义务等，多为无心疏忽。
She had neglected her child. 她疏于照管自己的孩子。
The police officer was accused of neglecting his duty.
那位警官被控渎职。

ignore 忽视，对…置之不理
指假装没有看见或听到某事，多为故意忽视。
She ignored the rude man. 她不理睬那个无礼的男人。
His suggestions were ignored. 他的建议无人理会。

disregard 无视，不重视
指忽视或轻视某事物。
Mary totally disregarded my advice.
玛丽完全不听我的建议。
The jury disregarded his last statement.
陪审团对他的最后陈述不予采信。

61. 文章，段落 paragraph, passage, article, essay, paper, novel, fiction, story

story 小说；故事
可以指虚构的故事、小说；也可以指对已发生事情的叙述。
adventure /detective /love, etc. stories
历险、侦探、爱情等小说
The police didn't believe her story.
警方不相信她对事情的描述。

paper 论文，研究报告
多指在学术刊物上发表或在学术会议上宣读的专题论文，也指高等学校的学期论文等。
The professor wrote a paper on psychology.
教授写了一篇心理学论文。

paragraph （文章的）自然段
The length of a paragraph depends on the information it conveys. 段落的长度取决于它所传达的信息。

passage （书中的）章节；段落
Read the following passage and answer the questions below.

阅读下面这段文章并回答后面的问题。

article （报刊上的）文章，论文，报道
多指在报刊上发表的非小说类文章，如新闻报道、学术论文等。
Did you read the article on the information revolution?
你读了有关信息革命的那篇文章没有？

essay 文章，论说文，小品文
（作为课程作业，学生写的）文章，短文
an essay on the causes of the First World War
一篇关于第一次世界大战起因的文章
（关于某一方面的）论文，杂文，散文
指任何一种非小说性的，篇幅不长、结构简练的文章，如论说文、报道、评论、讽刺性杂文等。
This essay needs polishing. 这篇文章需要润色。

novel n. 长篇小说
the novels of Jane Austen 简·奥斯汀的小说

fiction 虚构；虚构的事
The series will include both fiction and non-fiction.
本系列将包括小说和非小说。

62. 除…之外 except, except for, apart from, aside from, besides

这一组词都可作介词，表示"除…之外"。

besides 表示"除…之外（还有）"，相当于 in addition to，表达的是一种"相加"的关系。
What other sports do you like besides football?
除足球外你还喜欢哪些运动？

except 表示某事物不被包括在内，要从前面相同的事物中除去这一个，表达的是"排除"关系。
I like all sports except football.
我喜欢除足球外所有的运动。

except for 用于引出使某陈述不能完全成立的事物，但其排除的是构成前面事物的某一个方面。
The classrooms were silent, except for the scratching of pens on paper.
除了钢笔在纸上写字的沙沙声，教室里一片安静。
His novel is good except for a few spelling mistakes.
除去一些拼写错误，他的这本小说还是不错的。
except 一般不用于句首，在句首时通常用 **except for** 来表示 except 的意思。
Except for me, everyone is tired.
除了我之外，所有人都累了。

apart from 和 **aside from** 都可表示"除…之外"，既可表示"加"的关系，又可表示"排除"关系。也就是说，它们既可以替代 besides 又可替代 except。aside from 常用于美国英语。
What other sports do you like apart from football?
除足球外你还喜欢哪些运动？
I like all sports apart from football.
我喜欢除足球外所有的运动。

63. 职业，工作 career, profession, occupation, vocation

career 职业，事业
指从事的职业或希望毕生从事的事业。
His first concern while looking for a job is career prospects.
他找工作时首先关注的是职业前景。
She sacrificed a promising career to take care of her family.

她为了照顾家庭而牺牲了很有前途的事业。

profession 职业，行业

指需要经过专业培训的职业，尤指需要较高的受教育水平的职业。 the professions 统称需要较高教育水平的传统职业，如医生、律师等。

He hopes to enter the medical profession.
他希望能从事医务工作。

occupation 工作，职业

泛指任何一种工作，通常不用来谈论自己的职业，多用于表格填写或正式书面语中。（不要用 occupation 一词来谈论自己的职业，如可以说 I'm a teacher，但不能说 My occupation is a teacher。）

Please state your occupation in the box below.
请把你的职业写在下面的方框内。

Unskilled manual occupations usually don't earn much.
没有技术含量的体力工作通常挣钱不多。

vocation 工作，职业；使命

He believed that to be a writer was his true vocation.
他认为当作家是他真正的使命。

The girl missed her vocation—she should have been an actress. 那姑娘入错行了，她本该当演员。

64. 宣布 declare, announce, proclaim

declare 宣布，声明

指公开而郑重地宣布某事，通常用于正式场合。

The government has declared a state of emergency.
该政府已宣布进入紧急状态。

The US administration declared war on Japan in 1941.
美国政府于 1941 年对日本宣战。

announce 通知，宣告（消息，决定，计划等）

They haven't formally announced their engagement yet.
他们还没有正式宣布订婚。

Has our flight been announced yet?
广播通知了我们的航班没有？

用 declare 还是 announce？

declare 较常用于表明意见、看法；announce 较常用于说明事实。

~~The painting was announced to be a forgery（伪造）.~~
~~They haven't formally declared their engagement yet.~~

proclaim 宣布，宣告

指官方宣布重大政治事件，如国家独立、国王即位等。

The President proclaimed the independence of the Republic of South Sudan. 总统宣布南苏丹共和国独立。

The young princess was later proclaimed queen.
年轻的公主后来被宣布为女王。

65. 旅行 trip, journey, excursion, expedition, tour, travel, voyage

trip 旅行

普通用词，常指短途往返的旅行或不常为之的旅行，强调目的地或出行原因。

The manager has gone on a business trip. 经理出差去了。

His new job requires frequent trips to Shanghai.
他的新工作需要他经常去上海。

journey 旅行

主要指时间较长、距离较远的单程旅行，旅程长且艰难。

They are going on a journey to a strange country.
他们要去一个陌生的国家旅行。

tour 旅游，观光

指以游乐为目的、最后返回出发地的观光游览，途中走访数个不同地点，距离可长可短。

He has gone on a tour to Europe. 他去欧洲旅游了。

voyage 航行，旅行

指乘船或宇宙飞船的长途航行，尤用于书面语。

The ship will start its maiden voyage next Monday.
这艘船将于下周一开始它的处女航。

This is a voyage into space. 这是一次太空旅行。

travel 旅行

泛指旅行的行为而非某次具体的旅行。

This job involves a fair amount of travel.
这份工作需要经常出差。

He met many interesting people in his travels.
旅行中他遇到了许多有趣的人。

expedition 远征，探险；远征队，探险队

指有组织的、有特定目的的旅行，尤指去探明一个人们不很了解的地方。

the first expedition to the South Pole 首次去南极的探险

Three members of the Everest expedition were killed.
三名珠穆朗玛峰探险队员遇难。

excursion 远足，短途旅行

尤指有组织的集体远足或短途旅行。

We went on an all-day excursion to the island.
我们去岛上游览了一整天。

66. 绑架；劫持 abduct, kidnap, hijack

abduct 和 **kidnap** 都有"绑架，诱拐，劫持"之意，但 kidnap 多用于日常生活，而 abduct 常用于媒体报道中。

hijack 多指劫持交通工具，尤指飞机。

The plane was hijacked by two armed men on a flight from London to Rome.
飞机在从伦敦飞往罗马途中遭到两名持械男子劫持。

67. 垃圾 rubbish, garbage, trash, refuse, litter, waste

refuse 废物；垃圾（主要用于官方语言）

The District Council made a weekly collection of refuse.
区政务委员会每周收取一次垃圾。

refuse 为正式用语，用于英国英语和北美英语中。refuse collector 为 dustman 或 garbage collector 的正式说法。

rubbish 常用于英国英语中，指垃圾、废物。

garbage 和 **trash** 均用于北美英语。生活垃圾中，garbage 多指废弃的食物和其他湿物质，而 trash 则指废弃的纸、硬纸板和干物质。

在英国英语中，垃圾为 rubbish，街上的垃圾桶为 dustbin，清除垃圾的工人叫 dustman。在北美英语中，垃圾为 garbage 和 trash，街上的垃圾桶为 garbage/trash can，清除垃圾的工人叫 garbage man/collector。

litter 垃圾，废弃物

尤指在公共场所散落于地、有碍观瞻的废弃物。

Don't drop litter anywhere. 请不要乱扔垃圾。

waste 废弃物，废料

普通用词，多指已无使用价值的材料或陈旧的、破损的物品，也可指任何被丢弃之物。

household/industrial waste 家庭垃圾；工业废料

Put all the waste in this bag. 把所有垃圾放进这只袋子里。

68. 禁止 forbid, ban, bar, prohibit

forbid 禁止，不准
指通过下命令、制定规则等禁止某事，或禁止某人做某事。
My mum forbade me to play computer games.
我妈妈不准我玩电脑游戏。
Parking here is forbidden. 这里禁止停车。
The law strictly forbids racial discrimination.
法律严格禁止种族歧视。

ban 禁止；取缔
强调不可抗拒性，语气较强。
Gambling is banned in this country. 这个国家禁止赌博。
Why has he been banned from driving for two years?
为什么他被禁止驾车两年？

bar 禁止；阻止
指正式禁止某人出入某地或做某事。
He was barred from leaving the country. 他被禁止出境。
The players are barred from going out after 11 pm.
夜里 11 点之后运动员不得外出。

prohibit 禁止
正式用语，尤指以法令禁止做某事或使用某物，通常用被动语态。
Students are prohibited from smoking on campus.
学生不准在校内吸烟。
Never do what is prohibited by law.
永远不要做法律禁止的事情。

69. 高智力的，聪明的 intelligent, intellectual

intelligent 有智力的，聪明的，有理解力的；智能的
不仅用于人类，亦可用于动物或物品。
A dolphin is an intelligent animal. 海豚是很聪明的动物。
The girl looked intelligent. 这女孩看起来聪明伶俐。
Are there intelligent life forms on other planets?
其他行星上是否存在着有智慧的生物？
An intelligent computer will be an indispensable diagnostic tool for doctors.
智能计算机将成为医生不可或缺的诊断工具。

intellectual 智力发达的，思维理解力强的
尤指高等智力的，不用于小孩和动物。
He is an intellectual person. 他是个智力很高的人。

70. 电梯 lift, elevator, escalator

elevator [美] 电梯
可载人或物，通常设在高层住宅、办公楼等地。
I took the elevator to the top floor. 我乘电梯到了顶层。

lift [英] 电梯
词义同 elevator，可换用。

escalator 自动扶梯；电动楼梯；滚梯

71. 山 mount, mountain, hill

mountain 高山，山岳
通常指大山，比 hill 高。
She lives over the mountain. 她住在大山那边。
It is hard to climb up a mountain. 登山很艰苦。

hill 小山，小丘
通常指不如 mountain 那样高大的小山、小丘和丘陵。

mount …山，…峰
用作山名的一部分，通常首字母大写，或略作 Mt。在文学作品中与 mountain 同义。

Mount Tai 泰山
He decided to climb the Mount Tai with others.
他决定与其他人一起爬泰山。

72. 复杂的 complicated, complex, intricate, sophisticated

complex 复杂的
指各部分的内在关系复杂的。
the complex structure of the human brain
错综复杂的人脑构造
The government is an extremely complex organization.
政府是一个极其复杂的组织。

complicated 复杂的，难懂的
与 complex 的词义接近，但语气更强，强调因极其复杂或非常烦琐而很难理解或处理的。
This problem is too complicated for me to solve.
这道数学题太复杂了，我解不出来。
The machine is complicated in structure.
这台机器结构复杂。

intricate 复杂的, 错综的, 难以理解的
语气最强，指许多关系、部分相互缠绕、纵横交错，使人迷惑不解。
This intricate web of interactions is vital to the maintenance of soil, air and water quality.
这相互作用、错综复杂的网络对于维持土壤、空气和水的质量至关重要。

sophisticated（设备）先进的，精密的；（人）老练的
指事物发展到或到达高级程度所表现出的复杂，尤指高级、精确、尖端技术发展的复杂。
Medical techniques are becoming more sophisticated all the time. 医疗技术日益复杂精妙。

73. 由…组成 make up, consist of, compose, constitute, comprise

这些词都可以表示"由…组成"，但 consist of 是这组词中最通用也是唯一可与动词-ing 形式连用，表示"包含…活动"的词：
My work at that time just consisted of typing letters.
我那时的工作只有打字信件。

将整体作为主语，部分作为宾语的词有：
The group consists of/ comprises/ is made up of/ is composed of/is comprised of ten people. 这个小组由 10 个人组成。

将部分作为主语，整体作为宾语的词有：
Ten people make up/constitute/comprise/compose the group.
这个小组由 10 个人组成。

注意：只有 comprise 一词可以在不用被动的情况下既可以用部分作主语也可以用整体作主语，但以整体作主语最为常见。
The collection comprises 327 paintings.
这部画册收有 327 幅画。
Older people comprise a large proportion of those living in poverty.
在那些生活贫困的人中，老年人占有很大的比例。

74. 同意 assent, consent, accede, approve

assent 同意，赞成
正式用语，指审慎考虑后同意某项建议、要求、意见、计划等，常后接介词 to。
He assented to the committee's proposal.

他同意委员会的建议。
Have they assented to the terms of the contract?
他们同意合同的条款了吗？

consent 同意，允许
较正式用语，指同意别人的请求、建议或满足他人的愿望，常后接介词 to 或带 to 的动词不定式。
After hours of persuasion they consented to abandon the strike. 经过几个小时的劝说，他们同意放弃罢工。
Her father reluctantly consented to the marriage.
她父亲勉强答应了这桩婚姻。

accede 同意，答应
正式用语，尤指最初不同意后又应允的要求、请求、计划等，常后接介词 to。
We all acceded to the demands for his resignation.
我们大家都同意要他辞职的请求。

approve 同意，赞同
指认为某人或某事是好的、对的、合适的，常后接介词 of。
Did your father approve? 你父亲同意了吗？
I strongly approve of your proposal.
我十分赞同你的提议。

75. 保护 reserve, preserve, conserve

从构词上来看，这三个词都含有 serve（服务）。

reserve 预订；保留（权利）
The refreshments are reserved for the guests.
这些点心是留给客人的。
All rights reserved. 版权所有。

reserve 还可作名词，意为"保护区"。

preserve 保护，保存
The ancient vase was preserved well by the archaeologists.
这个古代花瓶被考古学家保存得很好。
She believed it's the most important thing to preserve her reputation. 她认为维护自己的声誉是最重要的事情。

preserve 还可作名词，意为"保护区"。

conserve 节省；保护（资源、水土、古建筑等）
You can set the temperature to 26 degrees centigrade in order to conserve energy.
你可以把温度设置成 26 摄氏度以节约能源。
Government should enforce laws to conserve wildlife animals in this area.
政府应该实施法律保护这个地区的野生动物。
Conservation programs cannot function without local support.
没有地方的支持，保护项目就无法运作。

服务本身是什么并不重要，重要的是面对服务本身需要做的事情。reserve，表示先留在那里，随后再服务，所以有预约、保留之意。preserve 表示享受服务之前或享受服务的同时要保护享受服务的对象。conserve 是指通过节约的途径来"保护"享受的权利，但是这种保护并非真正意义上的保护，而 preserve 更加贴近"保护"的真正含义。

reserve 和 preserve（US）都可以作"保护区"讲。
We have helped set up new nature reserves for pandas.
我们帮助建立起了新的大熊猫自然保护区。
The local government has built a preserve to protect this kind of animal.
为了保护这种动物，当地政府已建立了保护区。

76. 居住 reside, inhabit, dwell, live, settle, stay

reside 居住，定居

指在某处居住，含合法、长久之意。（"resident 居民"可以帮助理解此义）
I plan to reside in Salt Lake City. 我打算在盐湖城定居。

live 居住
最普通用词，指人在某处生活或动植物在某地生长，时间可长可短。
I have been living here since my childhood.
我打小就一直住在这里。

settle 定居
指开始在某一国家、地区或城镇生活，通常不接具体的住所。
They got married and settled near New York.
他们婚后定居在纽约附近。

inhabit 居住于（某地）
指人或动植物生活在某个地区，并已适应该地区的特殊环境。inhabit 是这一组词中唯一一个及物动词。
Fish inhabit the sea. 鱼栖息于海中。
They inhabit the tropical forests. 他们居住在热带森林中。

dwell 居住，栖身
指在某一地方居住。
For ten years, she dwelt in the forest.
她在森林里生活了 10 年。

stay 留宿，暂住
指到访或作客时短期居住。
If you ever visit Moscow, you must come and stay with us.
你要是到莫斯科来，一定要到我们这里住住。

77. 怀疑 doubt, suspect

doubt 怀疑，不确定
指不相信或不确定某事的真实性，可后接从句。
I doubt whether he will come to my birthday party.
我不确定他是否会参加我的生日聚会。
She never doubted her husband's stories.
她从未怀疑过丈夫的各种假话。

suspect 猜想，怀疑
指有疑问，觉得有某种可能，尤指坏事属实或有发生的可能，不用进行时，在肯定句和否定句中如接从句均用 that 引导。
He suspected that the woman staying in the flat above was using heroin.
他怀疑楼上公寓里的那个女人正在吸食海洛因。
They suspected him of betraying state secrets.
他们怀疑他泄露了国家机密。

简单地说，doubt 表示"不相信某事的真实性"，suspect 则表示"相信可能有不好的事情"。

78. 限制 limit, confine, restrict

limit 限制，限定
指在时间、数量、水平等方面加以限制，侧重事物的限度。
We must limit our spending. 我们必须限制开支。
His talk is limited to 30 minutes. 他的谈话限定在 30 分钟内。

confine 限制；使局限于
指将某人或某事物限制在某活动、主题、地区等范围之内，通常用被动语态。
They confined their study to 12 cases.
他们把研究限定在 12 个案例以内。
The work will not be confined to this area.
此项工作不会局限于这一地区。

restrict 限制，限定

指控制某事物的大小、数量或范围，侧重限制行为。
You can restrict access to certain files.
你可以限制某些文档的传阅人数。
The deal will restrict competition. 这个协议将限制竞争。

79. 限制 *limit, restriction, constraint, restraint*

limit 指极限，限量，限额。
The EU has set strict limits on pollution levels.
欧盟对污染程度订下了严格的限制。
the speed limit 速度限制

restriction 指掌权者所作的限制规定或法规，偏向于人为的限制。
There are no restrictions on the amount of money you can withdraw. 取款没有限额。

constraint 指受客观存在的某种限制，使不能自由做想做的某事情。
We have to work within severe constraints of time and money. 我们必须在时间紧迫、资金紧张的限制下工作。
He would have liked to travel overseas but his budget was a constraint. 他本想出国旅行，但预算有限。
When I worked in China it was a constraint that I could not speak the language.
当我在中国工作时，我不能说这种语言是一种限制。

constraint 也可表示"控制，限制"，比 restraint 更正式，口气也更重，所表达的"控制"之意近乎于 restriction，表示"使某人不能自由做自己想做的事情"。
This decision will impose serious constraints on all schools.
这项决定将使所有的学校受到各种严格的限制。
Northern Ireland has been an integral part of the UK, in which there is no constraint on movement of people and no constraint on movements of goods.
北爱尔兰一直是英国不可分割的一部分，英国对人员流动没有限制，对货物流动也没有限制。

restraint 克制（自己的行为）；限制、控制（使不能移动）
A car seatbelt is a restraint. 汽车安全带是一种约束装置。
They behaved with more restraint than I'd expected.
他们表现得比我预料的更为克制。
the physical restraint of prisoners 对囚犯的人身限制

下面这几句话，可以帮助我们理解 restriction、constraint 和 restraint 的区别：

• While outside restrictions like laws and customs cause constraints, restraints are inside restrictions that an individual places upon himself.

• You restrain yourself from eating favorite junk food as you know it is harmful for your health.

• Shortage of funds and shortage of time are often described as budgetary constraints and time constraints.

80. 克制 *restrain, refrain*

restrain 阻止，克制，抑制
restrain 是及物动词，常用作 restrain sb/sth from (doing) sth，含义广泛，通常指以武力阻止某人做某事，也指克制情绪、行为或控制、限制某事物。
I restrained tears with difficulty. 我好不容易才忍住眼泪。
The doctors restrained the patient from hurting himself.
医生制止了病人的自残行为。

refrain 克制，抑制
refrain 是不及物动词，常用于 refrain from (doing) sth，指

忍住不做自己想做的事情。
It's difficult for us to refrain from laughing when we are seeing a comedy.
当我们看喜剧的时候很难控制自己不笑出来。
The doctor suggested my father refrain from smoking.
医生建议我父亲戒烟。

81. 顾客 *client, consumer, customer*

client 客户，委托人
指接受专业人士、公司、组织等提供的服务或建议的人。
The client was too poor to pay his lawyer.
委托人太穷了，付不起律师的诉讼费用。
It will enable us to serve our clients even better in the future.
这将使我们以后能更好地服务客户。

consumer 消费者
Consumers need the best products and the best services.
客户需要最好的产品和服务。
Nowadays, many consumers prefer to shop on the Internet.
如今，许多消费者更愿意在网上购物。

customer 顾客
多指从某一商场或公司购买东西的人或机构。
Several customers came in and bought the same jackets.
几名顾客走进来买了同样的夹克。
The new shop across the street has taken away some of my customers.
街对面新开张的商店挖走了我的一些顾客。

82. 推测，假定 *assume, presume, suppose*

assume 设想，假定
指想当然地将未经证实的事当真，比较武断。
I didn't see your cell phone, so I assumed you'd left.
我没看见你的手机，所以我以为你离开了。
Assuming that Dad agrees, when do you want to shop for a new car? 假设爸爸同意，你打算什么时候买新汽车？

presume 假设，假定
常指以已有的经验、信息等为依据进行合乎逻辑的推测、推断，但结论可能有误。
I presume that this price includes all transportation and accommodation fees.
我猜测，这个价格包括了一切交通费用和住宿费。

suppose 假定；猜想
指在某一前提条件下或根据已有知识、信息等进行推测，有时用于表达意见。
What makes him suppose they're going to quit?
他凭什么认为他们要离职？
Public spending is supposed to fall, not rise, in the next few years.
在接下来的几年里，政府开支应该会下降，而不是上升。

83. 获得 *acquire, attain, obtain, gain*

acquire 获得，取得（知识、技能、名声、爱好等）
指通过努力、能力、行为表现等，得到日积月累获得的知识、技能、名声、爱好等。
Step by step he acquired job experience.
他逐步获得了工作经验。
She has acquired a good knowledge of English.
她英语已经学得很好。
He has acquired a reputation for dishonesty.
他得到了不诚实的名声。
I have recently acquired a taste for olives.

我最近开始喜欢吃橄榄了。

acquire 还可指 "购得；获得（something big or expensive）"，日常生活中，人们常用 get。

I've suddenly acquired a stepbrother.
我突然有了一个继兄弟。

The company has just acquired new premises.
公司刚购得新办公楼。

attain（经过努力）得到，获得
指通过长时间的艰苦努力而得到所需或盼望已久的东西，你可以 "attain" 一个你为自己设定的目标，或者在工作中 "attain" 一个高职位。

He attained the position of President of Ford Motors.
他终于当上了福特汽车公司的总裁。

His painstaking efforts to attain his pilot's licence is praiseworthy.
他为获得飞行员执照所下的苦功是值得赞扬的。

After six months, I attained my goal of losing 15 pounds.
6 个月后，我达到了减掉 15 磅的目标。

obtain 得到，获得
日常生活中常用 get。指得到自己想要的东西，可以是经过努力得来的，可以是没有经过努力而得到的。（而 attain 一定是指经过努力而得到的）

You can obtain a copy of this leaflet in your local library.
你可在当地图书馆获取一份这种小册子。

The robbers obtained weapons to commit the crime.
强盗们获得了作案的武器。

Police obtained a warrant to search the house.
警方获得搜查这所房子的搜查令。

试比较：
In college you work hard to attain a degree.
在大学里，你通过努力学习获得学位。

Once you graduate you will obtain your diploma.
你一毕业就能拿到毕业证书。

Many countries are working to attain nuclear technology, but the nuclear weapons themselves can only be obtained.
类似的，许多国家正在努力获得核技术，但核武器本身只能获得。

gain 获得，取得
指通过后天努力或有目的的行动逐渐获得某种想要或需要的东西，如成就、利益等。

No pains, no gains. 不劳无获。（这个谚语更能帮助我们理解 gain 的词义。）

I've gained a lot of useful experience.
我获得了许多有用的经验。

The research helped us gain an insight into how a child's mind works.
这项研究有助于我们深入了解孩子的思维方式。

84. 满足的 content 与 contented

content 多用作表语，后面可接不定式；contented 可用作表语或定语，表示安于现状无他求。

Now that she has apologised, I am content.
既然她已经道了歉，我也就满意了。

She was gazing at him with a soft, contented smile on her face. 她注视着他，脸上带着温柔而满足的微笑。

She is not content with her present lot and wishes to take steps to improve it.
她对自己目前的生活并不满意，希望能采取措施改善它。

85. 目的，意图 intention 与 intent

intention 意图，目的
普通用词，指做某事的打算或计划。

I came to London with the intention of studying English literature. 我来伦敦是为了学习英国文学。

intent 意图
指某人做某事的目的；也可作法律术语，指犯罪意图。

The company has declared its intent to get a bank loan.
该公司已宣布打算向银行贷款。

He broke the window with the intent to enter and steal.
他打破窗户意图入室行窃。

86. 乡村，地貌 country, countryside, landscape, terrain

country 乡下，乡村
（常作 the country）尤指具有自然特征的乡下、乡村。
She lives in the country. 她住在乡下。

countryside 乡村，农村
强调乡村地区的美丽或宁静时通常用 countryside。
a little village in the French countryside 法国乡间的小村庄

landscape（乡村的）风景，景色
This pattern of woods and fields is typical of the English landscape. 这是具有典型英格兰风景特征的森林与田野。

terrain 地带；地形
描述某地区的地形或地势时用 terrain。
The truck bumped its way over the rough terrain.
卡车在崎岖不平的地面上颠簸行进。

87. 特性 quality, attribute, characteristic, trait, feature, peculiarity, property

quality 特性，特征
普通用词，指有形或无形的特性，也可指个性或共性的特征。
She has a childlike quality. 她有着孩子般的天真特质。
One quality of wood is that it can burn.
木材的一个特性是可以燃烧。

attribute 特性，特质
指某人或某物特有的性质或属性，尤指好的、有用的特质。
What attributes should a good leader possess?
一名优秀的领导者应具备哪些素质？
Jake has all the attributes of a first-class athlete.
杰克拥有一流运动员应具备的所有特质。

characteristic 特性，特点
指有别于其他人或事物的典型的、特殊的、本质的特性或特征，含易于辨认之意，通常用复数。
These two groups of patients have quite different characteristics. 这两组患者具有截然不同的特点。
The physical characteristics of objects should also be taken into account. 物体的物理特征也应考虑进去。

feature 特征，特色
指引人注目的显著特征或细节，多用于说明人或事物的主要特征，也可用于说明地理特征等。
This is a key feature of our community college.
这是我们社区大学的一个主要特点。
What are the important features of the landscape in Holland?
荷兰重要的景观风貌是什么？

peculiarity 特性，特点
指地方、人、情况等的独特之处。

The lack of a written constitution is a peculiarity of the country. 没有一部成文宪法是该国的一大特点。

property 特性，性质
正式用语，多指同类事物所共有的特性，通常用复数。
Let's compare the physical properties of the two substances. 让我们来比较一下这两种物质的物理特性。
This container has good heat-retaining properties. 这种容器保温性能很好。

trait 特征，特性
正式用语，指人的性格或性情特征，尤指先天的性格特征。
The medical research was based on particular personality traits. 该医学研究以某些性格特征为基础。

88. 消失 vanish, disappear, evaporate

vanish 消失
强调莫名其妙地突然消失。
The magician waved his hand and the dove vanished. 魔术师挥了一下手，鸽子就消失了。
My skirt seems to have vanished. 我的裙子似乎不翼而飞了。

disappear 消失，不见
强调从视线中暂时地、突然地或永久地消失。
My English book has disappeared from the table where I left it. 我放在桌子上的英语书不见了。
His cellphone disappeared again. 他的手机又不见了。

evaporate 消失，消散
指感觉等逐渐消逝。
Her confidence has now completely evaporated. 她的信心已消失殆尽。

89. 躲避，回避 avoid, evade, elude

avoid 避开，躲避
指回避某人、某物或不使用某物，也指有意避开不好的、危险的事物，不能接动词不定式。
Why does everyone avoid Nick? 为什么所有人都躲着尼克？
Pregnant women should avoid raw eggs. 孕妇忌吃生鸡蛋。
This is an effective way for you to avoid overspending. 这是一种使你避免超支的有效办法。

evade 逃避，躲避
指回避谈论某事物，尤指试图隐瞒，也指不做该做的事，后不能接动词不定式。
He evaded the question. 他避开了那个问题。
You can't go on evading your responsibilities. 你不能继续逃避责任。

elude 逃避，躲避
尤指用计谋机敏地避开某人或某事物。
a criminal who eluded the authorities for 8 years
逃避当局追捕 8 年之久的罪犯
He eluded the police by using a series of false names.
他用了一连串假名逃脱了警方的追捕。

90. 相反 inverse, reverse, converse

inverse（在数或量上呈）反向变化的；上下颠倒的，倒置的
侧重数量关系、所处位置的相反。
例如：a+b=k，其中 a,b 是变量，k 是常数，很明显 a 越大 b 就越小；ab=k 的情形也一样（后者在数学上叫反比例函数关系）。常见短语：in inverse proportion to 与…成反比；

inverse function 反函数。

reverse 逆向的；逆序的；背面的
侧重顺序、方向上的相反。
例如：作动词时，"倒车"用 reverse the car，"颠倒顺序"用 reverse the order；作形容词时，"背面"用 the reverse side。

converse（性质）相反的；对立的
侧重事物性质上的相反。
例如：物质和反物质、命题和反命题、安装和反安装（卸载）、侦察和反侦察，等等，是指事物的性质、状态跟目前完全相反、对立的情况下所表现出的特征。常见短语：a converse example 反例；the converse is equally true 反之亦然；conversely=on the contrary 反之，相反地。

91. 感染；传播 infect, contract, transmit

infect 传染；使感染
~ sb/sth (with sth) "使某人感染上…"，被感染的对象常作宾语。
After work, the doctor washed his hands so he did not infect anyone else.
下班后，医生洗了手，这样他就不会传染别人了。
One of my roommates infected me with a bad cold.
我的一个室友使我染上了重感冒。
Be careful not to be infected with flu. 小心不要染上流感。

contract 感染（疾病）；得（病）
contract 指的是 "the action of receiving or getting a disease or illness"。
The girl had contracted the illness from her sick friend.
这个女孩从她生病的朋友那里感染了这个病。

transmit 传播；传染
China's National Health Commission has confirmed the virus can be transmitted from person to person through "droplet transmission".
中国国家卫生委员会证实，病毒可以通过"飞沫传播"在人与人之间传播。

92. 战争，战斗 war, battle, combat, fight

war 战争
通常指敌对国家之间或国内敌对势力之间进行的大规模武力斗争，其中可包括多个战役（battle）。
the Second World War 第二次世界大战
the war between England and Scotland
英格兰和苏格兰之间的战争

battle 战役，战斗
通常指敌对双方的军队之间的交战，尤指大型战争中的某一次战役。
It was the most crucial battle in the whole war.
那是整个战争中最为关键的一次战役。
We won the war after a decisive battle.
经过一场决战后，我们取得了战争的胜利。

combat 战斗，作战；格斗
指战争中的军事行动，尤指小规模的战斗，常可与 action 换用；也可指人或群体间的打斗。
Corporal Jill was killed in combat/action.
吉尔下士在战斗中阵亡了。
The soldiers were trained in unarmed combat.
士兵们接受了徒手格斗训练。

fight 战斗；打斗
普通用词，尤指敌对军队间为争夺某一地块或位置而进行

的战斗，也可指人或帮派之间的争斗。

After a fierce fight, the enemy yielded to our army.
经过一场激战，敌人向我军投降了。

Tom's always getting into fights at school.
汤姆老是在学校打架。

93. 流行病，传染病 endemic，epidemic, pandemic

endemic 地方性的；（某地或某集体中）特有的
指属于某个具体的地理环境（geography）、种族（race）、地区（area）、环境（environment）、人群（people）等的，可以翻译为"地方性的""特有的"等。如，diseases endemic to the tropics "热带特有的疾病"。

epidemic 流行病
通常指高度传染性（highly contagious），同时影响很多人，迅速广泛传播的疾病。如，an epidemic outbreak of influenza "流感流行"。它的定义具有一定的主观性，和人们的预期有关。如果仅局限于某个地点（local），那么它叫 outbreak；如果影响更大，就叫 epidemic；如果达到全世界范围，那么可以叫 pandemic。

pandemic 大规模流行性传染病
流行范围可能覆盖整个大洲甚至全球，可翻译为"大规模流行性传染病"。如，pandemic influenza "流感大流行"。

The prospect is daunting. A pandemic—an ongoing epidemic on two or more continents—may well have global consequences.
前景令人望而生畏。大流行——在两个或两个以上大陆上持续的流行病——很可能会造成全球后果。

94. 幻想 fantasy, illusion, delusion

fantasy 想象，幻想
指对刺激或异乎寻常的事情的臆想，此类事情基本不可能在现实中发生。

He used to have fantasies about living with a fairy in a wooden house near the sea.
他过去常幻想自己和仙女居住在海边的一座小木屋里。

illusion 幻想；错误的想法
尤指自己持有的错误观念或想法。

She suffers from the illusion that she can't possibly meet the deadline. 她误以为自己不能按时完成任务。

He is under the illusion that he will get an extra bonus.
他心存幻想，认为他将得到一笔额外的奖金。

delusion 错觉；妄想
指对自己或自身所处境况的错误看法。

The patient lives under the delusion that he is the president.
那个病人生活在他就是总统的错觉中。

95. 可怜的 pitiful, piteous, pitiable

pitiful 令人同情的，可怜的
指外表或经历令人同情的。

The refugees whose houses were ruined in the tsunami were a pitiful sight.
这些难民的房屋在海啸中被毁，看上去真可怜。

That little boy was in a very pitiful condition.
那个小男孩处于非常可怜的境况中。

piteous 可怜的，让人怜悯的
指表达苦难或悲伤的方式让人心生怜悯的。

Why did she give a long piteous cry?
为什么她发出一声长长的哀号？

pitiable 令人怜悯的，可怜的

指让人心生怜悯、值得同情的。

Women and children are prone to become pitiable victims of war. 妇女和儿童很容易成为可怜的战争受害者。

96. 汽油，石油 petroleum, gas, gasoline

petroleum 原油，石油
指埋藏于地下或海底的原油，用来生产汽油（英国英语用 petrol，美语用 gas 或 gasoline）和煤油（英国英语用 paraffin，美语用 kerosene）。

gasoline 汽油
常用于美语，也可拼作 gasolene。也常简写作 gas。

gas 汽油（美语）
gas 除去作"汽油"解之外，还可指"气体；天然气；毒气；瓦斯；肠气"等。

97. 压制，克制 suppress, repress

suppress 与 repress 有着相似的含义，但也有一些微妙的差异值得注意。

suppress 镇压；忍住
常表示采取武力控制。
The government suppressed the rebellion. 政府镇压了叛乱。

repress 压制；克制
常表示控制住某事物以维持或维护正常秩序。
The government repressed the rebellion. 政府平息了叛乱。

98. 名声 fame, renown, repute, reputation

fame 名誉，名气
指人、地方、机构等的知名度。
She gained fame as a critic before she published the popular novel.
在出版这本畅销小说之前，她作为评论家已经有了名气。
He came to fame in the eighties. 他成名于 80 年代。

renown 名誉，声誉
指因特殊才能、成就或品质而赢得的知名度和赞誉。
She has won world renown for her excellent acting.
她因出色的演技而享誉全球。

repute 和 **reputation** 都是名词，意为"名誉，名声"，词义相同，指以往发生的事情使人们形成的对某人或某事物的看法，此看法可好可坏。但 repute 是不可数名词，reputation 是可数名词。
She has a reputation for being fair. 她以公正著称。
He has gaind considerable repute. 他已相当出名。

99. 地区 zone, area, district, region, stretch, belt

zone 地区，地带
指具有某种区别性特征而被划分出来的区域、地带；用作科技术语时，多指地球上依据温度划分的气候带。
a commercial/parking/residential zone
商业/停车/住宅区
a danger/safety zone 危险/安全区
They are pulling their troops out of the battle zone.
他们正把部队调离战区。
Most of China is in the temperate zone.
中国的大部分地区处于温带。

area 地区，区域
普通用词，指国家、市镇等的区域，或建筑、处所等中作特定用途的场地。
There're large areas in Australia still unpopulated.

在澳大利亚还有大片地区至今仍然无人居住。

belt 区域，地带
指具有某种特色或某类人居住的地区或地带。
the corn/forest/green belt 玉米/森林/绿色地带
the Bible Belt《圣经》地带（指美国南部新教教义极具影响的地区）
the Belt and Road initiative "一带一路" 倡议

district 地区，行政区
多指由政府等机构出于行政管理等目的而明确划分的地区。
Do you know the postal code of this district?
你知道这个地区的邮政编码吗？
The basic laws of Hong Kong and Macao special administrative regions have been carried out to the letter.
《香港特别行政区基本法》和《澳门特别行政区基本法》得到了严格执行。

region 地区，区域
通常指界线不明的较大地区或一国的行政分区；the regions 则指某国除首都以外的所有区域。
The inhabitants of mountainous regions live more happily than ever before. 山区居民的生活比过去幸福多了。
I have visited the Basque region of Spain.
我去过西班牙的巴斯克区。

stretch 一片地域，一段水域
My hometown is located on a beautiful stretch of land.
我的家乡位于一片美丽的土地上。
Ships are rarely seen on this stretch of the river.
这一河段少有船只经过。

100. 决定 decide, determine, resolve

decide 决定，下决心
指经过考虑或协商后作出判断或选择，拿定主意做某件事而不做另外一件。

She has decided to buy a car. 她决定买辆汽车。
They decided to set out right away. 他们决定立刻出发。

determine 决定，决心
语义比 decide 强，表示非常明确地决定做某事，常后接介词 on 或动词不定式。
The whole group determined on an early start.
全队人都决定早点出发。
He determined to stay. 他决定留下来。

resolve 决定，决意
语义比 determine 强，指下定决心做某事，常有贯彻决定的坚定意志。
He resolved to get up earlier the next morning.
他决意第二天早一点起床。
She resolved that she would give up smoking. 她决心戒烟。

101. 报仇，报复 revenge, avenge

revenge常作名词，在正式文体中也可用作动词；而**avenge**只能作动词。
Dawson takes revenge on the man by knifing him to death.
道森用刀杀死了他的仇人。
There are few things quite as sweet as revenge.
几乎没有比复仇更痛快的事情了。

作动词时，**avenge**可以表示"报某事之仇"，也可以表示"报复某人"，**revenge**只能表示"报复某人"。在表示"报复某人"时，**avenge**只有"avenge oneself on sb"一种用法，而**revenge**有"revenge oneself on sb"和"be revenged on sb"两种用法。
He wanted to avenge his sister's death.
他要为死去的姐姐报仇。
She never thought to avenge herself on her husband who had had an affair. 她从未想过报复有外遇的丈夫。
The prince was later revenged on his father's killer.
王子后来向杀害他父亲的凶手报了仇。

附录 单词索引

F